THE HERITAGE GUIDE
TO THE CONSTITUTION

The Heritage Foundation
214 Massachusetts Avenue NE
Washington, DC 20002
(202) 546-4400
heritage.org

Regnery books may be purchased in bulk at special discounts for sales promotion, corporate gifts, fund-raising, or educational purposes. Special editions can also be created to specifications. For details, contact the Special Sales Department, Skyhorse Publishing, 307 West 36th Street, 11th Floor, New York, NY 10018 or info@skyhorsepublishing.com.

Regnery® is a registered trademark of Skyhorse Publishing, Inc. ®, a Delaware corporation.

Visit our website at skyhorsepublishing.com.

10 9 8 7 6 5 4 3 2 1

Library of Congress Cataloging-in-Publication Data is available on file.

Jacket design by David Ter-Avanesyan

Print ISBN: 978-1-5107-8335-5
eBook ISBN: 978-1-5107-8349-2

Printed in the United States of America

THE HERITAGE GUIDE TO THE CONSTITUTION

FULLY REVISED THIRD EDITION

JOSH BLACKMAN
SENIOR EDITOR

JOHN G. MALCOLM
EXECUTIVE EDITOR

FOREWORD BY THE HONORABLE EDWIN MEESE III
PREFACE BY JUSTICE SAMUEL A. ALITO, JR.

Since 1947
REGNERY
An Imprint of Skyhorse Publishing, Inc.

THE CONSTITUTION
OF THE UNITED STATES

THE CONSTITUTION OF THE UNITED STATES

Preamble			
		We the People of the United States, in Order to form a more perfect Union, establish Justice, insure domestic Tranquility, provide for the common defence, promote the general Welfare, and secure the Blessings of Liberty to ourselves and our Posterity, do ordain and establish this Constitution for the United States of America.	Essay #4: The Preamble
Article I			
Sec. 1		All legislative Powers herein granted shall be vested in a Congress of the United States, which shall consist of a Senate and House of Representatives.	Essay #5: Legislative Vesting Clause
Sec. 2	*Cl. 1*	The House of Representatives shall be composed of Members chosen every second Year by the People of the several States, and the Electors in each State shall have the Qualifications requisite for Electors of the most numerous Branch of the State Legislature.	Essay #6: House of Representatives Clause Essay #7: Elector Qualifications Clause
	Cl. 2	No Person shall be a Representative who shall not have attained to the Age of twenty five Years, and been seven Years a Citizen of the United States, and who shall not, when elected, be an Inhabitant of that State in which he shall be chosen.	Essay #8: Qualifications for Representatives Clause
	Cl. 3	[Representatives and direct Taxes shall be apportioned among the several States which may be included within this Union, according to their respective Numbers, which shall be determined by adding to the whole Number of free Persons, including those bound to Service for a Term of Years, and excluding Indians not taxed, three fifths of all other Persons.]* The actual Enumeration shall be made within three Years after the first Meeting of the Congress of the United States, and within every subsequent Term of ten Years, in such Manner as they shall by Law direct. The number of Representatives shall not exceed one for every thirty Thousand, but each State shall have at Least one Representative; and until such enumeration shall be made, the State of New Hampshire shall be entitled to chuse three, Massachusetts eight, Rhode-Island and Providence Plantations one, Connecticut five, New-York six, New Jersey four, Pennsylvania eight, Delaware one, Maryland six, Virginia ten, North Carolina five, South Carolina five, and Georgia three. * Changed by Section 2 of the Fourteenth Amendment.	Essay #9: Three-Fifths Clause Essay #10: Enumeration Clause Essay #11: Apportionment Clause

(Continued . . .)

Sec. 2	*Cl. 4*	When vacancies happen in the Representation from any State, the Executive Authority thereof shall issue Writs of Election to fill such Vacancies.	Essay #12: Executive Writs of Election Clause
	Cl. 5	The House of Representatives shall chuse their Speaker and other Officers; and shall have the sole Power of Impeachment.	Essay #13: Speaker of the House Clause Essay #14: House Impeachment Clause
Sec. 3	*Cl. 1*	The Senate of the United States shall be composed of two Senators from each State, [chosen by the Legislature thereof,]* for six Years; and each Senator shall have one Vote. *Changed by the Seventeenth Amendment.	Essay #15: Senate Clause
	Cl. 2	Immediately after they shall be assembled in Consequence of the first Election, they shall be divided as equally as may be into three Classes. The Seats of the Senators of the first Class shall be vacated at the Expiration of the second Year, of the second Class at the Expiration of the fourth Year, and of the third Class at the Expiration of the sixth Year, so that one third may be chosen every second Year; [and if Vacancies happen by Resignation, or otherwise, during the Recess of the Legislature of any State, the Executive thereof may make temporary Appointments until the next Meeting of the Legislature, which shall then fill such Vacancies.]* *Changed by the Seventeenth Amendment.	Essay #16: Senatorial Classes and Vacancies Clause
	Cl. 3	No Person shall be a Senator who shall not have attained to the Age of thirty Years, and been nine Years a Citizen of the United States, and who shall not, when elected, be an Inhabitant of that State for which he shall be chosen.	Essay #17: Qualifications for Senators Clause
	Cl. 4	The Vice President of the United States shall be President of the Senate, but shall have no Vote, unless they be equally divided.	Essay #18: Vice President as Presiding Officer Clause
	Cl. 5	The Senate shall chuse their other Officers, and also a President pro tempore, in the Absence of the Vice President, or when he shall exercise the Office of President of the United States.	Essay #19: President Pro Tempore Clause
	Cl. 6	The Senate shall have the sole Power to try all Impeachments. When sitting for that Purpose, they shall be on Oath or Affirmation. When the President of the United States is tried, the Chief Justice shall preside: And no Person shall be convicted without the Concurrence of two thirds of the Members present.	Essay #20: Senate Impeachment Trial Clause

(Continued . . .)

Sec. 3	*Cl. 7*	Judgment in Cases of Impeachment shall not extend further than to removal from Office, and disqualification to hold and enjoy any Office of honor, Trust or Profit under the United States: but the Party convicted shall nevertheless be liable and subject to Indictment, Trial, Judgment and Punishment, according to Law.	Essay #21: Impeachment Judgment Clause
Sec. 4	*Cl. 1*	The Times, Places and Manner of holding Elections for Senators and Representatives, shall be prescribed in each State by the Legislature thereof; but the Congress may at any time by Law make or alter such Regulations, except as to the Places of chusing Senators.	Essay #22: Elections Clause
	Cl. 2	The Congress shall assemble at least once in every Year, and such Meeting shall be [on the first Monday in December]*, unless they shall by Law appoint a different Day. * Changed by Section 2 of the Twentieth Amendment.	Essay #23: Congressional Assembly Clause
Sec. 5	*Cl. 1*	Each House shall be the Judge of the Elections, Returns and Qualifications of its own Members, and a Majority of each shall constitute a Quorum to do Business; but a smaller Number may adjourn from day to day, and may be authorized to compel the Attendance of absent Members, in such Manner, and under such Penalties as each House may provide.	Essay #24: Judge of Elections Clause Essay #25: Quorum Clause
	Cl. 2	Each House may determine the Rules of its Proceedings, punish its Members for disorderly Behaviour, and, with the Concurrence of two thirds, expel a Member.	Essay #26: Rules of Proceedings Clause Essay #27: Punishment and Expulsion Clause
	Cl. 3	Each House shall keep a Journal of its Proceedings, and from time to time publish the same, excepting such Parts as may in their Judgment require Secrecy; and the Yeas and Nays of the Members of either House on any question shall, at the Desire of one fifth of those Present, be entered on the Journal.	Essay #28: Journal Clause
	Cl. 4	Neither House, during the Session of Congress, shall, without the Consent of the other, adjourn for more than three days, nor to any other Place than that in which the two Houses shall be sitting.	Essay #29: Congressional Adjournment Clause

(Continued . . .)

Sec. 6	*Cl. 1*	The Senators and Representatives shall receive a Compensation for their Services, to be ascertained by Law, and paid out of the Treasury of the United States. They shall in all Cases, except Treason, Felony and Breach of the Peace, be privileged from Arrest during their Attendance at the Session of their respective Houses, and in going to and returning from the same; and for any Speech or Debate in either House, they shall not be questioned in any other Place.	Essay #30: Congressional Compensation Clause Essay #31: Privilege from Arrest Clause Essay #32: Speech or Debate Clause
	Cl. 2	No Senator or Representative shall, during the Time for which he was elected, be appointed to any civil Office under the Authority of the United States, which shall have been created, or the Emoluments whereof shall have been encreased during such time; and no Person holding any Office under the United States, shall be a Member of either House during his Continuance in Office.	Essay #33: Ineligibility Clause Essay #34: Incompatibility Clause
Sec. 7	*Cl. 1*	All Bills for raising Revenue shall originate in the House of Representatives; but the Senate may propose or concur with Amendments as on other Bills.	Essay #35: Origination Clause
	Cl. 2	Every Bill which shall have passed the House of Representatives and the Senate, shall, before it become a Law, be presented to the President of the United States; If he approve he shall sign it, but if not he shall return it, with his Objections to that House in which it shall have originated, who shall enter the Objections at large on their Journal, and proceed to reconsider it. If after such Reconsideration two thirds of that House shall agree to pass the Bill, it shall be sent, together with the Objections, to the other House, by which it shall likewise be reconsidered, and if approved by two thirds of that House, it shall become a Law. But in all such Cases the Votes of both Houses shall be determined by Yeas and Nays, and the Names of the Persons voting for and against the Bill shall be entered on the Journal of each House respectively. If any Bill shall not be returned by the President within ten Days (Sundays excepted) after it shall have been presented to him, the Same shall be a Law, in like Manner as if he had signed it, unless the Congress by their Adjournment prevent its Return, in which Case it shall not be a Law.	Essay #36: Presentment Clause Essay #37: Pocket Veto Clause
	Cl. 3	Every Order, Resolution, or Vote to which the Concurrence of the Senate and House of Representatives may be necessary (except on a question of Adjournment) shall be presented to the President of the United States; and before the Same shall take Effect, shall be approved by him, or being disapproved by him, shall be repassed by two thirds of the Senate and House of Representatives, according to the Rules and Limitations prescribed in the Case of a Bill.	Essay #38: Order, Resolution, or Vote (ORV) Clause

Continued . . .

(Continued . . .)

Sec. 8	Cl. 1	The Congress shall have Power To lay and collect Taxes, Duties, Imposts and Excises, to pay the Debts and provide for the common Defence and general Welfare of the United States; but all Duties, Imposts and Excises shall be uniform throughout the United States;	Essay #39: Taxing Clause Essay #40: Spending Clause Essay #41: Uniformity Clause
	Cl. 2	To borrow Money on the credit of the United States;	Essay #42: Borrowing Clause
	Cl. 3	To regulate Commerce with foreign Nations, and among the several States, and with the Indian Tribes;	Essay #43: Foreign Commerce Clause Essay #44: Interstate Commerce Clause Essay #45: Indian Commerce Clause
	Cl. 4	To establish an uniform Rule of Naturalization, and uniform Laws on the subject of Bankruptcies throughout the United States;	Essay #46: Naturalization Clause Essay #47: Bankruptcy Clause
	Cl. 5	To coin Money, regulate the Value thereof, and of foreign Coin, and fix the Standard of Weights and Measures;	Essay #48: Federal Money Clause Essay #49: Weights and Measures Clause
	Cl. 6	To provide for the Punishment of counterfeiting the Securities and current Coin of the United States;	Essay #50: Counterfeiting Clause
	Cl. 7	To establish Post Offices and post Roads;	Essay #51: Postal Clause
	Cl. 8	To promote the Progress of Science and useful Arts, by securing for limited Times to Authors and Inventors the exclusive Right to their respective Writings and Discoveries;	Essay #52: Copyright and Patent Clause
	Cl. 9	To constitute Tribunals inferior to the supreme Court;	Essay #53: Inferior Tribunals Clause

(Continued . . .)

Sec. 8	*Cl. 10*	To define and punish Piracies and Felonies committed on the high Seas, and Offenses against the Law of Nations;	Essay #54: Piracies and Felonies Clause Essay #55: Offenses Against the Law of Nations Clause
	Cl. 11	To declare War, grant Letters of Marque and Reprisal, and make Rules concerning Captures on Land and Water;	Essay #56: Declare War Clause Essay #57: Federal Marque and Reprisal Clause Essay #58: Captures Clause
	Cl. 12	To raise and support Armies, but no Appropriation of Money to that Use shall be for a longer Term than two Years;	Essay #59: Armies Clause
	Cl. 13	To provide and maintain a Navy;	Essay #60: Navy Clause
	Cl. 14	To make Rules for the Government and Regulation of the land and naval Forces;	Essay #61: Military Regulations Clause
	Cl. 15	To provide for calling forth the Militia to execute the Laws of the Union, suppress Insurrections and repel Invasions;	Essay #62: Calling Forth the Militia Clause
	Cl. 16	To provide for organizing, arming, and disciplining, the Militia, and for governing such Part of them as may be employed in the Service of the United States, reserving to the States respectively, the Appointment of the Officers, and the Authority of training the Militia according to the discipline prescribed by Congress;	Essay #63: Militia Organization Clause
	Cl. 17	To exercise exclusive Legislation in all Cases whatsoever, over such District (not exceeding ten Miles square) as may, by Cession of particular States, and the Acceptance of Congress, become the Seat of the Government of the United States, and to exercise like Authority over all Places purchased by the Consent of the Legislature of the State in which the Same shall be, for the Erection of Forts, Magazines, Arsenals, dock-Yards and other needful Buildings; — And	Essay #64: Federal District Clause Essay #65: Federal Enclave Clause
	Cl. 18	To make all Laws which shall be necessary and proper for carrying into Execution the foregoing Powers, and all other Powers vested by this Constitution in the Government of the United States, or in any Department or Officer thereof.	Essay #66: Necessary and Proper Clause

(Continued . . .)

Sec. 9	*Cl. 1*	The Migration or Importation of such Persons as any of the States now existing shall think proper to admit, shall not be prohibited by the Congress prior to the Year one thousand eight hundred and eight, but a Tax or duty may be imposed on such Importation, not exceeding ten dollars for each Person.	Essay #67: Migration or Importation Clause
	Cl. 2	The Privilege of the Writ of Habeas Corpus shall not be suspended, unless when in Cases of Rebellion or Invasion the public Safety may require it.	Essay #68: Habeas Corpus Clause
	Cl. 3	No Bill of Attainder or ex post facto Law shall be passed.	Essay #69: Federal Bill of Attainder Clause Essay #70: Federal Ex Post Facto Clause
	Cl. 4	No Capitation, or other direct, Tax shall be laid, [unless in Proportion to the Census or Enumeration herein before directed to be taken.]* * See the Sixteenth Amendment.	Essay #71: Direct Taxes Clause
	Cl. 5	No Tax or Duty shall be laid on Articles exported from any State.	Essay #72: Export Taxation Clause
	Cl. 6	No Preference shall be given by any Regulation of Commerce or Revenue to the Ports of one State over those of another: nor shall Vessels bound to, or from, one State, be obliged to enter, clear, or pay Duties in another.	Essay #73: Port Preference Clause
	Cl. 7	No Money shall be drawn from the Treasury, but in Consequence of Appropriations made by Law; and a regular Statement and Account of the Receipts and Expenditures of all public Money shall be published from time to time.	Essay #74: Appropriations Clause
	Cl. 8	No Title of Nobility shall be granted by the United States: And no Person holding any Office of Profit or Trust under them, shall, without the Consent of the Congress, accept of any present, Emolument, Office, or Title, of any kind whatever, from any King, Prince, or foreign State.	Essay #75: Federal Title of Nobility Clause Essay #76: Foreign Emoluments Clause

(Continued . . .)

Sec. 10	*Cl. 1*	No State shall enter into any Treaty, Alliance, or Confederation; grant Letters of Marque and Reprisal; coin Money; emit Bills of Credit; make any Thing but gold and silver Coin a Tender in Payment of Debts; pass any Bill of Attainder, ex post facto Law, or Law impairing the Obligation of Contracts, or grant any Title of Nobility.	Essay #77: State Treaty Clause Essay #78: State Marque and Reprisal Clause Essay #79: State Money Clause Essay #80: State Bill of Attainder Clause Essay #81: State Ex Post Facto Clause Essay #82: Obligation of Contracts Clause Essay #83: State Title of Nobility Clause
	Cl. 2	No State shall, without the Consent of the Congress, lay any Imposts or Duties on Imports or Exports, except what may be absolutely necessary for executing its inspection Laws: and the net Produce of all Duties and Imposts, laid by any State on Imports or Exports, shall be for the Use of the Treasury of the United States; and all such Laws shall be subject to the Revision and Controul of the Congress.	Essay #84: Import-Export Clause
	Cl. 3	No State shall, without the Consent of Congress, lay any Duty of Tonnage, keep Troops, or Ships of War in time of Peace, enter into any Agreement or Compact with another State, or with a foreign Power, or engage in War, unless actually invaded, or in such imminent Danger as will not admit of delay.	Essay #85: Tonnage Clause Essay #86: Troops, Ships of War, Compact, and Invasion Clause
Article II				
Sec. 1	*Cl. 1*	The executive Power shall be vested in a President of the United States of America. He shall hold his Office during the Term of four Years, and, together with the Vice President, chosen for the same Term, be elected, as follows:	Essay #87: Executive Vesting Clause Essay #88: Presidential Term Clause Essay #89: Vice Presidential Term Clause

(Continued . . .)

Sec. 1	*Cl. 2*	Each State shall appoint, in such Manner as the Legislature thereof may direct, a Number of Electors, equal to the whole Number of Senators and Representatives to which the State may be entitled in the Congress: but no Senator or Representative, or Person holding an Office of Trust or Profit under the United States, shall be appointed an Elector.	Essay #90: Presidential Electors Clause Essay #91: Elector Incompatibility Clause
	Cl. 3	[The Electors shall meet in their respective States, and vote by Ballot for two Persons, of whom one at least shall not be an Inhabitant of the same State with themselves. And they shall make a List of all the Persons voted for, and of the Number of Votes for each; which List they shall sign and certify, and transmit sealed to the Seat of the Government of the United States, directed to the President of the Senate. The President of the Senate shall, in the Presence of the Senate and House of Representatives, open all the Certificates, and the Votes shall then be counted. The Person having the greatest Number of Votes shall be the President, if such Number be a Majority of the whole Number of Electors appointed; and if there be more than one who have such Majority, and have an equal Number of Votes, then the House of Representatives shall immediately chuse by Ballot one of them for President; and if no Person have a Majority, then from the five highest on the List the said House shall in like Manner chuse the President. But in chusing the President, the Votes shall be taken by States, the Representation from each State having one Vote; A quorum for this Purpose shall consist of a Member or Members from two thirds of the States, and a Majority of all the States shall be necessary to a Choice. In every Case, after the Choice of the President, the Person having the greatest Number of Votes of the Electors shall be the Vice President. But if there should remain two or more who have equal Votes, the Senate shall chuse from them by Ballot the Vice President.]* * Changed by the Twelfth Amendment.	Essay #92: Electoral Meeting Clause Essay #93: Electoral Vote Counting Clause Essay #94: Presidential Majority and Contingent Elections Clause
	Cl. 4	The Congress may determine the Time of chusing the Electors, and the Day on which they shall give their Votes; which Day shall be the same throughout the United States.	Essay #95: Presidential Electors Timing Clause
	Cl. 5	No Person except a natural born Citizen, or a Citizen of the United States, at the time of the Adoption of this Constitution, shall be eligible to the Office of President; neither shall any person be eligible to that Office who shall not have attained to the Age of thirty five Years, and been fourteen Years a Resident within the United States.	Essay #96: Presidential Eligibility Clause

Sec. 1	*Cl. 6*	[In Case of the Removal of the President from Office, or of his Death, Resignation, or Inability to discharge the Powers and Duties of the said Office, the Same shall devolve on the Vice President, and the Congress may by Law provide for the Case of Removal, Death, Resignation or Inability, both of the President and Vice President, declaring what Officer shall then act as President, and such Officer shall act accordingly, until the Disability be removed, or a President shall be elected.]* * Changed by the Twenty-Fifth Amendment.	Essay #97: Presidential Succession - Devolve Clause Essay #98: Presidential Succession - Congress Clause
	Cl. 7	The President shall, at stated Times, receive for his Services, a Compensation, which shall neither be increased nor diminished during the Period for which he shall have been elected, and he shall not receive within that Period any other Emolument from the United States, or any of them.	Essay #99: Presidential Compensation Clause Essay #100: Domestic Emoluments Clause
	Cl. 8	Before he enter on the Execution of his Office, he shall take the following Oath or Affirmation: "I do solemnly swear (or affirm) that I will faithfully execute the Office of President of the United States, and will to the best of my Ability, preserve, protect and defend the Constitution of the United States."	Essay #101: Presidential Oath of Office Clause
Sec. 2	*Cl. 1*	The President shall be Commander in Chief of the Army and Navy of the United States, and of the Militia of the several States, when called into the actual Service of the United States; he may require the Opinion, in writing, of the principal Officer in each of the executive Departments, upon any Subject relating to the Duties of their respective Offices, and he shall have Power to grant Reprieves and Pardons for Offenses against the United States, except in Cases of Impeachment.	Essay #102: Commander in Chief Clause Essay #103: Commander of the Militia Clause Essay #104: Opinion Clause Essay #105: Pardon Clause
	Cl. 2	He shall have Power, by and with the Advice and Consent of the Senate, to make Treaties, provided two thirds of the Senators present concur; and he shall nominate, and by and with the Advice and Consent of the Senate, shall appoint Ambassadors, other public Ministers and Consuls, Judges of the supreme Court, and all other Officers of the United States, whose Appointments are not herein otherwise provided for, and which shall be established by Law: but the Congress may by Law vest the Appointment of such inferior Officers, as they think proper, in the President alone, in the Courts of Law, or in the Heads of Departments.	Essay #106: Treaty Clause Essay #107: Appointments Clause Essay #108: Inferior Officers Appointments Clause

(Continued . . .)

Sec. 2	*Cl. 3*	The President shall have Power to fill up all Vacancies that may happen during the Recess of the Senate, by granting Commissions which shall expire at the End of their next Session.	Essay #109: Recess Appointments Clause
Sec. 3		He shall from time to time give to the Congress Information of the State of the Union, and recommend to their Consideration such Measures as he shall judge necessary and expedient; he may, on extraordinary Occasions, convene both Houses, or either of them, and in Case of Disagreement between them, with Respect to the Time of Adjournment, he may adjourn them to such Time as he shall think proper; he shall receive Ambassadors and other public Ministers; he shall take Care that the Laws be faithfully executed, and shall Commission all the Officers of the United States.	Essay #110: State of the Union Clause Essay #111: Recommendation Clause Essay #112: Presidential Convening Clause Essay #113: Presidential Adjournment Clause Essay #114: Ambassadors Clause Essay #115: Take Care Clause Essay #116: Commissions Clause
Sec. 4		The President, Vice President and all civil Officers of the United States, shall be removed from Office on Impeachment for, and Conviction of, Treason, Bribery, or other high Crimes and Misdemeanors.	Essay #117: Impeachment Clause
Article III			
Sec. 1		The judicial Power of the United States, shall be vested in one supreme Court, and in such inferior Courts as the Congress may from time to time ordain and establish. The Judges, both of the supreme and inferior Courts, shall hold their Offices during good Behaviour, and shall, at stated Times, receive for their Services, a Compensation, which shall not be diminished during their Continuance in Office.	Essay #118: Judicial Vesting Clause Essay #119: Supreme Court Vesting Clause Essay #120: Inferior Courts Clause Essay #121: Good Behavior Clause Essay #122: Judicial Compensation Clause

(Continued . . .)

Sec. 2	*Cl. 1*	The judicial Power shall extend to all Cases, in Law and Equity, arising under this Constitution, the Laws of the United States, and Treaties made, or which shall be made, under their Authority; — to all Cases affecting Ambassadors, other public Ministers and Consuls; — to all Cases of admiralty and maritime Jurisdiction; — to Controversies to which the United States shall be a Party; — to Controversies between two or more States; — [between a State and Citizens of another State;]* — between Citizens of different States; — between Citizens of the same State claiming Lands under Grants of different States, [and between a State, or the Citizens thereof, and foreign States, Citizens or Subjects.]* *Changed by the Eleventh Amendment.	Essay #123: Judicial Power - Law & Equity Clause Essay #124: Judicial Power - Arising Under Clause Essay #125: Judicial Power - Treaties Clause Essay #126: Judicial Power - Ambassadors Clause Essay #127: Judicial Power - Admiralty Clause Essay #128: Judicial Power - Federal Party Clause Essay #129: Judicial Power - Interstate Controversies Clause Essay #130: Judicial Power - Citizen–State Diversity Clause Essay #131: Judicial Power - Diversity of Citizenship Clause Essay #132: Judicial Power - Land Grant Jurisdiction Clause Essay #133: Judicial Power - Foreign Diversity Clause

(Continued . . .)

Sec. 2	*Cl. 2*	In all Cases affecting Ambassadors, other public Ministers and Consuls, and those in which a State shall be Party, the supreme Court shall have original Jurisdiction. In all the other Cases before mentioned, the supreme Court shall have appellate Jurisdiction, both as to Law and Fact, with such Exceptions, and under such Regulations as the Congress shall make.	Essay #134: Original Jurisdiction Clause Essay #135: Appellate Jurisdiction Clause
	Cl. 3	The Trial of all Crimes, except in Cases of Impeachment; shall be by Jury; and such Trial shall be held in the State where the said Crimes shall have been committed; but when not committed within any State, the Trial shall be at such Place or Places as the Congress may by Law have directed.	Essay #136: Criminal Trials Clause
Sec. 3	*Cl. 1*	Treason against the United States, shall consist only in levying War against them, or in adhering to their Enemies, giving them Aid and Comfort. No Person shall be convicted of Treason unless on the Testimony of two Witnesses to the same overt Act, or on Confession in open Court.	Essay #137: Treason Clause
	Cl. 2	The Congress shall have Power to declare the Punishment of Treason, but no Attainder of Treason shall work Corruption of Blood, or Forfeiture except during the Life of the Person attainted.	Essay #138: Punishment of Treason Clause

Article IV

Sec. 1		Full Faith and Credit shall be given in each State to the public Acts, Records, and judicial Proceedings of every other State. And the Congress may by general Laws prescribe the Manner in which such Acts, Records and Proceedings shall be proved, and the Effect thereof.	Essay #139: Full Faith and Credit Clause
Sec. 2	*Cl. 1*	The Citizens of each State shall be entitled to all Privileges and Immunities of Citizens in the several States.	Essay #140: Privileges and Immunities Clause
	Cl. 2	A Person charged in any State with Treason, Felony, or other Crime, who shall flee from Justice, and be found in another State, shall on Demand of the executive Authority of the State from which he fled, be delivered up, to be removed to the State having Jurisdiction of the Crime.	Essay #141: Fugitive from Justice Clause
	Cl. 3	[No Person held to Service or Labour in one State, under the Laws thereof, escaping into another, shall, in Consequence of any Law or Regulation therein, be discharged from such Service or Labour, but shall be delivered up on Claim of the Party to whom such Service or Labour may be due.] * * Changed by the Thirteenth Amendment.	Essay #142: Fugitive Slave Clause

(Continued . . .)

Sec. 3	*Cl. 1*	New States may be admitted by the Congress into this Union; but no new State shall be formed or erected within the Jurisdiction of any other State; nor any State be formed by the Junction of two or more States, or Parts of States, without the Consent of the Legislatures of the States concerned as well as of the Congress.		Essay #143: Admissions Clause
	Cl. 2	The Congress shall have Power to dispose of and make all needful Rules and Regulations respecting the Territory or other Property belonging to the United States; and nothing in this Constitution shall be so construed as to Prejudice any Claims of the United States, or of any particular State.		Essay #144: Territories Clause Essay #145: Property Clause Essay #146: Claims Clause
Sec. 4		The United States shall guarantee to every State in this Union a Republican Form of Government, and shall protect each of them against Invasion; and on Application of the Legislature, or of the Executive (when the Legislature cannot be convened) against domestic Violence.		Essay #147: Guarantee Clause

Article V

		The Congress, whenever two thirds of both Houses shall deem it necessary, shall propose Amendments to this Constitution, or, on the Application of the Legislatures of two thirds of the several States, shall call a Convention for proposing Amendments, which, in either Case, shall be valid to all Intents and Purposes, as Part of this Constitution, when ratified by the Legislatures of three fourths of the several States, or by Conventions in three fourths thereof, as the one or the other Mode of Ratification may be proposed by the Congress; Provided that no Amendment which may be made prior to the Year One thousand eight hundred and eight shall in any Manner affect the first and fourth Clauses in the Ninth Section of the first Article; and that no State, without its Consent, shall be deprived of its equal Suffrage in the Senate.		Essay #148: Amendments - Congressional Proposal Clause Essay #149: Amendments - Convention Proposal Clause Essay #150: Amendments - Ratification Process Essay #151: Prohibition on Amendment - Migration, Importation, and Apportionment Essay #152: Prohibition on Amendment - Equal Suffrage of the States

(Continued . . .)

		Article VI	
	Cl.1	All Debts contracted and Engagements entered into, before the Adoption of this Constitution, shall be as valid against the United States under this Constitution, as under the Confederation.	Essay #153: Debts and Engagements Clause
	Cl. 2	This Constitution, and the Laws of the United States which shall be made in Pursuance thereof; and all Treaties made, or which shall be made, under the Authority of the United States, shall be the supreme Law of the Land; and the Judges in every State shall be bound thereby, any Thing in the Constitution or Laws of any State to the Contrary notwithstanding.	Essay #154: Supremacy Clause
	Cl. 3	The Senators and Representatives before mentioned, and the Members of the several State Legislatures, and all executive and judicial Officers, both of the United States and of the several States, shall be bound by Oath or Affirmation, to support this Constitution; but no religious Test shall ever be required as a Qualification to any Office or public Trust under the United States.	Essay #155: Oath or Affirmation Clause Essay #156: Religious Test Clause
		Article VII	
	Cl. 1	The Ratification of the Conventions of nine States, shall be sufficient for the Establishment of this Constitution between the States so ratifying the Same.	Essay #157: Ratification Clause
	Cl. 2	Done in Convention by the Unanimous Consent of the States present the Seventeenth Day of September in the Year of our Lord one thousand seven hundred and Eighty seven and of the Independence of the United States of America the Twelfth. In Witness whereof We have hereunto subscribed our Names, Attest William Jackson Secretary	Essay #158: Attestation Clause

(Continued . . .)

G°. Washington
Presidt and deputy from Virginia

Delaware {
Geo: Read
Gunning Bedford jun
John Dickinson
Richard Bassett
Jaco: Broom

New Hampshire {
John Langdon
Nicholas Gilman

Maryland {
James McHenry
Dan of St Thos. Jenifer
Danl. Carroll

Massachusetts {
Nathaniel Gorham
Rufus King

Virginia {
John Blair
James Madison Jr.

Connecticut {
Wm. Saml. Johnson
Roger Sherman

North Carolina {
Wm. Blount
Richd. Dobbs Spaight
Hu Williamson

New York {
Alexander Hamilton

South Carolina {
J. Rutledge
Charles Cotesworth Pinckney
Charles Pinckney
Pierce Butler

New Jersey {
Wil: Livingston
David Brearley
Wm. Paterson
Jona: Dayton

Georgia {
William Few
Abr Baldwin

Pennsylvania {
B Franklin
Thomas Mifflin
Robt. Morris
Geo. Clymer
Thos. FitzSimons
Jared Ingersoll
James Wilson
Gouv Morris

THE AMENDMENTS

Am. I	Congress shall make no law respecting an establishment of religion, or prohibiting the free exercise thereof; or abridging the freedom of speech, or of the press; or the right of the people peaceably to assemble, and to petition the Government for a redress of grievances.	Essay #159: Establishment Clause Essay #160: Free Exercise of Religion Clause Essay #161: Freedom of Speech and of the Press Clause Essay #162: Freedom of Assembly Clause Essay #163: Freedom of Petition Clause
Am. II	A well regulated Militia, being necessary to the security of a free State, the right of the people to keep and bear Arms, shall not be infringed.	Essay #164: Right to Keep and Bear Arms Amendment
Am. III	No Soldier shall, in time of peace be quartered in any house, without the consent of the Owner, nor in time of war, but in a manner to be prescribed by law.	Essay #165: Quartering Troops Amendment
Am. IV	The right of the people to be secure in their persons, houses, papers, and effects, against unreasonable searches and seizures, shall not be violated, and no Warrants shall issue, but upon probable cause, supported by Oath or affirmation, and particularly describing the place to be searched, and the persons or things to be seized.	Essay #166: Unreasonable Searches and Seizures Clause Essay #167: Warrant Clause
Am. V	No person shall be held to answer for a capital, or otherwise infamous crime, unless on a presentment or indictment of a Grand Jury, except in cases arising in the land or naval forces, or in the Militia, when in actual service in time of War or public danger; nor shall any person be subject for the same offence to be twice put in jeopardy of life or limb; nor shall be compelled in any criminal case to be a witness against himself, nor be deprived of life, liberty, or property, without due process of law; nor shall private property be taken for public use, without just compensation.	Essay #168: Grand Jury Requirement Clause Essay #169: Grand Jury Exceptions Clause Essay #170: Double Jeopardy Clause Essay #171: Self-Incrimination Clause Essay #172: Due Process Clause Essay #173: Takings Clause

(Continued . . .)

		Essay #174: Speedy Trial Clause
Am. VI	In all criminal prosecutions, the accused shall enjoy the right to a speedy and public trial, by an impartial jury of the State and district wherein the crime shall have been committed, which district shall have been previously ascertained by law, and to be informed of the nature and cause of the accusation; to be confronted with the witnesses against him; to have compulsory process for obtaining witnesses in his favor, and to have the Assistance of Counsel for his defence.	Essay #175: Public Trial Clause
		Essay #176: Jury Trial Clause
		Essay #177: Vicinage Clause
		Essay #178: Informed of Accusation (Arraignment) Clause
		Essay #179: Confrontation Clause
		Essay #180: Compulsory Process Clause
		Essay #181: Right-to-Counsel Clause
Am. VII	In suits at common law, where the value in controversy shall exceed twenty dollars, the right of trial by jury shall be preserved, and no fact tried by a jury, shall be otherwise reexamined in any Court of the United States, than according to the rules of the common law.	Essay #182: Civil Jury Trial Clause
		Essay #183: Re-examination Clause
Am. VIII	Excessive bail shall not be required, nor excessive fines imposed, nor cruel and unusual punishments inflicted.	Essay #184: Excessive Bail Clause
		Essay #185: Excessive Fines Clause
		Essay #186: Cruel and Unusual Punishments Clause
Am. IX	The enumeration in the Constitution, of certain rights, shall not be construed to deny or disparage others retained by the people.	Essay #187: Ninth Amendment
Am. X	The powers not delegated to the United States by the Constitution, nor prohibited by it to the States, are reserved to the States respectively, or to the people.	Essay #188: Tenth Amendment
Am. XI	The Judicial power of the United States shall not be construed to extend to any suit in law or equity, commenced or prosecuted against one of the United States by Citizens of another State, or by Citizens or Subjects of any Foreign State.	Essay #189: Eleventh Amendment

(Continued . . .)

Am. XII	The Electors shall meet in their respective states and vote by ballot for President and Vice-President, one of whom, at least, shall not be an inhabitant of the same state with themselves; they shall name in their ballots the person voted for as President, and in distinct ballots the person voted for as Vice-President, and they shall make distinct lists of all persons voted for as President, and of all persons voted for as Vice-President, and of the number of votes for each, which lists they shall sign and certify, and transmit sealed to the seat of the government of the United States, directed to the President of the Senate; — the President of the Senate shall, in the presence of the Senate and House of Representatives, open all the certificates and the votes shall then be counted; — The person having the greatest number of votes for President, shall be the President, if such number be a majority of the whole number of Electors appointed; and if no person have such majority, then from the persons having the highest numbers not exceeding three on the list of those voted for as President, the House of Representatives shall choose immediately, by ballot, the President. But in choosing the President, the votes shall be taken by states, the representation from each state having one vote; a quorum for this purpose shall consist of a member or members from two-thirds of the states, and a majority of all the states shall be necessary to a choice. [And if the House of Representatives shall not choose a President whenever the right of choice shall devolve upon them, before the fourth day of March next following, then the Vice-President shall act as President, as in case of the death or other constitutional disability of the President.]* — The person having the greatest number of votes as Vice-President, shall be the Vice-President, if such number be a majority of the whole number of Electors appointed, and if no person have a majority, then from the two highest numbers on the list, the Senate shall choose the Vice-President; a quorum for the purpose shall consist of two-thirds of the whole number of Senators, and a majority of the whole number shall be necessary to a choice. But no person constitutionally ineligible to the office of President shall be eligible to that of Vice-President of the United States. * Changed by Section 3 of the Twentieth Amendment.	Essay #190: Twelfth Amendment

(Continued . . .)

Am. XIII	*Sec. 1*	Neither slavery nor involuntary servitude, except as a punishment for crime whereof the party shall have been duly convicted, shall exist within the United States, or any place subject to their jurisdiction.	Essay #191: Thirteenth Amendment
	Sec. 2	Congress shall have power to enforce this article by appropriate legislation.	
Am. XIV	*Sec. 1*	All persons born or naturalized in the United States, and subject to the jurisdiction thereof, are citizens of the United States and of the State wherein they reside. No State shall make or enforce any law which shall abridge the privileges or immunities of citizens of the United States; nor shall any State deprive any person of life, liberty, or property, without due process of law; nor deny to any person within its jurisdiction the equal protection of the laws.	Essay #192: Citizenship Clause Essay #193: State Action Clause Essay #194: Privileges or Immunities Clause Essay #195: Due Process Clause Essay #196: Equal Protection Clause
	Sec. 2	Representatives shall be apportioned among the several States according to their respective numbers, counting the whole number of persons in each State, excluding Indians not taxed. But when the right to vote at any election for the choice of electors for President and Vice-President of the United States, Representatives in Congress, the Executive and Judicial officers of a State, or the members of the Legislature thereof, is denied to any of the male inhabitants of such State, being twenty-one years of age, and citizens of the United States, or in any way abridged, except for participation in rebellion, or other crime, the basis of representation therein shall be reduced in the proportion which the number of such male citizens shall bear to the whole number of male citizens twenty-one years of age in such State.	Essay #197: Apportionment of Representatives Clause
	Sec. 3	No person shall be a Senator or Representative in Congress, or elector of President and Vice-President, or hold any office, civil or military, under the United States, or under any State, who, having previously taken an oath, as a member of Congress, or as an officer of the United States, or as a member of any State legislature, or as an executive or judicial officer of any State, to support the Constitution of the United States, shall have engaged in insurrection or rebellion against the same, or given aid or comfort to the enemies thereof. But Congress may by a vote of two-thirds of each House, remove such disability.	Essay #198: Insurrection or Rebellion Clause

(Continued . . .)

		The validity of the public debt of the United States, authorized by law, including debts incurred for payment of pensions and bounties for services in suppressing insurrection or rebellion, shall not be questioned. But neither the United States nor any State shall assume or pay any debt or obligation incurred in aid of insurrection or rebellion against the United States, or any claim for the loss or emancipation of any slave; but all such debts, obligations and claims shall be held illegal and void.	Essay #199: Public Debt Clause
Am. XIV	*Sec. 4*		
	Sec. 5	The Congress shall have the power to enforce, by appropriate legislation, the provisions of this article.	Essay #200: Enforcement Clause
Am. XV	*Sec. 1*	The right of citizens of the United States to vote shall not be denied or abridged by the United States or by any State on account of race, color, or previous condition of servitude.	Essay #201: Fifteenth Amendment
	Sec. 2	The Congress shall have the power to enforce this article by appropriate legislation.	
Am. XVI		The Congress shall have power to lay and collect taxes on incomes, from whatever source derived, without apportionment among the several States, and without regard to any census or enumeration.	Essay #202: Income Tax Amendment
Am. XVII	*Cl. 1*	The Senate of the United States shall be composed of two Senators from each State, elected by the people thereof, for six years; and each Senator shall have one vote. The electors in each State shall have the qualifications requisite for electors of the most numerous branch of the State legislatures.	Essay #203: Popular Election of Senators Amendment
	Cl. 2	When vacancies happen in the representation of any State in the Senate, the executive authority of such State shall issue writs of election to fill such vacancies: Provided, That the legislature of any State may empower the executive thereof to make temporary appointments until the people fill the vacancies by election as the legislature may direct.	Essay #204: Senate Vacancies Amendment
	Cl. 3	This amendment shall not be so construed as to affect the election or term of any Senator chosen before it becomes valid as part of the Constitution.	
Am. XVIII*	*Sec. 1*	After one year from the ratification of this article the manufacture, sale, or transportation of intoxicating liquors within, the importation thereof into, or the exportation thereof from the United States and all territory subject to the jurisdiction thereof for beverage purposes is hereby prohibited.	Essay #205: Prohibition Amendment
	Sec. 2	The Congress and the several States shall have concurrent power to enforce this article by appropriate legislation.	

(Continued . . .)

Am. XVIII*	*Sec. 3*	This article shall be inoperative unless it shall have been ratified as an amendment to the Constitution by the legislatures of the several States, as provided in the Constitution, within seven years from the date of the submission hereof to the States by the Congress. * Repealed by the Twenty-First Amendment.	
Am. IX		The right of citizens of the United States to vote shall not be denied or abridged by the United States or by any State on account of sex. Congress shall have power to enforce this article by appropriate legislation.	Essay #206: Suffrage Amendment
Am. XX	*Sec. 1*	The terms of the President and the Vice President shall end at noon on the 20th day of January, and the terms of Senators and Representatives at noon on the 3d day of January, of the years in which such terms would have ended if this article had not been ratified; and the terms of their successors shall then begin.	Essay #207: Presidential Terms Amendment
	Sec. 2	The Congress shall assemble at least once in every year, and such meeting shall begin at noon on the 3d day of January, unless they shall by law appoint a different day.	
	Sec. 3	If, at the time fixed for the beginning of the term of the President, the President elect shall have died, the Vice President elect shall become President. If a President shall not have been chosen before the time fixed for the beginning of his term, or if the President elect shall have failed to qualify, then the Vice President elect shall act as President until a President shall have qualified; and the Congress may by law provide for the case wherein neither a President elect nor a Vice President shall have qualified, declaring who shall then act as President, or the manner in which one who is to act shall be selected, and such person shall act accordingly until a President or Vice President shall have qualified.	
	Sec. 4	The Congress may by law provide for the case of the death of any of the persons from whom the House of Representatives may choose a President whenever the right of choice shall have devolved upon them, and for the case of the death of any of the persons from whom the Senate may choose a Vice President whenever the right of choice shall have devolved upon them.	
	Sec. 5	Sections 1 and 2 shall take effect on the 15th day of October following the ratification of this article.	

(Continued . . .)

	Sec. 6	This article shall be inoperative unless it shall have been ratified as an amendment to the Constitution by the legislatures of three-fourths of the several States within seven years from the date of its submission.	
Am. XXI	Sec. 1	The eighteenth article of amendment to the Constitution of the United States is hereby repealed.	Essay #208: Repeal of Prohibition Amendment
	Sec. 2	The transportation or importation into any State, Territory, or Possession of the United States for delivery or use therein of intoxicating liquors, in violation of the laws thereof, is hereby prohibited.	
	Sec. 3	This article shall be inoperative unless it shall have been ratified as an amendment to the Constitution by conventions in the several States, as provided in the Constitution, within seven years from the date of the submission hereof to the States by the Congress.	
Am. XXII	Sec. 1	No person shall be elected to the office of the President more than twice, and no person who has held the office of President, or acted as President, for more than two years of a term to which some other person was elected President shall be elected to the office of President more than once. But this Article shall not apply to any person holding the office of President when this Article was proposed by Congress, and shall not prevent any person who may be holding the office of President, or acting as President, during the term within which this Article becomes operative from holding the office of President or acting as President during the remainder of such term.	Essay #209: Presidential Term Limit Amendment
	Sec. 2	This article shall be inoperative unless it shall have been ratified as an amendment to the Constitution by the legislatures of three-fourths of the several States within seven years from the date of its submission to the States by the Congress.	
Am. XXVIII	Sec. 1	The District constituting the seat of Government of the United States shall appoint in such manner as Congress may direct: A number of electors of President and Vice President equal to the whole number of Senators and Representatives in Congress to which the District would be entitled if it were a State, but in no event more than the least populous State; they shall be in addition to those appointed by the States, but they shall be considered, for the purposes of the election of President and Vice President, to be electors appointed by a State; and they shall meet in the District and perform such duties as provided by the twelfth article of amendment.	Essay #210: District of Columbia Electors Amendment
	Sec. 2	The Congress shall have power to enforce this article by appropriate legislation.	

(Continued . . .)

Am. XXIV	*Sec. 1*	The right of citizens of the United States to vote in any primary or other election for President or Vice President, for electors for President or Vice President, or for Senator or Representative in Congress, shall not be denied or abridged by the United States or any State by reason of failure to pay poll tax or other tax.	Essay #211: Poll Taxes Amendment
	Sec. 2	The Congress shall have power to enforce this article by appropriate legislation.	
Am. XXV	*Sec. 1*	In case of the removal of the President from office or of his death or resignation, the Vice President shall become President.	Essay #212: Twenty-Fifth Amendment - Sections 1 and 2
	Sec. 2	Whenever there is a vacancy in the office of the Vice President, the President shall nominate a Vice President who shall take office upon confirmation by a majority vote of both Houses of Congress.	
	Sec. 3	Whenever the President transmits to the President pro tempore of the Senate and the Speaker of the House of Representatives his written declaration that he is unable to discharge the powers and duties of his office, and until he transmits to them a written declaration to the contrary, such powers and duties shall be discharged by the Vice President as Acting President.	Essay #213: Twenty-Fifth Amendment - Section 3
	Sec. 4	Whenever the Vice President and a majority of either the principal officers of the executive departments or of such other body as Congress may by law provide, transmit to the President pro tempore of the Senate and the Speaker of the House of Representatives their written declaration that the President is unable to discharge the powers and duties of his office, the Vice President shall immediately assume the powers and duties of the office as Acting President. Thereafter, when the President transmits to the President pro tempore of the Senate and the Speaker of the House of Representatives his written declaration that no inability exists, he shall resume the powers and duties of his office unless the Vice President and a majority of either the principal officers of the executive department or of such other body as Congress may by law provide, transmit within four days to the President pro tempore of the Senate and the Speaker of the House of Representatives their written declaration that the President is unable to discharge the powers and duties of his office. Thereupon Congress shall decide the issue, assembling within forty-eight hours for that purpose if not in session. If the Congress, within twenty-one days after receipt of the latter	Essay #214: Twenty-Fifth Amendment - Section 4

(Continued . . .)

Am. XXV		written declaration, or, if Congress is not in session, within twenty-one days after Congress is required to assemble, determines by two-thirds vote of both Houses that the President is unable to discharge the powers and duties of his office, the Vice President shall continue to discharge the same as Acting President; otherwise, the President shall resume the powers and duties of his office.	
Am. XXVI	*Sec. 1*	The right of citizens of the United States, who are eighteen years of age or older, to vote shall not be denied or abridged by the United States or by any State on account of age.	Essay #215: Minimum Voting Age Amendment
	Sec. 2	The Congress shall have power to enforce this article by appropriate legislation.	
Am. XXVII		No law, varying the compensation for the services of the Senators and Representatives, shall take effect, until an election of representatives shall have intervened.	Essay #216: Congressional Compensation Amendment

Summary of Contents

CONTENTS

Part 3: Article III   439

Part 9: The Correction Amendments 711

Part 10: The Reconstruction Amendments 725

CONTRIBUTORS

John Acton. Former law clerk to Judge Britt C. Grant. *Essay No. 118*

Professor J. Joel Alicea. St. Robert Bellarmine Professor of Law; Director, The Center for the Constitution and the Catholic Intellectual Tradition, Catholic University of America. *Academic Advisory Board*

Justice Samuel A. Alito, Jr. Associate Justice, U.S. Supreme Court. *Essay No. 1*

Francis Aul. Former law clerk to Judge Elizabeth L. Branch. *Essay No. 167*

Professor Stephanie Barclay. Professor, Georgetown University Law Center; Faculty Co-Director, Georgetown Center for the Constitution. *Essay No. 159*

Professor Randy E. Barnett. Patrick Hotung Professor of Constitutional Law, Georgetown University Law Center; Faculty Co-Director, Georgetown Center for the Constitution. *Essay No. 44*

Hon. John F. Bash, III. Co-Chair, Quinn Emanuel's National Appellate Practice; former U.S. Attorney for the Western District of Texas and Assistant Solicitor General. *Essay No. 179*

Professor William Baude. Harry Kalven, Jr. Professor of Law, University of Chicago Law School; Faculty Director of the Constitutional Law Institute. *Essay No. 173*

Judge Carlos T. Bea. Circuit Judge, U.S. Court of Appeals for the Ninth Circuit. *Essay No. 125*

Professor David E. Bernstein. University Professor of Law, Antonin Scalia Law School; Executive Director, Liberty & Law Center. *Essay No. 163*

Judge Stephanos Bibas. Circuit Judge, U.S. Court of Appeals for the Third Circuit. *Judicial Advisory Board*

Joseph Bishop-Henchman. Executive Vice President, National Taxpayers Union Foundation; Adjunct Scholar, Cato Institute. *Essay Nos. 84, 85*

Professor Josh Blackman. Centennial Chair of Constitutional Law, South Texas College of Law Houston; President, The Harlan Institute. *Essay Nos. 33, 34, 76, 91, 98, 100; Senior Editor*

Michael D. Bopp. Partner, Gibson, Dunn & Crutcher LLP; Chair, Congressional Investigations Subgroup; Co-Chair, Public Policy Practice Group. *Essay Nos. 32, 74*

Professor Gerard V. Bradley. Professor Emeritus, Notre Dame Law School; Co-Director, James Wilson Institute. *Essay No. 156*

Judge Elizabeth L. Branch. Circuit Judge, U.S. Court of Appeals for the Eleventh Circuit. *Essay No. 167; Judicial Advisory Board*

Judge Andrew Brasher. Circuit Judge, U.S. Court of Appeals for the Eleventh Circuit. *Essay No. 174*

Judge Michael B. Brennan. Circuit Judge, U.S. Court of Appeals for the Seventh Circuit. *Essay No. 178*

Roy E. "Reb" Brownell II. Author about separation of powers; former Deputy Chief of Staff and Counsel to U.S. Senator Mitch McConnell. *Essay Nos. 18, 19, 89*

Judge Patrick J. Bumatay. Circuit Judge, U.S. Court of Appeals for the Ninth Circuit. *Essay No. 67; Judicial Advisory Board*

James Burnham. President, Vallecito Capital, LLC; Principal at King Street Legal, PLLC; Former General Counsel, U.S. DOGE Service. *Essay Nos. 29, 36, 113*

Judge John K. Bush. Circuit Judge, U.S. Court of Appeals for the Sixth Circuit. *Essay No. 119; Judicial Advisory Board*

Judge Jay S. Bybee. Circuit Judge, U.S. Court of Appeals for the Ninth Circuit. *Essay No. 50*

GianCarlo Canaparo. Senior Legal Fellow, Edwin Meese III Center for Legal and Judicial Studies, The Heritage Foundation. *Essay Nos. 30, 216*

Louis J. Capozzi III. Solicitor General of Missouri; Lecturer in Law, University of Pennsylvania Carey School of Law. *Essay Nos. 29, 36, 113*

Judge Joel M. Carson III. Circuit Judge, U.S. Court of Appeals for the Tenth Circuit. *Essay No. 180*

David W. Casazza. Senior Associate, Appellate and Constitutional Law Practice Group, Gibson, Dunn & Crutcher LLP. *Essay No. 83*

Lee A. Casey. Partner, BakerHostetler; former Office of Legal Policy (1986–90) and Office of Legal Counsel (1992–93). *Essay Nos. 64, 65*

Professor Paul G. Cassell. Distinguished Professor, University of Utah College of Law; former District Court Judge, U.S. District Court for the District of Utah. *Essay No. 171*

Professor Nathan S. Chapman. Associate Dean for Faculty Development & A. Gus Cleveland Distinguished Chair of Law, University of Georgia School of Law. *Essay No. 195*

Jacob B. Chefitz. Associate, Simpson Thacher & Bartlett LLP; former intern to Judge Matthew H. Solomson. *Essay No. 72*

Professor Eric A. Chiappinelli. Frank McDonald Endowed Professor of Law Emeritus, Texas Tech School of Law. *Essay No. 49*

Hon. Paul D. Clement. Partner, Clement & Murphy PLLC; Adjunct Professor, Georgetown University Law Center; Forty-Third Solicitor General of the United States. *Practitioner Advisory Board*

Hon. Charles J. Cooper. Chairman and Founding Partner, Cooper & Kirk, PLLC; former

Assistant Attorney General, Office of Legal Counsel. *Essay No. 188*

Professor Michael R. Dimino. Professor of Law, Widener University Commonwealth Law School. *Essay Nos. 11, 203, 215*

Jack Buckley DiSorbo. Former law clerk to Judges Jennifer Walker Elrod and Charles R. Eskridge. *Essay No. 122*

Professor Tabatha Abu El-Haj. Professor of Law, Drexel University, Kline School of Law. *Essay No. 162*

Judge Jennifer Walker Elrod. Chief Judge, U.S. Court of Appeals for the Fifth Circuit. *Essay No. 122; Judicial Advisory Board*

Hon. Steven A. Engel. Partner, Dechert LLP; former Assistant Attorney General, Office of Legal Counsel. *Practitioner Advisory Board*

Judge Kurt D. Engelhardt. Circuit Judge, U.S. Court of Appeals for the Fifth Circuit. *Essay Nos. 136, 176*

Professor Richard A. Epstein. Laurence A. Tisch Professor of Law, NYU School of Law; Director, Classical Liberal Institute. *Essay No. 82*

Jack Fitzhenry. Legal Fellow, Edwin Meese III Center for Legal and Judicial Studies. *Associate Editor*

Professor John D. Feerick. Professor and former Dean, Fordham University School of Law; Helped craft and frame the Twenty-Fifth Amendment. *Essay Nos. 97, 212, 213, 214*

Ethan Foster. Former law clerk to Judge Lawrence VanDyke. *Essay No. 132*

Hon. Noel J. Francisco. Partner, Jones Day; Forty-Seventh Solicitor General of the United States. *Practitioner Advisory Board*

C. Towner French. Managing Director, Cozen O'Connor Public Strategies. *Essay Nos. 13, 28*

Todd F. Gaziano. President, Center for Individual Rights; former Office of Legal Counsel and U.S. Commission on Civil Rights. *Essay No. 104*

Greta Gieseke. Former law clerk to Judge Kurt D. Engelhardt. *Essay No. 176*

Professor Michael J. Gerhardt. Burton Craige Distinguished Professor of Jurisprudence, University of North Carolina School of Law. *Essay Nos. 14, 20, 21, 117*

Patrick J. Glen. Adjunct Professor, Georgetown University Law Center; Senior Litigation Counsel, Office of Immigration Litigation, U.S. Department of Justice. *Essay No. 46*

Martin B. Gold. Partner, Capitol Counsel, LLC; former Floor Adviser and Counsel, Office of Senate Majority Leader Bill Frist. *Essay Nos. 15, 16, 17, 37*

Judge Britt C. Grant. Circuit Judge, U.S. Court of Appeals for the Eleventh Circuit. *Essay No. 118; Judicial Advisory Board*

Professor Christopher R. Green. Associate Director, Salmon P. Chase Center for Civics, Culture, and Society; Professor of Law, Moritz College of Law, The Ohio State University. *Essay No. 196*

Professor Andy Grewal. Orville L. and Ermina D. Dykstra Professor in Income Tax Law, University of Iowa College of Law. *Essay Nos. 35, 39, 71, 202*

Jenna Hageman. Program Assistant, Institute for Constitutional Government, The Heritage Foundation. *Managing Editor*

Stephen J. Hammer. Associate, Appellate and Constitutional Law Practice Group, Gibson, Dunn & Crutcher LLP. *Essay No. 83*

Chase T. Harrington. Associate, Torridon Law PLLC; former Deputy Associate Counsel to the President (2019–21). *Essay Nos. 114, 126*

Sarah M. Harris. *Practitioner Advisory Board*

Ian Brinton Hatch. Former law clerk to Judge Kurt D. Engelhardt. *Essay No. 176*

Tara Helfman. Partner, Torridon Law PLLC; former Associate Counsel and Special Assistant to President Trump; former Tenured Associate Professor, Syracuse University College of Law. *Essay No. 99*

James A. Heilpern. Research Fellow, Georgetown Center for the Constitution; President, Judicial Education Institute. *Essay No. 4*

Professor Arthur D. Hellman. Professor of Law (Emeritus), University of Pittsburgh School of Law. *Essay No. 124*

Professor Andrew Hessick. Judge John J. Parker Distinguished Professor of Law, University of North Carolina School of Law. *Essay Nos. 53, 120*

Allyson N. Ho. Co-Chair, Appellate and Constitutional Law Practice Group, Gibson, Dunn & Crutcher LLP. *Essay Nos. 75, 83; Practitioner Advisory Board*

Judge James C. Ho. Circuit Judge, U.S. Court of Appeals for the Fifth Circuit. *Judicial Advisory Board*

Judge Ryan T. Holte. Judge, U.S. Court of Federal Claims; Jurist-in-Residence Professor of Law, University of Akron School of Law. *Essay No. 145*

Thomas G. Hungar. Partner, Gibson, Dunn & Crutcher LLP; former General Counsel, U.S. House of Representatives (2016–19). *Essay Nos. 32, 74*

William M. Jay. Partner, Appellate & Supreme Court Litigation, Goodwin Procter LLP; former Assistant Solicitor General. *Practitioner Advisory Board*

Judge Edith H. Jones. Circuit Judge, U.S. Court of Appeals for the Fifth Circuit. *Essay No. 206; Judicial Advisory Board*

Professor Brian C. Kalt. Professor of Law and the Harold Norris Faculty Scholar, Michigan

State University College of Law. *Essay Nos. 177, 207*

Professor John P. Kaminski. Director, Center for the Study of the American Constitution, University of Wisconsin-Madison; Co-Editor of The Documentary History of the Ratification of the Constitution (1970-present). *Essay Nos. 157, 158*

Judge Gregory G. Katsas. Circuit Judge, U.S. Court of Appeals for the D.C. Circuit. *Essay Nos. 101, 155; Judicial Advisory Board*

Scott A. Keller. Partner, Lehotsky Keller Cohn LLP; former Chief Counsel, Senator Ted Cruz. *Essay No. 96; Practitioner Advisory Board*

Professor Orin S. Kerr. Professor, Stanford Law School. *Essay No. 166*

Elizabeth A. Kiernan. Senior Associate, Appellate and Constitutional Law Practice Group, Gibson, Dunn & Crutcher LLP. *Essay No. 75*

Professor Eugene Kontorovich. Professor of Law, Antonin Scalia Law School; Senior Research Fellow, Margaret Thatcher Center for Freedom, The Heritage Foundation. *Essay Nos. 43, 54, 55*

Professor Julian G. Ku. Maurice A. Deane Distinguished Professor in Constitutional Law, Maurice A. Deane School of Law at Hofstra University. *Essay Nos. 77, 86*

Hon. Christopher T. Landau. United States Deputy Secretary of State; former United States Ambassador to Mexico. *Essay Nos. 114, 126*

Paul J. Larkin. Rumpel Senior Legal Research Fellow, Edwin Meese III Center for Legal and Judicial Studies, The Heritage Foundation. *Essay Nos. 105, 205, 208*

Judge Joan L. Larsen. Circuit Judge, U.S. Court of Appeals for the Sixth Circuit. *Judicial Advisory Board*

Professor Kurt T. Lash. E. Claiborne Robins Distinguished Professor of Law, University of Richmond School of Law. *Essay Nos. 191, 192, 194*

Professor Gary S. Lawson. Levin, Mabie & Levin Professor of Law, University of Florida Levin College of Law. *Essay Nos. 5, 66, 143, 144, 154, 172; Academic Advisory Board*

Professor Thomas H. Lee. Leitner Family Professor of International Law, Fordham University School of Law; Special Counsel, Hughes, Hubbard & Reed LLP. *Essay No. 127*

Judge Kenneth K. Lee. Circuit Judge, U.S. Court of Appeals for the Ninth Circuit. *Essay No. 128*

Professor Robert Leider. Professor, Antonin Scalia Law School. *Essay Nos. 59, 60, 61, 62, 63, 103, 169*

Sarah Leitner. Associate, Supreme Court and Appellate Litigation Group, Skadden, Arps, Slate, Meagher & Flom LLP. *Essay No. 173*

Professor Renée Lettow Lerner. Legal historian and the Donald Phillip Rothschild Research Professor of Law, George Washington University Law School. *Essay Nos. 182, 183*

Seth J. Lucas. Former Senior Research Associate, Edwin Meese III Center for Legal and Judicial Studies, The Heritage Foundation. *Essay No. 133; Associate Editor*

Professor Nelson Lund. Distinguished University Professor, Antonin Scalia Law School. *Essay Nos. 41, 73, 164; Academic Advisory Board*

Robert Luther III. Distinguished Professor of Law, Antonin Scalia Law School; former Associate Counsel to the President; former Counsel on the U.S. Senate Judiciary Committee. *Essay No. 116*

J. Andrew Mackenzie. Former law clerk to Judge Jennifer Walker Elrod. *Essay No. 122*

Judge Gregory E. Maggs. Judge, U.S. Court of Appeals for the Armed Forces; Professorial

Lecturer in Law, George Washington University Law School. *Essay Nos. 59, 60, 61, 62, 63, 103, 169*

Professor Gerard N. Magliocca. Distinguished Professor, Samuel R. Rosen Professor, Indiana University Robert H. McKinney Law School. *Essay Nos. 197, 198, 199*

John G. Malcolm. Vice President, Institute for Constitutional Government, The Heritage Foundation; Director of Edwin Meese III Center for Legal and Judicial Studies; Ed and Sherry Gilbertson Senior Legal Fellow. *Essay No. 3; Executive Editor*

Professor Joyce Lee Malcolm. Professor Emerita of Law, Antonin Scalia Law School. *Essay Nos. 137, 138*

Professor Earl M. Maltz. Distinguished Professor, Rutgers Law School (Camden). *Essay No. 201*

Jeremy Evan Maltz. Partner, Lehotsky Keller Cohn LLP. *Essay No. 96*

Brennan Mancil. Former law clerk to Judge John K. Bush. *Essay No. 119*

Professor Jennifer Mascott. Associate Professor of Law and the Founder of the Separation of Powers Institute, Catholic University of America. *Academic Advisory Board*

Judge Paul B. Matey. Circuit Judge, U.S. Court of Appeals for the Third Circuit. *Essay No. 153*

Austin Mayron. Former law clerk to Judge Elizabeth L. Branch. *Essay No. 167*

Michael W. McConnell. Professor, Stanford Law School; former Circuit Judge, U.S. Court of Appeals for the Tenth Circuit. *Essay No. 195*

Trent McCotter. Partner, Boyden Gray PLLC; Director of the Separation of Powers Clinic, The Catholic University of America. *Essay No. 163*

Professor John O. McGinnis. George C. Dix Professor in Constitutional Law, Northwestern

Pritzker School of Law; former Deputy Assistant Attorney General, Office of Legal Counsel. *Essay No. 107; Academic Advisory Board*

Meaghen McManus. Program Assistant, Institute for Constitutional Government, The Heritage Foundation. *Managing Editor*

Taylor Meehan. Partner, Consovoy McCarthy PLLC; Lecturer, University of Chicago Law School. *Essay No. 68; Practitioner Advisory Board*

Hon. Edwin Meese III. Ronald Reagan Distinguished Fellow Emeritus, The Heritage Foundation; Seventy-Fifth Attorney General of the United States. *Essay No. 2; Chairman Emeritus*

Judge Steven J. Menashi. Circuit Judge, U.S. Court of Appeals for the Second Circuit. *Essay No. 129; Judicial Advisory Board*

Professor Michael T. Morley. Election Law Professor and Faculty Director of the Election Law Center, Florida State University College of Law. *Essay Nos. 92, 93, 94, 95, 190*

Professor Andrew P. Morriss. Professor, The Bush School of Government & Public Service and the School of Law, Texas A&M University. *Essay No. 165*

Professor Adam Mossoff. Professor of Law, Antonin Scalia Law School; Visiting Intellectual Property Fellow, The Heritage Foundation. *Essay No. 52*

Professor Derek T. Muller. Professor of Law, Notre Dame Law School. *Essay Nos. 7, 8, 22, 24, 90, 210, 211*

Professor Vincent Phillip Muñoz. Tocqueville Professor of Political Science and Concurrent Associate Professor of Law, The University of Notre Dame. *Essay No. 160*

Erin E. Murphy. Partner, Clement & Murphy, PLLC; Adjunct Professor, Georgetown University Law Center; former Bristow Fellow, Office of Solicitor General. *Practitioner Advisory Board*

Eli Nachmany. Associate, Covington & Burling LLP; former law clerk to Judge Steven J. Menashi. *Essay No. 129*

Professor Robert G. Natelson. Professor of Law (ret.), The University of Montana Blewett School of Law; Senior Fellow in Constitutional Jurisprudence, Independence Institute. *Essay Nos. 51, 109, 147, 148, 149, 150, 151, 152*

Andy Nolan. Career clerk to Judge Chad A. Readler. *Essay Nos. 88, 209*

Judge Kevin C. Newsom. Circuit Judge, U.S. Court of Appeals for the Eleventh Circuit. *Judicial Advisory Board*

Judge Andrew S. Oldham. Circuit Judge, U.S. Court of Appeals for the Fifth Circuit. *Essay No. 123; Judicial Advisory Board*

John Osorio. Research Associate, Edwin Meese III Center for Legal and Judicial Studies, The Heritage Foundation. *Managing Editor*

Alexandria Overcash. Former law clerk to Judge Lawrence VanDyke. *Essay No. 181*

Mitchell K. Pallaki. Former law clerk to Judge Carlos T. Bea. *Essay No. 125*

Jameson Payne. Former Research Associate, Edwin Meese III Center for Legal and Judicial Studies, The Heritage Foundation. *Managing Editor*

Professor James C. Phillips. Director and Associate Professor, Constitutional Government Initiative, Wheatley Institute, Brigham Young University. *Essay Nos. 40, 42, 200*

Alexander Phipps. Former Research Associate, Edwin Meese III Center for Legal and Judicial Studies, The Heritage Foundation. *Managing Editor*

Judge William H. Pryor Jr. Chief Judge, U.S. Court of Appeals for the Eleventh Circuit. *Essay Nos. 134, 135; Judicial Advisory Board*

William Poole. Senior Editor, Policy Publications, The Heritage Foundation. *Associate Editor*

Michael D. Ramsey. Warren Distinguished Professor of Law, University of San Diego School of Law. *Essay No. 106; Academic Advisory Board*

Michael D. Rappaport. Hugh and Hazel Darling Foundation Professor of Law, University of San Diego Law School; Director, Center for the Study of Constitutional Originalism. *Academic Advisory Board*

Judge Neomi J. Rao. Circuit Judge, U.S. Court of Appeals for the D.C. Circuit. *Judicial Advisory Board*

Judge Allison Jones Rushing. Circuit Judge, U.S. Court of Appeals for the Fourth Circuit. *Judicial Advisory Board*

Judge Chad A. Readler. Circuit Judge, U.S. Court of Appeals for the Sixth Circuit. *Essay Nos. 88, 209*

Professor Bradley Rebeiro. Associate professor, Brigham Young University's J. Reuben Clark Law School *Essay No. 142*

Judge Julius N. Richardson. Circuit Judge, U.S. Court of Appeals for the Fourth Circuit. *Essay No. 168*

Professor Stephen E. Sachs. Antonin Scalia Professor of Law, Harvard Law School. *Essay Nos. 131, 139; Academic Advisory Board*

Timothy Sandefur. Vice President for Legal Affairs, Goldwater Institute's Scharf-Norton Center for Constitutional Litigation; Adjunct Scholar, Cato Institute. *Essay No. 45*

Jefferson F. Serfass. Former law clerk to Judge Joel M. Carson III. *Essay No. 180*

Professor Ryan W. Scott. Louis F. Niezer Faculty Fellow, Indiana University Bloomington Maurer School of Law. *Essay No. 121*

Athanasius Sirilla. Former law clerk to Judge Matthew H. Solomson. *Essay No. 72*

Tyler Shannon. Former law clerk to Judge Patrick R. Wyrick. *Essay No. 175*

Erica Shuler. Former law clerk to Judge John K. Bush. *Essay No. 119*

Andrew W. Smith. Former law clerk to Judge Gregory G. Katsas. *Essay No. 155*

Professor Bradley A. Smith. Blackmore/Nault Professor, Capital University Law School; former Chairman, Federal Election Commission. *Essay No. 6*

Zack Smith. Senior Legal Fellow and Manager, Supreme Court and Appellate Advocacy Program, Edwin Meese III Center for Legal and Judicial Studies, The Heritage Foundation. *Essay Nos. 141, 146*

Judge Matthew H. Solomson. Chief Judge, U.S. Court of Federal Claims. *Essay No. 72*

Professor Andrew C. Spiropoulos. Professor, Oklahoma City University School of Law. *Essay No. 10*

Professor Chad Squitieri. Assistant Professor of Law, Catholic University of America; Managing Director, Center for the Constitution and the Catholic Intellectual Tradition; Director, Separation of Powers Institute. *Essay Nos. 110, 111*

Adam I. Steene. Of Counsel, Gibson, Dunn & Crutcher LLP. *Essay No. 123*

Professor Matthew Steilen. Professor, University at Buffalo School of Law. *Essay Nos. 69, 80*

Adam Steinhilber. Former law clerk to Judge Timothy Tymkovich. *Essay No. 170*

Michael Stern. Former Senior Counsel, U.S. House of Representatives (1996–2004). *Essay Nos. 23, 27, 31*

Professor John F. Stinneford. Edward Rood Eminent Scholar Chair, University of Florida Levin College of Law. *Essay Nos. 184, 185, 186*

Lee J. Strang. Executive Director, Salmon P. Chase Center for Civics, Culture, and Society; Professor of Law, Moritz College of Law, The Ohio State University. *Essay No. 193*

Judge David R. Stras. Circuit Judge, U.S. Court of Appeals for the Eighth Circuit. *Essay Nos. 53, 120, 121*

William J. Strench. Former law clerk to Chief Judge William H. Pryor Jr. *Essay No. 134*

Nathaniel C. Sutton. Former law clerk to Chief Judge William H. Pryor Jr. *Essay No. 134*

Paul B. Taylor. Visiting Fellow, National Security Institute, Antonin Scalia Law School; former Counsel and Chief Counsel, House Judiciary Committee Subcommittee on the Constitution, Civil Rights, and Civil Liberties. *Essay Nos. 12, 26*

Jacob J. Thackston. Former law clerk to Judge Kurt D. Engelhardt. *Essay No. 136*

Judge Amul R. Thapar. Circuit Judge, U.S. Court of Appeals for the Sixth Circuit. *Judicial Advisory Board*

Professor Seth Barrett Tillman. Associate Professor, Maynooth University School of Law and Criminology, Ireland; Scoil an Dlí agus na Coireolaíochta Ollscoil Mhá Nuad. *Essay Nos. 25, 33, 34, 38, 76, 91, 98, 100, 112*

Kate Comerford Todd. Partner, Torridon Law PLLC; former Deputy Counsel to President Donald J. Trump, Associate Counsel to President George W. Bush. *Essay No. 99; Practitioner Advisory Board*

Jack Tucker. Former law clerk to Judges Andrew Brasher and William H. Pryor Jr. *Essay No. 174*

Judge Timothy M. Tymkovich. Circuit Judge, U.S. Court of Appeals for the Tenth Circuit. *Essay No. 170*

Professor David R. Upham. Associate Professor of Law, St. Thomas University's Crump College of Law; Senior Fellow in Politics and Law, University of Dallas. *Essay No. 140*

Judge Lawrence VanDyke. Circuit Judge, U.S. Court of Appeals for the Ninth Circuit. *Essay Nos. 132, 181*

Seanhenry VanDyke. Former law clerk to Judge Gregory G. Katsas. *Essay No. 101*

Professor Eugene Volokh. Thomas M. Siebel Senior Fellow, Hoover Institution; Gary T. Schwartz Distinguished Professor of Law Emeritus, UCLA School of Law. *Essay No. 161; Academic Advisory Board*

Jeffrey B. Wall. Partner and Head of Supreme Court and Appellate Practice, Sullivan & Cromwell LLP; former Principal Deputy Solicitor General. *Essay No. 108; Practitioner Advisory Board*

Jacob R. Weaver. LTJG, U.S. Navy; former law clerk to Judges Edith H. Jones and Charles R. Eskridge. *Essay No. 206*

Dexter Webster. Former judicial intern to Judge Kurt D. Engelhardt. *Essay No. 136*

Professor John W. Welch. Robert K. Thomas Professor of Law (retired), Brigham Young University's J. Reuben Clark Law School; *Essay No. 4*

Professor Ryan Williams. Associate Professor, Boston College Law School. *Essay No. 187*

Judge Patrick R. Wyrick. District Court Judge, U.S. District Court for the Western District of Oklahoma. *Essay No. 175*

Katherine C. Yarger. Partner, Lehotsky Keller Cohn LLP. *Practitioner Advisory Board*

Professor John C. Yoo. Emanuel S. Heller Professor of Law, Berkeley Law; Senior Research Fellow, Civitas Institute, University of Texas at Austin. *Essay Nos. 56, 57, 58, 78, 87, 102, 115; Academic Advisory Board*

Professor Ernest A. Young. Alston & Bird Distinguished Professor, Duke University School of Law. *Essay Nos. 130, 189*

Michael A. Zarian. Deputy Solicitor General of Idaho. *Essay No. 75*

Professor Rebecca E. Zietlow. Dean, Distinguished University Professor, and Charles W. Fornoff Professor of Law and Values, University of Toledo College of Law. *Essay No. 9*

Professor Evan C. Zoldan. Professor of Law and Director of the Legal Institute of the Great Lakes, University of Toledo College of Law. *Essay Nos. 70, 81*

Professor Todd J. Zywicki. George Mason University Foundation Professor of Law, Antonin Scalia Law School. *Essay Nos. 47, 48, 79, 204*

ESSAY NO. 1: PREFACE

"*We* the people" adopted the Constitution, and it is important that all Americans understand what our founding document means. Since the publication of the first edition twenty years ago, the *Heritage Guide to the Constitution* has been an invaluable resource for judges, lawyers, and the public at large. It marries scholarly depth and sophistication with prose that is readily accessible. The new third edition of the *Guide* retains the virtues of its predecessors while deepening the discussion of how constitutional provisions were understood when they were adopted.

This new focus reflects a profound and beneficial change in constitutional interpretation that has taken place over the past half-century. In 1975—which, by chance, was the year when I graduated from law school—constitutional interpretation was in disarray. During the 1960s and early 1970s, groundbreaking Supreme Court decisions had elicited sharp debate, and both supporters and critics of those decisions were hard-pressed to defend their positions on grounds other than approval or disapproval of the results that the Court had reached. A response based on neutral principles required a theory of constitutional interpretation, and neither side had a crisp candidate readily at hand.

For defenders of the Court's work, a fundamental problem was that the Court's opinions had not articulated and consistently applied any neutral theory. Decisions had relied willy-nilly on the text of the constitutional provision at issue, its history, the structure of the Constitution, precedent, and what amounted more or less to a view about sound public policy. Why a particular recipe was selected for each case had not been explained.

Nor had the Court attempted to reconcile its new work with the broad consensus about the proper role of federal courts that had been forged during the New Deal era. That established consensus was that unelected judges should rarely if ever second-guess the judgment of legislators when the constitutionality of economic and social legislation was challenged. To do otherwise was seen as contrary to our nation's fundamental commitment to democratic self-government. The most academically minded jurists of the 1950s and 1960s, most notably Justice Felix Frankfurter and Judge Learned Hand, thought that a similar stance should be taken in cases involving provisions of the Bill of Rights. But the majority, confident in its views about sound public policy and the arc of history, brushed that concern aside. Thus, when popular opinion turned sharply against the results that were attributed to some of the Court's decisions, defenders were set back on their heels. This was most apparent with respect to decisions that were seen as hampering law enforcement. Beginning in the 1960s, the rate of violent crime climbed rapidly, and the Court was blamed.

Critics sought to change the direction of the Court's work, but they also struggled to find a neutral theory. In the 1968 presidential campaign, Richard Nixon promised to do something about the crime problem and to appoint Supreme Court justices who were "strict constructionists." But what did that term mean? Adhering strictly to the literal meaning of the Constitution's text? Strictly refusing to modify existing precedents? President Nixon appointed four Supreme Court justices during his five years in office. All but one of them joined the decision in *Roe v. Wade* (1973), which did not strictly follow anything other than the majority's view on what represented wise public policy.

Opponents of the work of the Warren Court (and to some extent the Burger Court as well) charged that the justices had become "activists," were behaving like legislators, and should have exercised "judicial self-restraint." These were often valid criticisms, but these phrases left important questions unanswered. Surely there are occasions when judges should be stirred into action. So what is the test for determining whether such an occasion is at hand?

What we now call "originalism" arose to fill this void, and three men led the charge. If we can envision a Mt. Rushmore of originalism, the three visages we would see carved in stone are those of Robert Bork, Edwin Meese III, and Antonin Scalia.

In 1972, when I entered Yale Law School, Robert Bork was a member of the faculty and a renowned antitrust scholar who was just turning to constitutional law. As of that date, his sole contribution in that field was a 1971 article in the *Indiana Law Journal* that bore the modest title

"Neutral Principles and Some First Amendment Problems." In the field of antitrust, Professor Bork championed an overarching theory, namely, that the antitrust laws should be interpreted to promote economic efficiency, and he brought this same theoretical bent to constitutional law. As most fully developed in his best-selling books *The Tempting of America* and *Slouching Towards Gomorrah*, he argued vigorously that judges should heed what the text of the Constitution would have been under-stood to mean at the time of adoption. Although his nomination to the Supreme Court failed, Robert Bork paved the way for the eventual rise of what we now call originalism.

The second key originalist was Edwin Meese III, who served as Attorney General from 1985 to 1988. Under General Meese's leadership, the Department of Justice sought to make up for the legal academy's disinterest in (and indeed, hostility toward) originalism. Justice Department attorneys enthusiastically studied, discussed, and wrote monographs on the original meaning of key constitu-tional provisions. And in a series of highly publicized speeches, General Meese took the originalist case to the general public. His effective speeches prompted an unusual response by Justice William J. Brennan, Jr., who charged that originalism was "little more than arrogance clothed as humility." General Meese was undeterred, and the growing influence of originalism was not halted.

The final pivotal originalist was Justice Antonin Scalia. The brilliant and engaging opinions he wrote during his thirty years on the Supreme Court provided a model that will guide originalist judges for many years to come.

Since these three men laid the foundations for originalism, other jurists (including my colleague Clarence Thomas) and several generations of scholars have worked to deepen the foundations of originalism and explore the original meaning of our founding document. Support for originalism has grown—to such an extent that there is now sometimes as much disagreement between original-ists of different stripes as there is between originalists and non-originalists.

In the 1980s, when I was an Assistant to the Solicitor General, I drafted a brief on a Sixth Amendment Confrontation Clause question that relied heavily on the original understanding of that provision. The deputy who reviewed the draft advised me that a different pitch would be more effective with the Court, which at the time did not include any committed originalists. As a matter of litigation strategy, he was probably correct. The brief was revised, and the Court's opinion was based on non-originalist grounds.

Today, no savvy attorney would disregard original meaning in briefing or arguing an unsettled constitutional question in federal court. For attorneys involved in such cases—and for all other Americans who want to understand what our Constitution means—the new edition of the *Heritage Guide* is a great place to start.

—Justice Samuel A. Alito, Jr.
U.S. Supreme Court

ESSAY NO. 2: FOREWORD

*T*he Constitution of the United States has endured for more than two centuries. And, for most of that history, the Supreme Court has tried—with varying degrees of success—to follow the intent of the Framers and the original meaning of the Constitution. Regrettably, during the Warren and Burger Courts, the so-called living Constitution became ascendant. The history of our foundational charter was no longer deemed relevant. Judges of all stripes would rewrite the Constitution based on "evolving standards" to address contemporary problems. Living Constitutionalism reached its pinnacle in *Roe v. Wade* (1973), in which a 7-2 Court invented out of thin air a right to abortion.

During the last half-century, however, we have witnessed something of a constitutional revolution—or perhaps it is better called a constitutional restoration. Starting in the late 1970s and early 1980s, jurists like William Rehnquist, Robert Bork, Antonin Scalia, and others pushed back against the living Constitution. At the time, many progressive judges and academics scoffed at the notion that courts should somehow channel the Framers' original intent. But the power of reason would gain ground, inch by inch and case by case.

In 1985, this process entered a new phase. That year, President Ronald Reagan was sworn in for his second term, and I was honored to be confirmed as the Seventy-Fifth Attorney General. In July of 1985, I delivered a speech to the American Bar Association. I announced that the Department of Justice would press for "a Jurisprudence of Original Intention." And the DOJ would "endeavor to resurrect the original meaning of constitutional provisions and statutes as the only reliable guide for judgment." Apparently, my remarks struck a nerve.

Three months later, Justice William Brennan, the longtime leader of the Court's liberal wing, felt compelled to respond. In a speech at Georgetown, Brennan charged that originalism was "little more than arrogance cloaked as humility." Brennan endorsed living constitutionalism and rejected originalism. He said, "[T]he genius of the Constitution rests not in any static meaning it might have had in a world that is dead and gone, but in the adaptability of its great principles to cope with current problems and current needs."

I felt the need to reply to Justice Brennan. In November 1985, I gave a speech to the District of Columbia chapter of the Federalist Society. In my view, originalism was not difficult to describe. First, where the language of the Constitution is specific, it must be obeyed. Second, where there is a demonstrable consensus among the Framers, it should be followed. And third, where the Constitution has ambiguity, it should be interpreted and applied in a manner so as not to contradict the text. I then laid out the terms of this ongoing discourse between the originalists and the living constitutionalists. I said, "We and our distinguished opponents carry on the old tradition, of free, uninhibited, and vigorous debate." I concluded, "Out of such arguments come no losers, only truth. It's the American way. And the Founders wouldn't want it any other way."

Over the ensuing four decades, that so-called vigorous debate would unfold in ways that were difficult to anticipate. In 1986, the Court's originalist core would double. Justice William Rehnquist was elevated to Chief Justice, and Judge Antonin Scalia was confirmed as an associate justice. Both of these jurists were committed to a jurisprudence of originalism. Justice Scalia, in particular, published scholarship defending originalism and delivered that message to law students and lawyers across the country. Regrettably, in 1987, Judge Robert Bork was nominated to the Supreme Court but was not confirmed. Had Bork made it through, the Court would have had three committed originalists. Ultimately, that troika would be established in 1991 with Justice Clarence Thomas's confirmation.

Throughout the 1990s, under the leadership of Chief Justice Rehnquist, the Court pushed the pause button on the living constitutional jurisprudence that had prevailed for decades. And with the new federalism, the Court identified restraints on the central government's powers. These changes were incremental but were foundational. The case of *United States v. Lopez* (1995) imposed the first new limits on Commerce Clause authority in six decades. *Printz v. United States* (1997) held that Congress could not commandeer state officials to implement federal policies. And *United States v.*

1

Morrison (2000) found that the federal government could not regulate local crimes like domestic violence. With these decisions, and others, the Court pushed closer to a jurisprudence of originalism.

By the early 2000s, The Heritage Foundation perceived an important relationship between the courts, lawyers, and scholars. In order for courts to write originalist decisions, lawyers had to provide originalist briefing. And in order for lawyers to make originalist arguments, they had to be familiar with originalist scholarship. Admittedly, this task is not always simple. Legal scholarship is often not accessible by practicing attorneys. Thus, the *Heritage Guide to the Constitution* was born. This volume would include originalist essays about every clause in the Constitution. The essays would be written by leading scholars and practitioners in an easy-to-understand fashion. The *Heritage Guide* would provide a one-stop resource for lawyers, professors, students, and ordinary citizens to learn about the Constitution.

The first edition of the *Heritage Guide* was published in 2005. I was honored to chair the Editorial Advisory Board. Matthew Spalding served as the Executive Editor and David Forte was the Senior Editor. The *Guide* caught on quickly and was used widely. And in time, the *Guide* would find an increasingly receptive audience for originalist scholarship.

That same year, President George W. Bush nominated John Roberts and Samuel Alito to the Supreme Court. Over the next decade, the Roberts Court would continue to push the Court closer to a jurisprudence of originalism. In the cases of *District of Columbia v. Heller* (2008) and *McDonald v. Chicago* (2010), the Supreme Court restored the Second Amendment to its equal station in the Bill of Rights. And *NFIB v. Sebelius* (2012), though largely a disappointment with respect to Congress's commerce and taxing power, still enforced limits on Congress's spending power. In 2014, Heritage published the second edition of the *Guide*, again under the leadership of Spalding and Forte. This revised volume accounted for recent judicial decisions, novel legal scholarship, and the expanded expertise of new authors.

During the presidency of Donald Trump, the Supreme Court, and indeed the entire federal judiciary, would take a strong turn toward originalism. Justice Antonin Scalia would be replaced by Justice Neil Gorsuch. Justice Anthony Kennedy would be replaced by Justice Brett Kavanaugh. And Justice Ruth Bader Ginsburg would be replaced by Justice Amy Coney Barrett. For the first time in generations, there was a majority of originalist Justices on the Supreme Court. And that shift in jurisprudence furthered the constitutional restoration. In *Dobbs v. Jackson Women's Health Organization* (2022), after five long decades, *Roe v. Wade* was finally overruled. *New York State Rifle & Pistol Association v. Bruen* (2022) endorsed a historical approach to interpreting the Second Amendment. And *Kennedy v. Bremerton School District* (2022) followed a historical approach to interpreting the Establishment Clause. These holdings would have been nearly unimaginable four decades ago when I sparred with Justice Brennan. But with the benefit of hindsight, I submit that Rehnquist, Bork, Scalia, Thomas, and others have won that "vigorous debate."

The time is now right for a third edition of the *Heritage Guide to the Constitution*. The project continues under the leadership of Josh Blackman and John G. Malcolm. They are building on the proud legacy of the prior editions. I am honored to serve as the Chairman Emeritus of the advisory board, which includes more than three dozen judges, practitioners, and scholars. I am confident that this volume will serve a new generation of lawyers, professors, students, and ordinary citizens who are deeply committed to the jurisprudence of originalism I spoke about four decades ago.

—Edwin Meese III
Chairman Emeritus, Advisory Board

ESSAY NO. 3: EDITORS' NOTE

I. PURPOSE

The first edition of the *Heritage Guide to the Constitution* was published in 2005. The second edition was published in 2014. The third edition is now published in 2025. This once-a-decade publication strives to be the definitive compendium about each provision of the Constitution. We have four primary audiences. First, the book is written for a general audience with an interest in the Constitution. Second, this book will be a useful resource for students and scholars who want a quick reference for their research. Our essays are perfectly suited for a *See generally* footnote in a scholarly article. Third, practicing lawyers are increasingly expected to make arguments based on text, history, and tradition in constitutional litigation. The *Guide* will provide a helpful starting point for originalist briefing. Fourth, the lower courts, following the Supreme Court's precedents, now focus more on text, history, and tradition. This *Guide* will provide a neutral and thorough accounting of the Constitution.

II. STRUCTURE

Over the past two decades, the federal judiciary has taken more seriously originalist scholarship. Even those judges who are otherwise skeptical of originalism have begun to incorporate text, history, and tradition into their opinions. Accordingly, all attorneys are well-advised to present arguments that are grounded in originalism. And increasingly, scholars across the ideological spectrum—whether they identify as originalists or not—are crafting articles that take original meaning seriously. The structure of the third edition of the Guide reflects this approach to judging, advocacy, and scholarship. Most of the essays separate history and modern precedent and are arranged roughly chronologically.

First, the essays track the history before 1787. The Constitution was not written on a blank slate. The essays begin with any relevant history that predated the federal Constitution, including the English common law, the natural law tradition, the law of nations, practices in the colonies, the Declaration of Independence, practices in the states post-independence, the shortcomings of the Articles of Confederation, and so on.

Second, the essays provide a deep dive into the records of the Constitutional Convention. We provide a detailed sequence of the various drafts, debates, and revisions during the summer of 1787.

Third, the essays cover the ratification debates, including a careful study of the Federalist Papers and the equally important Anti-Federalist Papers. Our essays also make use of the Documentary History of the Ratification of the Constitution, corpus linguistics, and other compendiums.

Fourth, where relevant, we discuss practice from the early congresses and presidencies. These formative bodies established many of the traditions that helped give meaning to the Constitution.

Fifth, we finally turn to judicial precedent. This choice is deliberate. Far too often, judges, attorneys, and scholars start with the precedents of the Supreme Court. While these decisions are no doubt important, they tell only part of the story about the Constitution's original meaning. Moreover, Supreme Court precedents change from time to time. It is impossible to provide a definitive account of all relevant judicial decisions. By contrast, the Founding-era sources can be stated definitively and will endure forever.

III. THE PROCESS

Due to the size of this project, we established a fairly rigorous process to ensure that essays of the highest quality were reviewed, edited, and revised in a timely fashion. Josh Blackman served as the Senior Editor and John G. Malcolm served as the Executive Editor. Our editors at Heritage included Seth Lucas, Jack Fitzhenry, Jenna Hageman, Meaghen McManus, John Osorio, Jameson Payne, and Alexander Phipps. We were also fortunate to have student editors who served on the Harvard Journal of Law & Public Policy, NYU Journal of Law & Liberty, Georgetown Journal of Law & Public Policy, and Texas Review of Law & Politics, as well as the Heritage Foundation intern program. We also assembled three external advisory boards. The Judicial Advisory Board included eighteen federal circuit courts of appeals judges, the Practitioner Advisory Board included thirteen Supreme Court advocates, and the Academic Advisory Board included ten law professors. All of the editors and advisors are listed on the masthead.

The publication process went through six rigorous phases. Phase 1 began in early 2022. Over the course of a year, every essay from the second edition was carefully scrutinized by our internal and external reviewers. During this process, we invited back authors to revise their essays and also invited many new authors to join the project. Moreover, we subdivided some essays that covered several clauses, thus creating more opportunities for new authors. We tried to develop a mix of senior professors, junior scholars, practitioners with relevant experience, and distinguished jurists. In Phase 2, authors were asked to deliver the first draft of their revised essays by the middle of 2023. We provided the authors with detailed guidelines to ensure that the essays were roughly uniform in structure and style and provided the proper focus on originalism. We are grateful to the authors for following our standards.

In Phase 3, throughout late 2023 and 2024, the substance of the first drafts was carefully reviewed by Blackman, Malcolm, and our internal editors at Heritage. Each essay was also referred to our external board for a double-blind review: Reviewers did not know the identity of the authors, and the authors did not know the identity of the reviewers of their respective essays. The external reviewers provided line edits, suggestions to add or remove material, and broader comments.

In Phase 4, during 2024, feedback was provided to the authors in an anonymized fashion so that they did not know who provided the comments. We are again thankful to the authors for considering and implementing many of our proposed edits.

Phase 5 began in mid-2024. Here, the essays were closely proofread, cite-checked, and bluebooked by Bill Poole, Heritage Senior Editor extraordinaire. External sources were digitized and archived to ensure citation accuracy.

Phase 6 commenced in 2025 as the essays were finalized and prepared for publication. We exerted our best efforts to catch all possible errors but still take responsibility for any mistakes that may have slipped through the process. The final text spanned approximately 500,000 words—more than fifty times the length of the Constitution and amendments. The complete Guide was delivered to the publisher in July 2025.

IV. JOSH BLACKMAN'S NOTE

In late 2021, my good friend John G. Malcolm asked me if I wanted to serve as the Senior Editor for the third edition of the *Heritage Guide to the Constitution*. On our initial call, which I remember like it was yesterday, John told me that Heritage wanted to "update" the Guide with some recent cases, but thought that the structure of the book would remain more or less the same.

My initial reaction was a combination of shock and humility. I considered the *Heritage Guide* to be the gold standard of constitutional scholarship. I couldn't fathom why I, of all people, was being asked to carry the torch first lit by Attorney General Edwin Meese decades ago. John assured me that he thought I was up to the task and that he had been impressed with my past work. I remained skeptical, but I considered the project in earnest. Over the course of several weeks, I carefully read through the second edition with the recognition that it was written in a very different time. In the early 2000s, originalism was still something of a fringe theory with minimal support in the judiciary and the academy. But times have changed, and I realized that the third edition could speak to the current generation.

I returned to John and said I would take the job but would do more than simply "update" it. Over the ensuing months, I laid out an ambitious agenda. I would recruit external boards of advisors who would blindly review each essay. I would invite nearly one hundred new authors who represented the leading lights of originalist scholarship, advocacy, and jurisprudence. I would ask the authors to separate their essays carefully so that text, history, and tradition came *before* judicial precedent. (This task was much harder than it may seem.) I would require authors to provide full citations for all of their work so that scholars, practitioners, and jurists could rely on the material in the book. And all of this would be completed in the span of about four years.

This project was daunting, but we did it. I sincerely thank John for believing in me and supporting this generational project. It would have been very easy for Heritage to simply "update" the second edition to keep things as they were. But John backed my vision. I think the state of constitutional law will be improved for these efforts. I owe a sincere debt to Attorney General Meese. Even at the age of ninety-three, he remains actively involved with the *Heritage Guide* and so many other activities. One of the highlights of my professional career was visiting Mr. Meese in his home, as we recorded him reading aloud the text of the entire Constitution. I would also like to thank all of the staff at Heritage, in particular Seth Lucas, whose careful editing and comprehensive planning helped keep the project moving along apace.

Finally, I want to thank my loving family, Militza, Miriam, and Clara. Every minute I spent on this project was time you generously let me share with the world. I hope we can all keep the Constitution close to our hearts.

—Josh Blackman
Senior Editor

V. JOHN G. MALCOLM'S NOTE

Working on the third edition of the *Heritage Guide to the Constitution* has been both a Herculean task and a labor of love. The second edition was published shortly after I arrived at Heritage, and I long hoped that I would be around to work on the third edition. I am pleased with the final product and proud to have my name associated with it.

There are two people in particular whom I would like to acknowledge.

The first is Josh Blackman. The best decision that I made with respect to this undertaking was to ask Josh to serve as Senior Editor. Josh proved to be a whirling dervish of ideas, passion, and energy who devoted countless hours to corralling authors and advisors, ensuring the completeness and accuracy of each essay, making sure that steady progress was being made, and coming up with new ideas for how to make the *Guide* more useful and accessible to a broad audience.

The second is former Attorney General Edwin Meese III. Although my highest title at Heritage is Vice President of the Institute for Constitutional Government, I have always said that other than husband to my wife and father to my children, the title that has meant the most to me throughout my professional career has been Director of the Meese Center for Legal and Judicial Studies. In addition to being a mentor, Ed Meese has been an inspiration to me and supporter of mine during my tenure at Heritage. Ed was a dedicated public servant and a stalwart protector of the Constitution. It was a series of seminal speeches that he delivered as our nation's Seventy-Fifth Attorney General that sparked the revival of originalism. Those speeches pointed out just how far the judiciary had strayed from remaining faithful to the Framers' intentions and the public's understanding of the Constitution at the time it was written and ratified. The seeds that Ed Meese planted have grown into a mighty forest, transforming the judiciary and the Academy, arresting the erosion of our rights and liberties, and ensuring that the Constitution that was ordained and established in 1787 continues to serve "We the people" and not "We the judges." The President under whom Ed Meese served, Ronald Reagan, once said, "If Ed Meese is not a good man, then there are no good men." I wholeheartedly agree.

I would also like to thank all the authors and reviewers who worked on this project, with special thanks to Seth Lucas and Bill Poole, two of the most hard-working and meticulous professionals with whom I have been privileged to work. The timely completion and quality of the *Guide* owes much to their efforts, for which I am deeply grateful.

Finally, I would like to thank my wife Mary Lee, who has always supported me and who has put up with my working more nights and weekends than she desired or deserved.

—John G. Malcolm
Executive Editor

CITATION ABBREVIATIONS

Blackstone	Sir William Blackstone, Commentaries on the Laws of England in Four Books. Notes selected from the editions of Archibold, Christian, Coleridge, Chitty, Stewart, Kerr, and others, Barron Field's Analysis, and Additional Notes, and a Life of the Author by George Sharswood. In Two Volumes. (George Sharswood ed., 1893)
Cannon's Precedents	Cannon's Precedents of the House of Representatives (1935).
DHRC	The Documentary History of the Ratification of the Constitution, published by the Center for the Study of the American Constitution at the University of Wisconsin-Madison
Deschler's Precedents	Deschler's Precedents of the U.S. House of Representatives (1970).
Elliot's	The Debates in the Several State Conventions on the Adoption of the Federal Constitution (Jonathan Elliot ed., Philadelphia, J.B. Lippincott 1836)
Farrand's	The Records of the Federal Convention of 1787 (Max Farrand, ed., 1911)
Hinds' Precedents	Asher C. Hinds., Hinds' Precedents of the House of Representatives of the United States (1907).
RA	Reconstruction Amendments: Essential Documents (Kurt T. Lash, ed., 2021)
Storing	The Complete Anti-Federalist (Herbert J. Storing ed., 1981).
Story's Commentaries	Joseph Story, Commentaries on the Constitution of the United States 1833).

PART 1

ARTICLE I

ESSAY NO. 4: THE PREAMBLE

We the People of the United States, in Order to form a more perfect Union, establish Justice, insure domestic Tranquility, provide for the common defense, promote the general Welfare, and secure the Blessings of Liberty to ourselves and our Posterity, do ordain and establish this Constitution for the United States of America.
—John W. Welch & James A. Heilpern

INTRODUCTION

The Preamble to the United States Constitution, though often considered merely ornamental, has long served as a vital interpretive tool in the hands of lawmakers, judges, and scholars. This essay first traces the Preamble's origins and enduring resonance in the American consciousness from its succinct crafting in the Constitutional Convention to its roles in shaping the American identity and defining the nation's core values. It will then consider the Preamble's historical usage by all three branches of government, including the shifting jurisprudence surrounding it as exemplified by cases like *Jacobson v. Massachusetts* (1905), and the ongoing debates among scholars about the Preamble's potential as a source of substantive law and its role in constitutional interpretation.

HISTORY BEFORE 1787

The Constitution was not the first legal document to begin with a preamble. Many ancient laws began with a prologue or preamble, which Plato strongly recommended in his *Laws*. Edward Coke wrote that preambles provide a "good mean to find out the meaning of a statute" and the "key" to understanding the law.[1] Thomas Hobbes advised lawmakers to state concisely "why the Law was made," for "a Declaration of the Causes, and Motives, for which it was made" shows "us the meaning of the Legislator."[2] Blackstone stated that such purpose statements can be "called in to help in the construction" of a legal document and thus should be given legal effect at least in some circumstances.[3] Courts on both sides of the Atlantic followed this interpretive practice.[4]

Preambles were common in early state constitutions as well. The constitutions of Massachusetts (1780), Vermont (1777), and Pennsylvania (1776) contained lengthy political discussions of the need to protect natural rights or justifications for breaking away from Great Britain. A majority of state constitutions contained statements about the legitimate purposes of government, many employing phrases that would be mirrored in the federal Preamble a decade later. The preambles of the constitutions of Pennsylvania (1777), Virginia (1776), and North Carolina (1776) mention the "blessings of liberty." The Massachusetts constitution (1780) contains the phrase "for ourselves and posterity."

THE CONSTITUTIONAL CONVENTION

The records of the Constitutional Convention contain almost no references to the Preamble. The Preamble was not debated on the Convention floor but instead was drafted as a final summation. Edmund Randolph of Virginia and John Rutledge of South Carolina stated that a preamble was *not* the place to opine on "the ends of government and human polities."[5] They acknowledged that such political statements might have been common in state constitutions but contended that the preamble to a *federal* charter should only emphasize the inadequacies of the Articles of Confederation, outline the historical circumstances leading to the Convention, and express confidence that the new Constitution solved its predecessor's shortcomings.

The Committee of Detail—which included both Randolph and Rutledge—was then charged with the task of synthesizing "the proceedings of the Convention" and producing a draft.[6] The committee's first draft included a Preamble that was even more concise than Randolph and Rutledge had originally suggested: "We the people of the States . . . do ordain, declare, and establish the following Constitution for the Government of Ourselves and our Posterity."[7]

This version of the Preamble was read to the entire Convention and was approved unanimously.[8] But the text was scrapped when it went to the Committee of Style. It is thought that Gouverneur Morris of Pennsylvania was tasked with revising the Preamble.[9] The Committee of Style's initial draft read as follows:

> We the People of the United States, in order to form a more perfect union, to establish justice, insure domestic tranquility, provide for the common defence, promote the general welfare, and secure the blessings of liberty to ourselves and our posterity, do ordain and establish this Constitution for the United States of America.[10]

This new version of the Preamble was included in the final text of the Constitution with only one change: the deletion of the word "to" from the string of clauses beginning with "to establish justice." Otherwise, Morris's version was adopted in the final document.

THE RATIFICATION DEBATES

The Preamble played a very influential role during the ratification process. In headlines, the Preamble captured the public's attention and strongly influenced the perception of what the Constitution promised to deliver.[11] However, the Preamble's exact influence and legal weight remained subjects of debate among the Founders. On the one hand, Anti-Federalists raised concerns about the Preamble's broad and sweeping language. Writers like Brutus and Luther Martin feared that the Preamble's expansive language could be used to grant unlimited power to the federal government and possibly lead to the absorption of the states.[12] On the other hand, James Madison and Alexander Hamilton assumed that the Preamble's broad phrases should be understood naturally in conjunction with the specific enumerated powers

and limitations outlined in the body of the Constitution.[13]

The Preamble was discussed during eight of the thirteen state ratification conventions, although never at the center of debate. Its opening phrase, "We the People," was accepted or passed over by most debaters, and the details of its language were not extensively contested. Instead, discussions focused on principles of federalism and the need for a bill of rights. Some delegates expressed concerns that the Preamble's language undermined the independence of the states; others believed it served as a restraint on federal power.[14]

During the Virginia ratification convention, James Monroe straddled between the Federalist and Anti-Federalist camps. In 1788, he published two extensive explanations of the proposed Constitution in which he justified the absence of a written bill of rights. He stated that, in 1776, the American people did not require a bill of rights to choose the form of government they deemed suitable. According to Monroe, such a declaration of rights could be used to curtail liberties rather than preserve them. He argued that the Constitution itself should be the arbiter in disputes concerning any exercise of power. If a particular power or prerogative was granted by the Constitution, the federal government could exercise it; otherwise, the people and the states retained that right.[15]

Within this context, Monroe highlighted the significance of the Preamble, referring to it as the "key of the Constitution." He considered the Preamble to be the most foundational and indispensable element of the Constitution, giving insights into its intended public purposes. Monroe believed that any exercise of federal power contrary to the spirit expressed in the Preamble would be unconstitutional and should be resisted by the people.[16]

EARLY PRACTICE

Throughout the eighteenth century, the Preamble was treated as an authoritative source of law by influential political actors in all three branches of government. As a rule, these figures accepted Monroe's view that the preamble was the "key to the Constitution." Joseph Story, for example, used the Preamble as an interpretive lens to focus and explain the rest of the document.[17]

This view of the Preamble became most notable in 1830. During the nullification crisis, South Carolina attempted to declare that federal tariffs were null and void. Senators on all sides of the issue—especially Daniel Webster from Massachusetts and Robert Hayne from South Carolina—turned to the Preamble to support their preferred constitutional interpretations. Hayne selectively employed the Preamble's language to argue against national debt and foreign interference. In his view, the Preamble emphasized the importance of individual liberties and state sovereignty. Webster used the Preamble to support his view of a consolidated government and the Union's role in promoting a more perfect unity among the states. Though the two sides did not agree on much, they did agree that the Preamble was a rich, essential source of insights for settling constitutional questions that gripped the nation.[18]

JUDICIAL PRECEDENTS

The Preamble was cited in a number of early Supreme Court decisions, primarily to help define and balance the limits of federalism and federal powers. *Chisolm v. Georgia* (1793), which rejected principles of state sovereignty, sparked a constitutional debate that culminated in the passage of the Eleventh Amendment. Chief Justice John Jay's seriatim opinion relied on two parts of the Preamble ("We the People" and "establish justice") to support his conclusion that federal courts have jurisdiction to hear cases between a state and a citizen of another state.[19] In *Martin v. Hunter's Lessee* (1816), Justice Joseph Story's majority opinion referenced the Preamble in holding that the Constitution vested the U.S. Supreme Court with the authority to review decisions of state appellate courts.[20] Story emphasized that the Constitution had been written by "the people of the United States" rather than by the states.

But the Court did not always use the Preamble as the federal imprimatur that some Anti-Federalists feared it would become. In *Barron v. Baltimore* (1833), Chief Justice John Marshall invoked the Preamble to *limit* the reach of the Constitution and show that the Bill of Rights applied only to the federal government, not the states.[21]

The Preamble's influence in Supreme Court opinions waned sharply after the Court decided *Jacobson v. Massachusetts*,[22] which upheld states' authority to impose a nominal fine on unvaccinated people. Henning Jacobson refused to receive the smallpox vaccination, asserting, among other claims, a Fourteenth Amendment right to liberty. On appeal to the Supreme Court, Jacobson asserted that the law was "contrary to the preamble of the Constitution."[23] Jacobson's argument was not well-developed. He simply concluded without any support that the "blessings of liberty" in the Preamble were secured *through* the Fourteenth Amendment.[24]

The Court ruled in favor of Massachusetts. Justice John Marshall Harlan's majority opinion rejected Jacobson's brief invocation of the Preamble. The Court "pass[ed] without extended discussion the suggestion that the . . . statute . . . is in derogation of rights secured by the Preamble." Harlan acknowledged that the "Preamble indicates the general purposes for which the people ordained and established the Constitution," but countered that the Preamble "has never been regarded as the source of any substantive power conferred on the government of the United States." Rather, "[s]uch powers embrace only those expressly granted in the body of the Constitution."[25]

In the century after *Jacobson*, members of the Court have continued to invoke the Preamble, primarily in concurrences and dissents.[26] Although the Court has never explicitly reaffirmed *Jacobson*'s treatment of the Preamble, lower courts have cited *Jacobson* as support for the proposition that the Preamble does not guarantee any substantive rights.[27]

OPEN QUESTIONS

Scholars continue to debate what (if any) substantive role the Preamble should play in constitutional interpretation. Most scholars continue to agree with Justice Harlan's dictum that the Preamble does not and cannot confer substantive rights.[28] Others, however, have identified several potential functions of the Preamble: (1) that it can and should be used to clarify otherwise ambiguous terms or purposes found in the body of the Constitution; (2) that the exercises of federal power must conform to at least one of the purposes undertaken in the Preamble; and (3) that the Preamble imposes duties on all people, states, and federal officers to work for the good of the country as a whole.[29] Some scholars across a broad political spectrum have argued for more muscular interpretations of the Preamble to justify various policy preferences, such as mobilizing the war on terrorism, protecting the unborn, or providing universal health care.[30] Still others have used the Preamble to argue either for natural law–based or progressive jurisprudence writ large.[31]

Cite as: John W. Welch & James A. Heilpern, *The Preamble, in* THE HERITAGE GUIDE TO THE CONSTITUTION 2 (Josh Blackman & John G. Malcolm eds., 3d ed. 2025).

Notes

1. Edward Coke, Institutes of the Lawes of England 79 (1628). **2.** Thomas Hobbes, Leviathan 388–89 (C.B. MacPherson ed., 1968) (1651). **3.** 1 Blackstone 59–60. **4.** *Brett v. Brett*, 162 Eng. Rep. 456, 458–59 (1716); *Cox v. Edwards*, 14 Mass. 491, 493 (1782). **5.** 2 Farrand's 137–38. **6.** *Id.* at 95, 97. **7.** *Id.* at 177. **8.** *Id.* at 193, 196; John Welch & James Heilpern, *Recovering Our Forgotten Preamble*, 91 S. Cal. L. Rev. 1021, 1033, n.44 (2018). **9.** 3 Farrand's 499. **10.** 2 Farrand's 590. **11.** Welch & Heilpern, *supra* at 1050–51. **12.** 2 Storing 2.9.141; Supplement, Farrand's 291–92. **13.** Welch & Heilpern, *supra* at 1053 & n.149 (quoting Federalist No. 41 (Madison) and Federalist No. 84 (Hamilton)). **14.** *Id.* at 1054–61. **15.** James Monroe, *Observations on the Federal Government, in* 1 The Writings of James Monroe 349, 356 (Stanislaus Murray Hamilton ed., 1898). **16.** Welch & Heilpern, *supra* at 1057. **17.** 1 Story's Commentaries § 459. **18.** Welch & Heilpern, *supra* at 1084–90. **19.** 2 U.S. 419, 470–79 (1793) (Jay, C.J.). **20.** 14 U.S. 304, 324–25 (1816). **21.** 32 U.S. 243, 247 (1833). **22.** 197 U.S. 11 (1905). **23.** Josh Blackman, *The Irrepressible Myth of* Jacobson v. Massachusetts, 70 Buff. L. Rev. 131, 162, 170 (2022); Brief for Plaintiff in Error at 5, *Jacobson v. Mass.*, 197 U.S. 11 (1905) (No. 70-175), https://perma.cc/EUK9-TX4V. **24.** Brief for Plaintiff in Error at 20. **25.** *Jacobson*, 197 U.S. at 22. **26.** Welch & Heilpern, *supra* at 1116. **27.** *Tinsley v. Methodist Hosp. of Ind., Inc.*, 70 F.3d 1275 (7th Cir. 1995); *Virginia v. Ferriero*, 525 F. Supp. 3d 36, 60 (D.D.C. 2021); *Hart Coal Corp. v. Sparks*, 7 F. Supp. 16, 27 (W.D. Ky. 1934); *Gallogly v. Att'y Gen. of U.S.*, No. 1:18-cv-571, 2018 WL 11452319, at *5 (W.D. Tex. Nov. 19, 2018). **28.** Peter Beck, *The Parts We Skip: A Taxonomy of Constitutional Irrelevancy*, 34 Const. Comm. 223 n.118 (2019); Welch & Heilpern, *supra* at 1123–26. **29.** Welch & Heilpern, *supra* at 1132–35. **30.** C. Dean McGrath Jr., *The Genius of the Constitution: The Preamble and the War on Terror*, 3 Geo. J.L. & Pub. Pol'y (2005); Raymond Marcin, *"Posterity" in the Preamble and a Positivist Pro-Life Position*, 38 Am. J. Juris 273, 281, 283 (1993); Kenneth Shuster, *Because of History, Philosophy, the Constitution, Fairness & Need: Why Americans Have a Right to National Health Care*, 10 Ind. Health L. Rev. 75, 89–91 (2013). **31.** Josh Hammer, *Common Good Originalism*, 44 Harv. J.L. & Pub. Pol'y 917 (2021); Eliot Tracz, *Towards a Preamble Based Theory of Constitutional Interpretation*, 56 Gonz. L. Rev. 95 (2021).

~~~

ESSAY NO. 5: THE LEGISLATIVE VESTING CLAUSE
ART. I, § 1

All legislative Powers herein granted shall be vested in a Congress of the United States, which shall consist of a Senate and House of Representatives.

—Gary S. Lawson

INTRODUCTION

The Legislative Vesting Clause defines the bicameral legislature; indicates, in conjunction with the other vesting clauses, that there are distinct kinds of governmental powers; and suggests that Congress has only limited powers that are "herein granted." The Legislative Vesting Clause may also define which branches of the federal government can exercise the different types of federal power.

CONSTITUTIONAL FUNCTIONS OF THE LEGISLATIVE VESTING CLAUSE

The Legislative Vesting Clause performs several critical constitutional functions. First, it defines the Congress as "a Senate and House of Representatives." This bicameral (two-chamber) structure was proposed in the earliest days of the Constitutional Convention and carried through to the final version of the document, notwithstanding an unsuccessful proposal for a unicameral legislature in the New Jersey Plan.[1] Nine of the 11 states that adopted constitutions before 1787 provided for bicameral legislatures, and the two holdouts (Pennsylvania and Georgia) went bicameral by 1791.[2] Today, every state except Nebraska has a bicameral legislature.

Second, by vesting a specific kind of power in a specific institution, the Legislative Vesting Clause, along with its counterpart vesting clauses in Articles II and III, communicates that there are distinct types of governmental powers. Madison explained in Federalist No. 48 that these powers "may *in their nature* be legislative, executive or judiciary." John Adams agreed, declaring that the "three branches of power have an unalterable foundation in nature; that they exist in every society natural and artificial. . . ."[3] The Constitution's entire scheme is built around this tripartite classification of governmental powers. However, Madison also acknowledged in Federalist No. 37 that not every exercise of governmental power can be neatly and easily placed into a legislative, executive, or judicial category. Rather, the Framers, along with contemporaneous framers of state constitutions, seemed to assume that such a distinction can be drawn in enough cases to make the constitutional system function.

Third, the Legislative Vesting Clause refers to "[a]ll legislative Powers herein granted" rather than to "[a]ll legislative Powers" in the abstract. This phrasing could be taken to mean that Congress is not vested with *all* legislative powers in the abstract, but only with those particular legislative powers "herein granted" by the Constitution. On this reading, the Legislative Vesting Clause serves as a textual reminder that Congress can exercise only an enumerated subset of the general category of "legislative Powers."

This reading of the "herein granted" language as a source for the doctrine of enumerated powers has been vigorously challenged. Some scholars contend that this approach overreads the language, begs important textual questions, and has little historical support in Founding-era materials.[4] On July 17, 1787, by a margin of 8 to 2, the Convention voted in favor of a version of the Legislative Vesting Clause that gave Congress power, among other things, "[t]o make laws binding on the People of the United States in all cases which may concern the common interests of the Union: and moreover to legislate in all cases for the general interests of the Union. . . ."[5] This resolution could be read as endorsing a grant of general legislative power, or it might have been a placeholder and guide for the more specific enumerations of power that later emerged from the Committee of Detail and ultimately became Article I, Section 8 of the Constitution.

In any event, as Chief Justice John Marshall observed in *McCulloch v. Maryland* (1819), the federal government "is acknowledged by all to be one of enumerated powers"[6] even if the precise role of the Legislative Vesting Clause as support for that doctrine remains uncertain. Other provisions of the Constitution, including the overall structure of Article I, the language of the Tenth Amendment, and background principles of constitutionalism, may play a role in supporting the doctrine of enumerated powers. *United States v. Lopez* (1995) reaffirmed that "[t]he Constitution creates a Federal Government of enumerated powers."[7] In doing so, the Supreme Court cited Article I, Section 8, which lists Congress's expressly enumerated powers, rather than the Legislative Vesting Clause in Article I, Section 1.

Fourth, one might also conclude that the Legislative Vesting Clause specifies *who* can exercise any constitutionally granted legislative powers within the federal government. Those powers can be exercised only by Congress, the body in whom those powers are vested, and not by any other federal actor such as the President, a federal judge, or an administrative agency. The Constitution, however, does not expressly circumscribe the lines that separate the legislative, executive, or judicial powers. Few laws can be crafted so precisely as to leave nothing of consequence to the discretion of executive or judicial actors. It is commonplace, and perhaps unavoidable, for executive and judicial actors to need to *interpret* enacted laws in the course of their duties. But the formal exercise of executive or judicial interpretation could become so extensive in shaping the meaning of a law that the executive or judicial actor in reality becomes the lawmaker. That is the essence of the delegation problem.

Some scholarship has questioned whether

and how the Constitution constrains the kind and quality of discretion that Congress may grant to other actors. Scholars have pointed out that the sparse language of the Legislative Vesting Clause does not expressly forbid or permit delegation and that no other clause expressly addresses the question. In the absence of a specific text, much of the scholarship has focused on early congressional practice. Some of that scholarship argues that early practice does not support a broad nondelegation principle that would lead to sweeping changes in current doctrine.[8] Other originalist scholarship is more supportive of a vigorous delegation principle.[9]

Scholars sometimes look to background principles as well as practice. John Locke, for example, wrote that "[t]he legislative cannot transfer the power of making laws to any other hands: for it being but a delegated power from the people, they who have it cannot pass it over to others."[10] In the language of the private law of agency, Locke's principle describes *subdelegation* rather than delegation.[11] Justice Neil Gorsuch, in particular, has cited Locke as "one of the thinkers who most influenced the framers' understanding of the separation of powers."[12] The Constitution undeniably delegates legislative powers from "We the People" to Congress, so perhaps the better framing of the issue is whether the Constitution then permits subdelegation from Congress to others. The cases, however, consistently speak of congressional delegation and nondelegation.

LEGISLATIVE DELEGATION ON THE MARSHALL COURT

Wayman v. Southard (1825) was the Supreme Court's first major encounter with the question of legislative delegation (or subdelegation).[13] A congressional statute fixed court rules for such matters as serving process and executing judgments, but it also authorized the judiciary to make "such alterations and additions as the said courts respectively shall in their discretion deem expedient. . . ."[14] Congress's enumerated legislative power under the Necessary and Proper Clause surely allows it to make laws "for carrying into Execution" the judicial power by specifying forms of process and the manner of execution of judgments. In a lengthy dictum, Chief Justice John Marshall, for a unanimous Court,

seemed to place a limit on Congress's powers to transfer legislative authority to the judiciary: "It will not be contended that Congress can delegate to the Courts, or to any other tribunals, powers which are strictly and exclusively legislative."[15] But Marshall also noted that some actions are not, in their nature, exclusively legislative. The fact that Congress could properly legislate in the area of judicial procedure did not mean that the *courts* could not also exercise power over those matters and that Congress could not enlist the courts to help establish the rules of procedure. This point is crucial to an understanding of the Legislative Vesting Clause, the Constitution's essential structure, and the lines drawn by the document among the various governmental powers.

The Constitution divides and allocates governmental *powers*, not governmental *functions* or *actions*. There may be some *actions*—such as passage of a bill, direction of troops in battle, or entry of a criminal judgment—that are uniquely the exercise of legislative, executive, or judicial *powers*, respectively, but other *actions* can easily fall within the scope of more than one of the three vested constitutional *powers*. For example, Congress has the exclusive *power* of establishing in law the right of persons to present claims against the government, but it can vest the *action* of adjudicating those claims in each of the three branches: in the courts as part of their judicial power of deciding cases, in the executive as part of its power to execute the laws faithfully, or in Congress itself as part of its own legislative power by passing private bills for the relief of individuals. Thus, the legislative, executive, and judicial powers are partially overlapping rather than mutually exclusive categories with regard to the actions that fall within these three categories.

Thus, *Wayman* reasoned, if the courts could promulgate rules of procedure under their "judicial Power," it would not constitute a delegation of legislative power for Congress to channel that power through a statute even if the statute provided no clear guidelines. Because this discussion was *dictum*, it was not necessary for the Court to determine precisely which procedural rules had to be fixed by Congress and which could be set by courts under a vague authorization from Congress. As Marshall noted, "there is some difficulty in discerning the exact limits within which the legislature may avail itself of the agency of its Courts."[16]

Similar difficulty arises when Congress seeks to "avail itself" of the aid of the executive in implementing statutes, perhaps by having agencies promulgate regulations or conduct adjudications to determine the meaning of a statute. The First Congress enacted a law that provided for the payment of military pensions "under such regulations as the President of the United States may direct."[17] Another such law required that licensed Indian traders be governed "by such rules and regulations as the President shall prescribe."[18] "The difference between the departments," explained Marshall, "undoubtedly is, that the legislature makes, the executive executes, and the judiciary construes the law; but the maker of the law may commit something to the discretion of the other departments, and the precise boundary of this power is a subject of delicate and difficult inquiry. . . ."[19] As for how to resolve this "delicate and difficult inquiry" when necessary, "[t]he line has not been exactly drawn which separates those *important* subjects, which must be entirely regulated by the legislature itself, from those of *less interest*, in which a general provision may be made, and power given to those who are to act under such general provisions, to fill up the details."[20]

LEGISLATIVE DELEGATION BEFORE AND DURING THE NEW DEAL

Courts have spent two centuries trying to improve on Chief Justice Marshall's analysis. The courts since 1825 have not expressly tried to distinguish between "important" matters and matters of "less interest" as the touchstone for determining the kind and quality of discretion that Congress can permissibly vest in executive or judicial actors. It is unclear what replaced that line for the first century after 1825.

Before the New Deal in the 1930s, there were many challenges to statutes as impermissible delegations of legislative authority. In all of those cases, the Court treated the challenges as constitutionally serious, although it was never clear about precisely how one should try to resolve such challenges. Only two of those cases found a statute unconstitutional, and neither

involved an executive agency.[21] More common was the outcome in *J. W. Hampton, Jr. & Co. v. United States* (1928), in which the Court upheld a statute authorizing the President to adjust tariff rates to "equalize the . . . costs of production" in the United States and the exporting country.[22] In oft-quoted language, the Court set out a standard that has governed for the ensuing century: A statute vesting very broad discretion in executive or judicial actors is constitutional if "Congress shall lay down by legislative act an *intelligible principle* to which the person or body . . . is directed to conform."[23]

In 1935, during the early years of the New Deal, the Court decided two cases that found an absence of "intelligible principle[s]" in two provisions of the National Industrial Recovery Act: *Panama Refining Co. v. Ryan* (1935) and *A.L.A. Schechter Poultry Corp. v. United States* (1935). For the first and (thus far) only times in the nation's history, the Court found statutes to be unconstitutional delegations of legislative authority to federal agencies.[24] The sheer scope of power over national affairs granted by the statute was unprecedented, and many scholars have speculated that this feature of the statute played a role in the decisions.

LEGISLATIVE DELEGATION AFTER THE NEW DEAL

In the nine decades since *Panama Refining* and *Schechter Poultry*, the Court has not declared a statute unconstitutional on delegation grounds. The Court has found valid "intelligible principle[s]" in a wide range of statutes: for example, laws that require agencies to determine "excessive profits"; to grant licenses as "public interest, convenience, or necessity" require; to set "fair" and "equitable" prices; and to prohibit corporate structures that "unfairly or inequitably" distribute voting power among security holders. In *Mistretta v. United States* (1989), the Court all but declared the delegation doctrine *non-justiciable*—that is, a dispute incapable of being resolved by the courts. *Mistretta* upheld an open-ended grant of authority to the U.S. Sentencing Commission to set ranges for criminal sentences. The Court explained that "our jurisprudence has been driven by a practical understanding that in our increasingly complex society, replete with ever changing and more technical problems, Congress simply cannot do its job absent an ability to delegate power under broad general directives."[25]

In *Whitman v. American Trucking Association* (2001), the Court unanimously upheld, with relatively little discussion, a statute instructing the Environmental Protection Agency to set ambient air quality standards "which in the judgment of the Administrator . . . are requisite to protect the public health" with "an adequate margin of safety."[26] From *Mistretta* through *Whitman,* the Supreme Court rejected all fifty-three delegations challenges before it.

The consequences of the Court's reluctance to police the boundaries of the legislative, executive, and judicial powers cannot be overstated. Since the New Deal, Congress has routinely enacted statutes that place the vast bulk of responsibility for promulgating binding norms in administrative agencies. Derivatively, courts review the decisions of these administrative agencies. With these sweeping delegations of authority, by any relevant measure, agencies are far more important instruments of governance than Congress is.

The Court has signaled a potential change in its approach. In *Gundy v. United States* (2019), upholding a statute that let the Attorney General determine the retroactive effects of a criminal law, three Justices vigorously dissented, calling for revival of a serious delegation principle.[27] Justice Gorsuch, joined by Chief Justice John Roberts and Justice Clarence Thomas, rejected the toothless "intelligible principle" inquiry that has governed for the past century. Justice Gorsuch located the delegation principle in the structure of enumerated institutional powers on the theory that "[i]f Congress could pass off its legislative power to the executive branch, the '[v]esting [c]lauses, and indeed the entire structure of the Constitution,' would 'make no sense.'"[28] Justice Samuel Alito expressed a willingness to reconsider the Court's jurisprudence in a future case. "If a majority of this Court were willing to reconsider the approach we have taken for the past 84 years," he wrote, "I would support that effort."[29] Shortly thereafter, Justice Brett Kavanaugh, who did not participate in the *Gundy* case, wrote in a concurrence to a denial of certiorari that "Justice Gorsuch's thoughtful *Gundy* opinion raised important points that may warrant further consideration in future cases."[30]

OPEN QUESTIONS

- If the Court chooses to reconsider the governing "intelligible principle" doctrine, "What's the test"[31] to determine whether a statute violates the delegation doctrine?
- Does the Constitution impose a categorical ban on all legislative grants of executive or judicial discretion? Or does it provide a categorical approval of all legislative grants of executive or judicial discretion? Or does it support a calibrated doctrine that applies differently in different contexts—and possibly across different clauses?[32]
- Does history provide good answers to any of the foregoing questions? Which history is most relevant? For example, does the history of early Congresses count for more, for less, or the same as the history of the common law of principal and agent?
- Do delegations to private parties raise more serious concerns than delegations to other government actors raise?

Cite as: Gary S. Lawson, *The Legislative Vesting Clause, in* THE HERITAGE GUIDE TO THE CONSTITUTION 5 (Josh Blackman & John G. Malcolm eds., 3d ed. 2025).

Notes

1. 1 Farrand's 20–21; Aaron T. Knapp, *The New Jersey Plan and the Structure of the American Union,* 15 Geo. J.L. & Pub. Pol'y 615, 620 (2017).   **2.** Penn. Const. of 1790, art, I, § 1; Ga. Const. of 1789, art. I, § 1.   **3.** 4 The Works of John Adams 579 (Charles Francis Adams ed., 1851).   **4.** John Mikhail, *The Constitution and the Philosophy of Language: Entailment, Implicature, and Implied Powers,* 101 Va. L. Rev. 1063, 1080–81 (2015); Richard Primus, *Herein of "Herein Granted": Why Article I's Vesting Clause Does Not Support the Doctrine of Enumerated Powers,* 35 Const. Comment. 301 (2020).   **5.** 2 Farrand's 21.   **6.** 17 U.S. (4 Wheat.) 316, 405 (1819).   **7.** 514 U.S. 549, 552 (1995).   **8.** Kevin Arlyck, *Delegation, Administration, and Improvisation,* 97 Notre Dame L. Rev. 243 (2021); Julian Mortenson & Nicholas

Bagley, *Delegation at the Founding*, 121 Colum. L. Rev. 277 (2021); Nicholas Parillo, *A Critical Assessment of the Originalist Case Against Administrative Regulatory Power: New Evidence from the Federal Tax on Private Real Estate in the 1790s*, 130 Yale L.J. 1288 (2021). **9.** Aaron Gordon, *Nondelegation Misinformation: A Reply to the Skeptics*, 75 Baylor L. Rev. 152 (2023); Ilan Wurman, *Nondelegation at the Founding*, 130 Yale L.J. 1490 (2021). **10.** John Locke, Second Treatise on Civil Government § 141. **11.** Philip Hamburger, Is Administrative Law Unlawful? 377 (2015); Gary Lawson, *A Private-Law Framework for Subdelegation, in* The Administrative State Before the Supreme Court 123 (Peter J. Wallison & John Yoo eds., 2022). **12.** *Gundy v. United States*, 588 U.S. 128, 153 (2019) (Gorsuch, J., dissenting). **13.** 23 U.S. (10 Wheat.) 1 (1825). **14.** Act of May 8, 1792, ch. 36, § 2, 2 Stat. 275, 276. **15.** *Wayman*, 23 U.S. (10 Wheat.) at 42. **16.** *Id.* at 46. **17.** Act of Sept. 29, 1789, ch. 24, 1 Stat. 95. 18. Act of July 22, 1790, ch. 33, § 1, 1 Stat. 137. 19. *Wayman*, 23 U.S. (10 Wheat.) at 46. **20.** *Id.* at 43 (emphasis added). **21.** *United States v. L. Cohen Grocery Co.*, 255 U.S. 81 (1921); *Knickerbocker Ice Co. v. Stewart*, 253 U.S. 149 (1920). **22.** 276 U.S. 394 (1928). **23.** *Id.* at 409. **24.** 293 U.S. 388 (1935); 295 U.S. 495 (1935). **25.** 488 U.S. 361, 372 (1989). **26.** 531 U.S. 457, 472 (2001). **27.** 588 U.S. 128, 149 (2019) (Gorsuch, J., dissenting). **28.** *Id.* at 155 (Gorsuch, J., dissenting) (quoting Gary Lawson, *Delegation and Original Meaning*, 88 Va. L. Rev. 327, 340 (2002)). **29.** 588 U.S. at 149 (Alito, J., concurring in the judgment). **30.** *Paul v. United States*, 140 S.Ct. 342 (2019). **31.** *Gundy*, 588 U.S. at 157 (Gorsuch, J., dissenting). **32.** Michael B. Rappaport, *A Two Tiered and Categorical Approach to the Nondelegation Doctrine, in* The Administrative State Before the Supreme Court: Perspectives on the Nondelegation Doctrine 195 (Peter J. Wallison & John C. Yoo eds., 2022); Chad Squitieri, *Towards Nondelegation Doctrines*, 86 Mo. L. Rev. 1239 (2021).

ESSAY NO. 6: THE HOUSE OF REPRESENTATIVES CLAUSE
ART. I, § 2, CL. 1

The House of Representatives shall be composed of Members chosen every second Year by the People of the several States . . .

—Bradley Smith

INTRODUCTION

The House of Representatives, unlike the Senate, is elected every two years "by the People of the several States." The direct election for the lower house was deeply rooted in colonial and post-independence practice. During the Constitutional Convention and the ratification process, there was broad agreement that members of the House would be elected by the people rather than by the state legislatures, but there was some disagreement about the duration: One year was too short, three years was too long, so two years was something of a compromise. In the early years of the Republic and well into the twentieth century, there was no suggestion that congressional districts must have equal populations. That practice changed with a series of decisions by the Warren Court in the early 1960s. Though not based on original understanding, there is little evidence that the Court is prepared to reassess its core jurisprudence in this area or that there is public demand for it to do so.

HISTORY BEFORE 1787

England's first representative parliament, the "Model Parliament" of 1295, based representation on geography. Every borough and every county was represented by two members, and this system was still in place at the time of the American settlement. Naturally, the early colonists tended to bring this system of geographic parliamentary representation with them.[1]

In 1619, Virginia convened the first representative assembly in colonial America.[2] The following year, to the north, the Pilgrims signed the Mayflower Compact before coming ashore, committing themselves to popular election of a "civil Body Politick" for the Plymouth Colony.[3] By the end of the seventeenth century, most colonies held regular elections. By 1776, the precedent was established, and elections to the lower house were the norm throughout colonial America. By contrast, the practice for upper houses was appointment, either directly by the king or by the colony's proprietor or governor. In Rhode Island and Connecticut, however, the upper chambers were elected. The importance placed on direct elections of the lower chambers can be seen in the frequency of elections—annually in most of the colonies and even semiannually in some.[4]

Generally, representatives in colonial America were apportioned by town or other geographic area. The early legislatures in Virginia and the Plymouth Colony set the standard with two delegates from each town or constituency regardless of population.[5] By 1787, some lawmakers recognized the desirability of some measure of population equality across districts but geographic considerations remained dominant.[6] For example, the Northwest Ordinance of 1787 did not require equally populated districts in the Northwest Territories. Representation was based on "counties or townships," and there would be one representative per 500 persons in the legislative assembly.[7]

THE CONSTITUTIONAL CONVENTION

On May 29, 1787, Edmund Randolph of Virginia presented the Virginia Plan to the Constitutional Convention. The Plan provided that "members of the first branch of the National Legislature ought to be elected by the people of the several states. . . ." Randolph's proposal left the term of office blank.[8]

Despite the tradition of popular elections, the proposal to choose representatives through direct election by the people met immediate opposition from Roger Sherman of Connecticut and Elbridge Gerry of Massachusetts. On May 31, both expressed concerns about the people being "misled" by demagogues. Gerry proposed a system in which state legislatures would choose representatives to the House from candidates nominated by popular election.[9]

James Wilson of Pennsylvania "contended strenuously" for direct election of "the most numerous branch of the Legislature" and argued that direct election was essential to the success of the federal government, which must have the "confidence" of the people and not be subservient to the state legislatures.[10] George Mason of Virginia agreed that direct election was necessary to assure that the House "sympathise with every part of the community."[11] Mason further worried about the "indifference of the superior classes" to the bulk of society absent direct

election.[12] James Madison of Virginia likewise argued that popular election was "essential to every plan of free government." Popular election, Madison contended, would make the government "more stable and durable" and more attentive to the concerns of all classes.[13] The views of Wilson, Mason, and Madison prevailed in the Committee of the Whole.[14]

On June 21, the matter was taken up by the full Convention. Charles Cotesworth Pinckney of South Carolina proposed that representatives to the House would be "elected in such manner as the Legislature of each State should direct."[15] The earlier debate largely repeated itself, with Mason and Wilson, now joined by Alexander Hamilton of New York and Rufus King of Massachusetts, arguing for direct election. Sherman again expressed his preference for election by legislatures but indicated that he would not oppose direct election. Pinckney's motion was defeated. The Convention then ratified an amendment that would provide for election to the lower house "by the people."[16]

Debate at the Convention centered around proportional representation of the states, not on equality of population between districts within a state. Wilson's arguments on the subject could certainly be considered supportive of equally populated districts,[17] but at no point during these debates was it suggested that election "by the people" meant that districts would be *required* to have equal populations. Rather, it was presumed that the remedy, if any, for large population disparities would lie in the Elections Clause. This provision would grant Congress the power to alter the "Times, Places, and Manner" of choosing members.[18]

The Convention compromised on the terms for House seats. Some delegates preferred annual elections, and others favored a longer, three-year term. Madison argued that three years would provide for greater stability in government.[19] At the time, most states held annual legislative elections. Madison suggested that representatives to Congress would need longer terms to develop knowledge of the federal government and of the other states. He observed that one-year terms would be largely taken up with travel to and from the capital. Gerry replied that the citizens of New England would "never" give up annual elections and that frequent elections were a vital check on tyranny.[20]

On June 21, Oliver Ellsworth of Connecticut moved for one-year terms. Wilson argued that the shorter terms were necessary to make the lower house an "effectual representation" of the people, but Madison pressed the argument for three-year terms, citing travel costs.[21] Hamilton expressed concern that frequent elections made the people "listless to them" and so facilitated "little cabals."[22] Mason noted that because of travel time, annual elections would benefit the middle states that were close to the capital.[23]

Sherman again expressed his preference for annual elections, fearful that if representatives remained too long at the seat of government, they would "acquire the habits of the place." But, having said his piece, Sherman, pragmatic and conciliatory as always, indicated that he would "be content" with biennial elections, and the Convention ultimately settled on a two-year term as a compromise.[24]

THE RATIFICATION DEBATES

Despite considerable debate at the Convention, the requirement for election of the House "by the people" received almost no mention during the ratification debates. Most opponents of the Constitution criticized the document for containing too few, not too many, democratic features. In Federalist No. 39, Madison wrote that the House of Representatives "is elected immediately by the great body of the people," a practice "like that of one branch at least of all the State legislatures." The House of Representatives Clause was a less than profitable point of attack for the Anti-Federalists.

The term of office received somewhat more attention. Centinel, an Anti-Federalist, argued that two-year terms were too long to "preserve a due dependence and accountability to their constituents."[25] Nathaniel Barrell, another Anti-Federalist, wrote that two-year terms made it too difficult to oust representatives who "behave[] ill."[26] Nevertheless, the duration was not a major point of debate, and alteration was not proposed in the post-ratification amendments that became the Bill of Rights.

EARLY PRACTICE

In the early years of the Republic, representation in the House was commonly based on towns and geographic districts rather than strictly on population.[27] Many state constitutions, like Pennsylvania's and Alabama's, required some degree of population equality in state legislative districts.[28] As a result, states usually drew congressional districts with some intent to equalize population across districts, but strict population equality was not the norm.[29] In 1872, Congress required states to draw equally populated districts "as nearly as practical."[30] Five decades later, this provision was removed in the Reapportionment Act of 1929.[31] Nevertheless, at any given time from ratification through the middle of the twentieth century, the overwhelming majority of states redistricted without regard to having equally populated districts.[32]

JUDICIAL PRECEDENT

Until the mid-twentieth century, Congress's power to set the "manner" of congressional election was widely considered the sole constitutional guarantee against excessive malapportionment. By that time, enormous population disparities, often exceeding a 10-to-1 ratio, existed in every state.[33]

This practice would change after the landmark decision in *Baker v. Carr* (1962). The U.S. Supreme Court reversed precedent and held for the first time that courts could hear claims that districts were malapportioned.[34] Two years later, *Wesberry v. Sanders* (1964) held that Article I, Section 2, Clause 1 mandated that congressional districts be equal in population "as nearly as is practicable."[35] To support its holding, the Court relied on statements that Madison and Wilson made at the Convention in favor of representation according to population.[36] These comments, however, were made during debate over the proportional representation of states in Congress, under which larger states would have more members and smaller states would have fewer members, and did not concern the issue at hand in *Wesberry*: whether districts within a state were required to be equal in population. As Justice John Marshall Harlan observed in dissent, this evidence from the Convention was tangential to the question before the Court.[37] Nevertheless, in *Reynolds v. Sims* (1964), the Court extended the equal population principle to redistricting of state legislatures on the basis of the Fourteenth Amendment.[38]

Since *Wesberry*, the Court has held to a

principle of mathematical equality of population in congressional redistricting. Notably, *Karcher v. Daggett* (1983) declared unconstitutional New Jersey congressional districts with an average population variation of just 726 people, or 0.1384 percent, a figure well within the margin of error in the census count.[39] The Court's dictation of a singular theory of representation undermined both state and congressional power and flexibility in redistricting. For example, requiring near-perfect population equality is often incompatible with following fixed city and county lines, or natural barriers such as mountains or rivers, that might be used to limit the practice of gerrymandering or otherwise drawing districts for partisan gain. This theory may also force legislative mapmakers either to divide natural communities of interests, such as ethnic enclaves, or to submerge them into larger communities. More broadly, this theory hampers the ability of legislative mapmakers to accommodate regional interests and political demands that call for compromise and the careful balancing of political power.

OPEN QUESTIONS

Despite its shaky constitutional grounding, *Wesberry* has not proven to be particularly controversial.[40] *Evenwel v. Abbott* (2016) reaffirmed *Wesberry*'s principle that states can use total population numbers when drawing districts. However, *Evenwel* left open the possibility that states could satisfy the *Wesberry* principle by using "eligible voters" rather than total population: Children, non-citizens, and others ineligible to vote, in other words, would not be considered in determining the size of the district. As a result, each district would have roughly the same number of eligible *voters* rather than the same number of *people*.[41] Under that approach, districts with more minors, aliens, and other people who cannot vote would lose representation.

Nevertheless, no state redistricting after the 2020 census attempted to base representation on the number of eligible voters rather than total population, most likely because the Census Bureau did not include a citizenship question, which would have made gathering citizenship data costly and time-consuming for individual states.[42] Further, nothing in *Evenwel* suggests that the Court is prepared to depart from its requirement of equal numbers, whether of voters or of population.

Cite as: Bradley Smith, *The House of Representatives Clause, in* THE HERITAGE GUIDE TO THE CONSTITUTION 10 (Josh Blackman & John G. Malcolm eds., 3d ed. 2025).

Notes

1. William Edwards, Crown, People, and Parliament 1760–1935, at 68 (1937). **2.** Harry M. Ward, Colonial America 1607–1763, at 27 (1991). **3.** *Id.* at 41. **4.** *Biennial Elections*, U.S. House of Representatives: History, Art & Archives, https://perma.cc/UN43-NR7V. **5.** Ward, *supra* at 46. **6.** N.C. Const. of 1776, arts. II, III. **7.** Ordinance for the Government of the Territory of the United States North-West of the River Ohio, 32 J. Cont. Cong. 334, 337 (July 13, 1787). **8.** 1 Farrand's 20. **9.** *Id.* at 48, 50. **10.** *Id.* at 49. **11.** *Id.* at 48. **12.** *Id.* at 49. **13.** *Id.* at 49–50. **14.** *Id.* at 46. **15.** *Id.* at 358. **16.** *Id.* at 360. **17.** *Id.* at 179, 183. **18.** *Wesberry v. Sanders,* 376 U.S. 1, 29–30 (1964) (Harlan, J., dissenting); Federalist No. 59 (Hamilton). **19.** 1 Farrand's 214. **20.** *Id.* at 214–15. **21.** *Id.* at 361. **22.** *Id.* at 362. **23.** *Id.* **24.** *Id.* **25.** Storing 2.7.22. **26.** 2 Debate on the Constitution 16–17 (Bernard Bailyn ed., 1993). **27.** 1791 Pa. Laws 20; 1801 Mass. Acts 386. **28.** Penn. Const. of 1790, art. I, § 4; Ala. Const. of 1819, art. III, § 9. **29.** Henry N. Williams, Congressional Appointment in Tennessee, 1796–1941, 4 J. Pol. 507, 508 (1942). **30.** Act of February 2, 1872, § 2, 17 Stat. 28. **31.** Pub. Law No. 71-13, 46 Stat. 21 (1929). **32.** *Baker v. Carr,* 369 U.S. 186, 301 (1962) (Frankfurter, J., dissenting). **33.** Stephen Ansolabehere & James M. Snyder, Jr., The End of Inequality: One Person, One Vote, and the Transformation of American Politics 26–27, Table 2.1 (2008). **34.** 369 U.S. 186 (1962). **35.** 376 U.S. 1, 7–8 (1964). **36.** *Id* at 10–18. **37.** *Id.* at 24–27 (Harlan, J., dissenting). **38.** 377 U.S. 533, 577 (1964). **39.** 462 U.S. 725, 727–28 (1983). **40.** Nelson Lund, *From* Baker v. Carr *to* Bush v. Gore, *and Back*, 62 Case W. Res. L. Rev. 947, 948 (2012). **41.** 578 U.S. 54, 74–75 (2016). **42.** *Dept. of Comm. v. New York*, 588 U.S. 752 (2019).

~

ESSAY NO. 7: THE ELECTOR QUALIFICATIONS CLAUSE
ART. I, § 2, CL. 1

. . . the Electors in each State shall have the Qualifications requisite for Electors of the most numerous Branch of the State Legislature.

—Derek T. Muller

INTRODUCTION

Under the Constitution, the voters would elect members of the House of Representatives. The Constitution refers to these voters as *electors*, not to be confused with *presidential electors*. The Framers gave the states wide latitude to define the qualifications of these electors. The power to determine who would elect members of Congress would not be with Congress, but with the states. In short, the qualifications to vote for representatives in Congress would mirror the qualifications to vote for members of the most numerous branch of the state's legislature. The Fifteenth, Nineteenth, Twenty-Fourth, and Twenty-Sixth amendments have restricted the types of qualifications states may enact. Courts have often acknowledged the broad power of states to determine elector qualifications. These cases have affirmed this power while recognizing some federal constraints on that power, including Congress's limited power to override those qualifications.

HISTORY BEFORE 1787

After the Declaration of Independence was signed, eleven states ratified constitutions.[1] Nine of those constitutions included specific elector qualifications.[2] Two referenced those qualifications already in place in their respective states.[3]

Age and residency were common requirements, and many states limited voting to property owners ("freeholders") or taxpayers.[4] North Carolina, for instance, limited voting in its lower house to "freemen" (those who were not enslaved) who were twenty-one years of age, had been inhabitants of the state for twelve months, and "paid public taxes."[5] Pennsylvania restricted the vote to those who "paid public taxes" or were the "sons of freeholders."[6] Massachusetts required that voters own "a freehold estate within the same town" as their residence "of the annual income of three pounds, or any estate of the value of sixty pounds."[7] New York limited voting outside of the cities of Albany and New York to "freeholder[s], possessing a freehold of the value of twenty points . . . or [who] have rented a tenement therein of the yearly value of forty shillings, and been rated and actually paid taxes to this state."[8]

Several state constitutions also included religious qualifications for voters. South Carolina, for example, required voters to believe in God and "in a future state of rewards and punishments."[9] Rhode Island restricted the vote to Christian freemen.[10] Connecticut also restricted the vote to freemen, who were required to be "trusted pillars of the commonwealth."[11] In practice, the franchise was essentially limited to Protestants in Connecticut, because Judaism and Roman Catholicism were not tolerated.[12] Other states made religion a precondition for the protection of inhabitants' rights that may have indirectly affected the right to vote.[13] New Hampshire guaranteed equal protection to Christians, New Jersey ensured the rights of Protestants, and Pennsylvania protected the rights of those who believed in God.[14]

THE CONSTITUTIONAL CONVENTION

By 1787, state restrictions on electors based on age, residency, property ownership, and religion had been widely adopted. These state restrictions on the franchise likely informed how the Framers would have understood federal elector voter qualifications.

During the Constitutional Convention, the Framers agreed to a House of Representatives that would be chosen by the people of the several states, but they debated how voter eligibility for the lower chamber would be determined. James Wilson of Pennsylvania observed that "[i]t was difficult to form any uniform rule of qualifications for all the States."[15] Some states might oppose a national rule of voter eligibility, which could have threatened ratification of the Constitution.[16] The states already imposed qualifications for their own voters. It would be difficult to restrict the franchise for federal officeholders to a set of voters narrower than those allowed under the existing state qualifications. Wilson argued that "[i]t would be very hard & disagreeable for the same persons, at the same time, to vote for representatives in the State Legislature and to be excluded from a vote for those in the Natl. Legislature."[17] James Madison of Virginia warned that "[t]he qualifications of electors and elected were fundamental articles in a Republican Govt." and that "[i]f the Legislature could regulate those of either, it can by degrees subvert the Constitution."[18] Over the entire course of the constitutional debates, several delegates, including John Dickinson of Delaware and Gouverneur Morris of Pennsylvania, proposed requiring that the electors of the House be limited to freeholders, but a majority of the delegates ultimately preferred to defer to the states.[19]

On August 8, delegates voted to approve the Elector Qualifications Clause as it had been presented by the Committee of Detail.[20] The Committee of Style later modified the clause slightly without controversy.[21] The clause provides that in each state, the voters for the members of the House of Representatives shall have the same qualifications as those permitted to vote for the "most numerous Branch of the State Legislature."[22] The "most numerous" branch would generally be the larger, lower house. The Constitution thus gave the states authority for determining elector qualifications.

THE RATIFICATION DEBATES

The Elections Clause granted Congress the power to "make or alter such [state] Regulations" regarding "[t]he Times, Places and Manner of holding Elections for Senators and Representatives."[23] As a textual matter, however, this power was limited to "holding Elections"—not the qualifications for voting. Both Alexander Hamilton and James Madison contended that the Elections Clause and the Elector Qualifications Clause were independent and did not overlap. In Federalist No. 60, Hamilton wrote that the national government's authority under the Elections Clause "would be expressly restricted to the regulation of the *times*, the *places*, and the *manner* of elections" and that under the Elector Qualifications Clause, the "qualifications of the persons who may choose . . . are defined and fixed in the Constitution, and are unalterable by the [national] legislature."

In Federalist No. 52, Madison wrote that, because of its place "as a fundamental article of republican government," it "would have been improper" for the Constitution to "have left [the suffrage right] open for the occasional regulation of the Congress." Madison also thought it would have been improper for the same reason to place this power entirely in the hands of state legislatures. Instead, the Elector Qualifications Clause struck something of a compromise. Qualifications for "that branch of the federal government which ought to be dependent on the people alone" would generally be set by state constitutions, which established suffrage rules, and likely not easily be modified by state legislatures. In Madison's view, the House should not be "rendered too dependent on the State [legislatures]."

There was no meaningful opposition to the Elector Qualifications Clause by the Anti-Federalists.

SUBSEQUENT AMENDMENTS

Four constitutional amendments have expressly prohibited denying or abridging the right to vote on specific grounds: the Fifteenth Amendment (race, color, or previous condition of servitude); the Nineteenth Amendment (sex); the Twenty-Fourth Amendment (failure to pay any tax); and the Twenty-Sixth Amendment (age). The Supreme Court of the United States has also held that the Equal Protection Clause of the Fourteenth Amendment forbids certain arbitrary voter qualifications. *Harper v. Virginia State Board of Elections* (1966) found that a state may not restrict the right to vote in state or local elections on the basis of ability to pay a tax.[24] Such a classification based on wealth has "no relation to voting qualifications" under the Equal Protection Clause.[25] The

Elector Qualifications Clause applies only to federal elections, but these amendments have affected qualifications of voters for both federal and state elections (although the Twenty-Fourth Amendment speaks only of federal elections).

The Seventeenth Amendment, which guaranteed the popular election of Senators, adopted the qualifications for the "Electors of the most numerous Branch of the State Legislature."

JUDICIAL PRECEDENT

The Supreme Court has taken different approaches to the Elector Qualifications Clause. One line of cases granted deference to the state's powers to set voter qualifications. For example, *Lassiter v. Northampton County Board of Elections* (1959) emphasized that states have "broad powers" under the Elector Qualifications Clause to impose a literacy test,[26] and *Richardson v. Ramirez* (1974) expressly held that a state may disqualify ex-felons from voting.[27]

However, a second line of cases has found limitations on state power to limit the franchise more generally under the Equal Protection Clause. *Kramer v. Union Free School District No. 15* (1969) reviewed restrictions on the franchise with skepticism.[28] The Court found unconstitutional a law that limited voting in local school board elections to parents of students or those who owned property. The Court has also held that the First Amendment right of association for political parties may restrict the authority of states to prescribe qualifications for primary elections.[29] For example, a state cannot require a *closed* primary limited to registered members of a political party if a political party's rules allow independents to vote.[30] Moreover, implementation of party rules that established different qualifications for voting in congressional elections than in elections for the more numerous house of the state legislature did not violate the Elector Qualifications Clause or the Seventeenth Amendment.[31]

OPEN QUESTIONS

- What is the relationship between the Elector Qualifications Clause and the Equal Protection Clause?
- What restrictions on voter qualifications are still permissible?
- Are the rules for political parties limiting the pool of voters who may participate in primary elections for members of Congress subject to any limitations?

Cite as: Derek T. Muller, *The Elector Qualifications Clause, in* The Heritage Guide to the Constitution 14 (Josh Blackman & John G. Malcolm eds., 3d ed. 2025).

Notes

1. Forrest McDonald, *Original Unintentions: The Franchise and the Constitution*, 40 Modern Age 344, 346 (1998). **2.** *Id.* **3.** *Id.* at 347. **4.** *Id.* at 346–48. **5.** N.C. Const. of 1776, art. VIII. **6.** Pa. Const. of 1776, ch. II, § 6. **7.** Mass. Const. of 1780, ch. I, § 3, art. IV. **8.** N.Y. Const. of 1777, art. VII. **9.** S.C. Const. of 1778, art. XIII. **10.** McDonald, *supra* at 347. **11.** *Id.* **12.** *Id.* at 346–47. **13.** *Id.* **14.** N.H. Const. of 1783, pt. I, art. VI; N.J. Const. of 1776, art. XIX; Pa. Const. of 1776, ch. I, § 2. **15.** 2 Farrand's 201. **16.** Alexander Keyssar, The Right to Vote: The Contested History of Democracy in the United States 23–24 (2000). **17.** 2 Farrand's 201. **18.** *Id.* at 250. **19.** 1 Farrand's 364, 368; 2 Farrand's 139, 151, 153, 163–64, 178, 209, 565, 590, 651. **20.** 2 Farrand's 216. **21.** *Id.* at 565, 590. **22.** Art. I, § 2, cl. 1. **23.** Art. I, § 4. **24.** 383 U.S. 663 (1966). **25.** *Id.* **26.** 360 U.S. 45, 50–51 (1959). **27.** 418 U.S. 24, 56 (1974). **28.** 395 U.S. 621, 622, 626–29 (1969). **29.** *Cal. Democratic Party v. Jones*, 530 U.S. 567, 577 (2000); *Clingman v. Beaver*, 544 U.S. 581, 591, 593–94 (2005). **30.** *Tashjian v. Republican Party of Conn.*, 479 U.S. 208, 216 (1986). **31.** *Id.* at 228–29.

~

ESSAY NO. 8: THE QUALIFICATIONS FOR REPRESENTATIVES CLAUSE
ART. I, § 2, CL. 2

No Person shall be a Representative who shall not have attained to the Age of twenty five Years, and been seven Years a Citizen of the United States, and who shall not, when elected, be an Inhabitant of that State in which he shall be chosen.
—Derek T. Muller

INTRODUCTION

The Constitution enumerates three qualifications for members of the House of Representatives: age, United States citizenship, and state inhabitancy. The Framers rejected more extensive qualifications for members of the House, and few disputes have arisen over these three. After the Framing, there were extensive debates about whether Congress or the states could add qualifications for members of the House, but in *Powell v. McCormack* (1969) and *U.S. Term Limits, Inc. v. Thornton* (1995), the Supreme Court concluded that neither may do so.

HISTORY BEFORE 1787

Rules about who was eligible to serve in elected office were common before the Constitution was adopted. Justice Joseph Story noted that, before ratification, "a great diversity of qualifications existed" for state representatives.[1] Delaware required only that members of its assembly be freeholders.[2] Georgia required representatives to be residents of the county from which they were elected for at least three months and residents of the state for twelve months; be members of the "Protestant religion"; be at least twenty-one years of age; and own at least 250 acres of land or property worth 250 pounds.[3] The Articles of Confederation imposed term limits on members of the national legislature: "[N]o person shall be capable of being a delegate for more than three years in any term of six years."[4]

THE CONSTITUTIONAL CONVENTION

Early in the Constitutional Convention, delegates added an age requirement for members of the House.[5] The Framers later considered but ultimately rejected property ownership and indebtedness.[6] Instead, they settled on three qualifications. Representatives must be at least twenty-five years of age, which presumes a minimum level of experience and maturity;[7] must have been U.S. citizens for seven years, which would prevent undue foreign influence;[8] and must be inhabitants of the states in which they are chosen.

The third standard was less onerous than a "residency" requirement would have been. As James Madison of Virginia explained, a residency requirement might "exclude persons absent occasionally for a considerable time on public or private business."[9] Inhabitancy would be ascertained for a candidate "when elected" and not beforehand. The Framers rejected proposals that would require one, three, or six-year inhabitance.[10]

John Dickinson of Delaware acknowledged that enumerating some qualifications meant that others could not be added. In fact, Dickinson opposed listing any qualifications precisely because it "would by implication tie up the hands of the Legislature from supplying the omissions."[11] His statement suggests that "the Framers were well aware of the *expressio unius* argument that would result from their wording of the Qualifications Clauses"—enumerating some qualifications meant that there were no other qualifications except those listed.[12]

The Constitution's structure supports this view. Article I, Section 5 provides that "[e]ach house shall be the Judge of the Elections, Returns and Qualifications of its own members." Each house of Congress may "punish its Members for disorderly behavior, and, with the Concurrence of two thirds, expel a Member." And the Elections Clause of Article I, Section 4 provides that "[t]he Times, Places and Manner of holding Elections for Senators and Representatives, shall be prescribed in each State by the Legislature thereof; but the Congress may at any time by Law make or alter such Regulations. . . ."[13] The structural separation of these provisions suggests distinct roles in administering elections. Congress's power over the "Times, Places, and Manner of holding Elections" is separate from the power over qualifications. The Constitution does not expressly grant states and Congress the power to regulate qualifications, which are fixed and enumerated elsewhere.[14]

Another structural argument further suggests that these qualifications are exclusive. As Article I, Section 5 states, Congress has the power to judge the qualifications enumerated in the Constitution, which takes place by a simple majority vote, and to expel seated members with a two-thirds vote. It would be inconsistent to allow a house to impose additional qualifications by a simple majority vote when the Constitution requires a supermajority vote to expel a member on grounds not enumerated in the Constitution. This structure suggests that a house can judge only the qualifications that are set forth in Article I, Section 2.[15]

THE RATIFICATION DEBATES
During the state ratification process, the debate over qualifications continued. These records arguably furnish more evidence for the inability of states or Congress to add qualifications beyond those mentioned in Article I, Section 2. Both the Constitution's promoters and its critics noted the minimal qualifications set out for Representatives. For instance, in Federalist No. 52, Madison praised the fact that there were few qualifications: "[T]he door of this part of the Federal Government, is open to merit of every description, whether native or adoptive, whether young or old, and without regard to poverty or wealth, or to any particular profession of religious faith."

In Federalist No. 60, Alexander Hamilton emphasized that the legislature had no power to add to these qualifications. He explained that the power under the Elections Clause "would be expressly restricted to the regulation of the *times*, the *places*, and the *manner* of elections," adding that "[t]he qualifications of the persons who may choose or be chosen . . . are defined and fixed in the Constitution, and are unalterable by the legislature."

Others condemned these few qualifications. The Federal Farmer, an Anti-Federalist, would have imposed far more qualifications for serving in Congress. He charged that the Constitution allows "pagans," "convicts," "beggar[s]," "absentee[s]," and "many men . . . who cannot be electors" to serve as "elected representatives."[16] In Massachusetts, some delegates complained that there were no property qualifications for members of Congress. One delegate remarked that the system was "democratic." He asked, "[W]hy should we bridle the people in their elections?"[17]

EARLY PRACTICE
Shortly after the Constitution was ratified, some states added qualifications for federal candidates.[18] Virginia, for example, required that members of Congress be "freeholder[s],"[19] one of two provisions that, according to St. George Tucker, "require[d] qualifications which the constitution does not" and therefore might "possibly be found to be nugatory" (of no force) in practice.[20] Five states in this early period required members of Congress to reside in the districts they sought to represent.[21] While the Constitution required only "inhabitancy" in the state, these states required establishing residency in a particular part of the state, and residency, as noted, was potentially a more onerous requirement than inhabitancy.

By contrast, Thomas Jefferson contended that the Constitution chose "the middle way" on the qualifications of candidates. In an 1814 letter, Jefferson wrote that the Constitution mandates "some disqualifications" (age, inhabitancy, and citizenship) while allowing states to impose other, non-uniform disqualifications that are otherwise constitutional.[22]

In 1833, Justice Story wrote that the Constitution's specifically enumerated qualifications "exclude[d] all others." He explained that states do not have powers that "spring out of the existence of the national government, which the constitution does not delegate to them."[23] Story rejected Jefferson's contrary view.[24] The Constitution established the federal government and federal elections. Therefore, Story argued, the power to add qualifications could not have been "reserved" to the states when the Constitution was adopted, because state power over federal elections did not exist before 1788.[25]

JUDICIAL PRECEDENT

There was no material judicial interpretation of the clause until the late twentieth century. The question of whether the House of Representatives could add to what constituted "qualifications" reached the U.S. Supreme Court in *Powell v. McCormack* (1969). The House refused to seat Representative-elect Adam Clayton Powell, Jr., because of Powell's serious misconduct even though Powell met the qualifications enumerated in Article I, Section 2.[26] The Court held that "the Constitution leaves the House without authority to *exclude* any person, duly elected by his constituents, who meets all the requirements for membership expressly prescribed in the Constitution."[27] In other words, the House could not refuse to seat Powell by adding a qualification to those enumerated in the Constitution.

However, *Powell* left open the question whether the states could add to the qualifications stated in the Constitution. This issue came to a head in the 1990s during a popular movement for congressional term limits. *United States Term Limits, Inc. v. Thornton* (1995) held that the Constitution's qualifications were in fact exclusive and that the states could therefore neither add to nor alter them.[28]

Justice John Paul Stevens's majority opinion reaffirmed the historical argument in *Powell* that Congress did not have the power to alter qualifications and extended that rationale to the states.[29] The Court relied on the Founding-era debates, which focused on the fact that the enumeration of some qualifications suggested that they were an exclusive list. The Court also considered the structure of the Constitution's other election provisions to find that states lacked the power to add qualifications. The majority relied heavily on the historical analysis from *Powell*, along with interpretations of Federalist Nos. 52 and 60 and Story's *Commentaries*, among other sources.

Justice Clarence Thomas, writing on behalf of four dissenting Justices, proposed a different historical argument. He contended that the federal government was created by the people not as a whole, but of the several states.[30] Thomas further argued that whatever powers were not given to the federal government were thus retained by the states and the people—a view confirmed by the Tenth Amendment.[31] Consequently, he reasoned, the states retained the power to add qualifications for Representatives.[32] If the Constitution did not remove the power to add qualifications from the states or the people, then it could not bar any action by the people of the states to add qualifications. Thomas carefully distinguished *Powell*, because the power of Congress is circumscribed in ways that the power of states is not.

Since *Term Limits*, there have been other occasional successful challenges to state laws on the basis that they improperly add to the qualifications for seeking federal office. For instance, California law required candidates for Congress to be registered voters in the state and residents of the state when filing paperwork to run for office. The Ninth Circuit held that this law unconstitutionally added to the qualifications that candidates for federal office are required to meet.[33] Furthermore, the Constitution specifies that the inhabitancy qualification attaches "when elected." A member of Congress need not be an "inhabitant" of a state before Election Day.

OPEN QUESTIONS

- Early records suggest that some states appeared to add qualifications for congressional candidates. Were those qualifications ever actually enforced or disputed?
- Does the *Term Limits* rule extend to qualifications for the office of President?[34]
- States provide rules over who may or may not appear on the ballot. When do these rules function to add qualifications to candidates? When are they simply rules regulating the "manner of holding elections"?[35]

Cite as: Derek T. Muller, *The Qualifications For Representatives Clause, in* THE HERITAGE GUIDE TO THE CONSTITUTION 17 (Josh Blackman & John G. Malcolm eds., 3d ed. 2025).

Notes

1. 2 Story's Commentaries § 614. **2.** Del. Const. of 1776, art. III. **3.** Ga. Const. of 1777, art. VI. **4.** Articles of Confederation, art. V, § 2. **5.** 1 Farrand's 375. **6.** 2 Farrand's 116–17, 121–26. **7.** 1 Farrand's 375. **8.** 2 Farrand's 268–72. **9.** *Id.* at 216–17. **10.** *Id.* at 218–19, 590. **11.** *Id.* at 123. **12.** *U.S. Term Limits, Inc. v. Thornton*, 514 U.S. 779, 793 n.9 (1995). **13.** Art. I, § 4, cl. 1. **14.** Derek T. Muller, *Weaponizing the Ballot*, 48 Fla. St. U.L. Rev. 61, 76 (2020); Robert G. Natelson, *The Original Scope of the Congressional Power to Regulate Elections*, 13 U. Pa. J. Const. L. 1, 22 (2010). **15.** Muller, *supra* at 76; Josh Chafetz, Congress's Constitution: Legislative Authority and the Separation of Powers 258–59 (2017). **16.** Storing 2.8.150. **17.** 6 DHRC 1240–41. **18.** Polly J. Price, *Term Limits on Original Intent? An Essay on Legal Debate and Historical Understanding*, 82 Va. L. Rev. 493, 509–12 (1996). **19.** Acts Passed at a General Assembly of the Commonwealth of Virginia, ch. 2, § 2 (Richmond, 1788). **20.** St. George Tucker, *View of the Constitution of the United States*, *in* View of the Constitution of the United States with Selected Writings 116 (Clyde N. Wilson ed., 1999), https://perma.cc/LJM8-TXAC. **21.** *U.S. Term Limits*, 514 U.S. at 826–27 & n.41. **22.** Letter from Thomas Jefferson to Joseph C. Cabell (Jan. 31, 1814), https://perma.cc/DT5U-Q2EN. **23.** 1 Story's Commentaries §§ 624, 626. **24.** 2 Story's Commentaries §§ 614–15, 625. **25.** *Id.* at § 625. **26.** *Powell v. McCormack*, 395 U.S. 486, 490 (1969). **27.** *Id.* at 522 (footnote omitted; emphasis in original). **28.** 514 U.S. 779, 783 (1995). **29.** *Id.* at 789–93. **30.** *Id.* at 846 (Thomas, J., dissenting). **31.** *Id.* at 847. **32.** *Id.* at 926. **33.** *Schaefer v. Townsend*, 251 F.3d 1031 (9th Cir. 2001) (O'Scannlain, J.). **34.** *U.S. Term Limits*, 514 U.S. at 861 (Thomas, J., dissenting); *Chiafalo v. Washington*, 591 U.S. 578, 589 n.5. **35.** Muller, *supra* at 2.

~

ESSAY NO. 9: THE THREE-FIFTHS CLAUSE
ART. I, § 2, CL. 3

Representatives and direct Taxes shall be apportioned among the several States which may be included within this Union, according to their respective Numbers, which shall be determined by adding to the whole Number of free Persons, including those bound to Service for a Term of Years, and excluding Indians not taxed, three fifths of all other Persons.

—Rebecca E. Zietlow

INTRODUCTION

The Three-Fifths Clause is among the most notorious provisions of our Constitution. For purposes of taxation and representation, "other Persons" were counted as only sixty percent of a person. Although the Three-Fifths Clause does not include the word "slave," its phrasing implies that "other people" were neither free nor white—and thus were enslaved.[1] Along with the so-called Fugitive Slave Clause,[2] the Three-Fifths Clause represented an acknowledgment of the institution of slavery in our original Constitution.[3] This provision was effectively repealed by the ratification of the Thirteenth Amendment.

THE ARTICLES OF CONFEDERATION

Under the Articles of Confederation, the national government's only source of revenue was the money it derived from "requisitions" that it submitted to the states.[4] These requisitions were based on "the value of all land within each state." However, an amendment to the Articles that was debated in 1783 provided that requisitions would be calculated based on a state's population. Under this proposal, advanced by James Madison, an enslaved person would be counted as three-fifths of a person for purposes of the requisitions.[5]

The resolution was controversial, as some southern states preferred taxation to be based on land values. It was a compromise between northerners, who thought it undervalued enslaved people, and southerners, who thought it overvalued enslaved people, for the purpose of determining taxation.[6] Madison's proposal faced some opposition, and because amendments to the Articles required unanimous consent, it was never adopted.

THE CONSTITUTIONAL CONVENTION

One of the first issues that the Framers of the Constitution considered in 1787 was the question of how representation would be apportioned in Congress. Under the Articles, each state had one vote in Congress. Now, Governor Edmond Randolph of Virginia proposed that the House of Representatives be apportioned based on population.[7] However, the population in the northern states was not equal to the population in the southern states. At the time, southern states had large numbers of enslaved persons but had smaller populations of free people than northern states had.[8]

The southern delegates to the Convention wanted to count enslaved people as full persons to increase their states' representation in the national government. Some northern delegates, on the other hand, resisted counting enslaved people at all. Why, asked Elbridge Gerry of Massachusetts, should "the blacks, who were property in the South, be in the rule of representation more than the cattle & horses of the North?"[9] Northern delegates were also concerned that counting slaves as full persons would incentivize southern slaveholders to import still more slaves. However, some southern delegates even threatened that they would "never confederate" unless enslaved people were counted under at least a three-fifths ratio.[10]

The Three-Fifths Clause represented a compromise between northern and southern delegates. It was introduced by James Wilson and Charles Pinckney on June 11, 1787.[11] "Free persons" would be counted at a ratio of 100 percent, and enslaved persons would be counted at a ratio of sixty percent. The clause excluded "Indians not taxed" because they were subject to tribal, not state, sovereignty.[12] It would also provide roughly equivalent population numbers between the North and the South and augmented the political power of southern states, giving the South a "strong claim to special treatment for its peculiar institution."[13]

By itself, however, the three-fifths compromise for representation was not enough to win approval by the delegates. On July 12, facing deadlock at the Convention, Gouverneur Morris of Pennsylvania moved to add a "proviso that taxation shall be in proportion to Representation" without regard to a three-fifths ratio for enslaved persons.[14] Representation, however, would still be subject to the three-fifths ratio. This proviso was later limited to direct taxation. James Madison of Virginia wrote that the purpose of this proviso was to "lessen the eagerness on one side, & the opposition on the other, to the share of Representation claimed by the [Southern] States on account of the Negroes."[15] In other words, southern states with larger enslaved populations would face a much larger tax burden. Morris said he meant his motion only "as a bridge to assist us over a certain gulph."[16] This proviso ultimately did not succeed. Instead, tying apportionment to both taxation and representation turned out to be crucial.

Under the Three-Fifths Clause as adopted, enslaved people were to be counted as less than free people for representation, which was not in the interests of the South, but also were to be counted as less than free people for measuring a state's apportioned direct-tax liability, which benefitted the South. Furthermore, applying the ratio to taxation as well as to representation protected the integrity of the census. As Madison explained in Federalist No. 54, "the States should feel as little bias as possible to swell or to reduce the amount of their numbers. . . . By extending the rule to both [taxation and representation], the States will have opposite interests which will control and balance each other and produce the requisite impartiality."

THE THREE-FIFTHS CLAUSE AND ABOLITIONISM

The Three-Fifths Clause recognized and, in a way, condoned the institution of slavery. It also insulted the human dignity of enslaved people by treating them as only three-fifths of a person—an insult that was not diminished by the counterintuitive regional divisions whereby southern slaveholders actually favored full representation for enslaved persons, while northern abolitionists opposed any representation at all. However, it is notable that the word "slave" is absent from the clause. Like its companion Fugitive Slave Clause, the Three-Fifths Clause employs the term "person" to refer to enslaved persons.

During the early nineteenth century, antislavery activists engaged in a fierce debate over the constitutionality of slavery. Some, most notably William Lloyd Garrison, referred to the Three-Fifths Clause as evidence that the Constitution was marred by slavery.[17] Others, such as Lysander Spooner and Joel Tiffany, argued that the Framers deliberately avoided using the term "slave" because they did not want to constitutionalize slavery.[18] These antislavery constitutionalists argued that the Framers hoped that slavery would die of its own accord.[19] They also advocated a textualist reading of the Constitution, claiming that the intent of those Framers who hoped to protect slavery was irrelevant to proper constitutional interpretation.

THE THREE-FIFTHS CLAUSE AND REPRESENTATION

Counting enslaved people for purposes of representation even at a three-fifths ratio gave southern states significant political advantages in the House of Representatives and the Electoral College. As a result, during the Antebellum Era, the southern states were largely able to elect Presidents who favored, or at least were not opposed to, slavery (the two notable exceptions being John Adams and John Quincy Adams). These Presidents, in turn, largely selected members of the Supreme Court who favored, or at least were not opposed to, slavery. This trend would continue until the election of Abraham Lincoln and the coming of the Civil War.

THE THREE-FIFTHS CLAUSE AND THE RECONSTRUCTION AMENDMENTS

After the Civil War, the Thirteenth Amendment was ratified. The amendment abolished slavery and in turn invalidated the Three-Fifths Clause. As a result, the population of southern states for purposes of apportionment increased substantially. Ironically, because the freedmen could not vote, the Thirteenth Amendment increased the power of the former Confederate states as their representatives returned to Congress.

Now that formerly enslaved people were counted as full people for the purposes of representation, debates began about efforts by the former Confederate states to deny their right to vote.[20] To prevent the disenfranchisement of the formerly enslaved, the Reconstruction Congress adopted Section 2 of the Fourteenth Amendment. Under this provision, if males over the age of twenty-one were denied the right to vote, they would not be counted for purposes of representation (men could be disenfranchised if they had participated in the rebellion "or other crime"). However, Section Two was never enforced.

After the ratification of the Thirteenth and Fourteenth Amendments, the irony continued: Formerly enslaved people and their descendants were still denied the right to vote even as they counted fully for purposes of representation, and for nearly a century, the power of the southern states in the federal government would continue to increase. The passage of the Voting Rights Act of 1965 would begin to reverse this trend, protecting the right to vote of people of color throughout the country, but especially in the former Confederate states.

OPEN QUESTIONS

The three-fifths rule does not directly affect litigation today, but it does affect how scholars interpret the apportionment requirement for direct taxes. It has been argued, for example, that the clauses dealing with direct taxation should be ignored because they are tainted by slavery or because, with slavery ended, there is no reason to honor any part of the compromise. In light of the entire history that led to the Revolution and the Constitution, however, it would be going too far to assume that in a world without slavery, the Founders would have been indifferent to the dangers of national taxation.

Cite as: Rebecca E. Zietlow, *The Three-Fifths Clause*, *in* The Heritage Guide to the Constitution 20 (Josh Blackman & John G. Malcolm eds., 3d ed. 2025).

Notes

1. Mark Graber, Dred Scott and the Problem of Constitutional Evil 13 (2006).   **2.** Art. IV, § 2, cl. 3.   **3.** Paul Finkleman, Slavery and the Founders: Race and Liberty in the Age of Jefferson 7 (2d. ed. 2001).   **4.** Articles of Confederation, art. VIII.   **5.** Digital History, *The Three-Fifth Compromise*, https://perma.cc/S7KN-3A76.   **6.** Finkleman, *supra* at 13.   **7.** *Id.* at 10.   **8.** Graber, *supra* at 101.   **9.** 1 Farrand's 201.   **10.** Finkleman, *supra* at 19.   **11.** 1 Farrand's 193, 201, 205.   **12.** Brad Tenant, *"Excluding Indians Not Taxed"*:
Dred Scott, Standing Bear, Elk and the Legal Status of Native Americans in the Latter Half of the Nineteenth Century, 86 Int'l Soc. Science Rev. 24 (2011).   **13.** *Id.* at 7.   **14.** 1 Farrand's 592.   **15.** 2 Farrand's 106.   **16.** *Id.*   **17.** Finkleman, *supra* at 3.   **18.** Rebecca E. Zietlow, The Forgotten Emancipator: James Mitchell Ashley and the Ideological Origins of Reconstruction 38 (2017).   **19.** *Id.* at 36.   **20.** Franita Tolson, *The Constitutional Structure of Voting Rights Enforcement*, 89 Wash. L. Rev. 379 (2014).

ESSAY NO. 10: THE ENUMERATION CLAUSE
ART. I, § 2, CL. 3

The actual Enumeration shall be made within three Years after the first Meeting of the Congress of the United States, and within every subsequent Term of ten Years, in such Manner as they shall by Law direct.

—Andrew C. Spiropoulos

INTRODUCTION

Under the Constitution, representation in the House of Representatives is based on population. The Enumeration Clause requires that an "actual Enumeration" be taken every decade. There are two possible bases for the enumeration: The *actual* enumeration would rely on the physical count of people, while an *estimated* enumeration would supplement the physical count with estimating or sampling methods. The legitimacy of measuring population with estimating methods was a subject of serious debate in England and its American colonies.

Although delegates to the Constitutional Convention did not discuss this question directly, revisions of the draft language by the Committee of Style support the actual enumeration position. The first census in 1790 relied only on the actual count and did not employ estimates, but doubts nevertheless emerged about inaccurate population counts, and these doubts had important political and policy consequences. Over time, expert statisticians argued that estimating or sampling methods would yield more accurate results. In 2002, the Supreme Court held that the Constitution permits the use of a sampling methodology and does not confine the government to its actual count.

ENGLISH AND COLONIAL PRACTICE

In the eighteenth century, the distinction between actual counting and estimating was well known and thoroughly discussed in controversies between the American colonies and England.[1] For example, in 1769, Richard Price, a writer known for his expertise on actuarial matters, applied estimating methods to show that the population in England and Wales had declined.[2] Critics excoriated him for relying on conjecture instead of actual evidence.[3] They insisted that the only way to count the population was to conduct an *actual* enumeration.[4] This phrase was crafted directly in response to the call for the use of estimates. The debate culminated in the passage of the Census Act of 1800, which rejected the use of estimates in favor of a full and actual enumeration.[5]

THE CONSTITUTIONAL CONVENTION

During the Constitutional Convention, there was no direct discussion regarding whether apportionment would be based on an actual count or on estimates. The Committee of Detail's draft of the section stated that the number of inhabitants "shall . . . be taken in such manner as . . . [Congress] shall direct."[6]

Then, echoing the language used by Price's critics, the Committee of Style added "actual Enumeration."[7]

Gouverneur Morris of Pennsylvania served on the Committee of Style. There is an emerging scholarly debate about whether, contrary to the stylistic charge of the Committee, Morris used his position to alter the substance of the Constitution. Professor William Michael Treanor, for example, has observed that the "'actual enumeration' language advanced the same underlying goals at the core of [Morris's] constitutional vision: limiting the power of new states and weakening the slave states."[8] Morris thus favored the actual count arguably required by the revised language rather than estimates.

The Convention also rejected a proposal that apportionment should be based on wealth and population. Several delegates argued that a rule based on population alone would provide a more certain basis for apportionment because a wealth rule would necessitate the use of estimates.[9]

THE RATIFICATION DEBATES

During the ratification debates, critics warned that through political chicanery, the taxing power could be used to discriminate against particular states. In Federalist No. 36, Alexander Hamilton reassured his audience that the population figures for taxes would be based on an actual enumeration that was not subject to political manipulation. He wrote that "an actual census or enumeration of the people must furnish the rule, a circumstance which effectually shuts the door to partiality or oppression."

EARLY PRACTICE

Following ratification, the Census Act of 1790 established the first census. The law required an actual counting. Census takers were required to swear an oath that they would "truly cause to be made, a just and perfect enumeration and description of all persons resident within [their] districts."[10]

Under the original design of the Constitution, the census counted the number of "free Persons" as well as the number of "other Persons." This latter number referred to slaves, three-fifths of whom would be included in the number used to apportion representatives. The

Thirteenth and Fourteenth Amendments superseded the Three-Fifths Clause, ensuring that representation is now based on the "whole number of persons" in each state.

JUDICIAL PRECEDENT

In 1996, the U.S. Supreme Court declared that the text of the Enumeration Clause "vests Congress with virtually unlimited discretion in conducting the decennial 'actual Enumeration'" and that Congress "has delegated its broad authority over the census to the Secretary [of Commerce]."[11] In the Census Act of 1954, as amended in 1974, Congress had delegated to the Secretary of Commerce the broad authority to conduct the census "in such form and content as he may determine, including the use of sampling and special surveys."[12]

Then, in 1999, *U.S. Department of Commerce v. U.S. House of Representatives* held that the Census Act prohibited the use of statistical sampling to calculate population numbers.[13] However, the majority did not reach the constitutional question. Justice Antonin Scalia wrote a concurrence in which he found that statistical sampling violated the Enumeration Clause and that the words "actual Enumeration" mean "counting 'singly,' 'separately,' 'number by number,' 'distinctly.'"[14] In dissent, Justice John Paul Stevens found that the use of statistical sampling was consistent with the phrase "actual Enumeration."

Three years later, the Court held in *Utah v. Evans* (2002) that an inferential counting methodology did not violate the Enumeration Clause.[15] Writing for the majority, Justice Stephen Breyer concluded that the Framers "did not write detailed census methodology into the Constitution."[16] Therefore, the inferential method used in this case, which did not involve actual counting, was constitutionally valid. Justice Clarence Thomas dissented. He observed that the Framers, "[w]ell familiar with methods of estimation . . . chose to make an 'actual Enumeration' part of our constitutional structure" but that "[t]oday, the Court undermines their decision, leaving the basis of our representative government vulnerable to political manipulation."[17]

In *Department of Commerce v. New York* (2019), the Supreme Court opined that the

Enumeration Clause permits the federal government "to use the census for more than simply counting the population."[18] This power includes the ability to inquire about citizenship on the census questionnaire. The Court, however, ultimately held that the decision by the Secretary of Commerce to inquire about citizenship must be set aside because he offered a pretextual rationale for the decision.

OPEN QUESTIONS

- *Utah v. Evans* upheld a relatively narrow sampling methodology. The 2020 census, by contrast, relied on broader sampling methodologies.[19] Such approaches have not been tested in the courts. A future case may consider whether other forms of sampling violate the Enumeration Clause.
- In *Department of Commerce v. New York*, Justice Breyer's dissent favorably cited Justice Thomas's dissent in *Utah v. Evans*. Breyer warned that counting methods employed must limit "political chicanery" and prevent the census from being "skewed for political purposes."[20] What sorts of methodologies may cross this line?
- Does the government exceed its authority under the Enumeration Clause when it employs the census to seek other demographic information, including race and family relationships?[21]

Cite as: Andrew C. Spiropoulos, *The Enumeration Clause*, in THE HERITAGE GUIDE TO THE CONSTITUTION 23 (Josh Blackman & John G. Malcolm eds., 3d ed. 2025).

Notes

1. Thomas R. Lee, *The Original Understanding of Census Clause: Statistical Estimates and the Constitutional Requirement of An "Actual Enumeration"*, 77 Wash L. Rev. 1, 39–47 (2002). **2.** *Id.* at 26–27. **3.** *Id.* at 28–32. **4.** *Id.* at 34–39. **5.** *Id.* at 21–41. **6.** 2 Farrand's 182–83, 571–72. **7.** *Id.* at 590–91. **8.** William Michael Treanor, *The Case of the Dishonest Scrivener: Gouverneur Morris and the Creation of the Federalist Constitution*, 120 Mich. L. Rev. 1, 71 (2021). **9.** 1 Farrand's 582. **10.** 1 Stat. 101. **11.** *Wisconsin v. City of New York*, 517 U.S. 1, 19 (1996). **12.** 13 U.S.C. § 141(a). **13.** 525 U.S. 316 (1999). **14.** *Id.* at 347. **15.** 536 U.S. 452 (2002). **16.** *Id.* at 479. **17.** *Id.* at 510. **18.** *Dept. of Comm. v. New York*, 588 U.S. 752, 769–70 (2019). **19.** American Statistical Association, 2020 Census State Population Totals: A Report from the American Statistical Association Task Force on 2020 Census Quality Indicators (Sept. 2021), https://perma.cc/UF6W-AK25. **20.** *Dept. of Comm. v. New York*, 588 U.S. at 803. **21.** Stephen Kruger, The Decennial Census (Apr. 6, 2025), https://ssrn.com/abstract=1985554.

ESSAY NO. 11: THE CONGRESSIONAL APPORTIONMENT CLAUSE
ART. I, § 2, CL. 3

The Number of Representatives shall not exceed one for every thirty Thousand, but each State shall have at Least one Representative; and until such enumeration shall be made, the State of New Hampshire shall be entitled to chuse three, Massachusetts eight, Rhode-Island and Providence Plantations one, Connecticut five, New-York six, New Jersey four, Pennsylvania eight, Delaware one, Maryland six, Virginia ten, North Carolina five, South Carolina five, and Georgia three.

—Michael R. Dimino

INTRODUCTION

The Framers' "Great Compromise" yielded a Senate with equal representation for all states and a House of Representatives with seats allocated by population. The adoption of a population-based House led to two important questions: How many Representatives would there be in the new Congress, and how many people would a state have to gain, or lose, before its allocation of congressional seats would be altered? The Apportionment Clause established the states' initial allocation of House seats pending the first census, which would be conducted in 1790. The clause mandated that at least one Representative be allocated to each state. It also provided that a congressional district must have at least 30,000 persons, although, because of the Three-Fifths Clause (see Essay No. 9), not every resident was counted as a full person.

HISTORY BEFORE 1787

Under the Articles of Confederation, each state was represented in Congress by between two and seven delegates, yet the Articles specified that "each state shall have one vote."[1] Thus, the number of delegates representing each state did not affect the state's voting power in Congress, as each state's voting power was equal to that of every other state. This system created some resentment because it meant that more populous states had the same voting power as less populous states. The Constitution would remedy this problem, at least in part.

THE CONSTITUTIONAL CONVENTION

Early in the Philadelphia Convention, Edmund Randolph's Virginia Plan proposed that states be allocated votes in Congress based on their respective populations.[2] Small states objected that population-based apportionment would result in a national government that favored the interests of more populous states. The competing New Jersey Plan offered by William Paterson would have created a one-house Congress in which each state had equal representation.[3] The conflict was resolved with the adoption of the so-called Great Compromise, which called for a two-house Congress: a House of Representatives with representation based on population and a Senate with equal representation for each state.[4]

The draft version of the Apportionment Clause had provided that Congress would "regulate the number of representatives by the number of inhabitants, according to the rule hereinafter made for direct taxation. . . ."[5] When the Committee on Style subsequently combined the Apportionment and Direct Taxation Clauses, the result was the language that appears in the ratified Constitution.[6]

The Apportionment Clause provides that population should be the basis for representation in the House but does not specify how population is to be used to allocate seats. Instead, the clause places some limits on the method of apportionment, including the requirement that each state be allocated at least one Representative.

Further, the clause provides that "[t]he Number of Representatives shall not exceed one for every thirty Thousand." By contrast, some of the state legislatures in the late eighteenth century had much-smaller districts. For example, in 1776, the New Hampshire House of Representatives had 87 members—one for every 100 families.[7]

The meaning of "shall not exceed one for every thirty Thousand" is not entirely clear. Professor David Currie has argued that the "most natural reading" of the Apportionment Clause is as a limit on "the total number of seats" in the House.[8] For example, if the population of the United States was three million people, the House could have no more than 100 members, and Congress could allocate those members however it saw fit as long as each state had at least one member.

The generally accepted view, however, is that 30,000 represents the smallest number of constituents that can be assigned to a single Representative. In other words, a district with a single Representative cannot have fewer than 30,000 constituents. Under this prevailing interpretation, the Apportionment Clause not only effectively places an upper limit on the size of the House, as Professor Currie suggested, but also imposes a lower limit on the size of each district.

As a result of a compromise among the Convention's delegates, the House of Representatives in the First Congress would have sixty-five members: eight each for Massachusetts and Pennsylvania; one each for Delaware and Rhode Island; three each for New Hampshire and Georgia; four for New Jersey; five each for Connecticut, North Carolina, and South Carolina; six each for New York and Maryland; and ten for Virginia.[9]

THE RATIFICATION DEBATES

Some opponents of the Constitution complained that the Apportionment Clause would require districts to be so large that Representatives would be unable to reflect the variety and interests of their constituents. One New York Anti-Federalist, the Federal Farmer, argued that "free and good government" required "full and equal representation of the people in the legislature."[10] As a result, he contended, the legislature should have "the same interests, feelings, opinions, and views [of] the people themselves."[11] More specifically, he argued that the House should be much larger so that it could include "a just proportion" of "professional men, merchants, traders, farmers, mechanics, etc."[12] In Pennsylvania, members of the minority anti-ratification faction warned that the people chosen for service in a small House would disproportionately be "men of the most elevated rank in life."[13] They argued that even the most democratic part of the proposed national government—the House—would not sufficiently represent the interests of the common people.

Still other Anti-Federalists warned that the House could have even fewer members. While there could not be *more* than one Representative for every 30,000 people under the Apportionment Clause, there was nothing in the Constitution to prevent House districts from being even larger (for example, one representative for every 100,000 residents), meaning that the House could have even *fewer* than 65 members after the first census.[14] Melancton Smith, another prominent Anti-Federalist, argued that a small House "would be more liable to corruption" than a larger one would be.[15]

James Madison responded to these arguments. In Federalist No. 58, he argued that the size of the House was likely to increase greatly as the population of the United States grew over the ensuing decades. More importantly, he defended large House districts that represented many constituents in terms that echoed his famous defense of large republics in Federalist No. 10. Contrary to Smith's argument that a large legislative body would be security against corruption, Madison maintained that a large legislative body would be controlled by a small number of leaders. In Federalist No. 55, Madison observed that a larger number of districts would have a greater tendency to be consumed with "the confusion and intemperance of a multitude." With an increase in the number of members of the legislature, he added in Federalist No. 58, "[t]he countenance of the government may become more democratic; but the soul that animates it will be more oligarchic." The optimal number, then, required a balance, as Madison explained in Federalist No. 55. On the one hand, a House with too few members could make it easy for Representatives to act corruptly and would fail to represent the country's different interests. On the other hand, a House with too many members would risk the "confusion and intemperance of a multitude." Madison memorably warned that in large assemblies, "passion never fails to wrest the sceptre from reason. Had every Athenian citizen been a Socrates; every Athenian assembly would still have been a mob."

Responding to the Anti-Federalists' argument that a larger House would better represent society's differing interests, Madison argued in Federalist No. 58 that "the larger the number [of Representatives], the greater will be the proportion of members of limited information and of weak capacities." Madison also made an argument grounded in federalism. He explained in Federalist No. 56 that members of the House needed to represent their constituents' views only as to matters within the jurisdiction of the national government. In Federalist No. 45, he contended that the national government would be limited to its "few and defined" powers. He surmised that because the number of congressional seats would be small, the chosen Representatives would likely be experienced politicians familiar with attitudes and interests throughout their states. That small number of elite Representatives, Madison wrote in Federalist No. 56, would have a "sufficient degree" of knowledge concerning the matters within the national government's competence.

EARLY PRACTICE

The first census was taken in 1790 and 1791 and reported a U.S. population of 3.9 million.[16] The sixty-five members of the House that assembled in 1789 increased to 105 members in 1791. The first proposed amendment to the Constitution would have required an expansion of the House as the nation's population grew, but that amendment was never ratified.[17]

Congress sought to allocate one Representative for every 30,000 people—the smallest districts (and therefore the greatest number of Representatives) permitted by the clause. Because state populations were not evenly divisible by 30,000, however, the question arose of what to do with the remainder. If a state had a population of 135,000, should it receive four Representatives or five? Should a state with 90,000 residents receive the same representation as a state with 119,999 residents?

Congress's 1792 apportionment bill granted an extra Representative to nine states with the largest "remainders"—that is, those whose populations were more than the number necessary to entitle them to a certain number of representatives but not quite large enough to entitle them to another.[18] That bill was vetoed by President George Washington.[19] (In fact, it was the first bill vetoed under the Constitution and one of only two that Washington vetoed during his presidency.) Washington's veto message explained that the bill exceeded the ratio of one Representative for every 30,000 constituents.[20] The apportionment that was subsequently adopted awarded one Representative for every 30,000 people, disregarding fractional remainders.

MODERN PRACTICE

America's population expansion soon made it impractical to have one Representative for every 30,000 people. As a result, the total number of Representatives was limited to 105 Representatives and periodically raised to account for population expansion. The limit was set at 435 in 1929 and, except for a brief period when Alaska and Hawaii were admitted as states, has remained in place ever since then.[21] Accordingly, the number of constituents per district has increased significantly: The average size of a congressional district is now more than 750,000 persons.

There is no danger that the Apportionment Clause will ever be violated by congressional districts that have too few people. To the contrary, the vast increase in population since 1787 has rendered that provision almost ludicrous in the twenty-first century. If there still was one Representative for every 30,000 people, the House of Representatives would contain 11,000

members. The Apportionment Clause provides only a minimum number of constituents; there is no upper limit on the number of people the districts may contain.

The 435-Representative cap also does not mandate how many Representatives each state shall have. The Apportionment Clause requires that each state have at least one Representative, but there are several ways that the remaining 385 Representatives might be allocated. For example, a system might require each district to have 1,000,000 people, with states not receiving a second Representative until their populations reached 2,000,000. In such a system, a state with 1,000,000 people and a state with 1,999,999 people would each receive one Representative. Alternatively, a state's population could be rounded up or down so that states with fewer than 1,500,000 people would receive one Representative, while states with between 1,500,000 and 2,499,999 people would receive two members each.

In 1941, after a century of wrangling over the matter, Congress adopted the "method of equal proportions" for allocating House seats.[22] Under this complicated method, the goal is to minimize the relative (not absolute) difference in average population per district.[23] "Relative" in this sense means that the population of the smaller district is subtracted from the population of the larger district and the difference is then divided by the size of the smaller district.[24] Thus, the method of equal proportions would require a seat to be moved from State A to State B if that would reduce the relative difference in the average sizes of the states' districts.

To understand the method of equal proportions, consider a simplified version of the facts of *Department of Commerce v. Montana* (1992), which is discussed below. After the 1990 census, the population of the 50 states was divided by 435 members to yield an average *ideal* district size of 570,000. Montana had a population of 800,000 and was given one Representative. Its single district thus had 230,000 more people than the ideal district. Had Montana been given two Representatives, each of those 400,000-person districts would have been closer to the ideal district than its actual single district was. Washington State, on the other hand, was given eight districts with an average population of 540,000 people—only 30,000 fewer than the ideal size. If Washington had seven districts, each of those districts would have had 610,000 people—40,000 more than the ideal. Accordingly, a different method of allocating Representatives could have improved *absolute* population equality by giving Montana an extra district and taking one away from Washington. This would have meant that the two states' districts would have had a population difference of 210,000 (610,000 minus 400,000) rather than the actual difference of 260,000 (800,000 minus 540,000). Nevertheless, such a shift would have increased the *relative* difference because the relative difference between Washington and Montana districts would have been 0.525 with a second Montana district, compared to 0.481 with a single Montana district. Given these numbers, under the method of equal proportions, Montana properly received one member, and Washington received eight members.

JUDICIAL PRECEDENT

In *Department of Commerce v. Montana*, the U.S. Supreme Court considered a challenge to the equal-proportions method.[25] Montana demonstrated that the method resulted in the state receiving one fewer Representative than it would have received if Congress had used a different formula for dealing with fractional remainders.

The Court unanimously held that Congress had the constitutional authority to use the method of equal proportions. Inevitably, some methods produce smaller disparities in *absolute* numbers of district residents, and other methods produce smaller disparities in *relative* sizes of districts. As a result, the Court observed, the choice of one method over the other is bound to lead to an allocation of congressional seats that leaves some states unhappy. The Court explained that "[t]he polestar of equal representation does not provide sufficient guidance to allow us to discern a single constitutionally permissible course."[26] The choice was left to Congress's discretion.

There also have been legal disputes over the status of Department of Defense employees who temporarily lived overseas. The 1990 census counted those employees as residents of the states where they lived before their overseas assignments, but Massachusetts argued that these employees should not be counted as residents for purposes of apportionment. The Supreme Court upheld the Census Bureau's decision.[27] The Court explained that the decision to count those employees as if they were still living in the states of their prior homes did "not hamper the underlying constitutional goal of equal representation."[28] To the contrary, "assuming that employees temporarily stationed abroad have indeed retained their ties to their home States," counting those employees would "actually promote[] equality."[29]

The Apportionment Clause allocates congressional seats among states but does not give any representation to residents of territories such as Puerto Rico or to residents of the District of Columbia. That difference in representation has been attacked as violating the equal protection component of the Fifth Amendment's Due Process Clause. These challenges, however, have failed.[30] The reviewing courts have noted that it would be anomalous for the allocation of members of Congress (and, relatedly, the Electoral College)—which is, after all, specified in the Constitution itself—to be found unconstitutional.

OPEN QUESTIONS
- Who must be included in the population tally that is the basis of apportionment? Under Section 2 of the Fourteenth Amendment, districts are allocated to states based on their "respective Numbers" of "Persons." The clause thus implies that the allocation should be made based on the total number of residents rather than on, for example, a more limited subset of people who are eligible to vote. In *City of San Jose v. Trump* (2020),[31] a three-judge district court held that the Constitution demanded that a state's population include all residents, including those present in the United States illegally. The case was not appealed to the Supreme Court.

- Can a 435-member House ably represent the diversity of people and interests in the United States? On the other hand, would a larger House dilute the quality and accountability of the Representatives and, as Madison feared, further increase the power of the leadership at the expense of individual members? In an age when members of the House already give voice to widely divergent governing philosophies, would increasing the number of Representatives exacerbate polarization and make governance even more difficult?

Cite as: Michael R. Dimino, *The Congressional Apportionment Clause, in* THE HERITAGE GUIDE TO THE CONSTITUTION 25 (Josh Blackman & John G. Malcolm eds., 3d ed. 2025).

Notes

1 Articles of Confederation, art. V, § 4.   **2.** 1 Farrand's 20–22.   **3.** 3 Farrand's 611–14.   **4.** 1 Farrand's 196.   **5.** 2 Farrand's 566.   **6.** *Id.* at 590.   **7.** New Hampshire House of Representatives, *House History,* https://perma.cc/Z2XT-6ZES.   **8.** David P. Currie, *The Constitution in Congress: The Second Congress, 1791–1793,* 90 Nw. U. L. Rev. 606, 613 (1995).   **9.** *Congress Profiles: 1st Congress (1789–1791),* U.S. House of Representatives: History, Art & Archives, https://perma.cc/9M9K-6ZMQ; 1 Farrand's 566–70.   **10.** Storing 2.8.15.   **11.** *Id.*   **12.** *Id.*   **13.** Storing 3.11.35.   **14.** Storing 4.13.25, 6.12.8.   **15.** Storing 6.12.9.   **16.** National Archives, *1790 Census Records,* at https://perma.cc/R59M-EXGM; U.S. Dep't of Commerce, United States Census Bureau, *Decennial Census History* (Oct. 31, 2023), https://perma.cc/YZ49-2L9R.   **17.** National Archives, *The Bill of Rights: A Transcription,* https://perma.cc/L4XD-24MP.   **18.** 3 Annals of Cong. 482–83 (1792); Currie, *supra* at 607–15.   **19.** 3 Annals of Cong. 539 (1792).   **20.** H.R. Jour., 2d Cong., 1st Sess. 563–64 (Apr. 5, 1792).   **21.** Permanent Apportionment Act of 1929, 2 U.S.C. § 2a.   **22.** *Id.*   **23.** Laurence F. Schmeckebier, *The Method of Equal Proportions,* 17 L. & Contemp. Probs. 302 (1952).   **24.** *Dep't of Com. v. Montana,* 503 U.S. 442, 455 n.29 (1992).   **25.** 503 U.S. 442 (1992).   **26.** *Id.* at 463.   **27.** *Franklin v. Massachusetts,* 505 U.S. 788 (1992).   **28.** *Id.* at 806.   **29.** *Id.*   **30.** *Igartua v. United States,* 626 F.3d 592 (1st Cir. 2010); *Castanon v. United States,* 444 F. Supp. 3d 118 (D.D.C. 2020); *Adams v. Clinton,* 90 F. Supp. 2d 35 (D.D.C. 2000).   **31.** 497 F. Supp. 3d 680 (N.D. Cal. 2020).

ESSAY NO. 12: THE EXECUTIVE WRITS OF ELECTION CLAUSE
ART. I, § 2, CL. 4

When vacancies happen in the Representation from any State, the Executive Authority thereof shall issue Writs of Election to fill such Vacancies.

—Paul Taylor

INTRODUCTION

Normally, members of the House of Representatives are elected for two-year terms, but, what if a vacancy arises because of death or resignation? Unlike what happens when there is a vacancy in the Senate, governors cannot make a temporary appointment. Instead, the state "Executive Authority . . . shall issue Writs of Election to fill such Vacancies."

A writ of election is a legal command for an election to be held. The Constitution does not specify how quickly the writ must be issued and the election itself must be held. However, the courts have held that a governor cannot decline to issue the writ. The clause vests the governor with the responsibility of calling such special elections to fill vacant House seats. "It is obvious," Justice Joseph Story wrote of the clause, "that such a power ought to reside in some public functionary" and that the Constitution vests such power with "the State Executive, which is best fitted to exercise it with promptitude and discretion."[1]

The House of Representatives is unique because it is the only part of the federal government that the Constitution specifies must be composed only of those who are elected. To that end, regarding the filling of vacancies in House membership, Article I, Section 2, Clause 4 does not allow for temporary appointments; it provides instead for mandatory elections, stating that governors "shall" issue "Writs of Election" (writs being a form of legal command). That is in contrast to the Seventeenth Amendment, which provides that "the legislature of any State may empower the executive thereof to make temporary appointments [to the Senate] until the people fill the vacancies by election as the legislature may direct." (The Seventeenth Amendment is discussed in Essay No. 204).

HISTORY BEFORE 1787
During the colonial era, King George III would delay calling for special elections to fill vacancies in colonial legislatures. This practice was so unpopular in the colonies[2] that it was listed as one of the grievances against the English king in the Declaration of Independence: "He has dissolved representative houses repeatedly, for opposing with manly firmness his invasion of the rights of the people. He has refused for a long time, after such dissolutions, to cause others to be elected. . . ."

The wording of the clause drew from colonial precedents. The 1776 Pennsylvania constitution provided for the filling of legislative "vacancies" by "certain and regular elections" but was not clear regarding who had the authority to call such elections.[3] The 1776 Virginia constitution provided that each house of the legislature should issue writs for the filling of "intermediate vacancies."[4] The 1778 South Carolina constitution allowed the legislative houses to issue writs for legislative vacancies "occasioned by death."[5] The 1777 New York constitution had no provision at all for the filling of legislative vacancies but did provide for the filling of vacancies occasioned by the resignation of the governor or lieutenant governor.[6] The 1777 Vermont constitution allowed the filling of vacancies created by the resignation of state "officers" but said nothing about filling legislative vacancies.[7] The 1786 Vermont constitution allowed for the replacement of "officers" whose positions were vacant because of "death or otherwise" but still said nothing about filling legislative vacancies.[8]

Of the remaining early state constitutions, some had provisions allowing legislative bodies to fill vacancies.[9] Others had vacancy provisions that were silent on the subject of who had the authority to call elections to fill vacancies.[10] And under the Articles of Confederation, congressional delegates were "annually appointed, in such manner as the legislature of each state shall direct."[11]

THE CONSTITUTIONAL CONVENTION
On July 26, 1787, Virginia delegate Edmund Randolph, a member of the Committee of Detail, produced a "draft sketch" of a constitution.[12] That draft provided that the filling of "Vacancies *by death disability or resignation* shall be supplied by a writ from the . . . *governor of the state, wherein they shall happen.*"[13] Randolph's draft was taken up by the Committee of Detail.[14]

However, that was the last time during the Convention that this wording appeared. The draft reported by the Committee of Detail to the full Convention provided that "Vacancies in the House of Representatives shall be supplied by writs of election from the executive authority of the State, in the representation from which it shall happen."[15] The Convention unanimously agreed to the provision for filling House vacancies.[16] At the end of the Convention, the Committee of Style tweaked the wording so that the House provision read, "When vacancies happen in the representation from any state, the Executive authority thereof shall issue writs of election to fill such vacancies."[17]

EARLY PRACTICE
In 1790, William Pinkney was elected to the House of Representatives from Maryland, but he never took his seat and in September 1791 sent a letter to the governor and council of Maryland seeking to resign.[18] The governor then issued a writ for a new election.[19] Governors also issued writs of election to fill House seats left vacant by Joshua Seney,[20] John Fracis Mercer,[21] and Uriah Forrest.[22]

JUDICIAL PRECEDENT
The U.S. Court of Appeals for the Seventh Circuit ruled in 1970 that the clause imposes a mandatory duty on governors to issue writs of election to fill vacancies in the U.S. House of Representatives.[23] More specifically, the court held that in performing that duty, the governor

has the discretion to choose the day of the week on which writs of election will be issued. However, the governor does not have the discretion to decide against issuing the writs of election altogether. The people's right to choose representation in the House of Representatives is "a continuing right, which is not to be defeated by death of a Representative once chosen, or other cause of vacancy."[24]

The U.S. Court of Appeals for the Sixth Circuit has held that the clause imposes a mandatory duty, leaving only the possibility that a

governor could avoid such duty when the time remaining in the congressional term "is truly de minimis."[25] The rule had been articulated earlier in *United States Term Limits, Inc. v. Thornton*[26] when Justice Clarence Thomas indicated in his dissenting opinion that the clause prescribes an affirmative duty of the state executive to issue a writ whenever a vacancy occurs.

Cite as: Paul Taylor, *The Executive Writs of Election Clause*, *in* The Heritage Guide to the Constitution 30 (Josh Blackman & John G. Malcolm eds., 3d ed. 2025).

Notes

1. Joseph Story, A Familiar Exposition of the Constitution of the United States, § § 87 (1840).   **2.** A General Meeting of the Freeholders of the County of Mecklenburg on the 29th Day of July, 1774, in Archibald Henderson, *An Interesting Colonial Document*, 28 Va. Mag. Hist. & Biography 54, 56 (1920).   **3.** Pa. Const. of 1776, art. I, § 6.   **4.** Va. Const. of 1776, art. II, para. 27.   **5.** S.C. Const. of 1778, art. XVIII.   **6.** N.Y. Const. of 1777, arts. XX–XXI.   **7.** Vt. Const. of 1777, ch. 2, § XVIII; *id.* ch. 2, § XX.   **8.** Vt. Const. of 1786, ch. 2, § 11.   **9.** Del. Const. of 1776, art. 5; Ga. Const. of 1777, arts. VII, XVII; N.C. Const. of 1776, arts. X, XXV–XXXIII; Md. Const. of 1776, art. VII ; *id.* art. XIX..   **10.** Mass. Const. of 1780, pt. 2, ch. 1, § 2, art. IV;.N.H. Const. of 1784, pt. 2, para.

14.   **11.** Articles of Confederation, art. V, § 1.   **12.** Farrand's Supp. 183–93.   **13.** *Id.* at 185.   **14.** 2 Farrand's 137, 140, 142.   **15.** *Id.* at 179.   **16.** *Id.* at 231.   **17.** *Id.* at 591.   **18.** H.R. Jour., 2d Cong., 1st Sess. 461 (Nov. 23, 1791) (reprinting the report of the Committee of Elections describing the situation).   **19.** *Id.*   **20.** H.R. Jour., 2d Cong., 2d Sess. 677 (Jan. 23, 1793).   **21.** H.R. Jour., 3d Cong., 1st Sess. 192–93 (May 31, 1794).   **22.** H.R. Jour., 3d Cong., 2d Sess. 279 (Jan. 1, 1795).   **23.** *Jackson v. Ogilvie*, 426 F.2d 1333 (7th Cir. 1970).   **24.** *Id.* at 1333, 1336.   **25.** *ACLU of Ohio, Inc. v. Taft*, 385 F.3d 641, 649 (6th Cir. 2004).   **26.** 514 U.S. 779 (1995) (Thomas, J., dissenting).

◦‿◦

ESSAY NO. 13: THE SPEAKER OF THE HOUSE CLAUSE
ART. I, § 2, CL. 5

The House of Representatives shall chuse their Speaker and other Officers. . . .
—C. Towner French

INTRODUCTION

The people elect the members of the House of Representatives, and the members in turn can choose their Speaker and other officers. Unlike earlier practices in England, the Executive has no role over the selection of the Speaker. Over the centuries, the role of the Speaker of the House has evolved. The Speaker has gained and lost powers and duties as the issues of the day have moved Representatives to grant or remove them. Generally, the courts treat the selection of the Speaker and other House officers as political questions that are not subject to judicial resolution.

ENGLISH PRACTICE

The "Speaker of the House" position has a long history that dates back in England to at least 1377, when the Rolls of Parliament first noted that Sir Thomas Hungerford was Speaker of the House of Commons.[1] Over time, various English kings sought to control Parliament by influencing the choice of the Speaker when Parliament was in session. During the Tudor era (1485–1603), the influence of the House of Commons "reached its lowest point."[2] In a period when the monarch dominated the government, the sovereign could exert greater control over Parliament. In particular, this control could lead to greater taxation and other streams of revenue to fund the monarch, the civil list, and the military list as well as taxation, appropriations, and spending outside of parliamentary control and even parliamentary scrutiny.[3]

Starting in the seventeenth century, the House of Commons began to assert full control of the selection of a Speaker.[4] This process would continue as the House of Commons fought for independent legislative power. Eventually, the House of Commons won the right to select the Speaker without hindrance from the Crown.[5] As a formality, the monarch confirmed, and to this day confirms, the Commons' choice of Speaker. Not since the late seventeenth century has a monarch, for political reasons, dared to challenge the House of Commons' selection of a Speaker.

COLONIAL AND ARTICLES-ERA PRACTICE

Before American independence, the selection of the Speaker in colonial lower legislative houses mirrored the earlier British process. Although colonial assemblies chose their own Speakers, the colonial governors appointed by the Crown often sought to control the result and also claimed the power to reject candidates put forward by the lower house.[6]

Following independence, the Articles of Confederation created a unicameral legislature. Article IX authorized the Congress "to appoint one of their number to preside, provided that no person be allowed to serve in the office of president [of Congress] more than one year in any term of three years."[7] This position was referred to as the "president." The root of the word "president" is "preside," and the President of the Articles Congress generally performed the sorts of duties that a presiding officer would perform in a legislative body. The President was perhaps akin to the modern Speaker of the House in that respect.[8]

One of the more influential state constitutions was the Massachusetts constitution of 1780. It provided that "the House of Representatives . . . shall choose their own Speaker, appoint their own officers, and settle the rules and order of proceeding in their own House."[9] The words "their own" emphasized that the legislature was free from the gubernatorial control under which colonial assemblies had struggled.

THE CONSTITUTIONAL CONVENTION

At the Constitutional Convention, the Framers drew on the Massachusetts model. Several drafts from the Committee of Detail gave the House of Representatives the power to choose its own Speaker and other officers.[10] On August 6, 1787, the Committee of Detail delivered its proposal, which provided that the House "shall choose its Speaker and other officers."[11] On August 9, this provision was adopted unanimously without any recorded debate.[12] No further substantive changes were made.[13]

The succinct language of the Speaker of the House Clause established the House's power to choose its leadership free from the influences of Executive and Senate power. The Speaker was now an internal House of Representatives officer, relieved of the burden of pleasing the Executive as a prerequisite for assuming the Speakership. The Appointments Clause in Article II does not permit the President to appoint the Speaker or the holders of non-apex legislative positions.[14] The clause also permits the House to appoint the holders of other, non-apex legislative positions, such as the Clerk of the House.[15]

SELECTING THE SPEAKER

The House of Representatives elects its Speaker as the first order of business at the start of each two-year term or when a Speaker dies or resigns during the legislative term.[16] The practice is customary, for it occurs before the House formally adopts its rules of procedure for the legislative term. Until 1839, the House elected the Speaker by ballot, but since that year, elections for Speaker have been conducted by roll call.[17] With a roll call, each member's name is called out, and the member announces his or her vote.

The party caucuses, however, attempt to predetermine the result by meeting and selecting the candidates to be voted upon. The successful candidate must obtain a majority of the votes cast. When there is no majority, the House continues to vote until someone wins a majority. A Speaker election has proceeded to multiple ballots sixteen times, with thirteen of which were before the Civil War.[18] The possibility of multiple ballots arises only when party discipline breaks down or a third party has sufficient strength.

On two occasions, the House has agreed

by resolution to allow a Speaker to be elected by a plurality. The resolution of both contests required agreement from a majority of the whole House. In 1849, there were sixty-three failed ballots, and in 1856, when neither party controlled the House, there were 133 failed ballots.[19] That Speaker election lasted for two months before Nathaniel Banks, a Massachusetts Republican, was elected by a plurality.[20] In 1923, when the Progressive Party held a number of seats, the House took nine ballots before Frederick Gillett, another Republican from Massachusetts, received a majority of the votes.[21]

In January 2023—for the first time in 100 years—the House required more than one round of voting to elect a Speaker. It took fifteen very public rounds of voting over the course of five days. Kevin McCarthy, a California Republican, received a majority vote from the members of the House. During this contested process, there were traditional backroom discussions.[22] However, many negotiations with various factions of McCarthy's own party were publicly captured during live telecasts while other Republicans made demands, concessions, and suggestions through social media.

Ten months later, in October 2023, there was another contested Speaker election that stretched nine days after the House voted to vacate McCarthy's speakership. It was the first time an incumbent Speaker had been removed during an active session.[23] Mike Johnson, a Louisiana Republican, was elected after the fourth ballot.

THE SPEAKER'S POWERS

The Constitution does not define the Speaker's powers. Those authorities would be developed through practice. The first Speaker, Frederick Muhlenberg, led a House of Representatives that was devoid of parties.[24] As Speaker, Muhlenberg attempted to construct the basic institutions of government described in the Constitution.[25] Even during the first session of Congress, the Speaker assumed a critically important power: the ability to appoint members of the House to the various committees.[26] In the early nineteenth century, Henry Clay demonstrated the extraordinary power that an active Speaker could assume by skillfully filling committees to build support for his preferred policies.[27]

Unlike British practice or the President Pro Tempore of the Senate, the Speaker of the House is the primary legislative leader of the body.[28] As the leader of the majority party, the Speaker declares and defends the legislative agenda of the majority party, but the Speaker traditionally refrains from debating, voting, or introducing legislation in most circumstances.[29]

By the early twentieth century, the Speaker was widely considered to be the second most powerful person in Washington after the President. He possessed the power to appoint members and chairmen of all committees. The Speaker, who also chaired the House Committee on Rules, was able to control the timing and content of bills brought before the House.[30] However, in 1910, that authority was significantly diminished during a revolt orchestrated by progressive Republicans and Democrats against Speaker Joseph Cannon (R–IL).[31] As a result of the uprising, the House voted to remove the Speaker's power to chair the Rules Committee. Chairmen would now be appointed primarily by reason of seniority.[32] Thereafter, the chairmen of the various committees became the center of power.

This trend would change in the 1970s when Congress undertook a comprehensive legislative reorganization that restored several of the Speaker's prior prerogatives.[33] But in modern times, the Speaker does not sit on any standing committees in the House.

"OTHER OFFICERS"

The Constitution empowers the House to "chuse their . . . other Officers." On April 1, 1789, in one of its first actions, the first House of Representatives chose the first Clerk.[34] The Clerk of the House serves as the presiding officer until the election of the new Speaker and is empowered to "call the House to order, preserve order and decorum, and decide all questions of order subject to appeal by any Member."[35] The House elects its other officers, such as the Sergeant-at-Arms, Chief Administrative Officer, and Chaplain.[36] However, under current rules, the Speaker can appoint the Historian of the House, the General Counsel, and the Inspector General.

Courts have afforded discretion to the House in appointing its officers. In *Murray v. Buchanan* (1983), the D.C. Circuit dismissed an Establishment Clause challenge to the payment of salaries to chaplains of the House of Representatives and the Senate.[37] Judge George MacKinnon concurred in the dismissal, laying out "the constitutional and unique historical base which supports [the] decision."[38] In MacKinnon's view, the decision to compensate chaplains "is a judgment made pursuant to and in execution of the powers conferred on the Senate and the House [under Article I, Section 2, Clause 5] to 'chuse their . . . officers' and to 'determine the Rules of [their] proceedings.'"[39] (See Essay No. 26.) Because these powers were textually committed to Congress by the Constitution, the political questions doctrine barred legal challenges to their exercise.[40]

OPEN QUESTION

Historically, the Speaker has always been a member of the House.[41] In 1997, 2013, 2015, 2019, 2021, and 2023, some House members voted for candidates who were not then members of the House, including several sitting Senators. Whether a non-member can serve as Speaker remains an open question.

Cite as: C. Towner French, *The Speaker of the House Clause, in* THE HERITAGE GUIDE TO THE CONSTITUTION 32 (Josh Blackman & John G. Malcolm eds., 3d ed. 2025).

Notes

1. John Smith Roskell, The Commons and Their Speakers in English Parliaments, 1376–1523, at 157 (1965).   **2.** 1 Josef Redlich, The Procedure of the House of Commons: A Study of Its History and Present Form 33 (1908).   **3.** Paul Einzig, The Control of the Purse: Progress and Decline of Parliament's Financial Control 50–55, 74 (1959).   **4.** *History of the Speaker*, Legislative Assembly of Manitoba, https://perma.cc/78PP-6GQ6.   **5.** *Id.*   **6.** Jack P. Greene, The Quest for Power: The Lower Houses of Assembly in the Southern Royal Colonies, 1689–1776, at 206–07 (1963); Mary Patterson Clarke, Parliamentary Privilege in the American Colonies 61–92 (1943).   **7.** Articles of Confederation, art. IX, § 5.   **8.** Seth Barrett Tillman & Josh Blackman, *Offices and Officers of the Constitution Part IV: The "Office . . . Under the United States" Drafting Convention*, 62 S. Tex. L. Rev. 455, 478 (2023).   **9.** Mass. Const. of 1780, ch. 1, § III, art. X.   **10.** 2 Farrand's 154, 158, 165.   **11.** *Id.* at 179.   **12.** *Id.* at 231.   **13.** *Id.* at 566, 591, 652.   **14.** Josh Blackman & Seth Barrett Tillman, *Offices and Officers of the Constitution, Part III: The Appointments, Impeachment, Commissions, and Oath or Affirmation Clauses*, 62 S. Tex. L. Rev. 349, 444–48 (2023); Josh Blackman & Seth Barrett Tillman, *Offices and Officers of the Constitution, Part VI: The Ineligibility Clause*, 64 S. Tex. L. Rev. 209, 218–19 (2025).   **15.** Josh Blackman & Seth Barrett Tillman, *Offices and Officers of the Constitution, Part II: The Four Approaches*, 61 S. Tex. L. Rev. 321, 389 (2022).   **16.** Richard S. Beth & Valerie Heitshusen, Cong. Rsrch. Serv., RL30857, Speakers of the House: Elections, 1913–2015, at 1 (2015).   **17.** *Id.*   **18.** *Speaker Elections Decided by Multiple Ballots*, U.S. House of Representatives, History, Art & Archives, https://perma.cc/H3MY-BGFJ.   **19.** *Id.*   **20.** Jeffrey A. Jenkins & Timothy P. Nokken, *The Institutional Origins of the Republican Party: Spatial Voting and the House of Speakership Election of 1855–56*, 25 Legis. Stud. Q. 101, 102 (2000).   **21.** Beth & Heitshusen, *supra* at 2.   **22.** Lindsey McPherson et al., *McCarthy Wins Speaker Election, Finally*, Roll Call (Jan. 7, 2023), https://perma.cc/J57V-XUU2.   **23.** John T. Bennett, *McCarthy Becomes First Speaker in History Ousted*, Roll Call (Oct. 3, 2023), https://perma.cc/6VMZ-3KT8.   **24.** *The First Speaker of the House, Frederick A.C. Muhlenberg of Pennsylvania*, U.S. House of Representatives, History, Art & Archives, Historical Highlights, https://perma.cc/GR4H-8H8Q.   **25.** Randall Strahan et al., *From Moderator to Leader: Floor Participation by U.S. House Speakers, 1789–1841*, 30 Social Sci. Hist. 51, 56 (2006).   **26.** Eric D. Lawrence et al., *The Politics of Speaker Cannon's Committee Assignments*, 45 Am. J. of Pol. Sci. 551, 551 (2001).   **27.** Randall Strahan et al., *The Clay Speakership Revisited*, 32 Polity 562, 580 (2000).   **28.** Art. I, § 3, cl. 5.   **29.** Lawrence et al., *supra*; Valerie Heitshusen, Cong. Rsrch. Serv., 97-780, The Speaker of the House: House Officer, Party Leader, and Representative 7–8 (2017), https://perma.cc/5W9M-UAXL.   **30.** *History of the Chairs of the Standing House Committee on Rules*, Committee on Rules, U.S. House of Representatives, https://perma.cc/JC3B-KJPX.   **31.** *Too Fast Too Furious: Uncle Joe Gets Driven Out*, U.S. House of Representatives, History, Art & Archives, https://perma.cc/Q7CC-JVS7.   **32.** Susan M. Miller & Peverill Squire, *Who Rebelled? An Analysis of the Motivations of the Republicans Who Voted Against Speaker Cannon*, 41 Am. Pol. Rsch. 561 (2012).   **33.** James D'Angelo & David King, *The Legislative Reorganization Act of 1970*, Cong. Rsrch. Inst. (Nov. 12, 2023), https://perma.cc/S4QS-DQXJ.   **34.** 1 Annals of Cong., 1st Cong., 1st Sess. 100 (1789); Tillman & Blackman, *Offices and Officers of the Constitution Part II*, *supra* at 321, 335–36.   **35.** 1 Hinds' Precedents § 64.   **36.** Beth & Heitshusen, *supra* at 16.   **37.** 720 F. 2d 689, 690 (D.C. Cir. 1983).   **38.** *Id.* at 690–91 (MacKinnon, J., concurring).   **39.** *Id.* at 697.   **40.** *Id.* at 691, 697.   **41.** *Speaker of the House*, U.S. House of Representatives, History, Art & Archives, https://perma.cc/J4LZ-T4R9.

~

ESSAY NO. 14: HOUSE IMPEACHMENT CLAUSE
ART. I, § 2, CL. 5

The House of Representatives . . . shall have the sole Power of Impeachment.
—Michael J. Gerhardt

INTRODUCTION

Article I, Section 2, Clause 5 vests the House of Representatives with the "sole Power of Impeachment," and Article I, Section 3, Clause 6 vests the Senate with the "sole Power to try all Impeachments" (See Essay No. 20). This two-stage process was common in both England and the colonies before the drafting of the Constitution: the lower chamber of the legislature had the authority to impeach or charge someone with impeachable misconduct and the upper chamber was empowered to try impeachments. The division of impeachment authority between the House and the Senate was one of the most important safeguards the Framers established against its abuse. Of the twenty-two federal officers (primarily corrupt federal judges) impeached by the House, only eight have been convicted and removed from office by the Senate.

HISTORY BEFORE 1787

In 1376, the British Parliament invented impeachment as a means to guard against monarchical tyranny and remove ministers who implemented the King's most dangerous tyrannical orders or policies. In practice, Parliament's lower chamber, the House of Commons, had the authority to initiate impeachments of government officials and other individuals for various offenses against the State. The House of Lords, the upper chamber, had the power to try these cases. Until the formation of formal cabinets in the nineteenth century, impeachment was the only means for removing malicious or corrupt ministers. Edmund Burke described the impeachment power as "the great guardian of the purity of the Constitution."[1] But, in England, where everyone but the King was subject to impeachment, impeachment also became a means by which Parliament sought to punish political opponents.[2] Parliament asserted the authority to charge private citizens with any kind of misconduct and impose any sanction if they were found guilty in the House of Lords.

Before 1776, the American colonies experimented with impeachment for criminal offenses and increasingly deviated from the early English practice. According to historians Peter Hoffer and N.E.H. Hull, "[b]etween 1776 and 1787, state politicians drafted and tested various provisions for impeachment."[3] The state constitutions uniformly rejected the worst features of the English impeachment practice. States with bicameral legislatures tended to follow the same two-step process for impeachment that was used in England, but only public officials were subject to impeachment, and the scope of impeachable offenses was narrowed. For example, the Virginia constitution (1776) and the Massachusetts constitution (1780) defined impeachable offenses as "misconduct and maladministration."[4]

THE CONSTITUTIONAL CONVENTION

The delegates to the Constitutional Convention did not agree immediately on which authorities should wield the powers to impeach and to try impeachments. On June 2, 1787, John Dickinson of Delaware tried to break an impasse. He proposed "that the Executive be made removable by the National Legislature on the request of a majority of the Legislatures of individual States."[5] James Madison of Virginia initially opposed the idea because he thought this approach would subject the executive to the "intrigues" of the states.[6] A draft of the Committee on Detail, however, placed the power of impeachment in the national legislature: The House of Representatives would have "the sole Power of Impeachment."[7]

On September 4, the Convention approved a text specifying that the President "shall be removed from his office on impeachment by the House of representatives, and conviction by the Senate, for treason or bribery."[8] The two-stage process on which the delegates settled was familiar to them because it mirrored the practices in England and the colonies. The Committee of Style would divide the powers for the House and Senate into different sections. The first step in the process now provided that "[t]he House of Representatives shall have the sole power of impeachment."[9]

THE RATIFICATION DEBATES

During the ratification process, there were extensive debates about the vesting of impeachment authority in the Senate, but the House Impeachment Clause drew far less attention. For example, Alexander Hamilton argued in Federalist No. 77 that the nation would find "republican" safety from a presidential abuse of power in the mode of his election and his "being at all times liable to impeachment." In Federalist No. 65, Hamilton further elaborated on why the delegates chose the Senate as the venue for impeachment trials. Hamilton noted that it made no sense to entrust the House with both the power of impeachment and the power to try impeachments.

Cincinnatus, an Anti-Federalist, observed that the House has "power to controul the representative in this high democratic right; to screen from punishment, or rather from conviction, all high offenders, being their creatures, and to keep in awe all opponents to their power in high office."[10]

HOW THE HOUSE EXERCISES THE IMPEACHMENT POWER

The Constitution does not specify how impeachment proceedings are to be initiated. Instead, according to Article I, Section 5, "each House" of Congress has the power to "determine the Rules of its proceedings." (See Essay No. 26.) One such proceeding is impeachment. During the early Republic, the House would craft rules or procedures for each impeachment proceeding it conducted. Usually, a Member would propose an impeachment, which would then be assigned to a committee. This process was followed with two early impeachments.

In the first impeachment, the Jefferson Administration and its partisan allies in Congress seriously explored using impeachment to retaliate against Federalist judges. These Adams Administration appointees had used the Sedition Act to punish their Republican critics. President Jefferson asked Treasury Secretary Albert Gallatin to collect evidence that John Pickering, a Federalist judge, had been acting erratically and issuing dubious rulings. On February 3, 1803, Jefferson sent Congress a special message that included a "letter and affidavits exhibiting matter of complaint" against Pickering. In response, the House formed a committee to explore possible charges against Pickering. The committee made its recommendation to the full House, which impeached Pickering on March 2, 1803.[11] The Senate trial started the next day, and Pickering was convicted on March 12. The Senate made Pickering the first federal officer in United States history to be removed from office.

The Pickering impeachment helped set the stage for the next serious deployment of the House's "sole power of impeachment." Jefferson urged his allies in the House to target Justice Samuel Chase, a Washington appointee to the Supreme Court.[12] The ardent Federalist judge was targeted based on his harsh rulings and statements while overseeing trials of Republicans for violating the Sedition Act. Representative John Randolph of Virginia asked the House to initiate an impeachment inquiry into Chase's alleged abuse of his judicial authority. The House authorized the inquiry and then formed a committee to study possible charges against Chase. The committee recommended that the House impeach Chase.

Randolph presented to the full House articles of impeachment against Chase, which the House approved. The House appointed several representatives as managers who would be responsible for prosecuting the articles in the Senate. The managers delivered the articles to the Senate on December 7, 1804, and the trial began. On March 1, 1805, at least six Jeffersonian Republicans voted with the Senate's nine Federalists to acquit Chase on each of the eight articles of impeachment.

Over time, the House developed a more formal procedure. In 1813, it established a standing

Committee on the Judiciary.[13] This committee would initiate impeachment proceedings and then make recommendations for consideration by the whole House. For example, impeachment hearings were held by the House Judiciary Committee for the impeachments of Presidents Andrew Johnson (1868); William Jefferson Clinton (1998–99); and Donald Trump (2019–20 and again in 2021). In 1974, the committee approved three impeachment articles against Richard Nixon, who resigned shortly thereafter.

Under the modern practice, if a majority of the House votes in favor of an impeachment resolution, the Chairman of the House Judiciary Committee recommends a slate of "managers" to serve as prosecutors in the Senate trial. The House subsequently approves these managers by resolution.

THE ROLE (OR NON-ROLE) OF THE FEDERAL JUDICIARY

The Constitution uses the word "sole" only twice, both times with respect to impeachment. As a textual matter, the fact that the House has the "sole power" over impeachment suggests that the federal courts cannot review impeachment proceedings.

Walter Nixon v. United States (1993) held that the Senate's "sole power" to try impeachments is not subject to review by the courts.[14] Chief Justice William Rehnquist explained for a unanimous Court that the word "sole" obviously indicated that no other authority, including the courts, had any role in second-guessing or reviewing House or Senate impeachment-related decisions. Judicial review of congressional impeachment procedures would undermine the finality of those proceedings. Supreme Court justices and other federal judges would also have the opportunity to review impeachment—the primary mechanism used to discipline judges. Rehnquist stressed that other safeguards were available to check the abuse of the impeachment power. Primarily, the Constitution divides the impeachment authority between the House and the Senate; thus, the final decision-making is in the hands of politically accountable members of Congress.

OPEN QUESTIONS

- Does the House Impeachment Clause impose an affirmative duty on the House to monitor the conduct of those who are subject to impeachment and, when evidence of impeachable offenses is manifest, to initiate proceedings? In the criminal law context, prosecutors have considerable discretion in determining whether to indict a defendant. By analogy, does the House have complete discretion in determining whether to initiate impeachment proceedings?
- In 2021, the House impeached President Trump *before* his constitutional term concluded. A majority of the Senate determined that the Senate still had jurisdiction over his impeachment even though he was no longer in office at the time of his Senate impeachment trial. One argument supporting the Senate's judgment was that the Constitution empowered the Senate "to try all impeachments" and that, because Trump had been impeached while he was still president, his impeachment properly fell within the jurisdiction of the Senate. Are there good counter-arguments against this reading of the Constitution?
- Can a former official who is out of office be impeached for conduct that occurred while he was in office?
- As a general matter, the House has oversight power to investigate the executive and judicial branches as well as, under the right circumstances, private citizens in connection with a legislative purpose.[15] However, this investigatory power is enhanced when connected to an impeachment proceeding. Does the House have to authorize an impeachment investigation formally by a majority vote to trigger this broader power? In 2019 and 2020, the Trump Administration's Justice Department argued that it would respond to investigative information requests only after such a vote.[16]

- If impeachment is unavailable as a sanction for the misconduct of an officer after he has left office, what, if any, are the constitutional options for holding such an official accountable for his conduct?

Cite as: Michael J. Gerhardt, *The House Impeachment Clause, in* The Heritage Guide to the Constitution 36 (Josh Blackman & John G. Malcolm eds., 3d ed. 2025).

Notes
1. Edmund Burke, The Works of Edmund Burke 397 (1839).   **2.** House of Commons Library, Impeachment, Briefing Paper No. CBP7612 (June 6, 2016), https://perma.cc/W9JE-66XX.   **3.** Peter Charles Hoffer & N.E.H. Hull, Impeachment in America: 1635–1805, at 68 (1984).   **4.** *Id.* at 76; Mass. Const. of 1780, ch. I,§ II, art. VIII; Va. Const. of 1776.   **5.** 1 Farrand's 85.   **6.** *Id.* at 86.   **7.** 2 Farrand's 164.   **8.** *Id.* at 495.   **9.** *Id.* at 566.   **10.** Storing 6.1.27.   **11.** 3 Hinds' Precedents §§ 2319–41.   **12.** *Id.* at §§ 2342–63.   **13.** House Judiciary Committee, *About the Committee: Committee History*, https://perma.cc/9SPJ-FAZA.   **14.** *Nixon v. United States*, 506 U.S. 224 (1993).   **15.** *Trump v. Mazars USA LLP*, 591 U.S. 848 (2020).   **16.** Steven A. Engel, Ass't Att'y Gen., Off. of Legal Counsel, U.S. Dep't of Justice, House Committees' Authority to Investigate for Impeachment, Memorandum Opinion for the Counsel to the President (Jan. 19, 2020), https://perma.cc/4GQ4-HTY2.

ESSAY NO. 15: THE SENATE CLAUSE
ART. I, § 3, CL. 1

The Senate of the United States shall be composed of two Senators from each State, chosen by the Legislature thereof for six Years; and each Senator shall have one Vote.

—Martin Gold

INTRODUCTION
Under the Articles of Confederation, the unicameral legislature had four distinct features: Delegates from each state voted as a unit, delegates rotated over time, delegates could be recalled by the states, and each state had equal representation. The Framers of the Constitution chose a different path. There would be a bicameral legislature. The House of Representatives would have proportional representation, and the Senate would have equal representation. Moreover, Senators would vote individually and not as a unit. State legislatures would have the power to elect Senators but not to recall them.

George Haynes, a leading Senate historian, observed that the House "would be elected immediately by the people and would represent them and their personal rights individually," while "the Senate would be elected by state legislatures and represent the States in their political capacity." In this way, Haynes wrote, "each [house] would form a proper and independent check upon the other and the legislative power would be advantageously balanced."[1] The Seventeenth Amendment, ratified in 1913, provided for the direct election of Senators.

HISTORY BEFORE 1787
The Articles of Confederation Congress was a unicameral legislature that had four prominent features: unit voting, rotation, recall, and equal representation. Although the Articles permitted states to send delegations of no fewer than two but no more than seven persons, the size of the delegation was irrelevant to a state's strength in Congress.[2] Each delegation participated as a unit, and each state had one vote.[3] However, unit voting created problems when delegates were absent and when delegations were divided. Delegates were appointed annually in a manner the state directed.[4]

The Articles observed the principle of rotation in office, so no delegate could serve more than three years out of every six.[5] In addition, delegates were subject to recall at any time, although none were ever recalled.[6] In creating a federal Congress, delegates would abandon unit voting, rotation, and recall but, after immense struggle, would retain equal representation for the Senate.

THE CONSTITUTIONAL CONVENTION

Early in the proceedings of the Constitutional Convention, delegates considered two major plans for the organization of Congress. The Virginia Plan called for a bicameral legislature with both chambers subject to proportional representation: that is, the number of representatives would be determined based on a state's population.[7] By contrast, the New Jersey Plan proposed a unicameral legislature in which states were represented equally regardless of their population.[8] On June 19, by a vote of seven states to three with one divided, the Convention supported the Virginia Plan.[9]

Under Convention rules, any question voted upon could later be reconsidered.[10] One such question was how the Senate would be constituted. Delegates initially approved proportionality for both chambers, but upon reconsideration, they deadlocked on whether the Senate should be proportional.

On June 25, by a vote of nine states to two, delegates determined that state legislatures should elect Senators.[11] Thus, the Framers gave state governments a seat at the federal table. While the people would be directly represented in the House of Representatives, states would be represented in the Senate. John Dickinson of Delaware, who proposed the motion, "wished the Senate to consist of the most distinguished characters, distinguished for their rank in life and their weight of property, and bearing as strong a likeness to the British House of Lords as possible." Dickinson "thought such characters more likely to be selected by the State Legislatures than in any other mode."[12]

One of the most divisive issues at the Constitutional Convention concerned whether the Senate would be constructed proportional to populations or be based on equality between states. Smaller states were determined to achieve the latter. Accustomed to equality of representation in the Articles of Confederation Congress and in the Constitutional Convention itself, these states feared being dominated in a proportional Congress. They could accept proportionality in the House but threatened not to confederate if the Convention imposed such arrangements on them in the Senate.

On June 11, Roger Sherman of Connecticut moved that every state should have one vote in the Senate. "Everything he said depended on this. The smaller states would never agree to the plan on any other principle than equality of suffrage in this branch."[13] Under the proportional plan, delegates discussed an arrangement in which the number of Senators would range from one to five, leaving a total of thirty-six members.[14]

On July 2, to break the impasse, the Convention appointed a committee composed of one representative from each of the 11 states then in attendance.[15] On July 5, the committee reported a compromise that provided for equality of representation in the Senate.[16] It is known as the Great Compromise or the Connecticut Compromise, because two of the strongest advocates of equality, Roger Sherman and Oliver Ellsworth, represented Connecticut in the Convention. Sherman had originally proposed such an arrangement on June 11, but the Convention rejected it several times before acting on the committee report in July.

This result dismayed James Madison, an advocate of the Virginia Plan. In opposition, he contended that the minority could impose policies on the majority and extort outcomes by making its assent conditional on other measures. Moreover, he predicted, such evils would be compounded with the addition of new, lightly populated states.[17]

Such arguments did not persuade the Convention. On July 16, 1787, it agreed to the committee's recommendation.[18] The vote was five states in favor, four opposed, and one deadlocked.[19] The five states in favor were Connecticut, New Jersey, Delaware, Maryland, and North Carolina. The four in opposition were Pennsylvania, Virginia, South Carolina, and Georgia. Massachusetts was divided, and New York, New Hampshire, and Rhode Island were not present.[20] The small states prevailed because their intense commitment on the issue made their walkout threats credible.[21]

The Convention would resolve several other issues regarding the upper House. First, the delegates agreed without dissent that every state would have two Senators so that the first Senate would have twenty-six members.[22] Second, delegates wanted the Senate to bring stability to the federal Congress, so they gave Senators six-year terms, three times as long as those for members of the House.[23] In so doing, the delegates followed the general example of five states that granted members of their upper chambers longer terms than they granted those of their lower chambers.[24] Third, to enhance the independence of the Senate, the delegates omitted the power to recall members of Congress and provided that Senators would be paid from the federal treasury and not by the states.[25] As a result, the Constitution preserved the stability of the six-year term, which the states could not cut short. Fourth, through staggered terms, delegates provided for the possible replacement of one-third of the Senate every two years while maintaining stability.[26] However, unlike in the Articles of Confederation, they did not mandate rotation in office. Fifth, the two Senators from each state would vote individually, not as a unit.[27] For the delegates, per capita voting was not controversial. It prevented the absenteeism and deadlocked delegations that had characterized the Articles of Confederation Congress.[28]

RATIFICATION DEBATES

Large states were deeply troubled by equal representation in the Senates. As James Madison recounted in 1830, "The difficulty in reconciling the larger States to the equality of the Senate is known to have been the most threatening that was encountered in framing the Constitution."[29] Yet, in Federalist No. 62, he defended the compromise. Publius recognized that "in a compound republic, partaking both of the national and federal character, the government ought to be founded on a mixture of the principles of proportional and equal representation." States would be represented in the Senate as states.

Madison justified equality of representation in the Senate as "a constitutional recognition of the portion of sovereignty remaining in the individual States and an instrument for preserving that residuary sovereignty." He further defended creation of the Senate as a response to "the propensity of all single and numerous assemblies to yield to the impulse of sudden and violent

passions, and to be seduced by factious leaders into intemperate and pernicious resolutions." The antidote, Publius argued, was a less numerous body that would "possess great firmness and consequently ought to hold its authority by a tenure of considerable duration."

In June 1788, Alexander Hamilton offered a similar defense of the Senate to the New York. "The main design of the Convention in forming the Senate," he said, "was to prevent fluctuations and cabals. With this in view, they made that body small and to exist for a considerable time."[30]

Opponents of the Constitution cited the absence of recall power as one of its failures. Federal Farmer, a prominent Anti-Federalist, presented letters to the Pennsylvania Convention. He argued that "[t]he exercise of sovereignty does not consist of chusing masters, such as Senators would be, who, when chosen, would be beyond controul, but in the power of dismissing, impeaching, or the like, those to whom authority is delegated."[31]

Luther Martin of Maryland was a delegate to the Constitutional Convention but dissented from the Constitution. He complained that "for six years the senators are rendered totally and absolutely independent of their States, of whom they ought to be representatives, without any bind or tie between them." Martin warned that Senators "may join in measures *ruinous* and *destructive* to *their States*, even such as should *totally annihilate* their *State governments*, and their States *cannot recall them* nor *exercise any controul over them*."[32]

Ultimately, New York, Rhode Island, and Pennsylvania futilely recommended that Congress pass a constitutional amendment to permit the recall of Senators.[33] However, such an amendment was never even proposed by the First Congress. Until early in the twentieth century, some state legislatures would instruct Senators on how to vote on federal legislation.[34] The instructions were not binding, and the long Senate terms, not subject to curtailment by recall, diminished the likelihood of Senators being held accountable for disregarding those instructions.

Opponents of the Constitution also criticized the lack of rotation among Senators. The Anti-Federalists claimed the Senate would create a permanent political elite. In the New York convention, leading Anti-Federalist Melancton Smith declared that "[a]s the clause now stands, there is no doubt that the senators will hold their office perpetually; and in this situation, they may of necessity lose their dependence and attachment to the people."[35] Smith warned that this design "is certainly inconsistent with the established principles of republicanism that the Senate should be a fixed and unchangeable body of men." Along with other anti-Federalists, Smith favored a constitutional amendment requiring rotation.[36] However, the First Congress did not propose such an amendment.

There was not much opposition to allowing each Senator to vote individually. Charles Cotesworth Pinckney, who attended the Federal Convention, defended this practice to the South Carolina House of Representatives. "Now that the Senators vote individually, and not by States," he argued, "each state will be anxious to keep a full representation in the Senate; and the Senate now has the power to compel attendance of its own members." Pinckney saw a pragmatic benefit from this plan: "We shall thus have no delay, and business will be conducted in a fuller representation of the States than it hitherto has been."[37]

DIRECT ELECTION OF SENATORS
Election by state legislatures proved to be problematic. Deadlocks between two chambers of some legislatures delayed or prevented the election of Senators. Between 1891 and 1905, there were 45 deadlocks in 20 states.[38] And even when

these impediments did not exist, there were periodic allegations of bribery and vote-buying for Senate elections.[39]

In 1893, 1894, 1898, 1900, and 1902, the House of Representatives passed proposals to amend the Constitution so that Senators could be elected by popular vote.[40] All of these proposals died in the Senate.[41]

Outside the Senate, agitation for reform became pronounced. By the end of the nineteenth century, thirty-one states had petitioned Congress to submit an amendment, in several cases after overwhelming public referenda.[42] By 1912, twenty-nine states had senatorial primaries, attempting to bind their legislatures to elect the winner of the popular vote.

Concerned that the Senate would not act on an amendment, states began to agitate for Congress to call a constitutional convention. By 1904, nineteen states had petitioned Congress for that purpose.[43] On May 13, 1912, Congress passed a direct election amendment, which was approved by a sufficient number of states by April 13, 1913.[44] On May 31, 1913, Secretary of State William Jennings Bryan issued a notification that the Seventeenth Amendment to the Constitution had been ratified; the people, not state legislatures, were now directly responsible for electing Senators.[45] The Seventeenth Amendment is discussed in Essay No. 203.

Cite as: Martin Gold, *The Senate Clause, in* THE HERITAGE GUIDE TO THE CONSTITUTION 39 (Josh Blackman & John G. Malcolm eds., 3d ed. 2025).

Notes
1. George Haynes, The Election of Senators 12 (1906). 2. Articles of Confederation, arts. V, §§ 2, 4. 3. *Id.* at §§3, 4. 4. *Id.* at § 1. 5. *Id.* at § 2. 6. *Id.*at § 1; Timothy Zick, *The Consent of the Governed: Recall of United States Senators*, 103 Dickinson L. Rev. 567, 571 (1999). 7. 1 Farrand's 20. 8. 3 Farrand's 613. 9. 1 Farrand's 322. 10. *Id.* at 9–10. 11. *Id.* at 395. 12. *Id.* at 150; Elaine K. Swift, The Making of an American Senate 11 (2002). 13. *Id.* at 201. 14. 2 Farrand's 5–11. 15. *Id.* at 519–20. 16. *Id.* at 526. 17. *Id.* at 9. 18. *Id.* at 15. 19. *Id.* 20. *Id.* 21. Michael J. Klarman, The Framers' Coup 201 (2016). 22. 2 Farrand's 94. 23. 1 Farrand's 418. 24. Federalist No. 39 (Madison); 2 Story's Commentaries § 718. 25. 1 Farrand's 427–28. 26. *Id.* at 418. 27. 2 Farrand's 179, 234. 28. Jay S. Bybee, Ulysses at the Mast: Democracy, Federalism, and the Sirens' Song of the Seventeenth Amendment 350 (1997). 29. James Madison to James Hillhouse, 17 May 1830, https://perma .cc/YU4H-6VB9. 30. New York Ratifying Convention Remarks (Francis Childs's Version), [24 June 1788], https://perma.cc/C8LZ-FSUM. 31. Storing 3.14.6. 32. *Id.* at 2.4.42. 33. Bybee, *supra* at 529. 34. *Id.* at 316–28. 35. Storing 6.12.27. 36. *Id.* at 6.12.27–.28. 37. 4 Elliot's 277–86. 38. 1 Robert C. Byrd, The Senate 1789–1989: Addresses on the History of the United States Senate 393 (1988). 39. Haynes, *supra* at 59–63. 40. *Id.* at 97. 41. Byrd, *supra* at 398; Lindsay Rogers, The American Senate 113 (1926). 42. Haynes, *supra* at 98. 43. *Id.* at 108–09. 44. Byrd, *supra* at 402. 45. *Id.* at 403.

ESSAY NO. 16: THE SENATORIAL CLASSES AND VACANCIES CLAUSE
ART. I, § 3, CL. 2

Immediately after they shall be assembled in Consequence of the first Election, they shall be divided as equally as may be into three Classes. The Seats of the Senators of the first Class shall be vacated at the Expiration of the second Year, of the second Class at the Expiration of the fourth Year, and of the third Class at the Expiration of the sixth Year, so that one third may be chosen every second Year; and if Vacancies happen by Resignation, or otherwise, during the Recess of the Legislature of any State, the Executive thereof may make temporary Appointments until the next Meeting of the Legislature, which shall then fill such Vacancies.
—Martin Gold

INTRODUCTION

Members of the House of Representatives serve two-year terms, and members of the Senate serve six-year terms. Every two years, new members are elected to the House, and new Senators are elected to the Senate. As a result, every two years, there is a new House comprised entirely of newly elected members.

The Senate, however, serves as a continuing body. Every two years, one-third of its membership will be newly elected, and two-thirds will return. As Massachusetts Senator Henry Cabot Lodge observed, "Administrations come and go, Houses assemble and disperse, Senators change, but the Senate is always there in the Capitol, and always organized, with an existence unbroken since 1789. . . ."[1]

The Senatorial Vacancies Clause also provided that state executives could "make temporary Appointments" while the state legislature was in recess. When they convened, the state legislatures could make formal appointments. The process of filling vacancies was altered by the Seventeenth Amendment, which provided for the direct election of Senators.

THE CONSTITUTIONAL CONVENTION: DIVIDING THE CLASS

During the Constitutional Convention, the delegates disagreed about the appropriate length of Senate terms. Different proposals would have specified four, six, seven, and even nine years. The delegates debated how to divide the Senate

into multiple classes. With a nine-year term, for example, one of three classes would stand for election every third year; with a four-year term, one of four classes would stand for election annually.

The seven-year term was approved on June 12, 1787, but was later rejected as being impractical to divide. Ultimately, on June 26, by a vote of seven states to four, the delegates settled on a six-year term.[2] The Senate would be divided into three classes, and one-third of the Senators would stand for election every two years. Under this design, a quorum of the Senate—a simple majority—would remain in office at all times. The Senate would endure as a continuing body. By contrast, every member of the House of Representatives must stand for election every two years. Though Representatives can be re-elected, each new House is a distinct body.

The Framers also addressed a problem that the first Senate would face: How would the initial batch of Senators be sorted into three classes? The text provides that these Senators should be "divided as equally as may be into three Classes." The Senatorial Classes Clause modified the terms for members of the first Senate: One-third would serve a two-year term, one-third would serve a four-year term, and one-third would serve the full six-year term.

THE CONSTITUTIONAL CONVENTION: SENATE VACANCIES

During the Convention, delegates determined that Senators would be elected by state legislatures. This raised a foreseeable issue: What would happen in the event of Senate vacancies? Members of the House were elected directly by the people, and if vacancies arose, the state executive authority would "issue Writs of Election to fill such Vacancies." (See Essay No. 12.) In other words, a special election would be scheduled to fill the former member's unexpired term. If a Senate vacancy arose, legislators could fill the vacancy while the legislature was in session, and that appointment would last for the unexpired term of the former Senator. But what if the state legislature was not in session? Would the seat remain vacant until the state legislature convened, or could the state executive make a temporary appointment?

On August 6, the Committee of Detail proposed that state Executives be able to fill such vacancies until the next meeting of the state legislature. The draft stated that "[v]acancies may be supplied by the Executive until the next meeting of the Legislature." James Wilson of Pennsylvania objected to this proposal.[3] At the time, Wilson observed, most Executives were elected by state legislatures and not by popular vote, so temporary gubernatorial appointments would not be accountable to the people. He also believed that such appointments would be unnecessary because legislatures convened annually, and vacancies would not be of extended duration.

Wilson, however, stood alone. Edmund Randolph of Virginia argued that because the Senate would be smaller than the House, even short vacancies could be consequential. Randolph contended that a temporary appointment power would be needed to prevent "chasms" in the Senate's membership. Hugh Williamson of North Carolina proposed that state legislatures should have the discretion to deny an Executive the power to fill vacancies. On August 9, delegates voted to reject Wilson's amendment to strike the provision for Executive appointment by a vote of eight to one with one state divided.[4] Delegates also rejected Williamson's proposal by a vote of four to six.[5]

After these votes, doubts remained about the Committee of Detail's proposal. James Madison of Virginia offered an amendment to clarify what would happen if Senators resigned or individuals refused election to a Senate seat. Madison's proposal read, "Vacancies happening by refusals to accept, resignations, or otherwise may be supplied by the Legislature of the State in the representation of which such vacancies shall happen, or by the Executive thereof until the next meeting of the Legislature." Gouverneur Morris of New York supported Madison's amendment, noting that the Committee of Detail's draft barred Senators from being appointed to certain federal positions during the time for which they had been elected and for another year thereafter. As a result, Morris explained, state legislatures could effectively disqualify persons from federal service by electing them to the Senate against their will.[6]

Madison's amendment passed without opposition.[7] The clause was modified into its present form in the September 12 report of the Committee of Style.[8]

RATIFICATION DEBATES

In Federalist No. 62, James Madison urged the "necessity of some stable institution in the government." The House of Representatives, like state legislatures, would be subject to frequent turnover, but the Senate would have continuity. Madison explained that "a continual change, even of good measures, is inconsistent with every rule of prudence."

While agreeing that the Senate should be structured to provide stability, Anti-Federalist Melancton Smith from New York opposed the absence of term limits. "It is certainly inconsistent with the established principles of republicanism," he wrote, "that the Senate should be a fixed and unchangeable body of men. There should be then some constitutional provision against this evil. A rotation I consider as the best possible mode of affecting a remedy."[9]

Cato, another Anti-Federalist from New York, criticized the Senate under the proposed Constitution. He wrote that the Framers gave "the executive the unprecedented power of making temporary senators, in case of vacancies, by resignation or otherwise."[10] In Federalist No. 67, Alexander Hamilton defended this provision, though he charged that Cato wrote that the President of the United States ("the Executive thereof") could fill Senate vacancies as a type of recess appointment.[11] Here, Hamilton did not fairly read Cato, who was referring to the power of appointment vesting in state Executives.

EARLY PRACTICE

The First Congress was supposed to convene on March 4, 1789. However, primarily because of transportation difficulties, a quorum of the Senate did not assemble until April 6.

Under the Constitution, Senators had to be divided into three classes. The Senate made the division on May 15, by which time twenty of the twenty-six Senators representing the original thirteen states had assembled.[12] Names were drawn from lots with no two Senators from the same state in the same lot. Seven Senators were designated for an initial two-year term, seven were designated for an initial four-year term, and six were designated for an initial six-year term. The Senate further provided that "when Senators shall take their seats from States that have not yet appointed Senators, they shall be placed by lot in the foregoing classes, but in such manner as shall keep the classes as nearly equal as may be in numbers."[13]

THE SEVENTEENTH AMENDMENT

The Senatorial Vacancies Clause was altered by ratification of the Seventeenth Amendment in 1913. (See Essay Nos. 203 and 204.) Senators would now be elected by popular vote instead of by state legislatures. The Amendment also adopted Hugh Williamson's rejected proposal from the Constitutional Convention to empower state legislatures to deny Executives the power to appoint Senators temporarily. This provision is contrary to the original Constitution, under which legislatures were not able to deny such authority to the Executives.

JUDICIAL PRECEDENT

The Supreme Court of the United States has not had occasion to interpret the original Senatorial Classes and Vacancies Clause.

Cite as: Martin Gold, *The Senatorial Classes and Vacancies Clause, in* THE HERITAGE GUIDE TO THE CONSTITUTION 43 (Josh Blackman & John G. Malcolm eds., 3d ed. 2025).

Notes

1. Henry Cabot Lodge, *The Senate*, 34 Scribner's Magazine 541, 541, 549–50 (1903).   **2.** 2 Farrand's 426.   **3.** *Id.* at 231.   **4.** *Id.*   **5.** *Id.* at 232.   **6.** *Id.*   **7.** *Id.*   **8.** *Id.* at 591.   **9.** 22 DHRC 2015–16   **10.** Storing 2.6.37.   **11.** Seth Barrett Tillman & Josh Blackman, *Offices and Officers of the* *Constitution, Part III: The Appointments, Impeachment, Commissions, and Oath or Affirmation Clauses*, 62 S. Tex. L. Rev. 349, 439–440 (2023).   **12.** 1 Annals of Cong. 16 (1789).   **13.** *Id.* at 26.

ESSAY NO. 17: THE QUALIFICATIONS FOR SENATORS CLAUSE
ART. I, § 3, CL. 3

No person shall be a Senator who shall not have attained to the Age of thirty Years, and been nine Years a Citizen of the United States, and who shall not, when elected, be an Inhabitant of that State for which he shall be chosen.

—Martin Gold

INTRODUCTION

The federal Constitution imposes three specific qualifications for Senators: A Senator must (1) be at least thirty years old, (2) have been a citizen for nine years, and (3) be an "Inhabitant" of the state in which he was elected. Despite these requirements, the Senate has administered the oath to several Senators who were under the age of thirty, and other underage Senators have delayed taking the oath until they turned thirty. Essay No. 8 discusses whether the House of Representatives and states can impose additional qualifications for serving in Congress.

THE CONSTITUTIONAL CONVENTION

The issue of a minimum age for Senators came up early during the Constitutional Convention.

Resolution 5 of the Virginia Plan provided that "members of the second Branch of the National Legislature ought to be selected by those of the first, out of a proper number of persons nominated by the individual legislatures." The Virginia Plan was presented to the Committee of the Whole on May 29, 1787, but although Resolution 5 conceived that there should be a minimum age, it left the number blank for later consideration.[1]

On June 12, the Convention rejected a proposal to eliminate the minimum age requirement, and without further controversy, delegates set the age at thirty years by a vote of seven states to four. That age was five years older than the twenty-five-year age requirement for the House of Representatives.[2] The higher minimum age was consistent with James Madison's concept that "[t]he use of the Senate is to consist in its proceeding, with more coolness, with more system, and with more wisdom than the popular branch."[3]

Later during the Convention, the delegates turned to the citizenship and residence requirements. In early August, the Committee of Detail presented its report, which added two additional qualifications for serving in the Senate: A Senator would have to have been a U.S. citizen for at least four years and would have to be a resident of the state in which he was elected.[4] The age requirement was not particularly controversial, but the citizenship and residency requirements generated spirited debate on August 9.

Gouverneur Morris of Pennsylvania proposed to replace the four-year citizenship requirement with fourteen years.[5] He warned against the danger of admitting strangers into public councils. Charles Pinckney of South Carolina seconded the motion. He spoke of the Senate's anticipated role in approving treaties and cautioned about the problem of subjecting them to persons with foreign attachments.[6]

James Madison of Virginia opposed placing citizenship requirements in the Constitution, believing that it would give that document "a tincture of illiberality" and discourage meritorious foreigners from immigrating to the United States. He further contended that because Congress would be responsible for setting immigration and naturalization rules,

citizenship requirements would be addressed more appropriately in that forum.[7] Benjamin Franklin of Pennsylvania was open to a citizenship threshold covering a "reasonable time," but argued that a fourteen-year requirement was excessive. He observed that "during the course of the Revolution, we found that many strangers served us faithfully and that many natives took part against their Country."[8] James Wilson of Pennsylvania spoke of the discouragement and mortification that foreign-born persons would feel from such "degrading discrimination."[9]

However, Morris remained skeptical of trusting foreigners. He was open to admitting them to many privileges in the United States but dubious about their serving in public office. "The men who would shake off their attachments to their own country can never love another," he claimed.[10] Morris's motion for a fourteen-year citizenship requirement failed by a vote of four states to seven. His further motion to impose a thirteen-year citizenship requirement failed by the same vote, as did a ten-year restriction proposed by Charles Cotesworth Pinckney of South Carolina.[11]

John Rutledge of South Carolina and Hugh Williamson of North Carolina noted that delegates had already set the citizenship requirement for the House of Representatives at seven years and thought that the Senate's should be longer.[12] By a vote of six states to four, with one state divided, delegates agreed to the requirement of nine years. Then, without dissension, they agreed to substitute the word "inhabitant" for "resident."[13] According to Professor Eugene D. Mazo, this change would "defeat efforts to adopt state durational residency requirements."[14]

Finally, the Committee of Detail's report included a recommendation that would have given Congress the discretion to add a property qualification for membership: "The Legislature of the United States shall have authority to establish such uniform qualifications of the members of each House, with regard to property, as to the said Legislature shall seem expedient." Madison opposed this recommendation. On October 10, he argued that "[T]he qualifications of electors and elected were fundamental articles in a Republican Government . . . and ought to be fixed by the Constitution." Madison observed that "[i]f the Legislature could regulate those of either, it can by degrees subvert the Constitution." He explained that "limiting the number of people capable of being elected, as the number authorized to elect" may convert a Republic "an aristocracy or oligarchy."[15]

Notwithstanding this admonition, Morris moved to strike "with regard to property," which would have given Congress complete discretion to set additional qualifications, and not just qualifications regarding property. However, Morris's motion was opposed by a vote of seven states to four. Accepting Madison's view, the Convention then rejected the Committee of Detail's recommendation outright by a vote of three states to seven.[16]

COMMENTARY

The Federalist Papers defended the Senate qualifications. In Federalist No. 64, John Jay wrote that "[b]y excluding men under thirty from the" Senate, the Constitution "confines the elections to men of whom the people have had time to form a judgment, and with respect to whom they will not be liable to be deceived by those brilliant appearances of genius and patriotism, which, like transient meteors, sometimes mislead as well as dazzle."[17] And in Federalist No. 62, Madison explained that "the term of nine years appears to be a prudent mediocrity between a total exclusion of adopted citizens, whose merits and talents may claim a share in the public confidence, and an indiscriminate and hasty admission of them, which might create a channel for foreign influence on the national councils."[18]

Later, Justice Joseph Story would praise the qualifications for Senators. "[I]f counsels are to be wise," he wrote, "the ardor and impetuosity and confidence of youth must be chastened by the sober lessons of experience; and if knowledge and solid judgment and tried integrity are to be deemed indispensable qualifications for senatorial service, it would be rashness to affirm that thirty years is too long a period for a due maturity and probation."[19]

CONGRESSIONAL PRACTICE

The express provisions of the Qualifications for Senators Clause have not been the subject of judicial review. However, the Senate has taken actions bearing on the implementation of this clause. For example, the Senate has administered oaths to people who had not yet reached the age of thirty. In 1806, Henry Clay of Kentucky was elected to the Senate by his state legislature.[20] He took the oath and began serving while he was still twenty-nine years old. In 1816, the Senate administered the oath to Armistead Mason of Virginia, who was elected by the state legislature to fill a vacancy.[21] The unexpired term would stretch about a year. At the time of his election, Mason was twenty-eight years old, and he was still several months shy of his thirtieth birthday when his term ended in March 1817. In 1818, the Senate administered the oath to John Henry Eaton of Tennessee,[22] who was only twenty-eight years old. According to the Senate Historical Office, "Apparently no one asked John Eaton how old he was."

The Senate has also delayed administering the oath to members who had not yet reached the age of thirty. In 1934, Rush Holt of West Virginia defeated incumbent Senator Henry Hatfield. Holt was elected to the Senate at the age of twenty-nine and pledged to wait until after his thirtieth birthday before taking the oath. Hatfield filed a petition with the Senate, contending that Holt did not meet the minimum age requirement. The Senate dismissed Hatfield's petition on the grounds that "the age requirement applies at the time of oath-taking rather than the time of election, or the time the term [to which the candidate is elected] begins."[23] For example, twenty-nine-year-old Russell B. Long of Louisiana was elected to the Senate on November 2, 1948, a day before his thirtieth birthday, and was sworn in on December 31, 1948, after he had turned thirty. Similarly, Joseph R. Biden of Delaware was twenty-nine on November 7, 1972, when he won election to the United States Senate. He turned thirty on November 20, 1972, and took the oath of office on January 3, 1973.

OPEN QUESTIONS

- Senators must be "nine Years a Citizen of the United States." When the first Senate assembled in 1789, who had been a "Citizen of the United States" for nine years? Did that period stretch back before the ratification of the Articles of Confederation or to the signing of the Declaration of Independence?[24]
- Does the Constitution permit the Senate to issue an oath to a member-elect who has not yet reached the age of thirty if no one objects? Does the Constitution impose a duty on Senators to inquire about a member-elect's age?
- Does the Constitution permit a member-elect who is under the age of thirty to delay taking the oath until he turns thirty?
- Does the residency requirement apply to a Senator who is "appointed" by a governor empowered by a state legislature to make such appointments?[25]

Cite as: Martin Gold, *The Qualifications for Senators Clause, in* THE HERITAGE GUIDE TO THE CONSTITUTION 45 (Josh Blackman & John G. Malcolm eds., 3d ed. 2025).

Notes

1. 1 Farrand's 20.   **2.** 2 Farrand's 217–18.   **3.** *Id.* at 151.   **4.** 2 Farrand's 179.   **5.** *Id.* at 235.   **6.** *Id.*   **7.** *Id.* at 235–36.   **8.** *Id.*   **9.** *Id.* at 237.   **10.** *Id.* at 237–38.   **11.** *Id.* at 238–39.   **12.** *Id.* at 239.   **13.** *Id.*   **14.** Eugene D. Mazo, *Residency and Democracy: Durational Residency Requirements from the Framers to the Present*, 43 Fla. State U.L. Rev. 611, 622 (2016).   **15.** 2 Farrand's 249–50.   **16.** *Id.* at 250–51.   **17.** Federalist No. 64 (Jay).   **18.** Federalist No. 62 (Madison).   **19.** 3 Story's Commentaries § 727.   **20.** *Henry Clay: A Featured Biography*, United States Senate, https://perma.cc/FV96-VS5V.   **21.** *Youngest Senator*, United States Senate, https://perma.cc/3QTQ-ER8Q.   **22.** *Id.*   **23.** *Id.*   **24.** Josh Blackman, *Original Citizenship*, 159 U. Penn. L. Rev. PENNumbra 95 (2010).   **25.** Stephen E. Sachs, *Can a Marylander Be the Senator from California?*, Volokh Conspiracy, Oct. 3, 2023, https://perma.cc/S78G-3P6B; Josh Blackman, *Laphonza Butler Better Hope Other Senators Are Textualists*, Volokh Conspiracy, Oct. 3, 2023, https://perma.cc/J2G9-FDYS.

ESSAY NO. 18: THE VICE PRESIDENT AS PRESIDING OFFICER CLAUSE
ART. I, § 3, CL. 4

The Vice President of the United States shall be President of the Senate, but shall have no Vote, unless they be equally divided.

—Roy E. Brownell II

INTRODUCTION

The position of Vice President is something of a hybrid with its constitutional functions alternating between the executive and legislative branches depending on context.[1] The officeholder is elected along with the President for a four-year term and is first in the line of succession. But he also presides over the Senate, where he can cast tie-breaking votes. In modern times, Vice Presidents spend most of their workday focusing on executive branch tasks and political assignments with their appearances in the Senate typically limited to ceremonial functions or breaking tie votes.

HISTORY BEFORE 1787

Several colonial charters and state constitutions included antecedents to the vice presidency.[2] The New York Constitution of 1777 seems to have been particularly influential.[3] It stated that the "lieutenant governor shall, by virtue of his office, be president of the senate, and, upon an equal division, have a casting voice in their decisions, but not vote on any other occasion." The officeholder also was to "exercise all the power and authority" of the governor in the event of an executive vacancy or absence.[4]

48

THE CONSTITUTIONAL CONVENTION

Alexander Hamilton appears to have been the first delegate at the Constitutional Convention to address executive succession.[5] On June 18, 1787, Hamilton proposed as part of his plan that the President of the Senate serve as successor. "On the death[,] resignation or removal of the [national] Governour his authorities [are] to be exercised by the President of the Senate till a Successor be appointed."[6] Perhaps following Hamilton's lead, the Committee of Detail also included the President of the Senate as its proposed successor on August 6, providing that "[i]n case of his removal . . . death, resignation, or disability to discharge the powers and duties of his office, the President of the Senate shall exercise those powers and duties. . . ."[7] This prompted concern from delegates, including James Madison who believed that having a Senator as successor might lead to mischief in the upper chamber.

Matters involving succession were placed on hold until September 4, when the Committee of Eleven put forward its work, which included introduction of the vice presidency.[8] The proposal required electors to vote for two candidates, including one from outside their home state.[9] It was thought that this procedure would encourage the election of chief executives who would enjoy countrywide prominence.[10] The candidate with a majority of electoral votes would become President, and the candidate with the second-highest total would become Vice President. (See Essay No. 94.) This mode of election was later changed by the Twelfth Amendment. (See Essay No. 190.)

To give officeholders some regular responsibility, the revised plan also proposed that the Vice President preside over the Senate except during presidential impeachment trials and "when he shall exercise the powers and duties of" the chief executive.[11] (See Essay Nos. 19 and 97.) The position was also granted the authority to break tie votes in the upper chamber.[12]

Later that month, the Committee on Style modified the Committee of Eleven's handiwork, muddying the waters with respect to the Vice President's status following a presidential vacancy or inability episode. This change would lend some support to the notion that the Vice President *became* chief executive under such circumstances instead of merely exercising the latter's powers and duties. This position would complicate situations involving presidential incapacity. The delegates also did not include a means of providing a new Vice President if the office became vacant.[13] These problems would later be remedied by the Twenty-Fifth Amendment.

THE RATIFICATION DEBATES

In Federalist No. 68, Alexander Hamilton offered three defenses of the office: (1) the Vice President's tie-breaking power assured that the Senate would always reach a decision; (2) if a Senator were to serve as President of the Senate, he would only have a "contingent" tie-breaking vote and would no longer be able to cast his vote regularly, leaving his home state in most cases with only one voting Senator instead of two; and (3) it made sense for a Vice President to serve as a "substitute for the President," analogizing the office to that of the lieutenant governor under the New York Constitution.

During the state ratification conventions, delegates focused attention on the office seeming to straddle the separation of powers.[14] In this regard, George Mason expressed concern that "the legislative and executive are hereby mixed and incorporated together."[15]

THE FIRST CONGRESS

John Adams, the first Vice President, was confounded by his office. He stated to the first Senate, "I am possessed of two separate powers . . . . I am Vice-President. In this I am nothing, but I may be everything. But I am president also of the Senate."[16] To the upper chamber, he posed the question, "what shall I be?" Lawmakers were unable to offer much guidance. Reflecting the office's ambiguity, some early statutes treated the position as part of the legislative branch, while others as part of the executive branch.[17]

THE VICE PRESIDENT AND THE SENATE

The Vice President is not a Senator. He is elected nationally, serves a four-year term, can be impeached, and can vote only when there is a tie. Nonetheless, in carrying out his duties in the upper chamber, the Vice President is part of the legislative branch and receives his salary from Senate funds.[18] The Constitution seems to suggest that the Vice President is *required* to preside over the Senate, the text providing that the Vice President "*shall* be president of the Senate." But for decades, officeholders have presided very little.[19] In such cases, the Constitution empowers the Senate, in the Vice President's absence, to select a "President pro tempore."

After World War I, Presidents began to ask Vice Presidents to join Cabinet meetings on a regular basis.[20] Other executive branch delegations soon followed, and by the 1950s, the Vice President's participation in the Senate had greatly diminished.[21] In modern times, the Vice President typically appears in the upper chamber only on ceremonial occasions and to break ties. Most of his workday is usually devoted to executive branch tasks and political assignments.[22]

There are two circumstances in which the Vice President cannot preside over the Senate. He may not do so while serving as acting President,[23] and the Chief Justice replaces the Vice President as presiding officer during presidential impeachment trials.[24] (See Essay Nos. 20, 207, and 214.)

The Vice President can make parliamentary rulings, which can be overruled by the Senate.[25] For instance, Vice President John Nance Garner made a series of pronouncements to the chamber in the 1930s. He formalized the custom whereby the Majority Leader would be recognized before all other Senators seeking to address the body. These statements, which went unchallenged by the Senate at the time, today undergird the Majority Leader's principal formal power, which is to be recognized first and to propose the Senate schedule.[26]

As a practical matter, the Parliamentarian has narrowed the presiding officer's authority over Senate procedure. This nonpartisan position was created in 1935 and provides technical advice on rules and precedents that the Vice President rarely ignores.[27]

In his Senate role, the Vice President is covered by the Speech or Debate Clause.[28] In 2023, a federal district court concluded that some of Vice President Mike Pence's actions in the leadup to the January 6, 2021, electoral vote count, were protected by the provision.[29]

TIE-BREAKING VOTES

In the Senate, the Vice President enjoys the authority to break tie votes. Constitutional text places no restrictions on the types of measures on which he can vote, and the Senate has never circumscribed this power.[30] Hamilton noted in Federalist No. 68 that the Vice President was given this assignment in order "to secure *at all times* the possibility of a definitive resolution of the body."[31]

Officeholders have cast tie-breaking votes in numerous contexts other than legislation: executive and judicial branch nominations; non-binding Senate resolutions; Senate officer appointments; adjournment efforts; and modifications to treaties and constitutional amendments. Vice Presidents have also decided whether the Senate will request information from the executive branch; if the chamber will uphold the Vice President's own parliamentary ruling; and how a committee will initiate an investigation.[32] In 1881, 2001, and 2021, when the Senate was evenly divided, the Vice President's tie-breaking votes essentially decided which party would control the chamber.[33] A Vice President is even permitted not to vote, in which case the measure is defeated.[34] In the modern era, officeholders have cast their votes consistent with their administration's policy, but this is not constitutionally prescribed. In the nineteenth century, it was not uncommon for a Vice President to vote contrary to the views of the President.[35]

The officeholder's ability to break tie votes is generally influenced by the partisan and ideological composition of the Senate. Not surprisingly, Vice Presidents have exercised this authority frequently when the Senate has been closely divided. As of May 2025, there have been a total of 303 tie-breaking votes. Vice President John C. Calhoun's record of thirty-one tie-breaking votes was broken by Vice President Kamala Harris, who cast thirty-three.[36]

OPEN QUESTIONS

- Could a Vice President claim the chair while he is the subject of a Senate impeachment trial?[37]
- Could the Vice President preside (and break tie votes) when, under the Twelfth Amendment, the Senate is deciding who should be Vice President if the Electoral College failed to produce a majority and the incumbent is a candidate?[38]

Cite as: Roy E. Brownell II, *The Vice President as Presiding Officer Clause, in* THE HERITAGE GUIDE TO THE CONSTITUTION 48 (Josh Blackman & John G. Malcolm eds., 3d ed. 2025).

Notes

1. Roy E. Brownell II, *A Constitutional Chameleon, Part I*, 24 Kan. J.L. & Pub. Pol'y 1, 4–5 (2014).   **2.** John D. Feerick, From Failing Hands 23–38 (1965).   **3.** Jamin Soderstrom, *Comment, Back to the Basics*, 35 Pepp. L. Rev. 967, 982 (2008).   **4.** N.Y Const. of 1777, art. XX.   **5.** Feerick, at 41–43.   **6.** 1 Farrand's 292.   **7.** 2 Farrand's 186.   **8.** *Id.* at 493.   **9.** *Id.* at 494.   **10.** Joel K. Goldstein, *The New Constitutional Vice Presidency*, 30 Wake Forest L. Rev. 505, 512–13 (1995).   **11.** 2 Farrand's 495.   **12.** *Id.* at 498.   **13.** Goldstein, at 510–18.   **14.** Feerick, at 51–56.   **15.** 3 Elliot's 487.   **16.** Journal of William Maclay 2–3 (1927 ed.).   **17.** 1 Stat. 23 (1789); 1 Stat. 72 (1789); Seth Barrett Tillman & Josh Blackman, *Offices and Officers of the Constitution, Part III*: The Appointments, Impeachment, Commissions, and Oath or Affirmation Clauses, 62 S. Tex. L. Rev. 349, 419, 425–28 (2023).   **18.** 2 U.S.C. § 4591.   **19.** Joel K. Goldstein, *Constitutional Change, Originalism, and the Vice Presidency*, 16 J. Con. Law 369, 383–403 (2013).   **20.** Roy E. Brownell II, *A Constitutional Chameleon, Part II*, 24 Kan. J.L. & Pub. Pol'y 294, 329–37 (2015).   **21.** Martin B. Gold, Senate Procedure and Practice 13 (2004).   **22.** Joel K. Goldstein, The White House Vice Presidency 301–15 (2016).   **23.** Art. I, § 3, cl. 5; Am. XX, § 3; Am. XXV, §§ 3, 4.   **24.** Art. I, § 3, cl. 6.   **25.** Christopher M. Davis, Cong. Rsrch. Serv., RL 30960, The President Pro Tempore of the Senate: History and Authority

of the Office 9 (2015), https://perma.cc/8L6C-UFGX.   **26.** 81 Cong. Rec. 8839–40 (1937); 83 Cong. Rec. 1062, 2202 (1938); Gold, *supra* at 40.   **27.** James Wallner, *Parliamentary Rule*, https://perma.cc/9Q7G-FLQ4.   **28.** Art. 1, § 6, cl. 1.   **29.** *In re Grand Jury Subpoena*, Case No. Redacted (JEB) (Under Seal D.D.C, Mar. 27, 2023), https://perma.cc/9LJR-779U.   **30.** Dan McLaughlin, *Yes, Kamala Harris Can Break a Senate Tie on Biden's Supreme Court Pick*, Nat'l Rev. (Jan. 28, 2022), https://perma.cc/5FWD-9GQ5; Riddick's Senate Procedure 1395 (1992 ed.).   **31.** Federalist No. 68 (Hamilton) (emphasis added); William Josephson, *Senate Election of the Vice President and House of Representatives Election of the President*, 11 J. Con. Law 597, 621 n.64 (2009).   **32.** Riddick's, at 1395; 96 Cong. Rec. 6245 (1950); 22 Senate J. 138–39 (1832); 52 Cong. Rec. 3780–81 (1915).   **33.** 12 Cong. Rec. 33–34 (1881); 147 Cong. Rec 75–88 (2001); Henry Barrett Learned, *Casting Votes of the Vice-Presidents, 1789-1915*, 20 Amer. Hist. Rev. 571, 573–74 (1915).   **34.** Riddick's, at 1395.   **35.** Roy E. Brownell II, *The Independence of the Vice Presidency*, 17 N.Y.U. J. of Legis. & Pub. Pol'y 297, 323–40 (2014).   **36.** *Votes to Break Ties in the Senate*, United States Senate, https://perma.cc/SCJ7-AQVK.   **37.** *Amalgamated Transit Union v. Laidlaw Transit*, 448 F.3d 1092, 1100 & n.5 (9th Cir. 2006) (Bybee, J., dissenting); Joel K. Goldstein, *Can the Vice President Preside at His Own Impeachment Trial?*, 44 St. Louis U.L.J. 849 (2000).   **38.** Josephson, *supra* at 618–21.

ESSAY NO. 19: THE PRESIDENT PRO TEMPORE CLAUSE
ART. I, § 3, CL. 5

The Senate shall chuse their other Officers, and also a President pro tempore, in the Absence of the Vice President, or when he shall exercise the Office of President of the United States.

—Roy E. Brownell II

INTRODUCTION

The Constitution provides presiding officers for both houses of Congress. In the House of Representatives, members "chuse their Speaker." (See Essay No. 13.) By contrast, the Senate—with the rare exception of a Twelfth Amendment contingent election—does not name its default presiding officer, the Vice President, because he is nationally elected. (See Essay No. 18.) In the "absence of the Vice President," the Constitution adds that the Senate shall choose a temporary replacement, the President pro tempore ("for the time being"). By tradition, the President pro tempore has always been a Senator, but—as with the Speaker—it is not required that he be a lawmaker.

The Senate, rather than the judiciary, has resolved most constitutional questions about the office. These include defining "absence" that triggers the President pro tempore's presiding officer role, outlining his Senate responsibilities, and determining when he can preside over impeachment trials.

HISTORY BEFORE 1787
At the time of the U.S. Constitution's framing, there was some precedent for a temporary presiding officer in the British Parliament. A Speaker presided over the House of Commons, but if the Speaker was absent, the body could choose a Speaker pro tempore with the monarch's blessing.[1]

Closer to home, New York State offered a template of its own for the Framers.[2] Under the state's 1777 constitution, the Lieutenant Governor was "president of the senate." If he assumed "the power and authority" of the governor's office or was "unable to attend as president of the senate," lawmakers were "to elect one of their own members to the office of president of the senate, which he shall exercise *pro hac vice* ['for this occasion only']."[3] The state charter also provided that the temporary President of the Senate would serve as the next in line of gubernatorial succession.[4] The document itself was even signed by the "President pro tempore" of the state constitutional convention. Thus, the New York Constitution offered the clearest state forerunner of the President pro tempore of the U.S. Senate.[5]

THE CONSTITUTIONAL CONVENTION
On June 18, 1787, Alexander Hamilton put forward his governmental plan at the Constitutional Convention. His presentation marks the first recorded mention of the President of the Senate during the proceedings.[6] On August 6, the Committee of Detail offered its own blueprint, which provided that "[t]he Senate shall chuse its own President and other Officers."[7] Under this proposal, as well as Hamilton's, the President of the Senate was made the Executive's immediate successor.[8]

However, on September 4, the Committee of Eleven introduced the vice presidency, which altered the dynamics of the Senate President position.[9] Whereas earlier plans had specified that the Senate would choose its own presiding officer, the Committee suggested that a nationally elected Vice President would now serve as "ex officio, President of the Senate," and could break tie votes.[10] In addition, the Vice President was made next in line for the presidency.[11] At the same time that it unveiled the vice presidency, the Committee also proposed his replacement in the chamber: "[I]n case of" the Vice President's "absence, the Senate" would "chuse a President pro tempore."[12]

Three days later, the Convention approved the Vice President to serve as "ex officio President of the Senate."[13] Later, the Committee of Style shortened the title to "President of the Senate."[14] While the vice presidency attracted some attention from the delegates, the President pro tempore occasioned no debate either at the Constitutional Convention or during the state ratifying conventions.[15]

WHEN DOES THE PRESIDENT PRO TEMPORE PRESIDE?
The President pro tempore can chair Senate proceedings under two circumstances: when the Vice President "shall exercise the Office of President of the United States" and "in the Absence of the Vice President." The Constitution, however, does not define "Absence." Does the President pro tempore position vanish the moment the Vice President appears in the Senate? Does it cease to exist only when the Vice President takes the presiding officer's chair? Or does the position continue irrespective of vice presidential actions?[16]

For its first hundred years, the Senate construed absence as meaning absence from the chamber itself: the President pro tempore's tenure terminating upon the arrival of the Vice President on the Senate floor. Consequently, with Vice Presidents chairing proceedings fairly regularly during the period, the President pro tempore's time in office was often brief.[17] In 1890, the upper chamber changed its mind about tenure, overturning a century of constitutional interpretation because of concerns about the disruptions to Senate proceedings caused by intermittent President pro tempore elections. Henceforth, the Senate would choose a President pro tempore who would serve irrespective of whether the Vice President was in the chamber.[18]

Related to the President pro tempore's role as backup Senate presiding officer is his responsibility to fill in for the Vice President if the latter is absent from the electoral vote count under authority of the Twelfth Amendment. As of 2021, the President pro tempore had assumed these responsibilities more than one-third of the time.[19]

SENATE ROLE

The President pro tempore exercises all of the powers in the chair that the Vice President does, except for breaking tie votes. Early on, it was determined that the President pro tempore—like any other Senator—would vote on all measures even though he was presiding.[20] He is responsible for recognizing Senators who wish to speak to the chamber, although he has less leeway than the House Speaker, who may ask about the subject of the intended remarks before recognizing the lawmaker.[21] He also rules on points of order, though the full chamber may overrule him.[22]

In addition, the President pro tempore has the authority to designate his replacement in the chair—a power the Vice President does not enjoy because it would conflict with the constitutional command that the Senate choose his replacement.[23] Moreover, unlike the Vice President, the President pro tempore has no constitutional successor to restrict his handoff of the gavel.

In the first half of the nineteenth century, Presidents pro tempore exercised some leadership in the chamber as the Senate delegated them authority to make committee assignments, but their erratic and often short tenures—coupled with the establishment and growth of Senate party institutions later in the century—doomed the office's prospects for an enduring de facto leadership role.[24] The position of President pro tempore therefore should not be confused with the position of the modern Majority Leader, who is responsible for proposing the Senate's agenda.

The chamber has authorized creation of an Acting President pro tempore to assume the chair when a President pro tempore has yet to

be elected.[25] This temporary position reflects the Senate's role in constitutional interpretation of the office. Similarly, the chamber has created other honorific adaptations of the title to bestow on lawmakers.[26]

During the twentieth century, both the Vice President and the President pro tempore began to preside less often, coming to see the role as essentially optional rather than mandatory.[27] As a result, other than at the daily opening of Senate proceedings, the task of presiding is usually performed by junior members of the majority party.[28]

Beginning in earnest in 1945, the Senate began to elect Presidents pro tempore based on seniority within the majority party.[29] With two exceptions, this tradition has continued.

IMPEACHMENT TRIALS

Under the Constitution, the Chief Justice presides over presidential impeachment trials in the Senate. In 2021, the question arose as to who would preside during the impeachment trial of a *former* president, Donald Trump. Chief Justice John Roberts decided against taking the gavel as did Vice President Kamala Harris.[30] Instead, President pro tempore Patrick Leahy chaired the proceedings. Presidents pro tempore had presided over impeachment trials before, but Leahy's actions established a precedent regarding the trials of former chief executives.[31]

As it is with respect to former Presidents, constitutional text is silent as to who will preside over vice presidential impeachment trials, and history provides no guidance. Presumably, an impeached Vice President would not preside as a matter of constitutional interpretation or political prudence. Otherwise, Congress (through a statute) or the upper chamber (through a rule or parliamentary precedent) could potentially replace him with the President pro tempore.[32] The Chief Justice could also assert a competing claim to preside, although that seems unlikely given Roberts' 2021 stance.[33]

PRESIDENTIAL SUCCESSION

Under a 1792 statute, the President pro tempore was made second in line to the presidency after the Vice President.[34] (See Essay No. 97.) Presidential deaths occurred in 1841, 1850, 1865, and 1881, and Vice Presidents passed away or otherwise left office in 1812, 1814, 1832, 1853, 1875, and 1885.[35] Each of these episodes therefore brought the President pro tempore within a heartbeat of the presidency. Yet even with these vacancies, a President pro tempore seems never to have sought nor been accorded formal recognition as Vice President or Acting Vice President, despite regular references to this effect in congressional debate.[36]

In 1886, Congress removed lawmakers as potential presidential successors.[37] But, in 1947, they were reinserted with the President pro tempore positioned third in line after the Vice President and the Speaker.[38]

The Vice President and President pro tempore have been linked together ever since the Constitutional Convention. Given the hybrid, executive-legislative nature of the vice presidency and the institutional relationship between the Senate's two constitutional presiding officers, the President pro tempore has often displayed a curious connection to the executive branch.

During vice presidential vacancies, for example, the President pro tempore is paid the Vice President's salary.[39] In fact, for a time, vice presidential funds from executive branch coffers were used to fill the pay gap.[40] In the early decades under the Constitution, no fewer than eleven Presidents pro tempore filled in for absent Vice Presidents as members of the executive branch's Sinking Fund Commission.[41] Finally, as a presidential successor, the President pro tempore has long had a White House "hotline" to facilitate communication in a crisis.[42]

OPEN QUESTION

- During a vice presidential absence, could a non-Senator President pro tempore break tie votes?

Cite as: Roy E. Brownell II, *The President Pro Tempore Clause, in* THE HERITAGE GUIDE TO THE CONSTITUTION 51 (Josh Blackman & John G. Malcolm eds., 3d ed. 2025).

Notes

1. Thomas Jefferson, A Manual of Parliamentary Practice IX (1801); 21 Cong. Rec. 2147 (1890). **2.** Federalist No. 68 (Hamilton); Jamin Soderstrom, *Comment, Back to Basics*, 35 Pepp. L. Rev. 967, 984–85 (2008). **3.** N.Y. Const. of 1777, arts. XX, XXI, XXXII; Soderstrom, *supra* at 984–85. **4.** N.Y. Const. of 1777, art. XXI. **5.** N.H. Const., Executive Power (1784). **6.** 1 Farrand's 292, 300. **7.** 2 Farrand's 155, 158, 179. **8.** *Id.* at 172, 186. **9.** *Id.* at 493. **10.** *Id.* at 495. **11.** *Id.* **12.** *Id.* **13.** *Id.* at 538. **14.** *Id.* at 592 n.9. **15.** 2 Story's Commentaries § 739. **16.** Joel K. Goldstein, *Can the Vice President Preside at His Own Impeachment Trial?: A Critique of Bare Textualism*, 44 St. Louis U. L.J. 849, 860–62 (2000). **17.** *About the President Pro Tempore | Presidents Pro Tempore*, United States Senate, https://perma.cc /FC5J-74PZ. **18.** 21 Cong. Rec. 2144–48, 2150–53 (1890). **19.** Joel K. Goldstein, *The Ministerial Role of the President of the Senate in Counting Electoral Votes*, 21 U.N.H. L. Rev. 369, 412–20 (2023). **20.** S. Journal, 2d Cong., 1st Sess. 429, (1792). **21.** Floyd M. Riddick, The United States Congress 80 (1949). **22.** Riddick's Senate Procedure 987 (1992). **23.** Senate Rule I(3), U.S. S. Comm. on Rules & Admin., https://perma.cc/T746-DC55. **24.** Gerald Gamm & Stephen S. Smith, *Last Among Equals*, in Esteemed Colleagues 105–14, 129–30 (Burdett A. Loomis, ed., 2000). **25.** Senate Rule I(2), U.S. S. Comm. on Rules & Admin., https://perma. cc/T746-DC55. **26.** Christopher M. Davis, Cong. Rsrch. Serv., RL 30960, The President Pro Tempore of the Senate: History and Authority of the Office 22–23 (2015), https: //perma.cc/24AR-YMSN. **27.** Senate Historical Office, Pro Tem 96 (2008); Joel K. Goldstein, *Constitutional Change, Originalism, and the Vice Presidency*, 16 J. Con. L. 369, 390–403 (2013). **28.** Martin B. Gold, Senate Procedure and Practice 223 n.4 (2004). **29.** Robert C. Byrd, 2 The Senate 1789–1989: Addresses on the History of the United States Senate 180 (1991). **30.** Nicholas Fandos, *Patrick Leahy, the Longest- Serving Democrat, Will Preside over Trump's Impeachment Trial*, N.Y. Times (Jan. 25, 2021), https://perma .cc/75XJ-N2YR. **31.** 13 Annals of Cong. 362–66 (1804); 4 Cong. Rec. 2578 (1876); Patrick Leahy, The Road Taken 423–37 (2022). **32.** Goldstein, *supra* at 859–63. **33.** *Id.* at 860–69. **34.** 1 Stat. 239 (1792). **35.** John D. Feerick, From Failing Hands 315–16 (1965). **36.** Mitch McConnell & Roy E. Brownell II, The U.S. Senate and the Commonwealth 55–58, 294–97 (2019); Ruth C. Silva, Presidential Succession 23–24 (1951). **37.** 24 Stat. 1 (1886); Seth Barrett Tillman & Josh Blackman, *Offices and Officers of the Constitution, Part II*: The Four Approaches, 61 S. Tex. L. Rev. 321, 418–23 (2021). **38.** 3 U.S.C. § 19. **39.** 2 U.S.C. § 6111. **40.** 24 Stat. 178 (1886); 24 Stat. 600 (1887). **41.** No. 116, *Sinking Fund*, Dec. 4, 1797, in 9 American State Papers: Finance, Class III, at 497 (1832), https://perma.cc/GVC6-LDAM; *Work of the Scientists*, Wash. Times, Jan. 25, 1900. **42.** Byrd, *supra* at 182.

〜

ESSAY NO. 20: THE SENATE IMPEACHMENT TRIAL CLAUSE
ART. I, § 3, CL. 6

The Senate shall have the sole Power to try all Impeachments. When sitting for that Purpose, they shall be on Oath or Affirmation. When the President of the United States is tried, the Chief Justice shall preside: And no Person shall be convicted without the Concurrence of two thirds of the Members present.

—Michael J. Gerhardt

INTRODUCTION

The Constitution vests the Senate with the "sole power to try all impeachments," and the Senate Impeachment Trial Clause provides several basic procedures for such trials. First, Senators must take an "Oath or Affirmation." Second, the Chief Justice of the United States is the presiding officer for presidential impeachment trials, and the Vice President, as President of the Senate, presides in all other impeachment trials. Third, a two-thirds supermajority vote is required for conviction and removal from office. This requirement's impact is apparent in the fact that the Senate has convicted only eight of the twenty-two people whom the House has impeached (all eight were federal judges). Beyond these specific procedures, the Rules of Proceedings Clause in Article I, Section 5 vests the Senate, as it does the House, with the power "to determine the Rules" for its internal governance. (See Essay No. 26.) This provision empowers the Senate to establish the procedures for impeachment proceedings.

HISTORY BEFORE 1787

In Parliament, impeachment authority was divided between the lower and upper chambers. The House of Commons (the lower chamber) had the authority to charge, or impeach, someone for impeachable misconduct. The House of Lords (the upper chamber) had the crucial power to try impeachments and impose sanctions. It was given this authority because its members were regarded as better educated than their counterparts in the lower chamber and less prone to the passions of the moment. The upper chamber also functioned as a check against an intemperate, ill-considered impeachment rendered by the lower chamber. Each legislative chamber had the power to determine the rules for its proceedings; the lower chamber tended to delegate authority to committees for investigations of possible misconduct of public officials, and the upper chamber modeled its trials on courtroom trials. There were presiding officials and rules of basic procedures to govern the proceedings.

A similar structure was adopted in the colonies. Bribery, extortion, and misuse of funds were the most common grounds for impeachment; purely or predominately partisan impeachments often failed. This model continued following independence. For example, in Virginia, an attempt to impeach Governor Thomas Jefferson for his performance in office failed. In Pennsylvania, the lower house impeached Frances Hopkinson for abusing his authority as chief of the Admiralty Court, but the State Council, which was responsible for trying the impeachment, found that the charges brought by his political foes were largely baseless and acquitted him on all counts.

Based on this record, historians Peter Charles Hoffer and N.E.H. Hull have determined that "conviction upon trial required that the impeachment managers establish the elements of mens rea (the guilty mind), actual causation of the offense, and damage of some kind to persons or the state itself."[1] The authors added that "the offense need not be a crime, but the elements of evil intention, causation, and actus reus [a bad act] were drawn from the criminal law."[2]

THE CONSTITUTIONAL CONVENTION

To varying degrees, the four features of the Senate Impeachment Trial Clause were discussed during the Constitutional Convention. First, the Framers debated which body should try impeachments. Under one proposal from the Committee of Detail, the House would have the "power of impeachment" and the "Senators and Judges of the foederal Court [would] be a Court for trying Impeachments."[3] Another proposal from the Committee of Detail provided that the President could be "removed from his Office on Impeachment by the House of Representatives, and Conviction in the Supreme (National) Court."[4]

On August 6, John Rutledge of South Carolina delivered the latter proposal to the Convention.[5] However, on September 4, the Committee of Eleven proposed that the Senate "shall have power to try all impeachments."[6] The Convention postponed voting on this issue until it resolved "the mode of electing the President."[7] Gouverneur Morris of Pennsylvania, pointing to "[t]he difficulty of establishing a Court of Impeachments, other than the Senate," argued that the Senate should be "the Judge of impeachments." He continued that the U.S. Supreme Court would "try the President after the trial of the impeachment" for any criminal offenses.[8]

On September 8, the Convention returned to the issue of impeachment. James Madison of Virginia "objected to a trial of the President by the Senate, especially as he was to be impeached by the other branch of the Legislature," and said he "prefer[red] the supreme Court for the trial of impeachments."[9] Morris repeated his point that "no other tribunal than the Senate could be trusted" and warned that "[t]he Supreme Court were too few in number and might be warped or corrupted."[10] Roger Sherman of Connecticut "regarded the Supreme Court as improper to try the President, because the Judges would be appointed by him."[11] Madison's proposal was defeated by a vote of nine to two with Virginia and Pennsylvania in the minority.[12]

Second, the delegates considered the oath as a possible safeguard that could ensure fair, credible impeachment trials in the Senate. On September 8, Morris proposed that "every member shall be on oath" during an impeachment trial.[13] This motion passed by a vote of nine to two.[14] The oath that Senators took upon entering office presumably applied to all of their duties as

Senators, but the requirement of a second oath underscored the heightened need for impartiality and even-handedness when exercising their responsibilities in presidential impeachment trials.

Third, the delegates chose the Chief Justice to preside during the impeachment trial of the President.[15] This decision would avoid the conflicts of interest that Vice President would have in presiding over the trial of the one person standing between him and the presidency. The prevailing wisdom was that no other official was likely to have the stature and commitment to the rule of law that characterized the Chief Justice, who was also immune to any direct political reprisals for any of his decisions during a presidential impeachment trial.

Fourth, the choice of a two-thirds supermajority for conviction was a significant innovation. There is not much debate or other evidence to indicate why the delegates eventually agreed to this requirement.[16] It appears to have derived from a growing awareness among the delegates that a simple majority vote would have made conviction too easy. The supermajority voting requirement had the virtue of ensuring widespread agreement among the Senators in the extraordinary instance of a conviction or removal, especially one involving the Chief Executive.

Hoffer and Hull suggested that requiring two-thirds majority approval for conviction and removal "ensured that the Senate would be as thoughtful and deliberate in its hearing and determining of cases as the House of Lords, without any of the aristocratic trappings of the English body."[17] In other words, the two-thirds majority requirement ensured the rarity and difficulty of convicting and removing the Executive.

Supermajority voting requirements were not new to the delegates. For example, the constitution New York specified a two-thirds requirements for impeachments.[18] The Articles of Confederation required nine of the thirteen states—a two-thirds majority—to approve treaties and other important business such as entry into war.[19] The Constitution would requires a two-thirds majority for a house to expel a member[20] or to ratify a treaty.[21] (See Essay Nos. 27 and 106.)

THE RATIFICATION DEBATES

In Federalist No. 65, Alexander Hamilton defended the Senate Impeachment Trial Clause. He believed that the Senate, rather than the judiciary, should try impeachments. Rather than having a single judge or panel of judges, Hamilton favored a "numerous court for the trial of impeachments." He believed such a large body would be well suited to the procedural demands of an impeachment trial. Unlike judges, the Senate should "never be tied down by such strict rules, either in the delineation of the offence by the prosecutors, or in the construction of it by the judges." Hamilton explained further that "[t]he awful discretion, which a court of impeachments must necessarily have, to doom to honor or to infamy the most confidential and the most distinguished characters of the community, forbids the commitment of the trust to a small number of persons."

During the Maryland ratifying convention, James McHenry explained that the delegates regarded the Senate as the only authority that would "more likely be governed by cool and candid investigation, than by those heats that too often inflame and influence more populous Assemblys."[22]

The Anti-Federalists opposed placing the impeachment power in the Senate. Cato, for example, warned that the Senate, being political, could not "be an impartial judicature" and would "serve as a screen to great public defaulters."[23] Luther Martin of Maryland added that the Senate serves as "a privy council to the President," and many influential Senators "may have advised or concurred in the very measures for which [the President] may be impeached."[24] Martin also charged that Senators would be "unduly under the influence of" and dependent on the President "since they also are appointable to offices."[25] In Martin's view, the President was "constitutionally empowered to bribe his judges" through the appointment power and could nominate as Chief Justice "a person of whose voice and influence he shall consider himself secure," In which case "there will be but little probability of the President ever being either impeached or convicted."[26]

POWERS OF THE CHIEF JUSTICE

In the normal course, the Senate's presiding officer would preside at impeachment trials, and that presiding officer would be either the Vice President or another Senator chosen by the Senate. However, the Constitution requires that the Chief Justice preside over the President's impeachment trial.

Three Presidents have been impeached. Andrew Johnson was impeached in 1868, and Chief Justice Salmon P. Chase presided over that trial. Bill Clinton was impeached in 1999, and Chief Justice William Rehnquist presided over that trial. And Donald Trump was impeached twice. The first trial, which began in 2020, was presided over by Chief Justice John Roberts. The second, which began in 2021 after Trump was no longer in office, was presided over by Senate President Pro Tempore Patrick Leahy.[27] Apparently, Chief Justice Roberts declined to preside over the trial of a former official.[28]

None of these trials led to a conviction. In the Johnson trial, the majority fell one vote short of removing him from office. In the Clinton and Trump impeachment trials, there never was any doubt that both would be acquitted. There were enough members of the Presidents' parties to ensure that, if they remained united in favor of acquittal, the Senate would not be able to meet the two-thirds threshold for conviction.

What is the extent of the Chief Justice's powers as presiding officer? In 1868, Chief Justice Chase claimed the authority to decide procedural issues on his own, but the Senate overruled him twice.[29] In President Clinton's impeachment trial, Chief Justice Rehnquist ruled on several procedural questions. For example, the Republican House managers referred to Senators as "jurors." A Democratic Senator objected, Rehnquist ruled that "[t]he Senate is not simply a jury. It is a court in this case."[30] The Senate did not challenge, much less vote to overrule, any of Rehnquist's rulings.[31]

In 2020, Chief Justice Roberts made several substantive rulings. He reprimanded House managers and lawyers for President Trump for their language. He admonished the lawyers to "avoid speaking in a manner and using language that is not conducive to civil discourse."[32] Roberts also refused to read a question posed by a Senator that named a whistleblower.[33] Finally, he declined to break any tie vote.[34] With regard to procedure, Roberts closely monitored the timing of each side's arguments. The Senate did not challenge any of his rulings.

SENATE RULES FOR IMPEACHMENT TRIALS

The Senate has formulated its own special impeachment trial procedures. These procedures were first written by Thomas Jefferson when he was Vice President.[35] In Andrew Johnson's impeachment trial, the Senate formulated an additional set of rules. These rules have remained largely intact and were followed by the Senate in the Clinton and Trump impeachment trials.

In 1936, the Senate added Rule XI, which allows the appointment of a small number of Senators to operate as a trial committee to gather evidence and take testimony. Rule XI was adopted as a response to poor attendance and preparation by Senators in impeachment trials in the early twentieth century.

During the 1980s, three federal district judges were impeached. For each trial, the Senate used trial committees to assist with fact-finding. Several Senators claimed that they had not prepared before earlier impeachment trials, as such proceedings diverted their energies from legislative business of greater concern to their constituents. Other Senators questioned whether they have the requisite competence to try impeachments. All three judges challenged the legitimacy of trial committees, first in the Senate and later in federal court. They argued that the Senate's "Power to try Impeachments" imposed on the full Senate—that is, all members—the obligation to conduct the full trial. The Senate countered that it had complete authority over how to fashion proceedings and that Senators' political accountability was the only check on this authority.

Ultimately, *Walter Nixon v. United States* (1993) held that the Senate's power to try impeachments includes the final discretion to determine how to conduct its trials—a discretion that is not reviewable by judges.[36] The Supreme Court did not address whether the judiciary could review possible deviations from any explicit safeguard required by the Constitution for impeachment trials. The Court has yet to make clear what it might do, for example, if someone other than the Chief Justice presided over a presidential impeachment trial.[37]

CONSTITUTIONAL CONSTRAINTS ON IMPEACHMENT TRIALS

What constraints, if any, does the Constitution impose on impeachment trials? In the 1980s, the Senate settled some procedural issues regarding the Fifth Amendment Due Process Clause. (See Essay No. 172.) Specifically, does the Due Process Clause limit the requisite rules of evidence and burden of proof for impeachment trials? The Senate ruled that adopting a uniform rule on these questions was impractical because it lacked the means for enforcing any such rule against Senators. The Fifth Amendment had no bearing on the question. Rather, the Senate decided that each question was a matter for individual Senators to decide for themselves.

There is also some question about whether the First Amendment constrains the impeachment power. For example, can a President be impeached for engaging in arguably protected speech?[38] This issue arose during the impeachment trials of Presidents Johnson and Trump.[39]

LATE IMPEACHMENT

Can an officer who was impeached while in office but later resigned still be tried by the Senate? In other words, does the Constitution permit so-called late impeachment?[40] In England, anyone except for the king could be impeached for anything at any time. The Framers rejected such a free-wheeling form of impeachment and restricted it to "Officers of the United States." Private citizens could not be impeached for their conduct as private citizens. In 1797, the House of Representatives impeached Senator William Blount of Tennessee. One day after the House impeached Blount, the Senate expelled him by a vote of 25 to 1. By the time impeachment proceedings began in the Senate, Blount was no longer in office. One of the House managers and Blount's lawyer agreed that Blount was subject to impeachment even after leaving office,[41] and the Senate proceeded to hold a trial.

A similar question arose eight decades later. In 1876, the House of Representatives was on the verge of impeaching Secretary of War William Belknap for bribery. Hoping to preempt his impeachment, Belknap rushed to the White House to submit his resignation, which President Ulysses S. Grant accepted. The

House impeached Belknap anyway. Could the Senate try an officer who was no longer in office when he was impeached? The Senate voted 37 to 29 that Belknap was "amenable to trial by impeachment for acts done as Secretary of War, notwithstanding his resignation before he was impeached."[42] After the trial, the Senate voted to convict Belknap by a similar vote, which fell short of the two-thirds required for conviction.

The issue of late impeachment arose a third time more than a century later. On January 13, 2021, the House voted to impeach President Donald Trump. However, the articles of impeachment were not delivered to the Senate until January 25, five days after Trump left office. The first order of business confronting the Senate upon receiving the impeachment articles was whether it had jurisdiction to hold a trial for a President who was no longer in office.

The House managers, Representatives Jamie Raskin and Joe Neguse, pointed to the Blount and Belknap precedents to support the Senate's proceeding with a trial against Trump.[43] They argued that if the Senate did not retain jurisdiction over Presidents after they left office, they would be able to escape constitutional accountability for misconduct committed or discovered in the last few months, weeks, or days of their presidencies. David Schoen, counsel for President Trump, countered that the Framers rejected the British practice in which private citizens and former officials were subject to impeachment.[44] Rather, the Framers expressly restricted impeachment to "the President, Vice President, and all civil Officers of the United States."[45] The Senate voted 56 to 44 to proceed with the trial; six Republican Senators joined all fifty Democrats.[46]

OPEN QUESTIONS

- Is an official impeached when the impeachment vote is cast or when the articles are delivered to the Senate?[47]
- What happens if the President is impeached and the Chief Justice cannot preside because of death, disability, resignation, recusal, or otherwise? Can the Senate designate another person to serve as Chief Justice?[48] Presumably, it can, because Senate rules allow for designation of the Senate President Pro Tempore as presiding officer when the Vice President is not available. In President Trump's second impeachment trial, the Senate followed that procedure in recognizing President Pro Tempore Patrick Leahy as presiding officer. Would that designation be reviewable in federal court?[49]
- During a presidential impeachment trial, does the Chief Justice or the presiding officer have the power to break a tie vote during a presidential impeachment trial? When the presiding officer is the Vice President, the Constitution settles that question by expressly empowering him or her to cast the tie-breaking vote in the Senate. When Senator Leahy presided over the second Trump impeachment trial, he followed Senate precedent, which allowed Senators when acting as presiding officers to cast separate votes.
- Does the Senate have a duty to hold an impeachment trial? Could the Senate simply ignore the articles entirely and not hold a trial? The clause does not clearly vest the Senate with discretion to hold a trial. Historically, in each instance in which a person has been impeached, the Senate has agreed to receive articles of impeachment and to take some action. In 2024, however, the Senate dismissed articles of impeachment against Secretary of Homeland Security Alejandro Mayorkas without holding a trial and resolved the matter based on briefs.

Cite as: Michael J. Gerhardt, *The Senate Impeachment Trial Clause, in* THE HERITAGE GUIDE TO THE CONSTITUTION 55 (Josh Blackman & John G. Malcolm eds., 3d ed. 2025).

Notes

1. Peter Charles Hoffer & N.E.H. Hull, Impeachment in America 1635–1805, at 78 (1984).   **2.** *Id.*   **3.** 2 Farrand's 159.   **4.** *Id.* at 172.   **5.** *Id.* at 177, 185–86.   **6.** *Id.* at 493, 497.   **7.** *Id.* at 499.   **8.** *Id.* at 500.   **9.** *Id.* at 551.   **10.** *Id.*   **11.** *Id.*   **12.** *Id.*   **13.** *Id.* at 552.   **14.** *Id.* at 552–53.   **15.** *Id.* at 495.   **16.** *Id.* at 493, 592, 653.   **17.** Hoffer & Hull, *supra* at 106.   **18.** N.Y. Const. of 1777, art. XXXIII.   **19.** Articles of Confederation, art. IX, § 6.   **20.** Art. I, § 5, cl. 2.   **21.** Art. II, § 2, cl. 2.   **22.** 3 Farrand's 148.   **23.** Storing 2.6.45   **24.** *Id.* at 2.4.88.   **25.** *Id.*   **26.** *Id.*   **27.** Your author served as Special Counsel to Senator Leahy during the second Trump impeachment trial.   **28.** Joan Biskupic, *John Roberts Ducks the Spotlight by Skipping the Second Trump Impeachment Trial*, CNN (Jan. 26, 2021), https://perma.cc/YB58-AAT3.   **29.** Michael J. Gerhardt, The Law of Presidential Impeachment: A Guide for the Engaged Citizen 59–60 (2024).   **30.** Joan Biskupic, *How the Last Chief Justice Handled an Impeachment Trial of the President of the United States*, CNN (Dec. 1, 2019), https://perma.cc/U8VV-XMYS.   **31.** Gerhardt, *supra* at 108–09.   **32.** Biskupic, *supra*.   **33.** Phil Mattingly et al., *John Roberts Publicly Rejects Rand Paul's Whistleblower Question in Senate Impeachment Trial*, CNN (Jan. 30, 2020), https://perma.cc/2CSZ-YRFM.   **34.** Pete Williams, *Chief Justice John Roberts Says He Won't Break Tie Votes in Senate Impeachment Trial*, NBC News (Jan. 31, 2020), https://perma.cc/TYN8-YFBC.   **35.** Jefferson's Manual of Parliamentary Practice, in H. Doc. 117-161, 17th Cong., 131–345

(2023).   **36.** 506 U.S. 224, 230 (1993).   **37.** Adam Liptak, *Can Trump Challenge His Impeachment in the Supreme Court?*, N.Y. Times (Nov. 25, 2019), https://perma.cc/5QSN-BTSN.   **38.** Katherine Shaw, *Impeachable Speech*, 70 Emory L.J. 1 (2020).   **39.** Josh Blackman & Seth Barrett Tillman, *We Should Not Forget the Free Speech Lessons from President Johnson's Impeachment Trial*, Volokh Conspiracy (Jan. 14, 2021), https://perma.cc/6SDL-YGVK; Keith E. Whittington, *Is There a Free Speech Defense to an Impeachment?*, Lawfare (Jan. 19, 2021).   **40.** Brian C. Kalt, *The Constitutional Case for the Impeachability of Former Federal Officials: An Analysis of the Law, History, and Practice of Late Impeachment*, 6 Tex. Rev. L. & Pol. 13, 17 (2001).   **41.** Laurence H. Tribe, *The Senate Can Constitutionally Hold an Impeachment Trial After Trump Leaves Office*, Wash. Post (Jan. 13, 2021).   **42.** The Impeachment and Trial of William W. Belknap, *in* 3 Hinds' Precedents §§ 2444–68.   **43.** 167 Cong. Rec. S591–97 (2021).   **44.** *Id.* at S601–08.   **45.** Art. II, § 4; 167 Cong. Rec. S606 (2021).   **46.** 167 Cong. Rec. S609 (2021).   **47.** Adam Liptak, *A Law Professor's Provocative Argument: Trump Has Not Yet Been Impeached*, N.Y. Times (Dec. 20, 2019), https://perma.cc/8W7D-7V8J.   **48.** Josh Blackman & Seth Barrett Tillman, *Could Justice Thomas Preside over President Trump's Impeachment Trial?*, Balkinization Blog (Nov. 17, 2019), https://perma.cc/J7L4-BSUU.   **49.** Josh Blackman, *What Happens If the Chief Justice Cannot Serve at the Presidential Impeachment Trial?*, Volokh Conspiracy (Nov. 25, 2019), https://perma.cc/BR7Z-7HJH.

∿

ESSAY NO. 21: THE IMPEACHMENT JUDGMENT CLAUSE
ART. I, § 3, CL. 7

Judgment in Cases of Impeachment shall not extend further than to removal from Office, and disqualification to hold and enjoy any Office of honor, Trust or Profit under the United States: but the Party convicted shall nevertheless be liable and subject to Indictment, Trial, Judgment and Punishment, according to Law.

—Michael J. Gerhardt

INTRODUCTION

The Impeachment Judgment Clause specifies the limited scope and nature of the judgments that the Senate may impose following conviction in impeachment trials. The Framers deliberately distinguished impeachment in this country from the British system. There were no limits to the punishments that the House of Lords could impose in impeachment proceedings—even death. The Framers limited the sanctions in the federal Constitution to those typically found in state constitutions: removal from the current office and disqualification from holding

future office. The Constitution further provided that neither of these sanctions precluded civil or criminal legal liability for officials' misconduct. *Trump v. United States* (2024) observed that "[t]he Clause both limits the consequences of an impeachment judgment and clarifies that notwithstanding such judgment, subsequent prosecution may proceed."[1]

HISTORY BEFORE 1787

In the British system of impeachment, Parliament could impose any sanction it wished, including death and imprisonment. During the

1600s, with virtually every impeachment conviction, the House of Lords imposed some kind of criminal punishment, including but not limited to loss of office, prison, fines, and forfeiture of property. In the sixteenth and seventeenth centuries, the House of Lords imposed death sentences on impeached officials. However, the king was exempted from impeachment.

The colonies initially modeled their impeachment procedures on the English system, but they had imperfect knowledge regarding particular impeachments and convictions in the eighteenth century. As the colonists learned more, they increasingly crafted impeachment proceedings that deviated from the English system.

After independence, the states identified limits to the relative scopes of impeachable offenses, impeachable officials, and sanctions. For example, the Massachusetts constitution of 1780 provided that the "judgment" in an impeachment trial "should not extend further than to removal from office disqualification to hold or enjoy any place of honor, trust, or profit, under this Commonwealth."[2] The delegates to the Constitutional Convention, being familiar with the features of the English impeachment process that they disliked, would follow the predominant practice within the states to restrict the sanctions following conviction.

THE CONSTITUTIONAL CONVENTION

On August 6, 1787, the Impeachment Judgment Clause was presented in the Committee of Detail's report: "Judgment, in cases of Impeachment, shall not extend further than to removal from Office, and disqualification to hold and enjoy any office of honour, trust or profit, under the United States. But the party convicted shall, nevertheless be liable and subject to indictment, trial, judgment and punishment according to law."[3] On August 28, the proposal was adopted without debate.[4] The only change made by the Committee of Style was to remove a comma after "profit."[5] No further changes were made. The Office of Legal Counsel in the Department of Justice would later observe that "the records [of the Constitutional Convention] do not reflect any substantive discussion of the [Impeachment Judgment Clause's] meaning."[6]

For much of the Constitutional Convention, the delegates considered having the Supreme Court of the United States try impeachments, but this proposal was rejected. Gouverneur Morris of Pennsylvania remarked that "[a] conclusive reason for making the Senate instead of the Supreme Court the Judge of impeachments, was that the latter was to try the President after the trial of the impeachment."[7] That way, the courts could hear the prosecution of those who were impeached, including themselves or their colleagues.

THE RATIFICATION DEBATES

In Federalist No. 65, Alexander Hamilton explained that the "punishment" for "conviction upon impeachment" is not limited to "the chastisement of the offender." After a person is "sentenced to a perpetual ostracism from the esteem and confidence and honors and emoluments of his country, he will still be liable to prosecution and punishment in the ordinary course of law." In Federalist No. 77, Hamilton observed that "the President is at all times liable to impeachment, trial, dismission [*sic*] from office . . . and to the forfeiture of life and estate by subsequent prosecution in the common course of law."

THE IMPEACHMENT PROCESS

The Constitution lays out several steps in the impeachment process. First, the House of Representatives has the "sole Power" to impeach "the President, Vice President and all civil Officers of the United States." It takes a simple majority to impeach an official. (See Essay No. 14.) Second, the "Senate shall have the sole Power to try all Impeachments." (See Essay No. 20.) A conviction in the Senate requires the "Concurrence of two thirds of the Members present." Under the Senate's current practices, after an official is convicted by a two-thirds vote, he is automatically removed from office.[8] However, "in earlier impeachment trials," such as that of John Pickering in 1804, "the Senate took separate votes on guilt and removal."[9] The Senate dropped the bifurcated vote after a consistent string of votes on guilt and conviction that were identical.

If the official is convicted and removed, the Senate can take one more vote to disqualify that person from holding certain positions in the future. The Senate has disqualified three officials, all of whom were federal judges. In each case, the Senate took separate votes to remove and disqualify them. A disqualified person cannot "hold and enjoy any Office of honor, Trust or Profit under the United States." During President Donald Trump's second impeachment trial, the scope of the Impeachment Disqualification Clause was discussed but not resolved.[10]

The Constitution clearly provides that a conviction requires a two-thirds vote, but, as Professor Akhil Reed Amar has observed, "[does] not explicitly specify whether disqualification would require a two-thirds vote or a simple majority."[11] The three instances in which the Senate disqualified officials may inform this inquiry. In 1862, the vote to disqualify Judge West H. Humphreys was unanimous.[12] In 1913, Judge Robert Archbald was convicted on several articles by more than a two-thirds vote but disqualified by a simple majority vote of 39 to 35.[13] And in 2010, Judge Thomas Porteous's disqualification vote was 94 to 2. Moreover, it is not clear that Judge Archbald ever sought to hold some covered office, so despite the intentions of the Senate, his disqualification vote may have been insufficient.[14] In any event, a disqualification is permanent. The President can grant pardons "except in cases of impeachment."[15] (See Essay No. 105.)

SEQUENCING OF IMPEACHMENTS AND CRIMINAL PROSECUTIONS

The Impeachment Disqualification Clause provides that "the Party convicted [in an impeachment trial] shall nevertheless be liable and subject to Indictment, Trial, Judgment and Punishment, according to Law." This text gives rise to two primary questions.

First, can Congress impeach and remove an officer who was already convicted in a civil or criminal proceeding? The sequencing question became relevant in the late 1980s. Judges Harry Claiborne and Walter Nixon were convicted of federal offenses and imprisoned. Subsequently, Congress began impeachment proceedings against Claiborne and Nixon, who *still* received their judicial salaries while incarcerated. Could the House impeach judges who were already convicted? It could be argued that once the

judges were convicted in a criminal court, they could no longer be impeached, but Congress adopted the alternate reading: The judges were impeached and removed following their criminal convictions.

Second, can an official who was impeached but not convicted still be subject to civil or criminal proceedings? President Trump, who was acquitted during his second impeachment trial, contended that he could not be prosecuted for conduct arising from his acquittal. In *Trump v. United States* (2024), the former President argued that an "un-convicted President is immune from prosecution."[16] Trump, citing Alexander Hamilton in the Federalist Nos. 65, 69, and 77, argued that "prosecution of the President can only come 'after[]' and 'subsequent' to Senate conviction."[17] In Federalist No. 69, for example, Hamilton wrote that, unlike the king, the president "would be liable to be impeached and removed" from office and "would *afterwards* be liable to prosecution and punishment in the ordinary course of law."

However, Chief Justice John Roberts, writing for the majority, rejected Trump's reading of Hamilton. The Court stated that "Hamilton did not endorse or even consider whether the Impeachment Judgment Clause immunizes a *former* President from prosecution."[18] The Court stated clearly that "[t]he President is not above the law" but also emphasized that "Congress may not criminalize the President's conduct in carrying out the responsibilities of the Executive Branch under the Constitution." Accordingly, "[t]he President . . . may not be prosecuted for exercising his core constitutional powers" and "is entitled, at a minimum, to a presumptive immunity from prosecution for all his official acts.'"[19]

CENSURE AS AN ALTERNATIVE TO IMPEACHMENT

The Impeachment Disqualification Clause provides that "Judgment in Cases of Impeachment shall not extend further than to removal from Office," but could the judgment fall short of removal and disqualification in its severity? For example, could Congress censure an officeholder either as an alternative to impeachment or in condemnation of misconduct that falls short of an impeachable offense?

In 1834, the Senate censured then-President Andrew Jackson for trying to destroy the National Bank.[20] Jackson protested that the Constitution did not expressly authorize censuring Presidents and that impeachment therefore was the only constitutional means for holding him accountable for misconduct in office. In 1837, the Democrat-controlled Senate expunged his censure.[21] (See Essay No. 28.) In 1848, the House condemned President James Polk for initiating an illegal war against Mexico,[22] but this resolution did not call itself a censure.

During the impeachments of Presidents William Jefferson Clinton and Donald Trump, members of Congress floated the idea of a censure resolution to express Congress's disapproval. The censure would have been an alternative to subjecting either Clinton or Trump to the impeachment process. In both cases, Congress ultimately decided against a censure. Some opponents of the censure argued that it was effectively a bill of attainder.[23] The Constitution expressly prohibits such a legislative determination of guilt in the absence of a judicial trial.[24] (See Essay No. 69.) Members of the House argued that any tangible effect as a result of a censure effectively transformed it into an illegal bill of attainder.[25]

LATE IMPEACHMENT

Can a former officer be convicted and disqualified after he has left office?[26] In the cases of Judges Humphreys, Archbald, and Porteous, the Senate proceeded with disqualification votes after it had convicted and removed each of them from office. Thus, as a technical matter, disqualification could be said to have applied after the officials were no longer in office.

The House of Representatives voted to impeach President Trump before his term ended on January 20, 2021.[27] However, the articles of impeachment were not delivered to the Senate until after Trump left office.[28] (There was some dispute about whether former President Trump was impeached until the articles were delivered.[29])

The Senate held an impeachment trial in February 2021 amid considerable debate about whether the Senate still had jurisdiction to hold such a trial. The House Managers and some scholars maintained that the Senate retained jurisdiction over Trump's impeachment because disqualification was a potential sanction.[30] They argued that disqualification could be imposed at any time against any impeachable officer, including a President, regardless of whether they were still in office. Trump and other scholars contended that the Senate could not hold an impeachment trial of a former official.[31] Nonetheless, the Senate voted 56 to 44 that it had jurisdiction over Trump's second trial even though he had left office before it had begun. The vote was consistent with the Constitution's directive for the Senate "to try all impeachments," which could be read as legitimizing a trial for an official who left office after being impeached.[32]

OPEN QUESTION

- A disqualified person cannot hold "any Office of honor, Trust or Profit under the United States." Does this category include all elected positions? Professors Akhil Reed Amar and Vikram David Amar argue that the Senate cannot disqualify a convicted official from serving in Congress.[33] Professors Seth Barrett Tillman and Josh Blackman contend that the Senate can disqualify a convicted official from holding some future *appointed* position but not from holding an *elected* position like the presidency or a seat in Congress.[34] Within our constitutional framework, who has the authority to resolve these different constitutional constructions, and how should they do so?

Cite as: Michael J. Gerhardt, *The Impeachment Judgment Clause*, in THE HERITAGE GUIDE TO THE CONSTITUTION 60 (Josh Blackman & John G. Malcolm eds., 3d ed. 2025).

Notes

1. 603 U.S. 593, 633 (2024). **2.** Mass. Const. of 1780, ch. I, § II, art. VIII; N.H. Const. of 1784, art 39. **3.** 2 Farrand's 187. **4.** *Id.* at 438. **5.** *Id.* at 576. **6.** Whether a Former President May Be Indicted and Tried for the Same Offenses for Which He Was Impeached by the House and Acquitted by the Senate, 24 Op. O.L.C. 110, 122 (2000), https://perma. cc/CG28-8QPY. Mary C. Lawton, Acting Ass't Att'y Gen., Off. of Legal Counsel, Presidential or Legislative Pardon of the President, Mem. Op. for the Deputy Att'y Gen. (Aug. 5, 1974). **7.** 2 Farrand's 500. **8.** Elizabeth B. Bazan, Cong. Rsrch. Serv., 96-186, Impeachment: An Overview of Constitutional Provisions, Procedure, and Practice 10 (2010), https://perma.cc/6CLD-AS39. **9.** Michael J. Gerhardt, Federal Impeachment Process: A Constitutional and Historical Analysis 189 (2000); 3 Hinds' Precedents § 2341. **10.** Josh Blackman & Seth Barrett Tillman, *New Evidence and Arguments About the Scope of the Impeachment Disqualification Clause: A Response to the House of Representatives' Managers' Trial Memorandum*, Volokh Conspiracy (Feb. 7, 2021), https: //perma.cc/G45B-DM2A. **11.** Akhil Reed Amar, America's Constitution: A Biography 567 n.52 (2005). **12.** 3 Hinds' Precedents § 2397. **13.** Michael J. Gerhardt, Impeachment: What Everyone Needs to Know 111 (2018). **14.** Seth Barrett Tillman & Josh Blackman, *Offices and Officers of the Constitution, Part V: The Electoral Incompatibility, Impeachment Disqualification, Foreign Emoluments, and Incompatibility Clauses*, 64 S. Tex. L. Rev. 237, 269 (2023). **15.** Art. II, § 2, cl. 1. **16.** Brief of Petitioner President Donald J. Trump, *Donald J. Trump v. United States*, No. 23-939 (Mar. 19, 2024), at 17, https: //perma.cc/324R-P75M. **17.** *Id.* at 17–18. **18.** 603 U.S. at 633 (emphasis in original) **19.** *Id.* at 642. **20.** Jane A. Hudiburg & Christopher M. Davis, Cong. Rsrch. Serv., R45087, Resolutions to Censure the President: Procedure and History 4–5, 14 (2021), https://perma.cc/Q5R7-T9XS. **21.** *Id.* at 5, 14. **22.** *Id.* at 9, 14. **23.** Neil A. Lewis, *Censure of Clinton May Be Unconstitutional, Scholars Warn*, N.Y. Times (Nov. 2, 1998), https://perma.cc/B6J6-FP94. **24.** Art. I, § 9. **25.** Hudiburg & Davis, *supra* at 17 n.58. **26.** Brian C. Kalt, *The Constitutional Case for the Impeachability of Former Federal Officials: An Analysis of the Law, History, and Practice of Late Impeachment*, 6 Tex. Rev. Law & Pol. 13 (2001). **27.** Jeremy Herb et al., *House Impeaches Trump for "Incitement of Insurrection,"* CNN (Jan. 13, 2021), https://perma.cc/RKA9-TDGF. **28.** Jeremy Herb & Manu Raju, *House Delivers Impeachment Article to Senate, Triggering only 4th Impeachment Trial of a President in US History*, CNN (Jan. 25, 2021), https://perma. cc/RS2R-HCLM. **29.** Adam Liptak, *A Law Professor's Provocative Argument: Trump Has Not Yet Been Impeached*, N.Y. Times (Dec. 20, 2019), https://perma.cc/8W7D-7V8J. **30.** Brian Kalt, *Trump Claims My Research Supports His Case Against Impeachment*, Slate (Feb. 9, 2021), https://slate. com/news-and-politics/2021/02/trump-late-impeachment-brief-research-wrong.html. **31.** J. Michael Luttig, *Once Trump Leaves Office, the Senate Can't Hold an Impeachment Trial*, Wash. Post (Jan. 12, 2021), https://perma.cc/F8XR-4ZEN. **32.** Michael C. McConnell, *Impeachment and Trial After Officials Leave Office*, 87 Mo. L. Rev. 793 (2022). **33.** Akhil Reed Amar & Vikram David Amar, *Is the Presidential Succession Law Constitutional?*, 48 Stan. L. Rev. 113, 115 n.14 (1995). **34.** Tillman & Blackman, *supra* at 264.

ESSAY NO. 22: THE ELECTIONS CLAUSE
ART. I, § 4, CL. 1

The Times, Places and Manner of holding Elections for Senators and Representatives, shall be prescribed in each State by the Legislature thereof; but the Congress may at any time by Law make or alter such Regulations, except as to the Places of chusing Senators.

—Derek T. Muller

INTRODUCTION

The Elections Clause provides that state legislatures have the power to determine the "times, places and manner of holding elections" for Senators and Representatives, but Congress itself may alter those regulations or make its own. During the ratification process, this clause was the source of heated debate over the balance between state and federal power. For decades after ratification, Congress did not exercise its Elections Clause authority, but it used this power more actively following the Civil War and during the civil rights era. The Supreme Court of the United States has been called on to interpret the clause's meaning in several landmark cases.

HISTORY BEFORE 1787

The phrase "manner of elections" appeared in a number of earlier sources from the British Isles. The Dublin Society's Royal Charter described its "manner of election" broadly as a power that included time limits, elector qualifications, and a process for determining a voting location.[1] *A Digest of the Laws of England*, published in 1780, described the "Manner of Election" for members of Parliament as including when and where voting took place, the identity of election officials, and their responsibilities. The *manner* included *how* voting took place: by voice, show of hands, or a poll (a process of identifying which voters were qualified or not). The *manner* also provided the penalties for election officials who violated their duties.[2]

Colonial legislation used the phrase similarly. An election code from South Carolina in 1721 set forth the "Manner and Form of electing Members" of the state's lower house. That manner included, among other things, the method of choosing election officials, their responsibilities, penalties for violating election rules, and qualifications for voters and candidates.[3] Rhode Island's royal charter described the "manner" of its gubernatorial elections. That manner included the date of elections, which were to be held at town meetings where votes would "be sealed up by the moderators and town clerks," and the manner in which votes would be counted.[4]

After the Revolutionary War, several states adopted constitutions and laws laying out the "manner" of elections. These laws used the word "manner" in ways that were similar to its meaning in colonial times, including requirements regarding times of elections, method of voting, election officials and their duties, and elector qualifications.[5]

Taken as a whole, these pre-1787 sources suggest that the "manner" power was quite broad. "Manner" typically included qualifications for both electors and candidates, the times and places of elections, election rules, the threshold of votes required to win, the method of casting votes or ballots, the method for resolving contested elections, enforcement of election laws, and all of the practical mechanics of carrying out an election.[6]

THE CONSTITUTIONAL CONVENTION

The Elections Clause proved to be one of the more contested clauses during the Constitutional Convention. An early draft of the Pinckney Plan, shared on May 29, 1787, allowed the states to regulate the time and manner of holding elections with no role for Congress.[7] A subsequent version from the Committee of Detail expanded that state legislature's power to regulate "the times and places and [the] manner of holding the elections of the members of each House." This version, which gave the "Legislature of the United States" the power to "alter[]" these regulations, was presented to the Convention on August 6.[8]

On August 9, the proposed clause was debated by the full Convention.[9] Charles Pinckney and John Rutledge, both of South Carolina, opposed language that would have permitted Congress to alter state regulations. They argued that the "States . . . could & must be relied on."[10]

Rufus King of Massachusetts warned that the houses' "right of judging the returns of their members" would be frustrated if Congress lacked authority over the manner of state elections.[11] According to King, Congress's power to regulate the manner of elections would reinforce Congress's power to judge the results of those elections. Gouverneur Morris of Pennsylvania further predicted that if Congress lacked this power, the states could "make false returns and then make no provisions for new elections."[12]

James Madison of Virginia argued that, inevitably, "State Legislatures will sometimes fail or refuse to consult the common interest at the expense of their local conveniency."[13] Because the states were granted authority over federal elections with "words of great latitude . . . [i]t was impossible to foresee all the abuses that might be made of the discretionary power."[14] The national legislature could be trusted with the power to intervene. In particular, Senators were elected by the very state representatives that were entrusted with authority over elections. Moreover, members in the House of Representatives were elected by the same population that chose the state legislatures.[15]

The text would be finalized on September

14. The final clause provided, "The Times, Places and Manner of holding Elections for Senators and Representatives, shall be prescribed in each State by the Legislature thereof; but the Congress may at any time by Law make or alter such Regulations, except as to the Places of chusing Senators." This text granted Congress authority to create election regulations in a scenario in which the states failed or refused to do so. Congress would also have the power to alter existing state regulations.[16] But Congress would not have the power to regulate "the Places of chusing Senators." Under the Constitution, Senators would be elected by state legislatures in their state capitols. (See Essay No. 15.) The last clause was designed "to exempt the seats of Gov[ernment] in the States from the power of Congress." This uncontroversial addition came very late in the process.[17]

THE RATIFICATION DEBATES

Contentious debate continued during the state ratification process.[18] The Federalist Papers dedicated significant time to defending the Elections Clause. In Federalist No. 59, Alexander Hamilton emphasized that "every government ought to contain in itself the means of its own preservation." It was too dangerous to leave the process to the states alone. Hamilton wrote that "an exclusive power of regulating elections for the national government, in the hands of the State legislatures, would leave the existence of the Union entirely at their mercy." If Congress lacked the power to revise state laws, the states "could at any moment annihilate [the Union] by neglecting to provide for the choice of persons to administer its affairs."

Hamilton acknowledged that putting power over elections in the hands of the federal government could lead to violations of the right of certain groups to vote "in certain turbulent and factious seasons." But he denied in Federalist No. 60 that this federal power could ever lead to Congress intentionally depriving "the great mass of the people" of their vote, at least without risking revolution.

Anti-Federalists offered a litany of objections to the Elections Clause. For example, Cincinnatus noted that state constitutions regulated elections instead of leaving such power to the legislature.[19] Centinel, writing to the people of Pennsylvania, warned that the wide range of powers would permit Congress to "abolish the suffrage by ballot"[20] and "revoke[] every other part of the constitution that may be tolerable."[21] Centinel also feared that Congress would abuse its power to regulate the "times" of elections by postponing them indefinitely on flimsy excuses about political unrest or threat of invasion.[22] Federal Farmer found "no valuable purposes" in giving power to Congress to interfere with state power over elections.[23]

Dissenters in Pennsylvania warned that once the federal government had been "firmly established" and "a numerous standing army" was in place, members of Congress could "comple[te] the system of despotism" by holding office for life and handing their positions to their children.[24] Anti-Federalists like Cato and Cornelius also predicted that federal legislators could "destroy the rights of election" using such tactics as placing voting locations in out-of-the-way places or holding elections at inconvenient times.[25]

EARLY PRACTICE

For about five decades after ratification, states provided the rules for elections without congressional intervention. Congress first enacted legislation pursuant to the Elections Clause with the Apportionment Act of 1842.[26] The law required that each district must elect a single representative. As a result, states with more than one representative were not permitted to elect all of its representatives in one state-wide election.[27]

During Reconstruction, Congress sought to protect the right to vote and the integrity of elections with new legislation. The Enforcement Act of 1870 prohibited individuals from committing fraud in congressional elections or interfering with voters or election officials in congressional elections.[28]

The Elections Clause is much broader than other election-related provisions of the Constitution in one respect and much narrower in another. Congress's power to "enforce" the Fifteenth Amendment, for example, extends to protecting the right to vote regardless of "race, color, or previous condition of servitude." The Elections Clause is much broader because it extends to all "manner of holding elections."

But the Elections Clause also applies only to congressional elections. Congress's power elsewhere often extends to enforcing "the right of citizens of the United States to vote," regardless of who administers the election and regardless of whether the election is federal, state, or local. Because the Elections Clause applies only to congressional elections, Congress must rely on other powers to extend its election rules to presidential, state, and local elections.

JUDICIAL PRECEDENT

In *Ex parte Siebold* (1879), the U.S. Supreme Court recognized the breadth of Congress's power under the Elections Clause as "paramount."[29] This power "may be exercised as and when Congress sees fit to exercise it," and a federal rule "necessarily supersedes" any state regulations.[30]

United States v. Classic (1941) explained that the Elections Clause is a "constitutional command" "without restriction or limitation."[31] This provision empowers Congress to regulate general elections, which are *public* activity, as well as primary elections, which affect the private organization and operation of a political party choosing its nominee.

Where Congress has not regulated congressional elections, states may freely regulate them, subject to other constitutional provisions like the First Amendment and the Equal Protection Clause. Still, there are outer bounds to state power under the Elections Clause. *U.S. Term Limits, Inc. v. Thornton* (1995) declared unconstitutional an Arkansas law that imposed term limits for those seeking to run for Congress.[32] The Court held that qualifications for members of Congress were enumerated in Article I

of the Constitution. (See Essay Nos. 8 and 17.) As a result, such qualifications fell outside of the scope of the state's power to regulate the "manner of holding elections," which were limited to "procedural regulations."

The Elections Clause provides that these rules "shall be prescribed in each State by the Legislature thereof" unless Congress makes or alters them. The Elections Clause expressly grants the "Legislature" the power to prescribe rules in congressional elections. Yet, the Supreme Court has found that other actors may participate in a state's lawmaking process. First, *Ohio ex rel. Davis v. Hildebrant* (1916) held that the "Legislature" may be checked by a popular referendum.[33] Second, *Smiley v. Holm* (1932) concluded that the "Legislature" may be checked by gubernatorial veto.[34] Third, *Arizona State Legislature v. Arizona Independent Redistricting Commission* (2015) held that the people could pass a ballot initiative creating an independent commission responsible for congressional redistricting, effectively taking the power out of the hands of the legislature.[35] And fourth, *Moore v. Harper* (2023) found that state constitutions could limit state legislatures.[36] The legislature exercises a federal responsibility when it is setting the rules for federal elections, but a state legislature could still be constrained to issue election rules that comply with state constitutional law. *Moore* recognized that federal courts should defer to how state courts interpret their state constitutions in these cases. Still, the Court cautioned that "state courts do not have free rein" and "may not transgress the ordinary bounds of judicial review such that they arrogate to themselves the power vested in state legislatures to regulate federal elections."[37]

OPEN QUESTIONS

- May Congress abrogate state sovereign immunity under the Elections Clause?[38]
- May Congress commandeer state officials to implement laws enacted pursuant to the Elections Clause?[39]
- What is the relationship between the "qualifications" for office, which are beyond the power of Congress and the state to regulate, and the state's power to implement rules about the "manner of holding elections"?[40]
- Under *Moore v. Harper* (2023), what are the "bounds" of state judicial review and when do state courts "arrogate" power from the state legislature?

Cite as: Derek T. Muller, *The Elections Clause*, *in* THE HERITAGE GUIDE TO THE CONSTITUTION 64 (Josh Blackman & John G. Malcolm eds., 3d ed. 2025).

Notes

1 The Royal Charter of the Dublin Society (1785). **2.** 5 John Comyns & Anthony Holland, A Digest of the Laws of England 255–259 (1822). **3.** 3 The Statutes at Large of South Carolina 135–38 (Thomas Cooper ed., 1838). **4.** 6 The Federal and State Constitutions, Colonial Charters, and Other Organic Laws of the State[s], Territories, and Colonies Now or Heretofore Forming the United States of America (6 Thorpe) 3214, 3230 (Francis Newton Thorpe ed., 1909). **5.** N.J. Const. of 1776, art. VII; Mass. Const. of 1780, ch. 1, § 2, arts. II, IV; Md. Const. of 1776, arts. II, IV, VI, IX, XII, XIV, XVII; 2 Thorpe 780; 5 Thorpe 2793. **6.** Robert G. Natelson, _The Original Scope of the Congressional Power to Regulate Elections_, 13 Univ. Pa. J. Const. L. 1, 17–18 (2010). **7.** 2 Farrand's 135; 3 Farrand's 597. **8.** 2 Farrand's 153, 155, & 179. **9.** _Id._ at 239. **10.** _Id._ at 240. **11.** _Id._ at 241. **12.** _Id._ **13.** _Id._ at 240. **14.** _Id._ at 240–41. **15.** _Id._ at 241. **16.** _Id._ at 240–42. **17.** _Id._ at 613. **18.** Jamal Greene, Note, _Judging Partisan Gerrymanders Under the Elections Clause_, 114 Yale L.J. 1021, 1034–39 (2005).

19. Storing 6.1.54. **20.** Storing 2.7.73. **21.** _Id._ at 2.7.100. **22.** _Id._ **23.** _Id._ at 2.8.161. **24.** Storing 3.11.25. **25.** Storing 2.6.47; Storing 4.10.10. **26.** 5 Stat. 491 (1842). **27.** Franita Tolson, _The Spectrum of Congressional Authority over Elections_, 99 Bost. U. L. Rev. 317, 347 (2019). **28.** 16 Stat. 140 (1870). **29.** 100 U.S. 371, 384 (1879). **30.** _Id._ at 384. **31.** 313 U.S. 299, 315 (1941). **32.** 514 U.S. 779, 834 (1995). **33.** 241 U.S. 565 (1916). **34.** 285 U.S. 355 (1932). **35.** 576 U.S. 787 (2015). **36.** 600 U.S. 1 (2023). **37.** _Id._ **38.** _Public Interest Legal Found. v. Matthews_, 589 F. Supp. 3d 932, 937–39 (C.D. Ill. 2022). **39.** Evan H. Caminker, _Printz, State Sovereignty, and the Limits of Formalism_, 1997 Sup. Ct. Rev. 199, 237–38 (1997); Paul E. McGreal, _Unconstitutional Politics_, 76 Notre Dame L. Rev. Online 519, 553–54 (2001). **40.** _Greene v. Sec. of State_, 52 F.4th 907 (11th Cir. 2022); _Cawthorn v. Amalfi_, 35 F.4th 245, 266–85 (4th Cir. 2022); Derek T. Muller, _Weaponizing the Ballot_, 48 Fla. St. U. L. Rev. 61 (2021).

ESSAY NO. 23: THE CONGRESSIONAL ASSEMBLY CLAUSE
ART. I, § 4, CL. 2

The Congress shall assemble at least once in every Year, and such Meeting shall be on the first Monday in December, unless they shall by Law appoint a different Day.

—Michael Stern

INTRODUCTION

In Britain, the monarch had broad powers to convene and adjourn Parliament. The U.S. Constitution gave Congress the primary role in convening and adjourning itself; the President's role is extremely limited. The Congressional Assembly Clause requires Congress to assemble at least once a year on the first Monday in December or on another date that Congress can set by statute. The Congressional Adjournment Clause allows each house unilaterally to adjourn for three days; a longer adjournment requires both House and Senate consent. (See Essay No. 29.) The Presidential Convening Clause allows the President to convene either or both houses of Congress "on extraordinary Occasions." (See Essay No. 112.) Under the Presidential Adjournment Clause, if the House and Senate disagree about the "Time of Adjournment," the President "may adjourn them to such Time as he shall think proper." (See Essay No. 113.) Over time, a regular schedule emerged for odd-numbered years, and its timing created several problems that would be addressed by the Twentieth Amendment, which was ratified in 1933. (See Essay No. 207.)

HISTORY BEFORE 1787

Sir William Blackstone explained that Parliament could not be "convened by its own authority."[1] Rather, the power to convene Parliament was a "royal prerogative" of the Crown, and "this prerogative [was] founded upon very good reason." Blackstone observed that it would be "impossible to conceive that all the members, and each of the houses, would agree unanimously upon the proper time and place of meeting." If only some of the members were present, Blackstone asked, "who shall determine which is really the legislative body, the part assembled, or that which stays away?" To avoid that problem, the king, a "single person, whose will may be uniform and steady" and is "superior to both houses in dignity," could call together the assembly "at a determinate time and place." Critically, the monarch was "the only branch of the legislature that has a separate existence, and is capable of performing any act at a time when no parliament is in being."

Colonial governors enjoyed comparable powers with regard to convening and dismissing their elected assemblies. In Maryland, for example, the colonial governor "could summon, dissolve, adjourn, or prorogue the Assembly."[2] Early state constitutions, on the other hand, sharply reduced or eliminated executive control of the legislative schedule. Typically, they required that the legislature assemble at least once a year and a specified date on which the meeting was to occur.[3]

The Articles of Confederation did not include any clause that provided when or how the unicameral legislature would convene.

THE CONSTITUTIONAL CONVENTION

During the Constitutional Convention, the delegates made three decisions regarding Congress's assembly: the default date on which Congress would meet, whether Congress could change that date, and how often Congress must assemble. The Committee of Detail's report proposed that the "Legislature shall meet on the first Monday in December in every year."[4] By fixing a date in the Constitution, this proposal avoided the uncertainty that Blackstone described in the English system: In the case of disagreement, there was a default rule.

However, there was some debate about what the starting date should be. On August 7, Gouverneur Morris of Pennsylvania argued for a May date.[5] This schedule would allow the United States time to respond to new measures from European countries, which were typically adopted during the winter. James Madison of Virginia also preferred May, as travelling in December would be during "the most inconvenient seasons of the year."[6] Oliver Ellsworth of Connecticut thought meeting in the summer would "interfere . . . with agriculture."[7] Ultimately, the Convention stuck with the December date by a vote of eight to two.[8]

The Convention also gave Congress the power to set a different assembly date. Madison proposed that the date could "be fixed or varied by law."[9] The Convention later settled on this language: "[S]uch meeting shall be on the first Monday in December unless a different day shall be appointed by law."[10] The Committee of Style altered the language slightly: "[S]uch meeting shall be on the first Monday in December, unless they shall by law appoint a different day."[11] Because "by law" means by statute, the President, armed with his veto, had some role in setting the date on which Congress would assemble.[12]

The final issue concerned whether Congress actually had to meet at any regular interval. Rufus King of Massachusetts suggested that yearly meetings were not necessary because there would not be enough legislative business for Congress to deal with annually.[13] Nathaniel Gorham, also of Massachusetts, countered that annual meetings were necessary as a "check on the Executive department."[14] He argued that the time should be fixed both to prevent disputes from arising within the legislature and to allow the states to adjust their elections to correspond with the fixed date. The Convention ultimately proposed that "[t]he Legislature shall meet at least once in every year."[15] The Committee of Style changed "meet" to "assemble": "The Congress shall assemble at least once in every Year."[16]

Like the similar provisions of early state constitutions, the Congressional Assembly Clause protected the legislative schedule from executive control and interference. In addition, as Justice Joseph Story would observe, it placed the requirement for annual legislative sessions "beyond the power of faction and of party, of power and of corruption."[17]

THE EARLY CONGRESSES

The First Congress did not initially assemble on the first Monday in December as provided by the Congressional Assembly Clause. Instead, following the new Constitution's formal ratification on June 21, 1788, the Confederation Congress resolved "that the first Wednesday in March next be the time and the present seat of Congress the place for commencing proceedings under the said constitution."[18] Accordingly, the First Congress assembled on March 4, 1789. The House and Senate wished to proceed immediately to count the electoral votes, but they did not do so because a quorum was absent; it was not until April 6 that both houses had a quorum and the electoral votes were counted.[19] (See Essay No. 25.) George Washington took his inaugural oath as President on April 30, 1789.[20] (See Essay No. 101.)

Congress continued to meet until September 29 and, before adjourning, enacted a law providing that its next meeting would be on the first Monday in January 1790.[21] The second session of the First Congress accordingly began on January 4, 1790; it adjourned on August 12.[22] There was some discussion about whether the Constitution required an additional meeting in 1790.[23] Congress decided to meet again on the constitutional assembly date of December 6 without enacting an additional law.[24] The third session of the First Congress began on December 6, 1790, and adjourned on March 3, 1791.

Before adjourning its third and final session, the First Congress enacted a law providing that the first annual meeting of the new Congress would be on the fourth Monday of October 1791.[25] Despite this precedent and others, however, there are those who question whether one Congress can change the constitutional assembly date for a future Congress.[26]

Pursuant to the aforementioned law, the Second Congress assembled on October 24, 1791. It continued to meet through the constitutional assembly date until May 8, 1792, when it adjourned and ended its first session. Other early Congresses also followed this practice that the constitutional assembly date would not interrupt or otherwise affect a session that had commenced earlier (whether by law or by presidential proclamation).[27] However, later precedent holds that a pre-existing Congress expires by operation of law and a new session begins on the constitutional assembly date.[28] This interpretation is consistent with Thomas Jefferson's Manual of Parliamentary Practice, which explains that a meeting of Congress on the constitutional assembly date "must begin a new session."[29] On the other hand, one modern scholar argues that Congress is not required to begin a new session every year and could hold just one session over a two-year period if it chose to do so.[30]

The Third Congress began its first session on the constitutional assembly date of December 2, 1793.

THE TIMING OF NEW CONGRESSES AND NEW SESSIONS

The resolution of the Confederation Congress that established March 4, 1789, as the date for "commencing proceedings" under the Constitution had some unintended and unfortunate consequences. Although the Constitution did not specify when the terms of elected officials would begin, it did specify the length of those terms: four years for President and Vice President, six years for Senators, and two years for Representatives. Because the Confederation Congress's action meant that these terms began on March 4, 1789, it followed that they would all end on a future March 3 and that the next terms would begin the following day.

The combination of the March 4 start of congressional and presidential terms and the constitutional assembly date of the first Monday in December created an odd congressional schedule.[31] Congressional elections would be held in every even-numbered year. In every odd-numbered year, there were three important dates: The old Congress would conclude on March 3; the new Congress would begin on March 4, and the President would take his inaugural oath; and, absent a statutory change, the first session of the new Congress would begin on the first Monday in December.

This timing led to three potential problems. First, it created the possibility of a lame-duck Congress. For example, the Sixth Congress was elected in 1798 with a Federalist Party majority. By the time its second session began in December 1800, it was clear that Thomas Jefferson, a Democratic-Republican, had won the presidency. Jefferson, however, would not take his oath until March 4, and the Democratic-Republican party would take control of the new Congress on that same day. Between December 3, 1800, and March 3, 1801, the Federalist Congress would enact sweeping legislative programs. One of these bills was the Judiciary Act of 1801, also known as the Midnight Judges Act,[32] which led to *Marbury v. Madison* (1803).[33] (See Essay No. 134.)

Second, more than a year could elapse between the congressional election and the start of the new session. In the thirteen-month gap between 1860 and 1861, the Civil War broke out. In 1930, congressional elections were held on

November 4 and yielded a slight majority for the Republican party. However, the 72nd Congress would not begin its first session until December 7, 1931—more than thirteen months later. During that period, fourteen members-elect died, including former Speaker of the House Nicholas Longworth, a Republican from Ohio. Special elections were held to fill the vacancies. As a result, when the 72nd Congress finally assembled in December 1931, the Democratic party had a slight majority.[34]

Third, with this schedule, a new President would be in office for nearly nine months until the new Congress begins its first session. However, the President does have the power "on extraordinary occasions" to "convene both Houses or either of them." For example, on March 4, 1933, President Franklin Roosevelt convened Congress in a special session to consider urgent legislative components of the New Deal.

Each of these three problems would be addressed by the Twentieth Amendment, which was ratified in 1933. Under the amendment, the new Congress would begin and would meet for its first session on January 3 of every odd-numbered year, and the President would take the inaugural oath of office on January 20 of every fourth year. As a result, the lame-duck Congress would stretch only from (about) November until January, and when the new President entered office, the new Congress would already be in session. Moreover, the new Congress rather than the old Congress would preside over the joint session of Congress that formally elects the President.

OPEN QUESTIONS

- Are there limits to the authority of one Congress to change the assembly dates for future Congresses? For example, could Congress pass a law saying that all future Congresses shall assemble on May 1?
- What happens if the House or Senate lacks a quorum on the constitutional assembly date of a year when a new President is to be inaugurated? Would the absence of a quorum in either house or the inability of the House to organize for any reason preclude the counting of electoral votes and thereby prevent the inauguration of a new President on January 20?
- Is Congress constitutionally required to begin a new session on the constitutional assembly date? Could it instead choose to hold a single session that lasted for more than a year? Could a single session last for two years or even longer?

Cite as: Michael Stern, *The Congressional Assembly Clause, in* THE HERITAGE GUIDE TO THE CONSTITUTION 68 (Josh Blackman & John G. Malcolm eds., 3d ed. 2025).

Notes

1. 1 Blackstone 150.   **2.** Paul H. Giddens, *Governor Horatio Sharpe and His Maryland Government*, 32 Md. Hist. Mag. 156, 160 (1937).   **3.** Ga. Const. of 1777, art. II; Md. Const. of 1776, art. XXIII; N.J. Const. of 1776, art. III.   **4.** 2 Farrand's 177.   **5.** *Id.* at 199.   **6.** *Id.*   **7.** *Id.* at 200.   **8.** *Id.*   **9.** *Id.* at 197.   **10.** *Id.* at 565.   **11.** *Id.* at 592.   **12.** William Montgomery Meigs, The Growth of the Constitution in the Federal Convention of 1787, at 337 (1900).   **13.** 2 Farrand's 198.   **14.** *Id.*   **15.** *Id.* at 565.   **16.** *Id.* at 592.   **17.** 1 Story's Commentaries § 829.   **18.** 34 J. Cont. Cong. 523 (Sept. 13, 1788).   **19.** S. Jour., 1st Cong., 1st Sess. 5–8 (Mar. 4–Apr. 6, 1789).   **20.** *Id.* at 18.   **21.** 1 Hinds' Precedents § 5.   **22.** *Id.*   **23.** *Id.*   **24.** *Id.*   **25.** *Id.* at § 6.   **26.** 1 Precedents (Wickham), ch. 1, § 2.1.   **27.** 1 Hinds' Precedents §§ 6–10.   **28.** 1 Deschler's Precedents ch. 1, § 3; 2 Hinds' Precedents § 1160.   **29.** House Rules and Manual § 590.   **30.** Saikrishna Bangalore Prakash, *Of Synchronicity and Supreme Law*, 132 Harv. L. Rev. 1220, 1264 (2019).   **31.** Edward J. Larson, *The Constitutionality of Lame-Duck Lawmaking: The Text, History, Intent and Original Meaning of the Twentieth Amendment*, 2 Utah L. Rev. 707, 716–17 (2012).   **32.** 2 Stat. 89.   **33.** 5 U.S. (1 Cranch) 137 (1803).   **34.** Andrew Glass, *The 72nd Congress Convenes, Dec. 7, 1931*, Politico (Dec. 7, 2009), https://perma.cc/RH3Y-VEJP.

~

ESSAY NO. 24: THE JUDGE OF ELECTIONS CLAUSE
ART. I, § 5, CL. 1

Each House shall be the Judge of the Elections, Returns and Qualifications of its own Members. . . .

—Derek T. Muller

INTRODUCTION

For centuries before America gained its independence, legislative bodies had judged their members' elections and qualifications. The Judge of Elections Clause in the Constitution reflects this long-standing tradition. Since ratification, the House and Senate have exercised this power on numerous occasions, but they have done so much less frequently in recent years. Precedent indicates that the judgments of the House and Senate in these matters are not subject to review in the courts. However, both houses lack the power to add to the qualifications for serving in Congress that are enumerated in Article I, Sections 2 and 3. (See Essay Nos. 8 and 17.)

Justice Joseph Story observed that the power to judge elections was a necessary attribute of the separation of powers. If that power, he wrote, were "lodged in any other, than the legislative body itself, its independence, its purity, and even its existence and action may be destroyed, or put into imminent danger."[1] Further, Story declared, the power allowed each house to "sustain the free choice of its constituents."[2]

HISTORY BEFORE 1787

By the fifteenth century, the Crown had long informally exercised power over parliamentary elections. Starting in 1405, the Court of Chancery, which was beholden to the Crown, formerly exercised power over those elections.[3] Yet, by the mid-sixteenth century, Parliament began to assert control over the elections of its own members.[4] And, by the early seventeenth century, Parliament's privilege of examining the election returns was undisputed.[5]

Before the American Revolution, to prevent encroachment by royal governors, the colonies insisted on the right of legislatures to judge the qualifications of their own members.[6] Under the Articles of Confederation, the state legislatures retained the power to judge their own elections.[7] By 1789, nearly all states had ratified their own constitutions spelling out this authority of their legislatures,[8] and several others soon followed suit.[9]

THE CONSTITUTIONAL CONVENTION

The Constitutional Convention approved the Judge of Elections Clause with minimal debate. The clause was presented by the Committee of Detail on August 6 and adopted without controversy on August 10.[10] The clause anticipated that each house of Congress would act as "judge," which suggests a kind of judicial power in this context. "Elections" related to the mode of choosing candidates; "returns," to the results of elections; and "qualifications," to the age, inhabitance, and citizenship requirements for members.

The Elections Clause gave Congress the power to make or alter the times, places, and manner of holding elections. (See Essay No. 22.) The Judge of Elections Clause was invoked to explain why the Elections Clause was necessary. Rufus King of Massachusetts explained that without the Elections Clause, "their right of judging of the returns of their members may be frustrated."[11] Gouverneur Morris of Pennsylvania likewise worried that "States might make false returns and then make no provisions for new elections."[12] The Judge of Elections Clause recognized the importance of the legislature's power to judge elections and returns. Members of the Convention thought a predicate power, to make or alter the rules for those elections, should also reside in the legislature.

THE RATIFICATION DEBATES

During the ratification debates, Anti-Federalists expressed concerns that placing the authority to judge member qualifications with each house would threaten the right of citizens' chosen candidates to be seated in the national legislature. "By this Federal Constitution," worried Cornelius, "each House is to be the judge, not only of the elections, and returns, but also of the *qualifications* of its members; and that, without any other rule than such as they themselves may prescribe." Cornelius wrote that "[t]his power in Congress, I take to be equal to that of a negative on elections in general."[13] The clause attracted little attention in the Federalist Papers. Federalist No. 53 observed that "[e]ach house is, as it necessarily must be, the judge of the elections, qualifications and returns of its members. . . ."

EARLY PRACTICE

In the decades after the Founding, both houses of Congress routinely judged the elections, returns, and qualifications of their members. One early and contested instance arose in 1793. The Pennsylvania legislature elected Albert Gallatin to the Senate. Gallatin, a member of the Democratic-Republican party, was a rival of Alexander Hamilton, a prominent Federalist.[14] Doubts arose about Gallatin's eligibility for the Senate. He was born in Switzerland[15] and had resided in the United States for thirteen years. But it was unclear whether Gallatin had been a U.S. citizen for the requisite nine years.[16] Two Senate committees dominated by Federalists found against Gallatin, and he was barred from the seat.[17]

A different controversy arose during the Civil War. The Senate judged whether James H. Lane of Kansas was entitled to be a Senator even though President Lincoln had appointed him a Brigadier General in the Union Army.[18] Lane's election apparently violated of the Incompatibility Clause.[19] (See Essay No. 34.) Although the Judiciary Committee found against Lane, the Senate decided to uphold his election, perhaps out of a sense of patriotism in the midst of the war.[20]

Another notorious contest during Reconstruction came from the election of Hiram Revels, the first black Senator. Opponents first charged that his election was improper because the governor of Mississippi who signed his certificate

of election was only the provisional governor and therefore not authorized to certify the legislature's selection of Revels. Challengers also claimed that Revels was not "nine years a citizen" because he was not a citizen under the Supreme Court's decision in *Dred Scott* until the ratification of the Fourteenth Amendment in 1868. Defenders noted that Revels had previously resided in Ohio, where he had voted in that state and must have been a citizen. In the end, the Senate seated him over the objection of a few Democrats.[21]

Over the years, Congress has considered hundreds of challenges. It developed a body of precedent and procedure for adjudicating these disputes that was consistent with its role as "judge."[22]

MODERN PRACTICE

Under modern practice, the power to judge elections is broad. It extends to investigations of fraud and voter intimidation.[23] It also includes the power to issue arrest warrants for witnesses to testify without a previous subpoena. Each house can also impose punishment for perjury.[24]

In 1935, West Virginia elected Rush D. Holt as Senator even though he would not be thirty years of age for another seven months.[25] Holt promised that he would not present his credential to the Senate to take the oath until his thirtieth birthday.[26] Holt's defeated opponent, an incumbent Senator, filed a petition before Holt presented his credentials and argued to the Senate that Holt did not meet the minimum age requirement. The Senate engaged in a long and contested investigation. Eventually, Holt was seated on the ground that the age requirement applied when the candidate took office, not at the time of election.[27]

By the late twentieth century, Congress had begun to disfavor exercising its independent judgment in elections. States adopted more robust election canvassing and recount procedures, which the federal courts approved and which gave Congress more confidence in election results.[28] The Federal Contested Elections Act of 1969 sets narrow rules to govern how contestants may challenge the outcomes of elections in the House.[29]

The last election overturned by Congress was a contest nicknamed the "Bloody Eighth." In 1984, Republican Rick McIntyre appeared to defeat Democrat Frank McClosky in Indiana's Eighth Congressional District election. Indiana certified McIntyre as the winner by thirty-four votes, a margin that expanded to 418 once some counties finished their recount. However, the Democratic-controlled House kept the seat vacant on a party-line vote while the Committee on House Administration conducted its own recount. After a series of bitterly contested and hotly partisan recount rules adopted by the committee, McClosky was deemed the winner by just four votes and was seated by the House on May 1, 1985.[30]

JUDICIAL PRECEDENT

The manner in which the House and Senate have decided qualification and election cases suggests that the power is unreviewable in the courts. In *Morgan v. United States* (1986), then-Circuit Judge Antonin Scalia declared that the House's determination in the McClosky–McIntyre dispute was nonjusticiable under the Judge of Elections Clause.[31] This holding found support from the fact that each house was "*the* judge," a definite article that excluded all others, and in dicta from previous Supreme Court cases that each house was the "sole" judge of its members' qualifications.[32] Nevertheless, *Powell v. McCormack* (1969) held that a house of Congress lacks the power to judge qualifications beyond those enumerated in the Constitution and that such questions are justiciable in the federal courts.[33]

The Supreme Court of the United States has emphasized that states cannot thwart Congress's power to judge elections. In *Roudebush v. Hartke* (1972), Indiana conducted a recount after its Senate election, which was challenged as a violation of the Judge of Elections Clause. The Court held that a state's law cannot "usurp" the function of Congress, which can occur if the law "frustrates" a house of Congress's "ability to make an independent final judgment."[34] Here, however, the Senate could still independently evaluate the election or conduct its own recount, and state law did not usurp Congress's power.[35]

OPEN QUESTIONS

Should a newly elected candidate whose credentials are challenged be seated in the House? The House of Representatives adjourns at the end of a session, and an entirely new House of 435 members-elect assembles to be sworn in. Historically, all members would be sworn in, but a contested member could be seated provisionally, and that candidate's seat could become vacant or be awarded to a contestant. However, with increasing frequency in recent contests, including in *Powell v. McCormack* (1969) and in the "Bloody Eighth," all of the other members take the oath of office while they ask the contested candidate to stand aside. The rest of the chamber then subsequently votes to decide whether to seat the member. Even if seated, the member may lose that seat if a later contest is successful. The decision of the House to ask members to "stand aside" in this fashion is of relatively recent vintage and merits further exploration to determine whether it is consistent with this clause.[36]

Do states have any power to judge qualifications of candidates for federal office? On the one hand, states have the power to regulate the "manner of holding elections" for Congress under Article I, Section 4, Clause 1. That power includes ballot access rules, or determining who appears on the ballot. On the other hand, Congress is "*the* judge" of the qualifications of its members. That power is seemingly reserved to Congress, and the power over the "manner of holding elections" does not necessarily extend to adjudications about qualifications.

Federal courts have been asked to address this issue but with limited analysis so far. In the 2022 election, challenges arose in states as to whether certain congressional candidates had engaged in insurrection under Section 3 of the Fourteenth Amendment and were ineligible to serve. (See Essay No. 198.) Challengers tried to keep those candidates' names off the ballot. Among the many contested questions was whether states had the power to do so or only Congress could do so. Federal courts mostly dodged the question, but some judges separately expressed doubt that states had this power.[37] In *Trump v. Anderson* (2024), the Supreme Court held that states may not unilaterally enforce Section 3 of the Fourteenth Amendment against federal candidates, but did not address other qualifications.[38]

Cite as: Derek T. Muller, *The Judge of Elections Clause*, in THE HERITAGE GUIDE TO THE CONSTITUTION 72 (Josh Blackman & John G. Malcolm eds., 3d ed. 2025).

Notes

1. 2 Story's Commentaries § 831.   **2.** *Id.*   **3.** Graeme Orr & George Williams, *Electoral Challenges: Judicial Review of Parliamentary Elections in Australia*, 23 Sydney L. Rev. 53, 55–57 & n.10 (2001).   **4.** *Id.* at 57.   **5.** *Id.* at 58.   **6.** Paul E. Salamanca & James E. Keller, *The Legislative Privilege to Judge the Qualifications, Elections, and Returns of Members*, 95 Ky. L. J. 241, 271–72 (2005).   **7.** Articles of Confederation, art. II.   **8.** Pa. Const. of 1776, § 9; N.C. Const. of 1776, art. X; Del. Const. of 1776, art. V; N.J. Const. of 1776, art. V; Md. Const. of 1776, art. IX; N.Y. Const. of 1777, art. IX; Vt. Const. of 1777, ch. II, § 8; Mass. Const. of 1780, pt. 2, ch. 1, § 2, art. IV.   **9.** Ga. Const. of 1789, art I, § 13; S.C. Const. of 1790, art. I, § 11; N.H. Const. of 1793, art. XXII.   **10.** 2 Farrand's 155, 180, 254.   **11.** *Id.* at 241.   **12.** *Id.*   **13.** Storing 4.10.10.   **14.** Anne M. Butler & Wendy Wolff, United States Senate Election, Expulsion and Censure Cases: 1793–1990, at 3 (1995).   **15.** *Id.*   **16.** 4 Annals of Cong. 19, 47–62 (1855).   **17.** Butler & Wolff, *supra* at 3–4.   **18.** Cong. Globe, 37th Cong., 1st Sess. 82 (1861); Cong. Globe, 37th Cong., 2nd Sess. 359–64 (1862).   **19.** Cong. Globe, 37th Cong., 2nd Sess. 363 (1862).   **20.** *Id.* at 364; Salamanca & Keller, *supra* at 285–88.   **21.** Cong. Globe, 41st Cong., 2d Sess. 1503–14, 1542–44, 1557–68 (1870).   **22.** A Historical Digest of All the Contested Election Cases in the House of Representatives of the United States from the First to the Fifty-Sixth Congress. 1789–1901 (Chester H. Rowell ed., 1901); Anne M. Butler & Wendy Wolff, United States Senate Election, Expulsion, and Censure Cases, 1793–1990 (1995).   **23.** 1 Hinds' Precedents § 336 (1907).   **24.** *Barry v. United States ex rel. Cunningham*, 279 U.S. 597, 614–18 (1929).   **25.** 79 Cong. Rec. 5916 (1935).   **26.** *Id.* at 9651.   **27.** *Id.* at 9840–42.   **28.** *Roudebush v. Hartke*, 405 U.S. 15 (1972).   **29.** 2 U.S.C. §§ 381 *et seq.*   **30.** Edward B. Foley, Ballot Battles 259–267 (2016).   **31.** 801 F.2d 445, 446–49 (D.C. Cir. 1986).   **32.** *Id.* at 447; *Jones v. Montague*, 194 U.S. 147, 153 (1904); *Burton v. United States*, 202 U.S. 344, 366 (1906).   **33.** *Powell v. McCormack*, 395 U.S. 486, 489–94, 550 (1969).   **34.** 405 U.S. 15, 25 (1972).   **35.** *Id.* at 25–26.   **36.** Brian C. Kalt, *Swearing in the Phoenix: Toward a More Sensible System for Seating Members of the House of Representatives at Organization*, 105 Marq. L. Rev. 1 (2021).   **37.** *Greene v. Raffensperger*, 599 F. Supp. 3d 1283 (N.D. Ga. 2022); *Greene*, 52 F.4th at 910–916 (Branch, J. concurring); *Cawthorn v. Amalfi*, 35 F.4th 245, 266–85 (4th Cir. 2022) (Richardson, J., concurring in the judgment); Derek T. Muller, *Scrutinizing Federal Electoral Qualifications*, 50 Ind. L.J. 559, 594–98 (2015).   **38.** 601 U.S. 100 (2024) (per curiam).

~

ESSAY NO. 25: THE QUORUM CLAUSE
ART. I, § 5, CL. 1

A Majority of each shall constitute a Quorum to do Business; but a smaller Number may adjourn from day to day, and may be authorized to compel the Attendance of absent Members, in such Manner, and under such Penalties as each House may provide.

—Seth Barrett Tillman

INTRODUCTION

The Constitution requires that each house of Congress have a majority of members in attendance to conduct business. If there is less than a majority in attendance, the available members (even if less than a quorum) can adjourn from day to day. And the available members (even if less than a quorum) may, if authorized by a prior statute or rule, compel absent members to attend. The Framers adopted a majority quorum rule rather than a submajority or supermajority rule. They also rejected a quorum rule that would have allowed each house to set its own quorum rule. As a result, a minority of members cannot easily frustrate the ability of a house to pass legislation or conduct other business—assuming the majority actively attends. This majority rule departed from the practice in the English House of Commons and some colonial legislatures, which allowed a submajority to make a quorum. Under long-standing practice, each house is "presumed" to have a quorum during a session unless a member or the presiding officer objects.[1] As Thomas Jefferson explained, if "it is observed that a quorum is not present, any member may call for the House to be counted, and being found deficient, business is suspended."[2] However, at the start of a two-year Congress or of a subsequent session, House practice has customarily required a majority's presence, absent any reliance on a presumption of a continuous quorum from any prior Congress or prior session.[3] And obviously, when members attended the first session of the First Congress, there could be no presumption of a continuous quorum from any prior session.

HISTORY BEFORE 1787

The size of the House of Commons has varied over time. In the early seventeenth century, the English House of Commons had between 450 and 500 seats.[4] In the late seventeenth century, with the exception of the Cavalier Parliament, the English House of Commons had between 500 and 560 seats.[5] In 1641, the English House of Commons adopted, by order, a sub-majority quorum rule of forty members.[6] That order remains in force in the Commons.[7]

Colonial practice sometimes followed English and subsequent British parliamentary precedents, but it was uneven, as was practice among the American states after the Revolution. Some state constitutions, like Maryland's and North Carolina's, had a majority quorum rule.[8] Other Revolutionary-era state constitutions, including Virginia's, had no express quorum rule at all,[9] which would have left the issue to be settled by statute, rule, or perhaps by custom.

Under the Articles of Confederation, there was no express quorum rule. Each state delegation voted separately; individual delegates only had a vote within their state's delegation. Moreover, to vote, a state delegation had to be represented by between two and seven delegates.[10] As a result, a state delegation might be unable to vote: because none of its delegates were present; or because only one of its delegates was present; or because its delegates were evenly divided. The Articles adopted several supermajority rules controlling much of the most important business before Congress. For example, under Article IX, support from nine of the thirteen state delegations was necessary to appoint a commander in chief of the army or navy.[11] Article XI generally required support from nine state delegations to admit new territory to the Union.[12] Article X controlled the structure and voting rules for the standing committee that was empowered to act for the Articles Congress when it was in recess.[13] Other business (except

for an adjournment) required the support of an absolute majority: seven state delegations. This was an absolute majority voting rule, and not a quorum rule per se. For example, on June 19, 1788, a motion was reported as lost, with five ayes, two noes, one divided state delegation, and with four other delegations represented by a single member, and Delaware entirely absent.[14]

These provisions, and the supermajority provisions in particular, functioned much as a traditional quorum rule functions. These rules allowed dissenting minorities of state delegations to stop public business merely by physically absenting themselves from the floor of the legislature and may well have contributed to the perceived weakness, ineffectiveness, and imbecility of the Articles government. When the Framers showed up for the Philadelphia Convention, supermajority quorum rules were likely disfavored.

THE CONSTITUTIONAL CONVENTION

At the Philadelphia Convention, a variety of views were expressed in regard to legislative quorums. On August 6, 1787, the Committee of Detail returned a draft Constitution with a majority quorum provision: "In each House a majority of the members shall constitute a quorum to do business; but a smaller number may adjourn from day to day."[15] This rule is a floating quorum: the size of the quorum changes or floats depending on the number of members. This measure was debated on August 10.[16] Gouverneur Morris of Pennsylvania proposed two fixed quorum rules: thirty-three members for the House and fourteen for the Senate. The choice of thirty-three and fourteen would have been a majority quorum rule under the assumption that all thirteen states ratified the Constitution and sent timely members to the First Congress. The first House would have had sixty-five authorized members, and the first Senate would have had twenty-six authorized members for thirteen states. But when the First Congress met in 1789, only eleven of thirteen states had ratified the Constitution. In those circumstances, had the Morris proposal been in effect, a fixed quorum of thirty-three House members and fourteen Senate members would have been a supermajority quorum. Likewise, as new states entered the Union beyond the original thirteen states, had the Morris proposal been in effect, a quorum of thirty-three House members and fourteen Senate members would have been a submajority quorum rule. Perhaps unsurprisingly, Morris's proposal failed by a vote of two to nine.

The August 10 debate revealed other divisions. Nathaniel Gorham of Massachusetts favored a submajority quorum rule that would have allowed each house to conduct business with less than fifty percent of its members present. Gorham argued that a majority quorum rule could cause a "great delay . . . in business, and great inconvenience from the future increase of numbers."[17] In other words, a majority quorum rule would be difficult to satisfy as the nation expanded and new members had to travel greater distances to the nation's capital. John Francis Mercer of Maryland supported, in principle, a submajority quorum rule, but he would have let Congress fix the quorum. In the British parliament, Mercer observed, "the requisite number is small & no inconvenienc[e] has been experienced." Mercer believed that if the Constitution fixed a majority or supermajority quorum rule, it would "[em]power . . . a few [members] by [their] seceding [from the legislative chamber] at a critical moment to introduce convulsions, and endanger the Government."[18]

George Mason of Virginia opposed a submajority quorum.[19] A submajority quorum rule, he said, would allow members from the "Central States," who lived close to the capital, to "meet[] earlier" and stay longer during the session. These centrally located members could "carry such measures as they pleased." Members from "distant" states might arrive later and have to leave earlier. Rufus King of Massachusetts proposed a complex alternative quorum rule using the fixed numbers proposed by Morris as a floor but otherwise leaving the legislature with discretion to raise that floor.[20]

These and other proposed amendments to the majority quorum rule all failed to garner support, but one amendment did pass: Oliver Ellsworth of Connecticut indicated that the threat of "secessions may be guarded against by giving to each House an authority to require the attendance of absent members."[21] In these debates, "secessions" related to members'

coordinating their failing to attend legislative sessions in order to frustrate legislative business and to accomplish political ends. James Wilson of Pennsylvania supported Ellsworth's position. Edmund Randolph and James Madison, both of Virginia, put forward a motion providing that a submajority of each house "(may) be authorized to compel the attendance of absent members in such manner & under such penalties as each House may provide."[22] This additional safeguard against the power of a minority to abuse the quorum process was approved almost unanimously, and the proposed majority quorum rule as amended passed without recorded dissent.

COMMENTARY

In Federalist No. 58, Madison defended the majority quorum provision and warned that under a supermajority provision, "[i]t would be no longer the majority that would rule; the power would be transferred to the minority." Under a supermajority quorum rule, absent members could frustrate legislative business and "facilitate and foster the baneful practice of secessions." In Federalist No. 59, Hamilton wrote that a quorum of the Senate would be sixteen members. However, Hamilton erred; if all thirteen states ratified the Constitution, there would be twenty-six Senators, and a quorum would be fourteen. In any event, the Constitution did not impose a fixed quorum number.

Justice Story praised each house's power to compel attendance. He explained that "[i]t was a defect in the articles of confederation, sometimes productive of great public mischief, that . . . no power of compelling the attendance of the requisite number [for enacting a resolution] existed."[23]

THE QUORUM RULE IN THE FIRST CONGRESS

In 1789, the First Congress was scheduled to convene in the then-capital New York, to begin the business of the government under the new Constitution. However, there would be a delay before the House and Senate were properly constituted: A quorum of members had yet to arrive. During those early days, the House and Senate could not select their presiding officials. Moreover, only eleven of the original thirteen states—all except Rhode Island and North Carolina—had ratified the Constitution. Among the eleven ratifying states, fifty-nine House seats and twenty-two Senate seats were authorized.[24] The House and Senate would not organize until thirty Representatives and twelve Senators were in attendance.

Based on these twin precedents, some scholars have assumed that the Quorum Clause's "majority" language refers to a majority of all authorized seats, and not to a majority of actual members.[25] For example, where an election for a seat is not held, or when an election is held but the member-elect fails to attend the house to which he was elected or attends without recognized credentials, the number of authorized seats remains constant, but the number of actual members is reduced by one. Under the former reading, that member's seat would still be part of the denominator for which a majority was necessary to make a quorum. In short, under this interpretation of the Quorum Clause, a quorum requires the attendance of members from a majority of all authorized seats, whether those seats have been filled by election or not. Under the alternate reading, if a state fails to hold an election for a seat, then that seat does not count towards the denominator. Thus, a majority quorum would be determined as a majority of actual members, and not a majority of all authorized seats.

Although these two precedents from the first session of the First Congress tell one story, the second session of the First Congress tells a somewhat different one. The first session ended on September 29, 1789. The second was scheduled to begin on January 4, 1790.[26] On November 21, 1789, during the recess between the two sessions, North Carolina ratified the Constitution, and the North Carolina legislature proceeded to elect its two Senators over the course of November and December.[27] In short, North Carolina's ratification and the election of its senators all took place well prior to the start of the second session. By January 1790, there would be twenty-four authorized Senate seats. On January 4, 1790, when the second session began, ten Senators were in attendance. The Senate's journal reflects an absence of a quorum.[28] An eleventh Senator was in attendance on January 5, and a twelfth was present on January

6 when the Senate first recognized the existence of a quorum during the second session.

At this juncture, however, there were twelve ratifying states and twenty-four authorized Senate seats. If the Constitution's majority quorum provision referred to the number of authorized seats, a quorum should have been thirteen Senators, not twelve. This Senate precedent reflects what would later be called a "floating quorum" rule.[29] A floating quorum rule does not count the number of authorized seats; it counts the number of actual members whose credentials have been accepted by the legislative body. Thus, the "majority" requirement floats upwards as new members attend for the first time. In other words, as each new state's members would show up to Congress for the first time, the denominator for purposes of the quorum would increase. When the quorum was established in the second session, the members from North Carolina had not yet presented their credentials. Therefore, the North Carolina Senators were not counted for purposes of the denominator. By contrast, the majority requirement would float downward, and the denominator would decrease as members were lost to the chamber because of death, resignation, expulsion, etc.

HOW A QUORUM IS DETERMINED

Generally, the presiding officer or a member of each house can, at his discretion, call for a vote to determine the presence or absence of a quorum.[30] That vote would determine if enough members are in attendance to transact business. But in the absence of such a quorum call, the number of members present could be determined in another way. Whenever the legislative body is divided by casting votes, for example, those votes may themselves reveal the presence of a quorum.

It is easy enough to tally the members' *ayes* and *noes*, as well as the other members who vote merely *present*. Speaker Thomas Reed's nineteenth-century procedural reforms empowered the House to count members who are physically present in the House, even if they have refrained from voting, as present for the purpose of determining the presence of a quorum.[31] The Supreme Court upheld that procedure in *United States v. Ballin* (1892).[32] If the total number of votes cast is fewer than the minimum for a quorum, the motion has failed. A federal district court has observed that "once a vote reveals that a quorum is lacking, the House and Senate must either obtain a quorum or adjourn—they cannot ignore the demonstrated absence by unanimous consent."[33] The available members can invoke a prior rule or statute to compel absent members to attend, thereby facilitating the House's reaching a quorum.

JUDICIAL PRECEDENT

Federal courts traditionally have been reluctant to declare unconstitutional congressional proceedings based on a lack of quorums or other asserted procedural defects relating to bill passage, even when those alleged defects are grounded in the Constitution. The enrolled bill rule bars courts from examining alleged procedural defects in the passage of a bill. Instead, the rule cautions courts to rely on the signatures of each chamber's presiding officer on the face of the enacted or engrossed bill as an assurance that all constitutional requirements have been met.

This rule was tested in the wake of the COVID-19 pandemic. In May 2020, the House of Representatives authorized remote proxy voting.[34] Under this rule, one member could authorize a second member to vote on the first member's behalf and in the first member's absence. The House rules permitted both members to count toward the House's quorum. As a result, a member would not need to be physically present in the chamber to cast a vote. House Republicans sought declaratory and injunctive relief against the rule's enforcement. Their lawsuit was dismissed, and that district court's decision was affirmed on appeal.[35] In this case, the plaintiffs did not allege that any particular bill's enactment was unconstitutional.

In December 2022, the House voted on the Pregnant Workers Fairness Act. When the House voted, a quorum of members was not physically present. The House's position was that a quorum existed under its proxy voting rule. The State of Texas challenged the enforcement of this bill on the grounds that the House voted on the bill without a quorum being present. In 2024, a federal district court ruled that a member must be physically present in the legislative chamber to count toward a quorum.[36] Here, the number of members who were physically present when the bill was passed by the House was less than a quorum.

OPEN QUESTIONS

- Is it possible to reconcile the competing precedents established at the start of the first and second sessions of the First Congress with regard to the quorum rule? Which is the "correct" one? Both precedents are consistent with the Constitution's text. Could it be that both precedents are correct with one concept of "majority" applicable at the start of each two-year Congress and another applicable on all other occasions?
- How much deference (if any) must the other branches of government give to the determination by a house's presiding officer that a quorum was present?
- How frequently must the presiding officer permit members to object to ongoing proceedings based on the alleged absence of a quorum? Repeated quorum objections are dilatory: They unfairly deny the elected majority the power to govern. On the other hand, a presiding officer's refusal to recognize a member's quorum objection, particularly if the presiding officer no longer has a working majority, allows business to go forward in violation of the minority's (and, arguably, the public's) constitutional rights.
- Both houses, in the absence of a member's objection, will routinely hold sessions and conduct business in the absence of a "quorum" (that is, without a majority of members being physically present). Does the Speaker or do members have a duty to object to proceedings if they believe that a quorum is absent?[37] Jefferson's *Manual* suggests that the answer is "no"; objections are discretionary, and the presence of a majority quorum, once established, is presumed to continue.[38]

- Can a member count toward the quorum for purposes of voting if he is participating in the proceedings by electronic video link? Here the issue is not proxy voting; it is whether physical presence in the legislative chamber is required by the Quorum Clause in circumstances where the member can individually cast his vote, debate, and otherwise interact with other members by electronic means. There is no developed case law on this point, but one jurist has suggested that this practice is constitutional.[39]

Cite as: Seth Barrett Tillman, *The Quorum Clause, in* THE HERITAGE GUIDE TO THE CONSTITUTION 75 (Josh Blackman & John G. Malcolm eds., 3d ed. 2025).

Notes

1. 6 Cannon's Precedents, §§ 564, 624. **2.** Thomas Jefferson, Manual of Parliamentary Practice § VI (2d ed. 1812). **3.** *Texas v. Garland*, 719 F. Supp. 3d 521, 591–92 (N.D. Tex. 2024). **4.** *The Composition of the House of Commons: 1604–1629*, The History of Parliament, https://perma .cc/W9JN-A2AS. **5.** *The Composition of the House: 1660–1690*, The History of Parliament, https://perma.cc /CRP7-SW9F. **6.** Charles Henry Parry, The Parliaments and Councils of England 345 (London, J. Murray 1839); William Paul White, The History and Philosophy of the Quorum as a Device of Parliamentary Procedure (Master of Arts, University of Montana 1967), https://perma.cc /Y59W-LJMT; 2 Story's Commentaries § 832. **7.** *Quorum of the House*, Erskine May, https://perma.cc/HPX7-D42N. **8.** Md. Const. of 1776, arts. VIII & XX; N.C. Const. of 1776, art. XLVI. **9.** The Constitution [of Virginia] as Adopted by the Convention, [29 June 1776], Founders Online, https: //perma.cc/5H3N-BHT9. **10.** Articles of Confederation, art. V, § 2. **11.** *Id.* art. IX, § 6. **12.** *Id.* art. XI. **13.** *Id.* art. X. **14.** 34 J. Cont. Cong. 1774–1789: January 21, 1788, to March 2, 1789, at 242–43 (June 19, 1788) (Roscoe R. Hill, ed., Washington, GPO 1937). **15.** 2 Farrand's 180. **16.** *Id.* at 251–54. **17.** *Id.* at 252. **18.** *Id.* at 251. **19.** *Id.* at 251–52. **20.** *Id.* at 251–53. **21.** *Id.* at 253. **22.** *Id.* at 253–54. **23.** 2 Story's Commentaries § 836. **24.** Art. I, § 3. **25.** John Bryan Williams, *How to Survive a Terrorist Attack: The Constitution's Majority Quorum Requirement and the Continuity of Congress*, 48 Wm. & Mary L. Rev. 1025, 1051–57 (2006). **26.** *Dates of Sessions of the Congress*, United States Senate, https://perma.cc/47HD-T5HA. **27.** *HAWKINS, Benjamin, 1754–1816*, https://perma.cc /QP5C-K8CJ; *JOHNSTON, Samuel, 1733–1816*, https://perma .cc/4DGT-2FP5. **28.** S. Jour., 1st Cong., 2d Sess. 101 (Jan. 4, 1790). **29.** 26 Cong. Rec. 2006 (1894). **30.** Josh Blackman & Seth Barrett Tillman, *Sweeping and Forcing the President into Section 3*, 28 Tex. Rev. L. & Pol. 350, 372, 378–80 (2024). **31.** House Rule XX 4(a), 6(b). **32.** 144 U.S. 1 (1892). **33.** *Garland*, 719 F. Supp. 3d at 592–93. **34.** John Bresnahan, *Pelosi Announcement Allows Proxy Voting on House Floor Next Week*, Politico (May 20, 2020), https: //perma.cc/4H9A-KY32. **35.** *McCarthy, v. Pelosi*, 5 F.4th 34, 37 (D.C. Cir. 2021), *affirming* 480 F. Supp. 3d 28 (D.D.C. 2020), *cert. denied*, 142 S.Ct. 897 (2022). **36.** *Garland*, 719 F. Supp. 3d at 592–93. **37.** Blackman & Tillman, *supra* at 376–378. **38.** Jefferson, *supra* § VI. **39.** Joseph R. Quinn, *COVID-19, Constitutions, and a Connected World: Assessing the Constitutionality of Remote Voting in Legislatures*, 100 Neb. L. Rev. 549 (2021).

ESSAY NO. 26: THE RULES OF PROCEEDINGS CLAUSE
ART. I, § 5, CL. 2

Each House may determine the Rules of its Proceedings . . .

—Paul Taylor

INTRODUCTION

The Constitution grants the House and Senate the power to determine the rules of their respective proceedings. This provision occasioned no debate during the Constitutional Convention, but it would prove essential for the operation of Congress. Justice Joseph Story wrote that without this power, "it would be utterly impracticable to transact the business of the nation at all, or at least, to transact it with decency, deliberation, and order."[1] Story added, "Without rules, no public body can suitably perform its functions." The U.S. Supreme Court has interpreted the Rules of Proceeding Clause to grant each house broad discretion in determining the rules of its own internal operations. The courts generally will not scrutinize the validity of those rules unless they "ignore constitutional restraints or violate fundamental rights."[2]

HISTORY BEFORE 1787

In 1629, King Charles I adjourned the House of Commons. Eleven years later, the Short Parliament in England criticized Charles for adjourning the House in violation of that body's cameral authority over its own proceedings. At about the same time, English jurist Sir Edward Coke wrote that "judges ought not to give any opinion of a matter of parliament, because it is not to be decided by the common laws, but *secundum legem et consuetudinem parliamenti*," meaning according to the law and usage of Parliament.[3] In the eighteenth century, Sir William Blackstone wrote that "as every court of justice hath laws and customs for its direction . . . so the high court of parliament hath also its own peculiar law."[4] Parliament's own peculiar law was called the "*lex et consuetudo parliamenti*," which Blackstone explained was a law discerned "out of the rolls of parliament, and other records, and by precedents, and continual experience."[5]

"As a general matter," Josh Chafetz observed, "the colonial assemblies tended to model themselves after the House of Commons, especially on matters relating to their privileges and procedures."[6] Colonial legislatures in America also asserted their own privileges to govern themselves when faced with encroachments on their power by state executives. In the 1650s, the Virginia House of Burgesses claimed for itself the authority to elect legislative officials formerly appointed by the king.[7] In 1705, the Massachusetts House of Representatives continued to work with its chosen Speaker over the objections of the governor, who refused to approve him.[8] In 1758, North Carolina's lower house refused to accede to the governor's instructions regarding the necessary quorum for doing business, insisting that at least half its members must be present.[9] In the early 1770s, a dispute between the Georgia House of Commons and the governor over who should be Speaker dragged on for two years with the House insisting that the selection of Speaker was integral to the House's independent legislative power.[10]

The Articles of Confederation did not create an executive, but they still included provisions recognizing Congress's authority to appoint its own presiding officer and any committees it might want to create.[11] Subsequently, six early state constitutions explicitly provided that their legislatures would determine the rules of their own proceedings.[12]

THE CONSTITUTIONAL CONVENTION

The Rules of Proceedings Clause first appeared in several drafts from the Committee of Detail. Draft IV stated: "The house shall have power to make rules for its own government."[13] Draft VI stated: "Each house shall have Authority to (settle) *determine* the Rules and Order of its Proceedings. . . ."[14] Draft VII stated: "Each House shall . . . settle its own Rules of Proceedings. . . ."[15] And Draft IX: "Each House (shall have Authority to) *may* determine the Rules of its Proceedings . . . ."[16] On August 6, 1787, the version of the Constitution presented by the Committee of Detail read: "Each House may determine the rules of its proceedings. . . ."[17]

During debate on August 10, 1787, there was no discussion regarding the meaning or purpose of this clause. Rather, the debate focused on another provision in the same clause dealing with a house's power to expel a Member. On September 12, 1787, the Committee of Style submitted another draft without any modifications to the Rules of Proceedings Clause. Such language was retained in the Constitution as ultimately ratified by the states. Throughout the process, there was no debate on this clause, perhaps because the background principle of parliamentary self-government was well accepted by that time.

EARLY PRACTICE

In the first Congress, the standing rules of both the House and the Senate provided for the appointment of committees. The House made all committees and committee chairmen subject to appointment by the Speaker "unless otherwise specially directed by the House."[18] The Senate made all committees subject to appointment by ballot of the full Senate.[19] By 1815, house committees had the authority to report out bills on their own without having to obtain permission from the full House.[20] The next year, the Senate created twelve standing committees of its own.[21]

JUDICIAL PRECEDENTS

United States v. Ballin (1892) provided the Supreme Court's formative discussion of the Rules of Proceedings Clause.[22] The Court explained that Congress's rules may not "ignore constitutional restraints or violate fundamental rights" and declared that "there should be a reasonable relation" between the rule of proceeding "and the result which is sought to be attained." But "all matters of method are open to the determination of the house." This "continuous power" is, when "within the limitations suggested, absolute and beyond the challenge of any other body or tribunal." Despite the admonition in *Ballin*, however, there have been many attempts to challenge congressional rules over the years.

For two primary reasons, challenges to congressional rules are usually beyond the scope of judicial review. The first rationale is based on the doctrine of standing. Federal courts can only hear controversies where a party is injured.[23] Regular citizens cannot challenge a congressional rule because they are not directly injured by the rule. For example, litigants have tried to challenge the Senate filibuster rule many times, yet "[n]o court has reached the merits of the dispute."[24] Moreover, members of Congress will have difficulty challenging congressional rules in court: The House or Senate would already have rejected such a challenge by virtue of adopting the rule. Also, there is no cognizable injury when a member is on the losing end of a congressional vote. The Supreme Court has recognized that a legislator might have standing if the challenged rule has "completely nullified" the votes of federal legislators,[25] but that standard has not yet been met.

There is a second reason why the courts usually cannot hear challenges to congressional rules. Under the so-called political question

doctrine, federal courts will not hear a case if it presents sufficient separation of powers concerns. *Baker v. Carr* (1962) observed that the political question doctrine may apply when a particular issue is committed by constitutional text to a "coordinate political department."[26] The Rules of Proceedings Clause would seem to be a "textually demonstrable constitutional commitment" of the rulemaking power to each house under the Constitution.

In rare cases, the courts have reviewed alleged violations of congressional rules. In *Morgan v. United States* (1986), the D.C. Circuit "found no absolute prohibition of judicial review in the [Rules of Proceedings] clause."[27] For example, in *United States v. Smith* (1932), the Supreme Court reviewed the Senate's decision to reconsider a presidential nominee who had already been confirmed. The Court found that because the case "affects persons other than members of the Senate, the question presented is of necessity a judicial one."[28] And in *Christoffel v. United States* (1949), the Supreme Court permitted a challenge to a perjury conviction resulting from testimony before a House committee where the committee failed to maintain a quorum under its rules.[29] Review was proper, the Court held, because the violation of the rule resulted in denial of a fundamental right. However, in *United States v. Rostenkowski* (1995), the D.C. Circuit refused to hear a case about an ambiguous House or Senate Rule.[30] Such a difficult interpretation "would effectively be making the Rules—a power that the [Rules of Proceedings] Clause reserves to each House alone."

Finally, the Court has made clear that the Rules of Proceedings Clause only grants Congress the power to make rules regarding its internal proceedings. *INS v. Chadha* (1983) ruled that this power "only empowers Congress to bind itself."[31]

Cite as: Paul Taylor, *The Rules of Proceedings Clause, in* THE HERITAGE GUIDE TO THE CONSTITUTION 80 (Josh Blackman & John G. Malcolm eds., 3d ed. 2025).

Notes

1. Joseph Story, A Familiar Exposition of the Constitution of the United States, § 137 (1840).   **2.** *United States v. Ballin*, 144 U.S. 1, 5 (1892).   **3.** Sir Edward Coke, The Fourth Part of the Institutes of the Laws of England: Concerning the Jurisdiction of Courts 15 (1797).   **4.** 1 Blackstone

163.   **5.** *Id.*   **6.** Josh Chafetz, *Leaving the House: The Constitutional Status of Resignation from the House of Representatives,* 58 Duke L.J. 177, 196 (2008).   **7.** Warren M. Billings, A Little Parliament: The Virginia General Assembly in the Seventeenth Century 35 (2004).   **8.** Evarts

Boutell Greene, The Provincial Governor in the English Colonies of North America 150 (1966). **9.** Jack P. Greene, The Quest for Power: The Lower Houses of Assembly in the Southern Royal Colonies, 1689–1776, at 217–19 (1963). **10.** *Id.* at 433–36. **11.** Articles of Confederation, art. IX, § 5. **12.** Del. Const. of 1776, art. V; Ga. Const. of 1777, art. VII; Md. Const. of 1776, art. XXIV; Mass. Const. of 1780, pt. 2, ch. 1, § 2, art. VII; *id.*, § 3, art. X; N.H. Const. of 1784, pt. 2, Senate, para. 12; *id.*, House of Reps., para. 12; Va. Const. of 1776, para. 4. **13.** 2 Farrand's 140. **14.** *Id.* at 156. **15.** *Id.* at 158. **16.** *Id.* at 166. **17.** *Id.* at 180. **18.** H. Journal, 1st Cong., 1st Sess. 140 (Jan. 13, 1790). **19.** S. Journal, 1st Cong., 1st Sess. 13 (Apr. 16, 1789). **20.** Ralph Volney Harlow, The History of Legislative Methods in the Period Before 1825, at 222, 225–26 (1917). **21.** Gerald Gamm & Kenneth Shepsie, *Emergence of Legislative Institutions: Standing Committees in the House and Senate, 1810–1825*, 14 Legis. Stud. Q. 39, 53–57 (1989). **22.** 144 U.S. 1 (1892). **23.** *Allen v. Wright*, 468 U.S. 750 (1984). **24.** *Common Cause v. Biden*, 748 F.3d 1280, 1282 n.2 (D.C. Cir. 2014). **25.** *Raines v. Byrd*, 521 U.S. 811, 824 (1997). **26.** 369 U.S. 186, 217 (1962). **27.** 801 F.2d 445, 449 (D.C. Cir. 1986). **28.** 286 U.S. 6, 33 (1932). **29.** 338 U.S. 84, 92 (1949). **30.** 59 F.3d 1291, 1306–07 (D.C. Cir. 1995). **31.** 462 U.S. 919, 956 n.21 (1983).

⁓

ESSAY NO. 27: THE PUNISHMENT AND EXPULSION CLAUSE
ART. I, § 5, CL. 2

Each House may . . . punish its Members for disorderly Behaviour, and, with the Concurrence of two thirds, expel a Member.

—Michael Stern

INTRODUCTION

The British Parliament, colonial assemblies, and early state legislatures claimed and exercised the power to discipline and expel members of their respective bodies for a variety of offenses or causes. The Punishment and Expulsion Clause of the Constitution vests each house of Congress with this power with respect to its own members but limits it in two ways. First, the power of punishment is limited to "disorderly Behaviour." The meaning of this term has been subject to longstanding debate. In modern times, both houses have construed "disorderly Behaviour" to encompass a wide range of misconduct found to be inconsistent with the public trust or to reflect discredit upon Congress.

Second, the power of expulsion, while not expressly limited to disorderly behavior, may be exercised only by a two-thirds vote. This structural limitation has ensured that expulsion is employed only in the most serious of cases. There have been only six expulsions in the House and fifteen in the Senate, and the vast majority of those expelled were members who supported the Confederacy during the Civil War.

HISTORY BEFORE 1787

Since the mid-sixteenth century, the English Parliament has exercised the power to punish its own members, often in retaliation for unpopular or intemperate speech in parliamentary debate. For example, in 1621, Thomas Sheppard, a member of Parliament, was expelled because of "his vehement opposition to a bill for keeping the Sabbath," which angered the Puritan sponsors of the legislation.[1] Parliament also had the general power to punish private citizens and others for perceived breaches of parliamentary privilege, although only members could be expelled. By the eighteenth century, internal parliamentary discipline had developed into a distinct practice that targeted members who accepted bribes or otherwise violated parliamentary rules or norms.[2] This discipline most often entailed expulsion, sometimes combined with other punishment such as imprisonment in the Tower of London.[3]

In America, colonial assemblies often asserted and exercised the power to punish or expel members.[4] Although there was little if any formal authority for this power, it was claimed as an inherent legislative function and was only occasionally challenged by royal governors.[5] American attitudes toward parliamentary discipline were strongly influenced by the mid-eighteenth-century case of John Wilkes, a radical and controversial member of Parliament. The House of Commons repeatedly expelled or refused to seat him for various offenses, mostly offenses involving libelous or inflammatory speech and writings. However, his constituents, despite knowing the accusations against him, continued to reelect him to Parliament.[6] American colonists were outraged by the treatment of Wilkes, which reminded them of their own grievances against the British government. Joseph Warren of the Boston Sons of Liberty, for example, wrote to Wilkes in 1769 that "[y]our expulsion from the seat in the House of Commons to which you was so Honorably elected and for which you are so eminently qualified has filled America with Grief."[7]

Although the Wilkes case did not cause Americans to reject the power of legislative punishment and expulsion altogether, it influenced a number of early state constitutions to limit the power of re-expulsion.[8] For example, Pennsylvania provided that its house of representatives "may expel a member, but not a second time for the same cause."[9]

Under the Articles of Confederation, the national legislature lacked the power to punish or expel delegates. Instead, states retained the power to recall delegates at will: "[D]elegates shall be annually appointed in such manner as the legislature of each State shall direct . . . with a power reserved to each State, to recall its delegates, or any of them, at any time within the year, and to send others in their stead for the remainder of the year."[10]

THE CONSTITUTIONAL CONVENTION

During the Constitutional Convention, a draft from the Committee of Detail stated that "[t]he house of delegates shall have power over its own members" but raised for discussion the question of "how far the right of expulsion may be proper."[11] Another draft stated that "[e]ach House shall have Authority . . . to punish its own Members." Alterations were made in the text: The words "for disorderly and indecent Behaviour" were added after "own Members," but the words "and indecent" were later crossed out.[12] The same draft also stated that "[e]ach House may expel a Member, but not a second Time for the same Offence."[13] However, the prohibition on repeat expulsions, designed to prevent the type of abuse decried by supporters

of Wilkes, did not advance. The Committee of Detail's report to the Convention simply stated that "[e]ach House . . . may punish its members for disorderly behaviour; and may expel a member."[14]

When the proposed language came before the Convention, James Madison of Virginia objected that expulsion could be "dangerously abused" and "was too important to be exercised by a bare majority of a quorum."[15] Gouverneur Morris of Pennsylvania countered that a majority could be trusted with the power of expulsion and that a supermajority requirement might lead to abuse by the minority. However, the Convention overwhelmingly supported Madison's amendment to require a two-thirds vote for expulsion.[16] With that revision, the clause was approved in its final form.

There is no record of further debate about the Punishment and Expulsion Clause either during the Convention or during ratification.[17]

DEFINING "DISORDERLY BEHAVIOUR"

There has been long-standing debate over the scope of "disorderly Behaviour" punishable under the clause. Justice James Wilson explained in his 1791 *Lectures on Law* that "indecency or licentiousness of language, in the course of debate" was an example of "disorderly behavior" punishable under the clause.[18] The Speech or Debate Clause prevents a member from being "questioned in any other Place" for his "Speech or Debate." (See Essay No. 32.) The member *can* be punished for "Speech or Debate" in his own house, but what of misconduct outside of debate? William Rawle, an early constitutional commentator, asserted that "misbehaviour out of the walls of the house or within them, when it is not in session, would not fall within the meaning" of disorderly behavior as that term is used in the Constitution.[19]

Justice Joseph Story wrote that Congress's power to make rules about misconduct would be ineffective unless Congress also had "a power to punish for disorderly behavior, or disobedience [of] those rules."[20] However, Story did not necessarily accept Rawle's narrow view of what constituted "disorderly behavior." Story contended that the scope of "disorderly Behaviour" does "not appear to have been settled by any authoritative adjudication of either house of congress."[21]

In 1797, the Senate expelled Senator William Blount for his participation in a conspiracy involving Aaron Burr. Story contended that this precedent established that "expulsion may be for any misdemeanor, which, though not punishable by any statute, is inconsistent with the trust and duty of a senator."[22] One century later, the Supreme Court later adopted a similar position: "The right to expel extends to all cases where the offense is such as in the judgment of the Senate is inconsistent with the trust and duty of a member."[23] Story did not take a firm position on how to define this standard, but he doubted the practicability of trying "to draw a clear line of distinction between the right to inflict the punishment of expulsion, and any other punishment upon a member, founded on the time, place, or nature of the offence."[24]

A narrow construction of the term "disorderly behavior" might exclude conduct that did not directly disrupt legislative proceedings or was committed outside the halls of Congress or at a time when it was not in session. But Congress has not taken this narrow view of the expulsion power. According to the Congressional Research Service, "[e]ach house of Congress has disciplined its own Members for conduct which has not necessarily violated any specific rule or law, but which was found to breach its privileges, demonstrate contempt for the institution, or which was found to discredit the House or Senate."[25] As a general matter, purely personal conduct is sometimes said to be beyond the scope of congressional discipline. Nevertheless, even nonofficial acts can be punished if the body considers that they are reprehensible or discredit the institution.[26]

TYPES OF PUNISHMENT A HOUSE CAN IMPOSE

Historically, the primary punishment imposed on members has been in the form of a formal rebuke by the legislative body. In the Senate, this can take the form of a censure by the full body or, in the case of lesser infractions, a letter of admonition from the Ethics Committee.[27] A censure in the House is imposed by the full body and generally requires the censured member to stand in the well of the House to be verbally rebuked by the Speaker.[28] A reprimand is a less severe rebuke that is also imposed by a vote of the House but does not include the ignominy of a verbal rebuke.[29] For infractions that do not merit action by the full House, the Ethics Committee may issue a letter of reprimand.[30]

Other possible sanctions include fines and monetary assessments.[31] These are imposed infrequently and often have been in the nature of restitution rather than fines of a punitive nature.[32]

PUNISHING OR EXPELLING A MEMBER FOR MISCONDUCT BEFORE HIS CURRENT TERM BEGAN

Early precedents of the House found that there was no constitutional power to punish or expel for misconduct in a prior Congress.[33] *Powell v. McCormack* (1969) Court cited these precedents without expressing a view on the issue.[34] *Powell's* dicta may reflect a constitutional limitation on the power to punish or expel.[35] However, in modern practice, both the House and the Senate have clearly asserted disciplinary jurisdiction over offenses committed in prior Congresses.

In 2023, the House of Representatives expelled first-term Congressman George Santos for conduct that largely preceded his election, although the investigatory subcommittee noted that his "misrepresentations and lack of transparency continued during his tenure in Congress."[36] The subcommittee rejected the argument that the conduct was beyond its jurisdiction, stating that the Ethics Committee "has determined on several occasions that misconduct that occurs in connection with a successful election to the House is subject to review by the Committee and may be the basis for a finding that a Member has violated the Code of Official Conduct."[37] Thus, acts committed before a member's first election may constitute disorderly behavior subject to congressional discipline, at least if the misconduct relates to the election and particularly if it involves deceiving the electorate (as in Santos's case).

Furthermore, even if a member's misconduct does not constitute disorderly behavior, the member might nonetheless be subject to expulsion. Read literally, the constitutional text does not limit the grounds for expulsion to disorderly behavior or any particular conduct; it merely requires a two-thirds vote. Professor David Currie has observed that "it is hard to imagine why the House should be licensed to employ only the extreme sanction of expulsion, and not lesser penalties, in other cases [not involving disorderly behavior]."[38] One possible explanation is that punishment is simply designed to deter behavior that actually disrupts the legislative process, while expulsion aims to remove members who are deemed unfit to serve.

THE APPLICABILITY OF JUDICIAL REVIEW

The courts have rarely had occasion to pass on congressional discipline matters. Expulsion, the most serious penalty, is uncommon. *Powell v. McCormack* did not involve expulsion. Rather, Representative Adam Clayton Powell was "excluded" based on the House's authority to judge qualifications. However, dicta in *Powell* and in other cases suggest that a congressional expulsion would present a nonjusticiable political question.

Other punishments, while they may not raise political questions, present different justiciability challenges. Censure and reprimand, the most common punishments, likely do not present injuries that can be redressed by a court. Under the Speech or Debate Clause and separation of powers principles, courts lack the power to order Congress to rescind these measures. Other punishments, like fines, present closer justiciability issues.[39]

OPEN QUESTIONS

- Could the House or Senate impose a suspension on members that would prohibit them from voting or performing other legislative functions for a period of time? Would such a punishment unconstitutionally deprive the member's constituents of representation (without the two-thirds vote required for expulsion)?
- Could a member be expelled for conduct that does not amount to disorderly behavior or for any reason (or no reason) at all? Could such an expulsion be subject to judicial review?
- Could the House or Senate impose punitive fines or even imprisonment as a punishment of members? Could members challenge such punishments in court?

Cite as: Michael Stern, *The Punishment and Expulsion Clause, in* THE HERITAGE GUIDE TO THE CONSTITUTION 83 (Josh Blackman & John G. Malcolm eds., 3d ed. 2025).

Notes

1. Josh Chafetz, Congress's Constitution: Legislative Authority and the Separation of Powers 234 (2017). **2.** Josh Chafetz, Congress's Constitution, *supra* at 232–38; Josh Chafetz, Democracy's Privileged Few: Legislative Privilege and Democratic Norms in the British and American Constitutions 193–96 (2007). **3.** 6 William Cobbett, The Parliamentary History of England 1071 (1810). **4.** Mary Patterson Clarke, Parliamentary Privilege in the American Colonies 173–204 (1943). **5.** *Id.* at 200–01. **6.** Benjamin Cassady, *"You've Got Your Crook, I've Got Mine:" Why the Disqualification Clause Doesn't (Always) Disqualify*, 32 Quinnipiac L. Rev. 209, 223–37 (2014). **7.** Pauline Maier, *John Wilkes and American Disillusionment with Britain*, 20 Wm. & Mary Q. 373, 383 & n.31 (1963). **8.** Cassady, *supra* at 238–39. **9.** Pa. Const. of 1776, § 9; Cassady, *supra* at 230, 237–42; Chafetz, Congress's Constitution, at 238–39. **10.** Articles of Confederation, art. V, § 1. **11.** 2 Farrand's 140. **12.** *Id.* at 156. **13.** *Id.* **14.** *Id.* at 180; Chafetz, Congress's Constitution, at 240. **15.** 2 Farrand's 254. **16.** *Id.* **17.** Chafetz, Democracy's Privileged Few, at 208 & n.9. **18.** James Wilson, Lectures on Law: Part Two: Of the Constitutions of the United States and of Pennsylvania—Of the Legislative Department (1791). **19.** 2 William Rawle, A View of the Constitution of the United States of America, ch. IV (2d ed. 1829). **20.** 3 Story's Commentaries § 835. **21.** *Id.* at § 836. **22.** *Id.* **23.** 166 U.S. 661, 669–70 (1897). **24.** 3 Story's Commentaries § 836. **25.** Jack Maskell, Cong. Rsrch. Serv., RL31382, Expulsion, Censure, Reprimand, and Fine: Legislative Discipline in the House of Representatives 2 (2016), https://perma.cc/2SMH-GWHU. **26.** *Id.* at 10–11. **27.** Senate Ethics Manual 15 (2003), https://perma.cc/HJT8-JZAJ. **28.** Maskell, *supra* at 10. **29.** *Id.* at 12. **30.** *Id.* at 16. **31.** Id. at 13–15. **32.** *Id.* at 15. Senate Ethics Manual 15. **33.** *Powell v. McCormack*, 395 U.S. 486, 508–09 & n.29 (1969). **34.** *Id.* **35.** *The Constitutional Framework for Congress's Ability to Uphold Standards of Member Conduct*, Hearing Before Subcomm. on the Const., Civil Rights, and Civil Liberties of the Comm. on the Judiciary, U.S. H. of Rep., 117th Cong., 1st Sess., 43–45 (Mar. 11, 2021). **36.** In the Matter of Allegations Relating to Representative George Santos, Report of an Investigative Subcomm. of the House Comm. on Ethics 11 (Nov. 9, 2023), https://perma.cc/TB2A-MFY4. **37.** *Id.* at 15. **38.** David P. Currie, The Constitution in Congress: Democrats and Whigs 1829–1861, at 218 (2005); Michael Stern, *George Santos, the Expulsion Power, and Fun with Textualism*, Point of Order Blog (May 10, 2023), https://perma.cc/F7HX-C2X4. **39.** *Massie v. Pelosi*, nex72 F.4th 319 (D.C. Cir. 2023).

⌒〜

ESSAY NO. 28: THE JOURNAL CLAUSE
ART. I, § 5, CL. 3

Each House shall keep a Journal of its Proceedings, and from time to time publish the same, excepting such Parts as may in their Judgment require Secrecy; and the Yeas and Nays of the Members of either House on any question shall, at the Desire of one fifth of those Present, be entered on the Journal.

—C. Towner French

INTRODUCTION

In the English Parliament, the practice of keeping a journal of legislative activities dates from the thirteenth century, and the tradition carried over to the colonies and to the states. The Journal Clause reflects this long-standing practice and has four primary elements: (i) The House and Senate are required to keep a journal; (ii) they are required to publish the journal only from "time to time"—a period not defined in the Constitution; (iii) the House and Senate have nearly complete discretion as to whether to hold sessions in secret; and (iv) with a one-fifth vote, the "Yeas and Nays" on "any question" shall be published in the journal. During the Constitutional Convention and ratification debates, only the second and third elements caused debate. Critics warned that Congress could shroud its proceedings in secret and would rarely publish the journal. To this day, some congressional proceedings are still held as closed sessions—that is, closed to the public, and only open to members and their staff. But over time, more sessions became open to the public. In the early years of the Republic, very little information was entered into the journal. During the nineteenth century, private records provided accounts of congressional proceedings in more depth. Following the Civil War, however, Congress began to publish the official *Congressional Record*. And in modern times, members of Congress can "revise" remarks in the *Record*, and even enter speeches that were never actually delivered on the floor.

HISTORY BEFORE 1787

The *Parliament Rolls of Medieval England* were compiled as far back as the thirteenth century, and the official *House of Lords Journal* and *House of Commons Journal* date from the early sixteenth century.[1] Parliament's journals historically contained a very basic record of proceedings that summarized the activities of each house: bills proposed and passed, votes counted, messages to and from each house, and communications with the Crown.[2]

During the colonial period, parliamentary officers were Crown officers. As a result, the Executive had power to control the Journal Clerk and the *Journal*, which was the official record of parliamentary proceedings. In the thirteen colonies, local lower houses attempted to appoint and control their own journals and journal clerks, as well as to exclude royal governors from the floor during debate.[3] It was widely believed that only in this fashion could freedom of speech in debate in colonial assemblies be maintained without interference by the monarch and colonial governors. This history also explains in part why parliamentary houses did not report debate and did not want it reported.[4] Members feared punishment or reprisals not by voters but by royal officers.

Around 1771, some members of Parliament sought to expand the scope of the journals to include a record of the actual debates.[5] Parliament formally acceded to this approach in 1803 with the introduction of *Hansard*, or the Official Report.[6]

The Articles of Confederation required Congress "to publish the Journal of their proceedings monthly."[7] However, there was an exception for "such parts thereof relating to treaties, alliances, or military operations, as in their judgment require secrecy," and "any delegate" could request the entering into the journal of the "the yeas and nays of the delegates of each State." Delegates could also request a "transcript" of the Journal, which would be laid "before the legislatures of the several states."

THE CONSTITUTIONAL CONVENTION

By 1787, the practice of keeping and publishing a journal of the legislature's activities was well-entrenched and uncontroversial. Two drafts from the Committee of Detail included a version of the Journal Clause.[8] On August 6, the Committee delivered this text to the Convention: "The House of Representatives, and the Senate, when it shall be acting in a legislative capacity, shall keep a Journal of their proceedings, and shall, from time to time, publish them: and the yeas and nays of the members of each House, on any question, shall[,] at the desire of one-fifth part of the members present, be entered on the journal."[9]

The delegates debated this issue on August 10.[10] Gouverneur Morris of Pennsylvania thought the one-fifth requirement would "disadvantage" the "small States" and argued that "any individual ought to be authorized to call for [the yeas and nays]."[11] Roger Sherman of Connecticut preferred to "strike out the yeas & nays altogether," arguing that "they never have done any good" because members do not list the "reasons" for their votes. Nathaniel Gorham pointed to "abuses" in his home state of Massachusetts where the "yeas & nays" were "misleading the people who never know the reasons determining the votes."[12] Morris's motion was rejected unanimously. Edmund Randolph of Virginia would have allowed "any member of the Senate . . . to enter his dissent" on a vote; Morris and James Wilson of Pennsylvania countered that the majority would also have a right to record their votes, and the Journal would be filled "like the records of a Court, with replications [and] rejoinders."[13] This motion was defeated. Elbridge Gerry of Massachusetts

proposed an exception: The proceedings would be published "except such parts thereof as in their judgment require secrecy."[14]

The following day, the delegates returned to the clause. Gerry and Sherman proposed that the House and Senate should not be required to publish matters that "related to treaties & military operations."[15] They would have given the House "discretion in such cases." This motion was defeated. Oliver Ellsworth of Connecticut would have struck the Journal Clause altogether. He thought "[t]he Legislature will not fail to publish their proceedings from time to time," and if the journal were "improperly omitted," the people would "call for it."[16] Wilson defended the clause. He thought "[t]he people have a right to know what their Agents are doing or have done, and it should not be in the option of the Legislature to conceal their proceedings."[17] Ellsworth's proposal failed, but the secrecy requirement passed by a vote of six to four with one state divided.

The Committee of Style made some slight edits.[18] On September 14, Gerry and George Mason of Virginia argued that the secrecy exception should be limited to the Senate, but "[i]t was intimated on the other side that cases might arise where secrecy might be necessary in both Houses." For example, the House might vote on "Measures preparatory to a declaration of war."[19] This proposal was defeated, and no further changes were made.[20]

The Journal Clause did not require that the content of debates be recorded. The Framers presumably only intended that the basic proceedings and rules be recorded as had been the previous British practice. However, the Journal Clause did represent a significant break from British practice.[21] Under the Constitution, the executive branch was excluded from exercising power over the journal, and the Incompatibility Clause barred appointed executive branch officials from being a member of either house. (See Essay No. 91.) However, this separation of powers meant that the Journal was "captured" by the presiding officers and the majorities in each house, and whoever controls the journal can control the house's agenda.

THE RATIFICATION DEBATES

At the Virginia ratifying convention, the secrecy provision proved controversial. Patrick

Henry charged that "[t]he liberties of a people never were, nor ever will be, secure, when the transactions of their rulers may be concealed from them."[22] Mason said the clause "enables [Congress] to keep the negotiations about treaties secret" and added that "under this veil they may conceal any thing and every thing."[23] Mason contrasted the Journal Clause with the Articles of Confederation, which required that the journal be published monthly and specified that only certain matters could be excluded for secrecy. By contrast, under the Constitution, Congress "may conceal what they please."[24] James Madison assured his fellow Virginians that the discretion was only designed to allow flexibility for the purposes of accuracy and convenience.[25]

In the North Carolina ratifying convention, William R. Davie explained that the phrase "from time to time" meant that it was the "sense of the Convention" that the journal would be "published at the end of every session."[26] However, he added, "there could be no doubt of their publishing [journals] as often as it would be convenient and proper, and that [Congress] would conceal nothing but what it would be unsafe to publish."[27]

EARLY PRACTICE

During the early years of the Republic, the congressional journal primarily contained a very basic record of proceedings. It generally included only a list of members' rules, votes, and the titles of bills and resolutions that were introduced but did not normally include the text of those bills or resolutions.

Professor Seth Barrett Tillman wrote that in the antebellum period, "legislative journals functioned much like (contemporaneous and modern) court dockets—journals reported a very limited range of information and events."[28] According to Tillman, "it is not surprising that one gleans very little substantive history from these [j]ournal entries [from the Early Republic]." Rather, he concluded, "[t]he [j]ournal[s] simply do[] not meaningfully report [on] the debate, arguments, or evidence [in election contests] put forward by the members. . . ."

Justice Joseph Story observed that "[t]he object of the whole clause is to ensure publicity to the proceedings of the legislature, and a

correspondent responsibility of the members to their respective constituents."[29] Given the fact that early journals did not include the content of debates, their ability to foster popular understanding and accountability was limited. However, attendance was recorded, and votes related to party agendas and other divisive issues could be recorded at the discretion of any one-fifth minority. These standards provided at least some public accountability.

Early Congresses also chose to hold some proceedings in secret. The Senate held its legislative sessions in secret until 1794.[30] Senate executive sessions to consider nominations and treaties were also closed to the public.[31] However, since the War of 1812, both houses have kept most of their proceedings open to the public. The U.S. Supreme Court ruled that each house has complete discretion with respect to which proceedings will be made publicly available in the journal.[32]

PUBLISHED JOURNALS

From the early decades of the Republic, newspaper reporters have attempted to record or summarize the content of bills and debates for their publications.[33] In 1834, Joseph Gales, Jr., and William Seaton started publishing the *Annals of Congress*. Its formal title was *The Debates and Proceedings in the Congress of the United States*. Part of the *Annals* consisted of reports of the First Congress from Thomas Lloyd, a shorthand writer whose record of debates in *The Congressional Register* has been considered incomplete and unreliable.[34] Unfortunately, Lloyd was sometimes intoxicated when he took notes, and a later comparison of his notes to what he published in *The Congressional Register* shows "only slight resemblance" between the two.[35] The *Annals* also compiled selected paraphrased remarks of members in their speeches and debates gathered from newspaper accounts.

The *Annals* project took twenty-two years to complete, and, when finished, it covered the years from 1789 to 1824. Congress began to underwrite the project in 1849. Meanwhile, in 1824, Gales and Seaton attempted to record contemporaneous debates and publish them in the *Register of the Debates in Congress*. Both publications reported members' remarks in the third person.[36] The *Register* ceased publication in 1837.[37]

A competitive private publication, *The Congressional Globe*, began in 1833. It was published by Francis Blair, Sr., and John C. Rives. At first, *The Globe* did not attempt to transcribe debates verbatim and only included summaries. Later, *The Globe* attempted to record members' statements verbatim and in the first person. However, partisanship marred the objectivity of the editing of both the *Annals of Congress* and *The Globe*: Gales and Seaton were associated with the Whigs, and Blair and Rives were affiliated with the Democrats during the 1830s and early 1840s.[38] *The Globe* ceased publication in 1873.[39]

In 1873, Congress began to publish the *Congressional Record*.[40] The official *Record* reports the debates on the floor of each house nearly verbatim and can also include undelivered remarks and documents.[41]

MODERN PRACTICE
In modern times, the Senate has been more likely than the House to hold secret sessions. For example, the Senate continued to hold certain executive sessions in secrecy until 1929 and did not open most of its committee sessions to the public until the 1970s. Even today, many committee sessions and business meetings concerning appropriations for national defense are held in secret. The Senate also holds secret sessions during debates over classified information, treaties, and national security. Moreover, during impeachment trials, the Senators deliberate in closed session.[42]

There is a somewhat controversial practice in Congress known as "revise privilege." This privilege allows members to revise their speeches (in form or substance) and even to add a speech to the *Congressional Record* that was never actually delivered on the floor. This practice was challenged in the 1980s, but the D.C. Circuit held that the rules allowing a member of Congress to edit his remarks before publication are unreviewable by the courts.[43]

OPEN QUESTIONS

- In 1834, the Senate censured President Andrew Jackson. In 1837, the Senate retrieved the 1834 Senate Journal and proceeded to expunge the prior Senate's censure of President Jackson.[44] What was the effect of this expungement?

Cite as: C. Towner French, *The Journal Clause*, in THE HERITAGE GUIDE TO THE CONSTITUTION 87 (Josh Blackman & John G. Malcolm eds., 3d ed. 2025).

Notes

1. C. Given-Wilson et al., The Parliament Rolls of Medieval England, 1275–1501 (2005). **2.** Elizabeth Read Foster, *Procedure in the House of Lords During the Early Stuart Period*, 5 J. of Brit. Stud. 56, 56–73 (1966). **3.** Mary Patterson Clarke, Parliamentary Privilege in the American Colonies 231–32 (1971); Jack P. Greene, The Quest for Power: The Lower Houses of Assembly in the Southern Royal Colonies, 1689–1776, at 205, 207–12 (1963). **4.** Greene, *supra* at 213–14. **5.** Robin Eagles, *John Wilkes, Parliament and the Freedom of the Press 1771–2021*, UK Parliament, Parliamentary Archives: Inside the Act Room Blog (Mar. 29, 2021), https://perma.cc/7S24-KT4A. **6.** *Hansard (Parliamentary Debates)*, UK Parliament, Parliamentary Archives, https://perma.cc/5RBN-49P6. **7.** Articles of Confederation, art. IX, § 7. **8.** 2 Farrand's 156, 166. **9.** *Id.* at 180. **10.** *Id.* at 254–56. **11.** *Id.* at 255. **12.** *Id.* **13.** *Id.* **14.** *Id.* at 256. **15.** *Id.* at 260. **16.** *Id.* **17.** *Id.* **18.** *Id.* at 568, 592. **19.** *Id.* at 613. **20.** *Id.* at 653. **21.** Seth Barrett Tillman, *A Note on the Constitution's Journal Clause*, New Reform Club Blog (Oct. 12, 2023), https://perma.cc/Q66M-CUEP. **22.** 3 Elliot's 170, 315, 396–98. **23.** *Id.* at 404. **24.** *Id.* **25.** *Id.* at 460. **26.** 3 Elliot's 72. **27.** *Id.* **28.** Seth Barrett Tillman, *A Religious Test in America?: The 1809 Motion to Vacate Jacob Henry's North Carolina State Legislative Seat—A Re-Evaluation of the Primary Sources*, 98 N.C. Hist. Rev. 1, 6–7 (2021). **29.** 1 Story's Commentaries § 638. **30.** Christopher M. Davis, Cong. Rsrch. Serv., R42106, Secret Sessions of the House and Senate: Authority, Confidentiality, and Frequency 3 n.11 (2014), https://perma.cc/NXV8-72G4. **31.** *Id.* at 3. **32.** *Marshall Field & Co. v. Clark*, 143 U.S. 649, 671 (1892). **33.** Nicholas Handler, *Rediscovering the Journal Clause: The Lost History of Legislative Constitutional Interpretation*, 21 J. of Const. L. 1219, 1268 n.270 (2019). **34.** Joseph Gales & William Seaton, The Debates and Proceedings in the Congress of the United States (1834); Historical Soc'y of Pa., Pennsylvania and the Federal Constitution, 1787–1788, at 14 (1888). **35.** Marion Tinling, *Thomas Lloyd's Reports of the First Federal Congress*, 18 Wm. & Mary Q. 519, 532, 536 (1961); James H. Hutson, *The Creation of the Constitution: The Integrity of the Documentary Record*, 65 Tex. L. Rev. 1, 38 (1986).

36. Richard J. McKinney, An Overview of the Congressional Record and Its Predecessor Publications: A Research Guide (May 2020), https://perma.cc/8HBU-W3KT.   **37.** *Register of Debates*, Library of Congress, A Century of Lawmaking for a New Nation: U.S. Congressional Documents and Debates 1774 to 1875, https://perma.cc/G5EF-X6SZ.   **38.** William E. Ames, *The National Intelligencer: Washington's Leading Political Newspaper*, 66 Records of Columbia Hist. Soc'y of Wash., D.C., 71, 71–83 (1966).   **39.** John J. Patrick et al., The Oxford Guide to the United States Government 143 (2001).   **40.** *Id.*   **41.** Michelle M. Springer, *The Congressional Record: "Substantially a Verbatim Report?"*, 13 Gov't Pub. Rev. 371, 371–78 (1986).   **42.** Cong. Rsrch. Serv., *supra* at 3.   **43.** *Gregg v. Barrett*, 771 F.2d 539, 547–49 (D.C. Cir. 1985).   **44.** *Senate Reverses a Presidential Censure*, U.S. Senate, About the Senate, https://perma.cc/T56K-YGXH.

ESSAY NO. 29: THE CONGRESSIONAL ADJOURNMENT CLAUSE
ART. I, § 5, CL. 4

Neither House, during the Session of Congress, shall, without the Consent of the other, adjourn for more than three days, nor to any other Place than that in which the two Houses shall be sitting.

—James Burnham & Louis J. Capozzi III

INTRODUCTION

Under the Twentieth Amendment, Congress must convene each year on January 3 or another date "set by law." (See Essay No. 207.) That date marks the beginning of Congress's annual session. From that point, "during the Session of Congress," the Congressional Adjournment Clause governs the ability of each house to "adjourn," which the Founders understood to mean "decisions to end [a] session and to take breaks during a session."[1] The clause gives each house the unilateral ability to adjourn for three days or less. In that respect, the clause is another example of the Constitution's empowerment of each house of Congress to manage its internal affairs, just as each can "determine the Rules of its Proceedings."[2] (See Essay No. 26.) Under the rules that Congress has established, a simple majority is required in each house on a motion to adjourn. Notably, the Senate's rules have long treated a motion to adjourn as one that cannot be filibustered,[3] and the Constitution expressly exempts adjournment votes from the President's veto power.[4] (See Essay No. 38.)

THE CONSTITUTIONAL CONVENTION

The clause places two limits on the unilateral adjournment power: One house cannot adjourn (1) to a different location or (2) for more than three days without the other house's consent. Both limitations reflect the Framers' fear of potential legislative mischief.

First, during the Philadelphia Convention, the potential for one or both houses of Congress to obstruct the operation of the government by convening away from the seat of government sparked some anxiety.[5] A draft from the Committee of Detail's thus prohibited a single house from adjourning to meet away from the seat of government without the other house's consent.[6] Some delegates wanted to tie Congress's hands even further. When the committee's proposal was debated by the entire Convention, Rufus King of Massachusetts proposed that Congress should have to pass a law—thus involving the President—to meet away from the seat of government.[7] However, Elbridge Gerry, also of Massachusetts, thought it would be improper for the President to interfere with the choice of where the two houses would meet.[8]

During further debate, some delegates expressed concern that King's proposal could result in Congress being forced to meet in an improper location. Ultimately, the Committee of Detail's language was left in place.[9] With minor stylistic edits by the Committee of Style, that language remained in the final Constitution.[10]

Second, the Framers worried that a majority in one house could try to prevent the legislature from functioning by adjourning and refusing to convene for an extended period. James Madison of Virginia explained at the Virginia convention that "it would be very exceptional to allow [either house] to adjourn without the consent of the other house, at any season whatsoever, without any regard to the situation of public exigencies."[11] Several state constitutions dealt with that concern by limiting the ability of a single house of the state legislature to adjourn without the other's consent. For example, Massachusetts, New Hampshire, and New York permitted unilateral adjournment only for two days or less.[12]

Within the Committee of Detail, Edmund Randolph's draft would have given each house the ability to adjourn unilaterally for seven days or less,[13] but John Rutledge edited the draft to impose a three-day limit. That revised limit made it into the committee draft presented to the entire Convention and the finalized Constitution with no recorded debate.[14]

RATIFICATION DEBATES

The Congressional Adjournment Clause generated relatively little controversy during the ratification debates. Nevertheless, some opponents of the Constitution feared that the Senate could manipulate the clause to prevent members of the House of Representatives from returning home.

At the Virginia convention, George Mason warned that the clause would give the Senate the "power of worrying the house of representatives into a compliance with any measure."[15] Specifically, the Senate could "stop[] the other house from adjourning." While the Senators would "feel no inconvenience from long sessions," the Representatives would be "on a different ground, from their shorter continuance in office." James Monroe made a similar objection.[16]

Mason's and Monroe's concerns reflected the assumption that serving in the House of Representatives was a part-time job and that its members would be home for substantial parts of the year.[17] As mentioned above, however, Madison addressed this concern by arguing that the clause was needed to ensure that Congress could function.[18]

HISTORICAL PRACTICE:
TIME OF ADJOURNMENT

The Framers recognized that the two houses of Congress could disagree on adjournment.

In such cases, Article II, Section 3, Clause 1 vests the President with authority to "adjourn [the houses of Congress] to such Time as he shall think proper." (See Essay No. 113.) Perhaps somewhat surprisingly, Congress has never failed to agree on adjournment, and the President has thus not yet had the opportunity to exercise his power to adjourn Congress.

Congress's agreement on adjournment has persisted despite marked evolutions in its annual schedule. In Federalist No. 84, Hamilton predicted that the House of Representatives would be in session only for "a fourth" of the year and the Senate for "a third, or perhaps a half" of the year. Until the Civil War, Congress met for three to six months a year.[19] Congress would take a lengthy *intersession* recess—that is, a recess between sessions—in the latter half of the year.[20] Congress took relatively few recesses in the middle of sessions.[21] These short breaks were known as *intrasession* recesses.[22] That general pattern continued in the latter half of the nineteenth century, except that Congress generally scheduled an intrasession recess of ten to fourteen days around Christmas.[23] In the twentieth century, Congress began to take a much shorter intersession recess along with roughly six intrasession recesses per year.[24]

The risk of disagreement about adjournment has decreased in recent years because Congress now typically remains in session year-round with only brief intrasession recesses of under three days and effectively no intersession recess. As the Congressional Research Service explains, "to avoid the need for a concurrent resolution" adjourning Congress under the clause, either chamber may hold *pro forma* sessions "at least once every three days."[25] The House and Senate rarely conduct legislative business during these *pro forma* sessions, though each is constitutionally capable of doing so by unanimous consent.[26]

HISTORICAL PRACTICE:
LOCATION OF ADJOURNMENT

It is hard to imagine Congress voting to meet away from the seat of government today, but this prerogative was important during the First Congress. In 1789 and 1790, Congress fiercely debated the location of the nation's capital.[27] Seeking to boost their state's chances, Pennsylvania's congressional delegation planned to adjourn Congress from New York to Philadelphia, believing the legislators would never want to leave once they moved to Philadelphia.[28] The House agreed to the adjournment, but Vice President John Adams cast three tie-breaking votes against the move in the Senate.[29] (See Essay No. 18.) Ultimately, rather than relying on adjournment, Congress passed a law designating Philadelphia as the temporary capital and a territory along the Potomac River as the permanent seat of government.[30] (See Essay No. 64.)

JUDICIAL PRECEDENTS

The Congressional Adjournment Clause has sparked almost no litigation, and few judicial decisions have addressed it. *NLRB v. Noel Canning* (2014) discussed the clause when addressing the scope of the President's power to "fill up all Vacancies that may happen during the Recess of the Senate."[31] (See Essay No. 109.) The Court considered how long the Senate must be out of session for a "Recess of the Senate" to occur. The majority drew from the Congressional Adjournments Clause to hold that a break of three days or less is never a "Recess of the Senate" and a break of ten days or less is presumptively not a recess.[32]

The Court also held that a legislative house is "in session" whenever it convenes a *pro forma* session.[33] The Senate can thus disable the President from making recess appointments by simply convening *pro forma* sessions every three days throughout extended breaks, ensuring that no "Recess of the Senate" arises.[34]

OPEN QUESTIONS

If the Senate convenes to handle only business in which the House has no constitutional role, such as confirming presidential nominees, would the Senate need the House's consent to adjourn for more than three days? At least one scholar suggests that it would not.[35] And indeed, Hamilton in Federalist No. 84 predicted that the Senate would be in session longer each year than the House. On the other hand, at several points, the Committee of Detail's draft of the Congressional Adjournments Clause included an exception to the three-day limit for the Senate when it performed such duties.[36] This exception was subsequently struck without recorded debate.[37] One potential explanation is that the Committee of Detail originally proposed giving the Senate the unilateral power to make treaties, appoint ambassadors and Supreme Court Justices, and resolve inter-state land disputes.[38] If the Senate needed to shoulder these additional unilateral duties, then giving it greater discretion with respect to its schedule would have made even more sense.

The clause authorizes Congress to adjourn to a location away from the capital, but it presumably would want to do so only if there were a severe emergency affecting Washington, D.C. If that circumstance arose while Congress was in recess and its members were scattered across the country, could it meet elsewhere without first reconvening in Washington so that it could vote to adjourn to another location? This situation arose in 1793. An outbreak of yellow fever beset the nation's temporary capital, Philadelphia. Congress was in recess but due to return soon. President Washington questioned whether he could convene Congress in Trenton, New Jersey, where he had moved some executive departments. Secretary of State Thomas Jefferson advised that the President had no power to convene Congress away from the seat of government.[39] Congress ultimately reconvened in Philadelphia, when the outbreak was less severe.

Cite as: James Burnham & Louis J. Capozzi III, *The Congressional Adjournment Clause*, *in* THE HERITAGE GUIDE TO THE CONSTITUTION 91 (Josh Blackman & John G. Malcolm eds., 3d ed. 2025).

Notes

1. Michael Rappaport, *The Original Meaning of the Recess Appointments Clause*, 52 UCLA L. Rev. 1487, 1551 n.198, 1557 (2005). **2.** Art. I, § 5, cl. 2. **3.** Standing Rules of the Senate 15 (2013) (R. XXII(1)), https://perma.cc/QS6L-77RS; Samuel Issacharoff & Trevor Morrison, *Constitution by Convention*, 108 Cal. L. Rev. 1913, 1939 n.121 (2020). **4.** Art. I, § 7, cl. 3. **5.** 2 Farrand's 261. **6.** *Id.* at 140, 180. **7.** *Id.* at 261. **8.** *Id.* at 262. **9.** *Id.* **10.** *Id.* at 262, 568, 593. **11.** 3 Farrand's 312. **12.** Mass. Const. of 1780, ch. 1, arts. VI, VIII; N.H. Const. of 1776; N.Y. Const. of 1777, art. XIV. **13.** 2 Farrand's 140, 142. **14.** *Id.* at 156, 180. **15.** 2 The Founders' Constitution 293–94 (Phillip B. Lerner & Ralph Lerner eds., 1987). **16.** 3 Farrand's 312. **17.** Federalist No. 84 (Hamilton). **18.** 3 Farrand's 312. **19.** Rappaport, *supra* at 1500–01. **20.** *Id.* **21.** *Id.* **22.** *Id.* **23.** *Id.* at 1501. **24.** *Id.* **25.** Valerie Heitshusen, Cong. Rsrch. Serv., R42977, Sessions, Adjournments, and Recesses of Congress 13 (2016). **26.** *Id.* at 19. **27.** Fergus M. Bordewich, The First Congress 144–45 (2016). **28.** *Id.* at 149. **29.** *Id.* at 233. **30.** *Id.* at 247–48. **31.** 573 U.S. 513 (2014). **32.** *Id.* at 538. **33.** *Id.* at 550. **34.** *Id.* at 614 (Scalia, J., concurring in the judgment). **35.** David J. Arkush, *The Original Meaning of Recess*, 17 U. Pa. J. Con. L. 161, 174 n.42 (2015). **36.** 2 Farrand's 142, 156, 180. **37.** *Id.* at 262. **38.** *Id.* at 183–85. **39.** Samantha Snyder, *A Philadelphia Story*, Mt. Vernon Magazine (Fall 2020), https://perma.cc/2SN7-3NNN.

ESSAY NO. 30: THE CONGRESSIONAL COMPENSATION CLAUSE
ART. I, § 6, CL. 1

The Senators and Representatives shall receive a Compensation for their Services, to be ascertained by Law, and paid out of the Treasury of the United States.

—GianCarlo Canaparo

INTRODUCTION

The Constitution limits Congress's ability to modify the compensation received by the President and federal judges. The President's compensation cannot be increased or decreased during his term in office,[1] and compensation for federal judges cannot be decreased during their tenure.[2] (See Essay Nos. 99 and 122.) But Article I imposes no limits on how much Senators and Representatives can pay themselves. The Congressional Compensation Clause, also known as the Ascertainment Clause, ensures that the federal government, not the states, provides the salaries for members of Congress.

This proposal represented a break from the Articles of Confederation. Under that system of government, the states would pay their own delegates' compensation. Justice Joseph Story observed that paying members for their services had the benefit of "removing a virtual disqualification, that of poverty, from that large class of men, who, though favoured by nature, might not be favoured by fortune."[3] Otherwise, poor members of Congress might "be compelled by their necessities, or tempted by their wants, to yield up their independence, and perhaps their integrity, to the allurements of the corrupt, or the opulent."[4]

In modern times, Congress has empowered an outside commission and the executive branch to set congressional salaries. This regime may be vulnerable to a challenge brought under the Congressional Compensation Clause and the nondelegation doctrine.

HISTORY BEFORE 1787

During the colonial era, members of certain legislatures were required to own property and to pay election expenses.[5] Moreover, they did not receive any wages from Parliament but instead were paid by the relatively poorer and occasionally cash-strapped colonial governments.[6] This made it difficult for men without wealth to win their seats. Wealthy candidates promised voters that they would take no wages or would even personally pay for local improvements like roads.[7] Colonial governments widely perceived these practices as corrupt.[8]

After independence, states took different approaches to property requirements. Some had significant requirements, others had small ones, and a few had none at all.[9] The states also paid the compensation for their delegates to the First Continental Congress, a practice that would continue in the Articles of Confederation Congress.[10] This power gave states leverage over their delegates. States could threaten to withhold members' salaries if they did not vote the way the states wanted them to vote. States also could recall any delegate for any reason.[11]

THE CONSTITUTIONAL CONVENTION

During the Constitutional Convention, there was some debate about whether the states or the national government should pay the compensation for members of Congress. Piece Butler of South Carolina argued that the states should pay. Senators, in particular, would "be so long out of their respective States, that they will lose sight of their Constituents unless dependent on them for support."[12] However, James Madison of Virginia contended that members would have "an improper dependence" if their states paid.[13] Alexander Hamilton of New York likewise reasoned that "[t]hose who pay are masters of those who are paid."[14] Edmund Randolph of Virginia added that the whole nation had an interest in members' services and therefore that the whole nation should pay them.[15] Randolph warned that allowing the states to pay would "vitiate the whole System."[16]

Exactly how members should be paid was also a subject of debate. Madison identified a conflict of interest if members of Congress could set their own salaries. He said it would be "indecent to put their hands into the public purse for the sake of their own pockets."[17] Madison suggested that the Constitution fix the amount of compensation to some benchmark, like the price of wheat.[18] (He made the same proposal for judicial salaries.) Hamilton worried that pegging compensation to a commodity would produce "inconsistency."[19] Gouverneur Morris of Pennsylvania argued that Congress should have discretion to set its own members' pay. He saw "no reason to fear that they would overpay themselves."[20] Roger Sherman of Connecticut was concerned about underpayment. He echoed concerns from the colonial legislatures: "men ever so fit could not serve unless they were at the same time rich."[21]

On August 14, by a vote of nine states to two, the Convention decided that Congress should set the compensation.[22] The compensation would have to be "ascertained by law," that is, set by statute. A single house could not set the salaries for its own members. Rather, the House and Senate would have to agree to a compensation rate, and the President would have to sign that bill into law. In this regard, there is some check on Congress's ability to increase or decrease its members' compensation.

RATIFICATION DEBATES

During the ratification debates, the Congressional Compensation Clause became a lightning rod for criticism. Anti-Federalists argued that the clause proved that the Constitution weakened the states and gave the federal government unrestrained power.[23] Even Edmund Randolph derided Congress's discretion to set salaries as "obnoxious."[24] Patrick Henry of Virginia railed against the clause during the Virginia ratifying convention, arguing that it would not stop members from enriching themselves at public expense.[25] James Madison responded that the people would never tolerate that behavior from their representatives.[26]

When the Virginia convention voted to ratify the Constitution, it submitted a proposed amendment that would delay the effect of any law changing compensation until after the next election of the House of Representatives.[27] Similar proposals were submitted by the New York and North Carolina conventions.[28] In the First Congress, on June 7, 1789, Representative Madison would include this proposal in a list of proposed amendments.[29] It provided that "[n]o law, varying the compensation for the services of the Senators and Representatives, shall take effect, until an election of Representatives shall have intervened." Ten amendments would be ratified by 1791, but the congressional pay amendment would not be ratified until 1992 when it became the Twenty-Seventh Amendment. (See Essay No. 216.)

THE FEDERAL SALARY ACT

From 1789 until 1967, Congress set the salaries of its members directly.[30] Congress would enact specific legislation that set specific rates of pay. The Executive had no formal role in the process apart from signing or vetoing the legislation.

That practice would be changed by the Federal Salary Act of 1967, which was amended in 1985.[31] Under this statute, every four years, a commission is established that includes members appointed by the President, the Chief Justice, the Speaker of the House, and the President of the Senate. The commission reviews compensation of different federal officials and recommends changes in congressional salaries to the President. The President, in turn, transmits his recommendations to Congress. Then, if Congress takes no action within 30 days, the President's recommendations are printed in the Statutes at Large. The only way to block those changes during the 30-day window is for both houses of Congress to enact a joint resolution disapproving the recommendation. Alternatively, Congress can enact a statute setting compensation at a different rate.

In 1987, six members of Congress challenged the constitutionality of the Federal Salary Act, claiming that the statute violated the Congressional Compensation Clause and the nondelegation doctrine.[32] In *Humphrey v. Baker*, the D.C. Circuit Court of Appeals rejected the Congressional Compensation Clause claim. The panel would not read the clause "inflexibly so as to require Congress to establish specific figures in specific legislation."[33] Congress could set members' salaries however it wanted to set them as long as its chosen method was "ascertained by law."[34] The court rejected the nondelegation claim because "[r]ecent delegations as broad (or broader) than the one at issue here have survived delegation doctrine attack."[35] The Supreme Court of the United States denied certiorari in *Humphrey*.

COST-OF-LIVING ADJUSTMENTS

The Cost-of-Living Adjustment Act of 1975 provided for automatic cost-of-living adjustments for members' salaries.[36] A member of Congress challenged this statute, arguing that it violates the Congressional Compensation Clause. In *Pressler v. Simon*, the D.C. District Court held that the Clause permitted any "rational procedures" for setting salaries.[37] The Supreme Court affirmed the decision in a per curiam order without any written opinion.[38] Then-Justice William Rehnquist wrote a concurrence cautioning that the unexplained affirmance did not signal that the Court agreed with the lower court's analysis of the constitutional claim.[39]

OPEN QUESTIONS

- Do the Federal Salary Act and the Cost-of-Living Adjustment Act violate the Congressional Compensation Clause?
- Do the Federal Salary Act and the Cost-of-Living Adjustment Act violate the nondelegation doctrine?[40]
- *Humphrey v. Baker* (1988) and *Pressler v. Blumenthal* (1978) predate the Twenty-Seventh Amendment. Does the Twenty-Seventh Amendment have the effect of prohibiting Congress from delegating its power to set members' compensation to any other body?[41] Are *Humphrey* and *Pressler* still good law?

Cite as: GianCarlo Canaparo, *The Congressional Compensation Clause, in* The Heritage Guide to the Constitution 94 (Josh Blackman & John G. Malcolm eds., 3d ed. 2025).

Notes

1. Art. II, § 1, cl. 7. **2.** Art. III, § 1. **3.** 1 Story's Commentaries § 854. **4.** *Id.* **5.** Richard B. Bernstein, *The Sleeper Wakes: The History and Legacy of the Twenty-Seventh Amendment*, 61 Fordham L. Rev. 497, 500–01 (1992) (citing 1 Edward Porritt & Annie G. Porritt, The Unreformed House of Commons: Parliamentary Representation Before 1832, at 155–66 (1909)). **6.** *Id.* **7.** *Id.* **8.** *Id.* at 501–02. **9.** Donald S. Lutz, Popular Consent and Popular Control: Whig Political Theory in the Early State Constitutions 90 (1980). **10.** Bernstein, *supra* at 501–02. **11.** Articles of Confederation, art. V, § 1. **12.** 2 Farrand's 290. **13.** 1 Farrand's 215–16. **14.** *Id.* at 373. **15.** *Id.* at 372;

1 Story's Commentaries § 854. **16.** 1 Farrand's 372. **17.** *Id.* at 374. **18.** *Id.* at 216. **19.** *Id.* at 373. **20.** 2 Farrand's 290. **21.** *Id.* at 291. **22.** *Id.* at 292–93. **23.** Storing 4.10.1–.22; *id.* at 4.14.1–.10; *id.* at 3.14.1–.23. **24.** *Id.* at 2.5.41. **25.** 3 Farrand's 313, App. A, CCX. **26.** *Id.* at 314. **27.** Contexts of the Bill of Rights 137 (Stephen L. Schechter & Richard B. Bernstein eds., 1990). **28.** *Id.* at 119 (New York), 143 (North Carolina). **29.** Creating the Bill of Rights: The Documentary Record from the First Federal Congress 11–14 (Helen E. Veit et al. eds., 1991). **30.** *Humphrey v. Baker*, 848 F.2d 211, 212 (D.C. Cir. 1988). **31.** Pub. L. 90-206, Title II, § 225(a) (1967). **32.** *Humphrey*,

848 F.2d at 213. **33.** *Id.* at 215. **34.** *Id.* **35.** *Id.* at 217. **36.** 2 U.S.C. § 4501. **37.** *Pressler v. Simon,* 428 F. Supp. 302, 305–06. (D.D.C. 1976). **38.** *Pressler v. Blumenthal,* 434 U.S. 1028 (1978). **39.** *Id.* (Rehnquist, J., concurring). **40.** *Gundy v. United States,* 588 U.S. 128, 149 (2019) (Gorsuch, J., dissenting); *Paul v. United States,* 140 S. Ct. 342 (2019) (statement of Kavanaugh, J.). **41.** GianCarlo Canaparo & Paul J. Larkin, Jr., *The Twenty-Seventh Amendment: Meaning and Application,* 2021 Harv. J.L. & Pub. Pol'y Per Curiam 10, 15–16 (2021).

ESSAY NO. 31: THE PRIVILEGE FROM ARREST CLAUSE
ART. I, § 6, CL. 1

The Senators and Representatives . . . shall in all Cases, except Treason, Felony, and Breach of the Peace, be privileged from Arrest during their Attendance at the Session of their respective Houses, and in going to and returning from the same . . .
—Michael Stern

INTRODUCTION

To ensure that members of Congress are not unduly hindered in the performance of their legislative duties, the Constitution provides them with limited immunity from arrest both during their attendance at and in traveling to and returning from the legislative session. This privilege from arrest, however, does not apply in cases of "Treason, Felony and Breach of the Peace," which effectively limits the privilege's scope to the largely obsolete practice of arrest in civil cases.

Historically, the Privilege from Arrest Clause has given rise to two primary questions. First, what types of cases are covered by the exception for treason, felony, and breach of the peace? And second, do legal processes that stop short of physical restraint or incarceration, but nonetheless could interfere with the performance of legislative duties, constitute "arrests?" The generally accepted answer to the first question is that this exception broadly covers all criminal offenses, leaving the privilege applicable only in civil cases. Thomas Jefferson and Justice Joseph Story answered "yes" to the second question, but in the twentieth century, the U.S. Supreme Court suggested that the answer is "no." As a consequence, the clause has little modern relevance, although courts will often follow the spirit of the clause by adjusting their schedules to avoid unnecessary conflict with a member's legislative duties.

HISTORY BEFORE 1787

In eighteenth-century England, it was not uncommon for defendants to be arrested in civil lawsuits to vindicate private rights, such as actions to collect debts. Members of Parliament long enjoyed a privilege against arrest in these civil cases during the period when Parliament was in session and for a period of time before and after the session to allow their arrival and return. Members also claimed a broad and somewhat ill-defined privilege against other types of legal process, such as subpoenas.[1] These claims were often successful, and the privilege could be extended even to a member's servants. In time, "it became almost impossible to get any justice out of a member of parliament."[2] However, Sir William Blackstone observed that this privilege applied only in civil cases and not to "any crime whatsoever."[3]

Arrest in civil cases was also practiced in America during colonial times and into the nineteenth century. Some early state constitutions expressly recognized a privilege from arrest for legislators. For example, the Massachusetts constitution of 1780 provided that a member of the legislature could not be "arrested, or held to bail . . . during his going unto, returning from, or his attending the general assembly."[4] The Articles of Confederation similarly provided that "the members of Congress shall be protected in their persons from arrests and imprisonments, during the time of their going to and from, and attendance on congress, except for treason, felony, or breach of the peace."[5]

THE CONSTITUTIONAL CONVENTION

Article V of Charles Pinckney's draft plan, submitted on May 29, 1787, provided that "Members of both Houses shall in all cases except for Treason[,] Felony[,] or breach of the Peace be free from arrest during their attendance at Congress [and] in going to [and] returning from it."[6] This proposal, which closely tracked the similar provision of the Articles of Confederation, attracted little discussion and was ultimately adopted with only minor changes by the Convention. There was no recorded debate about the clause at the ratifying conventions.[7]

EARLY COMMENTARY AND CONGRESSIONAL PRACTICE

During his time as President of the Senate, Thomas Jefferson pointed to the limited scope of the Privilege from Arrest Clause as evidence that the Framers wisely rejected the broad "encroaching character of privilege" that members of Parliament enjoyed.[8] Jefferson understood the concept of arrest quite broadly. He explained that the privilege against arrest attaches to "all process the disobedience to which is punishable by the attachment of the person."[9] A member would even be immune from the enforcement of a subpoena or a jury summons because he "has superior duties to perform" in Congress. Jefferson's understanding was consistent with Samuel Johnson's definition of arrest as a "stop or stay."[10] Likewise, English poet Abraham Fraunce's defined arrest as "a certain restraint of a man's person, depriving him of his own will and liberty, and binding it to become obedient to the will of the law" that "may be called the beginning of imprisonment."

Three decades later, Justice Joseph Story expressed a similar view. He wrote that "all crimes are offenses against the peace."[11] As a result, he explained, "breach of the peace" would include "all indictable offenses, as well those which are in fact attended with force and violence. . . ." The clause would also privilege against arrest for "constructive breaches of the peace of the government, inasmuch as they violate its good order." Jefferson and Story both

contended that the term "arrest" should be given a broad construction beyond mere physical restraint or incarceration.

Congressional practice in the nineteenth century was to avoid conflicts with judicial process where possible. Still, many members agreed with Jefferson's and Story's view that courts could not force them to appear while Congress was in session. In 1846, for example, the House debated whether to give a member permission to comply with a subpoena to testify as a witness in a pending criminal case. Ultimately, the House voted to grant the permission requested, but a number of members agreed with the view expressed by Representative Robert Winthrop that "there was no power in any judicial tribunal in the land to compel the attendance of a member of Congress, for the purpose of giving testimony."[12] Representative John Quincy Adams, however, warned that there was "a very grave question, whether the privileges of the Constitution would save [a member] from arrest for refusal to attend."[13]

In 1848, the House Judiciary Committee issued a report regarding the case of a member who had been arrested on state criminal charges of bribery. The committee noted that "the question to what extent, if any, a Member of Congress enjoys immunity from arrest under criminal process, State or Federal, was now presented for the first time since the organization of the Government."[14] The report concluded that the Privilege from Arrest Clause's exception for "treason, felony, or breach of the peace" was "intended to embrace the entire range of indictable crimes;" hence, the arrest did not violate any of the rights and privileges of the House.[15]

MODERN JUDICIAL PRECEDENT AND CONGRESSIONAL PRACTICE

The Supreme Court has addressed two principal questions about the Privilege from Arrest Clause: What types of offenses fall within the exception for "treason, felony, or breach of the peace," and what constitutes an "arrest"?

The answer to the first question is relatively straightforward. *Williamson v. United States* (1908) held that all criminal offenses are encompassed within the exception—regardless of whether they are felonies at common law or fall within the ordinary definition of breaches of the peace.[16] The Court noted that the "exact" same three categories of offenses appear in the Articles of Confederation and were used throughout the proceedings of the Philadelphia Convention without debate or controversy. This history "demonstrate[s] that these words were then well known as applied to parliamentary privilege, and had a general and well-understood meaning which it was intended they should continue to have."[17] A review of English legal sources "leave[s] no doubt that the words were used in England for the very purpose of excluding all crimes from the operation of the parliamentary privilege, and therefore to leave that privilege to apply only to prosecutions of a civil nature."[18] *Williamson* was consistent with the view of Justice Story and the report of the House Judiciary Committee in 1878. *Williamson* is also an example of a type of originalist methodology that involves viewing the Constitution as written in the language of the law and containing technical terms of art that may differ from the ordinary meaning of those words.

The second question has been somewhat more controversial. The Supreme Court's approach to this second question departed from the views of Jefferson and Story. *Long v. Ansell* (1934) suggests that "arrest" was limited to physical restraint or incarceration.[19] In this case, Senator Huey Long of Louisiana was issued a summons in a civil action for libel. The Court held that the privilege did not block enforcement of the summons.

In a brief opinion, Justice Louis Brandeis rejected the argument that the privilege prohibited service of process, even though the refusal to comply with the summons could result in contempt and even incarceration. Rather, Justice Brandeis found that the language of the clause is "exact" and "leaves no room for a construction which would extend the privilege beyond the terms of the grant." The Court concluded that "[h]istory confirms the conclusion that the immunity is limited to arrest."

Justice Brandeis did not even cite the views of Jefferson and Story. In fact, *Long* arguably undermined Jefferson's and Story's position, although practice in the House suggests otherwise.[20] In 1941, Representative Hamilton Fish III of New York was issued a subpoena to testify before a federal grand jury. The subpoena also restricted his movement: He could "not depart the court without leave of the court or district attorney," even while Congress was in session. Had the member disregarded those instructions, he could have been held in contempt of court and incarcerated.

The majority of the House Judiciary Committee contended that the subpoena constituted an outside interference with the right of members to attend legislative proceedings during the session. This conclusion was bolstered by the separation of powers: An Article I member of Congress was unable to attend a session of Congress without permission from an Article II prosecutor or an Article III judge. Other members disagreed with this view. Representative Estes Kefauver of Tennessee led a group who argued that a violation of the clause would occur only "when action is taken to forcibly enforce the attendance in court of the Member." According to Kefauver, the text of the subpoena did not violate the clause, but enforcement of the subpoena could trigger the privilege against arrest.

Nevertheless, almost all members agreed that a court could not force a member to testify or otherwise absent himself while the House was in session, except in cases where the member himself was charged with a criminal offense. One member suggested that such judicial process would conflict with the House's own constitutional authority to "compel the attendance of absent members." (See Essay No. 25.)

Three decades later, the Supreme Court reaffirmed *Long* in *Gravel v. United States* (1972).[21] The Court observed that "freedom from arrest [does not] confer immunity on a Member . . . as a witness in a criminal case." As a result, it is generally thought that the clause does not provide a privilege against testimonial subpoenas in criminal cases, and probably not in civil cases either.

As a practical matter, members will rarely need to rely on the Privilege from Arrest Clause for ordinary judicial process. Courts will normally adjust dates for responding to subpoenas or other process to ensure that there is no interference with legislative duties. Federal courts have also recognized as a matter of comity and judicial policy that high-ranking government officials, including members of Congress, should not be compelled to appear as witnesses unless their testimony is essential and the same information cannot be obtained elsewhere.[22]

OPEN QUESTIONS

- Members of Congress are exempted from jury duty by statute, regardless of whether Congress is in session.[23] What is the constitutional basis of this statute? Is this legislation to enforce the Privilege from Arrest Clause? *Long* and *Gravel* suggested that the privilege would not extend to a jury duty summons.
- Would the Privilege from Arrest Clause immunize a member from arrest who refused to testify in a criminal case as a material witness?[24]
- Some constitutional scholars have argued that the broader view of "arrest" held by Jefferson and Story squares with the purpose and function of the Privilege from Arrest Clause better than the narrow reading given to that term by the Supreme Court.[25]

Cite as: Michael Stern, *The Privilege from Arrest Clause, in* THE HERITAGE GUIDE TO THE CONSTITUTION 97 (Josh Blackman & John G. Malcolm eds., 3d ed. 2025).

Notes

1. Josh Chafetz, Democracy's Privileged Few: Legislative Privilege and Democratic Norms in the British and American Constitutions 122–24 (2007). 2. F.W. Maitland, The Constitutional History of England 244 (1963); Chafetz, *supra* at 111–33. 3. 1 Blackstone 166; *Williamson v. United States*, 207 U.S. 425, 440 (1908). 4. Mass. Const. of 1780, pt. II, ch. I, § 3, art. X; N.H. Const. of 1784, pt. II, ¶ II. 5. Articles of Confederation, art. V, § 5. 6. 3 Farrand's 597. 7. Chafetz, *supra* at 135. 8. Constitution, Jefferson's Manual, and Rules of the House of Representatives § 288. 9. *Id.* at § 290. 10. Arre'st, Samuel Johnson, A Dictionary of the English Language (1755), https://perma.cc/QBR2-6KRE; Peter Goodrich, Rhetoric and Somatics: Training the Body to Do the Work of Law, 5 Law Text Culture 241 (2001). 11. 2 Story's Commentaries § 862. 12. Cong. Globe, 29th Cong., 1st Sess., 767 (1846); 3 Hinds' Precedents, § 2660; *id.* at § 2666. 13. Cong. Globe, *supra* at 769. 14. 3 Hinds' Precedents, § 2673. 15. *Id.* 16. 207 U.S. 425 (1908). 17. *Id.* at 438. 18. *Id.* 19. 293 U.S. 76 (1934). 20. 87 Cong. Rec. 8934, 8949–58 (1941); 2 Deschler's Precedents, ch. 7, § 18.1. 21. 408 U.S. 606 (1972). 22. *In re Graham*, 621 F.Supp.3d 1324, 1323–25 (N.D. Ga. 2022). 23. 2 U.S.C. § 30a. 24. 18 U.S.C. § 3144. 25. Akhil Reed Amar & Neal Kumar Katyal, *Executive Privileges and Immunities: The Nixon and Clinton Cases,* 108 Harv. L. Rev. 708, 711–13 & n.44 (1995).

~

ESSAY NO. 32: THE SPEECH OR DEBATE CLAUSE
ART. I, § 6, CL. 1

. . . for any Speech or Debate in either House, [the Senators and Representatives] shall not be questioned in any other Place.

—Thomas G. Hungar & Michael Bopp

INTRODUCTION

The Speech or Debate Clause immunizes Senators and Representatives from prosecution and civil suits based on things they say or do in their legislative capacities. This immunity traces its roots to a parliamentary privilege that was enshrined in the English Bill of Rights of 1689. The clause helps to preserve the separation of powers by enabling members of Congress to legislate without fear of reprisals by the executive or judicial branches or by state governments. Justice James Wilson observed that the privilege was "indispensably necessary" for a representative to "enjoy the fullest liberty of speech" in order to "discharge his publick trust with firmness and success."[1] The Speech or Debate Clause also allows members to focus their time and energy on legislating instead of defending themselves against lawsuits brought by private individuals. The courts have addressed three primary questions with regard to the Speech or Debate Clause: What does the clause protect? How does the clause provide protections? Whom does the clause protect?

HISTORY BEFORE 1787

The Speech or Debate Clause has its origins in England's parliamentary privilege, which sometimes protected members' right to freedom of speech and debate in Parliament. According to Sir William Blackstone, the privilege "was principally established . . . to protect [Parliament] members . . . from being oppressed by the power of the crown."[2] Over the centuries, members of the House of Commons were prosecuted, imprisoned, and even sentenced to death for speeches or legislation that offended the Lancastrian, Tudor, and Stuart monarchs.[3] In these cases, the privilege was asserted with mixed success. In 1689, Parliament finally prevailed as the privilege was permanently enshrined in the English Bill of Rights.[4] It provided "[t]hat the freedom of speech and debates or proceedings in Parliament ought not to be impeached or questioned in any court or place out of Parliament."[5] After the Bill of Rights was adopted, the privilege "was never again seriously questioned or denied."[6]

Speech or Debate clauses were written into the charters or bills of rights of many of the thirteen colonies along with three state constitutions adopted before ratification of the Federal Constitution.[7] For example, the Massachusetts Constitution of 1780 provided that "[t]he freedom of deliberation, speech and debate, in either house of the legislature . . . cannot be the foundation of any accusation or prosecution, action, or complaint, in any other court or place whatsoever."[8] The Articles of Confederation copied the text of the English Bill of Rights nearly verbatim: "Freedom of speech and debate in Congress shall not be impeached or questioned in any Court, or place out of Congress."[9]

THE CONSTITUTIONAL CONVENTION AND RATIFICATION DEBATES

The Speech or Debate Clause was first introduced at the Constitutional Convention on May 29, 1787, by Charles Pinckney of South Carolina.[10] The Pinckney Plan provided that "[f]reedom of speech and debate in the Legislature shall not be impeached, or questioned, in any place out of it."[11] The Committee of Detail revised the clause, making it nearly identical to the language in the English Bill of Rights and the Articles of Confederation.[12] This version (with minor changes in capitalization) was adopted without debate on August

10, 1787.[13] The Committee of Style then revised the language of the clause to the version we have today.[14] Both Charles Pinckney and James Madison of Virginia proposed methods for interpreting the clause. Pinckney thought that "[e]ach House sh[ould]" have the power to be the "[j]udge of its own privileges," while Madison thought "it would be better" if the contours of the privilege were determined legally.[15] Neither proposal was adopted.

The clause was not controversial. During the ratification debates, there was no extensive discussion of the Speech or Debate Clause in The Federalist Papers or published opposition by the Anti-Federalists.

WHAT DOES THE SPEECH OR DEBATE CLAUSE PROTECT?

The text of the Speech or Debate Clause refers only to "Speech or Debate in either House," but the clause and its parliamentary antecedents have long been understood to encompass other conduct, albeit only legislative acts. Thomas Jefferson, who served as President of the Senate, explained that the acts protected by the privilege were "restrained to things done in the House in a Parliamentary course."[16] Justice Joseph Story added that the privilege "does not cover things done beyond the place and limits of duty."[17] For example, a "speech delivered in the house of commons" would be privileged, but if the same speech was published elsewhere, the member could be "liable to an action and prosecution" in court.[18] Story reasoned that these "same principles seem applicable to the privilege of debate and speech in congress."

The Massachusetts Supreme Judicial Court adopted a similar interpretation of the state's speech or debate clause. *Coffin v. Coffin* (1808) held that the privilege applied only to actions taken by a legislator "in the exercise of the functions of that office."[19] The Supreme Court of the United States has adopted this same view. *Kilbourn v. Thompson* (1880) held that the privilege extends "to things generally done in a session of the House by one of its members in relation to the business before it."[20]

In modern times, the Supreme Court has acknowledged that protected legislative acts are not actually "confine[d] . . . to words spoken in debate."[21] Rather, the Court held, this immunity extends to matters that are "an integral part of the deliberative and communicative processes" of "committee and House proceedings with respect to . . . proposed legislation or . . . other matters which the Constitution places within the jurisdiction of either House."[22] Under this precedent, immunity attaches to voting, drafting and proposing resolutions, engaging in committee or subcommittee hearings and meetings, preparing or authorizing publication of committee reports, and more.[23] Also covered are official investigations into subjects "on which legislation could be had," along with subpoenas issued pursuant to those investigations.[24] Even the motivation behind a legislative act is protected.[25]

Not everything that is regularly done by members of Congress is protected, however. Immunized legislative acts generally do not include speeches delivered outside Congress, constituent service efforts and communications, political activities, newsletters, press releases, and interactions with the media.[26] The Supreme Court has held that efforts to "influence the Executive Branch" outside of traditional legislative proceedings are likewise unprotected.[27] Other non-privileged activities include accepting bribes, promises by a member to perform an act (even if legislative) in the future, and the republication in a non-congressional setting of otherwise protected statements previously made in Congress.[28]

HOW DOES THE SPEECH OR DEBATE CLAUSE APPLY?

The privilege for protected legislative acts is absolute. The Supreme Court has explained that "the central role of the Speech or Debate Clause" is to shore up the separation of powers by "preventing intrusion by Executive and Judiciary into the legislative sphere."[29] Under Supreme Court doctrine, this means that legislators "are immune from liability for their actions within the legislative sphere . . . even though their conduct, if performed in other than legislative contexts, would in itself be unconstitutional or otherwise contrary to criminal or civil statutes."[30]

However, the scope of the privilege is not unlimited. The immunity extends only to core legislative activities so as to "free[] the legislator from executive and judicial oversight that realistically threatens to control his conduct as

a legislator."[31] But within that sphere, the clause is an "absolute bar to interference" that extends, for example, to the preclusion of civil litigation over legislative acts lest it "force[] Members to divert their time, energy, and attention from their legislative tasks."[32] The Court interprets the clause "broadly to effectuate its purposes."[33]

The clause has been construed to afford three distinct types of protection. First, the Clause provides immunity for members of Congress based on their legislative acts,[34] and this immunity applies in civil litigation and criminal prosecutions in both federal and state courts. Second, the clause creates an evidentiary privilege. In civil litigation and criminal prosecutions, opposing litigants cannot introduce evidence about legislative acts to prove their case against a member.[35] Third, the clause provides a testimonial privilege. Members cannot be "compelled to answer questions about legislative act[s] or produce legislative materials."[36] Because the clause confers immunity from suit, a decision by a trial court not to dismiss a lawsuit on Speech or Debate Clause grounds is immediately appealable.[37]

The Speech or Debate Clause protects against questioning "in any other Place," such as a court or grand jury. Members, however, are *always* accountable to their respective houses, which can punish or expel them for "disorderly Behaviour."[38] (See Essay No. 27.) And of course, members remain politically accountable to their constituents, who can vote them out of office on election day.

WHOM DOES THE SPEECH OR DEBATE CLAUSE PROTECT?

The text of the Speech or Debate Clause mentions only "Senators and Representatives," but the courts have extended that privilege to others, including congressional aides. *Gravel v. United States* (1972) recognized that in light of the complexity of the modern legislative process, "it is literally impossible . . . for Members of Congress to perform their legislative tasks without the help of aides and assistants."[39] As a result, congressional aides "must be treated as [the Members'] alter egos" or "the central role of the Speech or Debate Clause . . . will inevitably be diminished and frustrated."[40] Thus, the Court held that "the Speech or Debate Clause applies not only to a Member but also to his aides insofar as the conduct of the latter would be a protected legislative act if performed by the Member himself."[41]

On the other hand, the clause does not immunize congressional staff for unlawful or unconstitutional actions taken in furtherance of congressional directives. *Powell v. McCormack* (1969) held that "although an action against a Congressman may be barred by the Speech or Debate Clause, legislative employees who participated in the unconstitutional activity are responsible for their acts."[42] *Dombrowski v. Eastland* (1967) held that the clause "is less

absolute, although applicable, when applied to officers or employees of a legislative body, rather than to legislators themselves."[43] *Gravel* summarized the doctrine: Legislative aides are not covered by the privilege when they personally execute Congress's illegal commands, since executing the law is not a legislative act.[44]

The Court has also extended immunity to former members of Congress with respect to conduct during their term of office.[45] The Speech or Debate Clause does not apply to state legislators,[46] but their legislative acts may be protected by state constitutions or by virtue of the common law.[47]

OPEN QUESTIONS

- Does the Speech or Debate Clause protect informal congressional information-gathering? The Second, Fourth, and Ninth Circuits have held that at least some types of informal information-gathering are covered by the privilege.[48] The Tenth Circuit took the opposite position.[49] The D.C. Circuit has explained that the relevant inquiry is whether something is a "legislative act" within the meaning of *Gravel* and not whether there is a separate category of protected acts labeled informal fact-finding.[50] The Supreme Court declined to block a state grand jury subpoena for Senator Lindsey Graham.[51] According to the Court, doing so "was not necessary to safeguard the Senator's Speech or Debate Clause immunity" because the lower courts had "assumed that the [Senator's alleged] informal fact-finding" constituted protected legislative activity."[52]
- Does the Speech or Debate Clause protect against the disclosure of non-privileged materials that were found among privileged materials? The D.C. Circuit has held that permitting prosecutors to sort through privileged legislative materials to find the non-privileged materials violated the Speech or Debate Clause but that in camera review by the court to resolve privilege claims was permissible.[53] By contrast, the Ninth Circuit has held that "the Clause does not incorporate a non-disclosure privilege."[54]
- Are members' employment decisions protected by the Speech or Debate Clause?[55]
- Is the Vice President, in his role as President of the Senate, covered by the Speech or Debate Clause?[56] In 2023, a federal district court held that some of Vice President Mike Pence's actions in the lead-up to January 6, 2021, were protected by the Speech or Debate Clause.[57] This decision was not appealed.

Cite as: Thomas G. Hungar & Michael Bopp, *The Speech or Debate Clause, in* THE HERITAGE GUIDE TO THE CONSTITUTION 100 (Josh Blackman & John G. Malcolm eds., 3d ed. 2025).

Notes

1. 1 The Works of James Wilson 421 (R. McCloskey ed., 1967). **2.** 1 Blackstone 164. **3.** Carl Frederick Wittke, The History of English Parliamentary Privilege 23–30 (1921). **4.** *Id.* at 30. **5.** 1 W. & M., ch. 2, sess. 2 (1688) (Eng.). **6.** *Id.* **7.** *Kilbourn v. Thompson*, 103 U.S. 168, 202–03 (1880); *Tenney v. Brandhove*, 341 U.S. 367, 373–74 (1951). **8.** Mass Const. of 1780, Part I, Art. XI. **9.** Articles of Confederation, art. V, § 5. **10.** Journal of the Constitutional Convention, Kept by James Madison 58, 64, 66 (E.H. Scott ed., 1893). **11.** *Id.* at 66. **12.** 2 Farrand's 166. **13.** *Id.* at 254. **14.** *Id.* at 593. **15.** *Id.* at 340–41, 503. **16.** Thomas Jefferson, A Manual of Parliamentary Practice: For the Use of the Senate of the United States (1801). **17.** 2 Story's Commentaries § 863. **18.** *Id.* **19.** *Coffin v. Coffin*, 4 Mass. 1, 27 (Mass. 1808). **20.** *Kilbourn*, 103 U.S. at 204. **21.** *Gravel v. United States*, 408 U.S. 606, 617–18 (1972). **22.** *Id.* at 625. **23.** *Id.* at 616, 624; *Doe v. McMillan*, 412 U.S. 306, 313 (1973); *Powell v. McCormack*, 395 U.S. 486, 502

(1969).   **24.** *Eastland v. U.S. Servicemen's Fund*, 421 U.S. 491, 504 n.15, 505, 508 (1975).   **25.** *Tenney*, 341 U.S. at 377. **26.** *United States v. Brewster*, 408 U.S. 501, 512 (1972). **27.** *Doe*, 412 U.S. at 313.   **28.** *Brewster*, 408 U.S. at 526; *United States v. Helstoski*, 442 U.S. 489 (1979); *Hutchinson v. Proxmire*, 443 U.S. 111, 127–29 (1979).   **29.** *Helstoski*, 442 U.S. at 477, 491.   **30.** *Doe*, 412 U.S. at 312–13.   **31.** *Gravel*, 408 U.S. at 617–18.   **32.** *U.S. Servicemen's Fund*, 421 U.S. at 503.   **33.** *Id.* at 501.   **34.** *Doe*, 412 U.S. at 306, 312; *Dombrowski v. Eastland*, 387 U.S. 82, 85 (1967). **35.** *Helstoski*, 442 U.S. at 477, 487, 489–90.   **36.** *Howard v. Office of Chief Admin. Officer of U.S. House of Representatives*, 720 F.3d 939, 946 (D.C. Cir. 2013).   **37.** *Helstoski v. Meanor*, 442 U.S. 500, 506–08 (1979).   **38.** U.S. Const. art. I, § 5, cl. 2.   **39.** *Gravel*, 408 U.S. at 616.   **40.** *Id.* at 616–17.   **41.** *Id.* at 618.   **42.** *Powell*, 395 U.S. at 486, 504.   **43.** *Dombrowski*, 387 U.S. at 85.   **44.** *Gravel*, 408 U.S. at 621.   **45.** *Brewster*, 408 U.S. at 501.   **46.** *United States v. Gillock*, 445 U.S. 360, 374

(1980).   **47.** *Tenney*, 341 U.S. at 378–79.   **48.** *United States v. Biaggi*, 853 F.2d 89, 103 (2d Cir. 1988), *United States v. Dowdy*, 479 F.2d 213, 223–25 (4th Cir. 1973); *Miller v. Transamerican Press, Inc.*, 709 F.2d 524, 530–31 (9th Cir. 1983).   **49.** *Bastien v. Off. of Senator Ben Nighthorse Campbell*, 390 F.3d 1301, 1305–06 (10th Cir. 2004).   **50.** *In re Sealed Case*, 80 F.4th 355 (D.C. Cir. 2023).   **51.** *Graham v. Fulton Cnty. Special Purpose Grand Jury*, 143 S.Ct. 397 (2022).   **52.** *Id.* at 398.   **53.** *United States v. Rayburn House Office Building, Room 2113*, 497 F.3d 654 (D.C. Cir. 2007).   **54.** *United States v. Renzi*, 651 F.3d 1012, 1039 (9th Cir. 2011).   **55.** *Davis v. Passman*, 442 U.S. 228, 249 (1979); *Howard*, 720 F.3d at 939, 947.   **56.** Roy E. Brownell II, *Vice Presidential Secrecy: A Study in Comparative Constitutional Privilege and Historical Development*, 84 St. John's L. Rev. 423, 568–86 (2010).   **57.** *In Re Grand Jury Subpoena*, No. [Redacted], D.D.C. (Mar. 27, 2023), https://perma.cc/533L-7473.

ESSAY NO. 33: THE INELIGIBILITY CLAUSE
ART. I, § 6, CL. 2

No Senator or Representative shall, during the Time for which he was elected, be appointed to any civil Office under the Authority of the United States, which shall have been created, or the Emoluments whereof shall have been encreased during such time. . . .

—Josh Blackman & Seth Barrett Tillman

INTRODUCTION

Two provisions in Article I, Section 6, Clause 2 prohibit members of Congress from holding some other federal offices. First, the Ineligibility Clause prohibits a Representative or Senator from being appointed to a federal statutory office "created" during the time for which he was elected or for which the "emoluments" were "increased" during his term. This ineligibility continues for the duration of a member's elected term, even if he resigns from Congress. Second, the Incompatibility Clause bars a member from concurrently holding certain offices regardless of when those positions were created or whether the compensation was increased. However, if the member resigns, the incompatibility is cured. (See Essay No. 34.) Justice Joseph Story observed that the "reason" for the Ineligibility Clause was to reduce "any improper bias in the vote of the representative, and to secure to the constituents some solemn pledge

of his disinterestedness."[1] However, Story acknowledged that the clause "does not go to the extent of the principle," as the member can be appointed after his congressional term concludes, "thus leaving in full force every influence upon his mind."[2]

HISTORY BEFORE 1787

The Ineligibility Clause traces its roots to British statutes enacted in the early eighteenth century. These statutes addressed a well-known problem: The monarch would reward loyal members of the House of Commons with appointments to lucrative positions under the Crown's control. Parliamentary reformers took steps to limit this practice, which many thought corrupt. The Articles of Confederation likewise barred delegates to Congress from holding certain appointed positions in the national government.[3] However, features of the Ineligibility Clause appear to be the Constitutional Convention's innovations and without precise British or colonial antecedents.

THE CONSTITUTIONAL CONVENTION

During the Constitutional Convention, the drafting histories of the Ineligibility and Incompatibility Clauses were closely intertwined.[4] On June 13, 1787, Edmund Randolph of Virginia presented the Committee of the Whole's report.[5] It provided that members of the first and second branches of the national legislature "ought . . . to be ineligible to any office established by a particular State, or under the authority of the U. States . . . during the term of service, and under the national Government for the space of one year after its expiration."[6] In other words, members of the House and Senate would be ineligible to hold either state or national government positions. However, that ineligibility did not extend to "those [offices] peculiarly belonging to the functions of the first [or second] branch." Apparently, members would have remained eligible for certain legislative positions, such as the clerk of each chamber.

On June 22, the Convention debated the Committee of the Whole's report.[7] Pierce Butler of South Carolina observed that in Britain, a "man takes a seat in Parliament to get an office for himself or friends, or both; and this is a great source from which flows its great venality and corruption."[8] James Madison of Virginia offered a compromise covering only certain positions: "[N]o office ought to be open to a member, which may be created or augmented while he is in the legislature." Madison's language was very similar to the language of the Ineligibility Clause as eventually adopted. On this day, no action was taken on Madison's motion.

On June 23, the Convention deleted the language about ineligibility for state positions. Also, Madison refined his proposal: Members of the legislature would be "ineligible during their term of service, & for one year after—to such offices only, as should be established, or the emoluments thereof, augmented by the Legislature of the U. States during the time of their being members." Madison warned "that the unnecessary creation of offices, and increase of salaries, were the evils most experienced, & that if the door was shut agst. them, it might

properly be left open for the appointt. of members to other offices as an encouragmt. to the Legislative service."[9]

John Rutledge of South Carolina disagreed. He "was for preserving the Legislature as pure as possible, by shutting the door against appointments of its own members to offices, which was one source of its corruption."[10] Madison viewed his own motion "as a middle ground between an eligibility in all cases, and an absolute disqualification."[11] During the Virginia convention, Madison would explain the purpose behind his proposal: The Federal Convention "conceived that the great danger was in creating new offices, which would increase the burdens of the people," and his proposal was "a mean between two extremes. It guards against abuse by taking away the inducement to create new offices, or increase the emoluments of old offices."[12] On June 23, the Federal Convention voted down Madison's motion by a vote of 8 to 2.[13]

On August 6, the Committee of Detail delivered a revised version of the clause. Ineligibility would now last "during the time for which [the members of each house of Congress] shall respectively be elected."[14] This newly added language can be read to suggest that even if a member resigned, the ineligibility would continue until his elected term concluded.

On September 1, David Brearley of New Jersey reported on behalf of the Committee of Eleven. The Ineligibility Clause now provided that "[t]he Members of each House shall be ineligible to any civil Office under the authority of the United States during the time for which they shall respectively be elected."[15] This proposal was adopted by a vote of 7 to 1 with one state divided.[16]

After that vote, Rufus King of Massachusetts moved to restrict the Ineligibility Clauses to "any civil Office under the authority of the United States created during the time for which they shall respectively be elected."[17] In other words, the prohibition would extend only to new positions created during the member's term. Roger Sherman of Connecticut suggested that "the incapacity ought at least to be extended to cases where salaries should be *increased*, as well as *created*, during the term of the member."[18] King and Sherman echoed Madison's "middle ground." King's motion failed by a vote of 5 to 5.[19]

Hugh Williamson of North Carolina made a related motion: Ineligibility would apply to "any civil Office under the authority of the United States created or the emoluments whereof shall have been encreased during the time for which they shall respectively be elected."[20] This proposal passed by a vote of 5 to 4. The Committee of Style would make several revisions. The prior draft simply referred to a person's being "ineligible" to hold office. Now, it was made clear that a "senator or representative" could not be "appointed" to "any civil office under the authority of the United States."[21] This text would be adopted by the Convention.[22]

THE RATIFICATION DEBATES

The Ineligibility Clause would prove to be quite controversial during the ratification debates. Critics of the Constitution argued that this provision was not strong enough to prevent "corruption."[23] During the Virginia convention, Patrick Henry warned that "[a]fter the first organization of offices, and the government is put in motion, [members of Congress] may be appointed to any existing offices which become vacant."[24] Luther Martin of Maryland wrote that members of Congress would be "unduly placed under the influence of the President," who has the "power to nominate to all offices" and thereby "expose [members] to bribery and corruption."[25]

Federalists defended the clause. In Federalist No. 76, Alexander Hamilton wrote that this provision "provide[s] some important guards against the danger of executive influence upon the legislative body." Madison tried to downplay the concerns of the Anti-Federalists. He predicted that after the organization of the government, when new members "go to Congress, the old offices will be filled."[26] Madison assumed that new members could not "make any probable calculation that the men [already] in [appointed] office will die, or forfeit their offices."[27] He saw "[t]he chance of [a member's] getting an office" as "so remote, and so very distant, that it cannot be considered as a sufficient reason to operate on their minds to deviate from their duty."[28]

Madison did not entirely persuade his colleagues. The Virginia convention proposed an amendment to the Constitution that would have made members "ineligible to, and incapable of

holding, any civil office under the authority of the United States, during the time for which they shall respectively be elected."[29] It did not matter whether the office was newly created or whether the emoluments were increased. Similar proposals were advanced by the New York and North Carolina ratification conventions.[30]

EARLY PRACTICE

The first controversy over the Ineligibility Clause arose during the Washington Administration. Senators who were elected for terms that began in 1789 would have been ineligible for any of the judgeships created by the Judiciary Act of 1789. Senator William Paterson's term would expire on March 3, 1793. Some Senators elected to the First Congress had two-year and four-year terms.[31] (See Essay No. 16.) Paterson resigned in 1790 to become governor of New Jersey, but his ineligibility for federal positions covered by the prohibition remained in force. President George Washington nominated Paterson to the Supreme Court on February 27, 1793, but Washington quickly realized that Paterson was still within the duration of the original term for which he had been elected as Senator. On February 28, 1793, Washington "declare[d] that [he] deem[ed] the nomination to have been null by the Constitution."[32] Arguably, that nomination would have violated the Ineligibility Clause—at least Washington thought so. He resubmitted the nomination on March 4, 1793, after the ineligibility ended.[33]

Over time, as patronage grew, many believed that the Ineligibility Clause proved to be less than fully effective. Between 1789 and 1850, more than thirty constitutional amendments were proposed that would have rendered all members of Congress ineligible to hold appointed federal civil positions during their elected terms, regardless of whether those positions were newly created or whether the emoluments were increased.[34] However, none of these proposals was adopted. In 1833, Justice Joseph Story observed that "[p]erhaps there is quite as much wisdom in leaving the provision, where it now is."[35]

WHAT POSITIONS TRIGGER AN INELIGIBILITY?

The Ineligibility Clause extends to "any civil Office under the Authority of the United States."

This category likely includes certain appointed positions in the legislative, executive, and judicial branches.[36] The authors of this essay contend that this category includes other irregular positions such as holders of letters of marque and reprisal and certain territorial officers, but it does not include state positions.[37]

The authors of this essay also contend that the President, Vice President, and members of Congress do not hold "civil Office[s] under the Authority of the United States." It might be argued that if the presidency were covered by the Ineligibility Clause, then George McGovern would have been ineligible for the presidency in 1972.[38] During McGovern's Senate term, Congress approved a pay raise for the President.[39] Moreover, Ulysses S. Grant's Vice President, Henry Wilson, and Harry S. Truman's Vice President, Alben Barkley, had served in the Senate when the compensation for the vice presidency had been increased.[40] If the vice presidency was a "civil Office under the Authority of the United States," then both of these Senators would have been ineligible for that position,[41] but no suggestion that they were ineligible appears to have been raised.

Others disagree and contend that there is no difference between appointed and elected federal positions.[42] They argue that all such positions are "office[s] under the Authority of the United States."[43] They might also contend that even if the President and Vice President hold an "Office under the Authority of the United States," they are *elected* to this position, not *appointed*, so these two positions would not be subject to the Ineligibility Clause.

A contrary example is the Senate seat that was held by Prentiss Marsh Brown of Michigan.[44] Brown served in the House when the compensation for members of Congress had been increased. At this time, prior to ratification of the Twenty-Seventh Amendment, it was lawful for Brown, as well as for other *elected* members of the House and Senate, to receive the authorized increased salary compensation. (See Essay Nos. 30 and 216.) During that House term, Brown was then *appointed* by his state's governor to fill a vacant Senate seat. Brown then received, as a Senator, the salary that had been increased while he had served in the House. This appointment, which occasioned no debate on the scope of the Ineligibility Clause, provides some support for the position of the authors of this essay. Again, Brown had been a member of the House. During the time for which he was elected, the compensation for Senators had been increased, and, during that House term, Brown was appointed to the Senate, and it appears that Senator Brown received the increased compensation. Accordingly, the Congressional Research Service contended that that the Ineligibility Clause only extends to appointed positions created by Congress.[45]

Furthermore, the inclusion of the word "civil" would exclude military positions from the scope of the Ineligibility Clause.[46] This provision would not bar a member of Congress from being commissioned as a military officer.[47]

WHAT DOES IT MEAN FOR EMOLUMENTS TO HAVE BEEN INCREASED?

The Ineligibility Clause applies if "the Emoluments [of a covered office] shall have been encreased during such time" "for which [the member] was elected." The term "emoluments" refers to "every species of compensation or pecuniary profit derived from a discharge of the duties of the office."[48] (See Essay No. 76.)

The concept of increased emoluments was raised in an unusual case concerning Justice Hugo Black.[49] In 1927, Black had been elected to the Senate from Alabama and he was reelected in 1932. In March 1937, while Black was in the Senate, a new pension was established for Supreme Court justices.[50] Under the law, Justices could "retir[e] from regular active service on the bench" and still receive their full salary.[51] Black was appointed to the Supreme Court in August 1937. If the emoluments of this office had been increased, then Black was not eligible to receive an appointment to the Supreme Court. Black's appointment was challenged by a pro se litigant in *Ex parte Levitt* (1937).[52] However, the Supreme Court ruled that the plaintiff did not have legal standing to bring the case. Therefore, the Court did not reach the merits.

At the time, the Roosevelt Administration concluded that the appointment did not violate the Ineligibility Clause.[53] Many Senators who voted to confirm Black reached the same conclusion.[54] However, some Senators argued that Black was ineligible.[55] More recently, one scholar contended that the new pension was best viewed as an increase in emoluments.[56] Another wrote that there was no ineligibility because Black would receive the pension at the age of seventy, long after his Senate term concluded.[57]

The Office of Legal Counsel (OLC) within the Department of Justice addressed a related issue. In 1979, Representative Abner Mikva was appointed to a federal judgeship. After Mikva was appointed, but still during his elected term, the salary for that judgeship was increased. OLC ruled that Mikva could lawfully "be appointed to a judgeship as to which the emoluments may be increased subsequent to his appointment," but during his elected term.[58] The Ineligibility Clause, OLC found, applies only "when an increase in the emoluments of an office precedes an appointment of that office."[59]

THE SAXBE FIX

It is clear enough that an ineligibility is created when Congress *increases* the emoluments of an office, but what happens if, after Congress *increases* the emoluments, Congress subsequently *decreases* the emoluments before the member is appointed to an office? In other words, can Congress "roll back" an ineligibility caused by an earlier increase in emoluments? The executive branch has taken different positions on this question over the years.

William Saxbe was elected to the Senate from Ohio for a term that began in January 1969 and would conclude in January 1974. In 1969, the compensation for the Attorney General position was increased. In 1973, President Richard Nixon intended to nominate Saxbe to serve as Attorney General, but Saxbe would have been ineligible for that position.

Acting Attorney General Robert Bork testified that Congress could roll back the salary increase to remove the ineligibility.[60] Bork contended that the purpose of the Ineligibility Clause was to ensure that the "expectation of a higher salary" will not influence members of Congress, but there will be no such expectation if the member knows he will "have to accept the lower salary." Congress reduced the Attorney General's salary to the pre-1969 level.[61] After the salary was reduced, Nixon nominated Saxbe. Saxbe was confirmed, though some Senators argued that an ineligibility could not be set aside

in this manner.[62] This "rollback" work-around became known as the *Saxbe Fix*.

However, in 1987, OLC concluded that a rollback would not remove the ineligibility.[63] The OLC opinion stated that Bork's prior position "simply ignore[d] the plain language of the Ineligibility Clause."[64] Moreover, the Bork approach grants the "executive the power to appoint legislators to lucrative and prestigious executive and judicial offices" even though the Framers had "tried to limit the instances in which the executive could offer such enticements to legislators."[65] The Saxbe Fix would "largely render [the Ineligibility Clause] a nullity."[66]

President Ronald Reagan had considered nominating Senator Orrin Hatch of Utah to replace Justice Lewis Powell.[67] However, Hatch was in Congress when the compensation for Supreme Court Justices was increased, and his appointment to the high court would have been during this elected term. Hatch was therefore deemed ineligible for the Supreme Court. Despite this opinion, in 1993, the George H.W. Bush Administration used a Saxbe Fix to appoint Senator Lloyd Bentsen to serve as Secretary of the Treasury.[68]

Two decades later, OLC would reverse course. Hillary Clinton had been elected to the Senate from New York in 2000 and reelected in 2006. In 2007, during Senator Clinton's elected term, the compensation for the Secretary of State position had been increased through a cost of living adjustment.[69] In December 2008, President-elect Barack Obama announced his intent to nominate Clinton as Secretary of State. That month, Congress reduced the compensation for the Secretary of State position to the pre-2007 level.[70] In May 2009, OLC determined that the Saxbe Fix was valid.[71] Even though the compensation had been increased and then decreased, "on net," it was unchanged.[72] Moreover, OLC found that "[o]n at least seven occasions since the Civil War, Congress ha[d] rolled back the salary paid for service in an office, and subsequent to such rollbacks, the Senate has confirmed and the President has appointed a member of Congress who would otherwise have been barred from that office."[73] A Foreign Service Officer challenged Clinton's appointment, but he was found to lack legal standing.[74]

OPEN QUESTIONS

- What is the date to determine whether there is an Ineligibility Clause violation: (i) when the person was nominated; (ii) when the Senate provided advice and consent; (iii) when the President completed the appointment; (iv) when the officer received his commission; or (v) when the officer accepts his position? *Marbury v. Madison* (1803) suggests the answer is the third option.[75] However, President Washington, in light of his actions regarding the Paterson nomination, may have viewed the first or second as the starting point. After all, Washington could simply have delayed completing the appointment until after March 3, 1793.

- Assume that Congress uses a Saxbe Fix to remove an ineligibility and the Senator is then appointed to the office. What happens if Congress, subsequent to the appointment, restores the salary increase? OLC opined that "post-appointment legislation restoring the salary of an office to its pre-rollback level would not promote the ability of the executive corruptly to wield influence over the legislative branch insofar as the appointment would already have been completed."[76] What if the statute that is used to effectuate the salary rollback also states that, post-appointment, the same salary increase should go back into effect? If this stratagem or work-around is ineffective, can Congress achieve a valid Saxbe Fix if it enacts two separate statutes and passes them concurrently with one another? What if Congress passes the two separate statutes one after the other, but both are enacted prior to the appointment? Are these and other constitutional work-arounds consistent with the Constitution or with the rule of law generally?

- The Ineligibility Clause is framed in the passive voice. What happens if Congress authorizes the President to establish a new position and the President establishes the position during a subsequent Congress? For the purposes of determining "ineligibility," when was the position "created": when the statute was enacted, when the statute went into effect, or when the President established the position per congressional authorization?

- The Ineligibility Clause is the only provision in the Constitution of 1788 to use the phrase "Office under the Authority of the United States." What positions (if any) are in this category but are not "office[s] under the United States," which is the language used in the neighboring Incompatibility Clause and elsewhere in the Constitution?[77] What positions (if any) are "Office[s] under the United States" but not "Office[s] under the Authority of the United States"?[78] Are federal civil servants in either category? Are the Clerk of the Supreme Court and the clerks of the other federal courts? Are the Clerk of the House and the Secretary of the Senate? Although these latter positions arguably are filled by "appointment," they are not filled under the aegis of the Appointments Clause or by the heads of executive branch departments acting under the Inferior Office Appointments Clause.[79] Are these positions covered by the Ineligibility Clause?

- Assume that a Senator-elect or Representative-elect does not attend Congress, does not take his Article VI oath, and does not become a member of Congress. Further assume that during the term for which he was elected, Congress creates a new office or increases the emoluments of an extant office. Does the Ineligibility Clause bar the member-elect from being appointed to that office?

- Is an Ineligibility Clause violation a "qualification" like citizenship, age, and inhabitancy or residence, or is it somehow different? Is an Incompatibility Clause violation a "qualification"? Federalist No. 52 explained that holding an incompatible office is a disqualification vis-a-vis House membership.

- OLC has pointed to a series of seven post-Civil War appointments that had gone forward using a Saxbe Fix. The first such statutory salary rollback was in 1876. Is this a persuasive history of the legitimacy of the Saxbe Fix given that the Ineligibility Clause is a provision of the Constitution of 1788?

Cite as: Josh Blackman & Seth Barrett Tillman, *The Ineligibility Clause, in* The Heritage Guide to the Constitution 104 (Josh Blackman & John G. Malcolm eds., 3d ed. 2025).

Notes

1. 2 Story's Commentaries § 864.   **2.** *Id.*   **3.** Articles of Confederation, art. V, § 2.   **4.** Seth Barrett Tillman & Josh Blackman, *Offices and Officers of the Constitution, Part VI: The Ineligibility Clause*, 64 S. Tex. L. Rev. 209 (2025).   **5.** 1 Farrand's 235.   **6.** *Id.*   **7.** *Id.* at 377.   **8.** *Id.* at 379; Articles of Confederation, art. V, § 2.   **9.** 1 Farrand's 386.   **10.** *Id.*   **11.** *Id.* at 388.   **12.** 3 Elliot's 370.   **13.** 1 Farrand's 390.   **14.** 2 Farrand's 180.   **15.** *Id.* at 483.   **16.** *Id.* at 484.   **17.** *Id.* at 487.   **18.** *Id.* at 490.   **19.** *Id.* at 491–92.   **20.** *Id.* at 487, 492.   **21.** *Id.* at 593.   **22.** *Id.* at 614.   **23.** 3 Farrand's 313.   **24.** *Id.*   **25.** Storing 2.4.48.   **26.** 3 Farrand's 311, 315.   **27.** *Id.*   **28.** *Id.* at 315–16.   **29.** 3 Elliot's 659.   **30.** 1 Elliot's 330; 2 Elliot's 245.   **31.** Art. I, § 3, cl. 2.   **32.** Message from George Washington to the Senate, with Jefferson's Note to Washington (Feb. 28, 1793), https://perma.cc/MXN9-LD55.   **33.** Letter from Tobias Lear to Thomas Jefferson, with Jefferson's Note (Feb. 28, 1793), https://perma.cc/CM84-PQH7.   **34.** Comment, *The Ineligibility Clause's Lost History: Presidential Patronage and Congress, 1787–1850*, 123 Harv. L. Rev. 1727 (2010).   **35.** 2 Story's Commentaries § 864.   **36.** Tillman & Blackman, *Offices and Officers of the Constitution, Part VI, supra* at 213.   **37.** Seth Barrett Tillman & Josh Blackman, *Offices and Officers of the Constitution, Part II: The Four Approaches*, 61 S. Tex. L. Rev. 321, 394 (2022).   **38.** Tillman & Blackman, *Offices and Officers of the Constitution, Part VI, supra* at 235.   **39.** Act of Jan. 17, 1969, Pub. L. No. 91-1, 83 Stat. 3.   **40.** 42nd Cong. Sess. III, ch. 224–226, 17 Stat. 485 (1873); Act of January 19, 1949, c. 2, § 1(a), 63 Stat. 4.   **41.** Josh Blackman & Seth Barrett Tillman, *In* Trump v. Anderson, *the Respondents' Theory Would Render Unconstitutional Every Speaker and President Pro Tempore Since 1789, as Well as President Grant's VP and Presidential Candidate George McGovern*, Volokh Conspiracy (Feb. 4, 2024), https://perma.cc/V2F6-JLUA.   **42.** Rick Hasen, *Keisler and Bernstein: Trump's Reply Brief "Officer" and "Office" Arguments Miss the Mark*, Election Law Blog (Feb. 26, 2024), https://perma.cc/M3BY-TNXN.   **43.** David Froomkin & Eric Eisner, Officers (Jan. 6, 2025), https://ssrn.com/abstract=5029416.   **44.** Tillman & Blackman, *Offices and Officers of the Constitution, Part VI, supra* at 239–40.   **45.** Morton Rosenberg, Cong. Rsrch. Serv., Applicability of the Emoluments Clause (Article I, Section 6, Clause 2) of the Constitution to the Office of Vice-President 9–10 (1973), https://perma.cc/7RCT-PXUT.   **46.** 2 Story's Commentaries

§ 789.   **47.** *United States v. Lane*, 64 M.J. 1, 8 (U.S. Court of Appeals for the Armed Forces 2006), *reversing* 60 M.J. 781 (U.S. Air Force Criminal Appeals 2004) (per curiam).   **48.** *Hoyt v. United States*, 51 U.S. (10 How.) 109 (1850).   **49.** William Baude, *The Unconstitutionality of Justice Black*, 98 Tex. L. Rev. 327 (2019).   **50.** Act of March 1, 1937, ch. 21, 50 Stat. 24.   **51.** *Id.*   **52.** 302 U.S. 633 (1937) (per curiam).   **53.** Baude, *supra* at 332.   **54.** John F. O'Connor, *The Emoluments Clause: An Anti-Federalist Intruder in a Federalist Constitution*, 24 Hofstra L. Rev. 89, 114–17 (1995).   **55.** 2 Deschler's Precedents, ch. 7, § 13.4.   **56.** Baude, *supra* at 334.   **57.** Todd B. Tatelman, Cong. Rsrch. Serv., R40124, The Emoluments Clause: History, Law, and Precedents 6 (2009).   **58.** 3 Op. O.L.C. 286, 287 (1979), https://perma.cc/C7GF-C9SP.   **59.** *Id.*   **60.** Office of the Attorney General: Hearing on S. 2673 Before the S. Comm. on Post Office and Civil Service, 93d Cong. 11 (1973).   **61.** Pub. L. No. 93-178, 87 Stat. 697.   **62.** Mary Russell, *Robert Byrd Sees Saxbe Job Illegal*, Wash. Post, Nov. 20, 1973, https://perma.cc/XL6G-KHZE.   **63.** Charles J. Cooper, Memorandum for the Counselor to the Attorney General, Re: Ineligibility of a Sitting Congressman or Congressman to Assume a Vacancy on the Supreme Court, Office of Legal Counsel (Aug 24, 1987).   **64.** *Id.* at 6.   **65.** *Id.*   **66.** *Id.* at 7.   **67.** Irvin Molotsky, *Inside Fight Seen Over Court Choice*, N.Y. Times, June 28, 1987.   **68.** Michael Stokes Paulsen, *Is Lloyd Bentsen Unconstitutional?*, 46 Stanford L. Rev. 907 (1994).   **69.** Eugene Volokh, *Hillary Clinton and the Emoluments Clause*, Volokh Conspiracy (Nov. 24, 2008), https://perma.cc/YGY2-PNSA.   **70.** Pub. L. No. 110-455, 122 Stat. 5036.   **71.** 33 Op. O.L.C. 201, 205–06 (2009), https://perma.cc/6BDT-BPQP.   **72.** *Id.* at 205–06.   **73.** *Id.* at 217.   **74.** *Rodearmel v. Clinton*, 666 F. Supp. 2d 123 (D.D.C. 2009).   **75.** 5 U.S. 137 (1803).   **76.** 33 Op. O.L.C. at 216.   **77.** Seth Barrett Tillman & Josh Blackman, *Offices and Officers of the Constitution, Part IV: The 'Office . . . Under the United States' Drafting Convention*, 62 S. Tex. L. Rev. 455 (2023).   **78.** Seth Barrett Tillman & Josh Blackman, *Offices and Officers of the Constitution, Part V: The Elector Incompatibility, Impeachment Disqualification, Foreign Emoluments, and Incompatibility Clauses*, 63 S. Tex. L. Rev. 237 (2024).   **79.** Seth Barrett Tillman & Josh Blackman, *Offices and Officers of the Constitution, Part III: The Appointments, Impeachment, Commissions, and Oath or Affirmation Clauses*, 62 S. Tex. L. Rev. 349 (2023).

ESSAY NO. 34: THE INCOMPATIBILITY CLAUSE
ART. I, § 6, CL. 2

. . . no Person holding any Office under the United States, shall be a Member of either House during his Continuance in Office.

—Josh Blackman & Seth Barrett Tillman

INTRODUCTION

The Incompatibility Clause bars members of Congress from concurrently "holding any Office under the United States." Such an office is an incompatible position. This provision was not designed primarily to protect the separation of powers between the legislative and executive branches. Rather, it prevents the President from unduly influencing members of Congress with appointments. Incompatibility provisions stretch back to eighteenth-century British statutes, colonial legislatures, post-independence state law, and the Articles of Confederation. The Incompatibility Clause's restrictions apply after a member takes his congressional oath and is recognized as a member. Its text does not prohibit a member from concurrently holding a position in state government, nor does it prevent a person from serving in both the executive and judicial branches of the federal government. It is generally accepted that the Incompatibility Clause bars a member of Congress from holding *appointed* positions in the federal government, but there is academic debate about whether it also bars a sitting member of Congress from serving as the President or Vice President, both of which are *elected* positions.

HISTORY BEFORE 1787

The Incompatibility Clause traces its roots to English and British statutes enacted in the early eighteenth century.[1] These statutes addressed a well-known problem: The monarch would reward loyal members of the House of Commons with appointments to lucrative positions under the Crown's control. Parliamentary reformers took steps to limit this practice, which many thought corrupt. A 1700 English statute provided that "no person who has an office or place of profit under the King, or receives a pension from the Crown, shall be capable of serving as a member of the House of Commons,"[2] and a British 1707 statute disqualified any person from holding a seat in the House of Commons if he held a "new office or place of profit whatsoever under the [C]rown."[3]

These statutes did not apply to members of the colonial legislatures. In the Massachusetts lower house, for example, it was "common" practice for members to be chosen as clerk.[4] Samuel Adams held both positions concurrently for several years and received compensation for both.[5] For parliamentary reformers, the primary risk was the Crown's domination of members through appointments to lucrative offices, including parliamentary clerk positions. In the colonial legislatures, there was an additional corruption-related risk: The position of legislative clerk was sometimes controlled by the popular assembly, and such bodies would give these positions to members.[6] Thus, "corruption" also took the form of self-dealing by and for members as opposed to the risk of domination of members by the executive.

The Founders addressed this problem following independence. The Pennsylvania constitution of 1776 specified that no member of the state House of Representatives "while he continues such, [can] hold any other office, except in the militia."[7] It is not clear whether this provision applied only to positions in the executive and judicial branches or whether it also included legislative positions. The Massachusetts constitution of 1780 prohibited a member of the state House of Representatives and Senate from "holding . . . at the same time" several appointed positions, including "Clerk of the House of Representatives."[8] It further specified that a member's accepting such a position "shall operate as a resignation of their seat in the Senate or House of Representatives; and the place so vacated shall be filled up."[9]

The Articles of Confederation also addressed concerns about conflicts and self-dealing through two incompatibility provisions. The Congress established by the Articles was a unicameral body. Each state would appoint delegates to that body.[10] The Articles Congress had the power to appoint "civil officers as may be necessary for managing the general affairs of the United States under their direction."[11] However, a delegate was not "capable of holding any office under the United States, for which he, or another for his benefit receives any salary, fees or emolument of any kind."[12] Moreover, delegates could not "be appointed a judge of any of the said courts" under the Articles concerning piracies, felonies on the high seas, and captures.[13]

The primary purpose of such provisions was to prohibit self-dealing: that is, delegates appointing themselves to lucrative positions created by and responsible to the Articles Congress and then concurrently holding both positions. In our view, the category of "office[s] under the United States" included only positions appointed by the central Articles government.[14] Under the Articles of Confederation, both delegates and officeholders, who were not otherwise subject to restrictions under state law, could concurrently hold positions in state governments.[15] Delegates also were not barred from holding an "office under the United States" that lacked any compensation.

The incompatibility provisions of the Articles of Confederation were not designed to facilitate the separation of powers between or among branches of the government. After all, that government had only one permanent branch: the Articles Congress. Rather, these provisions were intended primarily to prevent conflicts and self-dealing involving members and lucrative offices. By contrast, the Virginia constitution of 1776 expressly separated the three branches of government and provided that no person shall "exercise the powers of more than one of them, at the same time."[16] Scholars have observed that "the [Incompatibility] Principle seems to have been grounded less in separation-of-powers theory than in the Framers' vivid memory of the British Kings' practice of 'bribing' Members of Parliament . . . with joint

appointments to lucrative executive posts."[17] This concern about self-dealing continued through the Philadelphia Convention.

THE CONSTITUTIONAL CONVENTION

During the Constitutional Convention, the drafting histories of the Ineligibility Clause and the Incompatibility Clause were closely intertwined. These concepts are related but would operate in distinct ways under the Constitution. An incompatibility can be cured if the member resigns from Congress; he can then hold the appointed position. However, an ineligibility cannot be cured if the member resigns from Congress. Rather, the ineligibility will continue for a specific period of time.

An early articulation of these general principles appeared in a Committee of Detail draft in the handwriting of Edmund Randolph of Virginia. Randolph proposed that members of the legislative branch "shall be ineligible to and incapable of holding offices under the authority of the united states, during the term of service of the house of delegates."[18] This somewhat opaque text was not adopted.

On August 14, 1787, the Convention considered a draft ineligibility clause that would have barred Representatives from holding an appointed "office under the authority of the United States during the time for which they shall respectively be elected" and made Senators ineligible for one additional year.[19] Charles Pinckney of South Carolina "argued that . . . making the members ineligible to offices was *degrading* to them." He warned that the "Legislature would cease to be a magnet to the first talents and abilities."[20] Pinckney instead proposed an incompatibility clause: "The members of each House shall be incapable of holding any Office under the United States for which they, or any other for their benefit, receive any salary, fees, or emoluments of any kind—and the acceptance of such office shall vacate their seats respectively."[21] In short, the member could choose which position he would hold—a seat in the legislature or the appointed lucrative office—but he could not hold both concurrently. This draft resembled the language in the incompatibility clauses from the Massachusetts constitution and the Articles of Confederation. Elbridge

Gerry of Massachusetts countered that "disqualification was [not] degrading" and added that "[i]f men will not serve in the Legislature without a prospect of such offices, our situation is deplorable indeed."[22] After a lengthy debate, the Convention postponed consideration until "it should be seen what powers would be vested in the Senate."[23]

The Convention returned to the matter on September 1. David Brearley of New Jersey, chairman of the Committee of Postponed Parts, proposed a new draft that imposed both an ineligibility and an incompatibility: "The members of each House shall be ineligible to any civil office under the authority of the U. S. during the time for which they shall respectively be elected, and no person holding an office under the U. S. shall be a member of either House during his continuance in office."[24] The early eighteenth-century English statutory predecessors extended only to lucrative offices; by contrast, Brearley's proposed incompatibility provision also extended to offices to which no compensation was attached.

The Convention debated the Brearley proposal on September 3.[25] Pinckney "was strenuously opposed to an ineligibility of members to office, and therefore wished to restrain the proposition to a mere incompatibility."[26] Roger Sherman of Connecticut "was for entirely incapacitating members of the Legislature" and worried that "their eligibility to offices would give too much influence to the Executive."[27] As in the British system, it was feared that the President could reward loyal members of the legislature with lucrative appointments. The vote on the Committee of Postponed Parts' proposal failed with a tie vote of 5 to 5.[28]

Sherman had offered a compromise: that "the incapacity ought at least to be extended to cases where salaries should be *increased*, as well as *created*, during the term of the member."[29] In other words, members would be ineligible for two categories of positions: federal statutory positions that were created during their elected terms, and federal statutory positions for which the compensation was increased during their elected terms. Hugh Williamson of North Carolina followed Sherman's suggestion and narrowed the positions that would trigger an ineligibility: "The members of each House

shall be ineligible to any Civil office under the authority of the U. States, created, or the emoluments whereof shall have been increased during the time for which they shall respectively be elected." The text of the Incompatibility Clause remained unchanged: "And no person holding any office under the U. S. shall be a member of either House during his continuance in office."[30]

Williamson's proposal was adopted without any further debate.[31] The Incompatibility Clause was referred to the Committee of Style, and no further changes were made.[32]

In the end, the Framers adopted both an ineligibility provision and an incompatibility provision. The ineligibility would last for the member's elected term and apply to newly created positions as well as positions for which the emoluments were increased. The incompatibility would last while the member continued to serve in Congress. A member could eliminate the incompatibility by resigning from Congress, or an officeholder could resign from office and then take a seat in Congress. But a member's resignation could not eliminate ineligibility.

THE RATIFICATION DEBATES

During the ratification debates, the Ineligibility Clause generated a measure of controversy. Some critics of the Constitution warned that members should be ineligible for appointment to *any* offices during their elected terms and not just barred from newly created offices or offices for which the emoluments were increased. In other words, these critics wanted a *broad* ineligibility rather than a *qualified* ineligibility. (See Essay No. 33.)

There does not seem to have been much debate about the Incompatibility Clause. This provision created a *broad* incompatibility against concurrently being a member and holding an "Office under the United States." Supporters and critics of the Constitution did not seem to object to forcing members of Congress to make a choice about which position they would hold.

DUAL OFFICEHOLDING IN THE EXECUTIVE AND JUDICIAL BRANCHES

The Incompatibility Clause prohibits members of Congress from concurrently "holding any Office under the United States." It is clear enough that the position of member of Congress is not an "Office under the United States." Otherwise, Representatives and Senators would be barred from holding their seats in Congress.

Further, it has long been understood that this provision does not prohibit dual office-holding in the executive and judicial branches. For example, in 1799, President John Adams appointed Chief Justice Oliver Ellsworth to serve as an envoy to France.[33] Ellsworth held both positions concurrently. In 1801, Adams appointed Secretary of State John Marshall to serve as Chief Justice.[34] Adams requested and authorized Marshall "to continue to discharge all the Duties of Secretary of State, untill ulteriour Arrangements can be made."[35]

CONCURRENTLY HOLDING POSITIONS IN CONGRESS AND IN STATE GOVERNMENTS

It is generally accepted that the Incompatibility Clause does not prohibit a member of Congress from concurrently holding a position in a state government, though there is some contrary authority.[36] In Federalist No. 56, James Madison observed that "representatives of each state [in Congress] . . . will probably in all cases have been members, and may even at the very time be members of the state legislature." While serving in the First and Second Senate, Charles Carroll of Maryland concurrently held a seat in the Maryland Senate between 1789 and 1792.[37] Several other members of Congress also held state positions.[38] Such joint officeholding was subsequently barred by Maryland law.[39]

Nevertheless, as a matter of practice, members have regularly resigned their seats in Congress before assuming a state position. In 1790, Senator William Paterson became the first Senator to resign from Congress. He resigned after he was elected governor of New Jersey.[40] In the twentieth century, after Senate vacancies had arisen, several governors resigned and were then appointed to the vacant Senate seats by their successors.[41] In 1957, Jacob K. Javits resigned his position as New York Attorney General the day that he took his oath as Senator.[42]

However, the better view is that the Incompatibility Clause did not require them to resign, as the example of Charles Carroll,

who served concurrently in Congress and the Maryland legislature, demonstrates. Some scholars suggest that some state positions may in fact be "Office[s] under the United States" and therefore covered by the Incompatibility Clause.[43] The House has determined that "the duties of a Member of the House and of the governor of a State are absolutely inconsistent and may not be simultaneously discharged by the same person,"[44] but it does not appear that this determination was expressly affirmed in connection with the Incompatibility Clause.

In any event, state law may prohibit holders of state positions from concurrently holding federal positions. For example, Maryland amended its constitution to bar joint state-federal legislative service as well as joint state-federal office-holding.[45] In consequence of this state constitutional amendment, Senator Charles Carroll resigned from Congress to retain his state senate seat.[46]

CONCURRENTLY HOLDING POSITIONS IN CONGRESS AND IN THE EXECUTIVE AND JUDICIAL BRANCHES

It is generally accepted that the Incompatibility Clause bars a member of Congress from holding appointed positions in the executive and judicial branches. For example, in May 1800, President John Adams nominated Senator Samuel Dexter of Massachusetts to be Secretary of War. It appears that Dexter became the first Senator to resign to accept an executive branch appointment.[47]

However, there is some debate about whether the Incompatibility Clause bars a sitting member of Congress from serving as President or Vice President, and no court has resolved this issue. Joseph Story reasoned, based on several provisions of the Constitution, that the presidency and vice presidency are not "Office[s] under the United States." If that is correct, these positions are not subject to the Incompatibility Clause.[48] We agree with Story.[49] In our view, the phrase "Office under the United States" extends to *appointed* positions in all three Branches but not to *elected* positions.[50]

Our position is entirely consistent with the text of the Religious Test Clause. Article VI provides that "no religious Test shall ever be required as a Qualification to any Office or public Trust under the United States." We contend that the phrase "public Trust under the United States" includes elected positions, while "Office . . . under the United States" refers to appointed positions.[51] If "Office . . . under the United States" includes both appointed and elected federal positions, then "public Trust under the United States" would not refer to any positions. For these reasons, we suggest that the better reading is that "Office under the United States" refers only to appointed positions. This view is consistent with Story's reading of the Constitution.

To date, no sitting member of Congress has concurrently held the presidency or vice presidency. Three sitting Senators (Warren G. Harding, John F. Kennedy, and Barack Obama) have resigned their positions to become President. More than a dozen Senators (including J.D. Vance, Kamala Harris, Joe Biden, Al Gore, Dan Quayle, and Harry S. Truman) have resigned their positions to become Vice President. In our view, the Incompatibility Clause did not require these Senators to resign their seats in Congress.[52] This provision was not designed primarily to preserve the separation of powers, but to prevent the President from unduly influencing members of Congress with appointments.

One federal district court decision stated that the consequences of the President's also serving in Congress would be "bizarre."[53] Other scholars have taken the same position.[54] The federal judge and these scholars claim that "Office under the United States" refers to positions in the federal government, both appointed and elected. Even if the Incompatibility Clause does not textually bar concurrently holding a congressional seat and the presidency, it is still possible that such concurrent officeholding is otherwise barred, perhaps by an atextual or implied structural separation of powers principle.[55]

WHEN DOES AN INCOMPATIBILITY ARISE?
The Incompatibility Clause applies to "a Member of either House." The category of "member[s]" is narrower than the category of "Senators and Representatives."[56] Not all Senators and Representatives become members. Senators and Representatives begin their terms

as members-elect from the date of the start of their two-year or six-year constitutional terms. Customarily, before the start of their terms, a state secretary of state or other state elections official provides the Senator or Representative—that is, the member-elect—with bona fide credentials or a certificate of election. Then the member-elect travels to the Capitol and presents those credentials. But such a member-elect does not become a member until his house organizes and accepts him as a member. Each house is the "Judge of the Elections, Returns and Qualifications of its own Members."[57] (See Essay No. 24.)

The Incompatibility Clause bars "a member of either House" from holding "any Office under the United States." But this restriction applies only to actual members, and not to members-elect. Therefore, when a member-elect's two-year or six-year constitutional term begins, before he is recognized as a member, he could still hold an appointed position in the executive or judicial branch. It appears that in order to be recognized as a member, however, the member-elect must resign any incompatible office he holds.

These sorts of disputes are not hypothetical. In 1818, the House of Representatives drew this distinction between member and member-elect when it accepted the credentials of Samuel Herrick, a member-elect who was also a United States Attorney. The House decided that a member-elect "was not affected by the constitutional requirement that an officer . . . shall not be a Member."[58] As a result, Herrick was permitted to become a member after having resigned from the incompatible office. The practice has become that the Incompatibility Clause does not apply until the member takes his oath.[59] The courts have recognized this precedent.[60]

INCOMPATIBLE POSITIONS IN THE MILITARY
The Ineligibility Clause is limited to "civil" positions, and thus it does not apply to military positions. The Incompatibility Clause, however, applies to both civil and military offices. The House has declared vacant many seats of members who were commissioned as active-duty officers in the armed forces,[61] although the practice has not been uniform. For example, Congress

has not definitively resolved whether members can concurrently be officers in the armed forces reserves. A federal district court ruled that service in the reserves created an incompatibility.[62] However, on appeal, the U.S. Supreme Court reversed and found that the plaintiff lacked legal standing to bring the suit.[63]

Three decades later, this issue returned to the judiciary. Senator Lindsey Graham served as a lieutenant colonel in the Air Force Reserves. Graham sat on an Air Force Court of Criminal Appeals panel that reviewed an airman's conviction. The airman filed a motion to recuse Senator Graham on the ground that his service on the court violated the Incompatibility Clause. The U.S. Court of Appeals for the Armed Forces held that the position of judge on the Air Force Court of Criminal Appeals is an "office of the United States and cannot be filled by a person who simultaneously serves as a Member of Congress."[64] As a result, Graham should not have served on the panel, and the proceedings were invalidated. Despite this ruling, Senator Graham continued to serve in the Air Force Reserves until his retirement from the reserves in 2015, but he apparently did not sit on any other judicial panels.[65]

OPEN QUESTIONS

- Assume that a person is elected to a term in Congress that begins on January 3; however, he does not take the oath on that day and instead accepts an incompatible office in the executive branch. After accepting his appointment, he attempts to take the congressional oath. Does the member-elect surrender his appointment in the executive branch by taking the congressional oath, or does he lose his House seat by not giving up the executive office before taking the oath? Neither of these questions is answered directly by the text. In 1909, on facts analogous to this hypothetical situation, the House ruled that the congressional seat is automatically vacated.[66]

- What if the chronology in the example above were reversed and a person who already holds an executive branch office was afterwards elected to Congress and then attempted to take his congressional oath? Does he surrender the executive branch position by taking the congressional oath, or does his holding the executive branch position preclude his taking a valid congressional oath and so cause the member-elect to lose his House seat?

- It is clear that the House or the Senate can resolve an incompatibility conflict by declaring a seat vacant, but the courts could also review an action by a person holding a seat in Congress and an incompatible office either in the executive or judicial branch. Can the courts declare unlawful executive or judicial actions taken by a member holding an incompatible office? Can the courts remove such an officer? Can a court invalidate a legislative vote cast before a seat is declared vacant by the house of Congress to which the member was elected? In *Griffin's Case*, Chief Justice Salmon P. Chase suggested that such a legislative vote would remain valid.[67]

- Is an Incompatibility Clause violation a "qualification" like citizenship, age, and inhabitancy or residence, or is it somehow different? Is an Ineligibility Clause violation a "qualification"?

Cite as: Josh Blackman & Seth Barrett Tillman, *The Incompatibility Clause*, in THE HERITAGE GUIDE TO THE CONSTITUTION 111 (Josh Blackman & John G. Malcolm eds., 3d ed. 2025).

Notes

1. C. Ellis Stevens, Sources of the Constitution of the United States, Considered in Relation to Colonial and English History 109 (New York, Macmillan & Co. 1894); Benjamin Cassady, *"You've Got Your Crook, I've Got Mine": Why the Disqualification Clause Doesn't (Always) Disqualify*, 32 Quinnipiac L. Rev. 209, 279–80 (2014). **2.** The Act of Settlement, 12 & 13 Will. III, c. 2, § 3 (1700) (Eng.). **3.** Act for the Security of Her Majesty's Person and Government and of the Succession to the Crown of Great Britain in the Protestant Line of 1707, 6 Ann., c. 7, § 25 (Gr. Brit.), https://perma.cc/VN7A-X32T. **4.** William Tudor, Life of James Otis, of Massachusetts 270–71 (1823), https://perma.cc

/XK2C-FN9U. **5.** John K. Alexander, Samuel Adams: The Life of an American Revolutionary 50, 60, 126 (2011). **6.** Mary Patterson Clarke, Parliamentary Privilege in the American Colonies 229–31 (De Capo Press 1971) (1943); Jack P. Greene, The Quest for Power: The Lower Houses of Assembly in the Southern Royal Colonies, 1689–1776, at 207–12, 219 (1963). **7.** Pa. Const. of 1776, § 7. **8.** Mass. Const. of 1780, ch. VI, art. II. **9.** *Id.* **10.** Articles of Confederation, art. VI, § 1. **11.** *Id.* art. IX, § 5. **12.** *Id.* art. V, § 2. **13.** *Id.* art. IX, § 1. **14.** Seth Barrett Tillman & Josh Blackman, *Offices and Officers of the Constitution, Part IV: The 'Office . . . under the United States' Drafting Convention*, 62 S. Tex. L. Rev. 455, 471 (2023). **15.** Md. Const. of 1776, art. LXXX; Seth Barrett Tillman, *The Original Public Meaning of the Foreign Emoluments Clause: A Reply to Professor Zephyr Teachout*, 107 Nw. U. L. Rev. Colloquy 180, 199–200 (2013). **16.** Va. Const. of 1776, § 5. **17.** Steven G. Calabresi & Joan L. Larsen, *One Person, One Office: Separation of Powers or Separation of Personnel?*, 79 Cornell L. Rev. 1045, 1050–51 (1994). **18.** 2 Farrand's 137, 138, 140. **19.** *Id.* at 282, 283 n.1. **20.** *Id.* at 283–284. **21.** *Id.* at 282, 283 n.1. **22.** *Id.* at 285. **23.** *Id.* at 290. **24.** *Id.* at 484. **25.** *Id.* at 489–90. **26.** *Id.* at 490. **27.** *Id.* **28.** *Id.* at 492. **29.** *Id.* at 490. **30.** *Id.* at 492. **31.** *Id.* **32.** *Id.* at 568. **33.** John Adams, Message to the Senate on the Appointment of the Nomination of Envoys to France (Feb. 25, 1799), https://perma.cc/T3GK-ZQZY. **34.** Letter from John Adams to John Marshall (Feb. 4, 1801), https://perma.cc/T6HD-NVF5. **35.** *Id.* **36.** Josh Chafetz, *Leaving the House: The Constitutional Status of Resignation from the House of Representatives*, 58 Duke L.J. 177, 219 (2008). **37.** *CARROLL, Charles (of Carrollton) 1737–1832*, Biographical Directory of the United States Congress, https://perma.cc/LN53-CCYD. **38.** Tillman, *supra* at 200 n.66. **39.** *Id.* at 199–200. **40.** *PATERSON, William 1745–1806*, Biographical Directory of the United States Congress, https://perma.cc/VH79-V56L. **41.** Ken Rudin, *When Governors Appoint Themselves to the Senate*, NPR (Sept. 8, 2009), https://perma.cc/K5BQ-CDZJ. **42.** 2 Deschler's Precedents ch. 7, § 13.1. **43.** Zephyr Teachout, *Gifts, Offices, and Corruption*, 107 Nw. U. L. Rev. Colloquy 30 (2012); Lawrence Lessig, *A Reply to Professor Hasen*, 126 Harv. L. Rev. F. 61, 70 (2012). **44.** 6 Cannon's Precedents, § 65. **45.** Md. Const. of 1792, https://perma.cc/VHH2-XU3H. **46.** *CARROLL, Charles (of Carrollton) 1737–1832*, Biographical Directory of the United States Congress, https://perma.cc/LN53-CCYD. **47.** *From the Senate to the Cabinet, May 13, 1800*, United States Senate: Historical Highlights, https://perma.cc/7TWX-C8UW. **48.** 2 Story's Commentaries § 791. **49.** Tillman & Blackman, *Offices and Officers of the Constitution, Part IV, supra* at 526–29. **50.** *Id.* at 459; Seth Barrett Tillman & Josh Blackman, *Offices and Officers of the Constitution, Part V: The Elector Incompatibility, Impeachment Disqualification, Foreign Emoluments, and Incompatibility Clauses*, 63 S. Tex. L. Rev. 237 (2024). **51.** Seth Barrett Tillman & Josh Blackman, *Offices and Officers of the Constitution, Part II: The Four Approaches*, 61 S. Tex. L. Rev. 321, 396 (2022). **52.** Seth Barrett Tillman, *Senator and Vice President of the United States: Could J.D. Vance Hold Both Positions at the Same Time?*, Jurist (July 25, 2024), https://perma.cc/W9T9-XPQF; Seth Barrett Tillman, *Senator and Vice President of the United States: Can Kamala Harris Hold Both Positions at the Same Time?*, Jurist (Nov. 30, 2020), https://perma.cc/24BP-G6M3; Seth Barrett Tillman, *Member of the House of Representatives and Vice President of the US: Can Paul Ryan Hold Both Positions at the Same Time?*, Jurist (Aug. 15, 2012), https://perma.cc/6DH9-LFVN. **53.** *District of Columbia v. Trump*, 315 F. Supp. 3d 875, 884 n.17 (D. Md. 2018), *vacated*, 838 F. App'x 789 (4th Cir. 2021). **54.** Saikrishna Prakash, *Why the Incompatibility Clause Applies to the Office of the President*, 4 Duke J. Const. L. & Pub. Pol'y 143, 148–51 (2009). **55.** Tillman & Blackman, *Offices and Officers of the Constitution, Part V, supra* at 291. **56.** Josh Blackman & Seth Barrett Tillman, *Is the President an "Officer of the United States" for Purposes of Section 3 of the Fourteenth Amendment?*, 15 N.Y.U. J.L. & Liberty 1, 12 (2021). **57.** Art. I, § 5, cl. 1. **58.** 1 Hinds' Precedents § 499, https://perma.cc/B5V8-XFD6. **59.** John F. O'Connor, *The Emoluments Clause: An Anti-Federalist Intruder in a Federalist Constitution*, 24 Hofstra L. Rev. 89, 99 (1995). **60.** *United States v. Dietrich*, 126 F. 676, 683 (C.C.D. Neb. 1904). **61.** 2 Deschler's Precedents, ch. 7, §§ 14, 14.1. **62.** *Reservists Comm. to Stop War v. Laird*, 323 F. Supp. 833 (D.D.C. 1971). **63.** *Schlesinger v. Reservists Comm. to Stop the War*, 418 U.S. 208 (1974). **64.** *United States v. Lane*, 64 M.J. 1, 8 (U.S. Court of Appeals for the Armed Forces 2006), *reversing* 60 M.J. 781 (U.S.A.F. Crim. App. 2004) (per curiam). **65.** Craig Whitlock, *Sen. Graham Moved up in Air Force Reserve Ranks Despite Light Duties*, Wash. Post (Aug, 2, 2015), https://wapo.st/4088N7e. **66.** 6 Cannon's Precedents, § 65. **67.** *Griffin's Case*, 11 F. Cas. at 27; Josh Blackman & Seth Barrett Tillman, *Sweeping and Forcing the President into Section 3*, 28 Tex. Rev. L. & Pol. 350, 414 (2024).

ESSAY NO. 35: THE ORIGINATION CLAUSE
ART. I, § 7, CL. 1

All Bills for raising Revenue shall originate in the House of Representatives; but the Senate may propose or concur with Amendments as on other Bills.

—Andy Grewal

INTRODUCTION

In the bicameral British Parliament, bills to raise revenue could originate only in the House of Commons and not in the House of Lords.[1] After the United States achieved independence, several state constitutions followed this model and permitted only the more populous house to originate tax measures. Under the Articles of Confederation, the unicameral federal legislature had no power to impose taxes on people; the legislature could only submit requests, or *requisitions*, to the states. The Constitution follows the English model: Revenue bills must originate in the House of Representatives, although the Senate can adopt amendments to those bills. The Origination Clause has been enforced principally through the legislature rather than through the courts.

HISTORY BEFORE 1787

Pre-ratification practices among the states were influenced by the practice of the British Parliament, in which tax legislation could be introduced only by the House of Commons.[2] Delaware's constitution mandated that "[a]ll money-bills for the support of government shall originate in the House of Assembly [Delaware's lower house], and may be altered, amended or rejected by the Legislative Council [Delaware's upper house]."[3] Other states had similar origination requirements for tax legislation, and in some cases did not even allow the upper house to amend that legislation.[4] In Virginia, for example, the upper house could only accept or reject "money-bills" in their entirety.[5]

The Articles of Confederation established a unicameral legislature with authority to seek revenue from the states.[6] Without a division in the structure of Congress, there was no need to consider where revenue bills could originate.

THE CONSTITUTIONAL CONVENTION

During the Constitutional Convention, the Origination Clause took a winding path to approval, with only a minority of delegates expressing initial support.[7] The initial draft was introduced by Elbridge Gerry of Massachusetts on July 5.[8] This version gave the House substantial authority over financial matters. Under Gerry's proposal, all "bills for raising or appropriating money" would originate in the House.[9]

The Senate would not even have the power to amend those money-related bills.

Gerry's draft drew from his concerns that Senators would be disconnected from the people. Under the Constitution, Representatives would be elected by the people for two-year terms, but Senators enjoyed six-year terms and appointment through legislatures.[10] "It was a maxim," Gerry said, "that the people ought to hold the purse-strings."[11]

Skeptics like Thomas Pinckney of South Carolina expressed concerns about Gerry's proposal. Pinckney feared there would be "pernicious disputes" between the Senate and the House over taxation.[12] On August 13, Edmund Randolph of Virginia moved that the Origination Clause "be altered so as to read: 'Bills for raising money for the *purpose of revenue*, or for appropriating the same, shall originate in the House of Representatives.'"[13] James Madison of Virginia objected to the ambiguity over what counted as a bill for raising revenue. He noted that bills may have multiple purposes and that often "no line could be drawn" between revenue bills and non-revenue bills, especially in the case of economic trade legislation.[14]

The Convention ultimately reached a compromise on September 8.[15] Edmund Randolph of Virginia introduced what would become the final version of the Origination Clause.[16] This provision gave the House the sole power to originate bills for "raising Revenue,"[17] but all other money-related bills could originate in either house. Additionally, the Senate would enjoy the power to "propose or concur with Amendments" to bills raising revenue.[18]

Some delegates doubted whether the Origination Clause would serve any meaningful purpose.[19] James Wilson of Pennsylvania observed that "[i]f both branches were to say yes or no, it was of little consequence which should say yes or no first."[20] However, by giving authority over revenue to the House, where the large states had greater influence than they did in the Senate, the clause helped the Convention to reach a critical compromise between large and small states.[21]

THE RATIFICATION DEBATES

During the Convention, James Madison did not support the Origination Clause. Later, though, he would embrace its breadth. In Federalist No. 58, Madison remarked that the House "alone can propose the supplies requisite for the support of government." He contended that this "power over the purse" could be "the most complete and effectual weapon with which any constitution can arm the immediate representatives of the people."

Gerry, by contrast, voiced his concerns about the clause. He observed that his Convention committee proposed a strict origination rule. That strict rule would not allow the Senate to alter or amend revenue measures.[22] Without alterations or amendments in the Senate, the small states could not "take money from the pockets of [large states]."[23] The committee would have "never . . . agreed," said Gerry, to equal representation in the Senate without a strict origination rule.[24] Gerry maintained that he "never consented" to the final version of equal state representation in the Senate, which allowed amendments to revenue bills.[25]

Other Anti-Federalists expressed similar concerns about the Senate's power to amend revenue bills. George Mason of Virginia criticized the amendment power. Mason lamented that the Senate would have "the power of altering all money bills" even though Senators were not "the representatives of the people or amenable to them."[26] The Constitution also did not define the term "revenue bill." Luther Martin of Maryland argued that the Origination Clause would lead to "dispute and controversy between the two branches" over "what are or are not revenue bills."[27]

EARLY PRACTICE

In 1807, the Senate passed amendments that would have expanded a revenue bill.[28]

Subsequently, the House rejected those amendments. Representative John Randolph of Virginia stated that the Senate had tried to amend the bill "so as to affect the quantum of tax, or the object of taxation."[29] To Randolph, the Senate's amendment power under the Origination Clause was limited to the "details of the bill," and the Senate could not change its "leading principles."[30]

Since the House's rejection of the 1807 amendments, the Senate has respected the House's authority to originate revenue legislation. In 1830, Senator Thomas Hart Benton of Missouri introduced a bill that would have abolished some taxes, but he later withdrew the bill after questions arose about whether such a measure could properly originate in the Senate.[31] In 1831, Senator Benton was denied leave to introduce a bill that would have reduced taxes on salt. The debates revealed concerns about the Senate's authority to originate revenue legislation.[32]

JUDICIAL PRECEDENT

The Supreme Court has never determined that legislation violated the Origination Clause, but it has preserved its authority to make that determination. *United States v. Munoz-Flores* (1990) held that a challenge under the Origination Clause presented a justiciable question, rather than a political one beyond the Court's jurisdiction.[33]

The Court has understood the substance of the Origination Clause somewhat narrowly. *United States v. Norton* (1875) held that the term "bills for raising revenue" was "confined to bills to levy taxes in the strict sense of the words" and did not "extend to bills for other purposes which incidentally create revenue."[34] Thus, a bill can have revenue effects but nonetheless originate in the Senate.

OPEN QUESTION

The House has occasionally claimed that the Origination Clause applies not only to revenue measures, but also to appropriations (spending) measures.[35] In 1856, Senator William Seward observed that "the Senate has never originated an appropriations bill, but . . . it has always conceded to the House of Representatives the origination of appropriations bills."[36] Whether the Origination Clause applies to appropriations measures has generated considerable debate and study within Congress.[37]

Cite as: Andy Grewal, *The Origination Clause*, in THE HERITAGE GUIDE TO THE CONSTITUTION 117 (Josh Blackman & John G. Malcolm eds., 3d ed. 2025).

Notes

1. Robert G. Natelson, *The Founders' Origination Clause and the Implications for the Affordable Care Act*, 38 Harv. J.L. & Pub. Pol'y 629, 649 (2015). **2.** Natelson, *supra* at 649. **3.** Del. Const. of 1776, art. VI. **4.** Md. Const. of 1776, art X; N.H. Constitution of 1776; S.C. Const. of 1776, art. VII. **5.** Va. Const. of 1776. **6.** Articles of Confederation, art. II & VIII. **7.** Rebecca M. Kysar, *On the Constitutionality of Tax Treaties*, 38 Yale J. Int'l L. 1, 8 (2013). **8.** 1 Farrand's 524. **9.** *Id.* **10.** 2 Farrand's 274. **11.** 1 Farrand's 233. **12.** 5 Elliot's 189. **13.** *Id.* at 414. **14.** *Id.* at 417. **15.** 2 Farrand's 545. **16.** *Id.* at 273. **17.** *Id.* at 654. **18.** *Id.* at 654. **19.** 1 Farrand's 543–45. **20.** *Id.* at 544. **21.** 3 Farrand's 265; Chris Land, *The Origination Clause's Missing Piece*, 87 Tenn. L. Rev. 933, 943–45 (2020). **22.** 3 Farrand's 265. **23.** *Id.* **24.** *Id.* **25.** *Id.* at 267. **26.** Michael J. Zydney Mannheimer, *The Contingent Fourth Amendment*, 64 Emory L.J. 1229, 1265 (2015). **27.** 3 Farrand's 202. **28.** 2 Hinds' Precedents § 1481 (1907). **29.** 16 Annals of Cong. 630 (1807). **30.** *Id.* **31.** 2 Hinds' Precedents § 1482. **32.** *Id.* at § 1483. **33.** 495 U.S. 385 (1990). **34.** 91 U.S. 566, 569 (1875). **35.** James V. Saturno, Cong. Rsrch. Serv., R46558, The Origination Clause of the U.S. Constitution: Interpretation and Enforcement 12 (2011). **36.** Cong. Globe, 34th Cong., 1st Sess. 376 (1856). **37.** Saturno, at 13–14.

❧

ESSAY NO. 36: THE PRESENTMENT CLAUSE
ART. I, § 7, CL. 2

Every Bill which shall have passed the House of Representatives and the Senate, shall, before it become a Law, be presented to the President of the United States: If he approve he shall sign it, but if not he shall return it, with his Objections to that House in which it shall have originated, who shall enter the Objections at large on their Journal, and proceed to reconsider it. If after such Reconsideration two thirds of that House shall agree to pass the Bill, it shall be sent, together with the Objections, to the other House, by which it shall likewise be reconsidered, and if approved by two thirds of that House, it shall become a Law. But in all such Cases the Votes of both Houses shall be determined by yeas and Nays, and the Names of the Persons voting for and against the Bill shall be entered on the Journal of each House respectively.

—James Burnham & Louis J. Capozzi III

INTRODUCTION

The Presentment Clause prescribes the exclusive method for passing federal laws, indicating that all bills must be passed by both houses of Congress and be subject to the President's veto.

Ever since the Romans gave the Tribunes the power to veto legislation, political theorists have recognized that veto holders wield great power over lawmaking.[1] The Declaration of Independence condemned abuses of the veto by the King, his Privy Council, and colonial governors. Unsurprisingly, only the Massachusetts and New York constitutions permitted an executive veto when the Framers met in Philadelphia.[2] Yet, after significant debate, the Framers gave the President a qualified veto over legislation.

The Framers took this controversial step with the primary goal of making lawmaking harder. In recent years, however, the veto has functioned primarily to make unilateral lawmaking by the executive branch *easier*—by preventing Congress from overruling regulations. It is a pressing modern question whether the Constitution's veto and its lawmaking system more generally are functioning properly.

HISTORY BEFORE 1787

The Framers were familiar with vetoes under British law. Three overlapping vetoes limited the laws under which colonial citizens lived.

First, the king had an absolute veto over legislation passed by Parliament.[3] Where the king chose to "reject what bills" he pleased, that power was "absolute" and there was "no legal authority that [could] either delay or resist him."[4] As a practical matter, however, the veto had fallen into disuse well before the American Revolution. The last British monarch to veto a bill from Parliament was Queen Anne in 1708.[5] By 1742, David Hume observed that the king's veto had become "little better than a form."[6]

Second, royally appointed colonial governors could veto bills passed by colonial legislatures in ten of the thirteen colonies.[7] This led to governors abusing the power for personal gain. For example, in Pennsylvania, colonial governors routinely used veto threats to prevent interference with their orders to the colonial treasury.[8] Benjamin Franklin complained that "[n]o good law whatever could be passed without a private bargain with [Pennsylvania's governor]."[9]

Third, the king's Privy Council could review and veto legislation passed by most colonial legislatures.[10] The Privy Council, acting in the name of "the King in Council,"[11] understood itself to be exercising the delegated authority of the king's absolute veto to secure British interests and "to protect the colonies or any of their inhabitants from ill-advised legislation."[12] Notably, many of the Privy Council's vetoes came only long after the relevant laws had gone into effect, thereby effectively repealing a law that had already been in force.[13] One New Hampshire law, for example, was vetoed *fifty-one* years after passage.[14]

The first three grievances against the king in the Declaration of Independence focused on the veto, and memories of the abusive use of the veto power left Americans with a "deep antipathy" toward its integration into their post-Revolution state governments.[15] To most Americans, "the popular assemblies were the bulwark of popular liberties, [and] the executive departments were the instrumentalities of British control."[16]

In that context, it is unsurprising that the original state constitutions largely denied their governors a veto. South Carolina alone granted a single executive the veto power[17]—only to strip that power away two years later.[18] New York created a durable, hybrid veto system in its Council of Revision, but this body included not only the governor but also state senators and judges.[19] Only the Massachusetts constitution of 1780 gave its governor a sole veto over legislation, subject to a two-thirds override by both houses of the legislature.[20]

THE CONSTITUTIONAL CONVENTION

Despite the widespread opposition to vetoes under British rule and the absence of gubernatorial vetoes in the states, the delegates to the Philadelphia Convention—after much debate—empowered the President with a veto.

The Virginia Plan proposed allowing the executive to veto Congress's legislation as part of a Council of Revision that included judges.[21] This proposal would likely have operated similarly to New York's system.[22] But Elbridge Gerry and Rufus King, both of Massachusetts, successfully objected to involving judges in the lawmaking process.[23]

As the Convention settled on a single President (with no executive council), "a spirited debate" began "between those who favored an absolute veto, those who favored a veto with an override, and those who opposed the presidential veto altogether."[24] Benjamin Franklin argued against giving the President any veto, reminding delegates about how colonial governors had abused the veto in Pennsylvania.[25] Franklin cautioned that the President could use a veto threat to obtain "power and money" and then "influence and bribe the Legislature into a compleat subjection to the will of the Executive."[26] Pierce Butler of South Carolina argued that "in all countries the Executive power is in a constant course of increase," raising the risk that a tyrant like "Cataline or a Cromwell" might emerge.[27] George Mason of Virginia also expressed concerns about the "probable abuses of a [veto]," questioning whether the delegates were constituting a monarchy more dangerous than the British monarchy: "an elective one."[28]

Others believed a veto was essential to restrain excessive lawmaking. James Madison of Virginia described the veto as the "most cherished function for the President" because it would allow him to check excess lawmaking by Congress.[29] James Wilson of Pennsylvania agreed and proposed giving the President an absolute veto over Congress.[30] That proposal, however, was easily rejected.[31] Alexander Hamilton also agreed and proposed giving the President an absolute veto over state legislatures as well, though few were interested in that proposal.[32]

The Convention would agree to a qualified veto over Congress. The delegates accepted

Elbridge Gerry's proposal that the President's veto be subject to override by a two-thirds vote of each house of Congress.[33] More than two months later, the delegates revisited the question, and a fresh battle ensued. Gouverneur Morris of Pennsylvania advocated strengthening the veto to "prevent the hasty passage of laws."[34] Roger Sherman of Connecticut responded by questioning why "one man" should "be trusted better than all the others if they all agree."[35] At the close of the debate, Hugh Williamson of North Carolina moved to increase the override threshold to three-fourths; that motion passed by a six-state to four-state vote.[36] George Washington, who was widely expected to be the first President, favored this proposal.[37]

Then, mere days before the Convention ended, Hugh Williamson moved to revert to a two-thirds veto.[38] Williamson admitted he had changed his mind, and now argued that a stronger veto "puts too much in the power of the President."[39] Elbridge Gerry and George Mason supported the change, contending that the President should not have too much power to block laws or their repeal.[40] Gouverneur Morris and Alexander Hamilton, however, argued that the New York legislature was overriding too many vetoes with a two-thirds override.[41] James Madison also opposed the change, arguing that the veto was necessary to guard against majoritarian "injustice."[42] Ultimately, the full Convention voted to reduce the override back to two-thirds, which is where it remained in the final Constitution.[43]

Although Madison, Wilson, and Hamilton did not get as strong a President (or veto) as they wanted, the Convention's choice to give the President a veto ensured that the President would play a powerful role in lawmaking. Their victory—a substantial departure from prevailing state practice—is a testament to the delegates' deep fear of legislatures and lawmaking.

THE RATIFICATION DEBATES

Some responses to the veto power reflected the fear that the Constitution was "vesting discretionary powers in the hands of man, which he may, or may not abuse."[44] Luther Martin of Maryland, a member of the Convention who did not sign the final Constitution, argued that the President should not have a veto. He reasoned

that "the *sovereignty* was not in [the President], but in the *legislature*,"[45] and further charged that "as here constituted, [the President is] a *king*, in every thing but the name."[46] Others worried that the veto did not go far enough. For example, Anti-Federalist writer Centinel asked how a non-absolute veto could prove efficacious when "[e]ven the king of England . . . has not dared to exercise it for near a century past."[47]

Federalist writers, however, vigorously defended the veto as part of their larger argument that the president differed from the king of Great Britain.[48] In Federalist No. 69, Hamilton argued that the "qualified [veto] of the President differs widely from [the] absolute [veto] of the British sovereign." In Federalist No. 73, Hamilton specifically defended the veto as necessary to check "[t]he propensity of the legislative department to intrude upon the rights, and to absorb the powers, of the other departments." The veto, he explained, "furnishes an additional security against the enaction of improper laws." Hamilton acknowledged that the veto could be used to prevent "good" laws but reasoned that the "injury which may possibly be done by defeating a few good laws will be amply compensated by the advantage of preventing a number of bad ones." After all, Hamilton insisted, "every institution calculated to restrain the excess of lawmaking" is "much more likely to do good than harm; because it is favorable to greater stability in the system of legislation."

THE PROBLEM OF DELEGATION

As Hamilton explained, the primary reason the Framers gave the President a veto was to make lawmaking more difficult. In part, they succeeded in achieving that goal. Presidents have vetoed significant legislation throughout American history.[49] In such circumstances, only rarely has Congress overridden those vetoes. As of May 2025, Presidents have vetoed legislation 2,597 times, and Congress has overridden only 112 vetoes.[50]

But the veto's most important function has arguably shifted with the vast congressional delegation of lawmaking power to the executive branch.[51] In Federalist No. 73, Hamilton argued that without the veto, the President "might gradually be stripped of his authorities by successive resolutions, or annihilated by a single vote." In fact, the opposite has happened. From the 1940s through the 1970s, Congress passed the effective equivalent of blank-check statutes, giving the executive branch vast discretion to issue whatever regulations it deems reasonable.[52] For example, the Occupational Health and Safety Act allows the executive branch to make any rule it deems "reasonably necessary or appropriate to provide safe or healthful employment and places of employment."[53] Using statutes like these, the President and his agencies effectively make laws governing vast swaths of American life—often with no meaningful input from Congress.[54]

The veto protects that executive lawmaking status quo.[55] If Congress wants to stop an executive branch regulation from going into effect, it must comply with the Presentment Clause, which means the President can veto Congress's efforts to override his unilateral laws.[56] For example, Congress passed twelve laws purporting to "nullify" regulations issued by the Biden Administration, and the President vetoed all of them.[57]

The veto's modern *pro*-lawmaking function is diametrically opposed to the Framers' expectation that the veto would make lawmaking *harder*. That fact may lend support to those who argue that broad delegations of legislative power by Congress to the executive branch are inconsistent with the Framers' original design. As a solution, some have proposed that courts apply the nondelegation doctrine to hold broad delegations of legislative power unlawful.[58] Others have suggested that courts at least ought to require Congress to delegate major powers with especially clear language.[59] Either approach helps to ensure that new laws comply with the Presentment Clause.

THE LEGISLATIVE VETO

The Congresses that enacted broad delegations of power to the executive branch attempted to retain primacy over lawmaking by giving themselves a new veto.[60] Hundreds of statutes between the 1930s and 1980s included a so-called legislative veto that empowered a single house of Congress to block an executive branch regulation.[61]

In *INS v. Chadha* (1983), the Supreme Court held that legislative vetoes violate the Presentment Clause.[62] That decision had the effect of nullifying one-house veto provisions in hundreds of statutes delegating power to the executive branch—all while leaving the delegations in place.[63] *Chadha* thus represents an important part of the story of Congress losing its lawmaking powers to the executive branch.[64] Notably, in separate opinions in *Chadha*, Justices Powell and White predicted that this problem would come to pass.[65]

THE LINE ITEM VETO

Another departure from the traditional lawmaking process was Congress's attempt in 1996 to give the President the power to line-veto legislation. The Line Item Veto Act did this by giving the President a unilateral power to "cancel" certain spending provisions in bills passed by Congress.[66]

The Supreme Court found the line veto was unconstitutional in *Clinton v. New York* (1998). The Court reasoned that the power to cancel spending provisions in a law was the effective equivalent of repealing a law.[67] Because the Line Item Veto Act authorized the President to repeal legislation unilaterally without going through the Constitution's system for making law, the Court deemed it unconstitutional.

OPEN QUESTIONS

- Some scholars have argued that the Constitution permits Congress to delegate broad swaths of power to the executive branch.[68] If this is true, then the veto ensures that Congress will struggle to check executive lawmaking. As discussed, the Framers resuscitated the veto from British practice to make lawmaking *harder*. Does that paradox cast doubt on defenses of broad delegations?
- Few people question whether, as a formalist matter, *INS v. Chadha* was correctly decided,[69] but one-house veto provisions were included in bills that delegated broad legislative powers to the executive branch. By invalidating one-house vetoes while leaving the corresponding delegations in place, was *Chada* selectively formalist?[70] If

courts leave broad delegations in place for non-formalist reasons, should the Supreme Court restore one-house-veto provisions for non-formalist reasons?

- Members of Congress who worry about the transfer of legislative power from Congress to the executive branch have offered a potential solution: the Regulations from the Executive in Need of Scrutiny (REINS) Act.[71] This bill would require Congress to vote affirmatively (with no filibuster) on defined "major" executive branch regulations *before* they can take effect. Do you support this bill?

Cite as: James Burnham & Louis J. Capozzi III, *The Presentment Clause, in* THE HERITAGE GUIDE TO THE CONSTITUTION 120 (Josh Blackman & John G. Malcolm eds., 3d ed. 2025).

Notes

1. H.F. Jolowicz & Barry Nicholas, Historical Introduction to the Study of Roman Law 14, 54–55 (3d. ed. 1972). **2.** Richard A. Watson, *Origins and Early Development of the Veto Power*, 7 Presidential Stud. Q. 401, 405 (1987). **3.** Joseph Chitty, Jr., A Treatise on the Law of the Prerogatives of the Crown and the Relative Duties and Rights of the Subject 74 (1820). **4.** 1 Blackstone 250. **5.** William Everett, *The Last Royal Veto*, 25 Procs. Mass. Hist. Soc'y 156, 158–61 (1889). **6.** David Hume, Political Essays 69 (Charles W. Hendel ed., 1992). **7.** Watson, at 404. **8.** *Id.* **9.** 1 Farrand's 99. **10.** Charles M. Andrews, *The Royal Disallowance*, 24 Procs. Am. Antiquarian Soc'y 325 (1914). **11.** Oliver Morton Dickerson, American Colonial Government 1696–1765, at 227 (1912). **12.** Andrews, *supra* at 349. **13.** Dickerson, *supra* at 226–27. **14.** Andrews, *supra* at 349. **15.** Declaration of Independence ¶¶ 3, 4, 5; Richard Beeman, Plain, Honest Men: The Making of the American Constitution 137 (2009). **16.** Charles C. Thach, Jr., The Creation of the Presidency: A Study in Constitutional History 15 (Liberty Fund ed., 2007) (1923). **17.** S.C. Const. of 1776, art. VII. **18.** Eric Nelson, The Royalist Revolution 147–48 (2014). **19.** N.Y. Const. of 1776, art. III; Daniel J. Hulsebosch. Constituting Empire: New York and the Transformation of Constitutionalism in the Atlantic World, 1664–1830, at 175–80 (2005). **20.** Mass. Const. of 1780, ch. 1, § 1, art. II. **21.** 1 Farrand's 21. **22.** Michael W. McConnell, The President Who Would Not Be King 45–46 (2020). **23.** 1 Farrand's 97–98, 103. **24.** McConnell, *supra* at 46. **25.** 1 Farrand's 99. **26.** *Id.* **27.** *Id.* at 100. **28.** *Id.* at 101. **29.** McConnell, *supra* at 44–45. **30.** 1 Farrand's 94. **31.** *Id.* at 103, 108. **32.** *Id.* at 293, 300. **33.** *Id.* at 104. **34.** 2 Farrand's 299. **35.** *Id.* at 300. **36.** *Id.* at 295, 301. **37.** Pauline Maier, Ratification 37 (2010). **38.** 2 Farrand's 585. **39.** *Id.* **40.** *Id.* at 586. **41.** *Id.* **42.** *Id.* at 586–87. **43.** *Id.* at 583, 587. **44.** Mercy Otis Warren, Observations on the New Constitution, and on the Federal and State Conventions (1788), https://perma.cc/KA3Z-TQVW . **45.** Luther Martin's Letter on the Federal Convention of 1787, in 1 Elliot's 367. **46.** *Id.* at 379. **47.** Storing 2.7.49. **48.** Federalist No. 69 (Hamilton). **49.** Lawrence W. Reed, *The Ten Best Presidential Vetoes in American History*, Found. Econ. Educ. (July 24, 2018), https://perma.cc/C2Z7-3AMP. **50.** *Vetoes, 1789 to Present*, U.S. Senate, https://perma.cc/JQ6W-642V. **51.** Louis J. Capozzi III, *In Defense of the Major Questions Doctrine*, 100 Notre Dame L. Rev. 509, 512–13, 536–37, 552–62 (2025). **52.** Capozzi, *In Defense, supra* at 44–45. **53.** 29 U.S.C. § 652(8). **54.** *City of Arlington v. FCC*, 569 U.S. 290, 315 (2013) (Roberts, C.J., dissenting). **55.** Capozzi, *In Defense, supra* at 47–48. **56.** *Id.* **57.** *Vetoes by President Joseph R. Biden, Jr.*, U.S. Senate, https://perma.cc/5UXG-PFWX. **58.** *Gundy v. United States*, 588 U.S. 128, 149–79 (2019) (Gorsuch, J., dissenting); Ilan Wurman, *Nondelegation at the Founding*, 130 Yale L. J. 1490 (2021); Michael B. Rappaport, *A Two-Tiered and Categorical Approach to the Nondelegation Doctrine, in* The Administrative State Before the Supreme Court: Perspectives on the Nondelegation Doctrine 195 (Peter J. Wallison & John Yoo eds., 2022). **59.** *West Virginia v. EPA*, 597 U.S. 697, 735–42 (2022) (Gorsuch, J., concurring); *Paul v. United States*, 140 S.Ct. 342 (2019) (Kavanaugh, J., respecting denial of certiorari); Louis J. Capozzi III, *The Past and Future of the Major Questions Doctrine*, 84 Ohio State L.J. 191, 241–42 (2023). **60.** Capozzi, *In Defense, supra* at 554–55. **61.** Jonathan Adler & Chris Walker, *Delegation and Time*, 105 Iowa L. Rev. 1931, 1950–51 (2020). **62.** 462 U.S. 919, 951 (1983). **63.** Capozzi, *In Defense, supra* at 553–55. **64.** *Id.* **65.** *Chadha*, 462 U.S. at 960 (Powell, J., concurring); *id.* at 968 (White, J., dissenting). **66.** Line Item Veto Act, Pub. L. No. 104-130, § 2, 110 Stat. 1200, 1200–01 (1996) (codified at 2 U.S.C. § 691 (1994 ed., Supp. II)); *Clinton v. New York*, 524 U.S. 417, 436–41 (1998). **67.** *Clinton*, 524 U.S. at 438–39. **68.** Julian Davis Mortenson & Nicholas Bagley, *Delegation at the Founding*, 121 Colum. L. Rev. 277, 332–56 (2021). **69.** Robert L. Glicksman & Richard E. Levy, *The New Separation of Powers Formalism and Administrative Adjudication*, 90 Geo. Wash. L. Rev. 1088, 1100 (2022); Peter B. McCutchen, *Mistakes, Precedent, and the Rise of the Administrative State: Toward a Constitutional Theory of the Second Best*, 80 Cornell L. Rev. 1, 30 (1994). **70.** William N. Eskridge & John Ferejohn, *The Article I, Section 7 Game*, 80 Geo. L.J. 523, 526–27 (1992). **71.** Regulations from the Executive in Need of Scrutiny Act of 2023, H.R. 227, 118th Cong. (2023).

~

ESSAY NO. 37: THE POCKET VETO CLAUSE
ART. I, § 7, CL. 2

If any Bill shall not be returned by the President within ten Days (Sundays excepted) after it shall have been presented to him, the Same shall be a Law, in like Manner as if he had signed it, unless the Congress by their Adjournment prevent its Return, in which Case it shall not be a Law.

—Martin Gold

INTRODUCTION

The Constitution provides the President a period to review legislation and grants Congress the authority to override a veto. (See Essay No. 36.) These powers can be in tension with each other if Congress adjourns before the President's time for consideration has elapsed; either the President's rights would be curtailed or Congress would lose the opportunity for an override. This essay discusses the President's power to "pocket veto" legislation without being subject to congressional override and the meaning of "adjournment" as it affects the pocket veto.

THE CONSTITUTIONAL CONVENTION

On May 29, 1787, Resolution 8 of the Virginia Plan was presented to the delegates. It proposed that legislation should be subject to veto by a combination of the Executive and the Judiciary in a Council of Revision.[1] That resolution would be debated on June 4. Elbridge Gerry of Massachusetts opposed such a hybrid structure. He argued that the veto should rest only with the Executive with the possibility of a congressional override.[2]

James Wilson of Pennsylvania proposed that the President should have an absolute veto. Wilson stated that the power would seldom be used but contended that its presence would serve to limit the likelihood of extreme legislation.[3] However, the absolute veto garnered little support. Benjamin Franklin of Pennsylvania cited the Pennsylvania experience to argue that it would invite executive corruption.[4] Roger Sherman of Connecticut contended that no leader should have that much unchecked power.

"He thought" that "we ought to avail ourselves of his wisdom in revising the laws, but not permit him to override the decided and cool opinions of the Legislature."[5] George Mason of Virginia declared that granting an absolute veto would be tantamount to creating an elective monarchy. Franklin echoed this concern about accretion of power. "The first man, put at the helm will be a good one." It was widely assumed that George Washington would be the first President. However, continued Franklin, "No body knows what sort may come afterwards. The Executive will always be increasing here, as elsewhere, until it ends in a monarchy."[6] Delegates defeated the proposal to give the Executive an absolute veto by a vote of ten states to none.[7]

Gerry offered a motion to strike the judiciary from the veto power, and delegates approved the motion without dissent. The motion was amended to specify that two-thirds of each house would be needed to override the executive's conditional veto. In that form, delegates approved it by a vote of eight states to two.[8] On June 13, the Committee of the Whole reported a qualified veto, stating "that the national executive shall have the right to negative any legislative act; which shall not be afterwards passed unless by two third parts of each branch of the national Legislature."[9] Delegates approved the qualified veto without dissent. There were several more unsuccessful attempts to restore the judiciary back to the veto process.

The Committee of Detail's report, delivered on August 6, contemplated a circumstance where the Executive would have insufficient time to return a veto message: "If any bill shall not be returned by the President within seven days after it shall have been presented to him, it shall be a law, unless the legislature by their adjournment, prevent its return; in which case it shall not be a law."[10] On August 15, by a vote of nine states to two, the Convention decided to change seven days to ten days with "[S]undays excepted."[11] As a result, the President would have more time to consider vetoes and would not have to work on the Sabbath. On September 8, James Madison of Virginia moved to clarify that "the day on which the bill be presented" would not be "counted . . . as one of the ten" days.[12] Gouverneur Morris of Pennsylvania responded that the amendment was "unnecessary" because "the law knows no fractions of days."[13] In other words, the "day on which" the bill was presented would obviously not count toward the ten-day limit. Madison's proposal was defeated by a vote of eight to three.

The adopted text gave the President ten full days to consider a measure, Sundays excepted. If he signed it, the legislation would become law. If he did not sign but failed to return a veto message, it would also become law. But if Congress's adjournment prevented the President from returning a veto message in a timely manner, he could simply withhold his signature and the legislation would not become law. This practice would become known as a "pocket veto."

COMMENTARY

In Federalist No. 69, Alexander Hamilton noted that the British monarch possessed an absolute veto over acts of Parliament, but that power was dormant. Nevertheless, Hamilton said, "the disuse of that power for a considerable time past does not affect the reality of its existence." Federalist and Anti-Federalist commentators discussed the qualified veto, but neither addressed the pocket veto.

WHY WOULD THE PRESIDENT USE A POCKET VETO?

A President has limited discretion in his exercise of the pocket veto. He cannot use it except in circumstances that render it impossible for him to return a qualified veto. A President is entitled to the full time the Constitution grants him to review legislation. Congress cannot, in effect, reduce that time by passing legislation

within that period and shortly before adjourning. If Congress does so, it relinquishes its right to override a veto and leaves the President with the power of an absolute negative.

While the President may choose whether or not to approve legislation, it is entirely up to Congress whether he has the power to pocket veto the bill. If Congress wishes to avoid the possibility of a pocket veto, it must present a measure to the President with sufficient time for him to consider it and return a veto message.

WHEN CAN THE PRESIDENT USE A POCKET VETO?

The President can use a pocket veto when the "adjournment" of Congress prevents the return of the bill. The Constitution makes several references to "adjournments." When a house lacks a quorum, a "smaller number may adjourn from day to day."[14] (See Essay No. 25.) One house cannot "adjourn for more than three days" without the "Consent of the other" house.[15] (See Essay No. 29.) And the President can "adjourn" Congress "in case of Disagreement between them, with respect to the Time of Adjournment."[16] (See Essay No. 113.) Relatedly, the President can make recess appointments "that may happen during the Recess of the Senate."[17] (See Essay No. 109.)

Controversies have arisen over when the legislature can be said to have "adjourned" so as to prevent a bill's return, thus making a pocket veto possible. Without question, the veto can be exercised after the House and Senate adjourn a Congress *sine die*, meaning without return. For example, on December 23, 1982, the 97th Congress passed a bill and adjourned *sine die* the same day. President Reagan withheld his signature and the bill did not become law. On January 4, 1983, following expiration of the ten-day review period, the President published a Memorandum of Disapproval explaining his reasoning for not letting the bill become law.[18]

What about adjournments that happen within a two-year Congress and are not *sine die*? For example, what happens if Congress adjourns a few days for a holiday? These gaps can vary but are often brief. During such periods, it has been customary for Congress to appoint an agent (either the Secretary of the Senate or the Clerk of the House) to receive messages. In theory, at least, these agents can receive the President's return of a bill. The central question is whether the circumstances of an adjournment, even with an agent present, prevent the return of a veto.

JUDICIAL PRECEDENT

The first Supreme Court case addressing this question was *The Pocket Veto Case* (1929).[19] This case involved legislation to authorize proceedings before the U.S. Court of Claims. The measure was presented to President Calvin Coolidge on June 24, 1926. Excluding that day and Sunday, June 27, Coolidge should have had until Tuesday, July 6, to review the bill. However, the first session of the 69th Congress adjourned on July 3. Coolidge could have returned the veto at any time between June 24 and July 3, but he chose not to do so. Coolidge signed other legislation during this period but did not sign or veto the claims bill. He took no action at all, which triggered the question of whether he had exercised a pocket veto.

Congress did not reconvene for the second session until December 6, 1926, and litigation ensued over whether the bill Coolidge refused to sign had become law. The Court held that it had not become law because Congress, by its own adjournment, had prevented the return of a veto. Justice Edward T. Sanford, writing for the Court, stated that an adjournment "'prevents' the President from returning the bill to the House in which it originated within the time allowed."[20] The Court considered designation of an agent to receive messages to be irrelevant. "No return can be made to the House," the Court ruled, "when it is not in session as a collective body, and its members are dispersed . . . ."[21] In addition, keeping legislation in abeyance for months until Congress reconvened would be inconsistent with the Framers' intent. "It was plainly the object of the constitutional provision," the Court said, "that there should be a timely return of the bill . . . [that] should enable Congress to proceed immediately with its reconsideration."[22]

Eleven years later, *Wright v. United States* (1938) considered whether an adjournment under dramatically different circumstances precluded the return of a veto. On April 24,

1936, a Senate-originated bill was presented to President Franklin D. Roosevelt. On May 4, during the President's constitutional ten-day review period, the Senate commenced a recess that lasted until May 7. The House remained in session throughout that period. During the Senate's recess, the President returned a veto message, which the Secretary of the Senate received. The Court held that the veto was effective, notwithstanding the fact that the Senate was in recess at the time.[23]

The Court distinguished this case from *The Pocket Veto Case* in two material respects: first, constitutional reference to the adjournment of Congress means the adjournment of *both* chambers, not the interim recess of just one; second, the length of the recess was so short that the public policy concerns that animated the Court in *The Pocket Veto Case* were absent. In short, Congress was not "adjourned" when Roosevelt returned his veto. "When there is nothing but such a temporary recess," wrote Chief Justice Charles Evans Hughes, "the organization of the House and its appropriate officers continue to function without interruption, the bill is properly safeguarded for a very limited time, and is promptly reported and may be reconsidered immediately after the short recess is over."[24]

In *Kennedy v. Sampson* (1974), the D.C. Circuit ruled on the president's attempt to exercise a pocket veto during a six-day intrasession bicameral adjournment—that is, where both houses adjourned during a legislative session.[25] Legislation was presented to President Richard Nixon on December 14, 1970, and the President's ten-day review period expired on December 25. Under the terms of an adjournment resolution, Congress had adjourned on December 22 for the Christmas holiday and reconvened on December 29. The President issued a Memorandum of Disapproval on December 24, purporting to have pocket vetoed the bill. Again, a veto message could have been overridden by a two-thirds vote, whereas a pocket veto was final. If "the Christmas adjournment . . . 'prevented' the return of [the bill] . . . by the President," then "the President's failure to approve the bill within ten days of its presentation to him constituted a pocket veto." Alternatively, "[i]f the adjournment did not prevent the return of [the bill] . . . then the bill became law without the President's signature."[26] The court observed that the pocket veto represents a constitutional anomaly and "must be limited by the specific purpose it is intended to serve."[27] That purpose, the court wrote, was "to enforce respect on the part of each of the law-making branches of the government for the legislative authority of the other."[28]

Appellants argued that *Wright* was distinguishable. The 1970 recess was bicameral instead of involving just the Senate and lasted for five days rather than three. Nevertheless, the court considered these differences inconsequential and found that "reliance upon the *Pocket Veto Case* would be misplaced." The court explained that "[t]he modern practice of Congress with respect to intra-session adjournments creates neither of the hazards—long delay and public uncertainty—perceived in the *Pocket Veto Case*."[29] The short, bicameral adjournment from 1970 was not sufficient to trigger the pocket veto power. The veto could still be returned during that period and be accepted by the agent. So long as each house maintains

"appropriate arrangements . . . for receipt of presidential messages during the adjournment," the President cannot issue a pocket veto.[30]

The D.C. Circuit reached a similar outcome in *Barnes v. Kline* (1984). That case involved an attempted pocket veto during a nine-week adjournment between the first and second sessions of the 98th Congress.[31] The Senate had authorized the Secretary of the Senate to receive messages in the interim. In rejecting the pocket veto, the court considered the circumstances surrounding the adjournment, such as the fact that in the second session, Congress could complete action on any measures or matters carried over from the first, including veto messages. In light of the *Pocket Veto Cases* and *Wright*, the court stated a "simple" rule of what happens during an adjournment when there is "a duly authorized officer of the originating house" who can receive a veto message: the President can only issue a pocket veto "if, under the circumstances of that type of adjournment, such a procedure would not occasion undue delay or uncertainty over the returned bill's status."[32]

OPEN QUESTIONS

- During a short adjournment, if the House and Senate maintain agents to receive vetoes from the President, can the President ever use a pocket veto?
- How short must an adjournment be to fall within the rules set by the D.C. Circuit?
- Article II, Section 3 grants the President power to adjourn Congress if the two houses disagree between themselves as to the time of adjournment. Could the President adjourn Congress to prevent the return of a bill and thus be allowed to use a pocket veto that cannot be overridden by a two-thirds vote of each house?

Cite as: Martin Gold, *The Pocket Veto Clause, in* The Heritage Guide to the Constitution 125 (Josh Blackman & John G. Malcolm eds., 3d ed. 2025).

Notes

1. 1 Farrand's 21. **2.** *Id.* at 97–98. **3.** *Id.* at 98. **4.** *Id.* at 98–99. **5.** *Id.* at 99. **6.** *Id.* at 103. **7.** *Id.* **8.** *Id.* at 104. **9.** *Id.* at 230. **10.** 2 Farrand's 181. **11.** *Id.* at 295. **12.** *Id.* at 608. **13.** *Id.* **14.** Art. I, § 5, cl. 1. **15.** Art. I, § 6, cl. 4. **16.** Art. II, § 3. **17.** Art. II, § 2, cl. 3. **18.** 128 Cong. Rec. 33440 (1982). **19.** 279 U.S. 655 (1929). **20.** *Id.* at 681. **21.** *Id.* at 683–84. **22.** 279 U.S. 655, 685. **23.** 302 U.S. 583 (1938). **24.** *Id.* at 595. **25.** 511 F2d. 430 (D.C. Cir. 1974). **26.** *Id.* at 437. **27.** *Id.* **28.** *Id.* at 438. **29.** *Id.* at 440–41. **30.** *Id.* at 442. **31.** 759 F2d. 21 (D.C. Cir. 1984). **32.** *Id.* at 35.

ESSAY NO. 38: THE ORDER, RESOLUTION, OR VOTE (ORV) CLAUSE
ART. I, § 7, CL. 3

Every Order, Resolution, or Vote to which the Concurrence of the Senate and House of Representatives may be necessary (except on a question of Adjournment) shall be presented to the President of the United States; and before the Same shall take Effect, shall be approved by him, or being disapproved by him, shall be repassed by two thirds of the Senate and House of Representatives, according to the Rules and Limitations prescribed in the Case of a Bill.

—Seth Barrett Tillman

INTRODUCTION

The Presentment Clause (Article I, Section 7, Clause 2) requires that "Every Bill" passed by the House and Senate must be "presented to the President" for his approval before it can become law. (See Essay No. 36.) This two-step process is known as *bicameralism and presentment*. Article I, Section 7, Clause 3 imposes a further requirement: "Every Order, Resolution, or Vote to which the Concurrence of the Senate and House of Representatives may be necessary (except on a question of Adjournment) shall be presented to the President of the United States." This provision is known as the Order, Resolution, or Vote (ORV) Clause. It has also been called the Second or Residual Presentment Clause or Presentment of Resolutions Clause. The Presentment Clause mandated the requirements of bicameralism and presentment for all statutory lawmaking. *INS v. Chadha* (1983) held that the ORV Clause accomplished the same general purpose.[1] *Chadha* saw the ORV Clause entirely as an anti-evasion clause designed to prevent Congress from opting out of the Presentment Clause's bicameralism and presentment requirements merely by denominating a bill by some other name, such as an order, resolution, or vote.

The alternative view is that the ORV Clause was an alternative procedural mechanism for making binding law, but not in the form of traditional statutes. The ORV Clause procedure was used a single time by the First Congress and subsequently fell into desuetude or disuse.

THE CONSTITUTIONAL CONVENTION

On August 15, 1787, the Convention agreed on the outlines of the Presentment Clause.[2]

James Madison of Virginia observed that "if the negative of the President was confined to bills; it would be evaded by acts under the form and name of Resolutions, votes [etc.]"[3] In other words, Madison warned that Congress could evade the possibility of a presidential veto by simply denominating a "bill" as a resolution, vote, or something else. For that reason, Madison made a motion to insert the words "or resolve" after the word "bill" in the Presentment Clause. With Madison's revision, the Presentment Clause would have read in part: "Every Bill *or resolve* which shall have passed the House of Representatives and the Senate, shall, before it become a Law, be presented to the President of the United States." Madison characterized the debate on his motion as "short and rather confused."[4] It was the only such debate at the Convention that was characterized as "confused." Madison's motion was defeated by a vote of eight to three.[5] The Convention then approved a proposal to change the time limit provision in the Pocket Veto Clause from seven days to ten days.[6] (See Essay No. 37.)

The following day, on August 16, Edmund Randolph of Virginia proposed a freestanding clause:

> [E]very order, resolution or vote, to which the concurrence of the Senate and House of representatives may be necessary (except on a question of adjournment, and in the cases hereinafter mentioned) shall be presented to the President for his revision; and before the same shall have

force, shall be approved by him, or, being disapproved by him, shall be repassed by the Senate & House of Reps according to the rules & limitations prescribed in the case "of a Bill."[7]

Randolph's August 16 proposal was nearly identical to what would become the final language of the ORV Clause. The Convention, without recorded debate or explanation, approved Randolph's proposal nine to one.[8] Seven states that had voted against Madison's proposal the day before voted for Randolph's proposal, which Madison characterized as "a new form [of his own prior] motion, putting votes, Resolutions &c. on a footing [equal] with Bills."[9]

Several inferences can be drawn both from this drafting history of Article I, Section 7 and from the text of related provisions of the Constitution. First, it seems unlikely that Randolph's proposal and Madison's accomplished the same purpose. Whereas Madison merely added two words to the draft Presentment Clause, Randolph proposed a freestanding clause that was more than seventy-five words long.

Second, the two provisions apply in different circumstances. The Presentment Clause applies when a bill is "passed [by] the House of Representatives and the Senate." The ORV Clause applies when "the Concurrence of the Senate and House of Representatives may be necessary" for an "Order, Resolution, or Vote." The former provision expressly mandates bicameralism for bill passage; with the latter provision, unicameral action is implicitly recognized. In other words, orders, resolutions, and votes are primarily single-house instruments.

Third, Madison's proposal was *defeated* by a lopsided majority, and Randolph's proposal the very next day was *approved* by a lopsided majority. If the two clauses accomplished the same basic purpose, it seems unlikely that the seven states that had voted against Madison's proposal, after less than a day had passed and absent any record of substantive debate, suddenly changed their minds and voted for Randolph's proposal. The better explanation is that Randolph's proposal accomplished an end

that was substantively different from the one that was accomplished by Madison's proposal.

Fourth, Madison reported that the debate on his proposal was "confused." If it was clear that the two proposals accomplished the same basic purpose, then there should not have been any confusion. It is possible that Madison was "confused" because he had pigeonholed Randolph's proposal as accomplishing the same basic purpose that was accomplished by his own failed proposal.

Fifth, the Committee of Detail reported its draft Constitution on August 6. In that draft, the President was granted a general "Power to convene the Legislature on extraordinary Occasions."[10] The ORV Clause was added to the draft on August 16, and the President's convening power was expanded on September 8. The revised Convening Clause was amended to read: "[The President] may convene both or *either* of the Houses on extraordinary occasions."[11] If Madison's understanding of the Presentment Clause applied to the ORV Clause, there was little reason to grant the President a power to convene just the House of Representatives. In fact, the grant of this specific power would puzzle Alexander Hamilton in Federalist No. 77, written in response to the Anti-Federalist Cato's Letter No. VII.[12] (Hamilton was in attendance on September 8 and should have heard the debate on the clause's amendment on that day.) By contrast, the amendment to the Convening Congress Clause can be explained if the ORV Clause permits Congress by statute to delegate limited legislative powers to a single house of Congress.

Finally, nine provisions of the original Constitution and two provisions in the Bill of Rights provide that Congress must act "by law."[13] *Office of Personnel Management v. Richmond* (1990) explained that "by law" means "by statute."[14] However, most clauses authorizing congressional action have no such limiting "by law" language. If Madison was correct, and if bills and orders, resolutions, and votes are substantively the same legal instruments but merely titled differently, then this "by law" language in these nine provisions is superfluous. Such an interpretation is not favored. By contrast, if bills are different from orders, resolutions, and votes, then the "by law" limitation in these nine clauses is functional: This "by law" language restricts Congress to the traditional statutory lawmaking processes set down in the Presentment Clause for these particular nine clauses. But where the "by law" language is not present, Congress can pass a traditional statute, and that statute could authorize further lawmaking by a single house in the form of an order, resolution, or vote that would be subject to separate presentment to the President just as the prior authorizing statute would be.

In short, the default rule is that Congress can engage in lawmaking, broadly understood, either by the Presentment Clause's procedures in Article I, Section 7, Clause 2 or by the ORV Clause's procedures in Article I, Section 7, Clause 3. But where a constitutional provision demands congressional action "by law," then Congress can engage in lawmaking only by the Presentment Clause's traditional statutory lawmaking procedures: bicameralism and presentment.

THE ORV CLAUSE IN THE FIRST CONGRESS

What was the original public meaning of the ORV Clause? Was it, as Madison suggested in his personal convention *Notes*, a method to ensure that Congress could not evade the requirements of bicameralism and presentment by denominating a bill as something other than a bill? Or did the ORV Clause, per Randolph's proposal, do something else? The actions of the First Congress shed some light on these questions.

In 1789, the First Congress enacted An Act to Establish the Treasury Department.[15] This statute required the Secretary of the Treasury to "give information to either branch of the legislature, in person or in writing (as he may be required), respecting all matters referred to him by the Senate or House of Representatives . . . ." In short, Congress by statute prospectively authorized each house of Congress, acting separately, to request information from the Secretary of the Treasury, and the statute made it the secretary's duty to report to a single house of Congress. Congress certainly could impose such an obligation through bicameralism and presentment, but this statute did not do that. Rather, this statute delegated the power

to each house of Congress, acting separately, to compel the Secretary of the Treasury to report information to it. In other words, each house of Congress, through a unicameral or simple resolution, could impose a legal obligation on the executive branch: This resolution would not be a statute, but it would still have the force of law. That is what the ORV Clause states: Orders, resolutions, and votes are not characterized as "laws" but "take effect" as laws. One scholar has asserted that "[t]he Constitution itself avoids [a] grammatical ambiguity, always carefully referring to federal legislative output as 'Law' or 'legislation' (which Congress 'makes' or 'passes')."[16] However, he did not discuss the ORV Clause.

If Madison's understanding was correct, and if the ORV Clause was designed to prevent evasion of the Presentment Clause's requirements, then this reporting provision imposed by statute by the First Congress was unconstitutional. Under Madison's understanding of the Presentment Clause and the ORV Clause, Congress enacts bills, as well as orders, resolutions, and votes, into law via bicameralism and presentment. But through this statute, the first Congress delegated a share of its lawmaking authority to either house of Congress acting separately. This statute's reporting provision amounts to a rejection of Madison's reading of Article I, Section 7, Section 3. It is worth noting that in 1789, Madison served in the first Congress, and Hamilton was the Treasury Secretary. They both would have played some role in regard to the statute.

What was the original public meaning of the ORV Clause? In my view, the Clause permits Congress by statute to delegate some of its lawmaking power to a single house.[17] When a single house acts under that delegated authority, its statutory instrument (an order, resolution, or vote) must be *intra vires*—that is, the single-house statutory instrument must conform to the authorizing statute. Moreover, the single house's order, resolution, or vote must be separately presented to the President just as the prior authorizing statute was presented. In other words, in some circumstances, Congress can opt out of bicameralism, but it cannot opt out of presentment. In this limited sense, Madison was correct. Because both traditional statutes and statutory instruments (orders, resolutions, and votes) must be presented to the President, the latter are "on a footing [equal] with bills." But orders, resolutions, or votes that are not statutory instruments—that are not passed in compliance with a congressional delegation—are not on equal footing with bills and therefore do not have the force of law.

For all of these reasons, the better reading of the ORV Clause is:

> Every [final] Order, Resolution, or Vote [of a single house of Congress] to which the Concurrence of the Senate and House of Representatives may be necessary [as prior statutory authorization] (except on a question of Adjournment) shall be presented to the President of the United States; and before the [order, resolution, or vote] shall take Effect [as a statutory instrument or regulation per the prior statutory authorization], shall be approved by him, or being disapproved by him, shall be repassed by two thirds of the Senate and House of Representatives, according to the Rules and Limitations prescribed in the Case of a Bill [which is a different case].

MODERN CONGRESSIONAL PRACTICE INVOLVING RESOLUTIONS

Today, not all resolutions of Congress require presidential approval, because not all such resolutions are intended to be laws, statutes, or acts of Congress. In modern practice, there are three general types of resolutions: joint resolutions, concurrent resolutions, and single-house or simple resolutions.

Joint resolutions are passed by both houses, are presented to the President, and if approved have the force of law. Joint resolutions are simply statutes, but they usually apply to specifically designated persons or have a limited scope or have a one-time effect.[18] By contrast, statutes apply indefinitely into the future to persons and cases unknown. For these reasons, a declaration of war is passed as a joint resolution. For reasons that are not entirely clear, a

congressionally proposed amendment to the Constitution is also styled as a joint resolution even though it is not subject to the President's veto power. Perhaps this is because the Article V amendment process operates independently of the presentment strictures in Article I, Section 7, which apply to bills and other bill-like congressional instruments.[19]

Concurrent resolutions are passed by both houses but are not presented to the President. They are not intended to have the force of law. They are often expressions of the opinion of both houses of Congress or affect the procedures of one or both houses. In addition to the concurrent resolutions that express the opinions or "the sense of the Congress" on an issue, many other concurrent resolutions set revenue and spending goals or fix the time for adjournment.

Simple resolutions are passed by a single house but are not presented to the President. They are not intended to have the force of law. Customarily, such resolutions simply express the opinion of a single house of Congress. Additionally, these resolutions deal with a single house's internal procedures, such as fixing the time for a short adjournment, imposing censure on a Member, or setting spending limits for particular committees.

INS V. CHADHA AND THE ORV CLAUSE

Federal statutes often empower executive branch officers to make discretionary decisions. However, in some twentieth-century statutes,[20] Congress also expressly provided that such exercises of discretion could be reversed by both houses of Congress acting together in a concurrent resolution or even by a unicameral simple resolution. Such congressional expressions of disapproval, sometimes called legislative vetoes, would not be presented to the President for his signature or veto.

INS v. Chadha (1983) held that Congress could not use a resolution by one house and, by extension, a concurrent resolution by both houses, to "veto" an executive action.[21] The Supreme Court ruled that this "one house veto" violated the ORV Clause. The *Chadha* Court went further and accepted Madison's understanding of the provision: that the purpose of the clause was to prevent Congress from evading bicameralism and presentment, which is required for bills, by using a single-house instrument. In his opinion for a majority of the Court, Chief Justice Warren Burger wrote that "[d]uring the final debate on Art. I, § 7, cl. 2, James Madison expressed concern that [the Presentment Clause] might easily be evaded by the simple expedient of calling a proposed law a 'resolution' or 'vote' rather than a 'bill.'"[22] As a result, Burger continued, "Art. I, § 7, cl. 3 [the ORV Clause] was added."[23] The *Chadha* Court adopted Madison's view that Randolph proposed the ORV Clause to ensure that mechanisms laid out in the Presentment Clause were not circumvented.

The few modern scholarly sources that discuss the ORV Clause have consistently adopted

Madison's understanding that the purpose of the clause is to preclude Congress from evading the President's veto by denominating a bill as something other than a bill. Professor Akhil Reed Amar, for example, has affirmed the correctness of *INS v. Chadha*.[24] However, like *Chadha*, these modern sources do not account for the significant textual differences between Madison's proposal and Randolph's proposal, as well as the Treasury Act from the First Congress. Moreover, the Madisonian reading renders the Constitution's "by law" language, appearing in many provisions of the Constitution of 1788, surplusage. The Congressional Research Service has reported the view that the ORV Clause permitted statutory delegations to a single house.[25]

OPEN QUESTIONS

There is some evidence that *Chadha*'s interpretation of the ORV Clause was incorrect as an originalist matter. What kind of test case would allow the Supreme Court to revisit *Chadha*?[26] One suggestion would be a statute in which Congress delegated significant legislative powers to a single house when all of the members of the other house had been killed or incapacitated by war, natural disaster, or a pandemic. Likewise, where an executive order or regulation impinging on private rights is authorized by a single-house order and the latter single-house order is authorized by a prior statute, private litigants could test the validity of the regulation, which would implicitly test the constitutionality of congressional action under the aegis of Article I, Section 7, Clause 3.

Cite as: Seth Barrett Tillman, *The Order, Resolution, or Vote (ORV) Clause*, in THE HERITAGE GUIDE TO THE CONSTITUTION 129 (Josh Blackman & John G. Malcolm eds., 3d ed. 2025).

Notes
1. 462 U.S. 919 (1983). **2.** 2 Farrand's 295. **3.** *Id.* at 301. **4.** *Id.* at 302. **5.** *Id.* **6.** *Id.* at 302. **7.** *Id.* at 304–05. **8.** *Id.* at 305; Seth Barrett Tillman, *A Textualist Defense of Article I, Section 7, Clause 3: Why* Hollingsworth v. Virginia *Was Rightly Decided, and Why* INS v. Chadha *Was Wrongly Reasoned*, 83 Tex. L. Rev. 1265, 1314 n.106 (2005). **9.** 2 Farrand's 304. **10.** *Id.* at 158, 171, 185. **11.** *Id.* at 547 (emphasis added). **12.** Storing 2.6.45–48. **13.** Seth Barrett Tillman & Josh Blackman, *Offices and Officers of the Constitution, Part III: The Appointments, Impeachment, Commissions, and Oath or Affirmation Clauses*, 62 S. Tex. L. Rev. 349, 378–83 (2023). **14.** *Off. of Pers. Mgmt. v. Richmond*, 496 U.S. 414, 424 (1990). **15.** An Act to establish the Treasury Department, ch. 12, § 2, 1 Stat. 65, 65–66 (1789). **16.** Nicholas Quinn Rosenkranz, *The Subjects of the Constitution*, 62 Stan. L. Rev. 1209, 1216 (2010). **17.** Tillman & Blackman, *supra* at 424. **18.** Robert Luce, Legislative Procedure: Parliamentary Practices and the Course of Business in the Framing of Statutes 554–558 (1922); 1 Statutes at Large 96–98, 187, 224–25 (Richard Peters ed., Boston, Charles C. Little & James Brown 1845). **19.** *Hawke v. Smith*, 253 U.S. 221, 229 (1920); *Chadha*, 462 U.S. at 955 n.21. **20.** Akhil Reed Amar, America's Unwritten Constitution: The Precedents and Principles We Live By 371 (2012). **21.** 462 U.S. at 959. **22.** *Id.* at 947 (citing 2 Farrand's 301–02). **23.** *Id.* (citing 2 Farrand's 304–05). **24.** Amar, *supra* at 369–72. **25.** Cong. Rsrch. Serv., The Constitution of the United States of America: Analysis and Interpretation 301 n.2, S. Doc. No. 117-12, 117th Cong., 2d Sess. (2023). **26.** Seth Barrett Tillman, *Model Continuity of Congress Statute*, 4 Pierce L. Rev. 191 (2006).

~

ESSAY NO. 39: THE TAXING CLAUSE
ART. I, § 8, CL. 1

The Congress shall have Power to lay and collect Taxes, Duties, Imposts and Excises.

—Andy Grewal

INTRODUCTION

Under the Articles of Confederation, the legislature could only request money from the states. In contrast, the federal Constitution allows Congress to impose taxes directly on people. Congress's first enumerated power is the "Power To lay and collect Taxes, Duties, Imposts and Excises." This provision broadly refers to taxes and then three subsets of taxes: duties, imposts, and excises. Duties and imposts are taxes the government applies to the import or export of goods.[1] Excises are taxes levied on the enjoyment of a privilege, such as the right to produce a good or pursue a specific occupation.

While broad, the taxing power faces several specific constitutional limits. Under the Direct Taxes Clause, taxes, when "direct," must be apportioned according to population.[2] (See Essay No. 71.) Under the Uniformity Clause, "Duties, Imposts and Excises" must be "uniform" throughout the United States.[3] (See Essay No. 41.) And under the Export Taxation Clause, Congress faces a flat ban on the taxation of exports.[4] (See Essay No. 72.) Early Supreme Court decisions closely examined federal taxes to determine whether they circumvented other limits on congressional power or violated state sovereignty. More recently, the Court has largely deferred to Congress.

HISTORY BEFORE 1787

The Confederation Congress had no authority to tax individuals; it could only make requests, or "requisitions," to the states for funds.[5] These requests were often unsuccessful. For example, in 1786, the national Board of Treasury mandated that the states collectively contribute $3.8 million to the federal purse, but the states paid only $663.[6] In Federalist No. 15, Alexander Hamilton observed that the Confederation Congress had "an indefinite discretion to make requisitions for . . . money" but "no authority to raise" money "by regulations extending to the individual citizens. . . ." Hamilton added that attempts to raise revenue could prove fruitless because the states could "observe or disregard [the requisitions] at their option."

THE CONSTITUTIONAL CONVENTION

During the Constitutional Convention, two key plans embraced different visions for the federal taxation power. The New Jersey Plan "authorized [Congress] to pass acts for raising a revenue, by levying a duty or duties" on imports, stamps, and postage.[7] The New Jersey plan would also make federal law, including federal tax law, the "supreme law,"[8] enforceable against individuals.[9] As a result, Congress would have broad taxation authority over individuals and would no longer need to seek revenues from the states.

Under the Virginia Plan, the national legislature could impose "Quotas of contribution" on states[10] Those quotas, similar to requisitions, would affect a state's representation: A higher quota would lead to higher "rights of suffrage in the National Legislature."[11] The Virginia Plan, unlike the New Jersey plan, did not provide for federal taxation of individuals.[12]

The "Connecticut Compromise" resolved several debates, including those related to the federal taxation power. The compromise, which was ultimately reflected in the final Constitution, established a bicameral legislature with proportional representation in the House of Representatives and equal representation for each state in the Senate.[13] Taxation would not affect this design. That is, representation would not turn on quotas or requisitions.[14] However, after the compromise, the Constitution included the Taxing Clause and thus the power to tax individuals.[15]

THE RATIFICATION DEBATES

In Federalist No. 30, Hamilton emphasized that the revenue scheme established under the Articles of Confederation was a "fallacious and delusive system of quotas and requisitions." Hamilton believed that the new government established by the Constitution should "raise its own revenues by the ordinary methods of taxation authorized in every well-ordered constitution of civil government." Those methods included the power to tax individuals.

Anti-Federalists scoffed at the new federal taxation power. George Mason of Virginia feared that the power to tax individuals directly, including through duties, imposts, and excises, "does of itself, entirely change the confederation of the states into one consolidated government."[16] Mason claimed that the new taxing power would be "at discretion, unconfined, and without any kind of control," making it "totally subversive of every principle" that had previously governed the country.[17] In Pennsylvania, dissenters from the state's ratification convention argued that the Taxing Clause would force people to pay even the most "oppressive" taxes because "all resistance will be in vain."[18] The dissenters feared that the "standing army and select militia"[19] would be deployed to collect federal taxes.

The Federalists tried to assuage these concerns. They cautioned that heavy taxation of individuals would be unnecessary under the new government.[20] For example, James McHenry of Maryland said that the "government would seldom have recourse to direct Taxation" of individuals.[21] Rather, taxes on imports, such as duties and imposts, as well as excise taxes would provide adequate revenue.[22]

Edmund Randolph of Virginia argued that practical considerations supported the Taxing Clause. The new government would need to borrow to survive, and to borrow "any sum of a considerable amount," the government would need the "full scope, and complete command over the resources of the Union" as provided by the Taxing Clause.[23]

EARLY PRACTICE

Shortly after ratification, Congress had to decide whether it could use its taxation authority for purposes other than just raising revenue. The first Congress believed that it could. The Tariff Act of 1789 laid duties on imports not only for the "support of government," but also for the "protection of manufactures."[24] During congressional debates, the act raised policy concerns but no constitutional objections.[25]

Four decades later, Congress enacted tariff measures with strong protectionist purposes. This time, the tariffs generated constitutional objections from southern states.[26] Senator John C. Calhoun of South Carolina and his allies claimed that Congress could tax imports only for revenue, not to regulate trade.[27] They also argued that the states could *nullify* unconstitutional federal tariffs. Senator Henry Clay of Kentucky defended tariffs on policy grounds, arguing that their introduction had led to "the greatest prosperity which this people have enjoyed since the establishment of their present Constitution."[28] James Madison observed that the constitutional power to regulate commerce with foreign nations implied a power to tax imports.[29] Ultimately, under the Compromise of 1833, Congress would gradually reduce federal tariffs.[30]

JUDICIAL PRECEDENT

The U.S. Supreme Court has understood the taxing power expansively. *J.W. Hampton, Jr. & Co. v. United States* (1928) concluded that customs duties could be imposed for purposes other than the raising of revenue.[31] The Court added that the Constitution allows Congress to use its taxing power "'with the incidental motive of discouraging [specific activities] by making their continuance onerous.'"[32]

The Court has scrutinized tax measures that attempt to expand Congress's authority under the Constitution. *Hammer v. Dagenhart* (1918) held that Congress's powers under the Commerce Clause could not support a federal prohibition on the interstate shipment of goods produced by child labor.[33] Congress responded to *Hammer* by enacting a significant profits tax on manufacturers who used child labor. However, *Bailey v. Drexel Furniture Co.* (1922) declared that the profits tax was unconstitutional.[34] Though the profits tax was styled as a revenue raising measure, the "tax" was in substance a penalty designed to regulate activity. And, the Court concluded, Congress lacked Commerce Clause authority to enact that penalty. To uphold the profits tax would "break down all constitutional limitation of the powers of Congress and completely wipe out the sovereignty of the states."[35]

After *Drexel Furniture*, the Court took a more relaxed approach to taxes with a regulatory purpose. *United States v. Kahriger* (1953) upheld a federal tax on gamblers.[36] The Court emphasized that it often upheld congressional attempts to "curtail and hinder" activities, or tax those activities.[37] *NFIB v. Sebelius* (2012) acknowledged the trend, stating that "[m]ore often and more recently," the Court has "declined to closely examine the regulatory motive or effect of revenue-raising measures."[38]

In the nineteenth century, the Court found that state sovereignty imposed some limitations on the Taxing Clause, but in the twentieth century, those limits receded. For example, in 1870, the Court found that a federal income tax that applied to a state judge was unconstitutional because it infringed upon a state's sovereignty.[39] But in 1938, the Court upheld federal taxation authority over state employees.[40] The Court made a similar switch for the federal taxation of state or municipal bonds. *Pollock v. Farmers' Loan & Trust Co.* (1895) held that such taxation violated state sovereignty,[41] but *South Carolina v. Baker* (1988) reversed that position. Under the case law, principles related to state government sovereignty no longer impose major barriers to federal taxation.[42]

OPEN QUESTIONS

In *NFIB v. Sebelius*, the Court cautioned that "there comes a time in the extension of the penalizing features" of a tax "when it loses its character as such and becomes a mere penalty with the characteristics of regulation and punishment."[43] However, exactly when Congress crosses the line from "tax" to "penalty" remains unclear. *NFIB* found that a measure that was statutorily labeled a penalty and was designed to shape behavior did not cross the line. Whether the "penalty" limitation imposes any practical restraint on Congress's taxing power remains to be seen.

Cite as: Andy Grewal, *The Taxing Clause*, in The Heritage Guide to the Constitution 134 (Josh Blackman & John G. Malcolm eds., 3d ed. 2025).

Notes

1. *Flint v. Stone Tracy Co.*, 220 U.S. 107, 151 (1911). **2.** Art. I, § 9, cl. 4. **3.** Art. I, § 8, cl. 1. **4.** Art. I, § 9, cl. 5. **5.** Articles of Confederation, arts. II & VIII. **6.** Calvin H. Johnson, *Homage to CLIO: The Historical Continuity from the Articles of Confederation into the Constitution*, 20 Const. Comment. 463, 486 (2004). **7.** 1 Farrand's 243. **8.** *Id.* at 245. **9.** *Id.* **10.** *Id.* at 35. **11.** *Id.* **12.** *Id.* at 19–22. **13.** Louis J. Sirico, Jr., *How Law Employs Historical Narratives: The Great Compromise as an Example*, 2017 Pepp. L. Rev. 65, 66 (2018). **14.** *Id.* **15.** Aaron T. Knapp, *The New Jersey Plan and the Structure of the American Union*, 15 Geo. J.L. & Pub. Pol'y 615, 639–40 (2017). **16.** Storing 5.17.1. **17.** *Id.* **18.** Storing 3.11.47. **19.** *Id.* **20.** Calvin H. Johnson, *Apportionment of Direct Taxes: The Foul-Up in the Core of the Constitution*, 7 Wm. & Mary Bill of Rts. J. 1, 20 n.74 (1998). **21.** James McHenry, *Speech Before the Maryland House of Delegates* (Nov. 19, 1787), in 3 The Founders' Constitution 355 (Philip B. Kurland & Ralph Lerner eds., 1987). **22.** 2 Elliot's 42. **23.** 9 DHRC 1021. **24.** Tariff Act of 1789, 1 Stat. 24, § 1. **25.** Jonathan S. Sidhu, *For the General Welfare: Finding a Limit on the Taxing Power After* NFIB v. Sebelius, 103 Cal. L. Rev. 103, 115 (2015). **26.** William J. Rich, *Lessons of Charleston Harbor: The Rise, Fall and Revival of Pro-Slavery Federalism*, 36 McGeorge L. Rev. 569, 591 (2005). **27.** Richard S. Arnold, *How James Madison Interpreted the Constitution*, 72 N.Y.U. L. Rev. 267, 290 (1997). **28.** Senator Henry Clay, *The American System* (Feb. 2, 3, and 6, 1832), in Robert C. Byrd, 3 The Senate 1789–1989, Classic Speeches 1830–1993, 84 (1994), https://perma.cc/VLL5-A2RJ. **29.** *Letter from James Madison to Joseph C. Cabell* (Sept. 18, 1828), in 9 The Writings of James Madison 316–340 (1910). **30.** David P. Currie, *The Constitution in Congress: The Public Lands, 1829–1861*, 70 U. Chi. L. Rev. 783, 786 (2003). **31.** 276 U.S. 394, 411 (1928). **32.** *Id.* at 412 (quoting *Bailey v. Drexel Furniture Co.*, 259 U.S. 20, 38 (1922)). **33.** 247 U.S. 251 (1918). **34.** 259 U.S. 20 (1922). **35.** *Id.* at 38. **36.** 345 U.S. 22 (1953). **37.** *Id.* at 27. **38.** 567 U.S. 519, 573 (2012). **39.** *Collector v. Day*, 78 U.S. 113 (1870). **40.** *Helvering v. Gerhardt*, 304 U.S. 405 (1938). **41.** 158 U.S. 601, 630 (1895). **42.** 485 U.S. 505 (1988). **43.** 567 U.S. at 573.

~

ESSAY NO. 40: THE SPENDING CLAUSE
ART. I, § 8, CL. 1

The Congress shall have Power . . . to pay the Debts and provide for the common Defence and general Welfare of the United States. . . .

—James C. Phillips

INTRODUCTION

The Constitution contains no express general spending power. Article I, Section 8, Clause 1 authorizes Congress to "lay and collect Taxes" for two purposes only: "to pay the Debts and provide for the common Defence and general Welfare of the United States." Taken together, these purposes traditionally have been held to imply and constitute Congress's spending power.

As a matter of original meaning, there is some doubt that the federal spending power flows from this clause. The clause grants only the power to tax: Any inference of a spending power from the clause's language about the "general Welfare" leaves unexplained where Congress obtains the power to spend money not obtained from taxes, such as borrowed money or the proceeds from land sales. It is more plausible to locate the general federal spending power in the Necessary and Proper Clause. Many legal scholars and jurists today believe that the two purposes of the Spending Clause are so broad as to amount to no limitation at all. Under that view, Congress's power to provide for the "general Welfare" is a power to spend for virtually anything that Congress itself views as helpful.

HISTORY BEFORE 1787

Without a written constitution, Great Britain lacked a spending or taxing or general welfare clause. Instead, the idea of the government as a fiduciary held sway.[1] Thus, both the king and Parliament were deemed, as Oliver Cromwell put it, "servants and trustees of the people."[2] The notion of "public trust" began to appear in English constitutional documents around the mid-1600s, and the doctrine made its way across the Atlantic in royal charters, such as those for New England in 1662 and Georgia in 1732.[3]

Many of the political philosophers who influenced the American Founders, such as Locke, Montesquieu, and Blackstone, discussed the public trust doctrine.[4] The doctrine appeared in early state constitutions, such as those of Maryland, Pennsylvania, Virginia, and Vermont.[5] As one scholar has argued, the language of the so-called Spending Clause—"to pay the Debts and provide for the common Defence and general Welfare of the United States"—was actually *limiting* language. This text "implement[ed] the fiduciary duty of impartiality by assuring that Congress could acquire revenues designated only for projects of general benefit, not for projects benefiting primarily localities or special interests."[6]

The Americans' first effort to create a government beyond just the individual states, the Articles of Confederation, imposed few restrictions on spending. The charter provided that "[a]ll charges of war, and all other expenses that shall be incurred for the common defence or general welfare, and allowed by the united states in congress assembled, shall be defrayed out of a common treasury, which shall be supplied by the several states."[7] This text gave the national government an express power to spend money for two purposes: "common defence" and "general welfare." The primary limitation was politics: Congress could only "ascertain the sums and expences necessary for the defence and welfare of the united states" if nine of the thirteen states agreed.[8] Both this language and subsequent practice led one scholar to argue that "[u]nder the Articles of Confederation the central government[] . . . had ample authority to spend any funds it collected" and that this spending power was in fact "virtually unrestricted."[9] Thus, for example, in January 1778, Congress approved $1,000 for gifts for destitute but peaceful and friendly Pennsylvania Indians.[10]

THE CONSTITUTIONAL CONVENTION

At the Constitutional Convention, the issue of spending was first raised in the New Jersey Plan, which, declared that revenue raised by the federal government could "be applied to such federal purposes as [Congress] shall deem proper & expedient."[11] Similarly, notes from the Committee of Detail referred to paying for (besides past and future debts) the "necessities of the union."[12] And a committee with a member from each state—the "grand committee"—reported that the following language should be added after congressional authorization to raise revenue: "for payments of the debts and necessary expences of the United States."[13]

In the Committee of Detail's August 6 report, any reference to spending was eliminated. Several weeks later the "grand committee" proposed that, "The Legislature of the United-States shall have power to fulfil the engagements which have been entered into by Congress, and to discharge as well the debts of the United States, as the debts incurred by the several States during the late war, for the common defence and general welfare."[14] Some express, enumerated language authorizing spending was thought necessary by Edmund Randolph of Virginia. He argued that "the new Govt. will have no authority in the case unless it be given to them."[15] James Madison of Virginia "thought it necessary to give the authority in order to prevent misconstruction."[16]

After this proposal was rejected, the delegates approved language from Gouverneur Morris of Pennsylvania: "The Legislature shall fulfil the engagements and discharge the debts of the United States."[17] The next day, this language was added to the Taxing Clause: "The Legislature shall fulfil the engagements and discharge the debts of the United-States, and shall have the power to lay and collect Taxes, duties, imposts, and excises."[18] There was some objection to the word "shall," which seemed to impose an obligation. On August 25, the language was changed to "all debts contracted and engagements entered into, by or under the authority of Congress shall be as valid against the United States under this constitution as under the confederation."[19]

A few days later, the "general welfare" language was added to the Taxing Clause. Roger Sherman of Connecticut argued that the Taxing Clause and the provision on paying old debts should be connected. This led ultimately to a combination of the two provisions that was adopted with no discussion and is nearly identical to the Constitution's language: "The Legislature shall have power to lay and collect taxes, duties, imposts, and excises, to pay the debts and provide for the common defence and general welfare of the United States."[20] As one scholar has concluded, "the 'general Welfare' phrase in the Taxing Clause of the Constitution alludes to the vast generality of purposes to which tax revenues, as well as other federal receipts, might be put, but does nothing to empower Congress to spend."[21]

Not all viewed the clause that way. About a week after the Constitution was signed, Connecticut delegates Roger Sherman and Oliver Ellsworth took a broad view of the spending power. They wrote to their governor that "[t]he objects, for which congress may apply monies, are the same mentioned in" Article VII of the Articles of Confederation—"for the common defence and general welfare, and for the payment of the debts incurred for those purposes."[22] This broad reading, however, is in some tension with the fact that the Convention rejected giving Congress the power to legislate for the nation's "common interests," "general welfare," and "general interest."[23]

Alexander Hamilton also took a broad view and argued that Congress should be given plenary spending power, but his proposal did not include "general welfare" language.[24] Professor Robert G. Natelson has noted that the term "general welfare" had "appeared (1) in Benjamin Franklin's proposed articles of confederation of 1775, (2) in John Dickinson's first draft of the eventually-adopted Articles, (3) in the Articles themselves (and therefore, by reference, in the New Jersey Plan to strengthen the Articles), (4) in the centralized Virginia Plan, (5) in Roger Sherman's proposal for a government less powerful than that contemplated by the Virginia Plan, (6) in proposals to have the federal government pay confederation debts, and (7) in the finished Constitution." Therefore, Natelson concludes, the "general welfare" language was not included in Hamilton's plan because "it was essentially not a phrase of power, but of *limitation,*" and "Hamilton wanted the national legislature to have power to legislate on matters of local and private as well as general welfare."[25]

THE RATIFICATION DEBATES

In Federalist No. 41, James Madison noted the connection between the language in the Constitution and the language in the Articles of Confederation. Given that the Articles Congress had a limited spending power, Madison wrote, it was a "misconstruction" to assert that the Constitution gave Congress an unlimited spending power. Madison and Hamilton may have disagreed on the scope of the power, but both implied that Congress had the power to spend money: Madison in Federalist No. 58 and Hamilton in Federalist No. 78 referred to Congress's power of the "purse."

Other Framers from the Convention also disagreed over the scope of the spending power. For instance, New York's Robert Gates took a more Hamiltonian view. He argued that the "general welfare" language provided Congress with a plenary spending power.[26] In the Connecticut convention, however, Ellsworth expounded a Madisonian view that Congress's enumerated powers limited its spending power.[27] Ellsworth may have been recanting his position from the transmittal letter to his governor.

The Anti-Federalists warned primarily about the dangers of the taxing power and discussed how that taxed money would be spent. Melancton Smith observed "a general maxim, that all governments find a use for as much money as they can raise" and added as "a settled truth, that they will all spend as much as their revenue; that is, will live at least up to their income."[28] Another Anti-Federalist, a Federal Republican, warned that "Congress will be the judges of what is necessary for the general welfare of the United States, and this will open the door to any extravagant expence which they shall be pleased to incur."[29] An Anti-Federalist Impartial Examiner identified two limitations on the clause: (1) Congress could spend on the "general good" as opposed to "private interest" and (2) Congress must "take equal care of the whole body of the community, so as not to favor one part more than another."[30] Such limitations could stem textually from two different senses of the clause's term "general," although they seem to derive from a more general maxim of government.[31]

THREE VIEWS ON THE SPENDING POWER

In the early Republic, three competing views of the spending power were debated. First, Hamilton revived his broad view after its apparent defeat in the Constitutional Convention. He contended that the only limits on the tax-and-spend power were the requirements that duties be uniform, that direct taxes be apportioned by population, and that no tax should be laid on articles exported from any state. The power to raise money was otherwise "plenary, and indefinite," Hamilton argued in his *Report on Manufactures*, "and the objects to which it may be appropriated are no less comprehensive."[32]

Second, James Madison and Thomas Jefferson advanced the narrow view. They argued that the Constitution did not confer on Congress the power to do whatever it thought might be in the best interests of the nation. Rather, the power to tax and spend conferred on Congress only the power to further the ends specifically enumerated elsewhere in the Constitution. In the *Virginia Report*, Madison explained that "Whenever . . . money has been raised by the general authority, and is to be applied to a particular measure, a question arises whether the particular measure be within the enumerated authorities vested in Congress."[33] Jefferson articulated a similar perspective when advising President Washington that the national bank was unconstitutional: "The incorporation of a bank, and other powers assumed by this bill have not, in my opinion, been delegated to the U.S. by the Constitution" and "are not among the powers specially enumerated."[34]

There was also a third interpretation, recognized later even by Hamilton. According to this intermediate view, the "common Defence and general Welfare" language contains its own limitation: Spending under the clause must be for the "general" (that is, national) welfare and not for purely local or regional benefit. President James Monroe adopted this position, albeit with more teeth than Hamilton had been willing to give it. In 1822, Monroe vetoed a bill to preserve and repair the Cumberland Road. In Monroe's veto message, he contended that Congress's power to spend was restricted "to purposes of common defence, and of general, national, not local, or state, benefit."[35]

EARLY CONGRESSIONAL VIEWS ON THE SPENDING POWER

During the early Congresses, the relatively few debates about the scope of the spending power seem to reject the broad Hamiltonian view. For example, the First Congress refused to make a loan to a glass manufacturer after members "doubt[ed] the constitutionality of the power of Congress to loan the money" and argued that this was a matter for state government.[36] The Fourth Congress did not believe it had the power to provide relief to the citizens of Savannah, Georgia, after a devastating fire destroyed the entire city. Representative Macon of North Carolina epitomized this view, "wish[ing] gentlemen to put their finger upon that part of the Constitution which gave that House power to afford them relief. . . ." Macon "felt for the sufferers . . . but he felt as tenderly for the Constitution; he had examined it, and it did not authorize any such grant."[37]

It is true that early Congresses approved some appropriations for apparently local projects. In 1790, for example, the First Congress approved an appropriation for a lighthouse at the entrance of the Chesapeake Bay. Yet this lighthouse would benefit the coastal trade of the entire nation, was to be on property ceded to the United States, and would be directed by the President. Thus, it would be a federal lighthouse authorized under the Federal Enclave Clause.[38] (See Essay No. 65.) This project and other similar expenditures were arguably of general benefit or specifically tied to other enumerated powers and therefore within the authority conferred by Article I, Section 8.

To illustrate this principle, the Ninth Congress approved various appropriations to fund a road across the Cumberland Gap in the Appalachian Mountains. These appropriations were based on a compact in Ohio's Enabling Act that Congress had entered into with Ohio. The compact specified that the state would not tax any federal lands sold for five years in exchange for building the road, which Ohio would then have responsibility to maintain. Congressional

authority for this arrangement arguably flowed either from the Territories Clause or the fact that the road served the country's purposes.[39] (See Essay No. 144.) In debate over the bill, Representative Bedinger of Kentucky argued that the bill would serve the "general interests of the Union."[40] Similarly, President Washington had viewed a "smooth way" to the west as important for the national interest because it bound the western settlers to the nation and protected against encroachment from Great Britain and Spain.[41]

EARLY PRESIDENTIAL VIEWS ON THE SPENDING POWER

A key issue in the presidential election of 1800 between Jefferson and incumbent Federalist President John Adams was the different interpretations of the Spending Clause. Jefferson would explain that this issue was "almost the only landmark which now divides the federalists from the republicans."[42] Jefferson won that election and rejected the more expansive interpretation of the spending power. His successors usually adopted the narrow perspective. Jefferson's 1806 State of the Union Address proposed a constitutional amendment to permit funding for "the great purposes of the public education, roads, rivers, canals, and such other objects of public improvement as it may be thought proper to add to the constitutional enumeration of the federal powers." Jefferson stated that these objects were "not among those enumerated in the Constitution, and to which it permits the public moneys to be applied."[43] The proposed amendment was ignored by Congress.[44]

President James Madison vetoed an internal improvements bill because a broad reading of the Spending Clause would render "the special and careful enumeration of powers, which follow the clause, nugatory and improper."[45] President Monroe initially adopted the Madison–Jefferson position. But, as noted above, Monroe later adopted an intermediate position that "general" was a limitation on spending that did not benefit the entire nation, but Congress otherwise had spending authority under the clause.

President John Quincy Adams favored the Hamiltonian position. He argued that Article I, Section 8, Clause 1 provided a separate grant of spending authority to Congress.[46] In response to Adams's position, former President Madison advocated a constitutional amendment that either would remove the phrase "common defence & general welfare" or add to it "in the cases required by this Constitution."[47]

Every other antebellum President rejected the more expansive interpretation of spending power. President Andrew Jackson, for example, rejected as a "fallacy" and "dangerous doctrine" the contention that the Spending Clause conferred upon Congress the power to do whatever seemed "to conduce to the public good."[48] President James Buchanan likewise assumed that funds from taxation were "confined to the execution of the enumerated powers delegated to Congress."[49] Before the Civil War, some members of Congress advocated an expansive spending power, as evidenced by the improvement bills they passed. But at least in the executive branch, a narrow interpretation was the majority position for the first seven decades after ratification.

JUDICIAL PRECEDENT

Before the New Deal, fights over congressional spending power tended to be between Congress and the Executive, with the legislature favoring a broader reading and the President favoring a narrower reading. That dynamic changed with *United States v. Butler* (1936), which launched modern Spending Clause jurisprudence.[50] In *Butler*, both the federal government and those challenging the Agricultural Adjustment Act relied upon the Hamiltonian position. Both the majority and dissenting opinions of the Court facially accepted the correctness of Hamilton's position, but the Court also acknowledged Madison's federalism-based concerns. The majority found that the regulation of agricultural production was unconstitutional because its purpose was to regulate "a matter beyond the powers delegated to the federal government."[51]

Moreover, the Hamiltonian position purportedly adopted by the Court was not the expansive view that Congress could do whatever it deemed to be in the public interest. Rather, the Court favored the more limited view that

the limits on spending were contained in the Spending Clause itself and not in the remainder of Article I, Section 8. In other words, the only limitation on Congress's power to tax and spend was that the spending must be for the "general Welfare"—the intermediate position actually advocated by James Monroe. What really made *Butler* a departure from the early interpretation of the clause, then, was that it gave Congress virtually unlimited discretion to determine what was in the "general Welfare." This holding was much more in line with the expansive Hamiltonian position than it was with the positions advocated either by Monroe or by Madison and Jefferson.

For nearly eight decades after *Butler*, the courts treated whatever limitation the clause might impose as essentially a nonjusticiable political question.[52] Instead, the courts focused on whether various conditions imposed on the receipt of federal funds were constitutionally permissible. In other words, conditions designed to achieve ends concededly not within Congress's enumerated powers could still be valid.

South Dakota v. Dole (1987) adopted a four-pronged test to assess the constitutionality of spending conditions.[53] The Court also applied another test: whether the "financial inducement" is so coercive that it compels rather than pressures.

NFIB v. Sebelius (2012) held for the first time that a congressional spending program violated the coercion principle. By a 7–2 vote, the Court found that Congress's threat to withhold *all* existing Medicaid program funds from states that chose not to participate in the significant expansion of that program's mandate was unduly coercive. The 2010 Affordable Care Act was like a "gun to the head" of the states and amounted to "economic dragooning" that left "the States with no real option but to acquiesce in the Medicaid expansion."[54]

Cite as: James C. Phillips, *The Spending Clause*, in THE HERITAGE GUIDE TO THE CONSTITUTION 137 (Josh Blackman & John G. Malcolm eds., 3d ed. 2025).

Notes

1. Robert G. Natelson, *The Constitution and Public Trust*, 52 Buff. L. Rev. 1077, 1108–23 (2004). **2.** 5 David Hume, The History of England from the Invasion of Julius Caesar to the Revolution in 1688, at 529 (1983) (1778). **3.** Natelson, *The Constitution and Public Trust, supra* at 1108–12. **4.** *Id.* at 1113–34; Md. Const. of 1776, art. IV; Pa. Const. of 1776, art. IV; Va. Const. of 1776, § 2; Vt. Const. of 1786, ch. I, art. VI. **5.** *Id.* at 1134–36. **6.** *Id.* at 1169–70. **7.** Articles of Confederation, art. VIII. **8.** *Id.* at Art. IX, § 6. **9.** David E. Engdahl, *The Basis of the Spending Power*, 18 Seattle U. L. Rev. 215, 235 (1995). **10.** 7 Journals of the Continental Congress 62–63 (1777). **11.** 1 Farrand's 243; 2 Farrand's 157. **12.** 2 Farrand's 142. **13.** *Id.* at 366. **14.** *Id.* at 352. **15.** *Id.* at 377. **16.** *Id.* at 377. **17.** *Id.* at 368, 377. **18.** *Id.* at 382, 392. **19.** *Id.* at 408, 414. **20.** *Id.* at 495, 499. **21.** Engdahl, *supra* at 243. **22.** 3 Farrand's 99. **23.** 2 Farrand's 21. **24.** 1 Farrand's 291–93. **25.** Robert G. Natelson, *The General Welfare Clause and the Public Trust: An Essay in Original Understanding*, 52 Kan. L. Rev. 1, 29, 30 (2003). **26.** 1 The Debate on the Constitution 3–6, 167, 501 (1993); 2 The Founders' Constitution 419 (Philip B. Kurland & Ralph Lerner eds., 1987). **27.** 2 Elliot's 190–97. **28.** Storing 6.12.37. **29.** Storing 3.6.19. **30.** Storing 5.14.6. **31.** *Id.* **32.** 2 The Founders' Constitution, *supra* at 446–47. **33.** The Virginia Report of 1799–1800, at 201 (J.W. Randolph ed., 1850). **34.** Thomas Jefferson, Opinion on the Constitutionality of the Bill for Establishing a National Bank (Feb. 15, 1791), https://perma.cc/5C66-GECC. **35.** 46 Annals of Cong. 1838, 1849 (1822). **36.** 2 Annals of Cong. 1686–88 (1790). **37.** 6 Annals of Cong. 1717 (1796). **38.** Act of July 22, 1790, 1 Stat. 53, 54; Lighthouses Act of 1789, Pub. L. No. 1-54, 1 Stat. 137 (1790). **39.** 2 Stat. 173, 175 (Apr. 30, 1802); Act of Mar. 29, 1806, Pub. L. No. 9-280, 2 Stat. 357; 29 Annals of Cong. 1252 (1816); Theodore Skye, The National Road and the Difficult Path to Sustainable National Investment 15 (2011). **40.** Skye, *supra* at 16. **41.** *Id.* at 14. **42.** Letter from Thomas Jefferson to Albert Gallatin (June 16, 1817) *in* 2 The Founders' Constitution, *supra* at 452. **43.** 16 Annals of Cong. 14–15 (1806). **44.** Forrest McDonald, The Presidency of Thomas Jefferson 130 (1976). **45.** 32 Annals of Cong. 211, 212 (1817). **46.** Stephen Minicucci, *Internal Improvements and the Union, 1790–1860*, 18 Stud. in Am. Pol. Dev. 160, 165 (2004) (citing John Quincy Adams, First Annual Message to Congress (Dec. 6, 1825)). **47.** Letter from James Madison to Martin Van Buren (Sept. 20, 1826), *in* 9 The Writings of James Madison 255 (Gaillard Hunt ed., 1910). **48.** Andrew Jackson, Veto to an Act to Improve the Navigation of the Wabash River, 1834, State of the Union History, https://perma.cc/4HT7-549C. **49.** H.R. Journal, 35th Cong., 2nd Sess. 506 (Feb. 26, 1859). **50.** 297 U.S. 1 (1936). **51.** *Id.* at 68. **52.** *South Dakota v. Dole*, 483 U.S. 203, 207 n.2 (1987). **53.** *Id.* at 207–08. **54.** 567 U.S. at 581, 582.

⌁

ESSAY NO. 41: THE UNIFORMITY CLAUSE
ART. I, § 8, CL. 1

. . . all Duties, Imposts and Excises shall be uniform throughout the United States. . . .

—Nelson Lund

INTRODUCTION

The Confederation government lacked the power to regulate interstate and foreign commerce and had weak powers of taxation.[1] The Constitution cured these defects but thereby created a new danger: The national government might abuse its powerful regulatory and taxing powers in ways that would undermine the kind of beneficial economic competition the Framers hoped to promote. The Uniformity Clause was designed to reduce this risk by ensuring that federal duties, imposts, and excise taxes would be uniform in every state.

THE CONSTITUTIONAL CONVENTION

At the Constitutional Convention, the Uniformity Clause was joined initially with what is now the Port Preference Clause (Article I, Section 9, Clause 6), which bars Congress from giving preferences "by any Regulation of Commerce or revenue" to the ports of one state over those of another.[2] (See Essay No. 73.) The Port Preference Clause limits both the commerce and taxing powers, whereas the Uniformity Clause applies to the taxing power alone. Their common origin, however, is a sign of their common purpose: Each was meant to prohibit geographic discrimination that would give some states or regions a competitive advantage in their commercial relations with the others.[3]

The U.S. Supreme Court seems to have assumed that the uniformity requirement applies to all levies that are not "direct taxes" within the meaning of the Direct Taxes Clause (Article I, Section 9, Clause 4).[4] (See Essay No. 71.) Because the scope of that clause is notoriously indeterminate, this definition is imprecise.[5] Generally speaking, however, the Uniformity Clause's three overlapping categories of "indirect taxes" included levies on consumption, trade, and legislatively specified business and official transactions (such as fees on auction sales and license fees).[6]

Because the goods and activities that can be taxed are distributed unequally through the country, virtually all duties, imposts, and excises have nonuniform effects. Accordingly, the Constitutional Convention's committee on trade changed "uniform and equal" to "uniform," presumably to avoid an implication that these taxes must have identical effects in all states.[7] A tax on tobacco, for example, would obviously have affected certain regions more severely than others. Because the Constitution expressly empowers Congress to levy these taxes, it necessarily permits some of the nonuniform effects that inevitably accompany them. The principal challenge in interpreting the Uniformity Clause is to distinguish the kind of nonuniformity that is forbidden by the Constitution from the nonuniform effects that necessarily accompany permissible duties, imposts, and excises.[8]

JUDICIAL PRECEDENT

The Supreme Court's first significant exposition of the Uniformity Clause came in 1884. The *Head Money Cases* (1884) declared that a tax is uniform if it "operates with the same force and effect in every place where the subject of it is found."[9] This rule was meant to forbid geographically nonuniform *taxes* without outlawing all geographically nonuniform *effects*. But the Court's formula does not describe any limits on the legislature's discretion to define the "subjects" of taxation. Without such limits, Congress could simply define the subject of an excise tax as "tobacco grown in Maryland" or "tobacco grown anywhere except in Maryland."

United States v. Ptasynski (1983) unanimously upheld an excise tax on the production of crude oil, with an exception for oil produced in most areas north of the Arctic Circle. The Court observed that a concern with regional discrimination motivated the adoption of the Uniformity Clause, relying primarily on the detailed analysis in *Knowlton v. Moore* (1900) and a passage in Justice Joseph Story's *Commentaries*. *Ptasynski* presented an issue that the Court had not yet squarely addressed: "whether the Uniformity Clause prohibits Congress from defining the class of objects to be taxed in geographic terms."[10] The Court concluded (1) that any tax in which the subject is defined in nongeographic terms satisfies the Uniformity Clause and (2) that where the subject is defined in geographic terms, the tax will be scrutinized for "actual geographic discrimination."[11]

The first part of this test creates a very large safe harbor for discriminatory taxes, which can often be framed without using overtly geographic terminology, such as "oil whose production might disturb a population of caribou." Nor does the second part of the test put a meaningful limit on Congress's power to favor some states or regions over others. The Court nowhere defined "actual geographic discrimination," and it went out of its way to emphasize that review of statutes using such geographic terminology would be highly deferential.[12] The absence of any definition of "actual geographic discrimination," especially when combined with the promise of deferential review, has rendered the Uniformity Clause without effect, except to the extent that it might encourage congressional self-restraint.

OPEN QUESTIONS

- Might the Court borrow from the jurisprudence of the Privileges and Immunities Clause and the Court's "dormant commerce" cases to create a legal test that reflects the Uniformity Clause's goal of protecting free markets and economic competition from the influence of special interests in Congress?[13]

- Might the Court adopt a legal test under which a tax is unconstitutional if and only if it provides benefits to a majority of states at the expense of a minority of states?[14]
- Might the Uniformity Clause be interpreted to help justify a uniformity constraint on federal spending?[15]

Cite as: Nelson Lund, *The Uniformity Clause, in* The Heritage Guide to the Constitution 142 (Josh Blackman & John G. Malcolm eds., 3d ed. 2025).

Notes

1. Federalist No. 22 (Hamilton); Federalist No. 30 (Hamilton); Federalist No. 42 (Madison).   **2.** 2 Farrand's 417–18.   **3.** *Knowlton v. Moore*, 178 U.S. 41, 95–101 (1900); 1 Story's Commentaries § 957.   **4.** *Knowlton*, 178 U.S. at 83; *Nicol v. Ames*, 173 U.S. 509, 515 (1889); Federalist No. 12 (Hamilton); Federalist No. 21 (Hamilton); and Federalist No. 36 (Hamilton).   **5.** Nelson Lund, *The Uniformity Clause*, 51 U. Chi. L. Rev. 1193, 1194–95 n.5 (1984).   **6.** Robert G. Natelson, *What the Constitution Means by "Duties, Imposts, and Excises"—and "Taxes" (Direct or Indirect)*, 66 Case W. Res. L. Rev. 297, 318–29 (2015).   **7.** *Knowlton*, 178 U.S. at 104; 2 Farrand's 437.   **8.** Lund, *supra* at 1195; Philip Joseph Deutch, *The Uniformity Clause and Puerto Rican Statehood*, 43 Stan. L. Rev. 685 (1991).   **9.** *Edye v. Robertson*, 112 U.S. 580, 594 (1884).   **10.** *United States v. Ptasynski*, 462 U.S. 74, 83 (1983).   **11.** *Id.* at 82, 84–85.   **12.** *Id.* at 86.   **13.** Lund, *supra* at 1195.   **14.** Deutch, *supra* at 689.   **15.** Laurence Claus, *"Uniform Throughout the United States": Limits on Taxing as Limits on Spending*, 18 Const. Comment. 517 (2001).

ESSAY NO. 42: THE BORROWING CLAUSE
ART. I, § 8, CL. 2

The Congress shall have Power . . . To borrow Money on the credit of the United States. . . .

—James C. Phillips

INTRODUCTION

The Borrowing Clause gives Congress authority to borrow money on behalf of the United States. During the ratification debates, Federalists and Anti-Federalists alike viewed this power as a way to support the "national defense" during times of war. Early in the Republic, Secretary of the Treasury Alexander Hamilton invoked the Borrowing Clause to support the constitutionality of chartering a Bank of the United States. Jeffersonians disagreed with the bank's constitutionality, and dismantled the national bank when they came to power, but it was reestablished during the War of 1812. In the twentieth century, federal spending increased and federal debt reached unprecedented levels. Litigation over the clause has involved intergovernmental tax immunity, the government's power to make contracts, and Congress's powers to alter debt obligations.

HISTORY BEFORE 1787

The Articles of Confederation provided the power "to borrow money, or emit bills on the credit of the united states."[1] However, as St. George Tucker observed, because the government did "not possess[] any revenue independent of the states," these "loans were obtained with difficulty, and, very rarely in time to answer the purposes for which they were intended."[2]

THE CONSTITUTIONAL CONVENTION

During the Constitutional Convention, the Committee of Detail included the same language from the Articles of Confederation in its report. Congress would have the power to "borrow money, and emit bills on the credit of the United States." The delegates voted to strike the power to "emit bills."[3] This revision strongly suggests that Congress was not authorized to borrow by means of issuing paper money, although it appears that interest-bearing debt instruments were permissible. (See Essay No. 48.)

THE RATIFICATION DEBATES

In Federalist Nos. 15, 30, 34, and 41, Madison and Hamilton connected the power to borrow money to the "national defence" and to the raising of revenue through taxes. The Anti-Federalist Brutus linked the powers to borrow money and the power to raise and support armies to the power to lay and collect taxes. He considered the first two "together . . . because their extent, and the danger that will arise from the exercise of these powers, cannot be fully understood, unless they are viewed in relation to each other."[4] Federalists argued that the power to borrow money was necessary to handle the debts the nation had already undertaken.[5]

Federalists argued that borrowing money on the public credit was generally reserved for the emergencies of war. Still, Anti-Federalists lamented the lack of any limitation on the borrowing power provided to Congress. "The Congress, by the proposed system," wrote A Farmer, has "the power of borrowing money to what amount they may judge proper, consequently to mortgage all our estates, and all our sources of revenue."[6] Brutus raised the concern that "Congress may mortgage any or all the revenues of the union, as a fund to loan money upon . . . the interest of which will be equal to the annual revenues of the country" and thereby "create a national debt, so large, as to exceed the ability of the country ever to sink."[7] But while there may not have been any constitutional check on Congress, one scholar observed, "[i]t was undisputed [that] the executive would have no prerogative power to tax, spend, or borrow."[8]

EARLY PRACTICE

During the nation's early history, Congress was expected to keep expenditures equal to or less than revenues.[9] Thus, the Treasury Department assiduously earmarked all revenues for specific government programs.[10] The Borrowing Clause, however, had a practical corollary. The terms upon which a nation could borrow money depended on its credit standing. President George Washington's Farewell Address captured the general sentiment of the times. He urged

Americans to "cherish public credit," which was a "very important source of strength [and] security." Washington stressed that credit should be used "as sparingly as possible" and that the country should "avoid[] likewise the accumulation of debt."[11]

Although Federalists and Democratic-Republicans agreed on the need to maintain the public credit, they diverged considerably in their views on how the borrowing power should be implemented. Secretary of the Treasury Alexander Hamilton, for example, argued "[t]hat [because] loans in times of public danger, especially from foreign war, are found an indispensable resource . . . the necessity for borrowing in particular emergencies cannot be doubted."[12] Others, such as Benjamin Rush, worried that the money borrowed would be used only to finance "unjust and offensive wars" since "just [and] necessary" wars in a republic could "always be [supported] by annual taxes from a free people."[13]

In 1791, Hamilton sought to assure a strong central government through the chartering of the First Bank of the United States.[14] Relying on a broad interpretation of the Borrowing Clause, he contended that the bank could maintain federal control over the federal monetary reserves and issue debt instruments that circulated like money. Hamilton viewed the issuing of federal debt instruments as an essential stimulant to commerce. This debt would provide a source of capital to a capital-poor society and was equally important for purposes of revenue collection. The Constitution, however, did not expressly authorize Congress to charter corporations, and the constitutionality of the bank was widely debated. Representative James Madison opposed his old Federalist co-author on the House floor during debate over the bank bill. Madison questioned the constitutional authority for a national bank by asking and answering: "Is this a bill to borrow money? It does not borrow a shilling."[15] The bill to charter the bank went far beyond the scope of the Borrowing Clause. President Washington ultimately approved the national bank.

A decade later, President Thomas Jefferson and his Democratic-Republican party dismantled much of Hamilton's program.[16] To the Jeffersonians, a balanced budget reflected a popular desire to limit the size and power of the federal government and protect states' rights.

Congress repealed Hamilton's internal taxes, which provided security for the federal debt. Jefferson appointed Albert Gallatin as Secretary of the Treasury with a mandate to pay down the federal debt.

Wartime exigencies and economic crises inclined the country toward the modern interpretation of the Borrowing Clause. During the War of 1812, a financial emergency threatened national security. A bipartisan consensus formed around the need for the federal government to control its reserves through the Second Bank of the United States. Chief Justice John Marshall's opinion in *McCulloch v. Maryland* (1819) upheld the constitutionality of the bank.[17] Marshall specifically found that the bank could be supported based on Congress's enumerated powers, such as borrowing money, that had been entrusted to the federal government. He also cited the need for "ample means" to exercise these "ample powers."[18]

With a few exceptions, subsequent administrations prioritized balancing the federal budget. In 1835, President Andrew Jackson successfully paid down the federal debt, making the last two years of his presidency the only time our nation has been debt-free.[19] The early Presidents followed the advice of George Washington in his Farewell Address.

MODERN PRACTICE

From 1789 until 1917, the federal government's policy of incurring and repaying debt remained relatively consistent.[20] Congress borrowed money to pay for wars and to sustain the economy during a recession, but it began to pay down those debts upon the return to peace and financial stability. In 1917, Congress granted the Department of the Treasury standing borrowing authority without the need for particular federal laws authorizing the borrowing.[21] Nevertheless, for many years, Congress continued to manage the incurrence and repayment of debt in substantially the same manner as before.

That policy would change after World War II. Attitudes were changed based partly on the influence of economic thinkers such as John Maynard Keynes. Also, during the New Deal, there was an expansion of government-funded entitlements as well as a large standing military force. These expenditures produced sustained peacetime deficits and very few periods of debt reduction. Since the 1990s, there have been periodic but failed attempts to implement spending and debt limits, as federal debt has reached unprecedented levels. Congress attempted to give the President more control over spending through the Line-Item Veto Act, but the Supreme Court declared it unconstitutional in *Clinton v. New York* (1998).[22] (See Essay No. 36.)

JUDICIAL PRECEDENT

Legal disputes dealing with the Borrowing Clause involve three issues. The most litigated issue involves the principle of immunity from intergovernmental taxation: When is the federal government immune from the taxes imposed by state and local governments? The U.S. Supreme Court has held that the Supremacy Clause prohibits state and municipal governments from directly or indirectly taxing the interest income on federal government debt and thereby interfering with the federal government's power under the Borrowing Clause.[23] (See Essay No. 154.)

The Borrowing Clause also implicitly requires Congress to maintain the public credit. The Supreme Court has invoked the clause to treat the government like a private party in its contractual dealings. In addition, the clause vests Congress with the power to contract against subsequent repudiation or impairment of its obligations by future Congresses. *Perry v. United States* (1935) cautioned that the power to borrow money is vital and one upon which the government's very life may depend.[24] By making the promise to repay binding, the United States is able to maintain sufficient credit to borrow.

Congress also has the power to authorize the issuance of definite obligations for the payment of money borrowed, but it has not been vested with authority to alter or destroy those obligations. *United States v. Winstar Corp.* (1996) held that the government's contractual obligations would be enforced unless doing so blocked the exercise of one of the government's essential sovereign powers.[25]

THE DEBT CEILING

Starting with the Obama Administration, there have been intense political debates about the possibility of the federal government reaching its debt limit or ceiling—the congressionally authorized limit on how much the federal government can borrow. Today, the nation's debt is bigger than its gross domestic product.[26] In 2011, given the text of the Borrowing Clause, President Barack Obama determined that he could not unilaterally raise the debt ceiling.[27] Eventually, Congress acquiesced and raised the ceiling, enabling the government to borrow more money. In 2023, when the debt ceiling was reached without congressional action, the Department of the Treasury decided to "take well-established 'extraordinary measures' to borrow additional funds without breaching the debt ceiling."[28]

Because the Constitution imposes no express limits on the borrowing power, when and how much to borrow are political questions left to Congress with public opinion and elections remaining the only check on this power. As in the Founding era, the question of the extent to which the government should run deficits and maintain a large federal debt are at the heart of the debate about the proper scope of the federal government.

Cite as: James C. Phillips, *The Borrowing Clause*, *in* THE HERITAGE GUIDE TO THE CONSTITUTION 144 (Josh Blackman & John G. Malcolm eds., 3d ed. 2025).

Notes

1. Articles of Confederation, art. IX, § 5.   **2.** St. George Tucker, 1 Blackstone's Commentaries: With Notes of Reference to the Constitution and Laws of the Federal Government of the United States and of the Commonwealth of Virginia 247 (1803).   **3.** 2 Farrand's 168, 303.   **4.** Storing 2.9.93–.95.   **5.** William Rawle, A View of the Constitution of the United States 81 (2d ed., 1829).   **6.** Storing 3.14.12.   **7.** Storing 2.9.93–.95.   **8.** Michael W. McConnell, The President Who Would Not Be King: Executive Power Under the Constitution 101 (2020).   **9.** Kate Stith, *Rewriting the Fiscal Constitution: The Case of Gramm–Rudman–Hollings*, 76 Calif. L. Rev. 595, 601 (1988).   **10.** *Id.* at 603.   **11.** George Washington, Farewell Address (Sept. 19, 1796), https://perma.cc/Y7XS-U5FG.   **12.** Alexander Hamilton, Report Relative to a Provision for the Support of Public Credit (Jan. 9, 1790), https://perma.cc/NV8R-JUJQ.   **13.** To James Madison from Benjamin Rush (Mar. 10 1790), https://perma.cc/T2CR-STMQ; Tucker, at 246–47.   **14.** Robert J. Reinstein, *The Limits of Congressional Power*, 89 Temp. L. Rev. 1, 7 (2016).   **15.** James Madison, The Bank Bill (Feb. 2, 1791), https://perma.cc/L5S2-RB33.   **16.** Gergory May, Jefferson's Treasure: How Albert Gallatin Saved the New Nation from Debt 87–140 (2018).   **17.** 17 U.S. 316 (1819).   **18.** *Id.* at 408.   **19.** Chris Edwards, *Federal Debt in Historical Perspective*, *in* A Fiscal Cliff 24–26 (John Merrifield & Barry W. Poulson eds. 2020).   **20.** Edwards, at 24–26.   **21.** Second Liberty Bond Act, Pub. L. 65-43, 40 Stat. at 288.   **22.** 524 U.S. 417 (1998).   **23.** *State of Missouri ex rel. Missouri Insurance Co. v. Gehner*, 281 U.S. 313 (1930).   **24.** 204 U.S. 330 (1935).   **25.** 518 U.S. 839 (1996).   **26.** Drew DeSilver, *5 Facts About the U.S. National Debt*, Pew Research Center (Feb. 14, 2023), https://perma.cc/LV2V-VRGN.   **27.** David Jackson, *Obama Says He Can't Raise Debt Ceiling on His Own*, USA Today (July 22, 2011), https://perma.cc/Q2PB-MU3A.   **28.** Cong. Budget Office, Federal Debt and the Statutory Limit (Feb. 2023), https://perma.cc/D4CG-7L73.

~

ESSAY NO. 43: THE FOREIGN COMMERCE CLAUSE
ART. I, § 8, CL. 3

The Congress shall have Power . . . To regulate Commerce with foreign Nations. . . .

—Eugene Kontorovich

INTRODUCTION

Article I, Section 8, Clause 3 grants Congress the power to regulate commerce with foreign states, among the several states, and with Indian Tribes. (The second and third of these provisions will be discussed in Essay Nos. 44 and 45, respectively.)

Under the Articles of Confederation, Congress had no meaningful authority over foreign commerce. The Framers of the Constitution largely agreed that the central government should have this power. Moreover, James Madison in Federalist No. 42 viewed the interstate commerce power as "supplemental" to the "great and essential power of regulating foreign commerce." Early Congresses used this power to regulate the foreign slave trade.

The U.S. Supreme Court has not resolved many cases concerning the Foreign Commerce Clause. Many lower courts have extended the Court's expansive twentieth-century jurisprudence concerning interstate commerce to foreign commerce, leading to broad powers of extraterritorial regulation for the federal government.

HISTORY BEFORE 1787

The lack of a federal power over foreign trade was perceived as one of the principal defects of the Articles of Confederation.[1] Under the Articles, Congress lacked the power to impose tariffs and restrictions on goods from foreign nations and was expressly forbidden from entering into a "treaty of commerce . . . whereby the legislative power of the respective states shall be restrained from imposing [certain] imposts and duties on foreigners. . . ."[2] As a result, any trade policy required coordinated action by the states.

However, such coordination was impossible in practice. Great Britain imposed duties and tariffs to monopolize trade in its favor, and the United States was unable to retaliate. In 1781, Congress asked the states to delegate a limited temporary foreign commerce authority so the central government could respond to British tariffs on U.S. exports.[3] In 1783, Congress considered an amendment to the Articles of Confederation that would have given Congress power over foreign commerce.[4] This proposal, however, would not be adopted.

THE CONSTITUTIONAL CONVENTION

At the Philadelphia Convention, the delegates generally agreed on the need for a national power to regulate foreign commerce. The regulation of foreign commerce combined two broad federal roles: managing relations with other countries, of which trade was a part, and preserving trade from state interference.

During the Committee of Detail's proceedings, several proposals were advanced that would have given Congress the power to "regulate Commerce."[5] John Rutledge of South Carolina added that this power would extend to "both foreign and domestic" commerce.[6] On August 6, Rutledge delivered the Committee of Detail's report.[7] It granted Congress the power "to regulate commerce with foreign nations, and among the several States."[8] Ten days later, this proposal was adopted without debate.[9]

The only significant discussion about the Foreign Commerce Clause occurred on August 29. Charles Pinckney of South Carolina proposed that legislation to regulate "the commerce of the United States with foreign powers or among the several States" should require a two-thirds vote in each house of Congress.[10] He explained that the Southern states did not "need the protection of the Northern States at present."[11] But Pinckney and other Southern delegates worried that in the future, the Northern states would use the foreign commerce power to enact protectionist laws. These taxes would benefit Northern merchant shipping but would increase the costs of exporting Southern crops. More generally, the Southern delegates seemed concerned that organized industrial groups would succeed in pushing through special-interest legislation that would harm overall welfare.

Gouverneur Morris of Pennsylvania opposed the motion as "highly injurious."[12] James Madison of Virginia stated that a two-thirds majority would make it harder to enact "retaliating measures" on "foreign nations."[13] Pinckney's proposal was defeated by a vote of seven to four, with Maryland, Virginia, North Carolina, and Georgia in favor.[14]

The Commerce Clause was later amended to include a power to regulate Indian commerce.[15] No further changes were made.[16] Congress would have the power "To regulate Commerce with foreign Nations."

THE RATIFICATION DEBATES

In Federalist No. 11, Alexander Hamilton contended that the immediate goal of the foreign commerce power was to enact retaliatory and protectionist measures. He wrote that Congress "may oblige foreign countries to bid against each other, for the privileges of our markets."

In Federalist No. 42, Madison described the interstate commerce power as "supplemental" to the "great and essential power of regulating foreign commerce power." Without the former, the latter would be "incomplete" and "ineffectual." In order to ensure that foreign commerce flows through all the states, Congress must be able to prevent states from imposing costs on other states. Today, this view of the interstate commerce power as auxiliary to the foreign commerce power seems exaggerated. The problem of state restrictions on domestic trade was real enough, but Madison's discussion reflects his view of the importance of international trade. Madison also thought the foreign commerce power could be used to impose "considerable discouragement" on the transatlantic slave trade.

The Anti-Federalists did not object to the Foreign Commerce Clause. Agrippa, for instance, a prominent critic of the Constitution, wrote that "the intercourse between us and foreign nations, properly forms the department of Congress."[17]

EARLY PRACTICE

Two early statutes invoked Congress's foreign commerce powers, and both regulated the slave trade. In 1794, Congress banned the fitting out of ships in American ports for use in the slave trade.[18] Six years later, Congress banned the participation of American seamen in the slave trade.[19] Overall, however, the Foreign Commerce Clause was used primarily, as Hamilton predicted, to enact retaliatory and protectionist measures.[20] The Embargo Act of 1807, for example, broadly restricted all foreign trade. This statute provides some evidence that Congress regarded the power to "regulate" foreign commerce as including the power to prohibit it. A federal district court observed that Congress could use the foreign commerce power for "other purposes, than the mere *advancement* of commerce."[21]

THE FOREIGN, INTERSTATE, AND INDIAN COMMERCE CLAUSES

As noted, Article I, Section 8, Clause 3 grants Congress the power "To regulate Commerce with foreign Nations, and among the several States, and with the Indian Tribes." There are both similarities and differences among the three Commerce Clauses.

First, is the meaning of "Commerce" the same with regard to foreign nations, the several states, and the Indian tribes? In *Haaland v. Brackeen* (2023), the Supreme Court "declined to treat the Indian Commerce Clause as interchangeable with the Interstate Commerce Clause."[22] Justice Clarence Thomas, in dissent, rejected the argument that "the Commerce Clause could have a broader application with respect to Indian tribes than for commerce between States or with foreign nations."[23] Instead, Thomas "would naturally read the term 'Commerce' as having the same meaning with respect to each type of 'Commerce' the Clause proceeds to identify."[24] Lower courts have carried the broad interpretation of "commerce" that has prevailed in the Interstate Commerce Clause cases over to the Foreign Commerce Clause.[25]

Second, the text uses different prepositions: commerce *with* foreign nations, commerce *among* the several states, and commerce *with* the Indian tribes. Is there a difference between these prepositions? As a textual matter, *with* appears narrower than *among*.[26] Hamilton observed that "Congress . . . may regulate, by law, our own trade and that which foreigners come to carry on with us; but they cannot regulate the trade which we may go to carry on *in foreign* countries . . . ."[27] Representative Thomas Tucker (the uncle of St. George Tucker) argued that Congress's power over foreign commerce "can only mean *betwixt* this country and foreign countries."[28] He thought it obvious that Congress could not prohibit a person in a foreign country from "buy[ing] himself a shirt or a coat." Even at the peak of U.S. efforts to suppress the slave trade, Congress authorized the punishment only of American vessels or American nationals.[29]

Third, the Supreme Court has recognized that even when Congress does not regulate interstate commerce, the states are still prohibited from regulating it. This principle is known as the *Dormant* Commerce Clause. Is there a *Dormant* Foreign Commerce Clause? In other words, do states have the power to regulate commerce with foreign nations even when Congress has taken no action? St. George Tucker observed that state regulations of foreign commerce, such as quarantine and inspection regimes, were more likely to be preempted than was state regulation of interstate commerce.[30] Yet the Supreme Court has upheld state regulation of foreign vessels with Congress's clear acquiescence.[31] By contrast, the Court has restricted the power of states to tax foreign goods and companies.[32]

Fourth, the Supreme Court's modern Interstate Commerce Clause jurisprudence allows Congress to regulate local economic activity that has a substantial effect on interstate commerce. This raises the question of whether Congress has a corresponding power to regulate purely foreign activity based on claimed remote effects within the United States. The Supreme Court has never squarely answered this question. The lower courts have reached different conclusions on how to apply the Commerce Clause precedents in the Foreign Commerce context.[33] In dissent, Justice Thomas suggested that, regardless of whether the foreign commerce power was broader than the interstate commerce power at the time of the Founding, to give it the same expansive scope as the expanded post–New Deal commerce power would absurdly "permit Congress to regulate any economic activity anywhere in the world."[34]

OPEN QUESTIONS

- What is the original public meaning of "Commerce" in the Foreign Commerce Clause? What is the original public meaning of "Commerce *with* foreign Nations"?
- Is there a *Dormant* Foreign Commerce Clause?
- Should the Supreme Court's Interstate Commerce Clause jurisprudence apply to the Foreign Commerce Clause?

Cite as: Eugene Kontorovich, *The Foreign Commerce Clause, in* THE HERITAGE GUIDE TO THE CONSTITUTION 147 (Josh Blackman & John G. Malcolm eds., 3d ed. 2025).

Notes

1. Fredrick W. Marks III, Independence on Trial: Foreign Affairs and the Making of the Constitution (1973). **2.** Articles of Confederation, art. IX, § 1. **3.** Grant of Temporary Power to Collect Import Duties and Request for Supplementary Funds (Apr. 18, 1783), https://perma.cc/FRH4-WYVL. **4.** *Id.* **5.** 2 Farrand's 143, 157, 167. **6.** *Id.* **7.** *Id.* at 177. **8.** *Id.* at 181. **9.** *Id.* at 308. **10.** *Id.* at 449. **11.** *Id.* **12.** *Id.* at 450. **13.** *Id.* at 452. **14.** *Id.* at 453. **15.** *Id.* at 367, 493, 495, 497. **16.** *Id.* at 569, 595. **17.** Storing 4.6.54. **18.** David Currie, The Constitution in Congress: The Federalist Period 64–67 (1997). **19.** *Id.* **20.** 3 Farrand's 519. **21.** *United States v. The William*, 28 F. Cas. 614, 621 (D. Mass. 1808) (emphasis added). **22.** 599 U.S. 255, 273 (2023). **23.** *Id.* at 351–52 (Thomas, J., dissenting). **24.** *Id.* at 352. **25.** *United States v. Bollinger*, 798 F.3d 201, 213 (4th Cir. 2015). **26.** Anthony J. Colangelo, *The Foreign Commerce Clause*, 96 Va. L. Rev. 949, 954, 970–71 (2010). **27.** Alexander Hamilton, Camillus No. XXXVI (1796), *in* 6 The Works of Alexander Hamilton 168–69 (Henry Cabot Lodge ed., 1904). **28.** Currie, at 67 (emphasis added). **29.** An Act to Continue in Force "An Act to Protect the Commerce of the United States and Punish the Crime of Piracy," and Also to Make Further Provisions for Punishing the Crime of Piracy, Pub. L. 16-113, 3 Stat. 600 (1820). **30.** St. George Tucker, 1 Blackstone's Commentaries: With Notes of Reference to the Constitution and Laws of the Federal Government of the United States and of the Commonwealth of Virginia 251–52 (1803). **31.** *Compagnie Francaise de Navigation a Vapeur v. La. Bd. of Health*, 186 U.S. 380 (1902). **32.** *Barclays Bank PLC v. Franchise Tax Bd. of Cal.*, 512 U.S. 298, 314 (1994); *Japan Line, Ltd. v. L.A. Cnty.*, 441 U.S. 434, 454–55 (1979); *Complete Auto Transit, Inc. v. Brady*, 430 U.S. 274, 279 (1977); *Brown v. State of Md.*, 25 U.S. 419, 448 (1827). **33.** *United States v. Rife*, 33 F.4th 838, 843 (6th Cir. 2022); *United States v. Davila-Mendoza*, 972 F.3d 1264, 1274 (11th Cir. 2020); *United States v. Durham*, 902 F.3d 1180, 1212 (10th Cir. 2018). **34.** *Baston v. United States*, 137 S.Ct. 850, 851, 853 (2017) (Thomas, J., dissenting from denial of certiorari).

ESSAY NO. 44: THE INTERSTATE COMMERCE CLAUSE
ART. 1, § 8, CL. 3

The Congress shall have Power . . . To regulate Commerce . . . among the several States. . . .

—Randy E. Barnett

INTRODUCTION

The Interstate Commerce Clause operates both as a power delegated to Congress and as a constraint on state legislation. The clause is one of the two greatest sources of federal power along with Congress's power to tax. Its three operative terms are "commerce," "to regulate," and "among the several states." The Supreme Court has decided many cases over the years interpreting these three terms. This provision also operates as the so-called Dormant Commerce Clause, which imposes an external restraint on state legislation that may impede or intrude on interstate commerce.

THE ORIGINAL MEANING OF "COMMERCE"

Justice Clarence Thomas's concurring opinion in *United States v. Lopez* (1995) provides evidence of the original meaning of "commerce."[1] "At the time the original Constitution was ratified," he wrote, "'commerce' consisted of selling, buying, and bartering, as well as transporting for these purposes."[2] He further noted that the etymology of the word "commerce" meant "with merchandise." Although some scholars have disputed this definition,[3] it has been confirmed by others, including the present author.[4]

Perhaps the most important evidence of the more limited original meaning of "commerce" is how frequently "commerce" was listed alongside other productive activities such as "manufacturing" and "agriculture." At the Constitutional Convention, James Madison of Virginia proposed to grant Congress the power "[t]o establish public institutions, rewards, and immunities for the promotion of agriculture, commerce, trades and manufactures."[5]

At the Massachusetts ratification convention, Thomas Dawes, a prominent revolutionary and legislator, observed that "[w]e have suffered . . . for want of such authority in the federal head. This will be evident if we take a short view of our agriculture, commerce, and manufactures."[6] At the New York ratification convention, Governor George Clinton referred to "[t]he situation of [each state's] commerce, its agriculture, and the system of its resources."[7]

Such evidence consistently suggests that not all economic or gainful activity was considered "commerce." And this evidence is inconsistent with the claim that noneconomic activity was considered "commerce." Rather, commerce was the activity of buying, selling, trading, and moving the goods produced by such activities as manufacturing and agriculture. Given that commerce involves movement rather than production, the activity of transportation itself—often called "navigation" or the "carrying trade"—was also included in the original meaning of "commerce."

THE ORIGINAL MEANING OF "TO REGULATE"

The core meaning of "to regulate" is to make regular—that is, to specify *how* an activity should be done, not *whether* it can be done. A pure regulation specifies that "if you want to do X, this is how you do it." Did the power "to regulate" commerce also include the power to prohibit it? The Migration or Importation Clause suggests it did.[8] The Commerce Clause gave Congress the power to regulate—that is, "make regular"—the "Migration or Importation" of slaves from other nations. In other words, Congress could say how the slave trade should be conducted, which it did through the Slave Trade Act of 1794.[9] But because the Migration or Importation Clause expressly limited Congress's power to "prohibit[]" the slave trade altogether until 1808, this suggests that the power to "regulate" commerce included some power to prohibit it as well.[10]

James Madison once invoked the concept of a "prohibitory regulation" of trade in describing a measure adopted by Virginia before the Constitution. That law was enacted to induce a reciprocal easing of trade barriers by Great Britain. Madison observed that, in response to complaints against "the monopolizing navigation laws of [Great Britain], particularly in the trade between the U. S. & the British W. Indies, [Virginia] deliberated . . . on the experiment of forcing a reciprocity by *prohibitory regulations* of her own."[11] Thus it was contemplated that, at least for some purposes, a regulation of trade could take the form of a prohibition.

The U.S. Supreme Court did not affirm this interpretation of "to regulate" until *Champion v. Ames* (1903).[12] By a vote of 5 to 4, the Court upheld a congressional ban on the interstate transportation of lottery tickets. Writing for the majority, Justice John Marshall Harlan reasoned that Congress, like the states, "may prohibit the carrying of lottery tickets from one state to another" in order to "guard[] the people of the United States against the 'widespread pestilence of lotteries' and to protect the commerce which concerns all the states."[13] In essence, Harlan reasoned that Congress had the same plenary "police power" over interstate commerce that states have over activities within their borders.

The view that Congress's power "to regulate" interstate commerce includes the power to prohibit commerce remains good law. By the same token, however, just as the Fourteenth Amendment's Due Process of Law Clause restricts the police power of states, the Fifth Amendment's Due Process of Law Clause may likewise limit Congress's power to regulate or prohibit interstate commerce.

THE ORIGINAL MEANING OF "AMONG THE SEVERAL STATES"

The most obvious meaning of commerce "among the several states" is activity that is taking place between one or more states and another one or more states. For example, in 1791, Treasury Secretary Alexander Hamilton wrote an opinion concluding that the Bank of the United States was constitutional. Hamilton described "the province of the federal government" under the Commerce Clause as the power to regulate "the trade with foreign countries, or . . . *between* the States, or with the Indian Tribes."[14]

Constitutional historian William Crosskey advanced the most prominent objection to this view. Crosskey contended that the "natural meaning" of "among the several states" includes all commerce occurring *within* any state.[15] He read the clause to empower Congress to regulate commerce "*with the people of* foreign nations, commerce *with the people* of the Indian tribes, and commerce *among the people* of the several states."[16] Under this reading, "the clause covered the *societal* internal commerce of the country, plus its two kinds of *societally* external commerce. . . ."[17]

But Crosskey's method of establishing "original meaning" was distorted. He deliberately excluded any evidence of usage during the framing or ratifying of the Constitution.

Instead, his "samples of word-usage and juristic and political discussion" were all "drawn . . . from sources not connected with the Constitution."[18] Contemporary originalist methodology, however, identifies the meaning of words by reference to the context in which these words were used at the time they were adopted. Such contextual evidence of word and phrase usage is not susceptible to the type of "natural suspicions" for which Crosskey professed concern when he excluded statements made during the drafting and ratifying of the Constitution. Crosskey's skewed methodology is not consistent with now well-established principles of constitutional originalism.

The first Supreme Court case to interpret the Interstate Commerce Clause was *Gibbons v. Ogden* (1824). It decided that the power to regulate "commerce" included the power to regulate navigation or the carrying trade.[19] The Federal Coasting Act of 1793 gave the plaintiffs a monopoly license to carry passengers on boats from New York to New Jersey. The Court held that this statute was a proper exercise of the power to regulate commerce among the several states.

Under the original meaning of "commerce," *Gibbons* was an easy case. Congress clearly had power over the activity of interstate navigation. In this case, the activity being regulated took place between one state and another. Congress was merely regulating navigation, not prohibiting it. But Chief Justice John Marshall's majority opinion contained some capacious language that later led to an expansionist reading of the clause: "This power," for example, "like all others vested in Congress, is complete in itself, may be exercised to its utmost extent, and acknowledges no limitations, *other than are prescribed* in the Constitution."[20]

This passage has led some jurists and scholars to contend that the only restrictions on the powers of Congress must be based on one of the express prohibitions, such as those in the Bill of Rights, and not on the limited meaning of the terms of the power itself. But Marshall recognized an inherent limit to this power over "commerce." He reasoned that "[t]he enumeration" of powers over three types of commerce—with foreign nations, between states, and with Indian tribes—"presupposes something not enumerated, and that something, if we regard the language or the subject of the sentence, must be the exclusively internal commerce of a State." With this limit in mind, he considered the meaning of the particular words in the clause.

The meaning of "commerce." Commerce, Marshall wrote, is more than "traffic"—that is, more than mere trade. This claim is well supported by evidence of original meaning. But Marshall also referred repeatedly to the seemingly broader concept of "commercial *intercourse*." Professor Jack Balkin has claimed that the term "intercourse" is synonymous with "interaction."[21] When the Constitution was framed, however, "intercourse"—like "commerce"—referred to the movement of something from one place to another. Intellectual intercourse, for example, concerned the transmission of ideas between persons. By qualifying "intercourse" with "commercial," Marshall was not expanding the meaning of commerce. He was restricting the scope of the intercourse that fell within congressional power.

The meaning of "to regulate." Marshall defined "the power to regulate" as the power "to prescribe the rule by which commerce is to be governed."[22] In other words, Congress had the power to establish the manner in which commerce is to be conducted.

The meaning of "among the several states." Finally, Marshall addressed the meaning of "among the several states." He affirmed that Congress's claim over navigation between two states "implies no claim of a direct power to regulate the purely internal commerce of a State or to act directly on its system of police,"[23] but he adopted a potentially expansive interpretation of "among." "Comprehensive as the word 'among' is," he wrote, "it may very properly be restricted to that commerce which *concerns* more States than one."[24] Marshall then offered an even more expansive definition of "among" as "intermingled with." His statement that "[a] thing which is among others is intermingled with them" has led some scholars like Crosskey to contend that "among" meant amidst or even within a state.[25]

Yet Marshall himself rejected this reading. He insisted, as noted, that "[t]he enumeration presupposes something not enumerated; and that something, if we regard the language or the subject of the sentence, must be the exclusively

internal commerce of a State." Purely local activities therefore remained outside of the reach of Congress.

THE CLOSE RELATIONSHIP BETWEEN THE COMMERCE AND NECESSARY AND PROPER CLAUSES

Article I, Section 8, Clause 18 delegates to Congress the power "[t]o make all Laws which shall be necessary and proper for carrying into Execution the foregoing Powers, and all other Powers vested by this Constitution in the Government of the United States, or in any Department or Officer thereof." (See Essay No. 66.) In *Gibbons v. Ogden*, Chief Justice Marshall noted that there may be some "internal concerns" of a state with which it may be "*necessary* [for Congress] to interfere . . . for the purpose of executing some of the general powers of the government."[26] Thus, even if these local activities are neither commerce nor interstate, Congress may still be able to regulate them if such a law is necessary and proper to execute its power over interstate commerce.

Five years before *Gibbons*, the Court decided *McCulloch v. Maryland* (1819).[27] Marshall, writing for the Court, offered an important test to understand the Necessary and Proper Clause: "Let the end be legitimate, let it be within the scope of the constitution, and all means which are appropriate, which are plainly adapted to that end, which are not prohibited, but consist with the letter and spirit of the constitution, are constitutional."[28] During the twentieth century, most of the expansion of Congress's powers under the Commerce Clause came not from expanding the meaning of "commerce," but from expanding the meaning of "necessary and proper" in the Necessary and Proper Clause.

In *McCulloch*, however, Marshall articulated three limiting principles on how far the Necessary and Proper Clause reached. First, Congress cannot "adopt measures which are prohibited by the constitution."[29] Second, a law must be "*really* calculated to effect any of the objects intrusted to the Government."[30] This suggests that Congress must have some demonstrable reason for regulating a particular activity as a means of carrying into execution one of its enumerated powers.

Third, Congress cannot, "under the *pretext* of executing its powers, pass laws for the accomplishment of objects not entrusted to the government."[31] In such cases, Marshall wrote, "it would become the painful duty of this tribunal . . . to say that such an act was not the law of the land."[32] It follows that Congress can regulate a local activity only if its purpose for doing so comports with its delegated power to regulate commerce between the states and the regulation is plainly adapted to that purpose.

The first Supreme Court case to declare unconstitutional a regulation of interstate commerce was *United States v. Dewitt* (1869).[33] Federal law prohibited the sale of "illuminating oil" anywhere in the United States, including all local sales. Chief Justice Salmon P. Chase's majority opinion tracked the reasoning of *Gibbons*. Chase explained that the "express grant of power to regulate commerce among the states has always been understood as limited by its terms, and as a virtual denial of any power to interfere with the internal trade and business of the separate states."[34] Chase, however, also acknowledged an exception to this rule premised on the Necessary and Proper Clause: Congress could regulate such internal trade "as a necessary and proper means for carrying into execution some other power expressly granted or vested."[35]

But Chase then rejected the argument that such a ban was a necessary and proper means of exercising Congress's power to tax. Rather, the federal ban was not an appropriate and plainly adapted means for carrying into execution "the power of laying and collecting taxes."[36] Here, Chase paraphrased Chief Justice Marshall's opinion in *McCulloch v. Maryland*.[37] *Dewitt* highlights the close connection between the scope of the interstate commerce power and the scope of the Necessary and Proper Clause.

THE PROGRESSIVE-ERA COURT
Following *Gibbons* and *Dewitt*, the Supreme Court had little occasion to investigate the breadth of the federal commerce power. That would change during the Progressive Era in the late nineteenth century with the growth of national economic legislation. *United States v. E.C. Knight Co.* (1895) held that the Sherman Antitrust Act could not constitutionally be applied to monopolies in manufacturing because the word "commerce" did not embrace manufacturing.[38] Moreover, any effect manufacturing may have on commerce was merely "indirect" and could not be reached under the Necessary and Proper Clause.

This qualitative distinction between manufacturing and commerce held for forty years, although the Court was generally deferential in upholding federal regulatory legislation. For example, several cases established what later came to be called the "jurisdictional element" test.[39] Under this test, Congress can regulate or prohibit activity that employs any item that traveled across state lines regardless of whether the activity being regulated was itself commerce, or even economic.

The last restrictive applications of the commerce power by the Court came in 1935 and 1936. *A.L.A. Schechter Poultry Corp. v. United States* (1935) declared unconstitutional the National Industrial Recovery Act, which was the centerpiece of the Roosevelt Administration's New Deal legislation.[40] The Court held that this statute impermissibly regulated goods *after* their interstate transportation or movement had come to rest.[41] The following year, *Carter v. Carter Coal Co.* (1936) held that Congress could not regulate goods *before* their interstate transportation had begun.[42] In both cases, the Court found that the effect of the activity being regulated on interstate commerce was too "indirect" to be within Congress's Necessary and Proper Clause power to reach activity that was itself "commerce . . . among the several states."

THE NEW DEAL-ERA COURT
The law would start to shift one year later. *NLRB v. Jones & Laughlin Steel Corp.* (1937) upheld the National Labor Relations Act's regulation of factory working conditions.[43] This case did not squarely reject the direct-indirect test. Under the Necessary and Proper Clause, Congress could not reach activities that had only an "indirect and remote" effect on interstate commerce. But Congress could reach activities that had a "close and intimate effect" on interstate commerce. An industry organized on a national level, like the steel company, had such an effect. The Court also acknowledged a principle that was reminiscent of Chief Justice Marshall's limit in *Gibbons*:

"The authority of the federal government may not be pushed to such an extreme as to destroy the distinction, which the commerce clause itself establishes, between commerce 'among the several States' and the internal concerns of a State."[44] The Court stressed that the "distinction between what is national and what is local in the activities of commerce is vital to the maintenance of our federal system."[45]

Four years later, however, in *United States v. Darby* (1941), the Court abandoned any effort to draw such a line between what is national and what is local.[46] *Darby* rejected the direct-indirect test in favor of what came to be known as the "substantial effects" doctrine. Under this test, Congress has "the power . . . to regulate . . . activities intrastate which have a substantial effect on the commerce or the exercise of the Congressional power over it."[47] To justify this doctrine, the Court relied, not on the Commerce Clause case of *Gibbons v. Ogden*, but on the Necessary and Proper Clause standard articulated by Marshall in *McCulloch v. Maryland*: Congress could regulate "those activities intrastate which so affect interstate commerce . . . as to make regulation of them appropriate means to the attainment of a legitimate end."[48]

This passage is revealing. Contrary to how *Darby* is often read, this case did not expand the meaning of "commerce" beyond its original meaning. Instead, the Court held that Congress's power "is not confined to the regulation of commerce among the states."[49] Under what clause, then, could Congress regulate local activity? The Court cited *McCulloch v. Maryland* as authority for this expansive power. *Darby* signals that the "substantial effects doctrine" is a product of an expansion of the Necessary and Proper Clause, not an expansion of the original meaning of "commerce."

Yet *Darby* was not entirely faithful to everything Chief Justice Marshall held in *McCulloch*. In particular, *Darby* rejected Marshall's limiting principle that "pretextual" laws "for the accomplishment of objects not entrusted to the government" were beyond that power.[50] Rather, *Darby* held that "[t]he motive and purpose of a regulation of interstate commerce are matters for the legislative judgment upon the exercise of which the Constitution places no restriction, and over which the courts are given no

control."[51] The Court opined that "[w]hatever [Congress's] *motive and purpose*, regulations of commerce which do not infringe some constitutional prohibition are within the plenary power conferred on Congress by the Commerce Clause."[52] In other words, without saying so, *Darby* quietly reversed one of *McCulloch's* limits on the Necessary and Proper Clause.

The reasoning of *Wickard v. Filburn* (1942) further shows how the New Deal Court was not expanding the meaning of "commerce" but was expanding the scope of the Necessary and Proper Clause.[53] The Agricultural Adjustment Act sought to help farmers by raising the market price of wheat. The law did so by limiting the amount of wheat a farmer could grow and market.[54] *Wickard* upheld the constitutionality of this law. The original meaning of "commerce" did not include the activity of agriculture and *Wickard* did not deny this meaning. Instead, it held that if an "activity be local, and *though it may not be regarded as commerce*, it may still, whatever its nature, be reached by Congress if [that activity] exerts a substantial economic effect on interstate commerce. . . ."[55] In this way, *Wickard* stayed within the original meaning of "commerce" while expansively interpreting the Necessary and Proper Clause.

Wickard further held that, to assess whether an activity has a substantial effect on interstate commerce, one should consider the effect of all incidences of the activity. This rule has come to be known as the "aggregation principle."

Along with the "jurisdictional element" test, both the substantial effects doctrine and the aggregation principle remain good law. The Court has used all three tests to approve wider federal criminal legislation as well as major social reforms such as the Civil Rights Act of 1964.[56]

THE REHNQUIST COURT

United States v. Lopez (1995) and *United States v. Morrison* (2000) found a limit to the substantial effects doctrine by introducing a distinction between economic and noneconomic local activity.[57] In *Lopez*, the Court held that Congress could regulate local *economic* activity that, in the aggregate, had a substantial effect on interstate commerce and its regulation.[58] But local *noneconomic* activity was outside Congress's power regardless of its aggregate effect on interstate commerce.[59] Furthermore, unlike economic activity, noneconomic activity could not be aggregated to show a substantial effect on commerce.[60] Moreover, Chief Justice William H. Rehnquist asserted that it was the Court's independent duty to determine whether a regulated activity was economic in nature.[61] His opinion based these limits, not on the original meaning of the Commerce Clause, but on "first principles" and post-New Deal precedents.

In *Morrison*, Chief Justice Rehnquist stated that "thus far in our Nation's history our cases have upheld Commerce Clause regulation of intrastate activity only where that activity is economic in nature."[62] Therefore, by drawing this line, no post-New Deal case needed to be reversed. Instead, the Rehnquist Court adopted a stance that can be described as "this far and no farther without a judicially administrable limiting principle."

Five years later, however, the Rehnquist Court seemed to pivot in *Gonzales v. Raich* (2005). The Court held that the federal Controlled Substances Act (CSA) properly reached locally home-grown marijuana notwithstanding a California law that legalized marijuana for medicinal use.[63] The vote in *Raich* was 6 to 3. In one sense, *Raich* stayed within the economic-noneconomic line drawn by *Lopez* and *Morrison*. The majority relied on *Webster's Third New International Dictionary* to hold that "economics" refers to "the production, distribution, and consumption of commodities."[64] Therefore, the Court concluded that, under *Lopez* and *Morrison*, Congress could reach this local activity under the substantial effects doctrine and aggregation principle.

In *Raich*, both the majority opinion and Justice Antonin Scalia's concurrence also relied on a statement made in passing in *Lopez*. *Lopez* left the door open for Congress to regulate even noneconomic local activity if such regulation is "an essential part of a larger regulation of economic activity, in which the regulatory scheme could be undercut unless the intrastate activity were regulated."[65] In his concurring opinion in *Raich*, Justice Scalia correctly characterized this power as based on the Necessary and Proper Clause rather than the Commerce Clause.[66] Scalia would then have used deferential "rational

basis" scrutiny to review Congress's claim that the regulation of intrastate activity—whether economic or noneconomic—was an essential part of a broader regulatory scheme.

THE ROBERTS COURT

Raich did not signal the end of the Court's attempt to find some limit to Congress's power to regulate interstate commerce. *National Federation of Independent Business v. Sebelius* (2012) found another.[67] Unlike *Lopez*, *Morrison*, and *Raich*, *NFIB* did not involve the substantial effects doctrine, which expansively reads the "necessary" part of the Necessary and Proper Clause. Instead, *NFIB* raised the question of whether compelling persons to engage in economic activity by requiring them to purchase health insurance from a private company was a "proper" exercise of Congress's power "to regulate." Chief Justice Roberts's controlling opinion observed that "[t]he Framers gave Congress the power to regulate commerce, not to compel it, and for over 200 years both our decisions and Congress's actions have reflected this understanding."[68] The power to compel, he wrote, "would give Congress the same license to regulate what we do *not* do, fundamentally changing the relation between the citizen and the Federal Government."[69] The individual insurance mandate exceeded Congress's power under the Necessary and Proper Clause: "[L]aws that undermine the structure of government established by the Constitution . . . are not "consist[ent] with the letter and spirit of the constitution." Here, Roberts quoted *McCulloch*: Such laws "are not 'proper [means] for carrying into Execution' Congress's enumerated powers."

THE DORMANT COMMERCE CLAUSE

The Interstate Commerce Clause has a second constitutional role. This provision acts as an external restraint on state legislation that may impede or intrude upon interstate commerce. This principle is known as the Dormant Commerce Clause, which traces to *Willson v. Black-Bird Creek Marsh Co.* (1829).[70] Chief Justice John Marshall wrote that a state law placing a dam across a creek was not "repugnant to [Congress's] *power to regulate commerce in its dormant state,* or as being in conflict with any law passed on the subject."[71]

The phrase "commerce in its dormant state" is confusing. Chief Justice Marshall was not referring to commerce that was dormant. Rather, he was referring to when Congress has not exercised its Commerce power. In other words, Marshall was referring to Congress's *unexercised* or "dormant" "power to regulate commerce." Can states exercise power over intrastate commerce that Congress has chosen not to regulate, or is Congress's power exclusive so that its failure to regulate means that activity must go unregulated by the states as well?

Since the nineteenth century, the courts have vacillated on the scope of the Dormant Commerce Clause doctrine.[72]

Cite as: Randy E. Barnett, *The Interstate Commerce Clause,* *in* The Heritage Guide to the Constitution 150 (Josh Blackman & John G. Malcolm eds., 3d ed. 2025).

Notes

1. 514 U.S. 549 (1995). **2.** *Id.* at 585. **3.** Grant S. Nelson & Robert J. Pushaw, Jr., *Rethinking the Commerce Clause: Applying First Principles to Uphold Federal Commercial Regulations but Preserve State Control over Social Issues,* 85 Iowa L. Rev. 1 (1999); Jack M. Balkin, *Commerce,* 109 Mich. L. Rev. 1 (2010). **4.** Randy E. Barnett, *The Original Meaning of the Commerce Clause,* 68 U. Chi. L. Rev. 101 (2001); Randy E. Barnett, *Jack Balkin's Interaction Theory of "Commerce,"* 2012 U. Ill. L. Rev. 623 (2012); Robert G. Natelson & David Kopel, *Commerce in the Commerce Clause: A Response to Jack Balkin,* 109 Mich. L. Rev. First Impressions 55 (2010). **5.** 2 Farrand's 322. **6.** 2 Elliot's 57. **7.** *Id.* at 261. **8.** Art. I, § 9, ¶ 1. **9.** 1 Stat. 347. **10.** 2 Stat. 426. **11.** James Madison, Letter to Joseph C. Cabell, Sept. 18, 1828, https://perma.cc/LFW9-QEK6. **12.** 188 U.S. 321 (1903). **13.** *Id.* at 357. **14.** Alexander Hamilton, *Final Version of an Opinion on the Constitutionality of an Act to Establish a Bank,* (Feb. 23, 1791) (emphasis added), https://perma.cc/7NDR-HAK9. **15.** William Winslow Crosskey, 1 Politics and the Constitution in the History of the United States 50–83 (1953). **16.** *Id.* at 77. **17.** *Id.* **18.** *Id.* at 5. **19.** 22 U.S. (9 Wheat.) 1 (1824). **20.** *Id.* at 196 (emphasis added). **21.** Balkin, *supra* at 15. **22.** *Gibbons,* 22 U.S. (9 Wheat.) at 196. **23.** *Id.* at 204. **24.** *Id.* at 194 (emphasis added). **25.** Walton H. Hamilton & Douglass Adair, The Power to Govern: The Constitution—Then and Now 141–42 (1937). **26.** *Gibbons,* 22 U.S. (9 Wheat.) at 195 (emphasis added). **27.** 17 U.S. 316 (4 Wheat.) (1819). **28.** *Id.* at 421. **29.** *Id.* at 423. **30.** *Id.* (emphasis added). **31.** *Id.* (emphasis added). **32.** *Id.* **33.** 76 U.S. 41 (1869). **34.** *Id.* at 44. **35.** *Id.* **36.** *Id.* 17 U.S. 316 (4 Wheat.) at 407. **38.** 156 U.S. 1 (1895). **39.** *Hipolite Egg Co. v. United States,* 220 U.S. 45 (1911); *Hoke v. United States,* 227 U.S. 308 (1913); *Caminetti v. United States,* 242 U.S. 470 (1917). **40.** 295 U.S. 495 (1935). **41.** *Id.* at 548–50. **42.** 298 U.S. 238 (1936). **43.** 301 U.S. 1 (1937). **44.** *Id.* at 30. **45.** *Id.* **46.** 312 U.S. 100 (1941). **47.** *Id.* at 119–20. **48.** *Id.* at 118. **49.** *Id.* **50.** *Id.* at 121. **51.** *Id.* at 115. **52.** *Id.* (emphasis added) **53.** 317 U.S. 111 (1942). **54.** *Id.* at 113. **55.** *Id.* at 125 (emphasis added). **56.** *Heart of Atlanta Motel, Inc. v. United States,* 379 U.S. 241 (1964); *Katzenbach v. McClung,* 379 U.S. 294 (1964). **57.** 514 U.S. 549 (1995); 529 U.S. 598 (2000). **58.** *Lopez,* 514 U.S. at 565–68. **59.** *Id.* **60.** *Id.* **61.** *Id.* at 562–63. **62.** 514 U.S. at 613. **63.** 545 U.S. 1 (2005). **64.** *Id.* at 25. **65.** *Lopez,* 514 U.S. at 561. **66.** *Raich,* 545 U.S. at 38. **67.** 567 U.S. 519 (2012). **68.** *Id.* at 555 (emphasis removed). **69.** *Id.* (emphasis added). **70.** 27 U.S. (2 Pet.) 245 (1829). **71.** *Id.* at 252 (emphasis added) **72.** *Nat'l Pork Producers Council v. Ross,* 598 U.S. 356 (2023).

ESSAY NO. 45: THE INDIAN COMMERCE CLAUSE
ART. I, § 8, CL. 3

The Congress shall have Power . . . To regulate Commerce . . . with the Indian Tribes. . . .

—Timothy Sandefur

INTRODUCTION

The Constitution gives Congress power to "regulate commerce" with foreign nations, among the states, and with "the Indian tribes." The fact that this clause consists of a single unbroken sentence suggests that Congress's power to "regulate commerce" is the same—and thus subject to the same constitutional limits—with respect to all three types of entities. The Framers' primary concern was to restrict state authority and vest a single, central entity with the power of legislating with respect to Indian commerce so as to avoid multifarious, potentially conflicting policies. Just as America would speak with one voice when dealing with foreign nations, the Indian Commerce Clause would ensure that commerce with Indians was regulated by a single federal government.

In the years after the Civil War, Congress grew uncomfortable with viewing tribes as sovereign entities and began to treat them instead as conquered aliens and captive wards with federal officials serving as their teachers, overseers, and guardians. This history gave rise to the so-called plenary power doctrine, which purportedly gives Congress absolute authority over Indians. This power cannot be squared with the original meaning of the Indian Commerce Clause.

HISTORY BEFORE 1787

The Articles of Confederation granted Congress a broad power over Indians. The legislature had the power to "regulat[e] the trade *and manag[e] all affairs* with the Indians *[who were] not members of any of the states.*"[1] However, this central power was limited: Some Indians were members of states, and the Articles ensured that the "legislative right of any state" over such Indian affairs "within its own limits, [would] be not infringed or violated." As a result, the states could assert the power to regulate Indian affairs within their borders.[2]

Under the Articles, state governments' hostility toward tribes often precipitated violent clashes. In Federalist No. 3, John Jay observed that "[n]ot a single Indian war has yet been occasioned by aggressions of the present [Confederation] government." However, "there are several instances of Indian hostilities having been provoked by the improper conduct of individual States, who . . . have given occasion to the slaughter of many innocent inhabitants." Centralizing the authority to regulate Indian commerce would prevent these dangers.

THE CONSTITUTIONAL CONVENTION

On May 29, 1787, South Carolina's Charles Pinckney proposed that the Convention give Congress "exclusive power . . . of regulating Indian affairs."[3] This proposal tracked the language used in the Articles of Confederation. What happened next is something of a mystery. A Committee of Detail draft in the handwriting of Edmund Randolph of Virginia granted Congress many powers to which John Rutledge of South Carolina had added "Indian Affairs" in a marginal note.[4] Another Committee of Detail draft in the handwriting of James Wilson provided that the legislature had the power "of regulating Indian Affairs."[5] Yet the Committee of Detail's report, presented on August 6, included no power over Indian affairs.

Professor Lorianne Updike Toler contends that the Committee of Detail "seems to have accidentally omitted an Indian Affairs Clause in preparing the first working draft of the Constitution."[6] She writes that Wilson meant to comply with Rutledge's note and even "placed a check mark next to the Clause" but that Wilson "simply failed to include the power in his final draft."[7] As Justice Neil Gorsuch put it, "[t]he framers considered a general Indian Affairs Clause but left it on the cutting-room floor."[8]

The Convention did address Congress's powers over Indians in another provision. A draft of Article I, Section 7 granted Congress the power "[t]o regulate commerce with foreign nations, and among the several States."[9] On August 16, this provision was approved without debate.[10] On August 18, James Madison referred to the Committee of Detail a list of powers for Congress that included the power "[t]o regulate affairs with the Indians as well within as without the limits of the U. States."[11] Toler suggests that Madison was attempting "to correct the Committee of Detail's oversight."[12] Madison also omitted the language in the Articles that allowed the states to regulate Indians that were "members of states."

Madison's proposal was rejected, and on August 22, the Committee of Detail instead proposed that Section 7 be amended to include "and with Indians, within the Limits of any State, not subject to the laws thereof."[13] This language would have preserved the ability of states to regulate Indian tribes. This proposal was not adopted.

On September 4, the Committee of Eleven proposed a simpler method: adding the "and with the Indian tribes" to the foreign and interstate commerce clauses.[14] That proposal was approved without debate.[15] The draft referred to the Committee of Style therefore granted Congress the power "[t]o regulate commerce with foreign nations, and among the several States; and with the Indian tribes."[16] The Committee of Style changed the semicolon to a comma but made no further changes.[17]

In the end, where the Articles of Confederation had provided a "free-floating Indian-affairs power," the Constitution included only a "bundle of federal authorities" relating to Congress's power to regulate commerce.[18] Thus the central question: What constitutes "commerce"?

THE RATIFICATION DEBATES

The Indian Commerce Clause was discussed sparingly during the ratification debates. In Federalist Nos. 40 and 42, Madison used the phrase "trade with the Indians" to characterize Congress's power. Robert Yates, an opponent of the Constitution writing as "Sydney," warned that the "new government, will enervate their legislative rights, and totally surrender into the hands of Congress the management and regulation of the Indian trade to an improper government."[19] There is no evidence that the ratifiers discussed the significance of the shift from "Indian affairs" in the Articles of Confederation to "commerce" in the Constitution.[20] However, the Constitution's meaning does not depend on the views of any individual framers; as Madison himself observed, its meaning depends on the ratifiers' understanding.[21]

THE PLENARY POWER DOCTRINE

In a "long line of cases," the U.S. Supreme Court has "characterized Congress's power to legislate with respect to the Indian tribes as 'plenary and exclusive.'"[22] Plenary means absolute and unlimited. The origin of this doctrine traces back to *United States v. Kagama* (1886), even though the word "plenary" does not actually appear in the decision.[23] *Kagama*, moreover, expressly acknowledged that such a power could *not* be derived from the Indian Commerce Clause. Justice Samuel Miller even called it "a very strained construction of [the] clause."[24] Nevertheless, *Kagama* held that "the soil and the people" living on reservations were "under the political control of the Government of the United States" because the tribes were effectively a conquered people whose continued existence now rested on the mercy and charity of the conqueror.[25] *Kagama* cited Chief Justice John Marshall's decision in *Worcester v. Georgia* (1832), which characterized the tribes as "wards of the nation."[26] *Kagama* concluded that "[f]rom their very weakness and helplessness . . . there arises the duty of protection, and with it the power."[27]

Indian law scholar N. Bruce Duthu has explained that *Kagama*'s "plenary" theory "gave Congress a blank check to legislate" and "turned a blind eye and a deaf ear to constitutional principles and tradition that viewed federal power as a limited authority that operates lawfully and legitimately only within the safe harbor of enumerated constitutional provisions."[28] Moreover, the historical basis of this ward-like relationship is dubious. Justice Clarence Thomas has been "unable to locate any evidence that the Founders thought of the Federal Government as having a generalized guardianship-type relationship with the Indian tribes," as that relationship "at times involved warfare, not trust."[29]

Since *Kagama,* the "plenary power" theory has sowed confusion, partly because the Court has also said this "plenary" power "is not absolute."[30] That confusion became especially prominent in *Haaland v. Brackeen* (2023), in which Justice Amy Coney Barrett's majority opinion insisted that "plenary" power is "not absolute" but that its limits are "undefined."[31] In dissent, Justice Samuel Alito condemned this self-contradictory phrasing for "violating one of the most basic laws of logic."[32]

One manifestation of the plenary power was the Indian Reorganization Act of 1934, which expanded federal authority over tribes in unprecedented ways. Congress radically reorganized internal tribal politics by inducing tribes to establish formal governments complete with chiefs even where, as with the Navajo, this was contrary to their tradition. The tribes were also induced to write constitutions that were subject to the approval of the Secretary of the Interior. This requirement subordinated tribal self-government to federal control at the most fundamental level.

ORIGINAL MEANING OF "COMMERCE . . . WITH THE INDIAN TRIBES"

In *Brackeen*, Justices Gorsuch and Thomas disagreed about the original meaning of "Commerce . . . with the Indian Tribes." First, Thomas contrasted the language used in the Articles of Confederation with the language used in the Constitution. "[W]hatever the precise contours of a freestanding 'Indian Affairs' Clause might have been," he wrote, "the Founders' specific rejection of such a power shows that there is no basis to stretch the Commerce Clause beyond its normal limits."[33] Gorsuch, however, defined commerce broadly, contending that the word gives Congress "the authority to manage 'all interactions or affairs . . . with the Indian [T]ribes' and foreign sovereigns—wherever those interactions or affairs may occur."[34]

Second, Thomas wrote that "Commerce" must "naturally" have the "same meaning" with respect to interstate commerce, Indian commerce, and foreign commerce.[35] Thus, if "commerce" means "all interactions or affairs," Congress could control all interactions with foreign nations or among states—something that is plainly not true. Gorsuch countered that "Indian commerce was considered 'a special subject with a definite content,' quite 'distinct and specialized' from other sorts of 'commerce.'"[36] Indian commerce therefore has "a broader meaning than simple economic exchange."[37] Thomas responded that equating "commerce" with "intercourse" was based on "a few, fairly isolated references to 'commerce' outside the context of trade, usually in the context of sexual encounters."[38]

Even though Justices Gorsuch and Thomas reached diametrically opposed conclusions in *Brackeen*, they agreed on the more fundamental issue that the "plenary" power theory is inconsistent with the Constitution's text and principles. In short, the "plenary" power is stitched together from what Thomas called a "smorgasbord" of constitutional provisions, none of which actually gives Congress the breadth of power that the "plenary" theory claims.[39]

OPEN QUESTIONS

- If the Supreme Court were to reconsider the plenary power doctrine, how would the relationship between the Indian tribes and the federal government be changed? What other models might replace the current structure?

- What significance does the Indian Citizenship Act of 1924 have on the "plenary power," given (1) that this power was first articulated at a time when Indians were not citizens and (2) that Congress certainly does not have "plenary" power over citizens?

- If "commerce" means something more comprehensive with respect to Indians than it does with respect to states and foreign nations, what consequences does that have for other clauses in the Constitution? The Fourth Amendment, for example, refers to the right of the people to be "secure in their persons, houses, papers, and effects." Does "security" mean something different in each of those instances? Congress also has power to regulate the "land and naval forces." Is its regulatory power broader in one case than in another?

- If Congress has both a "plenary power" and a "trust" obligation to preserve the existence of tribes, could it pass a statute specifying that tribal members may not marry outside of the tribe, abandon their tribal citizenship, or write or speak to others encouraging them to do these things?

Cite as: Timothy Sandefur, *The Indian Commerce Clause*, *in* THE HERITAGE GUIDE TO THE CONSTITUTION 157 (Josh Blackman & John G. Malcolm eds., 3d ed. 2025).

Notes

1. Articles of Confederation, art. IX, § 4 (emphasis added). **2.** Gregory Ablavsky, *Beyond the Indian Commerce Clause*, 124 Yale L.J. 1012, 1021–22 (2015). **3.** 3 Farrand's 595, 607. **4.** 2 Farrand's 137, 143. **5.** *Id.* at 157, 159. **6.** Lorianne Updike Toler, *The Missing Indian Affairs Clause*, 88 U. Chi. L. Rev. 413, 419 (2021). **7.** Id. **8.** *Haaland v. Brackeen*, 599 U.S. 255, 318–19 (2023) (Gorsuch, J., concurring) (citing Toler, *supra* at 444–76). **9.** 2 Farrand's 177, 181. **10.** *Id.* at 308. **11.** *Id.* at 324–25. **12.** Toler, *supra* at 464. **13.** 2 Farrand's 366, 367. **14.** *Id.* at 493, 497. **15.** *Id.* at 495, 499. **16.** *Id.* at 565, 569. **17.** *Id.* at 595, 655. **18.** *Brackeen*, 599 U.S. at 319 (Gorsuch, J., concurring) (quoting *Worcester v. Georgia*, 315 U.S. 515, 559 (1832)). **19.** Storing 6.9.10. **20.** Toler, *supra* at 419. **21.** Letter to Thomas Jefferson, April 4, 1796, in *The Writings of James Madison*, ed. Gaillard Hunt, Vol. VI (New York: G.P. Putnam's Sons, 1906), p. 272, https://perma.cc/3THM -8VEH. **22.** *Brackeen*, 599 U.S. at 273 (2023) (quoting *United States v. Lara*, 541 U.S. 193, 200 (2004)). **23.** 118 U.S. 375 (1886). **24.** *Id.* at 378 **25.** *Id.* at 379. **26.** *Id.* at 382. **27.** *Id.* at 384. **28.** N. Bruce Duthu, American Indians and the Law 169 (2009). **29.** *Brackeen*, 599 U.S. at 358 (Thomas, J., dissenting). **30.** *Delaware Tribal Business Committee v. Weeks*, 430 U.S. 73, 84 (1977) (quoting *United States v. Alcea Band of Tillamooks*, 329 U.S. 40, 54 (1946) (plurality opinion)). **31.** *Brackeen*, 599 U.S. at 275–76. **32.** *Id.* at 374 (Alito, J., dissenting). **33.** *Id.* at 354–55 (Thomas, J., dissenting). **34.** *Id.* at 321 (Gorsuch, J., concurring) (quoting Jack Balkin, *Commerce*, 109 Mich. L. Rev. 1, 23 (2010)). **35.** *Id.* at 352 (Thomas, J., dissenting) (citing Sai Prakash, *Our Three Commerce Clauses and the Presumption of Intrasentence Uniformity*, 55 Ark. L. Rev. 1149, 1161–62 (2003)). **36.** *Id.* at 320 (Gorsuch, J., concurring) (quoting A. Abel, *The Commerce Clause in the Constitutional Convention and in Contemporary Comment*, 25 Minn. L. Rev. 432, 467–68 (1941)). **37.** *Id.* at 320 (Gorsuch, J., concurring) (citing Ablavsky, *supra* at 1013). **38.** *Id.* at 355 n.10 (Thomas, J., dissenting). **39.** *Id.* at 335 (Thomas, J., dissenting).

ESSAY NO. 46: THE NATURALIZATION CLAUSE
ART. I, § 8, CL. 4

The Congress shall have Power . . . To establish an uniform Rule of Naturalization . . . .

—Patrick Glen

INTRODUCTION

Naturalization authority is a hallmark of sovereignty, carrying with it the ability to "adopt[] a foreigner, and cloth[e] him with the privileges of a native citizen."[1] It is therefore not surprising that conflicts over colonial naturalization policies helped lead to the Declaration of Independence. Yet it was not until ratification of the Constitution that authority over naturalization was placed firmly with the central government. State experimentation and the shortcomings of the Articles of Confederation ultimately led to the adoption of the Naturalization Clause in its final form, and Congress has exercised exclusive authority over citizenship issues since at least 1802.

HISTORY BEFORE 1787

During the colonial era, the naturalization authority lay with Parliament. The colonial governments did not have an explicit grant of authority to enact naturalization policies.[2]

Nonetheless, colonial governments encouraged migration to the colonies and conferred certain rights on aliens.[3] Moreover, the colonies established liberal policies for the incorporation of aliens into the colonial body economic and politic. These colonial laws did not mandate compliance with the stricter requirements of British naturalization law.[4]

In response, Great Britain curtailed these actions. In 1767, the Crown began to veto the colonies' bounty and benefits schemes to attract migrants.[5] In 1740, Parliament enacted a new naturalization act that would govern the naturalization question uniformly throughout the empire.[6] Three decades later, in 1773, Parliament established the exclusivity of these naturalization procedures.[7] These acts limited the ability of the colonies to attract new migrants and normalize their legal status. These grievances found their way into the Declaration of Independence: The King "has endeavoured to prevent the population of these States; for that purpose obstructing the Laws for Naturalization of Foreigners; refusing to pass others to encourage their migrations hither[.]"[8]

Following independence, the new states devised a range of provisions to address naturalization. Certain states, including Pennsylvania and Vermont, enacted constitutional provisions that allowed foreigners to become "free denizen[s]" after a one-year residence in the state.[9] Other states, such as New York, granted citizenship to foreigners without imposing any temporal residency requirement.[10] Still others, such as Maryland, imposed longer periods of residence—as many as seven years—during which the individual gained progressively more rights.[11]

On the more restrictionist side, many New England states required specific legislation, known as a special bill, that would grant citizenship and rights for an individual coupled with temporal residency requirements.[12] While the British conception of citizenship was perpetual, many in the post-independence states believed that renouncing one's citizenship, known as *expatriation*, was an inherent and fundamental right. As a result, a former subject of Great Britain could expatriate, renounce his former citizenship, and become a citizen of the new states.[13]

The Continental Congress played no role in the enactment of naturalization policy.[14] After the Articles of Confederation were ratified, this lack of federal authority over naturalization continued, but the Articles did establish an important principle for migration. Article IV provided that "the free inhabitants of each of these states . . . shall be entitled to all privileges and immunities of free citizens in the several states[.]"[15] This provision permitted an alien to naturalize in a state with a liberal naturalization policy but then move to any other state in the Confederation—even one where he would not have qualified for naturalization under state law.[16] The naturalization policy of the most permissive state thus became a *de facto* national naturalization policy.

Critically, the Articles of Confederation did not grant the central government any power governing naturalization. The absence of such authority in the Articles contributed directly to the subsequent adoption of the Constitution's Naturalization Clause.

THE CONSTITUTIONAL CONVENTION

This defect of the Articles was the starting point of debate at the Constitutional Convention. The Virginia Plan did not include an explicit provision governing naturalization, but the New Jersey Plan provided that the "rule of naturalization ought to be the same in every State."[17] Before the Committee of Detail, the clause evolved. A draft simply gave Congress power "to regulate naturalization."[18] The Committee returned to the proposed language of the New Jersey Plan[19] before settling on the formulation that would become the Naturalization Clause: empowering Congress "to establish an uniform Rule for Naturalization throughout the United States."[20] The Committee of Style put the clause in its final form, joining naturalization with bankruptcy for the first time when it presented its report to the full Congress on September 12, 1787.[21]

The record of proceedings is silent with respect to any debate or controversy surrounding its inclusion, wording, and adoption.[22]

THE RATIFICATION DEBATES

The Federalist Papers made two observations about the naturalization power. In Federalist No. 42, James Madison remarked about the lack of uniformity in naturalization laws under the Articles of Confederation. He observed that "[t]he dissimilarity in the rules of naturalization, has long been remarked as a fault in our system, and as laying a foundation for intricate and delicate questions." Madison added that "[t]he new Constitution has . . . with great propriety made provision against [the shortcomings of the Articles of Confederation] by authorising the general government to establish an uniform rule of naturalization throughout the United States." In Federalist No. 32, Alexander Hamilton contended that *only* the federal government had power over naturalization, and the states had none. The naturalization authority, he wrote, "must . . . be exclusive; because if each State had power to prescribe a DISTINCT RULE, there could be no UNIFORM RULE."

CONGRESSIONAL PRACTICE

The first Congress promptly enacted the Naturalization Act of 1790. This law provided that "[f]ree white person[s]" who had "resided within the limits and under the jurisdiction of the United States for the term of two years" and had resided in a state for at least one year would be admitted as United States citizens upon proof of good character and taking of the prescribed oath.[23]

The Naturalization Act of 1795 tightened the eligibility criteria for citizenship, requiring five years of residence.[24] However, it operated only prospectively. Aliens who were residing in the United States before this new law took effect were still eligible to apply for citizenship under the 1790 Act.[25] In 1798, Congress imposed dramatically longer eligibility criteria, including fourteen years of residence.[26] Unlike the 1795 Act, the 1798 Act did not provide a carve-out for aliens already present in the United States.[27] In 1802, the Jefferson Administration repealed the 1798 Act and effectively reinstated the 1795 Act.[28] Prospectivity has been a hallmark of naturalization legislation ever since.

The 1802 Act also established that the federal government would exercise *exclusive* power over naturalization. The law provided that state naturalizations qualified *only if* they occurred "previous to the passing of any law on that subject, by the government of the United States."[29] In the future, the states would have no power over naturalization. Chief Justice John Marshall would opine "[t]hat the power of naturalization is exclusively in congress does not seem to be, and certainly ought not to be, controverted."[30]

Nevertheless, starting in 1839 Congress began to enact private bills that granted citizenship to individuals. Earlier Congresses seemed to believe, however, that private bills would be unconstitutional as naturalization of individuals could occur only through a "uniform rule."[31] Such bills became more common in the latter part of the nineteenth century.[32]

Operating in the background of this legislative practice was the far more common method of conferring citizenship: birthright or *jus soli* citizenship, whereby birth within the United States under appropriate conditions conveyed citizenship even if the parents were not themselves citizens. As early as 1830, Justice Joseph Story recognized that "[n]othing is better settled at the common law than the doctrine that the children even of aliens born in a country, while the parents are resident there under the protection of the government, and owing a temporary allegiance thereto, are subjects by birth."[33]

THE RIGHT OF EXPATRIATION

Congress has the power to provide for a uniform rule of naturalization, but could a naturalized citizen at birth choose to *expatriate* and renounce his or her foreign citizenship? Early courts were divided over the existence and scope of a right to expatriation. Some courts assumed that the consent of the foreign state was required or at least that some positive law was necessary to authorize expatriation.[34] Others found that expatriation was a natural right that existed independent of any statutory authority.[35]

In 1808 and 1818, Congress considered bills that would permit citizens to expatriate and renounce their foreign allegiances.[36] However, some members were concerned that expatriation was not a valid subject of *federal* legislation. Some members contended that allegiance was owed to the foreign state of residence and that federal control of repatriation meant federal control of this relationship and therefore would encroach on foreign state prerogatives.[37]

Congress would finally address this issue after the Civil War.[38] The Expatriation Act of 1868 recognized the expatriation of prior aliens upon becoming U.S. citizens and declared expatriation to be a "natural and inherent right of all people."[39]

INVOLUNTARY EXPATRIATION AND DENATURALIZATION

Expatriation can refer to a person's right to renounce his foreign allegiances. It can also refer to the federal government's power to revoke a person's citizenship.[40] Beginning in the early twentieth century, Congress provided express bases for expatriating certain citizens. In legislation enacted in 1907 and 1940, for instance, Congress directed expatriation where a U.S. citizen is naturalized by a foreign government, where a naturalized U.S. citizen has returned to his or her home country and resided there for a certain number of years, and where a soldier has deserted the armed forces, among other circumstances.[41] These laws connected expatriation to Congress's naturalization authority.

The U.S. Supreme Court subsequently

rejected many of these bases for expatriation and held that expatriation could not be imposed as punishment.[42] Under modern doctrine, expatriation must arise from a voluntary renunciation of citizenship, although the intent to expatriate may be inferred from actions taken by the citizen.[43]

Denaturalization, a related concept, refers to the federal government's power to *denaturalize* a naturalized citizen. A natural-born citizen can be expatriated, but not denaturalized. The concept of denaturalization turns on certain incidents related to the process of naturalization itself. Under the Naturalization Act of 1906, fraud and ineligibility were bases for denaturalization.[44] Current law provides for denaturalization in several circumstances: where citizenship has been procured illegally or by concealment of a material fact or where the individual was statutorily ineligible at the time citizenship was granted.[45]

Cite as: Patrick Glen, *The Naturalization Clause, in* The Heritage Guide to the Constitution 161 (Josh Blackman & John G. Malcolm eds., 3d ed. 2025).

Notes

1. *Boyd v. Nebraska ex rel. Thayer,* 143 U.S. 135, 162 (1892). **2.** James H. Kettner, The Development of American Citizenship, 1608–1870, at 78–80, 83 (1978). **3.** *Id.* at 83–90. **4.** James E. Pfander & Theresa R. Wardon, *Reclaiming the Immigration Constitution of the Early Republic: Prospectivity, Uniformity, and Transparency*, 96 Va. L. Rev. 359, 381–82 (2010). **5.** *Id.* at 377. **6.** An Act for Naturalizing Such Foreign Protestants, and Others Therein Mentioned, as Are Settled, or Shall Settle, in Any of His Majesty's Colonies in America, 13 Geo. 11, c. 7 (Eng. 1740). **7.** An Act Amending the Act for Naturalizing Foreign Protestants, 13 Geo. III, c. 21 (Eng. 1773). **8.** Declaration of Independence, ¶ 9. **9.** Pa. Const. of 1776, § 42; Vt. Const. of 1777, § XXXVIII; Kettner, *supra* at 214. **10.** *Id.* **11.** *Id.* at 215–16. **12.** *Id.* at 216–18. **13.** Josh Blackman, *Original Citizenship*, 159 U.Penn. L. Rev. PENNumbra 95, 104–08 (2010). **14.** Kettner, *supra* at 219. **15.** Articles of Confederation, art. IV, § 1. **16.** Pfander & Wardon, *supra* at 384. **17.** 1 Farrand's 242, 245. **18.** 2 Farrand's 144. **19.** *Id.* at 158. **20.** *Id.* at 167. **21.** Pfander & Wardon, *supra* at 386 n.122. **22.** Kettner, *supra* at 225; Pfander & Wardon, *supra* at 386. **23.** An Act to Establish an Uniform Rule of Naturalization, 1 Stat. 103 (1790). **24.** An Act to Establish an Uniform Rule of Naturalization, 1 Stat. 414 (1795). **25.** *Id.* at § 2. **26.** Naturalization Act of 1798, 1 Stat. 566 (1798). **27.** Pfander & Wardon, *supra* at 407. **28.** Naturalization Act of 1802, 2 Stat. 153 (1802). **29.** *Id.* at § 4. **30.** *Chirac v. Chirac's Lessee*, 15 U.S. 259, 269 (1817). **31.** Kettner, *supra* at 253; Pfander & Wardon, supra at 399–402. **32.** Pfander & Wardon, *supra* at 429. **33.** *Inglis v. Trs. of Sailor's Snug Harbour*, 28 U.S. (3 Pet.) 99, 164 (1830). **34.** Pfander & Wardon, *supra* at 271–73 (citing, inter alia, *United States v. Gillies*, 25 F. Cas. 1321, 1322 (U.S.C.C. 1815)). **35.** *Id.* at 273–74 (citing, inter alia, *Murray v. M'Carty*, 2 Munford 393, 396–97 (Va. 1811)). **36.** Kettner, supra at 281, 284. **37.** *Id.* at 282–83, 283–84. **38.** Daniel Rice, *The "Uniform Rule" and Its Exceptions: A History of Congressional Naturalization Legislation*, 40 The Ozark Historical Rev. 23, 50–51 (2011). **39.** Expatriation Act of 1868, 15 Stat. 223. **40.** *Nishikawa v. Dulles*, 356 U.S. 129, 133–36 (1958). **41.** Expatriation Act of 1907, 34 Stat. 1228 (1907); Nationality Act of 1940, 68 Stat. 1146 (1940). **42.** *Kennedy v. Mendoza-Martinez*, 372 U.S. 144 (1963); *Trop v. Dulles*, 356 U.S. 86 (1958). **43.** *Afroyim v. Rusk*, 387 U.S. 253 (1967); 8 U.S.C. § 1481. **44.** Naturalization Act of 1906 § 15, 34 Stat. 596 (1906). **45.** 8 U.S.C. § 1451(a).

ESSAY NO. 47: THE BANKRUPTCY CLAUSE
ART. I, § 8, CL. 4

The Congress shall have Power . . . To establish . . . uniform Laws on the subject of Bankruptcies throughout the United States. . . .

—Todd J. Zywicki

INTRODUCTION

Today, bankruptcy law is thought of primarily as a device to provide debtors with relief from excessive debt. The overwhelming majority of bankruptcy cases are filed by individual debtors, not businesses. Historically, however, the purpose of bankruptcy law was to protect creditors from debtor fraud (such as concealing assets) and to require creditors to cooperate in distributing a debtor's assets. Moreover, for centuries, "bankruptcy" relief was limited to merchants and traders, not consumers or farmers.

Congress's power to "establish . . . uniform Laws on the subject of Bankruptcies throughout the United States" is consistent with this procreditor history. Through this provision, the Framers empowered Congress to knit together the nation into a uniform common market. Congress accomplished this goal in large part by overriding state discriminatory barriers that prevented creditors from collecting debts efficiently. Justice Joseph Story claimed that granting the bankruptcy power to the federal government was a necessary response to the tendency of a "mass of politicians, who will deem it more safe to consult their own temporary interests and popularity" to prefer local creditors over providing a "fair share of a ruined debtor" to "distant creditors."[1] The Bankruptcy Act of 1800, which proved unpopular, was repealed in 1803, and Congress would enact several other bankruptcy codes throughout the nineteenth century. The present-day version traces its roots to the 1978 code. The U.S. Supreme Court has held that bankruptcy laws can apply to merchants and non-merchants alike but must be geographically uniform.

HISTORY BEFORE 1787

Bankruptcy law in the United States finds its roots in English commercial law.[2] The primary purpose of English bankruptcy law was to assist creditors in their efforts to collect debts, not to protect debtors from creditors. Traditionally, a debtor's insolvency, or failure to pay his debts, was seen as a form of fraud.

The first English bankruptcy law was enacted in 1542 during the reign of King Henry VIII.[3] The law enabled creditors to seize and sell a debtor's assets for purposes of distribution to creditors. The statute, however, did not provide for the debts to be discharged, or canceled. Only creditors could involuntarily commence a bankruptcy proceeding against a debtor.[4]

The Statute of Anne (1705) introduced the idea of enabling traders or merchants who cooperated with creditors to *discharge* their debts provided certain conditions were met. In the eighteenth century, English bankruptcy law

began to focus less on the idea of the debtor's culpability and fraudulent behavior and instead came to distinguish between "bankruptcies" on the one hand and "insolvency" on the other. Only merchants and traders could be declared "bankrupt," which enabled them to have their debts discharged upon the satisfaction of certain requirements. Sir William Blackstone observed that "the laws of bankruptcy are considered as laws calculated for the benefit of trade, and founded on the principles of humanity as well as justice."[5] Blackstone explained that the laws of England "allow the benefit of the laws of bankruptcy to none but actual *traders*; since that set of men are, generally speaking, the only persons liable to accidental losses, and an inability of paying their debts, without any fault of their own."[6]

By contrast, non-merchant debtors under English law were seen as fraudulent actors who had to seek refuge under so-called insolvency laws. These laws did little more than release a debtor from debtor's prison; they did not discharge his debts. This dichotomy suggests that the Constitution's grant of power to Congress to enact a "bankruptcies" law may have referred only to the power to adjust the debts of merchants, not individual debtors. On the other hand, some commentators have argued that by the end of the eighteenth century, the legal definition of "merchant" had expanded to the point that this traditional limitation on bankruptcy had largely disappeared, except as applied to farmers.[7] English law, however, retained distinct insolvency and bankruptcy acts until the 1860s.

Bankruptcy law in the colonies followed English law in a somewhat haphazard fashion. Some colonies had bankruptcy laws, and others had insolvency laws with varying degrees of liberality.[8] Under the Articles of Confederation, there was no national bankruptcy law. Thus, by 1787, the states had enacted a patchwork of different laws. Conflicts arose when one state purported to discharge a debt and then, when a debtor relocated to another state, a creditor tried to collect the same debt in the new state.[9] Pro-debtor state laws—particularly those protecting farmers over out-of-state creditors by creating obstacles to foreclosure—interfered with the reliability of contracts. Moreover, courts in these pro-debtor states made it difficult for creditors to collect their judgments, especially when debtors absconded to other states to avoid collection.

THE CONSTITUTIONAL CONVENTION

During the Constitutional Convention, the subject of bankruptcy received minimal discussion. The most pressing goal was to establish a national bankruptcy law to address conflicting state laws that discriminated against out-of-state creditors.

On September 3, 1787, the Convention briefly debated the Bankruptcy Clause. Roger Sherman of Connecticut observed that under English law, bankruptcies could be punishable by death in some cases, and he opposed granting such a power to Congress.[10] Gouverneur Morris of Pennsylvania supported the proposal because "he saw no danger of abuse of the power" by Congress.[11] On September 3, 1787, the proposal to empower Congress "[t]o establish uniform laws on the subject of bankruptcies" passed the Convention by a vote of 9 to 1.[12] Only Sherman's state of Connecticut voted in the negative.[13]

THE RATIFICATION DEBATES

During the ratification process, the bankruptcy power received minimal debate. In Federalist No. 42, James Madison observed that the "expediency" for uniform bankruptcy laws would "not likely . . . be drawn into question." He explained that these laws "will prevent so many frauds where the parties or their property may lie or be removed into different States." Madison added that federal court jurisdiction over bankruptcy mitigated the problems that arose from state court biases against out-of-state creditors. Madison further argued that the bankruptcy laws were "so intimately connected with the regulation of commerce" that they would not be controversial.

Unsurprisingly, some Anti-Federalists objected to this new federal power. Federal Farmer, for example, feared the bankruptcy power would "immediately and extensively interfere with the internal police of the separate states" and embody a massive transfer of power to the federal judiciary.[14]

The New York ratifying convention passed a resolution that the Constitution should be amended to limit the federal government's power over bankruptcy. Under the proposal, "the power of Congress to pass uniform laws concerning bankruptcy" would "only extend to merchants and other traders," and "the States respectively [might] pass laws for the relief of other insolvent debtors."[15] New York's proposal was consistent with the historical dichotomy in England: Merchants and traders could use the bankruptcy laws; debtors could use the insolvency laws. On the other hand, contemporary dictionaries suggest that by the late-eighteenth century, the term "bankrupt" was commonly used in its broader sense to refer to any person who was unable to pay his debts and that the terms "bankruptcy" and "insolvency" were synonymous.[16]

EARLY PRACTICE

Congress did not exercise its new power over bankruptcy immediately. In the absence of federal bankruptcy law, all debtor–creditor relations were governed by state law. Financial panics in 1792 and 1797, however, resulted in widespread ruin and the imprisonment of thousands of debtors.[17] They also produced political pressure from merchant interests. The Federalist-controlled Congress narrowly passed the Bankruptcy Act of 1800,[18] which was opposed by Anti-Federalist southerners and agricultural interests. The act was nearly identical to prevailing English law: Fraudulent bankruptcy was a criminal act but was not punishable by death.[19]

The 1800 Act was unpopular from the time of its enactment.[20] Debtors viewed the law as inefficient and subject to abuse by debtors, and farmers contended that it favored merchant interests. Moreover, involved parties were burdened by the obligation to travel to distant federal courts. In 1803, the Democratic-Republican-controlled Congress repealed the law.[21]

Other bankruptcy laws existed from 1841 to 1843 and from 1867 to 1878.[22] The first permanent bankruptcy law was enacted in 1898 and remained in effect, with amendments, for nearly a century.[23] In 1978, Congress enacted a comprehensive new law, the essential structure of which remains in effect today.[24]

JUDICIAL PRECEDENT

Sturges v. Crowninshield (1819) was an early Supreme Court decision that considered the line between the federal government's power over bankruptcy and state laws.[25] New York State enacted a law that liberated the debtor from prison and also purported to discharge the debtor from his debts. Historically, such discharges were characteristic of bankruptcy laws, as insolvency laws did not provide for discharges. Chief Justice John Marshall held that to the extent the state law purported to discharge the debtor from his debts, it constituted a state impairment of contracts and was therefore unconstitutional. The creditor in the case did not seek confinement of the debtor to prison, so that issue was not relevant. But Marshall also explained that a state could not pass a bankruptcy law that discharged a debtor, but the term "bankruptcies" in the Constitution did not limit Congress to the regulation of merchant bankruptcies, the traditional scope of bankruptcy law. Rather, Congress's authority could also reach individuals who were traditionally subject to state insolvency laws. As a result, Congress could legislate with respect to both merchants and non-merchants. Therefore, while the state law would be valid in protecting a debtor from confinement to prison for non-payment of debts (the traditional scope of a state insolvency law), the law was invalid to the extent that it purported to discharge the debtor's debts.

Ogden v. Saunders (1827) further restricted the states' concurrent power over bankruptcy.[26] A state's law could not discharge debts owed to citizens of another state, but states could discharge debts owed to a citizen of that same state as long as the law operated prospectively so as not to impair existing contract obligations.

The Supreme Court also maintained that any federal bankruptcy law must be "uniform throughout the United States."[27] The 1898 Bankruptcy Act recognized property exemptions under state law that vary widely from state to state. *Hanover National Bank v. Moyses* (1902) held that this "personal" nonuniformity in treatment among individuals was permissible as long as "geographical" uniformity was preserved.[28] Thus, debtors and creditors in different states may receive different treatment as long as the debtors and creditors within the same state are treated the same. The "uniformity" requirement, however, apparently does forbid "private" or "personal" bankruptcy laws that affect only particular debtors.[29]

The separation of powers and the nature of the judicial power under Article III place certain restraints on bankruptcy courts, which are units of the U.S. district courts. The Supreme Court has also addressed the status of bankruptcy proceedings. Bankruptcy judges are so-called Article I judges. They are appointed for a term of years rather than for life during good behavior and lack many of the formal protections for judicial independence under Article III.

Granfinanciera, S.A. v. Nordberg (1989) held that Seventh Amendment jury trial rights are preserved in bankruptcy court.[30] *Stern v. Marshall* (2011) held that a bankruptcy judge lacked the power to enter a final judgment because such an order violated the right to have a particular state-law counterclaim heard by an Article III judge.[31] *Wellness International Network v. Sharif* (2015) held that the right to an adjudication by an Article III tribunal is an individual right that can be waived (as in *Granfinanciera*), not a jurisdictional limit on the bankruptcy court.[32] As a result, parties can consent to allowing a non–Article III tribunal to enter a final order or judgment otherwise requiring Article III adjudication. The Court further held that such consent need not be express but may be implied.

Harrington v. Purdue Pharma (2024) arose from the manufacture and sale of the notorious opioid prescription pain reliever OxyContin.[33] The Supreme Court held that the Bankruptcy Code does not authorize a court to issue a release and injunction that effectively discharges claims against a non-debtor party without the consent of affected plaintiffs.[34] The Court did not decide whether the Bankruptcy Clause would authorize a protective injunction for the benefit of third parties. But some scholars have argued that such injunctions are not authorized.[35] Rather, they claim that the Bankruptcy Clause only permits Congress to readjust relationships between debtors and credits, not third parties.

OPEN QUESTIONS

- The first three bankruptcy laws (1800, 1841, and 1867) required the debtor's insolvency as a condition for filing bankruptcy. However, under the 1898 and 1978 Codes, proof of insolvency is not required as a jurisdictional condition for invoking bankruptcy protection, except in the case of municipal bankruptcies. As a matter of original meaning, does Congress's bankruptcy power extend only to insolvent debtors?[36]
- Does Congress's power to adjust the relationship between debtors and creditors also extend to relations with third parties?[37]

Cite as: Todd J. Zywicki, *The Bankruptcy Clause, in* THE HERITAGE GUIDE TO THE CONSTITUTION 164 (Josh Blackman & John G. Malcolm eds., 3d ed. 2025).

Notes

1. 3 Story's Commentaries, § 1102.   **2.** Charles Jordan Tabb, *The History of the Bankruptcy Laws in the United States,* 3 Am. Bankr. L. Inst. L. Rev. 5 (1995); Stephen J. Lubben, *A New Understanding of the Bankruptcy Clause,* 64 Case Western Res. L. Rev. 319 (2013).   **3.** An Act Against Such Persons as Do Make Bankrupts, 34 & 35 Henry VIII, c. 4 (Eng. 1542).   **4.** *The Case of Bankrupts (Smith v. Mills),* 2 Coke Report 25a, 76 ER 441–76 (1584).   **5.** 2 Blackstone 471–72.   **6.** *Id.* at 473 (emphasis in original).   **7.** Thomas E. Plank, *The Constitutional Limits of Bankruptcy,* 63 Tenn. L. Rev. 487, 508–09 (1996).   **8.** Tabb, at 12.   **9.** Kurt H. Nadelman, *On the Origin of the Bankruptcy Clause,* 1 Am. J. Legal Hist. 215 (1957).   **10.** 2 Farrand's 441.   **11.** *Id.*   **12.** *Id.* at 488.   **13.** *Id.*   **14.** Storing 2.8.221.   **15.** N.Y. Ratification Debates and Proceedings (July 25, 1788), https://perma.cc/F9M2-SCFP.   **16.** Plank, *supra* at 529–30.   **17.** Tabb, *supra* at 14.   **18.** Act of Apr. 4, 1800, ch. 19, 2 Stat. 19 (repealed 1803).   **19.** Tabb, at 14.   **20.** *Id.*   **21.** Act of Dec. 19, 1803, ch. 6, 2 Stat. 248 (repealed 1841).   **22.** Act of Aug. 19, 1841, ch. 9, 5 Stat. 440 (repealed 1843); Act of Mar. 2, 1867, ch. 176, 14 Stat. 517 (repealed 1878).   **23.** Act of July 1, 1898, ch. 541, 30 Stat. 544 (repealed 1978).   **24.** Act of Nov. 6, 1978, Pub. L. 95-598, 92 Stat. 2549.   **25.** 17 U.S. (4 Wheat.) 122 (1819).   **26.** 25 U.S. (12 Wheat.) 213 (1827).   **27.** 25 U.S. (12 Wheat.) at 313.   **28.** 186 U.S. 181 (1902).   **29.** *Id.* at 188.   **30.** 492 U.S. 33 (1989).   **31.** 564 U.S. 462 (2011).   **32.** 575 U.S. 665 (2015).   **33.** 603 U.S. 204 (2024).   **34.** *Id.* at 226–27.   **35.** Plank, *supra* at 560–62.   **36.** *Id.* at 546–47.   **37.** *Id.* at 560–62.

∼

ESSAY NO. 48: THE FEDERAL MONEY CLAUSE
ART. I, § 8, CL. 5

The Congress shall have Power . . . To coin Money, regulate the Value thereof, and of foreign Coin. . . .

—Todd J. Zywicki

INTRODUCTION

The State Money Clause provides that the states cannot "coin Money; emit Bills of Credit; [or] make any Thing but gold and silver Coin a Tender in Payment of Debts. . . ."[1] (See Essay No. 79.) By contrast, Congress's power to coin money is both exclusive and open-ended.

The Federal Money Clause authorizes Congress to "coin money" from precious metals such as gold and silver. Congress also can regulate the value of the coins struck domestically and set the value of foreign coins. However, the Constitution does not directly address whether the federal government can also issue paper money and declare it to be legal tender for payment of all public and private debts. During the Constitutional Convention, there was some debate over this question. After the Civil War, however, the Supreme Court invalidated and then upheld paper money as legal tender in a controversial pair of cases decided just one year apart.

HISTORY BEFORE 1787

During the Revolutionary War, the state governments issued paper money. The Continental Congress issued Continental Dollars, also known as Continentals, that technically were redeemable in silver Spanish Milled Dollars but were repeatedly devalued and never redeemed. Counterfeiting of Continentals also occurred.

This widespread circulation of paper money spurred rampant inflation and loss of confidence by lenders and investors. In 1787, George Washington wrote that paper money will "ruin commerce—oppress the honest, and open a door to every species of fraud and injustice."[2] Thomas Jefferson would later state that paper money was only "the ghost of money" and "not money itself."[3] Nevertheless, there was also populist support for the issuance of paper money as a way to devalue debts, especially by farmers, and deal with the chronic shortage of valuable metals, known as *specie*, in America.

The Articles of Confederation were ratified in 1781. Congress and the states had concurrent powers to "coin" specie money—that is, money backed by precious metals or "specie."[4] The Confederation Congress held the power to regulate the value of coins struck domestically but not to set the value of foreign coins, which circulated widely. As a result, the states could attach disparate valuations to circulating domestic and foreign coins.

THE CONSTITUTIONAL CONVENTION

The Federal Money Clause would give Congress three distinct powers: the power to "coin Money," the power to "regulate the Value" of the money coined by the federal government, and the power to "regulate the Value" of the money coined by foreign governments. Throughout the Convention, these three powers were not particularly controversial. An early draft of this proposal appeared in a report from the Committee of Detail.[5] In contrast to the Articles of Confederation, the Constitution granted the federal government the exclusive power to coin money. Relatedly, it also gave Congress the power to "provide for the Punishment of counterfeiting the Securities and current Coin of the United States."

There was some controversy over a fourth power that did not make it into the Constitution: a federal power to issue bills of credit. A bill of credit was non-interest-bearing paper money issued on the good credit of the United States with no tangible backing in precious metal.

The Committee of Detail's report also granted Congress the power to "emit Bills on the Credit of the United States."[6]

On August 16, Gouverneur Morris of Pennsylvania moved to strike out the power to issue paper money.[7] He argued that "if the United States had credit such bills would be unnecessary," and if the United States lacked credit, paper money would be "unjust and useless."[8] James Madison of Virginia suggested it would be "sufficient to prohibit making" the bills of credit "legal tender" rather than denying Congress the power to issue bills of credit completely.[9] This distinction would permit the federal government to issue paper money to fund its operations in the event of national "emergencies" but not to declare those notes to be "legal tender" for purposes of requiring private parties to accept them in satisfaction of privately contracted debts. Nathaniel Gorham of Massachusetts advocated striking out the power "without inserting any prohibition."[10] Oliver Ellsworth of Connecticut thought this was "a favorable moment to shut and bar the door against paper money."[11] John Langdon of New Hampshire said that he would "rather reject the whole plan than" emit bills of credit.[12] George Read of Delaware opined that if the power to "emit bills of credit" were not expressly "struck out," the words "would be as alarming as the mark of the Beast in [the Book of] Revelation[]."[13]

By a vote of 9 to 2, the Convention voted to strike out the power of Congress to emit bills of credit.[14] Only New Jersey and Maryland opposed the amendment. However, even though the Constitution did not expressly grant the federal government the power to issue paper money, it also did not expressly prohibit it. By contrast, the states were expressly barred from emitting bills of credit.

This provision was debated on August 16. George Mason of Virginia argued that this silence implied that Congress therefore could not issue paper money, and by implication could not declare it to be legal tender because the federal government "would not have the power unless it were expressed."[15] By contrast, Madison later noted that he acquiesced to Virginia's vote to strike the clause. He "became satisfied that striking out the words would not disable the [government] from the use of public notes as far as they could be safe & proper," such as by issuing interest-bearing Treasury Bonds to fund the government rather than bills of credit.[16] This issue would not be settled by the Convention.

THE RATIFICATION DEBATES

In Federalist No. 44, Madison observed that under the Articles of Confederation, the state and federal governments held concurrent power to coin money. The Constitution, however, would take that power from the states in order to standardize the "forms and weights" of coins and reduce the duplicative costs of running mints. A standardized federal currency would also ease the cost and inconvenience of tax collection by the federal government. Madison criticized state issuance of paper money and highlighted the Constitution's prohibition of states' issuance of bills of credit and the further prohibition of their "power to make any thing but gold and silver a tender in payment of debts." The essay is silent with respect to whether the federal government had the authority to issue bills of credit or pass legal tender laws.

Deliberator, an Anti-Federalist, expressed concern that the new Constitution would empower Congress to issue paper money, declare it legal tender, and then depreciate its value.[17]

EARLY PRACTICE

On April 2, 1792, Congress passed the Mint Act, which established the U.S. coinage system and the dollar as the principal unit of currency.[18] The first U.S. coins were struck in 1793 at the Philadelphia Mint.[19] In February 1793, certain foreign coins were also designated legal tender at prescribed rates.[20] Congress chartered the First and Second Banks of the United States, which operated from 1791–1811 and from 1816–1836, respectively. But neither bank operated like a modern central bank in terms of issuing currency or serving as a lender of last resort.[21]

Before the Civil War, the federal government did not try to issue bills of credit. During the War of 1812, the Financial Panic of 1837, and the Mexican-American War of 1846, however, the government issued Treasury Notes.[22] These notes generally bore interest and could be redeemed for payment of government obligations and taxes, but they were not legal tender.[23]

Although generally issued in large denominations to fund government operations, some issuances were in sufficiently small denominations that they could circulate as a medium of payment and as cash reserves for banks. Their utility in paying taxes made them widely accepted on a voluntary basis, including as later issuances during the War of 1812.[24] Before the Civil War, most circulating currency was issued by more than 1,600 private banks.[25]

PAPER MONEY AND LEGAL TENDER

To fund the Civil War, Congress passed the Legal Tender Act of 1862.[26] Earlier issuances of paper money were used to finance government obligations. By contrast, Civil War "greenbacks" were designed to circulate as currency. These notes were declared legal tender, bore no interest, and were not redeemable in gold or silver. Following the end of the Civil War, greenbacks continued to circulate as currency but at a highly discounted value relative to gold. Meanwhile, many private banks continued to issue notes, typically convertible into gold at par or backed by Treasury Bonds.[27]

To discourage continued circulation of private state banknotes, Congress imposed a ten percent tax on private notes issued by state banks.[28] *Veazie Bank v. Fenno* (1869) upheld the tax as a valid exercise of Congress's power under the Necessary and Proper Clause.[29] The Supreme Court concluded that Congress had the "undisputed constitutional powers" to "provide a circulation of coin."[30] Congress's power to "provide a currency for the whole country" was "settled by the uniform practice of the government and by repeated decisions" and implied that Congress was authorized to emit bills of credit. The Court did not identify what those "repeated decisions" and "uniform practice[s]" were.

Veazie Bank, however, specifically left open the question of whether the federal government could also declare its paper money as legal tender. The Court would address this issue in two cases that were decided less than a year apart. First, *Hepburn v. Griswold* (1870) held that Congress did not have an *implied* power under the Necessary and Proper Clause to declare paper money as legal tender.[31] Second, just one year later after a dramatic change in membership, *The Legal Tender Cases* (1871) overruled

Hepburn and upheld the Legal Tender Act as a valid exercise of implied powers under the Necessary and Proper Clause.[32]

The holding of the *Legal Tender Cases* was limited to the context of wartime, but thirteen years later, *Juilliard v. Greenman* (1884) upheld the validity of legal tender laws during peacetime.[33] The Court held that the federal government's monetary power was inherent in its sovereignty; thus, it was not necessary for the Constitution to enumerate this power.[34] Justice Stephen Field's blunt dissent declared that "[i]f there be anything in the history of the Constitution which can be established with moral certainty, it is that the framers intended to prohibit the issue of legal tender notes both by the general government and by the States; and thus prevent interference with the contracts of private parties."[35]

From 1863 to 1935, National Bank Notes were issued by nationally chartered private banks and backed by gold or U.S. Treasury bonds.[36] During the Great Depression, Congress retired National Bank Notes as a form of currency and forced private parties to surrender gold coin and gold certificates for other currency not redeemable in gold.[37] This law abrogated pre-existing gold clauses in private contracts. *Norman v. Baltimore & Ohio Railroad Co.* (1935) upheld this practice based on *The Legal Tender Cases* as valid exercises of implied powers under the Necessary and Proper Clause.[38]

OPEN QUESTIONS

- Does the Federal Reserve Act grant the federal government the statutory authority to issue a digital currency and declare it legal tender? Under current precedent, Congress apparently would have the power to issue such tender (or anything else) under the Federal Money Clause.
- Professor Robert Natelson has argued that the original public meaning of the power to "coin Money" included the power to issue paper currency at the federal level and that "regulate the Value thereof" included the power to establish legal tender.[39] Would there be any opportunity for courts to reconsider this issue?

Cite as: Todd J. Zywicki, *The Federal Money Clause, in* THE HERITAGE GUIDE TO THE CONSTITUTION 168 (Josh Blackman & John G. Malcolm eds., 3d ed. 2025).

Notes

1. Art. I, § 10, cl. 1. **2.** Letter from George Washington to Jabez Bowen (Jan. 9, 1787), https://perma.cc/F5RX-6XVL. **3.** Letter from Thomas Jefferson to Edward Carrington (May 27, 1788), https://perma.cc/QQB2-UV63. **4.** Articles of Confederation, art. IX, §§ 4, 6. **5.** 2 Farrand's 167. **6.** *Id.* at 168. **7.** *Id.* at 303. **8.** *Id.* at 308–09. **9.** *Id.* at 309. **10.** *Id.* **11.** *Id.* **12.** *Id.* at 310. **13.** *Id.* **14.** *Id.* **15.** *Id.* at 309. **16.** *Id.* at 310. **17.** Storing 3.13.5. **18.** *Coinage Act of April 2, 1792*, U.S. Mint, https://perma.cc/7ZPA-HXZV. **19.** *The History of U.S. Circulating Coins*, U.S. Mint, https://perma.cc/PB26-Y5G6. **20.** *Legislation to Allow Foreign Coins as Legal Tender (Act of Feb. 9, 1793)*, U.S. Mint, https://perma.cc/8PWF-J7DZ. **21.** Andrew T. Hill, *The Second Bank of the United States*, Federal Reserve History (Dec. 5, 2015), https://perma.cc/2RVZ-8N5G. **22.** Natl. Credit Union Admin., History of United States Currency (Feb. 8, 2023), https://bit.ly/4keY7vF. **23.** Craig Elwell, Cong. Rsrch. Serv., R41887, Brief History of the Gold Standard in the United States (June 23, 2011), https://perma.cc/4PJC-NEVW. **24.** Donald H. Kagin, *Monetary Aspects of the Treasury Notes of the War of 1812*, 44 J. Econ. Hist. 69 (1984). **25.** Kevin Dowd, *US Banking in the "Free Banking" Period, in* The Experience of Free Banking 332 (Kevin Dowd ed., 2023); Howard Bodenhorn, *Small-Denomination Banknotes in Antebellum America*, 25 J. Money, Credit, & Banking 812 (1993). **26.** Act of Feb. 25, 1862, ch. 33, § 1, 12 Stat. 345 **27.** George A. Selgin & Lawrence H. White, *Monetary Reform and the Redemption of National Bank Notes, 1863–1913*, 68 Bus. Hist. Rev. 205 (1994). **28.** Act of Mar. 3, 1865, ch. 78, § 7, 13 Stat. 484. **29.** 75 U.S. (8 Wall.) 533 (1869). **30.** *Id.* at 548–49. **31.** 75 U.S. (8 Wall.) 603 (1870). **32.** *Knox v. Lee*, 79 U.S. (12 Wall.) 457 (1871); Charles Fairman, *Mr. Justice Bradley's Appointment to the Supreme Court and the Legal Tender Cases*, 54 Harv. L. Rev. 977 (1941). **33.** 110 U.S. 421 (1884). **34.** *Id.* **35.** 110 U.S. at 451 (Field, J., dissenting). **36.** Bureau of Engraving and Printing, BEP History Fact Sheet, National Bank Notes (Apr. 2013), https://perma.cc/N8EG-M8Q3. **37.** *Nortz v. United States*, 249 U.S. 317 (1935). **38.** *Norman v. Balt. & Ohio R.R.*, 294 U.S. 240 (1935). **39.** Robert G. Natelson, *Paper Money and the Original Understanding of the Coinage Clause*, 31 Harv. J.L. & Pub. Pol'y 1017 (2008).

ESSAY NO. 49: THE WEIGHTS AND MEASURES CLAUSE
ART. I, § 8, CL. 5

The Congress shall have Power To . . . fix the Standard of Weights and Measures . . . .

—Eric Chiappinelli

INTRODUCTION

From time immemorial, governments have recognized the importance of fair standards for weights and measures. The Constitution grants Congress the power to set uniform weights and measures nationwide. In 1790, Thomas Jefferson proposed a system of measurements based on the decimal system, but it was not adopted. Later, Congress would authorize the use of both the English and Metric systems of measurement, but neither system is mandated.

HISTORY BEFORE 1787

The importance of fair weights and measures dates back to ancient times. In the Book of Leviticus, the Lord told Moses, "You shall not commit a perversion of justice with measures, weights, or liquid measures." The verse continues, "You shall have true scales [and] true weights. . . ." The Book of Proverbs warns that "[d]eceitful scales are an abomination of the Lord; when willful wickedness comes, then comes disgrace."

Since the late eleventh century, the English Crown or Parliament has had the power to establish national standards of weights and measures. However, it appears that official standards were frequently ignored throughout England.[1] The Articles of Confederation gave the central government "the sole and exclusive right and power of . . . fixing the Standard of Weights and Measures throughout the United States."[2] On July 6, 1785, the Confederation Congress resolved that the "money Unit" would be "one dollar" and that the "smallest coin [would] be of copper, of which 200 shall pass for one dollar."[3] This currency did not follow a decimal system of measurement.

THE CONSTITUTIONAL CONVENTION

During the Constitutional Convention, there was widespread agreement about the Weights and Measures Clause. A draft from the Committee of Detail provided that Congress would have the "exclusive Right of . . . fixing the Standard of Weights and Measures throughout [the United States].[4] Other drafts had similar language.[5] On August 6, John Rutledge of South Carolina delivered the Committee of Detail's report to the Convention.[6] The plan gave Congress the power "to fix the standard of weights and measures."[7]

On August 16, the Convention adopted this provision without any recorded debate.[8] The Weights and Measures Clause would permit the federal government to adopt and enforce national measurement standards based on the prevailing consensus.[9] This consensus would facilitate both domestic and international commerce.

THE RATIFICATION DEBATES

The Weights and Measures Clause seems not to have excited opposition during ratification. In Federalist No. 42, James Madison merely mentions the clause in a "cursory review" of powers intended to "provide for the harmony and proper intercourse among the states."

THE FIRST CONGRESS

In January 1790, President George Washington urged Congress to turn its attention to weights and measures in his first address to that body: "Uniformity in the Currency, Weights and Measures of the United States is an object of great importance, and will, I am persuaded, be duly attended to."[10] In response, Congress requested Secretary of State Thomas Jefferson to prepare a report. In July 1790, Jefferson submitted his "Plan for Establishing Uniformity in the Coinage, Weights, and Measures of the United States" to the House of Representatives.[11] Jefferson in fact offered two plans. The first set the measure of length (miles, feet, and inches); capacity (pints, quarts, gallons); and weights (ounces and pounds). The second proposed to reduce "every branch to the same decimal ratio already established in their coins, and thus bring[] the calculation of the principal affairs of life within the arithmetic of every man who can multiply and divide plain numbers." There would be 10 inches in a foot and 10,000 feet in a mile, an ounce would be one-tenth of a pound, and there would be 100 cents in a dollar.

Congress took no action on either of Jefferson's proposals.[12] On October 25, 1791, President Washington's message to Congress reiterated the importance of weights and measures, urging that "[a] uniformity in the weights and measures of the country is among the important objects submitted to you by the Constitution."[13] Again, no action was taken on the measure.

EARLY PRACTICE

The Coinage Act of 1792 set the value of one dollar as "the value of a Spanish milled dollar."[14] It also adopted a decimal system of currency: A "cent" would be a "hundredth part of a dollar."[15] But Congress still did not act on Jefferson's proposal. In 1799, Congress addressed weights and measures indirectly. A statute directed the surveyors of each port to calibrate their instruments for weights and measures, which were used to assess duties.[16] However, no standards had been adopted against which to calibrate those instruments.[17]

In 1816, President James Madison recommended in his State of the Union address that Congress provide for uniform weights and measures. He observed that "no adequate provision has yet been made, for the uniformity of weights and measures, also contemplated by the Constitution."[18]

Madison favored Jefferson's decimal system. The next year, the Senate requested a report on the matter from the Secretary of State.[19] In 1821, Secretary of State John Quincy Adams

presented a 250-page report to Congress.[20] Adams's report rejected adopting France's metric system and proposed no federal enforcement mechanism. Congress decided to remain on the English system, as a result of which the states would be responsible for applying the standards.

By 1830, Congress realized that different ports of entry used different weights and measures to assess duties.[21] This wide variation in duties resulted in a loss of considerable revenue. The Senate passed a resolution directing "the Secretary of the Treasury . . . to cause a comparison to be made of the standards of weight and measure now used at the principle [*sic*] custom houses in the United States."[22] In 1836, Congress passed a joint resolution, which President Martin Van Buren approved,[23] directing the Secretary of the Treasury to adopt a "complete set of all weights and measures," to be used in custom houses and delivered to each state, with the goal of establishing a "uniform standard of weights and measures . . . through[out] the United States."[24] Through this action, Congress indirectly adopted a system based on the traditional English units of weights and measures.

Congress has acquiesced in, though never formally authorized, use of the traditional English system of weights and measures in non-business activities. In 1866, Congress authorized but did not mandate use of the metric system.[25] In 1975, Congress adopted the metric system as the "preferred system" for trade and commerce.[26] The Office of Weights and Measures within the Commerce Department's National Institute of Standards and Technology publishes standards for both English and metric weights and measures.[27]

JUDICIAL PRECEDENT

There is very little judicial precedent about the Weights and Measures Clause. There has been litigation over whether states can define standard measures for trade purposes in the absence of congressional regulation. The Supreme Court has never explicitly held that the states have this power. *Massachusetts State Grange v. Benton* (1926) upheld the state's daylight savings act.[28] Justice Oliver Wendell Holmes's majority opinion suggested that the state did have this power. In 1855, Justice Robert Cooper Grier, while riding circuit, was perhaps more dubious. He found that "any interference of state legislation to change . . . the standard of weights" is "injurious."[29] Justice Joseph Story, writing in his *Commentaries*, suggested that the states could fix weights and measures in the absence of action by Congress.[30]

Cite as: Eric Chiappinelli, *The Weights and Measures Clause, in* THE HERITAGE GUIDE TO THE CONSTITUTION 172 (Josh Blackman & John G. Malcolm eds., 3d ed. 2025).

Notes

1. 1 Blackstone 273–74. **2.** Articles of Confederation, art. IX, § 4. **3.** 29 J. Cont. Cong. 499–500 (July 6, 1785). **4.** 2 Farrand's 136. **5.** *Id.* at 143, 159, 167. **6.** *Id.* at 177. **7.** *Id.* at 182. **8.** *Id.* at 308. **9.** Louis A. Fischer, *History of the Standard Weights and Measures of the United States, in* 1 Bull. of the Bur. of Standards 365, 365 (1905). **10.** Message from George Washington to the United States Senate and House of Representatives (Jan. 8, 1790), https://perma.cc/968H-SJYN [hereinafter Washington Message]. **11.** Thomas Jefferson, Plan for Establishing Uniformity in the Coinage, Weights, and Measures of the United States (July 4, 1790), https: //perma.cc/39V8-7QYV. **12.** Sarah Ann Jones, Weights and Measures in Congress: Historical Summary Covering the Period of the Continental Congress to and Including the Adoption of the Joint Resolutions of 1836 and 1838, 3–5 (1936), https://perma.cc/6PDH-8L95. **13.** Washington Message, *supra.* **14.** 1 Stat. 246, 248. **15.** 1 Stat. 250. **16.** Act of Mar. 2, 1799, ch. 22, § 21, 1 Stat. 627, 643. **17.** Fischer, *supra* at 367. **18.** James Madison, Annual Message to Congress (Dec. 3, 1816), https://perma.cc /B3XA-XPBX. **19.** Jones, *supra* at 9. **20.** John Quincy Adams, Report Upon Weights and Measures (1821), https: //perma.cc/LPG3-A8ES; Jones, *supra* at 9–11. **21.** Jones, *supra* at 14. **22.** S. Jour., 21st Cong., 1st Sess. 342 (May 29, 1830). **23.** 12 Reg. of Debates in Cong., 24th Cong., 1st Sess. app. xix (1836). **24.** Jones, *supra* at 16. **25.** 14 Stat. 339. **26.** 89 Stat. 1007. **27.** *OWM Background & History*, U.S. Dep't of Commerce, Nat'l Inst. of Standards & Technology, Off. of Weights & Measures (Feb. 7, 2025), https://perma.cc/2LAE-2MVD. **28.** 272 U.S. 525 (1926). **29.** *The Miantinomi*, 17 F. Cas. 254, 256 (C.C.W.D. Pa. 1855). **30.** 3 Story's Commentaries § 1117.

ESSAY NO. 50: THE COUNTERFEITING CLAUSE
ART. 1, § 8, CL. 6

The Congress shall have Power...To provide for the Punishment of counterfeiting the Securities and current Coin of the United States. . . .

—Judge Jay S. Bybee

INTRODUCTION

The counterfeiting of securities and coin presents two problems for any government. First, the knowing uttering of counterfeit money is fraud. Second, because money is a medium of exchange, counterfeiting undermines the stability of the marketplace. Gresham's Law follows: "Bad money drives out good." This essay examines the English common-law tradition with respect to counterfeiting, summarizes the development of the Counterfeiting Clause of the U.S. Constitution, and concludes by analyzing the Supreme Court's precedents interpreting the clause and highlighting questions about its scope that remain unanswered.

HISTORY BEFORE 1787

English law has punished the counterfeiting of currency at least since the fourteenth century.[1] By the time William Hawkins penned his influential treatise on English criminal law at the start of the eighteenth century, two discrete crimes concerning counterfeiting had emerged.[2] First, the uttering of counterfeit money was a form of theft.[3] Second, the act of making counterfeit money was a crime against the Crown and punishable as treason.[4] Men guilty of this latter offense would be drawn (tied to a horse and dragged to the execution site) and hanged; women would be drawn and burned alive.[5] The severity of these punishments was understood at the time. Sir William Blackstone advocated treating counterfeiters less harshly than other high treasonists, asserting that "affixing the same ideas of guilt upon the man who coins a leaden groat and him who assassinates his sovereign, takes off from that horror which ought to attend the very mention of the crime of high treason, and makes it more familiar to the subject."[6]

Across the Atlantic, the new American colonies started to issue their own currency in the late seventeenth century.[7] This currency took the form of bills of credit to finance the public fisc. However, colonial control of these fledgling funds was loose: A scholar observed that "at various times, the [pre-revolutionary] economy was close to operating on a barter basis."[8] During the Revolution, the states expanded their issuance of paper currency to finance the war effort. The British responded by counterfeiting American bank notes to depreciate their value and starve America's war machine.[9] This tactic proved devastatingly effective: $40 million worth of currency was replaced, rendering American money "worthless" by 1781.[10]

The states, still reeling from their wartime experiences, granted the Continental Congress power to regulate the "value of coin struck by" the United States and by each individual state.[11] However, the Articles did not grant Congress the power to punish counterfeiting.[12] As a consequence, when the Continental Congress asked the states to do so themselves, these requests were met with uneven results.[13] The failure of the Articles of Confederation to address counterfeiting would thus become a topic of discussion at the Constitutional Convention.

THE CONSTITUTIONAL CONVENTION

In May 1787, delegates from the various states gathered to discuss solutions to the shortcomings of the Confederation. On May 29, Charles Pinckney of South Carolina offered a plan for a federal Constitution.[14] One provision would have given Congress the power "[t]o declare the law and Punishment of piracies and felonies at sea & of counterfeiting Coin & of all offences against the Laws of Nations."[15]

On August 17, Gouverneur Morris of Pennsylvania, evidently agreeing with Pinckney

that Congress should have the authority to punish counterfeiting, raised the prospect of "extend[ing] th[is] authority."[16] Pinckney's proposal centered on "Coin," but Morris observed that counterfeiting might extend to other forms of currency (such as "[b]ills of exchange"), which "might be forged in one state and carried into another."[17] He therefore advocated for a legislative power to "punish[] . . . counterfeiting in general" but did not sketch its contours.[18]

"[O]ther members" who were unnamed in the Convention report voiced worries that the counterfeiting of "*foreign* paper" by Americans might undermine the young nation's relations with other countries.[19] Consistent with Morris's broad conception of national power in this arena, they therefore suggested vesting the national legislature with authority to punish the counterfeiting of foreign currency as well.

In the end, the Framers left the matter to the Committee of Style, which separated the power to punish counterfeiting from the piracy and "Laws of Nations" provisions found in Pinckney's original proposal.[20] The Counterfeiting Clause was instead slotted between Congress's coinage and postal powers.[21] This relocation occurred with little fanfare, counterfeiting having been an ancillary part of discussions focused more on the reach of the legislative powers to "declare," "define," and "punish" various enumerated crimes.[22] In keeping with Morris's view that counterfeiting may come in multiple forms, the final draft of the clause extended to both securities and coins.

However, the Counterfeiting Clause also came with certain limitations. First, it specified that congressional power reached only securities and coins "of the United States."[23] It thus did not give Congress power to punish the counterfeiting of other, nongovernmental securities—a concern raised at the Convention. Second, the clause extended only to "current Coin of the United States,"[24] which would not include the Spanish dollars, German thalers, or British pounds that had circulated during the colonial period.[25] Third, the clause authorized Congress to punish "counterfeiting" but did not make clear whether "counterfeiting" meant only the act of producing counterfeit money or included the passing of counterfeits as well. Fourth—and reminiscent of Blackstone's reservations—counterfeiting was not to be punished as treason under the new Constitution. That category of crimes would be limited to "levying War against [the United States], or in adhering to [its] Enemies, giving them Aid and Comfort."[26]

THE RATIFICATION DEBATES

In post-Convention debates, counterfeiting was a relatively minor issue, but it did reflect larger differences of opinion concerning the relationship between the states and the national government. In Federalist No. 42, James Madison highlighted the need for the United States to protect the integrity of its markets. He argued that the Counterfeiting Clause would "secure the value" of coinage in the United States and that the Federal Money and Counterfeiting Clauses together "supplied a material omission in the articles of confederation."

Anti-Federalists focused on counterfeiting as a common form of commercial fraud. Brutus, for example, wrote that "[p]rotection and defence" against ordinary criminals—"the murderer, the robber, the thief, the cheat, and the unjust person"—were properly "derived from the respective state governments."[27] An Old Whig took issue not with the enumerated powers of Congress—including that of "punish[ing] counterfeiters"—but with the "*undefined, unbounded and immense power*" contained in the Necessary and Proper Clause.[28] Similarly, Federal Farmer worried not about the national authority to punish counterfeiters *per se*, but about the prospect of litigants "drag[ging] each other many hundred miles into the federal courts."[29] Perhaps in light of our experiences during the Revolutionary War and Articles of Confederation eras, serious disputes over the propriety of some national authority over counterfeiting do not appear to have emerged.

EARLY PRACTICE

The First Congress exercised its power over counterfeiting in An Act for the Punishment of Certain Crimes Against the United States.[30] Both counterfeiting a government security *and* passing the counterfeit became capital crimes under the act.[31] However, this early statute did not address the counterfeiting of "current Coin of the United States." Congress would not create a mint until two years later.[32]

Following the establishment of a national mint, in 1806, Congress extended the prohibition to counterfeit coins.[33] Curiously, this statute also applied to foreign coins even though the Counterfeiting Clause concerned only the "current Coin of the United States." Congress also specified that the law would not "deprive the courts of the individual states of jurisdiction, under the laws of the several states, over offences made punishable by this act."[34] By doing so, Congress intimated an understanding that the Constitution does not give it the exclusive power to prohibit counterfeiting. However, this accommodative view of state power with respect to counterfeiting would not prove to be universal. Two decades later, Justice Joseph Story took a position contrary to early state court decisions.[35] He suggested that the power to punish counterfeiting of federal coins and securities might "be exclusive of that of the states" because it "naturally flow[s] . . . from the antecedent powers to borrow money[] and regulate the coinage."[36]

JUDICIAL PRECEDENT

In 1847, the U.S. Supreme Court held that states have the concurrent power to punish at least the passing of counterfeit federal money. In *Fox v. Ohio* (1847), the Court upheld the state conviction of an Ohio man for passing counterfeit U.S. coins, thereby recognizing the states' concurrent authority.[37] Finding the passing of counterfeit money to be "a private cheat effected by means of a base dollar," the Court held that the offense was "peculiarly and appropriately within [a state's] functions and duties."[38]

Subsequently, the Court has held that Congress has the power to punish the counterfeiting and passing of *foreign* coin, based on a combination of four other constitutional provisions: the Federal Money Clause, the Foreign Commerce Clause, the Necessary and Proper Clause, and the federal government's foreign affairs powers.[39] The Court also broadly approved of Congress's "suppressing and preventing the making and use of illegitimate coin."[40] It has been silent, however, as to the reach of state power in these areas.

OPEN QUESTIONS

- Much of the early debate around counterfeiting concerned what specific currencies Congress could reach. These questions have largely been answered; the current counterfeiting and forgery provisions are located in 18 U.S.C. §§ 470–514 and address both the making and uttering of counterfeit coins and documents. However, at least one question remains concerning the traditional relationship between federal and state power over counterfeiting: Can states punish the *manufacture* of counterfeit U.S. coins and securities, or does that power, which is distinct from the power to punish the *passing* of counterfeit money, belong exclusively to Congress?[41] Currently, many states prohibit both the manufacture and the passing of counterfeit U.S. money. Congress surely could preempt such state laws, but whether the Constitution implicitly does so with respect to U.S. securities and "current Coin" remains to be seen.

- Additionally, questions may arise in the future around the counterfeiting of cryptocurrencies, but those questions will not involve Congress's authority under the Counterfeiting Clause unless such currencies become "Securities or current Coin of the United States."

Cite as: Judge Jay S. Bybee, *The Counterfeiting Clause*, in THE HERITAGE GUIDE TO THE CONSTITUTION 174 (Josh Blackman & John G. Malcolm eds., 3d ed. 2025).

Notes

1. J.G. Bellamy, The Law of Treason in England in the Later Middle Ages 15 (D.E.C. Yale ed. 1970). **2.** 1 William Hawkins, A Treatise of the Pleas of the Crown §§ 55–56 (4th ed. 1762). **3.** *Id.* § 56. **4.** *Id.* § 55; 4 Select Cases in the Court of King's Bench Under Edward II 102 (G.O. Sayles ed., 1955); Bellamy, *supra* at 15, 207. **5.** 4 Blackstone 92–93. **6.** *Id.* at 89. **7.** Claire Priest, *Currency Policies and Legal Development in Colonial New England*, 110 Yale L.J. 1303, 1311 (2001). **8.** *Id.* **9.** Lynn Glaser, Counterfeiting in America: The History of an American Way to Wealth 37 (1960); Stephen Mihm, A Nation of Counterfeiters: Capitalists, Con Men, and the Making of the United States 34 (2007); Kenneth Scott, Counterfeiting in Colonial America 3–4 (1957). **10.** Ralph E. McKinney, Jr., et al., *The Evolution of Financial Instruments and the Legal Protection Against Counterfeiting: A Look at Coin, Paper, and Virtual Currencies*, 2015 U. Ill. J.L. Tech. & Pol'y 273, 300 (2015). **11.** Articles of Confederation, art. IX, §§ 4, 6. **12.** *Id.* **13.** Adam H. Kurland, *First Principles of American Federalism and the Nature of Federal Criminal Jurisdiction*, 45 Emory L.J. 1, 24, 39–41 (1996). **14.** 3 Farrand's at 595. **15.** *Id.* at 598. **16.** 2 Farrand's 315. **17.** *Id.* **18.** *Id.* **19.** *Id.* **20.** *Id.* at 595.

21. Art. I, § 8, cls. 5–7. **22.** Sarah H. Cleveland & William S. Dodge, *Defining and Punishing Offenses Under Treaties*, 124 Yale L.J. 2202, 2225 (2015); 2 Farrand's 314–19. **23.** Art. I, § 8, cl. 6. **24.** *Id.* **25.** Stephanie Meredith, *The History of U.S. Circulating Coins*, U.S. Mint (May 8, 2025), https://perma.cc/PB26-Y5G6. **26.** Art. III, § 3, cl. 1. **27.** Storing 2.9.86. **28.** Storing 3.3.12. **29.** Storing 2.8.41. **30.** 1 Stat. 112 (1790). **31.** *Id.* at ch. 9, § 14, 1 Stat. at 115. **32.** David P. Currie, The Constitution in Congress: The Federalist Period, 1789–1801, at 96 & n.324 (1997). **33.** An Act for the Punishment of Counterfeiting the Current Coin of the United States, ch. 50, §§ 1–2, 1 Stat. 404, 404–05 (1806). **34.** *Id.* at ch. 50, § 4, 1 Stat. at 405. **35.** *State v. Tutt*, 18 S.C. Eq. (2 Bail. Eq.) 44, 46 (S.C. 1831); *State v. Antonio*, 7 S.C.L. (2 Tread.) 776 (S.C. 1816); *State v. Randall*, 2 Aik. 89 (Vt. 1827). **36.** 3 Story's Commentaries § 1118. **37.** 46 U.S. (5 How.) 410, 435 (1847). **38.** *Id.* at 434. **39.** *United States v. Arjona*, 120 U.S. 479, 483 (1887); *United States v. Marigold*, 50 U.S. (9 How.) 560, 566, 568 (1850). **40.** *Baender v. Barnett*, 255 U.S. 224, 227 (1921). **41.** Kurland, *supra* at 28 n.90, 39 n.129.

❧

ESSAY NO. 51: THE POSTAL CLAUSE
ART. I, § 8, CL. 7

The Congress shall have Power . . . To establish Post Offices and post Roads. . . .
—Robert G. Natelson

INTRODUCTION

The history behind the Postal Clause explains its meaning to the Founders. This essay examines that history and then outlines subsequent developments during the early Republic and in the courts. It then delineates some constitutional questions arising from the clause, including the scope of the Necessary and Proper Clause and the nondelegation doctrine.

HISTORY BEFORE 1787

The postal system authorized by the Constitution is the direct successor to the unitary British imperial post office, which extended to British North America. One can understand the language of the Postal Clause only in light of the pre-existing imperial institution.[1] This institution functioned as a single integrated whole under a parliamentary statute enacted in 1711.[2] The system offered not merely carriage of letters and parcels, but also personal transportation and carriage of freight. It featured arterial and branch "post roads," courier services, professional travel guides, vehicle rental, and other facilities. It also included a fleet of packet boats for international and coastal transportation and delivery.

A post road was an intercity highway. The name "post road" was due to the road's punctuation by posts (also called stages). A post was what we now call a rest stop. It was a site for refueling man and beast; stabling, exchanging, and renting vehicles and horses; accepting letters and packages from an earlier courier and handing them to the next; and collecting tolls and payment for rentals and guides. Like many rest stops today, posts often featured taverns and inns. Unlike today's rest stops, they often included newspaper offices. Each post was overseen by a post master or post mistress who carried out his or her official functions in a post office. Because of the integrated nature of the postal system, the grant of authority to "establish Post Offices and post Roads" was not two discrete powers (as a modern reader might expect), but one larger power.

The laws organizing the imperial postal system tell us what it meant to "establish" such a system and its components. The 1711 statute was entitled "An Act for Establishing a General Post-Office for all her Majesty's Dominions." Similarly, a 1767 law extending postal service to the Isle of Man authorized the postmaster general to "establish Post Offices and Post Roads" there.[3]

Among other provisions, the 1711 statute authorized new letter offices in Edinburgh, Dublin, and New York; provided for the appointment of personnel and disqualified them from politics; created monopolies, with delineated exceptions, in carriage of letters and parcels and in certain transportation-related services; created postal routes and authorized extensions; specified postal rates in detail; authorized the postmaster general to operate a fleet of packet boats; prescribed rules governing letters; regulated North American ferrymen; and granted certain "franking" privileges (free mail service). This statute establishing a postal service also defined offenses against the system, listed their punishments, and identified the courts in which violations were to be prosecuted. Finally, the law authorized the executive to promulgate further regulations.

The North American branch of the imperial service centered on a single post road running from Falmouth, Massachusetts (now Portland, Maine), to Savannah, Georgia. The northern half of this route was administered from an office in New York; the southern half, which included service to the Caribbean, was administered from an office in Charleston, South Carolina.

The Anglo-American postal system served four principal purposes: to improve the ability of officials to monitor the movement of persons and messages, to raise government revenue, to facilitate travel and communication on government business, and to assist trade and commerce. The modern "public service" vision of the post office was a later development.

In 1776, the American branch of the imperial postal service was transferred to the management of the Continental Congress. In 1781, the Articles of Confederation became effective, granting the Confederation Congress the power of "establishing or regulating post offices from one State to another, throughout all the United States, and exacting such postage on the papers passing through the same as may be requisite to defray the expenses of the said office."[4] Throughout this period, the modes and philosophy of postal operation remained mostly unchanged. Congressional management was very hands on, with little delegation to the post-master general.

In 1782, Congress adopted an ordinance to govern the system.[5] This ordinance, which largely duplicated the terms of British postal legislation, was amended twice.[6] In 1787, a congressional committee proposed a revised ordinance, but it was not enacted.

THE CONSTITUTIONAL CONVENTION

The proceedings of the Constitutional Convention rarely referred to the Postal Clause. Several delegates emphasized the postal system's revenue potential. Charles Pinckney's plan for a Constitution specified that the national legislature "shall have exclusive power of establishing Post-Offices, and raising a Revenue from them."[7] In a June 11, 1787, speech, James Wilson of Pennsylvania said he thought the system "would be another substantial source of revenue."[8] On June 27, Luther Martin of Maryland also referred to it as a source of revenue.[9]

William Paterson's "New Jersey Plan" would have given Congress power over "Stamps—Post-Office."[10] The Committee of Detail's August 6 draft constitution stated, "The Legislature of the United States shall have the power . . . To establish Post-offices."[11]

On August 16, Elbridge Gerry of Massachusetts moved to add "and post-roads" to the Committee of Detail draft. John Francis Mercer of Maryland seconded the motion, and the Convention approved the amendment by a vote of six to five.[12] The dissent may have arisen because the comprehensive nature of a postal system seemed to render the additional wording unnecessary.

The Convention tabled three other proposed additions to the postal power. One was "[t]o regulate Stages on the post roads." Another was "to provide for (public securities) for stages on post-roads." The third was "to provide for cutting canals where deemed necessary."[13] Given the nature of a postal system, the first two additions would have been superfluous. The reason for rejecting canal-cutting is less clear.

THE RATIFICATION DEBATES

The two delegates who proposed adding "post-roads" to the Constitution, Elbridge Gerry and

John Francis Mercer, opposed the Constitution during the ratification debates. As their proposal illustrates, the postal power was popular even among the Constitution's opponents. They sometimes cited the post office as a power the central government ought to possess—as opposed to others it ought not to possess. The Constitution's advocates constricted the scope of potential controversy by distinguishing post roads from other roads, representing that only the state governments would continue to exercise jurisdiction over the latter.

At the New York ratification convention, Samuel Jones offered an amendment that would have narrowed the scope of the term "establish" by depriving Congress of the power to make or repair highways without local state consent.[14] This proposal was rejected, but the rejection did not prevent Jones from voting for the Constitution. Other objections to the postal power are hard to find.

PRACTICE IN THE EARLY REPUBLIC

In 1792, the Federal Congress adopted An Act to establish the Post-Office and Post Roads within the United States.[15] This law was squarely within the tradition of the institution's parliamentary and congressional predecessors. The law designated post roads, set postal rates, described postal officers and provided for their compensation, affirmed a monopoly on the carriage of letters and parcels, regulated the transmission of mail bags to and from ship masters, set franking privileges, and defined postal offenses and fixed punishments. The 1792 statute delegated relatively little discretion to postal officials, although it did grant the postmaster authority to approve extensions in existing post roads for up to eight years and to regulate, with some exceptions, terms of employment within post offices.

In 1796, Thomas Jefferson claimed that the "safest" construction of the power to establish post roads would deny Congress the power to create new roads.[16] Others also argued that the postal power did not include construction authority.[17] The broad sweep of eighteenth-century statutes establishing postal systems suggests that this claim had little merit. Some have contended that the power to establish post roads did not include eminent domain authority. This contention is not well founded because when the Constitution was adopted, eminent domain power was acknowledged to be incidental to road-making and road-widening authority.[18]

JUDICIAL PRECEDENT

In *McCulloch v. Maryland* (1819), Chief Justice John Marshall suggested in dicta that Congress's power to define postal crimes is derived from the Necessary and Proper Clause.[19] Two modern cases on the scope of that clause have cited his language.[20] The Necessary and Proper Clause seems superfluous in this instance because eighteenth-century practice shows that defining postal crimes was within the ambit of establishing postal systems.

Elsewhere, the Supreme Court has recognized the broad scope of establishing a postal system. *Ex Parte Jackson* (1877) held that the Postal Clause encompasses regulation of the country's entire postal system, including decisions governing what may and may not be mailed.[21] *Ex Parte Rapier* (1892) sustained a ban on mailing lottery materials,[22] *Masses Pub'g Co. v. Patten* (1917) upheld a ban on mailing seditious material during wartime,[23] and both *Roth v. United States* (1957) and *United States v. Reidel* (1971) held that Congress may bar obscene material from the mails.[24] Although the Supreme Court has recognized that the postal power is subject to the limits in the Bill of Rights, obscene matter is not protected by the First Amendment, so postal officials may bar it if they can do so without violating the Fourth Amendment.

Other cases have held that Congress may make enforceable compacts with states for allocation of post road repair costs,[25] prohibit placing non-mailed material in letter boxes,[26] and maintain a monopoly on letter delivery.[27]

OPEN QUESTIONS

- Several recent Supreme Court decisions have addressed the scope of the Necessary and Proper Clause. Some have cited Chief Justice Marshall's view that the power to define postal crimes derives from that clause. As we have seen, however, the Postal Clause itself authorizes such measures. If the Court finally recognizes that fact, this may encourage a narrower scope for the Necessary and Proper Clause.

- From time to time, the postal service has explored or engaged in entrepreneurial activities seemingly unrelated to mail delivery. A proper understanding of the scope of the Postal Clause as originally understood might be of assistance in resolving court challenges to those activities.

- It is unsettled how probative early postal legislation is on the extent to which Congress may sub-delegate its delegated power to executive branch agencies. This issue might raise concerns under the nondelegation doctrine. British legislation is not useful because Parliament exercised sovereign rather than delegated power and was unconstrained by relevant constitutional limits. However, the Confederation Congress's 1782 ordinance might be indirectly probative.

Cite as: Robert G. Natelson, *The Postal Clause, in* THE HERITAGE GUIDE TO THE CONSTITUTION 177 (Josh Blackman & John G. Malcolm eds., 3d ed. 2025).

Notes

1. Where not otherwise cited, the historical discussion in this essay comes from Robert G. Natelson, *Founding-Era Socialism: The Original Meaning of the Constitution's Postal Clause*, 7 Br. J. Am. Legal Studies 1 (2018). **2.** Post Office (Revenues) Act 1710, 9 Anne c. 10 (1711). **3.** Post Office Offences and Isle of Man Postage Act 1767, 7 Geo. 3, c. 50 (1767), § 5. **4.** Articles of Confederation, art. IX. **5.** 23 J. Cont. Cong. 670–78 (Oct. 18, 1782). **6.** *Id.* at 688–89 (Oct. 28, 1783); *id.* at 880 (Dec. 24, 1782). **7.** 3 Farrand's 607. **8.** 1 Farrand's 205. **9.** *Id.* at 442. **10.** 3 Farrand's 612. **11.** 2 Farrand's 167–68. **12.** *Id.* at 308. **13.** *Id.* at 322, 328, 615. **14.** 2 Elliot's 406. **15.** Act of Feb. 20, 1792, ch. 1, 1 Stat. 232.

16. Letter from Thomas Jefferson to James Madison (Mar. 6, 1796), https://perma.cc/FSU3-SU4E. **17.** Letter from Thomas Jefferson to James Madison (Mar. 6, 1796), https://perma.cc/Q8LY-ME5W. **18.** Robert G. Natelson, *Did the Constitution Grant the Federal Government Eminent Domain Power?*, 19 Fed. Soc'y Rev. 88 (2018). **19.** 17 U.S. 316, 385 (1819). **20.** *United States v. Comstock*, 560 U.S. 126, 136 (2010); *Sabri v. United States*, 541 U.S. 600, 605 (2004). **21.** 96 U.S. 727 (1877). **22.** 146 U.S. 110 (1892). **23.** 246 F. 24 (1917). **24.** 354 U.S. 476 (1957); 402 U.S. 351 (1971). **25.** 44 U.S. 151, 180 (1845). **26.** 453 U.S. 114 (1981). **27.** 439 U.S. 1345 (1978).

ESSAY NO. 52: THE COPYRIGHT AND PATENT CLAUSE
ART. I, § 8, CL. 8

The Congress shall have Power . . . To promote the Progress of Science and useful Arts, by securing for limited Times to Authors and Inventors the exclusive Right to their respective Writings and Discoveries. . . .

—Adam Mossoff

INTRODUCTION

Article 1, Section 8, Clause 8 is usually identified as the Copyright and Patent Clause, although it is also referred to as the Progress Clause or the Intellectual Property Clause. The Framers did not use the terms "copyright" or "patent," but this provision authorizes Congress to enact patent and copyright statutes, which were some of the first laws enacted by the First Congress in 1790. The American copyright and patent systems arose out of the English copyright and patent systems but departed significantly from the English model.

Early Americans uniquely protected patents and copyrights as property rights, following the constitutional authorization to Congress to "secure" to "Authors and Inventors" an "exclusive Right to their respective Writings and Discoveries."[1] In this respect, the American copyright and patent laws were influenced by John Locke's natural rights philosophy, which justified the protection of the fruits of the productive labors of innovators and creators.

In the early Republic, James Madison, Chancellor Kent, and others viewed patents and copyrights as property rights secured to inventors and authors. By contrast, Thomas Jefferson was equivocal about patents and copyrights but is largely known today for viewing patents as monopolies. Today, reliable and effective property rights in copyright and patent have been upended by the Internet and other new technologies, as well as by the long-standing tension between the monopoly and property perspectives of these intellectual property rights.

THE ENGLISH COPYRIGHT AND PATENT SYSTEMS

The Copyright and Patent Clause "was written against the 'backdrop' of [pre-Revolutionary] English patent practices."[2] The Crown granted royal monopolies by "letters patent," the legal device for exercising the royal prerogative. The Crown abused its prerogative, and Parliament ultimately enacted the Statute of Monopolies in 1623. This law eliminated these abuses by limiting the issuance of patents to inventors or importers of new trades, imposing a fourteen-year term limit, and conferring jurisdiction over patents in the common-law courts.[3] By the late eighteenth century, patents were still granted by the Crown, but they were grants of personal privilege to inventors and importers of new trades in the realm.

Copyright also finds its provenance in royal patent grants of monopolies to publishers. Modern copyright law begins in the early eighteenth century with Parliament's enactment of the Statute of Anne of 1709.[4] This statute, in conjunction with common-law court decisions, shifted the focus of the vesting of the exclusive right against unauthorized copies from publishers to authors.[5]

By the eighteenth century, English copyright and patent laws were influenced by John Locke's natural rights theory. Locke himself defended copyrights as property rights of authors in 1695,[6] and he wrote approvingly in the *Second Treatise* of "Inventions and Arts" as exemplars of property created through productive labor.[7] Applying these ideas, Sir William Blackstone wrote that the right authors have in their literary works is a "species of property" because it is "grounded on labour and invention," referring to "Mr. Locke" and citing the *Second Treatise*.[8] However, Blackstone was of two minds when it came to patents, which he still recognized as a "royal patent of privilege."[9]

FRAMING THE COPYRIGHT AND PATENT CLAUSE

The United States's copyright and patent systems were based on a foundation in Lockean political theory and thus represented the same fundamental break from the English system that other U.S. political and legal institutions represented.[10] Between 1776 and 1787, for example, several states enacted copyright statutes that restated the Lockean principle that there is "no property more peculiarly a man's own than that which is produced by the labour of his mind."[11] There were no general patent statutes enacted by the states under the Articles of Confederation, but the Constitution's unification of copyrights and patents in a single clause strongly suggests the unification of a common justification in Lockean property theory.

The Copyright and Patent Clause exemplifies American exceptionalism for at least two reasons: It is the first time in history that a country's founding document expressly authorizes the government to protect patents and copyrights, and it is the only provision in the original Constitution in which the federal government is authorized to "secur[e]" a "right."

Yet, during the Constitutional Convention, there was no official commentary by the Framers about copyrights or patents. According to James Madison, the copyright and patent "clause was agreed to nem. con" (without debate).[12] The Committee on Style was responsible for the specific phrasing of Article 1, Section 8, Clause 8 as it now exists in the Constitution.

The specific text of the clause and its placement in the Constitution reveal several other important choices made by the Framers. First, the Copyright and Patent Clause is in Article I, Section 8, which delegates all powers to Congress. The Framers' decision to authorize Congress rather than the Executive to secure patents and copyrights is a key difference from the English patent practice in which patents were granted by the Crown as personal privileges.[13]

Second, the clause authorizes the securing of copyrights and patents only for the "Writings and Discoveries" of "Authors and Inventors." The patent statutes enacted by the First Congress, an authoritative source on the original public meaning of the Constitution, secured patents only to first "inventors."[14] By contrast, the Crown granted English patents to any person who was first to file an application for these royal privileges without regard to whether this person was an inventor. The U.S. intellectual property system represented a shift away from discretionary royal grants of personal privileges toward the protection of property rights secured in legal institutions like courts defined by the rule of law and due process.[15]

MADISON ON COPYRIGHTS AND PATENTS

James Madison is the only Framer to comment on the original public meaning of Copyright and Patent Clause in an authoritative source. In justifying the protection of patents and copyrights, Madison stated in Federalist No. 43 that the "utility of this power will scarcely be questioned," which perhaps explains the dearth of commentary by Framers and the lack of debate in the Convention. The reason, Madison explained, was that "[t]he public good in both cases [patents and copyrights] coincides with the claims of individuals." This reflects the well-evidenced Lockean view in the Founding era that the protection of property rights benefits both individuals and the public good. The Framers authorized Congress to secure copyrights and patents as federal property rights because the "States cannot separately make effectual provisions for either of the cases."

Madison went beyond this prudential justification for securing patents and copyrights in the Constitution and further justified them as fundamental property rights. He observed that copyright was "solemnly adjudged, in Great Britain, to be a right of common law. The right to useful inventions seems with equal reason to belong to the inventors." In the eighteenth century, it was widely accepted that the common law secured natural rights.[16] Thus, the *equal reason* that justifies patents along with copyrights is the Lockean natural right to property that already informed English court decisions and Blackstone's discussion of copyright in his *Commentaries*. Just as civil rights are justified by natural rights philosophy, Madison made the point here that natural rights philosophy also justified the protection of patents as fundamental civil rights in property.[17]

Chancellor James Kent advanced the Lockean principle in his influential *Commentaries on American Law.* Kent, who worked closely with Alexander Hamilton in the Founding era before becoming a New York judge, classified copyrights and patents under the title "Original Acquisition by Intellectual Labor."[18] Kent explained that "literary property" is a form of "property acquired by one's own act and power."[19] Both authors and inventors "should enjoy the pecuniary profits resulting from mental as well as bodily labor."[20] Justice Joseph Story is recognized as one of the architects of American patent law given his many opinions in patent cases.[21] He also agreed with Madison that patents and copyrights are property rights as distinguished from the hoary English grants of personal privileges in commercial monopolies.[22]

Some early nineteenth-century judges and officials did view patents and copyrights as special privileges or monopolies,[23] but Madison's view of copyrights and patents informed the public meaning of the Copyright and Patent Clause and became the prevailing public meaning in the early Republic. The "exclusive right" in patents was secured as a property right, for example, against the government. Although the Crown claimed a prerogative power to use the royal privileges it bestowed in English patents, the "exclusive right" in the Constitution limited unauthorized government uses of patents through the Due Process and Takings Clauses.[24]

JEFFERSON ON PATENTS

The Founders were not all of one mind about patent rights. Although Thomas Jefferson did not comment on copyright, he vacillated between skepticism and opprobrium about patents.[25] Jefferson, who wrote the Patent Act of 1793, believed that "ingenuity should receive a liberal encouragement."[26] In an 1813 letter, Jefferson denies any natural rights justification for patents. He stated that the "embarrasment [sic] of an exclusive patent" is permitted only because these "monopolies of invention" serve the "benefit of society."[27] The Supreme Court has cited this letter.[28]

The public understanding in the Founding era was more in line with Jefferson's positive views of patents as well as Madison's views. Moreover, other prominent early American jurists endorsed the Framers' view of patents and copyrights as property rights. Justice Story and Chancellor Kent are two exemplars of jurists who endorsed this public meaning.

MODERN DOCTRINE

In copyright and patent cases, the modern Supreme Court has wavered between the monopoly and property perspectives. In patent law, the Supreme Court has quoted and cited Jefferson's view of patents as monopolies as expressed in his 1813 letter, despite Jefferson not being a Framer.[29] Since the turn of the century, the Court has decided patent cases at a rate not seen since the early twentieth century. Many decisions frame patents as monopolies or public franchises; this has resulted in significant limitations of the rights of inventors to do such things as, for example, obtain patents[30] and commercialize their patents in the marketplace.[31] In *Oil States Energy Services v. Greene's Energy Group* (2018), the Court held for the first time that patents are public rights or public franchises, not private rights, and are subject to cancellation by administrative fiat exercised in ways similar to the ways the English prerogative power was exercised.[32]

In copyright law, however, the Supreme Court has more consistently affirmed that copyright is a property right. *Harper & Row v. Nation Enterprises* (1985) held that "[b]y establishing a marketable right to the use of one's expression, copyright supplies the economic incentive to create and disseminate ideas."[33] *Eldred v. Ashcroft* (2003) rejected the argument that the sole justification for copyright is utilitarianism, acknowledging that both natural rights theory and utilitarianism are legitimate justifications for the rights of creators under copyright law.[34] The Court was incrementally delimiting the scope of copyright protection in creating an expansive notion of "fair use," which is a safe harbor from copyright infringement liability.[35] But a significant decision in *Warhol v. Goldsmith* (2023) seems to have ended this development, as the Court protected the copyright in a photograph and rejected the argument that some changes in an unauthorized sale of the photo made it a "fair use."[36]

OPEN QUESTIONS

The status of both copyrights and patents as either private rights or public rights/public franchises continues to remain unsettled and affects all aspects of these intellectual rights. This is especially important as the expanding administrative state raises new questions about administrative powers over or regulatory restrictions of these property rights. Closely related to the competing historical perspectives of patents and copyrights as either property rights or monopoly privileges, the relationship of these intellectual property rights to antitrust law remains unsettled.

Cite as: Adam Mossoff, *The Copyright and Patent Clause, in* The Heritage Guide to the Constitution 181 (Josh Blackman & John G. Malcolm eds., 3d ed. 2025).

Notes

1. Art. I, § 8, cl. 8. **2.** *Graham v. John Deere Co.*, 383 U.S. 1, 5 (1966). **3.** An Act Concerning Monopolies, 21 Jac. I, c. 3 (1623). **4.** Statute of Anne, 8 Anne c. 21 (1709). **5.** H. Tomas Gomez-Arostegui, *Copyright at Common Law in 1774*, 47 Conn. L. Rev. 1 (2014). **6.** John Locke, John Locke: Political Essays 330–38 (Mark Goldie, ed., 1997). **7.** John Locke, Second Treatise of Government, ch. 5 (1689). **8.** 2 Blackstone 405. **9.** *Id.* at 406 **10.** *McKeever v. United States (McKeever's Case)*, 14 Ct. Cl. 396 (1878); Adam Mossoff, *Institutional Design in Patent Law: Private Property Rights or Regulatory Entitlements*, 92 So. Cal. L. Rev. 921 (2019). **11.** Copyright Enactments of the United States, 1783–1906, Copyright Off. Bulletin No. 3, at 14, 18–19 (Thorvald Solberg comp., 1906). **12.** 2 Farrand's 509–10. **13.** *McKeever*, 14 Ct. Cl. at 420. **14.** *Id.* at 417–20. **15.** B. Zorina Khan, The Democratization of Invention: Patents and Copyrights in American Economic Development, 1790–1920, at 51 (2005). **16.** Richard H. Helmholz, Natural Law in Court: A History of Legal Theory in Practice 96–97 (2015). **17.** Adam Mossoff, *Who Cares What Thomas Jefferson Thought About Patents? Reevaluating the Patent "Privilege" in Historical Context*, 92 Cornell L. Rev. 953 (2007). **18.** 2 James Kent, Commentaries on American Law 497 (O.W. Holmes, Jr. ed., 1873). **19.** *Id.* **20.** *Id.* **21.** Frank D. Prager, *The Influence of Mr. Justice Story on American Patent Law*, 5 Am. J. Legal Hist. 254 (1961). **22.** *Reed v. Cutter*, 20 F. Cas. 435, 438 (C.C.D. Mass. 1841) (Story, Circuit Justice); *Ryan v. Goodwin*, 21 F. Cas. 110, 112 (C.C.D. Mass. 1839) (Story, Circuit Justice); *Mellus v. Silsbee*, 16 F. Cas. 1332, 1333–34 (C.C.D. Mass. 1825) (Story, Circuit Justice). **23.** *Washing Machine Co. v. Earle*, 29 F. Cas. 332 (C.C.E.D. Pa. 1861). **24.** *Allen v. Cooper*, 589 U.S. 248, 261–62 (2020); Adam Mossoff, *Patents as Constitutional Private Property: The Historical Protection of Patents Under the Takings Clause*, 87 B.U. L. Rev. 689 (2007). **25.** Justin Hughes, *Copyright and Incomplete Historiographies: Of Piracy, Propertization, and Thomas Jefferson*, 79 So. Cal. L. Rev. 993, 1026–34 (2006); Mossoff, *Who Cares What Thomas Jefferson Thought About Patents?*, at 959–67. **26.** Letter from Thomas Jefferson to Oliver Evans (May 2, 1897), https://perma.cc/7LKL-FQU3. **27.** Letter from Thomas Jefferson to Isaac McPherson (Aug. 13, 1813), https://perma.cc/88KQ-AVYC; *Bonito Boats, Inc. v. Thunder Craft Boats, Inc.*, 489 U.S. 141, 147–48 (1989); *Graham*, 383 U.S. at 7–11. **28.** *Diamond v. Chakrabarty*, 447 U.S. 303, 308–09 (1980). **29.** *Bonito Boats*, 489 U.S. 141; *Graham*, 383 U.S. at 5; Frank H. Easterbrook, *Intellectual Property Is Still Property*, 13 Harv. J. L. & Pub. Pol'y 108, 117 (1990). **30.** *Alice Corp. v. CLS Bank Int'l*, 573 U.S. 208 (2014); *Assoc. for Molecular Pathology v. Myriad Genetics*, 133 U.S. 2107 (2013); *Mayo Collaborative Servs. LLC v. Prometheus Labs., Inc.*, 566 U.S. 66 (2012); *Bilski v. Kappos*, 561 U.S. 593 (2010). **31.** *Impression Prods., Inc. v. Lexmark Int'l, Inc.*, 581 U.S. 360 (2017); *Quanta Computer, Inc. v. LG Electronics, Inc.*, 553 U.S. 617 (2008); *MedImmune, Inc. v. Genentech, Inc.*, 549 U.S. 118 (2007). **32.** *Oil States Energy Servs., LLC v. Greene's Energy Grp., LLC*, 584 U.S. 325 (2018). **33.** *Harper & Row Publishers, Inc. v. Nation Enters.*, 471 U.S. 539, 558 (1985). **34.** *Eldred v. Ashcroft*, 537 U.S. 186, 212 n.18 (2003). **35.** *Google LLC v. Oracle Am., Inc.*, 593 U.S. 1 (2021); *Campbell v. Acuff-Rose Music*, 510 U.S. 569 (1994); *Universal City Studios v. Sony Corp.*, 464 U.S. 417 (1984). **36.** *Andy Warhol Found. for the Visual Arts, Inc. v. Goldsmith*, 598 U.S. 508 (2023).

⌐∾

ESSAY NO. 53: THE INFERIOR COURTS CLAUSE
ART. I, § 8, CL. 9

The Congress shall have Power . . . To constitute Tribunals inferior to the supreme Court. . . .

—Judge David R. Stras & Andy Hessick

INTRODUCTION

The Inferior Courts Clause empowers Congress to create a federal court system subordinate to the Supreme Court. The design of the federal judiciary was a point of major contention during the Constitutional Convention. There was no dispute about the need for a federal judiciary to enforce federal rights and ensure uniformity in federal law, but there was significant disagreement about how to structure it. Some argued that the federal judiciary should consist of a single supreme court; others argued for a more robust judicial system that included "inferior tribunals."[1]

In 1789, and still today, "inferior tribunals" suggests a judicial hierarchy with higher appellate courts reviewing the decisions of the lower trial courts. Through the Judiciary Act of 1789, the First Congress promptly created the inferior federal courts. In modern times, Congress has relied on the Inferior Tribunals Clause to create the federal district courts, the federal circuit courts, and other Article III courts.

HISTORY BEFORE 1787

Sir William Blackstone used the term "inferior" to describe the system of English courts, which resembled a pyramid.[2] At the bottom were the *courts piepoudre*, which had limited jurisdiction to decide disputes in local fairs and markets. Each successive layer of this pyramid was a superior court with "larger jurisdiction" and "greater power," capable of hearing a broader swath of disputes and "correct[ing] the errors of the inferior" courts.[3] By the 1700s, however, the English judicial system no longer resembled a perfect pyramid. The lines between superior and inferior courts had blurred as the jurisdiction of courts had changed over time. Some superior courts exercised concurrent jurisdiction with inferior courts, and not all decisions of inferior courts were reviewable by superior courts.[4]

By the time of the Constitutional Convention, most states had hierarchical judiciaries with higher courts reviewing the decisions of lower courts. The precise arrangement, however, differed by state. Virginia, for example, had county and town courts and three courts with statewide jurisdiction: a General Court that had some appellate jurisdiction over local courts and original jurisdiction in some matters; a High Court of Chancery; and a Court of Admiralty.[5] Delaware, by contrast, had "common pleas and orphans' courts" in each county, a "judge of admiralty," a "supreme court," and a "court of appeals" that could review the decisions of the "supreme court."[6]

As in England, however, the state judicial hierarchies did not form perfect pyramids. In most states, the superior courts often acted as trial courts, not appellate courts, and heard cases that were more significant than those heard by inferior courts. Some commentators have described certain state judiciaries as having a horizontal instead of a vertical arrangement.[7] Georgia did not even have a statewide hierarchy; there was a supreme court in each county, and those courts operated only as trial courts.[8]

THE CONSTITUTIONAL CONVENTION

During the Constitutional Convention, Edmund Randolph of Virginia proposed a resolution that would establish a supreme court as well as "inferior tribunals to be chosen by the National Legislature."[9] The proposal, in effect, would have mandated Congress to establish inferior federal courts. Randolph's proposal met significant opposition, led by John Rutledge of South Carolina and Roger Sherman of Connecticut. Sherman argued that constitutionally mandated inferior federal courts would be an unnecessary expense because state courts could hear federal cases.[10] Rutledge focused on state sovereignty. He argued that establishing inferior federal courts would "encroach[] on the jurisdiction" of state courts.[11] "State Tribunals," in his view, could "decide in all cases in the first instance."[12] In response to the concern that state courts might be biased against federal law, he thought that "the right of appeal to the supreme national tribunal [was] sufficient to secure the national rights [and] uniformity" of judgments.[13]

James Madison of Virginia led the defense of inferior federal courts. He argued that leaving trials to state judiciaries with review by one federal Supreme Court would be an inadequate guard against biased or prejudiced judgments. Although the Supreme Court could vacate biased judgments on appeal, the process would serve "no purpose" because the state courts could simply reenter them on remand.[14] Nor would it be practical to order new trials in the

Supreme Court because that would require "the parties to bring up their witnesses, tho' ever so distant from the seat of the Court."[15] In Madison's view, the federal system needed inferior courts, not just a single Supreme Court. Consistent with English practice, the inferior federal courts could have "*final* jurisdiction in *many* cases" to prevent "appeals" that "would be multiplied to a most oppressive degree."[16]

Madison's efforts to mandate the creation of inferior federal courts proved to be unpersuasive. Rutledge made a motion, seconded by Sherman, to strike out the provision requiring the creation of inferior tribunals. That motion carried by a vote of 5 to 4 with two states divided.[17]

Having failed to guarantee inferior courts in the Constitution, Madison proposed a compromise that gave discretion to "the National Legislature . . . to institute" inferior courts.[18] Madison repeated his earlier argument that inferior tribunals were essential to ensuring an effective federal judiciary. The compromise still faced opposition, including from Pierce Butler of South Carolina. He argued that the mere possibility of inferior courts would be seen as an "encroachment" on the state. In the end, Madison's compromise was approved by a vote of 8 to 2 with one state divided.[19]

Madison was not writing on a blank slate. Some states had expressly left the design of state courts to their legislatures. The Massachusetts constitution, for example, conferred power on the legislature to "erect and constitute" courts.[20] The same was true for New Hampshire.[21]

Despite Madison's compromise, delegates continued to view inferior federal courts with suspicion, largely because of the widespread availability of state courts and the primacy of state interests. Luther Martin of Maryland said the interior courts would "create jealousies . . . as the Country becomes more populous."[22]

Madison's compromise ultimately was adopted as Article I, Section 8, Clause 9. The Inferior Tribunals Clause authorizes Congress "[t]o constitute Tribunals inferior to the supreme Court." The compromise also found its way into Article III, which provides that the "judicial Power of the United States, shall be vested in one supreme Court, and in such inferior Courts as the Congress may from time to time ordain and establish."[23]

THE RATIFICATION DEBATES

Many of the arguments about the Madisonian compromise that were advanced during the Convention made their way into the ratification debates. Proponents of the compromise argued that inferior federal courts were necessary to prevent an overwhelming number of appeals to the Supreme Court. In Federalist No. 81, for example, Alexander Hamilton wrote that the power to create "local courts subordinate to the supreme court" would "obviate the necessity of having recourse to the supreme court in every case of federal cognizance."

Opponents reiterated that inferior federal courts were unnecessary, state courts already being available, and would expand federal power at the expense of the states.[24] Anti-Federalist Brutus summed up the opposition when he said that he feared that inferior federal courts would "swallow up all the powers of the courts in the respective states."[25]

Little was said about Congress's power to regulate the jurisdiction of any inferior courts that it created. The assumption appeared to be that Congress could limit their jurisdiction. For example, in Federalist No. 81, Hamilton suggested that Congress had power to regulate the geographic jurisdiction of the courts and could divide the country into several regions, each with its own inferior court. Edmund Pendleton told the Virginia ratifying convention that the country should "expect that there will be an inferior court in each state."[26]

THE JUDICIARY ACT OF 1789

Following ratification, Congress promptly exercised its power to establish inferior courts. On September 24, 1789, during the first session of the First Congress, the Judiciary Act of 1789 was enacted. This law created thirteen federal district courts, one for each state, and allocated a single district judge to each district.[27] These federal district courts acted as trial courts of first instance in many cases.

The act also established three circuit courts, which had both original and appellate jurisdiction. The Eastern Circuit included the districts of New Hampshire, Massachusetts, Connecticut, and New York; the Middle Circuit included the districts of New Jersey, Pennsylvania, Delaware, Maryland, and Virginia; and the Southern

Circuit included the districts of South Carolina and Georgia. However, the Judiciary Act did not establish separate judges to staff the circuit courts.[28] Instead, Congress directed that each circuit court should consist of three judges. One would be the district judge of the district in which that circuit court sat. The other two would be Supreme Court Justices, who were expected to "ride circuit" twice a year.[29]

The constitutionality of circuit riding was tested in *Stuart v. Laird* (1803).[30] Stuart challenged a judgment that had been rendered against him by a circuit court. He argued that because Congress had established the circuit courts separately from the Supreme Court, circuit riding fell outside a Justice's office. The Supreme Court upheld circuit riding, but it did not address Stuart's argument. Instead, the Court simply declared that circuit riding was too well established to declare the practice illegal: "practice and acquiescence under it, for a period of several years commencing with the organization of the judicial system, affords an irresistible answer."[31] But by affirming the practice, the Court implicitly rejected Stuart's argument. To this day, Justices may still sit on lower federal courts.

The text of the Inferior Tribunals Clause expressly authorized Congress to create inferior courts, but the Judiciary Act of 1789 did far more than establish the tribunals. The law fixed the location of those courts, when they would meet, the number of judges they would have, and what their salaries would be. In this early statute, the First Congress probably relied on its powers under the Necessary and Proper Clause to work out these details.

LIMITING THE JURISDICTION OF THE INFERIOR COURTS

Article I gives Congress the plenary power to constitute inferior tribunals. Article III, Section 1 arguably vests the entire judicial power of the United States in the inferior federal courts by extending it to nine categories of cases and controversies. But there is no constitutional provision that specifically allows Congress to limit the jurisdiction of the inferior federal courts as it can for the Supreme Court. The question then becomes: Can Congress limit the jurisdiction of the inferior courts and thus limit the types of cases they can hear?

In *United States v. Hudson* (1812), the Court answered this question in the affirmative: "[T]he power which congress possess to create Courts of inferior jurisdiction, necessarily implies the power to limit the jurisdiction of those Courts to particular objects."[32] This decision was consistent with the Madisonian compromise, which was an effort to give Congress the authority to determine where, and in what circumstances, federal courts were necessary. To do so, Congress had to have the ability to determine the contours of their jurisdiction, including the proper division between state and federal courts.

NON–ARTICLE III TRIBUNALS

Over time, Congress has created a vast number of non-judicial tribunals. Falling into this category are adjudicatory bodies of administrative agencies such as the Internal Revenue Service and the Social Security Administration. These tribunals do not exercise the judicial power. Rather, they make executive decisions—for example, what taxes to assess and whether a particular person is entitled to welfare benefits. To create these non-judicial tribunals, Congress could not rely on its power to "constitute Tribunals inferior to the supreme Court." This clause only authorizes Congress to create judicial tribunals, and non-judicial tribunals are not inferior to the Supreme Court. To establish non-judicial tribunals, Congress relied on its other powers.[33]

Congress also has established judicial tribunals outside of Article III. The judges on these tribunals do not have the salary and tenure guarantees of Article III. In the early nineteenth century, the constitutionality of those tribunals was called into question based on the argument that the judicial power of the United States "shall be vested" in one Supreme Court and any inferior courts created by Congress. But *American Insurance Co. v. Canter* (1828) held that Congress could create territorial courts under the Territories Clause in Article IV, Section 3, Clause 2.[34] (See Essay No. 144.) Since that time, the Supreme Court has upheld the validity of non–Article III tribunals, ranging from military tribunals to bankruptcy courts.

Today, federal tribunals cover a variety of subject matters and come in all different forms. For example, the U.S. Court of Federal Claims is considered an Article I tribunal. Its judges serve terms of fifteen years.

OPEN QUESTIONS

One of the most significant questions is whether there are any limits on Congress's power to regulate the jurisdiction of the lower courts. Since 1789, it has been understood that Congress's ability to establish inferior tribunals includes the power to regulate jurisdiction. For example, the Judiciary Act of 1789 significantly limited the geographic jurisdiction of each district court to the district in which it sat. The Supreme Court explicitly recognized Congress's power to regulate inferior court jurisdiction in *Sheldon v. Sill* (1850).[35] Twenty-two years later, *United States v. Klein* (1872), held that Congress could not restrict jurisdiction in a way that effectively dictates how cases are resolved.[36] Although subsequent decisions have limited *Klein* to its facts, several Justices have suggested that they agree with its conclusion.[37]

Another significant question is the extent to which there are limitations on Congress's power to create judicial tribunals outside of Article III. Although the Court upheld Congress's power to create such tribunals more than two hundred years ago, the proliferation of non–Article III tribunals and their increasing displacement of Article III courts could prompt the Court to revisit the issue.

Cite as: Judge David R. Stras & Andy Hessick, *The Inferior Courts Clause, in* The Heritage Guide to the Constitution 184 (Josh Blackman & John G. Malcolm eds., 3d ed. 2025).

Notes

1. 1 Farrand's 21. **2.** 3 Blackstone 30. **3.** *Id.* at 31. **4.** *Id.* at 31, 32–37. **5.** Va. Const. of 1776; David E. Engdahl, *What's in a Name? The Constitutionality of Multiple "Supreme" Courts,* 66 Ind. L.J. 457, 469 (1991). **6.** Del. Const. of 1776, arts. XII, XVII, XX. **7.** Wilfred J. Ritz, Rewriting the History of the Judiciary Act of 1789, at 44 (Wythe Holt & L.H. LaRue eds., 1990). **8.** Ga. Const. of 1777, art. XL. **9.** 1 Farrand's 21. **10.** *Id.* at 125. **11.** *Id.* at 124. **12.** *Id.* at 119. **13.** *Id.* at 124. **14.** *Id.* **15.** *Id.* **16.** *Id.* **17.** *Id.* **18.** *Id.* at 125. **19.** *Id.* **20.** Mass. Const. of 1780, pt. 2, ch. I, § 1, art. III. **21.** N.H. Const. of 1784, pt. 2. **22.** 2 Farrand's 45–46. **23.** Art. III, § 1. **24.** 3 Farrand's App. A. at 207. **25.** Storing 2.9.7, 2.9.139. **26.** 3 Elliot's 547. **27.** The Judiciary Act of 1789, ch. 20, §§ 2–3, 1 Stat. 73, 73. **28.** *Id.,* § 4, at 74. **29.** *Id.* at 74–75. **30.** 5 U.S. (1 Cranch) 299 (1803). **31.** *Id.* at 309. **32.** 11 U.S. 32, 33 (1812). **33.** *Ex Parte Bakelite Corp.,* 279 U.S. 438, 458 (1929). **34.** 26 U.S. (1 Pet.) 511 (1828). **35.** 49 U.S. 441 (1850). **36.** 13 Wall. 128 (1872). **37.** *Patchak v. Zinke,* 583 U.S. 244, 274 (2018) (Roberts, C.J., dissenting).

~

ESSAY NO. 54: THE PIRACIES AND FELONIES CLAUSE
ART. I, § 8, CL. 10

The Congress shall have Power . . . To define and punish Piracies and Felonies committed on the High Seas. . . .

—Eugene Kontorovich

INTRODUCTION

The Piracies and Felonies Clause grants Congress the power to punish maritime crime and implies that other enumerated powers do not grant such a power. James Madison defined piracies, a "technical term of the law of nations," as robbery on the high seas.[1] As Justice Joseph Story observed, "felonies" was a broad umbrella term with "indeterminate" meaning.[2] The Framers appear to have singled out piracy because of its unique universal jurisdictional status. It could be punished by any nation, even one without any connection to the offense. During the Constitutional Convention, there was little debate about the propriety of this power. Many Supreme Court cases from the early nineteenth century considered the clause, but during the twentieth century, this power faded into obscurity with changes in maritime commerce and the expansion of Congress's Commerce Power doctrine. Questions have emerged about Congress's ability to use the power to legislate against maritime drug trafficking with no connection to the United States.

HISTORY BEFORE 1787

"Piracies and felonies" was a well-known English legal formula for maritime crimes used in statutes and leading treatises.[3] During the reign of King Henry VIII, a statute brought piracy within the common-law procedures and treated it as a felony.[4] Piracy was one of the few international law offenses applicable to individuals and incorporated into the common law. It was also unique in its jurisdictional aspects. Under international law, nations could punish crimes only within their territory, but piracy on the high seas could be punished by any nation that apprehended the wrongdoer.[5]

The Articles of Confederation granted Congress the exclusive power to "appoint[] courts for the trial of piracies and felonies committed on the high seas."[6] A 1781 ordinance instructed special panels of state judges to hear such cases.[7] However, a report to Congress noted that "the punishment of piracies and felonies has a different operation in some of the States" and sought to increase uniformity by providing detailed procedures.[8] Under the Articles, Congress could provide for the "punishment" of such offenses but could not define the conduct that would trigger such punishment—the substance of the offense.[9] As a result, conduct on U.S. vessels could be subject to different legal consequences if prosecuted in different states.

THE CONSTITUTIONAL CONVENTION

The need to strengthen Congress's legislative powers over these crimes was taken for granted by the delegates. James Madison of Virginia observed that the current system did not produce "uniformity or stability in the law."[10] The Piracies and Felonies Clause was adopted in almost the exact form that came out of the Committee of Detail. There was little substantive debate.

The Committee draft provided that Congress could "declare the law and punishment of piracies and felonies."[11] Madison moved successfully to strike Congress's power of "punishment" of these crimes. To avoid inconsistency among state laws, Madison explained, Congress

would need only the power to "define" piracies.[12] Gouverneur Morris of Pennsylvania secured the restoration of "punishment" to the draft as a replacement for "declare the law."[13]

James Wilson of Pennsylvania thought "felonies" were "sufficiently defined by Common law."[14] Madison thought the term was "vague." The delegates were apparently concerned about limiting Congress to some predefined meaning of "felonies," a term that they understood to be general. The definition and jurisdictional status of piracies, however, seem to have been so commonly understood that they were not discussed in Philadelphia.

After some discussion, Madison and Edmund Randolph, also of Virginia, convinced the delegates to reword the draft so that Congress would have the power to "define and punish piracies and felonies." The delegates did not understand this text as confining Congress to the "preexisting meaning" of felonies, but rather allowed the creation of new ones, though not necessarily novel "piracies" subject to universal jurisdiction. Oliver Ellsworth of Connecticut proposed expanding the text to give Congress the power "to define and punish piracies and felonies committed on the high seas. . . ."[15] His proposal was approved unanimously. "Piracies" and "Felonies" were understood by the Framers to be two separate powers or "cases," but "felonies on the high seas" was a catch-all category of which piracy was also one element. This may not be a redundancy: Piracy may have been mentioned specifically to grant Congress the universal jurisdiction over piracies.[16]

EARLY PRACTICE AND JUDICIAL PRECEDENT

In the Crimes Act of 1790, Congress first exercised its "define and punish" powers. The statute criminalized "murder or robbery" by "any person or persons" on the high seas, as well as various forms of maritime embezzlement and conversion by a ship's crew.[17]

In the early nineteenth century, there was a surge of maritime violence connected with South American revolts against Spain. These insurgent republics issued letters of marque authorizing privateers to attack enemy shipping. These conflicts led to the Supreme Court's formative decisions concerning the Piracies and

Felonies Clause. (See Essay No. 57.) In *United States v. Palmer* (1818), Chief Justice John Marshall's majority opinion held that Congress could not have intended the Crimes Act to apply to foreign piracy against foreign vessels.[18]

United States v. Furlong (1820) addressed the status of "felonies" on the high seas that were non-piratical crimes.[19] The Court held that Congress could not punish offenses that involved only foreigners on foreign vessels. For example, murder on the high seas was not universally cognizable in the law of nations. Thus, Congress could not punish murder without regard for the nationality of the vessel or offender. The Court ruled that piracy and a felony like murder are "things so essentially different in their nature, that not even the omnipotence of legislative power can" treat them identically. *United States v. Holmes* (1820) limited this holding so that Congress could punish such crimes on "stateless" vessels.[20]

In response to *Palmer*, Congress promptly revised the Crime Act. The statute would now punish with death "any person or persons [who] shall, upon the high seas, commit the crime of piracy as defined by the law of nations,"[21] regardless of the nationality of the vessels. In *United States v. Smith* (1820), the defendant argued that the new statute was also an unconstitutional exercise of Congress's power because it failed to "define" piracy.[22] Justice Joseph Story's majority opinion concluded that piracy had a well-established meaning in international law that Congress could incorporate by reference.

Aside from piracy and murder on the high seas, early Congresses' most notable exercise of the felonies power was to restrict, and ultimately in 1820 ban on pain of death, American involvement in the transatlantic slave trade.

MODERN PRACTICE AND JUDICIAL PRECEDENT

In the second half of the nineteenth century, the Piracies and Felonies Clause fell into disuse as maritime piracy sharply declined. In the twentieth century, the expansion of Congress's federal commerce powers combined with changes in maritime commerce and technology made the enumerated power over piracies and felonies less relevant to lawmaking. However, it still arises in certain contexts.

First, the Maritime Drug Law Enforcement Act (MDLEA) regulates international drug trafficking.[23] This law led to a long series of cases considering the scope of the "Felonies" power. The MDLEA extends U.S. drug trafficking laws extraterritorially to foreign vessels on the high seas even when they have no connection to the United States, such that foreigners with no connection to the United States can be prosecuted for smuggling in violation of U.S. narcotics laws.[24] Some MDLEA cases have allowed the prosecution of entirely land-based crimes in foreign countries.[25] These prosecutions are in tension with the text of the Piracies and Felonies Clause, which is limited to conduct on the high seas.[26]

Second, in 2008, a sudden surge in Somali piracy resulted in federal charges being brought against numerous captured attackers. These prosecutions raised novel questions about the piracy power. For example, land-based aiding and abetting could be punished even though it did not occur on the "High Seas."[27] In another case, pirates had mistakenly attacked a U.S. naval vessel. The pirates were promptly captured, although they never actually boarded the naval vessel. The defendants argued that the Crime Act of 1820, which criminalized "piracy against the law of nations," froze the law as it stood in 1820 when mere attempts to board a vessel arguably were not acts of "piracy." (The current statute uses essentially the same language as the 1820 law while reducing the maximum penalty to life in prison.[28]) The Fourth Circuit rejected this contention. The court held that the meaning of "piracy against the law of nations" under the statute could evolve with changes in its international legal definition.[29]

Third, since World War II, there have been attempts to extend "universal jurisdiction," which once was unique to piracy, to prosecute other international crimes, such as torture or genocide.[30] A land-based Somali pirate negotiator was involved in arranging a ransom for a hijacked Danish vessel. The negotiator was later charged in federal court with conspiracy to commit piracy after having been lured to the United States by federal agents. The D.C. Circuit ruled that *conspiracy* to commit piracy is not criminalized under international law and therefore cannot be punished universally.[31] This holding was consistent with the Piracies and Felonies Clause, which does not authorize universal jurisdiction over offenses that are not piratical. In *Hamdan v. Rumsfeld* (2006), the plurality found that conspiracy to commit war crimes was not an international law offense and thus could not be punished as an exercise of Congress's Law of Nations Power.[32] Yet the D.C. Circuit Court concluded that land-based *aiding and abetting* of piracy did fall within universal jurisdiction, not because it was a separate offense but because it was a mode of commission.[33]

OPEN QUESTIONS

- Can Congress apply universal jurisdiction under the MDLEA? Several judges have suggested that it cannot do so.[34]
- Is U.S. jurisdiction over a vessel under the MDLEA a question of subject-matter jurisdiction? Several federal courts of appeals have held that it is,[35] but the First Circuit Court of Appeals held that it was not, and the Supreme Court denied review on this issue.[36]

Cite as: Eugene Kontorovich, *The Piracies and Felonies Clause, in* THE HERITAGE GUIDE TO THE CONSTITUTION 188 (Josh Blackman & John G. Malcolm eds., 3d ed. 2025).

Notes

1. 3 Farrand's 331–32.   **2.** 3 Story's Commentaries § 1157.   **3.** 4 Blackstone § 71.   **4.** Sir Edward Coke, The Third Part of the Institutes of the Laws of England: Concerning High Treason; and Other Pleas of the Crown, and Criminal Causes 111 (1680).   **5.** 4 Blackstone § 71.   **6.** Articles of Confederation, art. IX, § 1.   **7.** 19 J. Cont. Cong. 274 (Mar. 11, 1781).   **8.** 29 J. Cont. Cong. 682 (Sept. 6, 1785), 797–805 (Oct. 3, 1785).   **9.** *Id.* at 798; 3 Story's Commentaries §§ 1153–55.   **10.** 2 Farrand's 316.   **11.** *Id.* at 315.   **12.** *Id.* at 316.   **13.** *Id.* at 315.   **14.** *Id.* at 316.   **15.** *Id.*   **16.** Eugene Kontorovich, *The "Define and Punish Clause" and the Limits of Universal Jurisdiction*, 103 Nw. U. L. Rev. 149, 162 (2008).   **17.** An Act for the Punishment of Certain Crimes Against the United States, ch. 9, §§ 8, 12, 1 Stat. 112 (1790).   **18.** 16 U.S. (3 Wheat.) 610, 611 (1818).   **19.** 18 U.S. (5 Wheat.) 184, 228 (1820).   **20.** 18 U.S. (5 Wheat.) 412, 414–15 (1820).   **21.** An Act to Protect the Commerce of the United States, and Punish the Crime of Piracy, ch. 77, § 5, 3 Stat. 510 (1819).   **22.** 18 US. 153, 159–63 (1820).   **23.** 46 U.S.C. ch. 705.   **24.** *United States v. Vargas*, 781 F. App'x 815, 819 (11th Cir. 2019); *United States v. Nueci-Pena*, 711 F.3d 191, 198 (1st Cir. 2013).   **25.** *United States v. Ballestas*, 795 F.3d 138, 147 (D.C. Cir. 2015).   **26.** *United States v. Bellaizac-Hurtado*, 700 F.3d 1245, 1248 (11th Cir. 2012); *United States v. Carvajal*, 924 F. Supp. 2d 219, 260 (D.D.C. 2013), *aff'd sub nom. United States v. Miranda*, 780 F.3d 1185 (D.C. Cir. 2015); *United States v. Barbosa-Rodriguez*, 680 F. Supp. 3d 121, 127–28 (D.P.R. June 28, 2023).   **27.** *United States v. Shibin*, 722 F.3d 233, 243 (4th Cir. 2013).   **28.** 18 U.S.C. § 1651.   **29.** *United States v. Dire*, 680 F.3d 446, 467 (4th Cir. 2012).   **30.** Eugene Kontorovich, *The Piracy Analogy: Modern Universal Jurisdiction's Hollow Foundation*, 45 Harv. Int'l L.J. 183 (2004).   **31.** *United States v. Ali*, 718 F.3d 929, 942 (D.C. Cir. 2013).   **32.** 548 U.S. 557, 563, 601 (2006).   **33.** *Ali*, 718 F.3d at 947.   **34.** *United States v. Angulo-Hernandez*, 576 F.3d 59, 60 (1st Cir. 2009) (Tourrella, J., dissenting); *United States v. Aybar-Ulloa*, 987 F.3d 1, 15 (1st Cir.) (en banc) (Barron, J., concurring).   **35.** *Miranda*, 780 F.3d at 1192.   **36.** *United States v. Davila-Reyes*, 84 F.4th 400 (1st Cir. 2023) (en banc), *cert. denied*, 144 S.Ct. 2634 (2024).

ESSAY NO. 55: THE OFFENSES AGAINST THE LAW OF NATIONS CLAUSE
ART. I, § 8, CL. 10

The Congress shall have Power . . . To define and punish Piracies and Felonies committed on the high Seas, and Offences against the Law of Nations. . . .
                                    —Eugene Kontorovich

INTRODUCTION

The Constitution expressly authorizes Congress to create only a narrow set of federal crimes. These include piracy, felonies committed on the high seas, and the domestic offenses of treason and counterfeiting. Another category of federal crimes that Congress can "define and punish" is "Offences against the Law of Nations." The term "law of nations" is synonymous with what is today called "customary international law." These rules are created not by treaty, but by the general consent and practice of states through their mutual dealings.[1]

HISTORY BEFORE 1787

Sir William Blackstone wrote that the law of nations recognized only a very limited number of "offences" that could be committed by private actors as opposed to states.[2] These offenses consisted of piracy and assaults on ambassadors and certain other foreigners bearing particular protection. In England, these crimes would be punished as common-law offenses in criminal courts and regulated by statute. The Founding generation was very familiar with the views of Blackstone, Vattel, and others on the law of nations.[3]

Following independence, there were assaults on foreign diplomats in the United States. In 1784, a Frenchman assaulted a French diplomat in public in Philadelphia. This incident could have complicated Franco–American relations, and the king of France took a personal interest in it. However, the Articles of Confederation Congress lacked power to respond to violations of treaties or the law of nations by individuals.[4]

THE CONSTITUTIONAL CONVENTION

At the Constitutional Convention, Edmund Randolph of Virginia cited the inability to punish "infractions of treaties or of the law of nations" as one of the Articles of Confederation's many deficiencies.[5] James Madison of Virginia echoed this theme, warning that the failure of states to punish such offenses could "involve [America] in the calamities of foreign wars."[6] No delegates contested the propriety of such a federal power. The motivation for giving Congress the power to punish such offenses focused entirely on acts (such as "infractions of treaties and conventions to which the United States are a party") for which the new country would be held accountable by other nations.[7] This power was not intended to advance a more general or cosmopolitan interest in upholding international norms.

On August 17, the delegates approved a provision granting Congress the power "to punish the counterfeiting of the securities and current coin of the United States, and offences against the law of nations."[8] While this draft gave Congress the power to "punish" such offenses, it did not empower Congress to "define" them. The Committee of Style revised the clause to grant Congress the power "[t]o define and punish piracies and felonies committed on the high seas, and punish offences against the law of nations."[9]

The Convention revisited this provision on September 14. Gouverneur Morris of Pennsylvania moved to strike the word "punish."[10] With this revision, Morris explained, offenses against the law of nations would be "*definable* as well as punishable."[11] Morris added that Congress needed the power to "define" offenses because the law of nations is "often too vague and deficient to be a rule."[12] At the time of the Framing, the word "define" would be used to mean expounding or specifying the content of such "offenses" rather than inventing new ones.[13] James Wilson of Pennsylvania worried that no one country could "define" international law. "To pretend to *define* the law of nations which depended on the authority of all the Civilized Nations of the World," Wilson said, "would have the look of arrogance, that would make us look ridiculous."[14] The concern was odd because the same text gave Congress the power to "define" piracy, which was already precisely specified in international law. (See Essay No. 54.) Morris's position prevailed.

THE RATIFICATION DEBATES

In Federalist No. 42, James Madison observed that the Articles of Confederation "contain[ed] no provision for the case of offences against the law of nations." As a result, any "indiscreet member [could] embroil the Confederacy with foreign nations." Madison explained that "[t]he power to define and punish . . . offences against the law of nations, belongs with equal propriety to the general government; and is a still greater improvement on the articles of Confederation." Anti-Federalists did not appear to take issue with the "Offences" power.

EARLY PRACTICE

After the Constitution was ratified, Congress promptly passed laws punishing certain international crimes. Among these crimes were violations of the protections that international law gave to diplomats. These were precisely the concerns that arose under the Articles of Confederation.[15] The Neutrality Act of 1794 also, arguably though less obviously, prohibited conduct that would violate international law.[16]

The U.S. Supreme Court did not consider questions about the scope of the Offenses Clause until nearly a century after ratification in *United States v. Arjona* (1887), which involved a law that prohibited counterfeiting foreign currency.[17] Clear constitutional tests of the "Offences" power have been rare. Many borderline applications of the power, like that in *Arjona,* can be justified separately by reference to some combinations of the Treaty Clause, the Foreign Commerce Clause, or various war powers.

DELEGATION OF THE POWER TO DEFINE OFFENSES

Can Congress delegate its power to define offenses against the law of nations to the other branches? The Offenses Clause did not grant Congress an exclusive power to interpret international law in every possible context. Rather, Congress's power of "defining" is limited to statutes penalizing individuals' conduct. James Madison suggested this limitation in his report on the Virginia Resolution.[18] Both courts and the Executive, for example, must interpret terms in the Constitution like "war" or "ambassadors" that are borrowed from international law.

In *The Paquete Habana* (1900), the Supreme Court commented that "international law is part of our law, and must be ascertained and administered by the courts of justice of appropriate jurisdiction."[19] But that decision concerned prize jurisdiction, where Congress can be understood as delegating the discernment of international law to the Court.[20] Justice Joseph Story, in *United States v. Smith* (1820), wrote that offenses against the law of nations could not be "completely ascertained and defined in any public code recognized by the common consent of nations."[21]

Recall that at the Convention, the premise for giving Congress the power to define was the underlying indeterminacy or vagueness of the law of nations. This history makes it hard to argue that the law of nations is somehow

incorporated into U.S. law as a form of common law, or even as a rule of statutory construction.[22]

Congress has also delegated the work of "defining" offenses against the law of nations in statutes authorizing military commissions to try war crimes. Such a law was enacted during World War II. In 1942, German saboteurs infiltrated Long Island, New York. They were convicted of "unlawful belligerence." *Ex parte Quirin* (1942) upheld their convictions.[23] The Supreme Court spent eight pages considering "whether any of the acts charged is an offense against the laws of war," a component of the law of nations, and concluded that "unlawful belligerence" was such an offense.

A similar law was enacted during the twenty-first-century global war on terrorism. In 2004, a military commission charged Salim Hamdan with "conspiracy" to commit acts of terrorism. *Hamdan v. Rumsfeld* (2006) held that the international precedents for such a crime must be "plain and unambiguous."[24] A plurality of the Court concluded that the conspiracy charge failed that test.[25]

Quirin and *Hamdan* did not involve direct exercises of the "Define" power. Rather, Congress delegated the definition of offenses against the law of war to the military commissions themselves. It may be that offenses defined through delegation must match external international law more precisely than is the case when Congress defines offenses directly.

LIMITS ON CONGRESS'S POWER TO DEFINE OFFENSES

An unresolved question about the clause is whether the content of "offenses against the law of nations" serves as an objective limit on Congress's power or whether Congress can designate any conduct it chooses as an offense. The courts have suggested that Congress cannot simply invoke the power without a real connection to international law, but they have disagreed as to the scope of Congress's discretion.

Arjona took a broad view of Congress's powers. The Court declared that Congress need not formally invoke "the law of nations" to criminalize counterfeiting foreign securities as long as it was punishing an action that was in fact contrary to customary international law.[26] Yet instead of undertaking any substantive inquiry to see whether there was such a norm, the Court found it sufficient that the conduct could antagonize other countries.

Modern courts have required a greater connection between crimes defined under the clause and actual international law as practiced by the nations of the world. This more searching inquiry is motivated in part by federalism concerns. As a general matter, the Constitution sharply limits federal criminal powers. A federal court of appeals has observed that if Congress could regulate conduct simply by claiming it violates international law, "its power would be limitless and contrary to our constitutional structure."[27]

In response to *Hamdan*, Congress expressly exercised its power in the Military Commissions Act (2006) to define "conspiracy" and "material support" for terrorism as offenses.[28] A sharply divided D.C. Circuit took a narrow view of Congress's power: "Congress cannot, pursuant to the Define and Punish Clause, declare an offense to be an international war crime when the international law of war concededly does not."[29] Other courts have not required that the specific offense exist in international law.[30] One court has found it sufficient that "the acts in question are recognized by at least some members of the international community as being offenses against the law of nations."[31]

The Maritime Drug Law Enforcement Act (MDLEA) allows the extraterritorial application of U.S. drug laws to foreign drug trafficking.[32] This law is often used to prosecute foreign defendants with no demonstrable nexus with the United States. The Eleventh Circuit concluded that "the word 'define' would not have been understood [by the Framers] to

grant Congress the power to create or declare offenses against the law of nations, but instead to codify and explain offenses that had already been understood as offenses against the law of nations."[33] The court rejected broad arguments that mere universal condemnation suffices to make drug trafficking a violation of the law of nations and thus found the statute unconstitutional as applied.[34]

Sosa v. Alvarez-Machain (2004) confronted the limits of the Supreme Court's power to define offenses.[35] The case dealt with the meaning of the Alien Tort Statute (ATS), enacted initially as part of the Judiciary Act of 1789. The law provided that "[t]he district courts shall have original jurisdiction of any civil action by an alien for a tort only, committed in violation of the law of nations, or a treaty of the United States."[36] Lower courts had concluded that this statute authorized the judiciary to fashion civil causes of action for violations of international law. The Supreme Court disagreed, finding that Congress intended to allow for jurisdiction only over the few specific offenses against the laws of nations that existed at the time of the Founding, and concluded that the ATS is not a "mandate to seek out and define new and debatable violations of the law of nations."[37]

The Supreme Court has since resisted efforts to apply the Alien Tort Statute extraterritorially to punish conduct that occurs outside the United States. Such punishments could invite "reprisals" against the United States.[38] The Court has also declined to recognize private causes of action for a "narrow class of international norms" with particularly "definite content" comparable to those that commanded the attention of the Framers.[39]

OPEN QUESTIONS

- Can Congress "define and punish only those violations of customary international law that were established at the Founding"?[40] Or does "the power granted under the Clause expand[] and contract[] with changes in customary international law"?[41]
- To what extent, if any, is Congress limited with respect to the offenses it defines by the law of nations, and how could this limitation be enforced?
- Could Congress justify domestic police powers on the basis of enforcing international human rights norms that govern the relations between a country and its citizens rather than the relations between states?[42] This power would have implications even more expansive than the use of the Treaty Power questioned in *Bond v. United States* (2014).[43]

Cite as: Eugene Kontorovich, *The Offenses Against the Law of Nations Clause, in* THE HERITAGE GUIDE TO THE CONSTITUTION 191 (Josh Blackman & John G. Malcolm eds., 3d ed. 2025).

Notes

1. Sarah Cleveland & William Dodge, *Defining and Punishing Offenses Under Treaties*, 124 Yale L. J. 2202 (2015).   **2.** 4 Blackstone 68.   **3.** E. de Vattel, The Law of Nations 165 (1758 ed., C. Fenwick transl. 1916).   **4.** 21 J. Cont. Cong. 1136 (Nov. 16, 1781).   **5.** 1 Farrand's 19.   **6.** *Id.* at 316.   **7.** 21 J. Cont. Cong. 1137 (Nov. 23, 1781).   **8.** 2 Farrand's 312.   **9.** *Id.* at 595.   **10.** *Id.* at 614.   **11.** *Id.*   **12.** *Id.* at 615.   **13.** Eugene Kontorovich, *Discretion, Delegation, and Defining in the Constitution's Law of Nations Clause*, 106 Nw. U.L. Rev. 1675, 1705–06 (2015).   **14.** Farrand's 615 (emphasis in original).   **15.** An Act for the Punishment of Certain Crimes Against the United States, ch. 9, §§ 26, 28, 1 Stat. 112 (1790).   **16.** 1 Stat. 381.   **17.** 120 U.S. 479 (1887).   **18.** 4 Elliot's 556–57.   **19.** 175 U.S. 677, 700 (1900).   **20.** Curtis A. Bradley & Jack L. Goldsmith, *Customary International Law as Federal Common Law: A Critique of the Modern Position*, 110 Harv. L. Rev. 815 (1997).   **21.** 18 U.S. 153, 160 (1820).   **22.** Curtis A. Bradley, *The* Charming Betsy *Canon and Separation of Powers: Rethinking the Interpretive Role of International Law*, 86 Geo. L.J. 479 (1998).   **23.** 317 U.S. 1 (1942).   **24.** 548 U.S. 557 (2006).   **25.** *Id.* at 602–10.   **26.** 120 U.S. 479 (1887).   **27.** *United States v. Bellaizac-Hurtado*, 700 F.3d 1245, 1250 (11th Cir. 2012).   **28.** 120 Stat. 2600.   **29.** *Al Bahlul v. United States*, 792 F.3d 1, 15 (D.C. Cir. 2015).   **30.** *United States v. Ahmed*, 94 F. Supp. 3d 394, 415 (E.D.N.Y. 2015).   **31.** *United States v. Laden*, 92 F. Supp. 2d 189, 220 (S.D.N.Y. 2000) (emphasis added).   **32.** 46 USC § 70502(c)(1) & 70503.   **33.** *Bellaizac-Hurtado*, 700 F.3d at 1250.   **34.** *Id.* at 1257.   **35.** 542 U.S. 692 (2004).   **36.** 1 Stat. 73, 77.   **37.** *Id.* at 728.   **38.** *Jesner v. Arab Bank, PLC*, 584 U.S. 241, 292 (2018) (Gorsuch, concurring).   **39.** *Nestle USA, Inc. v. Doe*, 593 U.S. 628, 637–38 (2021); *id.* at 644–45 (Gorsuch, concurring).   **40.** *Bellaizac-Hurtado*, 700 F.3d at 1253.   **41.** *Id.*; J. Andrew Kent, *Congress's Under-Appreciated Power to Define and Punish Offenses Against the Law of Nations*, 85 Tex. L. Rev. 843, 847 (2007).   **42.** Anthony J. Bellia, Jr., & Bradford R. Clark, *The Federal Common Law of Nations*, 109 Colum. L. Rev. 1 (2009); Ernest A. Young, *Historical Practice and the Contemporary Debate Over Customary International Law*, 109 Colum. L. Rev. Sidebar 31, 37–38 (2009).   **43.** 572 U.S. 844, 854 (2014).

ESSAY NO. 56: THE DECLARE WAR CLAUSE
ART. 1, § 8, CL. 11

The Congress shall have Power . . . To declare War. . . .

—John C. Yoo

INTRODUCTION

Few constitutional issues have been debated so consistently and heatedly by legal scholars and politicians as the distribution of war powers between Congress and the President. As a matter of history and policy, it is generally accepted that the executive takes the lead in the actual conduct of war. A single, energetic actor is better able to prosecute war successfully than a committee is: The enemy will not wait for deliberation and consensus. At the same time, the Founders plainly intended to establish congressional checks on the executive's war power. Between these guideposts is a question of considerable importance: Does the Constitution require the President to obtain specific authorization from Congress before initiating hostilities?

HISTORY BEFORE 1787

Well before American independence, jurists had discussed the significance of declaring war. In 1625, Grotius explained that declarations of war gave notice of the legal grounds for the war and the opportunity for enemy nations to make amends.[1] These declarations also served notice on the enemy's allies that they would be regarded as cobelligerents and their shipping would be subject to capture.[2] Grotius added that declarations of war triggered such legal actions as the internment or expulsion of enemy aliens, breaking of diplomatic relations, and confiscation of the enemy's property.[3] In 1758, Vattel wrote that "when one nation takes up arms against another, she from that moment declares herself an enemy to all the individuals of the latter."[4] Vattel explained that when a country declares war, its navy and privateers could not be treated as pirates by the enemy, but its citizens were subject to prosecution if they dealt with the enemy.[5]

Sir William Blackstone agreed with these writers of international law. He described two purposes for a declaration of war in Britain: It notified other nations that the state approved the hostilities, and it legally bound the citizens to the king's decision to wage war.[6] Blackstone also contemplated an "incomplete state of hostilities"—hostilities before or without a formal declaration of war.[7]

During this time, the British monarch, not Parliament, had the power to declare war.[8] Many contemporary thinkers understood the executive power to arise from the need for a part of government to act quickly, vigorously, and decisively in response to unforeseen dangers and events, the most serious being war. John Locke described the executive as a "power always in being," bearing the responsibility to "see to the execution of the laws that are made."[9] Montesquieu explained that the executive power "makes peace or war, sends or receives embassies, establishes the public security, and provides against invasions."[10] Blackstone thought that "[i]t would indeed be extremely improper, that any number of subjects should have the power of binding the supreme magistrate, and putting him against his will in a state of war."[11] A single executive should have this power.

In April 1775, hostilities broke out between British forces and the Americans at Lexington and Concord, but war was not declared immediately.[12] It was not until nearly a year later that the Continental Congress issued the Declaration of Independence, a formal declaration of war against Great Britain that asserted the "full Power to levy War, [and] conclude Peace."[13]

The Articles of Confederation gave Congress "the sole and exclusive right and power of determining on peace and war."[14] The Articles required the approval of nine states before the nation could "engage in a war."[15] They further provided that no state "shall . . . grant commissions to any ships or vessels of war, nor letters of marque or reprisal, except [if] it be after a declaration of war by the united states in congress assembled."[16] This text suggests that the power

to declare war was understood to be a subset of the power to make war.[17]

THE CONSTITUTIONAL CONVENTION

An early Committee of Detail draft in the handwriting of Edmund Randolph of Virginia granted Congress the power "[t]o make war" alongside the power to "raise armies."[18] The Committee of Detail's report was delivered to the Convention on August 6.[19] Congress would have the power "[t]o make war; [t]o raise armies; [and] to build and equip fleets."[20] The delegates debated this provision on August 17.

James Madison of Virginia and Elbridge Gerry of Massachusetts moved to replace "make war" with "declare war" and "leav[e] to the Executive the power to repel sudden attacks."[21] Roger Sherman of Connecticut favored "make" over "declare," as the "latter narrow[ed] the power too much." He thought the Executive should "be able to repel and not to commence war."[22] Gerry responded that he "never expected to hear in a republic a motion to empower the Executive alone to declare war."[23] George Mason of Virginia "preferred 'declare' to 'make'" as a means to "clog[] rather than facilitate war."[24] Madison's and Gerry's motion passed by a vote of 7 to 2 with one state absent.

On September 5, the Committee of Eleven proposed that the "declare war" clause should be amended to give Congress the power to "grant letters of marque and reprisal."[25] The proposal passed without debate. The Declare War Clause was then referred to the Committee of Style.[26] The Committee's report lumped together three separate powers: "[t]o declare war, grant letters of marque and reprisal, and make rules concerning captures on land and water."[27] Article I, Section 8, Clause 11 received no further edits.

Certain inferences can be drawn from the text of the Declare War Clause. First, Article I, Section 8, Clause 11 enumerates three specific powers: "[t]o declare War, grant Letters of Marque and Reprisal, and make Rules concerning Captures on Land and Water." If the power to "declare War" included the broad authority to authorize and define the boundaries of any military conflict, then there would be no reason to enumerate the lesser powers. The Marque and Reprisal Clause and the Capture Clause, as well as other provisions, would be redundant, inconsistent, or superfluous. (See Essay Nos. 57 and 58.) But if the Declare War Clause only gives Congress the power to define the legal state of relations with hostile countries, this arrangement makes perfect sense.[28] These other powers are useful in defining the legal rules of hostilities that fall short of being a major declared war.

Second, the Constitution forbids states from "engag[ing] in" war without the consent of Congress.[29] (See Essay No. 86.) This provision would suggest a difference between *starting* a war and *declaring* a war. The Constitution further provides that a state may "engage in War" if it is "actually invaded, or in such imminent Danger as will not admit of delay."[30] This text suggests that a state can start new hostilities if attacked even without seeking congressional approval. In other words, a state's power to "engage in war" includes the power to defend itself. It is generally agreed that the President may authorize hostilities without congressional action if the war is defensive. Yet Article I, Section 8 does not give Congress the power to "engage in war." It provides the power to "declare war," and with this narrow phrasing, there was no need to provide that the President has the power to use self-defense to repel an invasion.

Third, the Constitution uses different language to refer to powers of Congress and the powers of the President. Article I, Section 8 appears to be an explicit enumeration of Congress's limited powers, while Article II, Section 2 vests in the President a broad grant of authority as "Commander in Chief" of the Army, Navy, and Militia. As between Congress and the President, the grant of authority in Article II may imply that the Executive retains the larger portion of the war power.[31]

THE RATIFICATION DEBATES

During the ratification process, there were extensive debates about the relationship between Congress and the President with respect to war powers. In Federalist No. 70, Alexander Hamilton stressed that "[g]ood government" requires "energy in the executive" and that "[i]n the conduct of war, in which the energy of the Executive is the bulwark of the national security, every thing would be to be apprehended from its plurality." But there were limits to that energy.

In Federalist No. 69, Hamilton distinguished between the British king's powers and the President's executive powers. In Britain, the king had the power to declare war, and Parliament had the power to raise armies; Article I granted Congress *both* the power to declare war *and* the power to raise armies. Hamilton also recognized that there were undeclared wars in Britain. In Federalist No. 25, he observed that "the ceremony of a formal denunciation of war has of late fallen into disuse."

The Anti-Federalists criticized the Declare War Clause for "concentrating power in Congress."[32] For example, an Anti-Federalist from Pennsylvania observed that in England, "the king has only the power of declaring war, and the house of parliament, that of raising money for the support of it."[33] The Federal Republican wrote "that it seems to be wrong to give Congress this combined power independent of a check from a majority of the state legislatures."[34]

Patrick Henry made a similar point in the Virginia ratifying convention. Henry favored the British system in which the king's power to declare war was separated from Parliament's power to raise armies. He warned that "The Congress can both declare war, and carry it on; and levy your money, as long as you have a shilling to pay."[35] Yet Henry also warned that the President would use his army domestically to "enslav[e] America."[36] Scholars have debated how to reconcile these Anti-Federalist arguments.[37]

Madison responded that "the sword and purse are not to be given to the same member." Rather, in America, the President, like the king, has the sword, and Congress, like Parliament, has the purse.[38] Here, Madison did not seem to think the power of the sword was equivalent to the power to declare war. For example, he later explained in a letter to Thomas Jefferson that "the Executive is the branch of power most interested in war, and most prone to it." Madison observed that the Constitution "has accordingly with studied care, vested the question of war in the Legisl[ature]."[39]

PRACTICE BEFORE 1973

In the early Republic, Congress affirmatively authorized numerous conflicts with formal declarations of war and other instruments. There was broad consensus that such authorizations were constitutionally required in the case of offensive war. In the Quasi-War of 1798 with France, Congress authorized a naval conflict and also carefully regulated how America's ships would carry out that conflict.[40] In 1801, the first real war began against Tripoli. Congress authorized this conflict by statute, but there was no formal declaration.[41] President Thomas Jefferson arguably directed some offensive action against Tripoli prior to congressional authorization.

Hamilton defended these actions only on the ground that Tripoli had itself begun the war: "[W]hen a foreign nation declares or openly and avowedly makes war upon the United States, they are then by the very fact already at war, and any declaration on the part of Congress is nugatory; it is at least unnecessary."[42] Several years earlier, Hamilton had acknowledged Congress's role in a *Pacificus* essay: "It is the province and duty of the executive to preserve to the nation the blessings of peace," but "[t]he Legislature alone can interrupt them by placing the nation in a state of war."[43]

Since ratification of the Constitution, only five wars have been formally declared by Congress.[44] The War of 1812 was formally declared before the start of hostilities.[45] However, in four other conflicts, Congress merely declared the prior existence of a state of war: the Mexican-American War of 1846, the Spanish-American War of 1898, World War I, and World War II.[46] Each of these declarations was accompanied by an express authorization for the use of force. During these conflicts, limited budgets and a small peacetime military led Presidents to defer to Congress.[47] If the Presidents wanted to wage a war, they had to ask Congress to build them the armed forces to fight it.[48] Congress has not issued a formal declaration of war since 1942.

After World War II, the creation of a large standing military dramatically altered the balance of war powers between the two branches.[49] Modern Presidents have been more aggressive in asserting unilateral authority to use force abroad without a declaration of war or other congressional authorization. The United States intervention in Korea in 1950 received congressional support but no formal approval.[50] President

Harry S. Truman claimed independent authority to commit troops without congressional authorization because the United Nations Security Council had authorized U.N. members to use force in resisting the North Korean invasion.[51]

Congress also did not declare war in Vietnam.[52] Presidents Lyndon B. Johnson and Richard M. Nixon undertook military operations in Vietnam armed only with the vaguely worded congressional approval in the Gulf of Tonkin Resolution.[53] Congress ended U.S. involvement in Vietnam by passing funding restrictions in 1973 rather than merely ending the war by fiat.[54]

PRACTICE AFTER 1973

In 1973, Congress enacted the War Powers Resolution over President Nixon's veto.[55] The statute purports to limit the President's ability to engage U.S. forces in hostilities for more than sixty days without a declaration of war or specific congressional authorization. The law also requires the President to consult with Congress about military deployments. No President has ever conceded its constitutionality, although many have acted "consistent with" its sixty-day limit on foreign interventions.[56] Presidents have unilaterally authorized military action in Iran, Lebanon, Grenada, Libya, Somalia, Bosnia, Haiti, Kosovo, Afghanistan, and Iraq.[57]

President Jimmy Carter did not consult with Congress before attempting to rescue Iranian hostages.[58] President Ronald Reagan unilaterally dispatched American military forces to Lebanon, Grenada, Libya, and the Persian Gulf.[59] Before Operation Desert Storm, President George H.W. Bush sent reports to Congress in which he failed to acknowledge that he had to consult with Congress or had to remove the troops in sixty days.[60] Bush nevertheless sought an authorization from Congress that he barely received.[61] President William Jefferson Clinton followed these precedents in Somalia, Haiti, Bosnia, the Middle East, and Kosovo.[62]

On September 18, 2001, Congress authorized the use of military force against those who were responsible for the 9/11 terrorist attacks. President George W. Bush used this authority to engage in hostilities against Al-Qaeda in Afghanistan. In 2002, Congress authorized the use of military force against Iraq. President Bush used this authority to topple Saddam Hussein's government. In 2011, President Barack Obama unilaterally ordered an intervention in the Libyan civil war. Obama contended that these hostilities, which did not include ground troops, were too small to constitute a "war" under the Constitution.[63]

During President Donald Trump's first term, he continued the war against the Islamic State of Iraq and Syria (ISIS) and loosened the rules of engagement to allow U.S. forces to fight more aggressively.[64] Trump also invoked executive constitutional authority for multiple strikes against Syria.[65] One of those strikes killed Iranian General Qassem Soleimani.[66] In 2018, the Office of Legal Counsel (OLC) opined that the Constitution gives the President "the authority to direct U.S. military forces in engagements necessary to advance American national interests abroad."[67] OLC recognized that Presidents have authorized many hostilities abroad, but only Congress may commit the United States to a war in the constitutional sense. OLC concluded that attacking Syria did not rise to the level of a war because of the "anticipated nature, scope, and duration" of the conflict.[68] To be a war, a conflict must be "characterized by 'prolonged and substantial military engagements.'"[69] OLC grounded this position in past executive branch opinions dating from the Nixon Administration through the Obama Administration as well as authorities stretching back to the Framing. The text of the Constitution, however, does not suggest a definition of war based on the magnitude of the conflict or the potential for harm to U.S. forces. Under this standard, would a nuclear attack qualify as a war because it does not risk any U.S. troops and does not involve a "prolonged" engagement?

President Joseph R. Biden, relying on this authority, directed targeted airstrikes in Syria without seeking permission from Congress.[70] In 2022, following Russia's invasion of Ukraine, Biden deployed thousands of troops to Poland, Germany, and other nations. Biden cited the United States's NATO obligations, but pledged that the U.S. would not take part in the conflict directly.[71]

JUDICIAL PRECEDENT

The U.S. Supreme Court has never intervened to stop a war regardless of whether Congress had authorized it. *The Prize Cases* (1863) stated in dicta that the President "has no power to initiate or declare a war."[72] This decision upheld President Abraham Lincoln's military actions against the Confederacy that occurred before congressional authorization. The Court reasoned that "the President is not only authorized but bound to resist force by force . . . without waiting for any special legislative authority."[73]

Some federal courts have held or implied that at least some level of congressional authorization is constitutionally required before the President may conduct military hostilities. *Orlando v. Laird* (1971), for example, ruled that "the test is whether there is any action by Congress sufficient to authorize or ratify the military activity in question."[74] Other courts have found that the issue was not subject to review by the courts.[75]

Members of Congress and private citizens have periodically filed suit to enforce the War Powers Resolution, but the lower courts have generally avoided ruling on the merits of these cases. Instead, these cases were dismissed on procedural grounds. In *Campbell v. Clinton* (2000), the D.C. Circuit unanimously dismissed a challenge to President Clinton's airstrike campaign in the former Yugoslavia because members of Congress did not suffer a legally cognizable injury.[76] In *O'Connor v. United States* (2003), the Tenth Circuit dismissed a citizen's challenge to the war in Iraq.[77] The court reasoned that this case posed a political question and that "there are no judicially discoverable standards that would permit a court to determine whether the intentions of the President in prosecuting a war are proper."[78]

SCHOLARLY DEBATES

In modern scholarly debates, there are two general views about the Declare War Clause. Under the *Congressional View*, the clause requires congressional authorization of hostilities, which may be done by formal declaration or otherwise.[79] In other words, only Congress can decide whether and when the United States will initiate hostilities against a foreign power. Since Congress has the power to declare war, it has the sole power to initiate hostilities. War must occur within a legalistic, step-by-step process beginning with a declaration. This interpretation gained popularity during the Vietnam War and has been advanced by originalist presidential and foreign relations scholars as well as by non-originalists.[80]

Other scholars, including your author, favor the *Presidential View*.[81] Under this approach, the Declare War Clause gives Congress the power to define the legal state of relations with another country under international law. A declaration of war, originally understood, triggered certain rights, privileges, and protections under the laws of war but was not a prerequisite for engaging in hostilities. This view relies on Article II, which vests "the executive Power" in the President and designates him as "Commander in Chief of the Army and Navy of the United States."[82] (See Essay Nos. 87, 102, and 103.) However, Congress can check the President's powers through appropriations. The President is commander in chief, but he has nothing to command except that which Congress provides. (See Essay Nos. 59 and 60.) When Congress maintains a large standing Army and Navy, the President can engage in hostilities and Congress can use its power of the purse, oversight, impeachment, and the political process if it opposes him.

Cite as: John C. Yoo, *The Declare War Clause*, in THE HERITAGE GUIDE TO THE CONSTITUTION 195 (Josh Blackman & John G. Malcolm eds., 3d ed. 2025).

Notes

1. 3 Grotius, The Rights of War and Peace ch. III, pt. VII (A.C. Campbell trans., 1901). **2.** *Id.* at pt. IX. **3.** *Id.* at ch. IV, pt. III. **4.** E. de Vattel, The Law of Nations 399 (1797). **5.** 2 E. Vattel, The Law of Nations 23 (trans. 1759). **6.** 1 Blackstone 258. **7.** *Id.* **8.** 5 Cobbett's Parliamentary History of England 234–25 (1809). **9.** John Locke, The Second Treatise of Government §§ 143–45 (J.W. Gough ed., 3d ed. 1966) (1689). **10.** Montesquieu, The Spirit of Laws bk. XI, ch. 6, ¶ 2 (David W. Carrithers ed., 1977) (1748). **11.** 1 Blackstone 257. **12.** Bernard Bailyn, The Great Republic: A History of the American People (1977). **13.** Declaration of Independence ¶ 32. **14.** Articles of Confederation, art. IX, § 1. **15.** *Id.*, art. IX, § 6. **16.** *Id.*, art. VI, § 5. **17.** Robert J. Delahunty & John Yoo, *Making War*, 93 Cornell L. Rev. 123, 134 (2007). **18.** 2 Farrand's 137, 143. **19.** *Id.* at 177. **20.** *Id.* at 182. **21.** *Id.* at 318. **22.** Id. at 318. **23.** *Id.* **24.** *Id.* at 319. **25.** *Id.* at 505, 508. **26.** *Id.* at 565, 570. **27.** *Id.* at 590, 595. **28.** Delahunty & Yoo, *supra* at 127. **29.** Art. I, Sec. 10, Cl. 3. **30.** *Id.* **31.** Delahunty & Yoo, *supra* at 129. **32.** Cameron O. Kistler, *The Anti-Federalists and Presidential War Powers*, 121 Yale L.J. 459, 461 (2011). **33.** Storing 3.6.20. **34.** *Id.* **35.** 3 Elliot's 172. **36.** *Id.* at 60. **37.** Delahunty & Yoo, *supra* at 137–38; Michael D. Ramsey, *Text and History in the War Powers Debate: A Reply to Professor Yoo*, 69 U. Chi. L. Rev. 1685, 1712 n.95 (2002). **38.** 3 Elliot's 393. **39.** Letter from James Madison to Thomas Jefferson (Apr. 2, 1798), https://perma.cc/6AII7 -T6GV. **40.** John C. Yoo, *The Continuation of Politics by Other Means: The Original Understanding of War Powers*, 84 Cal. L. Rev. 167, 177 (1996). **41.** Saikrishna Bangalore Prakash, *The Separation and Overlap of War and Military Powers*, 87 Tex. L. Rev. 299, 343 (2008). **42.** Alexander Hamilton, The Examination [of Jefferson's Message to Congress] No. I (Dec. 7, 1801), https://perma.cc/A6LF -XJ7U. **43.** Alexander Hamilton, Pacificus No. I (Jun. 29, 1793), https://perma.cc/S6LT-YFN2. **44.** Yoo, *The Continuation of Politics by Other Means, supra* at 177. **45.** Barbara Salazar Torreon & Sofia Plagakis, Cong. Rsrch. Serv., R42738, Instances of Use of United States Armed Forces Abroad, 1798–2020, at 2 (2023), https://perma.cc /EC2U-C4QQ. **46.** *Id.* **47.** Yoo, *The Continuation of Politics by Other Means, supra* at 177. **48.** *Id.* **49.** *Id.* at 178. **50.** *Id.* **51.** *Id.* **52.** *Id.* **53.** *Id.* at 179–80. **54.** *Id.* at 180. **55.** 50 U.S.C. ch. 33. **56.** Yoo, *The Continuation of Politics by Other Means, supra* at 181–82 (quoting Letter to the Speaker of the House and the President Pro Tempore of the Senate Reporting on the Operation (Apr. 27, 1980), *reprinted in* Public Papers of the Presidents of the United States: Jimmy Carter 1980–81, at 777; Report of President George Bush (Dec. 21, 1989), *reprinted in* Thomas M. Franck & Michael J. Glennon, Foreign Relations and National Security Law 596–97 (2d. ed. 1993)). **57.** Yoo, *The Continuation of Politics by Other Means, supra* at 181–82, 187; John Yoo, *Trump at War*, 45 Vt. L. Rev. 641, 644, 660 (2021). **58.** Yoo, *The Continuation of Politics by Other Means, supra* at 181. **59.** *Id.* **60.** *Id.* at 181–82. **61.** *Id.* at 187. **62.** Yoo, *Trump at War, supra* at 660. **63.** *Id.* at 644. **64.** *Id.* at 648–49. **65.** *Id.* at 649. **66.** Elena Moore & Roberta Rampton, *Timeline: How the U.S. Came to Strike and Kill a Top Iranian General*, NPR (Jan.4, 2020), https://perma.cc/SEY2 -EZT9. **67.** April 2018 Airstrikes Against Syrian Chemical -Weapons Facilities, 42 Op. O.L.C. 1, 5 (2018). **68.** *Id.* at 22. **69.** *Id.* at 18 (quoting Memorandum Opinion for the Attorney General: Authority to Use Military Force in Libya, 35 Op. O.L.C. 1, 8 (Apr. 1, 2011)). **70.** John Yoo, *On Unilateral Presidential War Powers*, 45 Harv. J.L. & Pub. Pol'y 69, 70, 75 (2022). **71.** Zachary B. Wolf, *Here's What Biden Has Said About Sending US Troops to Ukraine*, CNN (Feb. 24, 2022), https://perma.cc/5VZU-NPA8. **72.** 67 U.S. 635 (1863). **73.** *Id.* at 668. **74.** *Orlando v. Laird*, 443 F.2d 1039, 1042 (2nd. Cir. 1971). **75.** *Mitchell v. Laird*, 488 F.2d 611, 615 (D.C. Cir. 1973). **76.** 203 F.3d 19 (D.C. Cir. 2000). **77.** 72 Fed. Appx. 768 (10th Cir. 2003). **78.** *Id.* **79.** Saikrishna Prakash, *Unleashing the Dogs of War: What the Constitution Means by "Declare War,"* 93 Cornell L. Rev. 45, 48 (2007). **80.** Michael W. McConnell, The President Who Would Not Be King: Executive Power Under the Constitution (2020). **81.** Yoo, *The Continuation of Politics by Other Means, supra* at 170; H. Jefferson Powell, The President's Authority Over Foreign Affairs: An Essay in Constitutional

Interpretation 122 (2002). **82.** Robert F. Turner, *The War Powers Resolution at 40: Still an Unconstitutional, Unnecessary, and Unwise Fraud that Contributed Directly to the 9/11 Attacks*, 45 Case W. Rsrv. Int'l L.J. 109 (2012); John Lehman, Making War: The 200-Year-Old Battle Between the President and Congress Over How America

Goes to War (1992); Robert H. Bork, Address, *Erosion of the President's Power in Foreign Affairs*, 68 Wash. U. L.Q. 693, 695–701 (1990); Stephen L. Carter, *The Constitutionality of the War Powers Resolution*, 70 Va. L. Rev. 101 (1984); Eugene V. Rostow, *"Once More Unto the Breach:" The War Powers Resolution Revisited*, 21 Val. U. L. Rev. 1 (1986).

ESSAY NO. 57: THE FEDERAL MARQUE AND REPRISAL CLAUSE
ART. I, § 8, CL. 11

The Congress shall have Power To . . . grant Letters of Marque and Reprisal. . . .
—John C. Yoo

INTRODUCTION

At the time of the Founding, the sovereign of any nation could authorize holders of letters of marque and reprisal to engage in hostile actions against enemies of the state.[1] These letters authorize private parties, known as privateers, to engage in reprisals for private, commercial gain.[2] The Constitution has two clauses concerning such letters. Congress has the power to grant them, but the states do not. (See Essay No. 78.) Although Congress has not issued a letter of marque and reprisal since the War of 1812, there is a scholarly debate about whether the Federal Marque and Reprisal Clause gives Congress authority over all forms of hostilities short of declared wars.[3]

HISTORY BEFORE 1787

The word "Marque" is the French equivalent of "Reprisal," and the original understanding of "Reprisal" is a seizure of property, or sometimes persons, by a foreign state as redress for an injury committed by that state.[4] Thus, "Marque and Reprisal" is best understood as a single phrase. Sir William Blackstone observed that "letters of marque and reprisal" are "words in themselves synonymous."[5] Blackstone wrote that the power to issue such letters was "plainly derived from" the power to make war and that the issuance of these letters would generally end "in a formal denunciation of war."[6]

During the Revolutionary War, the Continental Congress granted letters of marque and reprisal. These privateers seized $10 million

of British goods, harming British commerce and hastening the colonists' eventual victory. According to one scholar, "[t]he harm to British commerce was one of the most significant sources of internal dissent in Britain concerning continuation of the war."[7]

The Articles of Confederation empowered Congress to grant these letters "in time of peace," but only with the consent of nine states.[8] One scholar has observed that such letters of marque and reprisal "issued 'in times of peace' could constitute state-authorized private warfare short of declared war."[9]

THE CONSTITUTIONAL CONVENTION

On August 17, 1787, the delegates granted Congress the power to "declare war."[10] The following day, James Madison of Virginia proposed a list of "additional powers . . . to be vested in" Congress.[11] The list, referred to the Committee of Detail, included the power "to grant letters of marque and reprisal."[12] Elbridge Gerry of Massachusetts agreed with Madison: "[S]omething [should be] inserted concerning letters of marque, which he thought not included in the power of war."[13] Gerry's proposal was adopted without debate.[14]

On August 28, the Federal Marque and Reprisal Clause was coupled with the prohibition. On September 5, the Committee of Eleven proposed that the "declare war" clause should be amended to give Congress the power to "grant letters of marque and reprisal."[15] The proposal was approved without debate.[16]

THE RATIFICATION DEBATES

There were few mentions of letters of marque and reprisal in Federalist and Anti-Federalist writings. In Federalist No. 41, Madison grouped together several "powers conferred on the government of the union" that relate to "security against foreign dangers." These powers included "granting letters of marque." This provision does not seem to have been particularly controversial, perhaps because a close analogue already existed under the Articles of Confederation.

EARLY PRACTICE

Between 1797 and 1801, the United States was engaged in the Quasi-War with France. Congress authorized and the President issued letters of marque and reprisal to privateers. However, the privateers' effect on that war was "negligible."[17] The United States had limited itself to fighting a "basically defensive" war. As a result, Congress had barred privateers from doing what they did best: attacking "ordinary" French merchant ships.[18]

Congress issued letters of marque and reprisal to privateers again during the War of 1812.[19] Scholars have observed that "not a single American war aim had been attained" by the war's end.[20] But that was not a failure of the privateers, who had "wo[rn] down the British fighting spirit" by "capturing more than $40 million" of British goods[21] and have been described as "the only effective American offensive weapon in the war."[22] Justice Joseph Story explained that "[t]he power to declare war would of itself carry the incidental power to grant letters of marque and reprisal."[23] Since the War of 1812, the United States has not issued letters of marque and reprisal.[24] In addition, the 1856 Declaration of Paris prohibits privateering as a matter of international law.[25] The United States has not ratified the Declaration, but it has upheld the ban in practice.[26]

Over time, however, both the executive and legislative branches have considered using letters of marque and reprisal. For example, in the 1980s, a scandal arose over the funding of military operations in Nicaragua. During the so-called Iran–Contra controversy, members of Congress objected to President Reagan's private financing of hostilities absent prior congressional consent.[27] However, Congress did not expressly invoke the Federal Marque and Reprisal Clause. Nor did members argue that the President should issue such letters without legislative approval.

Following the terrorist attacks on September 11, 2001, members of Congress proposed issuing letters of marque and reprisal to punish the "air pira[tes]."[28] Letters of marque and reprisal have been advocated to fight old threats like Somali piracy.[29] They have also been raised as a means to address modern threats like cyberattacks[30] and foreign adversaries like the Islamic State and Russia.[31]

LETTERS OF MARQUE AND REPRISAL AND THE WAR POWER

Article I, Section 8, Clause 11 lists three of Congress's powers: "To declare War [see Essay No. 56], grant Letters of Marque and Reprisal, and make Rules concerning Captures on Land and Water [see Essay No. 58]." Scholars debate the relationship between these provisions and the war power.

One school of thought holds that the President lacks any power whatsoever to initiate hostilities, except perhaps defensively to repel invasions.[32] Advocates of this approach contend that the Declare War Clause requires Congress to authorize wars, whereas the Federal Marque and Reprisal Clause requires Congress to authorize lower-level hostilities, whether by public forces or by privateers.[33]

A second school of thought (which your author endorses) agrees that Congress has exclusive authority over all funding of military hostilities, whether through public appropriations for a national military or letters of marque and reprisal for private actors.[34] However, Congress has no power to control directly the President's ability to initiate hostilities with whatever resources Congress has previously made available to him. As a result, the Federal Marque and Reprisal Clause is best read in conjunction with Congress's power of the purse. Locating the Federal Marque and Reprisal Clause in Article I prevents the President from engaging in hostilities free from congressional control of resources, whether through public appropriations or through the issuance of letters of marque and reprisal to private actors.

OPEN QUESTIONS

- The text of Article I, Section 8, Clause 11 speaks only to Congress having the power to "grant Letters of Marque and Reprisal." It does not address the role of the President in that process. Must the bill authorizing the letter be presented to the President under the Presentment Clause (Article I, Section 7, Clause 2), or could Congress also invoke the process in the Order, Resolution, or Vote Clause (Article I, Section 7, Clause 3)? (See Essay Nos. 36 and 38.) Would a statute that authorized a single House to approve a letter of marque and reprisal, subject to presidential approval, run afoul of *INS v. Chadha* (1983)?[35]

- Can the President veto a bill authorizing a letter of marque and reprisal? Can he simply decline to issue the letter?

- Historically, the President has issued letters of marque and reprisal subject to statutory authority and guidance. Could Congress grant a letter of marque and reprisal through its own officers?

- Does the holder of a letter of marque and reprisal hold an "office under the United States"?[36] Does the Constitution's Foreign Emoluments Clause bar a privateer from having a foreign title or receiving foreign emoluments? (See Essay No. 76.) Does the Constitution's Incompatibility Clause bar a member of Congress from holding a letter of marque and reprisal? (See Essay No. 34.) If a member of Congress served in the Congress that increased the compensation attached to a letter of marque and reprisal, would the Constitution's Ineligibility Clause bar that member from holding that letter?[37] (See Essay No. 33.) Is a privateer "appointed" to his position?

- Could Congress authorize victims of cyberattacks to "hack back" at their opponents even when doing so would otherwise violate a federal law like the Computer Fraud and Abuse Act?

Cite as: John C. Yoo, *The Federal Marque and Reprisal Clause*, *in* THE HERITAGE GUIDE TO THE CONSTITUTION 201 (Josh Blackman & John G. Malcolm eds., 3d ed. 2025).

Notes

1. John C. Yoo, *The Continuation of Politics by Other Means: The Original Understanding of War Powers*, 84 Cal. L. Rev. 167, 206 (1996).   **2.** *Bas v. Tingy*, 4 U.S. 37 (1800).   **3.** Yoo, *supra* at 250–51.   **4.** *Id.* at 250.   **5.** 1 Blackstone 250; Grover Clark, *The English Practice with Regard to Reprisals by Private Persons*, 27 Am. J. Int'l L. 694, 700 (1933).   **6.** 1 Blackstone 250.   **7.** J. Gregory Sidak, *The Quasi War Cases—And Their Relevance to Whether "Letters of Marque and Reprisal" Constrain Presidential War Powers*, 28 Harv. J.L. & Pub. Pol'y 465, 475 (2005).   **8.** Articles of Confederation, art. VI, § 4; *id.* at IX §§ 1, 6.   **9.** Jules Lobel, *Covert War and Congressional Authority: Hidden War and Forgotten Power*, 134 U. Pa. L. Rev. 1035, 1059 (1986).   **10.** 2 Farrand's 318–19.   **11.** *Id.* at 321.   **12.** *Id.* at 324, 326.   **13.** *Id.* at 326.   **14.** *Id.* at 328.   **15.** *Id.* at 505, 508.   **16.** *Id.* at 328; Sidak, *supra* at 477.   **17.** Alexander Deconde, The Quasi-War: The Politics and Diplomacy of the Undeclared War with France 1797–1801, at 126–27 (1966), https://bit.ly/4mwshg0.   **18.** *Id.*   **19.** Dorothy Denneen Volo & James M. Volo, Daily Life in the Age of Sail 235 (2002), https://perma.cc/PCR2-YMN4.   **20.** *Id.*   **21.** *Id.*   **22.** *Id.*   **23.** 3 Story's Commentaries § 1170.   **24.** William Young, *A Check on Faint-Hearted Presidents: Letters of Marque and Reprisal*, 66 Wash. & Lee L. Rev. 895, 897 (2009).   **25.** Declaration Respecting Maritime Law Between Austria, France, Great Britain, Prussia, Russia, Sardinia and Turkey, Apr. 16, 1856, 115 Consol. T.S. 1.   **26.** Todd Emerson Hutchins, *Structuring a Sustainable Letters of Marque Regime: How Commissioning Privateers Can Defeat the Somali Pirates*, 99 Calif. L. Rev. 819 (2011).   **27.** H.R. Rep. No. 100-433, at 15–16 (1987).   **28.** H.R. 3076, 107th Cong. (2001); H.R. 3216, 110th Cong. (2007); Robert P. DeWitte, *Let Privateers Marque Terrorism: A Proposal for a Reawakening*, 82 Ind. L.J. 131 (2007).   **29.** Hutchins, *supra*.   **30.** Ian C. Rice & Douglas A. Borer, *Bring Back the Privateers*, The Nat'l Interest (Apr. 22, 2015), https://perma.cc/D57T-FPEU; Paresh Dave, *Some Companies Looking at Retaliating Against Cyber Attackers*, L.A. Times (May 31, 2013), https://perma.cc/GKA4-EYFY; Commander Jonathan L. Still, *Strategic Research Report: Resurrecting Letters of Marque and Reprisal to Address Modern Threats* (Mar. 2012), https://perma.cc/UDX6-E3P8.   **31.** H.R. 6869, 117th Cong. (2022).   **32.** Saikrishna Prakash, *Unleashing the Dogs of War: What the Constitution Means by "Declare War"*, 93 Cornell L. Rev. 45, 88–89 (2007).   **33.** Lobel, *supra* at 69–70.   **34.** John C. Yoo, *War and the Constitutional Text*, 69 U. Chi. L. Rev. 1639, 1667–68 (2002); C. Kevin Marshall, *Putting Privateers in Their Place: The Applicability of the Marque and Reprisal Clause to Undeclared Wars*, 64 U.

Chi. L. Rev. 953, 974–75 (1997).   **35.** 462 U.S. 919 (1983).
36. Seth Barrett Tillman & Josh Blackman, *Offices and Officers of the Constitution, Part II: The Four Approaches,* 61 S. Tex. L. Rev. 321, 340, 394, 418–19, 424 (2022); Seth Barrett Tillman & Josh Blackman, *Offices and Officers of the Constitution, Part VI: The Ineligibility Clause,* 64 S. Tex.

L. Rev. 209, 252–53 (2025).   **37.** Seth Barrett Tillman & Josh Blackman, *Offices and Officers of the Constitution, Part V: The Elector Incompatibility, Impeachment Disqualification, Foreign Emoluments, and Incompatibility Clauses,* 63 S. Tex. L. Rev. 237, 279 (2024).

ESSAY NO. 58: THE CAPTURES CLAUSE
ART. I, § 8, CL. 11

The Congress shall have Power To . . . make Rules concerning Captures on Land and Water. . . .

—John C. Yoo

INTRODUCTION

During armed conflicts, property seized from enemies are known as prizes of war. Under the Captures Clause, Congress has the power to make rules for the confiscation, disposition, and distribution of captured enemy property. The original understanding suggests that the clause covers the seizure of enemy shipping as prizes of war. However, the war on terrorism spurred debate over whether the concept of prizes extends to enemy prisoners. Three main arguments have developed over the reach of the Captures Clause: (1) that Congress's powers under the clause do not apply to enemy prisoners, so the power over enemy prisoners rests with the President; (2) that the clause applies only to property, not persons, but Congress can invoke its authority over the armed forces to regulate the treatment of prisoners; and (3) that Congress can regulate prisoners under the Captures Clause as well as under the Offenses Against the Law of Nations and Declare War Clauses.

HISTORY BEFORE 1787

Prizes of war in Britain were handled through a specialized Court of Admiralty system, which developed a sophisticated body of prize law that determined the legality of captures, ownership rights, and distribution of proceeds.[1] The High Court of Admiralty employed rigorous procedural requirements, including the examination of ship's papers and crew depositions, to establish whether captures were lawful under prevailing laws of war and international custom.[2] This judicial oversight operated within the framework established by Parliament's legislative authority over maritime prizes. The British Prize Acts of the eighteenth century referred to property that had been seized but not confirmed as a prize through the courts.[3] These statutory frameworks created a structured legal pathway that transformed physical captures into legally recognized prizes. Parliament granted the Admiralty courts exclusive jurisdiction over this process to ensure uniformity in the application of prize law principles.[4]

Building on British admiralty practice, the Continental Congress established its own system of prize law during the Revolutionary War.[5] For example, the Congress frequently issued letters of marque and reprisal exclusively to privateers "to make Captures of British Vessels and Cargoes" pursuant to rules established by Congress.[6] Under these rules, captors could not claim lawful title to captured property until after a prize court had granted it.[7] At the time, the term "captures" referred to property.[8] Such property would include enemy ships or vessels aiding the enemy and their valuable goods. The captors would be entitled to at least partial title of the prize. Before 1780, capture cases were determined by state courts, generally by jury. The Continental Congress retained the power to review appeals.[9] This arrangement, however, created tensions between the state and national governments. State courts often bristled at congressional oversight of their decisions.

In 1780, the Continental Congress created the Court of Appeals in Cases of Capture.[10] The Articles of Confederation did not establish a national judiciary, but Article IX, Section 1 addressed the capture issue. Congress had the power "of establishing rules for deciding, in all cases, what captures on land or water shall be legal" and the power of "establishing courts" and "receiving and determining finally appeals in all cases of captures." But there was an incompatibility: "no member of congress shall be appointed a judge of any of the said courts." One such case was *Miller v. The Ship Resolution* (1781).[11] These courts would operate until the Constitution was ratified. In 1795, the U.S. Supreme Court observed that "[t]he existence of the Court of Appeals terminated with the old government" once the Constitution was ratified.[12]

THE CONSTITUTIONAL CONVENTION

The Virginia Plan, proposed by Edmund Randolph on May 29, provided an overview of the powers for the national government.[13] Under the plan, inferior tribunals would hear cases about "all . . . captures from an enemy."[14] On June 12, the Convention voted to strike out that clause.[15] The New Jersey Plan, introduced on June 15, also included a national judiciary that would hear "all cases of captures from an enemy."[16] Alexander Hamilton's plan would have granted "original jurisdiction in all causes of capture" to the "Supreme Judicial authority."[17]

A Committee of Detail draft grouped together Congress's power "To declare the law of piracy, felonies and captures on the high seas, and captures on land."[18] The Committee of Detail's report was delivered to the delegates on August 6.[19] Its text included a standalone provision that was not coupled with any other powers: "To make rules concerning captures on land and water."[20] This provision was referred to the Committee of Style.[21] The Committee of Style's report lumped together three separate powers: "To declare war, grant letters of marque and reprisal, and make rules concerning captures on land and water."[22] That provision received no further edits.

There was no substantial discussion of the Captures Clause during the ratification process.

WHAT CAN BE CAPTURED?

When the Constitution was ratified, it was well established that property could be captured as a prize. *Brown v. United States* (1814) held that the executive's power to conduct war necessarily includes the power to seize persons and property on the battlefield.[23] Yet the Supreme Court has construed the Captures Clause to deny the executive constitutional power to seize enemy property outside of the battlefield.[24] *Brown* concluded that by virtue of the Captures Clause, the executive lacks inherent constitutional authority to confiscate property owned by subjects of enemy nations and must seek congressional authorization in order to do so.[25]

WHO CAN BE CAPTURED?

Does the Captures Clause apply to people? The original understanding of "captures" included only enemy property. The term could not include captured enemy soldiers, as persons can neither be "divided" nor "appropriated," nor can they be treated as legally awarded prizes. This approach is bolstered by the fact that the "capture" was understood under international law to be "the act or practice of taking any thing; a prize."[26]

However, there may be some contrary authority with regard to piracy. Pirates were individuals who committed robbery or other violent acts on the high seas without the authorization of a nation-state.[27] Piracy was "robbery upon the sea."[28] Historically, the capture of pirates by public or private ships of any nation was considered lawful. The Supreme Court, for example, found that "pirates may be lawfully captured on the ocean by the public or private ships of any nation."[29] Pirates were considered *hostes humani generis*, or "enemies of the human race."[30] As such, they were beyond legal protection because piracy was considered a crime against all nations. The treatment of pirates under the Law of Nations was different from the treatment of non-pirates. Vattel, for example, distinguished between two categories: *formal* warfare by non-pirates for political purposes that was sanctioned by recognized authorities and *unlawful* war by pirates solely for plunder. Vattel wrote that "such in general are the depredations of pirates."[31]

The Supreme Court followed this principle

in *The Marinna Flora* (1825).[32] Justice Joseph Story defined letters of marque to contain "an authority to seize the *bodies* or goods of the subjects of the offending state" until the injury is made whole again.[33] These sources do not textually include the treatment of people as prizes, but they do suggest that the Captures Clause at least authorizes the seizure of people incident to the physical capture of goods.

THE CAPTURES CLAUSE AND SEPARATION OF POWERS

The original understanding of the clause appears to be that Congress alone has the power to establish rules governing the circumstances of the capture.[34] The Supreme Court has invoked the Captures Clause to demonstrate the balance of powers between Congress and the President. For example, *Hamdan v. Rumsfeld* (2006) observed that the Captures Clause was a congressional power distinct from the President's powers in executing war, but it did not clarify the powers included in the Captures Clause.[35] Two years

earlier, *Hamdi v. Rumsfeld* (2004) found that the detention of enemy combatants for the duration of the conflict was "so fundamental and accepted an incident to war as to be an exercise of the 'necessary and appropriate force' Congress has authorized the President to use."[36] The Court apparently saw no need to clarify whether Congress even needed to authorize the President to execute his war powers in areas "so fundamental and accepted."

The lower courts have also addressed this issue. In *Kiyemba v. Obama* (2009), then-Judge Brett Kavanaugh suggested that the Captures Clause was evidence that the "President does not possess exclusive, preclusive authority over the transfer of detainees."[37] Kavanaugh observed that Congress may place judicially enforceable limits on the transfer of prisoners but also can choose not to do so for policy reasons. The "negotiated exchange of prisoners was 'a wartime practice well known to the Framers,' and '[j]udicial intervention might have complicated' those negotiations."[38]

OPEN QUESTIONS

- Does the Captures Clause authorize Congress to regulate captures by private parties only and not by the armed forces of the United States, or does the practice of the Continental Congress support a power of the Congress to control captures by both private and public vessels?[39] If the answer to the latter question is yes, would Congress have some constitutional authority to prescribe rules for at least some elements of military conflict?

- Should the Captures Clause play a role with new forms of warfare that mix private and public activity and resources? For example, would intentional damage to underwater intercontinental fiber optic cables constitute piracy? Would seizure of electronic assets in the cloud be a "[c]apture[] on Land and Water"?

Cite as: John C. Yoo, *The Captures Clause, in* THE HERITAGE GUIDE TO THE CONSTITUTION 204 (Josh Blackman & John G. Malcolm eds., 3d ed. 2025).

Notes

1. Henry J. Bourguignon, The First Federal Court: The Federal Appellate Prize Court of the American Revolution, 1775–1787, at 12–16 (1977). **2.** Carl E. Swanson, Predators and Prizes: American Privateering and Imperial Warfare, 1739–1748, at 27–29 (1991). **3.** Matthew P. Harrington, *The Legacy of the Colonial Vice-Admiralty Courts*, 26 J. Mar. L. & Com. 581, 584–85 (1995). **4.** William R. Casto, *The Origins of Federal Admiralty Jurisdiction in an Age of Privateers, Smugglers, and Pirates*, 37 Am. J. Legal Hist. 117, 124 (1993). **5.** Bourguignon, *supra* at 89. **6.** Cont. Cong., Instructions to the Commanders of Private Ships or Vessels of War, § 2 (Apr. 3, 1776). **7.** *Id.*, § 5. **8.** *Brown v. United States*, 12 U.S. 110, 122–23 (1814). **9.** 3 J. Cont. Cong. 374

(Nov. 25, 1775). **10.** 16 J. Cont. Cong. 61–64 (Jan. 15, 1780). **11.** 2 U.S. (2 Dall.) 1 (Fed. Ct. App. 1781). **12.** *Penhallow v. Doane's Administrators*, 3 U.S. 54, 86 (1795). **13.** 1 Farrand's 20. **14.** *Id.* at 22. **15.** *Id.* at 211, 220. **16.** *Id.* at 244. **17.** *Id.* at 282, 292. **18.** 2 Farrand's 143. **19.** *Id.* at 177. **20.** *Id.* at 182. **21.** *Id.* at 565, 570. **22.** *Id.* at 590, 595. **23.** *Brown v. United States*, 12 U.S. 110 (1814). **24.** *Id.* at 126. **25.** *Id.* at 127–28. **26.** Thomas Sheridan, A Complete Dictionary of the English Language (1790). **27.** *United States v. Smith*, 18 U.S. 153, 162 (1820). **28.** *Id.* **29.** *The Marianna Flora*, 24 U.S. 1, 2 (1825). **30.** *United States v. Windsor*, 570 U.S. 744, 798 (Scalia, J., dissenting). **31.** E. Vattel, The Law of Nations; or Principles of the Law of Nature, Applied to the Conduct and Affairs of Nations and Sovereigns 320 (6th Am. ed. 1844).   **32.** 24 U.S. 1 (1825).   **33.** 3 Story's Commentaries § 1171 (emphasis added).   **34.** Art. I, § 8, cl. 11; Michael D. Ramsey, The Constitution's Text in Foreign Affairs 224–29 (2007). **35.** *Hamdan v. Rumsfeld*, 548 U.S. 557, 591 (2006).   **36.** *Hamdi*

v. Rumsfeld, 542 U.S. 507, 518 (2004).   **37.** *Kiyemba v. Obama*, 561 F.3d 509, 518 (D.C. Cir. 2009) (Kavanaugh, J., concurring).   **38.** *Id.* at 520 (quoting *Boumediene v. Bush*, 553 U.S. 723, 748 (2008)).   **39.** Ingrid Wuerth, *The Captures Clause*, 76 U. Chi L. Rev. 1683, 1735 (2009).

ESSAY NO. 59: THE ARMIES CLAUSE
ART. I, § 8, CL. 12

The Congress shall have Power . . . To raise and support Armies, but no Appropriation of Money to that Use shall be for a longer Term than two Years. . . .
—Judge Gregory E. Maggs & Robert Leider

INTRODUCTION

Because many in the Framing generation feared that a standing army could lead to domestic tyranny, the power to raise an army was among the most controversial military provisions of the Constitution. To address this concern, the Framers established a militia separate from the standing army, with its officer corps appointed by states, and gave Congress the power to make the militia uniform and effective by providing for its organizing, arming, disciplining, and calling forth. Over time, many members of Congress became dissatisfied with how the Constitution limited federal power over the militia. Ultimately, the federal government settled on using Congress's plenary power under the Armies Clause to raise all forms of land forces. Congress's efforts to consolidate the militia into the army, however, have raised difficult constitutional questions. For example, is conscription into the national army constitutional, and can the federal government exercise near-plenary control over land forces such as the Army Reserve, whose members are civilian nonprofessional soldiers?

HISTORY BEFORE 1787

From the Norman Conquest to the seventeenth century, English armies were temporary institutions.[1] Armies were raised for specific conflicts, after which they were disbanded. Beginning around 1660, however, Britain began to keep a standing army—a substantial permanent corps of soldiers that continued to exist in peacetime.[2] In a temporary army, soldiers often served for the duration of a specific conflict; soldiers in a standing army enlisted for long periods, essentially making military service their career.[3]

British political thought traditionally shunned standing armies, which were thought to be dangerous to civil liberty and limited government. Professional soldiers constituted their own special-interest faction in society.[4] They lived under military law and lacked the civil liberty and common-law rights of English subjects. They were also armed and capable of acting against the civil government or against the population that they were supposed to protect. Many people feared that such an unrepresentative armed faction of society might overthrow the government or be used by an executive officer to oppress the population.[5]

Despite these fears, Britain gradually accepted the need for a standing army. For much of English history, the keeping of a standing army was thought to be unconstitutional.[6] However, the British constitution is conventional, not binding legally, so Parliament could still authorize the keeping of a standing army by statute—which is what Parliament ultimately did. Beginning in the late seventeenth century, Parliament reauthorized the standing army annually through the Mutiny Act.[7]

England did not recognize any general obligation of inhabitants to perform military service in the army,[8] but inhabitants did have a general duty to bear arms to perform defensive military service, exercised through the militia and its predecessor institutions. Impressment into the army "was normally illegal" and during the rare times it occurred fell only upon marginalized groups, such as criminals and the poor.[9] The "cherished principle"[10] of raising a British army was that "every soldier was supposed to be a volunteer."[11]

In the seventeenth and early eighteenth centuries, the British did not station any significant numbers of troops in the American colonies, but this changed in the 1750s during the French and Indian War. At the conclusion of that war, the British kept a permanent military presence in the colonies.[12] The British government imposed taxes to provide for these troops and quartered them in private homes. Colonials resented both the troops and the means of providing for them. Resistance to taxation and quartering became major contributing causes of the American Revolution.[13]

Once war broke out between the United States and Britain, Americans raised their own regular forces—the Continental Army. On June 14, 1775, the Continental Congress authorized the raising of regular forces at national expense.[14] During the war, Congress appointed senior officers and governed the forces directly, often through various committees.[15]

Under the Articles of Confederation, ratified in 1781, Congress had the power to raise and support an army, but it had to rely on the states to exercise this power. The Articles provided that "A Committee of the States" consisting of one delegate from each state would have to "agree upon the number of land forces" needed and then "make requisitions [requests for money] from each state for its quota, in proportion to the number of white inhabitants in such state."[16] Each state then would "appoint the regimental officers, raise the men, and clothe, arm, and equip them, in a soldierlike manner," all "at the expense of the united states." Thereafter, "the officers and men so clothed, armed, and equipped" would "march to the place appointed, and within the time agreed on by" Congress.

These powers left Congress without adequate military authority. Making the states responsible for raising regular forces permitted them to obstruct Congress.[17] During the Revolution, the United States frequently lacked sufficient numbers of regular soldiers in the field.[18] Moreover, Congress had difficulty paying and supplying the troops.[19]

As the war ended, the army began to mutiny. The most serious incident occurred in March 1783 when frustrated army officers, backed by public creditors and some nationalist political figures, threatened to march on Congress.[20] An anonymous officer at the army's camp in Newburgh, New York, circulated a letter calling for the officers to meet and plot their actions against Congress—a plan that may have included overthrowing the government.[21] General George Washington, Commander in Chief of the Continental Army, caught wind of the plot. He attended the officers' meeting and, through sheer force of personality, defused the conspiracy in a famous address to his officers.[22] This episode reinforced the dangers that regular forces posed to civilian control of the government and, according to military historian Richard H. Kohn, "was the closest an American army has ever come to revolt or coup d'etat."[23]

Following the conclusion of the Revolution in September 1783, Congress largely disbanded the army, leaving it with a residual force of "eighty men and a few officers"[24] that was not enough to provide for national defense or respond to domestic turmoil. Shays's Rebellion in 1786, during which "the Confederation proved unable to protect its own arsenal" at Springfield, Massachusetts, reinforced the appearance of military weakness.[25] Nor did the standing army have a firm legal basis. Once peace with Britain was concluded, the Framing generation repeatedly debated whether the Articles conferred upon Congress the power to keep a standing army in peacetime.[26] The need to strengthen national military power was a major motivating force behind calls for the Constitutional Convention.

THE CONSTITUTIONAL CONVENTION

At the Constitutional Convention, there was broad agreement on the need for professional troops. The Committee of Detail originated what would become the Armies Clause. The draft text provided that Congress shall have the power "[t]o make war (and) raise armies. (& equip Fleets.)."[27] From here, the Convention split into two main camps.

The first camp wanted a strong professional army based on the European model.

One-third of the delegates were veterans of the Revolutionary War, and they understood the advantage of having trained professionals conduct war.[28] Many Framers had been troubled by the recurring congressional debates about whether Congress could maintain a standing army under the Articles of Confederation. They wished the controversy would conclude in favor of national power.[29] The second camp generally feared a standing army. They grudgingly acknowledged its necessity in some cases, such as manning garrisons and guarding the frontier, but sought various restrictions, including limiting the size of the army during peacetime.[30]

At the Convention, the first camp prevailed. The Convention expanded the power to "raise armies" into the power to "raise *and support* Armies."[31] The delegates also rejected all substantive restrictions on Congress's power, such as limiting the army's size.[32] The Constitution thus spoke of Congress's power to raise regular forces in the broadest terms. The only significant limitation was that "no Appropriation of Money to that Use shall be for a longer Term than two Years." This prevented Congress from establishing a perpetual standing army.

Here, the Framers loosely followed the British tradition. The Mutiny Act would remain valid only for one year, and by reauthorizing it, Parliament provided its ongoing consent for the standing army. Similarly, each new Congress would need to consent to the continued existence of the American army by funding the troops. If Congress did nothing, the army would cease to exist for lack of funding.[33] The Framers selected a two-year window because Congress was elected every two years and might not have a session each year.[34]

THE RATIFICATION DEBATES

During the ratification debates, the Anti-Federalists objected to Congress's unlimited power to create a standing army. These objections followed traditional British Whiggish political theory.[35] The Anti-Federalists complained that the creation of an army would lead to domestic tyranny because government officials could use the army to enforce domestic law by force rather than by consent.[36] The Anti-Federalists also recognized that a standing army would be expensive to maintain and feared that burdensome taxation and invasive search and seizure policies might be necessary to support the forces.[37] Finally, the Anti-Federalists emphasized the complete lack of limits on Congress's authority to keep standing forces. There were no limits on the number of troops and no substantive limits on Congress's power. Patrick Henry observed that "the quartering of troops upon us . . . was one of the principal reasons for dissolving the connection with Great Britain." Yet under the Constitution, "we may have troops in time of peace" who "may be billeted in any manner—to tyrannize, oppress, and crush us."[38]

Anti-Federalists sought several amendments to limit Congress's power to keep a standing army, including by requiring Congress to have a supermajority to authorize a standing army.[39] They also sought declarations that "standing armies in time of peace are dangerous to liberty."[40]

The Federalists offered several defenses of Congress's power. In Federalist No. 25, Alexander Hamilton noted that regular forces were militarily superior to the militia because "[w]ar, like most other things, is a science to be acquired and perfected by diligence, by perseverance, by time, and by practice." In the Virginia ratifying convention, George Nicholas questioned the adequacy of "men unacquainted with the hardships, and unskilled in the discipline of war."[41]

Federalists used the expense of armies to their rhetorical advantage. Because professional forces were expensive, the American army would also be naturally limited in size. They argued that Congress could not raise enough revenue to have a large standing army.[42] In Federalist No. 26, Hamilton stressed that the two-year appropriation restriction ensured that Congress could not "vest in the executive department permanent funds for the support of an army." Rather, Congress must "once at least in every two years . . . deliberate upon the propriety of keeping a military force on foot," "come to a new resolution on the point," and "declare their sense of the matter, by a formal vote in the face of their constituents."

The Federalists also emphasized the democratic checks on the power to raise armies. In England, the Crown had the power to raise armies and declare war. However, as

Hamilton pointed out in Federalist No. 24, the Constitution assigned those powers to the legislature, "a popular body, consisting of the representatives of the people." Finally, as Madison noted in Federalist No. 46, the American people possessed their own arms, making it unlikely that the standing army could be deployed against the civilian population to usurp the government or oppress the population.

THE BILL OF RIGHTS

The Constitution was ratified in 1788. During the First Congress, two constitutional amendments were proposed that concerned the dangers created by standing armies. The Second Amendment secured a general individual right to bear arms, thereby preventing Congress from investing a standing army with a monopoly of the means of force. (See Essay No. 164.) However, the amendment did not limit Congress's power to raise an army or include any language opposing the idea of a standing army. Instead, Anti-Federalists secured only the milder declaration that "[a] well regulated Militia" is "necessary to the security of a free State."

In addition, the Third Amendment prevented Congress from quartering troops in private homes without consent in peacetime. (See Essay No. 165.) This amendment relieved homeowners of the financial obligation of subsidizing the housing for regular forces. It also prevented the government from quartering troops in private homes to intimidate the civilian population.[43]

THE PROVISIONAL ARMY DURING THE QUASI-WAR WITH FRANCE

The Constitution does not define the difference between an "army" and a "militia." Yet the distinction between them is critical because the Constitution creates separate regulatory regimes for these two types of land forces. The Armies Clause gives the federal government plenary authority over the armies of the United States. It stands in contrast to the Militia Clauses, which divided control of the militia between the federal and state governments and limited the ability of the federal government to call forth the militia to domestic defensive conflicts. (See Essay Nos. 62, 63, and 103.)

During the Quasi-War with France,

Congress began to raise land forces through the Army Clause instead of the Militia Clauses. In 1799, Federalists in Congress authorized the President to create a provisional army, and part of that law authorized the President to accept individuals and associations that volunteered for service.[44] The President, not the states, would appoint the officers for the volunteers.

The law occasioned great debate in Congress about whether Congress had the power to create the provisional army. The Federalists argued that the Armies Clause authorized Congress to create it. The Democratic-Republicans countered that the provisional army was an unconstitutionally organized militia.[45]

As part of this debate, Federalists and Democratic-Republicans clashed on how to distinguish an "army" from a "militia." The Federalists argued that army soldiers were volunteers and militiamen were conscripts. Because the provisional army comprised volunteers, Federalists contended that it was an "army." The Democratic-Republicans had a different conception: The militia were part-time forces unlike armies, which consisted of regular forces. Because the provisional army comprised nonprofessional soldiers, the Democratic-Republicans argued that it was a militia, and this militia was unconstitutionally organized because the federal government would appoint the officers and could call forth the units for purposes outside those enumerated in the Constitution.[46]

Early nineteenth-century legal commentators were also divided on the status of war volunteers. In 1803, St. George Tucker wrote that the provisional army was an unconstitutional militia.[47] But in 1825, Justice Joseph Story suggested that a national consensus had emerged to consider the volunteer soldiers to be part of the national army.[48]

THE CONSTITUTIONALITY OF CONSCRIPTION

The army/militia distinction is also relevant to the constitutionality of conscription. The efforts toward national conscription were prompted by constitutional limits on the militia that federal policymakers often found intolerable. The Constitution federalized the militia, and during wartime, the federal government had difficulty working through the states to secure necessary forces. Moreover, the Constitution limited the authority of the federal government to call forth the militia to domestic defensive conflicts. Particularly in the twentieth century, the federal government wanted to be able to conscript soldiers for offensive and overseas operations that fell outside its authority to call forth the militia.[49]

The United States first experimented with conscription during the Civil War and enacted its first workable system of conscription during World War I.[50] Conscription gave the federal government the power to call forth the entire able-bodied manpower of the country, but because the Armies Clause gives Congress plenary power to raise, govern, and deploy armies, conscription permitted Congress to raise this military manpower without the legal restrictions on militia service. These efforts to evade the Militia Clauses using national conscription prompted constitutional challenges on the theory that it constituted an unconstitutional calling forth of the militia.

Debates over the constitutionality of conscription look both to linguistic interpretation and to construction across the document as a whole. These methods of interpretation point in different directions. Linguistically, the power to "raise" armies could include the power to compel service in the army, but looking across provisions, the Constitution limits the federal government's authority to call forth and govern the militia. Those limits do not have much substance if Congress may avoid them simply by drafting citizens into the army.[51] Challengers to conscription have also relied on history, noting that England did not recognize any general obligation of inhabitants to perform military service in the army.[52]

The courts have generally upheld conscription laws against these constitutional challenges. During the Civil War, state courts generally upheld conscription, both under the U.S. Constitution and under analogous provisions of the Confederate Constitution.[53] There were, however, strong opinions from judges arguing that conscription was unconstitutional.[54]

JUDICIAL PRECEDENT

In 1918, the U.S. Supreme Court unanimously upheld the constitutionality of conscription during World War I.[55] The *Selective Draft Law Cases* (1918) treated Congress's power to raise armies as an authority additional to and separate from its power to organize the militia. The decision grounded conscription in the power to raise armies, the power to declare war, and the Fourteenth Amendment's primacy of national citizenship.

The Court has described Congress's power to raise armies in broad terms but has never explored its limits. During the Vietnam War, lower courts expanded the holding in the *Selective Draft Law Cases* by upholding the constitutionality of conscription without a declared war. The Supreme Court did not grant certiorari to decide whether those decisions were correct.[56]

The courts have broadly deferred to congressional power over the composition and means of raising the army. *Rostker v. Goldberg* (1981) rejected challenges to male-only draft registration.[57] In 2021, three Justices suggested that the male-only draft may be a form of unconstitutional sex discrimination.[58] The Supreme Court has also upheld a requirement that universities accepting federal funds must make their campuses available for military recruiting.[59]

OPEN QUESTIONS

- In the early twentieth century, Congress created organized reserve forces for the armed forces, including the Army Reserve. These reserve forces are composed of nonprofessional, volunteer citizen-soldiers. They generally train a minimum of one weekend a month and two weeks a year. Are reserve forces part of the constitutional armies or an unconstitutional national militia? This answer may depend on the 1790s debate between the Federalists and Democratic-Republicans. Is the correct distinction between armies and militia whether the troops are volunteers or conscripted, or is it whether the soldiers are full-time or part-time troops?

- Is there tension between a legal theory upholding the constitutionality of conscription and a legal theory upholding the constitutionality of military reserve forces? The Federalists contended that the correct distinction turned on whether the force has volunteer soldiers. If the Federalists were correct, does this mean that civilians drafted by the Selective Service System are actually militiamen, not regular forces? If the Democratic-Republicans were correct that the army/militia distinction was between full-time and part-time troops, are the reserve forces constitutional?
- Under either view, could Congress authorize conscription into the Reserves?

Cite as: Judge Gregory E. Maggs & Robert Leider, *The Armies Clause, in* THE HERITAGE GUIDE TO THE CONSTITUTION 207 (Josh Blackman & John G. Malcolm eds., 3d ed. 2025).

Notes

1. Michael Prestwich, *The English Medieval Army to 1485, in* The Oxford History of the British Army 1, 11 (David Chandler & Ian Beckett eds., 1996).   **2.** Correlli Barnett, Britain and Her Army 1509–1970: A Military, Political and Social Survey 115 (1970).   **3.** H.C.B. Rogers, The British Army of the Eighteenth Century 59 (1977).   **4.** David C. Williams, The Mythic Meanings of the Second Amendment 26–28 (2003).   **5.** *Id.*; Letter from Samuel Adams to James Warren (1776), https://perma.cc/U27E-N5XS; Simeon Howard, *A Sermon Preached to the Ancient and Honorable Artillery Company in Boston, in* 1 American Political Writing During the Founding Era 1760–1805, at 199 (Charles S. Hyneman & Donald S. Lutz eds., 1983).   **6.** John Phillip Reid, In Defiance of the Law: The Standing-Army Controversy, the Two Constitutions, and the Coming of the American Revolution 6–7 (1981).   **7.** *Id.* at 6–9.   **8.** Prestwich, *supra* at 15.   **9.** Barnett, *supra* at 140.   **10.** *Id.* at 397.   **11.** Alan J. Guy, *The Army of the Georges 1714–1783, in* The Oxford History of the British Army, at 92, 97.   **12.** Reid, *supra* at 10.   **13.** *Id.* at 67–69.   **14.** Russell F. Weigley, A History of the United States Army 29 (1984).   **15.** *Id.* at 30, 45–46.   **16.** Articles of Confederation, art. IX, § 5.   **17.** 3 Story's Commentaries § 1178.   **18.** John K. Mahon, History of the Militia and the National Guard 44 (1983).   **19.** Richard H. Kohn, Eagle and Sword: The Federalists and the Creation of the Military Establishment in America, 1783–1802, at 19 (1975).   **20.** *Id.* at 25, 29.   **21.** *Id.* at 29–30.   **22.** *Id.* at 30–32.   **23.** *Id.* at 17.   **24.** Allan R. Millett & Peter Maslowski, For the Common Defense: A Military History of the United States of America 86 (1984); Weigley, at 81.   **25.** Weigley, *supra* at 84.   **26.** 1 Farrand's 287; Kohn, *supra* at 77.   **27.** 2 Farrand's 143.   **28.** Kohn, *supra* at 77.   **29.** *Id.*   **30.** 2 Farrand's 323, 329–30, 633.   **31.** *Id.* at 329 (emphasis added); Kohn, at 77.   **32.** 2 Farrand's 329–30.   **33.** Kohn, *supra* at 78.   **34.** 2 Farrand's 509.   **35.** Reid, *supra* at 4.   **36.** 10 DHRC 1270–71, 1494.   **37.** 2 DHRC 639.   **38.** 3 Elliot's 411.   **39.** 22 DHRC 2088; 30 DHRC 27.   **40.** Storing 2.7.55, 2.9.126.   **41.** 3 Elliot's 389.   **42.** Federalist No. 46 (Madison); Federalist No. 28 (Hamilton).   **43.** William Rawle, A View of the Constitution of the United States of America 123 (1825).   **44.** An Act authorizing the President of the United States to raise a Provisional Army, ch. 47, § 1, 1 Stat. 558, 558 (1798).   **45.** 1 David P. Currie, The Constitution in Congress: The Federalist Period 1789–1801, 248–50 (1997).   **46.** 8 Annals of Cong. 1704–06, 1725–26, 1730, 1733, 1759–60, 1765 (1798).   **47.** 1 St. George Tucker, Blackstone's Commentaries with Notes of Reference to the Constitution and Laws of the Federal Government of the United States and of the Commonwealth of Virginia app. D at 311 (1803).   **48.** 3 Story's Commentaries § 1187.   **49.** Robert Leider, *Deciphering the "Armed Forces of the United States,"* 57 Wake Forest L. Rev. 1195, 1228–34 (2022).   **50.** An Act for Enrolling and Calling Out the National Forces, and for Other Purposes, ch. 75, § 1, 12 Stat. 731, 731 (1863); An Act to Authorize the President to Increase Temporarily the Military Establishment of the United States, Pub. L. No. 65-12, § 2, 40 Stat. 76, 77–78 (1917).   **51.** Leon Friedman, *Conscription and the Constitution: The Original Understanding,* 67 Mich. L. Rev. 1493, 1497–98 (1969); Robert Leider, *Federalism and the Military Power of the United States,* 73 Vand. L. Rev. 989, 1037–50 (2020).   **52.** Prestwich, *supra* at 15.   **53.** *Ex parte Hill,* 38 Ala. 429, 433–44 (1863); *Jeffers v. Fair,* 33 Ga. 347, 349–50 (1862); *Parker v. Kaughman,* 34 Ga. 136, 142–43 (1865); *Simmons v. Miller,* 40 Miss. 19, 22–24 (1864); *Gatlin v. Walton,* 60 N.C. 325, 331–34 (1864); *Ex parte Coupland,* 26 Tex. 386, 392–94 (1862); *Burroughs v. Peyton,* 57 Va. (16 Gratt.) 470, 473–78 (1864).   **54.** *Kneedler v. Lane,* 45 Pa. 238 (1863).   **55.** *Arver v. United States (Selective Draft Law Cases),* 245 U.S. 366, 376–78 (1918).   **56.** *Holmes v. United States,* 391 U.S. 936, 936 (1968); *Id.* at 936–49 (Douglas, J., dissenting); *Hamilton v. Regents of the Univ. of Cal.,* 293 U.S. 245, 265–66 (1934) (Cardozo, J., concurring).   **57.** *Rostker v. Goldberg,* 453 U.S. 57 (1981).   **58.** Nat'l Coal. for Men v. Selective Serv. Sys., 141 S.Ct. 1815 (2021) (Sotomayor, J., statement respecting the denial of certiorari).   **59.** *Rumsfeld v. Forum for Acad. & Institutional Rts., Inc.,* 547 U.S. 47 (2006).

⁓

ESSAY NO. 60: THE NAVY CLAUSE
ART. I, § 8, CL. 13

The Congress shall have Power . . . To provide and maintain a Navy. . . .
—Judge Gregory E. Maggs & Robert Leider

INTRODUCTION

The Navy Clause empowers Congress to "provide and maintain a Navy" without further elaboration or qualification. In Federalist No. 24, Alexander Hamilton explained that this clause gives Congress the ability "to build and equip a fleet" in the "customary and ordinary modes practiced in other governments." The Armies Clause restricts congressional appropriations for land forces to a period of two years.[1] (See Essay No. 59.) The Navy Clause places no time limit on appropriations. Despite vast technological changes, the character of the Navy as a service, unlike that of the Army, has not altered much. Today's sailor has much in common with his predecessor from two centuries ago, technical expertise excepted. The foundation of this Navy was laid by Alexander Hamilton, John Adams, Benjamin Stoddert, and other Federalists who recognized the shortcomings of a navy limited to coastal defense alone. Service reforms beginning in the latter decades of the nineteenth century created the powerful Navy that exists today.

HISTORY BEFORE 1787

The concept of the navy has ancient roots.[2] In antiquity, the Athenian navy had protected the city's democracy.[3] In Great Britain, King Henry VIII created the Royal Navy in 1546.[4] The Royal Navy was used initially to support the army and deter invasion.[5] Later, it protected commerce.[6] While there was great concern about a standing army in Great Britain, there was general acceptance of a permanent navy. It was believed that a standing army could be used domestically against the populace, but a standing navy could serve only to protect the populace from invaders.[7]

Before 1641, King Charles asserted that he had a right under royal prerogative to appropriate funds to develop a navy. However, in 1641,

Parliament firmly overruled that prerogative and asserted that the legislative branch had the power to impose taxes for support of the navy.[8]

John Adams deserves credit as a great patron of the United States Navy. From October 1775 to January 1776, he chaired the Naval Committee of the Continental Congress.[9] In October 1775, he persuaded Congress to begin outfitting ships to defend American interests in the nascent war with Great Britain.[10]

Article IX of the Articles of Confederation expressly empowered Congress "to build and equip a navy."[11] Although the Americans also relied heavily on privateers, the Continental Navy acquired and used about sixty vessels during the Revolutionary War.[12] In June 1785, Congress voted to sell the Continental Navy's one remaining ship.[13] The fledgling nation then had only a fleet of small Treasury Department revenue cutters.[14]

THE CONSTITUTIONAL CONVENTION

At the Constitutional Convention, there was substantial concern about the risks posed by a standing army, and the delegates limited any appropriation for the Army to a period of two years. The federal government's power over the Navy was far less controversial.

On August 6, 1787, the Committee of Detail presented a draft clause that was similar to Article IX of the Articles of Confederation. The draft gave Congress the power "[t]o build and equip fleets."[15] On August 18, the Convention agreed to revise this language slightly. Elbridge Gerry of Massachusetts proposed "'to provide & maintain a navy' . . . as a more convenient definition of the power."[16] This text was adopted without any dissent.

This text reflects two implicit choices. First, the Framers followed the English model. They made creating the navy a legislative rather than an executive function. Second, they decided that the United States could have a standing navy. The Founding generation was well versed in ancient and European history.[17] They were apparently aware of the English view that armies, not navies, were the preferred tools of tyrants; Madison explained in Federalist No. 41 that the people should not fear a standing navy in the way that they might fear a standing army because "[t]he batteries most capable of repelling foreign enterprises on our safety, are happily such as can never be turned by a perfidious government against our liberties."

THE RATIFICATION DEBATES

In the *Federalist Papers*, Alexander Hamilton and James Madison offered three distinct arguments for having a federal navy. In Federalist No. 11, Hamilton asserted that a navy would be a "resource for influencing the conduct of European nations towards us." He explained that without a navy, "[a] nation, despicable by its weakness, forfeits even the privilege of being neutral." In Federalist No. 34, Hamilton wrote that a navy would protect commercial shipping. "[I]f we mean to be a commercial people," Hamilton observed, "it must form a part of our policy to be able one day to defend that commerce." Finally, in Federalist No. 41, Madison explained that a navy would be "a principal source of . . . security against danger from abroad."

Anti-Federalists disputed the notion that the navy would actually defend American commerce or guarantee American neutrality. Instead, they claimed, establishing a navy would provoke the European powers and invite war.[18] For example, William Grayson argued during the Virginia ratifying convention that "maintaining a navy" would "irritate the nations of Europe against us."[19] Anti-Federalists were also concerned about the expense of maintaining a navy and the distribution of that expense. Melancton Smith argued at the New York ratifying convention that building a navy would be

"wild and ridiculous."[20] Grayson contended that the South would have to pay its share for a navy but that the navy would not appreciably reduce the vulnerability of southern ports.[21]

EARLY PRACTICE

In the first two decades after ratification, American merchantmen increasingly found themselves at the mercy of British and French warships and the pirates of the Barbary States.[22] In 1798, President Adams appointed Benjamin Stoddert as the first Secretary of the Navy.[23] Under Stoddert, the new department grew rapidly.[24]

The Navy enabled the United States to hold its own in the Quasi-War with France (1798–1800).[25] President Adams and former Secretary of the Treasury Alexander Hamilton disagreed vehemently on the need to raise an army during this war,[26] but they agreed on the value of a strong navy. Adams had long argued that the Army was less necessary than the Navy because he believed that the United States was best protected by the "wooden walls" of a well-funded navy.[27]

President Thomas Jefferson, whose term began in 1801, believed differently. In his view, attempting to build a navy to match those of European nations "would be a foolish and wicked waste of the energies of our countrymen."[28] Accordingly, under his Administration, the Navy remained largely unfunded.[29] A decade later, the United States was forced to fight the War of 1812 with a dilapidated navy that had "half a dozen frigates, and six or eight sloops and brigs."[30] Nevertheless, older American frigates like the U.S.S. *Constitution* from 1797 performed extraordinary feats.[31]

Starting with the Administration of James Monroe in 1817, American views changed. Secretary of State John Quincy Adams urged an expansion of the U.S. Navy.[32] Since then, there has been an unbroken consensus that a strong navy is essential to the preservation of American liberty.[33]

OPEN QUESTION

- Essay No. 59 discussed whether conscription was permissible in the Army. Conscription into the Navy is a separate and more difficult constitutional question. For centuries, the British government would conscript, or impress, seamen into naval service.[34] There was a long-standing debate about whether pressing sailors was lawful and constitutional or whether it was illegal but tolerated by necessity.[35] American jurists similarly debated whether the British precedent of impressing seamen into naval service would support a broad congressional power to conscript citizens for naval service.[36] Would this practice be constitutional?

Cite as: Judge Gregory E. Maggs & Robert Leider, *The Navy Clause*, in THE HERITAGE GUIDE TO THE CONSTITUTION 213 (Josh Blackman & John G. Malcolm eds., 3d ed. 2025).

Notes

1. Art. I, § 8, cl. 12.   **2.** Arthur MacCartney Shepard, Sea Power in Ancient History 40 (1924).   **3.** *Id.* at 211.   **4.** David Hannay, A Short History of the Royal Navy 1217–1588, at 36 (1898).   **5.** *Id.* at 16–18.   **6.** *Id.* at 206.   **7.** Sarah Kinkel, *Disorder, Discipline, and Naval Reform in Mid-Eighteenth-Century Britain*, 128 Eng. Hist. Rev. 1451, 1453 (2013).   **8.** *Ship Money*, Encyclopedia Britannica, https://perma.cc/KA9W-EVJL.   **9.** F.E. Cross, *The Father of the American Navy*, 53 U.S. Naval Inst. Proceedings 1296 (1927).   **10.** 3 J. Cont. Cong. 293–94 (Oct. 13, 1775).   **11.** Articles of Confederation, art. IX, § 5.   **12.** U.S. Navy, Naval History and Heritage Command, *Vessels of the Continental Navy* (published Aug. 23, 2017), https://perma.cc/GY4P-C6FD.   **13.** Louis Arthur Norton, *Alliance—The Last Navy Continental Frigate*, 22 Naval Hist. 60 (2008).   **14.** C. Douglas Kroll, *Prologue: A Historical Overview of the U.S. Revenue Cutter Service, 1790–1898*, in The Fighting Coast Guard: America's Maritime Guardians in the Twentieth Century 29–30 (Mark Snell ed., 2022).   **15.** 2 Farrand's 182.   **16.** *Id.* at 330.   **17.** Richard M. Gummere, The Classical Ancestry of the United States Constitution, 14 Am. Quarterly 3, 4–5 (1962).   **18.** Marshall Smelser, *Whether to Provide and Maintain a Navy (1787—1788)*, 83 U.S. Naval Inst. Proceedings 655 (1957).   **19.** 3 Elliot's 428.   **20.** 2 Elliot's 381.   **21.** 3 Elliot's 429.   **22.** David B. Stansbury, *The Quasi-War with France*, 6 Naval History 16 (1992).   **23.** Jonathan R. Dull, American Naval History, 1607–1865: Overcoming the Colonial Legacy 43 (2012).   **24.** *Id.*   **25.** *Id.* at 44, 47.   **26.** David McCullough, John Adams 624–25 (2001).   **27.** *Id.* at 624.   **28.** Denver Brunsman, *De-Anglicization: The Jeffersonian Attack on an American Naval Establishment*, in Anglicizing America: Empire, Revolution, Republic 218 (Ignacio Gallup-Diaz et al. eds., 2015).   **29.** *Id.* at 217.   **30.** Theodore Roosevelt, Naval War of 1812, at 23–24 (1902).   **31.** *Id.* at 48, 83–92.   **32.** Brennan J. Suffern, *Like Father, Like Son*, 38 Naval History (2024), https://perma.cc/YM4V-MEUQ.   **33.** *Id.*   **34.** F.W. Maitland, Constitutional History of England 280 (1920).   **35.** *Id.*; David Hume, *Of Some Remarkable Customs*, in Essays and Treatises on Several Subjects 207 (1758); 2 Thomas Erskine May, The Constitutional History of England Since the Accession of George the Third 272–74 (1863).   **36.** *Kneedler v. Lane*, 3 Grant 465, 518 (Pa. 1863) (Bead, J., dissenting); Roger B. Taney, *Thoughts on the Conscription Law of the United States*, in The Military Draft: Selected Readings on Conscription 209, 213–14 (Martin Anderson ed., 1982).

ESSAY NO. 61: THE MILITARY REGULATIONS CLAUSE
ART. I, § 8, CL. 14

The Congress shall have Power . . . To make Rules for the Government and Regulation of the land and naval Forces. . . .

—Judge Gregory E. Maggs & Robert Leider

INTRODUCTION

The Military Regulations Clause grants Congress the power to "make Rules for the Government and Regulation of the land and naval Forces." Justice Joseph Story described this power as "a natural incident to the . . . powers to make war, to raise armies, and to provide and maintain a navy."[1] Congress has exercised this power in enacting nearly all of the laws that organize and regulate the Department of Defense, Army, Air Force, Coast Guard, Marine Corps, Navy, and Space Force. Congress also has used this power to establish a separate military justice system that includes both courts-martial and appellate courts. The Supreme Court has addressed this system in leading cases. Under modern precedent, members of the armed forces can be subject to a trial by court-martial for offenses regardless of whether the charged offenses are related to their service.

HISTORY BEFORE 1787

Military law has a long history. The Romans, for example, used a military law distinct from their civil law to maintain discipline within their army, arguably contributing greatly to its strength.[2] In England, King Richard I and subsequent kings used the royal prerogative to issue orders regulating the military.[3] Kings also authorized "articles of war" defining offences.[4] In 1661, Parliament adopted Articles of War for the Navy, about nine years after it had first passed rules governing the entire Navy.[5] Parliament's first legislation for the Army was the Mutiny Act of 1689, which established capital punishments for certain offenses.[6] During colonial times, when American troops joined British troops, both followed the then-applicable British articles of war.[7]

In April 1775, shortly after the battles of Lexington and Concord, representatives from the colonies met in Philadelphia as the Second Continental Congress. On June 14, 1775, the Congress created the Continental Army.[8] The same day, Congress also formed a committee that included such leading figures as John Adams and George Washington and charged it with preparing "a dra[f]t of Rules and regulations for the government of the army."[9] The committee proposed sixty-nine "Articles of War" based on British and colonial military laws.[10] These articles were "virtually identical" to those in British law. On June 30, Congress approved these Articles of War, which established a military justice system for the Continental Army.[11] In November, Congress approved a similar set of "Rules for the Regulation of the Navy of the United Colonies."[12] Congress substantially amended the Articles of War on September 20, 1776, to make them more effective by increasing the number of offenses that were punishable and the punishments that were authorized.[13]

The Articles of Confederation also empowered the national legislature to establish regulations for the military. Article IX provided that Congress "shall also have the sole and exclusive right and power of . . . making rules for the government and regulation of the . . . land and naval forces" in service of the United States.[14] Congress exercised this power by making various amendments to the Articles of War.[15] For example, an amendment in 1786 reduced the minimum number of members serving on a general court-martial from thirteen to five to facilitate the trial of offenders in smaller units.[16]

THE CONSTITUTIONAL CONVENTION

During the Constitutional Convention, there was no meaningful disagreement over the legislature's power to regulate the armed forces. The Framers would copy the language from Article IX. On August 18, 1787, with no recorded debate, the delegates approved a clause granting Congress the power to "make rules for the government and regulation of the land and naval forces."[17] James Madison of Virginia observed in his notes that this clause was "added from the existing Articles of Confederation,"[18] which had nearly identical language. The Committee of Style made no significant changes.[19] "Land forces" referred to the Army, and "naval forces" referred to the Navy. A separate provision would give Congress the authority to regulate the militia.[20] (See Essay Nos. 62 and 63.)

THE RATIFICATION DEBATES

During the ratification debates, Congress's power to make rules and regulations for the Army and the Navy appears not to have been controversial. Neither Federalists nor Anti-Federalists said much about it. In Federalist No. 69, Alexander Hamilton mentioned this power during a broader discussion of how the Constitution divided military authority between the President and Congress. He acknowledged that the President is the "Commander in Chief of the army and navy" but said that his power is inferior to that of the "British King" whose power "extends to the *declaring* of war and to the *raising* and *regulating* of fleets and armies." Hamilton observed that all of these powers under the Constitution "would appertain to the Legislature" and not to the Executive.

THE ARTICLES OF WAR

In 1789, the first Congress passed a law that expressly continued the Articles of War in force.[21] These were an amended version of the Articles first adopted by the Continental Congress in 1775 and subsequently amended by it on several occasions. Here Congress invoked its powers under the Military Regulations Clause.

Over the years, the Articles of War were revised from time to time. They provided the military justice system for the Army but did not apply to the Navy.[22] In 1950, Congress adopted the Uniform Code of Military Justice (UCMJ). This system governs all of the armed forces, including the Navy, Marine Corps, Air Force, Space Force, and Coast Guard as well as the Army.[23]

WHO IS SUBJECT TO COURT-MARTIAL?

A court-martial is a military "tribunal convened to determine guilt or innocence and levy appropriate punishment" when a person subject to court-martial jurisdiction is charged with a criminal offense.[24] The U.S. Supreme Court has decided a series of cases involving the question of who can be subjected to a court martial. Under the Articles of War, Congress subjected persons currently on active duty in the armed forces to trial by court-martial for military and naval offenses. *Dynes v. Hoover* (1857) held that the Military Regulations Clause granted Congress this power.[25] In this case, the defendant was charged with "desertion," but was only convicted of "attempted desertion." Nevertheless, the Articles of War did not specifically include an offense of the lesser offense of "attempted desertion." The Court still upheld this conviction. In resolving this narrow issue, the Court carefully explained the broader constitutional basis for courts-martial.

Nearly a century later, the Court found a limit on the Military Regulations Clause. *United States ex rel. Toth v. Quarles* (1955) held that former servicemembers, who were in the military but had completed their military service, could not be subject to trial by court-martial for crimes committed when they were on active duty.[26] The Court explained that Congress's power "'To make Rules' to regulate 'the land and naval Forces' would seem to restrict court-martial jurisdiction to persons who are actually members or part of the armed forces."[27]

Reid v. Covert (1957) held that Congress could not use the Military Regulations Clause to subject the wife of a servicemember to trial by court-martial for a capital offense.[28] The plurality opinion explained that the clause's "natural meaning" does not "extend" Congress's power "to civilians—even though they may be dependents living with servicemen on a military base."[29] *Kinsella v. United States ex rel. Singleton* (1960) further held that the clause also does not allow Congress to subject a dependent to trial by court-martial for a non-capital offense.[30] The Court reasoned that "civilian dependents" are not "included in the term 'land and naval Forces' at all."[31]

WHAT OFFENSES ARE SUBJECT TO COURT-MARTIAL?

Until the Civil War, the Articles of War primarily covered offenses of a military character, such as desertion, disrespect to commanders, and so forth, as opposed to traditional common-law crimes that civilians also might commit.[32] During and after the Civil War, military law expanded to bring more traditional civilian crimes such as robbery, arson, burglary, and rape within the scope of the military justice system.[33]

In "an unbroken line of decisions" from the 1860s until the 1960s, the Supreme Court held that the Constitution authorized Congress to subject a member of the armed forces to trial by court-martial based solely on his or her military status regardless of whether the offense charged had a military character.[34] For example, *Coleman v. Tennessee* (1879) held that a court-martial could try a soldier for murder, an offense that otherwise would be triable in state court.[35] However, *O'Callahan v. Parker* (1969) broke with this long-standing precedent and held that Congress could not use the clause to subject a member of the Armed Forces to trial by court-martial for an offense unless the offense was "service-connected."[36] In that case, an assault and an attempted rape of a civilian off-post and after duty hours was not connected in any way to the soldier's duties.

This holding was short-lived. Two decades later, *Solorio v. United States* (1987) overruled *O'Callahan* and held that no service connection was required if the accused has a military status.[37] The Court read the Military Regulations Clause deferentially: "[D]etermination[] concerning the scope of court-martial jurisdiction over offenses committed by servicemen [is] a matter reserved for Congress."[38]

OPEN QUESTIONS

- The Supreme Court has held that Congress cannot use the Military Regulations Clause to subject civilians to trial by court-martial, but can Congress subject certain classes of military reservists and military retirees to trial by court-martial for conduct that occurs in their civilian life? Lower courts have held that Congress can subject retirees of the regular components to military jurisdiction in their retirements when not serving on active duty.[39]

- Does Congress's power to regulate the armed forces trump the President's powers as Commander-in-Chief?[40] Can Congress limit who the President can select as officers? Can Congress set rules governing the treatment of detainees? President George W. Bush, for example, approved such laws but issued a signing statement that objected to the binding nature of these provisions.[41]

- The Military Regulations Clause gives Congress the power "To make Rules for the Government and Regulation of the land and naval Forces." What is the original public meaning of "Rules," "Government," and "Regulation"? These words are used elsewhere in the Constitution. Do they have a consistent meaning in these other provisions?

Cite as: Judge Gregory E. Maggs & Robert Leider, *The Military Regulations Clause, in* THE HERITAGE GUIDE TO THE CONSTITUTION 215 (Josh Blackman & John G. Malcolm eds., 3d ed. 2025).

Notes

1. 3 Story's Commentaries § 1192.   **2.** C.E. Brand, Roman Military Law 9 (1968).   **3.** 1 William Winthrop, Military Law and Precedents 18 (2d ed. 1920).   **4.** *Id.* at 19; 2 Winthrop at 919–46 (reprinting early British Articles of War).   **5.** 2 William Laird Clowes, The Royal Navy: A History from the Earliest Times to the Present 102–03 (1898).   **6.** 1 Winthrop at 19–20.   **7.** Walter B. Huffman & Richard D. Rosen, Military Law: Criminal Justice & Administrative Process 27 (2018).   **8.** 2 J. Cont. Cong. 89–90 (June 14, 1775).   **9.** *Id.*   **10.** *Id.* at 111–22; Lawrence Morris, Military Justice 14 (2010).   **11.** *Id.* at 111.   **12.** 3 J. Cont. Cong. 378 (Nov. 28, 1775); *id.* at 378–87.   **13.** Huffman & Rosen, *supra* at 30–32.   **14.** Articles of Confederation, art. IX, § 4.   **15.** 1 Winthrop at 22–23.   **16.** *Id.* at 23.   **17.** 2 Farrand's 330.   **18.** *Id.*   **19.** *Id.* at 570.   **20.** Art. I, § 8, cl. 16.   **21.** Act of Sept. 29, 1789, § 4, *reprinted in* 1 *United States Statutes at Large* at 95–96 (Richard Peters, ed. 1845).   **22.** Huffman & Rosen, *supra* at 73.   **23.** 10 U.S.C. § 802.   **24.** *Ortiz v. United States*, 585 U.S. 427, 432 (2018).   **25.** 61 U.S. 65, 79 (1857).   **26.** 350 U.S. 11, 23 (1955).   **27.** *Id.*   **28.** 354 U.S. 1 (1957).   **29.** 354 U.S. 1, 19 (1957) (plurality opinion).   **30.** 361 U.S. 234, 246 (1960).   **31.** *Id.*   **32.** Huffman & Rosen, *supra* at 38; 2 Winthrop at 953–85.   **33.** Huffman & Rosen, *supra* at 40.   **34.** *Solorio v. United States*, 483 U.S. 435, 439 (1987).   **35.** 97 U.S. (7 Otto) 509, 513–14 (1879).   **36.** 395 U.S. 258, 272 (1969).   **37.** 483 U.S. at 436.   **38.** *Id.*   **39.** *Larrabee v. Del Toro*, 45 F.4th 81, 83 (D.C. Cir. 2022).   **40.** Saikrishna Bangalore Prakash, *Deciphering the Commander-in-Chief Clause*, 133 Yale L. J. 1 (2023); Zachary S. Price, *Congress's Power over Military Offices*, 99 Tex. L. Rev. 491 (2021); John Yoo, *Transferring Terrorists*, 79 N.D. L. Rev. 1183, 1202 (2004).   **41.** President's Statement on Signing of H.R. 2863, Dec. 30, 2005, https://perma.cc/2Q4B-CLXZ.

❧

ESSAY NO. 62: THE CALLING FORTH THE MILITIA CLAUSE
ART. I, § 8, CL. 15

The Congress shall have Power . . . To provide for calling forth the Militia to execute the Laws of the Union, suppress Insurrections and repel Invasions. . . .
—Judge Gregory E. Maggs & Robert Leider

INTRODUCTION

On certain occasions, Anglo–American law has recognized that able-bodied civilians may be required to perform military service. Those able-bodied civilians are referred to collectively as the militia. The power to call forth the militia was the power to summon all or part of the able-bodied manpower of the civilian community for emergency military purposes. The power to call forth the militia into federal service was the clearest expression of federal power to conscript citizens for military purposes in land warfare. If the Armies Clause does not support conscription into the Army, the calling-forth power might be the exclusive method for conscription.

HISTORY BEFORE 1787

Until the seventeenth century, England saw no need to maintain a standing army, and the English viewed such an institution as dangerous to civil liberty. Because of its geographic separation from Europe, England relied primarily on its navy for defense.[1] When land forces were needed for specific conflicts abroad, the Crown raised temporary armies, and when war came to England, the Crown could either raise temporary armies or call upon the able-bodied citizenry (the militia) to come to the realm's defense.

The English disliked mandatory military service and largely resisted it. Under traditional international law, war could be classified as either defensive or offensive.[2] England did not recognize a general duty to perform military service in offensive wars. Instead, it recognized only a more limited duty to perform defensive military service.[3] Over the succeeding centuries, Parliament enacted various preventative statutes that prohibited the Crown from calling militiamen outside their counties of residence except in cases of invasion and rebellion.[4]

Similar legal rules applied in England's colonies in America. Service in the militia was generally limited to defensive service within a person's colony.[5] The colonies also frequently limited active service to three months at a time. If the colonies wanted a person to serve a longer period—or if they wanted to send the person on an expedition or offensive operation outside the colony—they had to seek war volunteers.

The result was two tracks of military land service. First, Army service under enlistment contracts was not restricted. Professional soldiers could be used in defensive or offensive wars and could serve at home or abroad. Second, militiamen were liable to serve only in defensive conflicts, and their service was restricted to Britain or, in America, to their colony.

After the Declaration of Independence, the states quickly established their own constitutions, most of which contained clauses that served as predecessors of the U.S. Constitution's Calling Forth the Militia Clause. Under these constitutions, however, the governor typically had the power to call forth the militia, but some states restricted the governor's ability to embody the militia or send them out of state without the consent of the legislature or a privy council. For example, the Delaware Constitution of 1776 provided that "[t]he president, with the advice and consent of the privy council, may embody the militia."[6]

The Articles of Confederation did not empower Congress by itself to call forth the militia, but they did provide that "every state shall always keep up a well regulated and disciplined militia, sufficiently armed and accounted."[7] The Articles further allowed Congress "to make requisitions from each state for its quota" of troops for the Continental Army.[8]

THE CONSTITUTIONAL CONVENTION

During the Constitutional Convention, delegates debated about when the federal government should be allowed to call forth the militia and against whom. An early proposal authorized the federal government "to call forth the force of the Union agst. any member of the Union failing to fulfill its duty under the articles thereof."[9] James Madison of Virginia thought the provision should operate against individuals, not states, because "the use of force agst. a State would look more like a declaration of war, than an infliction of punishment."[10] Elbridge Gerry of Massachusetts additionally expressed concern that "this clause 'ought to be expressed so as the people might not understand it to prevent their being alarmed.'"[11]

Eventually, the Committee on Detail listed, among Congress's enumerated powers, "to (make laws for) call(ing) forth the Aid of the Militia, in order to execute the Laws of the Union, (to) enforce Treaties, (to) suppress Insurrections, and repel invasions."[12] The Convention struck the part about enforcing treaties as duplicative of enforcing federal laws.[13] So amended, the provision was agreed to without dissent.[14]

THE RATIFICATION DEBATES

Debates were more heated in the state ratifying conventions. These debates fell into three categories: the circumstances that would justify deploying the militia, what restrictions should be placed on federal exercise of the power, and the role of the states.

The militia could be used to fight both foreign and domestic enemies. With respect to foreign enemies, there was no significant debate in the state ratifying conventions about the propriety of using the militia to repel invasions. Domestic use of the militia, however, was more controversial.

At the Virginia ratifying convention, Anti-Federalists objected to allowing the federal government to use the militia for law enforcement. Contemporary political thought believed that obedience to the laws should generally be secured by consent, not by force.[15] Patrick Henry feared that allowing the federal government to use the militia (a military force) as the routine method of law enforcement would allow the implementation of oppressive and unconstitutional laws.[16] Moreover, the Constitution did not explicitly provide for civil officers to enforce the law. Madison responded that the clause provided Congress with the power to use the militia when necessary but that, in the ordinary course, the authority to use the militia would not displace civil officers as the principal means of law enforcement. Madison also argued that when resistance overwhelmed civilian authorities, it was better for the militia, a civilian army representative of the people, to enforce the laws than for a standing army of professional soldiers to do so.[17]

The Anti-Federalists were also afraid that Congress might abuse its power to call forth the militia—for example, by marching the militia of Georgia into the New England states.[18] George Mason particularly feared that the federal government might intentionally make militia duty so burdensome that the citizenry would appeal to Congress to raise a large standing army so that they would not have to perform military service.[19] Consequently, Anti-Federalists sought various limitations on this federal power.

When it came to state power, two major issues arose. First, Anti-Federalists sought to interject state governments into the process of calling forth the militia by requiring some form of state-level consent.[20] Second, Anti-Federalists sought assurances that the power to call forth the militia was not exclusive in Congress and that states could still use their militia forces for domestic law enforcement or to suppress insurrections.[21] The Anti-Federalists proposed various amendments to address their objections. As Justice Joseph Story would observe, these amendments "were never duly ratified, and have long since ceased to be felt, as matters of general concern."[22] Story apparently did not think that the Second Amendment principally addressed these concerns.[23] (See Essay No. 164.)

EARLY PRACTICE

Academics have long debated about whether the President's Commander-in-Chief power includes the power to deploy regular forces without Congress's advance consent. (See Essay Nos. 102 and 103.) For the militia, however, the Constitution explicitly grants deployment power to Congress. Initially, Congress exercised the power directly on a case-by-case basis. In 1789, for example, Congress authorized the President to call forth the militia only during that session "for the purpose of protecting the inhabitants of the frontiers of the United States from the hostile incursions of the Indians."[24]

Beginning in 1792, Congress enacted a broad delegation to the President to use the militia for the reasons enumerated in the Constitution. During the congressional debates, the breadth of Congress's delegation to the President created some controversy.[25] In case of invasion, Congress authorized the President "to call forth such number of the militia" as he thought necessary.[26] To respond to insurrections against a state, Congress authorized the President to call forth the militia of other states.[27] And for law enforcement, Congress authorized the President to call forth the militia of the state where the obstruction of the laws was occurring and, if that was insufficient, to call forth the militia of other states.[28]

Congress also imposed significant limitations on the President's authority. When calling forth the militia to repel an invasion, the President would have to call forth the militia "of the state or states most convenient to the place of danger or scene of action."[29] And before the

President could use the militia for domestic law enforcement, he would have to be notified by a judge that the resistance was "too powerful to be suppressed by the ordinary course of judicial proceedings."[30] Thus, in providing for calling forth the militia by statute, Congress addressed earlier Anti-Federalist objections that Congress might march the militia long distances or use the militia as the routine means of enforcing the laws.

CONFLICTS BETWEEN THE STATES AND FEDERAL GOVERNMENT
The militia was split between the national and state governments, and this duality has caused significant problems. During the War of 1812, Federalist governors in Connecticut and Massachusetts opposed the war and refused the President's call to deploy their militias. The Massachusetts Supreme Judicial Court ruled that state commanders-in-chief could determine whether an imminent emergency existed that was sufficient to justify deploying the militia.[31] The states, moreover, refused to place their militia forces under the command of regular army officers.[32] Some militia units refused to pursue the British into Canada, believing that this would be an unconstitutional use of the militia to invade another country.[33]

State interference in national military affairs met strong objections from the federal government. At the conclusion of the War of 1812, Secretary of War James Monroe sent a letter to the Senate rebuking the obstructionist actions of the Federalist governors in New England.[34] Justice Story later noted that if the Massachusetts court's opinion were correct, "the public service must be continually liable to very great embarrassments."[35] *Martin v. Mott* (1827) held that Congress gave the President sole and unreviewable authority to determine when an emergency exists that is sufficient to justify deploying the militia,[36]

PURPOSES OF THE MILITIA
In 1912, Attorney General George W. Wickersham opined that Congress could authorize use of the militia only for the three enumerated purposes: to enforce the laws, suppress insurrections, and repel invasions.[37] This position has become the general legal consensus. The militia might be sent outside the country incidental to repelling an invasion, but it could not be used offensively.[38] However, the consensus has seen occasional dissent. During the War of 1812, some Congressmen argued that Congress could deploy the militia abroad for offensive purposes incidental to its power to declare war.[39]

In the twentieth century, use of the Armies Clause rendered these legal disputes largely moot.[40] (See Essay No. 59.) Congress can now conscript the body of the militia into the Army using the Selective Service System and has effectively required the organized militia of the states (the state Army National Guard forces) to enroll in the Army. By using the Armies Clause, Congress has assumed the power to deploy nonprofessional soldiers abroad for offensive operations, rendering these limitations on the militia effectively nugatory. In addition, because officers and soldiers of the organized militia are also enrolled in the Army, Congress can exercise direct authority over them in their capacity as Army soldiers, bypassing state governmental officers when necessary.

OPEN QUESTIONS
- Although the Constitution expressly permits the federal government to use the militia for domestic law enforcement, it is silent with respect to whether the federal government may use the regular Army and Navy for the same domestic purposes.
- The Supreme Court has never determined the upper limits of Congress's authority to delegate to the President the power to call out the militia.
- It has not been authoritatively determined when Congress has the power to order the militia abroad incidental to fighting a defensive war.

Cite as: Judge Gregory E. Maggs & Robert Leider, *The Calling Forth the Militia Clause, in* THE HERITAGE GUIDE TO THE CONSTITUTION 218 (Josh Blackman & John G. Malcolm eds., 3d ed. 2025).

Notes

1. Ian Beckett, *The Amateur Military Tradition*, *in* The Oxford History of the British Army 385 (David Chandler & Ian Beckett eds., 1996). **2.** E. de Vattel, The Law of Nations 471, 187–91 (Bela Kapossy & Richard Whatmore eds., 2008) (1797). **3.** Correlli Barnett, Britain and Her Army 1509–1970: A Military, Political and Social Survey 41 (1970). **4.** Statute the Second 1326, 1 Edw. 3 c. 5 (Eng.), 1 Statutes of the Realm 255; Militia Act 1776, 16 Geo. 3 c. 3 (Gr. Brit.); F.W. Maitland, The Constitutional History of England 277 (1920). **5.** John K. Mahon, History of the Militia and the National Guard 32 (1983). **6.** Del. Const. of 1776, art. IX; Md. Const of 1776, art. XXXIII; Mass. Const. of 1780, pt. 2, ch. II, § I, art. VII; N.C. Const. of 1776, art. XVIII; Va. Const. of 1776. **7.** Articles of Confederation, art. VI, § 4. **8.** *Id.*, art. IX, § 5. **9.** 1 Farrand's 21. **10.** *Id.* at 54. **11.** *Id.* at 61. **12.** 2 Farrand's 168. **13.** *Id.* at 389–90. **14.** *Id.* at 390. **15.** John Phillip Reid, In Defiance of the Law 103–07 (1981). **16.** 10 DHRC 1300. **17.** *Id.* at 1302–03. **18.** *Id.* at 1269–70. **19.** *Id.* at 1271. **20.** David E. Young, The Origin of the Second Amendment 160, 476 (1995). **21.** *Id.* at 1270. **22.** 3 Story's Commentaries § 1197. **23.** *Houston v. Moore*, 18 U.S. (5 Wheat.) 1, 52–53 (1820) (Story, J., dissenting). **24.** Act of Sept. 29, 1789, ch. 25, § 5, 1 Stat. 95, 96. **25.** David P. Currie, 1 The Constitution in Congress: The Federalist Period 1789–1801, at 160–31 (1997). **26.** Act of May 2, 1792, § 1, 1 Stat. 264, 264. **27.** *Id.* **28.** *Id.*, § 2. **29.** *Id.*, § 1. **30.** *Id.*, § 2 (restriction removed in Act of Feb. 28, 1795, ch. 36, § 2, 1 Stat. 424). **31.** *Op. of Justices*, 8 Mass. 548 (1812). **32.** *Id.* **33.** Russell F. Weigley, History of the United States Army 120 (1967). **34.** Robert Leider, *Federalism and the Military Power of the United States*, 73 Vand. L. Rev. 1011–14 (2020). **35.** 3 Story's Commentaries § 1210. **36.** *Martin v. Mott*, 25 U.S. (12 Wheat.) 19, 28 (1827). **37.** Auth. of President to Send Militia into a Foreign Country, 29 U.S. Op. Atty. Gen. 322 (1912). **38.** *Id.* at 324. **39.** 23 Annals of Congress 735–37, 743–46 (1812). **40.** Leider, *Federalism and the Military Power*, *supra* at 1017–50; Robert Leider, *Deciphering the Armed Forces of the United States*, 57 Wake Forest L. Rev. 1195, 1228–33 (2022).

ESSAY NO. 63: THE MILITIA ORGANIZATION CLAUSE
ART. I, § 8, CL. 16

The Congress shall have Power . . . To provide for organizing, arming, and disciplining, the Militia, and for governing such Part of them as may be employed in the Service of the United States, reserving to the States respectively, the Appointment of the Officers, and the Authority of training the Militia according to the discipline prescribed by Congress. . . .

—Robert Leider & Judge Gregory E. Maggs

INTRODUCTION

The Framers had no conception of the modern armed forces, complete with large reserve forces. In their world, the militia *was* the nation's reserve military force. Because of problems with the militia during and after the Revolutionary War, the Framers agreed that the militia needed to be put on a solid footing, but there were debates about whether the federal or state governments should exercise primary control. As a political compromise, the delegates split control of the militia between the national and state governments. This compromise created political accountability problems that over the ensuing century would leave much of the militia untrained and disorganized.

Beginning in the twentieth century, the federal government largely took over the militia using its powers under the Armies Clause.

(See Essay No. 59.) Congress circumvented state authority over the militia and expanded the federal government's limited deployment power. The complete federal takeover of the militia is "prickly with doubt."[1] Yet the political compromises struck at the Constitutional Convention created such systemic dysfunction in the militia system that the nationalization of all military forces has become well-entrenched.

HISTORY BEFORE 1787

The English militia tradition can be traced back to the Anglo-Saxon *fyrd*.[2] The institution survived the Norman Conquest of England in the eleventh century, and a series of laws were enacted to regulate the militia. The Assize of Arms (1181) and the Statute of Winchester (1285) required all freemen to provide themselves with arms and to obey the call for service.[3]

The term "militia" came into use during the six-teenth century. During this time, the militia was organized nationally, but principal executive control lay with local county officers.[4] The militia was thus "[a] national force, organized by counties."[5]

When the British settled in North America, they brought the militia system with them.[6] In the early days, the British had no significant troop presence in America.[7] At the time, the colonists lacked the manpower and money for professional soldiers.[8] To provide for security, the colonies (except in Quaker Pennsylvania) organized a universal militia system.[9] All able-bodied men were required to provide themselves with arms, and they drilled routinely.[10]

However, a well-disciplined universal mili-tia system would not last long. As the seven-teenth century ended, many colonies faced less danger from Indians and competing European powers.[11] Consequently, more people were exempted from militia service.[12] Over time, training occurred less frequently, if at all.[13] In North Carolina, the militia went inactive for a quarter-century.[14] Many colonies also divided their militia into a volunteer component that received additional training and a general mili-tia that received only perfunctory training.[15] In Massachusetts, the Minutemen were an example of a volunteer unit.[16] For much of the eighteenth century, militia organization would ebb and flow depending on whether war was imminent.[17]

The entire militia was rarely called into active service. Instead, militia musters served as a recruiting ground for military service. Colonies would obtain militiamen for cam-paigns by first seeking volunteers at musters. If enough individuals did not volunteer, then authorities would impose a draft from the gen-eral militia to fill the remaining vacancies.[18] The remaining militiamen would return home.

During the Revolutionary War, the mili-tia performed many valuable functions. The Continental Army was often short of regular soldiers, especially when enlistments expired. In a pinch, the militia could quickly provide temporary soldiers.[19] But there were also many problems with the militia system. Colonial law required the frequent rotation of militia-men, usually after three months. The militia-men would often leave active service almost

as soon as they arrived.[20] American leaders also had significant problems coordinating separate state militias. For example, state mili-tias "were too different from each other to be interchangeable,"[21] and "contentious state militia officers squabbled with each other over relative rank and right of command."[22]

Article VI of the Articles of Confederation required the states to "keep up a well regulated and disciplined militia, sufficiently armed and accoutred."[23] However, after the Revolution, the states largely failed to do this.[24] Worse, during Shays's Rebellion in 1786, many Massachusetts militiamen sided with the rebels.[25] Faced with these deficits, the Constitutional Convention would undertake to strengthen national power over the militia.

THE CONSTITUTIONAL CONVENTION

The delegates to the Constitutional Convention were acutely aware of the shortcomings of the American militia during and after the Revolution. In principle, they widely agreed about the need for greater national control of the militia, but the devil was in the details, and, when it came to the details, there were bitter divisions over how far nationalization should go.

George Mason of Virginia proposed that the federal government should have the power "to make laws for the regulation and discipline of the Militia of the several States reserving to the States the appointment of the Officers."[26] Mason wanted better militia regulation to prevent the federal government from raising a standing army.[27] He "considered uniformity as necessary in the regulation of the Militia throughout the Union."[28]

The Convention fractured on this point. Some delegates, including James Madison of Virginia, wanted plenary federal control of the militia because the militia involved national defense.[29] Others fought for more decentraliza-tion. Several delegates offered proposals that would have preserved state power while still allowing Congress to impose a national sys-tem of militia discipline.[30] Oliver Ellsworth of Connecticut wanted uniformity in arms and discipline but warned against giving "[t]he whole authority over the Militia" to the federal government. He worried that the states "would pine away to nothing after such a sacrifice of power."[31] But Mason's initial compromise proposal largely stuck. With some edits from the Committee on Style, the clause reached its current form.[32]

The militia envisioned by the Constitution was federal in the literal sense with control divided among the national and state governments. The clause gave Congress plenary authority over the organization of the militia. Congress could also govern militiamen who had been called into federal service. The states had power to select the officers, to train the militia according to Congress's direction, and to control the militia when not in federal service. However, the Constitution did not answer many of the controversial questions of the day. For example, it was silent with respect to who would be enrolled in the militia or how frequently militia training should be conducted. These were political judgments left to Congress.

The term "militia" has created "confusion . . . owing to its indiscriminate use to designate both the whole military manpower potential of the country" and "organized military companies."[33] Dictionaries published near the Founding Era often used the second meaning. American lexicographer Noah Webster, whose work the Supreme Court frequently cites, defined the "militia" as "the body of soldiers in a state enrolled for discipline, but not engaged in actual service except in emergencies; as distinguished from regular troops, whose sole occupation is war or military service."[34] Webster further explained that members of the militia are "required by law to attend military exercises on certain days only, but at other times left to pursue their usual occupations."[35] British authors Thomas Dyche and William Pardon, who have also been cited by the Supreme Court, similarly defined the members of the military as a civil defense force "who are casually raised out of the inhabitants upon extraordinary occasions of riots, tumults, invasions &c. [and] who as soon as the disturbance is over return to their respective habitations and employments."[36] Other period dictionaries commonly cited by the Supreme Court provide less detail, briefly defining the "militia" as the "trainbands."[37] But legal usage

often favored the broader meaning. *District of Columbia v. Heller* (2008) observed that the "militia" of this clause was the entire military manpower, which this clause gave Congress the power to organize.[38] Regardless of this important ambiguity, these dictionary definitions agree that the militia was a force comprised of citizens who performed only part-time and emergency military service, as distinguished from regular forces.

THE RATIFICATION DEBATES

During the ratification debates, the Anti-Federalists vigorously attacked Congress's powers over the militia. First, the Anti-Federalists objected to Congress's plenary power to organize the militia. Congress was not obligated to enroll the whole able-bodied population in the militia. Rather, it might create unrepresentative armed factions in society. At the Virginia ratifying convention, George Mason warned that Congress might not organize the militia at all, relying instead on a standing army.[39] Alternatively, Mason stated, Congress might enroll only part of the militia, thereby creating a "select militia."[40] Further, the Constitution gave Congress exclusive power to organize the militia. Mason and Patrick Henry pointed out that the states could not even enroll individuals into the militia on their own authority.[41]

Second, the Anti-Federalists warned that Congress could abuse its power by disarming or refusing to arm the militia. Mason and Henry worried that states had no concurrent power.[42]

Third, the Anti-Federalists were concerned that Congress could abuse its power to provide for militia discipline. Mason and Henry argued that Congress could provide for ignominious and harsh punishments for breaches of militia discipline.[43] It might do this, they feared, to create political support for a standing army. Delegates at the Maryland ratifying convention were concerned that without an additional declaration of rights, Congress could even subject all able-bodied men to military law instead of civilian law.[44] The dissent of the Pennsylvania ratifying convention stated that "the personal liberty of every man probably from sixteen to sixty years of age, may be destroyed by the power Congress ha[s] in organizing and governing of the militia."[45]

Nationalists responded to these fears. James Madison responded that the national government would not likely impose unusually harsh punishments on militiamen.[46] Several Virginians, including Edmund Randolph and Henry Lee III, argued that Congress could not subject the able-bodied civilian population to military law. The federal militia power, they argued, was limited to those times when the militia was in active federal service.[47]

Similarly, with respect to militia organization, the Federalists countered that the Anti-Federalists read the Constitution incorrectly. In the Virginia convention, James Madison and George Nicholas pointed out that states had concurrent power over the militia.[48] John Marshall, the future Chief Justice, observed that if Congress refused to organize or arm the militias, the Constitution did not prevent the states from enacting their own laws concerning the militia.[49] Further, in Federalist No. 46, Madison explained that the militia would remain attached to state governments because, in part, states were empowered to select the officers. Madison contended further that state selection of officers also provided a second chain of military command should the standing army ever be used to usurp the constitutional government.

The Anti-Federalists' concerns led them to propose a variety of constitutional amendments that would have altered the federal–state balance. For example, the Pennsylvania dissent recommended that "the power of organizing, arming and disciplining the militia . . . remain with the individual states."[50] Proposals from the Virginia and North Carolina conventions would have granted states explicit concurrent power over the militia and allowed states to set penalties for violations of militia discipline.[51] These proposals were never adopted.

Other proposed amendments that touched on the militia system were ratified. The Second Amendment guaranteed a general, individual right to bear arms and declared that the militia was "necessary to the security of a free State." (See Essay No. 164.) The Fifth Amendment explicitly required that civilian law and civilian trial procedures apply to militiamen except when those militiamen were in active military service. (See Essay No. 169.)

EARLY PRACTICE

The Militia Act of 1792 required universal enrollment of all white men between the ages of eighteen and forty-five.[52] These individuals were obligated to furnish themselves with muskets and other military equipment.[53] Beyond these meager provisions, early Congresses could not reach consensus on the organization, funding, and discipline of the militia. These disagreements resulted in a disastrous lack of military preparation.

The militia performed poorly during the War of 1812. Following that war, states increasingly added exemptions to militia training and eventually stopped actively enrolling most able-bodied citizens.[54] In place of a universal militia, states began to rely on volunteer militia units. These units were independent fraternal societies, but they would receive charters making them officially government-sponsored militia organizations.[55] The remaining militia was left unorganized and untrained.

The militia system largely lapsed after the Civil War. During the Progressive Era, states reorganized militia units as a means to put down labor strikes.[56] States relied on a volunteer, organized militia, usually labeled the National Guard, alongside an untrained reserve militia, which consisted of the remaining able-bodied men eligible for military service.[57] These state laws were challenged as violations of the Militia Act of 1792 and the constitutional prohibition against states keeping "troops," but the courts rejected these challenges. Importantly, courts held that National Guard units were an organized component of the militia, not "troops," because they were nonprofessional soldiers.[58] In *Houston v. Moore* (1820), a fractured Supreme Court also had ruled that states have concurrent power with the federal government to organize and discipline their militia.[59]

Before the twentieth century, National Guard units were organized at the state level. Both their training and their combat performance were uneven. The Spanish–American war was a watershed for military policy; National Guardsmen volunteered for service, but they performed poorly.[60]

THE MILITIA ACT OF 1903 (THE DICK ACT)

The National Guard's performance during the Spanish-American War led President Theodore Roosevelt to pursue militia reform.[61] In 1903, Congress passed the Dick Act.[62] The act legally separated the militia into an organized and reserve militia. The organized militia would consist of the National Guard and naval militia. The reserve militia (later called the unorganized militia) would consist of remaining able-bodied men who were subject to militia service. Congress also authorized federal funds for the National Guard and naval militia, but only if their units met federal standards. In 1916, Congress required states, as a condition of receiving federal funds, to appoint only militia officers meeting certain standards and to dismiss officers who lose federal recognition.[63]

Congress also looked for ways to evade the limitations of the Calling Forth the Militia Clause, which limited deployment of the militia to domestic defensive conflicts. (See Essay No. 62.) During World War I, Congress authorized direct conscription into the national army. Through a draft into the army, Congress could make National Guardsmen (and other able-bodied men) deployable abroad for any kind of conflict, defensive or offensive.

The Supreme Court upheld conscription in the army. The Court found that the Militia Organization Clause does not limit Congress's power to deploy individuals abroad as soldiers in the army.[64] Through conscription into the national army, the Supreme Court authorized Congress to access the entire body of the militia for military purposes without obeying the constitutional limitations of either the Calling Forth Clause or the Militia Organization Clause.

DUAL ENLISTMENT

As applied to the National Guard, conscription created special problems. Under legislation from World War I, National Guardsmen were relieved of their status as "militia" upon being conscripted into the federal army. The Guardsmen did not automatically return to the militia when their service in the army was over.[65] Moreover, they were selected as individuals rather than as units.

To fix these problems, Congress created a system of "dual enlistment" in 1933.[66] This system required National Guardsmen to enlist in two coextensive organizations: the National Guard of their state, which was the organized militia of the state, and "the National Guard of the United States," which was a component of the Army Reserve.[67]

Under the dual enlistment system, the Militia Clauses do not have much practical application. Using its constitutional power to raise armies, Congress may activate entire units of the National Guard and send them abroad for offensive wars in their capacity as Army Reserve soldiers. The federal government also trains much of the militia in their capacity as officers and soldiers in the U.S. Army Reserve or U.S. Air Force Reserve. In theory at least, states formally commission militia officers, but in practice, the federal government exercises nearly plenary *de facto* control of the appointment of officers. It can even force states to dismiss militia officers who lose federal recognition.[68]

The Supreme Court effectively upheld the constitutionality of dual enlistment in *Perpich v. Department of Defense* (1990).[69] In that case, the federal government ordered National Guardsmen to train in Central America. Governors, however, tried to veto these missions. Congress responded by eliminating the authority of governors to veto Guard training on political grounds. The governors challenged this action but did not contest the constitutionality of dual enlistment. The Supreme Court upheld Congress's power to eliminate the governors' veto authority. The Constitution did not require governors to have a veto power over National Guard training, and Congress had the authority to require Guardsmen to train abroad in their capacity as soldiers in the Army Reserve.[70]

OPEN QUESTIONS

- Is *Perpich* correct as an originalist matter? The Supreme Court explained that Guardsmen were militiamen because they were nonprofessional soldiers. The Court did not explain, however, how these nonprofessional soldiers could also be soldiers in the "armies," a term that the Constitution arguably uses to denote the regular forces.[71] As both militiamen and army soldiers, Guardsmen occupy two arguably inconsistent legal statuses.[72]

- States have a power with the federal government to organize their militia. Can states *override* federal militia legislation? Before *District of Columbia v. Heller* (2008),[73] many courts held that the Second Amendment gave states such a preclusive authority, but in military law cases, courts have uniformly upheld federal supremacy.[74] The Supreme Court has never settled the limits of federal power over the militia.

Cite as: *Robert Leider & Judge Gregory E. Maggs, The Militia Organization Clause, in* THE HERITAGE GUIDE TO THE CONSTITUTION 222 (Josh Blackman & John G. Malcolm eds., 3d ed. 2025).

Notes

1. S.T. Ansell, *Legal and Historical Aspects of the Militia*, 26 Yale L.J. 471, 480 (1917).   2. James Biser Whisker, *The Citizen-Soldier Under Federal and State Law*, 94 W. Va. L. Rev. 947, 952 (1992).   3. Assize of Arms 1181, 27 Hen. 2, §§ 1–2 (Eng.); Statute of Winchester 1285, 13 Edw. c. 6 (Eng.).   4. Robert Leider, *Deciphering the Armed Forces of the United States*, 57 Wake Forest L. Rev. 1195, 1219 (2022).   5. F.W. Maitland, The Constitutional History of England 276 (1920).   6. John K. Mahon, History of the Militia and the National Guard 6 (1983).   7. *Id.* at 24.   8. Russell F. Weigley, A History of the United States Army 4 (1984).   9. *Id.* at 3–4.   10. Mahon, *supra* at 14–18; Robert L. Goldich, *Historical Continuity in the U.S. Military Reserve System*, 7 Armed Forces & Soc'y 88, 91–92 (1980).   11. Jerry Cooper, The Rise of the National Guard: The Evolution of the American Militia, 1865–1920, at 3 (1997).   12. Mahon, *supra* at 18; E. Milton Wheeler, *Development and Organization of the North Carolina Militia*, 41 N. Carolina Hist. Rev. 307, 309–10, 315–17, 319–20 (1964).   13. William L. Shea, The Virginia Militia in the Seventeenth Century 133–35 (1983).   14. Wheeler, *supra* at 311.   15. Weigley, *supra* at 8.   16. *Id.* at 8.   17. Mahon, *supra* at 18.   18. *Id.*; Mahon, *supra* at 19–20; Cooper, *supra*, at 2J.   19. Mahon, *supra* at 44.   20. *Id.* at 19.   21. *Id.* at 36.   22. Cooper, *supra* at 5.   23. Articles of Confederation, art. VI, § 4.   24. 2 Farrand's 387.   25. Leonard L. Richards, Shays's Rebellion: The American Revolution's Final Battle 11–12 (2002).   26. 2 Farrand's 330, 326.   27. *Id.* at 326.   28. *Id.* at 330.   29. *Id.* at 331–32.   30. *Id.* at 385–86.   31. *Id.* at 331.   32. *Id.* at 570, 595.   33. Weigley, *supra*, at 321.   34. Noah Webster, An American Dictionary of the English Language (1828), https://perma.cc/W4A4-XZXK.   35. *Id.*   36. Thomas Dyche & William Pardon, A New General English Dictionary (18th ed. 1781).   37. Samuel Johnson, A Dictionary of the English Language (10th ed. 1792), https://perma.cc/V2ZK-2VB2; 1 John Ash, New and Complete Dictionary of the English Language (1775); James Barclay, Complete and Universal English Dictionary (1792); 2 Thomas Sheridan, A Complete Dictionary of the English Language (3d ed. 1790); John Walker, A Critical Pronouncing Dictionary (1791); 2 Timothy Cunningham, A New and Complete Law-Dictionary (1764); Thomas Potts, A Compendious Law Dictionary (1803).   38. 554 U.S. 570, 596 (2008).   39. 10 DHRC 1272.   40. *Id.* at 1312–13.   41. *Id.* at 1270, 1276, 1306.   42. *Id.* at 1270, 1276.   43. *Id.* at 1289, 1301, 1304, 1312.   44. 2 The Bill of Rights: A Documentary History 729, 734 (Bernard Schwartz ed., 1971).   45. Storing 3.11.52.   46. 10 Documentary History of the Ratification of the Constitution 1303.   47. *Id.* at 1280, 1288, 1294, 1301.   48. *Id.* at 1280, 1304.   49. *Id.* at 1307, 1308.   50. Storing 3.11.13.   51. 10 DHRC 1550, 1554; 30 DHRC 456.   52. Act of May 8, 1792, ch. 33, 1 Stat. 271 (repealed 1903).   53. *Id.* § 2.   54. Frederick B. Wiener, *The Militia Clause of the Constitution*, 54 Harv. L. Rev. 181, 188–91 (1940); Mahon, *supra* at 81–82; *Perpich v. Dep't of Def.*, 496 U.S. 334, 341 (1990).   55. Cooper, *supra* at 15–16.   56. *Id.* at 23–24.   57. *Id.* at 44.   58. *State ex rel Madigan v. Wagener*, 77 N.W. 424, 425 (Minn. 1898); *Smith v. Wanser*, 52 A. 309, 312–13 (N.J. 1902); *Alabama Great S. R.R. Co. v. United States*, 49 Ct. Cl. 522, 537–38 (1914); Wiener, *supra* at 216–17.   59. Houston v. Moore, 18 U.S. 1 (1820).   60. Cooper, *supra* at 96–98, 108.   61. Leider, *supra* at 1227–32.   62. Militia Act of 1903 (Dick Act), ch. 196, 32 Stat. 775.   63. Act of June 3, 1916, 39 Stat. 166; Wiener, *supra* at 200–01.   64. *Arver v. United States (Selective Draft Law Cases)*, 245 U.S. 366, 376–78 (1918); *Cox v. Wood*, 247 U.S. 3, 4 (1918).   65. *Perpich*, 496 U.S. at 345; Wiener, *supra* at 208.   66. Wiener, *supra* at 207–09.   67. National Guard Act of 1933, Pub. L. No. 73–64, ch. 87, § 1, 48 Stat. 153.   68. Leider, *supra* at 1238–39.   69. *Perpich*, 496 U.S. at 347.   70. *Id.* at 349–52.   71. *Id.* at 348.   72. Robert Leider, *Federalism and the Military Power of the United States*, 73 Vand. L. Rev. 989, 1017–35 (2020).   73. 554 U.S. 570 (2008).   74. J. Norman Heath, Exposing the Second Amendment: Federal Preemption of State Militia Legislation, 79 Univ. Det. Mercy L. Rev. 39 (2001).

~

ESSAY NO. 64: THE FEDERAL DISTRICT CLAUSE
ART. I, § 8, CL. 17

The Congress shall have Power . . . To exercise exclusive Legislation in all Cases whatsoever, over such District (not exceeding ten Miles square) as may, by Cession of particular States, and the Acceptance of Congress, become the Seat of the Government of the United States. . . .

—Lee A. Casey

INTRODUCTION

The Framers of the Constitution recognized the need for a dedicated seat of government. The location of that district, however, would prove contentious. Through negotiations by Thomas Jefferson, James Madison, and Alexander Hamilton, the federal District of Columbia was sited along the Potomac River between Maryland and Virginia. The District has been governed directly by Congress and through home rule. But, to this day, residents of the District cannot elect members to Congress. Only through the Twenty-Third Amendment was the District afforded electoral votes. Debates continue about whether statehood for the District of Columbia would be constitutional. The courts, however, have rejected challenges to the lack of representation in Congress.

HISTORY

In June 1783, several hundred unpaid and angry Continental soldiers had menaced the Confederation Congress in Philadelphia. Pennsylvania refused all requests for assistance by the government pursuant to the Articles of Confederation. Congress then adjourned, and its members fled into New Jersey. The incident made a lasting impression. During the Constitutional Convention, the Federal District Clause was adopted unanimously and without debate.[1]

In Federalist No. 43, James Madison explained the need for a "federal district," subject to Congress's exclusive jurisdiction and separate from the territory and authority of any single state. Without having "compleat authority at the seat of government," Madison wrote, "the public authority might be insulted and its proceedings interrupted, with impunity." Moreover, if the "general government" became dependent on a state, that "might bring on the national councils an imputation of awe or influence . . . dissatisfactory to the other members of the Confederacy."

The Anti-Federalist Federal Farmer noted the incident in 1783 as the event that "first gave rise" to the notion of an independent federal town.[2] Anti-Federalists persisted in visualizing the federal seat of government as a sink of corruption and nursery for tyrants.[3] The Federalists, however, believed that our federal system itself necessitated a territory where the general government exercised full sovereignty, not beholden to any state.

LOCATION AND GOVERNANCE

The new capital's location was a contentious issue—far more contentious than the question of its necessity. New York and Pennsylvania were desperate for the plum, and the First Congress wrangled over the issue. The resultant Compromise of 1790, reached over Jefferson's dinner table by Madison, Hamilton, and the Sage of Monticello himself, provided for a southern site near the fall line of the Potomac River. In exchange, the southern states agreed to Hamilton's proposal that the new federal government should assume the states' Revolutionary War debts.[4] Maryland and Virginia ceded "ten miles square" on their respective sides of the river. In December 1800, shortly before Jefferson's inauguration, the government moved to its permanent seat. An Act Concerning the District of Columbia[5] organized the new capital.

In 1846, Congress returned, or *retroceded*, Virginia's portion of the original ten square miles, calculating that it "has not been, nor is ever likely to be," necessary for the seat of government.[6] The constitutionality of this act was highly dubious. But in *Phillips v. Payne* (1875), the U.S. Supreme Court dismissed a challenge brought by a Virginia taxpayer for lack of standing and affirmed the "*de facto* condition of things."[7]

Over time, Congress has experimented with varying methods of home rule for the District. From 1800 to 1871, the District's local government was "municipal" and largely administrative in character with Congress retaining legislative power.[8] In 1871, Congress created a "Legislative Assembly" for the District, but this initial experiment ended in 1874 when the "District's 'corrupt and debt-ridden' government" was replaced with an appointed Board of Commissioners. Commission government continued in one form or another until Congress established home rule in 1973. Up to that time, with the exception of the brief Legislative Assembly, Congress acted as the District's legislature. The District now has an elected mayor and city council. The D.C. City Council exercises legislative authority in the District, although it remains subject to Congress's ultimate authority.[9]

Today, the most controversial aspect of Congress's authority over the District is the fact that its residents cannot elect members to that body. The Twenty-Third Amendment gave the District the right to participate in presidential elections but not in congressional elections. Instead, the residents elect a non-voting "delegate" to the House of Representatives.

This was not an oversight. The Framers did not provide such voting rights for the District's inhabitants because of the District's unique character as the federal city. In exchange, however, it was argued that they would enjoy the benefits of the national capital. As Justice Joseph Story noted, "there can be little doubt, that the inhabitants composing [the District] would receive with thankfulness such a blessing, since their own importance would be thereby increased, their interests be subserved, and their rights be under the immediate protection of the representatives of the whole Union."[10]

Efforts to change this original design continue, including a proposed 1977 constitutional amendment that would have granted the District of Columbia congressional voting representation "as if it were a state." This amendment was not ratified, and legislative proposals to achieve the same result have not commanded the necessary support in Congress—and would be vulnerable to constitutional challenge even if enacted.

THE QUESTION OF STATEHOOD

Statehood is the clear preference of District voting-rights advocates. Congress has considered several bills introduced to this end. During the 117th Congress (2021–2023), H.R. 51 was approved by the House but not the Senate. H.R. 1, which included a series of findings relating to D.C. statehood, was also introduced but died when the 117th Congress ended in January 2023.[11] Together, these bills evidence both the form the new state would take and the legal theory propounded by statehood advocates. First, the Admissions Clause gives Congress the power to admit new states. (See Essay No 143.) Second, the Federal District Clause gives Congress the power to "reduce the size of the seat of the Government." Third, Congress would shrink the size of the District to the areas immediately surrounding Capitol Hill, the National Mall, and the White House. Fourth, Congress could then admit as a new state all other areas that were formerly part of the District of Columbia.

H.R. 1 is similar in effect to a 1963 plan that would have retroceded most of the District to Maryland while retaining a rump "seat of government." At that time, Attorney General Robert F. Kennedy gave Congress a memorandum explaining that the proposal would be both impractical and constitutionally suspect. Kennedy concluded that "[a] persuasive argument can be made that article I, section 8, clause 17 of the Constitution established, as a permanent part of our constitutional system, a Federal District constituting the seat of the government, having a substantial area and population."[12]

This conclusion was based on the Federal District Clause's text. The Constitution contemplated a "single act" to create the District by accepting the state cessions but "makes no provision for revocation of the act of acceptance or for retrocession."[13] Moreover, the purpose of this provision was to establish a federal district "large enough to serve as the location of a capital city having substantial population."[14] "Reduction of the District to [a] small strip of territory occupied almost wholly by federal buildings is thus clearly inconsistent with the concept of the Federal City held by the framers."[15] The Kennedy Memorandum also noted that the constitutionality of retrocession, including the 1846 Virginia enactment, has never been settled by "any authoritative precedent."[16] As noted above, the Supreme Court dodged the question in *Philips v. Payne*.

The Kennedy Memorandum also raised the critical issue of the Twenty-Third Amendment, which states that "[t]he District constituting the seat of Government of the United States shall appoint in such manner as Congress may direct" at least three presidential electors. (See Essay No. 210.) The Twenty-Third Amendment's text is mandatory—the District "shall appoint"—and was adopted with reference to the District of Columbia as it existed in 1961. Congress cannot now dismember that entity, creating a new state and reducing the seat of government to a collection of public buildings, museums, and parks devoid of any meaningful resident population. "[I]t would be hard to imagine a result more opposed to our basic political traditions" than permitting the Congress, the incumbent President, or both to appoint three presidential electors.[17]

JUDICIAL PRECEDENT

In more recent years, the courts have rejected a series of arguments suggesting that the District's inhabitants, on various constitutional and policy grounds, are entitled to voting representation in Congress without an amendment. In *Adams v. Clinton* (2000), the plaintiffs argued that the Equal Protection and Guarantee Clauses require that District residents be given the right to vote for members of Congress. (See Essay Nos. 147 and 196.) The district court rejected this position, concluding that "it *is* the Constitution itself that is the cause of plaintiffs' voting disability."[18] The Constitution, in other words, cannot itself be unconstitutional. *Castañon v. United States* (2020) reaffirmed that the District's lack of voting representation in the House of Representatives did not violate the Constitution. The district court noted that "[d]espite their protestations to the contrary, Plaintiffs *do* seek to establish that the Constitution is unconstitutional."[19] Both of these cases were summarily affirmed by the Supreme Court without an opinion.

Thus, so far, efforts to find a constitutional basis on which to require enfranchisement of the District of Columbia's residents in congressional elections have failed. It is true that the courts have not addressed the key question whether Congress can, without an amendment, admit the District to the Union as a state. Statehood proponents still face an uphill battle, since an independent federal territory with a meaningfully populated capital city controlled by Congress as the seat of government was a critical part of the Framers' original notion of an indestructible federal union of indestructible states.

Cite as: Lee A. Casey, *The Federal District Clause*, in THE HERITAGE GUIDE TO THE CONSTITUTION 228 (Josh Blackman & John G. Malcolm eds., 3d ed. 2025).

Notes

1. 2 Farrand's 117, 505, 509, 510   2. Storing 2.8.222.   3. 3 Elliot's 399–402.   4. Jacob E. Cooke, *The Compromise of 1790*, 27 Wm. & Mary Q. 523 (1970).   5. 2 Stat. 103 (1801).   6. An Act to Retrocede the County of Alexandria, in the District of Columbia, to the State of Virginia, 9 Stat. 35 (1846).   7. 92 U.S. 130, 134 (1875).   8. *Metropolitan R. Co. v. Dist. of Columbia*, 132 U.S. 1, 3–6 (1889).   9. *In re Crawley*, 978 A.2d 608, 611–12 (D.C. App. 2009).   10. 3 Story's Commentaries § 1214.   11. H.R. 1, 117th Cong., § 2201(8).   12. Constitutionality of Retroceding the District of Columbia to Maryland, in Hearings Before Subcommittee No. 6 of the Committee on The District of Columbia, House of Representatives, 88th Cong. 125 (1964).   13. *Id.* at 128.   14. *Id.* at 126.   15. *Id.* at 131.   16. *Id.*   17. *Id.* at 132.   18. 90 F. Supp. 2d 35, 62 (D.D.C. 2000), aff'd 531 U.S. 941 (2000) (mem.).   19. 444 F. Supp. 3d 118, 144 (D.D.C. 2020), aff'd 142 S.Ct. 56 (2021) (mem.).

~

ESSAY NO. 65: THE FEDERAL ENCLAVE CLAUSE
ART. I, § 8, CL. 17

The Congress shall have Power To . . . exercise like Authority over all Places purchased by the Consent of the Legislature of the State in which the Same shall be, for the Erection of Forts, Magazines, Arsenals, dock-Yards, and other needful Buildings. . . .

—Lee A. Casey

INTRODUCTION

The Federal District Clause grants Congress "exclusive" legislative authority over the permanent seat of government, which in 1800 was established as the District of Columbia. (See Essay No. 64.) The Federal Enclave Clause grants Congress "like Authority" over certain federal installations, both military and civilian. Today, these federal "enclaves" include such varying areas and establishments as the National Institutes of Health in Bethesda, Maryland, and Kennedy Space Center in Cape Canaveral, Florida. This power also extends to "other needful buildings." The U.S. Supreme Court has defined this category to include locks, dams, federal courts, customs houses, post offices, and "whatever [other] structures are found to be necessary in the performance of the functions of the Federal Government."[1]

Questions remain about what substantive law applies in any given federal enclave and whether jurisdiction lies with state or federal governments. The Supreme Court has explained that "the grant of 'exclusive' legislative power to Congress . . . bars state regulation without specific congressional action,"[2] but in practice, the situation is far more complex.

THE CONSTITUTIONAL CONVENTION

Like the Federal District Clause, the Federal Enclave Clause's purpose was to accommodate and guarantee the independence of both federal and state sovereignties. During the Constitutional Convention, an early version of the Federal Enclave Clause gave Congress the power "to exercise like authority [*i.e.*, exclusive legislative authority as in the Federal District Clause] over all places purchased for the erection of Forts, Magazines, Arsenals, Dock-Yards, and other needful buildings."[3] Elbridge Gerry of Massachusetts objected to this language. He warned that it gave Congress a sweeping authority over any property purchased from the states, that this power "might be made use of to enslave any particular State by buying up its territory, and that the strongholds proposed would be a means of awing the State into an undue obedience to the Gen'l Government."[4]

Gerry's concern was assuaged by the timely addition of language requiring state consent to such establishments.[5] In the final version, the Federal Enclave Clause would grant Congress authority only where the property was "purchased by the Consent of the Legislature of the State."

THE RATIFICATION DEBATES

The addition of a state consent requirement did not satisfy all critics. At the Virginia convention, Patrick Henry warned that the Federal Enclave Clause would effectively eliminate state power. He warned that the federal "garrisons, magazines, arsenals, and forts, which will be situated in the strongest places within the states . . . will reduce the power of the latter to nothing." Henry also warned that the "ten miles square" district with "all the fine ornaments of human life," would only "add[] to [the federal government's] powers."[6] John Tyler Sr., the father of the future President John Tyler, worried that criminals "might take refuge in the sanctuary of the ten miles square, and [in] the strongholds . . . [where] the states had no power to punish them."[7] An exasperated James Madison responded that these concerns were exaggerated and suggested that "the gentleman [should] read the clauses" again as "he might see that nothing could be done without the consent of the states."[8]

Madison offered a somewhat fuller justification in Federalist No. 43. He acknowledged that "[t]he public money expended on such places, and the public property deposited in them, require that they should be exempt from the authority of the particular state." It would not "be proper for the places on which the security of the entire union may depend, to be in any degree dependent on a particular [state]." Madison sought to address any lingering concerns: "All objections and scruples are here also obviated by requiring the concurrence of the states concerned, in every such establishment."

Other state conventions expressed concern over federal enclaves. The New York ratifying convention proposed an amendment to the Constitution: the Federal Enclave Clause could not be "construed to authorize the Congress to make any law to prevent the laws of the states in which they may lie, from extending to such places in all civil and criminal matters, except as to such persons as shall be in the service of the United States."[9] In other words, state law would apply fully in federal enclaves to everyone *except* federal officers. This amendment was not adopted.

CESSION AND REGULATION OF FEDERAL ENCLAVES

A federal enclave can be created at the time a state joins the Union. Congress can reserve exclusive legislative authority over a particular area as a condition of admission. Or a federal enclave can be created—like the District of Columbia—by a state legislature's cession of both territory and exclusive legislative authority to Congress and Congress's acceptance of that authority.[10] A state may separately consent to a transfer of its legislative jurisdiction over land the federal government has purchased or taken through eminent domain proceedings for its own use, thus "complet[ing] the 'exclusive' jurisdiction of the Federal Government over such an enclave. . . ."[11]

States retain some authority to regulate federal enclaves. Specifically, states may reserve various authorities at the time they cede the area to the federal government. These authorities

can even include concurrent legislative power with the federal government as long as Congress consents.[12] Most states have reserved at least the right in federal enclaves to deliver civil and criminal legal documents: that is, serving process. Apart from such reservations, within the enclave, state law as it existed at the time of a cession continues in force. This state law functions as a species of federal law unless and until Congress enacts changes.[13]

Paul v. United States (1963) considered the status of a state regulation over a federal enclave that Congress did not expressly reject. The Supreme Court held that such state regulatory programs will continue to apply in an enclave as long as the "basic state law authorizing" the program was in effect at the time of cession, even if there are subsequent updates.[14] As a general matter, a state's powers over a federal enclave depend on the terms of the original cession, but federal enclave residents are entitled to vote as residents of the surrounding state no matter what the terms of the original cession.[15]

Congress began to regulate federal enclaves from the start with the Federal Crimes Act of 1790. Beginning in 1825, a series of Assimilative Crimes Acts affirmatively adopted existing state criminal laws within federal enclaves as federal law, and after 1948, state criminal law enacted after the date of cession would still become federal law governing that enclave. *United States v. Sharpnack* (1958) upheld this adoption of *future* state laws against constitutional attack on improper delegation of congressional authority grounds.[16] Under the "Federal Enclave Doctrine," individuals working in federal enclaves generally cannot bring certain tort cases or state statutory employment and employment discrimination causes of action.[17]

JURISDICTION OVER FEDERAL ENCLAVES

As a general matter, state courts do not have jurisdiction over federal enclaves. Rather, federal enclaves are subject to the "special maritime and territorial jurisdiction of the United States."[18] That is, these enclaves are treated in the same fashion as federal territories such as Puerto Rico or Guam are treated. As a result, criminal offenses committed within an enclave are subject to federal prosecution in federal court.

However, these prosecutions have a unique wrinkle, as the substantive offense may well be grounded in the surrounding state's law pursuant to the Assimilative Crimes Act.[19] Federal prosecutors can choose to bring charges under federal or state law based on whether "federal law indicates [a congressional] intent to punish conduct such as the defendant's to the exclusion of the particular state statute at issue."[20]

Cite as: Lee A. Casey, *The Federal Enclave Clause, in* THE HERITAGE GUIDE TO THE CONSTITUTION 231 (Josh Blackman & John G. Malcolm eds., 3d ed. 2025).

Notes

1. *James v. Dravo Contracting Co.*, 302 U.S. 134, 143 (1937). **2.** *Paul v. United States*, 371 U.S. 245, 263 (1963). **3.** 2 Farrand's 505. **4.** *Id.* at 510. **5.** *Id.* **6.** 3 Elliot's 83. **7.** *Id.* at 419. **8.** *Id.* **9.** 2 Elliot's 410. **10.** *Allison v. Boeing Laser Tech. Servs.*, 689 F.3d 1234, 1236 n.1 (10th Cir. 2012) (citing *Kelly v. Lockheed Martin Servs. Grp.*, 25 F. Supp. 2d 1, 3 (D. Puerto Rico 1998)). **11.** *Paul*, 371 U.S. at 264. **12.** *Lake v. Ohana Mil. Communities, LLC*, 14 F.4th 993, 1002 (9th Cir. 2021). **13.** *Id.* **14.** 371 U.S. at 269. **15.** *Evans v. Cornman*, 398 U.S. 419 (1970). **16.** 355 U.S. 286 (1958). **17.** *Kennicot v. Sandia Corp.*, 314 F. Supp. 3d 1142 (D. N.M. 2018); Emily S. Miller, *The Strongest Defense You've Never Heard Of: The Constitution's Federal Enclave Doctrine and its Effect on Litigants, States, and Congress*, 29 Hofstra Labor & Emp. L.J. 73 (Fall 2011). **18.** 18 U.S.C. § 2243. **19.** 18 U.S.C. § 13(a). **20.** *Lewis v. United States*, 523 U.S. 155, 166 (1998).

ESSAY NO. 66: THE NECESSARY AND PROPER CLAUSE
ART. I, § 8, CL. 18

The Congress shall have Power . . . To make all Laws which shall be necessary and proper for carrying into Execution the foregoing Powers, and all other Powers vested by this Constitution in the Government of the United States, or in any Department or Officer thereof.

—Gary S. Lawson

INTRODUCTION

The first seventeen clauses of Article I, Section 8 enumerate legislative powers vested in Congress. (See Essay Nos. 39–65.) The Constitution sets forth additional congressional powers in Articles IV and V. Other provisions vest power in the President, federal judges, individual houses of Congress, and (occasionally) individual federal actors such as the Chief Justice or the Vice President. The Necessary and Proper Clause, also known as the Sweeping Clause, appears at the conclusion of Article I, Section 8. It authorizes and sets the criteria for laws that carry into effect all these other federal powers. Over time, the Supreme Court has interpreted the Necessary and Proper Clause to support a sweeping expansion of federal power.

HISTORY BEFORE 1787

The Necessary and Proper Clause had no direct antecedents in other governmental instruments. "Necessary and proper" appeared in only one pre-Convention state constitution. A provision of the Massachusetts constitution of 1780 authorized the legislature "to adopt such other measures as may be necessary and proper for insuring continuity of the government . . ." in the event of invasion.[1]

Article II of the Articles of Confederation had something of a mirror image of the Necessary and Proper Clause: "Each state retains its sovereignty, freedom and independence, and every Power, Jurisdiction and right, which is not by this confederation expressly delegated to the United States, in Congress assembled." In other words, Congress would have a power only if it was expressly delegated to the national government; otherwise, that power was retained by the states. The Confederation Congress did not have any implied or incidental powers. In Federalist No. 44, Alexander Hamilton observed that Congress had "constru[ed] the term 'expressly' with so much rigour, as to disarm the government of all real authority whatever."

THE CONSTITUTIONAL CONVENTION

At the Constitutional Convention, the Necessary and Proper Clause emerged, seemingly out of thin air, in a draft from the Committee of Detail. This committee included four prominent lawyers, Oliver Ellsworth of Connecticut, Edmund Randolph of Virginia, John Rutledge of South Carolina, and James Wilson of Pennsylvania, as well as a prominent businessman, Nathaniel Gorham of Massachusetts. This draft, which was written in Wilson's handwriting with certain parts crossed out, reads: "and to make all Laws that shall be necessary and proper for carrying into full and complete Execution the foregoing Powers, and all other powers vested, by this Constitution, in the Government of the United States, or in any Department or Officer thereof."[2]

The Committee of Detail's report was delivered to the Convention on August 6. The text provided that Congress would have the power "to make all laws that shall be necessary and proper for carrying into execution the foregoing powers, and all other powers vested, by this Constitution, in the government of the United States, or in any department or officer thereof."[3] The Committee omitted the first crossed-out portion ("full and complete") but retained the second ("the foregoing Powers").

The Convention considered the clause on August 20.[4] However, there was no discussion as to why this provision was introduced. In Federalist No. 33, Hamilton would write that the clause was added out of "great[] caution, and to guard against . . . curtail[ing] and evad[ing] the legitimate authorities of the union."

The only debate at the Convention about the Necessary and Proper Clause concerned whether Congress had the power to create and define federal offices by statute.[5] James Madison of Virginia would have granted Congress the express power to "establish all offices."[6] He thought it "liable to cavil" that this power was not already included in the Constitution. Gouverneur Morris, James Wilson, and others disagreed. They "urged that the amendment could not be necessary." Madison's motion failed by a vote of nine to two. The Committee of Detail's proposal was adopted unanimously without further debate.

No further changes were made by the Committee of Style.[7] On September 15, toward the end of the Convention, Elbridge Gerry of Massachusetts "stated the objections which determined him to withhold his name from the Constitution."[8] Among other concerns, he warned that the "rights of the Citizens were . . . rendered insecure . . . by the general power of the Legislature to make what laws they may please to call necessary and proper."[9]

The Necessary and Proper Clause was adopted.[10] Another provision of the Constitution used somewhat similar language: The President shall "recommend to [Congress's] consideration such Measures as he shall judge necessary and expedient."[11] (See Essay No. 111.)

THE RATIFICATION DEBATES

The Necessary and Proper Clause would prove to be extremely controversial during the ratification debates. Opponents dubbed the clause the "sweeping clause" or "general clause." An Anti-Federalist from New England derided it as the "*omnipotent* clause."[12]

Many Anti-Federalists argued that the clause imposed no limits on the federal government's powers. In practice, only Congress would be the judge of what the clause permits.[13] This clause, critics claimed, subverted the principle of enumerated powers by giving limitless general legislative competence to Congress. Centinel asked, "Does not this sweeping clause subject every thing to the controul of Congress?"[14] He added that Congress could use this "unlimited power" to "carry the coup de grace to the state governments, to swallow them up in the grand vortex of general empire."[15] At the Virginia ratifying convention, Patrick Henry warned that the "sweeping clause will fully enable [Congress] to do what they please."[16] Brutus charged that this power could "entirely . . . abolish the state legislatures" and "reduce this country to one single government."[17] For example, Congress could "repeal" any state tax "because it may prevent the collection of a [federal] tax which [Congress] may think proper and necessary to lay. . . ."[18]

Federalists sharply disagreed.[19] In Federalist No. 44, Hamilton wrote that "[f]ew parts of the constitution have been assailed with more intemperance than" the Sweeping Clause. Yet, "on a fair investigation of it . . . no part can appear more completely invulnerable." Indeed, "[w]ithout the substance of this power, the whole constitution would be a dead letter." In Federalist No. 33, Hamilton responded to Brutus's attack on "the unfortunate and calumniated provision." Hamilton said that the purpose of the Sweeping Clause "is expressly to execute these powers" enumerated in the Constitution, and "[i]f there be any thing exceptionable, it must be sought for in the specific powers, upon which this general declaration is predicated."

Federalists also defended the Sweeping Clause at the ratifying conventions. In Pennsylvania, Wilson stated that this provision is "saying no more than that the powers we have already particularly given, shall be effectually carried into execution."[20] In Virginia, Madison said the clause was "at most but explanatory" as it "only extended to the enumerated powers."[21] James Monroe argued that this "formidable clause" was "only inserted for greater caution, and to prevent the possibility of encroaching upon the powers of Congress."[22]

There is further textual support for the Federalist position. Five power-granting provisions of the Constitution use discretionary language like "shall think," "they think," "shall judge," and "shall deem." (See Essay Nos. 67, 108, 110, 113, 148.) These provisions "expressly bestow discretion on the pertinent actors to determine the necessity, propriety, or expediency of prescribed action."[23] The Necessary and Proper Clause, by contrast, does not contain such discretionary language. Rather, it requires that laws objectively "*shall be* necessary and proper for carrying into Execution" federal powers. Hamilton observed in Federalist No. 33 that "in the first instance" Congress is to "judge of the necessity and propriety of the laws to be passed for executing the powers of the union." George Nicholas of Virginia insisted that if Congress "exceed these powers, the judiciary will declare it void, or else the people will have a right to declare it void."[24]

A FIDUCIARY CLAUSE

The meaning and purpose of the Necessary and Proper Clause would have been reasonably clear to an eighteenth-century citizen. The enumeration of powers in the Constitution is similar to the enumeration of powers that one would find in an eighteenth-century private agency instrument or corporate charter. That

is not surprising, as the Founders viewed the Constitution as a fiduciary instrument. James Iredell of North Carolina said the Constitution "may be considered as a great power of attorney, under which no power can be exercised but what is expressly given."[25] The principal ("We the People") grants power to official agents (the government).[26]

Eighteenth-century agency law understood that enumerated grants of power to agents generally carried implied powers in their wake: the enumerated (principal) granted powers were presumptively accompanied by implied (incidental) powers that were needed to effectuate the principal powers. Sir William Blackstone wrote that "[a] subject's grant shall be construed to include many things, besides what are expressed, if necessary for the operation of the grant."[27] Authors of agency instruments could draft around this background rule to change the baseline of incidental powers. The Articles of Confederation directly ruled out implied powers by specifying that "[e]ach state retains . . . every power, jurisdiction, and right, which is not by this Confederation *expressly* delegated to the United States, in Congress assembled."[28] Private agency instruments of the time calibrated the power of agents by referring to "necessary," "proper," or (most restrictively) "necessary and proper" incidental powers.[29]

The clause was written by the Committee of Detail, whose four lawyers and a businessman would all have been familiar with agency law, and ratified by a public accustomed to serving as or employing agents in a wide range of everyday affairs. The Framers and ratifiers would likely have understood the Necessary and Proper Clause as a provision clarifying the scope of incidental powers accompanying the grants of principal (enumerated) federal powers.[30]

So understood, the clause serves two significant purposes. First, it facilitates organization of the government. It empowers Congress to organize the judicial department and create executive offices. The Framers rejected Madison's motion at the Convention to make explicit that the clause authorized the creation of federal offices. Others contended that such a specification "could not be necessary."[31] Second, and more fundamentally, the clause confirms, defines, and limits the incidental powers that impliedly accompanied other grants of power. The scope of these incidental or implied powers has been a subject of dispute ever since the Founding era.

Accordingly, as a matter of original meaning, every law enacted under the Necessary and Proper Clause must be (1) incidental to a principal power; (2) "for carrying into Execution" a principal power; (3) "necessary" for that purpose; and (4) "proper" for that purpose.

INCIDENTAL TO A PRINCIPAL POWER

Laws enacted under the Necessary and Proper Clause must be incidental to a principal power. In *McCulloch v. Maryland* (1819), Chief Justice John Marshall emphasized this aspect of the clause.[32] *McCulloch* concerned whether the Necessary and Proper Clause authorized Congress to incorporate a national bank. Congress lacks a principal, or enumerated, power to create a corporation or bank. Marshall explained why the power to incorporate a bank was an incidental rather than a principal power. Marshall identified principal powers, "like the power of making war or levying taxes or of regulating commerce" which were "great substantive and independent power[s] which cannot be implied as incidental to other powers."[33] Rather, the implied power of incorporation "must be considered as a means not less usual, not of higher dignity."[34] But if an incidental power is of the same "dignity" as the principal enumerated powers, then it cannot be implied under the Necessary and Proper Clause, no matter how convenient, useful, or even indispensable it might be for effectuating a principal power.[35]

This basic distinction between incidental and principal powers largely (and mysteriously) disappeared from the law for nearly two centuries.[36] Yet, it reemerged to play a key role in Chief Justice John Roberts' controlling opinion in *NFIB v. Sebelius* (2012).[37] *NFIB* found that the Affordable Care Act's "individual mandate" to purchase government-approved health insurance was not as a valid exercise of Congress's powers under the Necessary and Proper Clause, but it could be upheld as an exercise of the taxing power. Still, the Court's discussion of the Necessary and Proper Clause was a necessary step to the judgment. Relying on *McCulloch*,

Roberts wrote that the clause "vests Congress with authority to enact provisions 'incidental to the [enumerated] power'" but "does not license the exercise of any 'great substantive and independent power[s]' beyond those specifically enumerated."[38] Roberts concluded that a governmental power to force people to buy a product was equal in dignity to the principal powers and thus could not be considered "'incidental' to the exercise of the commerce power" or any other power.[39]

This revival of the distinction between incidental and principal powers generated a rash of academic criticism regarding the difficulty of drawing that distinction.[40] One response is that "[c]ourts, and the drafters of agency instruments, had been distinguishing principals from incidents for centuries."[41] This history left a rich body of analogues on which to draw.[42]

FOR CARRYING INTO EXECUTION

Any law enacted under the Necessary and Proper Clause must be "for carrying into Execution" some other federal power. The clause authorizes laws to help other federal actors carry out their functions, not to hinder them.[43] For example, Congress could not, under the guise of this clause, tell the President whom to pardon.

Some cases suggest that Congress can also pass laws to make the exercise of federal powers more effective,[44] but this conclusion has been challenged by some Justices and scholars.[45]

NECESSARY

Incidental laws that carry into execution federal powers must be "necessary" for that purpose. The requirement of necessity entails some degree of causal connection between the implementing law and the implemented power. The degree to which that required causal connection has been a contentious issue for more than two centuries.

In *McCulloch*, the State of Maryland argued that a "necessary" law must be indispensable to the achievement of a permissible governmental end.[46] Here, the state echoed Secretary of State Thomas Jefferson's opinion regarding the Bank of the United States.[47] Treasury Secretary Alexander Hamilton's opinion countered that necessity "often means no more than *needful, requisite, incidental, useful,* or *conducive to.*"[48]

Representative James Madison took a middle ground. He described necessity as requiring "a definite connection between means and ends" in which the executory law and the executed power are linked "by some obvious and precise affinity."[49] In 1791, Madison disapprovingly paraphrased the Hamiltonian understanding of necessity as meaning anything that "might be conceived to be conducive" to a desired end.[50]

In *McCulloch*, Chief Justice Marshall adopted Hamilton's formulation almost verbatim.[51] Marshall had done the same fourteen years earlier in *United States v. Fisher* (1805).[52] Elsewhere in *McCulloch*, however, Marshall used slightly less capacious language: "Let the end be legitimate, let it be within the scope of the constitution, and all means which are appropriate, which are plainly adapted to that end, which are not prohibited, but consist with the letter and spirit of the constitution, are constitutional."[53]

Modern cases have interpreted *McCulloch* and two centuries of subsequent precedents quite generously in line with Hamilton's formulation. Laws are valid under the Necessary and Proper Clause when they accomplish valid legislative ends "by rational means."[54] Such laws are also valid as "a means that is rationally related to the implementation of a constitutionally enumerated power."[55] In *United States v. Comstock* (2010), Justices Samuel Alito, Anthony Kennedy, Antonin Scalia, and Clarence Thomas expressed some measure of unease with this "rational basis" formulation of the required means-ends connection.[56] Originalist scholarship also raises serious doubts about whether Hamilton and Marshall accurately captured either the ordinary or the legal meaning of "necessary."[57] Nonetheless, the Court has *never* declared unconstitutional a congressional law on the ground that it was not "necessary" for effectuating federal powers.

PROPER

Finally, laws under the Necessary and Proper Clause must be "proper" for executing federal powers. In *McCulloch*, Daniel Webster argued that "necessary" and "proper" have the same meaning.[58] A scholar has suggested that "necessary and proper" might be a unitary phrase known as a "hendiadys" rather than two distinct terms.[59] In *NFIB v. Sebelius*, however, five Justices treated the requirement of propriety as separate from and in addition to the requirement of necessity.[60] There are both contextual and intratextual reasons to think *NFIB* was correct.[61]

The modern Supreme Court has not elaborated on this requirement of propriety in detail. However, several late twentieth-century cases held that laws were not "proper" if they violated principles of federalism. For example, a federal law that compelled state officials to enforce federal law was not proper.[62] Another federal law that wrongly used Article I powers to waive, or abrogate, state sovereign immunity, was not proper.[63] In *NFIB v. Sebelius*, four Justices clarified that "the scope of the Necessary and Proper Clause is exceeded not only when the congressional action directly violates the sovereignty of the States but also when it violates the background principle of enumerated (and hence limited) federal power."[64] A fifth member, Chief Justice Roberts, noted that laws are not "proper" when they "undermine the structure of government established by the Constitution."[65] These statements are consistent with scholarship arguing that "proper" laws do "not usurp or expand the constitutional powers of any federal institutions or infringe on the retained rights of the states or of individuals."[66]

OPEN QUESTIONS

- The Sweeping Clause refers to the "Government of the United States, or in any Department or Officer thereof." What specific elements of the federal government are covered by this language?[67]

Cite as: Gary S. Lawson, *The Necessary and Proper Clause, in* THE HERITAGE GUIDE TO THE CONSTITUTION 233 (Josh Blackman & John G. Malcolm eds., 3d ed. 2025).

Notes

1. Mass. Const. of 1780, art. LXXXIII. **2.** 2 Farrand's 168. **3.** *Id.* at 182. **4.** *Id.* at 344–45. **5.** Seth Barrett Tillman & Josh Blackman, *Offices and Officers of the Constitution, Part III: The Appointments, Impeachment, Commissions, and Oath or Affirmation Clauses*, 62 S. Tex. L. Rev. 349, 435 n.408 (2023). **6.** 2 Farrand's 345. **7.** *Id.* at 570, 596. **8.** *Id.* at 632. **9.** *Id.* at 633. **10.** *Id.* at 656. **11.** Art. II, § 3. **12.** Storing 4.13.28. **13.** Gary Lawson & Patricia B. Granger, *The "Proper" Scope of Federal Power: A Jurisdictional Interpretation of the Sweeping Clause*, 43 Duke L.J. 267, 282–83 (1993). **14.** Storing 2.7.37. **15.** *Id.* at 2.7.96. **16.** 3 Elliot's 437. **17.** Storing 2.9.8–9. **18.** *Id.* at 2.9.8. **19.** Lawson & Granger, *supra* at 281–82. **20.** 2 Elliot's 449. **21.** 3 Elliot's 438, 455. **22.** *Id.* at 307. **23.** Lawson & Granger, *supra* at 277. **24.** 3 Elliot's 443. **25.** 4 Elliot's 148. **26.** Gary Lawson & Guy Seidman, "A Great Power of Attorney": Understanding the Fiduciary Constitution (2017); Gary Lawson & Guy Seidman, *An Enquiry Concerning Constitutional Understanding*, 17 Geo. J.L. & Pub. Pol'y 491 (2019); Ethan J. Leib & Jed Handelsman Shugerman, *Fiduciary Constitutionalism: Implications for Self-Pardons and Non-Delegation,* 17 Geo. J.L. & Pub. Pol'y 463, 463–69 (2019). **27.** 2 Blackstone 347. **28.** Articles of Confederation, art. II (emphasis added). **29.** Robert G. Natelson, *The Legal Origins of the Necessary and Proper Clause, in* Gary Lawson et al., The Origins of the Necessary and Proper Clause 52 (2010). **30.** Robert G. Natelson, *The Agency Law Origins of the Necessary and Proper Clause,* 55 Case W. Rsrv. L. Rev. 243 (2004). **31.** 2 Farrand's 345. **32.** 17 U.S. (4 Wheat.) 316 (1819). **33.** *Id.* at 417. **34.** *Id.* at 421. **35.** *Id.* at 421–22. **36.** Lawson & Seidman, *"Great Power of Attorney," supra* at 90–91. **37.** 567 U.S. 519 (2012). **38.** *Id.* at 559 (quoting *McCulloch,* 17 U.S. (4 Wheat.) at 418, 421). **39.** *Id.* at 560. **40.** Lawson & Seidman, *"Great Power of Attorney," supra* at 98. **41.** *Id.* at 99. **42.** Natelson, *Legal Origins, supra* at 62–63. **43.** David E. Engdahl, *Intrinsic Limits of Congress' Power Regarding the Judicial Branch,* 1999 B.Y.U. L. Rev. 75, 170–74 (1999).

44. *Missouri v. Holland*, 252 U.S. 416 (1920); *Shreveport Rate Cases,* 234 U.S. 342, 351–55 (1914). **45.** *Bond v. United States,* 572 U.S. 844, 876 (2014) (Scalia, J., concurring in the judgment); Steven Gow Calabresi & Gary Lawson, The U.S. Constitution: Creation, Reconstruction, the Progressives, and the Modern Era 841–42 (2020); Nicholas Quinn Rosenkranz, *Executing the Treaty Power*, 118 Harv. L. Rev. 1867, 1882–88 (2005). **46.** 17 U.S. (4 Wheat.) at 367. **47.** Thomas Jefferson, Opinion on the Constitutionality of the Bill for Establishing a National Bank (Feb. 15, 1791), https://perma.cc/5C66-GECC. **48.** Alexander Hamilton, Final Version of an Opinion on the Constitutionality of an Act to Establish a Bank (Feb. 23, 1791), https://perma.cc/7NDR-HAK9. **49.** Letter from James Madison to Spencer Roane (Sept. 2, 1819), https://perma.cc/X4SE-DYAT. **50.** 2 Annals of Cong. 1948 (1791). **51.** 17 U.S. (4 Wheat.) at 413–14. **52.** 6 U.S. (2 Cranch) 358, 396 (1805). **53.** 17 U.S. (4 Wheat.) at 421. **54.** *Sabri v. United States,* 541 U.S. 600, 605 (2004). **55.** *United States v. Comstock,* 560 U.S. 126, 134 (2010). **56.** *Id.* at 151–52 (Kennedy, J., concurring); *id.* at 158 (Alito, J., concurring); *id.* at 160–61 (Thomas, J., and Scalia, J., dissenting). **57.** Steven Gow Calabresi, Elise Kostial & Gary Lawson, *What* McCulloch. v. Maryland *Got Wrong: The Original Meaning of "Necessary" Is Not "Useful," "Convenient," or "Rational,"* 75 Baylor L. Rev. 1 (2023). **58.** 17 U.S. at 324. **59.** Samuel L. Bray, *Necessary* AND *Proper and Cruel* AND *Unusual: Hendiadys in the Constitution,* 102 Va. L. Rev. 687, 689 (2016). **60.** 567 U.S. at 559. **61.** Calabresi, Kostial, & Lawson, *supra* at 31 n.143; Gary Lawson, *Discretion as Delegation: The "Proper" Understanding of the Nondelegation Doctrine,* 73 Geo. Wash. L. Rev. 235, 250–55 (2005). **62.** *Printz v. United States*, 512 U.S. 898, 923–24 (1997). **63.** *Alden v. Maine,* 527 U.S. 706, 732–33 (1999). **64.** 567 U.S. at 653 (Scalia, J., Kennedy, J., Thomas, J., and Alito, J., dissenting). **65.** *Id.* at 559. **66.** Lawson & Granger, *supra* at 271. **67.** Seth Barrett Tillman & Josh Blackman, *Offices and Officers of the Constitution, Part II: The Four Approaches,* 61 S. Tex. L. Rev. 321, 403–17 (2022).

~

ESSAY NO. 67: THE MIGRATION OR IMPORTATION CLAUSE
ART. I, § 9, CL. 1

The Migration or Importation of such Persons as any of the States now existing shall think proper to admit, shall not be prohibited by the Congress prior to the Year one thousand eight hundred and eight, but a Tax or duty may be imposed on such Importation, not exceeding ten dollars for each Person.

—Judge Patrick J. Bumatay

INTRODUCTION

To unite under a single Constitution, our Founding generation had to reach a compromise over the Atlantic slave trade. Northern states increasingly viewed the practice as unacceptable, while Southern economies relied on it. The eventual compromise—a twenty-year period during which Congress could not ban the trade—was met with criticism and grudging acceptance. Congress banned the slave trade on the first day the Constitution permitted, but the Slave Trade Clause continued to shape the debate over slavery, citizenship, and federal power.

HISTORY BEFORE 1787

Around the time of the Founding, opposition to the Atlantic slave trade grew in both Europe and the Americas. In *Somerset v. Stewart* (1772), Lord Mansfield of the English Court of King's Bench held that a slave on English soil had the right not to be forcibly removed from the country and sent abroad for sale.[1] Across the ocean, Rhode Island and Connecticut banned the importation of slaves in 1774, and other future states later followed suit.[2] Thomas Jefferson penned a draft of the Declaration of Independence that condemned the slave trade as "execrable Commerce" and slavery as a "cruel war against nature itself."[3] Even so, these clauses were ultimately dropped from the final document. Against this backdrop of growing opposition to slavery and the slave trade, the Framers weighed the nascent federal government's authority to regulate the importation of slaves.

THE CONSTITUTIONAL CONVENTION

During the Constitutional Convention, the first debate over slavery concerned representation and what became the Three-Fifths Clause.[4] (See Essay No. 9.) The second debate arose when southern delegates objected to an unrestricted congressional power to regulate foreign and interstate commerce. (See Essay Nos. 43 and 44.) They warned that this power could restrict or outlaw the slave trade.[5] Charles Cotesworth Pinckney of South Carolina, for example, stated flatly that "South Carolina can never receive the plan if it prohibits the slave trade."[6] This debate yielded the Migration or Importation Clause, which stands as the first independent restraint on congressional powers in the Constitution. It appears even before the restriction on the power to suspend the writ of habeas corpus.

The Committee of Detail, which was chaired by John Rutledge of South Carolina, proposed the Migration or Importation Clause. This provision dealt with trade issues as well as those relating to slavery. The draft permanently forbade Congress from outlawing or taxing the "emigration or Importation of such persons."[7] "Migration" generally referred to the movement of free persons and slaves, while "importation" would have referred only to slaves.[8] Yet even at this early juncture in the Convention, the delegates avoided the word "slave" and instead used "such persons."[9] Later in the Convention, James Madison of Virginia argued that it was "wrong to admit in the Constitution the idea that there could be property in men."[10] Several delegates strongly objected to the proposal, including Gouverneur Morris of Pennsylvania, who delivered one of the Convention's most spirited denunciations of slavery as a "nefarious institution" and "the curse of heaven."[11]

When the issue came up for a vote, the southern delegates were sharply divided. George Mason of Virginia condemned the "infernal traffic,"[12] but Luther Martin of Maryland saw the restriction on Congress's power over the slave trade as "inconsistent with the principles of the Revolution and dishonorable to the American character."[13] Delegates from Georgia and South Carolina announced that they would not support the Constitution without the restriction. Charles Cotesworth Pinckney argued that failing to include the clause would trigger "an exclusion of South Carolina from the Union."[14]

The serious split was referred to a Committee of Eleven, which was chaired by William Livingston of New Jersey. The Committee rewrote the clause to focus exclusively on Congress's power to regulate the migration or importation of slaves. It recognized a congressional power over the slave trade but recommended that it be restricted for twelve years while allowing a tax on the importation of slaves.[15] This language was a significant change from the Committee of Detail's original proposal.

Southern delegates accepted the new arrangement but extended the time period to twenty years, from 1800 to 1808.[16] Madison argued that the twenty-year exemption was "dishonorable" and would "produce all the mischief that can be apprehended from the liberty to import slaves."[17] Roger Sherman of Connecticut aptly summarized the necessity for the compromise: "[I]t was better to let the [Southern] States import slaves than to part with them."[18] The Migration or Importation Clause with the twenty-year period was adopted by the Convention.

THE RATIFICATION DEBATES

During the ratification debates, the Migration or Importation Clause was the subject of significant debate. Opponents of the slave trade denounced the clause as a major concession to slavery interests but still grudgingly accepted it as a necessary and prudent compromise. In Federalist No. 42, Madison declared that it was "a great point gained in favor of humanity that a period of twenty years may terminate for ever, within these states" an "unnatural traffic" that was "the barbarism of modern policy."[19] The Anti-Federalists, however, seized upon the clause as an unacceptable endorsement of slavery. A Federal Republican of Pennsylvania wrote that "[t]o prohibit the importation of slaves is not to abolish slavery."[20]

In the North Carolina ratifying convention, James Iredell, who would later serve on the Supreme Court, said that he wished the "great cruelties" of the slave trade would soon be abolished, but "we often wish for things which are not attainable." He said "[i]t was the wish of a great majority of the Convention to put an end to the trade immediately; but the states of South Carolina and Georgia would not agree to it."[21]

Some members of the South Carolina House of Representatives viewed the clause as a delayed attack on their "only natural resource."[22] Charles Cotesworth Pinckney defended the Constitution's protections of slavery, arguing that "we have made the best terms for the security of this species of property it was in our power to make." Pinckney added, "We would have made better if we could; but, on the whole, I do not think them bad."[23]

Others were more optimistic. James Wilson of Pennsylvania, for example, claimed that the Interstate and Foreign Commerce Clauses gave Congress the power to regulate, or prohibit, both the interstate and the foreign slave trade after the twenty-year period had lapsed: "[Y]et the lapse of a few years, and Congress will have power to exterminate slavery from within our borders."[24] In Federalist No. 54, James Madison found significance in the fact that the words "slave" and "slavery" were not used in the Constitution of 1787. Instead, the Framers used the word "person" rather than "property." This would ensure that a slave would be regarded "as a moral person, not as a mere article of property."[25]

EARLY PRACTICE

At the Constitutional Convention, southern delegates had hoped opposition to the slave trade would weaken with time, but the practical effect of the Migration or Importation Clause was to create a growing expectation of federal legislation against the practice. The Slave Trade Act of 1794 prohibited any citizen or resident of the United States from carrying on any trade or traffic in slaves from the United States to any foreign country.[26] As a result, U.S. citizens were prohibited from engaging in the transatlantic slave trade.[27] The Slave Trade Act of 1800 further prohibited Americans from investing in the slave trade or transporting slaves from one foreign country to another foreign country.[28] In 1807, Congress passed, and President Jefferson signed into law, legislation to officially prohibit the slave trade, which became effective on January 1, 1808.[29]

Which enumerated power authorized Congress to prohibit the slave trade? Justice Joseph Story posited that "the power to regulate commerce applies . . . to the regulation of vessels employed in transporting men."[30] But it was not clear that the power to "regulate" includes the power to prohibit altogether. Abraham Lincoln, for example, did not claim that congressional power to regulate commerce could be used to restrict interstate commerce in slaves. In his first inaugural address, he said, "*May* Congress prohibit slavery in the Territories? The Constitution does not expressly say. *Must* Congress protect slavery in the Territories? The Constitution does not expressly say."[31]

JUDICIAL PRECEDENT

After 1808, the Migration or Importation Clause still had an effect on Supreme Court opinions. *Groves v. Slaughter* (1841) avoided deciding whether slaves were articles of commerce for purposes of the Commerce Clause.[32] *Smith v. Turner* (1849) ruled that "migration" and "importation" referred to immigrants and slaves, respectively, as distinct classes of people.[33] As a result, the Migration or Importation clause would buttress Congress's exclusive power over immigration. In *Dred Scott v. Sandford* (1857), Chief Justice Roger B. Taney pointed to the Migration or Importation Clause, along with the Fugitive Slave Clause, as evidence that persons of African descent were not intended to be accorded citizenship.[34] Even so, as Justice Benjamin Robbins Curtis observed in dissent, free blacks were citizens in a number of northern states and had voted to ratify the new Constitution.[35] Moreover, modern observers agree that those clauses did not address the question of citizenship at all.

OPEN QUESTIONS

- In 1788, what exactly was the difference between "migration" and "importation"?[36]
- Even after 1808, does the Migration or Importation Clause grant Congress an affirmative enumerated power to restrict immigration?[37]
- Does a state's power to "admit" "such Persons" confer a parallel power to deny persons entry into its territory?

Cite as: Judge Patrick J. Bumatay, *The Migration or Importation Clause, in* THE HERITAGE GUIDE TO THE CONSTITUTION 238 (Josh Blackman & John G. Malcolm eds., 3d ed. 2025).

Notes

1. 98 Eng. Rep. 499 (K.B. 1772). **2.** An Act for Prohibiting the Importation of Negroes, Rhode Island General Assembly (June 1774); An Act for Prohibiting the Importation of Indian, Negro or Molatto Slaves, Connecticut General Assembly (1774). **3.** 1 The Papers of Thomas Jefferson 243–47 (Julian P. Boyd ed., 1950), https://perma.cc/89TT-76TX. **4.** 1 Farrand's 205–06. **5.** 2 Farrand's 220, 364, 369. **6.** *Id.* at 364 **7.** *Id.* at 169. **8.** 4 Elliot's 100–102. **9.** 2 Farrand's 168–69. **10.** *Id.* at 417. **11.** 1 Farrand's 221. **12.** 2 Farrand's 370. **13.** *Id.* at 364. **14.** *Id.* at 372. **15.** *Id.* at 396. **16.** *Id.* at 415. **17.** *Id.* **18.** *Id.* at 374. **19.** Federalist No. 42 (Madison). **20.** Storing 3.6.22. **21.** 4 Elliot's 100. **22.** *Id.* at 273. **23.** *Id.* at 286. **24.** 2 Elliot's 484. **25.** Federalist No. 54 (Madison). **26.** 1 Stat. 347–49. **27.** Michael Daly Hawkins, *John Quincy Adams and the Antebellum Maritime Slave Trade: The Politics of Slavery and the Slavery of Politics*, 25 Okla. City U.L. Rev. 1, 7–8 (2000). **28.** An Act to Prohibit the Carrying on the Slave Trade from the United States to any Foreign Place or Country, Pub. L. 6-51 (1800). **29.** An Act to Prohibit the Importation of Slaves, 2 Stat. 426 (1807). **30.** 3 Story's Commentaries § 1331. **31.** Lincoln's First Inaugural Address (Mar. 4, 1861), https://perma.cc/P7CC-4J5U. **32.** 40 U.S. 449, 464 (1841). **33.** 48 U.S. 283, 307 (1849). **34.** 60 U.S. 393, 411, 536 (1857). **35.** *Id.* at 572–73 (Curtis, J., dissenting). **36.** Robert G. Natelson, *The Power to Restrict Immigration and the Original Meaning of the Constitution's Define and Punish Clause*, 11 Brit. J. Am. Legal Stud. 209, 211 (2022). **37.** Geoffrey Heeren, *Immigration Law and Slavery: Rethinking the Migration or Importation Clause*, 2023 Wisc. L. Rev. 1125 (2023).

ESSAY NO. 68: THE HABEAS CORPUS CLAUSE
ART. 1, § 9, CL. 2

The Privilege of the Writ of Habeas Corpus shall not be suspended, unless when in Cases of Rebellion or Invasion the public Safety may require it.

—Taylor Meehan

INTRODUCTION

The Habeas Corpus Clause, also known as the Suspension Clause, touches the "very core of liberty" by warding off "indefinite imprisonment at the will of the Executive."[1] Habeas corpus roughly translates to a command to bring the body of the imprisoned to the court. The courts have long used a writ of *habeas corpus ad subjiciendum* to examine the grounds for a person's imprisonment and decide whether continued imprisonment is lawful. Sir William Blackstone wrote that the "Great Writ" of habeas corpus secured against the "dangerous engine of arbitrary government," whereby the king could indefinitely detain his subject without due process, "secretly hurrying him to jail, where his sufferings are unknown or forgotten."[2] The Suspension Clause assumes the continued existence of this preexisting right to petition for a writ of habeas corpus. The clause lets Congress decide when, if ever, the writ may be suspended "in Cases of Rebellion or Invasion." The implications of that power remain "elusive."[3]

HISTORY BEFORE 1787

A fundamental principle of English law was that there would be no imprisonment without due process. In the words of the Magna Carta (1215), no man would be imprisoned "except by the lawful judgment of his equals or by the law of the land." Imprisonment based on the whims of the Executive alone was generally unlawful.[4] Over time, the common-law writ of habeas corpus became the means by which a prisoner could insist on those due process protections. Parliament codified the writ and enumerated procedural protections for its exercise in the Habeas Corpus Act of 1679. It promised a speedy trial without exceptions for wartime.[5] Blackstone celebrated it as a "second *magna carta*, and stable bulwark of our liberties."[6]

The Great Writ crossed the Atlantic and was well-established in all thirteen colonies.[7] Even so, the Crown routinely denied the protections of England's Habeas Corpus Act for colonists. In 1777, Parliament suspended the writ after the colonies declared independence.[8]

After the Revolutionary War and leading up to the 1787 Constitutional Convention, habeas corpus rights were affirmatively enshrined in some state statutes and in the Georgia, Massachusetts, New Hampshire, and North Carolina state constitutions.[9] The Massachusetts constitution provided that "[t]he privilege and benefit of the writ of habeas corpus shall be enjoyed in this commonwealth, in the most free, easy, cheap, expeditious, and ample manner, and shall not be suspended by the legislature, except upon the most urgent and pressing occasions, and for a limited time, not exceeding twelve months."[10] Massachusetts was the model for the habeas corpus provision proposed at the Constitutional Convention.[11]

THE CONSTITUTIONAL CONVENTION

At the Constitutional Convention, it was generally assumed that habeas corpus was one of many preexisting and continuing rights. Perhaps for these reasons, it was not mentioned in the draft that was initially reported by the Committee of Detail,[12] just as other preexisting rights were not.

On August 20, 1787, Charles Pinckney of South Carolina submitted a habeas corpus provision to be referred to the Committee of Detail. Mirroring the Massachusetts provision, his proposal provided that the "privileges and benefit of the Writ of Habeas corpus shall be enjoyed in this government in the most expeditious and ample manner" and that the writ "shall not be suspended by the legislature, except upon the most urgent and pressing occasions, and for a limited time, not exceeding — months."[13] In committee, Pinckney proposed that the "limited time" should not exceed "twelve months."[14] Gouverneur Morris of Pennsylvania moved to revise the clause to read nearly as it does today without the twelve-month limitation.[15] It contains a general rule and one exception: "The privilege of the writ of Habeas Corpus shall not be suspended, unless where in cases of Rebellion or invasion the public safety may require it."[16]

Delegates unanimously approved the first half of Morris's proposal,[17] but there was dissension and debate about the exception. North Carolina, South Carolina, and Georgia voted against giving the government the power to suspend the writ.[18] John Rutledge of South Carolina objected to any mention of suspension and would have declared "Habeas Corpus inviolable." James Wilson of Pennsylvania questioned when suspension would ever be necessary if judges had the discretion to refuse bail for public safety reasons.[19] The dissenters feared that the power to suspend habeas would be an "engine of oppression" in the federal government's hands to be used against states.[20]

When proposed in August 1787, the clause appeared in what became Article III alongside the guarantee of criminal jury trials. However, at the end of the Convention, the Committee of Style moved the Suspension Clause to Article I, which defines the powers of the national legislature. There is no recorded debate by the Convention on this decision.[21]

THE RATIFICATION DEBATES

During ratification, the Suspension Clause became a central issue in the debate over whether to add a Bill of Rights. In Federalist No. 84, Alexander Hamilton wrote that "[t]he establishment of the writ of *habeas corpus*" and other protections would be "greater securities to liberty and republicanism" than any protections a Bill of Rights would contain. During the Virginia ratifying convention, Patrick Henry raised alarm about the Suspension Clause in a famous exchange over the Bill of Rights. He wrote that this provision and other express limitations on Congress's power could be read to suggest that other rights "not expressly reserved" in the Constitution were "given up" to a Congress of general power.[22] Edmund Randolph countered that inclusion of the Suspension Clause was a necessary "exception" to Congress's specifically enumerated power to regulate the courts, which Congress could otherwise use to suspend the writ.[23]

EARLY PRACTICE AND PRECEDENT

Can federal courts grant the writ of habeas corpus based on the Suspension Clause alone, without relying on a statute? The First Congress avoided his question by enacting the Judiciary Act of 1789, which gave the federal courts power to grant the writ of habeas corpus.[24]

Shortly thereafter, Congress contemplated suspending the writ during the Burr conspiracy. In 1807, Aaron Burr was suspected of treason. His alleged co-conspirators, including Erick Bollman, were arrested and petitioned for a writ of habeas corpus. In *Ex parte Bollman* (1807), the U.S. Supreme Court granted the writ because the evidence was too thin to support their continued detention.[25] In response, Congress contemplated suspending the writ. The bill to suspend the writ failed in the House, which was unwilling to give the President the power to detain on "bare suspicion."[26]

THE CIVIL WAR

In the early days of the Civil War, President Abraham Lincoln questioned whether Congress alone could suspend the writ. He famously declared the writ suspended, without Congress, as Union troops moved through Maryland.

In May 1861, military officers arrested and detained alleged Southern sympathizer John Merryman at Fort McHenry.[27] Chief Justice Roger B. Taney ordered the fort's commander to produce Merryman. General George Cadwalader refused on the grounds that the President had suspended the writ.[28] Taney responded "with some surprise" because he supposed "there was no difference of opinion, and that it was admitted on all hands, that the privilege of the writ could not be suspended, except by act of congress."[29] By virtue of its placement in Article I, the power to suspend the writ was with Congress.[30] The President, Taney explained, had no unilateral power to suspend the writ.[31] Taney did not actually order Merryman's release and instead directed the clerk to transmit a copy of his opinion to Lincoln, leaving it for the President to decide what to do with Merryman.[32]

Thus, contrary to a common misconception, Lincoln could not have defied Taney's order because no such order was given.[33] Soon thereafter, Merryman was transferred to civilian authorities, charged with treason, and released on bail, but he was never tried.[34] In September 1862, President Lincoln issued a formal proclamation purporting to suspend habeas corpus for all persons arrested during the war by military authorities.[35]

In March 1863, Congress averted a constitutional crisis by passing the Habeas Corpus Suspension Act.[36] Congress delegated to the President the power to decide when "the public safety" required suspension of the writ for as long as the war continued.[37] During Reconstruction, Congress again suspended the writ to quell rebellion by the Ku Klux Klan in South Carolina, thereby empowering the government to make preventive arrests of presumed Klan members.[38]

HABEAS CORPUS AFTER 9/11

The country's response to the September 11, 2001, terrorist attacks reignited debate over the Suspension Clause and Congress's power to limit habeas relief. In the wake of 9/11, Congress enacted laws that permitted detention of enemy combatants.[39] In a series of Supreme Court cases, detainees at a Navy facility in Guantanamo Bay,

Cuba, challenged their detentions as violating the Suspension Clause.

In *Hamdi v. Rumsfeld* (2004), the Court divided over whether Congress, absent suspension, could authorize the indefinite detention of a U.S. citizen. Writing for a plurality, Justice Sandra Day O'Connor concluded that "[t]here is no bar to this Nation's holding one of its own citizens as an enemy combatant."[40] But the plurality found that Hamdi was entitled to more procedural due process protections to rebut the Executive's factual assertions for his detention in court.[41] Justice Antonin Scalia and Justice John Paul Stevens dissented. They concluded that the government had two choices: "prosecute him in federal court for treason or some other crime" or "relax the usual protections temporarily" by formally suspending the writ.[42] There was no in-between, according to Justice Scalia, whereby the Constitution "merely guarantees that he will not be detained unless Congress by ordinary legislation says he can be detained."[43]

In the wake of *Hamdi*, Congress did not formally suspend the writ. Four years later, *Boumediene v. Bush* (2008) considered whether Congress could prohibit courts from considering habeas petitions from noncitizen detainees at Guantanamo. The Court held that the Suspension Clause applied extraterritorially at Guantanamo. As a result, the clause's protections extended to noncitizens. Absent suspension, detainees were "entitled to the privilege of habeas corpus to challenge the legality of their detention" or an "adequate and effective substitute for habeas corpus."[44]

THE SUSPENSION CLAUSE AND STATE PRISONERS

Beyond these prominent episodes, the habeas writ has been sought primarily by state prisoners challenging their criminal convictions. During Reconstruction, Congress empowered the federal courts to grant the writ to those who were in state custody.[45] That act began as proposed legislation to guarantee freedom for newly freed persons after the Civil War.[46] Over time, however, its broad text became the basis for state prisoners to challenge all types of criminal convictions or sentences imposed by state criminal courts, even after the criminal proceedings had ended.[47]

That system of post-conviction review departs from the historic limits of the habeas writ, whereby the existence of a final criminal judgment was generally sufficient to establish the legality of imprisonment.[48] The Supreme Court has clarified that post-conviction claims "would not have been cognizable in habeas at all" at the Founding.[49] Congress limited post-conviction relief available in such circumstances with the Antiterrorism and Effective Death Penalty Act (AEDPA) in 1996.[50] The Supreme Court rejected the claim that these limitations violate the Suspension Clause.[51] The Court distinguished "postconviction review after criminal proceedings" from cases of executive detention "where no trial has been held."[52]

OPEN QUESTIONS

- Does the Suspension Clause implicitly require that federal courts remain open for habeas relief? What about state courts?
- To what extent may Congress limit habeas relief? What limitations amount to a suspension of the writ? What constitutes a valid suspension? Who could challenge such a suspension? And what are the consequences: Can the imprisoned still redress an unlawful detention in other ways?
- Could courts still grant the writ even absent a statute saying they could do so?[53] Could there be a "permanent suspension" of the writ?[54] Would that suspension be "unthinkable"?[55] Scholars continue to debate these questions.[56]
- The text of the Constitution refers to "*the privilege* of the writ of habeas corpus." The Supreme Court has recognized that "[t]he suspension of the privilege of the writ of habeas corpus does not suspend the writ itself."[57] What is the difference between "the writ" and the "privilege of the writ"?[58]

Cite as: Taylor Meehan, *The Habeas Corpus Clause, in* The Heritage Guide to the Constitution 241 (Josh Blackman & John G. Malcolm eds., 3d ed. 2025).

Notes

1. *Hamdi v. Rumsfeld*, 542 U.S. 507, 555 (2004) (Scalia, J., dissenting). **2.** 1 Blackstone 135. **3.** David L. Shapiro, *Habeas Corpus, Suspension, and Detention: Another View*, 82 Notre Dame L. Rev. 59, 59–60 (2006). **4.** Amanda L. Tyler, *The Forgotten Core Meaning of the Suspension Clause*, 125 Harv. L. Rev. 901, 923–28 (2012). **5.** *Id.* at 928–30. **6.** *Hamdi*, 542 U.S. at 557 (Scalia, J., dissenting) (quoting 1 Blackstone 137). **7.** Dallin H. Oaks, *Habeas Corpus in the States*, 32 U. Chi. L. Rev. 243 (1965). **8.** Tyler, *supra* at 944–55. **9.** *Id.* at 247, 251. **10.** *Id.* at 247 (quoting Mass. Const. of 1780, ch. 6, art. VII). **11.** *Id.* at 247–48. **12.** *Id.* at 248. **13.** 5 Elliot's 445; 2 Farrand's 341. **14.** 2 Farrand's 438. **15.** *Id.* at 340–41, 438. **16.** *Id.* at 438. **17.** *Id.* **18.** *Id.* **19.** *Id.*; Tyler, *supra* at 969–72. **20.** 3 Farrand's 213. **21.** 2 Farrand's 438, 576, 596. **22.** 3 Elliot's 460. **23.** *Id.* at 464. **24.** Act of 1789, § 14, 1 Stat. 81. **25.** 8 U.S. (4 Cranch) 75 (1807). **26.** Tyler, *supra* at 980–85. **27.** *Ex parte Merryman*, 17 F. Cas. 144, 147 (C.C.D. Md. 1861) (No. 9487) (Taney, C.J.). **28.** *Id.* **29.** *Id.* **30.** *Id.* at 147–48. **31.** *Id.* at 148–50; *Hamdi*, 542 U.S. at 562. **32.** *Merryman*, 17 F. Cas. at 152. **33.** Seth Barrett Tillman, Ex Parte Merryman: *Myth, History, and Scholarship*, 224 Mil. L. Rev. 481 (2016). **34.** Amanda L. Tyler, Habeas Corpus in Wartime: From the Tower of London to Guantanamo Bay 160–67 (2017). **35.** Proclamation No. 1 (Sept. 24, 1862), 13 Stat. 760. **36.** Act of Mar. 3, 1863, 12 Stat. 755. **37.** *Id.* § 1; Amanda L. Tyler, *Suspension as an Emergency Power*, 118 Yale L.J. 600, 639–54 (2009). **38.** Act of Apr. 20, 1871, ch. 22, § 4, 17 Stat. 14; Tyler, *supra* at 655–62. **39.** *Boumediene v. Bush*, 553 U.S. 723, 733–36 (2008). **40.** 542 U.S. at 519 (citing *Ex parte Quirin*, 317 U.S. 1 (1942)). **41.** *Id.* at 525–26, 536–37. **42.** *Id.* at 554. **43.** *Id.* at 575. **44.** 553 U.S. at 771, 795. **45.** Act of Feb. 5, 1867, ch. 28, § 1, 14 Stat. 385. **46.** Lewis Mayers, *The Habeas Corpus Act of 1867: The Supreme Court as Legal Historian*, 33 U. Chi. L. Rev. 31, 34–39 (1965). **47.** Paul M. Bator, *Finality in Criminal Law and Federal Habeas Corpus for State Prisoners*, 76 Harv. L. Rev. 441 (1963). **48.** *Ex parte Watkins*, 28 U.S. (3 Pet.) 193, 202 (1830); Bator, *supra* at 466–78; Rex A. Collings, Jr., *Habeas Corpus for Convicts—Constitutional Right or Legislative Grace?*, 40 Cal. L. Rev. 335, 336–52 (1952). **49.** *Jones v. Hendrix*, 599 U.S. 465, 482–85 (2023). **50.** Pub. L. 104-132, 110 Stat. 1214. **51.** *Jones*, 599 U.S. at 482–85; *Felker v. Turpin*, 518 U.S. 651 (1996). **52.** *Boumediene*, 553 U.S. at 774. **53.** *Ex parte Bollman*, 8 U.S. 75, 94 (1807). **54.** *INS v. St. Cyr*, 533 U.S. 289, 304 n.24 (2001). **55.** *Id.* at 339–41 & n.5 (Scalia, J., dissenting). **56.** Lee Kovarsky, *Habeas Privilege Origination and* DHS v. Thuraissigiam, 121 Colum. L. Rev. 23, 25–29 (2021); Richard H. Fallon, Jr., *The Supreme Court, Habeas Corpus, and the War on Terror*, 110 Colum. L. Rev. 352, 378 (2010); Shapiro, *supra* at 61–65. **57.** *Ex parte Milligan*, 71 U.S. (4 Wall.) 2, 130–31 (1866). **58.** William Baude, *The Judgment Power*, 96 Geo. L.J. 1807, 1853 n.255 (2008); Seth Barrett Tillman, Merryman *Redux: A Response to Professor John Yoo*, 22 Chap. L. Rev. 1, 4 n.15 (2019).

ESSAY NO. 69: THE FEDERAL BILL OF ATTAINDER CLAUSE
ART. I, § 9, CL. 3

No Bill of Attainder . . . shall be passed.

—Matthew Steilen

INTRODUCTION

Bills of attainder are "legislative acts . . . that apply either to named individuals or to easily ascertainable members of a group in such a way as to inflict punishment on them without a judicial trial."[1] There are two Bill of Attainder Clauses in the Constitution. The clause in Article I, Section 9 applies to federal laws. The clause in Article I, Section 10 applies to state laws. Most of the cases involving bills of attainder to reach the U.S. Supreme Court have concerned the federal ban. This essay will consider the judicial precedent interpreting the federal ban and its relationship to the constitutional text. The history of bills of attainder is covered in Essay No. 80, the entry for the state ban.

UNITED STATES V. LOVETT

The Supreme Court's leading authority on the federal Bill of Attainder Clause is *United States v. Lovett* (1946). At issue was Section 304 of the Urgent Deficiency Appropriation Act of 1943. This law directed that no salary be paid to Dr. Robert Morss Lovett, Government Secretary to the Virgin Islands and a well-known left-wing activist, and two other named federal employees, Goodwin B. Watson and William E. Dodd.[2] Representative Martin Dies (D–TX), chairman of the House Special Committee on Un-American Activities, had accused them of being "'irresponsible, unrepresentative, crackpot, radical bureaucrats' and affiliates of 'Communist front organizations.'"[3] Lovett and

245

others named by Dies were invited to testify at a closed hearing. However, they were not allowed the assistance of a lawyer or an opportunity to inspect FBI reports containing evidence against them.[4] The Supreme Court declared Section 304 to be unconstitutional. Justice Hugo Black's majority opinion described Section 304 as "precisely within the category" of a bill of attainder. The law punished Lovett and the others by withholding their government salaries but without the "safeguards" of a judicial trial.[5]

The Court identified four elements of an unconstitutional bill of attainder: (1) a legislative act (2) that applies to named individuals or members of a group, (3) that inflicts punishment on them, and (4) does not provide a judicial trial.[6] The overall effect of this standard is to prohibit legislatures from sentencing and punishing as a court does. The Court's bill of attainder doctrine has become an arm of the Constitution's separation of powers.[7]

WHAT IS A LEGISLATIVE ACT?

An act must be "legislative" to count as a bill of attainder. This requirement is not explicit in the text of Section 9, which simply states that "No bill of attainder . . . shall be passed."[8] At the time the Constitution was ratified, the term "bill" possessed both legislative and judicial meanings.[9] "Bill" could also be used to describe private legislation, often called "private bills," which were legislative acts that concerned the rights or interests of a single person, group, or region. Private bills were passed in the legislature but often in a judicial-type proceeding. Such hearings might include the presentation of a written complaint or "petition," notice to other persons involved, a hearing, and the presentation of evidence.[10] Private bills were common in state legislatures at the time of ratification and remained common in Congress for some time after ratification.[11] The placement of the Bill of Attainder Clause in Section 9, which contains exceptions to congressional power, suggests that it bans one particular type of private legislation in Congress.

Would a similar type of proceeding in the executive branch be a bill of attainder? Like Parliament, some early American legislative "assemblies" could act both as legislatures and courts of law.[12] Whether or not such a body was acting as a legislature when it passed a bill of attainder was not always clear in the record and in some cases may not have a definite answer. Would a federal agency that is nominally in the executive branch but possesses both legislative and judicial powers be subject to the Bill of Attainder Clause?

In *Joint Anti-Fascist Refugee Committee v. McGrath* (1951), Justice Hugo Black's concurrence addressed this question. In this case, the Attorney General compiled a list of "totalitarian, fascist, communist and subversive organizations" at the direction of President Harry S. Truman.[13] This list was not based on an act of Congress. But according to Black, "officially prepared and proclaimed governmental blacklists" by the Attorney General "possess[ed] almost every quality of bills of attainder." Black thought it difficult to believe "that the authors of the Constitution, who outlawed the bill of attainder, inadvertently endowed the executive the power to engage in the same tyrannical practices."[14]

Black's view has never been adopted by a majority of the Court. Challenges to no-fly lists and kill lists maintained by the executive branch have been rejected for lack of a legislative act.[15]

TO WHOM DOES THE LEGISLATIVE ACT APPLY?

The paradigmatic bill of attainder condemns named individuals. Under Supreme Court precedent, however, this is not necessary for a bill to count as a bill of attainder within the meaning of the Constitution.[16] Even acts punishing a relatively large class of individuals have been held to be bills of attainder. For example, *Ex Parte Garland* (1866) found that a law that applied to former confederates in the Civil War was a bill of attainder.[17] Conversely, an act that applies to a single named individual is not necessarily a bill of attainder.[18] This was the case in *Nixon v. Administrator of General Services* (1977), which upheld a law that ostensibly required only one person—former President Richard Nixon—to return certain documents to the federal government.

Congress has the power to legislate with specificity or particularity without passing a bill of attainder.[19] What Congress cannot do is to punish a class of persons on the basis of a judgment that its members are prone to certain behaviors. Rather, Congress must punish the behavior generally.[20] In this respect, bill-of-attainder doctrine intersects with equal-protection doctrine, which contains similar ideas.[21]

WHEN DOES A LEGISLATIVE ACT INFLICT PUNISHMENT?

A legislative act must impose a punishment to count as a bill of attainder.[22] The Supreme Court wrestled with the question of what counted as a punishment in a string of cases involving anti-Communist legislation. *United States v. Brown* (1965), for example, concerned a federal labor law that prohibited Communists from serving as union officers. The *Brown* Court rejected the view that punishments were necessarily "retributive" rather than "preventive." Rather, sometimes punishment aimed to prevent future crimes.[23] Thus, bills of attainder might focus on future conduct, as did the legislation in *Brown*, by condemning a political group whose members were thought likely to endanger national security.

Nixon v. Administrator of General Services identified three tests for deciding whether the law regulating presidential records was punitive under the Bill of Attainder Clause: (i) whether a sanction was one historically imposed by bills of attainder in England or the United States; (ii) whether the sanction could reasonably be said to further nonpunitive legislative purposes; and (iii) whether the legislative record evinced an intent to punish.[24] The *Nixon* Court found that the federal law was not a punitive bill of attainder. Lower federal courts have tended to narrowly apply the *Nixon* tests. In *TikTok v. Garland* (2024), the D.C. Circuit held that a federal law requiring foreign divestment from a social media company did not count as a bill of attainder under these tests.[25] First, the court reasoned that divestment differed from the historically imposed sanction of confiscation. Second, the panel found that forced divestment was "a rather conventional response to a security risk" and thus did not function as a punishment.

Finally, in this case, there was insufficient evidence of a congressional intent to punish, which "is difficult to establish," despite dozens of statements from individual legislators in the record.

The Supreme Court's broad construction of the meaning of "punishment" touched off heated scholarly criticism. Raoul Berger, an early originalist, severely criticized the Court for departing from the historical understanding of bills of attainder, which he argued always imposed a death sentence and disinherited the target's heirs. This feature was called "corruption of blood."[26] A more recent examination of the issue from an originalist point of view, however, took a different view.[27] As discussed in Essay No. 80, medieval bills of attainder rarely included an explicit death sentence.

IS A JUDICIAL TRIAL PROVIDED?

One of the principal objections to bills of attainder is that the legislature does not provide accused persons with the same rights they would enjoy in a court of law.[28] For example, Lovett was denied the assistance of an attorney and an opportunity to confront the witnesses against him. As a historical matter, denying process was often the point. Bills of attainder were used when a court could not proceed because of the procedural rights it was required to extend to defendants—principally the right to appear and offer a defense. The defendant might be in hiding or dead and thus unable to appear.

In several respects, the Supreme Court's bill of attainder doctrine is actually broader than what is known as procedural due process. For example, *Lovett* implied that a legislature must provide "a judicial trial" before inflicting a punishment.[29] By contrast, the Due Process Clauses guarantee no such right. The Sixth and Seventh Amendments do provide a limited right to a jury trial, but a survey of the case law concluded that the *Lovett* mandate was rarely honored because administrative proceedings short of a full trial were routinely upheld.[30]

OPEN QUESTIONS
- Can an action taken by the executive branch in the absence of a federal statute be considered a bill of attainder?
- What is sufficient evidence of an intent to punish under *Nixon v. Administrator of General Services*?

- Does a legislatively directed sale of property count as punishment for purposes of the Bill of Attainder Clauses?[31]

Cite as: Matthew Steilen, *The Federal Bill of Attainder Clause, in* The Heritage Guide to the Constitution 245 (Josh Blackman & John G. Malcolm eds., 3d ed. 2025).

Notes

1. *United States v. Lovett*, 328 U.S. 303, 315–16 (1946). **2.** *Robert M. Lovett, Educator, Is Dead*, N.Y. Times, Feb. 9, 1956, at 31. **3.** *Id.* at 308–09 (quoting 89 Cong. Rec. 474, 479, 486). **4.** *Id.* at 310–11. **5.** *Id.* at 315, 317–18. **6.** Michael P. Lehmann, *The Bill of Attainder Doctrine: A Survey of the Decisional Law*, 5 Hastings L.Q. 767, 767 n.1 (1978). **7.** *United States v. Brown*, 381 U.S. 437, 446 (1965). **8.** *Barron v. City of Balt.*, 32 U.S. (7 Pet.) 243, 248 (1833). **9.** Samuel Johnson, A Dictionary of the English Language (1st ed. 1755) (bill, noun, definition 3). **10.** Zephaniah Swift, 1 A System of Laws of the State of Connecticut 81–82 (1795). **11.** Maggie Blackhawk, *Petitioning and the Making of the Administrative State*, 127 Yale L.J. 1538, 1555–66 (2018). **12.** Mary Patterson Clarke, Parliamentary Privilege in the American Colonies 54 (1943). **13.** 341 U.S. 123, 124–25 (1951). **14.** *Id.* at 143–44. **15.** *Al-Aulaqi v. Panetta*, 35 F. Supp. 3d 56, 81–82 (D.D.C. 2014); *Amiri v. Kelly*, No. 17-cv-12188, 2018 WL 623652 (E.D. Mich., Jan. 30, 2018). **16.** *United States v. Brown*, 381 U.S. 437, 461 (1965). **17.** *Ex Parte Garland*, 71 U.S. 333, 376–77 (1866). **18.** *Nixon v. Admin'r Gen. Servs.*, 433 U.S. 425, 571–72 (1977). **19.** *Bank Markazi v. Peterson*, 578 U.S. 212, 232–234 (2016). **20.** *Brown*, 381 U.S. at 455, 461. **21.** Akhil Reed Amar, *Attainder and Amendment 2:* Romer's Rightness, 95 Mich. L. Rev. 203, 203–04, 210–11 (1996). **22.** *Fleming v. Nestor*, 363 U.S. 603, 613 (1960). **23.** *Brown*, 381 U.S. at 456–58. **24.** *Nixon*, 433 U.S. at 473–84. **25.** *TikTok Inc. v. Garland*, 122 F.4th 930, 967–69 (D.C. Cir. Dec. 6, 2024). **26.** Raoul Berger, *Bills of Attainder: A Study of Amendment by the Court*, 63 Cornell L. Rev. 355 (1978). **27.** Anthony Dick, Note, *The Substance of Punishment Under the Bill of Attainder Clause*, 63 Stan. L. Rev. 1177, 1182–90 (2011). **28.** *Lovett*, 328 U.S. at 317–18. **29.** *Id.* at 315. **30.** Lehmann, *supra* at 901, 911, 916–19. **31.** *TikTok, Inc.*, 122 F.4th at 967–69.

∼

ESSAY NO. 70: THE FEDERAL EX POST FACTO CLAUSE
ART. I, § 9, CL. 3

No . . . *ex post facto Law shall be passed.*

—Evan C. Zoldan

INTRODUCTION

Article I, Section 9, Clause 3 provides that no "ex post facto Law shall be passed" by Congress. A companion clause, Article I, Section 10, Clause 1, similarly provides that no state shall "pass any . . . ex post facto Law."[1] The U.S. Supreme Court has interpreted these two clauses to prohibit, roughly speaking, retroactive criminal laws at both the federal and state levels. Both clauses arose out of the same historical experiences, support the same intuitive policies, and share the same modern judicial interpretations. This essay describes the conceptual background and judicial interpretations of these two clauses. Essay No. 81 describes the historical background surrounding the inclusion of these clauses in the Constitution, focusing on the events that bear most heavily on their meaning today.

RETROACTIVITY AND THE EX POST FACTO CLAUSES

A statute is retroactive when it changes the legal consequences of conduct that occurred before the statute's enactment. Retroactive legislation has long been viewed with suspicion and even hostility. In *Ogden v. Saunders* (1827), Justice Bushrod Washington denounced retroactive laws as "oppressive, unjust, and tyrannical."[2] Modern scholars are no kinder. Lon Fuller's view that retroactive laws are "truly a monstrosity" represents an almost universally held view.[3] The prohibition on retroactive statutes serves some intuitively attractive policies, including protecting the value of fair notice. When individuals are assured that their conduct will be governed by laws that already are in effect, they are better able to plan their conduct with reasonable certainty of the legal consequences of their actions.[4] Prohibiting retroactivity also reinforces the separation of powers,[5] ensures fundamental fairness,[6] and upholds the rule of law.[7]

Despite this consistent aversion to retroactivity, the Constitution's Ex Post Facto Clauses have never been interpreted by the Supreme Court to apply to all retroactive legislation. One reason is textual. Reading the clauses to cover all retroactive statutes would lead them to overlap significantly with other clauses of the Constitution. For example, the Contracts Clause, which bars the states from "impairing the Obligation of Contracts," itself prohibits some types of retroactive action.[8] (See Essay No. 82.)

Another reason is practical. Sometimes statutes are popular precisely because of their retroactive effect. New York, for example, retroactively extended a statute of limitation for civil suits and even revived claims of child abuse that were barred by a generally applicable statutes of limitations.[9] Perhaps for these textual and practical reasons, the Supreme Court has never read the Constitution's Ex Post Facto clauses for all they are worth, instead interpreting them to prohibit a subset of retrospective laws—perhaps the most odious—while excluding from their scope other kinds of retrospective laws.[10]

CALDER'S FOUR CATEGORIES OF PROHIBITED RETROACTIVE LAWS

Calder v. Bull (1798) was the Supreme Court's first and most enduring statement concerning the scope of the Ex Post Facto clauses. Justice Samuel Chase described four categories of retroactive laws that fall within the Constitution's prohibitions. Although the Supreme Court has used other formulations throughout the centuries, it has returned time and again to these categories.

Calder's first category includes statutes that attach criminal liability to an action that was innocent when it was done. This type of statute is perhaps the archetype of a retroactive law and calls to mind the reasons why retroactive laws have been thoroughly denounced over the centuries. This category is exemplified by *Cummings v. Missouri* (1866).[11] *Cummings* declared unconstitutional a state law that penalized anyone who

practiced certain professions without first taking an oath that he had not engaged in conduct that was, at the time, lawful. The Court held that a law directed at acts that "were not offences at the time they were committed" is an impermissible ex post facto law. Today, statutes that fall within the first category are rare.

The second category includes statutes that "aggravate[] a crime, or make[] it greater than it was, when committed." *Calder* did not clarify what it means to "aggravate" a crime, but later cases have explained that "aggravating" a crime includes making punishment available when it previously would not have been available "in the ordinary course of law."[12] For example, *Stogner v. California* (2003) declared unconstitutional a statute that extended the statute of limitations for the criminal prosecution of certain offenses, even as to conduct for which the statute of limitations already had expired. The Court held that because prosecution was not available after the expiration of the statute of limitations, there was no legal consequence to the conduct "in the ordinary course of law." Accordingly, a statute that purported to allow prosecution to resume impermissibly aggravated the crime by making prosecution available when it would not ordinarily have been available.

The third category includes laws that "change[] the punishment, and inflict[] a greater punishment, than the law annexed to the crime, when committed." In other words, laws cannot increase the quantum of punishment compared with what was available at the time the conduct was committed. This category, unlike the first, contemplates that the conduct already was unlawful even before the change in law; unlike the second, it contemplates that at least *some* punishment already was available under the old law. By contrast, this third category addresses the situation in which the change in law creates a "sufficient risk" that the person subject to punishment will receive more punishment than he would have received under the law in force at the time the unlawful conduct was committed.[13] *Peugh v. United States* (2013) held that amendments to the federal sentencing guidelines that raised the punishment guideline for an already committed offense violate the Ex Post Facto Clause. This was true, the Court reasoned, despite the fact that the guidelines are advisory and leave sentencing discretion to judges. Raising the punishment guideline creates a "sufficient risk" that judges would apply a harsher punishment. As a result, the retroactive application of the more severe guidelines was impermissibly ex post facto.[14]

The fourth category includes laws that "alter[] the legal rules of evidence" to require "less, or different, testimony, than the law required at the time of the commission of the offence" to secure a conviction. In short, the rules of evidence cannot be modified retrospectively to make it easier to convict the accused. The classic example of a statute in this category retrospectively reduces the number of witnesses required to convict from two to one. This reduction makes conviction easier by decreasing the work the state must do to convict.[15] For example, in *Carmell v. Texas* (2000), at the time the unlawful conduct was committed, the defendant could be convicted only on a record that included both the victim's testimony *and* corroborating evidence.[16] By the time he was convicted, an amendment had altered the rule of evidence to require only the victim's testimony, without corroborating evidence, to convict. The Court held that the change reduced the "quantum of evidence required to convict" and was therefore impermissibly ex post facto.[17]

OPEN QUESTIONS

- The Ex Post Facto clauses prohibit a law only if it is *punitive* in nature—but what precisely qualifies as punitive? A statute is punitive if either the legislature intended it to punish or the effect of the statutory scheme is to punish.[18] The Court has declined to frame a bright-line rule to determine whether a statute has a punitive effect, instead considering a number of factors to resolve whether a statutory scheme is sufficiently punitive to trigger the clauses.[19] These factors, because they are both malleable and indeterminate, fail to provide predictable results.[20]
- Are *Calder*'s four categories exemplary or exclusive? Justice Chase suggested that they are not exclusive.[21] However, two centuries later, *Collins v. Youngblood* (1990) implied that these categories are exclusive and may neither be augmented nor diminished.[22] Other recent cases, like *Peugh* and *Weaver v. Graham* (1981), have taken a less categorical approach. As a result, the precise contours of the clauses' protections are not wholly settled.
- Do the Ex Post Facto clauses apply only to legislative action? The Supreme Court has offered mixed signals on this question. Some cases suggest that the provision applies to legislative action alone,[23] but the Court has noted that "the Ex Post Facto Clause is not limited to legislative acts."[24] Extending the clauses to executive and judicial conduct would not only expand the scope of the clauses' protections but also create significant overlap between them and other constitutional clauses, like the Due Process clauses.

Cite as: Evan C. Zoldan, *The Federal Ex Post Facto Clause, in* THE HERITAGE GUIDE TO THE CONSTITUTION 248 (Josh Blackman & John G. Malcolm eds., 3d ed. 2025).

Notes

1. Art. I, §§ 9, 10.   **2.** *Ogden v. Saunders*, 25 U.S. 213 (1827).   **3.** Lon Fuller, The Morality of Law 53 (1969).   **4.** *Weaver v. Graham*, 450 U.S. 24, 30 (1981).   **5.** *Carmell v. Texas*, 529 U.S. 513, 530 (2000).   **6.** Charles B. Hochman, *The Supreme Court and the Constitutionality of Retroactive Legislation*, 73 Harv. L. Rev. 692, 693 (1960).   **7.** *Carmell*, 529 U.S. at 530.   **8.** *Landgraf v. USI Film Prods.*, 511 U.S. 244 (1994).   **9.** Child Victims Act, N.Y.C.P.L.R. 214-g.   **10.** Douglas Kmiec & John O. McGinnis, *The Contract Clause: A Return to the Original Understanding*, 14 Hastings Con. L. Q. 525, 528 (1987).   **11.** 71 U.S. (4 Wall.) 277, 327–28 (1866).   **12.** *Stogner v. California*, 539 U.S. 607, 613 (2003).   **13.** *Peugh v. United States*, 569 U.S. 530, 539 (2013).   **14.** *Id.*   **15.** *Carmell*, 529 U.S. at 530.   **16.** *Id.*   **17.** *Id.* at 532.   **18.** *Smith v. Doe*, 538 U.S. 84 (2003).   **19.** *Id.*   **20.** Wayne Logan, The Ex Post Facto Clause (2022).   **21.** 3 U.S (3 Dall.) at 391.   **22.** 497 U.S. at 42.   **23.** *United States v. Marcus*, 560 U.S. 258, 264 (2010); Nicholas Quinn Rosenkranz, *The Objects of the Constitution*, 63 Stan. L. Rev. 1005, 1019–20 (2011).   **24.** *Peugh*, 569 U.S. at 544–45.

ESSAY NO. 71: THE DIRECT TAXES CLAUSE
ART. I, § 9, CL. 4

No Capitation, or other direct, Tax shall be laid, unless in Proportion to the Census or enumeration herein before directed to be taken.

—Andy Grewal

INTRODUCTION

Congress's first enumerated power is the "Power To lay and collect Taxes, Duties, Imposts and Excises."[1] (See Essay No. 39.) This provision refers to taxes broadly and then refers to three subsets of taxes: duties, imposts, and excises. Duties and imposts are taxes the government applies to the import or export of goods. Excises are taxes levied on the enjoyment of a privilege, such as the right to produce a good or pursue a specific occupation. If a tax is not a duty, impose, or excise—that is, if the tax is a "direct tax"—the tax faces an apportionment requirement.[2]

Under the apportionment requirement, direct taxes must be laid "in Proportion to the Census or enumeration." Whether a tax qualifies as direct and thus must follow this apportionment requirement generated uncertainty in the early days of the Republic.[3] However, the Sixteenth Amendment, ratified in 1913, reduced the practical importance of the apportionment requirement. (See Essay No. 202.)

HISTORY BEFORE 1787

The Articles of Confederation were a "fiscal disaster."[4] They did not allow Congress to tax the population directly; instead, taxes could be collected only from the states themselves through voluntary "requisitions."[5] However, the states often resisted congressional attempts at taxation, and the Articles provided no enforcement mechanism.[6] Thus, attempts at taxation proved futile. For example, in 1786 the Board of Treasury mandated that the states collectively contribute $3.8 million to the federal purse, but the states paid only $663.[7]

THE CONSTITUTIONAL CONVENTION

The Framers, to avoid the revenue challenges experienced under the Articles of Confederation, included broad taxing powers in the new Constitution.[8] Instead of having to seek revenue from the states, Congress would be able to tax the people themselves, including through direct taxes.[9] The Constitution specified that capitation (head) taxes qualify as direct taxes.[10] The Convention records shed no further light on what might qualify as a direct tax.[11] On August 20, Rufus King of Massachusetts asked "what was the precise meaning of *direct* taxation?" According to Madison's notes, "No one answ[ere]d."[12]

Direct taxes, whatever they might include, must comply with an apportionment requirement.[13] This means that Congress must allocate a direct tax to the states according to their respective populations.[14] Under the original Constitution, a slave would count as three-fifths of a person for purposes of the population computation.[15] (See Essay No. 9.) Thus, the presence of slaves would increase the amount of tax allocated to a state, but not by as much as the presence of free persons.

A simple example illustrates the apportionment rule. Suppose Congress wants to raise $100 million through a real estate tax, and that tax is considered direct. Congress could not establish a single tax rate to apply to the value of all real estate in the country. Instead, it would need to apportion the $100 million figure to the states, based on their population. Thus, a state with ten percent of the population would need to raise $10 million, a state with five percent of the population would need to raise $5 million, and so on. Under this regime, taxpayers in different states would likely face different tax rates on their real estate. For a state with 10 percent of the population and valuable land, a low tax rate would be needed to collect $10 million; in a state with 10 percent of the population and low-value land, a higher rate would be needed to collect $10 million.

THE RATIFICATION DEBATES

In Federalist No. 36, Alexander Hamilton emphasized that the apportionment rule for real estate taxes would help to prevent abuse. The proportion of real estate taxes paid by the people of a state would not be "left to the discretion of the national legislature." Instead, if Congress imposed a real estate tax, the burdens would be "determined by the numbers of each state." The apportionment requirement, Hamilton believed, "effectually shut[] the door to partiality or oppression."[16]

The Anti-Federalists expressed skepticism about a national taxing power. Luther Martin of Maryland, for example, preferred that states enjoy the exclusive authority to levy direct taxes.[17] A Federal Republican did not find solace in the protections offered by the apportionment rule, calling it "a great and fundamental error" and stating that "the apportioning of taxes according to numbers is not just."[18]

EARLY PRACTICE

At various times in the country's early history, Congress imposed real estate taxes using the apportionment scheme contemplated by the Constitution,[19] but it did not establish an apportionment scheme for other revenue measures.[20] Thus, Congress may have understood that direct taxes include only capitation and real estate taxes.[21]

Some notable figures viewed "direct taxes" more broadly. When Congress considered an unapportioned personal property tax on the ownership of carriages, James Madison voted against the bill. He believed that the federal carriage tax was a direct tax that required apportionment.[22] Hamilton also believed that direct taxes went beyond only capitation and real estate taxes. In a judicial filing, he argued that direct taxes would include taxes on "the whole property of individuals, or on their whole real or personal estate."[23] Thus, to Hamilton, a wealth tax would have qualified as a direct tax.

JUDICIAL PRECEDENT

In *Hylton v. United States* (1796), the Supreme Court upheld the federal carriage tax, finding that it was not an unapportioned direct tax.[24] As was customary at the time, there was no official Court opinion. Instead, the Justices issued individual *seriatim* opinions. Justice William Paterson's influential individual opinion understood "direct taxes" narrowly. Paterson wrote that the direct tax clause had a limited purpose: to allay southern fears of targeted federal real estate taxes.[25] Thus, he believed, the direct tax limitation should not apply to a tax that reached personal property, like the federal carriage tax.[26]

Throughout most of the nineteenth century, the Court followed Justice Paterson's narrow approach, and held that the direct tax limitation applied only to capitation and real estate taxes.[27] The Court rejected claims that the direct tax limitation applied to taxes on insurance company receipts, the circulation of state bank notes, and real estate inheritances.[28] *Springer v. United States* (1880) also rejected a challenge to the unapportioned Civil War–era income tax, finding that it qualified as an excise or duty rather than as a direct tax.[29]

Later, the Court would find that a tax on personal property could qualify as a direct tax. In 1894, Congress imposed an unapportioned income tax, similar to the one upheld in *Springer*. But in *Pollock v. Farmers' Loan & Trust Co.* (1885), a deeply divided Court found that, through reaching rental income, the 1894 income tax imposed an unapportioned real property tax that violated the direct tax requirement.[30] *Pollock* extended similar reasoning to other aspects of the 1894 income tax. The Court concluded that by taxing income from personal property, Congress had taxed the property itself.[31] And, the Court now concluded, a tax on personal property qualified as a direct tax.[32] The Court then found that the unconstitutional portions of the 1894 income tax act could not be severed from the rest of the law. Thus, the whole act fell.[33]

Pollock proved severely unpopular, and many public officials and legal scholars excoriated the majority's decision. For example, a few days after the Supreme Court released its decision, Justice John Marshall Harlan wrote to his sons that *Pollock* would "become as hateful with the American people as the *Dred Scott* case was when it was decided."[34] Sylvester Pennoyer, the former governor of Oregon, called for Congress to "impeach the nullifying [*Pollock*] judges for the usurpation of legislative power, remove them from office, and instruct the President to enforce the collection of the income tax."[35] Fourteen years later, in 1909, President William Howard Taft remarked that "[n]othing has ever injured the prestige of the Supreme Court more than [the *Pollock*] decision."[36]

The fierce backlash against *Pollock* led Congress to propose the Sixteenth Amendment to the Constitution.[37] Under that amendment, ratified in 1913, "taxes on incomes," even if considered direct, face no apportionment requirement.[38] A key issue under the Sixteenth Amendment relates to whether "taxes on incomes" include taxes on unrealized gains. Unrealized gains typically arise when a taxpayer's property has increased in value, but the taxpayer has not sold it. *Eisner v. Macomber* (1920) concluded that the Sixteenth Amendment established a realization requirement.[39] However, *Moore v. United States* (2024) leaves open whether *Macomber*'s realization holding remains good law.[40]

OPEN QUESTIONS

Debates over whether a tax qualifies as direct became less important after the Sixteenth Amendment. That amendment authorizes an unapportioned federal income tax, whether or not that tax is considered direct. Today, the federal income tax has become the main driver of federal revenue.[41] Thus, Congress can exert substantial taxation authority without concern for apportionment restrictions.

Some interpretive issues may arise as Congress considers more aggressive invocations of Sixteenth Amendment authority. Many very wealthy persons, including billionaires, do not have incomes that correspond to their wealth. That is, their wealth is associated with huge increases in the values of their assets rather than huge salaries. Can Congress treat this "unrealized appreciation" as income and tax it without following an apportionment requirement? The Court in *Moore* left this question open.[42]

Related questions may arise over *Pollock*'s holding that direct taxes include taxes on personal property. The Sixteenth Amendment did not alter that holding, and the Court has repeatedly indicated that direct taxes include all property taxes.[43] But scholars have urged the Court to revisit *Pollock*'s holding about personal property.[44] If the Court does so, Congress could easily impose wealth taxes on billion-dollar stock holdings even if it cannot impose wealth taxes on real estate accumulations.

Cite as: Andy Grewal, *The Direct Taxes Clause, in* THE HERITAGE GUIDE TO THE CONSTITUTION 251 (Josh Blackman & John G. Malcolm eds., 3d ed. 2025).

Notes

1. Art. I, § 8, cl. 1.   **2.** Art. I, § 9, cl. 4.   **3.** *Hylton v. United States*, 3 U.S. 171, 177 (1796); *Pac. Ins. Co. v. Soule*, 74 U.S. 433 (1868); *Veazie Bank v. Fenno*, 75 U.S. 533 (1869); *Scholey v. Rew*, 90 U.S. 331 (1974); *Springer v. United States*, 102 U.S. 586 (1880).   **4.** Erik M. Jensen, *The Taxing Power, the Sixteenth Amendment, and the Meaning of "Incomes,"* 33 Ariz. State L.J. 1057, 1068 (2001).   **5.** Articles of Confederation, arts. VIII & IX § 4.   **6.** Federalist No. 15 (Hamilton).   **7.** Calvin H. Johnson, *Homage to CLIO: The Historical Continuity from the Articles of Confederation into the Constitution*, 20 Const. Comment. 463, 486 (2004).   **8.** Art. I, § 8, cl. 1; 2 Farrand's 143, 366, 572; 3 Farrand's 149, 360.   **9.** Art. I, § 8, cl. 1; 2 Farrand's 572.   **10.** Art. I, § 9, cl. 4.   **11.** Edwin R. A. Seligman, The Income Tax: A Study of the History, Theory, and Practice of Income Taxation at Home and Abroad 565–66 (1911).   **12.** 2 Farrand's 350.   **13.** Art. I, § 9, cl. 4.   **14.** Art. I, § 2, cl. 3.   **15.** *Id.*   **16.** Federalist No. 36 (Hamilton).   **17.** Storing 2.4.56.   **18.** Storing 3.6.45.

19. John R. Brooks & David Gamage, *Taxation and the Constitution, Reconsidered*, 76 Tax L. Rev. 201 (2023).   **20.** Joseph M. Dodge, *What Federal Taxes Are Subject to the Rule of Apportionment Under the Constitution?*, 11 J. Const. L. 839, 871–72 (2009).   **21.** Seligman, *supra*, at 534.   **22.** 4 Annals of Cong. 730 (1794).   **23.** 8 The Works of Alexander Hamilton 382 (Henry Cabot Lodge ed., 1904).   **24.** 3 U.S. 171 (1796).   **25.** *Hylton*, 3 U.S. at 177.   **26.** *Id.*   **27.** *Soule*, 74 U.S. 433; *Veazie Bank*, 75 U.S. 533; *Scholey*, 90 U.S. 331; *Springer*, 102 U.S. 586.   **28.** *Soule*, 74 U.S. 433; *Veazie Bank*, 75 U.S. 533; *Scholey*, 90 U.S. 331.   **29.** *Springer*, 102 U.S. at 602.   **30.** *Pollock v. Farmers' Loan & Tr. Co.*, 158 U.S. 601, 618, 637 (1895).   **31.** *Id.* at 628.   **32.** *Id.* at 625, 637.   **33.** *Id.* at 637.   **34.** David G. Farrelly, *Justice Harlan's Dissent in the* Pollock *Case*, 24 S. Cal. L. Rev. 175, 180 (1951).   **35.** Sylvester Pennoyer, *The Income Tax Decision, and the Power of the Supreme Court to Nullify Acts of Congress*, 29 Am. L. Rev. 550, 558 (1895); Nat'l Governors Ass'n, Oregon

Gov. Sylvester Pennoyer, https://perma.cc/X6JL-FAAT. **36.** Letter from Archibald Butt to Clara Butt (July 1, 1909), *in* Taft and Roosevelt: The Intimate Letters of Archie Butt, Military Aide 133–34 (1930). **37.** Jensen, *supra* at 1107–15. **38.** Amend. XVI. **39.** *Eisner v. Macomber*, 252 U.S. 189, 207, 211–12 (1920). **40.** *Moore v. United States*, 602 U.S. 572, 588 n.3 (2024). **41.** Erica York & Madison Mauro, *The Composition of Federal Revenue Has Changed over Time,*

Tax Foundation (Feb. 28, 2019), https://perma.cc/RYS9 -ZUWX. **42.** *Moore*, 602 U.S. at 599. **43.** *Nat'l Fed'n of Indep. Bus. v. Sebelius*, 567 U.S. 519, 571 (2012); *Moore*, 602 U.S. at 582. **44.** Dawn Johnson & Walter Dellinger, *The Constitutionality of a National Wealth Tax*, 93 Ind. L.J. 111, 137 (2018); Bruce Ackerman, *Taxation and the Constitution,* 99 Colum. L. Rev. 1, 58 (1999).

~ꝰ

ESSAY NO. 72: THE EXPORT TAXATION CLAUSE
ART. I, § 9, CL. 5

No Tax or Duty shall be laid on Articles exported from any State.
—Chief Judge Matthew H. Solomson, Athanasius Sirilla, & Jacob B. Chefitz

INTRODUCTION

The Constitution grants Congress a broad "Power To lay and collect Taxes, Duties, Imposts and Excises."[1] (See Essay No. 39.) However, the Export Taxation Clause imposes an absolute limit on this power: "No Tax or Duty shall be laid on Articles exported from any State." This provision was vigorously debated during the Constitutional Convention. Delegates from southern agrarian states worried that an export tax would unfairly burden the South, the economy of which depended on exports significantly more than the North. Delegates from northern commercial states stressed the importance of taxing exports as a simple way to collect revenue. The Export Taxation Clause was one of the many accommodations the Framers made to cement unity among the various sections of the Union. Modern litigation about the clause generally turns on whether various services related to exports are considered "Articles."

HISTORY BEFORE 1787

In the Declaration of Independence, the colonies, being unrepresented in Parliament, voiced resentment against the king of Great Britain for "imposing Taxes on us without our Consent."[2] The Articles of Confederation reflected the objection of "no taxation without representation."[3] Only the local state governments, and not the national government, were allowed to levy taxes.[4] Opponents of a centralized government often argued that America

was too large for a national legislature to represent all citizens adequately. Ultimately, the Articles of Confederation government failed, at least in part, because it was an underfunded, weak national government lacking a taxing power. James Madison, among many others, identified this failure in his April 1787 "Vices of the Political System of the United States" memorandum. The first vice on Madison's list was "Failure of the States to comply with the Constitutional requisitions."[5]

THE CONSTITUTIONAL CONVENTION

While the Framers of the Constitution ultimately did not expressly limit Congress's power to place tariffs on imports from foreign nations, there was vigorous disagreement about whether Congress and the states should be able to tax exports to foreign nations. On June 18, 1787, Alexander Hamilton of New York said that "national revenue" could be "drawn" from "exports which notwithstanding the common opinion are fit objects of moderate taxation."[6] These taxes would be paid by farmers and other businesses that exported goods. Unsurprisingly, this idea would prove unpopular in southern states that exported agrarian products. On August 16, George Mason of Virginia insisted that "no tax should be laid on exports" and expressed his hope that the "Northn. States did not mean to deny the Southern [states] this security."[7] Mason proposed that "no tax duty or imposition, shall be laid by the Legislature of the U[nited] States on articles exported from any State."[8] Gouverneur Morris of Pennsylvania objected to Mason's proposal as "so radically objectionable, that it might cost the whole system the support of some members."[9] Morris argued that it would not be "equitable to tax imports without taxing exports; and that taxes on exports would be often the most easy and proper of the two."[10]

Madison contended that national taxes on exports would be "proper," as "the States cannot with propriety exercise it separately."[11] He recognized that the "burden should be somewhat heaviest on" the southern states but said that "time will equalize the situation of the States in this matter."[12] Elbridge Gerry of Massachusetts thought that the federal government "could not be trusted" with the power to tax exports, which "might ruin the Country . . . raising one [part] and depressing another part of it."[13] Roger Sherman of Connecticut agreed: "A power to tax exports would shipwreck the whole."[14] The delegates did not vote on Mason's proposal at that time. They also did not resolve the question of whether states could tax exports.

On August 21, debate on Mason's proposal resumed. As a compromise, Madison proposed that Congress be empowered to tax exports with a two-thirds vote of each house.[15] All of the southern states voted against this proposal, which was defeated by a vote of six to five.[16] The Virginia delegation, however, was divided with George Washington and Madison voting in favor of the proposal. Washington, who served as President of the Convention, spoke only twice in Philadelphia and rarely registered his separate views. The fact that he felt the need to vote on this proposal indicates that this issue must have been very significant for him.

Ultimately, Mason's original proposal was approved by a vote of seven to four with Washington and Madison voting no.[17] Thus, the general southern view prevailed over Madison's and Washington's dissent.

THE RATIFICATION DEBATES

The Export Taxation Clause did not prove to be particularly controversial during the ratification debates. In Federalist No. 32, Hamilton discussed the relationship between the federal government and the state governments with regard to taxation. As noted, Congress has the "Power To lay and collect Taxes, Duties, Imposts and Excises." This power, Hamilton wrote, would seem to include an "*exclusive* power in the Union to lay duties on imports and exports." But "no tax or duty shall be laid on articles exported from any state; in consequence of which qualification, it now only extends to the duties on imports." In other words, Congress could impose tariffs on imports but could not tax exports.

The Anti-Federalist Brutus from New York wrote that a "duty on exports" would be "the best source of revenue to grant the general government" and could "be raised by simple laws, with few officers, with certainty and expedition." Brutus could not "perceive the reason of the restriction" in the Export Taxation Clause.[18]

JUDICIAL PRECEDENT

The U.S. Supreme Court has strictly enforced the Export Taxation Clause's prohibition against any tax on goods in the course of exportation. For example, the Court found unconstitutional a tax on baseballs and baseball bats that applied to a manufacturer after it agreed to ship some bats and balls to a buyer in Venezuela—but before the goods had been shipped.[19] This standard applies to both "discriminatory" and "nondiscriminatory" taxes.[20] The Court expressly rejected the argument that "the sole purpose of this constitutional restriction was to prevent discrimination between the states by imposing an export tax on certain articles which might be a product of only a few of the states. . . ."[21]

The Court has also declared unconstitutional taxes on certain services and activities "closely related to the export process"[22] but has refrained from clearly defining what is "closely related" to the export process and thus may not be taxed: "[T]he question [of] whether a particular assessment on an activity or service is so closely connected to the goods as to amount to a tax on the goods themselves must await another day."[23]

The Court has read the clause to prohibit only federal taxes or duties imposed on goods in the course of exportation but not before exportation. In other words, this constitutional restriction does not apply merely because the goods may be intended for export.[24] In the late 1800s, for example, the Court upheld a federal law that imposed a stamp charge on packages of tobacco that were to be exported and thus were exempt from an excise tax.[25] The charge was not considered an export tax because the goods were not actually in the course of exportation. The Court has similarly upheld other federal assessments on pre-export goods ultimately intended for exportation, such as a tax on manufacturing of filled cheeses.[26]

By contrast, the Court has declared unconstitutional taxes imposed on certain services and activities that are directly related to the export process, such as taxes on bills of lading, marine insurance policies, and harbor maintenance.[27] *United States v. International Business Machines Corp.* (1996) declared unconstitutional a tax on foreign insurance premiums. The Court concluded that the Framers sought to "completely deny[] to Congress the power to tax exports at all."[28] In a dissenting opinion, Justice Anthony Kennedy contended that the Export Taxation Clause, as understood by the Framers, would prohibit export taxes on "articles" but not on services like insurance that arguably have only an indirect effect on export costs.[29]

The Supreme Court has taken a relatively narrow view of Congress's power to tax exports, consistent with the plain language of the Export Taxation Clause, but Congress has found ways to regulate exports in other ways. For example, export taxes are imposed based on the goods or services exported, but user fees represent fair "compensation given for [governmental] services rendered."[30] The stamps on tobacco packages were upheld as permissible user fees because the price was a flat rate that did not depend on the quantity or type of tobacco. This fee was held not to constitute an impermissible export tax. Congress has also regulated exports through embargoes on goods for export power that are arguably more restrictive than an export tax.[31]

Taxpayers may sue the United States for violating the Export Taxation Clause in the Court of Federal Claims. These suits request a federal tax refund.[32] Jurisdiction for these cases is based on the Tucker Act, which grants jurisdiction to the Court of Federal Claims over certain monetary claims, including those founded on the Constitution.[33]

OPEN QUESTIONS

- What is the scope of the Export Taxation Clause's prohibition? How "closely related" to the export process must a tax be before it is prohibited?

Cite as: Chief Judge Matthew H. Solomson, Athanasius Sirilla, & Jacob B. Chefitz, *The Export Taxation Clause, in* THE HERITAGE GUIDE TO THE CONSTITUTION 254 (Josh Blackman & John G. Malcolm eds., 3d ed. 2025).

Notes

1. Art. I, § 8, cl. 1. **2.** Declaration of Independence, ¶ 19. **3.** Patrick Henry, Virginia Resolves on the Stamp Act (1765), https://perma.cc/6279-NRQJ. **4.** Articles of Confederation, art. VIII. **5.** James Madison, *Vices of the Political System of the United States* (Apr. 1787), https://perma.cc/589D-EXB6; George Anastaplo, *The Constitution at Two Hundred: Explorations*, 22 Tex. Tech. L. Rev. 967, 969 (1991). **6.** 1 Farrand's 286. **7.** 2 Farrand's 305. **8.** *Id.* at 306. **9.** *Id.* **10.** *Id.* **11.** *Id.* **12.** *Id.* at 307. **13.** *Id.* **14.** *Id.* at 308. **15.** *Id.* at 363. **16.** *Id.* **17.** *Id.* at 363–64. **18.** Storing 2.9.92. **19.** *A.G. Spalding & Bros. v. Edwards*, 262 U.S. 66 (1923). **20.** *United States v. IBM Corp.*, 517 U.S. 843, 845, 860–61 (1996). **21.** *Fairbank v. United States*, 181 U.S. 283, 292–93 (1901). **22.** *IBM*, 517 U.S. at 848–49. **23.** *Id.* at 863. **24.** *Pace v. Burgess*, 92 U.S. 372 (1876); *Turpin v. Burgess*, 117 U.S. 504, 507 (1886); *Cornell v. Coyne*, 192 U.S. 418 (1904). **25.** *Turpin*, 117 U.S. at 507. **26.** *Cornell*, 192 U.S. at 429. **27.** *Fairbank*, 181 U.S. at 294; *Thames & Mersey Marine Ins., v. United States*, 237 U.S. 19, 27 (1915); *United States v. U.S. Shoe Corp.*, 523 U.S. 360, 369 (1998). **28.** 517 U.S. at 860–61. **29.** *Id.* at 873 (Kennedy, J., dissenting). **30.** *Pace*, 92 U.S. at 375. **31.** Erik M. Jensen, *The Export Clause*, 6 Fla. Tax Rev. 1, 46 (2003). **32.** I.R.C. §§ 6511, 6532, 7422. **33.** 28 U.S.C. § 1491(a)(1); *Cyprus Amax Coal Co. v. United States*, 205 F.3d 1369, 1373 (Fed. Cir. 2000); *United States v. Clintwood Elkhorn Min. Co.*, 553 U.S. 1, 14 (2008).

ESSAY NO. 73: THE PORT PREFERENCE CLAUSE
ART. I, § 9, CL. 6

No Preference shall be given by any Regulation of Commerce or Revenue to the Ports of one State over those of another; nor shall Vessels bound to, or from, one State, be obliged to enter, clear, or pay Duties in another.

—Nelson Lund

INTRODUCTION

The Constitution includes several provisions designed to prevent the federal government from treating the states inequitably, especially with respect to taxation and the regulation of commerce. The Uniformity Clause, for example, requires that federal duties, imposts, and excises be uniform throughout the United States. (See Essay No. 41.) Similarly, the Port Preference Clause forbids Congress from granting special privileges to the ports of certain states or to funnel shipping through ports other than those in the state of its origin or destination. Like the Uniformity Clause, with which it was initially joined at the Constitutional Convention,[1] the Port Preference Clause was meant to interfere with the natural tendency of legislatures to become instruments through which powerful special interests injure their politically weaker rivals.

THE CONSTITUTIONAL CONVENTION

The impetus for the Port Preference Clause came from the Maryland delegation, whose members were especially worried that vessels bound to or from the port of Baltimore might be required to stop in Virginia.[2] Some other delegates objected that Congress should not have its hands tied lest it be unable to deal adequately with problems such as smuggling on long rivers like the Delaware.[3] The issue was referred to an eleven-member committee on trade, which recommended language nearly identical to the final versions of this clause and the Uniformity Clause.[4] There was no further recorded debate at the Convention.

THE RATIFICATION DEBATES

Maryland's Luther Martin, who became a leading Anti-Federalist, remained dissatisfied. Martin objected to the Port Preferences Clause during a lengthy address to his state's legislature. He objected that Congress might easily violate the spirit of the Port Preference Clause, perhaps by limiting Maryland to one inconvenient port of entry such as Georgetown, which is situated near the point where the Potomac ceases to be navigable. This would effectively require shipping bound to or from other ports, such as Baltimore, to clear and enter at a Virginia port.[5] Despite Martin's efforts, however, the clause did not become a significant point of contention in the ratification debates.

JUDICIAL PRECEDENT

Notwithstanding the broad language of the Port Preference Clause, the U.S. Supreme Court has construed it very narrowly. Congress is allowed to grant enormous "incidental" preferences to the ports of certain states. For example, Congress can make improvements, such as dredging, in one place but not another; it can also create obstructions, such as bridges, in a disfavored place rather than a favored place.[6] The Court has indicated that the clause would be violated only by overt discrimination between all the ports of one state and those of another.[7] Yet even this prohibition is essentially toothless. The Court has read the Clause to allow Congress to impose a tax that affected all the ports of some states and no ports in some others.[8] The Federal Circuit upheld a tax exemption that applied only to ports in Alaska and Hawaii.[9]

A dissent in the leading Supreme Court case objected that the majority's interpretation rendered the clause a dead letter.[10] More recently, Justice Clarence Thomas suggested in a concurrence that a natural reading of the clause "prohibits Congress from using its commerce power to channel commerce through certain favored ports."[11] As the case law stands, however, Congress is only on its honor to comply with the spirit of the clause by refraining from politically motivated favoritism that distorts the natural economic competition among American ports.

OPEN QUESTIONS

- Might the Court someday revisit its narrow interpretation of the Port Preference Clause as Justice Thomas suggested?[12]
- If the Supreme Court were to reinterpret the Port Preference Clause to impose a broader uniformity constraint on Congress, might it also reinterpret the Commerce Clause to ban non-uniform commercial regulations more generally?[13]

Cite as: Nelson Lund, *The Port Preference Clause, in* THE HERITAGE GUIDE TO THE CONSTITUTION 257 (Josh Blackman & John G. Malcolm eds., 3d ed. 2025).

Notes

1. 2 Farrand's 410.   **2.** *Id.* at 417–18.   **3.** *Id*. at 418, 480–81.   **4.** *Id.* at 418, 434.   **5.** 3 Farrand's 172, 213–14.   **6.** *Pennsylvania v. Wheeling & Belmont Bridge Co.*, 59 U.S. 421, 433–34 (1856) (*Wheeling Bridge II*); *South Carolina v. Georgia*, 93 U.S. 4, 12–13 (1876).   **7.** *Wheeling Bridge II*, 59 U.S. at 435.   **8.** *Augusta Towing Co., Inc. v. United States*, 5 Cl. Ct. 160, 165–66 (1984).   **9.** *Thomson Multimedia Inc. v. United States*, 340 F.3d 1355, 1364–66 (Fed. Cir. 2003).   **10.** *Wheeling Bridge II*, 59 U.S. at 443–44 (McLean, J., dissenting).   **11.** *United States v. Lopez*, 514 U.S. 549, 587 (1995) (Thomas, J., concurring).   **12.** Sam Heavenrich, *The Neglected Port Preference Clause and the Jones Act*, 132 Yale L.J. 559 (2022).   **13.** Thomas B. Colby, *Revitalizing the Forgotten Uniformity Constraint on the Commerce Power*, 91 Va. L. Rev. 249 (2005).

ESSAY NO. 74: THE APPROPRIATIONS CLAUSE
ART. I, § 9, CL. 7

No Money shall be drawn from the Treasury, but in Consequence of Appropriations made by Law; and a regular Statement and Account of the Receipts and Expenditures of all public Money shall be published from time to time.

—Thomas G. Hungar & Michael D. Bopp

INTRODUCTION

The Appropriations Clause is the cornerstone of Congress's "power of the purse." It assigns to Congress the role of final arbiter of the use of public funds, providing Congress with a mechanism to control or limit spending by the federal government. The clause also requires Congress to publish a statement of expenditures from "time to time." Throughout history, Congress and the executive branch have often disagreed about restrictions placed on expenditures. Generally, the courts have deferred to Congress's appropriations power.

HISTORY BEFORE 1787

The Framers of the Constitution were not the first to grapple with control of government spending. Parliamentary supremacy over public funding had been established in Britain after the Glorious Revolution. The English Bill of Rights of 1689 affirmed that "levying money for or to the use of the Crown by pretence of prerogative, without grant of Parliament . . . is illegal."[1]

Revolution-era state constitutions embraced legislative control of spending.[2] The Articles of Confederation granted the Confederation Congress the power to "appropriate and apply" public funds for "defraying the public expenses."[3]

THE CONSTITUTIONAL CONVENTION

The Appropriations Clause first appeared at the Constitutional Convention as part of a proposed division of authority between the House of Representatives and the Senate. A part of that proposal declared that all bills raising or appropriating money—"money bills"—were to originate in the House and were not subject to alteration or amendment in the Senate. Further, no money could be drawn from the "public Treasury, but in Pursuance of Appropriations that shall originate in the House of Representatives."[4] The Convention rejected both the provision vesting exclusive control of money bills in the House and the associated appropriations clause.[5]

Late in the Convention, the Committee of Eleven, appointed to consider unresolved parts of the Constitution, offered a compromise to permit the Senate to amend or concur in amendments of money bills, provided that "[n]o Money shall be drawn from the Treasury, but in Consequence of Appropriations made by Law."[6] The Convention incorporated the proposal, which became the final language of the first part of the Appropriations Clause, with only minor changes made by the Committee of Style.[7] The Convention also adopted the Origination Clause in Article I, Section 7, Clause 1, which required that bills that raised revenue must originate in the House but allowed those bills to be altered by the Senate.[8] (See Essay No. 35.)

The second part of the Appropriations Clause requires Congress to publish a statement of expenditures. This provision stemmed from an amendment offered by George Mason of Virginia in the final days of the Convention. Mason proposed that "an Account of the public expenditures should be annually published."[9] The Convention relaxed this requirement to "from time to time" and adopted it.[10]

The placement and phraseology of the Appropriations Clause are significant. The Framers chose the language of limitation, not authorization, for the part of the clause addressing Congress's authority over spending. In other words, the clause did not empower Congress to spend money, but rather limited how money could be spent. In particular, the clause prevents federal funds from being spent without prior appropriations legislation passed by Congress.

Moreover, the Framers inserted the Appropriations Clause in Section 9 of Article I, which includes other restrictions on the federal government's actions. The Appropriations Clause was not placed in Section 8 of Article I, which grants Congress powers. As one scholar has explained, "a primary significance" of the clause "lies in what it takes away from Congress: the option not to require legislative appropriations prior to expenditure."[11] Congress's affirmative power to spend does not derive from the Appropriations Clause; rather, it likely derives from the Necessary and Proper Clause.[12] (See Essay Nos. 40 and 66.) The U.S. Supreme Court has observed that the "phrasing and location" of the Appropriations Clause "in the Constitution make clear that it is not itself the source of" Congress's power of the purse, but rather "is phrased as a limitation."[13]

THE RATIFICATION DEBATES

In Federalist No. 58, James Madison emphasized the centrality of the power of the purse, which he characterized as "the most compleat and effectual weapon with which any constitution can arm the immediate representatives of the people, for obtaining a redress of every grievance, and for carrying into effect every just and salutary measure."[14]

At the New York ratifying convention, Alexander Hamilton assured the delegates that "where the purse is lodged in one branch, and the sword in another, there can be no danger."[15] John McHenry made a similar point when introducing the Constitution to the Maryland House of Delegates: "[T]here can be no regulation more consistent with the Spirit of Economy and free Government" than the Appropriations Clause.[16]

During the Virginia convention, Patrick Henry and George Mason—both opponents of ratification—criticized the "Statement and Account" provision. They charged that the requirement for publication only "from time to time" meant that, in practice, Congress could shroud public spending in perpetual secrecy.[17]

Even after ratification, Madison's and Hamilton's arguments endured. Justice Joseph

Story, for example, described Congress's appropriations power as an important means of self-protection for the legislature. Congress, he explained, has "a controlling influence over the executive power, since it holds at its own command all the resources by which a chief magistrate could make himself formidable." Congress's power to "grant or withhold supplies . . . can unnerve the power of the sword by striking down the arm which wields it."[18]

EARLY PRACTICE

Appropriations practice was unsettled in the early years after the Constitution was ratified.[19] Federalists, such as Treasury Secretary Alexander Hamilton, argued for lump-sum appropriations and broad executive discretion. The nation's first appropriations bill, which reflected Hamilton's influence, was a single paragraph long.[20] Meanwhile, Republicans pressed for greater congressional control and itemization. This period also saw the first example of impoundment. Under this practice, the President refuses to spend money already appropriated by Congress. In 1803, for example, President Thomas Jefferson declined to spend funds appropriated for naval vessels.[21]

CONGRESSIONAL AND EXECUTIVE BRANCH PRACTICE

Since the founding era, Congress has moved to strengthen its control of the appropriations process.[22] In 1809, Congress mandated that appropriations "shall be solely applied to the objects for which they are respectively appropriated."[23]

In 1849, Congress enacted the Miscellaneous Receipts Statute. This law required all funds received "for the use of the United States" to be paid into the Treasury. As a result, and with certain exceptions, the Executive could not circumvent Congress—for example, by routing federal receipts directly to the agencies that collected them without the need for intervening appropriation by Congress.[24] The Anti-Deficiency Act, a series of measures passed between 1870 and 1905, bars federal agencies from spending in excess of currently available appropriations.[25] Finally, the Impoundment Control Act of 1974 generally prohibits the President from unilaterally refusing to spend appropriated funds.[26]

Presidents of both parties have pushed back against congressional authority over appropriations, seeking to withhold, transfer, or condition funds for topics as varied as border security, health care, and foreign assistance.[27] Some scholarship has questioned the traditional assumption of congressional supremacy over spending, arguing for a greater presidential role.[28]

The executive branch has routinely objected to, and sometimes even disregarded, some funding restrictions set by Congress, citing separation of powers principles.[29] These contested restrictions generally concern issues like national security or foreign policy that are thought to be core executive prerogatives. For example, some within the Reagan Administration worked to circumvent congressional restrictions on funding the Nicaraguan Contra rebels. The Obama Administration arguably failed to comply with a funding restriction requiring notice to Congress for the transfer of detainees from Guantanamo Bay.[30] A federal court also ruled that the Obama Administration violated the Appropriations Clause by spending money on a program created by the Administration's health care reform law without congressional appropriation.[31]

The first Trump Administration criticized the Impoundment Control Act as "unworkable in practice" and argued that it should be "significantly reformed or repealed" because it unduly infringed on executive branch prerogatives.[32] The Trump Administration also diverted appropriations from various other funds for construction of a border wall, prompting inconclusive litigation.[33] The Biden Administration rescinded the diversion of funds for border wall funding and temporarily "paused" the obligation of such funding even when specifically appropriated by Congress—a practice it defended as a "programmatic delay" consistent with the Impoundment Control Act.[34]

The appropriations power, like all of Congress's powers, is subject to the Bill of Rights and other structural constraints in the Constitution.[35] Congress may not, for example, subject named individuals to unconstitutional bills of attainder under the guise of appropriations.[36] (See Essay No. 70.) Furthermore, Congress may not abridge an individual's First Amendment rights through appropriations.[37] (See Essay No. 161.)

There also are important interplays between the appropriations power and the pardon power.

(See Essay No. 105.) First, a presidential pardon may not authorize payment of a claim out of the Treasury barred by an act of Congress.[38] Second, a presidential pardon may not permit the recovery of the proceeds of confiscated property deposited in the Treasury.[39] And third, Congress cannot, through an appropriations rider, impair the power of the President to grant pardons.[40]

JUDICIAL PRECEDENT

The courts have recognized the primacy given to Congress by the Appropriations Clause in allocating the resources of the Treasury. *Cincinnati Soap Co. v. United States* (1937) declared that the Appropriations Clause "was intended as a restriction upon the disbursing authority of the Executive department" and means simply that "no money can be paid out of the Treasury unless it has been appropriated by an act of Congress."[41] *United States v. MacCollom* (1976) articulated an "established rule" that "the expenditure of public funds is proper only when authorized by Congress, not that public funds may be expended unless prohibited by Congress."[42] Moreover, "Congress has a plenary power to exact any reporting and accounting it considers appropriate in the public interest."[43]

The judiciary lacks the power to order the obligation or payment of funds for which there are no appropriations.[44] Courts may not order an appropriation,[45] and private litigants may not use principles of estoppel to require the payment of benefits for which there is no appropriation.[46] Congress has "wide discretion in . . . prescribing details of expenditures"[47] and has a long and consistent practice of setting conditions on the expenditure of appropriations.

CFPB v. CFSAA (2024) upheld a statutory scheme whereby the Consumer Financial Protection Bureau (CFPB), a powerful regulatory agency, funds itself through an annual requisition from the Federal Reserve without further congressional involvement.[48] The Court noted that "[b]y the time of the Constitutional Convention, the principle of legislative supremacy over fiscal matters engendered little debate and created no disagreement." Based on a survey of history, the Court "conclude[d] that appropriations need only identify a source of public funds and authorize the expenditure of those funds for designated purposes to satisfy the Appropriations Clause."[49]

OPEN QUESTIONS

- Although modern practice recognizes the primacy of Congress over the public fisc, the precise contours of the Appropriations Clause continue to be refined.
- Does an individual house of Congress have standing to sue over alleged violations of the Appropriations Clause? Would both houses acting jointly? This issue remains unclear, although some courts have ruled in favor of the House of Representatives.[50]
- The Judgment Fund provides for the automatic payment of most settlements and judgments against the federal government and pays out billions of dollars each year without congressional review.[51] Concerns have been raised regarding transparency and executive branch abuse in the administration of this fund.[52] The availability of the Judgment Fund can have significant fiscal and policy consequences. For example, the Supreme Court has held that when a statute provides that the federal government "shall pay" the beneficiaries of a health care program but Congress has not specifically appropriated any money to do so, the government still owes the unpaid sums, which may be paid out of the Judgment Fund upon suit.[53] Concerns have also been raised that the use of the Judgment Fund rather than agency budgets to pay plaintiffs' legal expenses in suits against government agencies may incentivize "sue and settle" behavior in which interest groups sue agencies to force regulatory changes via settlement.[54]
- To what extent, if at all, may the President unilaterally refuse to spend money appropriated by Congress? Does the Impoundment Control Act, which prevents the President from doing so, infringe on the President's constitutional authority, or

instead merely implement Congress's plenary authority over the expenditure of federal funds?

Cite as: Thomas G. Hungar & Michael D. Bopp, *The Appropriations Clause, in* THE HERITAGE GUIDE TO THE CONSTITUTION 258 (Josh Blackman & John G. Malcolm eds., 3d ed. 2025).

Notes

1. 1 W. & M., ch. 2, sess. 2 (1688) (Eng.).   **2.** Del. Const. of 1776, art. VII; Mass. Const. of 1780, ch. 2, § 1, art. XI; Md. Const. of 1776, arts. X–XI.   **3.** Articles of Confederation, art. IX, § 5.   **4.** 2 Farrand's 154, 164.   **5.** *Id.* at 280.   **6.** *Id.* at 508–10.   **7.** *Id.* at 568, 596, 657.   **8.** *Id.* at 552.   **9.** *Id.* at 618–19.   **10.** *Id.*   **11.** Kate Stith, *Congress' Power of the Purse*, 97 Yale L.J. 1343, 1349 (1988).   **12.** *Id.* at 1348–49.   **13.** *CFPB v. Cmty. Fin. Servs. Ass'n of Am., Ltd.*, 601 U.S. 416, 438 (2024).   **14.** Federalist No. 58 (Madison).   **15.** 2 Elliot's 349.   **16.** 3 Farrand's 149–50.   **17.** *Id.* at 326; Storing 5.16.8.   **18.** 3 Story's Commentaries § 531.   **19.** Gerhard Casper, *Appropriations of Power*, 13 U. Ark. Little Rock L.J. 1, 9–21 (1990); Gillian E. Metzger, *Taking Appropriations Seriously*, 121 Colum. L. Rev. 1075, 1087 (2021); J. Gregory Sidak, *The President's Power of the Purse*, 1989 Duke L.J. 1162, 1177–83 (1989).   **20.** Act of Sept. 29, 1789, 1 Stat. 95.   **21.** Zachary S. Price, *Funding Restrictions and Separation of Powers*, 71 Vand. L. Rev. 357, 434 (2018).   **22.** Casper, *supra* at 21; Metzger, *supra* at 1088–89; Stith, *supra* at 1363–77.   **23.** Act of Mar. 3, 1809, 2 Stat. 535.   **24.** Act of Mar. 3, 1849, 9 Stat. 398 (now codified at 31 U.S.C. § 3302(b)); Stith, *supra* at 1365.   **25.** 31 U.S.C. § 1341.   **26.** 2 U.S.C. §§ 682–88.   **27.** Metzger, *supra* at 1077–80, 1092–1103.   **28.** Sidak, *supra* at 1183–1202.   **29.** Price, *supra* at 373–78.   **30.** *Id.* at 374–75.   **31.** *U.S. House of Representatives v. Burwell*, 185 F. Supp. 3d 165, 174–88 (D.D.C. 2016), *injunction vacated pursuant to parties' settlement*, 2018 WL 8576647 (D.D.C. May 17, 2018).   **32.** Letter from Russell T. Vought, Director, Off, of Mgmt. and Budget, to John Yarmuth, Chairman, H. Comm. on the Budget (Jan. 19, 2021), https://perma.cc/2WGM-84H6.   **33.** *Sierra Club v. Trump*, 977 F.3d 853 (9th Cir. 2020), *judgment vacated*, 142 S.Ct. 56 (2021).   **34.** Letter from Samuel R. Bagenstos, Gen. Counsel, Off. of Mgmt. and Budget, to Thomas M. Armstrong, Gen. Counsel, Gov't Accountability Off. (May 6, 2021), https://perma.cc/6W54-4PNB; GAO, Off. of Mgmt. and Budget and U.S. Dep't of Homeland Sec.—Pause of Border Barrier Construction and Obligations, B-33310 (June 15, 2021), available at https://perma.cc/Y57N-U2JC.   **35.** Stith, *supra* at 1350–51.   **36.** *United States v. Lovett*, 328 U.S. 303, 315–18 (1946).   **37.** *Legal Serv. Corp. v. Velazquez*, 531 U.S. 533, 548–49 (2001).   **38.** *Hart v. United States*, 118 U.S. 62, 65–67 (1886).   **39.** *Knote v. United States*, 95 U.S. 149, 154–57 (1877).   **40.** *United States v. Klein*, 80 U.S. 128, 147–48 (1871).   **41.** 301 U.S. 308, 321 (1937).   **42.** 426 U.S. 317, 321 (1976).   **43.** *United States v. Richardson*, 418 U.S. 166, 178 n.11 (1974).   **44.** *Reeside v. Walker*, 52 U.S. 272, 291 (1850).   **45.** *Rochester Pure Water Dist. v. EPA*, 960 F.2d 180, 184 (D.C. Cir. 1992).   **46.** *Office of Pers. Mgmt.*, 496 U.S. at 433.   **47.** *Cincinnati Soap Co.*, 301 U.S. at 321.   **48.** *CFPB v. Cmty. Fin. Servs. Ass'n of Am., Ltd.*, 601 U.S. 416 (2024).   **49.** *Id.* at 426, 431.   **50.** *U.S. House of Representatives v. Mnuchin*, 976 F.3d 1, 6–15 (D.C. Cir. 2020), *vacated as moot sub nom. Yellin v. U.S. House of Representatives*, 142 S.Ct. 332 (2021); *Burwell*, 130 F. Supp. 3d at 66–77.   **51.** Paul F. Figley, *The Judgment Fund: America's Deepest Pocket & Its Susceptibility to Executive Branch Misuse*, 18 U. Pa. J. Const. L. 145, 147, 161–67, 179–207 (2015).   **52.** *Id.* at 179–211; Paul Larkin, Jr. & Zack Smith, *"Brother, Can You Spare a Million Dollars?": Resurrecting the Justice Department's "Slush Fund,"* 19 Geo. J.L. & Pub. Pol'y 44 (2021).   **53.** *Maine Cmty. Health Options v. United States*, 590 U.S. 296, 305–25 (2020).   **54.** Figley, *supra* at 174–75, 186–89.

⌐‿⌐

ESSAY NO. 75: THE FEDERAL TITLE OF NOBILITY CLAUSE
ART. I, § 9, CL. 8

No Title of Nobility shall be granted by the United States. . . .
—Allyson N. Ho, Elizabeth A. Kiernan, & Michael A. Zarian

INTRODUCTION

In the English system, hereditary titles of nobility afforded an elite class certain rights, but after the Revolutionary War, Americans broke sharply from that practice. State constitutions and the Articles of Confederation prohibited granting titles of nobility, and the Constitution would prohibit the federal and state governments from granting titles of nobility.

This principle was essential to the American ideal of republicanism. St. George Tucker observed that "[a] Franklin, or a Washington, need not the pageantry of honours, the glare of titles, nor the pre-eminence of station to distinguish them . . . . Equality of rights . . . precludes not that distinction which superiority in virtue introduces among the citizens of a republic."[1] Justice Joseph Story wrote that "[d]istinctions between citizens, in regard to rank" would "silently subvert the spirit of independence and personal dignity, which are so often proclaimed to be the best security of a republican government."[2]

Alexander Hamilton described the Federal Title of Nobility Clause as the "corner-stone of republican government." This provision did not occasion much debate during either the Constitutional Convention or the ratification debates, with the main criticism being that the provision did not go far enough. Even today, perhaps because of its absolute clarity, the Federal Title of Nobility Clause is rarely litigated.

HISTORY BEFORE 1787

By the mid-eighteenth century, English law divided society into two legal groups, the nobility and the commons. There were five ranks of nobility (Duke, Marquess, Earl, Viscount, Baron) in the United Kingdom, separated by precedence but generally enjoying the same legal rights and privileges.[3] These titles were granted by the Crown and were inherited from one generation to another. Holders of noble titles could sit in the House of Lords, one of the two constituent houses of Parliament, and therefore held positions of authority in the legislature by virtue of inheritance.[4] In addition to their seats in the House of Lords, members of the nobility enjoyed legal protections. These included in all criminal cases the right to be tried by the House of Lords, rather than by a jury of commoners. They also received immunity from arrest in civil cases, including immunity from imprisonment for debt.[5]

The legal rights and privileges of the nobility played little role in pre-revolutionary colonial law because, with a small handful of exceptions, there were very few members of the nobility residing in the Thirteen Colonies. Nevertheless, American commentators attacked the system of noble privileges as part of their rhetorical move against the monarchy and its hereditary principle. Thomas Paine argued in his widely read pamphlet *Common Sense* that "most wise men, in their private sentiments, have ever treated hereditary right with contempt; yet it is one of those evils, which when once established is not easily removed."[6] Revolutionary Americans would enact this sentiment against heritable privilege in constitutions throughout the newly formed states.

After independence, the American states quickly rejected the English system of nobility. John Adams explained to Abigail Adams that "Capacity, Spirit and Zeal in the Cause" rather than hereditary titles would "supply the Place of Fortune, Family, and every other Consideration, which used to have Weight with Mankind."[7] Many state constitutions prohibited titles of nobility or conditioned the ability to vote or hold office on relinquishing such titles. Massachusetts, for example, prohibited any person from having "any other title" with "exclusive privileges" that were "distinct from those of the community."[8] Georgia barred a person who held a title of nobility from voting or serving in government.[9]

The Articles of Confederation forbade "the united states in congress assembled" from "granting any title of nobility."[10] Indeed, the Articles, which placed very few limits on the power of states, also prohibited the states from granting titles of nobility.[11] This provision of the Articles of Confederation, which demonstrated the strength of the Founders' objections to titles of nobility, "directly regulated states' internal governance" more than any other.[12]

These prohibitions were put to the test shortly after independence in the debate over the Society of the Cincinnati. The Society was a private organization intended to serve as an honorary distinction for the officers who had served in the Continental Army during the Revolution.[13] The Society was open only to the former officers and to their direct descendants. Even though the Society was a private organization with no legal privileges, this hereditary element drew widespread and vociferous criticism.[14] John Adams, then serving as ambassador to France, criticized the Society as an "order of Chivalry" that was "against our Confederation and against the Constitutions of several States" and "against the Spirit of our Governments and the Genius of our People."[15] Opposition to the Society grew so vociferous that George Washington urged it to "[d]iscontinue the hereditary part in all its connexions," and threatened to resign if it was not reformed.[16] The Society agreed to reform, and the tumult died down, but the public controversy underscored the public opposition to the English system of heritable rights and distinctions.[17]

THE CONSTITUTIONAL CONVENTION

The Framers of the Constitution adopted the same prohibitions that appeared in the Articles of Confederation. Article I, Section 9 prohibits the federal government from granting titles of nobility, and Article I, Section 10 prohibits the states from granting titles of nobility. There was essentially no debate about these provisions at the Constitutional Convention.

THE RATIFICATION DEBATES

During the ratification debates, the Federalists praised the prohibition of titles of nobility. In Federalist No. 44, Madison wrote that the provision "is copied from the articles of confederation and needs no comment." In Federalist No. 84, Hamilton explained that the prohibition of titles of nobility was designed to affirm and protect the republican character of the new American government. He denominated this prohibition as "the corner-stone of republican government; so long as [these titles] are excluded, there can never be serious danger that the government will be any other than that of the people." And Madison observed in Federalist No. 39 that the "absolute prohibition of titles of nobility" is the "most decisive" proof that the Constitution conforms in "the most rigid sense" to a republican form of government. The republican government established by the Founders was animated by the ideal of a civil society where advancement is fueled by talent, virtue, and accomplishment—not predetermined by a hereditary aristocracy based on birth. David Ramsay, an eighteenth-century historian, wrote that "Equality" is the "life and soul of commonwealth,"[18] and Madison wrote that protecting "diversity in the faculties of men" is "the first object of government."[19]

The primary criticism of the clause was that it did not go far *enough*. Massachusetts and New York proposed that the Federal Title of Nobility Clause be amended to prevent Congress from consenting to the grant of foreign titles of nobility as well.[20] Anti-Federalists contended that so much power would reside in the federal government that its officeholders would inevitably become a *de facto* aristocracy. Old Whig, for example, warned that even if the President could not confer titles of nobility, he would "have the power of making all the *great men*, which comes to the same thing."[21] Federal Farmer argued that if the federal government had only enumerated powers, then it would lack the power to issue titles of nobility. The fact that the Constitution expressly barred granting such titles suggests that the federal government has broad powers.[22]

EARLY PRACTICE

After ratification, Congress acted promptly to banish titles of nobility from American life. In 1795, Congress forbade naturalization to titled foreigners unless they formally renounced their titles.[23] In 1810, concerns spread that Great Britain and Napoleonic France would subvert the nascent Republic by capturing the allegiance of politicians with titles of nobility and emoluments. In response to these threats, Congress went further. It voted overwhelmingly to pass an amendment to the Constitution that would have revoked the citizenship of any person who accepted or retained a foreign title or emolument.[24] The amendment fell short of the three-fourths of states required to approve it so was not ratified.[25] Yet this provision was nonetheless mistakenly listed as "The Thirteenth Amendment" in the United States Statutes at Large for several years until the error was corrected after a House resolution and presidential investigation.[26]

JUDICIAL PRECEDENT

As noted above, the Federal Title of Nobility Clause has rarely been litigated. Chief Justice John Marshall described the prohibition of titles of nobility as "complete and total," a constitutional rule from which there is "no exception."[27] Justice Henry Baldwin described the clause's reference to nobility as "a term which defines itself," with a meaning "as plain and definite as its language" such that "any comment is useless."[28] In modern times, the Supreme Court has mentioned the clause only in passing references.[29]

Cite as: Allyson N. Ho, Elizabeth A. Kiernan, & Michael A. Zarian, *The Federal Title of Nobility Clause, in* THE HERITAGE GUIDE TO THE CONSTITUTION 262 (Josh Blackman & John G. Malcolm eds., 3d ed. 2025).

Notes

1. Charles T. Cullen, St. George Tucker and Law in Virginia, 1772–1804, at 124 (1987). **2.** 3 Story's Commentaries § 1351. **3.** 1 Blackstone § 385. **4.** *Id.* **5.** *Id.* at 386. **6.** Thomas Paine, Common Sense 76 (Isaac Kramnick ed., 1986) (1776). **7.** Letter from John Adams to Abigail Adams (July 10, 1776), https://perma.cc/6SDT-YL2P. **8.** Mass. Const. of 1780, Part I, art. VI. **9.** Ga. Const. of 1777, art. XI. **10.** Articles of Confederation, art. VI, § 1. **11.** *Id.* **12.** Akhil Reed Amar, America's Constitution: A Biography 125 (2005). **13.** Carlton F.W. Larson, *Titles of Nobility, Hereditary Privilege, and the Unconstitutionality of Legacy Preferences in Public School Admissions*, 84 Wash. Univ. L. Rev. 1375, 1387 (2006). **14.** Minor Myers, Liberty Without Anarchy: A History of the Society of the Cincinnati 49 (1983). **15.** Letter from John Adams to the Marquis de LaFayette (Mar. 28, 1784), https://perma.cc/294C-88NA. **16.** George Washington, Observations on the Institution of the Society (c. 4 May 1784), https://perma.cc/JC55-2LTH; Larson, *supra* at 1398. **17.** Larson, *supra* at 1399. **18.** David Ramsay, Oration on the Advantages of American Independence (July 4, 1778), https://perma.cc/8MHV-F822. **19.** The Federalist No. 10 (Madison).

20. Reports of Committee of Twenty-Five (Feb. 3, 1788), ConSource, https://perma.cc/SNA5-NMNT; Amendments Proposed by the New Hampshire Convention (June 21, 1788), ConSource, https://perma.cc/E7FH-PTFF. **21.** Storing 3.3.31. **22.** Storing 2.8.198. **23.** Act of Jan. 29, 1975, ch. 20, § 1, 1 Stat. 414 (1795). **24.** Resolution Proposing an Amendment to the Constitution of the United States, 11 Res. No. 2, 2 Stat. 613 (1810); 20 Annals of Cong. 530, 549, 572–73, 635, 671–72 (1810); 21 Annals. of Cong. 2050–51 (1810). **25.** Jol A. Silversmith, *The "Missing Thirteenth Amendment": Constitutional Nonsense and Titles of Nobility*, 8 S. Cal. Interdisc. L.J. 577, 585 (1999) (citing 2 Documentary History of the Constitution of the United States of America 454–515 (1894)). **26.** *Id.* at 586–89; 1 Laws of the United States of America, 1789–1815, at 74 (1815); 31 Annals of Cong. 530–31 (1817). **27.** *Ogden v. Saunders*, 25 U.S. (12 Wheat.) 213, 335 (1827) (Marshall, C.J., dissenting). **28.** *Briscoe v. Bank of Commonwealth of Ky.*, 36 U.S. (11 Pet.) 257, 327 (1837) (Baldwin, J., concurring). **29.** *Adarand Constructors, Inc. v. Pena*, 515 U.S. 200, 239 (1995) (Scalia, J., concurring in part and concurring in the judgment); *Fullilove v. Klutznick*, 448 U.S. 448, 533 (1980) (Stevens, J., dissenting).

─◦⁓

ESSAY NO. 76: THE FOREIGN EMOLUMENTS CLAUSE
ART. I, § 9, CL. 8

And no Person holding any Office of Profit or Trust under them [the United States], shall, without the Consent of the Congress, accept of any present, Emolument, Office, or Title, of any kind whatever, from any King, Prince, or foreign State.

—Josh Blackman & Seth Barrett Tillman

INTRODUCTION

The Foreign Emoluments Clause limits the ability of certain federal officials to accept presents, emoluments, offices, or titles from foreign governments. The clause traces its roots to a Dutch law that banned Netherlands officials from accepting gifts from foreign governments. Although the Articles of Confederation had its own Foreign Emoluments Clause, little debate occurred during the Philadelphia Convention about the Constitution's analogous provision, which departed from its Articles predecessor. This provision gives rise to questions about the original public meaning of "emolument," how Congress can consent to a covered officer's accepting a foreign emolument, what constitutes a "foreign State," and which federal officers are covered by the clause.

HISTORY BEFORE 1787

Many provisions of the Constitution were premised on English statutes and parliamentary precedents. By contrast, the roots of the Foreign Emoluments Clause lie in the Netherlands. A 1651 Dutch law prohibited government officials from taking any gifts "of whatever sort" from foreign governments.[1] At the time, it was a common diplomatic practice for a host country to give expensive gifts to departing diplomats from foreign countries. The Dutch rule was something of an outlier. Abraham de Wicquefort, a Dutch political writer, criticized the rule. Because "[t]he custom of making a present . . . is so well established," he said, and "is of as great an extent as the law of nations itself, there is reason to be surprised at the regulation that has been made on that subject in Holland."[2]

The Articles of Confederation, ratified in 1781, apparently borrowed from this Dutch rule. Article VI, Section 1 provides that no "person holding any office of profit or trust under the United States, or any of them [i.e., any state], [shall] accept of any present, emolument, office, or title of any kind whatever, from any king, prince, or foreign state."[3] This text applied to certain officers in both the Articles and state governments. The authors of this essay take the position that delegates to the Confederation Congress held neither an "office . . . under the United States" nor an office under any state and therefore were not subject to this provision.[4]

The Articles' text imposed an absolute prohibition against covered officers accepting foreign gifts. However, one scholar suggests that the "accepted interpretation" followed the Dutch rule, under which the gift could be kept if the diplomat's home government granted permission.[5] In 1780, for instance, before the Articles were ratified, Arthur Lee was a minister from the United States to the Court of Versailles. When Lee departed from France, King Louis XVI gave him a gold snuffbox set with diamonds and a picture of the monarch as a "mark of his Majesty's esteem." This type of gift was not uncommon; it was the sort of gift the French king gave to other departing ministers.[6] Lee deposited the box with the President of the Continental Congress, as he did not think he could retain it "without express approbation of Congress." Congress "approve[d] of his retaining the picture" that was "set with the diamonds."[7]

Subsequent to the Articles' ratification, in 1785, Benjamin Franklin concluded his service as minister to France.[8] Upon Franklin's departure, King Louis XVI gave him a snuffbox similar to the one he had given Lee and set with more than 400 diamonds.[9] On March 3, 1786,

Congress approved Franklin's keeping the gift.[10] That same day, Congress also gave permission to John Jay, a minister to Spain, to keep a horse presented by the king of Spain.[11] This practice would inform the Foreign Emoluments Clause under the Constitution.

THE CONSTITUTIONAL CONVENTION

During the Constitutional Convention, there was little discussion about the Foreign Emoluments Clause. The Committee of Detail proposed that "[t]he United States shall not grant any Title of Nobility."[12] This provision was adopted unanimously.[13] Immediately after this vote, Charles Pinckney of South Carolina "urged the necessity of preserving foreign Ministers & other officers of the U. S. independent of external influence." He proposed an amendment after the Title of Nobility Clause: "No person holding any office of profit or trust under the U.S. shall without the consent of the Legislature, accept of any present, emolument, office or title of any kind whatever, from any King, Prince or foreign State."[14] The motion was passed unanimously without any recorded debate.[15]

This text was referred to the Committee of Style.[16] The Committee appears to have made slight alterations. For example, it changed "office of profit or trust under the United States" to "Office of Profit or Trust under them." Here, "them" refers back to "the United States" referenced in the Title of Nobility Clause. (See Essay No. 75.) At the time of the Framing, "the United States" was viewed as a plural entity—a grouping of states—rather than as a single collective entity.[17] The Committee also changed "consent of the Legislature" to "Consent of the Congress." The final, adopted text provided that "[n]o Title of Nobility shall be granted by the United States: And no Person holding any Office of Profit or Trust under them, shall, without the Consent of the Congress, accept of any present, Emolument, Office, or Title, of any kind whatever, from any King, Prince, or foreign State."[18]

THE RATIFICATION DEBATES

The Federalists and Anti-Federalists agreed that the Constitution would limit opportunities for foreign corruption. In Federalist No. 22, Alexander Hamilton wrote that "[o]ne of the weak sides of republics . . . is that they afford too easy an inlet to foreign corruption." In the Virginia convention, Edmund Randolph said that the Foreign Emoluments Clause "is provided to prevent corruption."[19] Randolph mentioned that "a box was presented to our ambassador by the king of our allies."[20] This was likely a reference to one of the snuffboxes given by King Louis XVI. The clause "was thought proper," Randolph explained, "in order to exclude corruption and foreign influence, to prohibit any one in office from receiving or holding any emoluments from foreign states."[21] Nevertheless, in both cases, the recipients were allowed to keep their diplomatic gifts.

EARLY PRACTICE

In May 1798, Congress held its first debate on the Foreign Emoluments Clause.[22] Thomas Pinckney had served as an ambassador to Great Britain and Spain. At the end of his service, he received gifts from those foreign governments. After Pinckney returned to the United States, he asked Congress for permission to keep those gifts. By the time the House considered the request, Pinckney had been elected to Congress.[23] Representative James A. Bayard of Delaware asked whether the former ambassador still needed permission. Representative John Claiborne of Virginia insisted that Pinckney still needed to obtain congressional consent. This debate reveals early disagreement about the scope of the Foreign Emoluments Clause.

THE ORIGINAL PUBLIC MEANING OF "EMOLUMENT"

The Foreign Emoluments Clause restricts the acceptance of "any present, Emolument, Office, or Title, of any kind whatever." During the first Trump Administration, one federal trial court contended that an "emolument" was "commonly understood by the founding generation to encompass any 'profit,' 'gain,' or 'advantage.'"[24] One scholar wrote that Founding-era dictionaries did not define an "emolument" as compensation tied to employment.[25]

We think these readings of "emolument" are too broad. The U.S. Supreme Court has observed that "the term emoluments" refers to "every species of compensation or pecuniary profit derived from a discharge of the duties of the office."[26] Under this definition, emoluments would not include profits from private business transactions that are not connected to the discharge of the duties associated with holding public office. A corpus linguistics study of Founding-era sources supports this more restricted definition.[27]

This understanding of the term is further supported by scholarship collecting evidence from the Founding era and the early Republic.[28] First, under the Articles of Confederation government, George Washington served as Commander in Chief of the Continental Army. During this period, Washington's accounts in England were paid dividends by the Bank of England, an instrumentality of a foreign government.[29] We think Washington was subject to the Foreign Emoluments Clause under the Articles of Confederation but did not violate it because the dividends he received were not "emoluments."[30] These profits were not tied to the discharge of the duties of an office.

Second, under the Constitution, President George Washington purchased four lots of land in 1793 at a public auction in the new federal capital.[31] The Domestic Emoluments Clause, also known as the Presidential Compensation Clause, provides that the President "shall not receive . . . any other Emolument from the United States."[32] (See Essay No. 61.) Washington paid for and received valuable land from the federal government beyond his regular salary.[33] If an "emolument" includes anything of value, then Washington would have violated the Domestic Emoluments Clause. The better reading, we contend, is that "emolument" is limited to the lawful compensation or profits that arise from the discharge of the duties of an office. Under this position, Washington was not a lawbreaker.[34]

HOW DOES CONGRESS PROVIDE CONSENT?

The text of the Articles of Confederation imposed an absolute ban on officials accepting any presents, emoluments, offices, or titles from foreign governments. Under the federal Constitution, the Foreign Emoluments Clause does not impose such an absolute ban. Rather, the covered officer must seek congressional consent. Congress provides consent by enacting a statute.

Based on past practice, it would appear that Congress can also consent by means of a "joint resolution," which under modern nomenclature is merely a statute by another name. For example, in 1896, Congress "authorized" by a joint resolution former President Benjamin Harrison "to accept certain medals presented to him by the Governments of Brazil and Spain during the term of his service as President of the United States."[35]

We are not aware of any instance in which Congress purported to consent to a covered officer's receiving a foreign state gift by approving a mere concurrent resolution that was not presented to the President. In whatever form congressional consent is presented, the President may veto such a bill or joint resolution, and Congress could override the President's veto.

WHAT IS A "FOREIGN STATE"?

The Foreign Emoluments Clause applies to any "present, Emolument, Office, or Title . . . from any King, Prince, or foreign State." The Office of Legal Counsel (OLC) has considered whether different entities related to foreign governments constitute a "foreign state." In 1986, OLC found that two National Aeronautics and Space Administration scientists could work at a foreign public university because that institution made employment decisions independent of the foreign government.[36]

In 2009, President Barack Obama was awarded the Nobel Peace Prize, which included a cash award of approximately $1.4 million.[37] At the time, scholars observed that the "five-member Nobel commission is elected by the Storting, the parliament of Norway."[38] However, OLC concluded that "the Norwegian Nobel Committee was not a 'King, Prince, or foreign State.'"[39] Therefore, the Nobel Prize was not subject to the Foreign Emoluments Clause. OLC also stated, absent evidence or argument, that "[t]he President surely 'hold[s] an[] Office of Profit or Trust'" and is subject to the Foreign Emoluments Clause.[40] (See *infra*, "Is the President Subject to the Foreign Emoluments Clause?")

ARE MEMBERS OF CONGRESS SUBJECT TO THE FOREIGN EMOLUMENTS CLAUSE?

Under the Articles of Confederation, both federal and state officers were subject to the Articles' Foreign Emoluments Clause; under the federal Constitution, the Foreign Emoluments Clause applies to those who hold "any Office of Profit or Trust under" the United States. It is generally accepted that this provision applies only to those holding positions in the federal government and not to those holding state positions. There is some support for the view that the Foreign Emoluments Clause applies at least to appointed positions in the legislative, executive, and judicial branches.[41] However, Professors Akhil Reed Amar and Vikram David Amar have suggested that the terms "office" and "officer" extend only to the executive and judicial branches and that such language does not include elected members of Congress. One can also infer that under their approach, the Foreign Emoluments Clause does not reach subordinate positions in the legislative branch, such as the Clerk of the House and Secretary of the Senate.[42]

Professor Zephyr Teachout and other scholars contend that the Foreign Emoluments Clause applies to members of Congress.[43] In Teachout's view, the phrase "Office . . . under the United States" refers to "elected and appointed officials."[44] In our view, "Office . . . under the United States" refers to appointed positions in the executive and judicial branches as well as to appointed positions in the legislative branch. The elected members of Congress do not hold an "Office . . . under the United States."[45] Thus, they are not subject to the Foreign Emoluments Clause. On this point, we agree with the Amars.[46]

Some historical evidence distinguishes members from those holding covered offices. In 1798, during the House debate about Pinckney's gift, Representative Edward Gallatin of Pennsylvania stated that members are situated differently from officers. Gallatin "did not believe that permission could legally be granted to any member of Congress to receive any such present[.]"[47] In short, Gallatin thought members were distinguishable from officers: The latter can get consent under the Foreign

Emoluments Clause, but members of Congress cannot. Gallatin appears to have been the lone supporter of this view.

If Senators and Representatives hold an "Office . . . under the United States," they would be subject to the Foreign Emoluments Clause. Under this view, a member of one house of Congress who wishes to accept a foreign state gift must seek consent both from his house and from the other house. This arrangement would violate principles of cameral autonomy: Generally, members of one house do not have to seek "consent" from the other house in regard to their official duties.[48] In any event, the Foreign Gifts and Decorations Act (1966) restricts the abilities of members of Congress, the President, and those holding other elected and appointed positions in the federal government from accepting foreign state gifts.[49]

IS THE PRESIDENT SUBJECT TO THE FOREIGN EMOLUMENTS CLAUSE?

During the first Trump Administration, a federal district court ruled that the President is covered by the Foreign Emoluments Clause.[50] The court posited that "the term 'United States' is used in the Constitution to distinguish between" officers in "the federal and state governments."[51] A "federal office holder" such as the "President holds his office 'under the United States.'"[52] Teachout reaches a similar conclusion based on debates from the Virginia convention. Edmund Randolph contended that the President "is restrained from receiving any present or emolument whatever. It is impossible to guard better against corruption."[53] George Mason worried that foreign governments could exert pressure on the American President. Mason said, "This very executive officer may, by consent of Congress, receive a stated pension from European potentates."[54] Mason and Randolph, neither of whom signed the Constitution, assumed that the President was subject to the Foreign Emoluments Clause.[55]

In our view, the question whether the "Foreign Emoluments Clause[] reaches any or all federal elected positions—i.e., Representative, Senator, Vice President, President, and presidential elector—poses a difficult interpretive challenge."[56] Our position is that the weight of the textual evidence supports the conclusion that the elected President does not hold an "Office . . . under the United States."[57] Presidential practice from the early Republic is consistent with our position that the President is not subject to the Foreign Emoluments Clause.[58]

President George Washington received, accepted, and kept a full-length portrait of King Louis XVI, with a valuable frame, from the French ambassador to the United States.[59] The framed portrait was a diplomatic gift from the French government. President Washington also received, accepted, and kept the main key to the Bastille, along with a picture of the Bastille, from the Marquis de Lafayette, who, at that time, was a French government official. Washington publicly displayed these gifts in the capital during his term. These gifts were later sent to Mount Vernon after Washington's term concluded, and they remain on display there. Washington never sought congressional consent to accept these gifts. We have found no records of any contemporaneous objections raised in Congress, by the press, or in contemporaneous private correspondence. We also have found no records of subsequent historians or other academics objecting to Washington's practice.

President Thomas Jefferson, like President Washington, openly accepted foreign state gifts without seeking congressional consent. Jefferson accepted gifts from Thaddeus Kosciuszko that may have been considered foreign state gifts.[60] President Jefferson received a bust of Czar Alexander I. It appears that this was a diplomatic gift from the Russian government. Jefferson received, accepted, and kept this gift. Jefferson also received presents from Indian tribes, which he considered diplomatic gifts from foreign nations. The Tunisian envoy gave President Jefferson several valuable horses as a gift. Jefferson did not keep the horses as his personal property, nor did he seek congressional consent to keep these gifts; rather, he sold the horses to fund the envoy's stay in the United States. If the horses were the federal government's property, and not Jefferson's property, he would have needed legal authority to sell them. We are not aware of any such authority, and Jefferson did not expressly ask Congress for permission to sell the horses.

Presidents James Madison and James

Monroe (the fourth and fifth Presidents, respectively) also received a foreign state gift.[61] The history here, however, is far more complex than the history of the Washington gifts. In 1816, the revolutionary government of the United Provinces of Rio de la Plata declared independence from Spain. The self-proclaimed ruler of that breakaway nation sent two pistols to President Madison through diplomatic channels. Madison never responded to the ruler, nor did he seek congressional consent to keep the pistols. When Madison's term concluded, he apparently gave the pistols to his successor, President Monroe. Monroe never sought congressional consent, and he did not deposit the pistols with the United States government. Today, the pistols are on display in the James Monroe museum.

The conduct of Madison and Monroe is consistent with our position that the President is not subject to the Foreign Emoluments Clause. We add that even if the President is not subject to the clause—or, better, *because* the President is not subject to that provision—it is highly prudent for a President to regift such objects promptly. Doing so would have the effect of muting objections by political opponents that he is exploiting his position or acting in any self-interested manner.

We have found no report or any evidence that any antebellum President has ever asked Congress for consent to accept a gift from a foreign state. Such a request would have been the clearest evidence possible that the President viewed himself as subject to the Foreign Emoluments Clause. However, we have identified four other Presidents who took related actions. Presidents Andrew Jackson, Martin Van Buren, and John Tyler received foreign state gifts. Jackson declined to accept a gold medal from Colombia and asked Congress to dispose of it. Van Buren and Tyler asked Congress to dispose of gifts that each had received from the Imam of Muscat. Additionally, President

Abraham Lincoln asked Congress to dispose of gifts he had received from the king of Siam.[62]

We have identified six other Presidents who (likely) accepted foreign state gifts and did not surrender them.[63] We say likely because the records are not entirely clear. President James K. Polk received a table of marble from Tunis. It is not clear whether the gift came from the American consul to Tunisia or was a foreign state gift from the Tunisian government. President Andrew Johnson accepted foreign state gifts from the queen of Hawaii. President Ulysses S. Grant received foreign gifts from the queen of Madagascar and the Samoan government. President Chester A. Arthur received foreign state gifts from a diplomatic delegation from Madagascar. President Woodrow Wilson received a valuable tapestry from the French government. And President Herbert Hoover received valuable gifts from the king of Siam. None of these Presidents sought congressional consent to accept these gifts.

It seems that presidential efforts to comply with the Foreign Emoluments Clause peaked in the 1830s—and went downhill thereafter. There is no singular, clear stream of authority in regard to practice under this provision. In our view, practices during the early Republic are more probative than later practices, and President Washington's practices are the most probative, particularly where they were public and uncontested.[64]

As of July 2025, OLC has not yet publicly considered this evidence. However, the Congressional Research Service and the Civil Division of the Department of Justice have taken notice of these practices from President George Washington and his administration and, more generally, the early Republic.[65] This seems to indicate that the Congressional Research Service and the Civil Division are of the view that the issue of the applicability of the Foreign Emoluments Clause to the presidency remains unsettled.

OPEN QUESTIONS

- Can the judiciary enforce the Foreign Emoluments Clause? Must such a suit be brought against a covered officer in his official, individual, or personal capacity?[66] Does the Constitution provide a cause of action to enforce the Foreign Emoluments Clause?[67] Would such an implied cause of action be consistent with *DeVillier v. Texas* (2024)?[68]

- What must a recipient do to "accept" a foreign state present, emolument, office, or title? Can the recipient deposit the present in a government facility until he leaves office and then claim it? The Office of Legal Counsel has suggested that this work-around may be permissible.[69]

- If a wholly-owned or majority-owned corporation or commercial entity accepts a foreign state present, is that present imputed to the majority stockholder? Is working control, even if less than majority control, sufficient to impute receipt of a foreign state present, emolument, office, or title?

- Can foreign statutory (or other) benefits that all receive on the same terms be construed as a foreign state present? Would a diplomat living abroad who receives fire, police, or state-provided medical services from the foreign government run afoul of the Foreign Emoluments Clause?

- If a foreign government or state is not recognized by the United States, or if it is a revolutionary government or amidst civil war, is it a foreign state for the purposes of the Foreign Emoluments Clause? Would the acceptance of a present from such a government amount to official diplomatic recognition of that foreign state?[70]

Cite as: Josh Blackman & Seth Barrett Tillman, *The Foreign Emoluments Clause*, *in* The Heritage Guide to the Constitution 265 (Josh Blackman & John G. Malcolm eds., 3d ed. 2025).

Notes

1. 4 John Bassett Moore, A Digest of International Law 579 (1906); Liam Edward Cronan, *"In Defiance of Gifts": The Dutch Origins of the Foreign Emoluments Clause*, 40 Touro L. Rev. 465 (2025), https://ssrn.com/abstract=4590349. **2.** Monsieur de Wicquefort, The Embassador and His Functions 292 (John Digby trans., London, Bernard Lintott 1716), https://bit.ly/3DSvB3o. **3.** Articles of Confederation, art. VI, § 1. **4.** Josh Blackman & Seth Barrett Tillman, *Offices and Officers of the Constitution, Part IV: The "Office . . . under the United States" Drafting Convention*, 62 S. Tex. L. Rev. 455, 475 (2023). **5.** Zephyr Teachout, *Gifts, Offices, and Corruption*, 107 Nw. U. L. Rev. Colloquy 30, 36 (2012). **6.** 18 J. Cont. Cong., 1780, September 7–December 29, at 1114–15 (Wash., GPO 1910) (entry for December 1, 1780). **7.** *Id.* at 1115. **8.** *Benjamin Franklin: First American Diplomat, 1776–1785*, U.S. Dep't of State, Off. of the Historian, https://perma.cc/QME8-G3TG. **9.** Letter from William Temple Franklin to Thomas Jefferson (Apr. 27, 1790), https://perma.cc/P9WB-D35U. **10.** 30 J. Cont. Cong., 1786, January 2–July 31, at 95 (Wash., GPO 1934) (entry for March 3, 1786). **11.** *Id.* **12.** 2 Farrand's 169, 183, 187. **13.** *Id.* at 384. **14.** *Id.* at 389. **15.** *Id.* **16.** *Id.* at 572. **17.** Minor Myers, *Supreme Court Usage and the Making of an "Is,"* 11 Green Bag 2d 457, 457–58 (2008). **18.** 2 Farrand's 657. **19.** 3 Elliot's 465. **20.** *Id.* **21.** *Id.* **22.** 5 Annals of Cong., 5th Cong., 2d Sess. 1582–95 (1798). **23.** *Pinckney, Thomas 1750–1828*, Biographical Directory of the United States Congress, https://perma.cc/4A56-PF89. **24.** *District of Columbia v. Trump*, 315 F. Supp. 3d 875, 891 (D. Md. 2018), *judgment vacated sub nom. Trump v. D.C.*, 141 S.Ct. 1262 (2021), *and vacated* 838 F. App'x 789 (4th Cir. 2021). **25.** John Mikhail, The Definition of "Emolument" in English Language and Legal Dictionaries, 1523–1806 (July 12, 2017), https://perma.cc/RS75-VQXL. **26.** *Hoyt v. United States*, 51 U.S.

(10 How.) 109 (1850). **27.** James Cleith Phillips & Sara White, *The Meaning of the Three Emoluments Clauses in the U.S. Constitution: A Corpus Linguistic Analysis of American English from 1760–1799*, 59 S. Tex. L. Rev. 181, 195 (2018). **28.** Amandeep Grewal, *The Foreign Emoluments Clause and the Chief Executive*, 102 Minn. L. Rev. 639 (2017); Robert G. Natelson, *The Original Meaning of "Emoluments" in the Constitution*, 52 Ga. L. Rev. 1 (2018). **29.** *National Banks—English and American*, 14 Am. Q. Rev. 493, 504 (1833). **30.** Tillman & Blackman, *Offices and Officers of the Constitution, Part IV, supra* at 476. **31.** Seth Barrett Tillman, *Business Transactions and President Trump's "Emoluments" Problem*, 40 Harv. J.L. & Pub. Pol'y 759 (2017). **32.** Art. II, § 1, cl. 7. **33.** Josh Blackman & Seth Barrett Tillman, Joint Written Statement Before the Subcomm. on Economic Development, Public Buildings and Emergency Management (Sept. 25, 2019), https://perma.cc/QG39-77MP. **34.** Josh Blackman & Seth Tillman, *Who Was Right About the Emoluments Clauses? Judge Messitte or President Washington?*, Volokh Conspiracy (Aug. 3, 2018), https://perma.cc/FU5R-4YHW; Josh Blackman & Seth Barrett Tillman, *The Inspector General, General Services Administration, Refuses to Acknowledge Her Plain Error About the Domestic Emoluments Clause*, Volokh Conspiracy (Oct. 7, 2019), https://perma.cc/VZ3U-JAZ6. **35.** J. Res. 39, 54th Cong., 29 Stat. 759 (1896). **36.** Memorandum from Samuel A. Alito, Jr., Off. of Legal Counsel, Re: Emoluments Clause Questions Raised by NASA Scientist's Proposed Consulting Arrangement with the University of New South Wales (May 23, 1986). **37.** Press Release, The Norwegian Nobel Comm., The Nobel Peace Prize for 2009 (Oct. 9, 2009), https://perma.cc/MU5H-FQPP. **38.** Ronald D. Rotunda & J. Peter Pham, *Obama Barred Constitutionally from Accepting Nobel*, Wash. Post (Oct. 16, 2009), https://perma.cc/KUC8-5C24. **39.** Applicability of the Emoluments Clause

& the Foreign Gifts and Decorations Act to the President's Receipt of the Nobel Peace Prize, 33 Op. O.L.C. 370, 370 (2009). **40.** *Id.* at 374. **41.** Seth Barrett Tillman & Josh Blackman, *Offices and Officers of the Constitution, Part II: The Four Approaches*, 61 S. Tex. L. Rev. 321 (2021). **42.** Akhil Reed Amar & Vikram David Amar, *Is the Presidential Succession Law Constitutional?*, 48 Stan. L. Rev. 113, 115 (1995). **43.** Teachout, *supra*; Lawrence Lessig, *A Reply to Professor Hasen*, 126 Harv. L. Rev. F. 61, 70 (2013); Raoul Berger, Impeachment: The Constitutional Problems 226 n.11 (1974). **44.** Teachout, *supra* at 47. **45.** Seth Barrett Tillman & Josh Blackman, *Offices and Officers of the Constitution, Part V: The Elector Incompatibility, Impeachment Disqualification, Foreign Emoluments, and Incompatibility Clauses*, 63 S. Tex. L. Rev. 237, 298 (2024). **46.** Tillman & Blackman, *Offices and Officers of the Constitution, Part II, supra* at 368. **47.** 5 Annals of Cong., *supra* at 1593. **48.** Aaron-Andrew P. Bruhl, *If the Judicial Confirmation Process Is Broken, Can a Statute Fix It?*, 85 Neb. L. Rev. 960, 996–1007 (2007). **49.** 5 U.S.C. § 7342(a)(1)(E); Tillman & Blackman, *Offices and Officers of the Constitution, Part V, supra* at 394–96. **50.** *District of Columbia v. Trump*, 315 F. Supp. 3d at 882. **51.** *Id.* at 884. **52.** *Id.* **53.** 3 Elliot's 486. **54.** *Id.* at 484. **55.** Seth Barrett Tillman & Josh Blackman, *Offices and Officers of the Constitution, Part III: The Appointments, Impeachment, Commissions, and Oath or Affirmation Clauses*, 62 S. Tex. L. Rev. 349, 402–03 (2023). **56.** Zephyr Teachout & Seth Barrett Tillman, *The Foreign Emoluments Clause: Article I, Section 9, Clause 8*, Nat'l Const. Ctr., https://perma.cc/SGQ6-ZHM4.

57. Tillman & Blackman, *Offices and Officers of the Constitution, Part IV, supra* at 458–60. **58.** Tillman & Blackman, *Offices and Officers of the Constitution, Part V, supra* at 305. **59.** *Id.* at 308–17. **60.** *Id.* at 318–37. **61.** *Id.* at 337–47. **62.** *Id.* at 353–55. **63.** *Id.* at 382–89. **64.** Josh Blackman, *Defiance and Surrender*, 59 S. Tex. L. Rev. 157 (2017); Tillman & Blackman, *Offices and Officers of the Constitution, Part V, supra* at 411–24. **65.** Tillman & Blackman, *Offices and Officers of the Constitution, Part V, supra* at 399–407; Josh Blackman & Seth Barrett Tillman, *Biden Office of Legal Counsel Departs from Obama-Era Opinions, and Reverts to Reagan-Era Opinions, on the Difference Between "Officer of the United States" and "Office under the United States,"* Volokh Conspiracy (Jan. 19, 2025), https://perma.cc/DMJ6-WVUJ. **66.** Josh Blackman, *The President's Three Bodies After* Trump v. United States, Volokh Conspiracy (July 4, 2024), https://perma.cc/KV94-W56R. **67.** Josh Blackman & Seth Barrett Tillman, *The Unresolved Threshold Issues in the Emoluments Clauses Litigation: The President Has Three Bodies and There Is No Cause of Action for Ultra Vires Conduct*, 20 Geo. J.L. & Pub. Pol'y 163 (2022). **68.** 601 U.S. 285 (2024). **69.** Memorandum Opinion, Off. of Legal Counsel, Regarding Proposal That the President Accept Honorary Irish Citizenship 278, 280–81 (May 10, 1963), https://perma.cc/QZS4-F2AN; Tillman & Blackman, *Offices and Officers of the Constitution, Part V, supra* at 369–70. **70.** Tillman & Blackman, *Offices and Officers of the Constitution, Part V, supra* at 337.

〜⁓

ESSAY NO. 77: THE STATE TREATY CLAUSE
ART. I, § 10, CL. 1

No State shall enter into any Treaty, Alliance, or Confederation. . . .

—Julian G. Ku

INTRODUCTION

The Constitution explicitly delegates to the President the power to "make Treaties" with the advice and consent of the Senate.[1] (See Essay No. 106.) The Constitution also expressly prohibits state treaty-making. This explicit textual prohibition reminds us that the Framers established bright-line rules to prohibit certain state government activities that were deemed most dangerous to the nation as a whole.

On this point, at least, the Framers appear to have been largely successful. States are barred from entering into treaties and can enter into interstate "compacts" only with congressional consent. However, states have unilaterally entered into "agreements" with foreign nations that, at least in some regards, function like treaties.

HISTORY BEFORE 1787

Under British rule, the colonies lacked the power to negotiate their own treaties. With the Declaration of Independence, the "Free and Independent States" asserted the "full Power to . . . conclude Peace" and "contract Alliances,"[2] and as independent states, these sovereigns could negotiate treaties.

However, the states would soon surrender their unilateral power to make foreign alliances. Under the Articles of Confederation, states could enter into "any conference, agreement, alliance, or treaty" with foreign powers or other states as long as Congress approved.[3]

THE CONSTITUTIONAL CONVENTION

The Framers would impose an absolute ban on state treaty-making. An early proposal from the Committee of Detail combined what would become the State Treaty Clause and the Compact Clause. It barred states from entering into treaties, alliances, or confederations with "any foreign power" but, if Congress consented, allowed them to enter into agreements or compacts with other states.[4] These provisions were later made separate provisions.[5]

It is not clear how the Constitution distinguished between the terms "treaties, alliances, and confederations" as international agreements and domestic "agreements and compacts." Eighteenth-century commentators of international law, who were read by the Framers, provide useful guidance on the original public meaning of these words. Vattel was the most influential international law authority among the Framers' generation. He wrote that treaties were "made with a view to the public welfare by the superior power, either for perpetuity, or for a considerable time."[6] On the other hand, Vattel defined compacts as "temporary matters" that "are accomplished by one single act, and not by repeated acts."[7] Christian de Wolff, another influential commentator, explained that "if two nations reciprocally agree to furnish troops to each other in time of war, this stipulation is called a treaty; but if one nation permits another, on account of the high price of grain, to purchase in its territory, this will be a compact."[8]

THE RATIFICATION DEBATES

In Federalist No. 44, James Madison wrote that the proposed State Treaty Clause was already "part of the existing articles of union; and for reasons which needed no explanation, is copied into the new constitution." This is a curious statement because, as noted above, the Constitution imposes a complete ban on "treaties, alliances, and confederations," whereas the Articles allowed states to engage in such activities with congressional consent. Madison may

have thought the change unimportant. The State Treaty Clause was not controversial in the state ratification conventions.

JUDICIAL PRECEDENT

During the early years of the Republic, the meaning or impact of the State Treaty Clause sparked no litigation and very little commentary. An early discussion of the clause came in *Holmes v. Jennison* (1840).[9] Chief Justice Roger B. Taney's plurality opinion noted that states were "positively and unconditionally" forbidden from entering treaties, even with congressional approval. Taney also recognized, however, that Congress could consent to state "compacts." But nothing in that case turned on the distinction between these terms. The Supreme Court's most detailed discussion of the issue simply concluded that "[t]he records of the Constitutional Convention . . . are barren of any clue as to the precise contours of the agreements and compacts governed by the Compact Clause."[10] The Court suggested that the original understanding of the terms has been historically "lost."

The Supreme Court has decided other cases involving the State Treaty Clause. In *Barron v. City of Baltimore* (1833), Chief Justice John Marshall pointed to the State Treaty Clause as evidence that the Constitution does not "apply to the state government, unless expressly stated in its terms."[11] *Williams v. Bruffy* (1878) held that the Confederate States of America could not "be regarded . . . as having any legal existence" because the Constitution "prohibits any treaty, alliance, or confederation by one State with another."[12]

In 2017, California entered into a cap-and-trade agreement with Quebec and Ontario to reduce greenhouse gas emissions.[13] In 2019, the United States sued California, arguing that the agreement was in fact a treaty, which violated the State Treaty Clause.[14] In March 2020, a federal district court ruled that "[n]ot all international agreements may be 'treaties' in the constitutional sense."[15] The court concluded "that the Agreement does not represent a 'treaty' within Article I of the Constitution."[16] While the case was on appeal, there was a change in administrations and the appeal was voluntarily dismissed.[17]

OPEN QUESTIONS

- States may not enter into "treaties," but may enter into interstate "compacts" with the consent of Congress, and have unilaterally entered into "agreements" with foreign nations.[18] How do these three terms differ from one another?[19]
- Is California's cap-and-trade agreement an unconstitutional "treaty"?

Cite as: Julian G. Ku, *The State Treaty Clause, in* THE HERITAGE GUIDE TO THE CONSTITUTION 272 (Josh Blackman & John G. Malcolm eds., 3d ed. 2025).

Notes

1. Art. II, § 2.   **2.** Declaration of Independence, ¶32.   **3.** Articles of Confederation, art. VI, § 1.   **4.** 2 Farrand's 169.   **5.** *Id.* at 577, 619.   **6.** E. de Vattel, The Law of Nations; or, Principles of the Law of Nature Applied to the Conduct and Affairs of Nations and Sovereigns, bk. II, § 152 (Joseph Chitty ed. & trans., 1863) (1758).   **7.** *Id.*   **8.** Christian de Wolff, Jus Gentium Methodo Scientifica Pertactatum (J.B. Scott ed., 1983) (1749).   **9.** 39 U.S. (14 Pet.) 540 (1840).   **10.** *U.S. Steel Corp. v. Multistate Tax Commission*, 434 U.S. 452, 461–63 (1978).   **11.** 32 U.S. 243, 248 (1833).   **12.** 96 U.S. 176, 177 (1877).   **13.** *United States v. California*, 444 F. Supp. 3d 1181, 1188 (E.D. Cal. 2020).   **14.** *Id.* at 1189–90.   **15.** *Id.* at 1192 (quoting *United States v. Curtiss-Wright Export Corp.*, 299 U.S. 304, 318 (1936)).   **16.** *Id.* at 1193.   **17.** *United States v. California*, No. 20-16789, 2021 WL 4240403, at *1 (9th Cir. Apr. 22, 2021).   **18.** Duncan B. Hollis, *Unpacking the Compact Clause*, 88 Tex. L. Rev. 741, 760 (2010).   **19.** Abraham C. Weinfeld, *What Did the Framers of the Federal Constitution Mean by "Agreements or Compacts"?*, 3 U. Chi. L. Rev. 453 (1936).

~

ESSAY NO. 78: THE STATE MARQUE AND REPRISAL CLAUSE
ART. I, § 10, CL. 1

No State shall . . . grant Letters of Marque and Reprisal. . . .

—John C. Yoo

INTRODUCTION

At the Founding, the sovereign of nations could authorize holders of letters of marque and reprisal to engage in hostile actions against enemies of the state.[1] These letters authorized private parties, known as privateers, to engage in reprisals for private commercial gain.[2] One scholar has observed that letters of marque and reprisal were originally "an important tool of national power for the federal government created by the Framers, who placed great import on the federal government's role in protecting international commerce and in enforcing international law."[3] But this was a power for the sovereign to exercise, not the states.

The Constitution has two clauses concerning letters of marque and reprisal. Congress has the power to grant them (see Essay No. 57), but the states do not. "That such a power ought to exist in the national government," wrote Justice Joseph Story, "is something that no one will deny," but it "could not be left without extreme mischief, if not absolute ruin, to the separate authority of the several states."[4] If it were left to the states, each one would have "the option . . . to involve the whole in the calamities and burthens of warfare."[5] Congress has not issued a letter of marque and reprisal since the War of 1812, and the states are absolutely barred from issuing them.

HISTORY BEFORE 1787

In British practice, the sovereign issued letters of marque and reprisal. During the Revolutionary War, the Continental Congress issued them. The Articles of Confederation centralized authority over war and foreign affairs in the national government. A single state could not plunge the Confederation into war.

Article IX of the Articles of Confederation

vested in Congress the sole power to grant letters of marque and reprisal "in times of peace."[6] States could grant letters of marque and reprisal only once Congress had declared war.[7] And even when Congress had declared war, the power of the states to grant letters of marque and reprisal was constrained. First, the states could issue letters of marque and reprisal only "against the kingdom or state and the subjects thereof, against which war has been so declared." Second, such letters could be issued only "under such regulations as shall be established by the united states in congress assembled." However, there was an exception to these rules: The states could issue letters of marque and reprisal whenever "such state be infested by pirates,"[8] even if there was no declaration of war.

THE CONSTITUTIONAL CONVENTION

A Committee of Detail draft listed several powers that states could not exercise.[9] Many of these powers concerned foreign policy. As relevant here, states could not "grant Letters of Marque and Reprisal." At this point in the Convention, the Framers had not yet granted Congress the power to issue such letters.

On August 6, the Committee of Detail's report was delivered to the Convention.[10] The prohibition on states issuing letters of marque and reprisal was paired with bans on states' coining money, entering into treaties, and granting titles of nobility.[11] On August 18, the delegates voted to grant Congress the power to issue letters of marque and reprisal.[12] On August 28, the delegates approved by a vote of eight to one the Committee of Detail's draft that included the prohibition on states' issuing letters of marque and reprisal.[13] No further changes were made to this provision.

THE RATIFICATION DEBATES

The State Marque and Reprisal Clause in the Constitution was not controversial. Like the Articles of Confederation, the Constitution banned states from issuing letters of marque and reprisal. Unlike Article IX of the Articles, however, this prohibition against the states was an absolute bar and could not be waived in times of war. In Federalist No. 44, James Madison explained that "[t]his alteration is fully justified" and cited "the advantage of uniformity in all points which relate to foreign powers." Madison also observed that Congress has the "immediate responsibility to the nation in all those, for whose conduct the nation itself is to be responsible."

One scholar has observed that "[t]he anti-federalists acknowledged the need for letters of marque within the general war power as a Congressional power."[14] Still, there was a concern that the states could not issue such letters even in times of war. In fact, the prohibition was more restrictive than the state's ability to engage in war. Under Article I, Section 10, Clause 3 of the Constitution, the state can engage in war if it is "actually invaded, or in such imminent Danger as will not admit of delay." (See Essay No. 86.) By contrast, a state cannot issue letters of marque and reprisal under any circumstances. There is also a complete prohibition on states' entering into treaties, coining money, enacting bills of attainder or ex post facto laws, impairing with the obligation of contracts, or granting titles of nobility.[15] (See Essay Nos. 77, 79, 80, 81, 82, and 83.)

For example, Candidus, a prominent Anti-Federalist, proposed an alternative to the Constitution. Candidus urged the legislatures of each state to "frame a treaty of Amity."[16] This treaty would be "united with *some parts* of the Constitution proposed by the respectable Convention."[17] Candidus favored the provision that appeared in the Articles of Confederation: The treaty "should expressly declare that no State (without the consent of Congress) should . . . grant letters of marque and reprisal.[18]

PRACTICE

Letters of marque and reprisal have played little if any role in modern times. Consequently, the State Marque and Reprisal Clause remains uncontroversial.

Cite as: John C. Yoo, *The State Marque and Reprisal Clause,* in THE HERITAGE GUIDE TO THE CONSTITUTION 274 (Josh Blackman & John G. Malcolm eds., 3d ed. 2025).

Notes

1. John C. Yoo, *The Continuation of Politics by Other Means: The Original Understanding of War Powers*, 84 Cal. L. Rev. 167, 206 (1996). 2. *Bas v. Tingy*, 4 U.S. 37 (1800). 3. Theodore M. Cooperstein, *Letters of Marque and Reprisal: The Constitutional Law and Practice of Privateering*, 40 J. Mar. L. & Com. 221, 221 (2009). 4. 3 Story's Commentaries § 1164. 5. *Id.* 6. Articles of Confederation, art. IX, § 1. 7. *Id.* art. VI, § 5. 8. *Id.* 9. 2 Farrand's 169. 10. *Id.* at 177. 11. *Id.* at 187. 12. *Id.* at 328. 13. *Id.* at 439. 14. Cooperstein, *supra* at 231. 15. *Id.* 16. Storing 4.9.22. 17. *Id.* at 4.9.21. 18. *Id.* at 4.9.22.

~

ESSAY NO. 79: THE STATE MONEY CLAUSE
ART. I, § 10, CL. 1

No State shall . . . coin Money; emit Bills of Credit; make any Thing but gold and silver Coin a Tender in Payment of Debts. . . .

—Todd J. Zywicki

INTRODUCTION

During the Revolutionary War and the period of the Articles of Confederation, state governments engaged in rampant inflationary practices to fund the war effort. The states also depreciated the debts of borrowers, particularly farmers, that were owed to out-of-state creditors. This dynamic led to retaliation and interstate friction. In response, the State Money Clause significantly limits the power of states to issue money, providing in relevant part, "No State shall . . . coin money; emit Bills of Credit; [or] make any Thing but gold and silver Coin a Tender in Payment of Debts."

HISTORY BEFORE 1787

During the Colonial Era, Britain's mercantilist policies resulted in a chronic shortage of precious metals and specie coins, and whatever coins were acquired tended to flow back to Britain in exchange for manufactured goods.[1] As a result, the colonies relied on coins imported from Europe, especially the Spanish dollar. America's currency was eventually denominated in dollars rather than pounds.[2] But foreign coins had different values in different colonies.[3] Depending on local circumstances, colonists also had to barter with such currencies as Indian wampum or such commodities as tobacco and beaver skins. Massachusetts and some other colonies also illegally coined money in violation of English law.[4] The lack of coins forced some colonial governments to collect taxes in commodity currencies such as corn and wheat.[5]

Commodity money proved to be a cumbersome medium of exchange. As a result, starting in 1690, colonial governments also issued paper money.[6] These bills of credit were a convenient medium of exchange for the payment of government debts and taxes, but they were not redeemable on demand in gold, silver, or other precious metal coins. And, unlike a government "note," paper money generally did not bear interest. The result was inflation and conflicts when colonists attempted to pay their debts to English creditors with depreciated paper currency.[7]

Throughout the eighteenth century, this uncertainty and multiplicity of circulating currencies generated confusion and impeded intercolony and international trade.[8] Despite these inconveniences, however, paper money had great popular appeal, especially among farmers and other debtors who favored inflation.[9]

To stabilize the value of money, the British Parliament enacted a series of laws that regulated colonial paper money.[10] The 1751 Currency Act provided that bills of credit could be used to pay public debts, such as taxes, but they were not deemed "legal tender," which meant they could not be used to pay private debts such as payments to merchants and creditors. The 1764 Currency Act prohibited the use of bills of credit as legal tender for the payment of public *and* private debts. In 1773, in response to opposition by the colonies, Parliament repealed the prohibition and once again permitted bills of credit to serve as legal tender for public (but not private) debts. Soon thereafter, some colonies resumed issuing paper money.

During the Revolutionary War, all of the new states and the Continental Congress issued paper money to pay for military expenses.[11] These bills of credit, which could not be converted into gold or silver and did not bear interest, caused dramatic inflation.

The Articles of Confederation, ratified in 1781, granted the central government "the sole and exclusive right and power of regulating the alloy and value of coin struck by [Congress's] own authority, or by that of the respective states."[12] Congress also had the power to "coin money" and "emit bills" of credit.[13] As a result, the central government and the states had a *concurrent* power to coin metal money and issue paper money.

In May 1786, the Rhode Island legislature succumbed to pressure by farmers to issue paper money to alleviate their debt burdens.[14] When merchants and creditors refused to accept that currency as payment, the legislature passed the Forcing Act, which declared the bills of credit to be legal tender.[15] The law levied a heavy fine on those who refused to accept it. And under the law, there was no right to trial by jury and no right to appeal. In 1786, the Rhode Island Supreme Court held in *Trevett v. Weeden* that the law violated the state constitution's guarantee of a jury trial.[16] In the state's next legislative session, the state legislature removed four of the Justices and replaced them with new Justices more amenable to paper money. Still, many merchants fled the state to evade the excess paper money and harsh measures to force its acceptance. Commerce soon ground to a halt.

Rhode Island also mandated that out-of-state creditors must accept payment in the local currency.[17] Merchants refused to accept the depreciated currency, even closing their shops. Farmers responded by refusing to sell their produce. This law led predictably to retaliatory currency laws in New Jersey, Pennsylvania, Delaware, New York, and other states.[18] In August 1786, Shays Rebellion erupted in Massachusetts as creditors refused to receive payment in farm commodities and the state legislature refused to issue paper money after seeing the disastrous events in Rhode Island.[19] In September 1786, the Paper Money Riot, also known as the Exeter Rebellion, broke out in New Hampshire when a group of armed farmers marched on Exeter to demand that the New Hampshire General Court immediately issue paper money.[20] In all, only Connecticut and Delaware escaped the paper money conflagration.[21]

In August 1786, James Madison wrote to Thomas Jefferson in the midst of this chaos. Madison explained that "at the head" of the problems plaguing the nation was "the general rage for paper money," which was "producing the same warfare and retaliation among the States as were produced by the State regulations of commerce."[22] When the Constitutional Convention began in 1787, state issuance of paper money and state legal tender laws had led to a growing sense of crisis.[23] Rhode Island's determined support for its 1786 paper money act was a major factor in its boycott of the Constitutional Convention and extended refusal to ratify the Constitution.

THE CONSTITUTIONAL CONVENTION

The Committee of Detail's proposal provided that "No State, without the consent of the Legislature of the United States, shall emit bills of credit."[24] Thus, states retained the power to issue paper money, but only when specifically authorized by Congress.

The Convention quickly moved to deny states even this conditional power of issuance. James Wilson of Pennsylvania and Roger Sherman of Connecticut proposed making the prohibition on state issuance of bills of credit "absolute" instead of "allowable" with the consent of Congress.[25] Under this proposal, states also could not coin money. Nathaniel Gorham of Massachusetts responded that making the prohibition absolute would prove politically controversial. He added that requiring Congress to assent to a state's issuance of paper money would amount to an effective veto on reckless issuance of paper money but would not "excite[]" opposition or "rouse the most desperate opposition from" partisans of paper money.[26]

Sherman replied that the current time provided "a favorable crisis for crushing paper money."[27] He said that if Congress retained the power to issue paper money, supporters would apply lobbying pressure for Congress to permit it. After this brief discussion, the motion was carried eight to one, with Virginia voting in opposition and Maryland's delegation divided. At least one Virginian, George Mason, expressed his "mortal hatred to paper money."[28]

Wilson and Sherman also proposed that states could make only "gold & silver coin a tender in payment of debts."[29] This proposal was adopted unanimously with no discussion.[30] By 1787, gold and silver had emerged as the global standard to facilitate international trade.

Sherman would later explain in a letter to the governor of Connecticut that both the prohibition on issuing bills of credit and the prohibition on impairing the obligation of contracts were "thought necessary as a security to commerce, in which the interest of foreigners, as well as of the citizens of different states, may be affected."[31]

THE RATIFICATION DEBATES
In Federalist No. 44, Madison condemned the "pestilent effects of paper money" issued by state governments "on the industry and morals of the people, and on the character of republican government." In addition, "[t]he subjects of foreign powers might suffer from the same cause, and hence the union be discredited."[32] At the South Carolina convention, Charles Pinckney similarly contended that paper money would undermine the trust of foreign merchants in the United States.[33] He further argued that eliminating mischievous issuance of paper money in other states would guarantee South Carolinians a fair and just price for their commodities.

Anti-Federalists largely shared the Convention's concerns regarding the dangers of paper money. Brutus supported the Constitution's prohibitions on state emission of bills of credit, limits on legal tender, and the Contracts Clause: "These prohibitions give the most perfect security against those attacks upon property which I am sorry to say some of the states have but too wantonly made, by passing laws sanctioning fraud in the debtor against his creditor."[34]

Luther Martin provided a report to the Maryland state legislature about the Convention's proceedings. He argued that because the Convention had stripped the federal government of the authority to emit bills of credit by other actions, the states should not also

be deprived of that power. In his view, depriving both the federal and state governments of the power to emit bills of credit in times of crisis was unwise; once public and private credit had been restored, it might be valuable to retain that discretion in the future. Nevertheless, "the convention was so smitten with the paper money dread, that they insisted the prohibition should be absolute."[35]

EARLY PRACTICE
During the early Republic, private banks issued banknotes that circulated widely as private currency. Unlike bills of credit, private banknotes were redeemable in gold or silver but were not designated as legal tender. Like bills of credit, private banknotes were negotiable and payable to the bearer.[36]

JUDICIAL PRECEDENT
Two decisions from the 1830s interpreted the meaning of "bills of credit." *Craig v. Missouri* (1830) involved state-issued certificates that could be used to pay state taxes. Chief Justice John Marshall, writing for the Court, defined the issuance of a bill of credit as "the emission of any paper medium, by a state government, for the purpose of common circulation."[37] The state certificates were therefore void as "bills of credit." Marshall observed that the Constitution's prohibition on bills of credit was separate from limits on legal tender. In dissent, Justice Smith Thompson wrote that the certificates, which bore interest and were not intended predominantly as a circulating medium but as a loan instrument, should not be classified as bills of credit.

In the second case, *Briscoe v. Bank of Commonwealth of Kentucky* (1837), a state-established bank issued a banknote. The Court held that this banknote was not a "bill of credit" because it was not "a paper issued by the sovereign power containing a pledge of its faith and designed to circulate as money."[38] Moreover, the banknote was not legal tender. Issuance of the banknote was a valid exercise of the legislature's power to incorporate entities to carry out socially valuable enterprises.

The *Virginia Coupon Cases* (1895) ruled that negotiable, state-issued coupon bonds that could be used to pay taxes did not constitute "bills of credit" because they were not issued with the intent to circulate as money between individuals and between the government and individuals.[39] Relying on *Craig* and *Briscoe*, the Court stressed that the purpose of the Constitution's limit was not to prohibit *any* effort by states to issue debt. Rather, the purpose of the clause was to prohibit the issuance of paper money backed by state credit "which had been so abused to the detriment of both private and public interests" during the War of Independence.[40]

OPEN QUESTIONS

- Several states recognize gold and silver coins as legal tender, and many others have considered similar legislation. Are these laws constitutional?
- Bitcoin and other cryptocurrencies plainly are not "gold and silver coin." Can a state designate these forms of currency as legal tender?

Cite as: Todd J. Zywicki, *The State Money Clause, in* THE HERITAGE GUIDE TO THE CONSTITUTION 276 (Josh Blackman & John G. Malcolm eds., 3d ed. 2025).

Notes

1. Owen F. Humpage, *Paper Money and Inflation in Colonial America*, Federal Reserve Bank of Cleveland Economic Commentary No. 2015-06 (May 13, 2015). **2.** Federal Reserve Bank of Philadelphia, *Money in Colonial Times*, https://perma.cc/9A9X-SB2X. **3.** Louis Jordan, *Colonial Currency: The Comparative Value of Money Between Britain and the Colonies*, https://perma.cc/WW4D-2CB4. **4.** Claire Priest, *Currency Policies and Legal Development in Colonial New England*, 110 Yale L.J. 1303 (2001). **5.** Alvin Rabushka, *The Colonial Roots of American Taxation, 1607–1700* (Aug. 1, 2002), https://perma.cc/7AHC-LLPP. **6.** Priest, *supra* at 1311. **7.** *Id.* at 1383–84. **8.** *Deering v. Parker*, 4 Dall. App. xxiii (Privy Council 1760). **9.** Robert G. Natelson, *Paper Money and the Original Understanding of the Coinage Clause*, 31 Harv. J. L. & Pub. Pol'y 1017, 1040 (2008). **10.** Joseph Ernst, Money and Politics in America, 1755–1775: A Study in the Currency Act of 1764 and the Political Economy of Revolution (1973). **11.** Ben Baack, *America's First Monetary Policy: Inflation and Seigniorage During the Revolutionary War*, 15 Financial Hist. Rev. 107 (2008). **12.** Articles of Confederation, art. IX, § 1. **13.** *Id.* **14.** Murray N. Rothbard, 5 Conceived in Liberty: The New Republic, 1784–1791, at 76 (2019). **15.** *Id.* **16.** Patrick T. Conley, The Story Behind Rhode Island's Most Important Legal Case: *Trevett v. Weeden* in 1786 (Jan. 26, 2019) (adapted from address given May 3, 1976), https://perma.cc/MK3M-3Q2C. **17.** Natelson, *supra* at 1051. **18.** *Id.* **19.** Michael J. Klarman, The Framers' Coup: The Making of the United States Constitution 73–125 (2016). **20.** Robert J. Steinfeld, Judicial Review and Legislative Supremacy in Rhode Island: The Case of *Trevett v. Weeden*, 1786, and Its Aftermath, *in* The Emergence of American Judicial Review, 1784–1787: Developing Judicial Reviews A Check on Legislatures and on the People 299 (2021). **21.** John Fiske, *The Paper Money Craze of 1786 and the Shays Rebellion*, The Atlantic 376, 378 (Sept. 1886). **22.** Letter from James Madison to Thomas Jefferson (Aug. 12, 1786), https://perma.cc/PMZ4-9ERG. **23.** Edward Stanwood, *A Glimpse at 1786*, The Atlantic 777, 780 (June 18860. **24.** 2 Farrand's 187. **25.** *Id.* at 439. **26.** *Id.* **27.** *Id.* **28.** 2 Farrand's 309. **29.** *Id.* at 439. **30.** *Id.* **31.** 3 Farrand's 99. **32.** Federalist No. 44 (Madison). **33.** 4 Elliot's 333–36. **34.** Storing 2.9.182. **35.** 3 Farrand's 214. **36.** Ali Khan, *The Evolution of Money: A Story of Constitutional Nullification*, 67 U. Cincinnati L. Rev. 393, 412–13 (1999). **37.** 29 U.S. 410 (1830). **38.** 36 U.S. 257 (1837). **39.** *Poindexter v. Greenhow*, 114 U.S. 270 (1885). **40.** *Id.* at 284.

ESSAY NO. 80: THE STATE BILL OF ATTAINDER CLAUSE
ART. I, § 10, CL. 1

No State shall . . . pass any Bill of Attainder. . . .

—Matthew Steilen

INTRODUCTION

A bill of attainder is "a legislative act which inflicts punishment without a judicial trial."[1] There are two Bill of Attainder Clauses in the Constitution. Article I, Section 9, Clause 3 applies to federal laws; Article I, Section 10, Clause 1 applies to state laws. Since most of the cases to reach the U.S. Supreme Court have concerned the ban on federal bills of attainder in section 9, we consider the Court's modern bill of attainder doctrine in Essay No. 69. Here, in the entry for section 10, we consider the history of the bills of attainder, which were relatively widespread in the American states during the Revolution.

HISTORY BEFORE 1787

The bill of attainder is conventionally dated to the late fourteenth or early fifteenth century.[2] Beginning in this period, Parliament would condemn individuals who could not be brought before ordinary common-law courts but whose crimes were sufficiently "notorious" that they might be convicted in a summary proceeding without presenting evidence.[3] Lords in Parliament asserted that "the law and course of Parliament" did not require the presence of the accused during proceedings.[4] The process could be used against those who had taken flight or were too strong to be captured. On other occasions, bills of attainder were employed to confiscate the property of rebellious nobles who had died. Parliamentary condemnation allowed the king to preempt legal challenges to the confiscation of their lands.

In this context, "attainder" (from the French *atteindre* or "attain") meant "to convict." A "bill of attainder" was a means of convicting an individual in Parliament by introduction of a "bill," which was an informal written complaint.[5] "Bills" were also used to introduce legislation. In 1641, Lord Digby attributed to Parliament "a double Power of Life and Death by bill, a Judicial Power, and a Legislative; the measure of the one, is what's legally just; of the other, what is Prudentially and Politically fit for the good and preservation of the whole."[6]

English legal treatises have been affected by confusions about the meaning and etymology of "attainder."[7] For example, according to Sir William Blackstone, the word "attaint" derived from *attinctus*, a Latin expression meaning "stained" or "blackened," which was applied to someone sentenced to death.[8] Blackstone therefore viewed the "bill of attainder" as a legislative death sentence. It had been used, he wrote, when a "criminal is no longer fit to live upon the earth, but is to be exterminated as a monster."[9]

It is worth noting that other English commentators, including some writing around the same time as Blackstone, framed bills of attainder quite differently.[10] Moreover, although some bills of attainder certainly did contain death sentences, this was not a universal feature.[11] Medieval bills of attainder, for example, rarely included an explicit death sentence because their targets were often already dead. Sometimes the condemned or their heirs were able to recover their confiscated property by obtaining a repeal and royal pardon.[12]

During the Revolutionary War, Massachusetts, New York, Pennsylvania, and Virginia enacted bills of attainder targeting named individuals.[13] Typically, these acts targeted British officials and American loyalists. For example, New York's "Act for the Forfeiture and Sale of the Estates of Persons who had adhered to the Enemies of this State" named the two most recent colonial governors, members of their executive council, judges of the colonial supreme court, and several dozen other prominent individuals. The act declared that "the public justice and safety of this state absolutely require, that the most notorious offenders should be immediately hereby convicted and attainted" of the crime of adhering to the king and then banished them from the state and confiscated their property.[14]

Bills of attainder of this type formed part of a much larger mass of legislation and executive action, examples of which can be found in every state, which subjected "enemies" to various disabilities, including loyalty oaths, disenfranchisement, removal from public office, bars on practicing a profession or owning property, arrest, quarantine, and banishment.[15] Not every Revolutionary-era bill of attainder was used to punish disloyalty, however. In Virginia, Thomas Jefferson authored "An act to attaint Josiah Philips and others." This bill targeted the leader and unnamed members of a gang of laborers and escaped slaves who hid in Virginia's Great Dismal Swamp and were thought to have murdered a militia captain.[16] Jefferson argued that to wait until Philips was captured by ordinary methods would subject the state to great danger.

Bills of attainder were controversial during the Revolution. As Jefferson's involvement suggests, some lawyers supported their use in cases where the ordinary judicial process was thought to be incapable of handling a dire threat to the state. In support, they could cite English precedents. According to John Hatsell's *Proceedings in the House of Commons*, first published in 1781, "Cases have arisen . . . and may arise again, where the public safety, which is the first object of all government, has called for this extraordinary interference," although "this deviation from the more ordinary forms of proceeding by indictment or impeachment, ought never to be adopted, but in cases of absolute necessity."[17] Jefferson defended the Philips attainder in these terms and later described the *Proceedings* as his primary source for the manual of parliamentary practice he wrote for the United States Senate.[18] Other commentaries, however, cast doubt on the value of English precedents. St. George Tucker, who taught law at the College of William and Mary, prepared an influential American edition of Blackstone's *Commentaries* that condemned bills of attainder and cited the Josiah Philips case.[19]

In New York Constitution of 1777, banned bills of attainder except "for crimes . . . committed before the termination of the present war."[20] The first draft had banned legislative attainders outright. Gouverneur Morris, who would later play a role in banning bills of attainder in the federal Constitution, persuaded the state's constitutional convention to permit them for future crimes. But John Jay successfully moved to limit that power to crimes committed during the Revolution, producing the final text.[21]

When New York passed its bill of attainder, however, Jay harshly condemned it. Writing to the government from Spain, where he held a federal diplomatic post, Jay declared that he felt "disgraced" by reports of the act.[22] Alexander Hamilton, who represented attainted individuals in legal proceedings, also criticized the confiscation of loyalist property in an influential pamphlet, *A Letter from Phocion*.[23] Jay and Hamilton were part of a group that has been termed America's "cosmopolitan minority," whose leading concern was reintegration of the United States into the Atlantic commercial community. They regarded the security of property rights as an essential part of this project.[24]

THE CONSTITUTIONAL CONVENTION

The Virginia Plan, which formed the basis of initial deliberations at the Constitutional Convention, contained nothing about attainder. After the Committee of Detail's draft of the Constitution was introduced on August 6, however, both the federal and state bans fell quickly into place. The ban on federal bills of attainder was introduced on August 22. Gouverneur Morris seconded the motion. Though he had advocated their limited use in New York, Morris now described the prohibition as "essential."[25] The ban on state bills of attainder was inserted on a motion by John Rutledge of South Carolina, who proposed to add it to language prohibiting the states from interfering in private contracts. The motion passed by a vote of 7 to 3, without any recorded objection.[26]

THE RATIFICATION DEBATES

In Federalist No. 78, Hamilton cited bills of attainder as evidence of the need for judicial review. According to Hamilton, the bans could "be preserved in practice no other way than through the medium of courts of justice, whose duty it must be to declare all acts contrary to the manifest tenor of the Constitution void." James Madison also mentioned bills of attainder in Federalist No. 44. Even though some state constitutions banned them, "[o]ur own experience has taught us nevertheless, that additional fences against these dangers ought not to be omitted" to protect "personal security and private rights."

In the state conventions, the two clauses were the subject of little recorded debate.[27] The notable exception was Virginia. Edmund Randolph denounced the Josiah Philips attainder.[28] Shortly after ratification, St. George Tucker condemned bills of attainder and cited the Josiah Philips case in his influential American edition of Blackstone's *Commentaries*.[29]

JUDICIAL PRECEDENT

In a series of early cases, the Supreme Court invoked the Bill of Attainder Clause to develop the Constitution's separation of legislative and judicial powers.[30] In *Fletcher v. Peck* (1810), Chief Justice John Marshall described a state statute purporting to declare a land grant legally invalid as equivalent to a bill of attainder.[31] The comparison framed bills of attainder as a usurpation of judicial power and suggested that legislatures could not decide questions of individual property rights. In language reminiscent of *Marbury v. Madison* (1803), Marshall wrote that "[i]t is the peculiar province of the legislature to prescribe general rules for the government of society; the application of those rules to individuals in society would seem to be the duty of other departments."[32] This description is hard to square with the large mass of particular legislation and judicial activity that remained in state legislatures. *Fletcher* is probably best read as Marshall's effort to reform those practices, particularly with respect to disputes over land.

The Supreme Court's first important precedent on the Bill of Attainder Clause came after the Civil War in *Cummings v. Missouri* (1866). The Missouri Constitution of 1865 imposed disabilities on people who supported the Confederacy during the Civil War. Anyone who sought to vote, hold office, teach, practice law, or serve as a clergyman was required to swear that he had always been "truly and loyally on the side of the United States." Disloyalty included not only having aided the Confederacy, but having "manifested . . . adherence to the cause" "by act or word."[33] Cummings, a Catholic priest, was fined $500 and jailed for teaching and preaching without taking the oath. By a 5 to 4 vote, the Court reversed the judgment and ordered Cummings discharged. According to Justice Stephen Field's majority opinion, the loyalty provisions "presume[d] the guilt of the priests and clergymen" and punished them by "deprivation of their right to preach or teach unless the presumption be first removed by their expurgatory oath."[34]

Cummings was the first case in which the Supreme Court found that a state law violated the ban on state bills of attainder in Section 10. The Court has done so only one other time. *Pierce v. Carskadon* (1872), an unsigned, two-sentence opinion, directed the lower court to apply *Cummings*.[35]

OPEN QUESTIONS

- Are the Bill of Attainder Clauses effectively limited to the kinds of punishments used in English history or the American Revolution?
- Do the Bill of Attainder Clauses ban summary executive action of the sort used during the Revolution?

Cite as: Matthew Steilen, *The State Bill of Attainder Clause, in* THE HERITAGE GUIDE TO THE CONSTITUTION 279 (Josh Blackman & John G. Malcolm eds., 3d ed. 2025).

Notes

1. *Cummings v. Missouri*, 71 U.S. (4 Wall.) 277, 323 (1866). **2.** Allen Boyer & Mark Nichols, The Rise and Fall of Treason in English History 98–99 (2024). **3.** John Collins, Martial Law and English Laws, c.1500–c.1700, at 12, 18 (2016). **4.** 7 The Parliament Rolls of Medieval England, Richard II, 1385–1397, at 100–01 (Chris Given-Wilson ed., 2005). **5.** John P. Collas, *Introduction* to 70 Selden Society, at ix, xxi–lx (1951); Alan Harding, *Plaints and Bills in the History of English Law, Mainly in the Period 1250–1350*, in Legal History Studies 1972, at 65, 74–77, 80–82 (Dafydd Jenkins ed., 1975). **6.** 1 John Rushworth, The Tryal of Thomas Earl of Strafford 53 (1680). **7.** Boyer & Nichols, *supra* at 98; Matthew Steilen, *Bills of Attainder*, 53 Hous. L. Rev. 767, 823 (2016). **8.** 4 Blackstone 380. **9.** *Id.* **10.** 4 John Hatsell, Precedents of Proceedings in the House of Commons 90 (1796); 2 John Reeves, History of English Law 430 (1869). **11.** Anthony Dick, Note, *The Substance of Punishment Under the Bill of Attainder Clause*, 63 Stan. L. Rev. 1177, 1182–90 (2011). **12.** Steilen, *Bills of Attainder*, *supra* at 781, 789. **13.** *Id.* at 827 & n.340. **14.** 1 Laws of the State of New York 26–27 (1792). **15.** Bradley Chapin, The American Law of Treason 75–80 (1964); Claude Halstead Van Tyne, The Loyalists in the American Revolution 318–41 (1902). **16.** 9 The Statutes at Large, Being a Collection of All the Laws of Virginia 463–64 (William Waller Hening ed., 1821); Matthew Steilen, *The Josiah Philips Attainder and the Institutional Structure of the American Revolution*, 60 Howard L.J. 413, 421–29 (2017). **17.** 4 Hatsell, *supra* at 90. **18.** Wilbur Samuel Howell, Jefferson's Parliamentary Writings 43 (1988). **19.** 1 St. George Tucker, Blackstone's Commentaries: With Notes of Reference to the Constitution and Laws of the Federal Government of the United States and of the Commonwealth of Virginia 292–93 (1803). **20.** N.Y. Const. of 1777, art. XLI. **21.** 1 Journals of the Provincial Congress 846, 881–82, 898 (1842). **22.** Letter from John Jay to George Clinton (May 6, 1780), *in* 1 William Jay, The Life of John Jay 112 (1972 ed.). **23.** 1 The Law Practice of Alexander Hamilton 224–27 (Julius Goebel, Jr. ed., 1964). **24.** Daniel

J. Hulsebosch, *A Discrete and Cosmopolitan Minority: The Loyalists, the Atlantic World, and the Origins of Judicial Review*, 81 Chi.–Kent L. Rev. 825, 826–29, 837 (2006).   **25.** 2 Farrand's 368, 375–76.   **26.** *Id.* at 435–36, 440.   **27.** Steilen, *Bills of Attainder, supra* at 893 n.760.   **28.** Steilen, *The Josiah Philips Attainder, supra* at 430–32.   **29.** 1 St. George Tucker, *supra* at 292–93.   **30.** *Calder v. Bull*, 3 U.S. (3 Dall.) 386, 388 (1798); *Vanhorne's Lessee v. Dorrance*, 2 U.S. (2 Dall.) 304, 310 (C.C.D. Pa. 1795) (opinion of Paterson, J.).   **31.** 10 U.S. (6 Cranch) 87, 138–39 (1810).   **32.** *Id.* at 136.   **33.** Missouri Constitution of 1865, art. II, §§ 3, 6, 9.   **34.** *Cummings*, 71 U.S. at 325.   **35.** 83 U.S. (16 Wall.) 234 (1872).

ESSAY NO. 81: THE STATE EX-POST FACTO CLAUSE
ART. I, § 10, CL. 1

No State shall . . . pass any . . . ex post facto Law. . . .

—Evan C. Zoldan

INTRODUCTION

The State Ex Post Facto Clause provides that no state shall "pass any . . . ex post facto Law." A companion clause, The Federal Ex Post Facto Clause similarly provides that no "ex post facto law shall be passed" by Congress. The U.S. Supreme Court has interpreted these two clauses to prohibit, roughly speaking, retroactive criminal laws at both the state and federal levels. These clauses arose out of the same historical experiences, support the same intuitive policies, and share the same modern judicial interpretations. This entry describes the historical background surrounding the inclusion of these clauses in the Constitution, focusing on the events that bear most heavily on their meaning today. Essay No. 70, which introduces the federal prohibition, describes the conceptual background and judicial interpretations of these two clauses.

HISTORY BEFORE 1776

The term "ex post facto" did not originate in the Constitution. Nor was it coined by those who debated the document in Philadelphia. Rather, this term was known to British writers before the American Revolution who themselves learned it from older sources.[1] As used in these British and ancient sources, "ex post facto" meant, roughly speaking, retroactive, with the core case being retroactive criminal laws.[2] Although there has been some dispute over the scope of the term, both British and ancient sources considered ex post facto laws to be dangerous and unjust.

Sir William Blackstone described "ex post facto laws" in the following language: "after an action is committed, the legislator then for the first time declares it to have been a crime, and inflicts a punishment on the man who has committed it."[3] Because, in this situation "it is impossible that the party could foresee that an action, innocent when done, should be afterwards converted to guilt by a subsequent law," a person in violation of the law "had therefore no cause to abstain from it; and all punishment for not abstaining must of consequence be cruel and unjust."[4]

This passage shows both the core meaning of the term "ex post facto" and the core concerns that ex post facto laws elicit. Ex post facto laws declare that a person's conduct, although innocent when done, is punishable as a crime. Ex post facto laws are "cruel and unjust" because they deny a person fair notice of what the law requires before attaching legal consequences to that conduct. In the decades before American independence, British sources other than Blackstone, including judicial opinions and law dictionaries, also used the term "ex post facto."[5] For example, in the British case of *Wilkinson v. Meyer* (1724), the court referred to a statute that retroactively impaired contract rights as an ex post facto act.[6] Like *Wilkinson*, many of these British sources used the term "ex post facto" to include civil statutes.[7]

EX POST FACTO LAWS AFTER INDEPENDENCE

Blackstone's aversion to ex post facto laws was widely shared in the new states after independence.[8] Several states prohibited ex post facto laws in their new constitutions.[9] Maryland's 1776 constitution declared that ex post facto laws are "oppressive, unjust, and incompatible with liberty."[10] Early state courts expressed a similar distaste for ex post facto laws. In diverse contexts, they adjudged ex post facto laws to be void, improper, and an affront to justice. For example, in *Republica v. Chapman* (1781), the Pennsylvania Supreme Court declined to apply a treason statute retroactively, opining that "ex post facto laws are unjust and improper."[11] But not every state explicitly prohibited ex post facto laws. And perhaps reflecting the triumph of exigency over principle, several state legislatures enacted retrospective laws, including debtor relief laws, during the Confederation period.[12] Indeed, the same Pennsylvania court that declared ex post facto laws "unjust and improper" also noted that a legislature "impressed with the necessity of the case" had the right to enact even ex post facto *criminal* laws.[13]

THE CONSTITUTIONAL CONVENTION

The Framers had experienced firsthand both the economic and social dislocations caused by retrospective laws and the exigencies that prompted some legislatures to continue to enact them. Accordingly, there was a robust discussion during the Convention about whether such laws should be prohibited and if so, to what extent. Elbridge Gerry of Massachusetts introduced language to prohibit the federal legislature from passing any ex post facto law.[14] James Wilson of Pennsylvania and Oliver Ellsworth of Connecticut, both future Supreme Court justices, objected to the inclusion of this language. Ellsworth argued that "ex post facto laws were void of themselves." Therefore, "[i]t cannot then be necessary to prohibit them."[15] Wilson agreed that ex post facto laws were so obviously invalid that specifically prohibiting them would "bring reflexions on the Constitution—and proclaim that we are ignorant of the first principles of Legislation."[16] Hugh Williamson of North Carolina concurred with Wilson and Ellsworth that ex post facto laws were inappropriate but agreed with Gerry that they should be prohibited explicitly, noting that North Carolina's constitution prohibited ex post facto laws.[17]

Although these early comments reflect the historical aversion to ex post facto laws, a later exchange highlighted that the scope of the term "ex post facto" remained unsettled. When Rufus King of Massachusetts moved to prohibit the interference with private contracts, Virginia's George Mason objected that unforeseeable situations sometimes justified laws that interfered with contract rights. For example, he argued, a state should be permitted to shorten a statute of limitations period for bringing an action on an open account.[18] Wilson countered that not all interferences with contracts would be prohibited, but rather only those that were retrospective.[19] Madison added that the proposed prohibition on ex post facto laws "will oblige the Judges to declare such interferences null and void."[20] At the end of this discussion, the Convention approved a motion to insert a prohibition on "retrospective laws."[21] The Committee of Style changed the phrase to the final form, "ex post facto" without noted objection.

The following day, John Dickinson of Delaware returned to the question implicitly raised by Madison, Mason, and Wilson. Dickinson reported that he had consulted his copy of Blackstone's *Commentaries* and concluded that "the term[] 'ex post facto' related to criminal cases only" and "would not consequently restrain the States from retrospective laws in civil cases."[22] Apparently unconvinced by this reference to Blackstone, Mason continued to believe that the clause would prohibit even necessary retrospective civil laws. In the last days of the Philadelphia Convention, he moved to strike the clause as overbroad; his motion was voted down unanimously.[23]

THE RATIFICATION DEBATES

State conventions and the public debated both of the questions that arose during the Philadelphia Convention: namely, whether retrospective laws were ever proper and whether the term "ex post facto" in the Constitution covered both criminal and civil laws or criminal laws only.

In the Virginia convention, Mason, now joined by Patrick Henry, again raised the concern that the clauses would prohibit salutary retroactive civil statutes. In Mason's estimation, northern speculators owned large amounts of Continental paper money that, due to depreciation, was worth far less than its face value. He was concerned that the absolute prohibition on ex post facto laws would allow the redemption of depreciated paper money at face value, enriching speculators and saddling the states with enormous debt.[24] Future Attorney General Edmund Randolph responded that this concern was unfounded. The term "ex post facto," he argued, referred "technically" to criminal laws and would be applied as such by judges.[25] Mason was unconvinced, concerned that the "general meaning" of the term ex post facto, which he claimed included all laws having retroactive effect, would prevail.[26]

The point was addressed in other state conventions as well. In North Carolina, future Supreme Court justice James Iredell, along with Stephen Carrabus, argued that the clauses would prevent Congress from diminishing the value of the state's paper currency. Although North Carolina initially rejected the Constitution following this discussion, Iredell and Carrabus's argument does suggest that they understood the term "ex post facto" to include civil laws.[27] By contrast, New York's ratification of the Constitution was accompanied by a declaration that its prohibition "against ex post facto laws, extends only to laws concerning crimes."[28]

The scope of the Ex Post Facto Clauses was debated in public settings as well. Newspaper articles from several states referred to laws interfering with property and contract rights as ex post facto.[29] Notably, Roger Sherman and Oliver Ellsworth, both prominent members of the Philadelphia Convention, wrote an open letter arguing that the prohibition of ex post facto laws would prevent the retroactive impairment of contract rights.[30] This reference to property and contract rights suggests that they believed the term "ex post facto" included civil laws.

In a pamphlet answering Mason's public objections to the Constitution, James Iredell opined that ex post facto laws "have been some of the grossest acts of tyranny that were ever exercised." Nevertheless, the future Supreme Court justice wrote that "a great and overruling necessity, acknowledged and felt by all" could justify the rare ex post facto law.[31] Similarly, the Anti-Federalist writing as Centinel objected to the Constitution on the ground that the Ex Post Facto Clauses would prohibit laws interfering with civil obligations.[32]

When advocating for the adoption of the draft Constitution, the authors of the Federalist Papers wrote extensively of their view of the Ex Post Facto Clauses. In Federalist No. 81, Alexander Hamilton explained that the prohibition on ex post facto laws was necessary to prevent the "creation of crimes after the commission of the fact, or in other words, the subjecting of men to punishment for things which, when they were done, were breaches of no law." And Madison wrote in Federalist No. 44 that ex post facto laws were "contrary to the first principles of the social compact, and to every principle of sound legislation." Accordingly, the Ex Post Facto Clauses, along with the Bill of Attainder clauses and the Contract Clause, stand as a "constitutional bulwark in favor of personal security and private rights" by preventing the worst kinds of abusive legislation. Madison's reference to private rights can be read to mean that the Ex Post Facto Clauses, in conjunction with other constitutional prohibitions on the states, were meant to reach civil laws. (See Essay Nos. 80 and 82.)

POST-RATIFICATION INTERPRETATIONS OF THE CLAUSES

Ratification of the Constitution did not entirely settle the interpretation of the Ex Post Facto Clauses. In the years immediately following ratification, state courts interpreted the prohibition of ex post facto laws to include civil statutes.[33] By contrast, James Madison, by then a U.S. Representative, argued that the prohibition applied to criminal laws only. In 1790, Madison argued in the House of Representatives that a bill that would have allowed the debts of the United States to be paid below face value was not unconstitutional because "ex post facto laws related to criminal" rather than civil cases.[34]

The debate, as a legal matter, was settled when the Supreme Court interpreted the Ex Post Facto Clauses in *Calder v. Bull* (1798).[35] In *Calder*, the Connecticut legislature had vacated a lower court judgment in a civil dispute. The Supreme Court upheld the law, with each justice writing separately. Three justices—Samuel Chase, William Paterson, and James Iredell— opined that Ex Post Facto Clause did not reach the state law because it related to a civil rather than a criminal matter. They relied on the "technical" meaning of the term "ex post facto," as they believed it was used by lawyers. Following this technical meaning, the clause applied only to criminal or penal laws. Justice Paterson went further. He recalled that as a delegate to the Philadelphia Convention, he "had an ardent desire to have extended the provision in the Constitution to retrospective laws in general" but was unable to persuade his fellow delegates.[36]

Despite *Calder*'s definitive legal ruling,[37] the scholarly debate over the proper scope of the Ex Post Facto Clauses continues. And because *Calder*'s opinions emphasized the original meaning of the Ex Post Facto clauses, the debate about their proper scope continues to revolve around the original meaning of the phrase used in the Constitution. Robert Natelson has argued that the original meaning of the Ex Post Facto clauses was limited to criminal laws and that, accordingly, *Calder* was correctly decided on historical grounds.[38] Professor Caleb Nelson, on the other hand, has argued that "the meaning of

the prohibition arguably depended on whether one read the key phrase as a lawyer or as a layperson."[39]

Most commentators who have revisited the historical record, however, have concluded that *Calder* was wrongly decided as a matter of original meaning.[40] Indeed, recent scholarship has continued to uncover historical evidence that supports the broader, criminal-and-civil side of the debate. According to Professor John Mikhail, the widely understood public meaning of "ex post facto" during the Confederation and early Republic included at least some civil laws affecting title to land.[41] The author of this essay has written that, contrary to the assertions of Dickinson and Randolph at the constitutional conventions, and those of Chase, Iredell, and Paterson in *Calder*, the "technical" meaning of "ex post facto" did not refer to criminal laws only. Rather, late colonial and early state cases described retrospective civil and criminal laws alike as ex post facto.[42]

OPEN QUESTIONS

- The history of the Ex Post Facto Clauses exemplifies how historical research can lead to indeterminate conclusions about legal questions. How legal interpreters should handle this historical indeterminacy is an open question. One well-articulated solution is the concept of liquidation, by which post-ratification interpretations can settle questions left open by historical analysis alone.[43]

- Courts and commentators have long criticized ex post facto laws in the harshest terms. Nevertheless, there is also a long tradition recognizing that, at least in some circumstances, retrospective laws can be justified.[44] Even if *Calder* is wrong as a matter of original meaning, whether a rule could be crafted that would more tightly restrict retroactive laws without unduly restricting legislative powers remains an open question.

Cite as: Evan C. Zoldan, *The State Ex-Post Facto Clause, in* THE HERITAGE GUIDE TO THE CONSTITUTION 283 (Josh Blackman & John G. Malcolm eds., 3d ed. 2025).

Notes

1. Adolph Berger, *Ex Post Facto in Roman Sources and Ex Post Facto Laws in Modern Juristic Terminology*, 7 Seminar (The Jurist) 49, 65 (1949). **2.** 1 Blackstone 46. **3.** *Id.* **4.** *Id.* **5.** *Satterlee v. Matthewson*, 27 U.S. (2 Pet.) 380, 416 app. at 683–84 (1829) (Johnson, J., concurring). **6.** *Wilkinson v. Meyer*, 2 Ld. Raym. 1350, 1352 (1724). **7.** William W. Crosskey, *The True Meaning of the Prohibition of the Ex Post Facto Clauses, in* 1 Politics and the Constitution in the History of the United States 324, 330–32 (1953). **8.** N.C. Const. of 1776, art. XXIV; Md. Const. of 1776, art. XV. **9.** Wayne Logan, The Ex Post Facto Clause 7 (2022). **10.** Md. Const. of 1776, art. XV. **11.** *Respublica v. Chapman*, 1 U.S. (1 Dall.) 53 (Pa. 1781). **12.** Harold Krent, *The Puzzling Boundary Between Criminal and Civil Retroactive Lawmaking*, 84 Geo. L. J. 2143, 2153 (1996). **13.** *Respublica*, 1 U.S. (1 Dall.) at 53. **14.** 2 Farrand's 376–77. **15.** *Id.* at 376. **16.** *Id.* **17.** *Id.* **18.** *Id.* at 439–440. **19.** *Id.* **20.** *Id.* **21.** *Id.* **22.** *Id.* at 448–49. **23.** *Id.* at 617. **24.** 3 Elliot's 471–74. **25.** *Id.* at 477, 481. **26.** Id. at 479. **27.** 4 Elliot's 184–85. **28.** 3 Elliot's 328. **29.** Crosskey, *supra* at 327–29. **30.** *Id.* at 329–30. **31.** Marcus [James Iredell], Answers to Mr. Mason's Objections to the New Constitution (1788), *in* Pamphlets on the Constitution of the United States 368 (Paul Leicester Ford ed., 1888). **32.** Storing 2.7.167. **33.** Crosskey, *supra* at 341–42. **34.** *Id.* at 338–39. **35.** 3 U.S. (2 Dall.) 386 (1798). **36.** *Id.* at 391–97. **37.** *Eastern Enterprises v. Apfel*, 524 U.S. 498, 538 (1998) (Thomas, J., concurring). **38.** Robert G. Natelson, *Statutory Retroactivity: The Founders' View*, 39 Idaho L. Rev. 489, 521, 523 (2003). **39.** Caleb Nelson, *Originalism and Interpretive Conventions*, 70 U. Chi. L. Rev. 519, 578 (2003). **40.** Oliver P. Field, *Ex Post Facto in the Constitution*, 20 Mich. L. Rev. 315, 321 (1922); Krent, *supra* at 2143; Jane Harris Aiken, *Ex Post Facto in the Civil Context: Unbridled Punishment*, 81 Ky. L.J. 323, 326 (1992). **41.** John Mikhail, *James Wilson, Early American Land Companies, and the Original Meaning of "Ex Post Facto Law,"* 17 Geo. J.L. & Pub. Pol'y 79 (2019). **42.** Evan C. Zoldan, *The Civil Ex Post Facto Clause*, 2015 Wis. L. Rev. 728 (2015). **43.** Nelson, *supra* at 578. **44.** Bernard W. Bell, *In Defense of Retroactive Laws*, 78 Tex. L. Rev. 235, 248 (1999).

ESSAY NO. 82: THE OBLIGATION OF CONTRACTS CLAUSE
ART. I, § 10, CL. 1

No State shall . . . pass any . . . Law impairing the Obligation of Contracts. . . .
—Richard A. Epstein

INTRODUCTION

Article I, Section 10 contains a list of prohibitions concerning the role of the states in political, monetary, and economic affairs. This section prohibits the states from "pass[ing] any . . . Law impairing the Obligation of Contracts." This provision's interpretation by the U.S. Supreme Court, both before and after the Civil War, has been filled with odd turns and surprises.

HISTORY BEFORE 1787

The protection of contracts was a prime objective of Roman and English law before the Founding period, but contracts were not *constitutionally* protected. The Roman system held that the constitutional dictates were those that pleased the king (*quod principi placuit legis habet vigorem*). Much constitutional theorizing sought to explain why the king normally would protect these arrangements. The English Bill of Rights (1689) again ignored contractual protection. This issue also was not taken up separately by the English colonies before the Revolutionary War. Instead, contractual protection came in silently through the back door. Natural law writings in the spirit of John Locke spoke of the protection of life, liberty, and property.[1]

In 1787, the Articles of Confederation Congress had adopted the Northwest Ordinance. Article II provided an express protection for the rights of contract: "In the just preservation of rights and property . . . no law . . . shall, in any manner whatever, interfere with or affect private contracts or engagements, bona fide, and without fraud, previously formed."[2]

THE CONSTITUTIONAL CONVENTION

On August 28, 1787, the delegates debated the Constitution's prohibition on states issuing paper money as legal tender. Rufus King of Massachusetts proposed "a prohibition on the States to interfere in private contracts."[3] King hoped to extend the provision from the Northwest Ordinance to the states. A brief debate followed. George Mason of Virginia feared the prohibition would prevent the states from establishing time limits with respect to lawsuits involving state-issued bonds.[4] James Wilson of Pennsylvania responded that the clause would prevent "retrospective interferences only"—that is, impair contracts already made.[5] Wilson may have intended to limit the clause to retroactive impairment of contracts. The text, however, is not limited to contracts that were previously formed; it also could be read to prohibit the prospective impairment of future contracts.

The scope of the clause is also quite broad. It is not limited to the debtor-relief laws that were common in the states. Rather, it covers all types of contracts between private persons, including partnerships and corporations.[6] This text was consistent with the Roman tradition.[7]

The term "obligation" was long understood to protect the debtor or obligor, but it also protects the full interests of the creditor. Both sides could seek the clause's protection, whether the "impairment" be partial or total. Moreover, the Obligation of Contracts Clause applies to contracts with interstate connections as well as to local contracts.

The clause also reads as a stern imperative: Obligations of contracts cannot be violated under any circumstances, and Congress cannot waive that prohibition. By contrast, Congress can override other prohibitions on the states in Article I, Section 10, including the Import-Export Clause and the Compact Clause. (See Essays Nos. 84 and 86.)

THE RATIFICATION DEBATES

The Obligation of Contracts Clause appears in Article I, Section 10 alongside the section prohibiting the states from issuing paper money. (See Essay No. 79.) The Anti-Federalists feared that the two clauses operating in tandem would prevent the states from assisting the debtor classes: The states could not debase the currency with new issues of paper tender and could not invalidate contracts to wipe out unpaid debts. Luther Martin of Maryland had voted against the clause at the Constitutional Convention, arguing that the states would no longer be able "to prevent the *wealthy creditor* and the *monied man* from *totally* destroying the *poor* though even *industrious* debtor."[8]

In Federalist No. 44, James Madison argued that the Obligation of Contracts Clause would "banish speculations on public measures, inspire a general prudence and industry, and give a regular course to the business of society." Madison seemed to fear that debtor relief would undermine the long-term stability of commercial operations.

In the South Carolina ratifying convention, Charles Pinckney contended that the prohibitions on contractual impairment and state currency would help to cement the Union by barring the states from discriminating against out-of-state commercial interests.[9] In the Virginia convention, Edmund Randolph declared that the Obligation of Contracts Clause was essential for enforcement of the peace treaty with Great Britain, which guaranteed private

British debts.[10] The clause therefore afforded both a protection to individuals against their states and a limitation on the states that prevented them from intruding on essential federal interests.

JUDICIAL PRECEDENT

In the antebellum period, the Obligation of Contracts Clause was the only general federal constitutional guarantee that imposed limitations on the state governments. The clause soon became the focus of efforts to protect economic liberties against state intervention.

The first seminal case on the clause was *Fletcher v. Peck* (1810).[11] The Georgia legislature had passed a law that transferred land to private parties, and the recipients had transferred the property to innocent purchasers. However, that initial grant of the property from the government was tainted by bribery. The next state legislature passed a statute that purported to repeal the legislation and thus to void the transfers to the innocent purchasers. The Supreme Court held that revoking these transfers violated the Obligation of Contracts Clause but did not fully address the fraudulent nature of the initial grant.

Nine years later, Chief Justice John Marshall wrote the majority decision in *Trustees of Dartmouth College v. Woodward* (1819).[12] This case held that the clause also prohibited state governments from violating contracts between the state and private parties. New Hampshire, acting through Woodward, tried to stack the Dartmouth Board of Trustees with its own trustees to convert the college into a public institution. The Court held that Dartmouth could invoke the clause to block the state's legislation. Here, the obligation stretched back to Dartmouth's royal charter. Marshall's broad reading of the Obligation of Contracts Clause fits well with the Framers' antipathy to corrupt self-dealing and unlimited state powers. *Dartmouth College* remains unchallenged to this day.

That same year, the Court decided *Sturges v. Crowninshield* (1819), which recognized that the Obligation of Contracts Clause protects rights that were already vested in private contracts.[13] Specifically, state insolvency laws could not order the discharge of contracts that were already formed before the state statute was passed. This retrospective principle was not controversial. The clause must apply to pre-existing contracts; otherwise, it would effectively be a dead letter. The legislature could not flip the background rules of the legal system to prejudice individuals who had advanced money on the faith of earlier arrangements.

Does the clause impose limitations on the power of the state to regulate contracts that are *not yet* formed? *Ogden v. Saunders* (1827), in which a divided Court upheld a prospective state bankruptcy statute, provided something of a mixed answer. Justice Bushrod Washington, writing for the majority, held that the clause's original design does not block any improvements in the administration of commercial justice, but the Court also recognized limits on this holding. For example, the state could not nullify, individually and at-will, any contracts that were thereafter formed.[14] The net effect of this legislation would be to nullify entirely the force of the clause. In short, the state may alter the rules governing future contracts in ways that offer greater security and stability to contractual obligations. In this regard, the Court disagreed with James Wilson, who had stated that the clause was purely retroactive. As a practical matter, however, *Ogden* left all general state economic regulation outside the scope of constitutional prohibition.

Over time, the yawning gap left by *Ogden* was filled by other constitutional provisions. The Court held that some future contracts were protected from state interference by the so-called Dormant Commerce Clause. (See Essay No. 44.) The Court has also invoked the doctrine of liberty of contract under both Due Process Clauses, and the Equal Protection Clause.

THE POLICE POWER

In the American legal system, there is a concept known as the *police power*. Under the police power, the state can override private rights of property to protect the public "safety, health, morals, and the general welfare." (See Essay No. 173.) Actions taken pursuant to this power do not require just compensation under the Takings Clause of the Fifth Amendment. Limits on the police power are nowhere mentioned explicitly in the Constitution, but they are read into every substantive guarantee that limits the exercise of state power. For example, laws stopping contracts to pollute, to bribe, or to fix prices have always been permissible under the police power.

Beginning in the 1930s, the Supreme Court expanded the scope of the police power beyond these limited objectives. *Home Building & Loan Association v. Blaisdell* (1934) significantly multiplied the police-power exceptions to the Obligation of Contracts Clause even when no compensation was supplied. During the Great Depression, Minnesota imposed a mortgage moratorium to prohibit home foreclosures. The moratorium was challenged as a violation of the Obligation of Contracts Clause. But the Court upheld the mortarium as a proper exercise of the police power to deal with the exigencies of the fiscal crisis, despite the traditional police-power limitations relating to health and safety.[15] This decision also unleashed many other legislative initiatives that sought to neutralize the protections secured by individual contracts. After *Blaisdell*, it was no longer possible to distinguish between the general welfare and special-interest laws benefiting certain groups.

Under modern doctrine, it is virtually certain that the Supreme Court will find a police-power justification for special legislation with interest-group support. For example, *Exxon Corp. v. Eagerton* (1983) found that a "broad societal interest" was sufficient to justify preventing a company from asserting its explicit contractual rights.[16] The Court has effectively gutted the clause insofar as it applies to broad classes of existing contracts.

While the Supreme Court is largely deferential when the state voids contracts between private parties, it has remained more suspicious when the state voids a contract between the state and private parties. There is an obvious risk of self-dealing when the government uses legislation to extricate the state from its own covenants. The Court declared unconstitutional a law that nullified bond covenants that prohibited the government from using bond proceeds to support mass transit.[17] It also refused to allow Minnesota to impose retroactively more stringent financial obligations on an employer in the winding up of the state's pension plan.[18] But in another case, the Court allowed Minnesota to apply retroactively a law revoking a spouse's life insurance beneficiary status upon divorce.[19]

By contrast, when dealing with private contracts, the modern age often affords little intellectual respect for freedom of contract or for the sanctity of contracts validly formed.

OPEN QUESTIONS

- Can state and local governments unilaterally restrict pension benefits for public employees, both union and nonunion?[20]
- Does the Obligation of Contracts Clause apply to a state's subdivisions and administrative agencies?[21]
- What is the relationship between the Obligation of Contracts Clause and the Takings Clause of the Fifth Amendment? Does the state's impairment of a contract require the payment of just compensation?[22]

Cite as: Richard A. Epstein, *The Obligation of Contracts Clause, in* The Heritage Guide to the Constitution 287 (Josh Blackman & John G. Malcolm eds., 3d ed. 2025).

Notes

1. 2 The Writings of Samuel Adams 350–59 (Harry Alonzo Cushing ed., 1904–08), https://perma.cc/9ZBK-ESQB. **2.** Ordinance for the government of the territory of the United States, North West of the river Ohio, 32 J. Cont. Cong. 334 (July 13, 1787). **3.** 2 Farrand's 439; James W. Ely Jr., *Whatever Happened to the Contract Clause?*, 4 Charleston L. Rev. 371, 372–73 (2010). **4.** 2 Farrand's 440. **5.** *Id.* **6.** Thomas W. Merrill, *Public Contracts, Private Contracts and the Transformation of the Constitutional Order*, 37 Case W. Rsrv. L. Rev. 597, 597–98 (1987). **7.** Barry Nicholas, Introduction to Roman Law (1976). **8.** Storing 2.4.75– 78. **9.** 4 Elliot's 333–36. **10.** 3 Elliot's 478. **11.** 10 U.S. 87 (1810). **12.** 17 U.S. 518 (1819). **13.** 17 U.S. 122 (1819). **14.** 25 U.S. 213, 266–268 (1827). **15.** 290 U.S. 398 (1934). **16.** 462 U.S. 176 (1983). **17.** *United States Trust Co. v. New Jersey*, 431 U.S. 1 (1977). **18.** *Allied Structural Steel Co. v. Spannaus*, 438 U.S. 234 (1978). **19.** *Sveen v. Melin*, 584 U.S. 811 (2018). **20.** *In re Pension Reform Litigation*, 32 N.E. 3d 1 (Ill. 2015). **21.** Rodney W. Harrell, *The Contract Clause of the Constitution and the Need for "Pass Any . . . Law" Rehabilitation in the Age of Delegation*, 22 Geo. Mason L. Rev. 1317 (2015). **22.** Richard A. Epstein, *Toward the Revitalization of the Contract Clause*, 51 U. Chi. L. Rev. 703 (1984).

ESSAY NO. 83: THE STATE TITLE OF NOBILITY CLAUSE
ART. I, § 10, CL. 1

No State shall . . . grant any Title of Nobility.
—Allyson N. Ho, Stephen J. Hammer, & David W. Casazza

The State Titles of Nobility Clause corresponds to its federal counterpart (Article I, Section 9, Clause 8). Both clauses derive from the same background and serve the same end: promoting republican self-government.[1]

After independence, only some state constitutions guarded against titles of nobility,[2] but the Articles of Confederation prohibited the issuing of such titles both by the central government and by the states.[3] A desire for uniformity on this point across the new Republic was thus suggested as another explanation for the inclusion of the prohibition on state titles of nobility in the Constitution.[4] Accordingly, the clauses prohibiting federal and state titles of nobility were considered together during the ratification debates and have occasioned little distinction. For further elaboration of the history of these clauses, see Essay No. 75.

Cite as: Allyson N. Ho, Stephen J. Hammer, & David W. Casazza, *The State Title of Nobility Clause, in* The Heritage Guide to the Constitution 290 (Josh Blackman & John G. Malcolm eds., 3d ed. 2025).

Notes
1. Federalist No. 39 (Madison). 2. Mass. Const. of 1780, art. VI; Ga. Const. of 1777, art. XI. 3. Articles of Confederation, Art. VI, § 1. 4. *One of the Middling-Interest*, Massachusetts Centinel (Nov. 28, 1787), https://perma.cc/ETQ4-K6PW.

❧

ESSAY NO. 84: THE IMPORT-EXPORT CLAUSE
ART. I, § 10, CL. 2

No State shall, without the Consent of the Congress, lay any Imposts or Duties on Imports or Exports, except what may be absolutely necessary for executing its inspection Laws: and the net Produce of all Duties and Imposts, laid by any State on Imports or Exports, shall be for the Use of the Treasury of the United States; and all such Laws shall be subject to the Revision and Controul of the Congress.
—Joseph Bishop-Henchman

INTRODUCTION

The Import-Export Clause is a detailed and stringent prohibition on state taxation of trade and was debated extensively at the Constitutional Convention. However, it is invoked only rarely in constitutional litigation. One reason is that the U.S. Supreme Court has concluded that the clause's term "imports or exports" covers only foreign trade, not state-to-state trade. Another reason is a series of court decisions concluding that the clause does not absolutely ban state taxes on trade and prohibits such taxes only in certain circumstances.

HISTORY BEFORE 1787

In the 1780s, states taxed neighboring states and engaged in interstate trade wars. The Articles of Confederation prohibited states from "lay[ing] any imposts [taxes on imports] or duties [taxes on exports or trade generally]" that conflicted with existing foreign treaties, but the prohibition was weak.[1] The Articles neither prohibited trade wars nor empowered Congress to stop them. States with ports taxed commerce bound for interior states, tariff wars proliferated, and the national economy was imperiled.

New York, for example, imposed certain fees on all vessels that were heading to or departing from New Jersey and Connecticut.[2] Benjamin Franklin described New Jersey as "a barrel tapped at both ends" between Philadelphia and New York.[3] New Jersey retaliated against the New York law by imposing a tax on a lighthouse that New York City had purchased in New Jersey.[4] James Madison described North Carolina, which was wedged between Virginia and South Carolina, as "a patient bleeding at both Arms."[5] Rhode Island profited so much from taxing imports bound for other states that it refused to attend the Constitutional Convention because of a correct fear that this power would be curtailed.[6] Fisher Ames, who served in the Massachusetts convention, warned, "Our discontents were fermenting into civil war."[7] The Import-Export Clause would serve as "[t]he proposed remedy for this exploitation of the inland states by the seaboard states."[8]

THE CONSTITUTIONAL CONVENTION

In modern times, the Commerce Clause is viewed as more significant than the Import-Export Clause, but "their roles were reversed at the Philadelphia Convention."[9]

The Import-Export Clause's comprehensive language resulted from numerous debates and votes over several days. The first draft prohibited the states from "lay[ing] imposts or duties on imports" without the consent of Congress. Madison attempted to transform this provision into an absolute ban but was unsuccessful.[10]

George Mason of Virginia objected to the clause generally on the grounds that it would limit states from using protective tariffs to encourage specific industries.[11] Madison responded that protective tariffs would be imposed not just on foreign imports, but also on imports from other states and that the lack of this provision "would revive all the mischiefs experienced from the want of a Genl. Government over commerce" under the Articles of Confederation.[12] The Import-Export clause was subsequently amended to prohibit states from taxing exports as well as imports.[13] The Federal Export Taxation Clause also prohibits Congress from laying taxes or duties on exports from any state.[14] (See Essay No. 72.) Roger Sherman of Connecticut added the provision that any state collections on imports or exports in violation of the clause would revert to Congress.[15]

Mason successfully pressed to add the carveout for inspection fees, proposing that states be permitted to collect "the usual duties on produce . . . for the sole purpose" of "inspecting, packing, storing, and indemnifying losses."[16] Madison agreed, but with the proviso that any cases of abuse be "subject to the revision and controul of Congress"—a rare congressional power to rewrite, not merely override, state law.[17] On the last working day of the Convention, the Committee of Style made two modifications. First, the states could collect imposts and duties "for executing its Inspection laws," but only when it was "absolutely necessary." Six clauses in the Constitution used the word "necessary," but only the Import-Export Clause used the phrase "absolutely necessary." (See Essay Nos. 38, 66, 94, 111, and 148.) Second, the committee clarified Sherman's language to specify that "net Produce" (any state collections in excess of the cost of inspections) would be deposited into the U.S. Treasury.[18] After a last attempt by Mason to remove the provision that gave Congress the power of "Revision and Controul" over state laws, the final version of the clause was adopted over Virginia's objection.[19]

THE RATIFICATION DEBATES

In Federalist No. 32, Alexander Hamilton argued that the Constitution would give the federal government exclusive power over the states in only limited ways. He listed three examples, including the Import-Export Clause. The other two were a uniform rule of nationalization and exclusive legislation over what became the District of Columbia. Anti-Federalist opponents of ratification worried about restrictions on state

taxing powers. Cincinnatus warned that transferring tariff power from states to the general government would result in more tariffs and a heavier tax burden.[20] Brutus predicted that states would rely on direct taxation if they were not able to tax imports.[21]

At the Virginia convention, George Mason continued his criticism of the Import-Export Clause, arguing that Virginia would lose easy revenue from taxes on imports and exports. Madison replied, as he did at the Federal Convention, that the danger of states heavily taxing each other required a centralized solution by the national government.[22]

EARLY PRACTICE

In March 1789, when the new federal government assembled, Rhode Island still had not yet ratified the Constitution. Rhode Island, which was "nominally independent," sought to impose tariffs on imports from other states.[23] In July 1789, Congress adopted a national tariff law, and threatened to enact duties on all Rhode Island exports to the rest of the Union, or even to embargo all trade. Rhode Island ratified the Constitution in May 1790, and the threatened trade war was dropped.[24]

Congress ultimately proved deferential to state inspection laws: The First Congress enacted legislation requiring all vessels to comply with state inspection laws and directing federal customs officials to enforce it.[25] Congress did not modify state laws or claim revenue from excessive state enactments. In doing so, Congress "arguably . . . delegate[d] to state legislatures the power that the Constitution had conferred on Congress."[26]

JUDICIAL PRECEDENT

The first important Supreme Court case concerning the Import-Export Clause was *Brown v. Maryland* (1827).[27] Maryland imposed a $50 license on all importers selling goods in the state, regardless of the quantity or value of goods sold. Maryland argued that the tax was not on importing but on the selling of goods. Chief Justice Marshall rejected that argument and declared the tax unconstitutional. He concluded that "Imposts or Duties" meant any tax on imports or exports and that "a tax on the occupation of an importer is in like manner a tax on importation."[28] Marshall evidently believed that the Import-Export Clause applied to both foreign and interstate trade. At the end of his opinion, he observed that "the principles laid down in this case . . . apply equally to importations from a sister state."[29] That principle is not obvious from the text of the clause, but Marshall's observation is consistent with the position that Madison advanced at the Federal Convention and the Virginia ratifying convention.

In *Almy v. California* (1860), Chief Justice Roger B. Taney took these conclusions as obvious.[30] He declared unconstitutional California's stamp tax on paperwork facilitating the export of gold to New York.[31] *Canton R. Co. v. Rogan* (1951), however, held that a state could impose a broadly applicable business tax on a marine terminal that is not imposed on the goods shipped through that terminal.[32] Courts have generally deferred to Congress or state legislatures to address the excessiveness of inspection fees.[33]

The Framers may well have expected the Import-Export Clause to be far more impactful than the Commerce Clause, but two key Supreme Court decisions have significantly reduced the clause's protections. The first, *Woodruff v. Parham* (1868), upheld a tax on goods sold in Mobile, Alabama, but brought in from other states. The Court held that the clause applies only to foreign commerce. The Court repudiated Marshall's "casual remark" in *Brown*, and held that the words "export," "import," and "impost" in the clause were used exclusively to describe trade with foreign countries.[34]

Woodruff has been questioned but has not been overruled. Professor William Crosskey has identified several examples of the word "import" being used in the context of interstate trade.[35] Justice Clarence Thomas criticized *Woodruff* for being "selective in its use of history" and urged the Court to "restor[e] the original Import-Export Clause check on discriminatory state

taxation" in lieu of the Dormant Commerce Clause.[36] To date, the Court has not done so.

The second key decision, *Michelin Tire Corp. v. Wages* (1976), adopted a new, more lenient, framework for the Import-Export Clause.[37] Justice William Brennan's majority opinion upheld the imposition of Georgia's inventory tax on imported tires. The Court overruled an earlier case holding that imported goods are exempt from tax until removed from their "original package" or "broke bulk."[38] Based on the constitutional history and Chief Justice Marshall's opinion in *Brown*, the Court held that a state tax is invalid only if it prevents the federal government from speaking with one voice in foreign relations, diverts import revenue from the federal government, or disturbs interstate harmony by taxing goods merely flowing through to other states.[39]

The Court acknowledged that this new interpretive framework allowed for nondiscriminatory state taxes on imports or exports that "increase the cost of goods purchased by 'inland' consumers."[40] As a result, the test would seemingly be at odds with the clause's text. Justice Brennan defended the decision by citing Professor Crosskey, observing that "imposts or duties" are narrower terms than "tax" and that modern transportation makes imposts or duties easier to avoid.[41]

The *Michelin Tire* framework has also been applied to exports. The Court upheld a Washington state business tax on loading and unloading cargo ships where the tax did not prevent the federal government from speaking with one voice or disturb interstate harmony.[42] The Court also upheld Tennessee's tax on revenue from leases from international cargo containers because the tax was not levied "on the containers themselves or on the goods being imported in those containers."[43]

OPEN QUESTIONS

- When is an import no longer an import? For example, does an import lose its status when shipping containers are transferred from a ship to a train for movement to other states? Or to storage within the state? What if some packages in the shipping container are used?
- Does the Import-Export Clause prohibit all taxation of imports and exports or only imposts and duties? What is the difference?

- Is *Michelin Tire Corp. v. Wages* an originalist decision? Should it be overruled?
- *Michelin Tire* dealt with generally applicable taxes on imports, but courts have not extended its reasoning to taxes on exports. State power to tax goods "entering the export stream" is therefore very restricted.[44] Does this make sense?
- Does modern transportation mean the Import-Export Clause matters less today than it did at the Founding?
- Is Justice Thomas right in thinking *Woodruff v. Parham* was wrongly decided? Would the Import–Export Clause as he describes it accomplish the same results as the Dormant Commerce Clause?
- Why has the Commerce Clause mattered more than the Import-Export Clause? Does it matter whether the Framers expected the reverse to be true?

Cite as: Joseph Bishop-Henchman, *The Import-Export Clause*, *in* THE HERITAGE GUIDE TO THE CONSTITUTION 291 (Josh Blackman & John G. Malcolm eds., 3d ed. 2025).

Notes

1. Articles of Confederation, art. VI, § 3; Robert G. Natelson, *What the Constitution Means by "Duties, Imposts, and Excises"—and "Taxes" (Direct or Otherwise)*, 66 Case W. Rsrv. L. Rev. 297, 323 (2015). **2.** Joseph Bishop-Henchman, *The History of Internet Sales Taxes from 1789 to the Present Day:* South Dakota v. Wayfair, 2017–18 Cato Sup. Ct. Rev. 269, 272. **3.** 3 Farrand's 542. **4.** Bishop-Henchman, *supra* at 272. **5.** 3 Farrand's 542. **6.** *Id.* at 546–47. **7.** Allan Nevins, The American States During and After the Revolution, 1775–1789, at 555–57 (1927). **8.** Boris I. Bittker & Brannon P. Denning, *The Import–Export Clause*, 68 Miss. L.J. 521, 521 (1998–99). **9.** *Id.* at 522. **10.** 2 Farrand's 441. **11.** *Id.* **12.** *Id.* **13.** *Id.* at 442. **14.** Art. I, § 9, cl. 5. **15.** 2 Farrand's 442–43. **16.** *Id.* at 588, 597 n.17, 607. **17.** *Id.* at 588–89, 597 n.17, 607. **18.** *Id.* at 624; Denning, *supra* at 187 n.158; *McCulloch v. Maryland*, 17 U.S. 316, 414–15 (1819). **19.** 2 Farrand's 624. **20.** Storing 6.1.43. **21.** Storing 2.9.5. **22.** 3 Elliot's 481–83. **23.** Denning, *supra* at 211–12 (citing Frank Greene Bates, Rhode Island and the Formation of the Union 172 (1898)). **24.** David P. Currie, The Constitution in Congress: The Federalist Period, 1789–1801, at 98–99 (1997). **25.** *Id.* at 63–64 (citing 1 Stat. 106 (Apr. 2, 1790)). **26.** *Id.* at 64. **27.** 25 U.S. (12 Wheat.) 419 (1827). **28.** *Id.* at 444. **29.** *Id.* at 449. **30.** *Almy v. California*, 65 U.S. 169 (1860). **31.** *Id.* at 173–74 (1860). **32.** 340 U.S. 511 (1951). **33.** *Neilson v. Garza*, 17 Fed. Cas. 1302, 1303 (C.C.E.D. Tex. 1876) (Bradley, Circuit Justice); *Patapsco Guano Co. v. N.C. Bd. of Agric.*, 171 U.S. 345, 354 (1898); *Hale v. Bimco Trading, Inc.*, 306 U.S. 375 (1939). **34.** *Woodruff v. Parham*, 75 U.S. 123, 139 (1868). **35.** 1 William Crosskey, Politics and the Constitution in the History of the United States 295–323 (1953). **36.** *Camps Newfound/Owatonna, Inc. v. Town of Harrison*, 520 U.S. 564, 609 (1997) (Thomas, J., dissenting). **37.** *Michelin Tire Corp. v. Wages*, 423 U.S. 285 (1976). **38.** *Id.* at 301 (overruling *Low v. Austin*, 80 U.S. 29 (1872)). **39.** *Id.* at 285; *Youngstown Sheet & Tube Co. v. Bowers*, 358 U.S. 534, 555–56 (1959). **40.** *Michelin*, 423 U.S. at 288–89. **41.** *Id.* **42.** *Dep't of Rev. of Wash. v. Assoc. of Wash. Stevedoring Cos.*, 435 U.S. 734 (1978). **43.** *Itel Containers Int'l Corp. v. Huddleston*, 507 U.S. 60, 77 (1993). **44.** *Dep't of Rev. of Wash. v. Ass'n of Wash. Stevedoring Cos.*, 435 U.S. 734 (1978); *Dulles Duty Free, LLC v. Cnty. of Loudoun*, 803 S.E.2d 54, 59 (Va. 2017); Brief of Tax Law Professors in *Loudoun County, Virginia v. Dulles Duty Free, LLC*, 138 S.Ct. 1440 (cert. denied 2018) (No. 17-904).

**ESSAY NO. 85: THE TONNAGE CLAUSE
ART. I, § 10, CL. 3**

No State shall, without the Consent of Congress, lay any Duty of Tonnage. . . .
—Joseph Bishop-Henchman

INTRODUCTION

Tonnage refers to the internal volume, or cubic capacity of a vessel, which is measured in tons. Following independence, state governments imposed taxes or duties on vessels based on their tonnage for "the privilege of arriving or departing from a port." Under the Tonnage Clause, such state or local taxes or duties are unconstitutional.[1] Other charges, such as user fees that compensate for specific services provided to a vessel, may be permissible.[2]

In 1870, Michigan Chief Justice Thomas Cooley offered a concise explanation of the Tonnage Clause: "Vessels are taxable as property . . . [but] a tax on vessels at a certain sum 'per ton' was forbidden."[3] Further, "a tax of a certain sum upon every vessel arriving in port is to be regarded as duty of tonnage, though demanded irrespective of the vessel's capacity." While the U.S. Supreme Court has allowed state taxes on imports and exports notwithstanding the Import-Export Clause, its interpretation of the Tonnage Clause remains strict. (See Essay No. 84.)

HISTORY BEFORE 1787

In the 1780s, states taxed neighboring states and engaged in trade wars. The Articles of Confederation prohibited states from "lay[ing] any imposts or duties" that conflicted with existing foreign treaties, but it did so only weakly.[4] States imposed "duties of tonnage and duties on imports . . . as levies upon the privilege of access by vessels or goods to the ports."[5] These duties "were distinct from fees or charges . . . for services facilitating commerce, such as pilotage, towage, charges for loading and unloading cargoes, wharfage, storage, and the like." In 1783, for example, the Port of Baltimore required different tonnage fees based on where the vessel was registered.[6] All Maryland-registered vessels had to pay six pence per ton; British-registered vessels had to pay 60 pence per ton; and all other vessels had to pay 12 pence per ton. Moreover, all vessels that cleared customs had to pay a duty of one pence per ton. Unlike fees to compensate for a particular service rendered to a vessel, tonnage duties were charges "imposed by virtue of sovereignty" on vessels for the purposes of raising revenue or impeding commerce.[7]

THE CONSTITUTIONAL CONVENTION

On September 15, 1787—the last working day of the Constitutional Convention—"the delegates made a variety of corrections and changes" in the draft Constitution.[8] The Maryland delegation, in an effort to ensure that Congress could not prevent a state from taxing vessels as long as the revenue was used for improvements that benefited all vessels, requested an amendment stating that "no State shall be restrained from laying duties of tonnage for the purpose of clearing harbours and erecting lighthouses."[9] George Mason of Virginia supported the motion, arguing that the Chesapeake Bay had unique needs that justified this form of taxation.[10]

Gouverneur Morris of Pennsylvania replied that the amendment was not necessary. He argued that the Constitution did not restrain states from laying tonnage duties and that adopting the Maryland delegation's language would imply otherwise. James Madison of Virginia countered that federal power to regulate commerce would restrain the states from imposing tonnage duties and that the regulation of commerce "was in its nature indivisible and ought to be wholly under one authority."[11]

Maryland's proposal backfired. By a vote of 6 states to 4, the delegates adopted explicit language prohibiting states from laying a duty of tonnage unless Congress consented.[12] However, Congress would have the power to impose duties of tonnage.

THE RATIFICATION DEBATES

In Federalist No. 44, Madison described the Tonnage Clause as one of several "restrictions on the authority of" the states and contended that such restrictions were necessary and "qualified," as Congress could authorize state actions.[13] At the Maryland ratifying convention, Samuel Chase, who would serve on the Supreme Court, warned that the Constitution had the "tendency" to "annihilate state governments" and that, because of the Tonnage Clause, "no state can pay its debts—or support its government but only by direct taxes on Property."[14] In South Carolina, Rawlins Lowndes observed that the Constitution's ban on tonnage or import duties in particular would benefit the northern states.[15]

EARLY PRACTICE

In 1789, Congress imposed federal tonnage duties on ships engaged in interstate and foreign commerce.[16] The next year, Congress consented to tonnage duties sought by three states after it had declined to fund navigation improvements along the Savannah River.[17] In 1808, Congress agreed to Pennsylvania's request to impose tonnage duties at Philadelphia to fund harbor improvements, although critics attacked it as an unfair "preference" for that port.[18] (See Essay No. 73.)

Within a few decades, "few states any longer asked permission to impose [tonnage duties]" because "experience had shown tonnage taxes drove ships to other ports."[19] In 1847, President James K. Polk vetoed an internal improvements bill, vainly urging states to seek congressional approval for tonnage clauses rather than direct appropriation of funds.[20]

In the nineteenth century, the Tonnage and Commerce Clauses were viewed as sweeping guarantees of free trade within the country. According to Justice Samuel Miller, the Tonnage Clause ensured that "vessels coming from abroad, or engaged in navigation among the States, or even if plying entirely within the boundaries of and owned by citizens of a single State, shall not be taxed, as vessels, for the privilege of navigating the inland waters of the country, or coming into any of its ports."[21] States or harbors could collect fees for actual services provided, such as "charges for wharfage or towage, or any other local port-charges."[22] However, any vessel "tax or duty that is imposed, whatever the subject, solely according to the rule of weight" was forbidden in order "to guard against local hindrances to trade and carriage by vessels."[23]

JUDICIAL PRECEDENT

In *Clyde Mallory Lines v. Alabama* (1935), the Supreme Court described the Tonnage Clause as a supplement to the Import-Export Clause and said that the prohibition against laying duties of tonnage prevents states from taxing vessels and indirectly taxing the merchandise on that vessel.[24] The Court has attempted to draw a line between forbidden and permissible taxes. Some cases have allowed user fees "that operate only to compensate a government for benefits supplied."[25] This analysis resembles the Dormant Commerce Clause and Import-Export Clause analyses: The Court asks whether the charge is nondiscriminatory, a fair approximation of benefits received, and not excessive.

To this day, states cannot impose taxes on vessels based only on their capacity, whatever their use may be. *Polar Tankers, Inc. v. Valdez* (2009) declared unconstitutional a state-authorized property tax on large ships that travelled to and from the port.[26] Justice Stephen Breyer's majority opinion observed that the tax was designed to apply primarily to oil tankers, which were ships with large cargo capacity. The Alaska law was dissimilar to permissible taxes on other property and taxes on unrelated services provided to the vessels.[27] Chief Justice John Roberts and Justices Clarence Thomas and Samuel Alito concurred. They would simply have found that the tax was related to the size of the vessel and was unrelated to services rendered.[28] Roberts wrote that "it does not matter" whether the city imposes similar taxes on other property.[29] Justices John Paul Stevens and David H. Souter dissented. They contended that the tax was permissible because it was levied based on value and not tonnage.[30]

OPEN QUESTIONS

- Should the view of Chief Justice Roberts and Justices Thomas and Alito in *Polar Tankers* carry a majority of the Court?
- If Alaska imposed a tonnage tax on all forms of transportation and not just vessels, would the tax in *Polar Tankers* be constitutional?
- How would textualists define the term "tonnage"? How would originalists define it?
- Can a state impose user fees based on tonnage to fund harbor dredging or lighthouse operations?
- What would congressional authorization of a tonnage charge look like?

Cite as: Joseph Bishop-Henchman, *The Tonnage Clause, in* THE HERITAGE GUIDE TO THE CONSTITUTION 294 (Josh Blackman & John G. Malcolm eds., 3d ed. 2025).

Notes

1. *Clyde Mallory Lines v. Alabama*, 296 U.S. 261, 265 (1935); *Cannon v. New Orleans*, 87 U.S. 577, 581 (1874); *Inman Steamship Company v. Tinker*, 94 U.S. 238, 243 (1876) (quoting Cowel's Law Dictionary (1708)). **2.** *Polar Tankers, Inc. v. City of Valdez*, 557 U.S. 1, 10 (2009). **3.** Thomas M. Cooley, A Treatise on the Law of Taxation 61–62 (1876) (citing *State Tonnage Tax Cases*, 79 U.S. 204 (1870), and others); Erik M. Jensen, *Quirky Constitutional Provisions Matter: The Tonnage Clause, Polar Tankers, and State Taxation of Commerce*, 18 Geo. Mason. L. Rev. 669, 672–73 (2011). **4.** Articles of Confederation, art. VI, § 3. **5.** *Clyde Mallory Lines*, 296 U.S. at 265 (citing *Cooley v. Board of Wardens*, 53 U.S. 299, 314 (1851)). **6.** Port of Baltimore, *Duties upon Exports, Duties upon Tonnage, Duties upon Exports* (1784). **7.** *Packet Co. v. Keokuk*, 95 U.S. 80, 85 (1877). **8.** Edward J. Larson & Michael P. Winship, The Constitutional Convention: A Narrative History from the Notes of James Madison 150–51 (2005). **9.** 2 Farrand's 625. **10.** *Id.* **11.** *Id.* **12.** *Id.* at 625–26, 633–34. **13.** Federalist No. 44 (Madison).

14. Storing 5.3.16. **15.** *Id.* at 5.12. **16.** David P. Currie, The Constitution in Congress: The Federalist Period, 1789–1801, at 58 n.26 (1997). **17.** *Id.* at 56 n.6 & 70 n.116. **18.** David P. Currie, The Constitution in Congress: The Jeffersonians, 1801–1829. at 154 n.214 (2001). **19.** David P. Currie, The Constitution in Congress: Democrats and Whigs, 1829–1861, at 27 n.101 (2005). **20.** *Id.* at 25. **21.** Samuel Freeman Miller, Lectures on the Constitution of the United States 253 (1891). **22.** *Cooley*, 53 U.S. at 314. **23.** *Inman Steamship*, 94 U.S. at 243; *Packet Co.*, 95 U.S. at 84–85. **24.** *Clyde Mallory Lines*, 296 U.S. at 264–65. **25.** *Massachusetts v. United States*, 435 U.S. 444, 462, 464 (1978). **26.** *Polar Tankers*, 557 U.S. at 6. **27.** *Id.* at 10–13. **28.** *Id.* at 17 (Roberts, C.J., concurring in part and concurring in the judgment); *id.* at 19 (Alito, J., concurring in part and concurring in the judgment). **29.** *Id.* at 17 (Roberts, C.J., concurring in part and concurring in the judgment). **30.** *Id.* at 20 (Stevens, J., dissenting).

ESSAY NO. 86: THE TROOPS, SHIPS OF WAR, COMPACT, AND INVASION CLAUSE
ART. I, § 10, CL. 3

No State shall, without the Consent of Congress . . . keep Troops, or Ships of War in time of Peace, enter into any Agreement or Compact with another State, or with a foreign Power, or engage in War, unless actually invaded, or in such imminent Danger as will not admit of delay.

—Julian G. Ku

INTRODUCTION

Article I, Section 10, Clause 3 imposes four conditional constraints on the states: (i) States cannot impose any taxes on vessels based on their size, known as "duties of tonnage," unless Congress consents (see Essay No. 85); (ii) states cannot "keep Troops, or Ships of War in time of Peace" unless Congress consents; (iii) states cannot "enter into any Agreement or Compact with another State, or with a foreign Power" unless Congress consents; and (iv) generally cannot "engage in War" unless Congress consents. However, a state can engage in war if it is "actually invaded, or in such imminent Danger as will not admit of delay."

HISTORY BEFORE 1787

The Articles of Confederation addressed the states' powers to keep troops and ships of war, enter into certain alliances with other states, and engage in war if invaded. Article VI, Section 2 provided that states could enter into a "treaty, confederation, or alliance" only with the "consent of the united states, in congress assembled." Before 1776, the Crown had to approve any intercolonial agreements.[1] The Articles substituted Congress for the Crown but changed past practice. Congressional consent was required only if two states made a "treaty, confederation, or alliance." "In certain cases," however, "the [authority] of the Confederacy was disregarded, as in violations not only of the treaty of Peace; but of Treaties with France & Holland, which were complained of to Cong[res]s."[2] Federal authority was similarly violated by "Treaties & wars with Indians" and compacts made without the consent of Congress between Pennsylvania and New Jersey and between Virginia and Maryland.

Article VI, Section 4 prohibited states from

keeping "vessels of war" in "time of peace" unless Congress deemed it "necessary" for "the defence of such state." Section 4 also barred states from keeping "any body of forces . . . in time of peace" unless Congress consented. But the Articles also mandated that states "shall always keep up a well regulated disciplined militia, sufficiently armed and accoutred." Thus, the legal regime that applied to a state military force depended on whether the force constituted an "army," a "navy," or a "militia."

Under Article VI, Section 5, the Confederation Congress had the power to declare war. However, the states retained certain war powers. As a general matter, states could not "engage in any war without the consent" of Congress, but there were two exceptions. First, a state could engage in war if it "received certain advice of a resolution being formed by some nation of Indians to invade such State, and the danger is so imminent as not to admit of a delay till the united states in congress assembled, can be consulted." Second, states could engage in war if "actually invaded by enemies," regardless of whether there was enough time to consult Congress. If the danger was already ongoing, states could take immediate action. In short, Article VI, Section 5 "laid out a coherent scheme in which Congress received general authority to declare and wage war for the Confederation" and "[s]tate war powers were reserved but limited."[3] All three of these reserved state war powers would be retained in the new Constitution.

THE CONSTITUTIONAL CONVENTION

An early version of Article I, Section 10, Clause 3 appeared in a draft by Charles Pinckney of South Carolina that would have prohibited states from entering into alliances or "keeping troops or ships of war in time of peace."[4] By contrast, states could "engage in war" if "in self-defence, when actually invaded or the danger of invasion is so great as not to admit of a delay until the government of the United States can be informed thereof."[5] States would retain the power they had under the Articles of Confederation, to engage in war without consulting Congress in case of invasion. There was no temporal limitation on such powers in the event of an invasion.

The Committee of Detail's draft made some modifications to Pinckney's proposal. First, the proposed national legislature's consent was required for states to enter into "any agreement or compact" with other states. This language was far broader than the terms of the Articles of Confederation, which applied only to a specific set of arrangements: a "treaty, confederation, or alliance." Second, states could not "keep Troops or Ships of War in Time of Peace" without the national legislature's consent. Third, "No State shall, without such Consent engage in any War, unless it shall be actually invaded by Enemies, or the Danger of Invasion be so imminent as not to admit of a Delay, until the Legislature of the United States can be consulted."[6]

The Committee's report, delivered to the Convention on August 6, tracked this draft.[7] The text, two scholars observed, "divided war powers between the federal government and the states by granting authority to the federal government and limiting the reserved authority of the states."[8]

On August 28, the delegates debated this provision but focused almost entirely on the states' powers to enact imposts and duties.[9] There was no discussion of troops and ships of war, compacts, and invasion. This text was referred to the Committee of Style, which made some minor changes.[10] The Convention considered this provision on September 15, only two days before the Constitution would be signed.[11] The delegates discussed the Tonnage Clause, but there was still no debate about troops, ships of war, compacts, and invasion. "The remainder of the paragraph was then remoulded and passed as follows viz— 'No State shall without the consent of Congress, lay any duty of tonnage, keep troops or ships of war in time of peace, enter into any agreement or compact with another State, or with a foreign power, or engage in war, unless actually invaded, or in such imminent danger as will not admit of delay.'"[12] No further changes were made.

THE RATIFICATION DEBATES

The Invasion Clause in Article I, Section 10, Clause 3 recognizes the states' reserved power to respond to an invasion. Tench Coxe, a Federalist essayist, wrote in the *Pennsylvania Gazette* that "[a]ny state may repel invasions or *commence a war* under emergent circumstances, without waiting for the consent of Congress."[13] Further, Article IV, Section 4 provides that the United States "guarantee[s] to every State . . . a Republican Form of Government" and "shall protect each [state] against invasion." In Federalist No. 43, Madison explained that this "protection against invasion . . . seems to secure each state not only against foreign hostility, but against ambitious or vindictive enterprizes of its more powerful neighbours" (other states). (See Essay No. 147.) In Federalist No. 44, Madison wrote that the "reasonings" behind Article I, Section 10, Clause 3 "are either so obvious, or have been so fully developed, that they may be passed over without remark."

During the Virginia ratifying convention, delegates discussed the risk of invasion. Madison said that "[a] republican government is to be guarantied to each state, and they are to be protected from invasion from other states, as well as from foreign powers."[14] Moreover, when states are "invaded, or *in imminent danger* . . . they are not restrained" in their response.[15] Future Chief Justice John Marshall observed that "[a]ll the restraints intended to be laid on the state governments . . . are contained in" Article I, Section 10.[16] He explained that this section does not prohibit states from "defend[ing] themselves without an application to Congress."[17] Rather, when states are "invaded, they can engage in war, as also when in imminent danger."[18] These two comments confirmed that states maintain a residual military power that it can use to defend against invasions and against other imminent dangers.

THE COMPACT CLAUSE

The Compact Clause was rarely invoked in the first century after ratification and attracted little judicial attention. When states made agreements with each other, they usually received congressional consent.[19] In the late nineteenth century, these sorts of agreements became more common. *Virginia v. Tennessee* (1893) held that congressional consent was needed only when an agreement would "encroach upon or impair the supremacy of the United States or interfere with their rightful management of particular subjects placed under their entire control."[20] This interpretation allowed states to make agreements that did not threaten federal interests. Modern practice has

favored a unitary practice that would subject foreign compacts to the same standard.[21]

The Supreme Court has never invalidated an interstate compact that lacked congressional consent, and the federal government has also taken a hands-off approach. States have tested the limits of the Compact Clause with increasingly elaborate interstate and international agreements. For instance, states entered into a multistate settlement for regulation of tobacco without federal approval.[22] They also have made agreements with foreign states on subjects as varied as trade, natural resources management, drivers' licenses, and climate change.[23] In 2019, the Trump Administration sued California to block the state's agreement with Quebec on greenhouse gas emissions. A federal district court rejected the challenge, finding that the "Agreement does not contain the first indicium of a compact because it does not require reciprocal action to take effect."[24]

THE TROOPS AND SHIPS OF WAR CLAUSE

The Constitution recognizes three categories of military forces: armies, navies, and militia. Article I, Section 8, Clause 16 grants Congress the power to organize, arm, and discipline the militia (see Essay No. 62), but that provision also reserved to the states substantial power to govern and use the militia. States could conduct militia training, appoint militia officers, govern the militia when not in federal service, and use militia for domestic purposes.

The Framers took a more nationalistic approach to armies and navies. Article I, Section 10, Clause 3 banned states from "keep[ing] Troops, or Ships of War in time of Peace" without congressional consent.

Members of the Founding generation were not suspicious of the militia, which was a nonprofessional defensive force, but professional armies could project power outside a state's borders and be used as instruments of domestic suppression. Members of the Founding generation were therefore very suspicious of them. Justice Joseph Story observed that the "setting on foot of an army, or navy, by a state in times of peace, might be a cause of jealousy between neighbouring states, and provoke the hostilities of foreign bordering nations."[25]

In *Houston v. Moore* (1820), Justice Story explained that since states were "expressly prohibited from keeping troops or ships of war in time of peace . . . the militia would be their natural and sufficient defence."[26] How else, he asked, "could the States sufficiently provide for their own safety against domestic insurrections, or the sudden invasion of a foreign enemy?" *United States v. Miller* (1939) observed that "[t]he Militia which the States were expected to maintain and train is set in contrast with Troops which they were forbidden to keep without the consent of Congress."[27]

In the nineteenth century, states replaced their universal militia systems with organized volunteer units, often called the National Guard. The courts used professionalism as a criterion to distinguish between a permissible state militia and a prohibited state standing army with "Troops." The Illinois Supreme Court, for example, explained that a militia is the "body of armed citizens trained to military duty, who may be called out in certain cases, but may not be kept on service like standing armies, in time of peace."[28] Moreover, the term "troops" "conveys to the mind the idea of an armed body of soldiers, whose sole occupation is war or service."[29] States retain concurrent power to organize their militia consisting of nonprofessional citizen soldiers, but if they want to raise professional troops in time of peace, they must seek congressional consent.

The proper constitutional classification of the naval militia poses additional difficulties. Federal law defines the organized militia in part to include the naval militia,[30] but whether the naval militia is constitutionally part of the militia is open to dispute. On the one hand, because a naval militia requires armed ships, it may be a separate state navy under Article I, Section 10.[31] Alternatively, the term "Ships of War" may include only armed vessels capable of projecting power abroad as distinguished from small armed vessels of a purely defensive nature.

WHAT IS AN INVASION?

The Supreme Court has recognized that under the Guarantee Clause, the federal government is charged with "protect[ing] each" state "against Invasion."[32] Justice Antonin Scalia observed that Article I, Section 10, Clause 3 serves as an "acknowledgment of the States' sovereign interest in protecting their borders" and "leaves intact [States'] inherent power to protect their territory."[33] The Supreme Court has not defined what constitutes an invasion, but several lower courts have interpreted "invasion" to mean an incursion by a foreign army.[34]

Some originalist scholars adopt a more expansive definition of "invasion." Robert Natelson and Andrew Hyman contend that invaders do not need to be organized, armed, or part of a foreign army. They point out that during the Founding era, "Pennsylvanians used [the] term [invasion] to describe the essentially peaceful immigration of Connecticut settlers into Pennsylvania's Wyoming Valley, because the settlers were relying on legal title that the Pennsylvania government did not recognize."[35] They conclude that "[a]n incursion qualifies as an invasion if it is unauthorized and uninvited and causes or threatens detriment beyond the mere fact of crossing."[36] Ilya Somin, on the other hand, argues that the term "invasion" refers only to "large-scale use of force (or at least threat of force) to seize territory."[37] Somin relies on James Madison's Report of 1800, authored for the Virginia legislature, which specifies that "[i]nvasion is an operation of war."[38]

WHO CAN DETERMINE WHETHER THERE IS AN INVASION?

Article IV, Section 4 provides that the United States "shall protect each [state] against Invasion." But if a state is "actually invaded," it can "engage in war" without obtaining congressional consent. Who can determine whether there is an invasion? Congress has the sole power to "declare war." It also has the power to "suspend[]" the "Privilege of the Writ of Habeas Corpus . . . in cases of Invasion."[39] (See Essay No. 68.) This text suggests that Congress likewise has the power to declare that there is an invasion.

Congress can establish the rules by which the President, as Commander in Chief of the Militia, can "repel Invasions."[40] Here the text suggests that the President can determine in the first instance when an invasion is occurring. President Franklin D. Roosevelt referred to the attack on Pearl Harbor as a "premeditated invasion."[41] In 2025, President Donald Trump declared an invasion at the southern border.[42]

It is an open question whether a state executive can also declare an invasion, which would trigger the state's war powers. In 1874, Texas Governor Richard Coke declared an invasion and said that Texas had "the same 'right to self-defense that would 'ordinarily reside in the United States.'"[43] In 2024, Texas Governor Greg Abbott declared an invasion along the southern border to justify installing barriers in the Rio Grande River.[44]

The judiciary has ruled that certain *political* questions cannot be resolved by the courts but instead must be settled by the elected branches. The courts have generally found that whether a President's use of military force requires a declaration of war is a *nonjusticiable* political question in the absence of "a coherent test for judges to apply to the question what constitutes war. . . ."[45] The Supreme Court also deferred to a governor's finding that there is an insurrection.[46]

The determination as to whether there is an invasion also appears to be a political question. A court of appeals has ruled that "there are no manageable standards to ascertain whether or when an influx of illegal immigrants should be said to constitute an invasion."[47] One judge has found that "[d]etermining where the present illegal immigration crisis falls along this spectrum [of invasions] is not a legal question for judges, but a political determination for the other branches of government."[48]

WHEN CAN A STATE ENGAGE IN WAR?

The text provides that "No State shall, without the Consent of Congress . . . engage in War, unless actually invaded, or in such imminent Danger as will not admit of delay." In other words, when a delay in engaging in war is feasible, the state must obtain congressional consent to "engage in war" against an "imminent danger." As a textual matter, does the phrase "will not admit of delay" also modify "actually invaded"? In *United States v. Abbott*, the federal government argued "that any right that a State may have to defend itself [against an invasion] is a 'time-limited emergency authority,' and that the right ceases once the federal government has had the opportunity to respond."[49] Although the *Abbott* court did not rule on this argument, one judge opined that a state can "engage in war" to stop an actual invasion immediately with "no such temporal restriction."[50]

OPEN QUESTIONS

- After congressional approval, must a foreign or interstate compact be presented to the President under Article I, Section 7, Clause 2? As a matter of practice, such compacts have been presented to the President in the same manner as ordinary legislation,[51] and the threat of a presidential veto has stalled compacts.[52] However, it is possible that an interstate compact could be approved through a concurrent resolution without presidential presentment under Article I, Section 7, Clause 3.[53]

Cite as: Julian G. Ku, *The Troops, Ships of War, Compact, and Invasion Clause, in* The Heritage Guide to the Constitution 297 (Josh Blackman & John G. Malcolm eds., 3d ed. 2025).

Notes

1. Felix Frankfurter & James M. Landis, *The Compact Clause of the Constitution—A Study in Interstate Adjustments*, 34 Yale L.J. 685, 692, 730–32 (1925). **2.** 3 Farrand's 548; Duncan B. Hollis, *Unpacking the Compact Clause*, 88 Tex. L. Rev. 741, 760 (2010). **3.** Robert G. Natelson & Andrew T. Hyman, *The Constitution, Invasion, Immigration, and the War Powers of States*, 13 Br. J. Am. Legal Studies 1, 13 (2024). **4.** 1 Elliot's 149. **5.** *Id.* **6.** 2 Farrand's 169. **7.** *Id.* at 187. **8.** Natelson & Hyman, *supra* at 14. **9.** 2 Farrand's 442. **10.** *Id.* at 565, 570, 597. **11.** *Id.* at 625. **12.** *Id.* at 626. **13.** 15 DHRC 510. **14.** 3 Elliot's 425. **15.** *Id.* **16.** *Id.* at 420. **17.** *Id.* at 419. **18.** *Id.* at 420. **19.** Frankfurter & Landis, *supra* at 735–54. **20.** *Virginia v. Tennessee*, 148 U.S. 503, 518 (1893). **21.** Letter from William H. Taft, IV, Legal Adviser, Dep't of State, to Senator Byron L. Dorgan of North Dakota Regarding a Memorandum of Understanding Signed by the State of Missouri and the Province of Manitoba (Nov. 20, 2001), https://perma.cc/Z895-LRQ4. **22.** The Master Settlement Agreement, https://perma.cc/VR9K-TKTX. **23.** Julian G. Ku, *Gubernatorial Foreign Policy*, 115 Yale L.J. 2380, 2392–98 (2006). **24.** *United States v. California*, 444 F. Supp. 3d 1181, 1194 (E.D. Cal. 2020). **25.** 3 Story's

Commentaries § 1398. **26.** *Houston v. Moore*, 18 U.S. 1, 52 (1820). **27.** *United States v. Miller*, 307 U.S. 174, 178–79 (1939). **28.** *Dunne v. People*, 94 Ill. 120, 138 (1879). **29.** *Id.* at 138–39. **30.** 10 U.S.C. § 246(b)(1). **31.** Robert Leider, *Federalism and the Military Power of the United States*, 73 Vand. L. Rev. 989, 1001 n.56 (2020). **32.** *Torres v. Texas Dep't of Pub. Safety*, 597 U.S. 580, 590 (2022). **33.** *Arizona v. United States*, 567 U.S. 387, 419 (2012) (Scalia, J., concurring in part and dissenting in part). **34.** *California v. United States*, 104 F.3d 1086, 1091 (9th Cir. 1997); *Padavan v. United States*, 83 F.3d 23, 28 (2nd Cir. 1996); *New Jersey v. United States*, 91 F.3d 463, 468 (3rd Cir. 1996). **35.** Natelson & Hyman, *supra* at 23–24. **36.** *Id.* at 36. **37.** Ilya Somin, *Immigration Is Not "Invasion,"* Volokh Conspiracy (May 18, 2023), https://perma. cc/GR6C-GBV8. **38.** James Madison, The Report of 1800 (Jan. 7, 1800), https://perma.cc/SYU5-BWY2. **39.** Art. I, § 9, cl. 2. **40.** Art. I, § 8, cl. 14. **41.** Franklin D. Roosevelt, Joint Address to Congress Leading to a Declaration of War Against Japan (Dec. 8, 1941), https://perma.cc/BE3K-QHKM. **42.** President Donald J. Trump, Proclamation Guaranteeing the States Protection Against Invasion (Jan. 20, 2025), https://perma.cc/W54Z-XUGM. **43.** *United States v. Abbott*, 110 F.4th 700, 726 (5th Cir. 2024) (Ho, J., concurring in part and dissenting in part) (quoting Texas Frontier Troubles, H.R. Rep. No. 44-343, at 166–67 (1876)). **44.** Governor Greg Abbott, Statement on Constitutional Right of Texas to Self-Defense (Jan. 24, 2024), https://perma. cc/EQM9-XDVF. **45.** *Campbell v. Clinton*, 203 F.3d 19, 26 (D.C. Cir. 2000) (Silberman, J., concurring). **46.** *Sterling v. Constantin*, 287 U.S. 378, 399 (1932). **47.** *California v. United States*, 104 F.3d 1086, 1091 (9th Cir. 1997). **48.** *Abbott*, 110 F.4th at 728. **49.** *Id.* at 730. **50.** *Id.* at 725 n.1. **51.** Bradford R. Clark, *Domesticating Sole Executive Agreements*, 93 Va. L. Rev. 1573, 1661 (2007); Edward T. Swaine, *Does Federalism Constrain the Treaty Power?*, 103 Colum. L. Rev. 403, 508 (2003). **52.** Dana Brakman Reiser, Note, *Charting No Man's Land: Applying Jurisdictional and Choice of Law Doctrines to Interstate Compacts*, 111 Harv. L. Rev. 1991, 2008 (1998). **53.** Josh Blackman, *Does the Compact Clause Require Presentment?*. Josh Blackman's Blog (Nov. 16, 2014), https://perma.cc/7AR5-EWQQ.

PART 2

ARTICLE II

ESSAY NO. 87: THE EXECUTIVE VESTING CLAUSE
ART. II, § 1, CL. 1

The executive Power shall be vested in a President of the United States of America.
—John C. Yoo

INTRODUCTION

The Article II Vesting Clause grants the President "executive power." Traditionally, this encompassed law execution and a host of powers often associated with law execution such as authority over foreign affairs and the appointment, direction, and removal of executive officers.[1] Crucially, the otherwise broad grant of "executive power" is qualified by other clauses in Article II and by significant grants to Congress in Article I. The result is a Constitution that grants rather important executive powers to Congress, such as declaring war, and qualifies several other crucial ones like appointments and treaties.

HISTORY BEFORE 1787

Before American independence, the terms "executive power" and "executive powers" commonly referred to a suite of powers deemed executive by virtue of their long association with executives. European writers like Baron de Montesquieu and John Locke spoke of the "executive power" as consisting of a related set of authorities. In 1778, several towns in Essex County, Massachusetts, produced a commentary on the proposed Massachusetts constitution. This document, known as *The Essex Result*, described two types of executive power: *internal* executive power, which comprehended territorial defense and law execution, and *external* executive power, which encompassed war, treaties, and foreign relations.[2] It was quite common for Americans to speak of "executive power" as a familiar and known concept with no need of any explanation or specification.

Several state constitutions granted specific powers to their chief executives, whether singular or plural, and also granted "other executive powers." In Delaware, the "president or chief magistrate . . . may exercise all the other executive powers of government limited and restrained as by this constitution is mentioned, and according to the laws of the State."[3] In Maryland, "the Governor . . . may alone exercise all other the executive powers of government."[4] Similar language was used in North Carolina.[5] These constitutions thereby adopted the practice of using a catchall term rather than specifying each strand of executive power.

Under the Articles of Confederation, the Continental Congress exercised the executive power. The legislature appointed and controlled various executive officers, including the secretaries of departments. Congress could "appoint such other committees and civil officers as may be necessary for managing the general affairs of the united states under their direction."[6] However, delegates to Congress were not "capable of holding any [appointed] office under the United States, for which he, or another for his benefit receives any salary, fees or emolument of any kind."[7]

However, law execution under the direction of a distracted, plural executive was hardly vigorous. Congress likewise proved a poor steward of foreign affairs. American diplomats complained that Congress could not act with the requisite speed or secrecy.

THE CONSTITUTIONAL CONVENTION

The concept of the Vesting Clause emerged early during the Convention. The Virginia Plan, proposed by Edmund Randolph, resolved "that a National Executive be instituted" and explained "that besides a general authority to execute the National laws, [the National Executive] ought to enjoy the Executive rights vested in Congress by the Confederation."[8] In other words, whatever "executive" powers were vested in the Confederation Congress would belong to the

National Executive; there was no reference to some broader concept of "the executive power."

The Convention debated this resolution on June 1.[9] James Wilson of Pennsylvania "moved that the Executive consist of a single person."[10] Elbridge Gerry of Massachusetts favored "annexing a Council to the Executive."[11] Edmund Randolph "opposed a unity in the Executive," which he "regarded . . . as the foetus of monarchy," and argued that having "more than one" Executive would "support its independence."[12] Wilson responded "that Unity in the Executive instead of being the fetus of Monarchy would be the best safeguard against tyranny."[13] James Madison of Virginia thought it important to "fix the extent of the Executive authority" before deciding "between a unity and a plurality in the Executive."[14] Consideration of Wilson's motion was postponed.[15]

On June 4, the Convention resumed debate about whether there would be a single executive or multiple executives.[16] Wilson argued that the "tranquility not less than the vigor of the Govt. . . . would be favored by" a single executive.[17] His motion passed by a vote of 7 to 3.[18] On June 22, the delegates considered a proposal specifying that the "national Executive" would "consist of a Single Person to be chosen by the National Legislature for the term of Seven years with power to carry into execution the National Laws."[19] Again, there was still no reference to "the executive power." Instead, the President could execute "the National Laws." This text was approved unanimously.[20]

The first mention of "the executive power" in a written proposal appeared in a Committee of Detail draft in Wilson's handwriting.[21] It provided that "[t]he Executive Power of the United States shall be vested in a single Person. His Stile shall be, 'The President of the United States of America;' and his Title shall be, 'His Excellency.'"[22] This reference to some body of executive powers was a significant change. Professor Michael W. McConnell has observed that the Committee of Detail's "reformation of the executive power was . . . audacious."[23] The Convention debated this provision on August 24, and the "question for vesting the power in a single person . . . was agreed to" unanimously.[24] There was no debate on what these powers were.

Three separate clauses referred to the Committee of Style provided that "[t]he Executive power of the United States shall be vested in a single person. His stile shall be, 'The President of the United States of America;' and his title shall be, 'His Excellency.'"[25] This text seems to emphasize *who* has the power rather than what powers that person has,[26] and those powers were limited to the "Executive power of the United States." Those powers certainly included the executive authorities enumerated in the Constitution, but they could also extend to the broader category of executive powers understood by European jurists.

The Committee of Style condensed these three clauses into a single sentence: "The executive power shall be vested in a president of the United States of America."[27] Scholars debate about whether this revision was stylistic or substantive.[28] The emphasis shifted from who had the power to what powers were vested in the President.[29] Moreover, the executive power was no longer limited to that of the United States. Now, the text could more easily extend to the British model of executive power.[30] This text was novel. Professor William Michael Treanor has observed that "[n]one of the state constitutions" or other plans proposed to the Convention "had that framework" adopted by the Committee of Style.[31] The Convention made no further changes in the Executive Vesting Clause.

THE RATIFICATION DEBATES

Many Anti-Federalists warned that the presidency would be kingly in fact if not in name. At the Virginia ratification convention, George Mason warned that the presidency would be "an elective monarchy."[32] The resemblance was obvious. The presidency was powerful, and some European monarchies were elective.

At times, Federalists downplayed the office's powers; at other times, they celebrated the creation of a powerful executive. James Wilson captured the spirit of the reform during the Constitutional Convention when he remarked that a "single magistrate" would supply the "most energy, dispatch, and responsibility" to the execution of the laws.[33] Alexander Hamilton echoed this view in Federalist No. 70: "[A]ll men of sense will agree in the necessity of an energetic Executive." Some Federalists also spoke of the President's significant role in foreign affairs. They discussed the Senate's check on treaty-making as an exception to the grant of executive power. Finally, Hamilton wrote in Federalist No. 72 of an array of administrative authorities granted to the President that included conducting foreign negotiations, expending funds pursuant to appropriations, and overseeing the military.

EARLY PRACTICE

In 1789, the First Congress considered legislation that would have restricted the President's ability to remove certain executive branch officers. The Constitution spells out the process by which the President can appoint officers, but Article II is silent about whether the President also has the power to remove those officers. Members of Congress vigorously debated this issue. Some argued that Congress can provide protection for the offices it creates. Others contended that such restrictions violated the President's "executive power," which includes the removal power.

During the debate, Representative Fisher Ames of Massachusetts acknowledged that "the Constitution is not explicit on the point" but added that it "strongly infers that the [removal] power is in the President alone."[34] He cited Article II, which "declared that the executive power shall be vested in the President."[35] The U.S. Supreme Court has cited the so-called Decision of 1789 as the basis for the President's removal power.[36] Scholars continue to debate about how this episode should inform the original meaning of the Executive Vesting Clause.[37]

Other early practices shed light on the scope of the President's powers. In 1793, President George Washington issued the neutrality proclamation, under which the United States would remain neutral in the war between Great Britain and France. Yet nothing in the Constitution expressly empowered the President to issue such a proclamation. Hamilton, writing under the pseudonym Pacificus, defended the proclamation, citing the Executive Vesting Clause: "The general doctrine then of our constitution is, that the Executive Power of the Nation is vested in the President; subject only to the exceptions and qualifications which are expressed in the instrument."[38] Madison, writing under the pseudonym Helvidius, countered that President Washington lacked the power to issue

the proclamation and charged that Hamilton's views, like those of John Locke, were "warped by a regard to the particular government of England, to which [Locke] owed allegiance."[39] Washington also relied on Article II to ask for the recall of French emissary Citizen Genet.

Congress also refused to correspond with foreign governments because members concluded that foreign communications were left to the President by virtue of the executive power, even though that power is not expressly enumerated. The first President also directed federal law execution and executives of various sorts—soldiers, customs officials, U.S. attorneys, and departmental secretaries.[40]

JUDICIAL PRECEDENT

The Executive Vesting Clause has played a limited role in constitutional litigation. As a general matter, the Supreme Court has accepted that the Clause grants powers beyond those specifically enumerated in Article II. *Myers v. United States* (1926) cited the Executive Vesting Clause as the source of the President's removal and supervisory powers over executive officers.[41] *Nixon v. Fitzgerald* (1982) cited the clause as a source of three powers: law enforcement, foreign affairs, and a supervisory power over the executive branch.[42]

American Insurance Association v. Garamendi (2003) affirmed that the Vesting Clause grants the President foreign affairs authority.[43] This case marked a departure from prior case law, which had grounded the executive's foreign-affairs powers in necessity and sovereignty.[44] Yet *Zivotofsky v. Kerry* (2015) conspicuously eschewed reliance on the Vesting Clause in concluding that the President had a power to recognize foreign nations and governments.[45]

Free Enterprise Fund v. Public Accounting Oversight Board (2010) declared that Congress could not create multiple layers of removal protection.[46] This structure was inconsistent with the President's removal power, which is grounded in the Vesting Clause.[47] Other removal cases, including *Seila Law v. CFPB* (2020), also have relied on the Vesting Clause.[48]

However, other judicial decisions have limited the clause's potential reach. After *Myers*, the Supreme Court essentially sanctioned the creation of a fourth branch of government in the form of numerous independent agencies that simultaneously exercise legislative, executive, and judicial powers. *Humphrey's Executor v. United States* (1935) held that the President could not remove at will a member of the Federal Trade Commission.[49] Five decades later, *Morrison v. Olson* (1988) acknowledged that the Vesting Clause granted the President control of prosecutions.[50] Yet at the same time, the Court upheld the constitutionality of independent counsels.[51] These special prosecutors could be removed only for good cause. The Court concluded that this removal restriction protecting independent counsels did not "unduly trammel on executive authority."[52]

That framework well describes the Supreme Court's case law on the Vesting Clause: The clause grants the President substantive power not found elsewhere in the Constitution, but those powers are often subject to congressional regulation and modification. Those cases are best understood as grounded on the Court's belief that there is some uncertain measure of congressional power to tinker with or modify the grant of executive power. This framework is further illustrated by Justice Robert H. Jackson's influential concurring opinion in *Youngstown Sheet & Tube Co. v. Sawyer* (1952),[53] in which he narrowly construed the President's executive powers when they were not supported by congressional legislation: "When the President takes measures incompatible with the expressed or implied will of Congress, his power is at its lowest ebb, for then he can rely only upon his own constitutional powers minus any constitutional powers of Congress over the matter."[54]

OPEN QUESTIONS

- How should we understand the alterations made in the Executive Vesting Clause by the Committee of Style?[55] Should originalists focus only on the final, ratified text rather than earlier, unadopted drafts?
- How should the Supreme Court resolve the long-standing debate about what powers the Vesting Clause grants the executive? Some have long asserted that the Vesting Clause vests nothing of substance, with presidential powers granted later in Article II. Others contend that the clause extends to law execution.[56] Still others say that "executive power" referred to a set of powers, including "the implementation of legal norms created by some other authority," but did not encompass any authority over foreign affairs.[57]
- Does the Executive Vesting Clause support an executive privilege that enables the President to shield executive communications from Congress and the judiciary?[58] Does the clause grant the President certain immunities in court, such as immunity from suits challenging official actions? Does the clause convey certain "emergency powers" to take extraordinary actions during exigencies of the sort that Abraham Lincoln took at the outset of the Civil War?

Cite as: John C. Yoo, *The Executive Vesting Clause, in* THE HERITAGE GUIDE TO THE CONSTITUTION 304 (Josh Blackman & John G. Malcolm eds., 3d ed. 2025).

Notes

1. Steven G. Calabresi & Saikrishna B. Prakash, *The President's Power to Execute the Laws*, 104 Yale L.J. 541 (1994); Saikrishna B. Prakash & Michael D. Ramsey, *The Executive Power over Foreign Affairs*, 111 Yale L.J. 231 (2001). **2.** *The Essex Result* (Apr. 29, 1778), *in* 1 The Founders' Constitution ch 4, doc. 8 (Philip B. Kurland & Ralph Lerner eds., 1987), https://perma.cc/F5JG-DTXC. **3.** Del. Const. of 1776, art. VII. **4.** Md. Const. of 1776, art. XXXIII. **5.** N.C. Const. of 1776, art. XIX. **6.** Articles of Confederation, art. IX, § 5. **7.** *Id.*, art. V, § 2; Seth Barrett Tillman & Josh Blackman, *Offices and Officers of the Constitution, Part IV: The "Office . . . Under the United States" Drafting Convention*, 62 S. Tex. L. Rev. 455, 469–71 (2023). **8.** 1 Farrand's 20, 21. **9.** *Id.* at 64. **10.** *Id.* at 65. **11.** *Id.* at 66. **12.** 1 Farrand's 66. **13.** *Id.* **14.** *Id.* **15.** *Id.* **16.** *Id.* at 96. **17.** *Id.* **18.** *Id.* at 97. **19.** *Id.* at 230; 2 Farrand's 22. **20.** 2 Farrand's 22. **21.** *Id.* at 163. **22.** *Id.* at 171. **23.** Michael W. McConnell, *James Wilson's Contributions to the Construction of Article II*, 17 Geo. J.L. & Pub. Pol'y 23, 40 (2019). **24.** 2 Farrand's 401. **25.** *Id.* at 565, 572. **26.** William Michael Treanor, *The Case of the Dishonest Scrivener: Gouverneur Morris and the Creation of the Federalist Constitution*, 120 Mich.

L. Rev. 1, 33 (2021). **27.** 2 Farrand's 597. **28.** Steven G. Calabresi & Saikrishna B. Prakash, _The President's Power to Execute the Laws_, 104 Yale L.J. 541, 576 (1994); Treanor, _supra_ at 61. **29.** Treanor, _supra_ at 61. **30.** _Id._ at 62. **31.** _Id._ at 60. **32.** 3 Elliot's 484. **33.** 1 Farrand's 65. **34.** 4 Elliot's 395. **35.** _Id._ **36.** _Seila Law LLC v. CFPB_, 591 U.S. 197, 204 (2020) (citing _Myers v. United States_, 272 U.S. 52, 142 (1926)). **37.** Aditya Bamzai & Saikrishna Bangalore Prakash, _The Executive Power of Removal_, 136 Harv. L. Rev. 1756 (2023); Andrea Scoseria Katz & Noah A. Rosenblum, _Removal Rehashed_, 136 Harv. L. Rev. F. 404 (2023); Aditya Bamzai & Saikrishna Bangalore Prakash, _How to Think About the Removal Power_, 110 Va. L. Rev. Online 159 (2024). **38.** Pacificus No. 1 (June 29, 1783), https://perma.cc/27YM-DJE8. **39.** Helvedius No. 1 (Aug. 24, 1793), https://perma.cc/3XQM-98K4; Steven G. Calabresi & Christopher S. Yoo, _The Unitary Executive During the First Half-Century_, 47 Case W. Rsrv. L. Rev. 1451, 1507 (1997). **40.** Saikrishna B. Prakash & Michael D. Ramsey, _The Executive Power over Foreign Affairs_, 111 Yale L.J. 231 (2001). **41.** _Myers_, 272 U.S. at 138. **42.** 457 U.S. 731, 753 (1982). **43.** 539 U.S. 396 (2003). **44.** _United States v. Curtiss-Wright Export Corp._, 299 U.S. 304, 320–21 (1936). **45.** 576 U.S. 1 (2015). **46.** 561 U.S. 477 (2010). **47.** _Id._ at 492. **48.** _Seila Law_, 591 U.S. 197. **49.** 295 U.S. 602 (1935). **50.** 487 U.S. 655 (1988). **51.** _Id._ at 690 n.29. **52.** _Id._ at 654. **53.** 343 U.S. 579 (1952) (Jackson, J., concurring). **54.** _Id._ at 637–38 (Jackson, J., concurring). **55.** Treanor, _supra_ at 60. **56.** Curtis A. Bradley & Martin S. Flaherty, _Executive Power Essentialism and Foreign Affairs_, 102 Mich. L. Rev. 545 (2004). **57.** Julian D. Mortenson, _Article II Vests the Executive Power, Not the Royal Prerogative_, 119 Colum. L. Rev. 1169 (2019). **58.** _Trump v. Vance_, 591 U.S. 786, 815 (2020) (Thomas, J., dissenting).

⌐⌐⌐

ESSAY NO. 88: THE PRESIDENTIAL TERM CLAUSE
ART. II, § 1, CL. 1

[The President] shall hold his Office during the Term of four Years. . . .

—Judge Chad A. Readler & Andy Nolan

INTRODUCTION

The Presidential Term Clause limits the President's term to four years before needing to face reelection. There is no real dispute about the meaning of this provision. Most scholarship about the clause centers on the debate, both at the Framing and during the ratification period, over how great a time limit (if any) should be placed on the President's service. Some argued that instead of a set term of years, the President's tenure should be subject to the approval of the legislature or some other body. Others, more suspicious of centralized power, argued that there should be a term of years and that it should be less than four.

HISTORY BEFORE 1787

From the early days of representative government, states have imposed some form of term limitation on their executive and legislative leaders. In Athens, individuals could hold various leadership roles for only one year.[1] In the Roman Republic, various limits were placed on the ability of executive officers to stay in power, again limiting their service to a single year.[2] The political heritage to which the Founders more immediately belonged—the English tradition—utilized term limitation less pervasively. Kings and queens served for life. Prime Ministers faced no limit on consecutive terms but were statutorily compelled to face reelection after a certain number of years. During most of the eighteenth century, the longest time a Parliament could go without facing new elections was seven years.[3]

Early American practice was mixed. Specific limitations on term length and limitations on multiple terms became more common, although the practice was rare, utilized in only two states and at the federal level under the Articles of Confederation. In addition, term limits in early America tended to take the form of compulsory rotation of office rather than prohibitions on holding office again after a particular number of terms. The Articles of Confederation, for example, prohibited any one person from serving as President for more than one year out of three and any one person from serving as a delegate more than three years out of six.[4] In the state constitutions, this rotational method was used in the minority of jurisdictions that imposed term limits at all. In Connecticut, no person could serve as governor more than one year out of two,[5] and in Pennsylvania, delegates to the General Assembly could not serve more than four years out of seven.[6] It was against this backdrop of rare limitations on terms that the Framers worked in the summer of 1787.

THE CONSTITUTIONAL CONVENTION

Among the more impassioned debates at the Constitutional Convention were those involving the contours of the contemplated executive branch. After consolidating around a single head of the branch and setting up the Electoral College, the Framers turned their focus to tenure. Some preferred to allow the President to hold office during good behavior—an idea that gained even more support when paired with a low bar for impeachment.[7] Others preferred fixed terms and themselves split over whether the President should serve a longer single term or shorter renewable terms.[8]

Lengthy terms with no prospect of reelection were thought to incentivize independent exercises of executive authority,[9] but there was a perceived cost. Allowing Presidents to serve only one term, some suggested, would discourage qualified candidates from running for President while at the same time removing the best motivator for the faithful exercise of power—reelection.[10] Based on the assumption that former Presidents would seek to join Congress after their terms expired, there was also fear that incumbent Presidents would be encouraged to delegate more and more of the Executive's power to the legislature.[11]

Shorter terms (with the ability to be reelected) had their own apparent shortcomings. The ability to be elected to numerous terms might become a gateway to "hereditary tenure."[12] Popular leaders, it was believed, would be elected and reelected in perpetuity, and upon their retirement or death, their children would be likely to take their place. Basing tenure on good behavior was thought to have the same flaw.[13]

Lacking a consensus on presidential tenure, the Framers deferred the matter. The Committee on Postponed Parts eventually settled on four-year terms.[14] Four years was seen to strike a balance—not "so long, as to create danger to the people"[15] but long enough to give a President time "to make the community sensible of the propriety of the measures he might incline to pursue."[16] The Committee's proposal was adopted and incorporated into the Constitution, but with constitutional ratification looming, the debate over the issue would soon resurface.

THE RATIFICATION DEBATES

The Anti-Federalist Cato argued that terms exceeding one year were dangerous to liberty. Invoking Montesquieu, Cato reasoned that "if the president is possessed of ambition, he has power and time sufficient to ruin his country."[17] Alexander Hamilton, in Federalist No. 72, saw ambition as more virtue than vice. Ambition, he wrote, "would prompt [the President] to plan and undertake extensive and arduous enterprises for the public benefit," and limiting the President's time to accomplish great tasks would make the President focus on "not doing harm" instead of on "doing good." Doing good, after all, takes time.

Old Whig, another Anti-Federalist, favored a "perpetual and hereditary" presidency as long as the office conveyed the powers described in the Constitution. His reasoning is somewhat unexpected. Old Whig worried that regular presidential elections would subject the country to "horror and confusion" and surmised that it would be better to have a king than, "under pretence of a republic, to lay the foundation for a military government, which is the worst of all tyrannies."[18]

Thomas Jefferson expressed a similar concern in a letter to James Madison. He predicted that the President "will always be re-elected if the Constitution permits it" and that once it was observed that the President would serve "for life," foreign nations, both "friend" and "foe," would "interfere" in the elections "with money & with arms." Jefferson noted that kings would invite global interference.[19] For example, England might support a President with ties to England and oppose a President with ties to France, just as France might support a President with ties to France and oppose one with ties to England. Like Old Whig, Jefferson believed that "if elections are to be attended with these disorders, the seldomer they are renewed the better." But unlike Old Whig, Jefferson favored term limits that, to his mind, would prevent a President from getting too close to our global counterparts.

PRESIDENTIAL PRACTICE

President George Washington rejected the idea of serving a third term, but he did so more out of an interest in retiring than because of an active rejection of the concept of a third term. Washington observed in his Farewell Address of 1796 that "I have the consolation to believe that, while choice and prudence invite me to quit the political scene, patriotism does not forbid it."[20] Washington's actions are perhaps most closely linked to Jefferson's view.[21] Jefferson was the first President who actively espoused a considered opposition to a third term. In 1805, Jefferson wrote to Virginia politician John Taylor that

"service for eight years, with a power to remove at the end of the first four, comes nearly to my principle as corrected by experience."[22] Jefferson added that he was "determined to withdraw at the end of [his] second term."[23] And so he did.

The Presidents that immediately followed Jefferson in the nineteenth century espoused support for presidential term limits, and none attempted reelection more than once.[24] That practice came to an end in 1880. Ulysses Grant attempted to break the no-third-term precedent,[25] but his efforts stalled as he lost the Republican nomination for President.[26] (See Essay No. 209.)

Cite as: Judge Chad A. Readler & Andy Nolan, *The Presidential Term Clause, in* THE HERITAGE GUIDE TO THE CONSTITUTION 308 (Josh Blackman & John G. Malcolm eds., 3d ed. 2025)

Notes

1. John Thorley, Athenian Democracy 29 (2d ed. 2005). 2. Mary T. Boatwright et al., The Romans: From Village to Empire 60–62 (2004). 3. Septennial Act 1715, 1 Geo. 1 St. 2 c. 38 (Gr. Brit.). 4. Articles of Confederation, art. V, §§ 2, 5. 5. Conn. Fundamental Orders of 1639, § 4. 6. Pa. Const. of 1776, § 8. 7. Letter from James Madison to Thomas Jefferson (Oct. 24, 1787), https://perma.cc/CK7D-3JRR. 8. *Id.*; 1 Farrand's 64, 68. 9. 1 Farrand's 71–72; Madison to Jefferson (Oct. 24, 1787), *supra*. 10. 2 Farrand's 33; Madison to Jefferson (Oct. 24, 1787), *supra*. 11. 2 Farrand's 52; Madison to Jefferson (Oct. 24, 1787), *supra*. 12. Madison to Jefferson (Oct. 24, 1787), *supra*. 13. 2 Farrand's 33. 14. *Id.* at 493. 15. 3 Story's Commentaries § 1435. 16. Federalist No. 71 (Hamilton). 17. Storing 2.6.25. 18. Storing 3.3.31. 19. Letter from Thomas Jefferson to James Madison (Dec. 20, 1787), https://perma.cc/8MCP-9DPC;

Letter from Thomas Jefferson to John Adams (Nov. 13, 1787), https://perma.cc/JK6P-DVXH. 20. *Washington's Farewell Address to the People of the United States*, S. Pub. 115-5 (Dec. 2017), https://perma.cc/G4J5-HJ45. 21. Bruce G. Peabody & Scott E. Gant, *The Twice and Future President: Constitutional Interstices and the Twenty-Second Amendment*, 83 Minn. L. Rev. 565, 578 (1999). 22. Letter from Thomas Jefferson to John Taylor (Jan. 6, 1805), https://perma.cc/QPJ6-32ZB. 23. *Id.* 24. Peabody & Gant, *supra* at 579–80; 8 Writings of James Monroe 81 (Stanislaus Hamilton ed., 1898). 25. Stephen W. Stathis, *The Twenty-Second Amendment: A Practical Remedy or Partisan Maneuver,* 7 Const. Comment. 61, 63–64 (1990). 26. Willis Thornton, The Third Term Issue: Hot Potato of American Politics 51–57 (1939).

***

ESSAY NO. 89: THE VICE PRESIDENTIAL TERM CLAUSE
ART. II, § 1, CL. 1

[The President] shall hold his Office during the Term of four Years, . . . and, together with the Vice President, chosen for the same Term. . . .

—Roy E. Brownell II

INTRODUCTION

The Constitution assigns the Vice President specific powers in the legislative branch. The officeholder serves as President of the Senate and can break tie votes. (See Essay No. 18.) In addition, the Constitution provides that the Vice President plays a key role in situations involving presidential inability. During the early Republic, the officeholder was generally limited to modest legislative branch functions, but during the twentieth century, the vice presidency became more of an executive branch post. Today, the modern officeholder undertakes tasks such as participating in Cabinet meetings, advising the President, traveling abroad on foreign policy assignments, and chairing executive branch task forces; his Senate role, meanwhile, is largely limited to presiding on ceremonial occasions and breaking ties.

HISTORY BEFORE 1787

Colonial charters and early state constitutions likely helped inform the Framers' handiwork regarding the vice presidency.[1] In this regard, the Massachusetts, South Carolina, and New York constitutions authorized election of their governors and lieutenant governors in the same fashion and for the same term, presaging similar ties that would exist between the President and Vice President.[2]

THE CONSTITUTIONAL CONVENTION

During the Constitutional Convention, the position of Vice President was created fairly late in the proceedings. On September 4, 1787, the Committee of Eleven, also known as the Committee on Postponed Parts, proposed that the President would serve for four years "and together with the Vice President, [be] chosen for the same term."[3] This language would remain unaltered throughout the rest of the Convention.

The Framers offered several rationales for creating the vice presidency. The position addressed two important matters by establishing a presidential successor and a presiding officer for the Senate with the power to break ties, although the creation of an entirely new position was not needed for either function.[4] The main reason appears to have been that the office was essential to the presidential election mechanism.[5] Under this system, the Constitution created electors, each of whom was granted two votes for President. Electors were also prohibited from casting both votes for candidates from their own state. This restriction prevented electors from voting only for home-state favorites. Instead, it was thought that the Electoral College system—coupled with the vice presidency—would promote presidential candidates with a national profile.[6]

A member of the Committee of Eleven, Hugh Williamson of North Carolina, noted the link between electoral procedures and the vice presidency, asserting that the Vice President "was not wanted" and "was introduced only for the sake of a valuable mode of election which required two to be chosen."[7] Under the original Constitution, the candidate with a majority of electoral votes would become President, and the candidate with the second most votes would become Vice President. The Twelfth Amendment would later require separate votes for each office. (See Essay No. 190.)

VICE PRESIDENTIAL TENURE

The Vice President's four-year term under the Constitution helps ensure that the officeholder cannot be removed from office by the President. Thus, the former's secure tenure partly underpins his legal independence, although in a practical sense, the President clearly holds the upper hand in the relationship.[8] While the Vice President is expected to serve four years concurrently with the President, fate has often intervened. Eighteen of the nation's fifty Vice Presidents never completed their terms: seven died in office, two resigned, and nine were elevated due to presidential vacancy.[9] No Vice President's tenure has been ended by impeachment and removal.

EVOLUTION OF THE VICE PRESIDENCY

Both Vice President John Adams and his successor Thomas Jefferson viewed the office as a Senate position.[10] In keeping with this view, the First Congress enacted a vice presidential oath requirement specifying the Vice President's role as President of the Senate.[11] At the same time, early Congresses also treated the Vice President as an executive branch figure with respect to his mode of resignation (a letter to the Secretary of State) and wage (a salary rather than a per diem like for lawmakers of the day).[12] On occasion, President George Washington discussed executive branch business with Adams.[13] The President also asked Adams to attend a Cabinet meeting in his absence, which would prove a rare occurrence for well over a century.[14]

Throughout the nineteenth century, Vice Presidents devoted the vast majority of their workday to generally mundane Senate tasks with fairly limited prospects for career advancement.[15] As a result, a number of prominent political figures refused to be considered for the vice presidential nomination.[16] During this period, as a sign of the vice presidency's weak political standing, Presidents who were nominated for a second term were often paired with a different vice presidential candidate. This trend began with President Thomas Jefferson, whose Vice Presidents during his first and second terms were Aaron Burr and George Clinton respectively.

Moreover, when nineteenth-century Vice Presidents succeeded to the presidency, their political parties declined to choose them as their presidential standard-bearers in the next election. This happened to John Tyler, Millard Fillmore, Andrew Johnson, and Chester Arthur.[17] Not until Theodore Roosevelt in 1904 did a Vice President secure his party's nomination for President after succeeding to office because of a presidential vacancy.

Toward the end of World War I, broad historical currents began to reshape the office. In 1918, President Woodrow Wilson left for the Versailles Peace Conference and asked Vice President Thomas Marshall to preside at Cabinet sessions.[18] Wilson's successor, President Warren Harding, requested that Vice President Calvin Coolidge join his Cabinet on a permanent basis.[19] With a single exception (Charles Dawes, who refused then-President Coolidge's invitation), all Vice Presidents since have attended Cabinet meetings.[20]

Cabinet participation heralded a new era in which the vice presidency gradually drew away from the Senate and became more of an executive branch post.[21] With the expansion of national governmental activity during the New Deal and World War II, Presidents concluded that their Vice Presidents could help them govern.[22]

In the 1930s and 1940s, presidential and congressional assignments of executive branch tasks grew more frequent and came to be seen as the norm in part because the Constitution does not prohibit the President from delegating work to the Vice President. Indeed, the Vice Presidential Term Clause, which ties the Vice President to the President, tacitly supports the notion that the Vice President can play an active role within the executive branch.[23] By the 1950s, Vice Presidents were regularly traveling abroad on presidential business and heading governmental task forces and commissions. Reinforcing these mid-century trends in governance, presidential nominees increasingly began to choose vice-presidential candidates, thereby helping ensure greater compatibility and loyalty between the two officeholders.[24] Two decades later, Vice President Walter Mondale, who served under President Jimmy Carter from 1977 to 1981, became a top presidential counselor and troubleshooter and the first officeholder to secure permanent office space within the West Wing, elevating the post to a true White House position.[25]

During the joint session of Congress on January 6, 2021, Vice President Michael Pence demonstrated that an officeholder could still act independently from the chief executive when he repudiated President Donald Trump's view that the Vice President had the constitutional authority to refuse to accept electoral votes from certain states.[26]

JUDICIAL PRECEDENT

The constitutional development of the vice presidency has taken place largely without assistance from the judiciary. When litigation has directly implicated vice presidential constitutional power, the courts have typically declined to intervene, permitting the political branches to resolve matters.[27] As a result, constitutional amendments and changing political expectations and customs have largely driven interpretation of the office.[28] A rare exception to this rule occurred in 2023 when a federal district court concluded that some of Vice President Pence's communications about his legislative-branch role leading up to the January 6, 2021, electoral vote count were protected by the Speech or Debate Clause.[29]

OPEN QUESTIONS
- Does the Vice President enjoy immunity from civil litigation resulting from the execution of his official responsibilities?[30]
- Can an incumbent Vice President, who is also a candidate for reelection, preside over

the Senate and break ties when the upper chamber is picking a Vice President during a contingent election pursuant to the Twelfth Amendment?[31]

- Is the Vice President permitted to serve as presiding officer when he is the subject of a Senate impeachment trial?[32]
- What happens if a Vice President becomes de facto incapacitated?[33]

Cite as: Roy E. Brownell II, *The Vice Presidential Term Clause*, in THE HERITAGE GUIDE TO THE CONSTITUTION 310 (Josh Blackman & John G. Malcolm eds., 3d ed. 2025).

Notes

1. John D. Feerick, From Failing Hands 23–38, 43 (1965). **2.** Mass. Const. of 1780, pt. 2, ch. 2, § 2, art. I; S.C. Const. of 1778, art. III; N.Y. Const. of 1777, art. XX; Jamin Soderstrom, *Comment, Back to the Basics*, 35 Pepp. L. Rev. 967, 986–87 (2008). **3.** 2 Farrand's 493. **4.** *Id.* at 537; Federalist No. 68 (Hamilton); Joel K. Goldstein, *The New Constitutional Vice Presidency*, 30 Wake Forest L. Rev. 505, 511–13 (1995). **5.** Goldstein, *The New Constitutional Vice Presidency, supra* at 510–15. **6.** *Id.* **7.** 2 Farrand's 537. **8.** Roy E. Brownell II, *The Independence of the Vice Presidency*, 17 N.Y.U. J. Leg. & Pub. Pol'y 297, 305–06 (2014). **9.** U.S. Senate, *About the Vice President*, https://perma.cc/8KCS-YZS4. **10.** Roy E. Brownell II, *A Constitutional Chameleon, Part II*, 24 Kan. J.L. & Pub. Pol'y 294, 297–314 (2015). **11.** 1 Stat. 23 (1789); Seth Barrett Tillman & Josh Blackman, *Offices and Officers of the Constitution*, Part III: The Appointments, Impeachment, Commissions, and Oath or Affirmation Clauses, 62 S. Tex. L. Rev. 349, 419 (2023). **12.** 1 Stat. 241 (1792); 1 Stat. 72 (1789). **13.** 8 The Works of John Adams 489–93, 496–500, 515 (Charles Francis Adams ed., 1853); Linda Dudik Guerrero, John Adams' Vice-Presidency, 1789–1797, at 161–87 (1978) (Ph.D. dissertation, University of California, Santa Barbara). **14.** Letter from Thomas Jefferson to Benjamin Rush (Jan. 16, 1811), https://perma.cc/AZ6E-QQD4. **15.** Brownell, *A Constitutional Chameleon, supra* at 314–25; Joel K. Goldstein, *Crossroads in Vice-Presidential History*, in The Presidency: Facing Constitutional Crossroads 180–83 (Michael Nelson and Barbara A. Perry eds., 2021). **16.** Michael Nelson, *Background Paper, in* A Heartbeat Away: Report of the Twentieth Century Fund Task Force on the Vice Presidency 29–30 (1988). **17.** Goldstein, *Crossroads, supra* at 182–84. **18.** *Marshall Heads Cabinet Session*, N.Y. Times, Dec. 11, 1918, at 1. **19.** *Harding Confers on the Campaign with Gen. Wood*, N.Y. Times, July 11, 1920, at 1. **20.** Brownell, *A Constitutional Chameleon, supra* at 334–36. **21.** Arthur M. Schlesinger, Jr., The Cycles of American History 349 (1986). **22.** Joel K. Goldstein, The Modern American Vice Presidency 15–45, 139 (1982). **23.** Memorandum for the Vice President from Nicholas deB. Katzenbach, OLC, Re: Constitutionality of the Vice President's Service as Chairman of the National Aeronautics and Space Council 1 (Apr. 18, 1961), https://perma.cc/32AU-7JFS; Joel K. Goldstein, The White House Vice Presidency 13 (2016). **24.** Goldstein, *Crossroads, supra* at 187. **25.** Goldstein, The White House Vice Presidency, *supra* at 36–104. **26.** Letter from Vice President Michael R. Pence to Members of Congress (Jan. 6, 2021), https://perma.cc/N2AU-XHFU. **27.** *Gohmert v. Pence*, 510 F. Supp.3d 435 (E.D. Texas, 2021); *Common Cause v. Biden*, 748 F.3d 1280 (D.C. Cir. 2014). **28.** Goldstein, *The New Constitutional Vice Presidency, supra* at 526–40; Goldstein, The Modern American Vice Presidency, *supra* at 15–45, 134–84, 300–21. **29.** *In re Grand Jury Subpoena*, Case No. [Redacted], D.D.C. (Mar. 27, 2023), https://perma.cc/533L-7473. **30.** James D. Myers, *Note, Bringing the Vice President into the Fold*, 50 Bos. Coll. L. Rev. 897 (2009). **31.** Todd Garvey & Jack Maskell, *Can the Vice President Elect Himself?* CRS Legal Sidebar (Oct. 11, 2012), https://perma.cc/CF4G-NVRK. **32.** Joel K. Goldstein, *Can the Vice President Preside at His Own Impeachment Trial?*, 44 St. Louis U. L.J. 849 (2000). **33.** Roy E. Brownell II, *Vice Presidential Inability*, 48 Hofstra L. Rev. 291 (2019).

ESSAY NO. 90: THE PRESIDENTIAL ELECTORS CLAUSE
ART. II, § 1, CL. 2

[The President] shall . . . together with the Vice President, chosen for the same Term, be elected, as follows: Each State shall appoint, in such Manner as the Legislature thereof may direct, a Number of Electors, equal to the whole Number of Senators and Representatives to which the State may be entitled in the Congress.
— Derek T. Muller

INTRODUCTION

Before the Constitutional Convention, most state legislatures appointed their executives, and during the Convention, there seemed to be a consensus that the Congress would elect the President. However, the Framers crafted a compromise: The state legislatures could choose how they would appoint electors who in turn would vote for the President. In the early Republic, some state legislatures appointed their electors, and some states held popular statewide elections. Following the Civil War, the nation's growing democratic ethos led to popular election of presidential electors in all states. Courts have continued to affirm that state legislatures maintain broad authority over the method of choosing presidential electors.

HISTORY BEFORE 1787

Following independence, states had various methods for choosing the executive. In some states, like Massachusetts and New York, the people chose the executive in a popular election.[1] In others, like Georgia and Virginia, the executive was chosen by the legislature.[2] Still others had hybrid arrangements. Pennsylvania, for example, created a Supreme Executive Council of twelve members chosen by eleven counties and the city of Philadelphia, and the Council chose its President.[3]

THE CONSTITUTIONAL CONVENTION

During the Constitutional Convention, delegates debated how the President should be elected. James Madison would later explain to Thomas Jefferson that under various proposals, the President would be elected by popular vote, by state governors, by a joint ballot of both houses of Congress, or by one house choosing a slate of candidates from which the other house would choose the winner.[4] By wide margins, the Convention consistently rejected popular election or election by state legislatures.[5] The plan to have Congress choose the President seemed to be more agreeable,[6] although Gouverneur Morris of Pennsylvania worried that the executive would be dependent on the legislature and that it could lead to "Legislative tyranny."[7]

By August 24, 1787, late in the Convention, a series of divided votes led to an unsatisfactory proposal: The President would be elected by joint vote of both houses of Congress.[8] Gouverneur Morris proposed the "abstract question" that the President should be chosen by electors, but the vote failed because the states were equally divided.[9] The matter was referred to a Committee of Eleven, which included representatives from each state.

On September 4, the Convention considered the Committee of Eleven's proposal, which built on Morris's suggestion that electors would choose the President. Electors would be appointed in a manner of each state legislature's choosing, and the number of each state's electors would equal the number of its Senators and Representatives.[10] Roger Sherman of Connecticut explained that the objective was "to render the Executive independent of the Legislature."[11] State representation in the selection of the President would mirror state representation in Congress, which already reflected compromises between large states and small states and between free states and slave states. (In the Senate, every state received two Senators regardless of size; in the House, representation would be based on the free population plus three-fifths of the enslaved population.) Under the committee's proposal, the states would decide for themselves whether their electors would be chosen by the legislature, by popular vote, or by some other method. Delegates acknowledged that the committee's proposal seemed reasonable.[12]

THE RATIFICATION DEBATES

In Federalist No. 39, James Madison defended the Electoral College. He wrote that several features of the system balanced state sovereignty and participation of the national government: states were assigned a designated number of electors based on the "compound ratio" of the total number of Senators and Representatives; the House of Representatives had the ultimate responsibility for the election of the President; and during a so-called contingent election, each state's representatives would function as a single delegation with one vote.

The Anti-Federalists were skeptical of this system and favored a popular vote. Cato wrote that "[i]t is a maxim in republics, that the representative of the people should be of their immediate choice."[13] Luther Martin of Maryland warned that larger states, with more electors, would "have a very undue influence" and that the states would have "an equal voice" in the President's election only in close elections that would be decided by the House of Representatives.[14] Anti-Federalists also worried about potential undue influence on electors. The fact that there were so few of them (just sixty-nine in the first presidential election)[15] meant that it would not be difficult to influence them before they cast their votes. A Georgian wondered, "How many offices, and how much money, will it take to buy the majority of [the electors], if ambitious men should attempt to set about it?"[16] Agrippa even proposed that the President should be elected each year by a different set of states.[17]

EARLY PRACTICE

In the first nine presidential elections after ratification, states appointed presidential electors in a variety of ways. In 1789, when the first presidential election was held, some states, including Pennsylvania and Maryland, held popular statewide elections for all of their electors.[18] In Delaware and Virginia, electors were appointed by popular election in individual districts.[19] In South Carolina and Connecticut, the legislatures directly appointed electors.[20]

By 1824, popular elections were held in eighteen of the twenty-four states,[21] and by 1828, only Delaware and South Carolina chose electors by legislative appointment.[22] The last two legislatures to appoint presidential electors were Florida (in 1868) and Colorado (in 1876).[23] After the Civil War, popular election of presidential electors became the standard. An increasingly democratic national ethos embraced popular elections on all fronts, including presidential elections.

JUDICIAL PRECEDENT

The U.S. Supreme Court has been very deferential with respect to state laws that regulate the manner of appointing electors. In 1892, for example, Michigan divided the award of electors among districts across the state instead of awarding them in a winner-take-all fashion. *McPherson v. Blacker* (1892) upheld this system, which was used by some states in the early

Republic.[24] Alabama presented voters with ballots that listed only the names of presidential candidates even though the votes for a candidate are really for his party's slate of electors. *Ray v. Blair* (1952) upheld this ballot.[25] The *Ray* Court also allowed the states to require elector candidates to pledge that, if chosen, they will vote for their party's candidate.[26] *Chiafalo v. Washington* (2020) further held that a state may penalize a "faithless elector" who pledges his vote for a candidate and then fails to vote for that candidate.[27] The state may even replace an elector who attempts to cast a vote for a candidate he was not pledged to support.[28]

Article II's grant of authority to states to appoint electors "in such manner" as the legislature may direct gives "'the broadest power of determination' over who becomes an elector."[29] However, the exercise of a state's federal constitutional power to direct the manner of appointing presidential electors must be consistent with other constitutional provisions, including the First and Fourteenth Amendments. For example, in *Williams v. Rhodes* (1968), the Court found that an Ohio law that required new political parties to obtain petitions signed by number of voters equal to fifteen percent of ballots cast in the previous election was too onerous a burden on the Socialist Labor Party's right of association when the party tried to run a presidential ticket in the state.[30] In *Bush v. Gore* (2000), the Court found that the Florida Supreme Court's rules for a recount created uneven treatment of voters across the state, and the recount needed to be halted because this uneven treatment ran afoul of the Equal Protection Clause of the Fourteenth Amendment.[31]

Bush v. Gore resolved the contested presidential election in Florida by a 5-to-4 vote. The majority opinion focused on the equal protection issue, but Chief Justice William H. Rehnquist, joined by Justices Antonin Scalia and Clarence Thomas, wrote a concurring opinion that provided a different ground to decide the case. Rehnquist argued that the Constitution imposed a duty on a particular branch of the state government—the legislature—to direct the manner of appointing electors. The concurring opinion noted specifically that the Florida Supreme Court had infringed on the legislature's authority when it disregarded the "clearly expressed intent of the legislature"[32] and had "significantly departed from the statutory framework" for recounts provided by the legislature.[33]

Typically, questions of state law are left to state courts. In Rehnquist's view, however, "appointing Presidential electors presents a federal constitutional question," and when there is a "significant departure from the legislative scheme" by a state court in such cases, the Supreme Court should decide that constitutional question.[34] In this case, the state court usurped the role of the "legislature" in appointing electors, and the U.S. Supreme Court could correct the state court's decision. (Hours before the Court decided *Bush v. Gore*, the Florida House of Representatives passed a measure that would have appointed a slate of electors, but after the Supreme Court resolved the recount, the Florida Senate did not consider it.[35])

During disputes that arose ahead of the 2020 presidential election, Justices Thomas, Samuel Alito, Neil Gorsuch, and Brett Kavanaugh seemed to agree with Rehnquist's approach (sometimes called the "independent state legislature doctrine" in academic literature).[36] Some matters of state law might be ripe for federal court review if state actors deviated from the legislature's preferences or tried to develop rules on their own. The Supreme Court, however, has not definitively resolved the meaning of "Legislature" in the Presidential Electors Clause and what involvement non-legislative actors may have in setting the rules for a presidential election.

The language of the Elections Clause in Article I is similar to the language in the Presidential Electors Clause in Article II. The Elections Clause provides that in each state "the Legislature thereof" shall prescribe the "Times, Places and Manner of holding Elections for Senators and Representatives."[37]

Moore v. Harper (2023) held that "Legislature" in the Elections Clause did not refer only to the state's institutional legislature—in that case, the North Carolina General Assembly and Senate.[38] Rather, consistent with other Supreme Court precedent, "Legislature" referred more broadly to the state's lawmaking process, in which the state judiciary can determine whether the legislature followed the state constitution, as long as the state court did not "transgress the ordinary bounds of judicial review."[39] *Moore* did not resolve the meaning of "Legislature" in the Presidential Electors Clause, but it seems likely that the Supreme Court would give "Legislature" the same meaning in both clauses, as *Moore* cited *Bush v. Gore* favorably.[40]

The Electors Clause in Article I expressly grants Congress the power to "make or alter" state regulations regarding the "manner of holding elections" for Senators and Representatives; the Presidential Electors Clause does not provide a similar power. Nevertheless, Congress has sometimes regulated both types of elections together. The Supreme Court has previously assumed that Congress must have the power to regulate both presidential and congressional elections,[41] but this assumption does not square with the text of the Presidential Electors Clause, and the appropriate scope of federal power over presidential elections remains an open question.[42]

Amendments to the Constitution may also grant Congress additional power to regulate the selection of presidential electors. Under the Fifteenth Amendment, Congress can enact "appropriate legislation" regarding state laws that deny the right to vote on the basis of race. The Fifteenth Amendment does not distinguish between the types of federal elections; Congress therefore has power to regulate both congressional and presidential elections.[43]

OPEN QUESTIONS

- Do other provisions of the Constitution–including the Fourteenth Amendment– prevent a state legislature from appointing electors without a popular election in the present day?[44]
- How broad is Congress's power to appoint electors? How do other provisions of the Constitution interact with Congress's power?[45]
- What are Congress's powers, if any, to regulate the manner of appointing presidential electors, and what is the source of those powers?

- Under the proposed National Popular Vote Interstate Compact, each state would agree to award its electoral votes to the person who received the most popular votes nationwide.[46] Does the Presidential Electors Clause allow electors to be appointed based on reference to popular sentiment outside of the state?[47]

Cite as: Derek T. Muller, *The Presidential Electors Clause, in* THE HERITAGE GUIDE TO THE CONSTITUTION 313 (Josh Blackman & John G. Malcolm eds., 3d ed. 2025).

Notes

1. Mass. Const. of 1780, pt. II, ch. II, § I, cl. III; N.Y. Const. of 1777, § 17.   2. Ga. Const. of 1777, § II; Va. Const. of 1776, ch. II, § IX.   3. Pa. Const. of 1776, ch. II, § 19.   4. 3 Farrand's 132.   5. 2 Farrand's 22, 402.   6. *Id.* at 401.   7. *Id.* at 403, 36.   8. *Id.* at 402–04.   9. *Id.* at 404.   10. *Id.* at 497.   11. *Id.* at 499.   12. *Id.* at 499–502.   13. Storing 2.6.30.   14. *Id.* at 2.4.83.   15. 1 Annals of Cong. 17 (1789).   16. Storing 5.9.9.   17. Storing 4.6.75.   18. 13 Statutes at Large of Pennsylvania 140–45; 2 The Documentary History of the First Federal Elections, 1788–1790, at 136–40 (1985).   19. 2 Documentary History at 69–71, 289–92.   20. 1 The Documentary History of the First Federal Elections, 1788–1790, at 201–03 (1976); 2 Documentary History at 48.   21. Svend Petersen, A Statistical History of the American Presidential Elections 18 (1980).   22. *Id.* at 20.   23. *Id.* at 41, 45.   24. 146 U.S. 1 (1892).   25. 343 U.S. 214 (1952).   26. *Id.* at 227.   27. 591 U.S. 578, 587–89 (2020).   28. *Colo. Dep't of State v. Baca*, 591 U.S. 655 (2020) (per curiam).   29. *Chiafalo*, 591 U.S. at 589 (quoting *McPherson v. Blacker*, 146 U.S. 1, 27 (1892)).   30. *Williams v. Rhodes*, 393 U.S. 23, 28–31 (1968).   31. *Bush v. Gore*, 531 U.S. 98, 105–06 (2000) (per curiam)   32. *Id.* at 120 (Rehnquist, C.J., concurring).   33. *Id.* at 122.   34. *Id.* at 113.   35. Jo Becker, *Florida Senate May Scrap Plan to Name Second Slate of Electors*, Wash. Post (Dec. 14, 2000), https://perma.cc /D9QX-3CQA.   36. *Democratic Nat'l Comm. v. Wis. State Legislature*, 141 S.Ct. 28, 34 n.1 (2020) (Kavanaugh, J., concurring); *Republican Party of Pa. v. Boockvar*, 141 S.Ct. 1, 2 (2020) (statement of Alito, J.).   37. Art. I, § 4, cl. 1.   38. 600 U.S. 1 (2023).   39. *Id.* at 36.   40. *Id.* at 35–36.   41. *Burroughs v. United States*, 290 U.S. 534, 548 (1934); *Buckley v. Valeo*, 424 U.S. 1, 90–91 (1976).   42. Derek T. Muller, *The Electoral College and the Federal Popular Vote*, 15 Harv. L. & Pol'y Rev. 129, 138–41 (2020); *Arizona v. Inter Tribal Council of Ariz.*, 570 U.S. 1, 35–36 n.2 (2013) (Thomas, J., dissenting).   43. *Ex parte Yarbrough*, 110 U.S. 651, 665 (1884).   44. David B. Froomkin & Eric Eisner, *The Second Coming of the Second Section: The Fourteenth Amendment and Presidential Elections*, 58 Ariz. St. L.J. 127 (2024).   45. *Williams v. Va. State Bd. of Elections*, 288 F. Supp. 622 (E.D. Va. 1968), *aff'd*, 393 U.S. 320 (1969); Note, *"As the Legislature Has Prescribed": Removing Presidential Elections from the* Anderson-Burdick *Framework*, 135 Harv. L. Rev. 1082 (2022).   46. Derek T. Muller, *The Compact Clause and the National Popular Vote Interstate Compact*, 6 Election L.J. 372 (2007).   47. Norman R. Williams, *Why the National Popular Vote Is Unconstitutional*, 210 BYU L. Rev. 1523, 1573–77 (2012).

⁓

ESSAY NO. 91: THE ELECTOR INCOMPATIBILITY CLAUSE
ART. II, § 1, CL. 2

. . . but no Senator or Representative, or Person holding an Office of Trust or Profit under the United States, shall be appointed an Elector.

—Josh Blackman & Seth Barrett Tillman

INTRODUCTION

In our constitutional system, members of the Electoral College, known as presidential electors, cast votes for the President on behalf of each state and the District of Columbia. Currently, the fifty states and the District of Columbia appoint presidential electors. In each of these fifty-one jurisdictions, the prevailing slate of electors meets and votes separately from the electors of the other fifty jurisdictions, but each slate meets on the same day. *Chiafalo v. Washington* (2020) recognized that the states can decide how presidential electors are appointed.[1] Those holding positions in state governments can serve as presidential electors, but the Constitution prohibits those holding certain positions in the federal government from being appointed presidential electors.

The Constitution expressly bars U.S. Senators, Representatives, and those who hold an "Office of Trust or Profit under the United States" from being appointed as presidential electors. The U.S. Supreme Court has never opined on the precise meaning of "Office of Trust or Profit under the United States" in the Elector Incompatibility Clause. In the view of the authors of this essay, the phrase "Office of Trust or Profit under the United States" extends to appointed officers in the executive, judicial, and legislative branches, and those holding such positions are barred from being appointed as presidential electors.[2] We further contend that this clause does not expressly bar the President and Vice President, who hold elected positions, from serving as electors.

THE CONSTITUTIONAL CONVENTION

During the Constitutional Convention, the structure of the federal executive branch and how the chief magistrate would be elected or appointed was a subject of significant and lengthy debate and division. However, the Elector Incompatibility Clause was introduced fairly late in that process. On September 6, 1787, Rufus King and Elbridge Gerry of Massachusetts proposed language specifying that "no Person shall be appointed an Elector who is a Member of the Legislature of the United States or who holds any office of profit or trust under the United States."[3] This text was approved without any recorded debate.[4]

This provision was referred to the Committee of Style,[5] which reworded the text to read that "no senator or representative shall be appointed an elector, nor any person holding an office of trust or profit under the United States."[6] The Committee changed "Member of the Legislature" to "senator or representative" and flipped the ordering from "profit or trust" to "trust or profit." On September 15, the phrase "shall be appointed an elector" was moved to "the end of the clause."[7] The final, adopted text provides that "no Senator or Representative, or Person holding an Office of Trust or Profit under the United States, shall be appointed an Elector."[8]

THE RATIFICATION DEBATES

Alexander Hamilton discussed the Elector Incompatibility Clause in Federalist No. 68. He wrote that the Constitution did not vest the choice of President "on any preexisting bodies of men, who might be tampered with beforehand to prostitute their votes." Hamilton explained that the Elector Incompatibility Clause was designed to preserve the electors' decisional independence. In other words, they could cast their votes without fear of federal officeholders controlling their decision.

Caroliniensis, a Federalist from South Carolina, expressed a similar sentiment. He wrote that "[t]he president cannot bribe or influence his electors, because it is impossible for him to know them." Caroliniensis added that "all popular tumult is effectually guarded against, by the election's being held in thirteen different states at the same time. . . ."[9]

REPRESENTATIVES AND SENATORS CANNOT SERVE AS ELECTORS

U.S. Senators and Representatives are expressly precluded from serving as electors. During the joint session of Congress, the electors' votes are counted "in the Presence of the Senate and House of Representatives."[10] If the Electoral College fails to choose a President and/or Vice President—for example, if the vote is a tie—the selection of a President falls to the House, and the choice of Vice President falls to the Senate.[11] Moreover, the two houses of Congress have (or at least have exercised) an implied power to resolve conflicts over disputed electoral votes.

For these reasons, it makes sense to prohibit members of Congress from serving as electors, as they would need to sit in judgment of electoral votes that were already cast. It would be problematic for a member of Congress to decide the validity of a vote that he personally cast.

This separation between presidential electors and members of Congress avoids some potential conflicts of interest. We say *some* conflicts because a sitting member of Congress can be a presidential candidate, and if the two houses of Congress need to adjudicate an electoral dispute, there is no constitutional provision that expressly bars such a member from voting for himself.

The text of the Elector Incompatibility Clause suggests that Senators and Representatives do not hold an "office . . . under the United States." Why? If members of Congress held an "office . . . under the United States," the express enumeration of Senators and Representatives would be redundant. The Framers chose to list Senators and Representatives separately, suggesting that these elected positions do not hold an "Office . . . under the United States."[12]

"OFFICE[S] OF TRUST OR PROFIT UNDER THE UNITED STATES"

In the Elector Incompatibility Clause, the words "Trust" and "Profit" describe different types of "Office[s] . . . under the United States." An office of *trust* under the United States has regular, non-delegable duties that require the exercise of discretion.[13] An office of *profit* under the United States has a regular salary or other authorized emoluments, such as fees or commissions.[14] Offices of profit and offices of trust may overlap.[15] Indeed, courts in Commonwealth countries routinely decide how to characterize a given office. For example, *Hodel v. Cruckshank* (1889) turned on whether a position was in fact an office of *profit* under the Crown.[16]

CAN HOLDERS OF APPOINTED EXECUTIVE AND JUDICIAL BRANCH POSITIONS SERVE AS ELECTORS?

The Supreme Court has never squarely addressed whether holders of appointed positions in the executive and judicial branches can serve as presidential electors. In our view, they cannot. Specifically, we believe that those who hold appointed positions in the executive and judicial branches are "officers of the United States."[17] These positions are also "office[s] . . . under the United States." This exclusion makes good sense.

As noted, Hamilton and other Federalists recognized that this provision was drafted to protect presidential electors' decisional independence. However, the Elector Incompatibility Clause does not forbid all appointments where the appointee is dependent on others. An elector can be an employee of a private commercial enterprise and dependent on the entity's president or governing board for his livelihood. A state executive officer also can be an elector—even if the officer is dependent on higher state authority such as a governor. But an elector who is dependent on a federal elected official would amount to the federal government electing *itself*. This type of dependency is uniquely dangerous.

The Secretary of State, for example, who serves at the pleasure of the President, would lack decisional independence. In Federalist No. 68, Hamilton observed that "all those who from [their] situation might be suspected of too great devotion to the President in office" would be "excluded from eligibility to this trust." Statutory officers appointed by the President are excluded from serving as presidential electors precisely because the President is in a position to remove them—or appoint or promote them to additional or higher offices. Holders of these positions, in Hamilton's words, could not enter upon the task free from any "sinister bias." Their livelihood would depend on the President's continuing support. Statutory officers could be persuaded, directed, or even ordered to cast an electoral vote for the sitting President or his favored successor.

Article III judges are also prohibited from serving as electors. Such judges cannot be removed by the President, but they can be appointed by the President to higher judicial posts or to lucrative posts in the executive branch, which might be held concurrently with their judicial post. Excluding such judges from serving in the Electoral College helps to preserve the electors' decisional independence. Moreover, it is eminently reasonable to keep federal judges out of the non-judicial aspects of the electoral process. Federal judges have been called upon to decide electoral disputes, but it would be extremely problematic for a judge to serve in the Electoral College and then have to resolve cases that implicate the very electoral vote he cast or the votes cast by other electors for candidates that the judge voted for or against.

CAN HOLDERS OF APPOINTED LEGISLATIVE BRANCH POSITIONS SERVE AS ELECTORS?

The Elector Incompatibility Clause provides

that a "[p]erson holding an Office of Trust or Profit under the United States" cannot be "appointed [as] an Elector." In our view, holders of appointed positions in the legislative branch—for example, the Secretary of the Senate, Clerk of the House, and parliamentarian of each house—hold "office[s] . . . under the United States." Therefore, they cannot be appointed as presidential electors.

It would be problematic if members of Congress cannot serve as electors but the subordinate officers that those members choose could serve as electors. All such congressional staff would lack decisional independence. They can be dominated and removed by the presiding member of their chamber if the presiding member has a removal power. Likewise, a factional legislative majority in each chamber could certainly persuade, direct, or even order subordinate appointed legislative officers, who are always subject to the chamber's omnipresent removal power, to vote as directed. Again, such circumstances would amount to the federal government electing *itself*, and this type of dependency is uniquely dangerous.

The Elector Incompatibility Clause forbids members of Congress from participating in the Electoral College process. Allowing their dependent appointees to serve in the Electoral College would create a glaring loophole. It is far worse to have the Clerk of the House serve in the Electoral College than for the Speaker to serve in the Electoral College. The Speaker is arguably independent, subject to election by the voters and by the House, and faces substantial transparency expectations in regard to his official conduct. Not so for the Clerk, who serves at the pleasure of the House.

The Elector Incompatibility Clause was designed to preserve decisional independence against control by federal officials. *Chiafalo v. Washington* (2020) is consistent with this principle.[18] *Chiafalo* held that, in certain circumstances, state governments can instruct electors on how to vote.[19] Congress, however, has no power to control how electors vote. Congress, however, has historically claimed that it has the power to count or not count purportedly irregular or otherwise unlawful electoral votes.

CAN THE PRESIDENT AND VICE PRESIDENT SERVE AS PRESIDENTIAL ELECTORS?

In our view, while appointed officers—that is, those holding "Office[s] . . . under the United States"—in all three branches cannot serve as electors, the President and Vice President do not hold an "office . . . under the United States."[20] Therefore, each could serve as a presidential elector, and potentially, each could vote for himself or for his favored successor. This result may seem counterintuitive and perhaps even unseemly, but it does not trigger the concerns that animated the Elector Incompatibility Clause. As Hamilton explained in Federalist No. 68, the President as an elector cannot "be tampered with beforehand to prostitute [his] vote[]."

If the President serves as an elector, he is not at risk of being pressured or coerced to change his vote by any superior; in fact, it is to be expected that the President, if also an active candidate, would vote for himself. In every election, we see the spectacle of all politicians—including the President and other presidential candidates—voting for themselves in the general election. There is no doubt how those votes will be cast. Relatedly, in 2016, former President Bill Clinton was selected as an elector in New York for his wife, presidential candidate Secretary Hillary Clinton.[21] There was no doubt about how he would vote.

We believe that the sitting Vice President can also serve as a presidential elector even when he is on the ballot for President. The Vice President is not subject to presidential appointment, removal, or supervision in the ordinary course of his duties. A President has substantial control over Cabinet positions, but in his capacity as President, he enjoys few legal controls over the Vice President. Such self-interested candidates might very well vote for themselves for opportunistic reasons, but no third parties would be pulling their strings.

WHAT IS AN ELECTOR?

The Presidential Electors Clause provides that "[e]ach State shall appoint, in such Manner as the Legislature thereof may direct, a Number of Electors, equal to the whole Number of Senators and Representatives to which the State may be entitled in the Congress[.]"[22] In our view, presidential electors are not "Officers of the United States" and do not hold an "Office . . . under the United States."[23] Rather, we contend that presidential electors hold a federal position: a "public Trust under the United States" as that phrase is used in the Religious Test Clause. That provision provides that "no religious Test shall ever be required as a Qualification to any Office or public Trust under the United States."[24] For example, in Federalist No. 68, Hamilton refers to electors as holding a "trust" as opposed to using the language of "office" and "officer."

OPEN QUESTIONS

- What happens if a person holding an incompatible position is appointed as an elector? Is the appointment void, or does the appointment work an automatic loss of the incompatible position? Would a federal court have the power to remove the elector before he casts his vote as a presidential elector? Could the joint session of Congress refuse to count that elector's vote? What if the elector's vote could not be identified or disaggregated from the other electoral votes cast by that state's slate of electors?

- If a member of the House (or Senate) attempted to resign his seat in order to cast a vote as a presidential elector, could his efforts to resign and vote be frustrated if the House (or Senate) actively refused to accept his resignation?[25] If a covered federal officer attempted to resign his post in order to cast a vote as a presidential elector, could his efforts to resign and vote be frustrated if the President (or other superior officer) refused to accept his resignation?

- If a person holds an "office . . . under the United States" position as an officer *de facto* but not *de jure*, is he subject to the Elector Incompatibility Clause? If a person is lawfully appointed by higher authority to an "office . . . under the United States" position but the recipient has not yet accepted the post, does he "hold[]" the position for purposes of the Elector Incompatibility Clause?

Cite as: Josh Blackman & Seth Barrett Tillman, *The Elector Incompatibility Clause*, *in* THE HERITAGE GUIDE TO THE CONSTITUTION 317 (Josh Blackman & John G. Malcolm eds., 3d ed. 2025).

Notes

1. 591 U.S. 578 (2020). **2.** Seth Barrett Tillman & Josh Blackman, *Offices and Officers of the Constitution, Part V: The Elector Incompatibility, Impeachment Disqualification, Foreign Emoluments, and Incompatibility Clauses*, 63 S. Tex. L. Rev. 237, 251 (2024). **3.** 2 Farrand's 517, 521. **4.** *Id.* **5.** *Id.* at 572–73. **6.** *Id.* at 597. **7.** *Id.* at 621. **8.** *Id.* at 658. **9.** Caroliniensis, *Charleston City Gazette*, April 1788, *in* 27 DHRC 238. **10.** Art. II, § 1, cl. 3; Amend. XII, cl. 2. **11.** Amend. XII. **12.** Asher Steinberg, *The Textual Argument That the President Does Not Hold an "Office Under the United States,"* The Narrowest Grounds (Sept. 21, 2017), https://perma.cc/Y7DK-53S2. **13.** Floyd R. Mechem, A Treatise on the Law of Public Offices and Officers § 16, at 9 (Chicago, Callaghan & Co. 1890), https://perma.cc/B2L5-W3PJ. **14.** *Id.* § 13, at 8. **15.** *Doty v. State*, 6 Blackf. 529, 530 (Ind. 1843) (per curiam). **16.** *Hodel v. Cruckshank* (1889) 3 Queensland LJ. 141, 142 (Austl.), https://perma.cc/VZ33 -SYVJ. **17.** Seth Barrett Tillman & Josh Blackman, *Offices and Officers of the Constitution, Part III: The Appointments, Impeachment, Commissions, and Oath or Affirmation Clauses*, 62 S. Tex. L. Rev. 349 (2023). **18.** 591 U.S. 578 (2020). **19.** *Id.* at 595–97. **20.** Seth Barrett Tillman & Josh Blackman, *Offices and Officers of the Constitution, Part IV: The "Office . . . under the United States" Drafting Convention*, 62 S. Tex. L. Rev. 455 (2023). **21.** Bill Mahoney, *Electoral Delegate Bill Clinton: "Never Cast a Vote I Was Prouder of,"* Politico (Dec. 19, 2016), https://perma.cc/XMN3-BJRR. **22.** Art. II, § 1, cl. 2. **23.** Seth Barrett Tillman & Josh Blackman, *Offices and Officers of the Constitution, Part II: The Four Approaches*, 61 S. Tex. L. Rev. 321, 394–401 (2022). **24.** Art. VI, cl. 3. **25.** Josh Chafetz, *Leaving the House: The Constitutional Status of Resignation from the House of Representatives*, 58 Duke L.J. 177 (2008).

$\backsim$

ESSAY NO. 92: THE ELECTORAL MEETING CLAUSE
ART. II, § 1, CL. 3

The Electors shall meet in their respective States, and vote by Ballot for two Persons, of whom one at least shall not be an Inhabitant of the same State with themselves. And they shall make a List of all the Persons voted for, and of the Number of Votes for each; which List they shall sign and certify, and transmit sealed to the Seat of the Government of the United States, directed to the President of the Senate.

—Michael T. Morley

INTRODUCTION

The Electoral Meeting Clause established the original procedure for casting electoral votes in presidential elections. It required presidential electors to "meet in their respective states." Each elector had to cast electoral votes for "two Persons, of whom one at least shall not be an Inhabitant of the same State with themselves." Each state's electors were then required to "make a List of all the Persons voted for, and of the Number of Votes for each," and send it to the President of the U.S. Senate. Under this provision, electors did not cast separate votes for presidential and vice presidential candidates. In 1804, the clause was superseded by the Twelfth Amendment, but several of the constitutional questions that the clause raised have endured.

HISTORY BEFORE 1787

The English government did not include any institution comparable to the Electoral College. The closest parallel from early American state constitutions was the mechanism in the Maryland Constitution of 1776 for electing the state Senate.[1] Every five years, the voters of each county chose two electors by majority vote, and the voters of Annapolis and Baltimore each chose a single elector.[2] The state's electors met in Annapolis "or such other place as shall be appointed for convening the legislature" on the third Monday in September to elect fifteen Senators.[3] Each elector was required to take an oath "to elect without favour, affection, partiality, or prejudice, such persons for Senators, as they, in their judgment and conscience, believe best qualified for the office."[4] Maryland retained this system until 1837 when it adopted direct popular election of state Senators.[5]

During the Constitutional Convention, Alexander Hamilton of New York stated that Maryland's senate had been "much appealed to" as a model for balancing the interests of the wealthy and the poor, although he did not raise that point specifically in connection with presidential elections.[6] Federalist No. 63 cited the Maryland senate as precedent for the appointment of U.S. Senators by state legislatures.

THE CONSTITUTIONAL CONVENTION

Early in the Constitutional Convention, on June 1, 1787, James Wilson of Pennsylvania proposed dividing states into districts, each of which would elect an unspecified number of electors for the "Executive Magistracy." The electors would "meet" at an unspecified place, "and they or any ____ of them so met shall elect by ballot, but not out of their own body, ____ Person in whom the Executive authority of the national Government shall be vested."[7] (The blanks were to be filled in later.) The Convention rejected Wilson's motion.[8] Other early proposals by Wilson, Luther Martin of Maryland, Gouverneur Morris of Pennsylvania, and Oliver Ellsworth of Connecticut to have the President chosen by electors did not discuss the electors' meeting or how they would cast their votes.[9]

On July 25, Hugh Williamson of North Carolina first raised the idea of voting for multiple presidential candidates.[10] He suggested that the people should elect the President with each person "vot[ing] for 3 candidates."[11] Williamson surmised that each voter was likely to cast one of his votes for someone from his own state; candidates from large and small states were equally likely to receive the remaining votes.[12] Morris endorsed this idea but suggested that each person should vote for only two candidates, including at least one who was not from the voter's own state.[13] James Madison of Virginia acknowledged that this approach would allow a voter to cast one vote for "his favorite fellow Citizen" from his own state and then "throw away his second vote on some obscure Citizen of another State, in order to ensure the object of his first choice."[14] He thought it unlikely, however, that voters would take such a risk.[15] The Convention declined to consider Williamson's proposal by a vote of 5 to 6.[16]

In late August, the Committee on Postponed Parts proposed that the President be chosen by an electoral college.[17] Its draft of the Electoral Meeting Clause was nearly identical to the version that the Convention would ultimately adopt.

Morris, along with Madison, Wilson, and George Mason of Virginia, contended that requiring presidential electors to cast their electoral votes within their respective states reduced the possibility of "cabal and corruption."[18] Morris further explained that having each elector cast at least one of his two electoral votes for someone from a different state would ensure that at least half of the electoral votes "will fall on characters eminent & generally known."[19] The Convention rejected an amendment mandating that the electors "meet at the seat of the Genl. Govt."[20] It likewise declined to direct electors to transmit their votes "under the seal of the State."[21] The Convention ultimately adopted the Electoral Meeting Clause with only minor, non-substantive changes in capitalization and punctuation.[22]

On September 17, after the Constitution was signed, the Convention adopted an accompanying resolution recommending that, following the Constitution's ratification, the Confederation Congress should direct states to appoint presidential electors.[23] In correspondence following the Convention, Gouverneur Morris argued that the system protected small states because

a candidate would seldom receive a majority of electoral votes. Presidential elections were therefore likely to be decided by the House of Representatives. Such contingent House elections greatly enhanced the influence of small states because each state's representatives collectively could cast only a single vote.[24]

THE RATIFICATION DEBATES
The state ratification conventions recognized that requiring each state's presidential electors to cast their votes in their respective states on the same day would reduce the risk of their being bribed or otherwise corrupted. This point was articulated by Edmund Randolph in Virginia, James Iredell in North Carolina, and Charles Cotesworth Pinckney in South Carolina.[25] Alexander Hamilton echoed this notion in Federalist No. 68: "Nothing was more to be desired than that every practicable obstacle should be opposed to cabal, intrigue, and corruption."[26]

PRESIDENTIAL ELECTIONS BEFORE THE TWELFTH AMENDMENT
The first presidential election was in 1788 and proceeded smoothly under the Electoral Meeting Clause. Each elector cast one of his two votes for George Washington, and John Adams received the most votes among the remaining candidates.[27]

In 1792, Congress enacted the Presidential Election and Succession Act. That law required electors to deliver a certificate of their electoral votes to the President of the Senate, mail him a second copy, and send a third to their district's federal judge.[28] Each certificate was to be accompanied by a list of the electors' names certified by the state's "executive authority."[29] The presidential election later that year again occurred without incident. Once again, Washington received the most electoral votes and Adams received the next-highest amount.[30]

The election of 1796 demonstrated that the Constitution's original electoral system did not contemplate the rise of political parties. Federalist John Adams received the most electoral votes and became President. Thomas Jefferson, who was Adams's staunch political opponent, received the second-highest number of electoral votes and became Vice President.[31]

The Election of 1800 revealed further defects in the system. Jefferson and his ostensible running mate Aaron Burr each received the same number of electoral votes.[32] The election fell to the U.S. House of Representatives with each state's congressional delegation casting a single vote. Some Federalists in the House opposed Jefferson, and it took thirty-six rounds of balloting until he finally received votes from enough states to become President.[33] Due to these experiences, Congress proposed and the states quickly ratified the Twelfth Amendment, which modified the rules governing voting in the Electoral College.[34] In anticipation of the amendment's ratification, Congress adopted technical amendments to the 1792 Election and Succession Act.[35]

THE ELECTORAL COUNT ACT

The Electoral Count Act (ECA) of 1887 was adopted in response to the disputed Hayes-Tilden election of 1876. In addition to existing requirements, this law directed each state's executive to transmit a certificate of ascertainment to the U.S. Secretary of State identifying the state's electors and the number of votes that had been cast for each candidate for elector.[36] The certificate was to be sent "as soon as practicable" following the electors' appointments.[37] The executive was similarly required to send a certificate memorializing the "determination" of any "controversy or contest concerning the electors' appointments . . . as soon as practicable" after such determination was made.[38] Congress later required electors to make six copies of the certificates listing their votes,[39] adjusted the dates set forth in the ECA to reflect the Twentieth Amendment's modification of Inauguration Day,[40] and transferred the U.S. Secretary of State's responsibilities to the Archivist of the United States.[41]

The Electoral Count Reform Act (ECRA) of 2022 requires Congress to accept as conclusive a certificate from a state's executive regarding "the determination of electors appointed by the State," as modified or superseded by any federal or state court order.[42] If a state's executive refuses to issue or transmit the required certificate, a candidate may sue before a three-judge federal district court panel.[43] The losing party may seek direct expedited review from the U.S. Supreme Court by petitioning for a writ of certiorari.[44]

ELECTOR BINDING

The Electoral Meeting Clause does not expressly address whether states may "bind" electors, requiring them to vote for their party's presidential and vice presidential candidates. Most early commentators concluded that the Constitution gave presidential electors discretion to vote for the candidates of their choice. In Federalist No. 64, John Jay wrote that electors' decisions would "bear at least equal marks of discretion and discernment." Hamilton echoed these sentiments in Federalist No. 68, explaining that electors would "possess the information and discernment requisite" to choosing a President. St. George Tucker, William Rawle, and James Madison also emphasized electors' independence.[45] Justice Joseph Story's *Commentaries* stated that electors would "act[] under circumstances favourable to deliberation, and to a judicious combination of all the inducements, which ought to govern their choice."[46]

The Supreme Court has observed that, notwithstanding these original intentions, "[e]lectors have only rarely exercised discretion in casting their ballots for President. From the first, States sent [electors] to the Electoral College . . . to vote for pre-selected candidates, rather than to use their own judgment."[47] The majority of states have enacted various types of "faithless elector" laws that require electors to vote for the candidate of the political party that nominated them.[48] *Ray v. Blair* (1952) held that states may permit political parties to require their candidates for presidential elector to pledge to cast their electoral votes for that party's presidential nominee.[49] *Chiafalo v. Washington* (2020), upholding the constitutionality of elector binding laws, affirmed that "[t]he Constitution's text and the Nation's history both support allowing a State to enforce an elector's pledge to support his party's nominee—and the state voters' choice—for President."[50]

OPEN QUESTIONS

- What should Congress do if an elector casts both of his electoral votes for candidates from his own state? Under modern circumstances, this could realistically occur only if an elector errs or deliberately chooses to cast at least one "faithless" electoral vote.

  The Electoral Meeting Clause was violated in the election of 1872 when two electors from Georgia voted for former Georgia Governor Charles Jenkins for President and former Confederate General Alfred H. Colquitt of Georgia for Vice President. During the joint session at which Congress counted electoral votes, Senator Oliver Norton objected that those votes violated the clause. The President of the Senate, presiding over the joint session, ruled that Senator Norton's objection was out of order because he had raised it too late.[51]

  In the election of 1792, four electors from Kentucky cast both of their electoral votes for candidates from Virginia: George Washington and Thomas Jefferson.[52] In the 2005 election, a Minnesota elector cast his electoral votes for both President and Vice President for John Edwards.[53] None of these votes violated the Electoral Meeting Clause, however, because the electors lived in different states from the candidates for whom they voted. Professor Derek Muller has argued that "Congress may have the power to refuse to count the votes of [an] elector[] who violate[s]" the Electoral Meeting Clause by casting both of his electoral votes for candidates from his state.[54]

- What should Congress do if electors do not transmit an accurate list of their electoral votes? The Electoral Meeting Clause provides that, after casting their electoral votes, electors must submit a signed and certified list specifying the number of electoral votes each candidate received. The Twelfth Amendment contains a modified version of this requirement.

  Congressional precedents conflict concerning the proper treatment of procedurally defective votes. On the one hand, following the election of 1800, Georgia's electors failed to provide a numerical tally of their electoral votes, and their filing was neither signed nor certified.[55] Instead, the electors simply listed their names under the headings "Jefferson" and "Burr" on the back of the certificate of ascertainment.[56] Vice President Thomas Jefferson, presiding over the joint session of Congress at which electoral votes were counted, did not raise any issue with the submission and no members of Congress objected; the votes were counted.[57] On the other hand, following the election of 1872, Arkansas filed its electoral votes without certification; the state's submission also erroneously included the seal of the Secretary of State rather than the state's official seal. By a vote of 28 to 24, the Senate rejected the votes.[58] Under Joint Rule 22, which governed the electoral count at the time, the Senate's decision was sufficient for Congress to omit Arkansas' procedurally defective votes from the results.[59]

- May Congress reject electoral votes from "faithless" electors? A faithless elector casts his electoral vote for a presidential and/or vice presidential candidate other than the ones who won the election within that elector's jurisdiction. For example, in 1969, Republicans Richard M. Nixon and Spiro T. Agnew won the popular vote in North Carolina for President and Vice President, respectively. An elector from that state nevertheless cast his electoral votes for George Wallace and Curtis E. LeMay instead.[60] An objection was lodged but was rejected by both the House and Senate, which accepted the "faithless" votes as valid.[61]

  The ECRA allows Congress to reject electoral votes that are not "regularly given."[62] The statute does not define that phrase, however. Professor Derek Muller has persuasively argued that "regularly given" means "'cast pursuant to law,' with 'law' referring to the federal Constitution, federal law, and state law."[63] Some state laws require state officials to disregard "faithless" electoral votes and appoint replacement electors to cast their votes consistent with the outcome of the popular vote.[64] Others require electors to cast their votes consistent with their state's popular vote outcome but do not provide any express statutory remedies for violations.[65] Congress might determine that electoral votes cast in direct violation of state law are not "regularly given" for purposes of the ECRA and therefore may be rejected. Still other states are silent as to electors' obligations. *Bush v. Gore* (2000) held that "[w]hen the state legislature vests the right to vote for President in its people, the right to vote as the legislature has prescribed is fundamental."[66] It is unclear whether Congress would deem it unconstitutional for an elector to cast his electoral vote—with no prior warning or notice—for someone who lost the election within the relevant jurisdiction or did not even run in the first place.

Cite as: Michael T. Morley, *The Electoral Meeting Clause, in* THE HERITAGE GUIDE TO THE CONSTITUTION 322 (Josh Blackman & John G. Malcolm eds., 3d ed. 2025).

Notes

1. Keith E. Whittington, *Originalism, Constitutional Construction, and the Problem of Faithless Electors*, 59 Ariz. L. Rev. 904, 924 (2017); James Harvey Robinson, *The Original and Derived Features of the Constitution*, 1 Annals Am. Acad. Pol. & Soc. Sci. 203, 218, 228 (1890). 2. Md. Const. of 1776, art. XIV. 3. *Id.* art. XV. 4. *Id.* art. XVIII. 5. Tyler Yeargain, *Maryland's Legislative Appointment Process: Keep It and Reform It*, 51 U. Balt. L.F. 1, 4 (2020). 6. 1 Farrand's 288–89. 7. *Id.* at 77, 80. 8. *Id.* at 77, 81. 9. 2 Farrand's 22, 32, 50, 57–58, 97, 99, 105, 107–09, 397, 404. 10. *Id.* at 113. 11. *Id.* 12. *Id.* 13. *Id.* 14. *Id.* at 114. 15. *Id.* 16. *Id.* at 115. 17. *Id.* at 493–94, 496–97. 18. *Id.* at 30, 111, 500, 501. 19. *Id.* at 512. 20. *Id.* at 518, 526; *id.* at 525 & n.21. 21. *Id.* at 517, 526. 22. *Id.* at 573, 597–98, 658. 23. *Id.* at 665. 24. 3 Farrand's 404–05; *id.* at 458–59. 25. 3 Elliot's 486; 4 Elliot's 105, 304–05. 26. 1 St. George Tucker, Blackstone's Commentaries, App. Note D at 326–27 (1803); 3 Story's Commentaries § 1451. 27. S. Jour., 1st Cong., 1st Sess. 8 (Apr. 6, 1789); H.R. Jour., 1st Cong., 1st Sess. 8–9 (Apr. 6, 1789). 28. Ch. 8, §§ 2, 4, 1 Stat. 239, 239–40 (Mar. 1, 1792); Annals of Cong., 1st Cong., 3d Sess. 1915–18 (1791). 29. Ch. 8, § 3, 1 Stat. at 240. 30. S. Jour., 2d Cong., 2d Sess. 485–86 (Feb. 13, 1793); H.R. Jour., 2d Cong., 2d Sess. 701–02 (Feb. 13, 1793). 31. S. Jour., 4th Cong., 2d Sess. 320–21 (Feb. 8, 1797); H.R. Jour., 4th Cong., 2d Sess. 685–86 (Feb. 8, 1797). 32. H.R. Jour., 6th Cong., 2d Sess. 799 (Feb. 11, 1801); S. Jour., 6th Cong., 2d Sess. 125 (Feb. 18, 1801). 33. H.R. Jour., 6th Cong., 2d Sess. 799–801 (Feb. 11, 1801); S. Jour., 6th Cong., 2d Sess. 127–28 (Feb. 18, 1801). 34. Nathan L. Colvin & Edward B. Foley, *Lost Opportunity: Learning the Wrong Lesson from the Hayes-Tilden Dispute*, 79 Fordham L. Rev. 1043, 1048–49 & n.25 (2010). 35. Ch. 50, 2 Stat. 295–96 (Mar. 26, 1804); Rev. Stat. §§ 131–45 (1874). 36. Ch. 90, §§ 1, 3, 24 Stat. 373, 373 (Feb. 3, 1887). 37. *Id.* 38. *Id.* 39. Act of May 29, 1928, ch. 859, §§ 2–4, 45 Stat. 945, 946

(1928); H.R. Rpt. No. 70-750, at 1–2 (Feb. 23, 1928). 40. Act of June 5, 1934, ch. 390, § 6(a), 48 Stat. 879, 879. 41. National Archives and Records Administration Act of 1984, Pub. L. No. 98-497, § 107(e), 98 Stat. 2280, 2291–92. 42. Pub. L. No. 117-238, Div. P, § 104(a), 136 Stat. 4459, 5234–35 (Dec. 29, 2022) (codified at 3 U.S.C. § 5(c)(1)). 43. *Id.* at 5235 (codified at 3 U.S.C. § 5(d)(1)(B)). 44. *Id.* (codified at 3 U.S.C. § 5(d)(1)(D)). 45. 1 St. George Tucker, *supra* App. Note D at 326–27; William Rawle, A View of the Constitution of the United States of America 52 (2d ed. 1822); 3 Farrand's 464. 46. 3 Story's Commentaries § 1451. 47. *Chiafalo v. Washington*, 591 U.S. 578, 593 (2020); Rawle, *supra* at 57–58; 3 Story's Commentaries § 1457. 48. *Presidential Elections*, FairVote, https://fairvote.org/resources/presidential-elections/. 49. 343 U.S. 214, 230–31 (1952). 50. 591 U.S. at 588. 51. Cong. Globe, 42d Cong., 3d Sess. 1299–1300 (Feb. 12, 1873). 52. H.R. Jour., 2d Cong., 2d Sess. 702 (Feb. 13, 1793); S. Jour., 2d Cong., 2d Sess. 485 (Feb. 13, 1793). 53. 151 Cong. Rec. 198 (Jan. 6, 2005). 54. Derek T. Muller, *Scrutinizing Federal Election Qualifications*, 90 Ind. L.J. 559, 569–70 (2015). 55. Bruce Ackerman & David Fontana, *Thomas Jefferson Counts Himself Into the Presidency*, 90 Va. L. Rev. 551, 589–92 (2004). 56. *Id.* 57. *Id.* at 614–15; H.R. Jour., 6th Cong., 2d Sess. 798–800 (Feb. 11, 1801); 6 Annals of Cong. 1023 (Feb. 11, 1801). 58. Cong. Globe, 42d Cong., 3d Sess. 1291–92 (Feb. 12, 1873). 59. Nathan L. Colvin & Edward B. Foley, *The Twelfth Amendment: A Constitutional Ticking Time Bomb*, 64 U. Miami L. Rev. 475, 498 (2010). 60. 115 Cong. Rec. 146 (1969). 61. *Id.*; *id.* at 171. 62. 3 U.S.C. § 15(d)(2)(B)(ii)(II). 63. Derek T. Muller, *Electoral Votes Regularly Given*, 55 Ga. L. Rev. 1529, 1534–35 (2021). 64. Mich. Comp. L. § 168.47; Nev. Rev. Stat. § 298.075(1), (2)(b); Va. Code § 24.2-244(C). 65. Ohio Rev. Code § 3505.40. 66. 531 U.S. 98, 104 (2000) (per curiam).

ᕮᕮᕮ

ESSAY NO. 93: THE ELECTORAL VOTE COUNTING CLAUSE
ART. II, § 1, CL. 3

The President of the Senate shall, in the Presence of the Senate and House of Representatives, open all the Certificates, and the Votes shall then be counted.

—Michael T. Morley

INTRODUCTION

The constitutional procedure for counting electoral votes in presidential elections is somewhat underspecified. The Electoral Vote Counting Clause establishes a two-step process. First, the President of the Senate (the Vice President) must open the certified lists of electoral votes from each state's electors "in the Presence of the Senate and House of Representatives." Second, the clause specifies that "the Votes shall then be counted." The consensus interpretation of this provision based on constitutional structure, historical practice, and pragmatic considerations, is that the chambers of Congress rather than the Vice President are responsible for resolving disputes concerning a state's electors or electoral votes. The Vice President's role is essentially ministerial. Some scholars, however, have argued otherwise. The Twelfth Amendment, which modified important aspects of the electoral college, retains this language about counting the votes.

THE CONSTITUTIONAL CONVENTION AND RATIFICATION

During June and July of 1787, the Framers considered various proposals to elect the President through an electoral college. None of those proposals discussed how states' electoral votes would be tallied.[1]

In late August, the Committee on Postponed Parts suggested provisions to establish an electoral college. They stated, in relevant part, that "[t]he President of the Senate shall in that House open all the certificates, and the votes shall be then and there counted. . . ."[2] On September 6, the Convention voted without debate to require that the electoral votes be "counted in the presence of the Senate and House of Representatives."[3] In adopting that amendment, the Convention eliminated the requirement that counting occur in the Senate chamber.[4] After the Committee on Style made a few nonsubstantive modifications to capitalization and punctuation, the clause was included in the Constitution.[5]

Neither the ratification debates nor The Federalist Papers specifically discussed either the process for counting electoral votes or the respective roles of the Vice President and Congress in that process. These sources do not appear to have contemplated the possibility of any conflicts or difficulties in counting electoral votes.

EARLY COMMENTARY

None of the jurists who wrote about the electoral count process in the early nineteenth century suggested that the Constitution grants the Vice President any substantive authority or discretion over the matter. William Rawle explained that electoral votes are "transmitted to the senate . . . to be opened by its president in the presence of the senate and house of representatives."[6] St. George Tucker made a similar point.[7] Neither suggested the Vice President played any role in resolving disputes.

Justice Joseph Story elaborated that the Constitution made "no provision" for resolving "any questions which may arise" concerning the validity of electors' appointments, the "regularity and authenticity" of their electoral votes, or "the manner and circumstances in which they ought to be counted."[8] Rather, "[i]t seems to have been taken for granted, that no question could ever arise on the subject; and that nothing more was necessary than to open the certificates which were produced, in the presence of both

327

houses, and to count the names and numbers, as returned."[9] Story suggested, however, that such "very delicate and interesting inquiries" should be "debated and decided by some deliberative body."[10] This approach would preclude the Vice President from unilaterally resolving disputes concerning electors or electoral votes.

Chancellor James Kent noted that "[t]he constitution does not expressly declare *by whom* the votes are to be counted, and the result declared."[11] He therefore "presume[d]" that "the president of the senate counts the votes, and determines the result, and that the two houses are present only as spectators."[12] Kent did not provide any explanation for his "presum[ption]," however. In any event, he construed the Electoral Vote Counting Clause as establishing a constitutional default rule,[13] applicable only "in the absence of all legislative provision on the subject."[14] Since 1865, Congress has adopted rules and statutes specifying how disputes relating to the electoral count would be resolved. Thus, even under Kent's view, the Vice President today cannot assert any constitutional prerogative to accept or reject electoral votes.

THE FIRST PRESIDENTIAL ELECTION

After the Constitution was signed, the Constitutional Convention passed an accompanying resolution declaring that, once the Constitution was ratified, states should elect Senators, Representatives, and presidential electors.[15] The resolution specified that, after those electors transmitted their electoral votes "to the Secretary of the United States in Congress assembled," the newly chosen Senators should "appoint a [temporary] President of the Senate, for the sole Purpose of receiving, opening and counting the Votes for President. . . ."[16] At that point, neither the President nor the Vice President would have been elected. The resolution did not mention the chambers of Congress participating in the electoral count, nor did it address how any potential problems with the count or controversies concerning electors would be resolved.

Fortunately, no such conflicts arose. On April 6, 1789, after the Senate achieved a quorum, it elected John Langdon of New Hampshire as Senate President "for the sole purpose of opening and counting the votes for President of the United States."[17] The Senate went on to elect William Paterson of New Jersey as "a teller on the part of the Senate" to "sit at the Clerk's desk to make a list of the votes as they shall be declared."[18] The House similarly appointed two members "to sit at the Clerk's table with the member of the Senate, and make a list of the votes as the same shall be declared."[19]

The Senate and House then met in joint session in the Senate chamber to count electoral votes. George Washington was "unanimously" elected President with sixty-nine votes, and John Adams was elected Vice President with thirty-four votes.[20] Following the joint session, the Senate reconvened and elected Langdon as its President pro tempore.[21] Langdon announced that "the Senate and House of Representatives had met, and that he, in their presence, had opened and counted the votes of the electors for President and Vice President."[22] He went on to list the candidates' tallies from each state.[23] Similarly, when the House reconvened, its two tellers "delivered in at the Clerk's table a list of the votes of all the electors . . . as the same were declared by the President of the Senate, in the presence of the Senate and of this House."[24] There is no record of any objections being raised or other problems or disputes arising during the count.

OTHER EARLY ELECTIONS

In 1792, before the second presidential election, Congress passed a statute to establish certain procedures for the electoral college. The Presidential Election and Succession Act of 1792 required each state to submit two certificates to the President of the Senate: one from the state's executive identifying its presidential electors, and the other from the electors containing their electoral votes.[25] Congress would convene "on the second Wednesday in February . . . and the said certificates . . . shall then be opened, the votes counted, and the persons who shall fill the offices of President and Vice President ascertained and declared, agreeably to the Constitution."[26]

Shortly before convening to count electoral votes from the election of 1792, Congress adopted a concurrent resolution stating that each chamber would appoint tellers to "make a list of the votes as they shall be declared."[27] At the count's conclusion, the tellers would deliver those lists to the President of the Senate to announce the results.[28] Congress has since adopted a concurrent resolution setting forth the procedures for the electoral count before each such joint session.

When Congress met to count the electoral votes from the 1792 election, Vice President John Adams presided over the joint session in his capacity as President of the Senate. Adams "opened, read, and delivered to the tellers" the electoral votes.[29] The tellers, in turn, "examined and ascertained the votes" and prepared a list of each candidate's vote tally.[30] At the end of the session, Adams read the tellers' list to the chamber, declaring that he and President Washington had been re-elected.[31]

Following the presidential election of 1796, Vice President Adams again presided over the joint session of Congress to count electoral votes. Adams and former Secretary of State Thomas Jefferson were the leading candidates for President. Allegations had arisen earlier that Vermont's electors had not been appointed properly,[32] but no one objected to Vermont's electoral votes or otherwise raised the issue during the joint session.[33]

Adams opened the packet from each state and read the certificate of election for its electors.[34] The Senate Clerk then read the electors' votes and gave the state's documents to the tellers.[35] At the conclusion of the count, the tellers "reported the result" to Adams.[36] Adams then announced the number of electoral votes each candidate had received: "By the report which has been made to me by the tellers . . . there are 71 votes for John Adams, 68 for Thomas Jefferson . . . . [T]he person who has 71 votes, which is the highest number, is elected President, and the person who has 68 votes, which is the next highest number, is elected Vice President."[37] This tally included Vermont's four electoral votes for Adams and four electoral votes for Thomas Pinckney.[38]

The Annals of Congress note that at this point, Adams "sat down for a moment."[39] He then rose again and declared that he had won the presidency and Jefferson was Vice President.[40] Some scholars have suggested that Adams's decision to sit down was intended to give political opponents an opportunity to object to Vermont's votes.[41] They contend that this action suggests Adams "harbored some doubts about his authority as President of the Senate to resolve disputed issues unilaterally."[42]

THE ELECTION OF 1800

In advance of the 1800 election, Congress considered a bill to resolve any disputes that might arise. As passed by the Senate, the bill would have established a Grand Committee comprised of Senators and Representatives with the "power to examine, and finally to decide all disputes relative to" the presidential election.[43] The House version of the bill would have allowed the committee to gather evidence but gave it "no decisive[] powers."[44] The chambers were unable to resolve their differences and the measure died.[45] Importantly, however, neither chamber even considered the possibility of allowing the Vice President to resolve disputes over electoral votes, and none of the bill's opponents suggested that the Constitution granted the Vice President such power.

Following the presidential election, Vice President Jefferson presided over the joint session of Congress to count electoral votes. After Jefferson opened the certificate from each state, its electoral votes were read aloud and the tellers added them to a running tally.[46] Georgia's electoral votes, which were dispositive to the election's outcome, were not formatted according to constitutional requirements.[47] Although the official journals do not mention the problem, a contemporaneous newspaper reported that "[t]he Tellers declared there was some informality in the votes of Georgia, but believing them to be the true votes, reported them as such."[48] Accordingly, Georgia's votes were counted for Jefferson and Aaron Burr.[49] Professors Bruce Ackerman and David Fontana speculate that Jefferson had likely "asserted his authority" as President of the Senate to "decisively resolve[] the issue by counting" the votes.[50] This conclusion reflects a substantial leap, however, because the tellers accepted the votes as valid, and there is no record of any member objecting to the votes once the defect was announced.[51] Thus, it is far from clear that Jefferson exercised—or even purported to exercise—any decision-making authority.

Largely in response to the election of 1800, the Twelfth Amendment was adopted, modifying several key aspects of the electoral college. Congress implemented those constitutional changes by making corresponding amendments to the 1792 Presidential Election and Succession Act.[52] The revised statute provided that electoral votes "shall be opened by the president of the Senate, for the purpose of being counted."[53] It did not otherwise reference the President of the Senate's role.

ANTEBELLUM VOTE COUNTS

The Election of 1804 was the first presidential election conducted under the Twelfth Amendment. President of the Senate Aaron Burr opened the electoral count by declaring to the tellers, "You will now proceed gentlemen . . . to count the votes as the Constitution and laws direct."[54] This announcement appears to disclaim any substantive power over vote counting. Objections were raised to electoral votes from Indiana in 1817 and Missouri in 1821 on the grounds that those territories had not become states in time for their votes to count.[55] Senate Presidents, however, played no role in resolving those unsuccessful objections.

The closest the President of the Senate came to exercising substantive authority was in 1857. Wisconsin's electors had cast their electoral votes in the state capitol one day late because of inclement weather.[56] Shortly before Congress began to count the electoral votes, it adopted a concurrent resolution to govern the proceedings as it had done before each count since 1793.[57] The resolution, like previous ones, directed tellers appointed by each chamber to "make a list of the votes as they shall be declared" and "deliver[]" the "result" to the President of the Senate *pro tempore*, who would announce "the state of the vote" and the "persons elected."[58]

During the joint session, Virginia Representative John Letcher objected to counting Wisconsin's votes.[59] Senate President Pro Tempore James Mason replied that the concurrent resolution governing the proceedings did not permit motions or debate during the vote count.[60] James Buchanan of Pennsylvania ultimately prevailed with 174 electoral votes, defeating John C. Fremont of California who had received only 114 votes, including Wisconsin's

five electoral votes.[61] Given the margin, Wisconsin's votes did not affect the outcome.

At the count's conclusion, Letcher nevertheless renewed his effort to have Wisconsin's votes excluded.[62] Mason again responded that, under the concurrent resolution Congress had adopted, "nothing can be done here but to count the votes by tellers, and to declare the vote" results to the joint session.[63] He added that "[w]hat further action may be taken . . . will devolve upon" the chambers of Congress.[64]

After the joint session dissolved, both chambers debated the validity of Wisconsin's votes. During the Senate debates, Mason clarified that he "utterly disclaims and never asserted" the power to rule on that issue.[65] Had the election's outcome turned on those votes, he "would have considered it his duty to have reported" that fact to the joint session to allow Congress to decide how to "canvass[] the [electoral] votes."[66] While numerous members in both chambers argued that Wisconsin's votes were invalid,[67] both chambers rejected resolutions declaring that they should have been rejected.[68]

LATE NINETEENTH-CENTURY ELECTORAL COUNTS AND CONGRESSIONAL ENACTMENTS

During the late nineteenth century, Congress adopted several measures to regulate the electoral count, but none of them granted the President of the Senate authority to either determine the validity of electoral votes or resolve disputes concerning competing slates of electors. In 1864, toward the end of the Civil War, federal elections were held in several areas of the Confederacy that were controlled by the Union Army. The following February, Congress adopted Joint Resolution No. 12 which declared that the eleven Confederate states—individually named in the resolution—had "rebelled" and therefore were "not entitled to representation in the Electoral College" in the 1864 election.[69] The resolution specified that "no electoral votes shall be received or counted" from those states.[70]

That year, Congress also adopted Joint Rule 22 to memorialize the procedure for counting electoral votes. The rule required the President of the Senate to open certificates of electoral votes and hand them to tellers appointed by the

House and Senate to read aloud and tally.[71] If "any question shall arise in regard to counting the votes" from a particular state, the joint session would dissolve to allow each chamber to vote separately on the issue.[72] The rule specified that "no question shall be decided affirmatively, and no vote objected to shall be counted, except by the concurring vote of the two Houses."[73] Thus, under Joint Rule 22, a single chamber of Congress could reject a proposed slate of electors or electoral votes, but the Vice President lacked the authority to do so.

During the joint session following the 1864 presidential election, President of the Senate Hannibal Hamlin refrained from opening or giving the tellers certificates of electoral votes from the Confederate states of Louisiana and Tennessee, which were largely under Union control.[74] At the count's conclusion, Senator Edgar Cowan of Pennsylvania asked "whether there [were] any further returns to be counted."[75] Hamlin replied that he had received returns from Louisiana and Tennessee, "but in obedience to the law of the land the Chair holds it to be his duty not to present them to the convention."[76]

Representative George H. Yeaman of Kentucky then moved that Hamlin open and present "all the returns before this joint convention . . . for its consideration."[77] Hamlin responded that "if either branch of Congress shall be disposed to order the returns now upon the table to be read, it is within their power to do so."[78] Once those returns were read, "then would arise another question, whether the vote in the return so read should be added to the count of the tellers."[79] Upon learning that the joint session would have to dissolve to allow each chamber to vote on his motion, Yeaman withdrew it.[80] Thus, the count concluded without including electoral votes from Louisiana or Tennessee. Those votes, however, would not have affected the results: President Abraham Lincoln beat General George B. McClellan decisively by a vote of 212 to 21.[81] Even here, the Vice President did not exercise any independent discretion, but rather performed a ministerial duty in compliance with Joint Resolution No. 12, which explicitly prohibited the acceptance of electoral votes from Louisiana, Tennessee, and other Confederate states.

The Senate rescinded Joint Rule 22 in early 1876.[82] In the presidential election later that year between Democrat Samuel Tilden and Republican Rutherford B. Hayes, disputes arose over competing slates of electors submitted by Louisiana, South Carolina, Florida, and Oregon.[83] As Chief Justice William H. Rehnquist has explained, "Hayes and some of his Republican supporters contended that the decision of the Senate president as to which set of returns to count should be final."[84]

Flatly rejecting that approach, Congress instead adopted the Electoral Commission Act of 1877.[85] The Act specified that if Congress received only a single certificate of electoral votes from a state, those votes had to be counted unless both chambers voted to reject them.[86] In contrast, when Congress received multiple certificates from competing sets of electors in a state, all of that state's returns had to be submitted to a special commission comprised of five representatives, five senators, and five Supreme Court justices.[87] The commission was to render its "judgment and decision as to which is the true and lawful electoral vote of such state."[88] Its determination would be final unless both chambers of Congress voted concurrently to overturn it.[89] The commission resolved all of the disputes in Hayes's favor and, consistent with those determinations, he prevailed by an electoral vote of 185 to 184.[90]

A decade later, Congress passed the Electoral Count Act of 1887 to establish a more permanent framework for resolving disputes concerning electoral votes. The statute governed electoral counts for almost a century and a half.[91] Neither the Electoral Commission Act nor the Electoral Count Act gave the Vice President substantive power to accept or reject either electors' appointments or electoral votes.

TWENTIETH-CENTURY PRESIDENTIAL ELECTIONS

Electoral counts throughout the early twentieth century generally occurred without incident. The two leading presidential candidates in the election of 1960 were Vice President Richard M. Nixon and Senator John F. Kennedy. In Hawaii, following the initial count of the popular vote, Nixon led by 141 votes.[92] Because the race was so close, a state court ordered a recount that remained ongoing by December 19, the date on which federal law required electors to cast their electoral votes. Accordingly, the governor of Hawaii certified the Republican electors as the victors.[93] They cast their three electoral votes for Nixon and submitted a certificate of their votes to the federal government.[94]

Due to the ongoing recount, however, the Democratic candidates for presidential elector also met that day and purported to cast their own electoral votes for Kennedy.[95] They submitted their certificate without any endorsement from state authorities. Nearly two weeks later, after the recount's completion, a state court determined that Kennedy had prevailed in Hawaii by 115 votes.[96] Hawaii's newly elected governor submitted a third certificate to Congress declaring the Democratic electors to be the winners.[97]

On January 6, 1961, Congress convened in joint session with Vice President Nixon presiding to count electoral votes.[98] Upon reaching Hawaii's votes, Nixon announced that he had received "three certificates from persons claiming to be the duly appointed electors from the State of Hawaii."[99] He handed each certificate to the tellers to read aloud.[100] After the certificates were read into the record, Nixon announced that he had "knowledge" and was "convinced that he [was] supported by the facts" that the third certificate, confirming that the Democratic electors had won, "properly and legally portrays the facts with respect to the electors chosen by the people of Hawaii at the election."[101] He noted that those electors had cast their three electoral votes for Kennedy.[102]

Nixon continued: "In order not to delay the further count of the electoral vote here, the Chair, without the intent of establishing a precedent, *suggests* that the electors named in the certificate of the Governor of Hawaii dated January 4, 1961, be considered as the lawful electors from the State of Hawaii."[103] He added that "[i]f there be no objection," he would instruct the tellers to count those electors' votes for Kennedy.[104] No such objections were raised, and the votes were counted.[105]

Thus, rather than asserting authority to resolve any dispute over Hawaii's electoral votes, Nixon instead "suggest[ed]" a solution to the joint session and acted only "without

objection."[106] In any event, Republicans had little incentive to challenge Hawaii's three electoral votes because they were not dispositive: Kennedy defeated Nixon in the Electoral College by a margin of 303 to 219 (with fifteen electoral votes cast for Senator Harry F. Byrd of Virginia).[107]

During the joint session following the hotly contested 2000 election that culminated in *Bush v. Gore*,[108] Vice President Al Gore declared several objections out of order and refused to recognize points of order because they did not comply with the Electoral Count Act's procedural requirements.[109] After the 2004 election, in contrast, when a procedurally valid objection to Ohio's electoral votes was lodged during the joint session, Vice President Dick Cheney directed the chambers to "withdraw" to "deliberate separately" and "report [their] decision[s] back to the joint session."[110] Both chambers rejected the objection.[111]

THE ELECTION OF 2020

Following the 2020 election, Vice President Michael Pence rejected efforts to persuade him to either determine the validity of electoral votes or otherwise delay the proceedings.[112] In a letter to Congress, Pence wrote that his role would be "largely ceremonial."[113] "I do not believe that the Founders of our country intended to invest the Vice President with unilateral authority to decide which electoral votes should be counted during the Joint Session of Congress," he explained, "and no Vice President in American history has ever asserted such authority."[114] He opened the joint session by announcing that:

> After ascertaining that the certificates [of electoral votes] are regular in form and authentic, the tellers will announce the votes cast by the electors for each State . . . which the Parliamentarians have advised me is the only certificate of vote from that State, and purports to be a return from the State, and that has annexed to it a certificate from an authority of that State purporting to appoint or ascertain electors.[115]

Thus, Vice President Pence declined to present

to the joint session any "competing" slates of purported electors that had not been certified by state executives.

In the wake of January 6, Congress passed the Electoral Count Reform Act (ECRA) of 2022.[116] This law eliminated any potential ambiguity about the President of the Senate's role. It expressly specifies that "the role of the President of the Senate while presiding over the joint session shall be limited to performing solely ministerial duties."[117] Moreover, "[t]he President of the Senate shall have no power to solely determine, accept, reject, or otherwise adjudicate or resolve disputes over the proper certificate of ascertainment of appointment of electors, the validity of electors, or the votes of electors."[118]

MODERN ACADEMIC COMMENTARY

Some scholars have argued that both the Framers' intent and early practice suggest that the Vice President may exercise at least some substantive power over the electoral count.[119] As noted, however, early history provides limited support at best for such an interpretation. Moreover, despite such evidence, Vasan Kesavan concluded that the "better interpretation" is that the chambers of Congress have such power.[120]

Professors Jack Beerman and Gary Lawson argue that the Constitution's delegation of power to the President of the Senate to open the certificates of states' electoral votes implicitly empowers him to resolve disputes concerning those votes.[121] One could just as easily contend, however, that the Constitution's limited grant of authority to the Senate President to "open" states' certificates implicitly precludes him from asserting any greater prerogatives. Professors Beerman and Lawson further suggest that the Senate President's rulings are reviewable in federal court,[122] but a lawsuit of that sort would face substantial obstacles such as the political question doctrine.[123]

Professors Robert J. Delahunty and John Yoo contend that the Senate President must have constitutional power to resolve disputes concerning competing slates of electors because, in their view, Congress lacks such authority.[124] While they correctly note that the Framers wanted the President to be independent of Congress, such concerns do not imply that the Framers authorized a single person—particularly the Vice President, who would often be a presidential candidate—to resolve electoral disputes instead.[125]

OPEN QUESTIONS

- The Electoral Count Reform Act of 2022 clarifies that the Vice President plays only a circumscribed "ministerial" role during the joint session at which Congress counts electoral votes.[126] It is unclear, however, what remedies would be available if the Vice President were to exceed that role, decline to present a particular certified slate of electoral votes from a state to the joint session, or entertain objections that the ECRA does not authorize. Specifically, it is unclear whether the Vice President's ruling or other action would be subject to appeal and, if so, whether a majority of each chamber would have to vote to uphold the appeal. It is similarly unclear whether mandamus or other judicial relief would be available in this context.
- The ECRA allows Congress to reject electoral votes if they are not "regularly given,"[127] but it does not define that term. The circumstances under which Congress may exercise this authority are unclear. For example, may Congress reject electoral votes cast in violation of a state "faithless elector" statute that specifies how electors must cast their votes? May Congress reject votes for a deceased candidate?

Cite as: Michael T. Morley, *The Electoral Vote Counting Clause, in* THE HERITAGE GUIDE TO THE CONSTITUTION 327 (Josh Blackman & John G. Malcolm eds., 3d ed. 2025).

Notes

1. 1 Farrand's 77, 80–81; 2 Farrand's 22, 32, 50, 57–58, 97, 99, 105, 107–09. **2.** 2 Farrand's 493–94, 497–98. **3.** *Id.* at 518, 520, 526. **4.** *Id.* at 521, 528. **5.** *Id.* at 598. **6.** William Rawle, A View of the Constitution of the United States of America 53 (2d ed. 1829). **7.** 1 St. George Tucker, Blackstone's Commentaries: With Notes of Reference to the Constitution and Laws of the Federal Government of the United States and of the Commonwealth of Virginia, App. Note D at 326–27 (1803). **8.** 2 Story's Commentaries § 1470. **9.** *Id.* **10.** *Id.* **11.** 1 James Kent, Commentaries on American Law 258 (1826). **12.** *Id.* **13.** Nicholas Quinn Rosenkranz, *Federal Rules of Statutory Interpretation*, 115 Harv. L. Rev. 2085, 2098 (2002). **14.** Kent, *supra* at 258. **15.** 2 Farrand's 665–66. **16.** *Id.* at 666. **17.** S. Jour., 1st Cong., 1st Sess. 7 (Apr. 6, 1789). **18.** *Id.* at 7–8. **19.** H.R. Jour., 1st Cong., 1st Sess. 7 (Apr. 6, 1789). **20.** S. Jour., 1st Cong., 1st Sess. 8 (Apr. 6, 1789); H.R. Jour., 1st Cong., 1st Sess. 8 (Apr. 6, 1789); Seth Barrett Tillman & Josh Blackman, *Offices and Officers of the Constitution, Part III: The Appointments, Impeachment, Commissions, and Oath or Affirmation Clauses*, 62 S. Tex. L. Rev. 349, 425–26 (2023). **21.** S. Jour., 1st Cong., 1st Sess. 8 (Apr. 6, 1789). **22.** *Id.* **23.** *Id.* **24.** H.R. Jour., 1st Cong., 1st Sess. 7 (Apr. 6, 1789). **25.** Presidential Election and Succession Act of 1792, Ch. 8, §§ 2–3, 1 Stat. 239, 239–40 (Mar. 1, 1792); 1 Annals of Cong., 1st Cong., 3rd Sess. 1915–18 (1791). **26.** Presidential Election and Succession Act of 1792, § 5, 1 Stat. at 240. **27.** S. Jour., 2d Cong., 1st Sess. 484 (Feb. 11, 1793); H.R. Jour., 2d Cong., 1st Sess. 699–700 (Feb. 11, 1793). **28.** S. Jour., 2d Cong., 1st Sess. 484 (Feb. 11, 1793); H.R. Jour., 2d Cong., 1st Sess. 699–700 (Feb. 11, 1793). **29.** S. Jour., 2d Cong., 2d Sess. 485 (Feb. 13, 1793); H.R. Jour., 2d Cong., 2d Sess. 701 (Feb. 13, 1793). **30.** S. Jour., 2d Cong., 2d Sess. 485 (Feb. 13, 1793). **31.** *Id.* at 485–86. **32.** Bruce Ackerman & David Fontana, *Thomas Jefferson Counts Himself Into the Presidency*, 90 Va. L. Rev. 551, 571–73 (2004). **33.** 6 Annals of Cong. 2095–98 (1797). **34.** *Id.* at 2096. **35.** *Id.* **36.** *Id.* at 2097. **37.** *Id.* at 2097–98. **38.** *Id.* at 2096–97. **39.** *Id.* at 2098. **40.** *Id.* **41.** Ackerman & Fontana, *supra* at 581 (citing Edward Stanwood, A History of the Presidency from 1788 to 1897, at 52 (rev. Charles Knowles Bolton, 1926)). **42.** *Id.* **43.** An Act Prescribing the Mode of Deciding Disputed Elections of President and Vice-President of the United States, S.9, 6th Cong., 1st Sess., § 1 (Mar. 31, 1800); 10 Annals of Cong. 146 (1800); *id.* at 176–77. **44.** 10 Annals of Cong. 691–92 (1800); *id.* at 697. **45.** *Id.* at 176–77, 179, 182, 713. **46.** H.R. Jour., 6th Cong., 2d Sess. 796–97 (Feb. 11, 1801); S. Jour., 6th Cong., 2d Sess. 124–25 (Feb. 11, 1801); 10 Annals of Cong. 1023–24 (1801). **47.** Ackerman & Fontana, *supra* at 588. **48.** *Id.* at 601 (quoting Aurora & Gen. Advertiser (Phila.), Feb. 11, 1801, at 2). **49.** 10 Annals of Cong. 1024 (1801). **50.** Ackerman & Fontana, *supra* at 603, 631. **51.** 10 Annals of Cong. 1023–24 (1801); Ackerman & Fontana, *supra* at 601 n.25. **52.** Ch. 50, 2 Stat. 295–96 (1804). **53.** *Id.* § 2, 2 Stat. at 296. **54.** 8 Annals of Cong. 56 (1805). **55.** 14 Annals of Cong. 944, 949 (1817); 16 Annals of Cong. 346, 1154, 1163–64 (1821). **56.** Cong. Globe, 34th Cong., 3d Sess. 652 (1857); *id.* at 660 (statement of Rep. James C. Jones). **57.** *Id.* at 587 (Feb. 5, 1857). **58.** *Id.* **59.** *Id.* at 652 (statement of Rep. John Letcher). **60.** *Id.* (statement of Senate President Pro Tempore James Mason). **61.** *Id.* **62.** *Id.* (statement of Rep. John Letcher). **63.** *Id.* (statement of Senate President Pro Tempore James Mason). **64.** *Id.* **65.** *Id.* at 645, 649 (statement of Senate President Pro Tempore James Mason). **66.** *Id.* at 645. **67.** Vasan Kesavan, *Is the Electoral Count Act Unconstitutional?*, 80 N.C. L. Rev. 1653, 1686 (2002). **68.** Cong. Globe, 34th Cong., 3d Sess. 650 (1857); *id.* at 674–75. **69.** Cong. Globe, 38th Cong., 2d Sess. App. 159 (1865); H.R. Jour., 38th Cong., 2d Sess. 191 (1865); S. Jour., 38th Cong., 2d Sess. 136 (Feb. 4, 1865); Cong. Globe, 38th Cong., 2d Sess. 595, 602 (1865). **70.** Cong. Globe, 38th Cong., 2d Sess. App. 159 (1865). **71.** *Id.* at 608, 628. **72.** *Id.* **73.** *Id.* **74.** *Id.* at 668. **75.** *Id.* **76.** *Id.* **77.** *Id.* **78.** *Id.* at 669. **79.** *Id.* **80.** *Id.* **81.** *Id.* **82.** William H. Rehnquist, Centennial Crisis: The Disputed Election of 1876, at 100 (2004). **83.** Edward B. Foley, Ballot Battles: The History of Disputed Elections in the United States 119, 123–24 (2016). **84.** Rehnquist, *supra* at 100. **85.** Ch. 37, § 1, 19 Stat. 227, 227 (Jan. 29, 1877). **86.** *Id.* at 227–28. **87.** *Id.* § 2, 19 Stat. at 228. **88.** *Id.* **89.** *Id.* at 229. **90.** Cong. Globe, 44th Cong., 2d Sess. 2068 (1877). **91.** An Act to Fix the Day for the Meeting of the Electors of President and Vice-President, and to Provide for and Regulate the Counting of the Votes for President and Vice-President, and the Decision of Questions Arising Thereon, Pub. L. No. 49-90, § 4, 24 Stat. 373, 373–74 (Feb. 3, 1887). **92.** Nathan L. Colvin & Edward B. Foley, *The Twelfth Amendment: A Constitutional Ticking Time Bomb*, 64 U. Miami L. Rev. 475, 519 (2010). **93.** *Id.* at 520. **94.** *Id.* **95.** *Id.* **96.** *Id.* (citing *Lum v. Bush*, Civ. No. 7029 (Haw. Cir. Ct. Dec. 30, 1960)). **97.** *Id.* **98.** 107 Cong. Rec. 288–89 (1961). **99.** *Id.* at 289. **100.** *Id.* **101.** *Id.* at 290. **102.** *Id.* **103.** *Id.* (emphasis added). **104.** *Id.* **105.** *Id.* **106.** *Id.* **107.** *Id.* at 291. **108.** 531 U.S. 98 (2000) (per curiam). **109.** 147 Cong. Rec. H32, H34–36 (2001); 163 Cong. Rec. H186–H189 (2017). **110.** 151 Cong. Rec. H86 (2005). **111.** *Id.* at H128. **112.** Annie Karni, *Pence Rejects Trump's Pressure to Block Certification Saying He "Loves the Constitution,"* N.Y. Times (Jan. 6, 2021), https://perma.cc/3VWH-365J. **113.** Vice President Mike Pence's Full Statement on the Electoral Count (Jan. 6, 2001), https://perma.cc/2NTS-SGQC. **114.** *Id.* **115.** 167 Cong. Rec. H76 (2021). **116.** Pub. L. No. 117-238, Div. P, § 1, 136 Stat. 4459, 5233 (Dec. 29, 2022). **117.** *Id.* § 109(a), 136 Stat. at 5238 (codified at 3 U.S.C. § 15(b)(1)). **118.** *Id.* (codified at 3 U.S.C. § 15(b)(2)). **119.** Kesavan, *supra* at 1706; Colvin & Foley, *supra* at 480 (citing C.C. Tansill, *Congressional Control of the Electoral System*, 34 Yale L.J. 511, 511 (1925), and David A. McKnight, The Electoral System of the United States 17 (1878)). **120.** Kesavan, *supra* at 1706. **121.** Jack Beerman & Gary Lawson, *The Electoral Count Mess: The Electoral Count Act of 1887 Is Unconstitutional, and Other Fun Facts (Plus a Few Random Academic Speculations) About Counting Electoral Votes*, 16 FIU L. Rev. 297, 304–05 (2022). **122.** *Id.* at 305. **123.** Michael T. Morley, *The Enforcement Act of 1870, Federal Jurisdiction Over Election Contests, and the Political Question Doctrine*, 72 Fla. L. Rev. 1153, 1206–08 (2020). **124.** Robert J. Delahunty & John Yoo, *Who Counts? The Twelfth Amendment, the Vice President, and the Electoral Count*, 73 Case W. Rsrv. L. Rev. 27, 61, 90 (2022); Beerman & Lawson, *supra* at 305–06. **125.** Derek T. Muller, *The President of the Senate, the Original Public Meaning of the Twelfth Amendment, and the Electoral Count Reform Act*, 73 Case W. Rsrv. L. Rev. 1023, 1025 (2023). **126.** 3 U.S.C. § 15(b). **127.** *Id.* § 15(d)(2)(B)(ii)(II).

~

ESSAY NO. 94: THE PRESIDENTIAL MAJORITY AND CONTINGENT ELECTIONS CLAUSE
ART. II, § 1, CL. 3

The Person having the greatest Number of Votes shall be the President, if such Number be a Majority of the whole Number of Electors appointed; and if there be more than one who have such Majority, and have an equal Number of Votes, then the House of Representatives shall immediately chuse by Ballot one of them for President; and if no Person have a Majority, then from the five highest on the List the said House shall in like Manner chuse the President. But in chusing the President, the Votes shall be taken by States, the Representation from each State having one Vote; A quorum for this purpose shall consist of a Member or Members from two thirds of the States, and a Majority of all the States shall be necessary to a Choice. In every Case, after the Choice of the President, the Person having the greatest Number of Votes of the Electors shall be the Vice President. But if there should remain two or more who have equal Votes, the Senate shall chuse from them by Ballot the Vice President.

—Michael T. Morley

INTRODUCTION

In elections held under the Presidential Majority & Contingent Elections Clause, each presidential elector cast two electoral votes. The candidate with the most electoral votes was generally elected President as long as he had received votes from a majority of electors. The runner-up was elected Vice President. If the Electoral College failed to elect a President, the House of Representatives would hold a contingent election for that office. Each state's Representatives collectively cast a single vote, and a candidate needed to receive a majority to prevail. If two or more candidates tied for the position of Vice President, the Senate would choose among them. Contingent elections for President were held following the elections of 1800 and 1824. The nation's only contingent election for Vice President occurred following the election of 1836. The Twelfth Amendment, ratified in 1804, changed most aspects of this clause.

THE MECHANICS OF COUNTING ELECTORAL VOTES

The constitutional provisions that originally governed the Electoral College differed substantially from the current rules established primarily by the Twelfth Amendment. Under the Constitution as originally adopted, each presidential elector cast two electoral votes. To be elected President through the Electoral College, a candidate had to receive the "greatest Number" of electoral votes, and that figure had to reflect electoral votes from a majority of the presidential electors who had been appointed. The person with the next-highest number of electoral votes generally became Vice President.

As noted, the number of electoral votes required to win the presidency was based on the number of electors appointed, not the number of electoral votes cast. This distinction was particularly important under the original constitutional rules because each elector cast two undifferentiated electoral votes that were all tallied together. Mathematically, a candidate who had accumulated barely more than a quarter of the total number of electoral votes cast necessarily would have received votes from a majority of electors. For example, if fifty electors each cast two electoral votes, a total of 100 votes would have been cast. A candidate would need to receive only twenty-six to have accumulated votes from a majority of the fifty electors appointed.

The Twelfth Amendment has rendered

this issue less salient because each elector now casts only a single electoral vote for the office of President (along with a distinct electoral vote for Vice President). Thus, the number of electors appointed and the total number of electoral votes cast are now generally equal.

Under both the original Constitution and the Twelfth Amendment, when a state fails to appoint one or more of its electors or Congress declines to accept their appointments as valid, the total number of "electors appointed" decreases. The number of electoral votes a candidate would need to win the presidency accordingly is subject to reduction as well. The fewer "electors appointed," the smaller the "Majority" a candidate needs to prevail.

However, if Congress seats a state's electors but rejects one or more of their electoral votes as invalid or otherwise declines to count them, those actions do not affect the number of "electors appointed." Similarly, if an elector abstains, declining to cast an electoral vote (where permitted by state law), that person is still deemed to have been "appointed." In these cases, the necessary "Majority" of electoral votes a candidate must receive to become President would be unaffected even though fewer electoral votes are available to be allocated among the candidates.[1]

THE MECHANICS OF A CONTINGENT ELECTION

The Presidential Majority and Contingent Elections Clause also provided for two possible contingencies in which the Electoral College failed to elect a President and the choice "immediately" devolved to the House of Representatives. First, when two or more candidates tied, each with votes from a majority of electors, the House of Representatives chose the President from between (or among) them. Second, when no candidate received electoral votes from "a Majority of the whole Number of Electors appointed," the House chose the President from among the "five highest on the List." The Constitution did not specify whether the House could consider more than five candidates when certain types of ties arose—for example, if two or more candidates each received the fifth-highest number of votes in the electoral college.

During either type of contingent election, the vote was "taken by States." In other words,

each state cast a single vote regardless of how many representatives it had. One or more representatives from at least two-thirds of the states had to be present to establish a quorum for this purpose.

When a contingent election is required, the House adopts rules to govern how each state's vote will be determined. Following the presidential election of 1800, when the House anticipated that Thomas Jefferson and Aaron Burr would tie in the electoral college,[2] it adopted rules for a two-person race. The rules specified that each state's representatives would "ballot among themselves" to determine how their state's vote would be cast.[3] Under the circumstances, the rules did not explicitly state whether a candidate had to receive ballots from a plurality or majority of those representatives in order to win the state's vote. If a state's representatives were "evenly divided," its vote would be recorded as "divided," which was effectively an abstention.[4] Pursuant to the Presidential Majority and Contingent Elections Clause, a candidate had to receive votes from a "Majority of all the States" to be elected President.

The only other contingent election for President in the House occurred after the Election of 1824, in which none of the candidates received votes from a majority of electors. Since that election occurred after the adoption of the Twelfth Amendment in 1804, the House was required to choose from among the candidates with the three highest vote tallies in the electoral college. The House's rules specified that a majority of the state's representatives had to cast their ballots for a particular candidate for that person to receive the state's vote; if no candidate received such a majority, the state's vote would be recorded as "divided."[5] Again, votes from a majority of states were required for a candidate to win the presidency.

The Twelfth Amendment changed the process established by the Presidential Majority and Contingent Elections Clause in three primary ways. First, electors no longer cast two undifferentiated electoral votes. Instead, they cast one vote for President and one for Vice President. Accordingly, it is no longer possible for multiple candidates to each receive electoral votes from a majority of electors. Second, during a contingent election, the House may now consider only candidates who received the three highest numbers of electoral votes for President (meaning more than three candidates may be considered if some of them are tied). Third, the Vice President also must now receive votes from a majority of electors to be elected. If no candidate receives the necessary majority, the Senate chooses the Vice President from among the candidates who received the two highest numbers of electoral votes for that office. (See Essay No. 190.)

THE CONSTITUTIONAL CONVENTION

Throughout the Convention, the delegates considered various methods for electing the President. None of the initial proposals for establishing an electoral college specified either the number of electoral votes a candidate needed to win or what would happen if candidates tied.[6]

In late August 1787, the Committee on Postponed Parts presented its own recommendation for an electoral college. A candidate would become President if he received the "greatest number of votes" and that figure reflected votes from a "majority of the Electors." If multiple candidates tied with the most votes, and that figure constituted such a majority, the Senate would choose one of them in a contingent election. Similarly, if no candidate received a majority in the proposed electoral college, the Senate would hold a contingent election to choose the President "from the five highest on the list."[7] Each Senator would have one vote. After the President was chosen, the remaining candidate "having the greatest number of [electoral] votes" would become Vice President. If two or more candidates had "equal votes" at that point, the Senate would choose the Vice President from between (or among) the tied candidates.[8]

Roger Sherman of Connecticut and Gouverneur Morris of Pennsylvania praised this proposal because it rendered the President "independent of the Legislature."[9] Sherman further explained that the system struck a balance between large and small states. Large states, which held more electoral votes, had an advantage in "nominat[ing]" candidates through the Electoral College. In the event of a contingent election, however, small states had an advantage since all states had the same number of

Senators regardless of population.[10] He further believed that requiring the Senate to choose the President from among the top five candidates in the Electoral College would prevent the election of "obscure characters."[11]

The Framers disagreed as to whether the contingent election process would be frequently invoked. George Mason of Virginia, for example, argued that a majority of electoral votes would "rarely . . . fall on any one candidate."[12] As a result, "nineteen times in twenty the President would be chosen by the Senate, an improper body for the purpose."[13] Several others shared this concern, including Charles Pinckney and John Rutledge of South Carolina as well as Alexander Hamilton of New York.[14] Under this view, the Electoral College in effect would nominate the candidates from among whom the Senate would choose the President.[15]

Other delegates such as James Madison of Virginia and Gouverneur Morris believed that contingent elections would be rare.[16] They warned against amendments to the Presidential Majority and Contingent Elections Clause that would turn the Electoral College into a nomination process with electors focusing "too much to making candidates" rather than directly choosing a President.[17] Abraham Baldwin of Georgia argued that as "intercourse" among the states grew, "important characters" would become "less & less unknown," and the Senate would become correspondingly less likely "to have the eventual appointment thrown into their hands."[18] Morris agreed that because each elector was required to cast at least one vote for someone from a different state, a majority would likely coalesce around "characters eminent & generally known."[19] He added that because a candidate could win the presidency with only a quarter of the votes cast in the Electoral College, most presidential elections were likely to be resolved there.[20] Incumbent Presidents who performed well were especially likely to be re-elected with a majority of electoral votes.[21]

The Convention's most important change in the Presidential Majority and Contingent Elections Clause was transferring the venue for contingent elections for President from the Senate to the House. Several members opposed entrusting the Senate with such power. Hugh Williamson of North Carolina warned that contingent elections in the Senate would lead to "corruption."[22] Edmund Randolph of Virginia, John Dickinson of Delaware, and Williamson also feared that Senators could "influence" the President's actions.[23] Pinckney and Mason warned that the Senate might conspire with the President.[24] Several delegates, including Williamson, Randolph, and James Wilson of Pennsylvania, emphasized that they wanted to prevent the Senate from becoming "aristocratic."[25]

Opponents initially attempted to reduce or even eliminate the Senate's role in presidential elections by making it easier for the Electoral College to choose the President. Mason, with the support of Williamson and Hamilton, proposed eliminating the requirement that a candidate receive votes from a majority of electors to win the Presidency.[26] This recommendation would have reduced the likelihood of contingent elections in the Senate. Elbridge Gerry of Massachusetts opposed this suggestion, however. He warned that, unless such a majority were required, three or four large states could join together to elect a President in the Electoral College.[27] Williamson retorted that in a contingent election in the Senate, small states with less than one-sixth of the population could elect the President.[28] Hamilton added that the Senate might elect the candidate with the fewest electoral votes.[29] Mason's motions failed, and the Convention retained the majority vote requirement in the Electoral College.[30]

Wilson then proposed unsuccessfully to transfer authority for contingent elections from the Senate to Congress as a whole.[31] He argued that the House's more frequent elections and turnover made it less susceptible than the Senate to "influence & faction."[32] Gerry later made a similar proposal, supported by Rufus King of Massachusetts, Williamson, and Morris. Gerry's amendment would have given Congress authority over contingent elections only when a President was seeking re-election and none of the candidates secured the necessary majority in the Electoral College.[33] Sherman and Williamson commented that if Congress were to choose the President, "it ought to vote in the case by States" because larger states "would have so great an advantage in nominating the candidates" through the Electoral College.[34]

Morris appeared to take inconsistent positions concerning the Senate's power over contingent elections. He opposed Wilson's motion to transfer the Senate's authority to Congress on the grounds that limiting contingent presidential elections to the Senate would make the President potentially beholden to fewer people.[35] He nevertheless supported Gerry's proposal concerning incumbents seeking re-election because transferring authority to Congress as a whole would supposedly reduce the Senate's influence on presidential appointments.[36]

On September 6, the Convention resolved the issue by voting overwhelmingly and with very little debate to transfer the Senate's role in contingent elections to the House of Representatives when no candidate received a majority.[37] The Representatives from each state would share a single vote.[38] The Convention then voted to empower the House to select the President in the same manner when the leading candidates tied in the Electoral College with a majority of electoral votes.[39] It also unanimously adopted a quorum requirement for contingent elections, requiring at least one Representative from two-thirds of states to be present,[40] but the delegates declined to mandate that a majority of Representatives be present.[41]

Toward the end of the Convention, the Framers considered several further amendments to the Presidential Majority & Contingent Elections Clause. For example, the Convention twice rejected motions to specify that only electors "who shall have balloted" would count when determining the number of electoral votes needed for a majority. Supporters of the proposal sought to prevent "non voting electors" from increasing the number of electoral votes necessary for a candidate to win.[42] The Convention instead clarified that the necessary majority was to be calculated based on "the whole number of Electors appointed"[43] in order to "remove ambiguity from the intention of the clause."[44] Thus, electors who abstain or cast electoral votes that are rejected as invalid are nevertheless counted in determining the number of votes a candidate must receive to win the presidency.

Gerry made two proposals. First, he suggested that at least three Representatives from a state should be required to participate in casting the state's vote during a contingent election. If a state lacked sufficient Representatives, its Senators could participate.[45] Second, he proposed that a candidate be required to receive votes from a majority of states to win a contingent election in the House.[46] Gerry explained that these changes would prevent the President from being chosen by as few as five Representatives in a contingent election.[47] Madison added that the Convention should seek to prevent "the representatives of a *Minority* of the people" from "revers[ing] the choice of a *majority* of the *States* and of the *people*."[48] George Reed of Delaware warned that under Gerry's proposal, a small state would be disenfranchised if its Representative or a Senator were ill.[49] Gerry withdrew the first part of his motion, and the Convention adopted the majority-vote requirement for contingent elections.[50]

The Convention further specified that when a contingent election for President is necessary, the House must hold it "immediately" after Congress has finished counting electoral votes.[51] Conversely, it rejected proposals to limit contingent elections to the top three candidates in the Electoral College or expand them to include the top thirteen candidates.[52]

With those changes, the provision was nearly in its final form.[53] On September 8, the Convention submitted its revised version to the Committee on Style.[54] The Committee made a few nonsubstantive modifications.[55] Most notably, in the part of the clause requiring that votes in contingent elections be "taken by states," the Committee suggested adding the clarifying phrase "and not per capita."[56] The Convention struck that new language as "superfluous."[57] This final version of the Presidential Majority and Contingent Elections Clause was adopted as part of the Constitution.[58]

THE RATIFICATION DEBATES
Contingent elections proved to be controversial during the ratification debates. In the Virginia ratification convention, James Monroe said that the process made the President beholden to the states rather than the people.[59] George Mason claimed that "this mode of election was a mere deception . . . on the American people" to trick them into believing they were electing the President when in fact the choice would usually devolve onto the House.[60] He warned that the House could choose a candidate who had

received few electoral votes.[61] William Grayson added that contingent elections were susceptible to foreign interference.[62] In Maryland, Luther Martin warned that large states would exercise "undue influence" over presidential elections in the Electoral College by either selecting the President or choosing the candidates for a contingent election in the House.[63]

During the North Carolina ratification convention, James Iredell supported the contingent election process. "It is probable," he argued, "that the choice will always fall upon a man of experienced abilities and fidelity."[64] At the Virginia ratification convention, Madison supported the Presidential Majority and Contingent Elections Clause on the grounds that the various stages of the presidential election process balanced the interests of both large and small states.[65] In Federalist No. 68, Hamilton explained that it was "unsafe" to "conclusive[ly]" allow a candidate who failed to receive a majority of electoral votes to become President. The Electoral College, combined with contingent elections in the House, "afford[ed] a moral certainty" that Presidents would be "in an eminent degree endowed with the requisite qualifications."

THE ELECTION OF 1800
The United States has held only two contingent elections for President: the elections of Thomas Jefferson in 1801 and John Quincy Adams in 1825. Following the presidential election of 1800, Democratic-Republican Thomas Jefferson and his ostensible running mate, Aaron Burr, tied in the Electoral College, each with votes from a majority of the electors.[66] The House of Representatives immediately held a contingent election, having adopted rules for that process shortly before the electoral votes were counted. Those rules required each state's Representatives to decide collectively the candidate for whom their state's vote would be cast. A state's vote would be recorded as "divided"—effectively an abstention—if its Representatives were equally split between the two candidates.[67] If a question arose during balloting that a majority of Representatives deemed "incidental to the power of chusing the President," the matter would be "decided by States, and without debate."[68]

At the time, there were sixteen states; a candidate needed votes from nine states to be elected President. In the first round of voting, Jefferson received votes from eight states, Burr received votes from six, and two were divided, effectively abstaining.[69] The same result occurred throughout the next thirty-four rounds of voting.[70] Finally, on the thirty-sixth ballot, Jefferson won ten states, Burr won four, and two states submitted blank ballots, allowing Jefferson to be declared President.[71] In December 1803, Congress proposed the Twelfth Amendment to prevent a recurrence and ensure that a political party's intended vice presidential candidate did not win the presidency instead. The amendment was ratified six months later.[72]

THE ELECTION OF 1824

In 1824, four major Democratic-Republican candidates ran for President.[73] None of them won a majority of electoral votes.[74] Andrew Jackson received ninety-nine votes; John Quincy Adams, eighty-four; William H. Crawford, forty-one; and Henry Clay, thirty-seven. The House adopted rules for the contingent election similar to those from 1801, except they expressly required a majority of a state's Representatives to cast their ballots for a candidate in order for that candidate to receive the state's vote.[75] At the time, there were twenty-four states; a candidate needed votes from thirteen to prevail. Because the Twelfth Amendment limited the House to the top three candidates, Henry Clay was ineligible to receive votes in the contingent election. After a single round of voting, John Quincy Adams was elected President with thirteen states' votes; Jackson received seven votes, and Crawford received four.[76]

THE ELECTION OF 1836

In 1836, Democratic presidential candidate Martin Van Buren and vice presidential candidate Richard Mentor Johnson ran against several different Whig candidates. Van Buren received a majority of electoral votes, winning the Presidency.[77] Although Virginia's Democratic electors voted for Van Buren for President, they refused to vote for Johnson as Vice President and instead cast their electoral votes for former South Carolina Senator William Smith.[78] These defections left Johnson just shy of a majority of electoral votes for Vice President,

triggering the only contingent election for that office in American history. Pursuant to the Twelfth Amendment, the Senate chose between Democrat Johnson and the runner up for Vice President in the Electoral College, Whig Francis Granger.[79] At the time, the Senate was comprised of fifty-two Senators. Johnson won in the first round of balloting by a vote of 33 to 16 with three Senators abstaining.[80]

EARLY COMMENTARY ON CONTINGENT ELECTIONS

Writing in 1803, St. George Tucker lauded the overall electoral process as "securing the tranquility of elections" and ensuring a "wis[e]" choice of President.[81] He cautioned, however, that affording each state a single vote in contingent elections regardless of population enables "intrigue and cabal [to] have their full scope."[82] He went so far as to speculate that a "bold and desperate party" with "command of an armed force, and of all the resources of government" might exploit the opportunity to "establish themselves permanently in power."[83] These observations may very well have been inspired by rumors of backroom dealings and mobilization of state militias by Democratic-Republican governors that may have contributed to Jefferson's victory.[84]

In 1829, William Rawle defended the Constitution's requirement that Representatives vote by state in contingent elections from a pragmatic perspective. He speculated that if a majority of electors were unable to agree on a candidate, then a majority of individual Representatives in the House would similarly be unlikely to do so.[85] Requiring Representatives to vote by state "remov[es] the difficulty."[86]

Writing after the elections of both 1800 and 1824, Justice Joseph Story claimed that the Electoral College had a "constant tendency, from the number of candidates, to bring the choice into the house of representatives."[87] He warned that Representatives "may[] be influenced by many motives, independent of [a candidate's] merits and qualifications."[88] Story further observed that the "discords" generated by a contingent election "will probably long outlive the immediate choice, and scatter their pestilential influences all over the great interest of the country."[89]

OPEN QUESTIONS

- Under the Presidential Majority Contingent Elections Clause as originally drafted, what would have happened if no candidate received a majority of electoral votes and two or more candidates tied for fifth place in the Electoral College?[90] The clause specified that only the "five highest [candidates] on the List" were eligible to participate in a contingent election for President in the House. If multiple candidates tied for fifth place or other comparable ties occurred, would this language have allowed six or more candidates to participate in a contingent election? Congress intended for the Twelfth Amendment to resolve this ambiguity. It states that the House may choose from among "the persons having the highest numbers, not exceeding three on the list of those voted for as President."[91] This change in phrasing was adopted to clarify that all presidential candidates who received the greatest, second-greatest, or third-greatest numbers of votes in the Electoral College, even if ties occurred, could participate in a contingent election.[92]

- May the House vote for a candidate who dies in the course of a contingent election? This has never occurred. The closest historical analogue is Congress's decision following the 1872 election to reject three electoral votes that had been cast for presidential candidate Horace Greeley after his death.[93] Members reasoned that the votes were invalid because a deceased candidate is constitutionally ineligible to serve as President; this reasoning would appear to apply equally to a contingent election. The Twelfth Amendment does not address this issue, but the Twentieth Amendment empowers Congress to pass legislation specifying what happens when a presidential or vice presidential candidate dies during a contingent election. Congress has yet to enact any such statutes, however. The most prudent course of action would be for Congress to authorize votes for deceased candidates in contingent elections for both President and Vice President to ensure that neither the House nor the Senate is compelled to vote for someone opposed by a majority of states.

Cite as: Michael T. Morley, *The Presidential Majority and Contingent Elections Clause, in* THE HERITAGE GUIDE TO THE CONSTITUTION 335 (Josh Blackman & John G. Malcolm eds., 3d ed. 2025).

Notes

1. Derek T. Muller, *Electoral Votes Regularly Given*, 55 Ga. L. Rev. 1529, 1545 (2021).   **2.** Letter from Alexander Hamilton to Oliver Wolcott, Jr. (Dec. 16, 1800), https://perma.cc/3QDR-UAMN.   **3.** H.R. Jour., 6th Cong., 2d Sess. 791 (Feb. 9, 1801); Annals of Cong., 6th Cong., 2d Sess. 1010 (1801).   **4.** *Id.*   **5.** H.R. Jour., 18th Cong., 2d Sess. 213 (Feb. 7, 1825); 1 Reg. of Debates in Cong., 18th Cong., 2d Sess. 510–11 (Feb. 7, 1825).   **6.** 1 Farrand's 77, 80–81; 2 Farrand's 22, 32, 50, 57–58, 97, 99, 105, 107, 108–09, 397, 404.   **7.** 2 Farrand's 494, 498.   **8.** *Id.*   **9.** *Id.* at 499, 500.   **10.** *Id.* at 512–14.   **11.** *Id.* at 499.   **12.** *Id.* at 512.   **13.** *Id.* at 500–01.   **14.** *Id.* at 501, 511, 524–25, 530.   **15.** *Id.* at 512–13.   **16.** *Id.* at 512–13, 523.   **17.** *Id.* at 500, 513.   **18.** *Id.* at 501.   **19.** *Id.* at 512.   **20.** *Id.* at 501, 512.   **21.** *Id.* at 512.   **22.** *Id.*   **23.** *Id.* at 501, 513, 522.   **24.** *Id.* at 511–12.   **25.** *Id.* at 512, 513, 515, 522, 524.   **26.** *Id.* at 507, 512–13.   **27.** *Id.* at 514.   **28.** *Id.*   **29.** *Id.* at 524–25.   **30.** *Id.* at 507, 513.   **31.** *Id.* at 502, 507, 513.   **32.** *Id.* at 502.   **33.** *Id.*   **34.** *Id.* at 502, 527.   **35.** *Id.* at 502.   **36.** *Id.* at 522.   **37.** *Id.* at 518–19, 520, 527, 531.   **38.** *Id.*   **39.** *Id.* at 519, 527.   **40.** *Id.* at 518–20, 526–28.   **41.** *Id.* at 519, 520, 528.   **42.** *Id.* at 507, 515, 518, 526.   **43.** *Id.* at 507, 515, 518, 526.   **44.** *Id.* at 515.   **45.** *Id.* at 532, 535.   **46.** *Id.*   **47.** *Id.* at 535.   **48.** *Id.* at 536 (emphasis in original).   **49.** *Id.*   **50.** *Id.* at 532, 536.   **51.** *Id.* at 518, 520, 526, 502.   **52.** *Id.* at 501–02, 507, 514–15.   **53.** *Id.* at 521, 529 & *note, 534, 536, 573.   **54.** *Id.* at 547, 553.   **55.** *Id.* at 598, 605, 607.   **56.** *Id.* at 598.   **57.** *Id.* at 598 & n.19, 621, 628.   **58.** *Id.* at 622, 633.   **59.** 3 Elliot's 488–90.   **60.** *Id.* at 493.   **61.** *Id.*   **62.** *Id.* at 490.   **63.** 1 Elliot's 378.   **64.** 4 Elliot's 107.   **65.** 3 Elliot's 495.   **66.** H.R. Jour., 6th Cong., 2d Sess. 799 (Feb. 11, 1801); S. Jour., 6th Cong., 2d Sess. 125 (Feb. 11, 1801); Annals of Cong., 6th Cong., 2d Sess. 1024 (1801).   **67.** H.R. Jour., 6th Cong., 2d Sess. 791–92 (Feb. 9, 1801); Annals of Cong., 6th Cong., 2d Sess. 1009–11 (1801).   **68.** H.R. Jour., 6th Cong., 2d Sess. 792 (Feb. 9, 1801); Annals of Cong., 6th Cong., 2d Sess. 1011 (1801).   **69.** H.R. Jour., 6th Cong., 2d Sess. 801 (Feb. 11, 1801); Annals of Cong., 6th Cong., 2d Sess. 1025 (1801).   **70.** H.R. Jour., 6th Cong., 2d Sess. 801–03 (Feb. 11, 1801); Annals of Cong., 6th Cong., 2d Sess. 1025–28 (1801).   **71.** H.R. Jour., 6th Cong., 2d Sess. 803 (Feb. 11, 1801); S. Jour., 6th Cong., 2d Sess. 127–28 (Feb. 11, 1801); Annals of Cong., 6th Cong., 2d Sess. 1028 (1801).   **72.** Nathan L. Colvin & Edward B. Foley, *Lost Opportunity: Learning the Wrong Lesson from the Hayes–Tilden Dispute*, 79

Fordham L. Rev. 1043, 1048–49 & n.25 (2010). **73.** Ronald J. Krotoszynski, Jr., *The Unitary Executive and the Plural Judiciary: On the Potential Virtues of Decentralized Judicial Power*, 89 Notre Dame L. Rev. 1021, 1056 n.124 (2014). **74.** H.R. Jour., 18th Cong., 2d Sess. 220–21 (Feb. 9, 1825); 1 Reg. of Debates in Cong., 18th Cong., 2d Sess. 526 (Feb. 9, 1825). **75.** H.R. Jour., 18th Cong., 2d Sess. 212–15 (Feb. 7, 1825); 1 Reg. of Debates in Cong., 18th Cong., 2d Sess. 509–15 (Feb. 7, 1825). **76.** H.R. Jour., 18th Cong., 2d Sess., 222 (Feb. 9, 1825); 1 Reg. of Debates in Cong., 18th Cong., 2d Sess. 527 (Feb. 9, 1825). **77.** Cong. Globe, 24th Cong., 2d Sess. 167 (1837); H.R. Jour., 24th Cong., 2d Sess. 358–59 (Feb 8, 1837). **78.** Cong. Globe, 24th Cong., 2d Sess. 167 (1837); H.R. Jour., 24th Cong., 2d Sess. 358–59 (Feb 8, 1837). **79.** Cong. Globe, 24th Cong., 2d Sess. 167 (1837); S. Jour., 24th Cong., 2d Sess. 229 (Feb. 8, 1837). **80.** Cong. Globe, 24th Cong., 2d Sess. 167 (1837); S. Jour., 24th Cong., 2d Sess. 229 (Feb. 8, 1837). **81.** 1 St. George Tucker, Blackstone's Commentaries: With Notes of Reference to the Constitution and Laws of the Federal Government of the United States and of the Commonwealth of Virginia, App. Note D, at 326 (1803). **82.** *Id.* at 327. **83.** *Id.* **84.** Bruce Ackerman, The Failure of the Founding Fathers: Jefferson, Marshall, and the Rise of Presidential Democracy 106 (2005); Ron Chernow, Alexander Hamilton 638–39 (2004); Joanne B. Freeman, *The Election of 1800: A Study in the Logic of Political Change*, 108 Yale L.J. 1959, 1963 (1999). **85.** William Rawle, A View of the Constitution of the United States of America 54, 321 (2d ed. 1829). **86.** *Id.* at 54. **87.** 3 Story's Commentaries § 1458. **88.** *Id.* **89.** *Id.* **90.** *Id.* at § 1465. **91.** Amend. XII. **92.** Annals of Cong., 8th Cong., 1st Sess. 93, 677–80, 725 (1803). **93.** Cong. Globe, 42d Cong., 3d Sess. 505 (1873).

ESSAY NO. 95: THE PRESIDENTIAL ELECTORS TIMING CLAUSE
ART. II, § 1, CL. 4

The Congress may determine the Time of chusing the Electors, and the Day on which they shall give their Votes; which Day shall be the same throughout the United States.

—Michael T. Morley

INTRODUCTION

The Presidential Electors Timing Clause allows Congress to control the timing of two different aspects of the presidential election process. First, it empowers Congress to "determine the Time of chusing [presidential] Electors." Under the Constitution, a state's electors are chosen "in such Manner as the Legislature thereof may direct," including through popular elections.[1] The Presidential Election Timing Clause enables Congress to designate when that selection must occur. Second, the clause gives Congress the authority to determine "the Day" on which presidential electors must cast their electoral votes, which must "be the same throughout the United States." Thus, Congress may impose national uniformity with respect to the timing of presidential elections. Throughout American history, Congress has enacted a series of laws establishing when states must choose their presidential electors and those electors must cast their electoral votes.

THE CONSTITUTIONAL CONVENTION

In June and July 1787, the Constitutional Convention considered various proposals concerning the Electoral College, but none addressed the timing of presidential elections.[2] On September 4, the Committee on Postponed Parts suggested specifying, "The Legislature [Congress] may determine the time of chusing and assembling the Electors, and the manner of certifying and transmitting their votes."[3] This proposal would empower Congress to prescribe when state legislatures could appoint electors, as well as when those electors must meet to vote for President. Gouverneur Morris of Pennsylvania explained that Congress would ensure that each state's electors "vote at the same time through out the U.S." at "a distance from each other."[4] This arrangement would "avoid[]" the "great evil of cabal" and make it "impossible . . . to corrupt" electors.[5]

Over the next two days, the Convention voted without debate or explanation to amend this language by clarifying that Congress may designate when electors will "giv[e] their votes" and declaring that such "election shall be on the same day throughout the United States."[6] On September 12, the Committee on Style reported an updated draft of the Constitution that omitted the phrase "and the manner of certifying or transmitting their votes."[7] The Convention records do not provide any explanation for this omission. Professor David Currie suggests that "[i]n light of the Framers' clear desire to minimize congressional influence on the selection of the President, the omission may not have been accidental."[8] Following minor stylistic changes, the final version of this clause read, "The Congress may determine the Time of chusing the Electors, and the Day on which they shall give their Votes; which Day shall be the same throughout the United States."[9]

THE RATIFICATION DEBATES AND COMMENTARY

The Federalist Papers did not specifically discuss the Presidential Electors Timing Clause. In Federalist No. 68, Alexander Hamilton explained that the Framers crafted the presidential election process to avoid "cabal, intrigue, and corruption."

The timing provisions came up rarely during the state ratification conventions. James Wilson in Pennsylvania and William Davie in North Carolina argued that requiring all electors to cast their electoral votes in their respective states on the same day would make it harder to corrupt them.[10] In South Carolina, Charles Cotesworth Pinckney argued that electors would be more susceptible to bribes from foreign powers if they all gathered in a single place to cast their electoral votes.[11] James Iredell and Richard Dobbs Spaight in North Carolina, as well as Edmund Randolph in Virginia, were among those who noted that the clause would also preclude electors from conspiring among themselves.[12] Spaight added that the provision would allow Congress to promote "regularity and uniformity."[13]

James Monroe of Virginia, in contrast, objected that Congress might give electors the opportunity to "form a combination" by imposing a substantial delay between electors' appointments and the date on which they cast their electoral votes.[14] Joseph Taylor of North Carolina went even further, expressing his fear that Congress might use the army, along with its power over the timing of presidential elections, to "control the election of the electors of the President" and "compel the electors to vote as [Congress] please[d]."[15]

Justice Joseph Story would later declare that the "propriety" of the Presidential Electors Timing Clause is "almost self-evident."[16] St. George Tucker and Chancellor James Kent explained that it helps to prevent intrigues, corruption, and cabal.[17]

THE FIRST PRESIDENTIAL ELECTION

After approving the proposed draft Constitution, the Framers adopted a resolution to accompany it. The resolution declared that once nine states had ratified the Constitution, the Confederation Congress should "fix a Day on which Electors should be appointed by the States which shall have ratified the same, and a Day on which the Electors should assemble to vote for the President. . . ."[18] The Confederation Congress did so in September 1788 following New Hampshire's ratification.[19] The states were required to appoint their electors on January 7, 1789, and the electors would cast their votes on February 4. Each elector cast one of his two votes for George Washington, and John Adams received a majority of the remaining votes.[20]

FEDERAL LEGISLATION

The Second Congress exercised its power under the Presidential Electors Timing Clause by enacting the Presidential Election and Succession Act of 1792.[21] This statute required presidential electors to "meet and give their votes" on the first Wednesday in December of presidential election years.[22] Congress did not similarly establish a single day on which states would choose their electors; rather, the Act directed each state to appoint its electors "within thirty-four days preceding" the date on which electors were required to cast their electoral votes.[23] Under this statute, electors were generally chosen at some point in November and cast their electoral votes in December. This arrangement was permissible under the Presidential Electors Timing Clause. While the clause requires electors to vote on the precise "day" set by Congress, it allows Congress to specify the "time" when electors must be appointed, which Congress construed to include a period of several weeks.

Over the decades that followed, nearly all states came to appoint their electors through a popular vote, and concerns grew about widespread voter fraud in presidential elections.[24] In 1845, the Presidential Election Day Act eliminated the thirty-four-day window for choosing electors. It instead specified that all states generally must appoint their respective electors on the same day: "the Tuesday next after the first Monday in the month of November."[25] This statutory formula required states to hold their popular votes for President—Election Day—on a designated day between November 2 and November 8. Electors still cast their electoral votes about a month later on "the first Wednesday in December" pursuant to the 1792 Act.

The Electoral Count Act (ECA) of 1887 changed the date on which electors would cast their electoral votes to "the second Monday in January next following their appointment."[26] This amendment created a roughly two-month gap between when the electors were chosen in early November and when they voted. An 1891 Michigan law nevertheless purported to require the state's electors to cast their electoral votes on the "first Wednesday in December," consistent with Congress's original 1792 Act. *McPherson v. Blacker* (1892) held that this requirement was "in conflict with" the ECA and "must necessarily give way."[27]

In 1928, Congress again moved the date on which electors cast their electoral votes, this time to "the first Wednesday in January."[28] In 1933, the Twentieth Amendment was ratified. It changed the beginning of the President's term from March to January 20.[29] As a result, the following year, Congress pushed up the date on which electors cast their electoral votes from January to the "First Monday after the second Wednesday in December."[30]

Nearly a century later, Congress modified the timing of the presidential election process yet again with the Electoral Count Reform Act (ECRA) of 2022.[31] Electors are still presumptively chosen "on election day," which, as in the 1845 Act, remains set for early November.[32] But the ECRA also provides for a "modified period of voting" in response to "force majeure events that are extraordinary and catastrophic, as provided under laws of the State enacted prior to such day."[33] Critically, a state may not statutorily change its voting period for a presidential

election after the originally scheduled election date has occurred. The ECRA also adjusted the date on which electors must cast their electoral votes to "the first Tuesday after the second Wednesday in December."[34]

SCOPE OF FEDERAL POWER OVER PRESIDENTIAL ELECTIONS

The Presidential Election Timing Clause gives Congress the power to "determine the Time of chusing the Electors" for President. The Elections Clause, in contrast, grants Congress authority to regulate the "Time, Place, and Manner" of congressional elections.[35] (See Essay No. 22.) As early as 1800,[36] questions arose as to whether this difference in language suggests that Congress cannot regulate the "Manner" of presidential electors' appointments, including the electoral process in states that choose electors by popular vote.[37] A draft Constitution prepared by Alexander Hamilton, which he discussed at the Convention, would have specifically authorized Congress to adopt "further regulations as may be necessary for the more orderly election of the President."[38]

McPherson v. Blacker (1892) declared that "Congress is empowered to determine the time of choosing the electors and the day on which they are to give their votes . . . but otherwise the power and jurisdiction of the State is exclusive. . . ."[39] The Supreme Court later rejected this interpretation, however, holding that the Constitution confers "broad congressional power to legislate in connection with the elections of the President and Vice President."[40] Pursuant to this authority, Congress has enacted laws such as the National Voter Registration Act and Help America Vote Act that regulate federal elections, including presidential elections.[41]

Neither federal law nor court rulings explain the particular acts that may or must occur on the statutorily designated Election Day. As noted, the Presidential Electors Timing Clause states that Congress may specify "the Time of chusing the Electors." Pursuant to this authority, the ECRA establishes the date on which electors "shall be appointed[] in each state."[42] Particularly in the modern era, however, electors are not actually appointed until several weeks after this statutorily designated

Election Day when results have been canvassed, any recounts and post-election contests have been completed, and certificates of election have been issued. Moreover, a person need not cast his vote on Election Day itself. Courts have generally held that election officials may accept ballots in advance of Election Day through early voting, vote-by-mail, and absentee voting,[43] and the Supreme Court has never questioned the validity of such votes.[44] *Foster v. Love* (1997) construed the analogous statutory provision governing the timing of U.S. House elections to prohibit states from "consummat[ing]" such elections "prior to federal election day" with

"no act in law or in fact to take place on the date chosen by Congress."[45]

Congress's creation of a presidential Election Day bars state legislatures from claiming constitutional power to appoint their own slates of presidential electors after that date because they disagree with the outcome of the popular vote.[46] Moreover, the Constitution's requirement that presidential electors throughout the nation cast their electoral votes on the same day effectively creates a deadline by which recounts, election contests, and other disputes over a presidential election's results within each state must be resolved.

OPEN QUESTIONS

- May an otherwise valid ballot be accepted and counted if election officials receive it after the statutorily designated Election Day? Many states accept absentee ballots that arrive within a few days of Election Day as long as they are postmarked by Election Day or if the postmark is illegible.[47] This issue arises frequently with military and overseas voters.[48] A handful of courts, including the U.S. Court of Appeals for the Fifth Circuit and the Montana Supreme Court, have held that allowing election officials to receive completed absentee ballots in presidential elections after the close of polls on Election Day violates the Presidential Election Day Act.[49]

- The Presidential Election Timing Clause provides that the "Day" on which electors "shall give their votes . . . shall be the same throughout the United States." In light of this requirement, may Congress count electoral votes that are cast after the date it specifies? Some scholars suggest that the answer is no.[50] The issue has arisen only once. Wisconsin's electors cast their electoral votes in the 1856 election one day late due to a "terrific storm."[51] After Congress concluded its joint session for counting electoral votes, both chambers debated whether Wisconsin's votes were valid. "Almost every Member of Congress who spoke on the subject agreed [they] should not have been counted."[52] Because the joint session was over and the challenged votes did not impact the outcome, however, neither chamber took further action.

Cite as: Michael T. Morley, *The Presidential Electors Timing Clause, in* THE HERITAGE GUIDE TO THE CONSTITUTION 342 (Josh Blackman & John G. Malcolm eds., 3d ed. 2025).

Notes

1. Art. II, § 1, cl. 2; *Bush v. Gore*, 531 U.S. 89, 104 (2000) (per curiam). **2.** 1 Farrand's 80; 2 Farrand's 57, 404. **3.** 2 Farrand's 494–95, 498. **4.** *Id.* at 500. **5.** *Id.* **6.** *Id.* at 507, 515, 518, 526. **7.** *Id.* at 598. **8.** David P. Currie, *The Constitution in Congress: The Second Congress, 1791–1793*, 90 Nw. U. L. Rev. 606, 618 n.62 (citations omitted). **9.** 2 Farrand's 598 n.21–22, 658. **10.** 2 Elliot's 512; 4 Elliot's 104. **11.** 4 Elliot's 304–05. **12.** 3 Elliot's 201, 486; 4 Elliot's 104–05, 122. **13.** 4 Elliot's 104–06. **14.** 3 Elliot's 488. **15.** 4 Elliot's 104, 106. **16.** 3 Story's Commentaries § 1469. **17.** 1 St. George Tucker, Blackstone's Commentaries, App. Note D at 327 (1803); 1 James Kent, Commentaries on American Law 236 (1826). **18.** 2 Farrand's 665. **19.** 1

Elliot's 333. **20.** S. Jour., 1st Cong., 1st Sess. 8 (Apr. 6, 1789); H.R. Jour., 1st Cong., 1st Sess. 7–8 (Apr. 6, 1789). **21.** Ch. 8, § 2, 1 Stat. 239, 239–40 (Mar. 1, 1792); Annals of Cong., 1st Cong., 3rd Sess., at 1915–18 (1791). **22.** Ch. 8, § 2, 1 Stat. 239, 239–40 (Mar. 1, 1792). **23.** *Id.* § 1, 1 Stat. at 239. **24.** Michael T. Morley, *Postponing Federal Elections Due to Election Emergencies*, 77 Wash. & Lee L. Rev. Online 179, 185 (2020). **25.** Act of Jan. 23, 1845, ch. 1, 5 Stat. 721. **26.** Ch. 90, § 1, 24 Stat. 373, 373 (Feb. 3, 1887). **27.** 146 U.S. 1, 41 (1892). **28.** Act of May 29, 1928, ch. 859, § 1, 45 Stat. 945, 945–46. **29.** Amend. XX, § 1. **30.** Act of June 5, 1934, ch. 390, § 6(a), 48 Stat. 879, 879. **31.** Pub. L. No. 117-238, Div. P, 136 Stat. 4459, 5233–41 (Dec. 29, 2022). **32.** *Id.* §

102(a), 136 Stat. at 5233 (codified at 3 U.S.C. § 1). **33.** *Id.* § 102(b), 136 Stat. at 5234 (codified at 3 U.S.C. § 21(1)). **34.** *Id.* § 106(a)(1), 136 Stat. at 5236 (codified at 3 U.S.C. § 7). **35.** Art. I, § 4, cl. 1; *Oregon v. Mitchell*, 400 U.S. 112, 211 (1970) (Harlan, J., concurring in part and dissenting in part); Vasan Kesavan, *Is the Electoral Count Act Unconstitutional?*, 80 N.C. L. Rev. 1653, 1750 (2002). **36.** 10 Annals of Cong. 128–29 (1800); 15 Cong. Rec. 5078 (1884). **37.** Currie, *supra* at 618–19. **38.** 2 Farrand's 291, 617, 624. **39.** 146 U.S. 1, 35 (1892); *In re Opinion of the Justices*, 107 A. 705, 706 (Me. 1919). **40.** *Buckley v. Valeo*, 424 U.S. 1, 14 n.16 (1976) (per curiam); *Burroughs v. United States*, 290 U.S. 534, 545 (1934); Michael T. Morley, *Dismantling the Unitary Electoral System? Uncooperative Federalism in State and Local Elections*, 111 Nw. U. L. Rev. Online 103, 108–10 (2017). **41.** Pub. L. No. 103-31, 107 Stat. 77 (May 20, 1993); Pub. L. No. 107-252, 116 Stat. 1666 (Oct. 29, 2002). **42.** 3 U.S.C. § 1. **43.** *Millsaps v. Thompson*, 259 F.3d 545, 546 (6th Cir. 2001); *Voting Integrity Proj., Inc. v. Keisling*, 259 F.3d 1169, 1174–75 (9th Cir. 2001); *Voting Integrity Proj., Inc. v. Bomer*, 199 F.3d 773, 776 (5th Cir. 2000); *Lamone v. Capozzi*, 912 A.2d 674, 691–92 (Md. 2006). **44.** *O'Brien v. Skinner*, 414 U.S. 524, 529 (1974); *Brnovich v. Democratic Nat'l Comm.*, 594 U.S. 647 (2021). **45.** 522 U.S. 67, 72 & n.4 (1997). **46.** William Josephson, *Senate Election of the Vice President and House of Representatives Election of the President*, 11 U. Pa. J. Const. L. 597, 654 n.216 (2009); Richard D. Friedman, *Trying to Make Peace with Bush v. Gore*, 29 Fla. St. U. L. Rev. 811, 816 (2001). **47.** Nat'l Conf. of State Legislatures, *Voting Outside the Polling Place*, tbl. 11 (Apr. 8, 2025), https://perma.cc/25Y4 -PYRB. **48.** Fla. Stat. § 101.6952(5). **49.** *Republican Nat'l Comm. v. Wetzel*, 120 F.4th 200, 207–08 (5th Cir. 2024), *en banc denied* 134 F.4th 775 (2025) (mem); *Maddox v. Bd. of State Canvassers*, 149 P.2d 112, 115 (Mont. 1944). **50.** Michael W. McConnell, *Two-and-a-Half Cheers for Bush v. Gore*, 68 U. Chi. L. Rev. 657, 676 n.93 (2001). **51.** Cong. Globe, 34th Cong., 3d Sess. 660 (1857). **52.** Kesavan, *supra* at 1686.

❧

ESSAY NO. 96: THE PRESIDENTIAL ELIGIBILITY CLAUSE
ART. II, § 1, CL. 5

No Person except a natural born Citizen, or a Citizen of the United States, at the time of the Adoption of this Constitution, shall be eligible to the Office of President; neither shall any Person be eligible to that Office who shall not have attained to the Age of thirty five Years, and been fourteen Years a Resident within the United States.

—Scott A. Keller & Jeremy Evan Maltz

INTRODUCTION

The Constitution imposes three eligibility requirements on the Presidency. First, the President must be at least thirty-five years old. By contrast, Senators and Representatives must be at least thirty and twenty-five, respectively. Justice Joseph Story wrote that the "character and talents" of a man in the middle age of life are "fully developed" and that the President would have had the opportunity "for public service and for experience in the public councils."[1] Second, the President must have been a "Resident" of the United States for fourteen years. Senators and Representatives, on the other hand, must only be "Inhabitant[s]" of their states "when elected." Third, the President must be a "natural born Citizen." Yet Senators and Representatives must be citizens for at least nine and seven years, respectively. The Twelfth Amendment imposes the same qualifications for the Vice President.[2]

The Framers established these qualifications to increase the chances of electing a person characterized by patriotism, judgment, and civic virtue.

Among these three qualifications, the "natural born Citizen" requirement has inspired the most debate. The English common-law conception of "natural born" *subjects* appears generally to have included only persons born within sovereign territory (other than children of enemy aliens or foreign diplomats). By the time of the Founding, however, Acts of Parliament recognized a broader definition of "natural born." This category included all persons obtaining subjecthood on the basis that they were born to English subjects—regardless of whether they were born within sovereign territory.

The First Congress, tracking these Acts of Parliament, deemed a child born to American citizens abroad to be a "natural born" citizen.

These laws provide strong originalist evidence that the Constitution's use of "natural born Citizen" adopted the then-prevailing, broader conception: Citizenship was granted at birth if a person was born to American citizens, regardless of where he was born. Controversies about presidential candidates Senators John McCain and Ted Cruz, both of whom were born abroad, have been resolved in a manner supporting this broader definition of "natural born Citizen."

HISTORY BEFORE 1787

The term "natural born" has its roots in the British tradition of conferring subjecthood. Under the British common law, persons born within the sovereign's territory were "natural born" subjects. William Blackstone observed that the "children of aliens, born here in England, are, generally speaking, natural-born subjects, and entitled to all the privileges of such."[3] These "[n]atural-born subjects . . . are born within the dominions of the crown of England" with "allegiance of the king."[4] In addition, "the children of the king's embassadors born abroad were always held to be natural subjects."[5] But children of enemy aliens or foreign diplomats born in the sovereign's territory were not "natural born" subjects.

By 1787, various Acts of Parliament had expanded "natural born" subjecthood beyond that common-law conception. Blackstone described how, "by several more modern statutes," Parliament had declared that "all children, born out of the king's [allegiance], whose fathers were natural-born subjects, are now *natural-born subjects* themselves."[6] In other words, children born to British citizens outside of British sovereign territory would be "natural born" subjects.

THE CONSTITUTIONAL CONVENTION

The qualifications for members of the national legislature were addressed at the outset of the Convention in the Virginia Plan,[7] but Presidential qualifications were not established until fairly late in the Convention. John Jay of New York, who was not at the Convention, wrote a letter on July 25, 1787, to Convention President George Washington. Jay argued that the Constitution should "declare expressly that the Command[er] in chief of the american army shall not be given to nor devolve on, any but a natural born Citizen."[8]

On August 22, John Rutledge of South Carolina proposed that the President "shall be of the age of thirty five years, and a Citizen of the United States, and shall have been an Inhabitant thereof for Twenty one years."[9] At that juncture, the text did not yet impose a natural-born citizenship requirement. On September 2, Washington thanked Jay "for the hints contained in [his] letter."[10]

Only two days later, on September 4, 1787, the Committee of Eleven delivered a report that added the third qualification for the presidency: the natural-born citizen requirement. It provided that only "a natural born citizen or a Citizen of the United States at the time of the adoption of this Constitution shall be eligible to the office of President."[11] The proposal did not define what "natural born citizen" meant, but the textual dichotomy between "natural born citizen" and "Citizen of the United States at the time of the adoption" of the Constitution suggests that Americans born before the Framing could not be "natural born citizens" of the United States. As a result, those who were citizens when the Constitution was adopted would be grandfathered into presidential eligibility. The report further provided, "nor shall any person be elected to that office, who shall be under the age of thirty five years, and who has not been in the whole, at least fourteen years a resident within the United States."[12] This qualification would apply when the President is *elected*, and thus before the time he would hold the office. The inhabitancy qualifications in Article I for Representatives and Senators also applied when members were "elected."[13] Three days later, this proposal was agreed to unanimously without any debate.[14]

The Committee of Style made two subtle but important changes. First, it modified the inhabitancy requirement. The prior version required that the person must have "been in the whole, at least fourteen years a resident," which suggests a *cumulative* residency requirement.[15] The Committee now required a person to have "been fourteen years a resident," which suggests a *consecutive* residency requirement.[16] This revision therefore arguably made it harder for a person to meet the eligibility standards.

Second, the Committee removed the requirement that the age and residency requirements must apply when "elected to that office."[17] Instead, a person would only need to meet the age and residency requirements to be "eligible to the office of president."[18] As Professors Josh Blackman and Seth Barrett Tillman have observed, "[e]ligible could mean either 'eligible to hold office' . . . or 'eligible to be elected to office.'"[19] Under the former reading, the qualification could apply as late as Inauguration Day. As a result, a candidate who was not yet thirty-five years old on Election Day but who turned thirty-five before Inauguration Day could be eligible for the presidency. It is unclear why the Committee made these two revisions.

The Convention adopted the text as revised by the Committee of Style: "No Person except a natural born Citizen, or a Citizen of the United States, at the time of the Adoption of this Constitution, shall be eligible to the Office of President; neither shall any Person be eligible to that Office who shall not have attained to the Age of thirty five Years, and been fourteen Years a Resident within the United States."

EARLY PRACTICE

The First Congress adopted a definition of "natural born" that included children of U.S. citizens born outside U.S. territory: "the children of citizens of the United States, that may be born beyond the sea, or out of the limits of the United States, shall be considered as natural born citizens."[20] This statute tracked the Acts of Parliament discussed above. The First Congress included eight members of the eleven-member committee that proposed the "natural born Citizen" requirement. Thus, its actions provide substantial originalist support for the idea that the Framers understood "natural born" citizenship to include children of U.S. citizens regardless of their birthplace. At a minimum, "natural born" citizens included persons declared to be citizens at birth by federal statute.[21]

However, some scholars posit that the First Congress's law demonstrates a *break* from the British common-law tradition that does not lend meaning to the Constitution's requirement. Mary Brigid McManamon, for example, has argued:

[T]he very existence of this provision

demonstrates that the early American notion of "natural born citizen" adopted the English common law only and did not include the eighteenth-century statutes. If it had been otherwise, there would have been no need for the 1790 statute because the children covered would have been natural born under then-current English law.[22]

In 1795, Congress removed the "natural born citizen" language from the citizenship statute. The statute then provided, in part, that "the children of citizens of the United States, born out of the limits and jurisdiction of the United States, shall be considered as citizens of the United States."[23]

PRESIDENTIAL ELIGIBILITY

During the 2008 and 2016 campaigns, two leading presidential candidates were born outside of the United States, and questions about their eligibility were answered in their favor. Senator John McCain was born on a military base in the Panama Canal Zone to American parents.[24] In 2008, McCain was the Republican nominee. The U.S. Senate unanimously approved a resolution deeming McCain eligible for the presidency. The resolution stated that other "previous presidential candidates were born outside of the United States of America" to American parents but were still "understood to be eligible to be President."[25] The resolution also added that any other view would be "inconsistent with the purpose and intent of the 'natural born Citizen' clause of the Constitution of the United States, as evidenced by the First Congress's own statute defining the term 'natural born Citizen.'"[26] Many courts suggested that they agreed with the Senate, although they ultimately did not reach McCain's eligibility on the merits.[27] Some scholars, however, have argued that Senator McCain was not eligible.[28]

In 2016, Senator Ted Cruz was a leading candidate for the Republican presidential nomination. Cruz was born in Canada, and his mother was a U.S. citizen. Under the naturalization laws in effect at the time, Cruz obtained U.S. citizenship at birth. Was Cruz a natural born citizen? The state courts and tribunals that considered this question on the merits concluded that Senator Cruz was a natural born citizen because he was a citizen at birth under federal law.[29] Former Solicitors General Paul Clement and Neal Katyal contended that Cruz was eligible.[30] Other law professors, including Einer Elhauge and Mary Brigid McManamon, contended that Cruz might not be eligible.[31]

The candidacies of Senators McCain and Cruz illustrate the importance of Congress's role in presidential eligibility. Congress cannot unilaterally define what "natural born" means under the Constitution,[32] but it does define the statutory parameters for U.S. citizenship eligibility at birth. These rules, in turn, may inform who satisfies the Constitution's "natural born" requirement.

OPEN QUESTIONS

- During and after World War I, Herbert Hoover lived in Western Europe. He did not return to the U.S. until 1917, which was less than fourteen years before his election in 1928.[33] Does the fourteen-year residency requirement apply to the fourteen years before the President takes office, or can it be satisfied cumulatively over the President's life?
- Assume that a presidential candidate is thirty-four years old on Election Day but will turn thirty-five before Inauguration Day. Is the candidate constitutionally eligible?
- The Twentieth Amendment provides that "[i]f a President shall not have been chosen before the time fixed for the beginning of his term, or if the President elect shall have failed to qualify, then the Vice President elect shall act as President until a President shall have qualified." Assume that a presidential candidate will turn thirty-five at some point after Inauguration Day but during the four-year term. Will that candidate have "failed to qualify"? Can the Vice President serve as Acting President under the Twentieth Amendment until the President reaches the age of thirty-five?
- Do Article II's qualifications for Presidents apply to *acting* Presidents under the Twenty-Fifth Amendment?[34]

Cite as: Scott A. Keller & Jeremy Evan Maltz, *The Presidential Eligibility Clause, in* THE HERITAGE GUIDE TO THE CONSTITUTION 346 (Josh Blackman & John G. Malcolm eds., 3d ed. 2025).

Notes

1. 3 Story's Commentaries § 1472. **2.** Amend. XII. **3.** 3 Blackstone 373. **4.** 1 Blackstone 365–66. **5.** 1 Blackstone 373. **6.** *Id.* (emphasis added). **7.** 1 Farrand's 20. **8.** 3 Farrand's 61. **9.** 2 Farrand's 367. **10.** Letter from George Washington to John Jay (Sept. 2, 1787), https://perma.cc/JC3S-H3YS. **11.** 2 Farrand's 498. **12.** *Id.* **13.** Art. I, § 2, cl. 2; Art. I, § 3, cl. 3. **14.** 2 Farrand's 536. **15.** 2 Farrand's 498 (emphasis added). **16.** *Id.* at 598. **17.** *Id.* at 498 (emphasis added). **18.** *Id.* at 598. **19.** Josh Blackman & Seth Barrett Tillman, *Sweeping and Forcing the President into Section 3*, 28 Tex. Rev. L. & Pol. 460–61 (2024). **20.** 1 Stat. 103, 104 (1790). **21.** Michael D. Ramsey, *The Original Meaning of "Natural Born,"* 20 U. Pa. J. Const. L. 199, 213–24, 230–34 (2017); James C. Ho, *Defining "American": Birthright Citizenship and the Original Understanding of the 14th Amendment*, 9 Green Bag 367, 370–72 (2006). **22.** Mary Brigid McManamon, *The Natural Born Citizen Clause as Originally Understood*, 64 Cath. U.L. Rev. 317, 332, 336 (2015). **23.** 1 Stat. 414, 415 (1795). **24.** Paul Clement & Neal Katyal, *On the Meaning of "Natural Born Citizen,"* 128 Harv. L. Rev. F. 161, 164 (2015). **25.** S. Res. 511, 110th Cong. (2008). **26.** *Id.* **27.** *Robinson v. Bowen*, 567 F. Supp. 2d 1144, 1146 (N.D. Cal. 2008); *Hollander v. McCain*, 566 F. Supp. 2d 63, 66 & n.3 (D.N.H. 2008); *Ankeny v. Governor of State of Ind.*, 916 N.E.2d 678, 685 n.10 (Ind. Ct. App. 2009). **28.** Gabriel J. Chin, *Why Senator John McCain Cannot Be President: Eleven Months and a Hundred Yards Short of Citizenship*, 107 Mich. L. Rev. First Impressions 1 (2008). **29.** *Elliott v. Cruz*, 137 A.3d 646 (Pa. Commw. Ct. 2016), *summarily aff'd*, 635 Pa. 212, 134 A.3d 51 (2016); *Williams v. Cruz*, No. OAL DKT. STE 5016-16, 2016 WL 1554252, at *17 (N.J. Adm. Apr. 12, 2016). **30.** Clement & Katyal, *supra* at 163–64. **31.** Brief Amicus Curiae of Professor Einer Elhauge on the Justiciability and Meaning of the Natural Born Citizen Requirement at 12, *Elliott v. Cruz*, 134 A.3d 51 (Pa. 2016) (No. 29 MAP 2016), 2016 WL 2732221; Mary Brigid McManamon, *Ted Cruz Is Not Eligible to be President*, Wash. Post (Jan. 12, 2016), https://perma.cc/Y5HQ-FXVA. **32.** *City of Boerne v. Flores*, 521 U.S. 507, 519 (1997). **33.** James Hart, *Mr. Hoover's Eligibility for the Presidency*, 15 Va. L. Rev. 476 (1929). **34.** James C. Ho, *Unnatural Born Citizens and Acting Presidents*, 17 Const. Comment. 575 (2000).

ESSAY NO. 97: THE PRESIDENTIAL SUCCESSION—DEVOLVE CLAUSE
ART. II, § 1, CL. 6

In Case of the Removal of the President from Office, or of his Death, Resignation, or Inability to discharge the Powers and Duties of the said Office, the Same shall devolve on the Vice President, and the Congress may by Law provide for the Case of Removal, Death, Resignation or Inability, both of the President and Vice President, declaring what Officer shall then act as President, and such Officer shall act accordingly, until the Disability be removed, or a President shall be elected.

—John D. Feerick

INTRODUCTION

The Presidential Succession Clause has a long history in America. The delegates to the Constitutional Convention drew on that history in developing Article II, Section 1, Clause 6 of the Constitution. In July 1965, Congress proposed the Twenty-Fifth Amendment that became part of the Constitution in February 1967.[1] The amendment added to the Constitution a procedure for filling a vacancy in the Vice Presidency and set forth procedures enabling a President to declare his own inability and a process by which the Vice President and the principal officers of the executive departments may declare a President unable to discharge the powers and duties of office.[2]

HISTORY BEFORE 1787

The idea of executive succession was a formative part of American colonial governance.[3] According to one estimate, nearly one-third of colonial governors died in office. Others became ill, resigned, were removed, or became incapacitated. Governors were often absent from their colonies, traveling considerable distances. These contingencies necessitated the choice of someone to assume the responsibilities of office. This role usually fell to a deputy or lieutenant governor, a member of the governor's council, or even the council itself.

In May 1754, commissioners from nine colonies met to consider issues regarding Indian affairs and military activities. They adopted a Plan of Union drafted by Benjamin Franklin that called for a council of delegates selected by colonial assemblies and a president general selected by the king. The plan also provided a succession policy: Upon the death of the President General of the Grand Council, the Speaker of the Council would assume the President's powers and duties until the king decided otherwise.[4] The plan was rejected by the colonial assemblies.[5]

Following independence, the state constitutions provided for executive succession.[6] The state constitutions of Massachusetts and New York offered important guidance to the Framers in crafting the succession provision. Massachusetts's constitution provided that the lieutenant governor would perform the duties of the governor in cases of "death, absence from the commonwealth, or otherwise" and further stated that if both offices were vacant for these reasons, the governor's council would "have full power and authority to do and execute all and every such acts, matters, and things, as the governor or the lieutenant-governor might or could, by virtue of this constitution, do or execute, if they, or either of them, were personally present."[7] New York's constitution provided that "in case of the impeachment of the Governor or his removal from office, death, resignation, or absence from the state, the Lieutenant-Governor shall exercise all the power and authority" of "the office of Governor until another be chosen, or the Governor absent, or impeached, shall return or be acquitted."[8] The Articles of Confederation did not include any provision concerning executive succession.

THE CONSTITUTIONAL CONVENTION

Neither the Virginia Plan nor the New Jersey Plan contained an executive succession provision.[9] Instead, both plans provided that the legislature would choose the executive or co-executives.[10]

Alexander Hamilton of New York offered a plan calling for three branches of government: an executive chosen by electors of the people, a bicameral legislature consisting of an assembly and a senate, and a judiciary. The executive was to serve for life with a provision for succession: In the event of his death, resignation, or removal from office, the President of the Senate would exercise the powers of the national executive until a successor was appointed.[11] The records of the Convention do not reflect that any serious consideration was given to Hamilton's plan, although its presentation appears to have taken several hours.[12]

On August 6, 1787, the Committee of Detail presented its report to the Convention. Under this proposal, the legislature would choose the President, and in the event of the President's "removal . . . death, resignation, or disability to discharge the powers and duties of his office, the President of the Senate [would] exercise those powers and duties, until another President of the United States be chosen, or until the disability of the President be removed."[13]

On August 27, the succession provision came up for discussion. Delegates debated who should be the President's immediate successor. Gouverneur Morris of Pennsylvania objected to the Senate's president standing in the line of succession. Morris favored the Chief Justice of the United States.[14] Hugh Williamson of North Carolina suggested that the legislature should have the power to choose "occasional successors."[15]

John Dickinson of Delaware seconded a motion by Williamson to postpone discussion of the Committee of Detail's succession provision, noting "that it was too vague. What is the extent of the term 'disability' & who is to be the judge of it?"[16] There is no recorded response to Dickinson's questions.

On September 4, the Committee of Eleven proposed that there be an office of Vice President and that the President and Vice President should be chosen by electors.[17] The Committee's report also provided that, in the event of the President's "removal . . . death, absence, resignation or inability to discharge the powers or duties of his office, the vice-president shall exercise those powers and duties until another President be chosen, or until the inability of the President be removed."[18]

On September 7, Edmund Randolph of Virginia moved to add a provision for executive succession specifying that "[t]he legislature may declare by law what officer of the U.S. shall act as President in case of the death, resignation, or disability of the President and Vice-President" and that "such officer shall act accordingly until the time of electing a President shall arrive."[19] Madison objected to the absence of a provision for filling a vacancy by means of a special election, suggesting as a provision "until such disability be removed or a President shall be elected."[20] Some delegates expressed concern that Congress was limited as to whom it could choose as a successor. Randolph's proposal, with Madison's amendment, was approved by a vote of 6 to 4.[21]

On September 12, the Committee of Style returned a draft of the succession provision. It provided that:

> In case of the removal of the president from office, or of his death, resignation, or inability to discharge the powers and duties of the said office, the same shall devolve on the vice-president, and the Congress may by law provide for the case of removal, death, resignation or inability, both of the president and vice-president, declaring what officer shall then act as president, and such officer shall act accordingly, until the disability be removed, or the period for chusing another president arrive.[22]

The Committee made several changes.[23] First, "Officer of the U.S." was changed to "officer." (See Essay No. 97.) Second, "the vice-president shall exercise those powers and duties" was changed to "the same shall devolve on the Vice President." Third, the Committee included Madison's proposal "until such disability be removed, or a President shall be elected" but placed these words only after the provision providing for successors beyond the Vice President.[24] After reviewing the step-by-step development of the succession provision at the Constitutional Convention, it is clear to me[25] that the words "the same shall devolve" referred to the "powers and duties of the office," and the words limiting tenure "until the disability be removed" referred to all successors, including the Vice-President.[26]

The delegates made no further changes in the Committee's report, which was adopted by the Convention.

THE RATIFICATION DEBATES

The Succession Clause was mentioned only in passing in Federalist No. 68. Hamilton remarked on the importance of the Vice President, who "may occasionally become a substitute for the President, in the supreme Executive magistracy."

Likewise, in the state ratification conventions, discussion of the vice presidency focused principally on the role of the Vice President as President of the Senate. There was limited discussion of issues related to presidential succession.[27] All of the drafts before the Committees of Detail and Style were explicit in regard to a Vice President's status as an Acting President in a case of inability. Another part of the original Constitution is consistent with this view. Article I, Section 3, Clause 5 provided that "[t]he Senate shall chuse their other Officers, and also a President pro tempore, in the Absence of the Vice President, or when he shall exercise the Office of President of the United States."[28]

However, the text created ambiguities. Article II, Section 1, Clause 6 provides that "[i]n Case of the Removal of the President from Office, or of his Death, Resignation, or Inability to discharge the Powers and Duties of Office, the Same shall devolve on the Vice President." What is the Vice President's status upon succession? The provision states that "the Same shall devolve on the Vice President." To what words does "the Same" refer, the presidency's "Power and Duties" or the "Office" itself? This distinction is important. If a Vice President took over the "Office," a President who suffered an "Inability" might not be able to come back to power upon recovery. There is another textual uncertainty: The Succession Clause does not provide a definition of "Inability" and does not create a process to declare a President unable to perform the powers and duties of the office.

THE PRESIDENTIAL SUCCESSION ACT OF 1792

In 1792, the Second Congress passed and President George Washington signed the first presidential succession act. This law placed the President pro tempore of the Senate and the Speaker of the House of Representatives next in the line of succession after the Vice President. The statute also provided for a special election to fill both offices when there was a dual vacancy.[29]

For the five decades following ratification, there was no application of the Succession Clause or the 1792 law, but there were several close calls. Both of the Vice Presidents under President James Madison died in office: George Clinton in 1812 and Elbridge Gerry in 1814.[30] Moreover, in 1813, Madison suffered from a serious illness.[31] Had Madison succumbed to his illness, with Gerry dying the following year, there would have been a double vacancy. In late 1832, Vice President John C. Calhoun resigned with less than three months left on his term to fill a Senate vacancy.[32] On March 4, 1841, President William Henry Harrison was inaugurated. One month later, on April 4, 1841, he died in office from pneumonia. Vice President John Tyler was notified by messenger the next day and immediately traveled to Washington by horseback and boat. Tyler arrived on April 6 and was sworn in as President by the chief judge of the Circuit Court for the District of Columbia. Questions were raised immediately concerning his succession to the title and office of the President. Former President John Quincy Adams and others asserted that under the succession provision, he was only an *Acting* President serving as Vice President.

Shortly after the Twenty-Seventh Congress convened for a special session in May 1841, both houses debated the issue. Several members argued that the Vice President was only acting as President and could become President only through election and not by succession.[33] Others argued that the Vice President takes over for an immobilized President, including succeeding to the title. Ultimately, both houses passed a resolution accepting Tyler's claim and appointed a committee to call on him as President.[34] During this debate, concern was expressed as to how a case of inability would be handled.[35]

The rest of the nineteenth century repeated

the earlier history. Three Presidents died in office: Zachary Taylor died from an illness in 1850, Abraham Lincoln was assassinated in 1865, and James A. Garfield was shot in 1881.[36] Garfield died after eighty days of wavering between life and death. During that period, Garfield's Cabinet encouraged Vice President Chester A. Arthur to assume presidential power. However, Arthur hesitated because of the ambiguities surrounding the succession provision.[37] Several Vice Presidents also died in office during the second half of the nineteenth century: William Rufus DeVane King in 1853, Henry Wilson in 1875, Thomas Hendricks in 1885, and Garret Hobart in 1899.[38]

THE PRESIDENTIAL SUCCESSION ACT OF 1886

After Arthur became President in 1881, he asked Congress to consider the legal and constitutional issues surrounding the succession provision.[39] The Presidential Succession Act of 1886 removed the legislative leaders from the line of succession and substituted in their place the heads of the executive departments.[40] The statute did not address presidential inability, nor did it create a mechanism for filling a vacancy in the vice presidency. Both areas remained unresolved.

In the six decades that followed, there would be several more vacancies and disabilities in the executive branch.[41] In 1901, President William McKinley was assassinated. In 1912, Vice President James S. Sherman died. In 1919–20, President Woodrow Wilson suffered a severe incapacity, or inability in office. Wilson's Cabinet made some internal arrangements to handle the functioning of the presidency, which led Wilson to dismiss his Secretary of State.[42] In 1923, President Warren G. Harding died from illness. In 1945, President Franklin D. Roosevelt died from illness. Less than two hours after his death, Chief Justice Harlan Fiske Stone administered the presidential oath of office to Vice President Harry S. Truman, who immediately convened a meeting of his Cabinet, asking them to continue to function in their positions.[43] On June 19, 1945, in a special message to Congress, Truman advocated for a change in the 1886 succession law, stating that the next in line to the presidency should be filled "insofar as possible" by an elective officer such as the Speaker of the

House of Representatives. Bills were introduced in Congress to achieve this goal, and after congressional hearings and debates in both houses, the succession law of 1947 was passed and signed by President Truman on July 18.[44]

THE PRESIDENTIAL SUCCESSION ACT OF 1947

The Presidential Succession Act of 1947 remains in effect to this day.[45] The statute placed the Speaker of the House and the Senate President Pro Tempore as next in the line of succession after the Vice President, followed by the heads of the executive departments in the order of their creation. This statute still did not address the issue of presidential inability or provide a mechanism to fill a vacant vice presidency, but it did provide for succession in a case of inability and limited the term of service to the duration of the disability.

In the late 1950s, after President Dwight D. Eisenhower had suffered three disabling illnesses, the Eisenhower Justice Department attempted to clarify the Constitution on the subject of inability, but these efforts failed to receive approval by Congress. In 1958, President Eisenhower and Vice President Richard Nixon reached an informal framework by letter agreement for handling a future case of inability. Similar writings were adopted by President John F. Kennedy and Vice President Lyndon Johnson in 1961 and by President Johnson and Speaker John McCormack in 1964.[46] The death of President Kennedy on November 22, 1963, incentivized Congress to focus again on the adequacy of Article II, Section 1, Clause 6.

THE TWENTY-FIFTH AMENDMENT

The Twenty-Fifth Amendment (see Essays Nos. 212–214) was ratified in 1967 and resolved many of the issues left unresolved by the Succession Clause. Section 1 of the amendment adopts the Tyler precedent: The Vice President "shall become President" if the President leaves office permanently because of removal, death, or resignation. However, when the President is "unable to discharge the powers and duties of his office," the Vice President is to discharge them as "Acting President." The "Acting President" designation allows an unable President to retain the office of the presidency and return to power upon recovery.

The Twenty-Fifth Amendment did not define the word "Inability" in the Succession Clause. Instead, it created processes for declaring the President unable to perform the powers and duties of office. Section 3 empowers a President to declare voluntarily that he is unable to perform the powers and duties of office. Section 4 empowers the Vice President, acting either with a majority of the Cabinet or with an "other body" created by Congress, to declare the President "unable to discharge the powers and duties of his office."

OPEN QUESTIONS

- The Twenty-Fifth Amendment did not treat inability cases involving a dual inability of both the President and Vice President, an inability of the President when there was no Vice President, or an inability of an Acting President. A political judgment was made that to delve into these additional situations would have doomed the whole effort of providing for a vice presidential vacancy and cases of presidential inability.

Cite as: John D. Feerick, *The Presidential Succession—Devolve Clause, in* THE HERITAGE GUIDE TO THE CONSTITUTION 350 (Josh Blackman & John G. Malcolm eds., 3d ed. 2025).

Notes

1. See John D. Feerick, The Twenty-Fifth Amendment: Its Complete History and Applications (3d ed. 2014). 2. *Id.* 3. John D. Feerick, From Failing Hands: The Story of Presidential Succession 23–39 (1965), https://perma.cc/GPL4-FRTG. 4. Albany Plan of Union, § 22 (1754), https://perma.cc/5RA8-9MYH. 5. Feerick, From Failing Hands, *supra* at 35. 6. Mass. Const. of 1780, ch. II, § 3, art. VI; N.Y. Const. of 1777, arts. XX–XXI. 7. Mass. Const. of 1780, ch. II, § 3, art. VI. 8. N.Y. Const. of 1777, art. XX. 9. 1 Farrand's 20–23, 242–45. 10. *Id.* at 21, 244. 11. *Id.* at 292. 12. 1 Farrand's 20–23, 92. 13. 2 Farrand's 186. 14. *Id.* at 427. 15. *Id.* 16. *Id.* 17. *Id.* at 493–94. 18. *Id.* at 498–99. 19. *Id.* at 535. 20. *Id.* 21. *Id.* 22. *Id.* at 598–99. 23. *Id.* at 599; William M. Treanor, *The Case of the Dishonest Scrivener: Gouverneur Morris and the Creation of the Federalist Constitution*, 120 Mich. L. Rev. 1, 78–83 (2021). 24. 2 Farrand's 598–99. 25. Feerick, From Failing Hands, *supra* at 51. 26. *Id.* 27. *Id.* at 51–56. 28. *Id.* at 50–51; Art. I, § 3, cl. 5. 29. Presidential Succession Act of 1792, ch. 8, 1 Stat. 239 (repealed 1886). 30. Feerick, From Failing Hands, *supra* at 79–84. 31. Feerick, The Twenty-Fifth Amendment, *supra* at 4–5. 32. Feerick, From Failing Hands, *supra* at 85–86. 33. Cong. Globe, 27th Cong., 1st Sess. 3–5 (1841). 34. Feerick, From Failing Hands, *supra* at 89–96. 35. *Id.* at 95–96. 36. Feerick, The Twenty-Fifth Amendment, *supra* at 8–9. 37. *Id.* 38. *Id.* at 314. 39. *Id.* at 10. 40. Presidential Succession Act of 1886, ch. 4, 24 Stat. 1 (repealed 1947). 41. Feerick, The Twenty-Fifth Amendment, *supra* at 14, 16–19, 24. 42. *Id.* at 198–199. 43. Feerick, From Failing Hands, *supra* at 198. 44. *Id.* at 198–99. 45. 61 Stat. 380. 46. Feerick, From Failing Hands, *supra* at 229.

ESSAY NO. 98: THE PRESIDENTIAL SUCCESSION—CONGRESS CLAUSE
ART. II, § 1, CL. 6

. . . and the Congress may by Law provide for the Case of Removal, Death, Resignation or Inability, both of the President and Vice President, declaring what Officer shall then act as President, and such Officer shall act accordingly, until the Disability be removed, or a President shall be elected.

—Josh Blackman & Seth Barrett Tillman

INTRODUCTION

Under the Constitution, the Vice President is next in line to succeed the President. But what happens if the Vice President is unable to serve, and there is a *double vacancy*? The Framers let Congress decide "what Officer shall then act as President" if the President and Vice President are unable to serve, creating a double vacancy. This question may seem mundane, but the orderly succession of power in the executive branch is central to the government's stability. The Presidential Succession Act of 1792 placed the Senate President Pro Tempore and the Speaker of the House in the line of presidential succession after the Vice President. The succession statute currently in force, enacted in 1947, places the Speaker first in line after the Vice President, followed by the Senate President Pro Tempore and then Senate-confirmed Cabinet officers. Some scholars contend that legislative positions like the Speaker are not "Officer[s]" as that term is used in the Presidential Succession Clause, and thus such apex legislative officers cannot stand in the line of succession. We disagree. In the view of the authors of this essay, the word "Officer" in the clause refers to all appointed positions in all three branches of government, as well as the apex presiding officers in Congress. Therefore, the Speaker and Senate President Pro Tempore may lawfully be placed in the statutory line of succession.

THE CONSTITUTIONAL CONVENTION

Significant debate on this clause began on September 7, 1787. (For more detail on the drafting of this clause, see Essay No. 97.) Edmund Randolph of Virginia proposed that "[t]he Legislature may declare by law what officer of the United States shall act as President in case of the death, resignation, or disability of the President and Vice President. . . ."[1] Randolph did not use "officer" standing alone and unmodified; rather, his proposal used "officer of the United States." The Convention adopted Randolph's proposal by a vote of 6 to 4 with one state divided.[2]

James Madison of Virginia recorded several somewhat cryptic comments. First, he wrote, "[i]t seemed to be an objection to [Randolph's] provision with some, that according to the process established for chusing the Executive, there would be difficulty in effecting it at other than the fixed periods."[3] Madison referred to "some" delegates but did not identify them; he merely opined on what led some (and apparently not even most) to object.

Second, Madison noted that, "[i]t seemed to be an objection . . . with others, that the Legislature was restrained in the temporary appointment to '*officers*' of the *U.S.*: <They wished it to be at liberty to appoint others than

such.>"[4] It is unclear what (if anything) Madison intended to convey by putting "officers" in italics and quotation marks. Was he referring to "officers" standing alone and unmodified or to the language in the proposal at that time: "officer of the United States"? Furthermore, Madison did not express entire confidence in his view as to the other delegates' objections. He started his discussion with a hedge: "It seemed." Finally, the material enclosed by "<" and ">" was added later by Madison or under his direction but was not written by Madison during the Convention.[5]

Later in the day on September 7, the Convention approved the Appointments Clause, which provided, in part, that the President "shall nominate . . . all other officers of the United States."[6] The Appointments Clause defined and fixed the meaning of "Officers of the United States."[7] This phrase refers to appointed positions in the executive and judicial branches. But when the Succession Clause was approved earlier that morning, the meaning of "Officers of the United States" was still in flux. For these reasons, we think it likely that once the language of the Appointments Clause had been agreed to, a coordinate change was needed to the draft Presidential Succession Clause.

On September 12, the Committee of Style returned a revised draft of the Presidential Succession Clause. The draft provision specified that "Congress may by law provide for the case of removal, death, resignation or inability, both of the president and vice-president, declaring what officer shall then act as president . . . ."[8] The committee changed "Officer of the U.S." to "officer." The committee may have felt compelled to make this change to keep the Succession Clause's meaning consistent with what had been agreed to earlier. Had the Committee of Style not made that change, the meaning of the Succession Clause would have been altered: Only those who were appointed pursuant to the Appointments Clause could stand in the line of succession. In other words, the Committee of Style ensured that Congress could select from a *broader* category of officers to succeed to the presidency, including within the category of "officer[s]" both "officers of the United States" and also others holding federal positions that were not filled pursuant to the Appointments Clause.

355

The delegates made no further changes in the draft Presidential Succession Clause, and its text was adopted in its final form by the Convention.

THE PRESIDENTIAL SUCCESSION ACT OF 1792

The First Congress considered a presidential succession bill.[9] Members debated whether the Secretary of State, the Chief Justice, or the Senate President Pro Tempore should stand in the line of succession. They were not able to reach agreement, and no bill was enacted.

During the Second Congress, a new succession bill was considered.[10] On November 30, 1791, the Senate approved a bill that placed the Senate President Pro Tempore and Speaker of the House in the line of succession.[11] When the House debated the bill on December 22,[12] Representative Jonathan Sturges of Connecticut argued that the bill was "unconstitutional" because he "could not find that the Speaker of the House, or President of the Senate *pro tem.* were officers of the Government in the sense contemplated by the Constitution."[13] Alexander White of Virginia stated that the Speaker "was not a permanent officer" and "was no more an officer of Government than every other member of the House."[14] William Giles of Massachusetts added that "if they had been considered as such, it is probable they would have been designated in the Constitution." Rather, "these persons are not permanent." Theodore Sedgwick, also of Massachusetts, countered that "he did not know what office could with propriety be said to be permanent." Rather, "[i]n common parlance . . . there was no difficulty in the matter"—in other words, the Speaker and Senate President Pro Tempore were officers. Elbridge Gerry, also of Massachusetts asked, "[if] the Speaker is not an officer . . . what is he?" Gerry pointed to Article 1, Section 2, Clause 5, which provides that "the House shall choose their Speaker *and other officers.*"[15]

On January 2, 1792, Representative Hugh Williamson of North Carolina moved to strike out the Senate President Pro Tempore, which would have left only the Speaker of the House in the line of succession. His motion was defeated by a vote of 27 to 24.[16] Next, the House voted on a proposal to strike out the sub-provision "and in case there shall be no President of the Senate, then the Speaker of the House of Representatives [will serve as President] for the time being." This proposal passed by a vote of 26 to 25.[17] Thus, under the House amendments, only the Senate President Pro Tempore was in the line of succession. Both of these proposals would have maintained some legislative officer succession.

The House debate on the Senate bill continued on January 7.[18] This debate was not recorded in the *Annals of Congress* but was reported in *Claypoole's Daily Advertiser*, a Philadelphia newspaper.[19] Giles argued further that the Senate President Pro Tempore is "not a permanent office" but is instead "accidental and transitory, and at best is a mere auxiliary to another office." For example, this position would not exist while Congress is in recess. The Secretary of State, however, has the "necessary relation and intimate connection" with the President. Giles "regretted the necessity of mentioning this office, because of the person [Thomas Jefferson] who accidentally fills it for the present." Giles would have preferred the "Chief Justice, Secretary of the Treasury, with all their inconveniences, rather than" the Senate President Pro Tempore.

On February 9, the House voted to strike the provision designating the Senate President Pro Tempore to act as President. The House debated adding the Senior Associate Judge (presumably of the Supreme Court) or the Secretary of State to the line of succession.[20] On February 10, the House voted to place the Secretary of State in the line of succession and to remove the Senate President Pro Tempore and Speaker. This time, the vote was 32 to 22.[21] The bill was sent to the Senate on February 15.[22]

The Senate rejected the House's changes. On February 21, the House voted to approve the Senate version by a vote of 31 to 24.[23] In this bill, the Senate President Pro Tempore was first in the line of succession after the Vice President, and the Speaker was second. Among those voting "no" was James Madison. The bill was signed by President Washington on March 1, 1792.[24] Under the controlling presidential succession law, only two persons were in the line of succession after the Vice President: first, the Senate President Pro Tempore, and then the Speaker of the House.

JAMES MADISON'S LETTER CONCERNING THE 1792 ACT

On February 21, 1792, after the succession bill had already passed the House and Senate, James Madison wrote a letter to Edmund Pendleton, then serving as presiding officer of the Supreme Court of Appeals of Virginia. Madison wrote that there was a "point [on which] the Bill certainly errs." He explained there were "various" objections to placing the Senate President Pro Tempore and the Speaker in the line of succession. Madison wrote, "It may be questioned whether these are *officers*, in the constitutional sense," and he concluded that "[t]he House of Reps. proposed to substitute the Secretary of State, but the Senate disagreed, & there being much delicacy in the matter it was not pressed by the former."[25]

Professors Akhil Amar and Vikram Amar have offered this interpretation of the letter: "Madison suggested that legislators were not '*officers*, in the constitutional sense' (again the italics are [Madison's]) and that Congress 'certainly err[ed]' in allowing legislators to succeed to the Presidency."[26] Thus, the Amars contend that the Second Congress unconstitutionally placed the Senate President Pro Tempore and the Speaker in the line of succession and that Madison's letter shows that he too adhered to that position.

We are not so certain. Not all errors are constitutional. Madison's writing that Congress "erred," however, is not coextensive with his asserting that an act of Congress is unconstitutional. Congress can make policy blunders as well as constitutional mistakes. Madison may simply have thought it was a bad decision to put legislators in the line of succession or he may simply have been unsure about this issue. Moreover, it is also not clear whether, in reporting that Congress "erred," Madison was putting forward his own view or reporting a view announced by others in floor debate.

No record exists to show that Madison publicly made the arguments that he flagged in his letter to Pendleton. We have no record that then-Representative Madison made any speeches on the House floor making these arguments. We also have no evidence that Madison lobbied President Washington to veto this bill on the grounds that it was unconstitutional (as he had done with respect to the Bank of the United States bill[27]). We also have no evidence that Madison revisited this issue either during his tenure in President Jefferson's cabinet or during his own two terms as President.

The authors of this essay think the better view is that Madison was summarizing and, to some extent, perhaps "improving" on the news of the day. He was reporting arguments he had heard during the House debate to Pendleton, who was in Virginia. That is not to say that Madison thought these arguments wrongheaded. Madison was likely sympathetic to these arguments, but it is not clear that these arguments were *his* arguments. It appears that Giles was the primary advocate in the House for the position that legislative officer succession was unconstitutional. Madison's letter made points that were substantially similar to those made by Giles during the January 7, 1792, debate reported in *Claypoole's Daily Advertiser*. Our view is that Madison's letter summarized Giles's arguments.

We should hesitate to conclude that Washington and the Second Congress enacted a facially unconstitutional law that could throw the entire country into chaos following a double vacancy. The constitutional decisions set by the Washington Administration and this early Congress are entitled to due deference. Moreover, this statute would remain in effect for nearly a century. This long-standing settled statutory history provides some further support for its validity.

THE PRESIDENTIAL SUCCESSION ACT OF 1886

In December 1885, in his first annual message to Congress, President Grover Cleveland said that recent vacancies in the presidency and vice presidency had "caused public anxiety" and "require[d] immediate amendment."[28] The Senate debated a new succession bill. Under this bill, only members of the President's cabinet would stand in the line of succession after the Vice President: first, the Secretary of State; second, the Secretary of the Treasury; third, the Secretary of War; fourth, the Attorney General; and so on. Most of the discussion focused on the policy problems attendant on having legislative officers stand in line for the presidency.

It is noteworthy that Senators raised the constitutional issue of whether the Senate President Pro Tempore and the Speaker could stand in the line of succession. Senator Samuel B. Maxey of Texas did not think that "the President of the Senate or the Speaker of the House was such an officer as the Constitution contemplated."[29] To support his position, Maxey cited Madison's letter to Pendleton.[30] Senator George Hoar of Massachusetts found it "questionable" whether "the President Pro Tempore of the Senate or the Speaker of the House is an officer of the United States."[31] Senator John Morgan of Alabama said that a Senator can "scarcely be called in any sense an officer of the United States," and is "far more an officer of his State. . . ."[32] Senator William Evarts of New York argued that Senators and Representatives were "excluded" and could not stand in the line of succession because they were not officers. Evarts thought this new bill "conformed to the absolute language of the Constitution."[33] Senator George Edmunds of Vermont replied that the Constitution expressly referred to the Senate President Pro Tempore as an officer.[34] And Senator Wilkinson Call of Florida argued that Senators and Representatives were Officers of the United States, since "Their sole existence and their sole function is derived entirely from their relation to the Constitution of the United States."[35]

The Amars contend that congressional debates illustrate that there was "widespread doubt as to the constitutionality of the 1792 Act, based in large part on the scope of the term 'Officer.'"[36] We think the arguments on both sides of this issue were more balanced. In 1792, 1886, and later, members of Congress would disagree about the meaning of "officer" as used in the Succession Clause and in other constitutional provisions.

The Senate and House passed the bill. In January 1886, President Grover Cleveland signed the new Presidential Succession Act.[37] This law removed the Senate President Pro Tempore and the Speaker of the House from the line of succession and would remain in effect until the Presidential Succession Act of 1947.

THE PRESIDENTIAL SUCCESSION ACT OF 1947

On June 19, 1945, after Victory in Europe Day, President Harry Truman sent Congress a special message urging members that "this is an appropriate time . . . to reexamine the question of the Presidential succession."[38] Truman recognized that the 1886 Presidential Succession Act effectively granted him, in the case of a double vacancy, the "power to nominate the person who would be [his] immediate successor in the event of [his] own death or inability to act." Truman did not "believe that in a democracy this power should rest with the Chief Executive." Instead, Truman was of the view that "the office of the President should be filled by an elective officer" and not by a Cabinet member. (Several members of President Franklin Roosevelt's cabinet had never held elective office.) Truman recognized that the Speaker is "elected to be the presiding officer of the House by a vote of all the Representatives of all the people of the country." In this capacity, the Speaker "is the official in the Federal Government, whose selection next to that of the President and Vice President, can be most accurately said to stem from the people themselves." Truman thought the Senate President Pro Tempore should be second in line because Senators "are not as closely tied in by the elective process to the people as are the members of the House of Representatives." If the Speaker and Senate President Pro Tempore cannot serve, Truman acknowledged, "then the succession might pass to the members of the Cabinet as now provided."[39]

Two years later, Congress approved the Presidential Succession Act of 1947.[40] As Truman requested, the Speaker of the House was placed first in line, and the Senate President Pro Tempore was placed second. These legislative officers were followed by Cabinet officers: the Secretary of State, Secretary of the Treasury, Secretary of War (now Defense), Attorney General, and so on.

Like the original 1792 statute, the current presidential succession act, enacted in 1947, also places the two presiding congressional officers in the line of succession after the Vice President. However, under the 1947 act, the order is reversed. After the Vice President, the Speaker is first and the Senate President pro tempore is second. After the two presiding congressional officers, Congress selected the Secretary of State as next in the line of succession, followed by other Cabinet members.

Several members of Congress doubted the bill was constitutional. They contended that the Speaker and Senate President pro tempore were not "officers" for purposes of the Succession Clause.[41] Representative Clarence Hancock of New York argued that the Speaker "is not an officer of the United States."[42] Representative John Gwynne of Iowa argued that the Incompatibility Clause demonstrates that members of Congress cannot be officers.[43]

Other members argued that legislative officer succession was constitutional. Representative Estes Kefauver of Tennessee countered that "[t]he Constitution does not say that [the Speaker] must be an officer of the executive branch in order to be eligible to be named in the line of succession." He added that "[n]owhere in the debate in 1792 was the argument made that the Speaker of the House and the President pro tempore were not officers within the meaning of the Constitution."[44] Representative Mike Monroney of Oklahoma argued that legislative officer succession was constitutional. He argued that the issue had been "resolved" because the 1792 Act was passed "only a few short years after the Constitution had been written" and "stood for almost 100 years."[45] Representative Francis May of Pennsylvania observed that the "first officer mentioned in the Constitution is the Speaker of the House of Representatives."[46]

Acting Attorney General Douglas W. McGregor wrote a letter defending the law's constitutionality.[47] He explained that the issue was whether "the Speaker of the House and the Senate President pro tempore . . . are officers within the meaning of" the Succession Clause, and not whether a rank-and-file member of Congress is a civil officer of the United States for purposes of the Impeachment Clause. McGregor added that the word "officer" in the Succession Clause is used "without qualification." In other words, the Attorney General distinguished between an "officer," as that term is used without modification, and an "officer of the United States." He further wrote that the word "officer" "presumably includes not only officers of the executive branch of the Government, but also officers of the judicial and legislative branches." McGregor also pointed to the 1792 statute: "This law represents a construction of article II by an early Congress, whose views of the Constitution

have long been regarded as authoritative, and reflects a long-continued acquiescence in such a construction."

The Amars described the Attorney General's reasoning as "shoddy."[48] They wrote that McGregor, writing in 1947, "failed to address the textual and structural criticisms of that construction raised" in their 1995 article.[49]

IS THE PRESIDENTIAL SUCCESSION ACT OF 1947 CONSTITUTIONAL?

The Amars argued that the Presidential Succession Act of 1947 is unconstitutional: that "Officer," as used in "the Succession Clause, "is merely shorthand for any of the[] . . . longer formulations" of the Constitution's "office"- and "officer"-language, such as "Officers of the United States" and "Office . . . under the United States."[50] The Amars explained that "[a]s a textual matter," the varied references to officers of the United States and office under the United States "seemingly describe[] the same stations."[51] They did entertain the possibility that the Framers drew a "civil/military distinction" among different types of officers but posited that "the modifying terms 'of,' 'under,' and 'under the Authority of' are essentially synonymous."[52] The Amars concluded that the Constitution's divergent "office" and "officer" language creates a "global officer/legislator distinction."[53] More than a few prominent scholars have adopted their position either in whole or in part.[54]

Our view is that the word "officer" or "office," standing alone and unmodified, simply refers to a "position" in the national government created by the Constitution, whether appointed or elected. Two categories of positions can be considered an "Officer" for purposes of the Succession Clause.[55] First, all holders of "Office[s] . . . under the United States"—that is, all appointed positions in all three branches of government—could lawfully be placed in the statutory line of succession to the presidency. Second, an "Officer" of "the Government of the United States"[56] also could lawfully be placed in the statutory line of succession. We contend that the apex presiding officers referred to in the Constitution—specifically, the "Officers" of the "Government of the United States"— can succeed to the presidency. This category includes the Speaker of the House, the Senate

President Pro Tempore, and the Chief Justice. It also includes the President and Vice President.

Of course, in the event of a double vacancy, it makes no sense to put the President and Vice President in the line of succession. We do not think that rank-and-file members of Congress—Senators and Representatives—could lawfully be placed in the statutory line of succession. They are not apex presiding officers. In fact, they are not "officers" of any stripe. Thus, in our view, the provision of the Presidential Succession Act of 1792 as well as the successor provision in the Presidential Succession Act of 1947, placing apex presiding legislative officers in the line of succession, were constitutional.[57]

OPEN QUESTIONS

- In October 2020, President Donald Trump was hospitalized for three days because of COVID-19.[58] Vice President Michael Pence had recently been exposed to Trump. At the time, there was a robust debate about who would have become President in the event of a double vacancy: Speaker Nancy Pelosi, a Democrat, or Secretary of State Mike Pompeo, a Republican.[59] Some leading constitutional scholars endorsed the Amars' 1995 view, and some further suggested that the Presidential Succession Act of 1947 was unconstitutional.[60] Professor John Yoo found the Amars' view "persuasive[]."[61] Yoo wrote that Pompeo, not Pelosi, would become President in the case of a double vacancy. Professor Jack Goldsmith likewise observed that both Pelosi and Pompeo "could make competing claims to the presidency." How would the courts have adjudicated this issue?
- The Succession Act of 1947 requires that the officer elevated to President must resign his current position. Is this requirement constitutional? If it is not constitutional, can this resignation provision be severed from the remainder of the 1947 act, including the sections which elevate a would-be successor?
- If the Speaker of the House or the Senate President Pro Tempore succeeds to the presidency, does the Succession Clause require that he resign his position as a presiding legislative officer and as a member of Congress? Would he have to resign by virtue of the Incompatibility Clause, or would his resignation take effect by operation of law when the Speaker or Senate President Pro Tempore assumes the presidency?
- If the Secretary of State succeeds to the presidency, does the Constitution preclude his holding both positions concurrently?
- Could Congress place a recess appointee in the statutory line of presidential succession? Is a recess appointee an "Officer" for purposes of the Succession Clause?
- Could Congress place an acting officer of the United States in the statutory line of presidential succession? Does it matter whether the acting officer also holds an office appointed by the President and confirmed by the Senate but that other office is not in the statutory line of succession? Is an acting officer an "Officer" for purposes of the Succession Clause?
- Under the 1947 act, in the case of a double vacancy, if the Speaker of the House and the Senate President Pro Tempore choose not to accept the presidency, a Cabinet member can accept the presidency. What happens if the Speaker or Senate President Pro Tempore changes his or her mind? Can the Cabinet member be *bumped*? Is the 1947 act's bumping provision constitutional?
- As a policy matter, is legislative officer succession desirable? There was legislative officer succession under the Delaware Constitution of 1776 and the New York Constitution of 1777.[62] Some scholars describe it as a "nightmare."[63] The authors of this essay counter that the "long-standing policy objection[s]" to legislative officer succession are "dangerously misguided."[64] Seth Barrett Tillman has suggested placing legislative officers at the bottom of the statutory line of succession to function as

a flexible backstop if all the Cabinet members (that is, the fixed line of succession) were to die, resign, become incapacitated, etc.[65]

- Akhil Amar has argued that, although legislative officer succession is unconstitutional, it may be permissible "in very, very highly unusual situations."[66] Dean John Feerick contended that the issue is "ambiguous," and he was "not entirely convinced that [legislative officer succession] is unconstitutional."[67] Professor Joel Goldstein suggests that "'Officer'. . . may have been understood to have a broader meaning than 'Officer of the United States,'" and the Speaker could be in the former category even if not in the latter.[68] Majorities of the House and Senate in the Second Congress, as well as in 1947, enacted a bill placing the two presiding legislative officers in the line of succession after the Vice President. Indeed, under the 1792 act, the two presiding legislative officers were the entire line of succession after the Vice President, and President Washington signed that bill.

Cite as: Josh Blackman & Seth Barrett Tillman, *The Presidential Succession—Congress Clause*, *in* THE HERITAGE GUIDE TO THE CONSTITUTION 354 (Josh Blackman & John G. Malcolm eds., 3d ed. 2025).

Notes

1. 2 Farrand's 532, 535. **2.** *Id*. at 535. **3.** 2 Farrand's 535. **4.** *Id*. **5.** 1 Farrand's xviii–xix. **6.** 2 Farrand's 533, 539. **7.** Seth Barrett Tillman & Josh Blackman, *Offices and Officers of the Constitution, Part III: The Appointments, Impeachment, Commissions, and Oath or Affirmation Clauses*, 62 S. Tex. L. Rev. 349, 353 (2023). **8.** 2 Farrand's 598–99. **9.** Annals of Cong., 1st Cong., 3d Sess. 1911–15 (1791). **10.** John D. Feerick, From Failing Hands: The Story of Presidential Succession 58–59 (1965); Ruth C. Silva, Presidential Succession (1951); Ruth C. Silva, *The Presidential Succession Act of 1947*, 47 Mich. L. Rev. 451, 475 (1949). **11.** Annals of Congress, 2d Cong., 1st Sess. 36–38 (1791). **12.** *Id*. at 278. **13.** *Id*. at 281. **14.** *Id*. **15.** *Id*. **16.** Annals of Congress, 2d Cong., 1st Sess. 302–03 (1792). **17.** *Id*. at 303. **18.** *Id*. at 302–03, 315. **19.** *Philadelphia, Jan. 10. House of Representatives of the United States, Friday, January 7*, The Mail, or Claypoole's Daily Advertiser, Jan. 7, 1792, at 2–3, https://perma.cc/22J7-HLH2. **20.** Annals of Cong., 2d Cong., 1st Sess. 401 (1792). **21.** *Id*. at 402. **22.** *Id*. at 406–07. **23.** *Id*. at 417–18. **24.** 1 Stat. 239 (1792). **25.** Letter from James Madison to Edmund Pendleton (Feb. 21, 1792), https://perma.cc/S8LZ-A442. **26.** Akhil Reed Amar & Vikram David Amar, *Is the Presidential Succession Law Constitutional?*, 48 Stan. L. Rev. 113, 116 (1995). **27.** Message from James Madison to George Washington (Feb. 21, 1791), https://perma.cc/K4AH-VHKT. **28.** 8 Messages and Papers of the Presidents (Dec. 8, 1885), https://perma.cc/9NJL-LX6E. **29.** 17 Cong. Rec. 214 (1885), https://perma.cc/B6GB-RCNQ. **30.** *Id*. at 215. **31.** *Id*. at 221. **32.** *Id*. at 222. **33.** *Id*. at 250. **34.** *Id*. at 251. **35.** *Id*. at 224. **36.** Amar & Amar, *supra* at 134. **37.** 24 Stat. 1. **38.** President Harry S. Truman, Special Message to the Congress on the Succession to the Presidency (June 19, 1945), https://perma.cc/GP57-3MYG. **39.** *Id*. **40.** 61 Stat. 380. **41.** 91 Cong. Rec. 7011–12, 7015, 7017–18, 7022 (1945). **42.** *Id*. at 7015. **43.** *Id*. at 7017. **44.** *Id*. at 7016. **45.** *Id*. at 7012. **46.** *Id*. at 7013. **47.** 93 Cong. Rec. 8621–22 (1947), https://perma.cc/53DF-S3SG.

48. Amar & Amar, *supra* at 134. **49.** *Id*. at 134 n.131. **50.** *Id*. at 115. **51.** *Id*. at 114. **52.** *Id*. at 115. **53.** *Id*. at 117. **54.** Joshua A. Chafetz, Democracy's Privileged Few: Legislative Privilege and Democratic Norms in the British and American Constitutions 280 n.68 (2007); Seth Barrett Tillman & Steven G. Calabresi, Debate, *The Great Divorce: The Current Understanding of Separation of Powers and the Original Meaning of the Incompatibility Clause*, 157 U. Pa. L. Rev. PENNumbra 134, 135–40, 141–45, 146–53, 154–59 (2008); Saikrishna Bangalore Prakash, Response, *Why the Incompatibility Clause Applies to the Office of the President*, 4 Duke J. Const. L. & Pub. Pol'y Sidebar 35, 41–42 (2009); Benjamin Cassady, *"You've Got Your Crook, I've Got Mine": Why the Disqualification Clause Doesn't (Always) Disqualify*, 32 Quinnipiac L. Rev. 209, 287–94 (2014); Vasan Kesavan, *The Very Faithless Elector?*, 104 W. Va. L. Rev. 123, 129 n.28 (2001). **55.** Seth Barrett Tillman & Josh Blackman, *Offices and Officers of the Constitution, Part II: The Four Approaches*, 61 S. Tex. L. Rev. 321, 414–20 (2021). **56.** Art. I, § 8, cl. 18. **57.** Josh Blackman & Seth Barrett Tillman, *The Weird Scenario That Pits President Pelosi Against Citizen Trump in 2020*, The Atlantic (Nov. 20, 2019), https://perma.cc/8EES-3NTX. **58.** Christina Morales et al., *A Timeline of Trump's Symptoms and Treatments*, N.Y. Times (Oct. 14, 2020), https://perma.cc/3HZM-7WS6. **59.** Josh Blackman, *Do Professors Akhil and Vikram Amar Still Think the Presidential Succession Act Is Constitutional?*, Volokh Conspiracy (Oct. 3, 2020), https://perma.cc/D2JW-6L5U. **60.** Nicholas Fandos & Nick Corasaniti, *What If Trump Can't Run? Many Steps Are Clear, but Some Are Not*, N.Y. Times (Oct. 2, 2020), https://perma.cc/A4DG-3834. **61.** John Yoo, *A Winding Constitutional Path from Trump to Pence to Pompeo*, Wall St. J. (Oct. 2, 2020), https://perma.cc/N9AF-N9ZJ. **62.** Del. Const. of 1776, art. VII; N.Y. Const. of 1777, art. XXI. **63.** Jack Goldsmith & Ben Miller-Gootnick, *A Presidential Succession Nightmare*, Lawfare (Mar. 25, 2020, 1:38 PM), https://perma.cc/3T4A-GBSE. **64.** Seth Barrett Tillman, *Why Strict Cabinet Succession Is Always Bad Policy: A*

Response to Professor Jack Goldsmith and Ben Miller-Gootnick, Harv. Nat'l Sec. J. Online (Apr. 8, 2020), https://perma.cc/D9V9-DA8F.   **65.** *Id.*; Seth Barrett Tillman, *A Defense of the Legislative "Officer" Succession Provisions*, 91 Fordham L. Rev. Online 23 (2022), https://perma.cc/KK7X-BDG9.   **66.** Presidential Succession Act: Hearing Before the Subcomm. on the Const. of the H. Comm. on the Judiciary, 108th Cong. 52 (2004), https://perma.cc/RX6G-BR4N.   **67.** John D. Feerick, *A Response to Akhil Reed Amar's Address on Application and Implications of the Twenty-Fifth Amendment*, 47 Hous. L. Rev. 41, 62 (2010); John D. Feerick, *Presidential Succession and Inability: Before and After the Twenty-Fifth Amendment*, 79 Fordham L. Rev. 907, 944 (2011).   **68.** Joel K. Goldstein, *Akhil Reed Amar and Presidential Continuity*, 47 Hous. L. Rev. 67, 86 (2010); Joel K. Goldstein, *Taking from the 25th Amendment: Lessons in Ensuring Presidential Continuity*, 79 Fordham L. Rev. 959, 1022 (2010).

ESSAY NO. 99: THE PRESIDENTIAL COMPENSATION CLAUSE
ART. II, § 1, CL. 7

The President shall, at stated Times, receive for his Services, a Compensation, which shall neither be increased nor diminished during the Period for which he shall have been elected. . . .

—Kate Comerford Todd & Tara Helfman

INTRODUCTION

The Presidential Compensation Clause requires that the President receive "a Compensation" for his services that cannot be changed during "the Period for which he shall have been elected." Although this clause may seem like a fairly anodyne provision, history shows that the clause acts as a vital safeguard of the separation of powers and our republican form of government. Two themes have emerged throughout its history: The clause safeguards the separation of powers by denying Congress any power to alter the compensation of a sitting President during his term in office, and it preserves the integrity of the Executive by preventing a sitting President from signing into law a pay raise that would take effect during his term in office.

HISTORY BEFORE 1787

The principles underlying the Presidential Compensation Clause originated in the difficult relationship between local assemblies and royal governors in the American colonies. By the 1750s, each of the thirteen colonies was governed, at least nominally, by a governor who was appointed by and answerable to the king.[1] Even though they represented the executive power of the Crown, the royal governors were wholly dependent on colonial legislatures for appropriations, and these assemblies, elected by local voters, were not shy about using the power of the purse to impose their will on an unelected executive.[2] In some cases, they even withheld governors' salaries when royal instructions conflicted with local interests.[3] "Some Remedy must be found," one royal official warned, "or the People will at last govern."[4] Thomas Pownall, a member of Parliament, observed that the "scepter is . . . reversed," and "the officers of the crown [were] dependent on and governed by the [colonial] assemblies."[5]

In 1766, Parliament attempted to reassert royal authority in the colonies. The Townshend Revenue Act imposed duties on goods imported into the colonies for the stated purpose of raising revenue "for the support of civil government" in America.[6] Charles Townshend, the measure's architect, argued that "[t]he salaries of governors and judges . . . must be made independent of their [colonial] assemblies."[7] The response in the colonies was fierce: This was a direct tax masquerading as a customs regulation, and Parliament had no authority to levy a direct tax on the colonies without their consent. Making matters even worse, as John Dickinson observed in *Letters from a Farmer in Pennsylvania*, the royal governors would now be paid with revenue raised without the consent of the governed.[8] During the Revolutionary Era, the question of executive compensation was bound up with colonial demands for self-government, political representation, and political accountability.

After independence, state constitutions established chief executives elected either directly by the voters or indirectly by the state legislatures. Some of these constitutions expressly provided for executive compensation. In Delaware, Virginia, and North Carolina, the executive's salary had to be "adequate."[9] The South Carolina constitution specified 9,000 pounds per annum.[10] Other constitutions were silent on the matter. The Massachusetts constitution of 1776 reflected the lessons of the Colonial Era and foreshadowed the Executive framed by the Constitution of 1788. It instructed the state legislature to establish for the governor "an honorable stated salary, of a fixed and permanent value, amply sufficient" to serve three purposes: to preserve the governor's independence from "the undue influence" of the legislature, to prevent his "private concerns" from distracting him from serving the common good, and to "maintain the dignity of the commonwealth in the character of its chief magistrate[.]"[11]

THE CONSTITUTIONAL CONVENTION

From the very outset of the Constitutional Convention, the delegates agreed that the federal Executive, whatever its form, should receive a fixed salary from Congress. The Virginia Plan proposed a National Executive that would "receive punctually at stated times, a fixed compensation for the services rendered, in which no increase or diminution shall be made so as to affect the Magistracy, existing at the time[.]"[12] The New Jersey Plan incorporated the Virginia Plan's Executive compensation provision almost verbatim even though the two proposals differed from each other in almost every other way.[13] In fact, while proposals for the configuration of Executive power changed over the course of the Convention, the salary requirement remained more or less the same.[14]

The Committee of Detail reformulated the compensation clause in a way that echoed similar provisions in state constitutions: The President "shall, at stated Times, receive for his Services, a fixed Compensation, which shall neither be encreased nor diminished during his Continuance in Office."[15] The Committee of Style changed "during his Continuance in

Office" to "during the period for which he shall have been elected."[16] Under this provision, a sitting President could not sign a bill that would increase his salary. However, it would be possible for a President who is re-elected to sign a bill that increases the compensation for his subsequent term.

Benjamin Franklin was the only delegate at the Convention who objected to allowing the Executive to receive a salary. In prepared remarks, he expressed concern that the temptation of both power and money would make the high office attractive to "the bold and the violent, the men of strong passions and indefatigable activity in their selfish pursuits."[17] "[M]aking our posts of honor places of profit," he explained, would "sow the seeds of contention, faction & tumult" and would "nourish the foetus of a King[.]"[18] Instead, he argued, the office should be occupied by "wise and good men" actuated by "public spirit."[19] Franklin therefore moved to amend the text to provide that the Executive "shall receive no salary, stipend fee or reward whatsoever for their services."[20] Alexander Hamilton seconded the motion "with the view . . . merely of bringing so respectable a proposition before the Committee."[21] The proposal was immediately tabled without debate.[22]

THE RATIFICATION DEBATES

During the ratification debates, several opponents of the Constitution reiterated Franklin's concerns, albeit far less eloquently. Cornelius, an Anti-Federalist from Massachusetts, warned that the President's compensation was not "far below that of an European Monarch."[23] In Federalist No. 73, Hamilton provided a full-throated defense of the Presidential Compensation Clause as a necessary safeguard of the separation of powers. Congress could not "weaken [the President's] fortitude by operating upon his necessities, nor corrupt his integrity by appealing to his avarice." Hamilton recognized that "a power over a man's support, is a power over his will." There may be some men who can resist this temptation, but "this stern virtue is the growth of few soils." Hamilton added in Federalist No. 79 that Congress could not control the sitting President's will because it could not raise or lower his salary or alter when he would be paid.

EARLY PRACTICE

At the time, some state constitutions required "honorable," "adequate," "modest," or even "amply sufficient" compensation for the executive. The Federal Constitution, however, simply required that the President's compensation be "fixed" and provided at pre-stated intervals. The First Congress debated whether the President's compensation should correspond to the style in which Congress wanted him to live or correspond to the value of his services.[24]

President George Washington's inaugural address further complicated the matter. He announced that he would "renounce every pecuniary compensation" for serving as President and instead asked Congress to provide funds to cover "such actual expenditures as the public good may be thought to require."[25] Congress declined Washington's gesture on the ground that the Presidential Compensation Clause imposed a clear duty on Congress to fix the President's compensation.[26]

Ultimately, Congress settled on an annual salary of $25,000, to be paid quarterly.[27] (This amount would be about $900,000 in present-day value.) However, the statute did not address whether the President should be reimbursed for expenses associated with his service in office.

APPLICABLE LEGISLATION

The President's salary has been adjusted only five times since 1790. It was increased to $50,000 in 1873, $75,000 in 1909, $100,000 in 1949, $200,000 in 1969, and $400,000 in 1999.[28] The increase of 1873 was enacted on March 3, 1873, and went into effect the following day when Ulysses S. Grant was sworn in for his second term.[29] The increase of 1949 was enacted on January 19, 1949, and also went into effect the following day when Harry S. Truman was sworn in for his second term.[30]

It could be argued that the plain text of the Presidential Compensation Clause prohibits a President from signing a pay raise into law on the eve of his own reinauguration. The clause uses the future perfect tense ("shall have been elected"), so the prohibition would appear to apply not only to the current term of a sitting President, but also to a second term to which he had been elected at the time of enactment. Whatever the case, the constitutionality of the Grant and Truman salary increases remains an open question, as the measures were not challenged in court.

The 1949 statute also established an annual allowance for the President of $50,000 "to assist in defraying expenses relating to or resulting from the discharge of his official duties."[31] The allowance is not included in the President's gross income, and the President must return any unused amount to the federal government.[32] While the allowance is not taxable, the President's income is subject to the federal income tax.[33] This allowance has not been increased or decreased since its creation in 1949.

OPEN QUESTIONS

- The Presidential Compensation Clause provides for the President's "compensation." The Domestic Emoluments Clause prohibits the President from accepting certain "emoluments." What is the difference between compensation and emoluments?
- Does the Constitution prohibit a Presidential salary increase that is signed into law after the President is elected to a second, consecutive term but before the President is sworn in a second time?

Cite as: Kate Comerford Todd & Tara Helfman, *The Presidential Compensation Clause, in* THE HERITAGE GUIDE TO THE CONSTITUTION 362 (Josh Blackman & John G. Malcolm eds., 3d ed. 2025).

Notes

1. Leonard W. Labaree, Royal Government in America: A Study of the British Colonial System Before 1783, at 179 (1958). **2.** *Id.* at 269–71. **3.** Edgar J. McManus & Tara Helfman, 1 Liberty and Union: A Constitutional History of the United States 23–25 (2014). **4.** Archibald Kennedy, *An Essay on the Government of the Colonies* (1752), *in* 2 Exploring the Bounds of Liberty: Political Writings of Colonial British America from the Glorious Revolution to the American Revolution 1286 (Jack P. Greene & Craig B. Yirush eds., 2018). **5.** Thomas Pownall, The Administration of the Colonies 47 (1764). **6.** 7 Geo. 3 c. 46. **7.** John Phillip Reid, Constitutional History of the American Revolution: The

Authority to Tax 219 (1987).   **8.** 1 The American Revolution: Writings from the Pamphlet Debate, 1764–1772, at 406, 464 (Gordon S. Wood ed., 2015).   **9.** Del. Const. of 1776, art. VII; Va. Const. of 1776; N.C. Const. of 1776, art. XXI. **10.** S.C. Const. of 1776, art. XXXIV.   **11.** Mass. Const. of 1776, art. 13.   **12.** 1 Farrand's 21.   **13.** *Id.* at 244.   **14.** 2 Farrand's 61, 116, 132, 146, 185, 575, 599.   **15.** *Id.* at 172. **16.** *Id.* at 599.   **17.** *Id.* at 82.   **18.** 1 Farrand's 83.   **19.** *Id.* at 85. **20.** *Id.* at 81.   **21.** *Id.* at 85.   **22.** *Id.*   **23.** Storing 4.10.12. **24.** 1 Debates and Proceedings in the Congress of the United States 657–662 (Jul. 13, 1789).   **25.** George Washington, First Inaugural Address (Apr. 30, 1789).   **26.** Saikrishna Bangalore Prakash, Imperial from the Beginning: The Constitution of the Original Executive 54–56 (2015). **27.** Act of Sept. 24, 1789, 1 Stat. 72.   **28.** Cong. Rsrch. Serv., RS20115, President of the United States: Compensation 3 (2012), https://perma.cc/BG3G-VX8B. James F. Vivian, The President's Salary: A Study in Constitutional Declension, 1789–1990 (1993).   **29.** 17 Stat. 485.   **30.** Act of Jan. 19, 1949, c. 2, §1(a), 63 Stat. 4.   **31.** *Id.*   **32.** 3 U.S.C. § 102.   **33.** *Id.*

ESSAY NO. 100: THE DOMESTIC EMOLUMENTS CLAUSE
ART. II, § 1, CL. 7

. . . and [the President] shall not receive within that Period any other Emolument from the United States, or any of them.

—Josh Blackman & Seth Barrett Tillman

INTRODUCTION

The Constitution limits Congress's ability to change its own compensation, the President's compensation, and Article III judges' compensation. The President's compensation cannot be increased or decreased during his elected term.[1] (See Essay No. 99.) Compensation for federal judges cannot be decreased but can be increased while they remain in office.[2] (See Essay No. 122.) Under the original Constitution, compensation for members of Congress could be increased or decreased at any time.[3] (See Essay No. 30.) The Twenty-Seventh Amendment now provides that any change in congressional compensation can take effect only after a new election. (See Essay No. 216.)

The Constitution also restricts certain federal government officials and officers from receiving other forms of compensation and benefits. For example, the Foreign Emoluments Clause provides that those holding an "Office of Profit or Trust under" the United States cannot receive an "Emolument . . . of any kind" from a foreign government.[4] (See Essay No. 76.) The Supreme Court has observed that the term "emoluments" refers to "every species of compensation or pecuniary profit derived from a discharge of the duties of the office."[5]

The Constitution further provides that the President "shall not receive within that Period" to which he was elected "any other Emolument from the United States, or any of them." This provision, known as the Domestic Emoluments Clause or the Presidential Emoluments Clause, prohibits the President from receiving any emoluments from the state governments and from receiving any emoluments from the federal government apart from his regular presidential compensation. It is the view of the authors of this essay that this provision does not restrict the President from receiving income or other benefits from other entities, including domestic and foreign private commercial entities, and furthermore, it does not squarely bar even any federal or state government office-related benefits unless such benefits take the form of "emoluments."

THE CONSTITUTIONAL CONVENTION

The Domestic Emoluments Clause was added to the Constitution only two days before the document was signed. On September 15, 1787, John Rutledge of South Carolina and Benjamin Franklin of Pennsylvania sought to "annex" the Presidential Compensation Clause.[6] As previously reported by the Committee of Style on September 12, that provision specified that "[t]he president shall, at stated times, receive a fixed compensation for his services, which shall neither be encreased nor diminished during the period for which he shall have been elected."[7] Rutledge and Franklin added that "he (the President) shall not receive, within that Period [to which he was elected], any other emolument from the U. S. or any of them." (The word "them" refers to any of the states in the Union.)

This proposal was adopted by a vote of 7 to 4. There was no recorded debate. Much earlier in the Convention, on June 2, Franklin had urged the delegates not to give the proposed "Executive" any salary or regular compensation and, instead, to grant him only expenses.[8] In 1981, the Department of Justice's Office of Legal Counsel (OLC) explained that "[t]he extant records of the Constitutional Convention are silent regarding the purposes which" the Domestic Emoluments Clause was "intended to serve."[9]

THE RATIFICATION DEBATES

In Federalist No. 73, Alexander Hamilton discussed the importance of the Presidential Compensation Clause and the Domestic Emoluments Clause. He stressed the importance of "providing for vigor of the executive authority" and "an adequate provision for its support." Once Congress "declare[s]" the President's compensation, the legislature will "have no power to alter it." Moreover, the federal government and the states will not "be at liberty to give, nor will [the President] be at liberty to receive, any other emolument than that which may have been determined by the first act." Congress "can neither weaken his fortitude by operating on his necessities, nor corrupt his integrity by appealing to his avarice."

At the Pennsylvania ratification convention, James Wilson likewise explained that the Domestic Emoluments Clause was designed "to secure the President from any dependence upon the legislature as to his salary. . . ."[10]

THE FOREIGN AND DOMESTIC EMOLUMENTS CLAUSES

The Foreign Emoluments Clause prohibits a person "holding any Office of Profit or Trust under" the United States from accepting "any present, Emolument, Office, or Title, of any kind whatever, from any King, Prince, or foreign State" without congressional consent.[11] The Domestic Emoluments Clause provides that the President "shall not receive within that Period any other Emolument from the United States, or any of them."

There are several differences between these provisions. First, the Foreign Emoluments Clause applies to those holding an "Office . . . under the United States." It is our view that this phrase refers to appointed positions in the executive and judicial branches as well as non-apex appointed positions in the legislative branch, but the President does not hold such an office.[12] The Domestic Emoluments Clause applies solely to the President.

Second, the Foreign Emoluments Clause applies to a wide range of compensation and benefits: presents, emoluments, offices, and titles. The Domestic Emoluments Clause applies exclusively to emoluments. It follows that the Domestic Emoluments Clause does not bar the President from receiving presents or from holding an uncompensated office. The language of the clause only bars drawing a second set of "emoluments." This suggests that the President may concurrently hold a second federal or state position but is prohibited from receiving the emoluments (if any) attached to the second position.

Third, the Foreign Emoluments Clause applies to "any" present, emolument, office, or title "of any kind whatever." This language arguably broadens the meaning of those terms.[13] The Domestic Emoluments Clause applies exclusively to "emolument[s]"—that is, compensation (apart from his regularly authorized presidential compensation) from the United States or from any state in connection with his holding a second, federal or state position.

Fourth, Congress can consent to the President's acceptance of foreign emoluments, but it cannot consent to the President's receipt of domestic emoluments beyond his regularly authorized presidential compensation.

Fifth, the Foreign Emoluments Clause applies to the *acceptance* of foreign emoluments. By contrast, the Domestic Emoluments Clause applies to the *receipt* of domestic emoluments. This difference in language makes some logistical sense. The President could receive a foreign gift and then seek congressional consent before formally accepting the gift. By contrast, the President could not receive, even temporarily, a prohibited domestic emolument. Such receipt could not be authorized by Congress or any other body.

PRESIDENT WASHINGTON AND THE DOMESTIC EMOLUMENTS CLAUSE

During the first Trump Administration, a federal district court contended that an "emolument" was commonly understood by the Founding generation to encompass "*any* profit, gain, or advantage."[14] One scholar wrote that Founding-era dictionaries did not define an "emolument" as compensation tied to office or employment.[15] In Essay No. 76, we explain why we think these definitions of "emolument" are far too broad. In our view, emoluments would not include profits from private business transactions that are not connected to the discharge of the duties of a government office.

Practices during the Washington Administration inform this debate. In 1793, President George Washington purchased four lots of land at a public auction in the new federal capital.[16] Washington paid for and received valuable land from the federal government: a financial benefit beyond his regular salary.[17] If an "emolument" includes anything of value, then Washington would have violated the Domestic Emoluments Clause. We have found no contemporaneous record, either from public debate or in private correspondence, suggesting that Washington's bidding at a public auction was wrongful, much less unconstitutional. It was only at the time litigation began against Trump during his first Administration that some began to suggest that Washington acted lawlessly.

For all of these reasons, we suggest that the better reading of the clause is that "emolument" is limited to authorized, lawful compensation that arises from the discharge of the duties of a government office. Under our view of the scope of the term "emoluments," Washington was not a lawbreaker.[18]

PRESIDENT KENNEDY AND THE DOMESTIC EMOLUMENTS CLAUSE

While President John F. Kennedy was in office, he did not receive his naval retirement pay. After Kennedy's death, his estate sought the amount of pay that had accrued. The Office of Legal Counsel determined that the Domestic Emoluments Clause should be interpreted to prevent the federal government from attempting to influence the President.[19] In this case, however, Kennedy had earned the pension before taking office and did not have to "perform any services or fulfill any other obligations as a condition precedent to receipt of such payments."[20] Ultimately, the General Accounting Office found that the President's receipt of compensation as commander in chief precluded his ability to receive retirement pay for the same period.[21] As a result, the late President's estate did not receive his unpaid naval retirement pay.

PRESIDENT LYNDON JOHNSON AND THE DOMESTIC EMOLUMENTS CLAUSE

While in Congress, Representative Lyndon B. Johnson had an ownership interest in a radio station and a television station in Austin, Texas.[22] While Johnson served as Vice President and later as President, he did not sell his interest in these stations. Instead, he set up what he described and others later characterized, accurately or not, as a "blind trust."[23] Biographer Robert Caro observed that there was a "twenty-year-long string of strikingly favorable rulings by the Federal Communications Commission" (FCC) in favor of the television station.[24] Biographer Robert Dallek wrote that Johnson's "involvement in a business that largely depended on the actions of a Federal agency for its success created a clear conflict between his private interests and public position."[25]

If an "emolument" is defined as anything of value, then maintaining and renewing the radio station's FCC licenses would likely have been covered by the Domestic Emoluments Clause; that is, President Johnson received a valuable license from the federal government. We are not aware that anyone, including Johnson's many critics, raised constitutional concerns with respect to the trust arrangement. This is some evidence that Johnson's business interests and the regulatory benefits he received from the federal government while President did not amount to prohibited "emoluments." To put it another way, a transaction might pose an ethical or legal conflict and might even appear to be corrupt, but that does not mean it involves an "emolument" as that term is used in the Domestic Emoluments Clause.

PRESIDENT NIXON AND THE DOMESTIC EMOLUMENTS CLAUSE

After President Richard Nixon resigned from office, the General Services Administration (GSA) took custody of certain materials from the Nixon presidency. Nixon sued the government to retain control of these papers, recordings, and other items. Nixon claimed that these materials were his property. But the government argued that "the salary and benefits provided to Mr. Nixon by the United States during his presidency were the only economic benefits the United States could have provided him."[26] As a result, the government claimed, the Domestic Emoluments Clause prohibited Nixon "from receiving any 'emolument' from the United States beyond the compensation fixed by Congress before he . . . took office."[27] Moreover, Nixon would be "precluded from taking materials and selling them for personal profit during, or after, his . . . presidency."[28] Thus, he was "not entitled to any [further] compensation by virtue of the Emoluments Clause."[29] Nixon countered "that since the presidential papers were never public property to begin with, the [Domestic] Emoluments Clause does not apply to them."[30]

In *Griffin v. United States* (1995), a federal district court recognized that the Domestic Emoluments Clause "addressed the Framers' concern that the President should not have the ability to convert his or her office for profit."[31] However, the court also found that the clause "does not bar the award of compensation." This provision applies while a President is in office, but the clause "would not be violated because Mr. Nixon would receive compensation subsequent to the expiration of his term of office."[32] Any "proceeds derived from the sale of Mr. Nixon's presidential papers do not constitute an emolument."[33] Past Presidents had negotiated "fancy sums" for "lucrative library deals," and the Library of Congress has "authorized purchases" of materials from Presidents.[34] The court declined to address whether "a sitting President could sell his or her papers while in office" because those facts were not presented.[35]

Griffin is in some tension with an earlier district court decision, *Nixon v. Sampson*

(1975).[36] That case held that Nixon's materials from the White House were "directly related to the performance of the Office of the President and are of incalculable value." The judge ruled that it would violate the Domestic Emoluments Clause if the President was "given or . . . permitted to assert a personal right to such materials." Nixon argued that this material was "not an emolument because his right of ownership does not come into existence until he leaves office."[37] The court rejected this argument: "[I]f [Nixon's] claim of ownership does not come into existence until he leaves office, then it can only be concluded that while he is in office the documents, papers, tapes and other materials were government property." *Sampson* was later vacated, and *Griffin* did not cite *Sampson*.

PRESIDENT REAGAN AND THE DOMESTIC EMOLUMENTS CLAUSE

Before serving as President, Ronald Reagan earned a pension from the State of California, where he had served as governor. In 1981, the Office of Legal Counsel found that President Reagan's continued acceptance of his state pension would not violate the Domestic Emoluments Clause. OLC sought to give effect to the purpose of the clause as construed in the 1964 opinion concerning President Kennedy's naval retirement pay. In this case, Reagan's pension had vested before he became President, and he "no longer ha[d] to perform any services." Reagan's receipt of the pension would not have any "improper influence" or "have any such effect" on the President. OLC also provided a textual analysis.

Based on the dictionary definition of emolument, OLC further concluded that the state retirement benefits were not emoluments, because they are "a gift or part of the retiree's compensation."[38] Here OLC seems to reject a broad definition of "emolument" that would include anything of value. Nearly four decades later, a federal district court disagreed with this reasoning.[39] The Comptroller General declined to rule whether Reagan's pension was an emolument, finding instead that the Domestic Emoluments Clause "does not extend to payments for services rendered prior to the occupancy of, and having no connection with the Presidency."[40]

PRESIDENT TRUMP AND THE DOMESTIC EMOLUMENTS CLAUSE

During President Donald Trump's first term, he was sued for allegedly violating the Domestic Emoluments Clause. Plaintiffs claimed that Trump received "profits . . . [in that] domestic governments . . . patronize[d] the Trump International Hotel for the express purpose of potentially currying favor with a sitting President. . . ."[41] Specifically, the plaintiffs asserted that Maine's "spending state funds for its Governor and his entourage to stay at the [Trump International] Hotel and to frequent its facilities during an official visit of those officials to Washington"[42] violated the Domestic Emoluments Clause. A federal court adopted that position, found that plaintiffs' position "plausibly state[d] a claim," and denied Trump's motion to dismiss. The court found that these business transactions "present[ed] a stark contrast to the fully vested retirement benefits that then-Governor Reagan earned from the State of California which the State of California was not free to withdraw."[43]

Also during the first Trump Administration, the GSA leased to the Trump Organization the building that housed the Trump International Hotel. GSA determined that Trump's interest in the hotel did not violate the lease. The same federal district court determined that these factual allegations "plausibly state[d] a claim under the Domestic Emoluments Clause, and it denied Trump's motion to dismiss.[44] Subsequently, the district court's decisions opining on the scope of "emolument" in the Domestic Emoluments Clause were vacated.

The court acknowledged that investments in mutual funds or stocks "that could be traced to a foreign or domestic government" were emoluments, but the President could hold them. The court determined that such payments or benefits accruing to the fund were *de minimis* (of little value). Here the court focused on the purpose of the clause rather than its plain meaning: "It is highly doubtful that instances such as these could be reasonably construed as having the potential to unduly influence a public official."[45] One scholar replied that "no dictionary has ever defined an emolument as 'anything of value but with some de minimis exceptions where [the] potential of corruption does not exist.'"[46]

OPEN QUESTIONS

- The Domestic Emoluments Clause prohibits the President from drawing a second set of "emoluments" from the federal government or from a state government. Can Congress appoint the President to a second position that comes with compensation? Can the President appoint himself to such a position,[47] or would such an appointment violate some general atextual separation of powers or incompatibility principle? Could a state appoint the President to a second position that comes with compensation? Would that appointment violate some general atextual principle of federalism? In other words, does the bar against the President's receiving a second set of emoluments enjoin him only from accepting that second stream of compensation, or does it act impliedly as a bar against the President's holding a second position that comes with compensation?
- Are payments made to cover fees, expenses, and other costs incurred by a President prohibited emoluments?
- Is the budget the President receives to renovate the White House a prohibited emolument?
- Are payments made to cover fees, expenses, and other costs incurred by the President's spouse (or other family) prohibited emoluments?
- Is delayed compensation, such as increased pension benefits, an emolument?
- During the first Trump Administration, it was alleged that the President was personally receiving emoluments from state governments. However, any proceeds from state governments were not being paid directly into his personal accounts. Rather, the states were paying a private commercial entity in which Trump had an interest. Assuming these payments in connection with private commercial transactions were emoluments, would such transactions still violate the Domestic Emoluments Clause?

In other words, does a private commercial entity's independent legal personality make it possible for the President to receive an otherwise prohibited "emolument" indirectly through a potential constitutional workaround? Does it matter how much equity the President owns in the commercial entity—100 percent, a majority, working control even if less than a majority interest, any interest at all? What if the President's spouse, rather than the President, owned an interest or equity in the private commercial entity and the payments were made to that entity?[48]

Cite as: Josh Blackman & Seth Barrett Tillman, *The Domestic Emoluments Clause, in* THE HERITAGE GUIDE TO THE CONSTITUTION 365 (Josh Blackman & John G. Malcolm eds., 3d ed. 2025).

Notes

1. Art. II, § 1, cl. 7. **2.** Art. III, § 1. **3.** Art. I, § 6, cl. 1. **4.** Art. I, § 9, cl. 8. **5.** *Hoyt v. United States,* 51 U.S. (10 How.) 109 (1850). **6.** 2 Farrand's 626. **7.** *Id.* at 599, 621. **8.** 1 Farrand's 82–83. **9.** President Reagan's Ability to Receive Retirement Benefits from the State of California, 5 Op. O.L.C. 187, 188 (1981). **10.** 2 Elliot's 446. **11.** Art. I, § 9, cl. 8. **12.** Josh Blackman & Seth Barrett Tillman, *Offices and Officers of the Constitution, Part V: The Elector Incompatibility, Impeachment Disqualification, Incompatibility, and Foreign Emoluments Clauses,* 63 S. Tex. L. Rev. 237, 298 (2024). **13.** *D.C. v. Trump,* 315 F. Supp. 3d 875, 886 (D. Md. 2018), *judgment vacated sub nom. Trump v. D.C.,* 141 S.Ct. 1262 (2021), *and vacated,* 838 F. App'x 789 (4th Cir. 2021). **14.** *D.C. v. Trump,* 315 F. Supp. at 894–95. **15.** John Mikhail, The Definition of "Emolument" in English Language and Legal Dictionaries, 1523–1806 (July 12, 2017), https://ssrn.com/abstract=2995693. **16.** Seth Barrett Tillman, *Business Transactions and President Trump's "Emoluments" Problem,* 40 Harv. J.L. & Pub. Pol'y 759 (2017). **17.** Josh Blackman & Seth Barrett Tillman, Joint Written Statement for Landlord and Tenant: The Trump Administration's Oversight of the Trump International Hotel Lease: Hearing Before the Subcomm. on Econ. Dev. Pub. Bldgs., & Emergency Mgt. of the H. Comm. on Transportation & Infrastructure (Sept. 25, 2019), https://perma.cc/D83Q-C2AN. **18.** Josh Blackman & Seth Tillman, *Who Was Right About the Emoluments Clauses? Judge Messitte or President Washington?,* Volokh Conspiracy (Aug. 3, 2018), https://perma.cc/Z598-LQKS; Josh Blackman & Seth Barrett Tillman, *The Inspector General, General Services Administration, Refuses to Acknowledge Her Plain Error About the Domestic Emoluments Clause,* Volokh Conspiracy (Oct. 7, 2019), https://perma.cc/7CWT-RFU8. **19.** Letter from Assistant Attorney General Norbert Schlei to General Counsel Robert Keller, General Accounting Office (Oct. 13, 1964), and attached staff memorandum (Oct. 12, 1964). **20.** OLC, *supra* at 189. **21.** Letter from General Counsel Robert Keller, General Accounting Office, to Assistant Attorney General Norbert Schlei (Nov. 1, 1964). **22.** 4 Robert A. Caro, The Passage of Power: The Years of Lyndon Johnson 286 (2013). **23.** Megan J. Ballard, *The Shortsightedness of Blind Trusts,* 56 Kan. L. Rev. 43, 55 (2007); Josh Blackman, *President Lyndon B. Johnson's TV Station and the "Blind Trust,"* Volokh Conspiracy (Jan. 1, 2025), https://perma.cc/L4V5-DGCF. **24.** Robert Dallek, Lyndon B. Johnson: Portrait of a President 52 (2004). **25.** *Id.* **26.** *Griffin v. United States,* 935 F. Supp. 1, 3 (D.D.C. 1995). **27.** *Id.* **28.** *Id.* at 4. **29.** *Id.* at 3. **30.** *Id.* at 4. **31.** *Id.* **32.** *Id.* at 6. **33.** *Id.* **34.** *Id.* **35.** *Id.* **36.** *Nixon v. Sampson,* 389 F. Supp. 107, 137 (D.D.C. 1975), *rev'd sub nom. Reps. Comm. for Freedom of Press v. Sampson,* 591 F.2d 944 (D.C. Cir. 1978). **37.** *Id.* at n.80. **38.** OLC, *supra* at 187. **39.** *D.C. v. Trump,* 315 F. Supp. at 901. **40.** Comp. Gen. B-207467, 1983 WL 27823 (1983). **41.** *D.C. v. Trump,* 315 F. Supp. at 903. **42.** *Id.* at 906. **43.** *Id.* **44.** *Id.* **45.** *Id.* at 899. **46.** Andy Grewel, *District Court Adopts Purpose-Based Approach in Emoluments Lawsuit,* Yale J. on Reg. Notice & Comment Blog (July 26, 2018), https://perma.cc/WM3R-EM5K. **47.** Josh Blackman, *Can President Trump Appoint Himself Chairman of the Kennedy Center Board of Trustees?,* Volokh Conspiracy (Feb. 9, 2025), https://perma.cc/T25X-5BFG. **48.** Steven Nelson, *Sen. Richard Blumenthal Denies Facing Same Legal Issue He's Suing Trump Over,* Wash. Examiner (Aug. 22, 2017), https://perma.cc/895G-4DVS.

ESSAY NO. 101: THE PRESIDENTIAL OATH OF OFFICE CLAUSE
ART. II, § 1, CL. 8

Before he enter on the Execution of his Office, he shall take the following Oath or Affirmation:—"I do solemnly swear (or affirm) that I will faithfully execute the Office of President of the United States, and will to the best of my Ability, preserve, protect and defend the Constitution of the United States."
—Judge Gregory G. Katsas & Seanhenry VanDyke

INTRODUCTION

The Constitution of the United States claims to be "the supreme Law of the Land,"[1] but no document is authoritative just because it says so. Why, therefore, should the President submit to the constraints and demands of the Constitution of 1788 instead of, say, some newer charter of government that might be more to his liking? The President's political and institutional constraints surely provide part of the answer, but the Framers also sought to bind the President's conscience by creating a moral duty to the Constitution. As Justice Joseph Story explained, "If a judge, or a juryman, or a witness, ought to take a solemn oath or affirmation, to bind his conscience, surely a President, holding in his hands the destiny of the nation, ought to do so."[2]

The Constitution thus provides that the President must commit himself to the Constitution by oath before assuming office. While the Article VI Oath or Affirmation Clause allows Congress to craft an oath for other state and federal officials, the Article II Presidential Oath Clause dictates the precise text of the President's oath: "I do solemnly swear (or affirm) that I will faithfully execute the Office of President of the United States, and will to the best of my Ability, preserve, protect and defend the Constitution of the United States."[3] Presidents have invoked the presidential oath as a source of executive authority, but some judges have suggested that the oath actually serves as a constraint on executive power.

HISTORY BEFORE 1787

Oaths have a prominent place in the Anglo-American legal and political tradition. Thomas Hobbes thought that mutual oaths represented an important stepping stone on the road from the state of nature to civil society.[4] Oaths played a vital role in facilitating the transition from trial by combat to trial by jury. Oaths presuppose a trust that jurors and witnesses will tell the truth.[5] The Coronation Oath Act of 1688 required the monarchs to swear an oath to govern "according to the Statutes in Parliament Agreed on and the Laws and Customs of the same."[6] King William III and Queen Mary II both swore this oath when crowned.

The Founding generation was intimately familiar with political oaths as a popular tool for inspiring obedience and justifying punishment for disloyalty.[7] For example, before 1776, George Washington (as a surveyor and militia officer) and Benjamin Franklin (as a postal official) both swore oaths of loyalty to King George III.[8]

Following Independence, state constitutions imposed oaths on their officials. The oath in the Pennsylvania constitution of 1776 required officeholders to "faithfully execute the office . . . and . . . do equal right and justice to all men, to the best of [their] judgment and abilities, according to law."[9] The Massachusetts constitution of 1780 provided a similar oath of office: "I, A. B., do solemnly swear and affirm that I will faithfully and impartially discharge and perform all the duties incumbent on me as __, according to the best of my abilities and understanding . . . So help me, God."[10]

The Articles of Confederation prescribed only one oath: A judge who decided disputes between states was required to swear "well and truly to hear and determine the matter in question, according to the best of his judgment, without favour, affection, or hope of reward."[11] The Articles did not require delegates to the national legislature to take an oath to the Confederation.

THE CONSTITUTIONAL CONVENTION

From the outset of the Convention, the Virginia Plan provided that state officials would take an oath to support the national Constitution.[12] On July 23, "the Officers of the National Government" were also required to take an oath to "support . . . the Natl. Govt."[13] Around that same time, a separate oath was being developed for the chief executive. A draft from the Committee of Detail in the handwriting of Edmund Randolph of Virginia provided that "the Governor of the united People & States of America" should be made to "swear fidelity to the union (as the legislature shall direct) by taking an oath of office."[14] But rather than leave the content of the oath up to Congress, the Framers decided to draft it themselves.

On August 6, 1787, John Rutledge of South Carolina announced the Committee of Detail's report.[15] The President's oath now read: "Before he shall enter on the Duties of his Department, he shall take the following Oath or Affirmation, 'I solemnly swear, (or affirm) that I will faithfully execute the

Office of President of the United States of America.'"[16] The same report also required "Members of the Legislatures, and the executive and judicial Officers of the United States, and of the several States" to take an oath to "support" the Constitution.[17]

On August 27, James Madison and George Mason, both of Virginia, "moved to add to the oath to be taken by the supreme Executive 'and will to the best of my judgment and power preserve protect and defend the Constitution of the United States."[18] James Wilson of Pennsylvania argued that this amendment to the President's oath was "unnecessary" because the "general provision for oaths of office" already applied to the President.[19] The Convention was apparently unmoved by Wilson's concern, as the Madison/Mason proposal passed by a vote of 7 to 1 with two states absent.

That text was referred to the Committee of Style, which changed "duties of his department" to "execution of his office."[20] The text of the oath remained the same.[21] The clause now provided: "Before he enter on the execution of his office, he shall take the following oath or affirmation: 'I ____, do solemnly swear (or affirm) that I will faithfully execute the office of president of the United States, and will to the best of my judgment and power, preserve, protect and defend the constitution of the United States.'"[22]

THE RATIFICATION DEBATES

During the ratification process, there were many debates about the Article VI Oath or Affirmation Clause, but there was little discussion of the precise wording of the President's oath. In Federalist No. 18, Madison shed some light on why he proposed to add "preserve, protect, and defend" to the oath. Madison discussed the Greek Amphictyonic council, the "most considerable" of the "confederacies of antiquity." Ancient Greek states "took an oath mutually to *defend and protect* the united cities" of the confederacy and would "punish the violators of this oath." Yet, Madison observed, despite being "bound by oath to exert this authority on the necessary occasions," the Amphictyonic council failed. Madison blamed its failure on the lack of a strong executive and a "stricter confederation." He remedied this problem by placing the duty to preserve, protect, and defend the Constitution in a singular executive accountable to the whole nation rather than only in each member state as the Amphictyonic council had done in vain.

PRESIDENT WASHINGTON'S CONSTITUTIONAL OATH

The U.S. House and Senate were supposed to assemble on March 4, 1789, but on that date, both lacked a quorum.[23] On April 6, when both houses had quorums, the joint session of Congress elected George Washington as the first President.[24] On April 30, 1789, President George Washington took the oath of office pursuant to the Article II Presidential Oath Clause.[25] In *Elk Grove Unified School District v. Newdow* (2004), Chief Justice William Rehnquist quoted from a leading account of Washington's inauguration:

> [Washington] stepped toward the iron rail, where he was to receive the oath of office. The diminutive secretary of the Senate, Samuel Otis, squeezed between the President and Chancellor [Robert] Livingston and raised up the crimson cushion with a Bible on it. Washington put his right hand on the Bible, opened to Psalm 121:1: "I raise my eyes toward the hills. Whence shall my help come." The Chancellor proceeded with the oath: "Do you solemnly swear that you will faithfully execute the office of President of the United States and will to the best of your ability preserve, protect and defend the Constitution of the United States?" The President responded, "I solemnly swear," and repeated the oath, adding, "So help me God." He then bent forward and kissed the Bible before him.[26]

The Article II oath does not include the phrase "So help me God," although that phrase appeared in the Massachusetts constitution of 1780 and other early constitutions.[27] Some modern scholars assert that there is "absolutely no extant contemporary evidence that President Washington altered the language of the oath,"[28] and scholars at Mount Vernon have concluded that Washington's adding "So help me God" to the oath is a "myth."[29] Yet, to this day, Presidents conclude their constitutional oaths with "So help me God."

THE PRESIDENTIAL OATH AS A SOURCE OF EXECUTIVE AUTHORITY

Most American Presidents have ascribed personal significance to the oath in their inaugural addresses.[30] Many have also invoked the oath as an independent source of executive authority, using it to justify wielding extraordinary powers in cases of national crisis or independently interpreting the Constitution's requirements. Andrew Jackson repeatedly invoked his sworn duty to defend and preserve the Constitution in resisting South Carolina's efforts to nullify federal laws: "The laws of the United States must be executed. I have no discretionary power on the subject-my duty is emphatically pronounced in the Constitution."[31] Jackson also cited his oath to justify his opposition to the National Bank: "Each public officer who takes an oath to support the Constitution swears that he will support it as he understands it, and not as it is understood by others."[32]

Abraham Lincoln famously relied on his presidential oath as a justification for taking extraordinary measures to preserve the Union and to fight a civil war. Lincoln explained that "my oath to preserve the constitution to the best of my ability, imposed upon me the duty of preserving, by every indispensable means, that government—that nation—of which that constitution was the organic law."[33] Lincoln "felt that measures, otherwise unconstitutional, might become lawful, by becoming indispensable to the preservation of the constitution, through the preservation of the nation."[34]

THE PRESIDENTIAL OATH AS A CONSTRAINT ON EXECUTIVE AUTHORITY

Some judges have suggested that the presidential oath actually serves as a constraint on executive power. The Supreme Court's most in-depth discussion of the presidential oath appears in *Cunningham v. Neagle* (1890).[35] In that case, a U.S. marshal killed a man who was about to attack Justice Stephen J. Field. The Court held that the marshal acted under color of federal law, notwithstanding the absence of a statute authorizing marshals to serve as bodyguards.[36]

Justice Lucius Q.C. Lamar dissented, opining that the presidential oath commits the President to upholding the Constitution's separation of powers. However, only Congress can exercise any implied powers, such as providing bodyguards for endangered Justices.[37] Justice Lamar explained that the "oath has great significance" and that the President is "sworn to preserve" Congress's powers under the Necessary and Proper Clause. He turned the views of Jackson and Lincoln on their heads and read the presidential oath as constraining rather than empowering the President.

SCHOLARSHIP ON THE PRESIDENTIAL OATH

Professor Michael Stokes Paulsen has forcefully defended the notion that the Presidential Oath Clause supports a "co-equal independent interpretive power" and a wide zone of discretion for the President.[38] By contrast, Professor Edward S. Corwin has criticized the notion "that the President's oath adds indeterminate cubits to his constitutional stature," instead treating the oath as a source of constraint on the President's prerogatives.[39] For Corwin, reading the Presidential Oath Clause in conjunction with the Take Care Clause and the President's veto power, "once a statute has been duly executed, whether over [the President's] protest or with his approval, he must promote its enforcement by all the powers constitutionally at his disposal," but the President's oath gives him no additional "power of self-defense."[40]

Professor Richard Re has focused on the temporal significance of the presidential oath, arguing that "the critical moment of constitutional obligation is the moment of taking the oath and thereby promising to adhere to a certain role defined by certain powers and duties."[41] For Re, it follows that Presidents "have a promissory obligation to adhere to the public meaning of 'the Constitution' that existed at the time they took their oaths."[42]

Professor Matthew Pauley concluded that "the President's oath can be compared to a keystone that links together the great arch of our constitutional government."[43] In our secular age, ascribing such a grand role to a moralistic and ceremonial constitutional provision may feel idealistic, even quaint. At the very least, however, the presidential oath has inspired a sense of sobriety and duty in countless Presidents and has provided a fertile source of scholarly reflection on the nature and limits of presidential power.

OPEN QUESTIONS

- Does the presidential oath of office merely bind the individual officeholder in conscience, or does it have determinable legal content?
- If the presidential oath has determinable legal content, does it confer power on the President or constrain him?
- Is there a difference between the President's oath to "preserve, protect and defend the Constitution" and the Article VI oath to "support the Constitution"?

Cite as: Judge Gregory G. Katsas & Seanhenry VanDyke, *The Presidential Oath of Office Clause*, in THE HERITAGE GUIDE TO THE CONSTITUTION 370 (Josh Blackman & John G. Malcolm eds., 3d ed. 2025).

Notes

1. Art. VI, cl. 2. **2.** Joseph Story, A Familiar Exposition of the Constitution of the United States 170 (1847). **3.** Art. II, § 1, cl. 8. **4.** Thomas Hobbes, Leviathan 118–19 (Bobbs-Merrill 1958). **5.** Sir Frederick Pollock & Frederic William Maitland, 2 The History of English Law Before the Time of Edward I 616–32, 641–59 (1898). **6.** Coronation Oath Act 1688, 1 W. & M. c. 6 (Eng.). **7.** Harold M. Hyman, To Try Men's Souls: Loyalty Tests in American History 1–60 (1959). **8.** *Id.* at 60. **9.** Pa. Const. of 1776, § 40. **10.** Mass. Const. of 1780, ch. VI. **11.** Articles of Confederation, art IX, para. 2. **12.** 1 Farrand's 22, 28. **13.** 2 Farrand's 87. **14.** *Id.* at 146. **15.** *Id.* at 177. **16.** *Id.* at 172. **17.** *Id.* at 185. **18.** *Id.* at 427. **19.** *Id.* at 185, 427. **20.** *Id.* at 565, 575, 590. **21.** *Id.* at 599. **22.** *Id.* **23.** S. Journal, 1st Cong., 1st Sess. 5 (Mar. 4, 1789); H.R. Journal, 1st Cong., 1st Sess. (Mar. 4, 1789). **24.** S. Journal, 1st Cong., 1st Sess. 7–8 (Apr. 6, 1789). **25.** S. Journal, 1st Cong., 1st Sess. 18 (Apr. 30, 1789). **26.** *Elk Grove Unified Sch. Dist. v. Newdow*, 542 U.S. 1, 26–27 (2004) (Rehnquist, C.J., concurring) (quoting M. Riccards, A Republic, If You Can Keep It: The Foundation of the American Presidency, 1700–1800, at 73–74 (1987)). **27.** Mass. Const. 1780, ch. VI, art. I; S.C. Const. of 1778, art. XXXVI; Ga. Const of 1777, art. XXIV. **28.** Peter R. Henriques, *"So Help Me God": A George Washington Myth that Should Be Discarded*, History News Network (Jan. 11, 2009), https://perma.cc/EEL7-62NW. **29.** Kevin Butterfield, *Second Inaugural Address*, George Washington's Mt. Vernon, https://perma.cc/47RW-QL89. **30.** Robert M. Blomquist, *The Presidential Oath, the American National Interest and a Call for Presiprudence*, 73 UMKC L. Rev. 1, 7–35 (2004). **31.** Andrew Jackson, Proclamation Regarding Nullification (Dec. 10, 1832), https://perma.cc/3H4Y-GBG6. **32.** Andrew Jackson, Veto Message Regarding the Bank of the United States (July 10, 1832), https://perma.cc/7REY-EKP4. **33.** Letter from Abraham Lincoln to Albert G. Hodges (Apr. 4, 1864), https://perma.cc/EBC8-A35L. **34.** *Id.* **35.** 135 U.S. 1 (1890). **36.** *Id.* at 58–59. **37.** *Id.* at 82–83 (Lamar, J., dissenting). **38.** Michael Stokes Paulsen, *The Most Dangerous Branch: Executive Power to Say What the Law Is*, 83 Geo. L.J. 217, 257–62 (1994). **39.** Edward S. Corwin, The President: Office and Powers 1787–1948: History and Analysis of Fact and Opinion 62–66 (1957). **40.** *Id.* at 66. **41.** Richard M. Re, *Promising the Constitution*, 110 Nw. U. L. Rev. 299, 304 (2016). **42.** *Id.* **43.** Matthew A. Pauley, I Do Solemnly Swear: The President's Constitutional Oath: Its Meaning and Importance in the History of Oaths 232 (1999).

~∽

ESSAY NO. 102: THE COMMANDER IN CHIEF CLAUSE
ART. II, § 2, CL. 1

The President shall be Commander in Chief of the Army and Navy of the United States. . . .

—John C. Yoo

INTRODUCTION

The Commander in Chief Clause assures civilian control of the military, which is an important principle for republican government. The clause forbids the creation of any federal military force that is beyond the President's control and prohibits subordinate officers or other branches, such as Congress, from interfering with his authority.[1] It also provides the chief source of textual authority for presidential claims involving military tactics and strategy in war and a right to initiate hostilities abroad. As commander in chief, the President has authority over the deployment and operations of the military in peacetime and over the conduct of military strategy, tactics, and objectives once war has begun.[2]

HISTORY BEFORE 1787

The British constitution recognized a traditional division of authority between the executive and legislative powers.[3] The Crown held the role of commander in chief and directed all military affairs. Sir William Blackstone described the king as the "generalissimo, or the first in military command, within the kingdom."[4] English seventeenth- and eighteenth-century constitutional history told the story of Parliament's effort to tame the king's authority over war and peace through the power of the purse. John Locke also maintained that the executive naturally possessed a "federative power" that contained "the power of war and peace" as well as foreign affairs powers, including authority over "leagues and alliances, and all the transactions with all persons and communities without the commonwealth."[5] Locke contended that these foreign affairs powers and the executive power as commander of the military were "really distinct in themselves" but were usually combined in the same branch.[6] The discretionary powers of war and foreign affairs naturally fell to the executive because they required prompt, decisive action and adaptability that could not be anticipated by predetermined laws.

During the Revolutionary War, American forces suffered from a committee structure in the Continental Congress that oversaw George Washington's role as the "General and Commander in Chief" of the Continental Army.[7] Washington exercised control over strategy, operations, and military tactics, but Congress regularly advised on matters of strategy and control of resources. Washington's appointment specified that he would "observe and follow such orders and directions, from time to time, as you shall receive from this or a future Congress."[8] This awkward command structure failed to keep the Revolutionary Army adequately paid or supplied and led to confusion on matters of broader strategy.[9] Congress also could not maintain a unified position because of constant changes in committee composition and policy.[10]

In their Revolutionary constitutions, states continued to recognize executive authority over war. The Pennsylvania constitution of 1776 declared that the president of the supreme executive council "shall be commander in chief of the forces of the state, but shall not command in person."[11] The 1776 Virginia constitution specified that "[the] Governor may embody the militia, with the advice of the Privy Council; and when embodied, shall alone have the direction of the militia, under the laws of the country."[12]

Later in the Revolutionary period, state constitutions were even more explicit in their recognition of executive control over war. The 1779 New York constitution, which became an important model for the federal Constitution, vested in the governor "the supreme executive power and authority of this State" and declared him to be "general and commander-in-chief of all the militia, and admiral of the navy of this State."[13] The Massachusetts constitution of 1780, another model for the Constitutional Convention, declared that "the president of this state for the time being, shall be commander in chief of the army and navy, and all the military forces of the state, by sea and land; and shall have full power by himself. . . ."[14]

States such as Georgia, New Jersey, Delaware, and Maryland generally followed the New York model. To the extent that the Revolutionary states reacted against the British constitution, they did not limit the substantive commander-in-chief power vested in the executive but instead sought to disrupt the unity of the executive branch by creating advisory councils or prohibiting standing armies.

Even as the Revolutionary War came to a close, the Articles of Confederation, ratified in 1781, maintained the traditional vesting of war powers in the executive. Article IX provided that the legislature could appoint a "commander in chief of the army or navy" with the "assent" of nine states.[15] Congress also had the power to declare war and make treaties.[16] Commentators sometimes conclude that vesting Congress with these powers signaled a desire to turn the war power into a legislative function. In fact, the unicameral Congress under the Articles of Confederation assumed the executive powers of the nation upon independence; its great handicap was its lack of effective legislative powers.[17]

THE CONSTITUTIONAL CONVENTION

During the Constitutional Convention, there was very little discussion of the President's role as commander in chief of the Army and Navy. The Framers were far more concerned about the President's power as commander in chief of the militia. (See Essay No. 103.) Several drafts from the Committee of Detail framed the commander-in-chief power with different language. One draft provided that the president's "powers shall be . . . to (command and superintend the militia,) (to be Commander in Chief of the Land & Naval Forces of the Union & of the Militia of the sevl. states)."[18] A second provided that the President "shall, by Virtue of his Office, be Commander in chief of the Land Forces of U. S. and Admiral of their Navy."[19] A third stated that "He shall be Commander in Chief of the Army and Navy of the United States, and of the Militia of the Several States."[20]

The report delivered to the Convention on August 6 followed the third model.[21] The Framers took inspiration from state constitutions that gave their governors control of the state military.[22] This text was approved without any debate on August 27.[23] The Committee of Style changed "He" to "President."[24] No further revisions were made.

THE RATIFICATION DEBATES

During the ratification debates, supporters and opponents of the Constitution offered very different characterizations of the Commander in Chief Clause. The Federalists downplayed the President's powers to minimize the risk of tyranny, and the Anti-Federalists exaggerated the President's powers to maximize the risk of tyranny.

In Federalist No. 69, Alexander Hamilton observed that in many "particulars, the power of the president will resemble equally that of the king of Great Britain. . . ." However, he observed, one "material point[] of difference" was the Commander in Chief Clause. Hamilton wrote that the President's authority over the army and navy "would be nominally the same with that of the king of Great Britain, but in substance much inferior to it." The President's power "would amount to nothing more than the supreme command and direction of the military and naval forces, as first general and admiral" under the Articles of Confederation. Hamilton seemed to view the President's power as commander in chief as comparable to the powers

that General Washington exercised under the Articles of Confederation.

In Federalist No. 74, Hamilton returned to the Commander in Chief Clause. He explained that the "propriety" of the President's power over the army, navy, and militia is "so evident" and "so consonant to the precedents of the state constitutions in general, that little need be said to explain or enforce it." These states had "concentrated the military authority" in the governor's "single hand." Hamilton concluded that "[t]he direction of war, implies the direction of the common strength: and the power of directing and employing the common strength, forms an usual and essential part in the definition of the executive authority." Hamilton understood that success in the conduct of war demands the unique presidential qualities of unity, decisiveness, speed, secrecy, and energy.[25]

Hamilton added in Federalist No. 72 that the "administration of government" falls "peculiarly within the province of the executive department." That power includes the conduct of foreign affairs, preparation of the budget, expenditure of appropriated funds, and direction of the military and "the operations of war."[26]

Anti-Federalists feared that the President might abuse his command of the military to impose a dictatorship. Cato warned that the President's powers over war were "substantially the same" as the king's. He referred to the President as "the generalissimo of the nation" who "of course, has the command and controul of the army, navy and militia."[27] An Old Whig proclaimed that the President's power as "commander in chief of the army, navy and militia" was "dangerous."[28] He predicted that the President will be "unwilling to part with" his "eminent powers." An Old Whig alluded to a "future President and commander in chief adored by his army and the militia to as great a degree as our late illustrious commander in chief," who "struggles to resign." Not everyone would have the virtue of George Washington to resign. Philadelphiensis said that the President was for "all intents and purposes" a king as "commander in chief of a standing army."[29]

Federalists responded that the constitutional structure would check the commander-in-chief power.[30] Drawing on their understanding of British constitutional history, Federalists argued that Congress could use its sole control of the raising and funding of the military to control presidential power. In the Virginia ratification convention, Anti-Federalist Patrick Henry claimed that the Constitution set up the President as a potential military dictator: "If your American chief be a man of ambition and abilities, how easy is it for him to render himself absolute!"[31] Henry asked: "Can he not, at the head of his army, beat down every opposition?"

Federalist George Nicholas responded that the division of the war power between Congress and the President would prevent Henry's predictions of doom from being realized. Citing the Appropriations Clause, he explained that "no appropriation of money, to the use of raising or supporting an army, shall be for a longer term than two years."[32] Nicholas acknowledged that "[th]e President is to command" as commander in chief but added that under the Constitution, "the regulation of the army and navy is given to Congress." Virginia's "representatives [in Congress] will be a powerful check here." Nicholas referred to the separation of powers in Great Britain. "The influence of the [House of] commons," he said, "is very predominant."

James Madison saw the same influence. Immediately after Nicholas spoke, Madison declared that "[t]he sword is in the hands of the British king; the purse in the hands of the Parliament" and argued that "[i]t is so in America, as far as any analogy can exist."[33] Parliament's long struggle with the Crown to subject the military to the power of the purse established a structure that also would govern the tension between the commander in chief and Congress in the New World.

JUDICIAL PRECEDENT

Traditionally, the U.S. Supreme Court has treated decisions made by the President as commander in chief with great deference. The *Prize Cases* (1862), for example, declined to review President Abraham Lincoln's actions during the Civil War.[34]

However, a series of cases decided during the war on terrorism afforded the President less deference. *Hamdi v. Rumsfeld* (2004) concluded that a U.S. citizen held as an "enemy combatant" at a naval base in Guantanamo Bay, Cuba, could seek judicial review through the writ of habeas corpus.[35] *Hamdan v. Rumsfeld* (2006) found that the President's unilateral creation of military commissions violated the Uniform Code of Military Justice enacted by Congress.[36] Such specialized war crimes tribunals had been used in most major American wars. And *Boumediene v. Bush* (2008) held that non-citizen detainees held at a naval facility in Guantanamo Bay, Cuba could seek judicial review through the writ of habeas corpus.[37] In each case, strong dissents argued that the Court was interfering with the President's traditional commander-in-chief power.[38]

THE COMMANDER IN CHIEF AND DECLARE WAR CLAUSES

The Constitution designates the President as commander in chief but grants Congress the power to declare war. The relationship between the Commander in Chief Clause and the Declare War Clause has been the subject of several long-simmering constitutional debates. Three of these questions are discussed in Essay No. 45 on the Declare War Clause. First, does the Commander in Chief Clause permit the President to initiate war without Congress's approval? Some scholars contend that the Declare War Clause gives the power to initiate war exclusively to Congress; others contend that the President can launch hostilities subject to Congress's funding and raising of the military. Second, does the Commander in Chief Clause give the President power to respond to attacks on the United States? Almost all scholars contend that it does. Third, does the Commander in Chief Clause grant the President the authority to engage in foreign military action of limited nature, scope, and duration absent congressional approval? Executive branch officials have argued that it does.

CONGRESSIONAL CONTROL OF THE MILITARY

The Constitution squarely grants Congress the power to appropriate money for the military,[39] and the legislature has no constitutional obligation to provide the weapons that the President wants. But can Congress, through its power of the purse, direct the way that the President controls the military? During the war on terrorism and the conflict in Iraq, Congress considered enacting restrictions on appropriations directing the President to take or refrain from taking specific actions.[40]

Some scholars contend that Congress's various powers over war and the military allow a full range of control akin to its authority over domestic policy. Under this view, the President's commander-in-chief authority is residual and can be exercised only where Congress has not provided any specific statutory direction.[41]

Other scholars believe the Commander in Chief Clause affords the President plenary power, which Congress lacks the power to regulate.[42] A third view holds that Congress has authority to restrict and direct the commander-in-chief authority in certain areas but not in others.[43]

Cite as: John C. Yoo, *The Commander in Chief Clause, in* THE HERITAGE GUIDE TO THE CONSTITUTION 374 (Josh Blackman & John G. Malcolm eds., 3d ed. 2025).

Notes

1. John Yoo, *Administration of War*, 58 Duke L.J. 2277 (2009). **2.** Saikrishna Bangalore Prakash, Imperial from the Beginning: The Constitution of the Original Executive 154 (2015). **3.** Andrew Kent, Ethan J. Leib, & Jed Handelsman Shugerman, *Faithful Execution and Article II*, 132 Harv. L. Rev. 2111, 2158–59 (2019) (citing 1 Blackstone 262); Jack DiSorbo, *On Executive Orders and the Royal Prerogative*, 26 Tex. Rev. L. & Pol. 555, 563–76 (2022). **4.** 1 Blackstone 262. **5.** John Locke, The Second Treatise of Government § 146 (J.W. Gough ed., 3d ed. 1966). **6.** *Id.* § 147. **7.** 3 Farrand's 94. **8.** 2 J. Cont. Cong. 96 (June 7, 1775). **9.** E. Wayne Carp, To Starve the Army at Pleasure: Continental Army Administration and American Political Culture, 1775–1783, at 18–24 (1984). **10.** John Ferling, Almost a Miracle: The American Victory in the War of Independence 114–18 (2007). **11.** Pa. Const. of 1776, ch. II, § 20. **12.** Va. Const. of 1777, ¶ 34. **13.** N.Y. Const. of 1779, §§ XVII, XVIII. **14.** Mass. Const. of 1780, pt. 2, cl. 2, § 1, art. VII. **15.** Articles of Confederation, art. IX, § 6. **16.** *Id.* art. IX, § 1. **17.** John C. Yoo, *The Continuation of Politics by Other Means: The Original Understanding of War Powers*, 84 Cal. L. Rev. 167, 238 (1996). **18.** 2 Farrand's 137, 145. **19.** *Id.* at 157, 158. **20.** *Id.* at 163, 172. **21.** *Id.* at 177, 185. **22.** Yoo, *The Continuation of Politics, supra* at 252–54; N.J. Const. of 1776, art. VIII; Va. Const. of 1776, art. XIII. **23.** 2 Farrand's 422. **24.** *Id.* at 577, 599. **25.** Yoo, *The Continuation of Politics, supra* at 304. **26.** *Id.* **27.** Storing 2.6.31. **28.** Storing 3.3.31. **29.** *Id.* at 3.9.97. **30.** Yoo, *The Continuation of Politics, supra* at 252, 278. **31.** 3 Elliot's 59. **32.** *Id.* at 391. **33.** *Id.* at 393. **34.** 67 U.S. 635, 670 (1862). **35.** 542 U.S. 507 (2004). **36.** 548 U.S. 557 (2006). **37.** 553 U.S. 723 (2008). **38.** *Hamdi*, 542 U.S. at 579 (Thomas, J., dissenting); *Hamdan*, 548 U.S. at 678 (Thomas, J., dissenting); *Boumediene*, 553 U.S. at 826 (Scalia, J., dissenting). **39.** Art. I, § 8, cl. 12. **40.** H.R. 1591, 110th Cong. (2007). **41.** Saikrishna Bangalore Prakash, *The Separation and Overlap of War and Military Powers*, 87 Tex. L. Rev. 299, 299 (2008); David J. Barron & Martin S. Lederman, *The Commander in Chief at the Lowest Ebb—A Constitutional History*, 121 Harv. L. Rev. 941, 1101–06 (2008). **42.** John C. Yoo, *War and the Constitutional Text*, 69 U. Chi. L. Rev. 1639, 1654 (2002). **43.** Michael D. Ramsey, *Response: Directing Military Operations*, 87 Tex. L. Rev. 29 (2009).

$$\sim$$

ESSAY NO. 103: THE COMMANDER OF THE MILITIA CLAUSE
ART. II, § 2, CL. 1

The President shall be Commander in Chief . . . of the Militia of the several States, when called into the actual Service of the United States. . . .
—Judge Gregory E. Maggs & Robert Leider

INTRODUCTION

In addition to being commander in chief of the regular Army and Navy (see Essay No. 102), the President is commander in chief of the militia when called forth for national purposes. The Framers had no conception of modern reserve forces; they expected that the militia, comprised of citizens who could be called to perform temporary military service, would be the nation's primary military reserve. This clause granted the President the same right of command over militia called into federal service that he had at all times over the regular Army and Navy. Dissatisfaction with the militia system, however, has led Congress to create a military system in which organized militiamen are also part of the armed forces. Statutorily, the organized component of the militia (primarily the National Guard) is organized ostensibly under the constitutional Army and Navy powers. As a result, the federal government has used its plenary military powers to bypass difficult constitutional questions about the operation of the militia.

HISTORY BEFORE 1787

In England, the Crown exercised principal control of the country's military forces. Parliament feared that King Charles intended to overthrow Parliament using the army. In 1642, Parliament claimed it had control of the militia.[1] This dispute over control of the militia was a precipitating cause of the English Civil War. Following the Restoration, Parliament passed a 1661 statute recognizing that the "sole supreme government of the militia and of all forces by sea and land is, and by the laws of England ever was, the undoubted right of the king and his predecessors, and that neither house of parliament could pretend to the same."[2] Ultimately, Parliament would wrest other military powers from the Crown. The 1689 English Bill of Rights declared that a standing army was illegal unless raised with Parliament's consent.

In the colonies, the militia remained decentralized. Each colony had its own separate militia, and the colonial executives were generally the commanders in chief of these forces. (See Essay No. 62.) Initially, the governors also had substantial power to organize and govern the forces, although colonial legislatures gradually assumed more control.[3]

This decentralized structure largely continued after independence. Upon separation from Britain, states adopted constitutions, many of which provided that state executives, often labeled governors, commanded the militia in their states. However, to cabin executive power, constitutions in some states required the executive to consult another body, such as a privy council.[4] In the Northwest Ordinance, Congress similarly vested the territorial governor with supreme command of the territory's militia.[5]

The existence of thirteen separate militia systems produced serious inconveniences during the Revolutionary War. These forces had difficulty fighting alongside one another,[6] and disputes arose over which officers had the right of command.[7] To remedy these defects, the delegates to the Constitutional Convention sought to partially nationalize control of the militia. (See Essay No. 63.)

THE CONSTITUTIONAL CONVENTION

During the Constitutional Convention, the delegates agreed that the militia should be nationalized when called into federal service. The least controversial aspect of this nationalization was to place the militia under the President's command. The Committee of Detail's proposal provided that the President "shall be Commander in Chief of the Army and Navy of the United States, and of the Militia of the Several States."[8] On August 27, the Convention limited this power: The President would be commander in chief of the militia only "when called into the actual service of the United States."[9] This amendment made clear that the President is the supreme commander of that portion of the militia that is called forth by Congress. Otherwise, principal command of the militia rested with the state commanders in chief.

The Constitution heavily circumscribed presidential power over the militia. It gave Congress the power both to provide for militia organization and to call forth the militia.[10] The President thus has no inherent power either to organize militia forces or to call them into federal service. He may act only pursuant to the authority of Congress.

THE RATIFICATION DEBATES

Alexander Hamilton discussed the Commander of the Militia Clause in Federalist No. 69. He explained that the President "will have only the occasional command of such part of the militia of the nation, as by legislative provision may be called into the actual service of the Union." This restricted power, Hamilton argued, gave the President less power than "[t]he King of Great-Britain and the Governor of New-York." They "have at all times the entire command of all the militia within their several jurisdictions."

THE WHISKEY REBELLION

On May 2, 1792, Congress enacted the Calling Forth Act.[11] The act delegated to the President the power to call forth the militia to execute the laws, suppress insurrections, and repel invasions. Congress conditioned this delegation in numerous ways. For example, in case of invasion, Congress instructed the President to "call forth such number of the militia of the state or states most convenient to the place of danger or scene of action, as he may judge necessary to repel such invasion."[12] The use of the militia for domestic law enforcement was a touchy subject at the Constitutional Convention with Anti-Federalists fearing a military government. In the Calling Forth Act, Congress conditioned the President's power to call forth the militia for domestic law enforcement on receiving notification from "an associate justice or the district judge" that federal law was being "obstructed . . . by combinations too powerful to be suppressed by the ordinary course of judicial proceedings, or by the powers vested in the marshals by this act."[13]

President George Washington's most notable use of the commander-in-chief power came in the summer of 1794 when opponents of liquor excise taxes imposed by Congress organized violent resistance to federal law.[14] Washington received notification from Justice James Wilson that the laws could not be enforced through regular process of law, and only then did he summon 12,500 militia from New Jersey, Pennsylvania, Maryland, and Virginia to suppress the rebellion.[15] This marked the first time that "the militia functioned as a national, rather than a local, institution."[16]

THE WAR OF 1812

Before, during, and after the War of 1812, several questions arose concerning the Commander of the Militias Clause. First, did the states have a role in calling forth the militia for federal service? Congress, anticipating an invasion from Great Britain, sought to have the militia enter federal service to provide for the defense, and governors in Connecticut, Massachusetts, and Rhode Island contested this authority.[17]

The Connecticut governor would not allow the Connecticut militia to enter federal service because the United States had neither been invaded nor was in imminent danger.[18] The Massachusetts governor similarly refused to place his state's militia into federal service.[19]

The Massachusetts Supreme Judicial Court addressed this issue in an advisory opinion. It found that the Constitution reserved to the "commanders in chief of the militia of the several states" the authority to determine whether a military exigency existed requiring the militia to be placed in federal service.[20] In 1814, Connecticut and Maine eventually placed some of their militia units into federal service for the limited purpose of securing their own coasts with the federal government funding the operation.[21]

After the war, federal officials widely condemned the states' actions. Secretary of War James Monroe maintained that Congress had the sole power to call forth the militia. Monroe argued that the militia would be useless if the federal government had to negotiate with each state's governor individually to get the forces transferred to federal control.[22] In his *Commentaries on the Constitution*, Justice Joseph Story doubted that the Massachusetts Supreme Judicial Court was correct. If it was, "the public service must be continually liable to very great embarrassments in all cases, where the militia are called into the public service in connexion with the regular troops."[23] *Martin v. Mott* (1827) held that Congress had the sole and unreviewable discretion to call forth the militia for federal service.[24]

Second, who would command the militia forces? Did the Commander in Chief Clause require the President to command militia forces personally, or could the President place the militia under the command of regular army officers? President James Madison argued that once the militia was called into federal service during defensive conflicts, he could command both the regular forces and the militia in the manner most conducive to successful prosecution of the war.[25] This authority included the power to delegate operational control to subordinate commanders, whether Army or militia.

By contrast, the Massachusetts Supreme Judicial Court's advisory opinion found that the President had to command the militia himself.[26] The Massachusetts court concluded that only the President and militia officers could command the militia when called into federal service.[27] These militia officers were appointed by the states.

Underneath these issues are two fundamentally different visions about the nature of the militia. The Massachusetts Supreme Judicial Court treated the militia as state military forces. These forces may be allied with the regular military of the United States, but they may not be fused with them.[28] The Madison Administration considered the militia, when in federal service, to be a constitutive part of the national military establishment.

MODERN DOCTRINE

The difficult legal questions that arose during the War of 1812 have never been firmly settled. The federal government found much of the militia system unworkable. Congress and the President have sought to bypass the militia system by recruiting temporary war volunteers under the control of the regular Army. Beginning in the twentieth century, the federal government used conscription, dual enlistment, and its Spending Clause authority to wrest operational control of nonprofessional forces from the states. (See Essays Nos. 59 and 63.) As a result, the federal government exercises virtual plenary control of all nonprofessional forces, and the U.S. Supreme Court has upheld this arrangement.

OPEN QUESTIONS

- Congress has delegated to the President the power to organize militia forces and call them into federal service, and the Supreme Court has upheld this delegation.[29] Is this delegation consistent with the text and history of the Constitution?
- Does the President have preclusive powers to make war without congressional authorization or to direct the military notwithstanding congressional acts attempting to regulate the armed forces?[30] Some scholars who deny that the President has such inherent power point to the militia provision as an example in which the President's right to command is subordinate to the regulations made by Congress.[31]
- The President is commander in chief of the District of Columbia militia at all times.[32] But what is the constitutional status of the District of Columbia's militia? This question has received occasional scholarly inquiry. William Winthrop argued that the "authority for and legal status of the District militia are not clear. It is no part of the militia referred to in the Constitution, which evidently contemplates a militia of the States."[33] Again, this objection gets to the nature of the militia. If the militia is a state military force, this objection may have merit because the District is not a state. But if the militia is the able-bodied citizenry who may be called into temporary military service, then the District has militiamen just like the states do. If this second option is correct, the President's plenary commander-in-chief power over the District's militia comes from his authority as President to command the militia in federal service and by Congress's authority to exercise exclusive power over the District.[34]

Cite as: Judge Gregory E. Maggs & Robert Leider, *The Commander of the Militia Clause, in* THE HERITAGE GUIDE TO THE CONSTITUTION 378 (Josh Blackman & John G. Malcolm eds., 3d ed. 2025).

Notes

1. F.W. Maitland, The Constitutional History of England 325–26 (1920).   **2.** *Id.* at 326 (quoting 13 Car. II, c. 6). **3.** Allan R. Millett, et al., For the Common Defense: A Military History of the United States from 1607 to 2012, at 5 (rev. ed. 2012).   **4.** David J. Barron & Martin S. Lederman, *The Commander in Chief at the Lowest Ebb—Framing the Problem, Doctrine, and Original Understanding*, 121 Harv. L. Rev. 689, 781–82 & n.299 (2008); Del. Const. of 1776, art. IX; Md. Const. of 1776, art. XXXIII; Mass. Const. of 1780, pt. 2, ch. II, § I, art. XVII; N.C. Const. of 1776, art. XVIII; Va. Const. of 1776.   **5.** Northwest Ordinance (1787), § 6. **6.** John K. Mahon, History of the Militia and the National Guard 36 (1983).   **7.** Jerry Cooper, The Rise of the National Guard: The Evolution of the American Militia, 1865–1920, at 5 (1997).   **8.** 2 Farrand's 172.   **9.** *Id.* at 422.   **10.** Art. I, § 8, cls. 15–16.   **11.** An Act to Provide for Calling Forth the Militia to Execute the Laws of the Union, Suppress Insurrections, and Repel Invasions, ch. 28, 1 Stat. 264.   **12.** *Id.* § 1.   **13.** *Id.* § 6.   **14.** Russell F. Weigley, History of the United States Army 100 (1967).   **15.** *Id.* at 100–01; David P. Currie, The Constitution in Congress: The Federalist Period 1789–1801, at 189 (1997).   **16.** Millet et al., *supra* at 87.   **17.** Marcus Armstrong, *The Militia: A Definition and Litmus Test*, 52 St. Mary's L.J. 1, 28 (2020).   **18.** *Id.* at 28–29.   **19.** *Id.*

at 31–32. **20.** *Op. of the Justices*, 8 Mass. (8 Tyng) 548, 550 (1812). **21.** Michael D. Doubler, I Am the Guard: A History of the Army National Guard, 1623–2000, at 79 (2001). **22.** Letter from Sec'y of War James Monroe, to Senate Military Affairs Comm. (Feb. 11, 1815), *in* 1 American State Papers: Military Affairs 604–06 (Walter Lowrie & Matthew St. Clair Clarke eds., 1832). **23.** 3 Story's Commentaries § 1210. **24.** *Martin v. Mott*, 25 U.S. (12 Wheat.) 19 (1827). **25.** James Madison, Fourth Annual Message to Congress (Nov. 4, 1812), https://perma.cc/PZE6-DR2H. **26.** 8 Mass. at 550–51. **27.** *Id.* **28.** *Id.* at 551. **29.** *Mott*, 25 U.S. (12 Wheat.) at 19. **30.** Saikrishna B. Prakash, *Deciphering the Commander-in-Chief Clause*, 133 Yale L.J. 1 (2023); Zachary S. Price, *Congress's Power over Military Offices*, 99 Tex. L. Rev. 491 (2021); John Yoo, *Transferring Terrorists*, 79 N.D. L. Rev. 1183, 1202 (2004); David J. Barron & Martin S. Lederman, *The Commander in Chief at the Lowest Ebb—A Constitutional History*, 121 Harv. L. Rev. 941 (2008); Barron & Lederman, *supra*; Robert J. Delahunty & John C. Yoo, *Making War*, 93 Cornell L. Rev. 123 (2007); John C. Yoo, Crisis and Command: A History of Executive Power from George Washington to George W. Bush (2010). **31.** Richard A. Epstein, *Executive Power, the Commander in Chief, and the Militia Clause*, 34 Hofstra L. Rev. 317 (2005). **32.** D.C. Code § 49-409. **33.** See William Winthrop, Military Law and Precedents 56 n.67 (2d ed. 1920) (citation omitted). **34.** Art. I, § 8, cl. 17; art. II, § 2, cl. 1; Robert Leider, *Deciphering the "Armed Forces of the United States*," 57 Wake Forest L. Rev. 1195, 1208 n.72 (2022).

ESSAY NO. 104: THE OPINION CLAUSE
ART. II, § 2, CL. 1

The President . . . may require the Opinion, in writing, of the principal Officer in each of the executive Departments, upon any Subject relating to the Duties of their respective Offices. . . .

—Todd F. Gaziano

INTRODUCTION

The Opinion Clause arose from the debates at the Constitutional Convention regarding whether the President would exercise executive authority singly or in concert with other officials or privy councilors. The primary disagreement was over whether the new President should be aided or constrained in important decisions by other officials or whether that would diminish his responsibility and democratic accountability for such decisions. Those who stressed the need for heightened accountability of a single executive prevailed. The resulting Opinion Clause augments the President's managerial authority even over Senate-confirmed department heads. That choice has enabled Presidents to form advisory cabinets that suit their particular needs and leadership styles.

HISTORY BEFORE 1787

In England, the king could secure the assistance of and seek advice from any of his subjects.[1] In modern times, the Prime Minister is an elected parliamentary leader, associated with parliamentary rule. Initially, however, the holders of these positions were ministers to the king.

Moreover, during the colonial era, the king could require any nobleman, judge, or Member of Parliament to serve in his Privy Council and request both official and personal advice from that body.[2]

Over time, the ministerial offices assumed greater practical and administrative power.[3] The transformation from royal servants and advisers to largely independent administrative officials was well under way during the reign of King George II. By the end of the eighteenth century, the king exercised fewer powers and thus had less need to seek ministerial guidance; in turn, the king's responsibility for actions taken by the government was greatly diminished. Thus, the king could do no legal wrong himself and was not politically responsible for his ministers' administrative wrongs.[4]

Following independence, many states adopted councils. Alexander Hamilton would observe in Federalist No. 70 that "[t]he idea of a council to the Executive, which has so generally obtained in the State constitutions, has been derived from that maxim of republican jealousy which considers power as safer in the hands of a number of men than of a single man." In many states, their executives required the concurrence of the Council.[5]

THE CONSTITUTIONAL CONVENTION

During the Constitutional Convention, the delegates debated whether there should be some sort of council to advise the President. James Wilson of Pennsylvania and James Madison of Virginia supported a Council of Revision that could veto legislation.[6] This Council would be composed of the President and judges. Rufus King of Massachusetts objected to Madison's proposal. He argued that "the Unity of the Executive was preferred for the sake of responsibility" and that the executive alone should therefore have the veto power.[7] However, vesting all executive power in one person was a break with English tradition and early state practice. King's position caused unease and initially failed to win sufficient support from the other delegates.

Several delegates, including Oliver Ellsworth of Connecticut, supported a constitutional "Privy Council." Such a council would not bind the President but would be obligated to provide him with advice.[8] Charles Pinckney of South Carolina objected to this proposal because he thought it would lessen presidential accountability.[9] Elbridge Gerry of Massachusetts also objected. He explained that heads of department would be able to blame the council for an unpopular decision and thus evade personal responsibility regarding matters for which they were responsible.[10]

The Opinion Clause was born from this concern. An August 20 proposal would have established a Council of State. Under this proposal, the President could "require the written opinions of any one or more of the [Council's] members," each of whom would be assigned a particular portfolio of matters on which to advise. The Chief Justice of the United States would propose changes regarding the "due administration of Justice." The Secretary of Domestic Affairs would "attend to matters of general police." The Secretary of Commerce and Finance would "superintend all matters relating to the public finances." The Secretary of Foreign Affairs would attend to "the Interests of the United States, in their connection with foreign Powers." The Secretaries of War and Marine would focus on military matters. And the Secretary of State would serve as Secretary of the Council of State. Critically, however, the President would "in all cases exercise his own judgment." Under the plan, "every officer" was "responsible for his opinion on the affairs relating to his particular Department." Finally, these officers would be "liable to impeachment & removal from office for neglect of duty, malversation, or corruption."[11]

The Convention, however, rejected even a weak advisory council. Pinckney's earlier warning summarized many delegate's thinking: "The President [should] be authorized to call for advice or not as he might chuse. Give him an able Council and it will thwart him; a weak one and he will shelter himself under their sanction."[12]

Toward the end of the Constitutional Convention, a Committee of the States was tasked with further consideration of this and other unresolved matters. On September 7, Gouverneur Morris of Pennsylvania explained that this committee also rejected the idea of a privy or other advisory council: "The Presidt. by persuading his Council to concur in his wrong measures, would acquire their protection for them."[13] In other words, the President could evade responsibility by hiding behind his council.

Instead, Morris proposed language that formed the basis of the current Opinion Clause. The text merely authorized the President "to call for the opinions of the Heads of Departments, in writing," and these written opinions could be obtained "upon any Subject relating to the Duties of their respective Offices."[14] Thus modified, the clause does not even encourage the President to seek a consensus from all department heads or any particular department head. In the end, the President, and not department heads, will bear the responsibility for his decisions.

THE RATIFICATION DEBATES

In Federalist No. 70, Alexander Hamilton criticized the executive councils in the states, arguing that "multiplication of the Executive is rather dangerous than friendly to liberty." Instead, he praised the single executive. In Federalist No. 74, Hamilton discussed the Opinion Clause:

"This I consider as a mere redundancy in the plan, as the right for which it provides would result of itself from the office." Hamilton was not clear what it meant for a power to "result of itself from the office," but it seems to suggest that this power was inherent in the office of the presidency. If this was Hamilton's view, then the Opinion Clause would seem to serve no independent function.

PRESIDENTIAL PRACTICE

As a result of the debates over the Opinion Clause and a privy council, the Constitution nowhere requires a formal Cabinet. Yet President George Washington still found it prudent to organize his principal officers into one.[15] This sort of presidential Cabinet has been part of the executive branch structure ever since, but this does not permit the President to deflect political accountability.

Presidents have used Cabinet meetings of selected principal officers to widely differing extents and for different purposes. For example, during the Civil War, Secretary of State William H. Seward advocated for the use of a parliamentary-style cabinet government. President Abraham Lincoln was viewed as a "political genius" for co-opting Seward and other rivals into a single Cabinet,[16] but Lincoln rebuffed any notion of shared responsibility. After one Cabinet vote, he supposedly said "Seven nays and one aye, and ayes have it."[17] Several twentieth-century Presidents pledged to use their Cabinets as deliberative bodies, but Dwight Eisenhower was one of the few who did so.[18]

In modern times, Cabinets have grown unwieldy for effective deliberations. Some Cabinets have as many as twenty-five members including the Vice President, fifteen department heads, and nine other agency heads. President Ronald Reagan even included in his Cabinet Edwin Meese III, the then-Deputy White House Chief of Staff.[19] President Reagan also formed seven sub-Cabinet councils to work with White House staff on formulating policy.[20] That number was later reduced to two. Subsequent Presidents have followed that practice. Most recent Presidents have met infrequently with their entire Cabinets. In an age when the President relies heavily on White House staff for advice and assistance, Presidents often use Cabinet meetings to make the members feel more a part of the President's inner circle or to increase their loyalty to the Administration.[21]

OPEN QUESTIONS
- Is the Opinion Clause, as Hamilton implied, redundant? Justice Elena Kagan embraced this negative inference in her dissenting opinion in *Seila Law LLC* v. *Consumer Financial Protection Bureau*.[22] Professor Akhil Reed Amar rejected such a negative inference. He argued that many clauses of the Constitution, including in the Bill of Rights, explicitly affirmed "what otherwise would have been the best reading 'by unavoidable *implication*.'"[23] Other scholars have pointed to the Opinion Clause as evidence that the President has enumerated executive powers and not unenumerated, inherent executive powers.[24]
- What is the relationship between the Opinion Clause and the Recommendations Clause? (See Essay No. 111.) Can Congress require presidential appointees to report to Congress instead of to the President?
- Can a federal court prohibit a department head from providing the President with his opinion? *Trump v. New York* (2020) reviewed an injunction that barred the Secretary of Commerce from informing the President about census data. The Supreme Court hinted that this injunction "implicat[es] the President's authority under the Opinions Clause."[25]

Cite as: Todd F. Gaziano, *The Opinion Clause, in* THE HERITAGE GUIDE TO THE CONSTITUTION 382 (Josh Blackman & John G. Malcolm eds., 3d ed. 2025).

Notes

1. Akhil Reed Amar, *Some Opinions on the Opinion Clause*, 82 Va. L. Rev. 647, 647, 654, 656 (1996).   **2.** *Id.* at 654; Steven Calabresi & Saikrishna Prakash, *The President's Power to Execute the Laws*, 104 Yale L.J. 541, 634 (1994).   **3.** HM Government, Ministerial Code (Nov. 2024), https://perma.cc/7QX4-SKHN.   **4.** 1 The Works of James Wilson 318–19 (Robert G. McCloskey ed., 1967).   **5.** Calabresi & Prakash, *supra* at 610 n.278.   **6.** 1 Farrand's 138–39.   **7.** *Id.* at 139.   **8.** 2 Farrand's 328–29.   **9.** *Id.*   **10.** *Id.*   **11.** *Id.* at 335–37.   **12.** *Id.* at 329.   **13.** *Id.* at 542.   **14.** *Id.* at 541.   **15.** James P. Pfiffner, The Modern Presidency 101–02 (6th ed. 2011).   **16.** Doris Kearns Goodwin, Team of Rivals: The Political Genius of Abraham Lincoln, Part II (2005).   **17.** Pfiffner, *supra* at 103.   **18.** *Id.* at 103–04.   **19.** Meese, Edwin, III: Files 1981–1985, Ronald Reagan Presidential Library & Museum, https://perma.cc/7QX4-SKHN.   **20.** Pfiffner, *supra* at 106–07.   **21.** *Id.* at 104, 110–14.   **22.** 591 U.S. 197, 266 n.3 (2020) (Kagan, J., dissenting).   **23.** Amar, *supra* at 648, 648–53.   **24.** Lawrence Lessig & Cass R. Sunstein, *The President and the Administration*, 94 Colum. L. Rev. 1 (1994); Zachary Murray, Note, *The Forgotten Unitary Executive Power: The Textualist, Originalist and Functionalist Opinion Clauses*, 39 Pace L. Rev. 229, 235–41 (2018).   **25.** *Trump v. New York*, 592 U.S. 125, 133 (2020).

~

ESSAY NO. 105: THE PARDON CLAUSE
ART. II, § 2, CL. 1

The President . . . shall have Power to grant Reprieves and Pardons for Offences against the United States, except in Cases of Impeachment.

—Paul J. Larkin

INTRODUCTION

The Framers vested the nation's chief executive with the authority, almost without limitation, to correct errors in the federal criminal justice system or to grant mercy at any time after a crime has been committed. The President generally may relieve someone charged with a federal offense of the burden of trial, the weight of a conviction, and the pain of punishment as he or she sees fit without interference from Congress or the federal judiciary. Clemency serves as "the fail safe in our criminal justice system."[1] Given the clause's breadth, the President's power to grant clemency is perhaps the last surviving royal prerogative.

HISTORY BEFORE 1787

Clemency has an ancient lineage in England.[2] Because a felony was considered "an act contrary to the peace and dignity of the crown," only the king or queen could excuse an offender from blame or punishment through clemency on whatever conditions the monarch deemed fit. Sir William Blackstone wrote that "the king may extend his mercy upon what terms he pleases, and may annex to his bounty a condition, either precedent or subsequent, on the performance whereof the validity of the pardon will depend; and this by the common law."[3] Lord Edward Coke explained that a pardon from the king was "a work of mercy, whereby the King, either before attainder, sentence, or conviction, or after, forgiveth any crime, offence, punishment [or] execution."[4]

Monarchs exercised the pardon power with alacrity and granted clemency for many reasons. Pardons would avoid sending a person to the gallows because of the primitive state of the common law of crimes. For example, a minor could be convicted of a capital crime because every felony was a capital crime, and there was no infancy defense. Moreover, the law of criminal procedure was not developed, and there was no right to counsel in felony cases. The king also recognized that every felony was a capital offense, and a commutation of the death sentence might be warranted in the interests of justice. The Crown may also have had other motives. Kings would offer a pardon to people willing to serve in the army or navy or would send them to populate colonies in America or Australia. Pardons could be sold to generate revenue without a need for an appropriation from Parliament. And in all cases, clemency could "curry favor with the Almighty."[5]

Over time, Parliament restricted the

Crown's pardon power. For example, the king could not grant clemency *before* a person committed a crime; such a preemptive pardon would amount to a suspension of the law. In 1689, Parliament won a long battle with the Crown over such legal supremacy by passing the English Bill of Rights, which eliminated a royal suspensionary power,[6] and the Act of Settlement of 1701 disallowed the Crown from using clemency to frustrate parliamentary impeachment.[7] Generally, however, the Crown's clemency authority was plenary.

Clemency accompanied the colonists to America. Colonial governors or other Crown officials had that power. For example, the Virginia Charter of 1609 granted the governor "full and absolute Power and Authority to correct, punish, pardon, govern, and rule" all English subjects in the colony.[8] Every colony and state placed the pardon power somewhere in the government.

THE CONSTITUTIONAL CONVENTION

Clemency was little discussed at the Constitutional Convention of 1787.[9] The two principal models for the new federal government—the Virginia Plan and the New Jersey Plan—created an office of the President, but neither one granted him a clemency power. Alexander Hamilton proposed granting the chief executive pardon authority.[10] Hamilton's proposal resembled the English Act of Settlement of 1701: the chief executive could excuse someone from a crime or its punishment, but he could not prevent Congress from removing a government official from office. The Convention accepted this proposal.

The Convention rejected proposals to limit the President's clemency authority. Roger Sherman sought to limit the power to grant a reprieve until only the next session of the Senate and to require the Senate to concur in the granting of a pardon.[11] Edmund Randolph would have exempted treason from the category of pardonable offenses.[12] The Convention rejected each proposal. Luther Martin proposed making the pardon power a purely post-conviction authority, but he withdrew his proposal once James Wilson pointed out that a pre-trial pardon might be necessary to secure the testimony of accomplices to

a crime.[13] Otherwise, the Convention spent little time on the Pardon Clause. It became part of the Constitution sent to the states for their consideration, and the states ratified it.

The laconic text of the Pardon Clause is deceptively simple. It vests the President with authority to grant "Reprieves and Pardons" but is not limited to those forms of relief. A President may also commute an offender's sentence—that is, nullify a death sentence or reduce the length of a prison sentence, even to zero. The President may remit, or cancel, whatever fine was imposed. The President may also return any property that was forfeited.[14] The President generally grants clemency on a case-by-case basis to correct "individual cases of injustice"[15] but may also award clemency to multiple offenders, a practice known as granting amnesty.[16]

There may have been so little discussion because the Framers relied on the well-known history from England. Chief Justice John Marshall would later observe that the pardon "power had been exercised, from time immemorial, by the executive of that nation whose language is our language, and to whose judicial institutions ours bear a close resemblance."[17] Marshall added that the Framers "adopt[ed] their principles respecting the operation and effect of a pardon, and look[ed] into their books for the rules prescribing the manner in which it is to be used by the person who would avail himself of it."[18] Another explanation for the lack of debate might be that everyone at the Convention of 1787 anticipated that George Washington would become the first President, and they had complete confidence in his judgment and character.[19]

THE RATIFICATION DEBATES

Alexander Hamilton discussed the clemency power in Federalist No. 74. Hamilton wrote, "The criminal code of every country partakes of so much necessary severity that that without an easy access to exceptions in cases of unfortunate guilt, justice would wear a countenance too sanguinary and cruel." Anti-Federalists warned that the pardon power was too broad. George Mason of Virginia stated that the President had the "unrestrained Power of granting pardon for Treason."[20] Mason even insinuated that the President might himself be implicated in the treason, and the pardon would "thereby prevent a Discovery of his own Guilt." Luther Martin of Maryland raised similar objections.[21] No objection carried the day, and the states ratified the Constitution, including the Article II Pardon Clause.

LIMITATIONS ON THE PARDON POWER

The clemency power is not unlimited. First, the President can pardon only federal crimes: The Pardon Clause is limited to "Offences against the United States." Second, the pardon power does not extend to "Cases of Impeachment." In other words, the President cannot prevent Congress from removing his appointed subordinates from office. Third, if a convicted person has already paid a fine, the President cannot return funds that were already paid into the federal treasury. The Appropriations Clause ensures that "[n]o money shall be drawn from the treasury, but in consequence of appropriations made by law."[22] Fourth, the U.S. Supreme Court stated in dicta that the President cannot deny relief on an arbitrary ground elsewhere forbidden by the Constitution, such as a person's race, religion, or political views.[23] Fifth, the President cannot grant someone clemency *before* he commits a crime. Such a preemptive pardon would be uncomfortably close to exempting that person from the law and would resemble the sort of suspensionary power that was prohibited by the English Bill of Rights. Under the Constitution, a preemptive pardon might violate the President's Article II obligation to "take Care that the Laws be faithfully executed."[24]

The Supreme Court has suggested in dicta that there might be other limitations as well,[25] but it also has explained that this power "cannot be modified, abridged, or diminished by the Congress."[26] Likewise, the Court has not created any procedural rules that a President must follow when acting on a clemency application. Nor has the Court placed any substantive restraints on when, how, and to whom a President can extend relief. The President's power to grant clemency is perhaps the last surviving royal prerogative.

EXECUTIVE BRANCH PRACTICE

Presidents have used clemency to correct mistaken convictions, to soften unduly onerous punishments, to end a period of domestic political turmoil, for "reasons of state," and for personal reasons, not all of which would have been legitimate. President George Washington granted amnesty to participants in the Whiskey Rebellion against federal whiskey taxes.[27] Presidents Abraham Lincoln and Andrew Johnson pardoned and granted amnesty for Confederate soldiers and officials.[28] President Warren G. Harding pardoned Eugene Debs, the prominent socialist who ran for President from prison.[29] Presidents Gerald Ford and Jimmy Carter granted amnesty to a large number of men who unlawfully failed to register for the Vietnam War draft.[30] Ford also pardoned former President Richard Nixon for his actions during the Watergate scandal.[31] President Joseph Biden used clemency as part of a prisoner exchange with Russia.[32]

JUDICIAL PRECEDENT

The Supreme Court has rarely discussed the Pardon Clause.[33] Chief Justice John Marshall characterized clemency as similar to an act of divine "grace."[34] In the twentieth century, however, the Court abandoned that description. According to Justice Holmes, clemency is "not a private act of grace from an individual happening to possess power." Rather, pardons are "the determination of the ultimate authority that the public welfare will be better served by inflicting less than what the judgment fixed."[35] The lack of precedent about the pardon power is likely due to standing doctrine. Under settled precedent, a third party lacks standing to challenge the grant or denial of clemency to an offender.[36]

OPEN QUESTIONS

- Some scholars have contended that clemency has fallen into desuetude.[37] Whether that remains true after Biden went nuclear with clemency before leaving office remains to be seen. Critics have faulted the U.S. Department of Justice, which has the power to strangle a clemency application in the cradle.[38] As a result, there have been calls to shift the pardon recommendation process to an independent clemency board or to transfer the process to the Executive Office of the President.[39]

- Some Presidents have used their clemency authority for allegedly corrupt purposes, and some critics have urged Congress to restrain such pardons.[40] Would such a statute infringe on the President's pardon power?

- Can a pardon be granted or denied based on an arbitrary ground elsewhere forbidden by the Constitution, such as a person's race, religion, or political views?

- Can the President pardon himself? This issue has arisen several times over the past half-century. There is disagreement over the legality of such pardons. The Justice Department's Office of Legal Counsel and some scholars have argued that the President cannot self-pardon.[41] Others (including the author of this essay) argue that the President can issue a self-pardon.[42] The Supreme Court has never addressed that issue.

- During President Biden's final days in office, he issued pardons to members of his family and government officials who had not yet been charged with any crimes.[43] Are such preemptive pardons valid?

Cite as: Paul J. Larkin, Jr., *The Pardon Clause, in* THE HERITAGE GUIDE TO THE CONSTITUTION 385 (Josh Blackman & John G. Malcolm eds., 3d ed. 2025).

Notes

1. *Herrera v. Collins*, 506 U.S. 390, 415 (1993) (citation and punctuation omitted). The author was one of the lawyers who represented the United States in *Herrera*. **2.** Naomi D. Hurnard, *The King's Pardon for Homicide Before A.D. 1307* (1969); K.J. Kesselring, *Mercy and Authority in the Tudor State* (2003). **3.** 4 Blackstone 401. **4.** Jonathan Harris & Lothlórien Redmond, *Executive Clemency: The Lethal Absence of Hope*, 3 Am. Univ. Crim. L. Brief 2, 12, n.15 (2007) (quoting 3 Edward Coke, Institutes of the Laws of England 233 (8th ed., 1680)). **5.** Paul J. Larkin, Jr., *Guiding Presidential Clemency Decision Making*, 18 Geo. J.L. & Pub. Pol'y 451, 477 (2020). **6.** 1 Wm. & M., Sess. 2, c. 2; Philip Hamburger, *Is Administrative Law Unlawful?* 65–73 (2014). **7.** 12 & 13 Will. 3, c. 2, § 3 (1700); William Duker, *The President's Power to Pardon: A Constitutional History*, 18 Wm. & Mary L. Rev. 475, 487–96 (1977). **8.** 7 The Federal and State Constitutions, Colonial Charters, and Other Organic Laws of the State, Territories, or Colonies Now or Heretofore Forming the United States of America 3801 (Francis Newton Thorpe ed., 1909). **9.** 2 Farrand's 419, 627; Duker, *supra*, at 476–77; Larkin, *supra*, at 480–81, 501–02. **10.** 1 Farrand's 292. **11.** 2 Farrand's 419. **12.** 2 Farrand's 564, 580, 626–27. **13.** 2 Farrand's 426. **14.** *Ex parte Wells*, 59 U.S. (18 How.) 307, 314–15 (1855). **15.** Barack Obama, *The President's Role in Advancing Criminal Justice Reform*, 130 Harv. L. Rev. 811, 835 (2017). **16.** *Knote v. United States*, 95 U.S. 149, 152–53 (1877); *United States v. Klein*, 80 U.S. (13 Wall.) 128, 147–48 (1871). **17.** *United States v. Wilson*, 32 U.S. (7 Pet.) 150, 160 (1833) (Marshall, C.J.). **18.** *Id.* **19.** Jack Rakove, *Original Meanings: Politics and Ideas in the Making of the Constitution* 244 (1996). **20.** Storing 2.2.9. **21.** *Id.* at 2.4.85. **22.** Art. I, § 9, cl. 7; *Knote*, 95 U.S. at 154–55; *United States v. Padelford*, 76 U.S. (9 Wall.) 531, 542–43 (1869). **23.** *Schick v. Reed*, 419 U.S. 256, 267 (1974). **24.** Art. II, § 3; *Kendall v. United States ex rel. Stokes*, 37 U.S. 524, 612–13 (1838). **25.** *Ex parte Wells*, 59 U.S. (18 How.) at 312. **26.** *Schick*, 419 U.S. at 266. **27.** Jeffrey P. Crouch, *The Presidential Pardon Power* 55–56 (2009). **28.** Jonathan Truman Dorris, Pardon and Amnesty Under Lincoln and Johnson, 1861–1898 (photo. reprt. 2018) (1953). **29.** James D. Robenalt, *100 Years Ago, a President Forgave His Opponent's Alleged Subversion*, Wash. Post (Jan. 6, 2022). **30.** U.S. Presidential Clemency Board, Report to the President (1975); Graham G. Dodds, *Mass Pardons in America: Rebellion, Presidential Amnesty, and Reconciliation* 143–78 (2021). **31.** *Murphy v. Ford*, 390 F. Supp. 1372, 1374 (W.D. Mich. 1975). **32.** Paul J. Larkin & Dakota Wood, *Clemency for Favored Constituents: The Brittney Griner–Viktor Bout Prisoner Swap*, 56 Int'l Law. 443 (2023). **33.** Paul J. Larkin, *Focusing Presidential Clemency Decision-Making*, 70 Buff. L. Rev. 1, 19 n.42 (2022). **34.** *Wilson*, 32 U.S. (7 Pet.) at 160. **35.** *Biddle v. Perovich*, 274 U.S. 480, 486 (1927) (Holmes, J.). **36.** *Linda R.S. v. Richard D.*, 410 U.S. 614, (619 (1973). **37.** Paul Rosenzweig, *Reflections on the Atrophying Pardon Power*, 102 J. Crim. L. & Criminology 593 (2012). **38.** Mark Osler, *Fewer Hands, More Mercy: A Plea for a Better Federal Clemency System*, 41 Vt. L. Rev. 465 (2017). **39.** Rachel E. Barkow & Mark Osler, *Restructuring Clemency: The Cost of Ignoring Clemency and a Plan for Renewal*, 82 U. Chi. L. Rev. 1 (2015); Paul J. Larkin, Jr., *Essay—A Proposal to Restructure the Clemency Process—The Vice President as Head of a White House Clemency Office*, 40 Harv. J.L. & Pub. Pol'y 237 (2017). **40.** Albert W. Alschuler, *Bill Clinton's Parting Pardon Party*, 100 J. Crim. L. & Criminology 1131 (2010). **41.** Mary C. Lawton, Acting Ass't Att'y Gen., Off. of Legal Counsel, Presidential or Legislative Pardon of the President, Mem. Op. for the Deputy Att'y Gen. (Aug. 5, 1974), https://perma.cc/93D8-XQS3; Brian C. Kalt, *Note, Pardon Me: The Constitutional Case Against Presidential Self-Pardons*, 106 Yale L.J. 779 (1996). **42.** Paul J. Larkin, Jr., *The Legality of Presidential Self-Pardons*, 44 Harv. J.L. & Pub. Pol'y 763, 782–824 (2021). **43.** Presidential Statement on Pardons of General Mark A Milley et al. (Jan. 20, 2025), https://perma.cc/3HTU-JRQQ; Presidential Statement on Pardons of Gerald G. Lundergan and Ernest William Cromartie and Commutation of Leonard Peltier's Sentence (Jan. 20, 2025), https://perma.cc/HW78-NG9A.

~

ESSAY NO. 106: THE TREATY CLAUSE
ART. II, § 2, CL. 2

The President . . . shall have Power, by and with the Advice and Consent of the Senate, to make Treaties, provided two thirds of the Senators present concur. . . .
—Michael D. Ramsey

INTRODUCTION

The Treaty Clause has a number of striking features. It gives the President and the Senate a shared role in treaty-making and requires a supermajority (two-thirds) of the Senate for approval of a treaty. However, the clause gives the House of Representatives no formal role in the process. Moreover, unlike Congress's law-making power, the Treaty Clause contains no express limits on its scope. This essay provides a brief history of the clause's development and considers several key issues relating to the clause including the use of executive agreements as substitutes for treaties, the termination of treaties, and possible limits on the subject matter of treaties.

HISTORY BEFORE 1787

In the English system, the monarch had sole power to make treaties, which Blackstone described as an aspect of the "executive part of government."[1] However, Parliament's action was required to make treaty provisions part of domestic law. After independence, the Continental Congress assumed the power to make treaties for the new nation, including the crucial 1778 alliance with France. The Articles of Confederation, adopted in 1781, confirmed Congress's power to make treaties but required the assent of nine of the thirteen states.[2] That supermajority requirement became critical in the principal treatymaking debate under the Articles.

In the mid-1780s, the Confederation Congress attempted to negotiate a treaty with Spain that would provide trading rights and free access to the Mississippi River through Spanish-controlled New Orleans. Spain offered favorable trade terms, but only if the United States would give up its demands on the Mississippi.[3]

The Northern states would have benefited most from the trade treaty and cared little about New Orleans; they had a majority—but not a supermajority—of votes in Congress. The Southern states, insisting on protecting access to the Mississippi, were able to block the treaty despite having only a minority of votes. The Southern states, and many people in the North, concluded that the supermajority requirement had prevented an unwise treaty. This experience undoubtedly encouraged the Constitution's Framers to carry over the supermajority principle from the Articles of Confederation.

THE CONSTITUTIONAL CONVENTION

The Virginia Plan proposed to give the national executive "a general authority to execute the National laws" in addition to "the Executive rights vested in Congress by the Confederation."[4] John Rutledge of South Carolina and James Wilson of Pennsylvania objected to the latter provision, which they thought would include "powers of war and peace."[5] Wilson argued that these powers should belong to the legislature.[6] James Madison of Virginia proposed that the Convention delete the clause conveying "Executive rights."[7] This motion was passed, leaving uncertainty as to whether the treaty-making power belonged to the legislative or executive branch.[8]

The Convention did not materially consider the treaty-making power further until the report of the Committee of Detail in August. A Committee draft in the handwriting of Edmund Randolph of Virginia defined "legislative powers" as including the power "to make treaties of commerce" and "to make treaties of peace or alliance." A note in parentheses, likely in Rutledge's handwriting, questioned whether the

Senate in particular should have these powers.[9] A Committee draft in Wilson's handwriting granted the Senate alone the power to "make Treaties of Peace, of Alliance, and of Commerce" as well as the authority to "send Ambassadors."[10] Another draft from Wilson simplified the language to give the Senate power to "make treaties, and to appoint Ambassadors."[11] This version was delivered to the Convention on August 6.[12] However, that proposal proved unsatisfactory to the Convention.

On August 23, Madison suggested that, as the Senate represented only the states, the President should "be an agent in Treaties."[13] The matter was then referred to the Committee of Eleven, which, apparently adopting Madison's suggestion, in September proposed essentially the final language: The President would "make treaties" and the Senate would approve treaties with the "Consent of two thirds of the Members present."[14] The Convention adopted this allocation with little recorded debate.

Wilson attempted to require the House's approval for treaties as well as the Senate's.[15] Roger Sherman of Connecticut worried that there is a "necessity of secrecy" for treaties that would prohibit referring them to the "whole Legislature."[16] He thought the smaller Senate could be "safely trusted." The small states, wary of being disadvantaged, also presumably preferred to keep the treaty-making power in the Senate where they had proportionally greater power. Wilson's proposal was rejected by a vote of 10 to 1, supported only by Pennsylvania.[17]

Treaty-making thus became a mixture of executive and legislative power. Most delegates likely recognized the actual conduct of diplomacy as an executive function.[18] However, under Article VI, treaties were part of the "supreme Law of the Land." The choice to involve both the President and the Senate in the process reflected the view that American interests might be undermined by treaties entered into without proper reflection. The Framers believed that treaties should be strictly honored, both as a matter of the law of nations and as a practical matter. The United States could not afford to give the great powers any cause for war, but this meant that the nation should be doubly cautious in accepting treaty obligations.

The Committee of Eleven's proposal also introduced the supermajority requirement for Senate approval of treaties.[19] Wilson thought the two-thirds requirement would "put[] it in the power of a minority to controul the will of a majority."[20] Elbridge Gerry of Massachusetts moved that a treaty could be made with a "majority of the whole number of the Senate."[21] This proposal was defeated by a vote of 6 to 5.

Although the Convention records do not indicate how the supermajority requirement first arose, it presumably derived from the Articles of Confederation's requirement of nine states to approve a treaty. The wisdom of retaining the Articles' rule was no doubt highlighted by the defeat of the Spanish treaty under the Articles.[22]

The Framers worried that, as with the proposed Spanish treaty, one region or interest constituting a bare majority within the nation would make a treaty that was to its advantage but prejudicial to other parts of the country and to the national interest. The ultimate purpose of the Treaty Clause was therefore to ensure that treaties would not be adopted unless most of the country stood to gain. Treaties would be more difficult to adopt than statutes would be, but the Framers realized that an unwise statute could simply be repealed, while an unwise treaty remained a binding international commitment that would not be so easy to unwind.

THE RATIFICATION DEBATES

During the ratification debates, the Treaty Clause drew attacks on two principal grounds. First, opponents objected to combining the executive and legislative branches in violation of the (supposed) principle of strict separation of powers. Alexander Hamilton addressed this objection in Federalist No. 75. He pointed to the role of treaties as both diplomatic instruments and (as a result of Article VI) part of the supreme law of the land. Hamilton also emphasized the importance of the Senate as a check on presidential treaty-making and defended the omission of the House from the process.

A more practical objection to the clause, especially in Virginia, was that the supermajority requirement was insufficiently demanding. Anti-Federalists, invoking the Spanish treaty episode under the Articles, wanted two-thirds of all Senators (not just those present) or three quarters of Senators present to approve a treaty. Federalists replied that the Constitution's requirement—two-thirds of Senators present—would be sufficient protection.[23]

PRESIDENTIAL PRACTICE

In August 1789, President George Washington visited the Senate to seek "advice and consent" for a treaty. Rather than giving Washington a clear answer, the Senate opted to consider the treaty further and referred it to a committee. Washington became visibly upset "in a violent fret."[24] After some debate, the Senate provided its consent to the treaty. Washington never again visited the Senate to obtain advice and consent. He found personal consultation with the Senate to be so awkward and unproductive that he abandoned it, and subsequent Presidents have followed his example.

The practice became that either the President or the President's emissaries negotiated and signed treaties independently, and the President then presented the signed treaty to the Senate for its consent. As a practical matter, there often has been consultation between the executive and members of the Senate before treaties are crafted and signed. Generally, the President will make clear to foreign nations that the President's signature on a treaty is only a preliminary commitment subject to Senate scrutiny. As long as the Senate takes seriously its constitutional role of reviewing treaties rather than merely deferring to the President, the check that the Framers sought to create remains in place.

The Senate at times has refused to consent to treaties. It also has approved treaties with conditions or refused to consent to particular parts of treaties. By going beyond a simple "up-or-down" vote, the Senate retains some of its power of "advice." The Senate not only disapproves the treaty proposed by the President but also suggests how the President might negotiate a better treaty.

TREATIES AND EXECUTIVE AGREEMENTS

The Treaty Clause does not say that it is the exclusive method for approving treaties, but its purpose was to avoid bare-majority approval of treaties that disadvantage one part of the nation, and this suggests that no other route was envisioned for approving treaties. Further, the drafting and ratifying debates reflect a broad consensus that the clause was the only constitutional avenue for treaty-making.

However, the Framers also apparently recognized a class of less important international agreements that did not rise to the level of treaties. Article I, Section 10 prohibits states from entering into "Treat[ies]" but allows them to enter into "Agreement[s] or Compact[s]" with the consent of Congress. This text indicates that not all international agreements are treaties and suggests that these other agreements would not need to go through the procedures specified in the Treaty Clause. Instead, the President, exercising the executive power, could make these agreements independently.[25] But this procedure would have to be limited to agreements of minor importance; otherwise, there would be too great an avenue for evading the protections the Framers placed in the Treaty Clause.[26]

Since the early Republic, Presidents have made executive agreements on their own authority without seeking Senate approval. For example, President John Adams made an executive agreement settling claims with the Netherlands in 1799. This practice continued intermittently during the nineteenth century.[27] However, during the twentieth century, this minor diplomatic tool increased in frequency of use and in importance. Executive agreements became even more commonplace during the New Deal and after World War II.

In modern practice, many more international agreements are made as executive agreements than as treaties.[28] In *United States v. Belmont* (1937) and *United States v. Pink* (1942), the U.S. Supreme Court embraced the idea that the President under some circumstances may make executive agreements,[29] but the scope of this independent presidential power remains a serious question. *Belmont* and *Pink* involved agreements settling claims as part of the recognition of a foreign government. The recognition power is closely tied to the President's power to receive ambassadors, under Article II, Section 3. Subsequent decisions have continued to accept the President's power to settle foreign claims by executive agreement, and *Dames & Moore v. Regan* (1981) emphasized that Congress has acquiesced in the practice.[30] It remains unclear what other subjects might be appropriately addressed by executive agreements.

There is another path for the approval of international agreements: The President submits so-called congressional-executive agreements for approval by a majority of both houses of Congress. These agreements, which became more common after World War II, do not require the Senate's supermajority approval. Congressional-executive agreements have largely replaced treaties in such areas as international trade. Examples include the United States-Mexico-Canada Agreement (USMCA); the agreement establishing the World Trade Organization (WTO); and other bilateral and regional free trade agreements. At least with respect to trade matters these agreements are now well established.[31] Two cases from the late nineteenth and early twentieth centuries in the trade area might provide support for these agreements.[32] The practice now appears so settled that it is unlikely to be overturned or even substantially questioned, but how these agreements can be squared with the Constitution's original meaning remains a difficult question.[33]

Presidents also increasingly claim that Congress has authorized the President to make international agreements in advance, often by general legislation. This approach to international agreement-making seems even more in tension with the Treaty Clause, at least if used for important matters, because Congress does not approve the actual text of the agreement.

Despite the rise of congressional-executive agreements, Article II, Section 2 treaties remain an important part of U.S. international obligations in such areas as arms control, human rights, the environment, tax, and extradition.

TERMINATION OF TREATIES

The Treaty Clause does not say who has power to terminate treaties, and the Framers do not appear to have discussed the question directly. Termination might be seen as an aspect of the President's executive powers to conduct foreign affairs and execute the laws.[34] The termination question first arose in 1793. President Washington asked his Cabinet whether he should suspend or terminate U.S. treaties with France to maintain U.S. neutrality. Secretary of the Treasury Alexander Hamilton argued that Washington should terminate the treaties. Secretary of State Thomas Jefferson opposed termination on policy grounds but did not say that the President lacked authority to do so.[35]

Treaty termination might also have been understood as a legislative power. In 1798, the first actual U.S. termination of a treaty was done by Congress at the request of President John Adams.[36] Congress presumably has authority to terminate treaties that are related to its enumerated powers. Congress might also have a general termination power based on its authority to enact laws that are "necessary and proper" to carry into effect the President's treaty power. Moreover, if a statute and a treaty conflict, for purposes of U.S. law the last expression of the sovereign controls. Thus, a statute enacted later overrides a treaty adopted earlier (and vice versa).[37] This "last-in-time" rule appears to be consistent with the Constitution's text and has at least some support in Founding-era materials.[38]

Modern Presidents have claimed an independent treaty termination power, at least when termination is permitted by a treaty's terms or by international law.[39] For example, in 1978, President Jimmy Carter terminated the Mutual Defense Treaty with Taiwan in accordance with its notice procedures. Some Senators objected to Carter's termination of this treaty, but *Goldwater v. Carter* (1979) found that challenge to be a "political question" that the judiciary could not review.[40]

Many scholars agree that this type of presidential treaty termination power is now well established, and it does not obviously depart from the original understanding as reflected in the consensus from the Washington Administration. There is much more debate about whether the President has the constitutional authority to terminate or suspend a treaty where the terms of the treaty restrict termination or suspension. The President's textual obligation to take care that the laws are faithfully executed would seem to include the obligation to follow any termination or suspension clauses.[41]

CONSTITUTIONAL LIMITS ON TREATIES

A treaty cannot alter the constitutional structure of government or violate individual rights protected by the Constitution.[42] Other subject-matter limits on treaties have been debated since shortly after ratification. The 1794 Jay Treaty with Britain addressed, among other matters, property ownership, which was usually a matter of state law. Republican opponents of the Jay Treaty argued that treaties could address only subjects that were part of Congress's powers under the Constitution; otherwise, the federal government's power was not limited, as it could be indefinitely expanded through the

treaty power. Hamilton replied that the treaty power was not so limited. Ultimately the Senate gave its consent to the Jay Treaty, and the House provided necessary funding to implement it.[43] *Missouri v. Holland* (1920) adopted Hamilton's view, upholding a treaty that was arguably beyond the enumerated powers of Congress.[44] Scholars disagree as to whether its conclusion on this point is consistent with the Constitution's original meaning.[45]

OPEN QUESTIONS

- In *Bond v. United States* (2014), Justice Clarence Thomas, joined by Justices Antonin Scalia and Samuel Alito, suggested that the original meaning of "treaty" extends only to agreements that "in their nature relate to intercourse with other nations . . . rather than to purely domestic affairs."[46] It is not clear how much this position would limit the treaty power or what the distinction would be between matters that relate to foreign nations and matters that do not.

- Can Congress pass legislation implementing treaties in areas not otherwise within its enumerated powers? In *Bond*, Justice Scalia, joined by Justices Thomas and Alito, argued on originalist grounds that Congress could not do so.[47] However, *Missouri v. Holland* indicates otherwise, and modern practice embraces the broader view of Congress's power.[48] A lower court, for example, found that Congress could implement a treaty to criminalize overseas conduct in an area beyond Congress's power over foreign commerce.[49] Scholars have disagreed as to the Constitution's original meaning on this issue.[50] Some contend that Congress has independent treaty-implementation power while favoring limits to prevent abuse.[51]

Cite as: Michael D. Ramsey, *The Treaty Clause*, *in* THE HERITAGE GUIDE TO THE CONSTITUTION 389 (Josh Blackman & John G. Malcolm eds., 3d ed. 2025).

Notes

1. 1 Blackstone 250.   **2.** Articles of Confederation, art. IX, §§ 1, 6.   **3.** Frederick W. Marks, Independence on Trial: Foreign Affairs and the Making of the Constitution 24–34 (1986).   **4.** 1 Farrand's 21.   **5.** *Id.* at 65–66.   **6.** *Id.*   **7.** *Id.* at 66–67.   **8.** Michael D. Ramsey, The Constitution's Text in Foreign Affairs 145–51 (2007); Jack N. Rakove, *Solving a Constitutional Puzzle: The Treatymaking Clause as a Case Study*, 1 Persp. Am. Hist. New Series 233–81 (1984).   **9.** 2 Farrand's 137, 143, 145.   **10.** *Id.* at 155, 169.   **11.** *Id.* at 169.   **12.** *Id.* at 183.   **13.** *Id.* at 392.   **14.** *Id.* at 495.   **15.** *Id.* at 538.   **16.** *Id.*   **17.** *Id.*   **18.** Saikrishna B. Prakash & Michael D. Ramsey, *The Executive Power over Foreign Affairs*, 111 Yale L.J. 231, 282 (2001).   **19.** 2 Farrand's 495.   **20.** *Id.* at 540.   **21.** *Id.* at 549.   **22.** Ramsey, The Constitution's Text, *supra* at 148; Charles Warren, *The Mississippi River and the Treaty Clause of the Constitution*, 2 Geo. Wash. L. Rev. 271, 285–90 (1934).   **23.** Warren, *supra* at 287–99; Lance Banning, *Virginia: Sectionalism and the General Good, in* Ratifying the Constitution 261 (Michael Allen Gillespie & Michael Lienesch eds., 1989); Federalist No. 75.   **24.** William Maclay, The Journal of William Maclay 127–31 (Edgar S.

Maclay ed., 1890).   **25.** Michael D. Ramsey, *Executive Agreements and the (Non)Treaty Power*, 77 N.C. L. Rev. 133, 162–71 (1999); Ramsey, The Constitution's Text, *supra* at 179–93.   **26.** Michael D. Ramsey, *Evading the Treaty Power? The Constitutionality of Non-Binding Agreements*, 11 FIU L. Rev. 371 (2016).   **27.** Ramsey, *Executive Agreements*, *supra* at 171–83.   **28.** Oona A. Hathaway, *Treaties' End: The Past, Present, and Future of International Lawmaking in the United States*, 117 Yale L.J. 1236 (2008).   **29.** 301 U.S. 324 (1937); 315 U.S. 203 (1942).   **30.** 453 U.S. 654, 680–81 (1981).   **31.** Curtis A. Bradley, Historical Gloss and Foreign Affairs: Constitutional Authority in Practice 72–98 (2024).   **32.** *Field v. Clark*, 143 U.S. 649 (1892); *B. Altman & Co. v. United States*, 224 U.S. 583 (1912).   **33.** Ramsey, The Constitution's Text, *supra* at 197–217.   **34.** Prakash & Ramsey, *supra* at 324–27.   **35.** *Id.*   **36.** David P. Currie, The Constitution in Congress: The Federalist Period, 1789–1801, at 244 (1997).   **37.** *The Cherokee Tobacco*, 78 U.S. 616, 620–21 (1870).   **38.** Julian G. Ku, *Treaties as Laws: A Defense of the Last-in-Time Rule for Treaties and Federal Statutes*, 80 Ind. L.J. 319 (2005).   **39.** Bradley, *supra* at 99–118.

40. 444 U.S. 996 (1979).   **41.** Derek Jinks & David Sloss, *Is the President Bound by the Geneva Conventions?*, 90 Cornell L. Rev. 97 (2004).   **42.** *Geofroy v. Riggs*, 133 U.S. 258, 267 (1890); *Reid v. Covert*, 354 U.S. 1, 15–19 (1957).   **43.** David Golove, *Treaty-Making and the Nation: The Historical Foundations of the Nationalist Conception of the Treaty Power*, 98 Mich. L. Rev. 1075 (2000).   **44.** 252 U.S. 416, 433 (1920). **45.** Gary Lawson & Guy Seidman, *The Jeffersonian Treaty Clause*, 2006 U. Ill. L. Rev. 1 (2006); Michael D. Ramsey, *Missouri v. Holland and Historical Textualism*, 73 Mo. L. Rev. 969 (2008).   **46.** 572 U.S. 844, 884–93 (2014) (Thomas, J., concurring).   **47.** *Id.* at 873–81 (Scalia, J., concurring). **48.** 252 U.S. at 434–35.   **49.** *United States v. Rife*, 33 F.4th 838 (6th Cir. 2022).   **50.** Michael D. Ramsey, *Congress's Limited Power to Enforce Treaties*, 90 Notre Dame L. Rev. 1539 (2015); Nicholas Quinn Rosenkranz, *Executing the Treaty Power*, 118 Harv. L. Rev. 1867 (2005).   **51.** Ramsey, *Congress's Limited Power, supra* at 1551–60.

ESSAY NO. 107: THE APPOINTMENTS CLAUSE
ART. II, § 2, CL. 2

The President . . . shall nominate, and by and with the Advice and Consent of the Senate, shall appoint Ambassadors, other public Ministers and Consuls, Judges of the supreme Court, and all other Officers of the United States, whose Appointments are not herein otherwise provided for, and which shall be established by Law. . . .

—John O. McGinnis

INTRODUCTION

The Appointments Clause contemplates three sequential acts for the appointment of principal officers: nomination by the President, advice and consent of the Senate, and appointment of the officer by the President. The requirements of this provision apply to principal officers but not to inferior officers. (See Essay No. 108.) Although the Senate must confirm principal officers, including ambassadors and Supreme Court justices, Congress may still require that any inferior officer whose office is "established by Law" also be confirmed by the Senate. The principal concern of the Framers regarding the Appointments Clause, as in many of the Constitution's other separation-of-powers provision, was to ensure accountability while avoiding tyranny.[1]

There are several important questions with respect to principal officers and their confirmation: (1) Does the President have plenary power of nomination, or does the Constitution limit this power by requiring the President to seek pre-nomination "advice" from the Senate? (2) Must the President nominate only those who meet qualifications set by Congress? (3) Does the Senate have plenary power to reject nominees, or is that power circumscribed by some standard? Both the debates among the Framers and subsequent practice confirm that the President has plenary power to nominate; Congress has imposed some (but not absolute) qualifications on nominees; and the Senate has exercised an absolute power to reject nominees for any reason.

HISTORY BEFORE 1787

The English monarch had unilateral authority to appoint colonial officers. Alexander Hamilton would charge in Federalist No. 69 that "The king of Great Britain . . . not only appoints to all offices, but can create offices." The Declaration of Independence charged that the Crown had "erected a multitude of New Offices, and sent hither swarms of Officers to harass our people, and eat out their substance."[2] The U.S. Supreme Court would observe that "'the [King's] power of appointment to offices' was deemed 'the most insidious and powerful weapon of eighteenth century despotism'" by "the American revolutionary generation[]."[3]

The Founders responded to this experience by vesting the appointment power in their state legislatures. The Virginia constitution of 1776 authorized the legislature to appoint the Attorney General, the Treasurer, and some judges.[4] Other states, like Massachusetts, gave the governor a limited appointment power. Under the New York constitution of 1777, appointments were made by the governor, subject to approval by a council of members of the legislature.[5] The Massachusetts constitution of 1780, written by John Adams, gave the governor somewhat greater power: "All judicial officers, the Attorney-General, the Solicitor-General, all Sheriffs, Coroners, and Registers of Probate, shall be nominated and appointed by the Governor, by and with the advice and consent of the Council,"[6] the members of which were appointed by the governor. This provision resembled language from the 1691 Charter of Massachusetts Bay.[7]

Under the Articles of Confederation, Congress was a unicameral body, and each state would appoint delegates to that body.[8] The Articles Congress had the power to appoint "civil officers as may be necessary for managing the general affairs of the United States under their direction"[9] and the power to "appoint[] all officers of the land forces in the service of the United States, excepting regimental officers."[10] Congress could also appoint judges to decide cases concerning piracies, felonies on the high seas, and captures.[11]

THE CONSTITUTIONAL CONVENTION

In the final version of the Constitution, Congress would not have the power to make appointments to the executive and judicial branches. However, earlier in the Convention, under the Virginia Plan, the "National Legislature" would appoint judges, and the "National Executive" would appoint "executive branch officers."[12]

On July 17, 1787, the Committee of the Whole modified what would become the Appointments Clause.[13] The new text provided that the "National Executive" would have the power "to appoint to offices in cases not otherwise provided for."[14] The legislature could appoint offices otherwise provided, including judges, as well as the Treasurer.[15]

On July 18, the Convention debated whether the legislature should appoint judges.[16] Nathaniel Gorham of Massachusetts thought that the legislature was "too numerous, and too little personally responsible, to ensure a

good choice."[17] He suggested that "Judges be appointed by the Executive with the advice & consent of" the Senate. "Advice and consent" suggests a simple majority vote. Gorham explained that this was "the mode prescribed by the [Massachusetts] constitution" and had been "found to answer perfectly well."[18] His comparison was not entirely apt, however, as the council that provided the governor with advice and consent was part of the executive branch. James Wilson and Gouverneur Morris of Pennsylvania supported Gorham's proposal.

Luther Martin of Maryland opposed the proposal, believing that the Senate, "[b]eing taken from all the States" would "be best informed of characters & most capable of making a fit choice."[19] Roger Sherman of Connecticut added that it "would be less easy for candidates to intrigue with [the Senate], than with the Executive Magistrate."[20] Gorham responded that "the Executive will be responsible in point of character at least, for a judicious and faithful discharge of his trust" and "will be careful to look through all the States for proper characters."[21] James Madison of Virginia suggested "that the Judges might be appointed by the Executives with the concurrence of" at least one-third of the Senate.[22] This approach would "unite the advantage of responsibility in the Executive with the security afforded in the" Senate against "any incautious or corrupt nomination by the Executive."[23]

After this debate concluded, the Convention voted on whether to move the appointment of judges to the executive instead of the Senate. This proposal was defeated by a vote of 6 to 2, supported only by Massachusetts and Pennsylvania.[24] Gorham then proposed "that the Judges be nominated and appointed by the Executive, by & with the advice & consent of the [Senate]."[25] He explained that this mode had been ratified by the experience of 140 years in Massachusetts.[26] Gorham's proposal failed by a vote of 4 to 4.

The Convention would later adopt Gorham's proposal. On September 4, 1787, the Committee of Eleven moved the power to appoint judges from Congress to the President in conjunction with Senate advice and consent.[27] The draft now provided, "The President ... shall nominate and by and with the advice and consent of the Senate shall appoint Ambassadors and other public Ministers, Judges of the supreme Court, and all other officers of the U.S. whose appointments are not otherwise herein provided for."[28] It appears that with this revision, "officers of the U.S." was added to the Appointments Clause.[29] Ten days later, on September 14, John Rutledge of South Carolina moved to strike out Congress's power to appoint the Treasurer.[30] That officer, Rutledge explained, should be "appointed in the same manner with other officers[]"—that is, by the President.[31] The motion was approved by a vote of 8 to 3.[32] The appointment of all "officers of the United States" was provided for in what would become Article II, Section 2.[33]

The initiative of choice would be the President's responsibility, but it was checked by advice and consent to forestall the possibility of abuse of this power. Morris described the advantages of this multistage process: "As the President was to nominate, there would be responsibility, and as the Senate was to concur, there would be security."[34]

Before the end of the Convention, the delegates made two final alterations in the Appointments Clause: A comma was added between "all other officers of the U.S." and "whose appointments," and an additional clause ("and which shall be established by Law") was added at the end. This clause refers to appointed offices that were created through bicameralism and presentment.[35]

The adopted text is an overly long single sentence, and its structure is grammatically complex. Chief Justice John Marshall would observe, "I feel no diminution of reverence for the framers of this sacred instrument, when I say that some ambiguity of expression has found its way into this clause."[36]

THE RATIFICATION DEBATES

In Federalist No. 76, Hamilton answered critics who would have preferred the whole power of appointment to be lodged in the President. Under the Constitution, the President had the sole power of nomination, but the Senate had to consent to the nominee's appointment. Hamilton asserted that the President's nomination power assured sufficient accountability and that an "absolute power of appointment in the hands of that officer [should] be avoided."

The President's "judgment alone would be exercised" with the "act of nomination." Hamilton added that the Senate's role "would be an excellent check upon a spirit of favoritism in the President, and would tend greatly to prevent the appointment of unfit characters."

The Federalists also argued that the Constitution would avoid an appointment that was the result of secret deals.[37] In Federalist No. 77, Hamilton contrasted the appointments process under the federal Constitution with New York's multi-member appointment council. He argued that such a council acting in secret would be "a conclave in which cabal and intrigue will have their full scope" and warned that "the desire of mutual gratification will beget a scandalous bartering of votes and bargaining for places."

The Senate was not understood to have any formal pre-nomination advisory role. Such a role might lead Senate leaders and the President to make a deal that would serve their parochial interests and then be insulated from all but pro forma scrutiny.[38] At the North Carolina ratification convention, James Iredell observed that "[a]s to offices, the Senate has no other influence but a restraint on improper appointments." The future Supreme Court justice said that if the Senate thinks the President's nominee is "improper, the President must nominate another, whose appointment ultimately again depends upon the Senate."[39]

THE PRESIDENT'S EXCLUSIVE POWER OF NOMINATION

The practice of the first President and Senate support the construction of the Appointments Clause that reserves the act of nomination exclusively to the President. In June 1789, President George Washington requested confirmation of his first nominee to be the *charge d'affaires* at the French embassy: "I nominate William Short, Esquire, and request your advice on the propriety of appointing him."[40] Two days later, the Senate notified the President of Short's confirmation: "Resolved, that the President of the United States be informed, that the Senate advise and consent to his appointment of William Short Esquire. . . ."[41] The Senate regarded "advice" as a post-nomination rather than a pre-nomination function.

Washington wrote in his diary that Thomas Jefferson and John Jay agreed with him that the Senate's powers "extend no farther than to an approbation or disapprobation of the person nominated by the President, all the rest being Executive and vested in the President by the Constitution."[42] Washington's construction of the Appointments Clause has been embraced by his successors and confirmed by *Marbury v. Madison* (1803), Justice Joseph Story's *Commentaries on the Constitution*, and modern Supreme Court precedent.[43]

Nevertheless, there is some role for consultation between the President and the Senate. The Congressional Research Service has observed that "U.S. Senators of the state in which the judicial districts are located" identify candidates for district court positions according to a "well-established custom" that stretches back to the "early 19th Century."[44] Also, Presidents at times have made deals with Congress about appointments. The disputed election of 1800 was purportedly settled after Thomas Jefferson promised to keep in place the holdover tax collector in the port of Wilmington, Delaware.[45] Presidents have consulted with Senators out of comity or political prudence and never with the understanding that they were constitutionally obliged to do so, and modern Presidents have rejected any notion that the Senate has a duty to provide "advice" about a potential nominee before a nomination is made.[46]

CONGRESS'S POWERS OVER PRESIDENTIAL NOMINEES

Congress has often used its powers under the Necessary and Proper Clause to establish qualifications for those who can serve in the offices it has created, thereby limiting the range of those the President can nominate.[47] For example, the Solicitor General must be "learned in the law."[48] But Congress may not give itself or its presiding officers the power to make appointments of "officers of the United States." *Buckley v. Valeo* (1976) held that the Speaker of the House and the Senate President Pro Tempore lacked the power to appoint officers to the Federal Election Commission.[49]

A new appointment is not necessary if Congress expands the duties of an office after the initial appointment takes place. *Weiss v. United States* (1994) held that military officers who served as judges in courts-martial did not need a separate act of appointment and Senate approval.[50] The Supreme Court declared that serving as military judge was not "so different" from the duties of a military officer that a separate appointment was necessary. In fact, it went so far as to say that being a military judge was "germane" to the duties of a military officer at the time of the original appointment.

It is unclear how many qualifications Congress can impose for principal officers without contravening the Framers' interest in assuring the President's accountability for the initial choice. In *Myers v. United States* (1926), Chief Justice William Howard Taft declared that the qualifications set by Congress may not "so limit selection and so trench upon executive choice as to be in effect legislative designation."[51] In *Public Citizen v. U.S. Department of Justice* (1989), Justice Anthony M. Kennedy, concurring, opined that the President's appointing power was exclusive and that the Ineligibility Clause is "the sole limitation on the President's power to nominate these officers."[52] The Supreme Court has not yet resolved this issue.

THE SENATE'S POWER TO REJECT NOMINEES

The Senate has independent constitutional authority to refuse to confirm a nominee for any reason. The Framers located the process of advice and consent in the Senate as a check to prevent the President from appointing people who have unsound principles as well as blemished characters and checkered histories.[53] Hamilton wrote in Federalist No. 66 that a nominee should be rejected only for "special and strong reasons." Ideology was likely not foremost on the Framers' minds. As the President has complete discretion in the use of his veto power, the Senate has complete and final discretion as to whether to accept or reject a nomination.

When a substantial number of Senators assert that there are strong and compelling political reasons to reject a nominee, the Constitution's structure ensures a confirmation battle. The Appointments Clause contains conflict within the republican process in order to protect against degeneration of the Republic's original ideals and thus ensure the

Republic's stability. This provision structures the confirmation process so that when two of the Republic's national governing branches are in fundamental disagreement, there will be a struggle to persuade the people of the correctness of their respective positions.[54]

If the Senate rejects a nominee, the President would generally be in a position to find a second candidate without these putative defects who generally shares the President's point of view.[55] George Mason recognized this salient fact at the Philadelphia Convention: "Notwithstanding the form of the proposition by which the appointment seemed to be divided between the Executive & Senate, the appointment was substantially vested in the former alone."[56]

OPEN QUESTIONS

- The consensus view is that "Officers of the United States" refers to appointed positions in the executive and judicial branches. The Supreme Court has observed that "[t]he people do not vote for the 'Officers of the United States.'"[57] Some scholars contend that members of Congress, the Speaker of the House, the President, and the Vice President may be "officers of the United States" whose appointments are provided for outside of Article II, Section 2.[58] But these positions are *elected* rather than appointed and are not "established by law."[59]

- Does the Senate have a constitutional duty to give a nominee a hearing or a confirmation vote? Following the death of Justice Antonin Scalia and nomination of Judge Merrick Garland to fill the vacancy, some scholars argued that the Senate had such a duty.[60] Is there any textual or historical basis for such an obligation?[61]

- The D.C. Home Rule Act provides that the President can select nominees for D.C. courts only from a list of three candidates generated by the D.C. Judicial Nominations Commission.[62] If the President fails to choose one of these candidates, the Nomination Commission appoints the candidate for Senate confirmation. Would these local territorial judges be considered "officers of the United States,"[63] and if so, does the Home Rule statute violate the Appointments Clause?[64] What would the remedy be if the President nominated and the Senate confirmed a judge who was not on this list? Could the courts invalidate the appointment, or would that be a political question?

- Does the President have any duty to nominate candidates to vacant positions? If the President fails to do so, is he subject to any sanctions and perhaps even impeachment?

Cite as: John O. McGinnis, *The Appointments Clause, in* The Heritage Guide to the Constitution 394 (Josh Blackman & John G. Malcolm eds., 3d ed. 2025).

Notes

1. John O. McGinnis, *The President, the Senate, the Constitution, and the Confirmation Process: A Reply to Professors Strauss and Sunstein*, 71 Tex. L. Rev. 633, 639 (1993). **2.** Declaration of Independence, ¶ 12. **3.** *Freytag v. Commissioner*, 501 U.S. 868, 883 (1991) (quoting G. Wood, The Creation of the American Republic 1776–1787, at 79 (1969)). **4.** Va. Const. of 1776. **5.** N.Y. Const. of 1777, art. XXIII. **6.** Mass. Const. of 1780, ch. II, § II, art. IX. **7.** The Charter of Massachusetts Bay (1691), https://perma.cc/G86J-L3KY. **8.** Articles of Confederation, art. VI, § 1. **9.** *Id.* at art. IX, § 5. **10.** *Id.* at art. IX, § 4. **11.** *Id.* at art. IX, § 1. **12.** 1 Farrand's 20–22. **13.** 2 Farrand's 21. **14.** *Id.* at 23. **15.** *Id.* at 177, 181–82, 315. **16.** *Id.* at 41. **17.** *Id.* **18.** *Id.* **19.** *Id.* **20.** *Id.* at 41, 43. **21.** *Id.* at 42. **22.** *Id.* **23.** *Id.* at 43. **24.** *Id.* at 44. **25.** *Id.* **26.** *Id.* **27.** *Id.* at 493, 495. **28.** *Id.* at 495, 539–40. **29.** Jennifer L. Mascott, *Who are "Officers of the United States,"* 70 Stan. L. Rev. 443, 472 (2018). **30.** 2 Farrand's 612, 614. **31.** *Id.* at 614. **32.** *Id.* **33.** Seth Barrett Tillman & Josh Blackman, *Offices and Officers of the Constitution, Part III: The Appointments, Impeachment, Commissions, and Oath or Affirmation Clauses*, 62 S. Tex. L. Rev. 349, 383–85 (2023). **34.** 2 Farrand's 539. **35.** Tillman & Blackman, *supra* at 378–83. **36.** *United States v. Maurice*, 26 F. Cas. 1211, 1213 (C.C.D. Va. 1823) (No. 15,747) (Marshall, C.J.). **37.** McGinnis, *supra* at 642. **38.** *Id.* **39.** 4 Elliot's 134. **40.** 1 S. Exec. J., 1st Cong., 1st Sess. 6 (June 16, 1789). **41.** *Id.* at 7. **42.** Diary entry (Apr. 27, 1790), *in* The Diary of George Washington from 1789 to 1791, at 128 (Benson J. Lossing ed., 1860). **43.** 5 U.S. (1 Cranch) 137 (1803); 3 Story's Commentaries § 1525; *Edmond v. United States*, 520 U.S. 651, 660 (1997); *United States v. Arthrex*, 594 U.S. 1, 11–12 (2021). **44.** Denis Steven Rutkus, Cong. Rsrch. Serv., R43762, The Appointment Process for U.S. Circuit and District Court Nominations:

An Overview 9 n.43 (2016), https://perma.cc/7K5E-S4RS. **45.** Bruce Ackerman, The Failure of the Founding Fathers: Jefferson, Marshall, and the Rise of Presidential Democracy 106 (2005). **46.** Patrick Leahy, *Supreme Court Preview: It Doesn't Have to Be Armageddon*, Vote Smart (June 25, 2003), https://perma.cc/XB6B-6H6X; David G. Savage, *Bush Spurns Proposal on Court Picks*, L.A. Times (June 19, 2003), https://perma.cc/DJR3-MFDW; Josh Blackman, *Foreword: SCOTUS After Scalia*, 11 N.Y.U. J.L. & Liberty 48, 140–43 (2017). **47.** Art. I, § 8, cl. 18. **48.** Act of June 22, 1870, ch. 150, § 2, 16 Stat. 162. **49.** 424 U.S. 1, 126–27 (1976). **50.** 510 U.S. 163 (1994). **51.** 272 U.S. 52 (1926). **52.** 491 U.S. 440, 484 (1989) (Kennedy, J., concurring); Art. I, § 6, cl. 2. **53.** McGinnis, *supra* at 653. **54.** *Id.* at 659. **55.** *Id.* **56.** 2 Farrand's 27. **57.** *Free Enter. Fund v. Pub. Co. Acct. Oversight Bd.*, 561 U.S. 477, 497–98 (2010). **58.** Thomas W. Merrill, *Rethinking Article I, Section 1: From Nondelegation to Exclusive Delegation*, 104 Colum. L. Rev. 2097, 2136 n.157 (2004); David Froomkin & Eric Eisner, *Officers* (Jan. 5, 2025), https://ssrn.com/abstract=5029416. **59.** Tillman & Blackman, *supra* at 443; Chad Squitieri, *Towards Nondelegation Doctrines*, 86 Mo. L. Rev. 1239, 1262 (2021). **60.** Peter J. Eckerstrom, *The Garland Nomination, the Senate's Duty, and the Surprising Lessons of Constitutional Text*, 21 U. Pa. J. Const. L. 33 (2018). **61.** Seth Barrett Tillman, *On the Senate's Purported Constitutional Duty to Meaningfully Consider Presidential Nominees to the Supreme Court of the United States*, 21 U. Pa. J. Const. L. 881 (2019). **62.** D.C. Code §§ 1-204.34(d)(1) & 1-204.33(a). **63.** William Baude, *Adjudication Outside Article III*, 133 Harv. L. Rev. 1511, 1540 (2020). **64.** *In the Matter of a Charge of Judicial Misconduct or Disability*, Judicial Council Complaint No. DC-21-90051, Judicial Council of the District of Columbia Circuit at 12 (Feb. 14, 2022) (Katsas, J., dissenting), https://perma.cc/9LEA-FGU3; Josh Blackman, *Judge Silberman Petitions the Judicial Council to Review His Misconduct Complaint Against Judge Sullivan*, Volokh Conspiracy (Nov. 19, 2021), https://perma.cc/5H2J-TX4X.

ESSAY NO. 108: THE INFERIOR OFFICERS APPOINTMENTS CLAUSE
ART. II, § 2, CL. 2

. . . but the Congress may by Law vest the Appointment of such inferior Officers, as they think proper, in the President alone, in the Courts of Law, or in the Heads of Departments.

—Jeffrey B. Wall

INTRODUCTION

Article II of the Constitution divides "officers of the United States" into two classes: principal officers and inferior officers. Both classes can be appointed "with the Advice and Consent of the Senate," but Congress can also vest the power to appoint inferior officers "in the President alone, in the Courts of Law, or in the Heads of Departments."[1] The Inferior Officers Appointments Clause, also known as the Excepting Clause, has become one of the Executive's chief powers.[2] It authorizes the President to exercise the power to appoint inferior officers directly or through heads of departments who are themselves the President's appointees. It also authorizes the courts of law, over whom the President has no power, to appoint inferior officers in the judiciary. The Supreme Court has rebuffed attempts by Congress to circumvent the Appointments Clause, either by making appointments directly or by "unilaterally appointing an incumbent to a new and distinct office."[3] At the same time, the clause prevents the President from appointing subordinates to high-level governmental posts without the Senate's consent.[4]

THE CONSTITUTIONAL CONVENTION

The Inferior Officers Appointments Clause was not introduced until September 15, 1787, two days before the Constitution would be signed.[5] Gouverneur Morris of Pennsylvania proposed an amendment to the end of the Appointments Clause: "but the Congress may by law vest the appointment of such inferior Officers as they think proper, in the President alone, in the Courts of law, or in the heads of Departments."[6] He seemed to recognize that the President should not be burdened with lower-level executive branch appointments. Moreover, the courts of law should be able to appoint their own subordinate officials without seeking consent from the President and the Senate. Roger Sherman of Connecticut seconded the motion.

James Madison of Virginia, however, argued

that the provision did "not go far enough." He thought that "Superior Officers below Heads of Departments ought in some cases to have the appointment of the lesser offices."[7] Morris dismissed Madison's proposal as unnecessary: "Blank Commissions can be sent."[8] Presumably, the heads of departments could rubber-stamp any appointments made by their subordinates.

Morris's motion failed by a vote of 5 to 5 with one state divided. According to Madison's journal records, "[i]t was urged that [the question] be put a second time, some such provision being too necessary, to be omitted."[9] The clause was then approved without further debate.

THE RATIFICATION DEBATES

The Inferior Officers Appointment Clause was not widely discussed during the ratification debates. Some Anti-Federalists feared that this provision would allow the President to bypass Senate confirmation. Federal Farmer asked, "Who are inferior officers?"[10] He warned that Congress could "vest the appointment of almost every officer in the president alone" and thereby "destroy the check" that is "lodged in the senate."[11] A Georgian wanted to strike out the clause and would have allowed the President to "nominate and appoint all officers, civil and military, by and with the advice of the senate, etc. only."[12]

The Framers were concerned that the Senate's advice-and-consent process might prove "inconvenient" "when offices became numerous, and sudden removals necessary."[13] The Excepting Clause ensured "that they had provided for all cases of offices" that might require appointments.[14] The Appointments Clause reflects the Framers' desire to divide the appointment power between the political branches. As the U.S. Supreme Court has explained, the "Framers understood . . . that by limiting the appointment power, they could ensure that those who wielded it were accountable to political force and the will of the people."[15] The Framers were specifically concerned that Congress might place its political supporters in high-level governmental posts and thereby undermine the President's control of the executive branch.[16] By preventing Congress from directly appointing either principal or inferior officers, the Appointments Clause functions

as a restraint on Congress and is an important structural element in the separation of powers.

Three major question recur under the Excepting Clause: (1) who are "inferior Officers" that may be appointed without the advice and consent of the Senate; (2) who qualifies as a "Head of Department" able to appoint an inferior officer; and (3) under what conditions can Congress limit the power of the President or the head of a department to remove inferior officers?

WHO ARE "INFERIOR OFFICERS" OF THE UNITED STATES?

The Appointments Clause does not actually refer to "principal" officers. Rather, the Opinion Clause provides that the President "may require the Opinion, in writing, of the _principal Officer_ in each of the executive Departments,"[17] and this term has carried over to the Appointments Clause. The Supreme Court has decided a number of cases drawing the line between principal and inferior officers. _Morrison v. Olson_ (1988) listed certain hallmarks of "inferior Officer" status, including accountability to a principal officer and limitations on the officer's duties, jurisdiction, and tenure.[18] _Edmond v. United States_ (1997) adopted a more formalist approach: An "inferior officer must be 'directed and supervised at some level by others who were appointed by Presidential nomination with the advice and consent of the Senate.'"[19] _Arthrex v. United States_ (2021) explained that an inferior officer is "directed and supervised" only when a superior officer has the power to remove the inferior officer or review the inferior officer's decisions.[20]

Edmond and _Arthrex_ did not overrule _Morrison's_ multifactored approach. Rather, there is no "exclusive criterion for distinguishing between principal and inferior officers for Appointments Clause purposes."[21] But those decisions nonetheless make clear that some level of supervision will be required before Congress can rely on the Excepting Clause to avoid the Senate's advice-and-consent process.

The Supreme Court has distinguished further between officers and employees.[22] First, in order to be an "officer of the United States," an "individual must occupy a 'continuing' position established by law."[23] Second, only officers can "exercise significant authority pursuant to the laws of the United States."[24] By contrast, non-officer employees who comprise "the broad swath of 'lesser functionaries' in the Government's workforce" do not need to occupy their positions consistent with the Appointments Clause.[25] However, "any appointee exercising significant authority pursuant to the laws of the United States is an 'Officer of the United States,' and must, therefore, be appointed in the manner prescribed by § 2, cl. 2, of that Article."[26]

In earlier cases, the Court focused on the nature of the duties performed as opposed to just continuity and significant authority. For example, governmental employees, such as clerks or surgeons, were not considered officers because they do not exercise "independent authority" or their duties were performed on a "temporary and episodic basis."[27] It seems that even if a person has regular duties but his position is not continuous, his position lacks *duration*, and he is not an officer. Duration, in the constitutional sense, does not simply refer to a substantial period of time; it demands continuity from one position's holder to his successor.[28] For example, with the Independent Counsel at issue in *Morrison v. Olson*, "when that [position's] task is over the office is terminated."[29] That position was not continuous.

WHO CAN APPOINT INFERIOR OFFICERS?

Congress has the discretion, as it "think[s] proper," to vest the appointment of inferior officers in the "President alone, in the Courts of Law, or in the Heads of Departments." This vesting must be done "by law" (that is, by statute).[30] First, Congress can grant this power to the President acting alone without the need to seek Senate consent.

Second, Congress traditionally has vested the power to appoint inferior judicial officers in individual federal courts or divisions of courts rather than in the federal judiciary as a whole or in the presiding officers alone.[31] The "Courts of Law" are not limited to Article III courts.

Third, *Freytag v. Commissioner of Internal Revenue* (1991) interpreted "Heads of Departments" to refer "to executive divisions like the Cabinet-level departments."[32] However, *Freytag* reserved the question whether the heads

of non-Cabinet executive branch agencies could also be deemed "Heads of Departments."

The Court would answer that question in *Free Enterprise Fund v. Public Company Accounting Oversight Board* (2010).[33] The Securities and Exchange Commission (SEC), which "is a freestanding component of the Executive Branch, not subordinate to or contained within any other such component," constituted a "Department" for purposes of the Appointments Clause.[34] "Heads of Departments" includes all freestanding agencies and departments exercising executive power under the supervision of the President. *Free Enterprise* also clarified that the "head of a department" does not need to be a single official; a multimember body like the SEC can be a "head of a department" within the meaning of the Appointments Clause.[35]

CAN CONGRESS LIMIT THE REMOVAL OF INFERIOR OFFICERS?

Courts and commentators have long disagreed about whether and under what circumstances Congress can prevent the President or the head of a department from removing inferior "officers of the United States." (See Essay No. 107.) Many of the Supreme Court's leading precedents on the removal power concern principal officers who were nominated by the President and confirmed by the Senate.[36] However, several cases have addressed limitations on the President's ability to appoint inferior officers.

It is generally understood that the President can remove only officers that he or his predecessor personally appointed.[37] The President cannot remove an inferior officer appointed by the head of a department, and Congress has imposed restrictions on the ability of heads of department to remove inferior officers. In *Morrison v. Olson*, a special division of the D.C. Circuit appointed an independent counsel who could be removed only by the Attorney General for "good cause."[38] The Court found that this restriction did not "interfere with the President's exercise of the 'executive power' and his constitutionally appointed duty to 'take care that the laws be faithfully executed' under Article II."[39]

The Court revisited the issue in *Free Enterprise Fund*, which involved a statute that empowered the SEC to appoint members of an oversight board.[40] In that case, the SEC appointed five members to the oversight board.[41] Those inferior officers could be removed by the SEC only for "good cause,"[42] and the parties agreed that the President can remove members of the SEC only for good cause.[43] There was, in effect, a double layer of "for-cause" removal protections between the President and the board members.[44] The Court ruled that these tenure protections for inferior officers "subvert[ed] the President's ability to ensure that the laws are faithfully executed."[45] The Court concluded that the "good cause" protection for the board members was therefore unconstitutional.

One decade later, *Seila Law v. Consumer Financial Protection Bureau* (2020) took a restrictive view of Congress's ability to place limits on the removal of principal or inferior officers.[46] According to *Seila Law*, there is a "general rule that the President possesses the authority to remove those who assist him in carrying out his duties."[47] That general rule has "only two exceptions." First, the Court has upheld limitations on the President's powers to remove members of "multimember expert agencies that do not wield substantial executive power." *Humphrey's Executor v. United States* (1935) viewed the Federal Trade Commission as such an entity.[48] Second, the Court has permitted restrictions on "inferior officers with limited duties and no policymaking or administrative authority."[49] The independent counsel in *Morrison* was deemed to be such an inferior officer.[50]

OPEN QUESTIONS

- The Fifth Circuit Court of Appeals declared unconstitutional the tenure protections for administrative law judges, who are inferior officers appointed by the Securities Exchange Commission.[51] On appeal, the Supreme Court decided *SEC v. Jarkesy* (2024) on other grounds.[52] Was the Court of Appeals correct?
- The Commissions Clause provides that the President "shall Commission *all* the Officers of the United States."[53] However, there is a long-standing tradition of inferior officers not receiving commissions from the President,[54] and the Office of Legal Counsel has concluded that not all officers of the United States must receive a commission: "[A]lthough the holder of an office usually receives a commission, that characteristic too, like an oath or pay, is incidental rather than essential."[55] How can this tradition be reconciled with the text of the Commissions Clause?
- Were Special Counsels Robert Mueller and Jack Smith principal officers or inferior officers?[56] Or is the Special Counsel an employee rather than an officer?[57]

Cite as: Jeffrey B. Wall, *The Inferior Officers Appointments Clause*, in THE HERITAGE GUIDE TO THE CONSTITUTION 399 (Josh Blackman & John G. Malcolm eds., 3d ed. 2025).

Notes

1. *Freytag v. Commissioner*, 501 U.S. 868, 878 (1991). 2. *Edmond v. United States*, 520 U.S. 651, 660 (1997). 3. *Weiss v. United States*, 510 U.S. 163, 188 (1994). 4. *Edmond*, 520 U.S. at 660. 5. Theodore Y. Blumoff, *Separation of Powers and the Origins of the Appointment Clause*, 37 Syracuse L. Rev. 1037, 1067–68 (1987). 6. 2 Farrand's 627. 7. *Id.* 8. *Id.* 9. *Id.* at 627–68. 10. Storing 2.8.45. 11. *Id.* 12. Storing 5.9.10. 13. *United States v. Germaine*, 99 U.S. 508, 510 (1878). 14. *United States v. Maurice*, 26 F.Cas. 1211, 1214 (C.C.D.Va.1823) (Marshall, C.J.). 15. *Freytag*, 501 U.S. at 884. 16. *Buckley v. Valeo*, 424 U.S. 1, 135–36 (1976). 17. Art. II, § 2, cl. 1 (emphasis added). 18. 487 U.S. 654, 671–72 (1988). 19. *United States v. Arthrex*, 594 U.S. 1, 13 (2021) (quoting *Edmond*, 520 U.S. at 663). 20. *Id.* at 13–14. 21. *Id.* at 23 (citing *Edmond*, 520 U.S. at 661). 22. *Lucia v. Sec. & Exch. Comm'n*, 585 U.S. 237 (2018) (citing *Germaine*, 99 U.S. at 511–512, and *Buckley*, 424 U.S. at 126). 23. *Lucia*, 585 U.S. at 245 (quoting *Germaine*, 99 U.S. at 511). 24. *Id.* (citing *Germaine*, 99 U.S. at 511–12, and *Buckley*, 424 U.S. at 126). 25. *Id.* (citing *Buckley*, 424 U.S. at 126, n.162); Dep't of Just., Off. of Legal Counsel, *Officers of the United States Within the Meaning of the Appointments Clause*, 31 Op. O.L.C. 122 (Apr. 16, 2007). 26. *Buckley*, 424 U.S. at 126. 27. *United States v. Hartwell*, 73 U.S. 385 (1867); *Germaine*, 99 U.S. at 510; *Lucia*, 585 U.S. at 247 & n.4. 28. *Morrison*, 487 U.S. at 672. 29. *Id.* at 572. 30. Seth Barrett Tillman & Josh Blackman, *Offices and Officers of the Constitution, Part III: The Appointments, Impeachment, Commissions, and Oath or Affirmation Clauses*, 62 S. Tex. L. Rev. 349, 378–79, 385 (2023). 31. *Morrison*, 487 U.S. at 678–79. 32. 501 U.S. 868, 886 (1991). 33. 561 U.S. 477 (2010). 34. *Id.* at 511. 35. *Id.* at 512. 36. *Myers v. United States*, 272 U.S. 52, 109–110 (1926); *Humphrey's Executor v. United States*, 295

U.S. 602, 631–32 (1935); *Seila L. v. U.S. Consumer Fin. Prot. Bureau*, 591 U.S. 197, 202 (2020).   **37.** *Free Enter. Fund*, 561 U.S. at 493; *Myers*, 272 U.S. at 238 (Brandeis, J., dissenting).   **38.** *Morrison*, 487 U.S. at 663.   **39.** *Id.* at 690.   **40.** 561 U.S. 477 (2010).   **41.** *Id.* at 484.   **42.** *Id.* at 486, 510.   **43.** *Id.* at 487; *id.* at 546 (Breyer, J., dissenting).   **44.** *Id.* at 488; *id.* at 526 (Breyer, J., dissenting).   **45.** *Free Enter. Fund*, 561 U.S. at 498.   **46.** *Seila L.*, 591 U.S. at 204–05.   **47.** *Id.* at 215.   **48.** 295 U.S. 602 (1935).   **49.** *Id.* at 218.   **50.** *Id.* at 218–20.   **51.** *Jarkesy v. SEC*, 34 F.4th 446, 463–64 (5th Cir. 2022).   **52.** *SEC v. Jarkesy*, 603 U.S. 109, 115 (2024).   **53.** Art. II, § 3 (emphasis added).   **54.** Tillman & Blackman, *supra* at 418.   **55.** *Officers of the United States Within the Meaning of the Appointments Clause, supra*.   **56.** *United States v. Trump*, 740 F. Supp. 3d 1245, 1267 (S.D. Fla. July 15, 2024); Steven G. Calabresi & Gary Lawson, *Why Robert Mueller's Appointment as Special Counsel Was Unlawful*, 95 Notre Dame L. Rev. 87 (2019).   **57.** *Trump*, 740 F. Supp. 3d at 1301 n.60; Seth Barrett Tillman & Josh Blackman, *Is Robert Mueller an "Officer of the United States" or an "Employee of the United States"?*, Lawfare (July 23, 2018), https://perma.cc/GA25-56MU.

ESSAY NO. 109: THE RECESS APPOINTMENTS CLAUSE
ART. II, § 2, CL. 3

The President shall have Power to fill up all Vacancies that may happen during the Recess of the Senate, by granting Commissions which shall expire at the End of their next Session.

—Robert G. Natelson

INTRODUCTION

The Constitutional Convention adopted the Recess Appointments Clause to prevent paralysis during periods when the Senate was not in session. The clause presents three important legal questions: (1) For the President to appoint without senatorial consent, must the vacancy arise during the recess or may it have arisen when the Senate was in session and continued into the recess? (2) Does "Recess of the Senate" include only inter-session recesses or also intra-session adjournments? (3) If it includes some intra-session adjournments, which ones qualify? The answers to these questions determine whether, when, and for how long a President may fill a vacant position.

HISTORY BEFORE 1787

Several colonial charters contained provisions governing appointments to vacancies in offices elected by the people or by colonial legislatures.[1] Early state constitutions contained more of these provisions,[2] and some early American statutes addressed vacancies as well.[3] The Confederation Congress's 1787 Northwest Ordinance included a vacancy-appointments clause for territorial legislative councils.[4]

These provisions contained certain common features that would appear in the Constitution's Recess Appointments Clause.

First, many were triggered when a "vacancy happens,"[5] an expression derived from English practice.[6] According to contemporaneous dictionaries, an occurrence "happened" when it arose.[7] This meaning is confirmed by many of the clauses themselves, which often provided examples of events that made a vacancy "happen," including death, resignation, departure from the jurisdiction, and removal from office.[8]

Second, provisions for filling vacancies typically required that the triggering vacancy arise within an identified time period. Thus, the Maryland constitution provided that a vacancy in the office of Register of Wills must occur "in the recess of the General Assembly."[9] A 1783 Massachusetts law authorized the governor to fill vacancies in the office of Collector of Excise if a vacancy "shall happen by reason of the death, resignation, removal out of the State, or non-acceptance of any person appointed" during "the recess of the General Court [legislature], or at so late a period in any session of the same Court, that the vacancy occasioned . . . shall not be supplied in the same session thereof. . . ."[10]

Third, as exemplified in the Maryland and Massachusetts provisions, "the recess" of the legislature often comprised all or part of the time during which the triggering vacancy had to arise. Although in other contexts "recess" might mean any pause in proceedings, in this context "*the* recess" specifically referred to the period between formal legislative sessions or "sittings."[11] In prevailing British and American legislative practice, no adjournments other than an adjournment *sine die* (or its equivalent) commenced "the recess."[12]

Finally, provisions for filling vacancies typically specified the duration of interim appointments. The 1776 Maryland constitution, for example, terminated them when the legislature met,[13] and the 1776 Delaware and 1778 South Carolina constitutions terminated them when the legislature elected replacements.[14]

THE CONSTITUTIONAL CONVENTION

Many of the delegates to the Federal Convention of 1787 derived their authority from documents that included vacancy-appointment clauses.[15] At least two, James McClurg of Virginia and William Blount of North Carolina, were themselves vacancy appointments.[16]

The Convention discussed at length whether the President should wield such traditionally executive powers as appointment to office or share those powers with one or both houses of Congress. Ultimately, the delegates decided to condition presidential appointments on Senate consent unless the office was an "inferior" one and a statute vested appointment in the President alone.[17]

That decision, however, necessitated a way to fill offices requiring senatorial consent when the Senate was not in session. On September 7, 1787, Richard Dobbs Spaight of North Carolina proposed the Recess Appointments Clause in substantially its current form. The Convention adopted it without dissent.[18] The Recess Appointments Clause thereby became one of the finished Constitution's three vacancy-appointment provisions. The other two addressed vacancies in the House of Representatives and the Senate.[19]

THE RATIFICATION DEBATES

The fact that the Recess Appointments Clause closely followed pre-existing patterns helps to explain why there were only isolated and undeveloped objections to it during the ratification debates. Governor Edmund Randolph of Virginia identified the Recess Appointments Clause as a defect in the Constitution but offered no reason for this conclusion.[20] James Monroe, the future President, criticized Randolph: "This inoffensive clause is made a ground of objection by Governor Randolph! I wish he had informed us wherefore."[21] Randolph did not pursue the matter. A South Carolina Anti-Federalist predicted possible "serious consequences" but failed to elaborate.[22] New York Governor George Clinton thought the clause granted the President power to appoint interim Senators,[23] but few, if any, agreed with this misreading.

Otherwise, reaction seems to have been favorable. Alexander Hamilton resoundingly rebutted Clinton's mistake in Federalist No. 67. Another Federalist writer labeled the clause "inoffensive,"[24] and still others touted it as proof that the new Senate would not be in continuous session.[25]

EARLY PRACTICE

In 1792, Congress created the office of Chief Coiner, but President George Washington did not fill the vacancy during the congressional session. After the session, Secretary of State Thomas Jefferson asked Attorney General Edmund Randolph for his opinion on whether the President could make a recess appointment. The answer depended on whether the vacancy in the Chief Coiner's office "happened" only when it arose during the session or continued to "happen" into the recess. Randolph responded that "happen" means "arise." The President could not fill the vacancy because it "happened" while Congress was still in session.[26] Randolph's conclusion was consistent with established meanings.

Yet more than three decades later, in 1823, Attorney General William Wirt opined that "happen" means "exist." He acknowledged that the more natural reading of the constitutional language is that "happen" means "arise" but concluded that the "spirit" of the Constitution supported the "exist" interpretation because unanticipated occurrences might cause the Senate to recess without confirming a nominee.[27] Wirt did not support his conclusion by citing any external authorities, but that has not deterred the Executive from adhering to the view that "happen" means "exist." By contrast, in 1863, the Senate Judiciary Committee issued a report strongly contending for the "arise" interpretation,[28] and Congress passed a statute prohibiting payment to officers filling vacancies arising during a senatorial session.[29] Only in 1940 did Congress amend the statute to permit payment to such appointees under certain circumstances.[30]

In 1921, Attorney General Harry M. Daugherty opined that "the Recess" included a month-long intra-session adjournment.[31] Like Wirt's opinion, Daugherty's opinion was devoid of Founding-era citation and emphasized instead the practical convenience of the Executive.[32] Since then, Presidents have maintained that "the Recess" encompasses intra-session breaks.

JUDICIAL PRECEDENT

The Supreme Court has addressed the Recess Appointments Clause only once—in *National Labor Relations Board v. Noel Canning* (2014).[33] As predicates for deciding on the validity of three recess appointments, the Court examined the following issues:

- Can "the Recess" include intra-session adjournments?
- Does a vacancy "happen" only when it arises or during the entire time it exists?
- Is the Senate in recess if its session is only "pro forma?"
- If the constitutional phrase "the Recess" refers to intra-session adjournments, does it include all or only some of them?

- If it refers only to some intra-session adjournments, what distinguishes those that qualify as "the Recess" from those that do not?

Writing for a 5-4 majority, Justice Stephen G. Breyer found that "the Recess" was ambiguous. This finding was based largely on lay usage of the term "recess" and inaccurate interpretations of historical events.[34] Nevertheless, it opened the way for the Court to rely on elements of post-ratification practice to conclude that "the Recess" encompassed intra-session adjournments. The same majority ruled that the "exist" view of "happen" was "a permissible reading of a doubtful phrase."[35] On the basis of this second reputed ambiguity, the Court again examined post-ratification practice and concluded that the "exist" view was more consonant with that practice.

The majority further determined that (1) a pro forma session of the Senate does not qualify as "the Recess," (2) "the Recess" encompasses only adjournments of more than three days, and (3) "the Recess" presumptively includes only adjournments of more than ten days. These determinations led the Court to void the challenged vacancy appointments.

Justice Antonin Scalia wrote for the four-person minority. He concurred with the invalidation of the vacancy appointments at issue in the case but enlisted both Founding-era and subsequent practice to show that "happen" means "arise" and "the Recess" includes only inter-session adjournments.

OPEN QUESTIONS

- What events can rebut the Supreme Court's presumption in *Noel Canning* that an adjournment shorter than ten days does not qualify as "the Recess of the Senate?"
- Does the recess appointment of Article III judges irreparably conflict with the Constitution's injunction that judges "shall hold their Offices during good Behaviour?"

Cite as: Robert G. Natelson, *The Recess Appointments Clause, in* THE HERITAGE GUIDE TO THE CONSTITUTION 403 (Josh Blackman & John G. Malcolm eds., 3d ed. 2025).

Notes

1. Conn. Charter (1662); Ga. Charter (1732). **2.** Del. Const. of 1776, art. 21; Ga. Const. of 1777, art. XXI; Md. Const. of 1777, art. XIII; Mass. Const. of 1780, pt. 2d, art. IV; Pa. Const. of 1776, § 19; S.C. Const. of 1778, art. XXXI. **3.** 1783 Mass. Acts & Resolves, c. 12, at 523. **4.** 32 J. Cont. Cong. 314, 317 (July 11, 1787). **5.** Mass. Const. of 1780, pt. 2d, art. VI; 1783 Mass. Acts & Resolves, *supra*; Pa. Const. of 1776, § 19; 32 J. Cont. Cong., *supra* at 317. **6.** Jean-Louis DeLolme, The English Constitution 309 (4th ed. 1784). **7.** Robert G. Natelson, *The Origins and Meaning of "Vacancies that May Happen During the Recess" in the Constitution's Recess Appointments Clause*, 37 Harv. J.L. & Pub. Pol'y 199, 227–28 (2014). This article is the source for material in this essay that is not otherwise footnoted. **8.** Art. I, § 3, cl. 2; Natelson, *supra* at 230–32. **9.** Md. Const. of 1776, art. XLI. **10.** 1783 Mass. Acts & Resolves, c. 12, at 523. **11.** Natelson, *supra* at 207–13; Michael B. Rappaport, *The Original Meaning of the Recess Appointments Clause*, 52 UCLA L. Rev. 1487 (2005). **12.** Natelson, *supra* at 213–27. **13.** Md. Const. of 1776, art. XLI. **14.** Del. Const. of 1776, art. 21; S.C. Const. of 1776, art. XXXI. **15.** *Ga. Act Electing and Empowering Delegates*, Feb. 10, 1787, *in* 1 DHRC 204. **16.** 3 Farrand 562–63; *id.* at 569–70. **17.** Art. II, § 2, cl. 2. **18.** 2 Farrand 540. **19.** Art. I, § 2, cl. 4; Art. I, § 3, cl. 2. **20.** Edmund Randolph, *Reasons for Not Signing the Constitution*, Dec. 27, 1787, *in* 8 DHRC 260, 273. **21.** "A Native of Virginia," *Observations upon the Proposed Plan of Federal Government*, April 2, 1788, *in* 9 DHRC 655, 682. **22.** "Cato," State Gazette of S.C., Nov. 26, 1787, *in* 27 DHRC 44, 46. **23.** "Cato V," N.Y.J., Nov. 22, 1787, *in* 14 DHRC 184, 185. **24.** "A Native of Virginia," *supra*. **25.** Remarks of Thomas McKean at the Pennsylvania Ratifying Convention, Dec. 10, 1787, *in* 2 DHRC 533, 537; Remarks of James Madison at the Virginia Ratifying Convention, Jun. 14, 1787, *in* 10 DHRC 1294, 1296; "A Federalist," Balt. Gazette, Jan. 18, 1788, *in* 11 DHRC 184, 185. **26.** Edmund Randolph, Opinion on Recess Appointments (July 7, 1792), https://perma.cc/H47Z-2XL4. **27.** 1 Op. Atty. Gen. 631 (1823). **28.** S. Rep. No. 37-80 (3d Sess. 1863), cited in Rappaport, *supra* at 1543 n.173. **29.** Rappaport, *supra* at 1543. **30.** *Id.* **31.** 33 Op. Atty. Gen. 20 (1921). **32.** *Id.* **33.** 573 U.S. 513 (2014). **34.** 573 U.S. at 577 n.2 (Scalia, J., concurring); Natelson, *supra*, at 222 n.120. **35.** 573 U.S. at 540.

~

ESSAY NO. 110: THE STATE OF THE UNION CLAUSE
ART. II, § 3

[The President] shall from time to time give to the Congress Information of the State of the Union. . . .

—Chad Squitieri

INTRODUCTION

Most years, the President makes the short trip down Pennsylvania Avenue from the White House to the U.S. Capitol to provide a State of the Union address to Congress. This tradition dates back to "speeches of the throne" by the English monarch in medieval times. After ratification, President George Washington followed the Constitution's instruction that the President "shall from time to time give to the Congress Information of the State of the Union." Justice Joseph Story explained that the President's constitutionally vested authority to "giv[e] information . . . to congress, is so consonant with the structure of the executive departments of the colonial and state governments . . . that it may well be presumed to be above all real objection."[1]

Washington and John Adams delivered their annual messages in person. However, Thomas Jefferson delivered his message in a letter. Jefferson began a new tradition that would continue until Woodrow Wilson's in-person address in 1913. In modern times, Presidents have delivered their State of the Union addresses in person by using the modern technologies of the day, including radio, television, the Internet, and social media.

HISTORY BEFORE 1787

The American conception of the State of the Union address finds historical support in the English monarch's practice of delivering speeches to Parliament.[2] This English practice can be traced back to the medieval period.[3] Following in the English tradition, at least one state required its executive to provide the state legislature with information; the New York constitution of 1777 provided that "it shall be the duty of the governor to inform the legislature, at every session, of the condition of the State."[4]

THE CONSTITUTIONAL CONVENTION

An early version of the State of the Union Clause, evidently from proceedings referred to the Committee of Detail by a July 23, 1787, resolution, included language that would become the Recommendation Clause.[5] The draft provided that the President "shall propose to the Legisl[ature] from Time to Time by Speech or Mess[a]g[e] such Meas[ures] as concern this Union."[6] The two provisions (the State of the Union Clause and Recommendation Clause) would be separated in the Constitution as ratified. By referring to both a "Speech or Mess[a]g[e]," this early language would more explicitly have given the President a choice between giving a speech (the modern norm) or delivering a letter (Jefferson's preference).

A document from the same proceedings referred to the Committee of Detail, believed to be part of the original plan proposed by Charles Pinckney, provided that "[i]t shall be [the President's] Duty to inform the Legislature of the Condition of [the] U.S. so far as may respect his Department."[7] This language would have imposed an explicit "Duty" on the President to keep the legislature informed. Other drafts, however, did not include such an express reference to duty. For example, a proposal found in James Wilson's papers stated that the President "shall from Time to Time give information (to the Legislature) of the State of the (Nation to the Legislature) (Union)."[8] A later version, from proceedings referred to the Committee on Style on September 10, 1787, stated that the President "shall, from time to time, give to the Legislature information of the State of the Union."[9] The final version of the Clause, as adopted, retained "shall" but replaced "Legislature" with "Congress."[10]

The ratified version of the State of the Union Clause gives rise to three primary questions: (1) Does the "shall" imply some sort of obligation, or does it merely suggest what the President would do in the normal course? (2) How often is "from time to time"? Does that mean annually or whenever the President deemed it necessary?[11] (3) Would the "information" be conveyed orally or in writing?

THE RATIFICATION DEBATES

There does not appear to have been any significant debate concerning the State of the Union Clause during the ratification process. In Federalist No. 77, Alexander Hamilton made a reference to a variety of constitutional provisions relating to the President's relationship with Congress, including the State of the Union Clause, and explained that "no objection has been made" regarding those provisions, "nor could" the provisions "possibly admit of any" objections.

EARLY PRACTICE

Washington gave the first State of the Union Message on January 8, 1790, just "a few days after the First Congress assembled for its second session."[12] The address was delivered in the Senate chamber of Federal Hall in New York City. John Adams continued Washington's practice and delivered each of his four State of the Union addresses in person. However, Adams's final address, delivered in 1800, would prove to be the last in-person address delivered for more than a century.[13]

The break in tradition began with President Thomas Jefferson. In 1801, Jefferson began the practice of delivering his State of the Union address to Congress by written letter. Jefferson explained that a letter could be read at "the convenience of the Legislature," and could respect "the economy of their time."[14] He concluded that a letter would also afford Congress "relief from the embarrassment of immediate answers on subjects not yet fully before them."[15]

MODERN PRACTICE

In 1913, Woodrow Wilson resumed the practice of delivering in-person addresses.[16] Wilson wanted to convey a personal connection: "[T]he President of the United States is a person, not a mere department of the Government hailing Congress from some isolated island of jealous power," and "is a human being trying to cooperate with other human beings in a common service" in "his own voice."[17]

Presidents have delivered their State of the Union addresses using the latest technologies of the day. In 1923, President Calvin Coolidge was the first President to broadcast his address over the radio; in 1947, President Harry Truman was the first President to broadcast his address on television; in 2002, President George W. Bush was the first President to use the Internet for a live presentation of his message; and in 2011, President Barack Obama was the first President to have his in-person address simultaneously live-tweeted on Twitter, the social media platform.[18]

OPEN QUESTIONS

- May Congress dictate when the President shall give the State of the Union address, or is that decision up to the President alone?
- May Congress impose limitations (or requirements) concerning the type of information that the President may (or must) convey to Congress pursuant to the State of the Union Clause?
- Must the President deliver the State of the Union address in person, or does a written version suffice?
- Who could enforce the clause if the President failed to give the message?

Cite as: Chad Squitieri, *The State of the Union Clause, in* THE HERITAGE GUIDE TO THE CONSTITUTION 406 (Josh Blackman & John G. Malcolm eds., 3d ed. 2025).

Notes

1. 3 Story's Commentaries § 1555.   **2.** Sudah Setty, *The President's Question Time: Power, Information, and the Executive Credibility Gap*, 17 Cornell J.L. & Pub. Pol'y 247, 272 (2008).   **3.** Henrik Woods, "My Lords and Gentlemen": A Study of British Origins and the Evolution of the Canadian Throne Speech Genre 4–5 (2011).   **4.** N.Y. Const. of 1777, art. XIX.   **5.** Vasan Kesavan & J Gregory Sidak, *The Legislator-in-Chief*, 44 Wm. & Mary L. Rev. 1 (2002); J. Gregory Sidak, *The Recommendation Clause*, 77 Geo. L.J. 2079 (1989).   **6.** 2 Farrand's 129, 137, 145.   **7.** *Id.* at 129, 157, 158.   **8.** *Id.* at 129, 163, 171.   **9.** *Id.* at 564–65, 574.   **10.** Art III, § 3, cl. 2.   **11.** Kesavan & Sidak, *supra* at 14–15.   **12.** *Id.* at 15.   **13.** President John Adams's Annual Message of 1800 (Nov. 22, 1800), https://perma.cc/9NN8-HKRM.

14. Thomas Jefferson, Letter to the President of the Senate and to the Speaker of the House of Representatives Regarding the President's Annual Message (Dec. 8, 1801), https://perma.cc/45W6-74LS.   **15.** *Id.*   **16.** List of In-Person Annual Message and State of the Union Addresses, U.S. House of Representatives: History, Art & Archives, https://perma.cc/7DW5-5FPG; Keith E. Whittington, *The State of the Union Is a Presidential Pep Rally*, 28 Yale L. & Pol'y Rev. Inter Alia 37, 48 (2010).   **17.** Woodrow Wilson, Address to a Joint Session of Congress on Tariff Reform (Apr. 8, 2013), https://perma.cc/4P8Z-98M6.   **18.** Kajal Singh, *This Day in History: One Huge Leap for Digital Communications at the White House*, The White House (Dec. 6, 2014), https://perma.cc/XG8D-RM55.

~

ESSAY NO. 111: THE RECOMMENDATION CLAUSE
ART. II, § 3

[The President] shall from time to time . . . recommend to [Congress's] . . . Consideration such Measures as he shall judge necessary and expedient. . . .

—Chad Squitieri

INTRODUCTION

The Constitution ensures that the President plays a role in the federal lawmaking process from beginning to end. Specifically, the Recommendation Clause ensures that the President has the authority not only to identify problems but also to offer legislative solutions to those problems at the start of the process. And at the end of the process, the President's veto authority (unless overridden) can halt legislation passed by both houses of Congress. In this regard, the Constitution "enables the President 'to point out the evil [of legislation], and to suggest the remedy.'"[1]

As Justice Joseph Story explained, the President's authority to "recommend[] measures to congress, is so consonant with the structure of the executive departments of the colonial, and state governments . . . that it may well be presumed to be above all real objection."[2] In modern times, Congress has attempted to restrict the ability of the executive branch to submit budget requests.

Presidents have countered that such limitations would violate the Recommendation Clause.

HISTORY BEFORE 1787

As St. George Tucker observed, "In England, the laws do, in fact, originate with the executive: a revenue bill is always proposed by the chancellor of the exchequer, or some member of that department; and . . . every other measure of considerable magnitude and importance is first discussed in the privy council, before it is brought into parliament."[3] The Recommendation Clause similarly permits legislative proposals to originate with a recommendation from the executive branch—subject, of course, to other portions of the Constitution, such as the Origination Clause.[4]

THE CONSTITUTIONAL CONVENTION

The drafting history sheds light on at least four important decisions with respect to the Recommendation Clause. The first decision separated the Recommendation Clause from the closely related State of the Union Clause.[5] Early in the Convention, the two clauses were coupled, but an early draft, evidently from proceedings referred to the Committee of Detail by a July 23, 1787, resolution, provided that the President "shall propose to the Legisl[ature] from Time to Time by Speech or Mess[a]g[e] such Meas[ures] as concern this Union."[6] The two provisions would later be separated, which suggests that the President can make recommendations outside of the limited State of the Union setting.

The second decision imposed what is arguably a presidential duty.[7] An August 6 draft document separating the State of the Union and Recommendation Clauses suggests that only the former would impose a presidential obligation: The President "*shall*, from Time to Time, give information to the Legislature" and "*may* recommend to their consideration such measures as he shall judge necessary, and expedient."[8] An August 24 draft changed the Recommendation Clause's "may" to "shall." As James Madison's records indicate, the change was made "in order to make it the *duty* of the President to recommend, & thence prevent umbrage or cavil at his doing it."[9]

The third decision was the choice of the word "measures."[10] A document evidently referred to the Committee of Detail on July 23

and found in James Wilson's papers, specifies that the President "may recommend (Matters) <such measures as he shall judge nesy. & expedt.> to their Consideration."[11] Later drafts, such as the one from August 6, continued to use "measures" rather than "matters."[12] The use of "measures" suggests that the Framers envisioned the President as doing more than simply pointing out societal ills ("matters") that Congress, in the President's opinion, should consider remedying.[13] Instead, the President was to recommend *solutions* ("measures") to those societal ills.[14] While "Matter" was defined as "Subject of . . . complaint,"[15] "Measure" was defined as "Means to an end."[16]

The fourth important decision was the decision to include "necessary and expedient" in the Recommendation Clause. A document evidently referred to the Committee of Detail on July 23, and believed to be part of the original plan proposed by Charles Pinckney, does not use "necessary and expedient."[17] Instead, it states that the President shall "recommend Matters to [Congress's] consideration."[18] But the July 23 document found in James Wilson's papers included a reference to "such measures as he shall judge nesy. & expedt."[19] Drafts from August 6,[20] and proceedings referred to the Committee of Style and Arrangement,[21] similarly use the phrase "necessary, and expedient." The Report of the Committee of Style dropped the comma and instead reads "necessary and expedient."[22] The comma-less "necessary and expedient" is what ultimately was ratified into law.[23]

THE RATIFICATION DEBATES

The Recommendation Clause does not seem to have attracted much attention during the ratification debates. In Federalist No. 77, Alexander Hamilton referred to a variety of constitutional provisions relating to the President's relationship with Congress, including the Recommendation Clause. He explained that "no objection has been made" regarding those provisions, "nor could" the provisions "possibly admit of any" objections.

EARLY PRACTICE

In 1789, George Washington delivered his first inaugural address to Congress. He explained that "[b]y the article establishing the executive department it is made the *duty* of the

President 'to recommend to your consideration such measures as he shall judge necessary and expedient.'"[24] He concluded, however, that "[t]he circumstances" of that first speech "acquit[ed]" him "from entering into that subject further than to refer to the great constitutional charter under which you [Congress] are assembled, and which, in defining your powers, designates the objects to which your attention is to be given."[25] A few months later, in January 1790, Washington directed Congress's attention to a variety of subjects (albeit in broad terms), including military preparations, foreign relations, immigration, national currency, the postal system, promoting science and literature, and the advancement of "Agriculture, Commerce and Manufactures by all proper means," although he was careful to note that he gave that last subject attention even though he "trust[ed]" it did "not . . . need recommendation."[26]

Like Washington, Joseph Story thought the Recommendation Clause imposed a duty. Story wrote that "[t]here is great wisdom . . . in not merely allowing, but in *requiring*, the president to lay before congress all facts and information, which may assist their deliberations."[27]

Recognizing the Recommendation Clause as a duty is consistent with the nature of the President's office. "[T]he nature and duties of the executive department," explained Story, indicate that the President "must possess more extensive sources of information, as well in regard to domestic as foreign affairs, than can belong to [C]ongress."[28] Moreover, this informational advantage is further strengthened by the President's authority to "require the Opinion, in writing, of the principal Officer in each of the executive Departments, upon any subject relating to the Duties of their respective Offices."[29]

MODERN PRACTICE
In the twentieth century, Congress has attempted to restrict the President's powers to submit budget requests, and Presidents have claimed that such restrictions violate the Recommendation Clause. For example, in 1912, Congress passed an appropriations rider that purported to restrict the form and timing of how the executive branch could submit budget requests.[30] President William Howard Taft announced that he would not interpret the rider

as having that effect, because such a restriction would "abridge the executive power in a manner forbidden by the Constitution."[31] Likewise, in 1966, Congress enacted an appropriations rider that purported to prohibit the executive branch from using appropriated funds to formulate certain budget requests. President Lyndon B. Johnson announced that the rider would "clearly intrude upon the Executive function of preparing the annual budget."[32] Presidents Ronald Reagan, Bill Clinton, George W. Bush, Barack Obama, and Donald Trump have similarly sought to defend their Recommendation Clause authority from congressional interference.[33]

JUDICIAL PRECEDENT
The U.S. Supreme Court has not interpreted the Recommendation Clause directly. Various courts, however, have considered the clause in passing. The U.S. Court of Appeals for the D.C. Circuit observed that "all executive branch authority to recommend legislation derives" from "the Recommendation Clause."[34] Taken literally, this conclusion would mean that the President has no authority to recommend legislation that the President concludes is not "necessary and expedient." The Supreme Court has spoken of the President's authority to propose legislation in looser terms, noting that the President has the authority to "recommend[] . . . laws he thinks wise."[35]

Although the Recommendation Clause speaks of presidential recommendations, some jurists have indicated that executive branch officials operating on behalf of the President may invoke the clause's authority as well. The D.C. Circuit has explained that the Recommendation Clause empowers "the U.S. Department of Labor" to "ask Congress to update" a "statute to cover . . . new situation[s]."[36] However, then-Judge Brett Kavanaugh used more precise terms: "The Framers specifically contemplated . . . that there would be situations where the *Executive Branch* confronts a pressing need that it does not have current authority to address" but that "[i]n those circumstances, the Constitution's Recommendation Clause provides that the *President* [and not the *Executive Branch*] may 'recommend' to Congress 'such Measures as he shall judge necessary and expedient.'"[37]

OPEN QUESTIONS

- May Congress enact a statute requiring the President to recommend legislation even when the President does not think a recommendation is "necessary and expedient"?
- May Congress prohibit the President from using government funds to research particular subjects, thereby limiting the President's ability to make recommendations pertaining to those subjects?
- May executive officials other than the President invoke the Recommendation Clause to recommend measures to Congress if the President does not approve of such recommendations?
- Are political disputes concerning the meaning of "necessary and expedient" subject to judicial review?

Cite as: Chad Squitieri, *The Recommendation Clause, in* THE HERITAGE GUIDE TO THE CONSTITUTION 408 (Josh Blackman & John G. Malcolm eds., 3d ed. 2025).

Notes

1. *Clinton v. City of New York*, 524 U.S. 417, 438 n.27 (1998) (quoting 3 Story's Commentaries § 1555).   **2.** 3 Story's Commentaries § 1555.   **3.** St. George Tucker, 1 Blackstone's Commentaries: With Notes of Reference to the Constitution and Laws of the Federal Government of the United States and of the Commonwealth of Virginia (1803), https://perma.cc/4SH8-G9JZ.   **4.** Art. 1, § 7, cl. 1.   **5.** Vasan Kesavan & J Gregory Sidak, *The Legislator-in-Chief*, 44 Wm. & Mary L. Rev. 1 (2002), and J. Gregory Sidak, *The Recommendation Clause*, 77 Geo. L.J. 2079 (1989).   **6.** 2 Farrand's 129, 137, 145.   **7.** Sidak, *supra* at 2081–85.   **8.** 2 Farrand's 185 (emphases added).   **9.** *Id.*   **10.** Sidak, *supra* at 2084.   **11.** 2 Farrand's 171.   **12.** *Id.* at 185.   **13.** Sidak, *supra* at 2084.   **14.** *Id.*   **15.** Noah Webster, An American Dictionary of the English Language 819 (1828), https://perma.cc/2G4V-YKMV.   **16.** *Id.* at 823.   **17.** 2 Farrand's 129, 157–58.   **18.** *Id.*   **19.** *Id.* at 171.   **20.** *Id.* at 185.   **21.** *Id.* at 565, 574.   **22.** *Id.* at 590, 600.   **23.** Art. II, § 3.   **24.** George Washington, First Inaugural Address (Apr. 30, 1789), https://perma.cc/LQ2M-PLUD (emphasis added).   **25.** *Id.*   **26.** George Washington, First Annual Address to Congress (Jan. 8, 1790), https://perma.cc/ZG6J-9KM8.   **27.** 3 Story's Commentaries § 1555 (emphasis added).   **28.** *Id.*   **29.** Art. II, § 2.   **30.** Act of Aug. 23, 1912, Pub. L. No. 62-299, § 9, 37 Stat. 360, 415.   **31.** Application of the Recommendations Clause to Sec. 802 of the Medicare Prescription Drug, Improvement, and Modernization Act of 2003, 40 Op. O.L.C. 66, 72 (2016) (quoting Letter Sent by the President to the Secretary of the Treasury Relative to the Submission of a Budget to Congress 5 (Sept. 19, 1912)).   **32.** Statement by the President Upon Signing the Department of Agriculture and Related Agencies Appropriations Bill (Sept. 8, 1966), *in* 2 Pub. Papers of Pres. Lyndon B. Johnson 980, 981 (1966).   **33.** Benjamin J. Schwartz, *The Recommendations Clause and the President's Role in Legislation*, 168 U. Pa. L. Rev. 767, 769, 784 (2020).   **34.** *Ass'n of Am. Physicians & Surgeons, Inc. v. Clinton*, 997 F.2d 898, 908 (D.C. Cir. 1993).   **35.** *Youngstown Sheet & Tube Co. v. Sawyer*, 343 U.S. 579, 587 (1952).   **36.** *Dist. of Columbia v. Dept. of Lab.*, 819 F.3d 444, 450 (D.C. Cir. 2016).   **37.** *Coal. for Responsible Reg., Inc. v. EPA*, 09-1322, 2012 WL 6621785, at *22 (D.C. Cir. Dec. 20, 2012) (Kavanaugh, J., dissenting from the denial of rehearing en banc) (emphases added).

ESSAY NO. 112: THE PRESIDENTIAL CONVENING CLAUSE
ART. II, § 3

. . . [the President] may, on extraordinary Occasions, convene both Houses, or either of them. . . .

—Seth Barrett Tillman

INTRODUCTION

In England, the king had broad powers to set the calendar and legislative agenda for both houses of Parliament. He could convene, prorogue, or dissolve parliament. The Constitution of 1788, like any number of Revolutionary-era state constitutions, substantially broke with the British model. The Framers restricted the Executive's control over Congress's calendar and legislative agenda. During the Constitutional Convention,

James Wilson of Pennsylvania observed that the President "could not like the Executive Magistrate in England interpose by a prorogation, or dissolution."[1] And just as the President had no unilateral power to dissolve Congress, he had no power to call new elections for its members. Congress was on a fixed two-year calendar cycle. The first day a new Congress would meet within its two-year term was determined by a statute enacted customarily by the preceding Congress; the last day would be fixed by a concurrent resolution.[2]

The President has no general power over congressional adjournments. Instead, the President has a limited adjournment power only if the two houses cannot agree on a common time of adjournment. (See Essay No. 113.) To this day, this limited presidential power over adjournment has gone unexercised.[3] Moreover, the President, unlike the king, has no unilateral power to control where Congress would reassemble. The Constitution does empower the President to convene either or both houses of Congress "on extraordinary Occasions."

PARLIAMENTARY PRACTICE BEFORE 1787

Under traditional British practice before the American War of Independence, unless otherwise controlled by statute, the king could convene or dissolve (terminate) a Parliament.[4] The king could also *prorogue* Parliament.[5] Prorogation, unlike dissolution, had the more limited effect of terminating legislative business then pending before both houses of Parliament. (Impeachments, as non-legislative business, could carry on notwithstanding a prorogation.) Thus, prorogation would permit the extant Parliament to start a new session during which legislative business could be resumed. All told, the king played an important role in setting the calendar and legislative agenda for both the House of Commons and the House of Lords.

This practice, however, was viewed as controversial and, by some, as less than desirable. Following independence, the North Carolina constitution of 1776 did not grant the governor any express power over the legislative calendar, including the timing of elections, or over each house's timing of its adjournments, recesses, and dissolution. By contrast, the Massachusetts

constitution of 1780 granted the governor, with the "advice of the [Executive] Council," a discretionary power to "adjourn or prorogue" the legislature for a limited period "[i]n cases of disagreement between the two houses, with regard to the necessity, expediency or time of adjournment, or prorogation."[6]

THE CONSTITUTIONAL CONVENTION

The records from the Constitutional Convention report little about the origin of the Presidential Convening Clause and the thinking behind it. It appears that this provision was first proposed in a Committee of Detail draft in the handwriting of Edmund Randolph of Virginia.[7] The draft provided that the President could "convene [the] legislature."[8] Another Committee of Detail draft granted the President the power to "convene the Legislature on extraordinary Occasions and the power to "prorogue, provided such Prorogation shall not exceed" a limited duration.[9] A blank space was left in the text, leaving it for the Convention to fix the durational limit of this power. In a subsequent draft in the handwriting of James Wilson of Pennsylvania, the prorogation language was dropped, but there was an emendation in the hand of John Rutledge of South Carolina: "(& in Case of a disagreemt between the 2 Houses with regard to the Time of Adj. he may adjourn them to such Time as he shall think proper.)."[10]

The Committee of Detail's report, which was delivered to the Convention on August 6, did not include an express proroguing power.[11] It provided in part that the President "may convene them on extraordinary occasions."[12] Here the word "them" refers back to the top of the section, which refers to "the Legislature." The very next sentence, which followed Rutledge's emendation, includes the Presidential Adjournment Clause: "In case of disagreement between the two Houses, with regard to the time of adjournment, he may adjourn them to such time as he thinks proper."[13] As the text was presented, it was not entirely clear whether the President had the power to convene only both houses of Congress (the "Legislature") or whether he could also convene a single house. On August 13, Wilson argued that the President "here could not like the Executive Magistrate in England interpose [his will against the Legislature] by a prorogation, or dissolution."[14]

On September 8, James McHenry of Maryland proposed language to amend the clause. He "observed that the President had not yet been any where authorized to convene the Senate" and proposed language specifying that the President "may convene both or either of the Houses on extraordinary occasions."[15] Wilson opposed the motion. He thought it "implied that the senate might be in Session, when the Legislature was not, which he thought improper."[16] McHenry's proposal was adopted by a vote of 7 to 4.

The text as referred to the Committee of Style provided that the President "may convene both or either of the Houses on extraordinary occasions, and in case of disagreement between the two Houses, with regard to the time of adjournment, he may adjourn them to such time as he shall think proper."[17] The Committee of Style modified the text: "[H]e may, on extraordinary occasions, convene both houses, or either of them, and in case of disagreement between them, with respect to the time of adjournment, he may adjourn them to such time as he shall think proper."[18] The Convention adopted this text with no further changes.[19]

THE RATIFICATION DEBATES

During ratification, the widely held view was that the President had no power to prorogue congressional proceedings. In Federalist No. 69, Alexander Hamilton observed that "[t]he British monarch may prorogue or even dissolve the Parliament" and that "[t]he governor of New York may also prorogue the legislature of this State for a limited time; a power which, in certain situations, may be employed to very important purposes." The President, however, has no similar power. He "can only adjourn the national legislature in the single case of disagreement about the time of adjournment."

The Federalists and Anti-Federalists also debated something of a puzzle. The clause speaks to the President's convening the two houses (collectively) or either of them. It is not difficult to understand why a President would need to convene both houses when they are out of session. The President might need a declaration of war, and it is both houses (collectively)

that enact such declarations by statute. Similarly, in the face of an unexpected calamity, the President may need new organic, legal authorities to deal with the crisis. It also makes sense for the President to need to call the Senate into session. Only the Senate can act on nominations to important offices and on treaties, and during a long recess, an office might become vacant or treaty negotiations might conclude. In both instances, decisive action is needed, and time may be of the essence. But why would the President need authority to convene the House alone? Cato, an Anti-Federalist, observed that "[n]o occasion can exist for calling the assembly without the senate."[20]

In Federalist No. 77, Hamilton offered something less than a full-throated defense of the provision. Characterizing Cato's critique as a mere "cavil," Hamilton acknowledged that in certain circumstances there would be "good reason" for exclusively convening the Senate, which "has a concurrent power with the Executive in the article of treaties." In addition, "it might often be necessary to call [the Senate] together . . . when it would be unnecessary and improper to convene the House of Representatives."

However, Hamilton's response is not entirely satisfactory. He only repeated what was already quite clear about the President's convening the Senate alone, but he did not answer Cato's challenge: Why does this clause grant the President the power to convene the House alone? Your author has offered one view as to the provision's original public meaning: In certain circumstances, the House alone, acting under the authority of a prior statute, could pass a resolution that would be separately presented to the President, and such a resolution of a single house, taken under prior statutory authority, would have the force of law.[21] (See Essay No. 38.)

SPECIAL SESSIONS ON "EXTRAORDINARY OCCASIONS"

There is little scholarly and judicial discussion of what constitutes an "extraordinary occasion." This would seem to be a political question wholly committed to the President's discretion. Furthermore, as a historical matter, the clause's "extraordinary occasion" language does not appear to impose a high bar. Past Presidents have used this power for reasons relating to economic crises, time-sensitive treaties, and war. However, during the antebellum period, outgoing Presidents regularly requested that the Senate should convene for the first day of the successor President's term. It is not clear that these requests formally invoked the convening power, but it also is not clear by what other authority the Senate could have convened.

On March 1, 1797, President George Washington asked the Senate to convene for the first day of John Adams's presidential term: "It appearing to me proper that the Senate of the United States should be convened on Saturday, the 4th of March, instant, you are desired to attend in the Chamber of the Senate, on that day, at 10 o'clock in the forenoon, to receive any communications which the President of the United States may then lay before you, touching their interests." Accordingly, "[i]n conformity with the summons from the President of the United States above recited, the Senate assembled in their Chamber, in the city of Philadelphia, and commenced their thirteenth session."[22] Four years later, President John Adams issued a similar request to the Senate to convene for the first day of President Thomas Jefferson's first term.[23] In each case, this request facilitated the new President's making nominations.

Perhaps the most famous invocation of the convening power occurred at the start of the Civil War. President Abraham Lincoln was sworn into office on March 4, 1861. Active hostilities began at Fort Sumter as early as April 12, 1861, but Congress was not due to meet until the first Monday in December. This date was set by Article I, Section 4, Clause 2. Faced with an eight-month recess, Lincoln took unilateral action, sometimes lacking clear statutory authorization. On April 15, 1861, he called Congress into session early to meet on July 4.[24] Lincoln sought new statutory authority to arm the government and to fight the war. Specifically, he sought authority to raise 400,000 men and authority to spend $400,000,000.[25]

OPEN QUESTIONS

- Thomas Jefferson published his influential *Manual of Parliamentary Practice for the Use of the Senate of the United States* in 1801. He explained that should a President convene Congress while both houses are in session, his doing so terminates that session and starts a new session.[26] Would the instantaneous break between the regularly scheduled session and the session convened by the President be an *intersession* recess or an *intrasession* recess?[27] (See Essay No. 113.) If that break is properly characterized as an intersession recess, did the Framers grant the President a limited, as opposed to a general, prorogation power that may be exercised only on an "extraordinary Occasion[]"? Jefferson's position has not been universally approved, and the modern practice appears to be that the President's convening the two houses while they are already in session does not terminate the extant session.[28] In those circumstances, there is no intersession break or intrasession break.

- Congress can grant its own officers the power to reconvene both houses, either collectively or separately, when they are not in session. This can be done by concurrent resolution or by statute. Does such a grant of power nullify or trespass upon the President's power to convene the houses of Congress?[29]

- The President can "convene" Congress "on extraordinary Occasions." Is the President's power to adjourn Congress limited to sessions that were convened as "extraordinary Occasions"? Both Justice Joseph Story and Justice John Marshall Harlan suggested that the answer is "no."[30] In 1834, President Andrew Jackson apparently considered using his adjournment power to adjourn Congress and to prevent the Senate from reauthorizing the Second Bank of the United States.[31] These questions were debated by the Democrats and Whigs. Some modern scholars have read the Convening Clause to limit the Adjournment Clause.[32]

Cite as: Seth Barrett Tillman, *The Presidential Convening Clause*, in THE HERITAGE GUIDE TO THE CONSTITUTION 411 (Josh Blackman & John G. Malcolm eds., 3d ed. 2025).

Notes

1. 2 Farrand's 275.   **2.** 1 Hinds' Precedents § 2.   **3.** S. Doc. No. 117-12, at 794 (2023).   **4.** 1 Blackstone §§ 150, 185–89.   **5.** Jefferson's Manual 306 (1801), https://perma.cc/J8FF-H8XA.   **6.** Mass. Const. of 1780, pt. II, ch. 2, § I, art. VI.   **7.** 2 Farrand's 137.   **8.** *Id.* at 146.   **9.** *Id.* at 158.   **10.** *Id.* at 163, 171.   **11.** *Id.* at 177, 185.   **12.** *Id.* at 185.   **13.** *Id.*   **14.** *Id.* at 275.   **15.** *Id.* at 546–47, 553.   **16.** *Id.* at 553.   **17.** *Id.* at 565, 574.   **18.** *Id.* at 590, 600.   **19.** *Id.* at 660.   **20.** Storing 2.6.45.   **21.** Seth Barrett Tillman, *A Textualist Defense of Article I, Section 7, Clause 3: Why* Hollingsworth v. Virginia *Was Rightly Decided, and Why* INS v. Chadha *Was Wrongly Reasoned*, 83 Tex. L. Rev. 1265 (2005).   **22.** S. Exec. J., 5th Cong., Spec. Sess. 233 (Mar. 4, 1797).   **23.** S. Exec. J., 7th Cong., Spec. Sess. 391 (Mar. 4, 1801).   **24.** Cong. Globe, 37th Cong., 1st Sess. 1 & 2 (1861).   **25.** *Id.* at app. 1–4; President Lincoln's Special Session Message (July 4, 1861), https://perma.cc/FZ3D-S84H.   **26.** Jefferson's Manual, *supra* at 306.   **27.** Seth Barrett Tillman, *Terminating Presidential Recess Appointments: A Reply to Professor Brian C. Kalt*, 101 Nw. U. L. Rev. Colloquy 94, 98 (2007); Josh Blackman, *Keep Calm About the Adjournment Clause and Read Tillman*, Volokh Conspiracy (Nov. 22, 2024), https://perma.cc/FB4X-CC9E.   **28.** *Ashley v. Keith Oil Co.*, 7 F.R.D. 589, 591–92 (D. Mass. 1947) (Wyzanski, J.); 1 Hinds' Precedents § 2 & n.3.   **29.** George T. Washington, Asst. Solicitor General, Mem. Op. for the Attorney General, Presidential Authority to Call a Special Session of Congress (Oct. 17, 1947), https://perma.cc/GLN5-KR66.   **30.** 3 Story's Commentaries § 1557; Brian L. Frye, Josh Blackman, & Michael McCloskey, *Justice John Marshall Harlan: Lectures on Constitutional Law, 1897–98*, 81 Geo. Wash. L. Rev. Arguendo 12, 230 (2013).   **31.** Jason Willick & Philip Huff, *How a Long-Ago Fight over a Dormant Constitutional Weapon Echoes Today*, Wash. Post (Dec. 16, 2024), https://perma.cc/5ZFZ-6JQM.   **32.** Allan Erbsen, *Constitutional Limits on the President's Authority to Adjourn Congress*, 2026 U. Ill. L. Rev. (forthcoming 2026).

ESSAY NO. 113: THE PRESIDENTIAL ADJOURNMENT CLAUSE
ART. II, § 3

. . . in Case of Disagreement between [both Houses] . . . with Respect to the Time of Adjournment, [the President] . . . may adjourn them to such Time as he shall think proper. . . .

—James Burnham & Louis J. Capozzi III

INTRODUCTION

Although the Framers of the Constitution largely gave each house of Congress the power to regulate its internal affairs, the Congressional Adjournment Clause requires that the Senate and House of Representatives must agree before adjourning for more than three days.[1] If the two houses disagree "with Respect to the Time of Adjournment," the Presidential Adjournment Clause gives the President the power to adjourn them until "such Time as he shall think proper." No President has ever exercised this power, but in *NLRB v. Noel Canning* (2014),[2] the U.S. Supreme Court recognized that a President could use the adjournment power to force the Senate into recess and make recess appointments.

HISTORY BEFORE 1787

The Presidential Adjournment Clause arose in part from British practice.[3] Traditionally, the king could unilaterally order Parliament to adjourn (a break within a session).[4] The king could also unilaterally end Parliament's session either by a writ of prorogation (ending the session but specifying when Parliament would meet again) or by dissolving Parliament and requiring a new election.[5] This broad authority reflected Parliament's medieval origin as a group of advisors to the monarch.[6]

As Parliament grew in importance and power, however, the king's practical ability to rule without Parliament diminished. In the mid-fourteenth century, King Edward III conceded that the monarch could not raise taxes without Parliament's consent.[7] In the seventeenth century, King Charles I challenged this arrangement by dismissing Parliament and ruling without it for eleven years.[8] The king's effort to raise revenues without convening Parliament was one cause of the English Civil War (1642–1651).[9] King James II likewise dismissed Parliament in 1685 and tried to raise money without it. These actions contributed to his overthrow in the

Glorious Revolution of 1688. The English Bill of Rights later reaffirmed that revenue measures required parliamentary assent.[10]

The colonies remained suspicious of the king's power to prevent the legislature from meeting. In 1765, King George III's royal governors dissolved the Virginia Assembly because it opposed the Stamp Act. And in 1768, the royal governors dissolved the Massachusetts and South Carolina legislatures over the Massachusetts Circular Letter, which challenged Parliament's taxation authority.[11] Consequently, the Declaration of Independence accused the king of abusing his power to prevent legislatures from meeting: "He has dissolved Representative Houses repeatedly, for opposing with manly firmness his invasions on the rights of the people. He has refused for a long time, after such dissolutions, to cause others to be elected . . . ."[12]

After independence, the states addressed this charge in their constitutions. Many early constitutions gave the governor no power to adjourn the state legislature,[13] and several explicitly denied the governor this power.[14] Only four gave the governor some power to adjourn the legislature temporarily: New York, Massachusetts, Maryland, and New Hampshire.[15] The Framers of the Constitution would follow this minority practice.

THE CONSTITUTIONAL CONVENTION

On May 28, Charles Pinckney of South Carolina proposed allowing the President to "prorogue" Congress on "special occasions" and to adjourn them in cases of disagreement.[16] James Wilson of Pennsylvania prepared a draft for the Committee of Detail that gave the President the power to "prorogue" Congress for a limited (but unspecified) number of days.[17] (Wilson omitted that power in his next draft.) Editing Wilson's draft, John Rutledge inserted what became, in substance, the final text.[18] It referred to the President's power to adjourn but not the power to prorogue.[19] The provision generated no recorded debate at the Philadelphia Convention. Considering the Framers' concern about the king's power over the legislature's schedule, it is unclear why the Constitution gave the President *any* power to adjourn Congress.

THE RATIFICATION DEBATES

Given their experience living under British rule, it is hardly surprising that the Framers allowed the President a much weaker power to prevent Congress from meeting. First, the king could prorogue or even dissolve Parliament at will. However, in Federalist No. 69, citing the governor of New York's limited adjournment power, Alexander Hamilton observed that "the President can only adjourn the national legislature in the single case of disagreement [between both houses] about the time of adjournment." Second, the king theoretically could rule without Parliament for lengthy periods of time. However, Article I, Section 4 provides that "The Congress shall assemble at least once in every year." As a result, the President's already restricted adjournment power is limited to periods of less than one year.

The Presidential Adjournment Clause received limited attention during the ratification debates. In South Carolina, Rawlins Lowndes complained that the President's "power of adjourning to any day he thought proper" was too "monarchical."[20] At the Virginia ratification convention, James Monroe questioned how legislative adjournment would work. In response, James Madison insisted that the President's role was necessary in situations where the two houses disagreed as to adjournment, and Edmund Randolph explained that "[i]f [the President] be honest, he will do what is right. If dishonest, the representatives of the people will have the power of impeaching him."[21]

EXECUTIVE BRANCH PRACTICE

Congress has never failed to agree on adjournment. Accordingly, the President has never used his adjournment power. In 2020, President Donald Trump raised the possibility of adjourning Congress in order to make recess appointments, citing the Senate's slow pace in confirming his nominees.[22] However, he ultimately declined to exercise this power.

JUDICIAL PRECEDENT

The Presidential Adjournment Clause received some attention in 2012. President Barack Obama attempted to make recess appointments during short, three-day breaks in the Senate calendar.

In *NLRB v. Noel Canning*, the Supreme Court ruled that Obama's appointments were invalid. However, the case was not a total loss for the executive branch. The Court also held that the Recess Appointments Clause empowered the President to fill vacancies that arose *both* before and during the Senate's recess.[23]

Justice Stephen G. Breyer wrote the majority opinion, and Justice Antonin Scalia concurred in the judgment. Both jurists observed that the Presidential Adjournment Clause could create a potential workaround if the Senate would not confirm the President's appointees. Specifically, the President could potentially ally with one house of Congress to create a disagreement on adjournment. Once the houses disagreed, the President could force an adjournment, and while the Senate was adjourned, even for a short period of time, the President could fill the executive branch with recess appointments. This workaround could circumvent the Senate's power to withhold "advice and consent" from executive branch nominees.[24]

Under Justice Breyer's broad interpretation of the Recess Appointments Clause, this maneuver could potentially fill every vacancy outstanding at the time of the forced adjournment. However, under Justice Scalia's narrower interpretation, the President could fill only those vacancies that arose after the President forced an adjournment.[25]

OPEN QUESTIONS

- The Congressional Adjournment Clause provides that one house cannot "adjourn for more than three days" without the consent of the other house.[26] Does this three-day time limit restrict the President's ability to adjourn Congress to three days?[27] Given the ability of each house to adjourn unilaterally for three days, would that restriction make the Presidential Adjournment Clause superfluous? Or does the President have the power to adjourn Congress for a period longer than three days until "such Time as He thinks proper"?

- What precisely needs to happen for the President to conclude that a disagreement as to adjournment exists between the houses? If the House votes to adjourn for ten days and the Senate ignores the House's vote and remains in session, could the President proceed to adjourn Congress—and for whatever period the President deems proper? Or would the house seeking to adjourn need to specify a deadline by which the other house must respond? Does a house wishing to adjourn need to notify the President of a disagreement? Is there any way to challenge the President's conclusion that a disagreement between the houses exists?

Cite as: James Burnham & Louis J. Capozzi III, *The Presidential Adjournment Clause, in* THE HERITAGE GUIDE TO THE CONSTITUTION 415 (Josh Blackman & John G. Malcolm eds., 3d ed. 2025).

Notes

1. Art. I, § 5, cl 2. **2.** 573 U.S. 513 (2014). **3.** Federalist No. 69 (Hamilton). **4.** Robert G. Natelson, *The Origins and Meaning of "Vacancies that May Happen During the Recess" in the Constitution's Recess Appointments Clause*, 37 Harv. J.L. Pub. Pol'y 199, 207–10 (2014); 1 Blackstone § 179. **5.** Natelson, *supra* at 207–10; 1 Blackstone § 179–801. **6.** John Baker, An Introduction to English Legal History 217 (2019). **7.** *Id.* at 218. **8.** *Id.* at 227. **9.** *Consumer Fin. Prot. Bureau v. All Am. Check Cashing*, 33 F.4th 218, 226 (CA5 2022) (en banc) (Jones, J., concurring). **10.** 1 Wm. & Mary c. 2, § 7, *in* 3 Eng. Stat. at Large 417 (1689). **11.** Andrew Roberts, The Last King of America: The Misunderstood Reign of George III, at 296 (2021). **12.** Declaration of Independence, ¶ 7. **13.** Ga. Const. of 1777, art. VII; N.C. Const. of 1776, art. X; N.J. Const. of 1776, arts. V & VI; Pa. Const. of 1776, § 9; Va. Const. of 1776. **14.** Del. Const. of 1776, art. X; S.C. Const. of 1778, art. XVII; Va. Const. of 1776. **15.** Md. Const. of 1776, art. XXIX; Mass. Const. of 1780, Pt. 2, ch. 2, § 1, art. VI; N.H. Const. of 1784; N.Y. Const. of 1777, art. XVIII. **16.** 3 Farrand's 111. **17.** 2 Farrand's 158. **18.** *Id.* at 171. **19.** *Id.* at 600. **20.** 4 Elliot's 310–11. **21.** 3 Farrand's 312. **22.** Josh Breshnahan, *Trump Threatens to Adjourn Congress to Push Through Nominees*, Politico (Apr. 15, 2020), https://perma.cc/969T-35VG. **23.** 573 U.S. at 538. **24.** *Id.* at 555; *id.* at 614 (Scalia, J. concurring in the judgment); Josh Chafetz, *A Fourth Way? Bringing Politics Back Into Recess Appointments (And the Rest of the Separation of Powers, Too)*, 64 Duke L.J. Online 161,

169 (2015).   **25.** Michael Rappaport, *The Original Meaning of the Recess Appointments Clause*, 52 UCLA L. Rev. 1487, 1490 (2005).   **26.** Art. 1, § 5, cl. 4.   **27.** Adam J. White, *The*

Flaw in the President's Newest Constitutional Argument, The Atlantic (Apr. 17, 2020), https://perma.cc/FMT6-UMXB.

ESSAY NO. 114: THE AMBASSADORS CLAUSE
ART. II, § 3

[The President] shall receive Ambassadors and other public Ministers. . . .
—Christopher T. Landau & Chase T. Harrington

INTRODUCTION

The Ambassadors Clause, also known as the Reception Clause, tasks the President with receiving other nations' foreign diplomats. As an original matter, reception appears to entail the ministerial duty under customary international law of receiving foreign diplomatic envoys. During the twentieth century, however, the reception power morphed into a substantive prerogative, and it is now the principal constitutional footing for the President's unilateral and unreviewable power to recognize foreign governments.

HISTORY BEFORE 1787

Since ancient times, international law has provided a specific means for the formal initiation of an envoy's diplomatic service: The envoy presents a letter of credence from the head of state of his or her country to the head of state of the host country.[1] Such a letter generally vouches for the envoy's *bona fides* (credentials) and asks the host government to give credence to the envoy's authority to speak on behalf of his or her government.[2]

After the United States declared independence, it was widely understood and accepted that the responsibility of receiving foreign envoys rested with the national government, not the states. In August 1778, the Second Continental Congress received French diplomat Conrad Alexandre Gérard de Rayneval, the first accredited minister to the United States from a foreign nation.[3] The following year, Congress received Gérard's successor, Anne-César de La Luzerne.[4]

Congress's power to receive foreign ministers was formalized by the Articles of Confederation, ratified in 1781. Under the

Articles, "The united states, in congress assembled, shall have the sole and exclusive right and power . . . of . . . receiving ambassadors."[5] The states also ceded their unilateral sovereign power to receive foreign envoys: "No State, without the Consent of the united States, in congress assembled, shall . . . receive any embassy from, or enter into any conference, agreement, alliance, or treaty, with any King prince or state."[6] During this period, as before, foreign envoys would present their credentials to Congress, and Congress would authorize state governments to interact with these ministers as necessary.[7]

THE CONSTITUTIONAL CONVENTION

During the Constitutional Convention, it was similarly understood and accepted that the job of receiving foreign diplomatic envoys should be transferred from Congress to the new national executive. On August 6, 1787, the Committee of Detail's draft charged the national executive with receiving foreign diplomatic envoys.[8] That draft provided that the Executive "shall receive Ambassadors, and may correspond with the supreme Executives of the several States."[9]

On August 25, without debate, the phrase "and other public ministers" was added after "Ambassadors." This change presumably recognized that some foreign diplomatic envoys would not hold the rank of ambassador. The delegates also struck the power to correspond with state executives, or governors, as unnecessary.[10] The clause was not the subject of any recorded discussion at the Convention and was ultimately located in Article II, Section 3, Clause 1 in a list of the President's duties.[11]

THE RATIFICATION DEBATES

In Federalist No. 69, Alexander Hamilton characterized the Reception Clause as a purely ceremonial power. This provision was "more a matter of dignity than authority," he wrote, "without consequence in the administration of the government." It was "far more convenient" for foreign envoys to present their credentials to the President than to "conven[e] the legislature, or one of its branches, upon every arrival of a foreign minister. . . ."

Although Hamilton asserted that the clause "ha[d] been a rich theme of declamation," it does not appear to have been controversial during the ratification debates and was not challenged by the Anti-Federalists.[12] In fact, what appears to be the sole recorded mention of the clause during the state ratification debates was by the Federalist Archibald Maclaine at the North Carolina Convention, who echoed Hamilton's view. He thought it was more practical to give this responsibility to the President, who "is perpetually acting for the public," as opposed to Congress, which was frequently not in session.[13]

EARLY PRACTICE

Hamilton's characterization of the clause as purely ceremonial would soon prove to be inaccurate. Starting in 1789, the French Revolution forced the new federal government to address a number of novel questions, including whether to recognize the new revolutionary government in France and how to determine the status of treaties with the former royal regime.[14] Controversy arose as to whether the power to answer these questions rested with Congress or the President. Hamilton (writing under the pseudonym "Pacificus") took the position that such power belonged to the President, partly because of the "right of the Executive to receive ambassadors and other public ministers." This power, he explained, "includes that of judging, in the case of a Revolution of Government in a foreign Country, whether the new rulers are competent organs of the National Will and ought to [be] recognised or not." And in cases when the United States has previously entered a treaty with a foreign country, the discretion to receive ambassadors "involves the power of giving operation or not to such treaty."[15]

James Madison (writing under the pseudonym "Helvidius") disagreed. He asserted that the Reception Clause intended "little if any thing more" than providing for "the ceremony of admitting public Ministers."[16] Here, Madison advanced the ministerial understanding of the clause that Hamilton had articulated in the Federalist Papers. According to Madison, "a right to refuse to acknowledge a new government cannot be implied by the right to refuse a public Minister." Rather, the power to recognize foreign governments and determine the status of treaty obligations, like the power to declare war, rested in Congress.[17]

As a historical and practical matter, Hamilton's view prevailed. President Washington received the diplomatic envoy of the revolutionary French government, Citizen Genêt, and thereby recognized that government.[18] The Washington Administration did not consult with Congress, and Congress did not object.[19] Moreover, Washington's Proclamation of Neutrality had the effect of nullifying the Treaty of Alliance signed by the Continental Congress and the deposed King Louis XVI of France.

EARLY COMMENTARY

Early commentators agreed with Hamilton that the President's power to receive ambassadors from foreign governments necessarily included the power to recognize the government sending the ambassador and the power *not* to recognize that government (by refusing to receive the putative ambassador). These commentators, however, left open the possibility that Congress might override such recognition decisions. Thus, Justice Joseph Story wrote that "[i]f the executive receives an ambassador . . . it is an acknowledgment of the sovereign authority de facto of such new nation, or party. If such recognition is made, it is conclusive upon the nation, unless indeed it can be reversed by an act of congress repudiating it."[20] Story cautioned, however, that Congress's authority to challenge a President's recognition decision was an "abstract statement[]" that was "still open to discussion."[21]

William Rawle went somewhat further in his treatise on the Constitution. He declared that Congress could override the President on the recognition of foreign governments if it chose to exercise that power. The power to receive foreign ambassadors, Rawles observed, includes "the right of judging . . . whether the new rulers ought to be recognised" after a revolution. Rawles contended that "[t]he legislature indeed possesses a superior power, and may declare its dissent from the executive recognition or refusal," but "until that sense [of Congress] is declared, the act of the executive is binding."[22]

JUDICIAL PRECEDENT

United States v. Palmer (1818) dodged the question of whether Congress had any legitimate role in a recognition decision.[23] In dicta, the U.S. Supreme Court observed that "the courts of the Union must view . . . [a] newly constituted government" following a civil war "as it is viewed by the legislative and executive departments of the government of the United States."

Once the Reception Clause is interpreted to give the President an implicit "recognition power," a question arises about the scope of that substantive power. *United States v. Belmont* (1937) and *United States v. Pink* (1942) held that the Reception Clause grants the executive branch the power to settle the claims of United States citizens against a foreign government, at least insofar as such claims are settled in the context of recognizing that government.[24] Both cases arose in the wake of President Franklin D. Roosevelt's 1933 recognition of the government of the Soviet Union. As part of that recognition and the subsequent exchange of ambassadors, the so-called Litvinov Assignment between the two nations settled the claims of United States nationals against the Soviet Union. *Pink* held

that the recognition power "is not limited to a determination of the government to be recognized" and "includes the power to determine the policy which is to govern the question of recognition," including conditions on recognition.[25] The President's recognition power necessarily included the power to enter into that agreement.[26]

The Court has held that the implicit executive recognition power provides exclusive authority to establish United States policy regarding a foreign nation's territorial boundaries. *Zivotofsky v. Kerry* (2015) involved the constitutionality of a 2002 statute that required the President to list Israel as the place of birth of a United States citizen born in the city of Jerusalem.[27] The Court held that the law unconstitutionally infringed on the President's recognition power, based in part on the Reception Clause. Both Justice Clarence Thomas's concurrence and Chief Justice John Roberts' dissent pointed out that reception of an ambassador is not generally understood under international law to encompass a recognition of the territorial claims of the foreign government sending that ambassador. For example, the United States has long recognized Argentina and exchanged ambassadors with that nation's government without recognizing that nation's claims over the Falkland Islands. After *Zivotofsky*, the Reception Clause is now deemed a source of exclusive executive power to recognize (or not recognize) a foreign government's claims to particular territory—an issue far removed from receiving an ambassador.

OPEN QUESTIONS

- As an original matter, who had the better of the argument between Pacificus (Hamilton) and Helvidius (Madison) over the question of whether the Reception Clause gives the President any substantive power, such as the power to determine which foreign governments to recognize? Even assuming that Hamilton had the better of that argument, does it follow that Congress lacks any power over recognition of foreign governments?
- Assuming the current interpretation of the President's recognition power is sound, how far does that power extend? Would *Belmont* and *Pink* have been decided the same way if Congress had purported to preserve the claims of U.S. citizens against the Soviet Union?
- Who had the better of the dispute in *Zivotofsky* on whether the recognition power extends to the boundaries of foreign countries—the Justices in the majority or the Chief Justice and Justice Thomas? Does the power to recognize foreign governments

have anything to do with the power to take a position on territorial claims asserted by those governments?

Cite as: Christopher T. Landau & Chase T. Harrington, *The Ambassadors Clause, in* THE HERITAGE GUIDE TO THE CONSTITUTION 418 (Josh Blackman & John G. Malcolm eds., 3d ed. 2025).

Notes

1. Hugo Grotius, The Rights of War and Peace 379 (Jean Barbeyrac ed., 1738); E. de Vattel, The Law of Nations, Bk. IV, §§ 55–68 (1758). **2.** Vattel, *supra* at § 76. **3.** 11 J. Cont. Cong. 752–57 (Aug. 5 & 6, 1778). **4.** 15 J. Cont. Cong. 1278–83 (Nov. 17, 1779). **5.** Articles of Confederation, art. IX, § 1. **6.** *Id.* at art. VI, § 1. **7.** 21 J. Cont. Cong. 940–41 (Sept. 7, 1781); 26 J. Cont. Cong. 79 (Feb. 11, 1784). **8.** 2 Farrand's 185. **9.** *Id.* **10.** *Id.* at 411. **11.** Robert J. Reinstein, *Recognition: A Case Study on the Original Understanding of Executive Power*, 45 U. Rich. L. Rev. 801, 812–13, 843 (2011). **12.** Reinstein, *supra* at 850. **13.** *Id.* at 846. **14.** From George Washington to the Cabinet (Apr. 18, 1793), https://perma.cc/QXS9-7F68. **15.** The Pacificus–Helvidius Debates of 1793–1794, 14–15 (Morton J. Frisch ed., 2007). **16.** *Id.* at 75. **17.** *Id.* at 77. **18.** Saikrishna Prakash & Michael Ramsey, *The Executive Power over Foreign Affairs*, 111 Yale L.J. 231, 312 –13 (2001). **19.** *Id.* **20.** 3 Story's Commentaries § 1560. **21.** *Id.* **22.** William Rawle, A View of the Constitution of the United States of America 195 (1829). **23.** *United States v. Palmer*, 16 U.S. (3 Wheat.) 610, 643–44 (1818). **24.** *United States v. Pink*, 315 U.S. 203 (1942); *United States v. Belmont*, 301 U.S. 324 (1937). **25.** *Belmont*, 301 U.S. at 229. **26.** *Id.* **27.** *Zivotofsky v. Kerry*, 576 U.S. 1, 7 (2015).

ESSAY NO. 115: THE TAKE CARE CLAUSE
ART. II, § 3

. . . [the President] shall take Care that the Laws be faithfully executed . . . .
—John C. Yoo

INTRODUCTION

The Article II Vesting Clause grants "the executive power" to the President. The Take Care Clause qualifies that power: The President must wield his executive power over law execution to "take Care that the Laws be faithfully executed." The President must use the constitutional and statutory resources at his disposal to see that Congress's laws are executed faithfully. Further, the President must execute the law without violating other federal laws, and the President cannot order his subordinates to do so. Finally, the Executive should not deliberately misread or twist statutes, which would be unfaithful execution.[1] The Supreme Court has addressed the Take Care Clause in a wide array of separation of powers cases but "almost never construes the clause, at least not in any conventional way."[2]

HISTORY BEFORE 1787

The Take Care Clause can be traced back as far as Magna Carta.[3] Chapter 61 provided that the barons "shall faithfully observe" that King John would observe his obligations under the Great Charter.[4] Sir William Blackstone observed that the king had "the whole executive power of the laws" but had a duty to execute those laws "in subservience to the law of the land" for "the care and protection of the community."[5] The king lacked the power *not* to execute, or to *suspend*, the law. The English Bill of Rights of 1689 repudiated "the pretended power of suspending the laws or the execution of laws by regal authority without consent of Parliament."[6]

This duty of faithful execution continued in the colonies. William Penn's Charter of Liberties for Pennsylvania provided that the governor "shall take Care, that all Laws Statutes and Ordinances which shall at any time be made within the said Province be duly and diligently executed."[7] Scholars have observed that "faithful execution was often tied to staying within authority and abiding by the law, following the intent of the lawgiver, and eschewing self-dealing and financial corruption."[8]

This understanding continued in the states following independence. Most of the new states required "that the chief magistrate govern according to law and take an oath of faithful execution of office."[9] The Virginia Declaration of Rights found that "all power of suspending laws, or the execution of laws . . . is injurious to [the people's] rights and ought not to be exercised."[10] In Pennsylvania, all government officials were required to swear or affirm "that I will faithfully execute the office . . . and will do equal right and justice to all men, to the best of my judgment and abilities, according to law."[11] In New York, the governor had the duty "to take care that the laws are faithfully executed to the best of his ability."[12]

These state executives understood that they had the power to execute the laws and a duty to ensure faithful execution. The Confederation Congress imposed similar oaths. For example, Secretary of Foreign Affairs John Jay took an oath "for the faithful execution" of his trust.[13]

THE CONSTITUTIONAL CONVENTION

During the Constitutional Convention, the Framers debated two provisions on faithful execution. The first, the Presidential Oath of Office Clause, provided that the President would "faithfully execute the Office of President of the United States."[14] (See Essay No. 101.) The second would become the Take Care Clause.

Edmund Randolph's Virginia Plan would have granted the President the "power to carry into execution the national laws,"[15] but the concept of faithful execution would be introduced by the Committee of Detail. Two members of that committee drafted different formulations.[16] James Wilson of Pennsylvania proposed that the President "shall take Care to the best of his Ability, that the Laws of the United States be faithfully executed." Wilson appears to have modeled this text after the Pennsylvania Constitution. John Rutledge of South Carolina proposed: "It shall be his duty to provide for the due & faithful exec — of the Laws to the best of his ability." The Committee's report, which was delivered to the Convention on August 6, largely followed Wilson's phrasing: "he shall take care that the laws of the United States be duly and

faithfully executed."[17] The words "to the best of his Ability," were removed.

The Convention approved this text, and it was referred to the Committee of Style.[18] However, the Committee shortened it: [H]he shall take care that the laws be faithfully executed."[19] The Committee dropped "duly and faithfully" and "of the United States." The Convention adopted this revised provision without further debate.

THE RATIFICATION DEBATES

During the ratification debates, there was little consideration of the Take Care Clause. In Federalist No. 69, Alexander Hamilton wrote that the President's "power . . . to take care that the laws be faithfully executed" would "resemble equally that of the king of Great Britain and of the governor of New York." In Federalist No. 77, Hamilton explained that "no objection has been made" to the "power[] of . . . faithfully executing the law."

During the Pennsylvania ratification convention, James Wilson referred to the Take Care Clause as "another power of no small magnitude intrusted to this officer."[20] These Framers seemed to view the Take Care Clause as a duty as well as a power. In the North Carolina ratification convention, Archibald Maclaine praised the Take Care Clause as "[o]ne of the best provisions contained in" the Constitution. If the President "takes care that the laws be faithfully executed," Maclaine said, "it will be more than is done in any government on the continent."[21]

Yet much about this provision was uncertain. William Symmes, an Anti-Federalist from Massachusetts, wrote that the Take Care Clause was "so *brief*, so *general*."[22] He asked a series of questions: "Can we exactly say how far a faithful execution of the laws may extend? or what may be called or comprehended in a faithful execution? . . . And should the legislature direct the mode of executing the laws, or any particular law, is [the President] obliged to comply, if he does not think it will amount to a faithful execution?"[23] The Federalists gave no clear answers.

EARLY PRACTICE

The First Congress established several great departments in the executive branch, including

Foreign Affairs, War, and Treasury, and placed a Secretary at the head of each department. Who would ensure that these departments executed federal law: the secretaries or the President? Congress assumed that the Executive would be responsible for law execution, as each secretary was subordinate to the President. The Take Care Clause obligates the President to ensure that those below him faithfully execute the law. Professor Robert Natelson explains that at the Framing, "take care" was a term of art employed in "power-conferring documents" in which officials assigned tasks to agents.[24] Over time, the President would direct and supervise the executive branch, including the military, the diplomatic corps, and domestic officers like prosecutors and tax collectors.

President George Washington, for example, directed both federal and state officers in their execution of federal law. In the midst of the Whiskey Rebellion, Washington observed that "it is my duty to see the Laws executed: to permit them to be trampled upon with impunity would be repugnant to" that duty.[25] Consistent with the notion that he had both power and duty, Washington repeatedly instructed officers.[26] He gave enforcement orders to state governors, prosecutors, revenue officers, and the departmental secretaries. Washington wrote that "[i]n light of '[t]he impossibility that one man should be able to perform all the great business of the State,' the Constitution provides for executive officers to 'assist the supreme Magistrate in discharging the duties of his trust.'"[27] During the Civil War, President Abraham Lincoln invoked the clause as one of the grounds for his duty to suppress the rebellion.[28]

EARLY JUDICIAL PRECEDENT

The U.S. Supreme Court has discussed the Take Care Clause in a wide range of cases. In *Little v. Barreme* (1804), Chief Justice John Marshall observed that the president's "high duty... is to 'take care that the laws be faithfully executed.'"[29] In that case, Congress "seemed to have prescribed that the manner in which this law shall be carried into execution ...."[30] *United States v. Tingey* (1831) found that the President is "enjoined" with the "trust" of faithful execution.[31] The President "not only may, but he is bound to avail himself of every appropriate

means not forbidden by law."[32] Accordingly, the Court concluded that the President could demand bonds from federal officers to ensure their faithful handling of federal funds.

The Court's most authoritative decision concerning the Take Care Clause came in *Kendall v. United States* ex rel. *Stokes* (1838).[33] Chief Justice Roger B. Taney's majority opinion held that the Postmaster General must comply with positive congressional edicts lest the duty to take care that the laws be faithfully executed become a "dispensing power" to suspend the law.[34] Taney added that "[t]o contend that the obligation imposed on the President to see the laws faithfully executed, implies a power to forbid their execution, is a novel construction of the constitution."[35] The Court later referred to these principles as "fundamental and essential" and said that without them, "the administration of the government would be impracticable."[36]

Chief Justice Taney invoked the clause again in *Ex parte Merryman* (1861).[37] During the Civil War, President Lincoln unilaterally suspended the writ of habeas corpus. John Merryman, who was imprisoned in Fort McHenry in Baltimore, challenged his detention. Taney found that only Congress had the power to suspend the writ. Regarding the Take Care Clause, Taney wrote that the President is "not authorized to execute [the laws] himself ... but he is to take care that they be faithfully carried into execution, as they are expounded and adjudged by the co-ordinate branch of the government to which that duty is assigned by the constitution."[38] The President "certainly does not faithfully execute the laws, if he takes upon himself legislative power, by suspending the writ of habeas corpus."[39]

Taney did not issue any sort of order against Lincoln—or anyone else for that matter—to release Merryman,[40] but he did instruct the clerk to transmit his opinion to the President. Taney stated, "It will then remain for that high officer, in fulfilment of his constitutional obligation to 'take care that the laws be faithfully executed,' to determine what measures he will take to cause the civil process of the United States to be respected and enforced."[41]

MODERN JUDICIAL PRECEDENT

The Supreme Court has relied upon the Take

Care Clause as the basis for the President's power to remove subordinates. In *Myers v. United States* (1926), Chief Justice William Howard Taft concluded that "as part of his executive power" to "take care that [the laws] be faithfully executed," the President "should select those who were to act for him under his direction in the execution of the laws."[42] This power, Taft found, implies that the President has the "power of removing those for whom he cannot continue to be responsible."[43] As a result, congressional restrictions on the President's removal power were unconstitutional.

In dissent, Justice Louis Brandeis wrote that the removal power could not be "spelled out of the direction" in the Take Care Clause.[44] Justice Oliver Wendell Holmes similarly concluded that "[t]he duty of the President to see that the laws be executed is a duty that does not go beyond the laws or require him to achieve more than Congress sees fit to leave within his power."[45] But the Roberts Court followed Taft's view in removal decisions: "'The President cannot 'take Care that the Laws be faithfully executed' if he cannot oversee the faithfulness of the officers who execute them."[46]

The Court has also relied upon the Take Care Clause to support the principle that the President cannot make laws, but can only enforce them. In *Youngstown Sheet & Tube Co. v. Sawyer* (1952), several justices cited the duty of faithful execution to find that the President could not seize American steel mills during the Korean War.[47] Justice Hugo Black's majority opinion stated that "[i]n the framework of our Constitution, the President's power to see that the laws are faithfully executed refutes the idea that he is to be a lawmaker." Congress makes the laws and the President enforces them. Justice Robert Jackson's influential concurrence observed that the Take Care Clause signifies the "principle that ours is a government of laws, not of men, and that we submit ourselves to rulers only if under rules."[48] The Take Care Clause "allows the President to execute the laws, not make them."[49]

The Supreme Court has cited the Take Care Clause as the basis for prosecutorial discretion.[50] The clause also supports modern standing doctrine.[51] Unlike the executive, the judiciary lacks a roving commission to ensure faithful execution of the laws. But courts have yet to answer whether the Take Care Clause prohibits Presidents from using prosecutorial discretion to reduce the enforcement of a federal law to zero. President Barack Obama, for example, imposed two controversial immigration programs, Deferred Action for Childhood Arrivals (DACA) and Deferred Action for Parents of Americans and Lawful Permanent Residents (DAPA), that granted lawful presence to large classes of illegal aliens. Texas and other parties challenged these policies as a violation of the President's duty of faithful execution.[52] The plaintiffs claimed that DACA and DAPA amounted to unconstitutional suspensions of the law. The lower courts found that DAPA and DACA violated statutory law and so did not decide the constitutional question.[53] The Supreme Court also did not reach this issue.[54]

OPEN QUESTIONS

- What does "faithful" execution require?[55] Does it imply a duty of good faith,[56] or does it create some sort of fiduciary interest?[57]
- When does the President actually violate the Take Care Clause? Did President Lincoln violate the clause by suspending the writ of habeas corpus or by refusing to order the release of John Merryman?[58]
- Does the Take Care Clause provide a basis for the President's ability to impound, or decline to spend, appropriated funds?[59] Or does the clause restrict the ability of the President to impound funds?[60]
- Presidents have declined to enforce laws that they have determined are unconstitutional. Does the Take Care Clause prohibit the President from even determining whether a statute is unconstitutional?[61] Is the President's role limited to determining whether to sign or veto the bill? Does the Take Care Clause support the President's issuance of signing statements, which explain why part of a law may be unconstitutional?[62] Or is the President barred from executing a law he determines

is unconstitutional because doing so would violate the Take Care Clause and the Presidential Oath of Office?[63]
- Does the Take Care Clause provide a basis for presidential criminal immunity,[64] or does it reject the basis for such immunity?[65]

Cite as: John C. Yoo, *The Take Care Clause, in* The Heritage Guide to the Constitution 421 (Josh Blackman & John G. Malcolm eds., 3d ed. 2025).

Notes

1. Saikrishna Bangalore Prakash, Imperial from the Beginning: The Constitution of the Original Executive 84–99 (2015).   **2.** Jack Goldsmith & John F. Manning, *The Protean Take Care Clause,* 164 U. Pa. L. Rev. 1835, 1853 (2016).   **3.** Andrew Kent, Ethan J. Leib, & Jed Handelsman Shugerman, *Faithful Execution and Article II,* 132 Harv. L. Rev. 2111, 2142 (2019).   **4.** *Id.* at 2142.   **5.** 1 Blackstone 267.   **6.** The Bill of Rights, 1 W. & M., c. 2 (1689).   **7.** Penn's Charter of Libertie (Apr. 5, 1682), https://perma.cc/C4M3-HJV4.   **8.** Kent et al., *supra* at 2169.   **9.** *Id.* at 2173.   **10.** Va. Decl. of Rts. of 1776, § 7.   **11.** Pa. Const. of 1776, § 40, https://perma.cc/BF3N-GZRZ.   **12.** N.Y. Const. of 1777, § XIX, https://perma.cc/6F8G-TWV8.   **13.** 19 J. Cont. Cong. 44 (Jan. 10, 1781).   **14.** Art. II, § 1, cl. 8.   **15.** 1 Farrand's 63, 226, 230, 236.   **16.** 2 Farrand's 171.   **17.** *Id.* at 185.   **18.** *Id.* at 574.   **19.** *Id.* at 600, 660.   **20.** 2 Elliot's 513.   **21.** 4 Elliot's 136.   **22.** Storing 4.5.2.   **23.** *Id.*   **24.** Robert G. Natelson, *The Original Meaning of the Constitution's "Executive Vesting Clause,"* 31 Whitt. L. Rev. 1, 14 & n.59 (2009).   **25.** Letter from George Washington to Alexander Hamilton (Sept. 7, 1792), https://perma.cc/8CC5-JDL2.   **26.** Steven G. Calabresi & Saikrishna B. Prakash, *The President's Power to Execute the Laws,* 104 Yale L.J. 541, 641 (1994).   **27.** *Free Enter. Fund v. Pub. Co. Acct. Oversight Bd.,* 561 U.S. 477, 483 (2010) (quoting 30 Writings of George Washington 334 (J. Fitzpatrick ed., 1939)).   **28.** Address to Congress (July 4, 1861), *in* 2 Abraham Lincoln: Speeches and Writings 252 (1989).   **29.** 6 U.S. (2 Cranch) 170 (1804).   **30.** *Id.* at 177–78.   **31.** 30 U.S. 115, 122 (1831).   **32.** *Id.*   **33.** 37 U.S. (12 Pet.) 524 (1838).   **34.** *Id.* at 608.   **35.** *Id.* at 613.   **36.** *U.S. ex rel. Goodrich v. Guthrie,* 58 U.S. 284, 304 (1854); *United States v. Midwest Oil Co.,* 236 U.S. 459, 505 (1915).   **37.** *Ex parte Merryman,* 17 F. Cas. 144 (1861) (No. 9487) (Taney, C.J., Md., in chambers).   **38.** *Id.* at 149.   **39.** *Id.*   **40.** Seth Barrett Tillman, Ex parte Merryman: *Myth, History, and Scholarship,* 224 Mil. L. Rev. 481, 511–13 (2016); John Yoo, *Merryman, Milligan, and McCardle,* 12 Chapman L. Rev.

505 (2009).   **41.** *Merryman,* 17 F. Cas. at 153.   **42.** *Myers v. United States,* 272 U.S. 52, 117 (1926).   **43.** *Id.*   **44.** *Id.* at 246 (Brandeis, J., dissenting).   **45.** *Id.* at 295 (Holmes, J., dissenting).   **46.** *Free Enter. Fund,* 561 U.S. at 484; *Seila L. LLC v. Consumer Fin. Prot. Bureau,* 591 U.S. 197, 214 (2020).   **47.** *Youngstown Sheet & Tube Co. v. Sawyer,* 343 U.S. 579, 587 (1952).   **48.** *Id.* at 646 (Jackson, J., concurring).   **49.** *Medellin v. Texas,* 552 U.S. 491, 532 (2008).   **50.** *United States v. Armstrong,* 517 U.S. 456, 464 (1996); *Heckler v. Chaney,* 470 U.S. 821 (1985).   **51.** *Allen v. Wright,* 468 U.S. 737, 761 (1984).   **52.** Robert J. Delahunty & John C. Yoo, *Dream On: The Obama Administration's Nonenforcement of Immigration Laws, the DREAM Act, and the Take Care Clause,* 91 Tex. L. Rev. 781, 820 (2013); Josh Blackman, *The Constitutionality of DAPA Part II: Faithfully Executing the Law,* 19 Tex. Rev. L. & Pol. 215, 216 (2015).   **53.** *Texas v. United States,* 809 F.3d 134, 146 n.3 (5th Cir. 2015); *Texas v. United States,* 328 F. Supp. 3d 662, 712 (S.D. Tex. 2018).   **54.** *United States v. Texas,* 579 U.S. 547 (2016).   **55.** Zachary S. Price, *Enforcement Discretion and Executive Duty,* 67 Vand. L. Rev. 671 (2014).   **56.** Blackman, *supra* at 230.   **57.** Kent et al., *supra.*   **58.** John Yoo, *Lincoln and Habeas: Of Merryman and Milligan and McCardle,* 12 Chap. L. Rev. 505, 513 (2009); Seth Barrett Tillman, Merryman Redux: *A Response to Professor John Yoo,* 22 Chap. L. Rev. 1 (2019).   **59.** *Impounding Appropriated Funds,* Constitution Annotated, https://perma.cc/PK48-H3SZ.   **60.** Zachary S. Price, *Funding Restrictions and Separation of Powers,* 71 Vand. L. Rev. 357, 439 (2018).   **61.** Christopher N. May, Presidential Defiance of "Unconstitutional" Laws: Reviving the Royal Prerogative (1998).   **62.** Nelson Lund, *Presidential Signing Statements in Perspective,* 16 Wm. & Mary Bill Rts. J. 95 (2007).   **63.** Saikrishna B. Prakash, *The Executive's Duty to Disregard Unconstitutional Laws,* 96 Geo. L.J. 1613 (2008).   **64.** *Trump v. United States,* 603 U.S. 593, 626–27 (2024).   **65.** *Id.* at 673 (Sotomayor, J., dissenting); *id.* at 698 (Jackson, J., dissenting).

ESSAY NO. 116: THE COMMISSIONS CLAUSE
ART. II, § 3

[The President] shall Commission all the Officers of the United States.

—Robert Luther III

INTRODUCTION

The Constitution does not define "Commission," but it is well-described in Founding-era dictionaries. John Kersey's *Dictionarium Anglo-Britannicum* (1736) defines "Commission" as "a Warrant for an Office of Place; a Charge to buy, or to do any Act for another,"[1] and Samuel Johnson's *Dictionary of the English Language* (1755) defines it as "[a] trust; a warrant by which any trust is held, or authority exercised."[2] In short, a commission is some act taken by the President, or perhaps under his direction, that produces a written record or evidence of an appointment. Although occasionally overlooked or mistaken for a "trifling" duty,[3] it is a necessary final step in the appointment of a federal officer.[4]

Three primary legal issues are associated with commissions. First, who does the President commission? The text provides that the President "shall Commission all the Officers of the United States." Second, when does the President issue a commission? The President can commission a principal "Officer of the United States" only after the Senate provides advice and consent. Third, how does the President issue a commission? Traditionally, the President has signed a commission, though Congress can set the "final act" to complete the appointment.

HISTORY BEFORE 1787

The Executive's power to commission officers derives from the English tradition. In Britain, the monarchy controlled the entire appointment process.[5] The king appointed royal governors to rule the American colonies and listed their duties and powers in royal commissions.[6]

In the years following independence, the new national and state governments rejected British norms and experimented with decentralized methods of appointing officers.[7] The Pennsylvania constitution of 1776, for example, specified that "[a]ll commissions shall be in the name, and by the authority of the freemen of the commonwealth of Pennsylvania, sealed with the state seal, signed by the president or vice-president, and attested by the secretary; which seal shall be kept by the council."[8] In Massachusetts, militia officers were "commissioned by the governor, who shall determine their rank."[9]

The Articles of Confederation granted the national legislature the power to select certain civil officers,[10] but because Americans feared the consolidation of power in the central government, the Articles split the selection power of military officers between Congress and state legislatures.[11] Regardless of who made the selection, the Confederation Congress ultimately commissioned "all officers whatever in the service of the United States."[12]

THE CONSTITUTIONAL CONVENTION

During the Constitutional Convention, the delegates vigorously debated the appointment power,[13] but the Commissions Clause was not subject to much debate. The Committee of Detail listed the power to commission among the President's other powers.[14] On August 25, 1787, there was a proposal that would have allowed Congress to designate that the "Executive[s] of the several States shall have the power" to appoint and commission certain officers.[15] This proposal was defeated, and the language proposed by the Committee of Detail was adopted without alteration.

THE RATIFICATION DEBATES

The Commissions Clause was not controversial during the ratification debates. In Federalist No. 69, Alexander Hamilton observed that the Commissions Clause, a "power of the president, will resemble equally that of the king of Great Britain, and of the governor of New York."

THE COMMISSION PROCESS

The President is obligated to issue a commission to a broad category of positions: "*all* the Officers of the United States." This category clearly includes the principal and inferior "Officers of the United States" that the President appoints.[16] For example, on September 11, 1789, President Washington nominated Alexander Hamilton as Secretary of the Treasury.[17] The Senate confirmed Hamilton, and Washington promptly issued the commission.[18] Similarly, Washington nominated John Jay to serve as the first Chief Justice of the U.S. Supreme Court on September 24.[19] The Senate confirmed the nomination two days later, and Washington promptly signed and mailed Jay's commission.[20] From the outset of the Republic, the commissioning process was diligently executed.

Does the President also have an obligation

to commission the inferior "Officers of the United States" who are appointed by the "Courts of Law" or the "Heads of Departments"? The text would seem to suggest that the President would commission *all* of the "Officers of the United States"—principal and inferior—but there is evidence that some early inferior officers, such as the first clerk of the Supreme Court, did not receive presidential commissions.[21] In *Marbury v. Madison* (1803), Chief Justice John Marshall recognized that the Constitution "requires the President to commission all the officers of the United States" but observed that it "may never have been applied to officers appointed otherwise than by himself. . . ."[22] In modern times, the Justice Department's Office of Legal Counsel (OLC) has observed that "although the holder of an office usually receives a commission, that characteristic too, like an oath or pay, is incidental rather than essential."[23]

There is no evidence that the President has ever commissioned a member of Congress, and congressional precedent reveals that Representatives and Senators do not receive commissions.[24] Likewise, there is no evidence that the President has ever commissioned a Vice President, himself, or his successor. Professors Josh Blackman and Seth Barrett Tillman reach the sound conclusion that these elected officials are not "Officers of the United States" and therefore do not receive commissions.[25]

Finally, the Recess Appointments Clause provides that the President shall "grant Commissions" to recess appointees.[26] (See Essay No. 109.) Because the Senate does not provide consent for recess appointees, the commission is the sole act of appointment.

JUDICIAL PRECEDENT

Presidential appointment of a principal "Officer of the United States" is a three-step process: (1) The President submits a nomination to the Senate, (2) the Senate provides its advice and consent, and (3) the President appoints the officer.[27] This third step is concluded when the President signs the presidential commission. However, after the Senate confirms a nominee, the President retains the discretion to withhold the actual appointment.[28] An officer's appointment is complete only when the President signs the commission.[29]

In *Marbury*, the Supreme Court deferred to the President's authority to make appointments, but drew a clear line that cut off the President's discretion at the end of the three-step process.[30] Chief Justice John Marshall wrote that "[s]ome point of time must be taken when the power of the Executive over an officer, not removable at his will, must cease." Specifically, this "point of time must be when the constitutional power of appointment has been exercised." When the appointment is complete, the President forfeits his discretion over the nominee. Even the subsequent death of the President before delivery does not affect the appointment.[31]

In January 2022, Justice Stephen Breyer announced that he intended to retire "when the Court rises for the summer recess . . . assuming that by then my successor has been nominated and confirmed."[32] President Joseph Biden nominated Judge Ketanji Brown Jackson to the seat, and she was confirmed on April 7, 2022. Biden signed Jackson's commission on April 8, 2022, despite the fact that Justice Breyer was still serving.[33] The Office of Legal Counsel took the position that the President has "appointment authority at the time [a] vacancy is expected to arise" and therefore "may perform in advance the 'last act' in the three-step appointment process." As a result, OLC reasoned, the President may commission an officer well before the officer is actually appointed.[34] OLC identified "several examples of judges who were appointed by the President prior to the effective date of the outgoing official's resignation."[35] OLC's reasoning is unsound, but this issue has not been tested in the courts.

In *Marbury*, the law provided that a presidential commission for a Justice of the Peace "shall have been signed by the President of the United States."[36] Chief Justice Marshall concluded that "the last act required from the person possessing the power . . . is the signature of the commission."[37] Delivery of the signed commission was not required to make an appointment effective, nor was any overtly public act. In this case, President John Adams signed the commission appointing William Marbury as Justice of the Peace. Even though then-Secretary of State John Marshall failed to deliver the commission to Marbury, his appointment was still final. The Supreme Court reaffirmed this analysis in *United States v. Le Baron* (1856).[38]

In *Marbury*, Marshall as Chief Justice suggested that Congress could choose a different "final act," other than a signature. He wrote that Congress has the power to chart a "precise course accurately marked out by law" to complete the appointment and that the President "has no control" over this process.[39]

OPEN QUESTIONS

- As an original matter, is the appointment of an "Officer[] of the United States" absent a commission invalid? Would that appointment be saved by the *de facto* officer doctrine?[40]

- Can Congress by law "automatically" appoint an officer after the Senate provides advice and consent?[41]

- By what authority was Justice Jackson appointed to a seat that was not yet vacant? Did the United States briefly have a Supreme Court composed of ten active Justices? Federal law limits the Court to nine members.[42] Could Justice Breyer have withdrawn his retirement letter?

- Could a President preemptively nominate and commission replacements for each member of the Supreme Court and lower federal courts? Would "stockpiled commissions" effectively finalize an appointment as soon as a vacancy arises?

Cite as: Robert Luther III, *The Commissions Clause*, in THE HERITAGE GUIDE TO THE CONSTITUTION 425 (Josh Blackman & John G. Malcolm eds., 3d ed. 2025).

Notes

1. John Kersey, Dictionarium Britannicum (2nd ed., 1776), https://bit.ly/3SlQmZn. **2.** Samuel Johnson, 1 A Dictionary of the English Language (1755), https://bit.ly/3FdKfDb. **3.** *Youngstown Sheet & Tube Co. v. Sawyer*, 343 U.S. 579, 641 n.9 (1952) (Jackson, J., concurring). **4.** Appointment of a Senate-Confirmed Nominee, 23 Op. O.L.C. 232, 233 (1999). **5.** David Loades, Power in Tudor Britain 70–71 (1997). **6.** *Commission to Sir Edmund Andros as Governor of the Dominion of New England*, in English Historical Documents: American Colonial Documents to 1776, 239 (Merrill Jensen ed., 1955). **7.** Articles of Confederation, art. IX. **8.** Pa. Const. of 1776, § 21. **9.** Mass. Const. of 1780, art. X. **10.** Articles of Confederation, art. IX. **11.** *Id.* at arts. VII, IX. **12.** *Id.* at art. IX. **13.** Joseph P. Harris, *Debates on the Appointing Power in the Constitutional Convention*, in The Advice and Consent of the Senate 17 (1953). **14.** 2 Farrand's 146, 171. **15.** *Id.* at 420. **16.** Seth Barrett Tillman & Josh Blackman, *Offices and Officers of the Constitution, Part III: The Appointments, Impeachment, Commissions, and Oath or Affirmation Clauses*, 62 S. Tex. L. Rev. 349, 415–16 (2023). **17.** S. Exec. Jour., 1st Cong., 1st Sess. 25 (Sept. 11, 1789). **18.** Appointment [of Alexander Hamilton] as Secretary of the Treasury (Sept. 11, 1789), https://perma.cc/MS9GJQZ4. **19.** *John Jay, 1789–1795*, Supreme Court Historical Society, https://perma.cc/Q8PE-KZFF. **20.** Letter from George Washington to John Jay (Oct. 5, 1789), https://perma.cc/KRN7-FL6H. **21.** The Documentary History of the Supreme Court of the United States, 1789–1800, at 158–60 (Maeva Marcus & James R. Perry eds., 1985). **22.** *Marbury v. Madison*, 5 U.S. 137, 156 (1803). **23.** Officers of the United States Within the Meaning of the Appointments Clause, 31 Op. O.L.C. 122 (2007). **24.** Asher C. Hinds, 1 Hinds' Precedents of the House of Representatives of the United States § 547 (1907), https://perma.cc/5GN7-C5NQ; Case of Brigham H. Roberts, of Utah, H.R. Rep. No. 56-85, at 36 (1900). **25.** Tillman & Blackman, *supra* at 416–21; Josh Blackman & Seth Barrett Tillman, *Sweeping and Forcing the President into Section 3*, 28 Tex. Rev. L. & Pol. 350, 549 (2024). **26.** Art. II, § 2. **27.** Appointment of a Senate-Confirmed Nominee, *supra* at 232. **28.** 2 Story's Commentaries § 1546. **29.** Appointment of a Senate-Confirmed Nominee, *supra* at 232. **30.** 5 U.S. 137, 157 (1803). **31.** *United States v. Le Baron*, 60 U.S. 73, 78–79 (1856). **32.** Letter from Justice Stephen Breyer to President Joseph Biden (Jan. 27, 2022), https://perma.cc/FM25-H9HG. **33.** Ed Whelan, *KBJ Appointment Follies*, Natl. Rev. Bench Memo (Apr. 14, 2022, 8:07 AM), https://perma.cc/B2HU-5MBT. **34.** Authority of the President to Prospectively Appoint a Supreme Court Justice, 46 Op. O.L.C. __, 5 (Apr. 6, 2022). **35.** *Id.* at 4–5. **36.** *Marbury*, 5 U.S. at 155. **37.** *Id.* **38.** 60 U.S. at 78–79. **39.** *Id.* at 158, 140. **40.** *Nguyen v. United States*, 539 U.S. 69, 77 (2003) (quoting *Ryder v. United States*, 515 U.S. 177, 180 (1995)). **41.** *Dysart v. United States*, 369 F.3d 1303 (Fed. Cir. 2004). **42.** 28 U.S.C. § 1.

~

ESSAY NO. 117: THE IMPEACHMENT CLAUSE
ART. II, § 4

The President, Vice President and all civil Officers of the United States, shall be removed from Office on Impeachment for, and Conviction of, Treason, Bribery, or other high Crimes and Misdemeanors.

—Michael J. Gerhardt

INTRODUCTION

In American constitutional law, impeachment can refer to (1) bringing charges against certain officials for misconduct and (2) the entire process set forth in the Constitution. The Impeachment Clause itself answers two primary questions: Who can be impeached, and what are the offenses for which a covered official may be impeached and removed from office? The clause specifies that the "President, Vice President and all civil Officers of the United States" may be impeached. The conventional understanding is that this provision does not apply to members of Congress, members of the military, or appointed positions that are not "Officers of the United States." The clause also specifies three specific types of conduct that can lead to impeachment and removal from office: "Treason, Bribery, or other high Crimes and Misdemeanors." Treason and bribery are relatively straightforward in terms of their meaning. The third category, however, has proven to be the hardest to define. Nonetheless, virtually all scholars agree that the impeachment process was designed primarily as a last resort to address misconduct that is not redressable through ordinary legal proceedings, such as civil and criminal trials.

HISTORY BEFORE 1787

In England, any person, whether a governmental official or private citizen, could have been impeached by Parliament for any reason. The House of Commons had the authority by majority vote to charge anyone other than the king with misconduct, and the House of Lords had the power to hold trials and impose sanctions for that misconduct. There was no limit to the punishments that could be imposed, including death.

Generally, people could be impeached for "high crimes and misdemeanors." Sir William Blackstone traced the understanding of the terms "high crimes and misdemeanors" to the ancient or classical concept of treason, which distinguished "high" treason (disloyalty to a superior authority such as the state) from "petit" treason (disloyalty to an inferior).[1] Blackstone further defined "high crimes" as offenses such as "treason, murder, and bribery" that "strike at the very being of society" and the rule of law.[2] Blackstone explained that the "first and principal" "high misdemeanor" is "the *mal-administration* of such high officers, as are in public trust and employment."[3] He explained further that such "misprision"[4] was "usually punished by the method of parliamentary impeachment."[5] The punishments, though "short of death," were "inflicted, as . . . the house of peers shall seem proper" and usually consisted of "banishment, imprisonment, fines, or perpetual disability."[6] Professor Raoul Berger has suggested that the English practice treated "high crimes and misdemeanors" as a "category of political crimes against the state."[7]

The American colonies, not having laws expressly vesting them with the power of impeachment, adapted the English procedures and precedents to their particular circumstances. The power to hold officials accountable for their misconduct was generally manifested in the form of an indictment by the lower house for misconduct. This power was also exercised as an *address*, which was an appeal to the governor to initiate some action to redress the alleged wrongdoing.

After independence, state constitutions included mechanisms for impeaching certain kinds of misconduct. These processes generally limited impeachment to officeholders for particular official acts. Offenses were not limited to crimes or felonies but instead included abuses of power and breaches or dereliction of duty. In England, as noted, anyone other than the king could be impeached for any reason; In contrast, the states created a uniquely American system of impeachment.[8]

One such impeachment occurred in North Carolina. In 1785, some legislators initiated impeachment proceedings against the Superior Court justices, including Chief Justice Samuel Ashe.[9] The articles charged various misconduct, including partisan rulings against Loyalist interests, misappropriating funds, and abusing judicial power. After a brief investigation, the Committee of the Whole found insufficient evidence to proceed with the impeachments. In retrospect, the failed proceedings reaffirmed judicial independence from political reprisals.

The Articles of Confederation had no mechanism of impeachment. This omission was not surprising, because the Articles had not provided for a chief executive or Supreme Court. However, delegates to the national legislature could be recalled by their states.

THE CONSTITUTIONAL CONVENTION

The federal impeachment process in the Constitution derives from two sources, both of which were familiar to the constitutional and ratification convention delegates: experience in England, where Parliament had wielded the impeachment authority for centuries, and the federal impeachment process in the colonies and then the states.

Shortly after the Convention opened, the delegates agreed that the chief executive would be subject to impeachment. The debate would turn on who would wield the power of impeachment and on what grounds the executive could be impeached. On June 2, 1787, John Dickinson of Delaware proposed "that the Executive be made removeable by the National Legislature on the request of a majority of the Legislatures of individual States."[10] This proposal did not include any standards or grounds that would justify the Executive's removal. George Mason of Virginia warned that "making the Executive the mere creature of the

Legislature" would violate "the fundamental principle of good Government."[11] Dickinson's proposal was rejected with only Delaware voting in favor of its adoption.[12] On June 18, the Committee of the Whole House proposed a different standard: "The Governour[,] Senators and all officers of the United States to be liable to impeachment for mal [*sic*] — and corrupt conduct."[13] ("Governour" would eventually become "President.")

On July 19, Gouverneur Morris of Pennsylvania declared that vesting the national legislature with impeachment authority was "dangerous" because "[i]t will hold him in such dependence that he will be no check on the Legislature, will not be a firm guardian of the people and of the public interest."[14] Instead, "[h]e will be the tool of a faction, of some leading demagogue in the Legislature." The next day, the Convention considered the draft from the Committee of the Whole House with some variations: The Executive would be "removeable on impeachment and conviction for malpractice or neglect of duty."[15]

A lengthy debate ensued. Morris again expressed skepticism with respect to allowing the national legislature to remove the Executive. He argued that the Executive "can do no criminal act without Coadjutors who may be punished."[16] James Madison of Virginia thought "it indispensable that some provision should be made for defending the Community [against] the incapacity, negligence or perfidy of the chief Magistrate."[17] Mason conceded "impeachment" was essential and asked, "Shall any man be above Justice?" He then answered his own question, "Shall the man who has practised corruption & and by that means procured his appointment in the first instance, be suffered to escape punishment, by repeating his guilt?"[18] By the end of the debate, Morris admitted that his "opinion had been changed" and he was "now sensible of the necessity of impeachments."[19] The Convention adopted the Committee's proposal by a vote of 8 to 2.[20]

The delegates also discussed the appropriate grounds for impeaching and removing the Executive. William Davie of North Carolina cautioned his fellow delegates that if the President "be not impeachable whilst in office, he will spare no effort or means whatever to get himself re-elected."[21] Mason stressed the need to make the Executive impeachable because he was the man "who can commit the most extensive injustice."[22] Madison agreed that a "president might pervert his administration into a scheme of peculation [stealing public funds] or oppression" or that he might "betray his trust to foreign powers."[23] Edmund Randolph of Virginia added that a President "will have great opportunitys of abusing his power; particularly in time of war when the military force, and in some respects the public money will be in his hands."[24] Morris observed that the President "may be bribed by a greater interest to betray his trust; and no one would say that we ought to expose ourselves to the danger of seeing the first Magistrate in foreign pay."[25] Elbridge Gerry of Massachusetts speculated that a good president "will not fear" impeachments, but "a bad one ought to be kept in fear of them."[26]

"Malpractice or neglect of duty" remained the favored constitutional standard for impeachment until September. On September 4, the Committee of Eleven proposed new language: the Executive "shall be removed from his office on impeachment by the House of Representatives, and conviction by the Senate, for Treason, or bribery . . . ."[27] This clause would be debated four days later. Mason asked why the text was limited to "treason and bribery only." He thought that treason would "not reach many great and dangerous offences" and moved to add "maladministration" after "bribery."[28] Gerry seconded Mason's motion,[29] but Madison objected that "[s]o vague a term" as "maladministration" "will be equivalent to a tenure during pleasure of the Senate."[30] Mason agreed to withdraw the term "maladministration" and substituted (with Madison's approval) "other high crimes & misdemeanors,"[31] which Mason and other delegates recognized as borrowed from the English standard. The Convention approved the new language by a vote of 8 to 3.[32]

Four days later, on September 8, the Convention expanded the class of officials who would be subject to impeachment. Under the British system, virtually any citizens were impeachable, whether they held public offices or not. Instead, the Framers limited impeachment to a select number of government officials. Before September 8, the Impeachment Clause applied only to the President; on that day, however, a motion was made to add "[t]he vice-President and other Civil officers of the U. S." to the scope of the clause.[33] The motion was adopted unanimously.[34]

Ultimately, the delegates agreed on a multi-step process. First, the Constitution requires a majority vote of the House of Representatives to bring impeachment charges.[35] This feature tracked both the Parliamentary and many state legislative schemes that placed the authority, by majority vote, in the lower house to wield the power of impeachment. (See Essay No. 14.) Second, impeachment charges, or articles, are then tried before the Senate, and a two-thirds vote is required to convict.[36] (See Essay No. 20.) Third, the Constitution expressly bars the President's pardon power from being used "in cases of impeachment."[37] (See Essay No. 105.) Fourth, if an official is impeached by the House and convicted by the requisite vote in the Senate, then the Senate may take another vote to disqualify him from holding any future "Office of honor, Trust, or Profit under the United States."[38] (See Essay No. 118.)

THE RATIFICATION DEBATES

In Federalist No. 64, John Jay argued that the threat of impeachment would encourage executive officers to perform their duties with honor. Impeachment, he explained, would be used as a last resort to remove those who betray the interests of their country. The Framers specified particular grounds for impeachment in the Constitution because they wished to prevent impeachment from becoming a politicized offense. In England, the impeachment power had been used to sanction political disagreement as treason. Nonetheless, in Federalist No. 65, Alexander Hamilton warned that during impeachment proceedings, it would be difficult for Congress to act solely in the interests of the nation and resist political pressure to remove a popular official. The expectation was that the Senate, elected by the state legislatures, would have the requisite independence from popular majorities to try impeachments, and the supermajority vote would militate against purely partisan House impeachments supported only by a factional majority.

There was some debate about the meaning of "high crimes and misdemeanors." In

Federalist No. 65, Hamilton explained that impeachable conduct involves offenses that "proceed[] from the misconduct of public men, or in other words from the abuse or violation of some public trust." Such offenses are political because "they relate chiefly to injuries done immediately to the society itself." Hamilton's phrasing was reminiscent of Blackstone's explanation of "high" as referencing injuries to the state. Brutus, a prominent Anti-Federalist, wrote that the phrase has a limited definition: "[C]ivil officers, in which the judges are included, are removable only for crimes" and added that "[e]rrors in judgement, or want of capacity to discharge the duties of the office, can never be supposed to be included in these words, high crimes and misdemeanors."[39]

In sharp contrast, the examples of impeachable misconduct given by the constitutional and ratification convention delegates were not limited to indictable crimes. Many if not most abuses of power, such as lying to the Senate to secure ratification of a treaty, are not crimes. For example, at the North Carolina ratification convention, James Iredell observed that high crimes and misdemeanors involved misconduct "arising from acts of great injury to the community."[40] The future Supreme Court justice declared that the "President is of a very different nature from a monarch. He is to be . . . personally responsible for any abuse of the great trust reposed in him."[41]

In the South Carolina ratification convention, Charles Cotesworth Pinckney contended that impeachment would be available for federal officers who "behave amiss, or betray their public trust."[42] Also in South Carolina, Edward Rutledge stated that "[i]f the President or the senators abused their trust, they were liable to impeachment and punishment."[43]

During the Virginia ratification convention, George Mason and Edmund Randolph argued that Senators could be impeached.[44] However, James Monroe observed "that the Senators are not impeachable, and therefore Governor Randolph's objection falls to the ground. I am surprised that a man of that gentleman's abilities should have fallen into this mistake."[45] This issue would be tested again within a decade of ratification.

WHO MAY AND MAY NOT BE IMPEACHED

The President and the Vice-President are indisputably impeachable officials because the Constitution expressly makes them so. Similarly, "civil Officers of the United States" who are appointed pursuant to the Appointments Clause can be impeached. However, military officers, who also are appointed pursuant to the Appointments Clause, cannot be impeached. Justice Joseph Story observed that the phrase "civil Officers" in the Constitution "seems to be in contradistinction to *military*."[46] Military officers are subject to court martial. Since the beginning of the Republic, there have been debates about whether members of Congress could be impeached.

This issue arose in the first impeachment proceeding. On July 7, 1797, the House of Representatives initiated an impeachment inquiry against Senator William Blount of Tennessee, who was alleged to have conspired with the British to take control of southwest territory owned by Spain. This conspiracy would have violated both America's policy of neutrality in British–Spanish relations and the Neutrality Act.[47] The next day, the Senate expelled Blount by a vote of 25 to 1.[48] Nonetheless, the House proceeded to impeach Blount, marking the first time that the House of Representatives had formally impeached a federal official.

When the matter moved to the Senate, Blount's defense counsel argued that the Senate lacked jurisdiction over Blount's impeachment because he was no longer in office and because members of Congress, being elected officials rather than officials who had been appointed pursuant to the Appointments Clause, were not "civil Officers of the United States."[49] The debate focused largely on the question of whether Senators were impeachable officials. Ultimately, the Senate voted 14 to 11 to reject a resolution stating that "Blount was a civil officer of the United States within the meaning of the Constitution of the United States, and, therefore, liable to be impeached by the House of Representatives[.]"[50] The standard view of the Blount impeachment and trial proceedings is that the case was dismissed because Senators are not "officers of the United States." Since the

Blount proceedings, no member of Congress has been impeached.

CATEGORIES OF IMPEACHABLE OFFENSES

The Constitution lists three categories of impeachable offenses: "Treason, Bribery, or other high Crimes and Misdemeanors." It defines the crime of treason as "levying War against" the United States "or in adhering to their Enemies, giving them Aid and Comfort." (See Essay No. 137.) Blackstone defined treason as "betraying, treachery, or breach of faith."[51] He explained that treason against the king was the "highest civil crime," which was regarded as "high treason."[52] Petty treason entailed subordinates' betrayals of the trust placed in them. Before ratification of the Constitution, the American common law in the states adopted a similar understanding of bribery. The first federal bribery statute was passed as part of the Crimes Act of 1790.[53]

The Constitution then lists a category apart from treason and bribery: "other high Crimes and Misdemeanors." This category has proved to be the most difficult to define. The historical record of impeachment in England, which furnished the term "high crimes and misdemeanors," does not support a limited interpretation. Rather, during the eighteenth century, "misdemeanor" meant "misdeeds" or violation of a public law rather than petty crimes as it now does.[54] The Constitution's text refers to "crimes" and "misdemeanors," but these terms, in context, are preceded by the term "high." Thus, "other high crimes and misdemeanors" must be on the same level of seriousness and magnitude as "treason" and "bribery," which are listed immediately before them.

Story acknowledged that impeachable offenses are "of a political nature." He explained that "it is impossible to fix any exact grade, or measure, either in the offences, or the punishments." Rather, "a very large discretion must unavoidably be vested in the court of impeachments." Story added that "[a]ny attempt to define the offences . . . would probably tend to more injustice and inconvenience, than it would correct; and perhaps would render the power at once inefficient and unwieldy."[55] Nonetheless, Story asserted that impeachable offenses were

likely "[s]uch kind of misdeeds . . . as peculiarly injure the commonwealth by the abuse of high offices of trust" and suggested that such offenses "were the most usual grounds for this kind of prosecution in parliament."[56]

There may also be a pragmatic standard for an impeachable offense. In 1970, then-Representative Gerald Ford of Michigan initiated an ultimately unsuccessful attempt to impeach Supreme Court Justice William O. Douglas. Ford contended that "high crimes and misdemeanors" were "whatever a majority of the House of Representatives considers them to be at a given moment in history." Thus, the House has the "sole" responsibility to define "other high crimes and misdemeanors."[57] The federal courts have treated appeals from impeachment convictions as not subject to judicial review,[58] but even if the courts cannot resolve these matters, there still may be appropriate standards for Congress to follow.

There have been twenty-two impeachments in the House and eight convictions in the Senate.[59] The most prominent impeachment trials were against Supreme Court Justice Samuel Chase and Presidents Andrew Johnson, Bill Clinton, and Donald Trump (twice). In each of these trials, Congress grappled with defining the grounds for impeachment, but none of them resulted in removals from office.

Perhaps not surprisingly, Presidents facing serious threat of impeachment in the House have interpreted the scope of impeachable offenses narrowly, thus making it harder for them to be impeached. By contrast, the House has pushed for broader constructions of the permissible range. In all cases, impeachment proceedings have turned on the gravity of the offense, its context, and the political composition of Congress. However, because neither the House nor the Senate is bound by either chamber's prior judgments in impeachment proceedings, the past is at most a guide, not a prediction or rule, for the future of impeachment in the United States.

THE IMPEACHMENT OF SAMUEL CHASE

One of the most serious impeachment proceedings after Blount's acquittal involved Samuel Chase. President George Washington had been warned about Chase's mercurial behavior before appointing him to the U.S. Supreme Court in 1796, and Chase had written the President that, if appointed, he would do nothing to embarrass the Administration.[60] In his early years on the Court, Chase kept his pledge and rendered several decisions clarifying the powers of the national government.[61]

When President John Adams sought reelection in 1800, his leading opponent was Vice President Thomas Jefferson. Chase took the unprecedented step of openly campaigning for Adams—a rare move for sitting judges even then—and soon earned the ire of Jefferson's emerging Republican Party.

In 1803, Chase continued his brazen conduct. In Baltimore federal court, while sitting as a circuit justice, Chase lamented the Jeffersonian restructuring of the federal judiciary. He also criticized the Jeffersonians in Maryland who abolished a state court and established universal male suffrage. Jefferson and his associates believed that to have a federal judge publicly articulating such views was harmful to the government. The Republicans decided to initiate impeachment proceedings against Chase.

The attempt to impeach Chase was part of a broader Jeffersonian assault on the judiciary. None of the eight impeachment articles approved in the House charged Chase with any criminal conduct.[62] Rather, they charged that Chase's legal rulings were simply not in accordance with the Jeffersonian theory of how trials should be conducted or how juries should function. However, there was substantial legal precedent behind each of Chase's rulings. He may have been guilty of having a hair-trigger temper, but it was clear that removing him would seriously—perhaps permanently—compromise the independence of the federal judiciary. The requisite two-thirds of the Senate could not be cobbled together to remove Chase. In fact, members of Jefferson's own party voted for acquittal, which came to be understood as a bar to removing a Supreme Court justice because of his political views.

There have been several subsequent attempts to bring impeachment proceedings against several Justices, but the House has impeached none. However, as discussed below, eight lower-court federal judges have been impeached, convicted, and removed, most of whom committed traditional crimes such as bribery.

THE IMPEACHMENT OF ANDREW JOHNSON

In 1865, Andrew Johnson succeeded to the presidency following Abraham Lincoln's assassination and became immensely unpopular. The radical Republicans recoiled at Johnson's hostility to their plans to protect the newly freed slaves. Congress enacted the Tenure of Office Act, which prohibited the firing of Cabinet officials without the Senate's consent. Despite this law, Johnson unilaterally fired Secretary of War Edwin Stanton.

On February 24, 1868, the House of Representatives impeached Johnson, making him the first President to be impeached.[63] In early March, the House approved eleven articles of impeachment against Johnson including one that charged him with violating the Tenure of Office Act. Johnson claimed the law was unconstitutional because it undermined the independence of the executive. Johnson contended that Article II of the Constitution granted him the power to control his subordinates to ensure that the Administration implemented his priorities. The Senate fell one vote short of convicting Johnson.

Myers v. United States (1926) declared unconstitutional a law similar to the Tenure of Office Act.[64] This decision provided at least some vindication for Johnson's defense. Johnson's acquittal, combined with *Myers*, has come to be widely understood as upholding the proposition that the impeachment power may not be used to sanction Presidents for having policy differences with Congress.

THE IMPEACHMENT OF WILLIAM JEFFERSON CLINTON

In 1994, Kenneth Starr was appointed as Independent Counsel to investigate possible criminal activity on the part of then-Governor Clinton in a failed land scheme.[65] Starr uncovered evidence that Clinton had lied during a deposition in a civil case. Starr questioned Clinton about the same matter before a grand jury, making Clinton the first President to testify as the subject before a grand jury. Starr issued a lengthy referral to Congress detailing what he contended were several impeachable offenses committed by Clinton.

Based on the referral, the House of Representatives approved two articles of impeachment against Clinton in December 1998. He thus became the second American President to be impeached. One article charged Clinton with committing perjury in his testimony before the grand jury, and the other charged him with obstruction of justice based on his efforts to hide evidence pertaining to the false testimony. The vote in the House was largely along party lines. Republicans argued that perjury and obstruction of justice were serious felonies that undermined the integrity of the administration of justice. Democrats responded that Clinton's indiscretions were not impeachable because they were minor and unrelated to the performance of his duties as President. The Senate acquitted Clinton, almost entirely by a straight party-line vote.

THE IMPEACHMENTS OF DONALD TRUMP

President Donald Trump faced two impeachment proceedings during his first term in office. In 2019, an impeachment inquiry began after Trump allegedly requested a "favor" from Ukraine's President.[66] The House impeached Trump largely on a party-line vote for abuse of power and obstruction of Congress. Neither charge was a criminal offense.

During the Senate trial, there was some debate about whether "abuse of power" was "a high crime or misdemeanor" for impeachment purposes.[67] Trump's counsel argued that only statutory offenses in the U.S. Code could count as "high crimes or misdemeanors."[68] His lawyers argued that the codification of felonies would give the President clear notice of the misconduct for which he could be impeached and would clearly establish the grounds for impeachment, and there was no statutory offense for "abuse of power." House Managers responded that abuse of power was the most common example of an impeachable offense cited during the Constitutional and Ratification Conventions.[69] The House prosecutors further explained that abuse of power was clearly illegal because it was a breach of, or deviation from, the Constitution's limits on executive power.

After the Senate trial, Trump was acquitted by a nearly party-line vote.

Trump's second impeachment proceeding began during his last few days in office. On January 6, 2021, hundreds of President Trump's supporters stormed the U.S. Capitol. One week later, on January 13, the House voted to impeach Trump for incitement of insurrection.[70] This charge did involve a criminal offense. At the time, the Senate was holding a series of pro forma sessions, and outgoing Republican Majority Leader Mitch McConnell of Kentucky said that he would not ask Senators to return without the unanimous consent of the Senate. Without such consent, the Senate was not in a position to begin the impeachment trial until January 20, the day of President Joe Biden's inauguration. At that time, a new Democratic majority led by Senator Charles Schumer of New York took control of the Senate.

When the Senate trial began on February 9, Trump was already out of office. There was some question whether an impeachment trial could be held for a former official. Chief Justice John Roberts declined to preside over this proceeding, as did newly sworn Vice President Kamala Harris.[71] The Senate voted 55 to 45 to accept jurisdiction over Trump's second impeachment trial.

On February 13, fifty-seven Senators voted to convict Trump—ten votes short of the two-thirds required for conviction and removal.

Trump's and Clinton's acquittals illustrate the extreme difficulty of mustering supermajority support for conviction and removal in the Senate as long as the members of the President's political party remain largely, if not wholly, united in opposition to the effort.

THE POTENTIAL IMPEACHMENT OF RICHARD NIXON

In 1972, President Richard M. Nixon won reelection by a landslide. However, the Democratic National Headquarters at the Watergate Hotel had been burglarized on June 17, and as evidence of Nixon's involvement in the cover-up mounted, his presidency unraveled. Some of the evidence came from Nixon's tape-recording system in the Oval Office.

On July 24, 1974, the Supreme Court decided *United States v. Nixon*.[72] In this case, the criminal defendants had issued a subpoena to President Nixon for the tapes. The Court unanimously ordered Nixon to comply with the subpoena and turn the tapes of White House conversations over to the defendants. Nixon largely complied with the order but refused to provide four of the most incriminating tapes to the House Judiciary Committee, which was considering his impeachment.[73]

On July 30, the House Judiciary Committee approved three articles of impeachment against Nixon.[74] The first article was for obstruction of justice by covering up the Watergate burglary. The second was for abuse of power. Nixon was alleged to have ordered the heads of various agencies to harass his political enemies. The third was for contempt of Congress. Nixon was charged with refusing to comply with four legislative subpoenas. On August 8, 1974, Nixon resigned from office before the full House had the opportunity to consider and vote on the proposed articles of impeachment. His resignation brought an end to the impeachment proceedings against him in the House.

At the time, some scholars argued that the actual commission of a crime was necessary to serve as a basis for an impeachment proceeding.[75] Others argued that it was not required. However, since Nixon resigned, these theories were never tested. Had Nixon remained in office, it is widely believed that he likely would have faced impeachment, conviction, and removal from office.

IMPEACHMENT FOR CRIMINAL AND NON-CRIMINAL OFFENSES

It is generally accepted that not all impeachable offenses are actual crimes or felonies and not all crimes or felonies are impeachable offenses. For example, jaywalking is a crime, but it is not as seriously injurious to the Republic as treason or bribery. Conversely, ordering department heads to harass a President's political enemies is a serious abuse of power, but it is not a criminal offense.

The Senate has convicted several judges for engaging in criminal misconduct.[76] For example, in 1986, Judge Harry Claiborne was

convicted for income tax fraud; in 1988, Judge Walter Nixon was convicted for perjury before a federal grand jury; and in 1989, Judge Alcee Hastings was convicted for perjury and bribery. (The Senate did not vote to disqualify Hastings, who was later elected to the House of Representatives.) Several other officials were impeached by the House for criminal misconduct but were acquitted by the Senate. In 1876, Secretary of War William Belknap was acquitted on charges of bribery.[77] (Belknap had resigned moments before he was impeached, but the Senate voted to retain jurisdiction over his impeachment.)

The Senate has also convicted several judges for non-criminal offenses. In 1936, Judge Halsted Ritter was impeached on several grounds, including embezzlement and tax evasion,[78] but he was convicted only on one non-criminal article: engaging in misconduct that brought the "judiciary into disrepute." Ritter later challenged his conviction in the Court of Claims, arguing that the Senate could not convict him solely for this non-criminal offense. That court found that it lacked jurisdiction to review a Senate conviction.[79] After the Civil War began, Judge West Hughes Humphreys left his federal judgeship without resigning and joined the Confederacy.[80] In 1861, he was impeached, convicted, removed, and disqualified for violating his oath of office.[81]

Only one official has been impeached and convicted based on misconduct before entering his office: Judge Thomas Porteous. Before joining the bench, Porteous had a "corrupt relation" with a law firm. During his background check, he failed to disclose both criminal conduct in which he had engaged before his nomination as a judge and the potential for blackmail. Porteous was impeached for making false statements to the Senate and the FBI, as well as for corrupt conduct.[82] The false statements he made on his paperwork for his judicial appointment provided a connection between his past misconduct and his federal office. In 2010, the Senate convicted and removed Porteous. It then voted separately to disqualify Porteous from holding future federal office.[83]

OPEN QUESTIONS

- How should the outcome of the Blount impeachment trial be understood? As an original matter, can a member of Congress be impeached?[84]

- At what point is an official impeached? Is he impeached when the House approves articles of impeachment or when the articles of impeachment are delivered to the Senate?[85]

- In December 1998, President Clinton was impeached by the lame-duck House at the end of the 105th Congress. He was tried by the Senate in the 106th Congress. At the time, it was argued that the articles of impeachment expired with the end of the 105th Congress?[86] Was this position correct?

- The second Trump impeachment followed the precedent established in the Belknap trial, but it did not clarify the answers to every conceivable instance of post-presidential impeachment.[87] Obviously, a private citizen who has never worked for the federal government can never be impeached, but can an official be convicted and disqualified (a) if the misconduct occurred while the official was in office but the official is out of office when the House approves articles of impeachment; (b) if the official is in office when the House approves articles of impeachment but leaves office before the articles are delivered to the Senate (this is similar to the Belknap trial and Trump's second trial); (c) if the official is in office when the articles are delivered to the Senate but leaves office before the Senate trial begins; (d) if the official is in office before the Senate trial begins but leaves office before the Senate votes to convict; (e) if the official is out of office before the Senate begins its trial; or (f) if the official is in office when the Senate votes to convict but is out of office before the Senate votes to disqualify?

- To what extent, if any, may someone be impeached for misconduct that was not known when he or she was appointed or elected to an office covered by the Impeachment Clause?

- To what extent, if any, may someone be impeached for misconduct that was known when he or she was elected or appointed to an office covered by the Impeachment Clause?

Cite as: Michael J. Gerhardt, *The Impeachment Clause, in* THE HERITAGE GUIDE TO THE CONSTITUTION 429 (Josh Blackman & John G. Malcolm eds., 3d ed. 2025).

Notes

1. 4 Blackstone 75.   **2.** 4 Blackstone 5.   **3.** 4 Blackstone 121.   **4.** *Id.*   **5.** *Id.*   **6.** *Id.*   **7.** Raoul Berger, Impeachment: The Constitutional Problems 64 (1974).   **8.** Peter Charles Hoffer & N.E.H. Hull, Impeachment in America, 1635–1805, at 96–106 (1984).   **9.** *Id.* at 89–90.   **10.** 1 Farrand's 85.   **11.** *Id.* at 86.   **12.** *Id.* at 87.   **13.** *Id.* at 292.   **14.** 2 Farrand's 53.   **15.** *Id.* at 61.   **16.** *Id.* at 64.   **17.** *Id.* at 65.   **18.** *Id.*   **19.** *Id.* at 68.   **20.** *Id.* at 69.   **21.** *Id.* at 64.   **22.** *Id.* at 65.   **23.** *Id.* at 65–66.   **24.** *Id.* at 67.   **25.** *Id.* at 68.   **26.** Id. at 66.   **27.** *Id.* at 499.   **28.** *Id.* at 550.   **29.** *Id.*   **30.** *Id.*   **31.** *Id.*   **32.** *Id.*   **33.** *Id.* at 552.   **34.** *Id.*   **35.** Art. I, § 2, cl. 5.   **36.** Art. I, § 3, cl. 6.   **37.** Art. I, § 2, cl. 1.   **38.** Art. I, § 3, cl. 7.   **39.** Storing 2.9.192.   **40.** 4 Elliot's 113.   **41.** *Id.* at 74.   **42.** *Id.* at 281.   **43.** *Id.* at 276.   **44.** 3 Elliot's 202, 402, 484, 486.   **45.** James Monroe writing as A Native of Virginia, Observations on the Proposed Plan of Federal Government 17 (1788), https://perma.cc/76RP-AGND.   **46.** 2 Story's Commentaries § 789.   **47.** 7 Annals of Cong. 459–62 (1797); Buckner F. Melton, Jr., The First Impeachment: The Constitution's Framers and the Case of Senator William Blount, app. 3 (1999).   **48.** 7 Annals of Cong. 43–44 (1797).   **49.** Proceedings on the Impeachment of William Blount, A Senator of the United States from the State of Tennessee, for High Crimes and Misdemeanors 70 (Philadelphia, Joseph Gales 1799).   **50.** 8 Annals of Cong. 2318 (1799).   **51.** 4 Blackstone 75.   **52.** 4 Blackstone 76.   **53.** Crimes Act of 1790, ch. 9, 1 Stat. 112.   **54.** 4 Blackstone 5.   **55.** 2 Story's Commentaries § 783.   **56.** *Id.* at § 788.   **57.** News release, Off. of Rep. Gerald R. Ford, Remarks by Rep. Gerald R. Ford (R–Mich.), Republican Leader, Prepared for Delivery on the Floor of the U.S. House of Representatives on April 15, 1970, https://perma.cc/G9PF-MZSW.   **58.** *Walter Nixon v. United States,* 506 U.S. 224 (1993).   **59.** *List of Individuals Impeached by the House of Representatives,* U.S. House of Representatives: History, Art & Archives, https://perma.cc/X7NN-TMX8.   **60.** Hoffer & Hull, *supra* at 228–63.   **61.** *Id.*   **62.** *Impeachment Trial of Justice Samuel Chase,*

1804–05, U.S. Senate, https://perma.cc/MT23-5CDX. **63.** Impeachment Trial of President Andrew Johnson, 1868, U.S. Senate, https://perma.cc/6ETZ-VL5F. **64.** 272 U.S. 52 (1926). **65.** Russell Riley, *The Clinton Impeachment and Its Fallout*, Miller Center, https://perma.cc/PV28-P4VV. **66.** Michael J. Gerhardt, The Law of Presidential Impeachment: A Guide for the Engaged Citizen 114 (2024). **67.** Victoria F. Nourse, The Impeachments of Donald Trump: An Introduction to Constitutional Interpretation 71–82 (2021). **68.** *Id*. at 78–80. **69.** *Id*. at 86–89. **70.** *Id*. at 189. **71.** Joan Biskupic, *John Roberts Ducks the Spotlight by Skipping the Second Trump Impeachment Trial*, CNN (Jan. 26, 2021), https://perma.cc/E3XM-EKQT. **72.** 418 U.S. 683 (1974). **73.** Gerhardt, *supra* ch. 3. **74.** *Articles of Impeachment Adopted by the House of Representatives Committee on the Judiciary*, The American Presidency Project (July 27, 1874), https://perma.cc/6DY6-SGWG. **75.** Berger, *supra*. **76.** *Impeachments of Federal Judges*, Federal Judicial Center, https://perma.cc/SBC8-DYQM. **77.** Impeachment Trial of Secretary of War William Belknap, 1876, U.S. Senate, https://perma.cc/J87H-DN4U. **78.** 3 Deschler's Precedents, ch. 14, § 18, 2205–46, https://perma.cc/5HGV-LZPG. **79.** *Ritter v. United States*, 84 Ct. Cl. 293 (1936). **80.** Kaitlin E. O'Brien & Ian Binnington, West H. Humphreys: A Civil War Impeachment, https://perma.cc/MD9L-562Z. **81.** 3 Hinds' Precedents §§ 2385–97. **82.** H. Rpt. 111-427 (2010), https://perma.cc/UV5W-UVNS. **83.** Ben Evans, *Senate Convicts Federal Judge, Removing Him from Office*, Wash. Times (Dec. 8, 2010). **84.** Seth Barrett Tillman & Josh Blackman, *Offices and Officers of the Constitution, Part III: The Appointments, Impeachment, Commissions, and Oath or Affirmation Clauses*, 62 S. Tex. L. Rev. 349, 403–410. **85.** Adam Liptak, *A Law Professor's Provocative Argument: Trump Has Not Yet Been Impeached*, N.Y. Times (Dec. 30, 2019), https://perma.cc/8W7D-7V8J. **86.** Bruce Ackerman, The Case Against Lameduck Impeachment 9–14 (1999). **87.** Brian Kalt, *The Constitutional Case for the Impeachability of Former Federal Officials: An Analysis of the Law, History, and Practice of Late Impeachment*, 6 Tex. Rev. L. & Pol. 13 (2001).

PART 3

ARTICLE III

ESSAY NO. 118: THE JUDICIAL VESTING CLAUSE
ART. III, § 1

The judicial Power of the United States shall be vested in one supreme Court, and in such inferior Courts as the Congress may from time to time ordain and establish.

—Judge Britt C. Grant & John Acton

INTRODUCTION

For many years, the federal judiciary has had a three-tiered structure: district courts, courts of appeals, and the Supreme Court. To a lawyer or court watcher, this structure might seem inevitable. But the question of whether the United States would have federal courts at all was contested at the Founding. And even today, the U.S. Supreme Court is the only constitutionally required federal court; the Constitution's text leaves the rest of the details to Congress.

HISTORY BEFORE 1787

The Articles of Confederation contained only narrow grants of judicial power, instead authorizing limited tribunals for specific types of controversies and specifying that members of Congress could not be appointed to any of these courts.[1] The Articles authorized Congress to create one national court—the Court of Appeals in Cases of Capture, which dealt with the capture of enemy ships and cargo.[2] But that body was not truly independent from Congress, which both constrained the court's powers and interfered in its disposition of particular cases.[3]

Beyond this single, limited court, the Articles authorized Congress to resolve disputes through two types of ad hoc tribunals. First, Congress could "appoint" state courts to adjudicate piracies and felonies committed on the high seas, but because these tribunals obviously depended on the state courts' cooperation, they were not independent federal entities.[4] Second, the Articles authorized ad hoc tribunals to handle disputes between the states, with the judges selected either by Congress or by the consent of the parties.[5] Even that process was used only once.[6] All in all, it became clear that these "courts" lacked the necessary independence and scope of authority to ensure that federal law was followed throughout the country.[7]

THE CONSTITUTIONAL CONVENTION

Delegates to the Constitutional Convention widely agreed that the United States needed a national judicial power, including a Supreme Court.[8] But the decision to create lower federal courts became fraught with controversy.

The Convention initially, and unanimously, approved a clause specifying that the national judiciary would "consist of One supreme tribunal, and of one or more inferior tribunals."[9] But that unanimity did not last—the next day, John Rutledge of South Carolina moved to reconsider the establishment of inferior tribunals.[10] He argued that Supreme Court review of state court decisions would ensure national uniformity in federal law and that the lower federal courts would encroach on the states' authority.[11] James Madison of Virginia countered that Rutledge's approach would create too many appeals to the Supreme Court.[12] Madison added that a Supreme Court with only appellate jurisdiction would be insufficient to root out systematic biases in the state judicial systems.[13] In a closely divided vote, the Convention agreed with Rutledge.[14]

Madison, together with James Wilson of Pennsylvania, immediately responded with a compromise proposal allowing, but not requiring, Congress to establish inferior federal courts.[15] Even giving Congress that option was controversial, but this "Madisonian compromise" had staying power. It won a divided vote and survived a final push to eliminate lower federal courts entirely.[16] The Committee on Style wrote the final language of the Judicial Vesting Clause that was ratified.[17]

THE RATIFICATION DEBATES

During ratification, the inferior federal courts were just as controversial as Rutledge and other delegates had predicted. In fact, the Anti-Federalist Brutus latched on to the issue in his very first essay against the Constitution. He warned that lower federal courts would "eclipse the dignity, and take away from the respectability, of the state courts."[18]

Brutus showed an even greater hostility toward the Supreme Court, warning that the judges on the Supreme Court would "not confine themselves to any fixed or established rules" when interpreting the Constitution, but instead follow what they viewed as "the reason and spirit of the constitution."[19] Brutus also drew a negative contrast between the proposed Constitution, in which legislative appeals were unavailable, and the English system, in which judicial decisions could be modified by the House of Lords. This unchecked judicial authority, he said, would encourage a complete consolidation of power in the federal government at the expense of the states.[20]

In Federalist No. 81, Alexander Hamilton directly addressed Brutus's criticisms, assuring his readers that there was "not a syllable" in the Constitution "which *directly* empowers national courts to construe the laws according to the spirit of the constitution" or "gives them any greater latitude in this respect, than the court of every state." And in Federalist No. 78, Hamilton praised the "wisdom" of separating the judiciary and the legislature: "liberty can have nothing to fear from the judiciary alone, but would have everything to fear from its union with either of the other departments." Hamilton further reasoned that, because federal judges "should be bound down by strict rules and precedents, which serve to define and point out their duty in every particular case that comes before them," the judiciary would be a relatively weak branch. He also reminded his readers that while the legislature could always impeach judges, judges did not have the same authority over legislators. Meanwhile, Hamilton reiterated Madison's concern that federal courts were necessary because state judges would be "too little independent" from the state legislatures to "be relied upon for an inflexible execution of the national laws."

EARLY FEDERAL JUDICIARY

Following the Constitution's ratification, the First Congress made the federal judiciary a reality when it enacted the Judiciary Act of 1789.[21] The Act set the Supreme Court at six Justices.[22] Congress also took the nationalist side of the Madisonian compromise, exercising its discretion to create lower federal courts.[23]

The structure of the original lower courts was convoluted. There were "district courts" not unlike today's district courts with individual judges presiding over cases.[24] But "the circuit courts" (Eastern, Middle, and Southern) did not have their own judges; instead, they had three-judge panels made up of one district court judge and two Supreme Court Justices.[25] Their caseload was also a mix because they both reviewed district court decisions and sat as trial courts in the first instance.[26] Defenders of this system thought that having Supreme Court Justices "ride circuit" would save money, keep the Court connected to the day-to-day administration of justice, and expose the whole country to America's most distinguished jurists.[27] But the Justices hated being, in the words of Justice James Iredell, "traveling postboys."[28]

According to Madison's Convention notes, it was "generally supposed" that the federal courts' jurisdiction "was constructively limited to cases of a Judiciary nature."[29] Hamilton famously opined in Federalist No. 78 that the judiciary "may truly be said to have neither Force nor Will, but merely judgment." But many practical questions about what judges and courts can and cannot do remained unanswered.

One example arose in 1793 when Secretary of State Thomas Jefferson asked the Supreme Court for its opinion on twenty-nine specific questions of law relating to United States–France relations and port management. He noted that the questions were "often presented under circumstances which do not give a cognizance of them to the tribunal of the country" and that President Washington "would . . . be much relieved" if the Court would answer them.[30]

This might sound like a reasonable request. After all, would it not be better if the President could ensure that he is following the law before taking action? But Chief Justice John Jay and his colleagues wrote to President Washington that the judicial power did not extend to "extrajudicially deciding the questions alluded to."[31] This refusal is an early example of modern *justiciability* doctrines—rules that federal courts use to ensure that they are exercising the judicial power rather than some sort of extrajudicial authority. Similar doctrines include *standing*, which broadly speaking refers to whether the parties have enough of a stake to be before the court; *mootness*, which asks whether there is still a live case to decide; and so-called *political questions*, which are issues that, although they may arise in litigation, are better decided by the political branches.

THE ROAD TO THE MODERN FEDERAL JUDICIARY

As the country expanded westward, Congress created new circuits, and as the number of circuits increased, Congress established new Justices to ride those circuits. By 1869, Congress settled on nine Justices, and the Court has had nine Justices ever since.[32] In 1891, Congress created the modern federal intermediate circuit courts of appeals and made circuit riding optional for Justices.[33] The original "circuit courts" were formally retired in 1911.[34]

As the population continued to grow and caseloads increased, Congress expanded federal jurisdiction and increased the number of district and circuit judges.[35] Today, federal district courts hear hundreds of thousands of cases every year.[36] These cases can either be civil or criminal and are generally heard by a single judge.[37] The federal circuit courts of appeals, in turn, hear tens of thousands of appeals from district court decisions, considering both factual findings and legal determinations, albeit under different standards of review.[38] Twelve separate courts of appeals cover twelve different regions, or "circuits," across the United States and decide most appeals in three-judge panels.[39] A subset of cases including patent appeals are consolidated in the Federal Circuit.[40]

At the top, the Supreme Court uses, for the most part, a discretionary process called certiorari to hear a comparatively small number of cases from the courts of appeals each year.[41] These cases usually involve issues of particular national importance or questions of federal law that have divided lower courts.[42] In addition, because it is the only federal court whose decisions have precedential effect in state courts, the Supreme Court plays a special role in ensuring the nationwide uniformity of federal law.

OPEN QUESTIONS

- Does the "judicial power" include the power to strike down or set aside laws?
- Does the "judicial power" include the doctrine of stare decisis?
- When does adjudication of controversies by Article II federal agencies infringe on the Article III judicial power?
- Are judicial concurrences that opine on matters beyond those presented by the case at issue consistent with the judicial power?

Cite as: Judge Britt C. Grant & John Acton, *The Judicial Vesting Clause, in* The Heritage Guide to the Constitution 440 (Josh Blackman & John G. Malcolm eds., 3d ed. 2025).

Notes

1. Articles of Confederation, art. IX, § 1. **2.** *Id.* **3.** Richard H. Fallon, Jr., et al., Hart and Wechsler's The Federal Courts and the Federal System 8 n.36 (7th ed., 2015). **4.** Articles of Confederation, art. IX, § 1; Hart & Wechsler, *supra* at 6 & n.35. **5.** Articles of Confederation, art. IX, § 2. **6.** Hart & Wechsler, *supra* at 8 n.34. **7.** Hart & Wechsler, *supra* at 7–8. **8.** 1 Farrand's 95, 104; Hart & Wechsler, *supra* at 6; *id.* at 7 & n.38. **9.** 1 Farrand's 95, 104. **10.** *Id.* at 124. **11.** *Id.* **12.** *Id.* **13.** *Id.* **14.** *Id.* **15.** *Id.* **16.** Hart & Wechsler, *supra* at 7 n.39, 7–8; 2 Farrand's 45–46. **17.** Hart & Wechsler, *supra* at 9. **18.** Storing 2.9.7. **19.** *Id.* at 2.9.138. **20.** *Id.* at 2.9.187 *et seq.* **21.** Act of Sept. 24, 1789, 1 Stat. 73 [hereinafter Judiciary Act]. **22.** *Id.* § 1. **23.** Russell R. Wheeler & Cynthia Harrison, Creating the Federal Judicial System 6–7 (3d ed., 2005). **24.** Judiciary Act § 3. **25.** *Id.* § 4. **26.** Hart & Wechsler, *supra* at 22. **27.** Wheeler & Harrison, *supra* at 7–8. **28.** *Id.* at 8. **29.** 2 Farrand's 430. **30.** Letter from Thomas Jefferson to the Justices of the Supreme Court (July 18, 1793), https://perma.cc/JN62 -WVSA. **31.** Letter from Justices of the Supreme Court to George Washington (Aug. 8, 1793), https://perma.cc/4MGY -ZEKF. **32.** Hart & Wechsler, *supra* at 9–11, 19. **33.** *Id.* at 16–18. **34.** *Id.* at 18. **35.** *Id.* at 21. **36.** 28 U.S.C. §§ 81–131; 2022 Year-End Report on the Federal Judiciary 6–7, https: //perma.cc/E3EM-GPWA. **37.** 28 U.S.C. § 132. **38.** 2022 Year-End Report on the Federal Judiciary, *supra* at 5–6. **39.** 28 U.S.C. § 41. **40.** *Id.* **41.** 28 U.S.C. § 1. **42.** 28 U.S.C. § 2101; Supreme Court Rule 10.

⌒

ESSAY NO. 119: THE SUPREME COURT VESTING CLAUSE
ART. III, § 1

The judicial Power of the United States shall be vested in one supreme Court. . . .
—Judge John K. Bush, Brennan Mancil, & Erica Shuler

INTRODUCTION

Article III, Section 1 creates "one supreme Court" and authorizes it, along with "such inferior Courts as the Congress may from time to time ordain and establish," to exercise the "judicial Power of the United States." The Supreme Court Vesting Clause ensures, among other things, that a single body separate from Congress and the President has the ultimate federal judicial authority, although Congress has constitutional power to regulate certain aspects of the Court.

HISTORY BEFORE 1787

In Great Britain, the House of Lords served as the court of last resort,[1] which meant that English judicial opinions were "subject to correction" by that legislative body.[2] The judiciaries of the American colonies also were not without oversight by a political body.[3] Colonial courts generally resembled the English judicial structure, and "appeals lay from each colony to the Privy Council in London."[4]

The appeal structure in the colonies changed when they became states. Most of the new states "committed the judicial power, in the last resort, not to a part of the legislature, but to distinct and independent bodies of men."[5] On the national level, the Articles of Confederation authorized a separate judiciary only for certain maritime cases and disputes between states.[6]

THE CONSTITUTIONAL CONVENTION

The Virginia Plan called for a "National Judiciary . . . to consist of one or more supreme tribunals, and of inferior tribunals to be chosen by the National Legislature."[7] On the same day that Edmund Randolph introduced the Virginia Plan,[8] Charles Pinckney of South Carolina proposed that Congress should establish federal courts "as shall be necessary" and that "[o]ne of these Courts shall be termed the Supreme Court."[9] Similarly, William Paterson's New Jersey Plan called for the creation of "a supreme Tribunal."[10]

Without recorded debate, the delegates unanimously approved the creation of one supreme tribunal.[11] This single judicial body, John Rutledge of South Carolina remarked, would hear appeals to "secure the national rights & uniformity of Judgm[en]ts."[12] The arrangement would help to ensure that federal law, particularly the Constitution, remained supreme.[13]

By vesting the ultimate exercise of judicial power in an independent Supreme Court, the delegates sought at the national level to keep the federal judiciary separate from both the executive and legislative branches. They rejected a "Council of Revision to be selected out of the ex[ecutive] and jud[iciary] Departments" with veto power over statutes from state or national legislatures.[14] The Framers also refused to adopt a "Council of State" that would have included the Chief Justice to "assist the President in conducting the Public affairs[.]"[15]

THE RATIFICATION DEBATES

Anti-Federalists objected to the guarantee of "one supreme Court" that would not be subject to revision by any other governmental body. According to Brutus, for example, "[f]rom this court there is no appeal. And I conceive the legislature themselves, cannot set aside a judgment of this court, because they are authorised by the constitution to decide in the last resort."[16] Supreme Court Justices who were "independent of the people, of the legislature, and of every power under heaven" would "generally soon feel themselves independent of heaven itself."[17]

There also was concern that a Supreme Court authorized to adjudicate questions of law, equity, and fact would exercise unchecked power, trampling individual rights. Federal Farmer wrote that he could "not see a spark of freedom" in a judicial system in which the powers to review questions of law, equity, and fact were "blended in the same hands."[18] Brutus warned that a written constitution would not effectively limit the Court's authority, as Justices empowered to "decide questions arising upon the meaning of the constitution in law, but also in equity" could interpret the document "according to the reasoning spirit of it, without being confined to the words or letter."[19] He further warned that creation of a Supreme Court could deprive citizens of their right to a jury trial because the Court would have authority to "re-examine the whole merits of the case, both with respect to the facts and the law which may arise under it, without the intervention of a jury."[20]

Not so, said Alexander Hamilton in Federalist No. 78. He argued that "the judiciary is beyond comparison the weakest of the three departments of power" and "can never attack with success either of the other two." Further, under a written constitution, the Court may disregard legislative authority only "where the will of the legislature declared in its statutes, stands in opposition to that of the people declared in the Constitution."

Anti-Federalists also feared that the Article III national judiciary would "melt down the states into one entire government, for every purpose as well internal and local, as external and national."[21] A related concern was that a single Supreme Court, likely to be located "in the centre of the union," would pose logistical problems for far-away litigants forced to suffer "great inconveniences and enormous expences" to litigate.[22]

Hamilton, on the other hand, argued in Federalist No. 81 that the efficiency and impartiality of a system of inferior courts subject to one Supreme Court far outweighed any resulting limitations on state authority. A Landowner, a supporter of the Constitution, likewise contended that a national Supreme Court was preferable to state courts for interpreting federal law because "[j]udges who owe their appointment and support to one state will be unduly influenced and not reverence the laws of the union."[23] Hamilton reiterated in Federalist No. 22 that

establishing "one SUPREME TRIBUNAL" as a court of last resort in the federal system was necessary to "produce uniformity in [judicial] determinations." A Landowner wrote similarly that to maintain "[a] perfect uniformity" throughout the Union and prevent "jealousy and unrighteousness," "one judiciary must pervade the whole."[24]

CONGRESS, THE PRESIDENT, AND REFORM PROPOSALS

The Judiciary Act of 1789 provided for a Supreme Court of six members.[25] Notably, the First Congress severely limited the Court's role by curtailing its jurisdiction. Under the Judiciary Act of 1789, "the Supreme Court had no appellate jurisdiction to review state court decisions of federal questions that upheld claims of federal rights, nor did it have appellate jurisdiction over lower federal court decisions in criminal cases."[26]

Congress and the President have regulated or attempted to regulate the Supreme Court many times since 1789. Congress changed the number of Justices seven times, for example, with the number ranging from five to ten, before settling on nine in 1869.[27]

President Franklin D. Roosevelt's Judicial Procedures Reform Bill of 1937 would have authorized the President to appoint an additional Justice for each sitting Justice over seventy years old.[28] At the time, passage of the bill would have enabled Roosevelt to nominate six new Justices, leading to a total of fifteen.[29] However, widespread opposition and Justice Owen Roberts's decision to uphold New Deal legislation led Roosevelt to abandon his effort to expand the Court's size.[30]

In 1972, the Study Group on the Caseload of the Supreme Court recommended creating a National Court of Appeals composed of seven active circuit court judges to "screen all petitions for review . . . fielded in the Supreme Court, and hear and decide on the merits many cases of conflicts between circuits."[31] Scholars subsequently challenged the proposed National Court of Appeals on constitutional grounds.[32] The bill to create that tribunal failed.[33]

The Supreme Court Vesting Clause also is relevant to debates surrounding an ethics code for the Supreme Court. Chief Justice John G.

Roberts[34] and Justice Samuel A. Alito[35] questioned Congress's authority to impose an ethics code. In 2023, the Court voluntarily adopted an ethics code.[36] Congressional efforts to create enforcement mechanisms for this code would need to comply with the Supreme Court Vesting Clause.[37]

JUDICIAL PRECEDENT

The Constitution establishes the Supreme Court as the highest federal court, both by using the term "supreme" in the Supreme Court Clause and by vesting the Supreme Court with appellate jurisdiction over "inferior" federal courts.[38] The Marshall Court cemented the Supreme Court's position within the federal judicial hierarchy by expounding constitutionally grounded concepts of judicial independence in *Marbury v. Madison* (1803)[39] and appellate review of state courts' decisions involving federal questions in *Martin v. Hunter's Lessee* (1813).[40]

OPEN QUESTIONS

- Were Anti-Federalists justified in their concern that the Constitution does not adequately limit the power of Supreme Court Justices?
- Notwithstanding constitutional limitations, how would a congressionally imposed ethics code differ from other ways that Congress shapes the judiciary, like affecting the Supreme Court's appellate jurisdiction, determining the judiciary's budget, or even specifying the number of Supreme Court Justices?

Cite as: Judge John K. Bush, Brennan Mancil, & Erica Shuler, *The Supreme Court Vesting Clause, in* The Heritage Guide to the Constitution 443 (Josh Blackman & John G. Malcolm eds., 3d ed. 2025).

Judge Bush acknowledges the assistance of Mark Scalzo in the preparation of this article.

Notes

1. 1 W.S. Holdsworth, A History of English Law 362–65 (3d ed., 1921). **2.** Storing 2.9.187; 3 Story's Commentaries § 1576; Federalist No. 47 (Madison). **3.** Erwin C. Surrency, *The Courts in the American Colonies*, 11 Am. J. Legal Hist. 253, 253 (1967). **4.** William S. Swindler, *Seedtime of an American Judiciary: From Independence to the Constitution*, 17 Wm. & Mary L. Rev. 503, 503–04 (1976); John A. Fairlie, *The Doctrine of Stare Decisis in British Courts of Last Resort*, 35 Mich. L. Rev. 946, 946 (1973). **5.** Federalist No. 81 (Hamilton); 3 Story's Commentaries § 1580; Storing 2.8.16. **6.** Articles of Confederation, art. IX. **7.** 1 Farrand's 21. **8.** *Id.* at 23. **9.** 3 Farrand's 600. **10.** 1 Farrand's 244. **11.** 2 Farrand's 37; 3 Story's Commentaries § 1574; Robert N. Clinton, *A Mandatory View of Federal Court Jurisdiction: A Guided Quest for the Original Understanding of Article III*, 132 U. Pa. L. Rev. 741, 767 (1984). **12.** 1 Farrand's 124. **13.** *Id.* at 221; Laurence Claus, *The One Court that Congress Cannot Take Away: Singularity, Supremacy, and Article III*, 96 Geo. L.J. 59, 69 (2007). **14.** 1 Farrand's 28, 97–98, 108–09; 2 Farrand's 73–80. **15.** 2 Farrand's 335, 342, 344. **16.** Storing 2.9.138. **17.** *Id.* at 2.9.189. **18.** *Id.* at 2.8.42. **19.** *Id.* at 2.9.137. **20.** *Id.* at 2.9.174. **21.** *Id.* at 2.9.194. **22.** *Id.* at 2.8.16. **23.** Essays on the Constitution of the United States 159 (Paul Leicester Ford ed., 1892). **24.** *Id.* **25.** Judiciary Act of 1789, ch. 20, §1, 1 Stat. 73.

26. Richard H. Fallon, Jr., *Jurisdiction-Stripping Reconsidered*, 96 Va. L. Rev. 1043, 1088 (2010). **27.** Federal Judicial Center, Congress and the Courts: Landmark Legislation, https://perma.cc/W7J6-DJCX. **28.** Joanna R. Lampe, Cong. Rsrch. Serv., LSB10562, "Court Packing": Legislative Control over the Size of the Supreme Court 3 (2020). **29.** *Id.* **30.** *Id.* **31.** Federal Judicial Center, Report on the Study Group on the Caseload of the Supreme Court 18–19 (1972), https://perma.cc/3FNP-4MLL. **32.** Charles L. Black, *The National Court of Appeals: An Unwise Proposal*, 83 Yale L.J. 883, 885–88 (1974). **33.** Jake Kobrick & Daniel S. Holt, Debates on the Federal Judiciary: A Documentary History, Volume III: 1939–2005, at 58–59, https://perma.cc/Y4JE-8DRB. **34.** 2011 Year-End Report on the Federal Judiciary 6, 8–9, https://perma.cc/Y6K9-E3RE. **35.** David B. Rivkin & James Taranto, *Samuel Alito, the Supreme Court's Plain-Spoken Defender*, Wall St. J. (Jul. 28, 2023), https://perma.cc/S3S4-EWA3. **36.** Code of Conduct for Justices of the Supreme Court of the United States 3 (Nov. 13, 2023), https://perma.cc/3AUN-N9VG. **37.** Joanna R. Lampe, Cong. Rsrch. Serv., LSB11078, The Supreme Court Adopts a Code of Conduct 3 (2023). **38.** Art. III, §§ 1–2. **39.** 5 U.S. (1 Cranch) 137 (1803). **40.** 14 U.S. (1 Wheat) 603 (1813).

~

ESSAY NO. 120: THE INFERIOR COURTS CLAUSE
ART. III, § 1

The judicial Power of the United States shall be vested in one supreme Court, and in such inferior Courts as the Congress may from time to time ordain and establish.

—Judge David R. Stras & Andy Hessick

INTRODUCTION

Article III, Section 1 of the Constitution provides that the "judicial Power of the United States shall be vested in one supreme Court, and in such inferior Courts as the Congress may from time to time ordain and establish." During the Constitutional Convention, there was broad agreement on the need for a single Supreme Court but vigorous disagreement about the need for inferior federal courts. To bridge the gap between the two camps, James Madison proposed a compromise under which Congress would have the discretion to establish inferior courts. The Inferior Courts Clause enshrines this so-called Madisonian compromise, and the First Congress relied on this power to establish the lower federal courts in the Judiciary Act of 1789.

HISTORY BEFORE 1787

Sir William Blackstone explained that under the "antient constitution," there were "as many courts of judicature [in England] as there [were] manors and townships in the kingdom."[1] These "little courts" at the base of the pyramid "communicated with others of a larger jurisdiction, and those with others of a still greater power."[2] Appeals would "ascend[] gradually from the lowest to the supreme courts, which were respectively constituted to correct the errors of the inferior ones."[3] Blackstone observed that this hierarchical system was similar to that "established in the Jewish republic by Moses."[4] Although the lines between superior and inferior courts had blurred by the eighteenth century, the English judiciary retained its basic hierarchical structure.[5]

Hierarchical judiciaries were common in the American colonies as well.[6] In Virginia, county and corporate courts heard local matters with appeals taken to a "general court."[7] After independence, most states had hierarchical judiciaries, but the precise arrangements varied. Some states followed a relatively strict hierarchy. Delaware, for example, established a supreme court as a court of first instance with appeals taken to a "court of appeals."[8] Others had looser hierarchies. Virginia limited review of lower-court decisions and empowered the superior courts to operate as trial courts.[9] Georgia did not have any appellate courts; all judicial matters were resolved by local courts.[10]

As John Marshall indicated in a speech to the Virginia Convention, the Articles of Confederation lacked a robust national judiciary.[11] Congress could only establish courts with jurisdiction over piracy, capture, and disputes involving state borders.[12] There were no national courts to hear interstate disputes or interpret laws enacted by Congress; state courts adjudicated most claims, including those arising under congressionally enacted laws; and there was no hierarchy that included lower national courts.

This arrangement had two major shortcomings. First, the protection of national interests was inadequate. State judges were more inclined to favor state interests over national ones. Second, without a single, final judicial body, there was a lack of uniformity in the interpretation and enforcement of national laws.

THE CONSTITUTIONAL CONVENTION

A central goal of the Constitutional Convention was the establishment of a federal judiciary that would correct the shortcomings of the Articles of Confederation.[13] The Framers broadly agreed that one Supreme Court was necessary to ensure the uniform interpretation of federal laws and to protect federal interests, but the need for inferior federal courts was controversial.

Two major proposals captured the disagreement: the Virginia Plan and New Jersey Plan. Virginia proposed the establishment of one Supreme Court and other "inferior tribunals to be chosen by the National Legislature."[14] This hierarchical structure with a system of inferior courts subordinate to a Supreme Court was common in the states. The New Jersey plan, by contrast, proposed the creation of a Supreme Court but no inferior courts.[15]

John Rutledge of South Carolina and Roger Sherman of Connecticut led the opposition to the establishment of inferior federal courts. Rutledge stated that state courts could adjudicate claims "in the first instance" and that "the right of appeal to the supreme national tribunal [was] sufficient to secure the national rights & uniformity."[16] He added that inferior federal courts would "encroach[] on the jurisdiction" of state courts.[17] Sherman warned about the "supposed expensiveness of having a new set of Courts, when the existing State Courts would answer the same purpose."[18]

James Madison, who drafted the Virginia Plan, was the key proponent of inferior federal courts. He argued that they were necessary because state judges might be biased against federal interests. Supreme Court review was insufficient, he said, because the sheer number of "appeals" filed "would be multiplied to a most oppressive degree."[19] Madison also argued that appeals of state court judgments would often serve "no purpose."[20] Although the Supreme Court could vacate biased state court judgments, they could be reentered on remand.[21] The Supreme Court could order a new trial, but that remedy would require "the parties to bring up their witnesses, tho' ever so distant from the seat of the Court."[22]

Madison's view failed by a vote of 5 to 4 with two states divided.[23] Undeterred, Madison promptly proposed a compromise that would confer "discretion" on "the Legislature . . . to establish or not establish" inferior courts.[24] This compromise garnered more support and passed by a vote of 8 to 2 with only one state divided.[25] Still, objections continued to be voiced throughout the Convention.[26] Eventually, however, even its most ardent opponents, like Roger

Sherman, were "willing to give the power to the Legislature but wished them to make use of the State Tribunals whenever it could be done with safety to the general interest."[27]

The Madisonian compromise ultimately became enshrined in Article III. The Inferior Courts Clause provides that the "judicial Power of the United States, shall be vested in one supreme Court, and in such inferior Courts as the Congress may from time to time ordain and establish."[28] The clause establishes a hierarchical judiciary with inferior courts subordinate to the Supreme Court. In other words, Congress had the power to create inferior courts and give them the jurisdiction to resolve certain cases. This grant of power reflects Madison's view that the inferior courts should have final say in some cases to prevent an overwhelming number of appeals to the Supreme Court.[29]

THE RATIFICATION DEBATES
Many of the same arguments against the Madisonian compromise reappeared in the ratification debates. Anti-Federalist Luther Martin of Maryland said that inferior federal courts were unnecessary because state courts were widely available.[30] Brutus feared that federal courts would "swallow up all the powers of the courts in the respective states."[31]

Proponents of the compromise repeated Madison's argument that inferior federal courts were necessary to prevent an overwhelming number of appeals to the Supreme Court. In Federalist No. 81, for example, Alexander Hamilton stated that "[t]he power of constituting inferior courts" would "obviate the necessity of having recourse to the supreme court, in every case of federal cognizance."

There was also some discussion of how the inferior courts would be structured. At the Virginia Ratifying Convention, Edmund Pendleton stated that the country should "expect that there will be an inferior court in each state."[32] Hamilton likewise observed in Federalist No. 81 that Congress could divide the country into several "districts," each with its own inferior court.[33]

EARLY PRACTICE
The Judiciary Act of 1789, passed during the first session of the First Congress, created thirteen

federal district courts, one for each state, and allocated a single district judge to each district.[34] It also established three regional circuit courts with several districts in each.[35] The circuit courts sat in each district twice a year. The Act did not create circuit judgeships. Instead, each circuit court consisted of three judges: two Supreme Court Justices and the district judge of the district in which the circuit court sat.[36] There appears to have been no doubt that Congress could create inferior federal courts based on geography.

CONGRESS'S POWER TO LIMIT INFERIOR COURTS' JURISDICTION

Article III, Section 2 empowers Congress to make "Regulations" about the Supreme Court's "appellate Jurisdiction," but Article III does not mention Congress's authority to regulate the jurisdiction of the inferior federal courts. Nevertheless, Congress's power to regulate the inferior courts has never been seriously doubted. For example, under so-called diversity jurisdiction, Article III empowers federal courts to resolve any dispute "between Citizens of different states," but the Judiciary Act of 1789 limited federal jurisdiction in diversity cases to disputes exceeding $500.[37] Under Article III, the "judicial Power" also extends to all cases "arising under" the Constitution or federal laws—in other words, to cases that present a question of federal or constitutional law—but the Judiciary Act of 1789 withheld jurisdiction over many cases presenting federal or constitutional questions from federal courts.[38] In fact, Congress has never conferred the full extent of Article III jurisdiction on inferior federal courts.

The Supreme Court has consistently recognized Congress's ability to limit the jurisdiction of inferior courts. *United States v. Hudson* (1812) accepted that "the power which congress possess to create Courts of inferior jurisdiction, necessarily implies the power to limit the jurisdiction of those Courts to particular objects."[39]

CONGRESS'S POWER TO ABOLISH INFERIOR COURTS

Article III gives Congress the power to "ordain and establish" inferior courts but is silent about the power to eliminate them. The Madisonian compromise itself, however, is inconsistent with a permanent, unalterable, inferior judiciary. For the compromise to work, Congress needed the power to eliminate inferior courts, especially those that had become obsolete.

Since the early Republic, Congress has abolished and reorganized inferior federal courts many times. For example, the Judiciary Act of 1801, known as the Midnight Judges Act, doubled the number of federal circuit courts from three to six[40] and established fifteen circuit judge positions.[41] One year later, Congress reversed course and abolished the three new circuits and eliminated all of the new judgeships.[42]

CONGRESS'S POWER TO CREATE NON–ARTICLE III TRIBUNALS

Article III provides that the judicial power "shall be vested" *only* in the Supreme Court and in any inferior courts that Congress may "ordain and establish." This text leaves no room for other bodies to exercise this power. Since the early Republic, however, Congress has created non–Article III tribunals with judges that lack salary and tenure guarantees, and the Supreme Court has upheld the validity of these tribunals.[43] *American Insurance Co. v. Canter* (1828) recognized that Congress has plenary regulatory authority over the territories under the Article IV Territories Clause (See Essay No. 144), which necessarily gives Congress the power to create non–Article III territorial courts.[44] *Kendall v. United States ex rel. Stokes* (1838) upheld Congress's power to create non–Article III courts in the District of Columbia based on Congress's power over the "seat of government."[45]

The Supreme Court has also recognized a complicated patchwork of other exceptions.[46] One prominent example relates to military tribunals.[47] Another is the consent exception, which permits a non–Article III court to decide a dispute if the parties consent as long as an Article III court maintains some degree of supervision.[48] A third is the public rights exception, under which non–Article III tribunals may adjudicate disputes if the United States is a party or if the dispute involves a statutorily created right closely related to a federal regulatory scheme.[49]

OPEN QUESTIONS

- Is senatorial advice and consent required for the appointment of judges of inferior courts?[50] Or are inferior court judges "inferior officers" who could be appointed by the President alone or by the Courts of Law?[51] Although all inferior court judges have been appointed with senatorial advice and consent, whether the Constitution requires senatorial approval for those appointments is debatable.
- To what can Congress authorize non–Article III tribunals to adjudicate disputes? The Supreme Court has recognized a number of exceptions to Article III's command that the judicial power be allocated in the Supreme Court and inferior Article III courts. However, the precise contours of these exceptions are not well-defined.

Cite as: Judge David R. Stras & Andy Hessick, *The Inferior Courts Clause, in* THE HERITAGE GUIDE TO THE CONSTITUTION 446 (Josh Blackman & John G. Malcolm eds., 3d ed. 2025).

Notes

1. 3 Blackstone 30.　**2.** *Id.*　**3.** *Id.*　**4.** *Id.* at 31.　**5.** *Id.* at 24, 32–37.　**6.** Erwin C. Surrey, *The Courts in the American Colonies,* 11 Am. J. Legal Hist. 253, 261 (1967). **7.** David E. Engdahl, *What's in a Name? The Constitutionality of Multiple "Supreme" Courts,* 66 Ind. L.J. 457, 468–69 (1991).　**8.** Del. Const. of 1776, art. XVII.　**9.** *Appendix* to 4 W. Blackstone, Commentaries, With Notes of Reference, To the Constitution and Laws, Of the Federal Government of the United States; And of the Commonwealth of Virginia 9–22 (St. George Tucker ed. 1803); Engdahl, *supra* at 469.　**10.** Ga. Const. of 1777, art. XL.　**11.** 3 Elliot's 551.　**12.** Articles of Confederation, art. IX, §§ 2–3.　**13.** Edward J. Larson and Michael P. Winship, The Constitutional Convention: A Narrative History from the Notes of James Madison 27 (2005).　**14.** 1 Farrand's 21.　**15.** *Id.* at 244.　**16.** *Id.* at 124.　**17.** *Id.*　**18.** *Id.*　**19.** *Id.*　**20.** *Id.*　**21.** *Id.*　**22.** *Id.*　**23.** *Id.*　**24.** *Id.* at 125.　**25.** *Id.*　**26.** 2 Farrand's 45–46.　**27.** *Id.* at 46.　**28.** Art. III, § 1.　**29.** 1 Farrand's 124.　**30.** 3 Farrand's 207.　**31.** Storing 2.9.7; *id.* at 2.9.139.　**32.** 3 Elliot's 547.　**33.** Federalist No. 81.　**34.** Judiciary Act of 1789, ch. 20, §§ 2–3, 1 Stat. 73.　**35.** *Id.* § 4, at 74–75.　**36.** *Id.* **37.** *Id.* § 4, at 74–75.　**38.** *Id.* § 11, at 78–79.　**39.** 11 U.S. 32, 33 (1812).　**40.** Act of Feb. 13, 1801, ch. 4, § 6, 2 Stat. 89.　**41.** *Id.,* ch. 4.　**42.** Act of Mar. 8, 1802, ch. 8, 2 Stat. 132.　**43.** William Baude, *Adjudication Outside Article III,* 133 Harv. L. Rev. 1511 (2020).　**44.** 1 Pet. 511 (1828).　**45.** 37 U.S. (12 Pet.) 524, 619 (1838); U.S. Const. Art. I, § 8, cl. 17.　**46.** F. Andrew Hessick, *Federalism Limits on Non-Article III Adjudication,* 46 Pepp. L. Rev. 725, 729–31 (2019).　**47.** *Solorio v. United States,* 483 U.S. 435, 436 (1987); *Ex parte Quirin,* 317 U.S. 1, 48 (1942).　**48.** *Wellness Int'l Network, Ltd. v. Sharif,* 575 U.S. 665, 678 (2015).　**49.** *Oil States Energy Servs., LLC v. Greene's Energy Grp., LLC,* 584 U.S. 325, 334–35 (2018); *Thomas v. Union Carbide Agric. Prods. Co.,* 473 U.S. 568 (1985).　**50.** *Weiss v. United States,* 510 U.S. 163, 191 n.7 (1994) (Souter, J., concurring); Josh Blackman & Seth Barrett Tillman, *Offices and Officers of the Constitution, Part II: The Four Approaches,* 61 S. Tex. L. Rev. 321, 390 n.251 (2022).　**51.** Akhil Reed Amar, *A Neo-Federalist View of Article III: Separating the Two Tiers of Federal Jurisdiction,* 65 B.U. L. Rev. 205, 235 n.103 (1985).

~

ESSAY NO. 121: THE GOOD BEHAVIOR CLAUSE
ART. III, § 1

The Judges, both of the supreme and inferior Courts, shall hold their Offices during good Behaviour. . . .

—Judge David R. Stras & Ryan Scott

INTRODUCTION

The Good Behavior Clause of Article III safeguards judicial independence by protecting federal judges against removal from office at the whim of the executive and legislative branches. Federal judges do not enjoy "life tenure." Rather, "good behavior" serves as a legal term of art that grants an office for life, at least in the absence of misbehavior. Federal judges can be removed following impeachment for "Treason, Bribery, or other high Crimes and Misdemeanors" but, under longstanding practice, not for their judicial acts. Congress may have the power to remove judges by eliminating the federal courts on which they sit. Some scholars also argue that Congress could create mechanisms other than impeachment to remove federal judges. Debates continue about whether term limits can be imposed on federal judges by statute.

HISTORY BEFORE 1787

In eighteenth-century England, tenure "during good behaviour" emerged to shield judges from removal at the pleasure of the king. The 1701 Act of Settlement required that judges hold their offices *quam diu se bene gesserint* (for as long as they conduct themselves well).[1] Further legislation in 1761 ensured that judges would continue in office notwithstanding the death of the monarch.[2] Sir William Blackstone wrote that those tenure protections safeguarded judicial independence: "In this distinct and separate existence of the judicial power, in a peculiar body of men, nominated indeed, but not removeable at pleasure, by the crown, consists one main preservative of the public liberty."[3]

In the American colonies, judges enjoyed no such protection. They could be removed from office by the king for any reason—a powerful incentive to favor the Crown's interests. In the Declaration of Independence, the Second Continental Congress cited the lack of tenure protections for judges as one of the "repeated injuries and usurpations" inflicted by the king: "He has made Judges dependent on his Will alone, for the tenure of their offices. . . ."[4]

After independence, early state constitutions overwhelmingly provided that judges should continue in office "during good behavior." John Adams wrote in *Thoughts on Government* that judges "should hold estates for life in their offices; or, in other words, their commissions should be during good behavior."[5] A few state constitutions, such as those of Virginia and North Carolina, included that language without elaboration.[6] The New York constitution provided for service "during good behavior or until they have respectively attained the age of sixty years."[7] Other constitutions explicitly addressed mechanisms for removal. Several states followed the English model. Delaware, Massachusetts, Maryland, South Carolina, and Vermont granted judges tenure "during good behavior" but authorized removal upon the address of the legislature.[8]

Some states, like Maryland, provided that "[j]udges shall be removed for misbehaviour, on conviction in a court of law."[9] In each of these formulations, the main protection for judges in the newly independent states was tenure during good behavior.

THE CONSTITUTIONAL CONVENTION

The Constitutional Convention adopted the Good Behavior Clause without controversy. Both the Virginia and New Jersey Plans called for judges "to hold their offices during good behaviour," and that language was approved without discussion.[10]

On August 27, John Dickinson of Delaware proposed an amendment to allow the removal of judges "by the Executive on the application by the Senate and House of Representatives."[11] Gouverneur Morris of Pennsylvania opposed the amendment, arguing that it would be "a contradiction in terms to say that the Judges should hold their offices during good behavior, and yet be removeable without a trial."[12] Roger Sherman of Connecticut observed that there was a similar provision in Great Britain.[13] Edmund Randolph of Virginia countered that this motion would "weaken[] too much the independence of the Judges." Dickinson's amendment was rejected by a vote of 7 to 1.

On September 8, the impeachment process was extended to the President as well as to "The Vice President and other civil Officers of the United States."[14] The Appointments Clause provides that judges of the U.S. Supreme Court and other judges appointed by the President are "Officers of the United States" and therefore subject to impeachment. Although Article III does not explicitly refer to the impeachment process, the Impeachment Clause is the only method described in the Constitution for the removal of "Officers of the United States." As a result, judges could be impeached only for "Treason, Bribery, or other high Crimes and Misdemeanors" and, as Morris stated, be removed only after a trial and conviction by two-thirds of the Senate.

THE RATIFICATION DEBATES

In Federalist No. 78, Alexander Hamilton explained that the "good behaviour" standard for "continuance in office of the judicial magistracy is certainly one of the most valuable of the modern improvements in the practice of government." He observed that "[i]n a republic," this standard is an "excellent barrier to the encroachments and oppressions of the representative body" and "the best expedient which can be devised in any government, to secure a steady, upright, and impartial administration of the laws."[15]

Although Article III does not grant judges "life tenure," the "good behaviour" clause was widely understood to confer tenure for life in the absence of impeachment and removal. Hamilton acknowledged that if federal judges "behave[d] properly," they would "be secured in their places for life."[16] Even opponents of the Constitution understood that the Constitution would grant a form of life tenure, warning that "[t]he same judge may frequently be in office thirty or forty years."[17] Hamilton further described impeachment as "the only provision on the point" for removing federal judges, one "which is consistent with the necessary independence of the judicial character."[18]

During the ratification debates, many Anti-Federalists argued that Congress should have greater power over the judiciary. Brutus, for example, warned that under the Constitution, the legislature would lack any power to reverse judicial decisions or remove judges for incapacity or "error[s] in judgement" and that this would make judges independent of "every power under heaven."[19] Hamilton responded that any means of removal outside of the impeachment process would "be liable to abuse."[20]

IMPEACHMENT OF JUDGES

Fifteen federal judges have been impeached by the House of Representatives and tried in the Senate. Eight were convicted and removed from office, three resigned before judgment by the Senate, and four were acquitted.[21] Not all impeachments have involved allegations of criminal misconduct. Judge John Pickering, for example, was impeached, convicted, and removed from office in 1803 for intoxication on the bench and mental instability. But most judges removed through impeachment were accused of criminal misconduct following either a criminal conviction or an acquittal.[22]

Samuel Chase was the only Supreme Court justice to be impeached. He was charged with being biased during two criminal cases, delivering a "political harangue" to a grand jury, and issuing a bench warrant instead of a summons.[23] Justice Chase's defense team argued that removal from office was inappropriate for "petty errors and indiscretions too insignificant to have a name in the penal code." The lawyers asked whether the Senate should "fix a standard of politeness in a judge, and mark the precincts of judicial decorum[.]"[24]

Although Republicans controlled twenty-five Senate seats—more than enough to convict—Justice Chase was acquitted of all charges.[25] A frustrated President Thomas Jefferson declared that "[t]his business of removing Judges by impeachment is a *bungling way*."[26] Two centuries later, however, Chief Justice William Rehnquist described Justice Chase's acquittal as establishing the "political precedent" that "a judge's judicial acts may not serve as a basis for impeachment."[27]

REMOVING JUDGES OUTSIDE OF IMPEACHMENT

Outside of impeachment, two other methods of removing federal judges from office may be available. Both are controversial.

First, might Congress remove federal judges from office by dissolving their courts entirely? The "Midnight Judges" Act of 1801 created sixteen new federal circuit court judgeships.[28] In 1802, the Republican Congress repealed the Judiciary Act of 1801, effectively removing the judges from those courts. Repeal was premised on Congress's power "to constitute" and "from time to time to ordain and establish" inferior federal courts. In *Stuart v. Laird* (1803), the Supreme Court appeared to accept the constitutionality of the repeal.[29] The decision held that Congress was free to transfer actions from one federal court to another, but it did not expressly address either the "good behaviour" clause or the separation of powers. Tellingly, it has been 150 years since Congress has tried to remove federal judges by eliminating a court.[30]

Second, might the judiciary itself remove judges upon a finding of misbehavior? Both before and after the Settlement Act of 1701, those holding office "during good behaviour" were subject to judicial proceedings to determine whether they had misbehaved. The common-law writ of *scire facias* allowed a plaintiff (typically the king) to seek an officeholder's removal for misbehavior. Professor Raoul Berger acknowledged that "this procedure found employment with respect to lesser officials" and that "there is no English case wherein a judge comparable to a federal judge was removed in a judicial proceeding."[31] Nevertheless, based on that historical practice, some scholars have suggested that Congress could constitutionally authorize the President, legislators, or others to strip judges of their office by suing them in federal court for misbehavior.[32]

Some scholars have suggested that term limits, age limits, and other limitations on life tenure can be imposed by statute without a constitutional amendment.[33] Others have disagreed, citing doubts about the historical evidence and maintaining that impeachment was understood to be the exclusive method for the removal of judges.[34]

The judiciary itself has done little to explore whether it can remove judges. The most high-profile test of that power involved Stephen Chandler, Chief Judge of the U.S. District Court for the Western District of Oklahoma. Chandler had been sued for malicious prosecution, criminally charged with conspiracy by the State of Oklahoma, and twice forced to recuse himself from cases by the U.S. Court of Appeals for the Tenth Circuit.[35] In 1965, the Judicial Council of the Tenth Circuit voted to bar Chandler from taking action in any cases. The Judicial Council found that Chandler was "presently unable, or unwilling, to discharge efficiently the duties of his office."[36]

Chandler asked the Supreme Court to find that the Judicial Council had usurped Congress's power to impeach and remove judges. The Court, in an opinion by Chief Justice Warren Burger, dismissed the suit because the order had been rescinded shortly after it was entered.[37] But three Justices would have reached the merits. Justice John Marshall Harlan II, concurring, opined that Congress had empowered judicial councils to exercise supervisory or disciplinary authority over district courts, including the power to prevent judges from hearing cases.[38] Justices William Douglas and Hugo Black dissented. In their view, "there is no power under our Constitution for one group of federal judges to censor or discipline any federal judge and no power to declare him inefficient and strip him of his power to act as a judge."[39]

The Judicial Councils Reform and Judicial Conduct and Disability Act of 1980, enacted ten years after the *Chandler* case, authorized judicial councils to suspend case assignments from judges who are mentally or physically unable to discharge their duties or who have engaged in inappropriate conduct.[40] However, the law also specifies that "[u]nder no circumstances may [it] order removal from office of any judge appointed to hold office during good behavior."[41]

COURT REFORM PROPOSALS

Throughout the nation's history, there have been repeated efforts to eliminate life tenure, and they tend to coincide with periods of political dissatisfaction with the Court's decisions. From 1807 to 1912, members of Congress introduced numerous proposals to amend the Constitution and impose term limits, age limits, or popular elections for federal judges.[42] President Franklin D. Roosevelt's failed "court packing" plan in 1937 was accompanied by a flurry of proposals to end life tenure by constitutional amendment.[43] At the height of the Warren Court, there were more than thirty proposals from Congress to end life tenure.[44]

In 2021, President Joe Biden established the Presidential Commission on the Supreme Court of the United States to investigate various proposals for reform. The final report declined to take "a position on the merits of term limits."[45]

OPEN QUESTIONS

- Can Congress impose term limits by statute in the absence of a constitutional amendment?[46]
- Could Congress assign "senior" members of the Supreme Court to hear only certain cases—for example, when an "active" Justice is recused?[47]

- Can the federal courts refuse to assign cases to a judge unless he or she consents to a medical examination?[48]

Cite as: Judge David R. Stras & Ryan Scott, *The Good Behavior Clause*, in The Heritage Guide to the Constitution 449 (Josh Blackman & John G. Malcolm eds., 3d ed. 2025).

Notes

1. Act of Settlement 1701, 12 & 13 Will. 3 c. 2. **2.** 1 Geo. 3, c. 23 (1761) (Ruffhead, 8 Statutes at Large 574 (1763)). **3.** 1 Blackstone 259. **4.** Declaration of Independence, ¶¶ 2, 11. **5.** 4 The Works of John Adams 198 (Charles Francis Adams ed., 1851). **6.** Va. Const. of 1776, *in* 2 The Federal and State Colonial Charters, and Other Organic Laws of the United States 1911 (Benjamin Perley Poore ed., 1877); N.C. Const. of 1776, art. XIII. **7.** N.Y. Const. of 1777, art. XXIV. **8.** Del. Const. of 1776, art. XXIII; Mass. Const. of 1780, ch. III, art. 1; Md. Const. of 1776, art. XXX; S.C. Const. of 1776, art. XX; Vt. Const. of 1777, ch. II, § XXVII. **9.** Md. Const. of 1776, art. XXX. **10.** 1 Farrand's 21, 126, 244. **11.** 2 Farrand's 428. **12.** *Id.* **13.** *Id.* at 429. **14.** *Id.* at 545. **15.** Federalist No. 78 (Hamilton). **16.** Federalist No. 79 (Hamilton). **17.** Storing 2.8.188; Benjamin Gale, On a Town's Choice of Delegates (Nov. 12, 1787), *reprinted in* 3 DHRC 428. **18.** Federalist No. 79. **19.** Storing 2.1.191–92. **20.** Federalist No. 79. **21.** *About Impeachment: Senate Trials*, U.S. Senate, https://perma.cc/DQ8N-NGFY. **22.** Michael J. Gerhardt, *The Lessons of Impeachment History*, 67 Geo. Wash. L. Rev. 603, 614, 619 n.81 (1998). **23.** 14 Annals of Cong. 85–88 (1804). **24.** R.W. Carrington, *The Impeachment Trial of Samuel Chase*, 9 Va. L. Rev. 485, 494 (1923). **25.** Jerry W. Knudson, *The Jeffersonian Assault on the Federalist Judiciary, 1802–1805; Political Forces and Press Reaction*, 14 Am. J. Legal Hist. 55, 67 (1970). **26.** Letter from John Langdon to Thomas Jefferson (Feb. 13, 1804), explanatory note, https://perma.cc/8WFQ-AGA6. **27.** Hon. William H. Rehnquist, *Judicial Independence*, 38 U. Rich. L. Rev. 579, 589 (2004) (emphasis omitted). **28.** Judiciary Act of 1801, ch. 4, 2 Stat. 89 (1801); Judiciary Act of 1802, 2 Stat. 156 (1802). **29.** U.S. (1 Cranch) 299 (1803). **30.** Charles Gardner Geyh, *Judicial Independence at Twilight*, 71 Case W. Rsrv. L. Rev. 1045, 1067–68 (2021). **31.** Raoul Berger, *Impeachment of Judges and "Good Behavior" Tenure*, 79 Yale L.J. 1475, 1479–80 (1970). **32.** Saikrishna Prakash & Steven D. Smith, *How to Remove a Federal Judge*, 116 Yale L.J. 72, 128–33 (2006); Berger, *supra* at 1526–28; Burke Shartel, *Federal Judges—Appointment, Supervision,* *and Removal—Some Possibilities Under the Constitution*, 28 Mich. L. Rev. 870, 891–98, 894 n.70 (1930). **33.** David R. Dow & Sanat Mehta, *Does Eliminating Life Tenure for Article III Judges Require a Constitutional Amendment?* 16 Duke. J. Const. L. & Pub. Pol'y 89, 107–09 (2021); Paul D. Carrington & Roger C. Cramton, *The Supreme Court Renewal Act: A Return to Basic Principles*, in Reforming the Court: Term Limits for the Supreme Court Justices 471 (Roger C. Cramton & Paul D. Carrington eds., 2006). **34.** James E. Pfander, *Removing Federal Judges*, 74 U. Chi. L. Rev. 1227, 1227–30 (2007); David R. Stras & Ryan W. Scott, *Retaining Life Tenure: The Case for a "Golden Parachute,"* 83 Wash. U. L.Q. 1397, 1402–38 (2005); Martin H. Redish, *Judicial Discipline, Judicial Independence, and the Constitution: A Textual and Structural Analysis*, 72 S. Cal. L. Rev. 673, 699 (1999); Irving R. Kaufman, *Chilling Judicial Independence*, 88 Yale L.J. 681, 691–703 (1979). **35.** *Chandler v. Jud. Council of Tenth Cir. of U.S.*, 398 U.S. 74, 77 & n.4 (1970); *Occidental Petroleum Co. v. Chandler*, 305 F.2d 55 (10th Cir. 1962) (en banc); *Texaco, Inc. v. Chandler*, 354 F.2d 655 (10th Cir. 1965) (en banc). **36.** *Chandler*, 398 U.S. at 77. **37.** *Id.* at 88–89. **38.** *Id.* at 104–06 (Harlan, J., concurring). **39.** *Id.* at 137 (Douglas, J., dissenting). **40.** Pub. L. No. 96-458, § 3, 94 Stat. 2035 (1980); 28 U.S.C. §§ 351(a), 354(a)(2)(A). **41.** 28 U.S.C. § 354(a)(3)(a). **42.** Michael J. Mazza, *A New Look at an Old Debate: Life Tenure and the Article III Judge*, 39 Gonzaga L. Rev. 131, 143-46 (2003). **43.** *Id.* at 149–50 (internal quotation marks omitted). **44.** *Id.* at 152–53. **45.** Presidential Commission on the Supreme Court of the United States Final Report 8 (2021), https://perma.cc/U55S-NNEC. **46.** Alicia Bannon & Michael Milov-Cordoba, *Supreme Court Term Limits*, Brennan Center for Justice (June 20, 2023), https://perma.cc/5XWY-CWXZ. **47.** *The Case for Supreme Court Term Limits*, U.S. Supreme Court Working Group (Oct. 25, 2023), https://perma.cc/7786-Q98R; Jack Balkin, *Don't Pack the Court. Regularize Appointments*, Balkinization Blog (Oct. 5, 2020), https://perma.cc/37YA-N26E. **48.** *Newman v. Moore*, 743 F. Supp. 3d 62 (D.D.C. 2024).

❦

ESSAY NO. 122: THE JUDICIAL COMPENSATION CLAUSE
ART. III, § 1

The Judges, both of the supreme and inferior Courts . . . shall, at stated Times, receive for their Services a Compensation, which shall not be diminished during their Continuance in Office.

—Chief Judge Jennifer Walker Elrod, Jack Buckley DiSorbo, & J. Andrew Mackenzie

INTRODUCTION

"Next to permanency in office," wrote Alexander Hamilton in Federalist No. 78, "nothing can contribute more to the independence of the judges than a fixed provision for their support." Concern over judicial compensation was a catalyst of the American Revolution and a rare point of consensus in the nation's early political debates, including the debate over the adoption of the Constitution. It continues to be a jealously guarded feature of the federal judiciary, at times raising unexpectedly thorny questions about indirect effects on the real wages of judicial officers.

The federal judiciary has resolved several questions concerning the Judicial Compensation Clause. Congress cannot diminish an incumbent judge's salary but can prospectively reduce the salaries of future judges. Congress may lawfully repeal a future increase in judicial compensation but cannot repeal a definite commitment to automatic cost-of-living adjustments. Early cases held that a federal judge's salary is immune from federal taxation, but those decisions have been overturned. The rising cost of living poses an ongoing concern about the significant compensation gap between judicial officers and private practitioners, which Chief Justice John Roberts has described as a "constitutional crisis" for the strength of the federal judiciary.

HISTORY BEFORE 1787

One of the "long train of abuses and usurpations"[1] that drove the American colonists to revolt was the issue of who paid colonial judges. In response to the Boston Tea Party, Parliament transferred the power to pay the salaries of Massachusetts' colonial courts from the local legislative body to King George III's royal governor, thus rendering those judges "dependent on [the king's] Will alone, for the tenure of their offices, and the amount and payment of their salaries."[2] This transfer of power was effected by the Massachusetts Government Act of 1774, one of the four edicts known collectively as the Intolerable Acts that were designed to break the rebellious spirit of Massachusetts and punish the "dangerous commotions and insurrections" that had been "fomented and raised in the town of Boston."[3]

Needless to say, the Intolerable Acts backfired. The colonists considered the Massachusetts Government Act to be a transparent attack on judicial independence and on their rights as Englishmen. The Declaration of Independence would charge that the Act was one more reason to conclude that the design of the British government was to "reduce [the colonies] under absolute Despotism."[4]

When it came time to organize the governments of the independent United States, salary and tenure protections were a staple concern. John Adams's April 1776 *Thoughts on Government* explained that judges "should not be dependant upon any man or body of men."[5] Rather, they "should hold estates for life in their offices, or in other words their commissions should be during good behaviour, and their salaries ascertained and established by law."

Early state constitutions provided such protections. Virginia's 1776 constitution declared that "[Judicial] officers shall have fixed and adequate salaries."[6] Maryland's 1776 constitution similarly stated that "all Judges . . . shall hold their commissions during good behavior, removable only for misbehavior, on conviction in a Court of law."[7]

CONSTITUTIONAL CONVENTION

The records of the Federal Convention reflect relative unanimity on the notion that judges' salaries ought to be secured in some manner. The only disagreement came when Gouverneur Morris of Pennsylvania sought to remove language from an early draft that would have prohibited increases in judicial salaries as well as decreases. Morris reasoned that "the Legislature ought to be at liberty to increase salaries as circumstances might require[.]"[8] The edit was seconded by Benjamin Franklin of Pennsylvania, who predicted that "Money may not only become plentier, but the business of the department may increase as the Country becomes more populous."[9]

James Madison of Virginia strenuously disagreed with the proposed change. He countered that "[w]henever an increase is wished by the Judges, or may be in agitation in the legislature, an undue complaisance in the former may be felt towards the latter." The resulting temptation to render rulings favorable to the legislature "ought not to [be] suffered, if it can be prevented."[10]

Nevertheless, recognizing that salaries might need to increase to account for changes in the cost of living and judicial workload, Madison proposed that "[t]he variations in the value of money, may be guarded agst. by taking for a standard wheat or some other thing of permanent value."[11] Madison made the same proposal for congressional salaries (See Essay No. 30.) Charles Pinckney of South Carolina aired a different concern: "The importance of the Judiciary will require men of the first talents: large salaries will therefore be necessary, larger than the U.S. can allow in the first instance."[12] Pinckney's objection foreshadowed future debates. Ultimately, Morris's motion carried by a vote of 6 to 2.[13]

RATIFICATION DEBATES

During the ratification debates, consensus over the idea of fixed salaries for judges largely continued. One outlier was the Anti-Federalist Federal Farmer, who worried that the legislature's inability to decrease judicial salaries might lead to unintended wealth as a result of rising and falling prices.[14] For the most part, however, even Anti-Federalists who were critical of the federal judiciary did not object to the Judicial Compensation Clause. It was the fact that judicial decisions, rather than judicial tenure and salaries, would be insulated from legislative review that caused Brutus to fear that the proposed Constitution would create a judiciary "independent of the people, of the legislature, and of every power under heaven."[15] Brutus did not object to giving judges good-behavior tenure and fixed salaries as long as their decisions could be overturned if they conflicted with the legislature's will.[16]

Prominent jurists subsequently cited the importance of guaranteed salaries for judges. Justice James Wilson stated that judges should be "completely independent" in "their salaries, and in their offices."[17] James Kent, future Chief Justice of the New York Supreme Court, wrote that "permanent support of the judges is well calculated, in addition to the tenure of their office, to give them the requisite independence."[18] Kent also cited the need to "secure a succession of learned men on the bench" by persuading the leaders of the legal profession "to quit the lucrative pursuits of private business for the important station" as a reason to support fixed salaries for judges.[19] Chief Justice John Marshall told the Virginia Convention that a judge "should be rendered perfectly and completely independent, with nothing to influence or countroul him but God and his conscience."[20]

JUDICIAL PRECEDENT

The federal courts have decided several cases arising under the Judicial Compensation Clause. First, while Congress cannot diminish an incumbent judge's salary, it can prospectively reduce the salaries of future judges. This principle was established during the early Republic. In 1801, Congress provided that federal justices of the peace in the District of Columbia would receive certain fees.[21] But Congress subsequently repealed those fees. Judge Benjamin More, a Jefferson appointee, was denied a fee of twelve-and-a-half cents. (Roughly $3.50 today.) The dispute gave rise to litigation, and the circuit court ruled for More. The court held that Congress could repeal the fee statute, but the repeal had to be prospective—*i.e.*, it could not apply to judges who were already on the bench.[22] The appeal before the Supreme Court was dismissed for lack of jurisdiction.

Second, the courts have recognized that the Judicial Compensation Clause does not protect compensation for judgeships "created by virtue of . . . Article I."[23] This principle logically extends to all non-Article III magistrate judges, bankruptcy judges, administrative law judges, District of Columbia Superior Court judges, Tax Court judges, and so on. The salaries of such federal officers may be diminished.[24]

Third, it was long argued that the Judicial Compensation Clause made federal judges immune from taxation. Justice Stephen Field suggested such an immunity in his concurrence in *Pollock v. Farmers' Loan & Trust Co.* (1895).[25] This noteworthy case held that a federal income tax was unconstitutional, precipitating ratification of the Sixteenth Amendment. *Evans v. Gore* (1920) held that a federal judge's compensation was indeed immune from federal taxes,[26] but over time, the Court eroded that general immunity.[27] Eight decades later, *Evans* was overturned in *United States v. Hatter* (2001).[28] Justice Stephen Breyer's majority opinion observed that "a nondiscriminatory tax . . .

upon judges" was constitutional "whether those judges were appointed before or after the tax law in question was enacted or took effect."[29] In dissent, Justice Clarence Thomas wrote that *Evans* was correct.[30]

Fourth, the courts have considered the relationship between the Judicial Compensation Clause and cost-of-living adjustments. *United States v. Will* (1980) held that Congress may lawfully repeal a specific future increase before it goes into effect.[31] But in *Beer v. United States* (2012), the *en banc* Federal Circuit held that Congress cannot repeal a "definite commitment to automatic yearly cost of living adjustments for sitting members of the judiciary."[32] The Supreme Court denied review in *Beer*.[33]

ONGOING ISSUES

In Federalist No. 79, Hamilton recognized that a judge's real wages may decrease in light of inflation: "It will readily be understood that the fluctuations in the value of money and in the state of society rendered a fixed rate of compensation in the Constitution inadmissible." But it would be up to Congress, with its power of the purse, to increase judicial compensation over time. The First Congress set the salary for a federal judge at $3,500 (roughly $122,000 today), but Congress let that amount stagnate. In 1812, Justice Joseph Story expressed reservations about accepting his Supreme Court nomination because Congress had not increased judicial salaries in more than two decades.[34]

The ongoing disparity between the compensation of judicial officers and private practitioners may create difficulties in recruiting *and* retaining talent.[35] In 2007, Chief Justice John Roberts wrote that the failure to raise judicial compensation "has now reached the level of a constitutional crisis that threatens to undermine the strength and independence of the federal judiciary."[36] It remains to be seen whether Congress will pass legislation to address these issues and, if so, whether such legislation would pose any constitutional questions.

Cite as: Chief Judge Jennifer Walker Elrod, Jack Buckley DiSorbo, & J. Andrew Mackenzie, *The Judicial Compensation Clause*, *in* THE HERITAGE GUIDE TO THE CONSTITUTION 453 (Josh Blackman & John G. Malcolm eds., 3d ed. 2025).

Notes

1. Declaration of Independence, ¶ 2. **2.** Massachusetts Government Act of May 20, 1774. **3.** Boston Port Act of March 31, 1774. **4.** Declaration of Independence, ¶ 2. **5.** 4 The Papers of John Adams 86–93 (Robert J. Taylor ed., 1979). **6.** Va. Const. of 1776. **7.** Md. Const. of 1776, art. 40, § xl. **8.** 2 Farrand's 44. **9.** *Id.* at 44–45. **10.** *Id.* at 45. **11.** *Id.* **12.** *Id.* at 429–30. **13.** *Id.* at 45. **14.** Storing 2.8.188. **15.** Storing 2.9.189. **16.** *Id.* **17.** 1 Works of James Wilson 363 (J. Andrews ed., 1896). **18.** 1 James Kent, Commentaries on American Law 319 (10th ed. 1860). **19.** *Id.* **20.** Proceedings and Debates of the Virginia State Convention, of 1829–1830, at 616 (1830). **21.** An Act Concerning the District of Columbia, 6th Cong., 2d Sess., 2 Stat. 103 (1801). **22.** *United States v. More*, 7 U.S. (3 Cranch) 159, 160 n.2 (1805). **23.** *Palmore v. United States*, 411 U.S. 389, 393 (1973). **24.** *Williams v. United States*, 289 U.S. 553 (1933); *Freytag v. Commissioner*, 501 U.S. 868, 901–15 (1991) (Scalia, J., concurring in part and concurring in the judgment). **25.** 157 U.S. 429, 604 (1895) (Field, J., concurring). **26.** 253 U.S. 245, 264 (1920). **27.** Jonathan L. Entin, *Getting What You Pay For: Judicial Compensation and Judicial Independence*, 2011 Utah L. Rev. 25, 31–36 (2011). **28.** 532 U.S. 557 (2001). **29.** *Id.* at 571. **30.** *Id.* at 586–87 (Thomas, J., concurring in the judgment and dissenting in part). **31.** 449 U.S. 200, 224–26 (1980). **32.** 696 F.3d 1174, 1177 (Fed. Cir. 2012). **33.** *United States v. Beer*, 569 U.S. 947 (2013). **34.** Charles Warren, The Supreme Court in United States History 416 (rev. ed. 1926). **35.** Michael J. Frank, *Judge Not, Lest Yee Be Judged Unworthy of a Pay Raise: An Examination of the Federal Judicial Salary "Crisis,"* 87 Marq. L. Rev. 55, 60–67 (2003); Jonathan L. Entin & Erik M. Jensen, *Taxation, Compensation, and Judicial Independence*, 56 Case W. Rsrv. L. Rev. 965, 1001–09 (2006). **36.** John G. Roberts, 2006 Year-End Report on the Federal Judiciary 1 (2006), https://perma.cc/9WCY-6JVS.

❧

ESSAY NO. 123: THE JUDICIAL POWER—LAW & EQUITY CLAUSE
ART. III, § 2, CL. 1

The judicial Power shall extend to all Cases, in Law and Equity . . .
—Judge Andrew S. Oldham & Adam I. Steene

INTRODUCTION

Individually, the words "law" and "equity" could be understood extremely broadly, allowing the judiciary to do almost anything. Taken together, they refer to the systems of justice found in the common-law courts and the courts of equity, respectively. Established in England and later carried over to the American colonies, these two sets of courts had different rules and offered litigants different kinds of remedies. Empowering the federal judiciary to hear "all Cases, in Law and Equity" therefore meant that federal courts were competent to hear all cases that came before them, regardless of whether, in England, the case would have been brought in a law court or a court of equity.

When the Constitution was proposed, the Anti-Federalists argued that the flexibility of equity—equitable remedies in particular—would undermine the rule of law. The Federalists insisted that equity would be limited to the principles that existed in England, where courts of equity were governed by well-settled rules. Today, the Supreme Court sometimes honors the promise of the Federalists, looking to see whether the requested equitable remedy was available in English equity courts at the Founding. Other times, the Court treats equity as flexible enough to permit innovation in those remedies. And sometimes it takes the view that, even without express statutory authorization, equity allows suits to prevent officials from violating the Constitution.

HISTORY BEFORE 1787

At the Founding, the word "law," in its most general sense, meant "[a] rule of action."[1] But when mentioned along with "equity," law would have been understood to refer to the system of justice administered in England in the common-law courts as opposed to the courts of equity.

Sir William Blackstone expressly distinguished between "the universally established courts of common law and equity."[2] Common-law courts first emerged in England no later than the thirteenth century as part of the monarchy's consolidation of power.[3] In the thirteenth century, English kings presided over the Court of King's Bench, the principal common-law court.[4] By the eighteenth century, that practice had fallen out of use.[5]

The remedies common-law courts could afford parties were fairly limited. Relief was often restricted to money damages, and lawsuits were procedurally complex. A litigant might discover—too late—that he had chosen the wrong procedure, or it might be that there was *no* procedure that would provide him with a remedy for the violation of his rights.[6] That is where courts of equity came in.

Before 1787, the word "equity" was used in two different ways. In its broader sense, it was a synonym for "justice" or the "soul and spirit of all law."[7] Courts would sometimes be said to interpret legislation "within the equity" of the statute—that is, not too broadly or narrowly, but "according to the true intent of the legislature."[8]

When used in contrast to "law," however, "equity ha[d] a more restrained and qualified meaning."[9] It connoted "[t]he rules of decision observed by the [C]ourt of Chancery,"[10] the principal court of equity in England. At least as far back as the fourteenth century, litigants who were unable to obtain relief in the common-law courts would turn to the king's chancellor for a remedy.[11] Over time, the chancellor and his court began to develop more formal rules. And, by the mid-eighteenth century, the system of equity was as well-settled as the system of law in the common-law courts.[12] Equity permitted litigants to obtain remedies unavailable in the law courts. The most famous remedy was the injunction—an order preventing the defendant from performing (or requiring the defendant to perform) a certain act.[13]

Equity had a mixed reception in the newly independent states. Some states retained courts of equity, relying on English chancery practice for guidance.[14] Some merged the courts of law and equity. Others abolished equity entirely.[15]

THE CONSTITUTIONAL CONVENTION

The inclusion of "in Law and Equity" received little attention during the Constitutional Convention. Toward the end of the Convention on August 27, 1787, William Samuel Johnson of Connecticut "suggested that the judicial power ought to extend to equity as well as law—and moved to insert the words 'both in law and equity.'"[16] George Read of Delaware "objected to vesting these powers in the same Court" (the U.S. Supreme Court), but the motion passed.[17] In mid-September, the word "both" was removed from the draft. That language was approved by the Convention.[18]

THE RATIFICATION DEBATES

The Anti-Federalists raised two principal concerns, both stemming from fears of federal judicial activism. First, they warned that "equity" might be given its broader meaning as synonymous with "justice." Federal Farmer wrote that this provision would afford federal judges a "discretionary power."[19] Brutus argued that judges would be free of "any fixed or established rules," able to interpret laws "according to what they conceive are their spirit."[20] In other words, the Anti-Federalists worried that federal courts would rely on their equity jurisdiction to justify interpreting laws and the Constitution according to the judges' subjective view of justice rather than the text of those documents.

Second, the Anti-Federalists had concerns about how federal courts would operate as courts of equity. Federal Farmer recognized that "in Great Britain, . . . chancery proceedings there [had been] reduced to [a] system."[21] But equity practice in the young United States differed from state to state, and some states had no equity courts at all. Without "precedents in this country . . . to regulate the divisions in equity as in Great Britain," Federal Farmer feared that

federal courts would exercise their equity powers according to nothing but "mere discretion."[22]

The Federalists argued that "equity" should be understood in its narrower, more technical sense. "[T]he word 'equity,'" Alexander Hamilton argued in Federalist No. 80, referred to matters that are "object[s] of equitable, rather than of legal jurisdiction." Hamilton added that this "distinction [was] known and established in several of the States."

The Federalists also sought to assuage fears that equity jurisdiction would afford judges unbounded power. Hamilton insisted in Federalist No. 83 that "the principles by which [equitable] relief is governed are now reduced to a regular system." Federalist politician Timothy Pickering argued that "[a]s our ideas of a court of equity are derived from the English jurisprudence," federal courts would be bound to follow "the practice of the Court of Chancery in England."[23]

EARLY PRACTICE

The First Congress promptly gave the new federal courts the powers of the English courts of law and equity. The Judiciary Act of 1789 gave the circuit courts jurisdiction over certain "suits of a civil nature at common law or in equity."[24] In 1792, Congress provided that the courts' equitable power would be governed "according to the principles, rules and usages which belong to courts of equity . . . as contradistinguished from courts of common law."[25] The Supreme Court soon explained that this provision meant that federal courts were to rely on the equitable principles of the English Court of Chancery at the time of Founding, not on the contemporaneous principles of state courts.[26]

In 1822, the Supreme Court prescribed thirty-three Equity Rules for the inferior federal courts.[27] In 1842, the Court prescribed ninety-two Equity Rules.[28] The 1842 rules lasted until the Court adopted the Equity Rules of 1912,[29] which were its last before the merger of law and equity in 1938.

JUDICIAL PRECEDENT

Over the years, the Supreme Court has often looked to Founding-era equity practice when determining the scope of federal equity power. *In re Debs* (1895) surveyed over a century of writing on equity to conclude that federal courts could enjoin striking unionists—a perceived public nuisance—from interfering with interstate commerce.[30] Fifty years later, the Court confirmed that, to invoke the equity power of the federal courts, "the suit must be within the traditional scope of equity as historically evolved in the English Court of Chancery."[31] In *Grupo Mexicano* (1999), the Court reaffirmed that the "prerequisites for obtaining an equitable remedy . . . depend on traditional principles of equity jurisdiction."[32]

Still, when it comes to equity, the Court has not always been a stickler for tradition. In *Osborn v. Bank of United States* (1824), the Court permitted the issuance of an injunction to remedy a trespass by state officials even though an injunction "ha[d] [n]ever been granted in such a case."[33] It was enough that the Court could draw analogies between *Osborn's* case and cases in which injunctions *had* been granted.[34] At the turn of the twentieth century, the Court went even further. *Ex parte Young* (1908) held that a state official could be sued in equity to prevent him from enforcing an allegedly unconstitutional law even though no law expressly permitted that kind of injunction.[35] In dissent, Justice John Marshall Harlan wrote that this was an unprecedented and unwarranted extension of federal equity power.[36]

OPEN QUESTIONS

- Is it permissible to deviate from the traditional forms of equitable relief? If so, how far? As two centuries of case law show, the answers to these questions remain unsettled. Chief Justice John Marshall, author of the *Osborn* opinion, apparently thought that some minor deviations were permissible.[37] Justice Antonin Scalia, writing for the majority in *Grupo Mexicano*, agreed with "the proposition that equity is flexible" but added that this "flexibility is confined within the broad boundaries of traditional equitable relief." Going beyond those boundaries, he cautioned, would replace "flexibility" with "omnipotence."[38] Even today, scholars continue to debate the appropriate role of equity.[39]

- The debate about equity's flexibility informs another much-debated issue: whether *Ex parte Young* was correctly decided. Some scholars say that equity *always* permitted suits against officials to prevent enforcement of a law.[40] In *Armstrong v. Exceptional Child Center, Inc.* (2015), Justice Scalia wrote that "[t]he ability to sue to enjoin unconstitutional actions by state and federal officers is the creation of courts of equity, and reflects a long history of judicial review of illegal executive action."[41] Other scholars contend that *Young's* holding was a novel but appropriate one.[42] We believe that the holding exceeded the authority of federal courts to afford traditional equitable relief.[43]

Cite as: Judge Andrew S. Oldham & Adam I. Steene, *The Judicial Power—Law & Equity Clause, in* THE HERITAGE GUIDE TO THE CONSTITUTION 457 (Josh Blackman & John G. Malcolm eds., 3d ed. 2025).

Notes

1. 1 Samuel Johnson, A Dictionary of the English Language (1755), https://perma.cc/ZJZ4-SV2C. **2.** 3 Blackstone 30. **3.** Frederic William Maitland, Equity, Also the Forms of Action at Common Law 2 (1910); Theodore F.T. Plucknett, A Concise History of the Common Law 80–81 (5th ed., 1956). **4.** 3 Blackstone, 41 & n.p. **5.** *Case of Prohibitions* (1607) 77 Eng. Rep. 1342; 12 Co. Rep. 64; 3 Blackstone 41 n.p. **6.** Maitland, *supra* at 298–99. **7.** Johnson, *supra*, https://perma.cc/XC2J-XNP6; 3 Blackstone 429. **8.** 3 Blackstone 430–31. **9.** 1 John Bouvier, A Law Dictionary, Adapted to the Constitution and Laws of the United States of America, and of the Several States of the American Union 368 (1st ed., 1839). **10.** Johnson, *supra*. **11.** Maitland, *supra* at 4–5. **12.** *Id.* at 8; Andrew S. Oldham, Adam I. Steene, & John W. Tienken, *The Ex Parte Young Cause of Action: A Riddle, Wrapped in a Mystery, Inside an Enigma*, 120 Nw. U. L. Rev. (forthcoming 2026) (manuscript at 6), https://ssrn.com/abstract=4204132. **13.** Maitland, *supra* at 254. **14.** 1 St. George Tucker, Blackstone's Commentaries: With Notes of Reference to the Constitution and Laws, of the Federal Government of the United States and of the Commonwealth of Virginia 429 (1803); Oldham, Steene, & Tienken, *supra* at 8–9. **15.** *Robinson v. Campbell*, 16 U.S. (3 Wheat.) 212,

222 (1818); Oldham, Steene, & Tienken, *supra* at 8–9.   **16.** 2 Farrand's 428.   **17.** *Id.*   **18.** *Id.* at 621–22.   **19.** Storing 2.8.195.   **20.** *Id.* at 2.9.138, 2.9.160.   **21.** *Id.* at 2.8.195.   **22.** *Id.* at 2.8.42.   **23.** Letter from Timothy Pickering to Charles Tillinghast (Dec. 24, 1787), *in* 2 Charles W. Upham, Life of Timothy Pickering 360 (1873 ed.).   **24.** Ch. 20, § 11, 1 Stat. 73, 78.   **25.** Act of May 8, 1792, ch. 36, § 2, 1 Stat. 275, 276.   **26.** *Robinson v. Campbell*, 16 U.S. (3 Wheat.) 212, 222–23 (1818); Oldham, Steene, & Tienken, *supra* at 9 & n.70.   **27.** 20 U.S. (7 Wheat.) xvii.   **28.** 42 U.S. (1 How.) xli.   **29.** 226 U.S. 627.   **30.** 158 U.S. 564, 586–93 (1895).   **31.** *Guaranty Tr. Co. v. York*, 326 U.S. 99, 105 (1945).   **32.** *Grupo Mexicano de Desarrollo S.A. v. All. Bond Fund, Inc.*, 527 U.S. 308, 318–19

(1999).   **33.** 22 U.S. (9 Wheat.) 738, 841 (1824).   **34.** *Id.* at 841–42.   **35.** 209 U.S. 123, 167 (1908).   **36.** *Id.* at 192 (Harlan, J., dissenting).   **37.** *Osborn*, 22 U.S. (9 Wheat.) at 841–42.   **38.** *Grupo Mexicano*, 527 U.S. at 322.   **39.** Samuel Bray, *Getting into Equity*, 97 Notre Dame L. Rev. 1763, 1795–99 (2022); Josh Blackman & Seth Barrett Tillman, *There Is No Cause of Action for Ultra Vires Conduct*, 19 Geo. J.L. & Pub. Pol'y 163, 211–14 (2022).   **40.** John Harrison, Ex parte Young, 60 Stan. L. Rev. 989 (2008).   **41.** 575 U.S. 320, 327 (2015).   **42.** James E. Pfander & Jacob Wentzel, *The Common Law Origins of* Ex parte Young, 72 Stan. L. Rev. 1269 (2020).   **43.** Oldham, Steene, & Tienken, *supra*.

ESSAY NO. 124: THE JUDICIAL POWER—ARISING UNDER CLAUSE
ART. III, § 2, CL. 1

The judicial Power shall extend to all Cases . . . arising under this Constitution, [and] the Laws of the United States. . . .

—Arthur D. Hellman

INTRODUCTION

Article III, Section 2 delineates the scope of the federal judicial power by listing nine kinds of "Cases" and "Controversies" to which the "judicial Power" of the United States "shall extend." First in the enumeration and, in the view of Chief Justice John Marshall, "first in the mind of the framers"[1] is the category encompassing "all Cases . . . arising under this Constitution, the Laws of the United States, and Treaties made, or which shall be made, under their Authority." This category is often referred to as the "federal question" jurisdiction, and although the Constitution does not use the term, it is a convenient label. The Framers intended the scope of this provision to be broad. The breadth of the constitutional grant was recognized during the ratification debates and confirmed by decisions of the Marshall Court and its successors.[2]

THE CONSTITUTIONAL CONVENTION

The federal question jurisdiction, in embryonic form, made its first appearance at the Constitutional Convention as part of the Virginia Plan. That proposal would have authorized federal courts to hear "questions which may involve the national peace and harmony."[3] Edmund Randolph of Virginia "observed the difficulty in establishing the powers of the

judiciary" but emphasized that one purpose was "to preserve the harmony of states and that of the citizens thereof."[4]

On July 18, 1787, James Madison of Virginia proposed adding to the Virginia Plan's language a grant of jurisdiction over "cases arising under laws passed by the general Legislature."[5] The proposal passed unanimously, but when the Committee of Detail reported to the Convention on August 6, the reference to "national peace and harmony" had disappeared; only the "arising under" language remained.[6]

The delegates devoted little more time to the federal question jurisdiction. In the course of a single day, on August 27, the Convention made three important changes. The delegates replaced the reference to "laws passed by the Legislature" with "laws of the United States."[7] And, on separate motions, the Convention extended the judicial power to cases arising under the Constitution and then to cases arising under treaties.[8] When the Committee of Style reported to the Convention in September, the provision read substantially the same as the ratified version: The federal judicial power extends "to all cases, both in law and equity, arising under this Constitution, the laws of the United States, and treaties made, or which shall be made, under their authority."[9]

Significantly, the evolution of the "arising

under" jurisdiction proceeded in parallel with that of the Supremacy Clause. The initial version of the Supremacy Clause was part of the New Jersey Plan. It provided that "Acts" of Congress and "Treaties" of the United States "shall be the supreme law of the respective states."[10] The New Jersey Plan was not adopted, but on July 17, immediately after the delegates rejected the Virginia Plan's provision allowing the legislature to "negative" state laws, Luther Martin of Maryland proposed a supremacy provision that closely tracked the one in the New Jersey Plan.[11] The proposal was adopted unanimously and appeared in streamlined language in the report of the Committee of Detail.[12]

On August 23, the Convention agreed to an amended version of the provision that accorded supremacy to the Constitution as well as statutes and treaties.[13] Four days later, on August 27, the Convention made the conforming change in the "arising under" clause. In the end, the Constitution, federal laws, and treaties would be the "supreme law of the land" (See Essay No. 154). And the federal courts would have jurisdiction to hear cases that arise under those three sources of supreme law.

THE RATIFICATION DEBATES

When the proposed Constitution came before the states for ratification, as Anthony Bellia has observed, "the meaning of Article III 'arising under' jurisdiction did not dominate [the] debates about the federal judicial power."[14] Nevertheless, some insights do emerge.

First, the connection between the Supremacy Clause and the Arising Under Clause was recognized both by supporters of ratification and by opponents. For example, Luther Martin, arguing to the Maryland legislature against ratification, insisted that with the Supremacy Clause in force, there was no reason to authorize federal courts to hear cases "that should arise under" federal law.[15] But, he reported, "a majority" at the Convention believed that the supremacy of federal law would be at risk if state judges were "intrusted with the administration of" federal laws.[16]

Second, opponents of ratification criticized the potential breadth of the language. For example, during the Virginia ratification convention, George Mason asked rhetorically,

"What objects will not this expression extend to?"[17] James Madison, a supporter of ratification, implicitly responded the following day, asserting that "the judicial power [of the national government] should correspond with the legislative [power]."[18] More broadly, Edmund Randolph emphasized the need for federal courts to enforce federal law, particularly to prevent encroachments by the states.[19]

Third, supporters of ratification emphasized that the jurisdictional grant would empower federal judges to strike down Acts of Congress that were "inconsistent with the Constitution."[20] Opponents agreed that the provision conferred that authority, but they argued that the jurisdictional grant—particularly for cases arising under the Constitution—would lead, in the words of the Anti-Federalist Brutus, to "an entire subversion of the legislative, executive and judicial powers of the individual states."[21]

Finally, as Hamilton explained in Federalist No. 80, the "arising under" jurisdiction was viewed as an essential means for securing uniformity in the interpretation of federal law.[22]

JUDICIAL CONSTRUCTION: THE MARSHALL COURT

When does a case "arise under" federal law so that it falls within the judicial power of the United States? The authoritative answer to this question is found largely in two decisions by Chief Justice Marshall in the 1820s.

The first, *Cohens v. Virginia* (1821), involved a challenge to the authority of the U.S. Supreme Court to review a case originating in state court.[23] The defendants were convicted of a crime under state law. They claimed that those state offenses were preempted, or trumped, by the supreme federal law.[24] When the state's highest court rejected their argument, they asserted that the Supreme Court could consider their appeal, both because an Act of Congress allowed it,[25] and because it was a case "arising under" federal law within the meaning of Article III. Virginia countered that a case could "arise under" federal law only if the party who initiated the lawsuit invoked that federal law.[26] This was a state criminal prosecution that did not meet this standard.

The state's interpretation is a plausible

reading of the Arising Under Clause, but the Supreme Court rejected it as "too narrow."[27] Marshall said that cases are defined by the rights of both parties, not just the plaintiff who filed the suit. Thus, a case "may truly be said to arise under the Constitution or a law of the United States whenever its correct decision depends on the construction of either."[28] Under *Cohens*, the Supreme Court has jurisdiction to hear appeals from state courts when those courts have decided federal questions.

The second and better-known decision is *Osborn v. Bank of the United States* (1824).[29] Marshall's analysis proceeded in two steps. First, he declared that a "question" is "federal" if "the title or right set up by the party, may be defeated by one construction of the Constitution or law of the United States, and sustained by the opposite construction. . . ."[30] In other words, a federal question is a question whose answer depends in some way on federal law. Second, Marshall stated that a case "arises under" the Constitution or laws of the United States if a federal question "forms an ingredient of the original cause"—that is, if the question is an element of the plaintiff's claim.[31]

The breadth of this definition is made clear by a companion case argued together with *Osborn* and decided the following day. This was *Bank of the United States v. Planters' Bank of Georgia* (1824).[32] In this case, the Bank of the United States brought a suit against a state bank. The defendant bank's liability depended entirely on state law. Nevertheless, the Court upheld the jurisdiction, saying simply that the jurisdictional issue "was fully considered" in *Osborn* and required no further discussion.

How did Marshall conclude that a federal question formed an "ingredient" of the "original cause"? Marshall explained in *Osborn* that there are some federal questions that necessarily exist in every case brought by the bank.[33] These questions include the bank's capacity to sue in federal court. *Osborn* thus establishes that as long as a proposition of federal law is a logical antecedent of the plaintiff's claim, it is sufficient as a constitutional matter to support federal judicial power over the case.

REMOVAL TO FEDERAL COURT

Cohens and *Osborn* provide two complementary tests for defining the "arising under" jurisdiction, each targeted to a different situation. *Cohens* is concerned with the Supreme Court's appellate jurisdiction over cases initially litigated in state courts. *Osborn* provides the test for cases in which the plaintiff seeks entry to a federal trial court.

But there is a third possibility. From the beginning, Congress has authorized a process by which a case can be *removed* from state court by the defendant to be litigated in federal court. If a federal question is an ingredient of the plaintiff's claim, the *Osborn* test, of itself, would allow the removal: Nothing in the definition turns on which party is seeking entry to federal court. But suppose the plaintiff's claim is grounded solely in state law and the federal question is raised by the defendant. The case would not fall within the *Osborn* test, nor would it meet the *Cohens* test: At the time of removal, there is no way to know whether the federal question will be dispositive.

In a series of nineteenth-century cases, the Supreme Court made plain that Article III empowers Congress to authorize removal of any case in which a defense under federal law has been invoked, even though the federal issue may prove not to be dispositive. The leading case is *Tennessee v. Davis* (1880).[34] In *Davis*, a federal revenue agent was prosecuted for killing one of several armed men who fired on him as he attempted to enforce federal revenue laws. A federal statute allowed removal based on his federal defense, and the Court, relying heavily on *Cohens*, held that the statute was constitutional. The Court emphasized that in order to preserve the supremacy of federal judicial power, it is essential that the national government be able to "take control" "whenever and wherever a case arises under the Constitution and laws or treaties of the United States . . . whether it be civil or criminal, *in any stage of its progress.*"[35]

SETTLED LAW AND OPEN QUESTIONS

The Supreme Court decisions summarized above have established that Congress can authorize federal courts to hear cases based on the Arising Under Clause under three circumstances: when a federal question is a logical antecedent of the plaintiff's claim, regardless of whether that question is contested; when the federal question is the basis of a defense actually raised, even though the defense may not be dispositive; and when the federal question is the basis of the decision actually made, typically by a state court.

Relying on the Court's decisions, Congress has deployed the jurisdiction in numerous statutes, creating a complex body of law that is made more complex by judicial interpretation.[36] Meanwhile, other constitutional issues remain unresolved:

Can Congress authorize jurisdiction over cases in which federal *interests* may be involved but a federal question is an element neither of the original cause nor of the defense—for example, a case in which a litigant is a member of a class that Congress seeks to protect, such as federal employees sued in state court?[37]

Osborn is sometimes read as allowing jurisdiction based on the mere possibility that a federal question will be presented.[38] Is that a correct reading, and should the Court go that far?

Article III provides that the federal judicial power "shall extend to *all* cases . . . arising under [federal law]." Does this mean that Congress must authorize "*some* federal court . . . to hear and resolve finally any given federal question [case]?"[39] Or can Congress leave final resolution of some federal-question cases to state courts?[40]

Cite as: Arthur D. Hellman, *The Judicial Power—Arising Under Clause, in* THE HERITAGE GUIDE TO THE CONSTITUTION 460 (Josh Blackman & John G. Malcolm eds., 3d ed. 2025).

Notes

1. John Marshall, *A Friend of the Constitution*, in John Marshall's Defense of *McCulloch v. Maryland* 155, 203–04 (Gerald Gunther ed., 1969) (1819).   2. Arthur D. Hellman, *The Federal Question Jurisdiction Under Article III: "First in the Minds of the Framers," But Today, Perhaps, Falling Short of the Framers' Expectations*, 104 B.U. L. Rev. 2143 (2024).   3. 1 Farrand's 22.   4. *Id.* at 238.   5. 2 Farrand's 39, 46.   6. *Id.* at 186.   7. *Id.* at 431.   8. *Id.* at 430, 431.   9. *Id.* at 600   10. 1 Farrand 245.   11. 2 Farrand 27–28; 3 Farrand's 286–87.   12. 2 Farrand's 183.   13. *Id.* at 381–82, 389.   14. Anthony J. Bellia, Jr., *The Origins of Article III "Arising Under" Jurisdiction*, 57 Duke L.J. 263, 305 (2007).   15. 3 Farrand's 206.   16. *Id.* at 207.   17. 3 Elliot's 521.   18. *Id.* at 532.   19. *Id.* at 570.   20. 2 Elliott's 489.   21. Storing 2.9.139.   22. Bellia, *supra* at 316.   23. 6 Wheat (19 U.S.) 264 (1821).   24. *Id.* at 375.   25. Judiciary Act of 1789, ch. 20, § 25, 1 Stat. 73, 85.   26. *Id.* at 378–79.   27. *Id.* at 379.   28. *Id.*   29. 22 U.S. (9 Wheat.) 748 (1824).   30. *Id.* at 822.   31. *Id.* at 823.   32. 22 U.S. (9 Wheat.) 904 (1834).   33. *Osborn*, 22 U.S. at 823–24.   34. 100 U.S. 257 (1880).   35. *Id.* at 266 (emphasis added).   36. Hellman, *supra*.   37. *Mesa v. California*, 489 U.S. 121 (1989).   38. *Verlinden B.V. v. Central Bank of Nigeria*, 461 U.S. 480, 492 (1983).   39. Akhil Reed Amar, *A Neo-Federalist View of Article III: Separating the Two Tiers of Federal Jurisdiction*, 65 B.U. L. Rev. 205, 206 (1985) (emphasis added).   40. Henry Hart, *The Power of Congress to Limit the Jurisdiction of Federal Courts: An Exercise in Dialectic*, 66 Harv. L. Rev. 1362, 1372–73, 1401 (1953).

ESSAY NO. 125: THE JUDICIAL POWER—TREATIES CLAUSE
ART. III, § 2, CL. 1

The judicial Power shall extend to all . . . Treaties made, or which shall be made, under the Authority [of the United States]. . . .

—Judge Carlos T. Bea & Mitchell K. Pallaki

INTRODUCTION

One theme unifies the Constitution's provisions: It is a document of liberty oriented toward protecting individual rights. The drafters did not limit these protections to domestic matters: They extended them even to areas historically reserved for sovereigns applying the law of nations. One unique and innovative example is the Constitution's grant of federal jurisdiction over cases brought to vindicate persons' rights arising under treaties. Contrary to historical practice, this provision recognized that individuals, not just nations or groups of nations, can acquire and enforce rights based on treaties in federal courts.[1] The legal force of such treaties still depends in part on the exercise of sovereign authority by signatory nations. But the creation of federal jurisdiction over individual claims involving treaty rights underscores the Constitution's novel approach: establishing a government that safeguards the rights of *individuals*.[2]

HISTORY BEFORE 1787

Treaties have their origins in ancient times with examples stretching as far back as the third millennium B.C. One of the earliest treaties resolved boundary and water disputes between warring Sumerian city-states.[3] Historically, treaty disputes were resolved not by lawsuits, but by sovereign action: Sovereigns either turned to war or enforced their treaties through the good faith of the people. As Hugo Grotius observed, such arrangements would "invoke the divine vengeance on their heads, if they violate[d] their engagements."[4]

English law followed this historical tradition. It regarded treaties as creating rights and obligations that explicitly bound the signatory sovereign nations.[5] Domestic common-law courts in Great Britain, such as the King's Bench, accordingly lacked authority under the treaties themselves to adjudicate claims by individuals whose rights were affected by a given treaty. For a private individual to vindicate his personal rights under the treaty, Parliament had to enact laws recognizing such rights before courts could take jurisdiction over claims that raised such rights.[6]

The admiralty and prize courts, which were physically separate from the common-law courts, were different. They enforced a unique body of law based on the recognition of natural law, justice, and the laws of nations. For admiralty and prize courts, Parliament did not need to enact enabling legislation. Instead, the treaties were eventually recognized as vesting rights in individuals.[7]

Early courts in colonial America inherited this English tradition regarding the law of nations and the treatment of treaties as matters of sovereign engagements.[8] However, because these colonial courts were subordinate to English courts, they had little occasion to apply these traditional rules of the law of nations.[9]

After 1776, the notions of sovereignty underlying the legal effect of treaties in English common law took on special relevance. The formal recognition of the United States as a sovereign vested it with the powers inherent in all civilized nations. The Continental Congress exercised that newly obtained sovereign authority to execute treaties with several countries.[10] And the Articles of Confederation gave the Confederation Congress the "sole and exclusive right and power of . . . entering into treaties and alliances."[11] But the Confederation Congress lacked direct enforcement authority; it could only encourage states and local legislatures to give effect to these agreements—efforts that were largely unsuccessful.

The most potent example followed the signing of the 1783 Treaty of Paris with Great Britain.[12] The Treaty of Paris ended the Revolutionary War and settled many of the disputes that had arisen between British loyalists and American revolutionaries. It required states to provide restitution to loyalists whose property was confiscated during the war. The states were also barred from imposing legal impediments to efforts by British creditors to collect money owed by American debtors.[13]

Yet the Revolutionary War–period hostility toward loyalists remained after the Treaty of Paris. Many states refused to comply with these treaty obligations.[14] The Confederation Congress, which lacked the power to compel compliance, failed to persuade the states to protect the loyalists' property rights as required.[15] State courts similarly took cues from the state legislatures, which had declined to protect loyalists' property rights. These courts also refused to enforce the treaty obligations.[16] Further complicating matters, the Articles of Confederation did not establish any national courts to enforce treaties. The flaws of the system were palpable.

THE CONSTITUTIONAL CONVENTION

These problems came to a head at the Constitutional Convention. On June 19, 1787, William Paterson of New Jersey observed that under the Articles of Confederation, the states had a "tendency" to "violat[e] . . . the laws of nations & of Treaties." Congress had received "complaints . . . from almost every nation with which treaties have been formed," which led Paterson to remark that "[t]his cannot be the permanent disposition of foreign nations."[17]

The Framers would address this problem partly through the federal judiciary. On August 27, John Rutledge of Virginia proposed that the judicial power should include the power to adjudicate claims arising under treaties. This provision would extend federal court jurisdiction to cases concerning "treaties made or which shall be made under the[] Authority" of the United States.[18] The Treaty Clause expressly extended to treaties made before 1787, including the Treaty of Paris, to ensure that preexisting obligations were enforced. This language resembles the protections found in the Debt Assumption Clause, which ensured that debts "contracted . . . before the Adoption of this Constitution" would remain valid. (See Essay No. 153.) There was no noted discussion of the Treaty Clause, which was adopted unanimously.

THE RATIFICATION DEBATES

During the ratification debates, Anti-Federalists were generally opposed to federal authority over treaty rights. They feared that this federal power would restrict the ability of state legislatures and state courts to interpret and enforce such treaties. Centinel, for example, warned that "[t]he objects of jurisdiction [in Article III, Section 2], are so numerous, and the shades of distinction between civil causes are oftentimes so slight, that it is more than probable that the state judicatories would be wholly superceded."[19] Brutus similarly warned that the vesting of jurisdiction under Article III, Section 2, including jurisdiction over treaties, "w[ould] operate to a total subversion of the state judiciaries, if not, to the legislative authority of the states."[20]

The Federalists, by contrast, argued that this provision was necessary. In Federalist No. 3, John Jay defended this grant of jurisdiction, which he said would ensure that "treaties and articles of treaties . . . will always be expounded in one sense and executed in the same manner."

EARLY PRACTICE AND JUDICIAL PRECEDENT

The Judiciary Act of 1789 granted the federal courts jurisdiction over cases concerning individual rights implicating treaty obligations, even if the party was an alien.[21] This statute, now known as the Alien Tort Statute, also granted the U.S. Supreme Court jurisdiction over appeals dealing with state judgments adverse to the rights of parties who made claims under treaties.[22] The Judiciary Act did not yet grant federal courts the full jurisdiction available under the Treaty Clause, but it enabled the Supreme Court to adjudicate important treaty-related cases.

The earliest conflicts implicated the 1783 Treaty of Paris. Virginia, for example, discharged debts owed to British subjects by treating them as enemy aliens who were incapable of contracting. *Ware v. Hylton* (1796) held that this state law was abrogated by the Treaty of Paris, which formed a part of the "Supreme Law of the Land."[23] Justice James Iredell's opinion provided an early articulation of the individual rights protections implicit in the Treaty Clause: Treaties could be read to vest rights in individuals that the judiciary could adjudicate.[24]

The Court applied this principle in *The Schooner Peggy* (1801).[25] There, a United States ship seized a French ship, and the French owners invoked a U.S.–France treaty to restore their possession and ownership. Because the treaty had taken effect before the seizure, the Court directed the lower court to order that the ship be returned to the French owners. Though treaties could vest rights in individuals, *Owings v. Norwood's Lessee* (1809) made clear that federal jurisdiction attached only if "a right grows out of, or is protected by, a treaty."[26] Hence, the Treaty of Paris did not furnish the source of the petitioner's property claim, because the property interest expired before the Treaty was signed.

FEDERAL AND STATE COURT JURISDICTION

Over time, lower courts played a larger role in resolving claims involving individual treaty rights. Before 1875, only the Supreme Court adjudicated cases arising under treaties that came up on appeal from state courts.[27] But the Jurisdiction and Removal Act of 1875 granted lower federal courts jurisdiction over all cases "arising under . . . treaties made, or which shall be made, under the[] authority [of the United States]."[28] In substance, that grant of jurisdiction is the equivalent of the current federal question jurisdiction statute, which affords federal courts the full Article III jurisdiction under the Treaty Clause.[29] This jurisdiction, however, is not exclusive. Individuals or nations can also enforce their treaty rights in state courts.[30] Today, most treaty cases are brought in federal court.[31]

TERMINATION OF TREATY RIGHTS

Even though the Constitution recognizes and protects individual treaty rights, sovereign nations must still exercise their authority to give those treaties legal force. This is generally clear when a treaty goes into effect, but the issue becomes more complicated when a treaty is no longer enforceable.

For example, war can suspend the treaty rights of individuals but not necessarily extinguish them. During the War of 1812, the treaty obligations of the United States and Britain were suspended, but the 1814 Treaty of Ghent, which ended hostilities, revived those nations' responsibilities under the 1783 Treaty of Paris. For this reason, the Supreme Court ruled that rights to a pre-Revolution land grant by the British crown were protected by the Treaty of Paris despite the War of 1812.[32]

If the United States repudiates its obligations under a treaty, the treaty and the rights it created lose legal force. For example, the Jay Treaty of 1794 granted Canadians the unrestrained right to immigrate to the United States, but the War of 1812 and border skirmishes had the effect of automatically voiding such rights.[33]

Similarly, if a foreign sovereign disavows its treaty obligations, the United States can terminate the treaty—likely by presidential decree, although the caselaw on this point is unsettled.[34] But if the United States still complies with its treaty obligations, the treaty is not voided and remains legally enforceable.[35] In 1910, for example, Italy petitioned the United States to extradite an American citizen accused of murdering his wife in Italy. The Supreme Court concluded that the accused had properly been remanded to federal custody for extradition under an enforceable 1868 extradition treaty.[36] The Court reached this conclusion even though Italy had disavowed *its* treaty obligation to extradite Italian citizens because the United States "elected to waive any right to free itself from the obligation to deliver up its own citizens."[37]

OPEN QUESTIONS

- Can Article II executive agreements reached by the President vest individuals with rights in the same manner as self-executing treaties do? (See Essay No. 106.) *Reid v. Covert* (1957) acknowledged some distinction between executive agreements and treaties but explained that the difference did not matter in that case.[38]

- Generally, states are immune from suits by citizens because of sovereign immunity, but what happens when a state violates a treaty? Can Congress abrogate state sovereign immunity and create federal causes of action that allow individuals to sue states in federal courts for violating rights arising under treaties? Justice Clarence Thomas has observed that "it is not likely that the Founders did, in fact, expect foreign creditor suits against States" under the 1783 Treaty of Paris.[39] Rather, as Professor Bradford R. Clark has written, "it is more likely that they expected creditors to sue their individual debtors and rely on the Treaty to defeat any state law defenses."[40]

- Under Article III, the federal courts have jurisdiction only over suits that have "a close historical or common-law analogue for the[] asserted injury."[41] How does this standing rule affect rights arising under treaties that deviate from those causes recognized at common law? Do these precedents constrain Congress's ability to consummate treaties that create causes of action for individuals to vindicate their treaty rights?[42]

Cite as: Judge Carlos T. Bea & Mitchell K. Pallaki, *The Judicial Power—Treaties Clause, in* THE HERITAGE GUIDE TO THE CONSTITUTION 463 (Josh Blackman & John G. Malcolm eds., 3d ed. 2025).

Notes

1. Carlos Manuel Vázquez, *Treaty-Based Rights and Remedies of Individuals*, 92 Colum. L. Rev. 1082, 1084–85 (1992). **2.** James Wilson, *Of the Natural Rights of Individuals*, in 2 Collected Works of James Wilson 1061 (Kermit L. Hall & Mark David Hall eds., 2007). **3.** Peter H. Sand, *Environmental Dispute Resolution 4,500 Years Ago: The Case of* Lagash v Umma, 30 Yearbook Int'l Envtl. L. 137 (2020). **4.** Grotius, The Rights of War and Peace 167 (A.C. Campbell trans., 1901). **5.** J.G. Collier, *Is International Law Really Part of the Law of England?*, 38 Int'l & Comp. L.Q. 924, 925–26 (1989). **6.** Harold H. Sprout, *Theories as to the Applicability of International Law in the Federal Courts of the United States*, 26 Am. J. Int'l L. 280, 282–85 (1932); Collier, *supra* at 925–28. **7.** *Lindo v. Rodney & Another*, (1781) 2 Doug. 613 (K.B.) (opinion of Lord Mansfield) (reported in *Le Caux v. Eden*, (1781) 99 E.R. 375, 385 n.10 (K.B.)). **8.** Edwin D. Dickinson, *The Law of Nations as Part of the National Law of the United States*, 101 U. Pa. L. Rev. 26, 32–33 (1952). **9.** *Id.* at 33. **10.** Treaties Between the United States of America and Foreign Nations: From the Declaration of the Independence of the United States to 1845, 8 Stat. 6–105 (Richard Peters ed., 1846). **11.** Articles of Confederation, art. IX, § 1. **12.** The Definitive Treaty of Peace Between the United States of America and His Britannic Majesty, Sept. 3, 1783, 8 Stat. 80 (Richard Peters ed., 1846) [hereinafter Treaty of Paris]. **13.** Treaty of Paris, arts. IV–V, 8 Stat. 82–83. **14.** James Westfall Thompson, *Anti-Loyalist Legislation During the American Revolution*, 3 Ill. L. Rev. 147, 168–71 (1908). **15.** *Id.*; *A Letter from Mr. Hammond, Minister Plenipotentiary of Great Britain, to Mr. Jefferson, Secretary of State* (Mar. 5, 1792), 1 Am. State Papers 193–200 (1833). **16.** Wythe Holt, *The Origins of Alienage Jurisdiction*, 14 Okla. City U. L. Rev. 547, 552, 561–62 (1989). **17.** 1 Farrand's 316. **18.** 2 Farrand's 423–24, 431. **19.** Storing 2.7.12. **20.** *Id.* at 2.9.133. **21.** Alien Tort Statute, Judiciary Act of 1789, § 9, 1 Stat. 73, 76 (codified at 28 U.S.C. § 1350). **22.** *Id.* at § 25, 1 Stat. 85. **23.** 3 U.S. (3 Dall.) 199 (1796); *accord Martin v. Hunter's Lessee*, 14 U.S. (1 Wheat.) 304, 355–62 (1816). **24.** 3 U.S. (3 Dall.) at 274–77 (opinion of Iredell, J.). **25.** 5 U.S. (1 Cranch) 103, 108–10 (1801). **26.** 9 U.S. (5 Cranch) 344, 348 (1809). **27.** William M. Wiecek, *The Reconstruction of Federal Judicial Power, 1863–1875*, 13 Am. J. Legal Hist. 333, 341–42, 348–49 (1969). **28.** Jurisdiction and Removal Act of 1875, § 1, ch. 137, 18 Stat. 470 (1875); Judicial Code of 1911, §§ 24, 289, Pub. L. No. 61–475, 36 Stat. 1087, 1091, 1167 (1911). **29.** 28 U.S.C. § 1331. **30.** *Scandinavian Airlines Sys., Inc. v. L.A. Cnty.*, 363 P.2d 25 (Ca. 1961); *In re Zalewski's Estate*, 55 N.E.2d 184 (N.Y. 1944); *San Lorenzo Title & Improvement Co. v. City Mortg. Co.*, 73 S.W.2d 513 (Tex. 1934); *King of Prussia v. Kuepper's Adm'r*, 22 Mo. 550 (1856). **31.** *Republic of Paraguay v. Allen*, 949 F. Supp. 1269 (E.D. Va. 1996); *Principality of Monaco v. Mississippi*, 292 U.S. 313, 323 n.2 (1934) (citing *The Sapphire*, 78 U.S. (11 Wall.) 164, 167–68 (1870)). **32.** *Soc'y for the Propagation of the Gospel in Foreign Parts v. New Haven*, 21 U.S. (8 Wheat.) 464, 493–94 (1823). **33.** *Karnuth v. United States*, 279 U.S. 231, 239–41 (1929). **34.** *Terlinden v. Ames*, 184 U.S. 270, 289 (1902); *Zivotofsky v. Kerry*, 576 U.S. 1, 13–14 (2015); *United States v. Curtiss-Wright Export Corp.*, 299 U.S. 304, 324 n.2 (1936); Jules Lobel, *The Limits of Constitutional Power: Conflicts Between Foreign Policy and International Law*, 71 Va. L. Rev. 1071, 1126 (1985). **35.** *Terlinden*, 184 U.S. at 286–87, 289–90. **36.** *Charlton v. Kelly*, 229 U.S. 447, 469–73 (1913). **37.** *Id.* at 470–71, 476. **38.** 354 U.S. 1, 17 n.33 (1957). **39.** *Torres v. Tex. Dep't of Pub. Safety*, 597 U.S. 580, 615 (2022) (Thomas, J., dissenting). **40.** Bradford R. Clark, *The Eleventh Amendment and the Nature of the Union*, 123 Harv. L. Rev. 1817, 1910 (2010). **41.** *TransUnion LLC v. Ramirez*, 594 U.S. 413, 424 (2021); *Spokeo v. Robins*, 578 U.S. 330, 341 (2016). **42.** *Farrell v. Blinken*, 4 F.4th 124, 133 (D.C. Cir. 2021).

ESSAY NO. 126: THE JUDICIAL POWER—AMBASSADORS CLAUSE
ART. III, § 2, CL. 1

The judicial Power shall extend . . . to all Cases affecting Ambassadors, other public Ministers and Consuls. . . .

—Christopher T. Landau & Chase T. Harrington

INTRODUCTION

The Ambassadors Clause of Article III extends the federal judicial power to "all Cases affecting Ambassadors, other public Ministers and Consuls."[1] The phrase "Ambassadors, other public Ministers, and Consuls" apparently derives from a similar phrase in the British Diplomatic Privileges Act of 1708 and encompasses the full range of foreign representatives who have rights under international law. The clause seems designed both to provide a federal forum for cases involving the law of nations, including the proper application of diplomatic immunity, and to protect the United States' international standing by ensuring proper respect for all members of foreign diplomatic missions.

HISTORY BEFORE 1787

Going back at least to Roman times, international law has recognized that foreign diplomats duly accredited in a host nation are generally immune from that nation's judicial process, absent a waiver of such immunity by the foreign sovereign.[2] Roman law disfavored permitting a lawsuit "against an ambassador . . . lest diplomacy be hampered."[3] The law of nations also obligated nations to ensure that offenses against a foreign sovereign's diplomats would be punished to "give full satisfaction to the sovereign who has been offended in the person of his minister."[4]

It was thus understood at the Founding that a failure to honor diplomatic immunity or to punish offenses against foreign diplomats could damage relations with other countries. For example, in 1708, the Russian ambassador to Great Britain was seized by creditors and jailed as a result of his debts. He was freed on bail, but Czar Peter of Russia demanded that the creditors responsible be severely punished. The creditors were put on trial and found guilty of violating the law of nations, but English law punished such infractions only as misdemeanors.[5] In response to these tensions, Parliament passed the Diplomatic Privileges Act of 1708.[6] This statute prohibited all judicial process against "Ambassadors or other publick Ministers" and prohibited their arrest.[7] Justice Joseph Story referenced this incident as the "well known" backdrop of Article III's Ambassadors Clause.[8]

After the United States declared independence from Great Britain, only state governments had authority to protect foreign diplomats and punish violations against the law of nations. The most the Continental Congress could do was implore states to carry out this responsibility. Thus, in 1781, Congress passed a resolution imploring states to "provide expeditious, exemplary and adequate punishment" for "infractions of the immunities of ambassadors and other public ministers."[9] The resolution also advised states to "authorise suits . . . for damages by the party injured, and for compensation to the United States for damage sustained by them from an injury done to a foreign power by a citizen."[10] Most states ignored this resolution.[11]

Congress's impotence led to crisis when a French adventurer, Charles Julian De Longchamps, assaulted the Secretary of the French legation in the United States, Francis Marbé-Marbois.[12] Following his arrest and release on bail, De Longchamps continued to harass Marbois, even threatening assassination, provoking international outrage.[13] When De Longchamps was eventually put on trial in Pennsylvania, all Congress could do was pass a resolution that it "highly approve[d]" that the law of nations was at last being enforced.[14]

THE CONSTITUTIONAL CONVENTION

Despite profound differences among the delegates over the scope of the proposed federal judicial power, there is no record of any controversy about extending that power to cases involving foreign diplomats. Edmund Randolph of Virginia, perhaps in reference to the Marbois incident, lamented that "[i]f the rights of an ambassador be invaded by any citizen it is only in a few States that any laws exist to punish the offender."[15] Both the Virginia Plan (which contemplated a relatively broad role for the federal judiciary) and the New Jersey Plan (which contemplated a relatively limited role) recognized that the federal judicial power should encompass cases involving foreign diplomats. There was a general concern that state courts could trigger diplomatic incidents by failing to accord such diplomats the immunity and respect due them under international law.[16] The ideal forum for such cases would be federal court.

The Committee of Detail therefore drafted Article III to extend the federal judicial power "to all Cases affecting Ambassadors, other public Ministers, and Consuls."[17] The provision was not the subject of any debate at the Convention, even in light of the heated discussion about the scope of federal judicial power. Nor did the Committee of Style make any changes.[18]

THE RATIFICATION DEBATES

The Ambassadors Clause similarly excited no controversy during the ratification debates. In Federalist No. 80, Alexander Hamilton noted that the extension of the federal judicial power to cases involving foreign diplomats has "an evident connection with the preservation of the national peace." Even the Anti-Federalists agreed that such cases belonged within federal jurisdiction. Brutus observed that "none but the general government, can, or ought to pass laws on their subjects."[19] Agrippa agreed that "[t]he judicial department" should decide "cases where Ambassadours are concerned."[20] George Mason, expressing his fear of federal courts at the Virginia ratification convention, nevertheless spoke in favor of "judicial cognizance in all cases affecting ambassadors, foreign ministers and consuls."[21]

STATUTORY LIMITS ON JURISDICTION UNDER THE AMBASSADORS CLAUSE

As noted, the Ambassadors Clause grants the federal courts jurisdiction over certain types of cases but does not purport to withdraw state court jurisdiction over such cases. Congress has never extended federal jurisdiction under the clause to its full limits. Article III establishes the outer bounds of federal jurisdiction but Congress is not required to extend such jurisdiction to those outer limits.[22]

Section 13 of the Judiciary Act of 1789 gave the Supreme Court original and "exclusive jurisdiction . . . of suits or proceedings *against* ambassadors, or other public ministers, or their domestics, or domestic servants, as a court of law can have or exercise consistently with the law of nations." This category concerned cases where the ambassadors and public ministers were the defendants. Section 13 also granted the Supreme Court "original but not exclusive jurisdiction of all suits *brought by* ambassadors, or other public ministers, or in which a consul, or vice consul, shall be a party."[23] Here, ambassadors and public ministers could bring suit as plaintiffs in the Supreme Court, invoking its original jurisdiction, or in a lower federal court. (See Essay No. 134.) Moreover, the Supreme Court would have original but not exclusive jurisdiction in cases where a consul or vice consul is a plaintiff or a defendant. Section 9 added that federal district courts "shall also have jurisdiction exclusively of the courts of the several States, of all suits against consuls or vice-consuls," subject to certain exceptions.

State courts continue to enjoy concurrent jurisdiction, apart from specific categories of cases involving foreign diplomats that Congress commits to the exclusive jurisdiction of federal courts.[24] For example, *State of Ohio ex rel. Popovici v. Agler* (1930) held that an American divorce suit against a Romanian official could be brought in Ohio because Congress had not divested state courts of family law matters involving foreign diplomats.[25]

WHAT SUITS "AFFECT" AMBASSADORS?

The Crimes Act of 1790 extended broad immunity to diplomatic personnel and their families.[26] This statute was based on the English Diplomatic Privileges Act of 1708. This immunity can be raised in federal court, but over what sorts of suits involving diplomats do federal courts have jurisdiction? In *Osborn v. Bank of the United States* (1824), Chief Justice John Marshall emphasized in dicta that this judicial power extends beyond cases in which a foreign diplomat is a party.[27] Marshall considered "a suit . . . [that] affects the interest of a foreign minister, or by which the person of his secretary, or of his servant, is arrested." In such a case, the "actual defendant pleads to the jurisdiction of the court, and asserts his privilege."[28] Under the immunity statute, Marshall suggested that "if the suit affects a foreign minister, it must be dismissed not because [the minister] is a party to it, but because it affects him."[29]

Just two years later, however, the Supreme Court suggested a far narrower interpretation of "affecting." *United States v. Ortega* (1826) held that a federal prosecution of a criminal defendant charged with assaulting a Spanish diplomat was not a case "affecting a public minister" that had to be brought in the Court's original jurisdiction.[30] Rather, this case "affects the United States, and the individual whom they seek to punish."[31] The minister was "injured by the assault, but has no concern, either in the event of the prosecution, or in the costs attending it."[32] As a result, the prosecution could be brought in the lower federal court.

MODERN DOCTRINE

Federal law today gives the district courts "original jurisdiction, exclusive of the courts of the States, of all civil actions and proceedings against consuls or vice consuls of foreign states."[33] That jurisdiction extends further to suits against "members of a mission or members of their families" as those terms are defined in the Diplomatic Relations Act of 1978.[34] The Supreme Court has "original but not exclusive jurisdiction" over "[a]ll actions or proceedings to which ambassadors, other public ministers, consuls, or vice consuls of foreign states are parties."[35]

The phrase "Ambassadors, other Public Ministers, and Consuls" refers to foreign diplomats accredited to the United States; it does not encompass diplomats or other government officials of the United States itself. *Ex parte Gruber* (1925) dismissed on jurisdictional grounds a proceeding brought against a United States consul general serving in Canada. As the Court explained, "[t]he provision, no doubt, was inserted in view of the important and sometimes delicate nature of our relations and intercourse with foreign governments."[36] This authority "is a privilege, not of the official, but of the sovereign or government which he represents, accorded from high considerations of public policy, considerations which plainly do not apply to the United States in its own territory."[37] In determining whether a particular party claiming diplomatic status in fact qualifies for that status, the Court has expressed a willingness to defer to the executive branch.

OPEN QUESTIONS

- What are the outer limits of suits "affecting" ambassadors? If Congress sought to extend federal jurisdiction to the outer limits of the Ambassadors Clause, could it establish federal jurisdiction over all suits in which a foreign diplomat may be called as a witness?

- Does the Ambassadors Clause provide Congress with any substantive powers, such as the power to pass a federal law punishing those who commit torts against foreign diplomatic personnel?

- Could Congress provide for exclusive federal jurisdiction over state criminal cases against foreign diplomats? In 1820, a South Carolina court held that a consul could be tried for violating a state criminal law in state court.[38] Was this case wrongly decided as a textual matter?[39]

Cite as: Christopher T. Landau & Chase T. Harrington, *The Judicial Power—Ambassadors Clause, in* THE HERITAGE GUIDE TO THE CONSTITUTION 467 (Josh Blackman & John G. Malcolm eds., 3d ed. 2025).

Notes

1. Art. III, § 2, cl. 1.   **2.** E. de Vattel, *The Law of Nations*, bk. IV, § 110 (1758).   **3.** Justinian's Digest. lib. v. tit. 1, De Judiciis, &c. leg. 24, § 2.   **4.** Vattel, *supra* § 80.   **5.** Margaret Buckley, *Origins of Diplomatic Immunity in England*, 21 U. Miami L. Rev. 349, 357 (1966).   **6.** *Id.*   **7.** Diplomatic Privileges Act, 1708, 7 Anne, c. 12, §§ 3–4.   **8.** 3 Story's Commentaries, § 1653; *Davis v. Packard*, 32 U.S. 276 (1833).   **9.** 21 J. Cont. Cong. 1136–37 (Nov. 23, 1781).   **10.** *Id.* at 1137.   **11.** *Sosa v. Alvarez-Machain*, 542 U.S. 692, 716 (2004).   **12.** *Respublica v. De Longchamps*, 1 U.S. (1 Dall.) 111 (1784).   **13.** William R. Casto, *The Federal Courts' Protective Jurisdiction over Torts Committed in Violation of the Law of Nations*, 18 Conn. L. Rev. 467, 491–94 (1986).   **14.** 27 J. Cont. Cong. 502–04 (June 1, 1784).   **15.** 1 Farrand's 25.   **16.** *Id.* at 21–22, 25, 242–45.   **17.** 2 Farrand's 422–26.   **18.** *Id.* at 576.   **19.** Storing 2.9.160.   **20.** Storing 4.6.75.   **21.** 3 Elliot's 523.   **22.** *Verlinden B.V. v. Central Bank of Nigeria*, 461 U.S. 480, 494–96 (1983).   **23.** Judiciary Act of 1789, ch. 20, § 13, 1 Stat. 73, 80–81.   **24.** *Plaquemines Tropical Fruit Co. v. Henderson*, 170 U.S. 511, 517 (1898).   **25.** 280 U.S. 379 (1930).   **26.** Crimes Act of April 30, 1790, ch. 9, §§ 25–27, 1 Stat. 112, 117–18.   **27.** 22 U.S. (9 Wheat.) 738 (1824).   **28.** *Id.* at 854–55.   **29.** *Id.*   **30.** 24 U.S. (11 Wheat.) 467, 469 (1826).   **31.** *Id.*   **32.** *Id.*   **33.** 28 U.S.C. § 1351; Diplomatic Relations Act, Pub. L. No. 95-393, 92 Stat. 808 (1978) (codified at 22 U.S.C. § 254a et seq. and 28 U.S.C. § 1364 (Supp. 11 1978)).   **34.** *Id.*   **35.** 28 U.S.C. § 1251.   **36.** *Ex parte Gruber*, 269 U.S. 302, 303 (1925).   **37.** *Id.*   **38.** *State v. De La Foret*, 2 Nott & McC. 217 (Const. App. Ct. S.C. 1820).   **39.** Josh Blackman, *State Judicial Sovereignty*, 2016 Ill. L. Rev. 2033, 2088–89, 2097–98 (2016).

~

ESSAY NO. 127: THE JUDICIAL POWER—ADMIRALTY CLAUSE
ART. III, § 2, CL. 1

The judicial Power shall extend . . . to all Cases of admiralty and maritime Jurisdiction . . . .

—Thomas H. Lee

INTRODUCTION

Admiralty and maritime jurisdiction, though a backwater today, was the most vital of the Article III judicial powers at the framing. First, uniform rules and neutral adjudication of admiralty and maritime cases were critical to the economy of the new coastal nation that depended on maritime trade. Second, state courts had adjudicated maritime captures, known as "prize" cases, that were contrary to the law of nations during the War of Independence. These decisions had created considerable friction both among the states and with foreign states and led to the establishment of the first national court of appeals under the Articles of Confederation. Third, because customs duties were the most important source of revenue for the early federal government, a system of federal courts located at key ports was critical for the effective enforcement of federal revenue laws to fund the new national government.

HISTORICAL ANTECEDENTS

The origins of Article III admiralty and maritime jurisdiction lay in England. Admiralty courts were formed in the fourteenth century to handle matters incidental to naval commands to the west, east, and south of England. In 1463, these courts were consolidated into one High Court of Admiralty. Because the disputes and issues the admiralty court decided necessarily occurred at sea, that court did not apply the domestic law of the land, English common law. Instead, it applied the law of the sea, which was part of the law of nations. This maritime law was anchored in Roman law and developed by jurists from the seafaring civil-law countries of continental Europe. For this reason, admiralty judges in England were called "civilians." The "law of nations" at the time encompassed general principles of law shared by civilized nations that applied both "internally" as "the public law of the state" and "externally" as to the "rights, intercourse, and obligations of nations" and among "their respective subjects."[1]

The High Court of Admiralty also employed procedures prevalent in the continental European civil-law countries that differed from the procedures in the common-law courts. Given the distances and diverse nationalities of parties often involved, admiralty courts relied on documentary evidence as opposed to live testimony at trial. Most significantly, there was no right to a jury trial in admiralty courts as there was in the English common-law courts. As the common-law courts grew in prestige and power, their judges expanded their jurisdiction by issuing writs of prohibition against the admiralty court's exercise of jurisdiction over any maritime contract made on land, as most were.[2] Moreover, the admiralty court was stripped of its jurisdiction to try crimes given the absence of a right to trial by jury. The result was a dramatic diminution in the judicial power of the English admiralty court.

The common-law courts' writs of prohibition, however, did not extend to the colonies. Consequently, admiralty courts established by royal governors *ex officio* as Vice-Admirals came to exercise jurisdiction not only over maritime disputes, but also over controversial cases ostensibly linked to maritime commerce including prosecutions to enforce revenue and navigation laws. Like the High Court of Admiralty, vice-admiralty courts operated without juries, enraging colonial Americans. An infamous example of the vice-admiralty courts' perceived overreach was their enforcement of the Stamp Act of 1765. This law levied taxes on paper products, which grounded the Declaration of

Independence's charge that the British Crown had "depriv[ed] us in many cases of the benefits of Trial by Jury."[3]

ADMIRALTY AND MARITIME JURISDICTION

The historical distinction between *admiralty* and *maritime* jurisdiction was geographic. *Admiralty* jurisdiction referred to criminal and civil cases arising upon or related to domestic internal navigable or territorial waters—what sailors call "brown water." Examples include suits seeking damages for loss of carried goods or persons, injuries, or collisions in navigable rivers or territorial seas as well as suits to enforce territorial fishing restrictions, trade and navigation laws, and duties on imports at ports of entry. In England, admiralty jurisdiction did not extend to internal waters outside the "ebb and flow" of ocean tides; admiralty jurisdiction in continental Europe generally covered rivers and other internal waters used by cargo-carrying or passenger-carrying vessels.

Maritime jurisdiction pertained to criminal and civil cases occurring on the high seas or international waters—what sailors call "blue water." Examples include civil actions related to the carriage of goods and persons on the high seas; prosecutions for crimes committed in international waters such as piracy; and adjudication of captures of foreign ships and cargoes during wars or armed encounters. Captures could occur in domestic or international waters, but the law of nations prescribed rules for condemnation of seized ships or cargoes, which were called "prizes" (from the French "prise" for "taken"). (See Essay No. 58.) The "law of prize" was thus viewed as falling within the maritime jurisdiction of admiralty courts and included captures by privately owned vessels known as privateers that a sovereign commissioned by issuing letters of marque.[4] The word "marine" was often used as an adjective to encompass both domestic and international waters.

The historical provenance of English admiralty and maritime jurisdiction thus indicates that Article III's expansive reference to "all Cases" of admiralty and maritime jurisdiction meant "all" criminal and civil "cases" in brown (domestic) or blue (international) waters. This jurisdiction included cases arising from or related to contracts for the carriage of goods or persons on the seas or navigable waters; cases arising out of collisions or other non-contract injuries to persons or property (torts) occurring upon the seas and navigable waters; criminal prosecutions for piracy or other crimes on the seas; cases adjudicating captures of foreign ships and cargoes at sea; and cases enforcing trade, navigation, fisheries, and revenue laws and import duties on ships and cargoes.

THE ARTICLES OF CONFEDERATION

During the War of Independence, some American states had set up admiralty courts with juries that awarded prizes to American captors without regard to the law of nations, thereby causing considerable friction with foreign neutral states. Article IX of the Articles of Confederation gave the "United States in Congress assembled" the "sole and exclusive power" of "appointing courts for the trials of piracies and felonies committed on the high seas and establishing courts for receiving and determining finally appeals in *all cases* of captures."[5] Congress sought to "giv[e] satisfaction to foreign nations complaining of a violation of neutralities, of treaties or other breaches of the law of nations. . . ."[6]

In January 1780, Congress established the first national court "for the trial of all appeals from the courts of admiralty in these United States, in cases of capture, to consist of three judges, appointed and commissioned by Congress" and "the trial therein [to] be according to the usages of the nations and not by jury."[7] Congress thus gave a national court the supreme power to review adjudications by state admiralty courts regarding when foreign ships and cargoes were lawfully seized by Americans—a lucrative and vital sphere of operations during the War of Independence. More than a year later, in April 1781, Congress vested trial of maritime crimes in "any two or more" state judges or justices with juries "as if the piracy or felony were committed upon the land."[8] These two models—creating new federal courts and vesting admiralty and maritime jurisdiction in existing state courts—would endure in discussions of Article III admiralty and maritime jurisdiction with some Anti-Federalists favoring the latter option.

THE CONSTITUTIONAL CONVENTION

The Virginia Plan—the sketch of a national government that framed debate during the opening weeks of the Constitutional Convention—enumerated four items that appeared to fall within the admiralty and maritime jurisdiction: "all piracies & felonies on the high seas," "captures from an enemy," "cases . . . which respect the collection of the National revenue [including import duties]," and "questions which may involve the national peace and harmony."[9] The Committee of Detail provided "that the jurisdiction shall extend to all cases arising under the Natl. laws; And to such other questions as may involve the Natl. peace & harmony."[10]

The Committee of Style produced a version of Article III, Section 2 enumerating several categories of federal judicial power including "all cases of admiralty and maritime jurisdiction."[11] The admiralty and maritime jurisdiction occasioned no debate during the Convention's final deliberations. Admiralty and maritime jurisdiction is the only category among the "Cases" and "Controversies" listed in Article III, Section 2 that the Continental Congress had vested in courts under the Articles of Confederation.[12]

THE RATIFICATION DEBATES

During state ratification conventions, two points of contention implicating Article III admiralty and maritime jurisdiction were raised, and both echoed innovations in Article IX of the Articles of Confederation. First, given the alternative of using state courts as the Continental Congress did for maritime crimes in implementing Article IX, there was pushback against setting up any new lower federal courts. However, even leading Anti-Federalists acknowledged that admiralty and maritime jurisdiction was the strongest case for having an independent system of federal courts to ensure uniform rules for maritime trade, crimes, and armed encounters. Brutus, for example, acknowledged that "cases affecting . . . admiralty and maritime jurisdiction . . . should be under the cognizance of the courts of the union, because none but the general government, can, or ought to pass laws on their subjects."[13] As Alexander Hamilton observed in Federalist No. 80, even the "most bigoted idolizers of state authority have not thus far shewn

a disposition to deny the national judiciary the cognizance of maritime causes."

Second, there was much criticism of Article III's provision that the U.S. Supreme Court should have appellate jurisdiction "both as to law and fact."[14] That provision, reflecting the Articles of Confederation concern about runaway juries in maritime capture cases, seemed to authorize Supreme Court review of jury fact-finding. For example, at the Virginia ratification convention, Patrick Henry stated that the Supreme Court's appellate jurisdiction would "in operation destroy the trial by jury."[15]

THE FIRST CONGRESS

In 1789, when the First Congress passed the original Judiciary Act and the Bill of Rights, it demonstrated sensitivity to concerns about preserving both state court jurisdiction and protecting the right to jury. The Judiciary Act of 1789 established lower district and circuit federal courts and vested in them a substantial portion of Article III admiralty and maritime jurisdiction.[16] Section 9 provided that:

> [T]he district courts shall have exclusive original cognizance of all civil causes of admiralty and maritime jurisdiction, including all seizures under laws of impost, navigation or trade of the United States, where the seizures are made, on waters which are navigable from the sea by vessels of ten or more tons burthen, within their respective districts as well as upon the high seas; saving to suitors, in all cases, the right of a common law remedy where the common law is competent to give it.[17]

The "saving to suitors" exception was enacted to preserve the overlapping jurisdiction of state courts to give common-law remedies in certain suits traditionally entertained in common-law courts (e.g., injuries to maritime workers) that also fell within the admiralty and maritime jurisdiction. Although the Seventh Amendment right to jury applies only "[i]n Suits at common law"[18] and therefore not to "civil cause of admiralty and maritime jurisdiction," it would necessarily be available in common-law suits that fall within the saving-to-suitors exception.

The Judiciary Act bifurcated admiralty and maritime jurisdiction with respect to "all crimes and offenses that shall be cognizable under the authority of the United States, committed . . . upon the high seas."[19]— Lesser crimes could be tried in the district courts and the circuit courts could try both lesser crimes and more serious crimes on the high seas. The Sixth Amendment preserves the right to a jury "[i]n all criminal prosecutions" without exception, including admiralty and maritime cases.[20]

JUDICIAL PRECEDENTS

Federal courts addressed some of the foundational questions left open regarding the meaning of the Article III grant of judicial power as to "all Cases of admiralty and maritime jurisdiction."

First, was the scope of the constitutional admiralty and maritime jurisdiction the same as it was in England at the time of the War of Independence? In *DeLovio v. Boit*, Justice Joseph Story, while riding circuit, answered that the Article III jurisdiction as implemented by Section 9 of the Judiciary Act was not limited to English law but rather was to be measured by the much larger scope recognized by continental European nations.[21] Federal courts were therefore not limited to the narrow definition of "maritime contracts" that prevailed in England because of the dominance of common lawyers over civilians there. The full Supreme Court affirmed Story's interpretation three decades later in *Waring v. Clarke* (1847).[22] Story had accepted the restrictive English rule confining admiralty jurisdiction to riverine "waters within the ebb and flow of the tide" of the oceans. But the Supreme Court overruled that doctrine in upholding a statute extending admiralty jurisdiction to the Great Lakes and connecting navigable waters.[23] This holding was later extended to all internal waters navigable in fact, including manmade canals.[24]

Second, could Congress make substantive rules of decision and watershed procedural changes for admiralty and maritime cases that departed from the maritime law of nations at the time the Constitution was adopted? The general answer was that it could. In *The Lottawanna* (1875), the Supreme Court held that "[i]t cannot be supposed that the framers of the Constitution contemplated that the law should forever remain unalterable."[25] The Court added that "Congress undoubtedly has authority under the commercial power, if no other, to introduce such changes as are likely to be needed." Later decisions identified the source of congressional power to change maritime law as the Article III grant of judicial power itself in conjunction with the Necessary and Proper Clause, not the Commerce Clause.[26]

Modern Commerce Clause precedents would surely support Congress's power to modify the maritime law of nations in admiralty and maritime cases. The Supreme Court has consistently held, however, that the federal courts have power to make federal common-law rules in admiralty and maritime civil cases in the absence of congressional legislation.[27] With respect to fundamental procedural rules, the Court has held that admiralty and maritime jurisdiction can be exercised *in personam*— a suit seeking personal liability against, for example, a vessel owner.[28] However, traditional admiralty suits were typically *in rem*—based on the court's having impounded the vessel (and cargoes) that are the subject of suit. The Court has also affirmed that Congress may require a jury for admiralty claims even though jury trials were not authorized in admiralty and maritime cases when the Constitution was adopted.[29]

Third, do the state courts have any residual role in admiralty and maritime cases given the breadth of Article III judicial power in "*all* Cases of admiralty and maritime Jurisdiction"? The answer is that they do and they don't. As a threshold matter, Congress generally cannot encroach upon state sovereign police powers. It could not, for instance, vest jurisdiction in federal courts for skating accidents on Walden Pond by invoking the judicial power in "all Cases of admiralty and maritime jurisdiction." Furthermore, states have concurrent power to regulate crimes on their navigable and territorial waters in the absence of congressional legislation.[30] The saving-to-suitors clause in the First Judiciary Act preserves common-law remedies, presumably under state laws. The Supreme Court has held that although Congress has the power to vest exclusive *in rem* admiralty jurisdiction over a vessel and its cargo in federal court,[31] a state court can entertain concurrent jurisdiction over an *in personam* cause of action arising from the same transaction or occurrence against the vessel's owners.[32] However, the Court has also clarified that the Constitution was not designed "to place the rules and limits of maritime law under the disposal and regulation of the several States, as that would have defeated the uniformity and consistency at which the Constitution aimed."[33]

There is a frequent collision between these two impulses: concurrent state power and "the uniformity and consistency at which the Constitution aimed" in the Article III admiralty and maritime jurisdiction. This tension was manifest in *Southern Pacific Co. v. Jensen* (1917), which held that New York could not apply its workers' compensation scheme to an employee killed on navigable waters.[34] The Supreme Court has not overruled *Jensen*, but it stands in tension with the holding in *Erie Railroad Co. v. Tompkins* (1938) that state law should prevail over "general" law in suits between citizens of different states in federal court.[35]

OPEN QUESTIONS

- To what extent does the robust federal judicial power to apply rules of decisions from the law of nations in cases of admiralty and maritime jurisdiction inform judicial power in other Article III cases and controversies?
- From an originalist perspective, how much does Article III admiralty and maritime jurisdiction borrow from English practice (e.g., "ebb and tide" of the oceans as its riverine limit) or reject it (e.g., the overreaching of the colonial vice-admiralty courts)?

Cite as: Thomas H. Lee, *The Judicial Power—Admiralty Clause*, in The Heritage Guide to the Constitution 471 (Josh Blackman & John G. Malcolm eds., 3d ed. 2025).

Notes

1. *Law of Nations*, in 9 Encyclopedia Americana 141–49 (Joseph Story; Francis Lieber ed., 1838); Thomas H. Lee, *The Law of Nations and the Judicial Branch*, 106 Geo. L.J. 1707, 1715–26 (2018). **2.** I Charles M. Gray, The Writ of Prohibition: Jurisdiction in Early Modern English Law xlvii–liii (1994). **3.** Declaration of Independence, ¶ 20. **4.** Henry Wheaton, A Digest of the Law of Maritime Captures and Prizes, ch. I (1815). **5.** Articles of Confederation, art. IX, § 1 (emphasis added). **6.** 13 J. Cont. Cong. 284 (Mar. 6, 1779). **7.** 16 J. Cont. Cong. 61 (Jan. 15, 1780). **8.** 19 J. Cont. Cong. 354–55 (Apr. 5, 1781). **9.** 1 Farrand's 22. **10.** 2 Farrand's 46. **11.** *Id.* at 600. **12.** Thomas H. Lee, *Article IX, Article III, and the First Congress: The Original Constitutional Plan for the Federal Courts, 1787–1892*, 89 Fordham L. Rev. 1895, 1901–07 (2021). **13.** Storing 9.160. **14.** Art. III, § 2, cl. 2. **15.** 10 DHRC 1420. **16.** Judiciary Act of 1789, ch. 20, 1 Stat. 73. **17.** *Id.* ch. 20, § 9, 1 Stat. at 76–77. **18.** Amend. VII. **19.** Judiciary Act of 1789, ch. 20, § 9, 1 Stat. at 76–77; § 11, 1 Stat. at 78–79. **20.** Amend. VI. **21.** 7 Fed. Cas. 418 (No. 3776) (C.C.D. Mass. 1815). **22.** 46 U.S. (5 How.) 441 (1847). **23.** *Gennessee Chief v. Fitzhugh*, 53 U.S. (12 How.) 443 (1851). **24.** *Ex parte Boyer*, 109 U.S. 629 (1884). **25.** 88 U.S. (21 Wall.) 558, 577 (1875). **26.** *Butler v. Boston & S. S.S. Co.*, 130 U.S. 527, 557 (1889). **27.** *Moragne v. States Marine Lines*, 398 U.S. 375 (1970). **28.** *Leon v. Galceron*, 78 U.S. (11 Wall.) 185, 187–188 (1870). **29.** *Gennessee Chief*, supra. **30.** *United States v. Bevans*, 16 U.S. (3 Wheat.) 336 (1818). **31.** *The Moses Taylor*, 71 U.S. (4 Wall.) 411 (1866). **32.** *Madruga v. Superior Court*, 346 U.S. 556 (1954). **33.** *The Lottawanna*, 88 U.S. (21 Wall.) at 574–75. **34.** 244 U.S. 205 (1917). **35.** 304 U.S. 64 (1938).

ESSAY NO. 128: THE JUDICIAL POWER—FEDERAL PARTY CLAUSE
ART. III, § 2, CL. 1

The judicial Power shall extend . . . to Controversies to which the United States shall be a Party. . . .

—Judge Kenneth K. Lee

INTRODUCTION

The Federal Party Clause was almost an after-thought for the Framers because its purpose—establishing jurisdiction for cases involving the United States as a party—was so obvious. It was added to Article III at the end of the Constitutional Convention without any debate or discussion, and during the ratification debates, Federalists and Anti-Federalists agreed that federal courts under the new Constitution must have jurisdiction to hear cases in which the United States is a party.

Today, the Federal Party Clause is discussed primarily in the context of sovereign immunity: Did the United States waive its immunity from being sued? The clause states that federal juris-diction extends to cases in which the United States is a "party." But does this clause apply only when the United States is the plaintiff, or also when the United States is the defendant? The historical record suggests that the original understanding of this provision did not encom-pass cases in which the United States was a defendant—unless, of course, it had waived sov-ereign immunity—and the U.S. Supreme Court has confirmed that understanding. Litigants still argue about whether Congress has waived sovereign immunity in a particular case and, if so, the scope of that waiver.

THE CONSTITUTIONAL CONVENTION

The Framers generally agreed that the new Constitution should feature an independent judiciary shielded from legislative meddling.[1] They also agreed in principle that federal juris-diction should extend to certain national mat-ters and international affairs. They parted ways, however, on the precise scope of jurisdiction. During the Constitutional Convention, the Framers added and excised the types of cases that belong in federal court.[2] For example, del-egates removed federal jurisdiction over pira-cies, felonies on the high seas, and captures—only to adopt draft language later that extended jurisdiction over "all cases arising under the Natl. laws: And to such other questions as may involve the Natl. peace & harmony."[3] That broad language was further modified by the time the Constitution was finalized.

On August 27, 1787, about three weeks before the Constitution was signed, James Madison of Virginia and Gouverneur Morris of Pennsylvania moved to insert language that would become the Federal Party Clause, extend-ing jurisdiction over controversies "to which the U– S– shall be a party."[4] The delegates adopted the amendment unanimously without debate.[5] This last-minute—and uncontroversial—amendment suggests that adding the Federal Party Clause merely corrected an oversight of an obvious proposition that the United States should have its case heard in federal court.

THE RATIFICATION DEBATES

While the Federalists and Anti-Federalists clashed on a wide range of issues, they agreed that federal courts should hear cases involving the United States as a party. In Federalist No. 80, Alexander Hamilton devoted only a single para-graph to arguing that cases "between the nation and its members or citizens, can only be "prop-erly referred to the national tribunals" and that "[a]ny other plan would be contrary to reason, to precedent, and to decorum." Brutus, a promi-nent Anti-Federalist, agreed. He explained that such cases belong in federal courts because "none but the general government, can, or ought to pass laws on their subjects."[6]

EARLY PRACTICE

The text of the Federal Party Clause refers only to the United States as a "party," and there is some evidence that the Founding generation would have understood this term to include only cases in which the United States is a plaintiff.[7] The Judiciary Act of 1789, for example, estab-lished jurisdiction for district courts for "all suits at common law where the United States sue."[8] Similarly, the act specified that circuit courts have jurisdiction in cases in which "the United States are plaintiffs, or petitioners."[9]

Why did the Framers' apparent under-standing of the clause seemingly deviate from its text? We must examine the text within the context of the historical and traditional under-standing of sovereign immunity. Under British common law, a sovereign enjoyed immunity, and the Framers agreed. As Hamilton explained in Federalist No. 81, "[i]t is inherent in the nature of sovereignty, not to be amenable to the suit of an individual *without its consent*." Thus, when the Federal Party Clause referred to the United States as a "party," it likely meant "plaintiff." The Framers seem to have presumed that the United States could not be a defendant unless it agreed to waive its immunity.

JUDICIAL PRECEDENT

Four years after ratification, the Supreme Court addressed the Federal Party Clause. In *Chisholm v. Georgia* (1793), Chief Justice John Jay observed that for "cases in which the whole people are interested, it would not be equal or wise to let any one State decide and measure out the justice due to others."[10]

Two decades later, *Dugan v. United States* (1818) recognized that the United States did not need specific congressional authorization to sue in federal court.[11] Conversely, *United States v. Clarke* (1838) held that private litigants needed specific congressional authorization to sue the United States.[12] In other words, a federal lawsuit against the United States could proceed only if Congress authorized the suit and if sovereign immunity was waived in that particular case.[13]

A waiver of sovereign immunity must be express and unequivocal in the statutory text; any ambiguity will be construed in favor of immunity.[14] While Congress need not use "magic words" to waive immunity, the "scope of Congress' waiver [must] be clearly discernable from the statutory text in light of traditional interpretive tools." If the waiver is not clear, then courts "take the interpretation most favorable to the Government."[15] Moreover, "when Congress attaches conditions to legislation waiving the sovereign immunity of the United States, those conditions must be strictly observed, and exceptions thereto are not to be lightly implied."[16]

Perhaps the most prominent example of such a waiver is found in the Federal Tort Claims Act, which waives immunity for certain torts committed by federal employees.[17] Also, in amending the Administrative Procedure Act in 1976, Congress allowed petitioners to seek relief (other than monetary damages) against federal agencies.[18]

OPEN QUESTIONS
- Is the Supreme Court's jurisprudence about waiver supported by the original meaning of the Constitution? How unequivocal must a waiver be?
- Is the United States an entity distinct from federal officers acting in their official capacity for purposes of the Federal Party Clause?

Cite as: Judge Kenneth K. Lee, *The Judicial Power – Federal Party Clause*, in THE HERITAGE GUIDE TO THE CONSTITUTION 475 (Josh Blackman & John G. Malcolm eds., 3d ed. 2025).

Notes
1. Robert N. Clinton, *A Mandatory View of Federal Court Jurisdiction: A Guided Quest for the Original Understanding of Article III*, 132 U. Penn. L. Rev. 741, 762 (1983). **2.** *Id.* at 764, 768–69, 773. **3.** *Id.* at 764, 769. **4.** 2 Farrand's 430. **5.** *Id.* **6.** Storing 2.9.160. **7.** Robert J. Pushaw, Jr., *Article III's Case/Controversy Distinction and the Dual Functions of Federal Courts*, 69 Notre Dame L. Rev. 447, 506 (1993). **8.** Judiciary Act of 1789, ch. 20, § 9, 1 Stat. 73, 76–77. **9.** *Id.*, § 11 at 1 Stat.78. **10.** 2 U.S. 419, 475 (1793). **11.** 16 U.S. 172 (1818). **12.** 33 U.S. 436, 444 (1834); *Cohens v. Virginia*, 19 U.S. 264, 380 (1821). **13.** *Fed. Aviation Admin. v. Cooper*, 566 U.S. 284, 290 (2012). **14.** *Id.* **15.** *Id.* at 291. **16.** *Block v. North Dakota ex rel. Board of Univ. and School Lands*, 461 U.S. 273, 287 (1983). **17.** 28 U.S.C. § 1346. **18.** 5 U.S.C. § 702.

⌐◦◦⌐

ESSAY NO. 129: THE JUDICIAL POWER—INTERSTATE CONTROVERSIES CLAUSE
ART. III, § 2, CL. 1

The judicial Power shall extend . . . to Controversies between two or more States . . . .

—Judge Steven J. Menashi & Eli Nachmany

INTRODUCTION

Following independence and under the Articles of Confederation, the states often disagreed. The Framers of the Constitution needed to decide how to adjudicate disputes between states. With a national government came a national court system, and under Article III, Section 2, the Constitution extended the judicial power of the United States to controversies between two or more states. The Constitution also gave the U.S. Supreme Court original jurisdiction over these disputes. The source of the judicial branch's power over these cases is known as the Interstate Controversies Clause.

HISTORY BEFORE 1787

Before the United States declared independence, disputes over boundary lines were among the most commonplace disagreements between colonies. The British Privy Council—a body of advisors to the king—would adjudicate these disputes, which concerned charters that the king had granted.[1] Legal scholar Charles Warren observed that "boundary disputes were frequent" because "[e]ach colony was more or less of a land-grabber from other colonies."[2] The "English charters and patents frequently overlapped in territory and displayed little knowledge of American geography," Warren wrote, and "[d]ifferences as to commerce and matters other than boundaries also aroused much bitterness of feeling between" the colonies.[3] The Privy Council resolved boundary disputes between Rhode Island and Connecticut in 1727, between New Hampshire and Massachusetts in 1741, and between Rhode Island and Massachusetts in 1746.[4]

When the Founders drafted the Articles of Confederation, they needed to devise a mechanism for resolving such territorial disputes.

They decided that Congress would "be the last resort on appeal, in all disputes and differences now subsisting, or that hereafter may arise between two or more states concerning boundary, jurisdiction, or any other cause whatever."[5] However, Article IX also "contained an elaborate procedure for selecting judges to decide interstate disputes if the state parties could not themselves agree on a tribunal, presumably because of their special sensitivity."[6] In this way, the Articles of Confederation assumed that "such controversies were political matters, a view which is consistent with the fact that the states were sovereign."[7] The procedure set forth in the Articles of Confederation "was not particularly effective, for methods of enforcement were tenuous," and "[a]t the inauguration of the Constitutional Convention, there were no less than eleven boundary disputes pending."[8]

THE CONSTITUTIONAL CONVENTION

Initially, the Convention delegates were unsure of what to do about controversies between two or more states. One early proposal from the Committee of Detail conferred jurisdiction on the Supreme Court over all controversies between two or more states, with the exception of those controversies concerning territory, which would be resolved in the Senate.[9] John Rutledge of South Carolina contended that the establishment of a national judiciary obviated the need for the Senate to resolve such disputes.[10] Some delegates responded that the justices might be too partial to their states to adjudicate disputes fairly. Nathaniel Gorham of Massachusetts, for example, said that "[t]he Judges might be connected with the States being parties."[11]

Nevertheless, the Convention decided that the Supreme Court should have original jurisdiction over all interstate disputes.[12] The final language read: "The judicial Power shall extend to . . . Controversies between two or more States."[13] Article III further provides that "[i]n all Cases . . . in which a State shall be Party, the supreme Court shall have original Jurisdiction."[14] (See Essay No. 134.) Accordingly, Congress has given the Supreme Court "original and exclusive jurisdiction of all controversies between two or more States."[15]

EARLY COMMENTARY

In Federalist No. 39, James Madison noted that the Interstate Controversies Clause was "an example of an exception to the general principle that the federal government under the Constitution operates on the people and not on the states."[16]

Justice Joseph Story observed that "[s]ome tribunal, exercising such authority, is essential to prevent an appeal to the sword, and a dissolution of the government."[17] Because "the States gave up a significant part of their ability to resolve any differences that might arise between them" when assenting to the Constitution, "it was essential that the Constitution provide them an alternative means of resolving disputes that would not require the use of the courts of one of the involved states."[18]

EARLY PRACTICE

The language of the Interstate Controversies Clause seems to encompass *all* disputes between states, including boundary disputes. Massachusetts challenged this proposition in *Rhode Island v. Massachusetts* (1838), an early boundary-dispute case.[19] Justice Henry Baldwin's majority opinion held that the Supreme Court had jurisdiction over such cases.[20] He acknowledged that "the constitution does not, in terms, extend the judicial power to *all* controversies between two or more states" but concluded that "it in terms excluded none, whatever may be their nature or subject."[21] Chief Justice Roger B. Taney dissented, describing boundary disputes as political questions that fell outside the grant of judicial power.[22] Taney's view followed from the pre-constitutional practice. In *Hans v. Louisiana* (1890), Justice Joseph

Bradley explained that "[s]ome things, undoubtedly, were made justiciable [by the Constitution] which were not known as such at the common law; such, for example, as controversies between States as to boundary lines."[23] Chief Justice Taney would come around in a later case, recognizing that "repeated decisions" had "settled . . . that a question of boundary between States is within the jurisdiction" of the Court.[24]

Disputes between states have sometimes threatened to lead to violence, but the constitutional mechanism has avoided that result. In the 1840s, for example, Iowa and Missouri disagreed about the sovereignty of 2,000 square miles between the two states. The dispute progressed to the point that "Missouri at one time had called out 1,500 troops and Iowa 1,100 to defend their respective alleged rights."[25] Missouri was a slave state, and Iowa was a free state, so the dispute could have expanded slavery across 2,000 square miles of the Midwest.[26] The Court ruled for Iowa,[27] and the states acquiesced in the judgment.[28] Professor Warren wrote, "just at a time when the dire question of slavery was threatening the stability of the Union in every political direction, a decision of the Court settled its fate for 2,000 square miles of American territory."[29]

This experience provides evidence for Justice Story's conclusion that "[t]his power [to resolve disputes between states] seems to be essential to the preservation of the peace of the Union."[30] Amos Peaslee, a lawyer and diplomat, described the Interstate Controversies Clause as "[o]ne of the smartest political actions ever taken in history" and praised the decision to "lif[t] the settlement of inter-state disputes out of the old Continental Congress—a deliberative body composed of diplomatic representatives of states in their political capacities—and ves[t] jurisdiction over such controversies in a supreme judicial body."[31]

JUDICIAL PRECEDENT

In the contemporary era, states continue to appear before the Supreme Court to resolve disputes. One commentator has described "[t]he state controversy cases" as "a small and specialized body of law."[32] But those precedents occupy a "significant enclave" of federal common law.[33] The Supreme Court has considered a range of issues by way of its original jurisdiction over controversies between states, including "such diverse matters as water rights, interstate pollution, and the apportionment of public debts."[34]

In these cases, the Court now routinely appoints a special master to recommend a disposition of the suit.[35]

OPEN QUESTIONS

- Justices Clarence Thomas and Samuel Alito have stated that the Supreme Court must exercise *mandatory* original jurisdiction over controversies between states.[36] They have cited the "virtually unflagging" obligation of a federal court to decide cases within its jurisdiction.[37] Yet they contend that the majority of the Court has improperly exercised discretionary review over these disputes.[38] Are Justices Thomas and Alito correct as an originalist matter?
- Does the word "States" in the clause encompass foreign states?[39] This position has not been adopted.

The views expressed in this essay do not necessarily reflect the views of Eli Nachmany's employer.

Cite as: Judge Steven J. Menashi & Eli Nachmany, *The Judicial Power—Interstate Controversies Clause, in* THE HERITAGE GUIDE TO THE CONSTITUTION 478 (Josh Blackman & John G. Malcolm eds., 3d ed. 2025).

Notes

1. Charles Warren, *The Supreme Court and Disputes Between States,* 34 Bull. of Coll. of Wm. & Mary in Va. 1, 7 (1940). **2.** *Id.* at 6–7. **3.** *Id.* at 7. **4.** *Id.* at 8. **5.** Articles of Confederation, art. IX, § 2. **6.** Thomas H. Lee, *Article IX, Article III, and the First Congress: The Original Constitutional Plan for the Federal Courts,* 89 Fordham L. Rev. 1895, 1905 (2021). **7.** William P. Murphy, *State Sovereignty and the Drafting of the Constitution,* 32 Miss. L.J. 155, 162 (1961). **8.** Henry W. Toll, *Modern Machinery for Interstate Cooperation,* 23 Iowa L. Rev. 573, 574 (1938). **9.** 2 Farrand's 170, 172–73; *South Dakota v. North Carolina,* 192 U.S. 286, 314 (1904); *Louisiana v. Texas,* 176 U.S. 1, 15 (1900). **10.** 2 Farrand's 400–01. **11.** *Id.* at 401. **12.** *Id.* at 163. **13.** Art. III, § 2, cl. 1. **14.** *Id.,* cl. 2. **15.** 28 U.S.C. § 1251(a). **16.** Robert D. Cheren, *Environmental Controversies "Between Two or More States,"* 31 Pace Env't L. Rev. 105, 116 (2014) (citing Federalist No. 39 (Madison)). **17.** 3 Story's Commentaries, § 1675. **18.** Kristin A. Linsley, *Original Intent: Understanding the Supreme Court's Original Jurisdiction in Controversies Between States,* 18 J. App. Prac. & Process 21, 26 (2017); *Hans v. Louisiana,* 134 U.S. 1, 15 (1890). **19.** *Rhode Island v. Massachusetts,* 37 U.S. 657 (1838); Harvey Hoshour, *Boundary Controversies Between States Bordering on a Navigable River,* 4 Minn. L. Rev. 463, 464–65 (1920). **20.** *Rhode Island,* 37 U.S. at 731–32.

21. *Id.* at 721. **22.** *Id.* at 752–54 (Taney, C.J., dissenting). **23.** 134 U.S. 1, 15 (1890). **24.** *Florida v. Georgia,* 58 U.S. 478, 491 (1855). **25.** Warren, *supra* at 14. **26.** *Id.* **27.** *Missouri v. Iowa,* 48 U.S. 660 (1849). **28.** Warren, *supra* at 14–15. **29.** *Id.* at 14. **30.** Story, *supra* at § 1673; *Louisiana v. Texas,* 176 U.S. 1 (1900). **31.** Amos J. Peaslee, *The Dumbarton Oaks Proposal,* 14 Fordham L. Rev. 55, 57 (1945). **32.** Cheren, *supra* at 107. **33.** Bradford R. Clark, *Federal Common Law: A Structural Reinterpretation,* 144 U. Pa. L. Rev. 1245, 1322 (1996). **34.** *Id.* **35.** Anne-Marie C. Carstens, *Lurking in the Shadows of the Judicial Process: Special Masters in the Supreme Court's Original Jurisdiction Cases,* 86 Minn. L. Rev. 625, 626–28 (2002). **36.** *Texas v. California,* 141 S.Ct. 1469 (2021) (Alito, J., dissenting); *Arizona v. California,* 140 S.Ct. 684 (2020) (Thomas, J., dissenting); *Nebraska v. Colorado,* 577 U.S. 1211 (2016) (Thomas, J., dissenting). **37.** *Texas v. California,* 141 S.Ct. at 1469–70 (Alito, J., dissenting) (quoting *Colo. River Water Conservation Dist. v. United States,* 424 U.S. 800, 827 (1976)). **38.** *Id.* at 1470. **39.** Thomas H. Lee, *The Supreme Court of the United States as Quasi-International Tribunal: Reclaiming the Court's Original and Exclusive Jurisdiction over Treaty-Based Suits by Foreign States Against States,* 104 Colum. L. Rev. 1765, 1793–95 & n.117 (2004).

❧

ESSAY NO. 130: THE JUDICIAL POWER—STATE-CITIZEN DIVERSITY CLAUSE
ART. III, § 2, CL. 1

The judicial Power shall extend . . . to Controversies . . . between a State and Citizens of another State. . . .

—Ernest A. Young

INTRODUCTION

Article III extends the federal judicial power "to Controversies between a State and Citizens of another State." This provision is generally known as the State-Citizen Diversity Clause. It is most often viewed in tandem with its neighbor, the Foreign Diversity Clause, which extends federal jurisdiction to controversies "between a state . . . and foreign states, citizens, or subjects." (See Essay No. 133.) Both clauses govern a variety of potential applications, but they have been discussed primarily for their role in enduring controversies involving the scope of state sovereign immunity in suits by private parties.

HISTORY BEFORE 1787

Sovereign immunity limits the ability of courts to entertain suits against government entities, especially when brought by private parties. The principle of sovereign immunity derives from both the English common-law background and writers on political theory, all of which formed part of the Founders' intellectual vocabulary. (See Essay No. 189.) As Alexander Hamilton put it in Federalist No. 81, "It is inherent in the nature of sovereignty not to be amenable to the suit of an individual without its consent. This is the general sense and the general practice of mankind; and the exemption, as one of the attributes of sovereignty, is now enjoyed by the government of every state in the Union." This view was widespread in the Founding era. Professor Caleb Nelson reports that "people of widely varying perspectives agreed that unconsenting states were not amenable to suit by individuals," and "[t]he consensus on this fact continued in later years."[1]

THE CONSTITUTIONAL CONVENTION

At the Philadelphia Convention, the draft State-Citizen Diversity Clause appeared to threaten this consensus about sovereign immunity. The Committee of Detail proposed an early version of the clause on August 6, 1787. It provided in part that "The Jurisdiction of the Supreme Court shall extend to . . . controversies . . . between a State and Citizens of another State . . . and between a State or the Citizens thereof and foreign States citizens or subjects."[2] This text at least raised the possibility that states could be sued in federal court. The final version included state-citizen diversity cases in the "judicial power" for all federal courts. This language, according to Professor Bradford Clark, "was adopted relatively late in the Convention without objection or discussion."[3]

THE RATIFICATION DEBATES

The State-Citizen Diversity Clause's text said nothing at all about the doctrine of sovereign immunity. Critics, however, feared that by extending the judicial power to cover suits involving state governments, the Clause implicitly subjected unwilling states to suit. These concerns surfaced in the various state ratifying conventions. Some delegates worried that by exposing states to suit in federal court, the State-Citizen Diversity Clause (and its state-alien analog) would undermine the states' dignity and subject them to disastrous liability for debts arising out of the Revolutionary War. In the Virginia Convention, George Mason inquired, "Is this state to be brought to the bar of justice like a delinquent individual? Is the sovereignty of the state to be arraigned like a culprit, or private offender?"[4] The Anti-Federalist writer Brutus warned that Article III would "produce the utmost confusion, and in its progress, will crush the states beneath its weight."[5]

Some proponents of Article III seemed to embrace this possibility as a means for ensuring that state governments would honor their debts. Edmund Randolph of Virginia, for example, asked, "Are we to say that we shall discard this government because it would make us all honest?"[6] James Wilson of Pennsylvania urged that employing federal courts to enforce state debts payable under the Treaty of Paris would "show the world that we make the faith of treaties a constitutional part of the character of the United States."[7]

Mindful of the states' financially precarious position following the Revolution, other leading Federalists sought to dispel these concerns by insisting that Article III left the states' preexisting immunities intact. At the Virginia Convention, James Madison explained that the State-Citizen Diversity Clause was designed to allow state governments to come into federal court as plaintiffs, not to allow private citizens to overcome a state's immunity as a defendant;

states could be brought into federal court only "if a state should condescend to be a party."[8] John Marshall agreed: "The intent is, to enable states to recover claims of individuals residing in other states."[9] In Federalist No. 81, Hamilton acknowledged the states' immunity prior to entering the Union and insisted that "[u]nless . . . there is a surrender of this immunity in the plan of the convention, it will remain with the States."

CHISHOLM, THE ELEVENTH AMENDMENT, AND SUBSEQUENT INTERPRETATION

Despite the leading Federalists' assurances that the State-Citizen Diversity Clause would not eliminate the states' traditional immunity from suit, the U.S. Supreme Court rejected that reading shortly thereafter in *Chisholm v. Georgia* (1793).[10] *Chisholm* involved a suit by a South Carolina citizen to recover Revolutionary War debts owed by the State of Georgia. The state insisted that it was immune from such suits, but the Court upheld its jurisdiction. Justice James Wilson rejected the very notion of state sovereign immunity on the broad ground that it was antithetical to republican government.[11] By contrast, Justices John Jay, John Blair, and William Cushing relied primarily on the State-Citizen Diversity Clause.[12] They argued that this provision had in fact done precisely what the Anti-Federalists feared: overridden the common-law immunity that the states would otherwise have enjoyed in a suit by a private individual. Only Justice James Iredell dissented, primarily on the ground that Congress had not passed any statute that clearly authorized private suits against state governments in the federal courts.[13]

Hans v. State of Louisiana (1890) would later observe that Chisholm "created such a shock of surprise throughout the country that, at the first meeting of Congress thereafter, the Eleventh Amendment to the Constitution was almost unanimously proposed, and was in due course adopted by the legislatures of the States."[14] That amendment provided that "[t]he Judicial power

of the United States shall not be construed to extend to any suit in law or equity, commenced or prosecuted against one of the United States by Citizens of another State, or by Citizens or Subjects of any Foreign State."

Several commentators have noted the extent to which the latter part of the Eleventh Amendment tracks the language of the State-Citizen Diversity Clause; the "diversity theory" of the amendment thus infers that it simply "repealed" the State-Citizen Diversity Clause in all cases in which a nonconsenting state is the defendant.[15] On this reading, federal courts could exercise jurisdiction over a state defendant if some other ground existed, such as a federal question. Although other scholars have endorsed different readings, most justices of the Supreme Court have construed the amendment's text in line with the diversity reading.[16]

However, the Supreme Court has also endorsed a broader principle of constitutional immunity extending beyond the amendment's text. (See Essay No. 189.) The text is limited to a suit by a citizen of one state against another state. *Hans* acknowledged the Amendment's textual limits, but still enforced a broader principle of immunity to also bar suit by a citizen against his own state when raising a federal question.[17] And *Seminole Tribe v. Florida* (1996) and *Alden v. Maine* (1999) have read the Eleventh Amendment's reversal of *Chisholm* to restore the broad baseline of state sovereign immunity that Madison, Hamilton, and Marshall accepted during the ratification debates.[18] Challenges to that view focus on whether that baseline is constitutional in stature or rather, like a form of federal common law, subject to alteration by Congress.[19] That debate, however, does not turn on any disagreement about the meaning or effect of the State-Citizen Diversity Clause.

Cite as: Ernest A. Young, *The Judicial Power—State-Citizen Diversity Clause*, *in* THE HERITAGE GUIDE TO THE CONSTITUTION 480 (Josh Blackman & John G. Malcolm eds., 3d ed. 2025).

Notes

1. Caleb Nelson, *Sovereign Immunity as a Doctrine of Personal Jurisdiction*, 115 Harv. L. Rev. 1559, 1577, 1578 (2002). **2.** 2 Farrand's 186. **3.** Bradford R. Clark, *The Eleventh Amendment and the Nature of the Union*, 123 Harv. L. Rev. 1817, 1852 (2010). **4.** 3 Elliot's 527. **5.** Storing 2.9.167. **6.** 3 Elliot's 575. **7.** 2 Elliot's 490. **8.** 3 Elliot's 533. **9.** John Marshall, Address to the Virginia Convention (June 20, 1788), *in* 10 DHRC 1430, 1433. **10.** 2 U.S. (2 Dall.) 419 (1793). **11.** *Id.* at 454–58 (Wilson, J.). **12.** *Id.* at 450–52 (Blair, J.); 466–68 (Cushing, J.); 475–77 (Jay, C.J.). **13.** *Id.* at 432–35 (Iredell, J.). **14.** 134 U.S. 1, 11 (1890). **15.** William A. Fletcher, *A Historical Interpretation of the Eleventh Amendment: A Narrow Construction of an Affirmative Grant of Jurisdiction Rather than a Prohibition Against Jurisdiction*, 35 Stan. L. Rev. 1033, 1058–63 (1983). **16.** *Franchise Tax Bd. v. Hyatt*, 587 U.S. 230, 1496 (2019); *Seminole Tribe v. Florida*, 517 U.S. 44, 54 (1996). **17.** 134 U.S. at 10–12. **18.** 517 U.S. 44 (1996); 527 U.S. 706 (1999); Kurt T. Lash, *Leaving the* Chisholm *Trail: The Eleventh Amendment and the Background Principle of Strict Construction*, 50 Wm. & Mary L. Rev. 1577, 1689–90 (2009). **19.** *Seminole Tribe*, 517 U.S. at 100, 137–42, 159 (Souter, J., dissenting).

ESSAY NO. 131: THE JUDICIAL POWER—DIVERSITY OF CITIZENSHIP CLAUSE
ART. III, § 2, CL. 1

The judicial Power shall extend . . . to Controversies . . . between Citizens of different States. . . .

—Stephen E. Sachs

INTRODUCTION

Article III, Section 2, Clause 1 extends the federal judicial power to "Controversies . . . between Citizens of different States." The Framers designed this form of jurisdiction, commonly called "diversity jurisdiction," to offer out-of-state litigants an independent federal tribunal and guard against home-field advantage in state courts. When federal courts hear state-law cases, however, they often face complex questions about the structure of our federal system.

HISTORY BEFORE 1787

At the time of Independence, "prejudice against those from other states was rampant."[1] In 1783, George Washington noted that Americans "from the different parts of the Continent" had entered the Continental Army with "the most violent local prejudices."[2] These prejudices did not stop at the courthouse door. In "state admiralty courts," for example, when the parties came from different states, "[o]ut-of-state or foreign litigants could be denied justice."[3] The pleas of out-of-state litigants to the Confederation Congress produced "little effective relief"[4] because the Articles of Confederation did not establish national courts to handle disputes between citizens of different states. State judges might refuse to enforce Congress's decrees or might retry cases before new juries until the local party won.[5] Nor were these juries themselves free from prejudice.[6]

THE CONSTITUTIONAL CONVENTION

Many of the Framers of the Constitution argued that there should be independent national courts to try cases of national interest. Early in the Constitutional Convention, the Virginia Plan suggested that federal courts should be able to hear cases "in which . . . citizens of other States . . . may be interested."[7] The Committee of Detail included diversity jurisdiction among those "questions [that] involve the National peace and harmony."[8]

Some delegates, such as Luther Martin of Maryland, opposed the creation of any federal trial courts.[9] Others, including James Madison of Virginia, contended that only these courts could prevent "improper Verdicts in State tribunals obtained under the biassed directions of a dependent Judge, or the local prejudices of an undirected jury."[10] The final version of the Constitution included both judicial power over "Controversies . . . between Citizens of different States"[11] and a power in Congress to create "inferior Courts . . . from time to time."[12]

THE RATIFICATION DEBATES

Diversity jurisdiction was a significant topic during ratification. Anti-Federalists such as George Mason of Virginia feared that defendants would be forced to litigate "a thousand miles from home."[13] Federalists defended diversity jurisdiction as a means of enforcing the Constitution's substantive protections. For example, the Constitution bars states from "coin[ing] Money" or "impairing the Obligation of Contracts."[14] Edmund Pendleton of Virginia argued that a state law violating these provisions might still be enforced by state courts. Without a federal trial court to hear the case in diversity jurisdiction, an out-of-state creditor might be forced to wait for long-delayed review from the Supreme Court—and, in the meantime, to accept payment in depreciated state currency.[15] By contrast, a federal trial court could be trusted to respect the Constitution from the outset.

Federalists also worried about the roadblocks facing out-of-state creditors.[16] In Federalist No. 80, Alexander Hamilton wrote that federal courts could secure the Constitution's parchment guarantees "against all evasion and subterfuge" and suggested that federal jurisdiction should extend to cases "in which the State tribunals cannot be supposed to be impartial and unbiased."

Some Anti-Federalists like Agrippa worried that the federal courts, sitting in diversity, would apply newly invented laws.[17] In the Virginia Convention, John Marshall belittled such arguments. He contended that federal courts would decide cases according to familiar choice-of-law rules—regulating contracts, for example, "[b]y the laws of the State where the contract was made," whether of Maryland or of "the East-Indies."[18]

WHAT ARE "CONTROVERSIES"?

Article III refers to "Cases" and "Controversies." The latter have long been read as purely civil, while the former may be civil or criminal.[19] Some scholarship suggests that "controversies" also require adverse parties.[20] But in certain cases concerning probate matters or domestic relations, the courts act *in rem*—that is, with regard to a particular property interest or legal status—and there need not be adversity among the parties.[21] Perhaps for this reason, courts have recognized long-standing "probate" and "domestic relations" exceptions to diversity jurisdiction.[22]

WHOM ARE "CONTROVERSIES . . . BETWEEN"?

The Judiciary Act of 1789 provided for jurisdiction in a suit "between a citizen of the State where the suit is brought, and a citizen of another State."[23] This rule is easy enough to follow when there is one plaintiff and one defendant, but what happens when there are multiple plaintiffs and multiple defendants? In *Strawbridge v. Curtiss* (1806), Chief Justice John Marshall held that this statute required *all* parties on one side of the case to be diverse from *all* their opponents on the other side of the case so that each party was "competent to sue, or liable to be sued," in federal court.[24] This reading might have made diversity jurisdiction less effective in resolving complex cross-state disputes.[25] However, *Strawbridge* was consistent with common-law rules that did not allow special jurisdictional privileges to be shared with unprivileged parties to joint actions.[26]

The modern diversity jurisdiction statute (28 U.S.C. § 1332) is still read to require "complete diversity": no plaintiff and defendant in a diversity case may be from the same state.[27] A few statutes require only "minimal diversity" with at least one plaintiff and defendant hailing from different states.[28] In 1967, the U.S. Supreme Court held that this minimal diversity was constitutional under the Diversity of Citizenship Clause.[29] However, the Court decided the point without briefing or argument, based on twentieth-century sources rather than original history. The Court also failed to explain why Chief Justice Marshall would have read the similar language of the Judiciary Act differently.[30]

WHO ARE "CITIZENS OF DIFFERENT STATES"?

Diversity jurisdiction is for citizens of "States."[31] The Marshall Court recognized that the District of Columbia was not a state in the sense of "a member of the union" and held that its residents therefore could not sue in diversity.[32] It soon reached the same result as to citizens of U.S. territories.[33] In 1940, however, Congress extended diversity jurisdiction to citizens of the District of

Columbia, Puerto Rico, and the territories.[34] A fractured Court upheld this extension of diversity jurisdiction in *National Mutual Insurance Co. of D.C. v. Tidewater Transfer Co.* (1949), whether as an exercise of Congress's territorial powers or by giving "States" a broader construction.[35] Scholars examining this case have proposed a variety of solutions for D.C. or territorial residents, but most regard the Court's suggestions as unsuccessful on originalist grounds.[36]

A harder question is posed by corporations and other legal entities that may sue or be sued under their own names. In 1799, both sides before the Supreme Court assumed that the "President, Directors, and Company of the Bank of North-America" could sue in diversity, noting that its president and directors were all Pennsylvania citizens.[37] In *Bank of the United States v. Deveaux* (1809), Chief Justice Marshall held that a corporation "is certainly not a citizen."[38] However, the Court again ruled that "the rights of the members" who compose the corporation may "be exercised in their corporate name" so that the Article III "controversy" is "between those persons" and the opposing party.[39] For diversity purposes, Marshall described "the universal understanding on the subject" as treating a corporation's lawsuit as if all of its members were suing or being sued together.[40]

Deveaux, however, made it difficult for widely held corporations to achieve complete diversity, because its rule required counting the citizenship of each member (equivalent to the modern shareholder). In 1844, the Taney Court suggested that Marshall had "regret[ted]" *Strawbridge* and *Deveaux*.[41] The Court abandoned *Deveaux* and presumed corporations to be citizens of their states of incorporation.[42] The Court soon declared this presumption irrebuttable.[43] *Deveaux*'s rule remains in place for non-corporate entities such as limited partnerships and limited liability corporations.[44] Some modern scholars, however, reject legal entities' use of diversity jurisdiction altogether.[45]

WHAT LAW WILL COURTS SITTING IN DIVERSITY APPLY?

Once a controversy between citizens of different states is properly before a federal court, what law should that court apply? The Constitution gives controversies involving federal laws their own route to federal court for all cases "arising under . . . the Laws of the United States."[46] Diversity cases typically involve some other type of law. Would it be the law of the plaintiff's state, or of the defendant's state, or of the state where the court is located? Or would the federal court follow a choice-of-law rule that depends on the events in the case? And what if the federal court and the state courts would understand that law differently?

In a provision of the Judiciary Act of 1789 known as the Rules of Decision Act, Congress declared "the laws of the several states" to be "rules of decision in trials at common law . . . in cases where they apply."[47] The instruction to apply state laws "where they apply" was not circular, because it presupposed an already existing system of choice-of-law rules. For example, a contract's substance was regulated by "the law of the country where it is made," but remedies for breaching the contract were determined by the local court's "modes of proceeding."[48] These standards were recognized under "the general rule admitted by the comity of nations."[49] Diversity jurisdiction thereby preserved whatever legislative powers the states had previously enjoyed "within the ordinary functions of legislation."[50]

In identifying those state laws, federal courts were expected to defer to state court decisions when interpreting a state's statutes or describing its local customs.[51] They were not, however, required to treat court decisions about state laws as if they were "laws" themselves.[52] Nor were federal judges required to take state judges' word as final on questions that were "not subject to state regulations" or that state law did not answer.[53] These might have included questions of English common law, international law, or other forms of "general" law to which a state's law might have cross-referred.[54] In *Swift v. Tyson* (1842), the Court addressed those cases that were governed neither by "local statutes" nor by "local usages" and that a state had left up to "general principles of commercial law."[55] In such cases, it held, the federal and state courts were to decide independently, with "the state tribunals . . . called upon to perform the like functions as ourselves."[56]

Erie Railroad Co. v. Tompkins (1938) overruled *Swift*, holding that "[t]here is no federal general common law" and that federal courts had no "power to use their judgment as to what the rules of common law are."[57] Federal courts had to assume that "the law of the state" was "'not the common law generally'" but whatever had been declared to be state law by the "highest [state] court in a decision."[58] The Court made no exceptions for cases in which a state's legislature had specified that the common law should be used[59] or in which the state's constitution had not granted its courts such declarative power.[60] The Court instead rooted its holding in a misreading of the Judiciary Act's legislative history and in its own view of the nature of law.[61]

The Court soon applied its new *Erie* doctrine to choice of law. In 1941, it held that federal courts should not make an impartial assessment

under the Rules of Decision Act of "where" state laws "apply" but should apply whichever laws would be applied by the courts of the state in which they sit.[62] This change promoted "vertical" uniformity between the federal and state courts in each state, but it destroyed the "horizontal" uniformity among different federal courts—something that diversity jurisdiction had previously guaranteed to out-of-state litigants across the country and that some scholars have identified as the main benefit of diversity jurisdiction.[63]

Cite as: Stephen E. Sachs, *The Judicial Power—Diversity of Citizenship Clause*, in THE HERITAGE GUIDE TO THE CONSTITUTION 483 (Josh Blackman & John G. Malcolm eds., 3d ed. 2025).

Notes

1. Deirdre Mask & Paul MacMahon, *The Revolutionary War Prize Cases and the Origins of Diversity Jurisdiction*, 63 Buff. L. Rev. 477, 508 (2015).   **2.** George Washington, Farewell Address to the Army (Nov. 2, 1783), https://perma.cc/8R3Z-FTDJ.   **3.** Henry J. Bourguignon, The First Federal Court: The Federal Appellate Prize Court of the American Revolution, 1775–1787, at 320 (1977).   **4.** *Id.*   **5.** Mask & MacMahon, supra at 506–07.   **6.** Robert L. Jones, *Finishing a Friendly Argument: The Jury and Historical Origins of Diversity Jurisdiction*, 82 N.Y.U. L. Rev. 997, 1041–43 (2007).   **7.** 1 Farrand's 22.   **8.** 2 Farrand's 39, 186.   **9.** *Id.* at 45–46.   **10.** 1 Farrand's 124.   **11.** Art. III, § 2, cl. 1.   **12.** Art. III, § 1; Art. I, § 8, cl. 9.   **13.** 10 DHRC 1387, 1405.   **14.** Art. I, § 10, cl. 1.   **15.** 10 DHRC 1428.   **16.** Henry J. Friendly, *The Historic Basis of Diversity Jurisdiction*, 41 Harv. L. Rev. 483, 496 (1928).   **17.** 4 DHRC 406, 407 (Agrippa); 10 DHRC 1422 (Patrick Henry).   **18.** 10 DHRC 1434.   **19.** St. George Tucker, 1 Blackstone's Commentaries: With Notes of Reference to the Constitution and Laws of the Federal Government of the United States and of the Commonwealth of Virginia app. E, at 420–21 (1803).   **20.** James E. Pfander & Daniel B. Birk, *Article III Judicial Power, the Adverse-Party Requirement, and Non-Contentious Jurisdiction*, 124 Yale L.J. 1346, 1424 (2015).   **21.** *Id.* at 1367, 1457–58; James E. Pfander & Emily K. Damrau, *A Non-Contentious Account of Article III's Domestic Relations Exception*, 92 Notre Dame L. Rev. 117, 147–48 (2016).   **22.** Pfander & Birk, *supra* at 1458 (citing *Gaines v. Fuentes*, 92 U.S. 10 (1875)); Pfander & Damrau, *supra* at 147–49.   **23.** Ch. 20, § 11, 1 Stat. 73, 78 (1789).   **24.** 7 U.S. (3 Cranch) 267, 267 (1806); Patrick Woolley, *Diversity Jurisdiction and the Common-Law Scope of the Civil Action*, 99 Wash. U. L. Rev. 573, 573–74, 587–93, 606–07 (2021).   **25.** Charles J. Cooper & Howard C. Nielson, Jr., *Complete Diversity and the Closing of the Federal Courts*, 37 Harv. J.L. & Pub. Pol'y 295, 310 (2014).   **26.** 1 Matthew Bacon, A New Abridgment of the Law 8 (Henry Gwillim ed., 5th corr. ed., 1798); Mark Moller, *Complete Diversity:*

The Origin Story, 76 Fla. L. Rev. 1224, 1236–59 (2024).   **27.** *Lincoln Prop. Co. v. Roche*, 546 U.S. 81, 84, 88–89 (2005).   **28.** 28 U.S.C §§ 1332(d), 1335.   **29.** *State Farm Fire & Cas. Co. v. Tashire*, 386 U.S. 523, 530–31 (1967).   **30.** *Id.* at 530, 531 n.7.   **31.** Art. I, § 2, cl. 1.   **32.** *Hepburn v. Ellzey*, 6 U.S. (2 Cranch) 445, 452–53 (1805).   **33.** *Corp. of New-Orleans v. Winter*, 14 U.S. (1 Wheat.) 91 (1816).   **34.** 28 U.S.C. § 1332(e); *Nat'l Mut. Ins. Co. of D.C. v. Tidewater Transfer Co.*, 337 U.S. 582, 584 (1949) (opinion of Jackson, J.).   **35.** *Tidewater*, 337 U.S. at 589; *id.* at 623–26 (opinion of Rutledge, J.).   **36.** Henry M. Hart, Jr. & Herbert Wechsler, The Federal Courts and the Federal System 371–72 (1953); James E. Pfander, *The Tidewater Problem: Article III and Constitutional Change*, 79 Notre Dame L. Rev. 1925, 1978–79 (2004); Mila Sohoni, *The Puzzle of Procedural Originalism*, 72 Duke L.J. 941, 977 (2023).   **37.** *Turner v. Bank of N. Am.*, 4 U.S. (4 Dall.) 8, 10–11 (1799).   **38.** 9 U.S. (5 Cranch) 61, 86 (1809).   **39.** *Id.* at 86–87.   **40.** *Id.* at 88.   **41.** *Louisville, Cincinnati & Charleston R.R. Co. v. Letson*, 43 U.S. (2 How.) 497, 555 (1844).   **42.** *Id.*   **43.** *Marshall v. Balt. & Ohio R.R. Co.*, 57 U.S. (16 How.) 314, 327–29 (1855); 28 U.S.C. § 1332(c)(1).   **44.** *Carden v. Arkoma Assocs.*, 494 U.S. 185 (1990).   **45.** Mark Moller & Lawrence B. Solum, *The Article III "Party" and the Originalist Case Against Corporate Diversity Jurisdiction*, 64 Wm. & Mary L. Rev. 1345 (2023).   **46.** Art. III, § 2, cl. 1; 28 U.S.C. § 1331.   **47.** Judiciary Act § 34, 1 Stat. at 92.   **48.** *Camfranque v. Burnell*, 4 F. Cas. 1130, 1131 (C.C.D. Pa. 1806) (No. 2342) (Washington, Circuit Justice).   **49.** *Golden v. Prince*, 10 F. Cas. 542, 543 (C.C.D. Pa. 1806) (No. 5509).   **50.** *Id.* at 543.   **51.** Caleb Nelson, *A Critical Guide to* Erie Railroad Co. v. Tompkins, 54 Wm. & Mary L. Rev. 921, 941–43 (2013).   **52.** *Id.* at 956–59 (rebutting Charles Warren, *New Light on the History of the Federal Judiciary Act of 1789*, 37 Harv. L. Rev. 49, 52, 88 (1923)).   **53.** *Golden*, 10 F. Cas. at 543.   **54.** Nelson, *supra* at 943–49, 959.   **55.** 41 U.S. (16 Pet.) 1, 18 (1842).   **56.** *Id.* at 19; William A. Fletcher, *The General Common Law and Section 34 of the Judiciary*

Act of 1789: The Example of Marine Insurance, 97 Harv. L. Rev. 1513, 1515 (1984).   **57.** 304 U.S. 64, 78 (1938).   **58.** *Id.*; *id.* at 79 (quoting *Black & White Taxicab & Transfer Co. v. Brown & Yellow Taxicab & Transfer Co.*, 276 U.S. 518, 533 (1928) (Holmes, J., dissenting).   **59.** Nelson, *supra* at 937 & n.49; Stephen E. Sachs, *Finding Law*, 107 Calif. L. Rev. 527, 573 (2019).   **60.** Nelson, *supra* at 980–84; Sachs, *supra* at 574–77; Michael Steven Green, *Erie's Suppressed Premise*, 95

Minn. L. Rev. 1111, 1112–13 (2011).   **61.** *Erie*, 304 U.S. at 73 n.5 (citing Charles Warren, *New Light on the History of the Federal Judiciary Act of 1789*, 37 Harv. L. Rev. 49 (1923)); *id.* at 79; Nelson, *supra* at 954–56.   **62.** *Klaxon Co. v. Stentor Elec. Mfg. Co.*, 313 U.S. 487, 496 (1941).   **63.** Nelson, *supra* at 967–68; Douglas Laycock, *Equal Citizens of Equal and Territorial States*, 92 Colum. L. Rev. 249, 282 (1992).

❧

ESSAY NO. 132: THE JUDICIAL POWER—LAND GRANT JURISDICTION CLAUSE
ART. III, § 2, CL. 1

The judicial Power shall extend . . . to Controversies . . . between Citizens of the same State claiming Lands under Grants of different States . . . .
—Judge Lawrence VanDyke & Ethan Foster

INTRODUCTION

The Land Grant Jurisdiction Clause vests the federal courts with jurisdiction to hear cases when two states purport to grant identical property to different citizens. This provision was an uncontroversial answer to protracted colonial disputes that had persisted at the Constitutional Convention. Its inclusion in the Constitution helped advocates to champion ratification. Although it has not been a serious subject of litigation since the 1950s, it serves as a reminder of the sacrifices made on the way to a more perfect union. Today, the provision is largely vestigial.

CONFLICTING CLAIMS IN THE COLONIES

Before forming a more perfect union, the North American colonies were not all fully bounded territories. The Atlantic Ocean provided a natural eastward limit to expansion, and neighboring colonies constrained most northern and southern expansion, but several colonies lacked firmly defined westward borders in their charters. Under these circumstances, colonial governments with royal authorization to do so encouraged widespread land speculation by granting land claims. In 1754, for example, Virginia Lieutenant Governor Robert Dinwiddie issued a proclamation granting land in the Kanawha Valley to veterans of the French and Indian Wars in partial repayment for their service.[1] Some colonies made expansive claims

to land outside their borders; others made few such claims.

A natural consequence was that disputes could emerge between states over competing grants to the same land. Not all Colonial charters specified how to resolve these sorts of land claims beyond their boundaries. For example, the charters of Massachusetts, Connecticut, Virginia, and Carolina (which later would subdivide into North Carolina and South Carolina) broadly defined their borders. These charters included provisions that claimed land extending from the Atlantic to the Pacific.[2] At the time, however, it was not known how much land separated the two oceans. Several states, including New York, Virginia, Massachusetts, and Connecticut, laid claim to the same pieces of land in the Northwest Territory (largely land northwest of the Ohio River).[3]

By contrast, Maryland, Rhode Island, New Jersey, and Delaware had fixed boundaries and were wary of the larger colonies' expansive claims.[4] These claims were fueled by the 1763 Treaty of Paris, which confirmed and increased England's sovereignty over western land as far as the Mississippi River. The ensuing efforts of the English Crown to recover financially from the French and Indian War led to increased taxes, which prompted a war for independence against the same authority that could have resolved the competing claims of the colonies. In other words, the very events that incentivized colonial westward expansion also set off the American Revolution. As a result, the colonies were forced to resolve competing land claims among themselves in an altogether new forum of their own making.

THE CONTINENTAL CONGRESS

Tensions between colonies with and without expansive land claims emerged at the very start of the Continental Congress. In July 1776, John Dickinson of Pennsylvania presented a draft of the Articles of Confederation for consideration and debate. Articles XIV, XV, and XVIII seemed to allow some colonies to expand westward indefinitely based on their charters.[5] Samuel Chase of Maryland, a future Supreme Court Justice, resisted this language. He argued that "[n]o Colony has a Right to go to the South Sea [Pacific Ocean]; they never had; they can't have. It would not be safe to the rest. It would be destructive to her sisters, and to herself."[6] James Wilson of Pennsylvania, also a future Supreme Court Justice, concurred. Such claims, he said, were "extravagant" because the charter grants were based on the assumption that "the South Sea [was] within one hundred miles of the Atlantic Ocean," and it "was not conceived that they extended three thousand miles." Accordingly, Wilson warned that Pennsylvania "will not confederate unless those claims are cut off."[7]

Chase later bristled to Richard Henry Lee of Virginia that conflicting "claims to the *South-Sea*" needed to be settled and that "[w]e do not all see the importance, nay, the necessity, of a Confederacy" if that question were to remain unresolved.[8] In August 1776, an amendment was proposed to "[l]imit[] the bounds of States, which by charter, &c. extend to the South Sea." But representatives of Virginia, which had expansive claims, aggressively opposed the proposal.[9]

In October 1777, Maryland proposed that the Continental Congress "shall have the sole and exclusive right and power to ascertain and fix the western boundary of such States as claim to the Mississippi or South Sea, and lay out the land beyond the boundary, so ascertained, into separate and independent States, from time to time, as the numbers and circumstances of the people may require." That proposal was roundly defeated with Maryland alone voting in favor.[10]

Rhode Island, New Jersey, and Delaware were less concerned with the jurisdictional sweep of other states and more interested in seeing that revenues from sales of western land be distributed or consolidated to defray war debts. Their proposed amendments to that end were also defeated.[11]

THE ARTICLES OF CONFEDERATION

On November 15, 1777, the Second Continental Congress adopted the Articles of Confederation, which depended on unanimous state ratification for their validity.[12] Article IX allowed states to petition Congress to resolve "[a]ll controversies concerning the private right of soil claims under different grants of two or more states."[13] The process used to deal with those petitions would be the same as the process used to "decid[e] disputes respecting territorial jurisdiction between different states." Such disputes over charter grants would be resolved by "commissioners or judges" selected by the states or by Congress, and during this process, states could not "be deprived of territory for the benefit of the United States."[14]

On September 19, 1778, the Committee on Finance recommended that states "having large uncultivated Territory, beyond what is in their Power to govern, be called on to cede the same to the United States."[15] By May 1779, Rhode Island, New Jersey, and Delaware ratified the Articles of Confederation,[16] but Maryland refused to ratify until 1781 because of conflicting land claims.[17] New York offered to cede her western lands in 1780, and Virginia began to offer cessions of its own in January 1781. In February 1781, Maryland ratified the Articles of Confederation.[18] (See Essay No. 146.)

States with larger claims continued to cede lands to the central government.[19] Such cessions reveal that the union's stability was built on a hidden foundation of voluntary sacrifices by several states. As the national territory expanded, states could have competed with each other for that land. Instead, the states gave the territory to the central government, which in turn could admit new states. In 1783, Virginia ceded land claims northwest of the Ohio River to the Confederation Congress.[20] In July 1787, the Northwest Ordinance was adopted by the

Confederation Congress, erecting a temporary government for that territory as well as establishing a framework for admitting new states.[21]

THE CONSTITUTIONAL CONVENTION

In July 1787, the Committee of Detail drafted language that would have authorized the Senate to resolve "[c]ontroversies concerning Lands claimed under different Grants of two or more States."[22] But on August 24, the provision containing that language was defeated as more properly belonging within the purview of the national judiciary.[23] On August 27, Roger Sherman of Connecticut inserted what is now the Land Grant Jurisdiction Clause—"between Citizens of the same State claiming lands under grants of different States"—without reported debate.[24] That text received no further changes. James Madison of Virginia observed that the Land Grant Jurisdiction Clause was relocated within the jurisdiction of the federal judiciary and without controversy.[25]

Given the history of conflicts between states, it is little surprise that the Land Grant Jurisdiction Clause found its home in Article III. A basic purpose envisioned for the federal judiciary—one sustained throughout the Constitutional Convention—was that jurisdiction would extend to "questions which involve the national peace or harmony."[26] With cessions still anticipated and boundary disputes not fully resolved at the time of the Convention, a federal forum to address future conflicts was needed.[27] Delegates from Delaware and Maryland, for example, intimated that questions about western lands were still on the minds of their constituents.[28]

THE RATIFICATION DEBATES

Federalists in Maryland promoted the Land Grants Clause as a welcome concession. A Maryland broadside by Aratus recited the clause and commented that "[i]t ought not to be overlooked in this frame of government, and it appears to me to be a most striking character in its composition, that the grand object is to preserve unanimity amongst the several states and the citizens thereof, by removing every probable cause of disagreement."[29]

Alexander Hamilton defended the federal judiciary in Federalist No. 80 as an impartial forum for resolving disputes where state courts might not be trusted. He had a salient example in mind: "Claims to land under grants of different states, founded upon adverse pretensions of boundary, are of this description." Hamilton observed that "[t]he courts of neither of the granting states could be expected to be unbiased." Indeed, he wrote, "[t]he laws may have even prejudged the question, and tied the courts down to decisions in favour of the grants of the state to which they belonged." As a general matter, land disputes between citizens of different states could be heard in federal court under the Citizen-State Diversity Clause, but the Land Grant Jurisdiction Clause provides jurisdiction only for disputes between citizens of the same state.[30] In such cases, the Land Grant Jurisdiction Clause was the only avenue to a neutral federal forum.

Another strategic advantage of the Land Grant Jurisdiction Clause was that its narrow specificity was cited to mollify the Anti-Federalists' fear that Article III courts would absorb and destroy the state judiciaries.[31]

JUDICIAL PRECEDENT

Congress promptly enacted legislation implementing the Land Grant Jurisdiction Clause in the Judiciary Act of 1789.[32] Relevant jurisprudence is sparse and largely concerns jurisdictional questions. In 1809, the U.S. Supreme Court refused to exercise jurisdiction under the Land Grants Clause if one of the parties was a corporation.[33] At the time, the Court had not yet settled that corporations were citizens. But it rejected that framework in 1844.[34]

In 1815, the Court exercised jurisdiction over a dispute between citizens of Vermont asserting competing land grants. When the dispute arose, Vermont was part of New Hampshire. Vermont issued one land grant, and New Hampshire issued the other.[35] Following the Judiciary Act of 1887, the Court made clear that a federal circuit court could take up a case under the Land Grants Clause without regard to the amount in controversy.[36]

In modern times, the land grant provision is codified at 28 U.S.C. § 1354. Minor border disputes have arisen involving citizens of the same state. In *Schroeder v. Freeland*, a private dispute erupted over ownership of land between Iowa (which lost land) and Nebraska (which gained land) as a result of changes in the Missouri River's boundaries.[37] The Eighth Circuit reasoned that because the property dispute did not arise from state or charter grants, federal jurisdiction was unavailable.[38] Nor is that holding surprising: It is now vanishingly rare for two states to purport to grant identical property to different citizens within the same state.

OPEN QUESTIONS

- If a state were to subdivide in the future, the Land Grant Jurisdiction Clause could become useful for a narrow transitional period. But the fact that it is not commonly invoked is, perhaps counterintuitively, its crowning achievement: The Land Grant Jurisdiction Clause helped to pave the way for our now firmly established Union.

Cite as: Judge Lawrence VanDyke & Ethan Foster, *The Judicial Power—Land Grant Jurisdiction Clause*, in THE HERITAGE GUIDE TO THE CONSTITUTION 487 (Josh Blackman & John G. Malcolm eds., 3d ed. 2025).

Notes

1. 7 The Statutes at Large, Being a Collection of All the Laws of Virginia 661–62 (William Waller Hening ed., 1820). **2.** Charter of Massachusetts Bay (1691); Charter of Carolina (1665); Charter of Connecticut (1662); Third Charter of Virginia (1611). **3.** Herbert Adams, *Maryland's Influence upon Land Cessions to the United States*, in Johns Hopkins University Studies in Political Science 9–22 (3d Ser., Herbert Adams, ed., 1885). **4.** Payson Jackson Treat, The National Land System 1785–1820, 4–5 (1910). **5.** 5 J. Cont. Cong. 549–51 (July 12, 1776). **6.** 6 J. Cont. Cong. 1076–77 (July 25, 1776). **7.** *Id.* at 1077. **8.** 1 American Archives 672 (5th Ser., Peter Force ed., 1839). **9.** 6 J. Cont. Cong. 1082–83 (Aug. 2, 1776). **10.** 9 J. Cont. Cong. 806–07 (Oct. 15, 1777). **11.** Adams, *supra* at 23–24; Treat, *supra* at 5. **12.** 9 J. Cont. Cong. 906–25 (Nov. 15, 1777). **13.** Articles of Confederation, art. IX, § 3. **14.** *Id.*, art. IX, § 2. **15.** 12 J. Cont. Cong. 931–32 (Sept. 19, 1778). **16.** Adams, *supra* at 24–25. **17.** *Id.* at 25. **18.** Treat, *supra* at 5. **19.** *Id.* at 6–7. **20.** 11 Statutes at Large *supra* at 567–70. **21.** An Ordinance for the Government of the Territory of the United States, North-West of the River Ohio (1787). **22.** 2 Farrand's 162–63, 171, 184–85. **23.** *Id.* at 400–01. **24.** *Id.* at 425–26. **25.** *Id.* at 431–32. **26.** 1 Farrand's 22, 223–24, 231–32, 237–38. **27.** *Id.* at 22. **28.** *Id.* at 405, 463, 471, 441; 2 Farrand's 455, 461–62; 3 Farrand's 575 n.6. **29.** 11 DHRC 30, 40. **30.** *Stevenson v. Fain*, 195 U.S. 165, 168–70 (1904). **31.** 3 DHRC 490, 527. **32.** 1 Stat. 73, 80. **33.** *Bank of U.S. v. Deveaux*, 9 U.S. 61, 85–87 (1809). **34.** *Louisville, C. & C.R. Co. v. Letson*, 43 U.S. 497, 555–56 (1844). **35.** *Town of Pawlet v. Clark*, 13 U.S. (9 Cranch) 292, 319–22 (1815); *Colson v. Lewis*, 15 U.S. 377, 378–79 (1817). **36.** *United States v. Sayward*, 160 U.S. 493, 497–98 (1895). **37.** 188 F.2d 517, 518–19 (8th Cir. 1951). **38.** *Id.* at 519–20.

❦

ESSAY NO. 133: THE JUDICIAL POWER—FOREIGN DIVERSITY CLAUSE
ART. III, § 2, CL. 1

The judicial Power shall extend . . . to Controversies . . . between a State, or the Citizens thereof, and foreign States, Citizens or Subjects.

—Seth J. Lucas

INTRODUCTION

The Foreign Diversity Clause defines the sixth and last of the "Controversies" to which the federal judicial power extends. It is also one of two clauses extending the judicial power to controversies in which the parties are diverse (meaning that they are not both citizens of the same state). But unlike the Citizen-State Diversity Clause (see Essay No. 130), the Foreign Diversity Clause extends the judicial power to controversies in which one side is made up entirely of foreign states or a foreign state's citizens or subjects. Because various questions about the Foreign Diversity Clause intersect with questions about the meaning of "controversies" in Article III, citizen-state diversity, and the Eleventh Amendment, the reader is advised to also consult Essays Nos. 124, 130, and 189.

HISTORY BEFORE 1787

By the American Revolution, it was settled practice that an alien from a friendly nation could generally sue an Englishman in England's courts.[1] As Sir William Blackstone explained in his *Commentaries*, however, "an alien enemy" could not bring suit in English courts.[2] Before the U.S. Constitution's ratification, aliens who were not enemies were able to sue Americans in the States' courts too.

At the same time, as a general rule, sovereign immunity barred individuals, including aliens, from suing a state itself without its consent.[3] Under the law of nations, this doctrine also barred sovereign states from suing other sovereigns in their courts.[4] This rule rested on the theory that sovereigns were, in the words of Professor James Pfander, "equal and independent and . . . therefore not obliged to submit to the jurisdiction of another's courts."[5] The usual means of dispute resolution were the exchange of ambassadors, treaty negotiations, and war if necessary.[6]

The Framers were likely very familiar with these principles. In 1781, for instance, when Pennsylvania's Court of Common Pleas issued a writ of foreign attachment against Virginia, Virginia secured dismissal of the case through diplomatic channels.[7] Virginia's delegates to Congress, believing the writ violated the law of nations, sought relief from Pennsylvania's Executive Council—not from the court.[8] At the Council's direction, Pennsylvania's attorney general successfully urged the court to dismiss the case.[9] Serving process on Virginia would violate the law of nations, he argued, because independent sovereigns are not subject to the other's jurisdiction.[10] Two Framers who would later defend the Foreign Diversity Clause were involved in the case: James Wilson of Pennsylvania represented the plaintiff, and James Madison of Virginia signed communications from Virginia to the Pennsylvania Executive Council.[11]

THE CONSTITUTIONAL CONVENTION

An early version of the Foreign Diversity Clause appeared in the Virginia Plan, which Edmund Randolph introduced on May 29, 1787. The draft proposed to give inferior federal tribunals and the supreme tribunal jurisdiction over "cases in which foreigners or citizens of other States applying to such jurisdictions may be interested."[12] Another recorded version would have conferred jurisdiction over "Disputes between Foreigners and Citizens."[13] On June 13, Randolph explained that "the object" of this jurisdiction was "to establish . . . the security of foreigners where treaties are in their favor, and to preserve the harmony of states and that of the citizens thereof."[14] The New Jersey Plan, however, introduced on June 15, proposed to give to the judiciary narrower "authority to hear . . . all cases in which foreigners may be interested, in construction of any treaty or treaties . . . ."[15] This proposed jurisdiction was also solely appellate.[16]

Delegates went with the Virginia Plan's draft clause. In one document from the Committee of Detail, the jurisdiction was extended to all "disputes" (a change from "cases") "in which subjects or citizens of other countries are concerned."[17] Another version read that it would encompass "all Cases in which Foreigners may be interested in the Construction of any Treaty, or which may arise on any Act for regulating Trade or collecting Revenue *or on the Law of Nations, or general commercial or marine laws*."[18] Yet another document from the Committee of Detail, likely written by James Wilson of Pennsylvania and marked up by John Rutledge of South Carolina, gave the Supreme Court appellate jurisdiction over "Controversies . . . between <a State or the> Citizens (of any of the States) <thereof> and foreign States, Citizens or Subjects."[19] (Angle brackets indicate Rutledge's emendations, and parenthesis indicate crossed-out material.)

On August 6, the Committee of Detail delivered a report to the full Convention that contained almost identical language: The Supreme Court would have appellate jurisdiction over controversies "between a State or the Citizens thereof and foreign States, citizens or subjects."[20] This language was referred to the Committee of Style,[21] which reported it back to the Convention on September 12 with no changes other than the addition of two commas, one after "state" and the other after "citizens thereof."[22] The engrossed copy of the Constitution capitalized the words "State," "Citizens," and "Subjects."[23] No other changes were made to the clause.

THE RATIFICATION DEBATES

The new federal judicial power provoked much controversy during the ratification debates, and the Foreign Diversity Clause was no exception. Federal Farmer, an Anti-Federalist, argued that "no action against a state government, by any citizen or foreigner, ought to be allowed. . . ."[24] He further contended that "no action in which a foreign subject is a party" should be permitted in the federal courts "unless it be of very considerable importance."[25] In his view, there was no reason for foreigners to "carry[] sixpenny causes into the federal courts" as "state courts will be found by experience, to be bottomed on better principles, and to administer justice better than the federal courts."[26]

The Constitution's supporters raised three arguments defending the clause. First, James Wilson emphasized that the clause merely gave foreigners a choice of venue.[27] This was necessary, he observed, "to restore either public or private credit" and "credit with . . . foreign states."[28] And the United States' commercial interests required providing "proper security . . . for the regular discharge of contracts," which in turn required that the general government have the power "of deciding upon those contracts."[29]

Second, Wilson argued that foreigners should enjoy "the same security against state laws . . . that the citizens have" lest unequal treatment threaten peace with foreign states.[30] Wilson hypothesized that a foreigner denied justice might appeal to his own government, which would then demand that Congress do justice.[31] In that instance, "[i]f the United States are answerable for the injury, ought they not to possess the means of compelling the faulty state to repair it? They ought; and this is what is done here."[32] If such a situation did arise, he concluded, Congress could simply respond to the aggrieved foreign government, "Why did not your subject apply to the General [Federal] Court, where the unequal and partial laws of a particular state would have had no force?"[33]

This argument was also raised by Alexander Hamilton in Federalist No. 80 and James Monroe.[34] The alternative, as Monroe contemplated, would be disaster: Might not angered foreign states say that "'we must take that redress by force which your feeble government denies us? We are under the necessity of seizing American property wherever we can lay our hands upon it, till the just demands of our subjects are satisfied.'"[35]

Third, defenders argued that the clause would not abrogate the States' immunity from suits. In the Virginia ratification convention, John Marshall pushed back on objections to extending the judicial power to cases involving a state and a foreign nation. He argued that "[t]he previous consent of the parties is necessary" to be sued in such cases.[36] Hinting at the desirability of a federal forum for resolving these disputes, Marshall then declared that "as the Federal Judiciary will decide, each party will acquiesce."[37] Marshall also underscored that "[i]t will be the means of preventing disputes with foreign nations."[38] James Madison similarly could "not conceive that any controversy can ever be decided, in these [federal] courts, between an American state and a foreign state, without the consent of the parties. If they consent, provision is here made."[39] And in Federalist No. 81, Hamilton emphasized that, at least in the context of contracts with private individuals residing in other states, the Constitution did not abrogate a State's immunity to suits by those individuals.

EARLY PRACTICE

The Judiciary Act of 1789 did not grant federal courts the full scope of jurisdiction possible under the Foreign Diversity Clause. Congress gave the newly created federal district courts jurisdiction over only "all causes where an alien sues for a tort only in violation of the law of nations or a treaty of the United States."[40] This provision became known as the Alien Tort Statute, which is discussed in more depth in Essay No. 55. The Judiciary Act also gave the circuit courts jurisdiction over "all suits of a civil nature at common law or in equity" in which the matter exceeded $500 (excluding costs) and "an alien is a party."[41] An alien defendant could also petition to remove the same cases from state court into federal court.[42]

STATE SOVEREIGNTY AND THE ELEVENTH AMENDMENT

The Foreign Diversity Clause also raised the question of whether a foreign state could sue a State without that State's consent. In *Chisholm v. Georgia* (1793), Justice John Blair Jr. remarked that if the Foreign Diversity Clause were read to allow a State to sue a foreign nation but not to allow a foreign nation to sue a State, that reading would "lose sight of the policy which, no doubt, suggested this provision, viz. That no State in the Union should, by withholding justice, have it in its power to embroil the whole confederacy in disputes of another nature."[43] Similarly looking back to arguments during the ratification debates, Justice William Cushing asserted that the states and foreign states were placed "without distinction upon the same footing" by the Constitution to ensure peaceful relations with other nations.[44]

Although the Eleventh Amendment has been read as repudiating the Court's holding in *Chisholm v. Georgia*, the Amendment's text does not mention a foreign state's suits against non-consenting States. After all, it applied only to suits brought "by Citizens of another State, or by Citizens or Subjects of any Foreign State."

Cherokee Nation v. Georgia (1831) indicated that the Eleventh Amendment did not bar a foreign nation from suing a State.[45] In that case, Georgia attempted to evict the Cherokee nation from land it then occupied. In response, the Cherokee nation sued Georgia in the U.S. Supreme Court's original jurisdiction (see Essay No. 134). The Court dismissed the suit on jurisdictional grounds, holding that the Cherokee nation was not a foreign state under the Foreign Diversity Clause.[46] No one disputed, however, that if the Cherokee nation were a foreign state, the Court would have had jurisdiction. In his majority opinion, Chief Justice John Marshall

never asked whether the Eleventh Amendment barred the suit.[47] Justice William Johnson Jr., dissenting, explained that the Court's original jurisdiction required "that a state of this union should be a party" and that "the other party must, under the control of the eleventh amendment, be another state of the union, or a foreign state."[48] Justice Smith Thompson, also dissenting, remarked that "[t]he controversy in the present case is alleged to be between a foreign state, and one of the states of the union; and does not, therefore, come within the eleventh amendment. . . ."[49] Justice Joseph Story agreed with Thompson's dissent.[50]

Nonetheless, a century later, *Principality of Monaco v. Mississippi* (1934) declared that a foreign state could not sue one of the United States without its consent.[51] The Court concluded that Madison's remarks at the Virginia Convention "correctly interpreted [the Clause] . . . as making provision for jurisdiction of a suit against a State by a foreign State in the event of the State's consent but not otherwise."[52] The Court stated that *Cherokee Nation* "is not opposed" to this holding because it only resolved whether the Cherokee nation was a foreign state.[53] Notably, however, *Monaco* also added that "[i]t cannot be supposed that it was the intention" of the Framers that an action of a State which harms a foreign state's interests and provokes a controversy of national concern "should be taken out of the sphere of international negotiations and adjustment through a resort by the foreign State to a suit under the provisions of § 2 of Article III."[54]

OPEN QUESTIONS

- Dissenting in *Seminole Tribe v. Florida* (1996), Justice John Paul Stevens remarked that "*Monaco* reveals little about the power of Congress to create a private federal cause of action to remedy a State's violation of federal law" because that case concerned only a State's federal defense to an equitable state-law action.[55] Is he correct, and if so, could Congress create a federal cause of action for foreign nations to sue a state for violating federal law?
- Disagreement exists about whether sovereign immunity limits federal courts' jurisdiction over this kind of controversy. One view of the Eleventh Amendment and the distinction between "cases" and "controversies" is that the Amendment reaffirmed that "state sovereign immunity would limit the judicial Power over . . . controversies."[56] Some scholars have argued, however, that the Eleventh Amendment *did not* extend to suits against a State brought by a foreign state, because the Amendment reflected contemporary international law that "presume[ed] no difference between the sovereign

dignity of a State and a nation-state."[57] Does a state lack immunity from suit by a foreign state under the clause's original meaning?

Cite as: Seth J. Lucas, *The Judicial Power—Foreign Diversity Clause*, in THE HERITAGE GUIDE TO THE CONSTITUTION 490 (Josh Blackman & John G. Malcolm eds., 3d ed. 2025).

Notes

1. *Omychund v. Barker* (1744), 125 Eng. Rep. 1310, 1317, [1744] Willes 551.   **2.** 3 Blackstone 301, 330–31, 343–45, 359–61.   **3.** James Pfander, *Rethinking the Supreme Court's Original Jurisdiction in State Party Cases*, 82 Cal. L. Rev. 555, 581 (1994).   **4.** *Id.* at 582–83.   **5.** *Id.* at 583.   **6.** *Id.* at 583–84.   **7.** *McCarty v. Nixon*, 1 U.S. (1 Dall.) 77, (Pa. C.P. 1781), https://perma.cc/7WFD-AXCJ.   **8.** *Id.* at 78.   **9.** *Id.* at 78, 80; Pfander, *supra* at 583–86.   **10.** *McCarty*, 1 U.S. at 78.   **11.** Pfander, *supra* at 586; Letter from Virginia Delegates to Supreme Executive Council of Pennsylvania (ca. July 9, 1781), https://perma.cc/4V4L-K883.   **12.** 1 Farrand's 22.   **13.** *Id.* at 28–29.   **14.** *Id.* at 238–39.   **15.** *Id.* at 243.   **16.** *Id.*   **17.** 2 Farrand's 147.   **18.** *Id.* at 157.   **19.** *Id.* at 163 n.17, 173 .   **20.** *Id.* at 186.   **21.** *Id.* at 576.   **22.** *Id.* at 582, 601.   **23.** *Id.* at 661.   **24.** Storing 2.8.224.   **25.** *Id.*   **26.** *Id.*   **27.** 2 Elliot's 491–92.   **28.** *Id.* at 492–93.   **29.** *Id.*   **30.** *Id.* at 493.   **31.** *Id.* at 493.   **32.** *Id.*   **33.** *Id.*   **34.** 4 Founder's Constitution 251.   **35.** *Id.* at 249.   **36.** *Id.*   **37.** *Id.*   **38.** *Id.*   **39.** 3 Elliot's 533.   **40.** 1 Stat. 73, 77.   **41.** *Id.* at 78.   **42.** *Id.* at 79.   **43.** 2 U.S. 419, 451 (1793) (Blair, J.).   **44.** *Id.* at 467–68 (Cushing, J.).   **45.** 30 U.S. 1 (1831).   **46.** *Id.* at 20.   **47.** *Id.* at 15–16 (Marshall, C.J.).   **48.** *Id.* at 21 (Johnson, J., dissenting).   **49.** *Id.* at 52 (Thompson, J., dissenting).   **50.** *Id.* at 80 (Thompson, J., dissenting).   **51.** 292 U.S. 313 (1934).   **52.** *Id.* at 330.   **53.** *Id.*   **54.** *Id.* at 331–32.   **55.** 517 U.S. 44, 88–89 (1996) (Stevens, J., dissenting).   **56.** Alexander Schultz, *Sovereign Immunity and the Two Tiers of Article III*, 29 Geo. Mason L. Rev. 287, 338–39 (2021).   **57.** Thomas Lee, *Making Sense of the Eleventh Amendment: International Law and State Sovereignty*, 96 Nw. U. L. Rev. 1027, 1028–29 (2002).

❧

ESSAY NO. 134: THE ORIGINAL JURISDICTION CLAUSE
ART. III, § 2, CL. 2

In all Cases affecting Ambassadors, other public Ministers and Consuls, and those in which a State shall be Party, the supreme Court shall have original Jurisdiction.
—Chief Judge William H. Pryor Jr., Nathaniel Sutton, & William Strench

INTRODUCTION

Article III of the Constitution makes all federal courts—both the U.S. Supreme Court and inferior courts—courts of limited jurisdiction. Congress does not have to grant federal courts the full jurisdiction that Article III provides, but its jurisdictional grant cannot exceed the limits of Article III.[1] One constraint on the Court is its limited ability to hear cases as an exercise of its original jurisdiction. Original jurisdiction refers to the power to hear and decide cases in the first instance as opposed to the power to review another court's judgment. Under Article III, the Supreme Court has original jurisdiction over only select interstate disputes and "cases affecting ambassadors, other public ministers and consuls," but its jurisdiction in such disputes does not require congressional authorization.[2] Article III grants the Supreme Court appellate jurisdiction to hear a broader class of cases, subject to exceptions provided by Congress.

HISTORY BEFORE 1787

Under the Articles of Confederation, "courts were a minor feature of the centralized government, which is unsurprising since it was a wartime constitution."[3] Article IX relied primarily on congressional designation of state tribunals for matters of continental concern with some appellate review by either congressional committees or a specially created court for capture cases.[4] The Articles did not create any original jurisdiction as of right in a national court: The closest they came was a process for adjudicating state-to-state disputes when the states could not agree to their own arbitration procedures.[5]

THE CONSTITUTIONAL CONVENTION

The Virginia and New Jersey Plans reflected a widely recognized deficiency of the Articles of Confederation: The central government lacked a national tribunal to adjudicate state-to-state and international disputes.[6] During the Convention, the original jurisdiction of the Supreme Court was kept narrow. On August 6, 1787, the Committee of Detail presented to the Convention the precise categories of the Court's original jurisdiction, which included cases affecting ambassadors, public ministers and consuls, and those in which a state was a party.[7] This draft also would have given the Supreme Court original jurisdiction over "the trial of impeachments of Officers of the United States."[8] Edmund Randolph's Virginia Plan had proposed the impeachment of "any National officers" as a category of jurisdiction for a "National Judiciary."[9] The House and Senate were later empowered to handle impeachments.[10] The limited scope of the Supreme Court's original jurisdiction may have been based on a pragmatic concern that litigants would be oppressed by the burden of traveling to the national capital for too many suits.[11]

Although the Original Jurisdiction Clause narrowly limited the Supreme Court's original jurisdiction, the Court would have appellate jurisdiction over "all the other Cases" mentioned in Article III, subject to "such Exceptions" as Congress might make.[12] (The Appellate Jurisdiction Clause is discussed in Essay No. 135.) A draft in Edmund Randolph's handwriting that was found in the papers of George Mason would have allowed Congress to shift at least some cases from the Supreme Court's appellate jurisdiction to its original jurisdiction, but this proposal was rejected.[13]

THE RATIFICATION DEBATES

In Federalist No. 81, Alexander Hamilton wrote that "[t]he Supreme Court is to be invested with original jurisdiction, only" in the cases listed in the Original Jurisdiction Clause. He reasoned that the limited class of disputes in that provision was "so directly connected with the public peace . . . that . . . it is both expedient and proper that such questions should be submitted in the first instance to the highest judicatory of the nation." Each of the disputes contemplated by the clause involved either the relationships of the United States with foreign countries or the rights of sovereign states.

During the Virginia Convention, two prominent delegates rejected interpreting the Exceptions Clause as empowering Congress to expand the original jurisdiction of the Supreme Court. Future Chief Justice John Marshall asked rhetorically, "What is the meaning of the term *exception*? Does it not mean an alteration and diminution?"[14] He then answered that "Congress is empowered to make exceptions to the appellate jurisdiction, as to law and fact, of the Supreme Court. These exceptions certainly go as far as the legislature may think proper for the interest and liberty of the people." Edmund Pendleton argued that "the legislature cannot extend its original jurisdiction, which is limited to these cases only."[15]

Marshall and Pendleton were perhaps influenced by what James Pfander has described as Virginia's "long struggle[] with the inconvenience of a centralized supreme court with broad original jurisdiction over civil and criminal proceedings at common law."[16] During the Pennsylvania Convention, James Wilson expressed a similar understanding of the Original Jurisdiction Clause: "In two cases the Supreme Court has original jurisdiction—that affecting ambassadors, and when a state shall be a party. It is true it has appellate jurisdiction in more, but it will have it under such restrictions as the Congress shall ordain."[17]

THE FIRST CONGRESS

Section 13 of the Judiciary Act of 1789, enacted by the First Congress, provided for the inferior federal courts to exercise concurrent jurisdiction with the Supreme Court with respect to some but not all of the categories of original jurisdiction.[18] This statute addressed the Supreme Court's original jurisdiction and confirmed the plain meaning of Article III: The Court may exercise original jurisdiction only in a narrow class of cases, although its jurisdiction over those cases need not be exclusive. Professor Akhil Amar has observed that "[n]othing in the explicit language or the geographic logic of Article III seems to prevent Congress from opting for original jurisdiction concurrent with the state courts, at least in state party cases."[19]

In 1793, Circuit Justice James Wilson and Judge Richard Peters ruled that Section 13's grant of concurrent jurisdiction was constitutional.[20] The Supreme Court would later reach the same conclusion.[21]

MARBURY V. MADISON

At the end of President John Adams's Administration, the lame-duck Federalist Congress enacted the Judiciary Act of 1801, which created a new system of appellate courts and judgeships.[22] Adams, a Federalist, then nominated members of his own party to the new positions.[23] After the Senate confirmed these judges, the President signed their commissions, which were records of their appointments, but not all these commissions were delivered before Adams left office.

William Marbury, who was confirmed by the Senate to serve as a justice of the peace, never received his commission. After President Thomas Jefferson was inaugurated, he discovered Marbury's commission and others and instructed Secretary of State James Madison not to deliver them. When Marbury failed to receive his commission, he bypassed the lower court and filed a petition for a writ of mandamus directly in the Supreme Court invoking its original jurisdiction. A writ of mandamus commands officials (like Madison) to perform duties required by law (such as delivering Marbury's commission). Congress had previously granted the Court the mandamus power in Section 13 of the Judiciary Act of 1789.[24]

Chief Justice John Marshall wrote the majority opinion in *Marbury v. Madison* (1803). The Court held that if Section 13's mandamus power was a grant of original jurisdiction, it was unconstitutional because Article III provides the exclusive bases for the Court's original jurisdiction.[25] (There is a textualist argument that Section 13 gave the Supreme Court the mandamus power only in a case over which it already had jurisdiction.) The Original Jurisdiction Clause would be "mere surplusage" if Congress could expand the Court's original jurisdiction to encompass a variety of other cases.[26] Marshall also concluded that the narrow class of cases in the Original Jurisdiction Clause was exclusive: By specifying a narrow subset of disputes, Article III implies the exclusion of other grounds for original jurisdiction.

Why did Marbury start his case in the Supreme Court? His attorney, former Attorney General Charles Lee, argued that the Court had already issued writs of mandamus in similar original actions on three occasions. Did Marshall ignore or misread this history, as some scholars have suggested?[27] Marshall acknowledged these isolated practices but treated their rarity as evidence of "how far the practice has conformed to the general doctrines" on which *Marbury* relied. In any event, the precedents Lee cited and others were cognizable under one of the enumerated bases of jurisdiction, were arguably appellate in nature, or did not involve mandamus.[28]

In the end, *Marbury* held that Congress cannot expand the Court's original jurisdiction.[29] Rather, the Original Jurisdiction Clause enumerates the only types of cases in which the Court may exercise original jurisdiction. *Marbury* was consistent with Hamilton's observation in Federalist No. 81, as well as Marshall's arguments during the Virginia Convention, that the Constitution defines the original jurisdiction of the Supreme Court.

Nevertheless, some modern critics argue that Congress's power to make exceptions to the Court's appellate jurisdiction necessarily implies the power to reallocate cases from the Court's appellate jurisdiction to its original jurisdiction.[30] By using the exceptions power, these critics argue, Congress can enlarge the Court's original jurisdiction. Professor Akhil Amar counters that "exceptions" leads to the opposite inference: Congress may withdraw disputes only from the Court's already existing jurisdiction; Article III contains no "Additions Clause."[31]

POST-*MARBURY* PRECEDENTS

Since *Marbury*, the Supreme Court has clarified how to determine the scope of its original and appellate jurisdiction. *Cohens v. Virginia* (1821) considered an appeal in a criminal case that was decided by a state court and in which the state was a party.[32] Virginia argued that the Supreme Court lacked appellate jurisdiction to review the state court's decision because the Constitution granted the Supreme Court original, not appellate, jurisdiction over cases in which a state is a party. Under this position, the Court had to hear the dispute involving a state as an original matter or not at all.[33]

Chief Justice Marshall, writing for the Court, rejected that argument. He reaffirmed the central holding of *Marbury*: "The original jurisdiction of this Court cannot be enlarged."[34] But he acknowledged that the Court did not have to hear every case contemplated by the Original Jurisdiction Clause in the first instance. Instead, he reasoned that the Court's appellate jurisdiction extends to "every case cognizable under" Article III of the Constitution, including questions "arising under . . . the Laws of the United States."[35] The appellate jurisdiction, therefore, includes cases in which a state is a party even though those cases would also qualify for the exercise of original jurisdiction.

Ex parte Bollman (1807) held that the Court could exercise appellate jurisdiction over a petition for a writ of habeas corpus that would not be cognizable as an exercise of original jurisdiction. In that case, the petition required, before it was filed, a lower court order of commitment.[36] Therefore, the Court was reviewing an inferior judicial determination through its appellate jurisdiction.

ORIGINAL JURISDICTION IN PRACTICE

At the Founding, boundary disputes between states were the disputes most likely to arise under the Court's original jurisdiction.[37] At the turn of the twentieth century, the Court's original jurisdiction docket began to diversify as water-rights disputes, pollution abatement, and Commerce Clause claims became more common.[38] Such disputes continue to this day.[39] More infrequently, the Court has allowed urgent constitutional challenges involving states to proceed on its original jurisdiction docket, such as disputes involving the Voting Rights Act.[40]

When the Court accepts a case on its original jurisdiction docket, it will ordinarily appoint a special master to gather evidence, take sworn testimony, and issue a report.[41] In some disputes, such as water-rights disputes, the Court reviews the special master's factual conclusions through a deferential lens.[42] Like a trial, the special master's review of a dispute is a time-consuming endeavor. For example, a water dispute involving Kansas, Nebraska, and Colorado took sixteen years to resolve.[43] Although appointing a special master is certainly the Court's preferred approach, it may conduct a jury trial itself. On at least one occasion, the Court has done so,[44] but that trial occurred before *Marbury*.

OPEN QUESTIONS

- Is the exercise of the Supreme Court's original jurisdiction mandatory? The Court has routinely exercised discretion to decline to hear cases falling within the terms of its original jurisdiction.[45] Some originalists criticize this practice in light of the text that the Court's original jurisdiction "shall" extend to certain controversies.[46]
- Can Congress restrict the Court's ability to hear original jurisdiction cases to less than what Article III grants? For example, could Congress create a court to hear interstate disputes and grant the Supreme Court only appellate jurisdiction? The Court has expressed skepticism with respect to this possibility but has never decided the issue.[47]
- Can the Supreme Court exercise original jurisdiction over disputes between the United States and a state? The Court has answered affirmatively.[48] However, individual Justices have criticized that understanding of the clause,[49] and modern scholarship discusses the issue.[50]

Cite as: Chief Judge William H. Pryor Jr., Nathaniel Sutton, & William Strench, *The Original Jurisdiction Clause, in* THE HERITAGE GUIDE TO THE CONSTITUTION 494 (Josh Blackman & John G. Malcolm eds., 3d ed. 2025).

Notes

1. *Sheldon v. Sill*, 49 U.S. 441 (1850). **2.** *Kentucky v. Dennison*, 65 U.S. (24 How.) 66, 74 (1860). **3.** Thomas H. Lee, *Article IX, Article III, and the First Congress: The Original Constitutional Plan for the Federal Courts, 1787–92*, 89 Fordham L. Rev. 1895, 1901 (2021). **4.** *Id.* at 1902–04. **5.** Articles of Confederation, art. IX, §§ 2–3. **6.** 2 Farrand's 21–22, 223–24; 3 Farrand's 600. **7.** 2 Farrand's 186. **8.** *Id.*; 1 Farrand's 237. **9.** 1 Farrand's 21–22. **10.** 2 Farrand's 493, 592. **11.** 3 Farrand's 220; Akhil Reed Amar, *Marbury, Section 13, and the Original Jurisdiction of the Supreme Court*, 56 U. Chi. L. Rev. 443, 475–78 (1989). **12.** 2 Farrand's 186. **13.** *Id.* at 147, 425, 430–32. **14.** 3 Elliot's 560. **15.** *Id.* at 518. **16.** James E. Pfander, *Marbury, Original Jurisdiction, and the Supreme Court's Supervisory Powers*, 101 Col. L. Rev. 1515, 1551–52 & n.153 (2001). **17.** 2 Elliot's 493. **18.** Act of Sept. 24, 1789, ch. 20, § 13, 1 Stat. 73, 80–81. **19.** Amar, *supra* at 492 n.219. **20.** *United States v. Ravara*, 2 U.S. (2 Dall.) 297, 298 (Cir. Pa. 1793). **21.** *Börs v Preston*, 111 U.S. 252, 256–61 (1884); *Ames v. Kan. ex rel. Johnston*, 111 U.S. 449, 463–71 (1884). **22.** Judiciary Act of 1801, 2 Stat. 89 (1801), repealed by Judiciary Act of 1802, ch. 8, §§ 1–2, 2 Stat. 132. **23.** Louise Weinberg, *Our Marbury*, 89 Va. L. Rev. 1235, 1236–38 (2003). **24.** Act of Sept. 24, 1789, ch. 20, § 13, 1 Stat. 73, 80–81. **25.** *Marbury v. Madison*, 5 U.S. (1 Cranch) 137, 174–75 (1803). **26.** *Id.* at 174. **27.** Susan Low Bloch & Maeva Marcus, *John Marshall's Selective Use of History in* Marbury v. Madison, 1986 Wis. L. Rev. 301 (1986). **28.** Weinberg, *supra* at 1321–1330. **29.** *Marbury*, 5 U.S. (1 Cranch) at 175. **30.** William W. Van Alstyne, *A Critical Guide to* Marbury v. Madison, 1969 Duke L. J. 1, 31–32 (1969). **31.** Amar, *supra* at 455, 465. **32.** 19 U.S. (6 Wheat.) 264 (1821). **33.** *Id.* at 392. **34.** *Id.* at 399. **35.** *Id.* **36.** 8 U.S. (4 Cranch) 75, 101 (1807). **37.** *Wisconsin v. Pelican Ins. Co.*, 127 U.S. 265 (1888). **38.** *Louisiana v. Texas*, 176 U.S. 1, 19 (1900); *Missouri v. Illinois*, 180 U.S. 208 (1901). **39.** *New Jersey v. New York*, 523 U.S. 767 (1998); *Florida v. Georgia*, 592 U.S. 433 (2021). **40.** *South Carolina v. Katzenbach*, 383 U.S. 301 (1966). **41.** *Mississippi v. Tennessee*, 595 U.S. 15, 22–23 (2021). **42.** *Texas v. New Mexico*, 485 U.S. 388 (1988). **43.** *Kansas v. Nebraska & Colorado*, 574 U.S. 445, 451–53 (2015). **44.** *Georgia v. Brailsford, Powell & Hopton*, 3 U.S. (3 Dall.) 1 (1794). **45.** *Ohio v. Wyandotte Chems. Corp.*, 401 U.S. 493, 505 (1971). **46.** *Arizona v. California*, 140 S.Ct. 684 (2020) (Thomas, J., dissenting from denial of motion for leave to file complaint). **47.** Thomas H. Lee, *The Supreme Court of the United States as Quasi-International Tribunal: Reclaiming the Court's Original and Exclusive Jurisdiction over Treaty-Based Suits by Foreign States*, 104 Col. L. Rev. 1765, 1778 (2004); *California v. Arizona*, 440 U.S. 59, 65–66 (1979); *Wisconsin v. Pelican Ins. Co.*, 127 U.S. 265, 300 (1888), *overruled by Milwaukee Cnty. v. M.E. White Co.*, 296 U.S. 268 (1935); *Kansas v. Colorado*, 556 U.S. 98, 109 (2009) (Roberts, C.J., concurring). **48.** *United States v. Texas*, 143 U.S. 621, 643–45 (1892). **49.** *Id.* at 648–49 (Fuller, C.J., dissenting); *Ex parte Republic of Peru*, 318 U.S. 578, 598 (1943) (Frankfurter, J., dissenting). **50.** Lochlan Shelfer, *The Supreme Court's Original Jurisdiction over Disputes Between the United States and a State*, 66 Buff. L. Rev. 193 (2018); James E. Pfander, *Rethinking the Supreme Court's Original Jurisdiction in State-Party Cases*, 82 Calif. L. Rev. 555 (1994).

ESSAY NO. 135: THE APPELLATE JURISDICTION CLAUSE
ART. III, § 2, CL. 2

In all the other Cases before mentioned, the supreme Court shall have appellate Jurisdiction, both as to Law and Fact, with such Exceptions, and under such Regulations as the Congress shall make.

—Chief Judge William H. Pryor Jr.

INTRODUCTION

Article III of the Constitution establishes two types of jurisdiction for the Supreme Court. First, there is "original Jurisdiction" over "all Cases affecting Ambassadors, other public Ministers and Consuls, and those in which a State shall be Party." (See Essay No. 134.) And second, there is "appellate Jurisdiction" in "all other Cases" listed in Article III, Section 2, Clause 1 that are not allocated to the Court's "original Jurisdiction," subject to congressional "Exceptions." The Appellate Jurisdiction Clause has raised four issues at various points in U.S. history: (1) What is the meaning of "Appellate" in the clause? (2) Does the Court's appellate jurisdiction extend to the judgments of state courts? (3) What is the effect of the extension of appellate jurisdiction to "both . . . Law and Fact"? And (4) what is the scope of Congress's power to make "Exceptions" to the Court's appellate jurisdiction?

HISTORY BEFORE 1787

The Articles of Confederation gave the United States in Congress the "exclusive right and power" of "establishing courts for receiving and determining finally appeals in all cases of captures."[1] In 1780, Congress created a Court of Appeals in Cases of Capture that was the "one permanent judicial body which the Confederation maintained."[2] This court's appellate jurisdiction permitted it to hear new evidence and did not require deference to state courts' "findings of fact or law, even when the case had been tried by jury."[3]

THE CONSTITUTIONAL CONVENTION

At the Constitutional Convention, the influential Virginia Plan would have established "One Supreme Tribunal" and allowed the "national Legislature [to] be empowered to appoint inferior Tribunals."[4] The supreme court would have exercised appellate jurisdiction in cases involving "the national peace and harmony" and a few enumerated categories.[5] But the Virginia Plan did not give the legislature power to make exceptions to that appellate jurisdiction. Nor did it give the supreme court jurisdiction to review law as well as the factual determinations of the lower courts.

The delegates later tinkered with the scope of appellate jurisdiction. The state-friendly New Jersey Plan proposed that the Supreme Court would hear appeals "in all cases touching the rights of Ambassadors," "cases of captures," "cases of piracies & felonies on the high seas," and "cases in which foreigners may be interested, in the construction of any treaty or treaties, or which may arise on any of the Acts for regulation of trade, or the collection of federal revenue."[6] Relatedly, some delegates argued that inferior federal courts were unnecessary. For example, John Rutledge of South Carolina argued that the creation of inferior courts would be "an unnecessary encroachment on the jurisdiction" of state courts.[7]

Nevertheless, there was widespread agreement that the Supreme Court would exercise appellate jurisdiction over state courts. Rutledge admitted that appeals to "the supreme national tribunal" were necessary "to secure the national rights & uniformity of Judgments."[8] Even the New Jersey Plan permitted appellate jurisdiction over state courts.[9] In the end, the Convention left it to the Committee of Detail to fill in the particulars as Edmund Randolph of Virginia proposed.[10]

A Committee of Detail draft in Randolph's handwriting gave Congress the power to make some exceptions to the Supreme Court's appellate jurisdiction: "But this supreme jurisdiction shall be appellate only, except in <Cases of Impeachmt. & (in)> those instances, in which the legislature shall make it original. and the legislature shall organize it."[11] The draft also specified that in certain classes of cases, the Supreme Court would have jurisdiction only as "the national legislature [would] assign."[12] Later, the Committee of Detail's report contained the final wording of the Exceptions Clause.[13] Exactly why the Committee chose this wording is not known.[14] The Committee's draft, however, did not grant the Supreme Court the power to review *both* "Law and Fact."[15] That language was added on the floor of the Convention. James Wilson of Pennsylvania stated that it was the Committee's intention to extend appellate jurisdiction to "facts as well as law."[16]

THE RATIFICATION DEBATES

The Appellate Jurisdiction Clause did not occasion much debate during the Constitutional Convention, but it would become controversial during the ratification debates. Brutus, a prominent Anti-Federalist, warned that "[t]he appellate jurisdiction granted to the supreme court" was "one of the most objectionable parts of the constitution."[17]

The principal controversy centered on the grant of appellate jurisdiction "both as to law and fact." The Anti-Federalist Federal Farmer contended that allowing the Supreme Court to review facts as determined by the inferior court would effectively abolish trial by jury— "the most noble and important principle of the common law."[18] In Federalist No. 81, Alexander Hamilton responded that appellate jurisdiction over law and fact might be limited to civil law and admiralty cases and added that, in any event, Congress could and would address this issue under its power to create exceptions to the Supreme Court's appellate jurisdiction so that it would not disturb facts found by juries.

In 1789, the First Congress proposed the Seventh Amendment, which addressed the Anti-Federalists' concerns.[19] It guaranteed that "no fact tried by a jury, shall be otherwise re-examined in any Court of the United States, than according to the rules of the common law."[20] (See Essay Nos. 182 and 183.)

APPELLATE VERSUS ORIGINAL JURISDICTION

In *Marbury v. Madison* (1803), William Marbury asked the Supreme Court in its original jurisdiction to order Secretary of State James Madison to deliver Marbury's judicial commission. The Court held that it lacked the power to grant a writ of mandamus because Article III fixed the Court's original jurisdiction.[21] Chief Justice John Marshall explained that Marbury had not invoked what was understood to be the appellate jurisdiction of the Supreme Court: "It is the essential criterion of appellate jurisdiction, that it revises and corrects the proceedings in a cause already instituted, and does not create that cause."[22] That is, Marbury's mandamus request was not directed to a lower court where a cause had been instituted; instead, it was directed in the first instance to the Secretary of State to deliver the commission. Marshall concluded that Marbury's request "seems not to belong to appellate, but to original jurisdiction."[23] *Marbury*'s definition of appellate jurisdiction would prove influential.

The Supreme Court would next address its appellate jurisdiction in *Ex parte Bollman*.[24] Erick Bollman was implicated in an alleged treason plot involving Aaron Burr. After a federal circuit court found probable cause to order Bollman to stand trial for treason, Bollman sought a writ of habeas corpus in the Supreme Court under Section 14 of the Judiciary Act of 1789.[25] Was Bollman's petition an appeal from the circuit court's ruling, or was his petition a new action within the Supreme Court's original jurisdiction? The Court held that the habeas petition fell within the Court's appellate jurisdiction.[26] Marshall relied on his discussion of original and appellate jurisdiction in *Marbury* and acknowledged that the writ was sought in the first instance in the Supreme Court. But that application still implicated the Court's appellate jurisdiction because the application sought "the revision of a decision of an inferior court, by which a citizen has been committed to jail."[27] Following *Bollman*, an "original" petition for a writ in the Supreme Court has been deemed to fall within the Court's appellate jurisdiction as long as the writ concerns or is directed to an inferior court proceeding previously instituted.[28]

APPELLATE JURISDICTION OVER STATE COURTS

During the Philadelphia Convention, "it was universally assumed that the Supreme Court would have jurisdiction to review the decisions of state courts on matters of federal concern."[29] Nonetheless, the issue was widely contested in early American history.[30] It also inevitably came before the Supreme Court, where it was resolved in two of the Court's most famous early decisions. First, *Martin v. Hunter's Lessee* (1816) upheld the constitutionality of Section 25 of Judiciary Act of 1789, which gave the Court appellate jurisdiction over state civil decisions that denied the validity of a federal claim.[31] And second, *Cohens v. Virginia* (1821) upheld the Supreme Court's appellate jurisdiction under Article III to review state criminal cases.[32]

In *Ableman v. Booth* (1858), the Supreme Court observed that "this ultimate appellate power in a tribunal created by the Constitution itself was deemed essential to secure the independence and supremacy of the General Government in the sphere of action assigned to it; to make the Constitution and laws of the United States uniform, and the same in every State."[33]

THE EXCEPTIONS CLAUSE

The Supreme Court's appellate jurisdiction is subject to "such Exceptions, and under such Regulations as the Congress shall make."[34] This provision, known as the Exceptions Clause, has raised two issues: how to construe statutory conferrals of appellate jurisdiction in light of the clause and the scope of Congress's power to create "Exceptions."

The Judiciary Act of 1789 provided that the Supreme Court might "re-examine[]" certain non-criminal federal circuit court decisions and state court decisions that denied a federal claim.[35] The act purported to grant the Court appellate review over these cases, but *Durousseau v. United States* (1810) held that the Court's appellate jurisdiction was established by the Constitution, not Congress.[36]

The seminal decision on the meaning of the Exceptions Clause is *Ex Parte McCardle* (1868). William McCardle, a Mississippi newspaper editor, was placed in military custody. A circuit court denied his habeas petition. McCardle thereafter appealed to the Supreme Court pursuant to the Habeas Corpus Act of 1867. After the Court heard oral argument, Congress repealed the provisions of the 1867 statute that had authorized Supreme Court review. The Court concluded that Congress had created an exception to its appellate jurisdiction. Therefore, even at that late date, the Court no longer had jurisdiction to decide the case. The Court stated, "We are not at liberty to inquire into the motives of the legislature. We can only examine into its power under the Constitution; and the power to make exceptions to the appellate jurisdiction of this court is given by express words."[37] *McCardle* provides the basis for the concept known as *jurisdiction stripping.*

The Court later affirmed Congress's broad power to make exceptions to its appellate jurisdiction.[38]

United States v. Klein (1871) may have qualified *McCardle.* In *Klein,* Congress purported to alter the Court's appellate jurisdiction to change the effect of a presidential pardon. The Court, however, held that Congress could not make such an exception or "prescribe rules of decision to the Judicial Department of the government in cases pending before it."[39] But *Klein* also made clear that if Congress had "simply denied the right of appeal in a particular class of cases, there could be no doubt that it must be regarded as an exercise of the power of Congress to make 'such exceptions from the appellate jurisdiction' as should seem to it expedient."[40]

OPEN QUESTIONS

- Professor Akhil Amar has argued that Congress cannot create exceptions for cases in the first three heads of Article III, Section 2, Clause 1 if such jurisdiction is denied to lower federal courts.[41] This view may find some support in dicta from *Martin v. Hunter's Lessee,*[42] but it finds little support in Supreme Court case law.
- The Habeas Corpus Clause, also known as the Suspension Clause,[43] grants Congress the power to "suspend" the "Privilege of the Writ of Habeas Corpus." (See Essay No. 68.) The relationship between the Exceptions Clause and the Suspension Clause remains uncertain.[44] Does the constitutional right to habeas corpus relief, as recognized in *Boumediene v. Bush* (2008), impose a limit on Congress's power to make exceptions to the Supreme Court's appellate jurisdiction?[45] *McCardle* and later cases went to great lengths to construe congressional abrogation of Supreme Court appellate review as not eliminating statutory habeas jurisdiction.[46]

Cite as: Chief Judge William H. Pryor Jr., *The Appellate Jurisdiction Clause, in* THE HERITAGE GUIDE TO THE CONSTITUTION 498 (Josh Blackman & John G. Malcolm eds., 3d ed. 2025).

Notes

1. Articles of Confederation, art. IX, § 1. **2.** J. Franklin Jameson, *The Predecessor of the Supreme Court, in* Essays in the Constitutional History of the United States in the Formative Period 1775–1789, 4 (J. Franklin Jameson ed., 1889). **3.** Thomas H. Lee, *Article IX, Article III, and the First Congress: The Original Constitutional Plan for the Federal Courts, 1787–92,* 89 Fordham L. Rev. 1895, 1903 (2021). **4.** 1 Farrand's 22. **5.** *Id.* **6.** *Id.* at 244. **7.** *Id.* at 124. **8.** *Id.* **9.** *Id.* at 243–44. **10.** *Id.* at 238. **11.** 2 Farrand's 147 (punctuation as in original). **12.** *Id.* **13.** *Id.* at 186. **14.** John Eidsmoe, *The Article III Exceptions Clause: Any Exceptions to the Power of Congress to Make Exceptions?,* 19 Regent U. L. Rev. 96, 106 (2006). **15.** 2 Farrand's 186. **16.** *Id.* at 431. **17.** Storing 2.9.169. **18.** *Id.* **19.** Edith Guild Henderson, *The Background of the Seventh Amendment,* 80 Harv. L. Rev. 289, 291–99 (1966). **20.** Amend. VII. **21.** 5 U.S. (1 Cranch) 137, 174–75 (1803). **22.** *Id.* at 175. **23.** *Id.* at 175–76. **24.** 8 U.S. (4 Cranch) 75 (1807). **25.** Act of Sept. 24, 1789, ch. 20, § 14, 1 Stat. 73, 81–82. **26.** *Id.* at 101. **27.** *Id.* **28.** *Felker v. Turpin,* 518 U.S. 651, 667 n.1

(1996) (Souter, J. concurring); *Ex parte* Yerger, 75 U.S. (8 Wall.) 85, 103 (1868); *Ex parte* Watkins, 32 U.S. (7 Pet.) 568, 572–73 (1833). **29.** Richard H. Fallon, Jr., et al., Hart and Wechsler's The Federal Courts and the Federal System 19 (7th ed. 2015). **30.** *Id.* at 474. **31.** 14 U.S. (1 Wheat.) 304 (1816). **32.** 19 U.S. (6 Wheat.) 264 (1821). **33.** 62 U.S. (21 How.) 506, 518 (1858). **34.** Art. III, § 2, cl. 2. **35.** Judiciary Act of 1789, ch. 20, §§ 22, 25, 1 Stat. 73, 84; *Id.* § 25. **36.** *Durousseau v. United States,* 10 U.S. (6 Cranch) 307, 314 (1810). **37.** *McCardle,* 74 U.S. (7 Wall.) at 514. **38.** *The Francis Wright,* 105 U.S. 381 (1881). **39.** 80 U.S. (13 Wall.) 128, 146 (1871). **40.** *Id.* at 145. **41.** Akhil Reed Amar, *A Neo-Federalist View of Article III: Separating the Two-Tiers of Federal Jurisdiction,* 65 B.U. L. Rev. 205 (1985). **42.** 14 U.S. (1 Wheat.) at 328–33. **43.** Art. I, § 9, cl. 2. **44.** Richard H. Fallon, Jr., *Jurisdiction-Stripping Reconsidered,* 96 Va. L. Rev. 1043, 1053 (2013). **45.** 553 U.S. 723 (2008). **46.** *McCardle,* 74 U.S. (7 Wall.) at 514; *Yerger,* 75 U.S. (8 Wall.) at 104–06; *INS v. St. Cyr,* 533 U.S. 289 (2001).

ESSAY NO. 136: THE CRIMINAL TRIALS CLAUSE
ART. III, § 2, CL. 3

The Trial of all Crimes, except in Cases of Impeachment, shall be by Jury; and such Trial shall be held in the State where the said Crimes shall have been committed; but when not committed within any State, the Trial shall be at such Place or Places as the Congress may by Law have directed.
—Judge Kurt D. Engelhardt, Jacob J. Thackston, & Dexter Webster

INTRODUCTION

Sir William Blackstone wrote that "the trial by jury ever has been, and I trust ever will be, looked upon as the glory of the English law."[1] The Founders agreed. In 1771, John Adams noted that the jury system was an essential feature of a government committed to securing the "fundamental rights" of the people: The jury ought to have "as complete a control, as decisive a negative, in every judgment of a court of judicature" as the populace had in the legislative branch.[2] In 1789, Thomas Jefferson stated that he would sooner omit the people from the legislative branch than abolish the jury system, for "[t]he execution of the laws is more important than the making them."[3] The Criminal Trials Clause of Article III reflects the importance with which the Framers regarded the jury system.

HISTORY BEFORE 1787

Clause 39 of Magna Carta stated that "[n]o free man shall be seized or imprisoned . . . except by the lawful judgment of his equals or by the law of the land." The U.S. Supreme Court has pointed to this clause as the foundational promise of the right to a jury trial in English law.[4] However, this provision appears to have applied mostly to trials directly involving the king and his noblemen.[5] Nonetheless, it reflected a deeply rooted value placed by the English legal system on judgment by peers. Five decades before Magna Carta, the first juries with twelve members and the authority to declare guilt or innocence were used under the reign of King Henry II.[6] In the remaining years of the thirteenth century, the convention of trial by jury continued to expand, and by the late fourteenth century, the jury had become "the dominant mode of trial."[7]

This English practice of using juries continued in America from the time of the very first settlements. The 1606 Charter of the Virginia Company declared that the colonists who were to settle there would enjoy all the rights of Englishmen, including the right to a jury trial.[8] King James I's directive for the government of the Colony of Virginia instructed that serious crimes were to be tried by juries, including rebellion, conspiracy, sedition, rape, and murder.[9]

Before the American Revolution, juries played a vital role in the colonial resistance to English authority. One particularly noteworthy case involved John Peter Zenger. The New York publisher accused the British governor of, among other things, "taking away trials by juries."[10] In 1735, Zenger was tried for seditious libel: that is, publishing material designed to cause scandal and vilify a member of government. Zenger's attorney, Andrew Hamilton (no relation to Alexander Hamilton), admitted that Zenger had published the materials in question but argued that no libel was committed because the accusations were true.[11] The judge rejected this legal argument and charged the jury that a true statement could still be libelous.[12] Hamilton, unbothered by the judge's contrary declamation, still argued to the jury that truth was a defense to a charge of libel. Ultimately, the jury seemed to reject the judge's instructions and found Zenger not guilty.[13]

The Zenger trial precisely illustrates the value of juries to our constitutional heritage. As Blackstone explained, the executive power has a tendency sometimes to imprison those it deems "obnoxious to the government," and judges, acting as arms of the executive, could often play a role in this.[14] It was therefore necessary to balance this dangerous tendency with a check by a jury of peers. Applying these insights to the Zenger trial, the jury acquitted Zenger against an executive government and a judge that perhaps were a little too overzealous in their desire to silence their political critics. Liberty was maintained thanks to the role of the jury.

In the decades that followed, the grievances about which Zenger published continued to fester. The "Declaration and Resolves of the First Continental Congress" of 1774 demanded the repeal of the so-called Intolerable Acts imposed by Parliament on the American colonists. That charter denounced various acts of Parliament that were said to "deprive the American subject of trial by jury." Additionally, among the grievances listed in the Declaration of Independence was the charge that the king had "depriv[ed] us in many cases, of the benefits of Trial by Jury."[15]

After the American Revolution, the right to a jury trial remained a central part of the American experiment. Pennsylvania's 1776 constitution, for example, stated that the "right to trial by jury . . . ought to be held sacred."[16] The Massachusetts constitution of 1780 drafted by John Adams provided that "the legislature shall not make any law, that shall subject any person to a capital or infamous punishment . . . without trial by jury."[17] In sum, trial by jury was a nearly universal part of the early American criminal justice system. The Articles of Confederation made no mention of the right to a jury trial, but the Confederation government did not establish any regular criminal courts.

THE CONSTITUTIONAL CONVENTION

During the Constitutional Convention, there was a broad consensus that the Constitution would require juries for criminal trials, and the Criminal Trials Clause seems to have been introduced without any controversy or debate.[18] After its introduction, the clause underwent only one substantial amendment, and that was to provide for a right to a jury trial for crimes committed outside of the United States.[19]

During the Convention, delegates debated whether the right to a jury should also extend to civil cases.[20] Charles Pinckney of South Carolina and Elbridge Gerry of Massachusetts moved to

add "[a]nd a trial by jury shall be preserved as usual in civil cases" to the end of the clause.[21] In response, some members of the committee raised concerns about how to distinguish civil cases for which juries are proper from those for which they are not. Nathaniel Gorham of Massachusetts noted that "[t]he constitution of Juries is different in different States and the trial itself is usual in different cases in different States."[22] Gorham made this same point earlier with better clarity: "It is not possible to discriminate equity cases from those in which juries are proper. The Representatives of the people may be safely trusted in this matter."[23]

In other words, the states did not have a uniform standard as to when juries applied in civil cases. Juries were not used in equity cases, as Gorham noted, but states themselves might differ as to when a case is in equity. It was best to leave it to the legislature to parse the details rather than impose a single, broad requirement. Pinckney and Gerry's motion was thus defeated.[24]

The Criminal Jury Trials Clause also requires that criminal trials "be held in the State where the said Crimes shall have been committed." The Framers sought to prohibit a recurrence of the English practice of transporting colonial defendants overseas to England for trial by juries of Englishmen. The Declaration of Independence specifically charged King George with "transporting us beyond Seas to be tried for pretended offences."[25]

THE RATIFICATION DEBATES

In Federalist No. 83, Alexander Hamilton observed that "[t]he friends and adversaries of the plan of the convention, if they agree in nothing else, concur at least in the value they set upon the trial by jury." But the omission of a jury trial right for civil cases became a point of controversy during the ratification debates. For example, at the Pennsylvania Convention, William Findley contended that "[p]ersonal liberty cannot be enjoyed without trial by jury" and warned that, because "trial by jury . . . in civil cases . . . is at the mercy of the legislature," the liberties of Americans under the proposed Constitution were "held on the most precarious tenures."[26]

At the Massachusetts Convention, Thomas

Dawes, responding to similar critiques, noted that the guarantee of the right in criminal trials was a direct response to the British government's "abuse of power" in taking away that right. He further explained that the reason "the Constitution [is not] as *explicit* in securing the right of jury in *civil*, as in criminal cases" is that "[t]he several States differ so widely in their *modes* of trial, some states using a jury in causes wherein other states employ only their judges, that the Convention have very wisely left it to the federal legislature to make sure regulations . . . accommodate the whole."[27] Dawes was simply repeating the same point the delegates at the Constitutional Convention had made. Because the states did not have a single, uniform standard for juries in civil cases, the Constitution would not have one. Nonetheless, the general right to a jury would be maintained.

In Federalist No. 83, Hamilton wrote that the Constitution's silence with regard to the right of a jury trial in civil cases was not meant to imply any prohibition of such a right. "[T]he trial by jury in civil cases [will] not be abolished," he declared. The Anti-Federalists were unpersuaded. Centinel wrote that "[w]hether the *trial by jury* is to continue as your birthright, the freemen of Pennsylvania, nay, all of America, are now called upon to declare."[28] In the end, these concerns prevailed, and the right to a jury trial in certain civil cases was enshrined in the Seventh Amendment. (See Essay Nos. 182 and 183.)

JURY NULLIFICATION

In criminal trials, judges explain the law to the jury, and the jury is expected to apply that law to the facts. However, the Zenger trial demonstrates that in the nation's early history, the jury not only applied the law to the facts it found, but sometimes also decided unsettled questions of law themselves. In the first few decades after the Founding, many federal judges refused to tell jurors that they were obliged to accept the judge's view of the law, and lawyers argued questions of law before the jury. The U.S. Supreme Court, for instance, opined in an early 1794 case that a jury has the right "to determine the law as well as the fact in controversy."[29] Alexander Hamilton, acting as counsel for a defendant in an 1804 criminal libel case, similarly argued that the jury has a right to judge the law in criminal matters insofar as the law is intertwined with facts.[30] When the jury rejects a law with which it disagrees, the process is known as *jury nullification.*[31]

Over time, however, the power of a jury to decide the law eroded. *Sparf v. United States* (1895) concluded that the jury did not have the right to decide legal questions. Rather, "it [i]s the duty of the court to expound the law, and that of the jury to apply the law as thus declared to the facts as ascertained by them."[32] The Court found that disregarding "this separation of the functions of court and jury" would endanger "the stability of public justice, as well as the security of private and personal rights."[33] In modern practice, judges instruct juries that they must accept the judge's view of the law, and lawyers are no longer allowed to argue the merits of the law to the jury.[34] Nevertheless, a jury retains the raw power to check general laws with which it disagrees in individual cases. Nullification is still possible because the jury can issue an unreviewable general verdict of acquittal.

WAIVER OF JURY TRIAL RIGHTS

The jury's power has eroded in a second respect as well. Before 1930, jury trials in federal court, like jurisdictional provisions, could not be waived. This practice reflected the mandatory language in Article III and in the Sixth Amendment: The trial of all crimes "shall" be by jury. (See Essay No. 176.) This obligatory practice may also have resulted from the common view that the citizenry itself benefits from sitting in jury trials.[35] However, *Patton v. United States* (1930) concluded that a defendant could waive a jury trial in favor of a bench trial before a judge.[36] The prosecutor may still insist upon, and the court must grant, a jury trial.[37]

Cite as: Judge Kurt D. Engelhardt, Jacob J. Thackston, & Dexter Webster, *The Criminal Trials Clause, in* THE HERITAGE GUIDE TO THE CONSTITUTION 502 (Josh Blackman & John G. Malcolm eds., 3d ed. 2025).

Notes

1. 3 Blackstone 379.   **2.** 2 John Adams, The Works of John Adams, Second President of the United States 252, 253 (Charles Francis Adams ed., 1850).   **3.** 15 Thomas Jefferson, The Papers of Thomas Jefferson 282–83 (Julian P. Boyd ed., 1958).   **4.** *Thompson v. State of Utah*, 170 U.S. 343, 349 (1898).   **5.** Barnaby C. Keeney, Judgment by Peers 68 (1952).   **6.** Lloyd E. Moore, The Jury 35 (2nd ed. 1988). **7.** *Id.* at 60.   **8.** *Id.* at 95.   **9.** American Bar Association, Sources of Our Liberties 34 (Richard L. Perry ed. 1959). **10.** 17 Thomas Bayly Howell, A Complete Collection of State Trials and Proceedings for High Treason and Other Crimes and Misdemeanors from the Earliest Period to the Year 1783, 695 (1813).   **11.** *Id.* at 694, 699.   **12.** *Id.*   **13.** *Id.* at 724. **14.** 4 Blackstone 343.   **15.** Declaration of Independence, ¶ 20.   **16.** Pa. Const. of 1776, Decl. of Rts. art. XI. **17.** Mass. Const. of 1780, pt. I, art. XII.   **18.** 2 Farrand's 144, 173, 187.   **19.** *Id.*   **20.** *Id.* at 587–588.   **21.** *Id.* at 628–29. **22.** *Id.* at 629.   **23.** *Id.* at 587.   **24.** *Id.*   **25.** Declaration of Independence, ¶ 15.   **26.** 2 DHRC 527–28.   **27.** 6 DHRC 1370.   **28.** Storing 2.7.1.   **29.** *Georgia v. Brailsford*, 3 U.S. (3 Dall.) 1, 4 (1794).   **30.** *People v. Croswell*, 3 Johns. Cas. 337, 355 (N.Y. Sup. Ct. 1804).   **31.** *United States v. Dougherty*, 473 F.2d 1113, 1130 (D.C. Cir. 1972).   **32.** *Sparf v. United States*, 156 U.S. 51, 106 (1895).   **33.** *Id.*   **34.** Fed. Jud. Ctr., Benchbook for U.S. District Court Judges 93 (6th ed. 2013).   **35.** Akhil Reed Amar, *The Bill of Rights as a Constitution*, 100 Yale L.J. 1131, 1196 (1991).   **36.** 281 U.S. 276, 299 (1930).   **37.** *Id.* at 312.

ESSAY NO. 137: THE TREASON CLAUSE
ART. III, § 3, CL. 1

Treason against the United States, shall consist only in levying War against them, or in adhering to their Enemies, giving them Aid and Comfort. No Person shall be convicted of Treason unless on the Testimony of two Witnesses to the same overt Act, or on Confession in open Court.

—Joyce Lee Malcolm

INTRODUCTION

This essay begins with a survey of the early development of the treason acts in England, which lays the groundwork for the Treason Clause in the American Constitution. It also examines the Constitutional Convention's definition of treason, the ratification debates, early practice in America, later cases, and treason trials. This essay concludes with questions to consider—most significantly why the trial for treason has become so rare.

HISTORY BEFORE 1787

The legal concept of treason, or betrayal, emerged from the Middle Ages. Early English law divided treason into high treason and petit treason.[1] High treason struck at the bond between subject and sovereign—the very basis of the state—and was regarded as the most heinous of crimes. It encompassed several crimes and therefore deserved the harshest punishment. Petit treason was the crime of betrayal of one subject by another. For example, if a servant killed his master or a priest killed his superior, that would be petit treason. It was also petit treason if a wife killed her husband, but not if a husband killed his wife.

The Treason Act of 1351 defined high treason in law for the first time and is one of the oldest pieces of legislation still on the statute books.[2] This act of King Edward III spelled out examples of high treason. A lead offense was conspiracy against the king or even "compassing or imagining" killing the sovereign, his queen, or the heir apparent. It was also an offense to kill certain officers of state (the Lord Chancellor, Lord High Treasurer, and judges) when they were carrying out their official functions. Other offenses included violating the royal blood line (rape, adultery); fighting against the sovereign within his kingdoms; helping his enemies; or giving aid and comfort to the king's enemies. The scope of high treason fluctuated with the exigency of the times.

The English Reformation and the separation from the Roman Catholic Church added new dangers and produced other treason acts. The 1534 Treason Act made anyone a traitor who deprived the king, queen, or their heirs of the "dignitie, title or name of heir royal estates."[3] The Treason Act of 1547 expanded treason to include religious treasons, treasonous thoughts, political plots, and revolutionary groups and for the first time required that two witnesses testify to the crime of treason.[4] However, this two-witnesses rule was not always followed. For example, Algernon Sydney was charged with high treason for the Rye House plot to kill Charles II and his brother James. During that notorious trial, there was no second witness against him. Instead, Sydney's unpublished manuscript, *Discourses Concerning Government*, was used as a second witness.

After the Glorious Revolution of 1688, more procedural guarantees were added. Those accused of high treason were provided a copy of their indictment, defense witnesses were required to testify in person, and the accused were permitted to have counsel. The offense itself, however, was still quite broad. Sir William Blackstone warned about the risks of this poorly defined crime: "[I]f the crime of high treason be indeterminate, this . . . is sufficient to make any government degenerate into arbitrary power."[5] Nevertheless, the English Treason Act of 1795 made it treason to "compass, imagine, invent, devise or intend the death or destruction, or any bodily harm tending to death or destruction, maim or wounding, imprisonment or restraint, of the person of . . . the King."[6] Although that act was meant to be temporary, it would remain in place until 1998 when punishment for treason was changed to life in prison.[7]

Colonial American treason laws generally mirrored English law. After 1763, however, tensions grew. American juries proved unwilling to find Americans guilty of treason and balked at the plan to move trials to England. The Declaration of Independence specifically criticized the king for "transporting us beyond Seas to be tried for pretended Offenses."[8]

During the American Revolution, state legislatures expanded the definition of treason and tried some individuals for treason with limited success.[9] Following the Revolution, in treason prosecutions, the courts had to determine whether the accused was an alien levying war against the United States or just a disloyal citizen who was engaged in sedition.[10]

THE CONSTITUTIONAL CONVENTION

During the Constitutional Convention, treason made an early appearance in a Committee of Detail draft that was "evidently an outline of the Pinckney Plan."[11] The text provided that the Senate and House of Delegates "shall have the exclusive Power of declaring what shall be Treason & Misp. [misprision] of Treason agt. U. S."[12] Another Committee of Detail draft in the handwriting of Edmund Randolph of Virginia granted Congress the power "[t]o declare it to be treason to levy war against or adhere to the enemies of the U. S."[13]

The Committee's report was delivered to the Convention on August 6.[14] The proposed Treason Clause had four elements: (1) "Treason against the United States shall consist only in levying war against the United States, or any of them" ("any of them" referred to any of the individual states); (2) "The Legislature of the United States shall have power to declare the punishment of treason"; (3) "No person shall be convicted of treason, unless on the testimony of two witnesses"; and (4) "No attainder of treason shall work corruption of bloods nor forfeiture, except during the life of the person attainted."[15]

The delegates debated this clause on August 20. James Madison of Virginia thought the "definition" of treason was "too narrow," as it "did not appear to go as far as the Stat. of Edwd. III."[16] George Mason of Virginia would have adopted the Statute of Edward III.[17] Edmund Randolph of Virginia would have added the "giving them aid and comfort" language from the British statute."[18] The delegates voted unanimously to remove "any of them."[19] Only treason against the United States would be prohibited. The delegates also added "to the same overt act" after "two witnesses." Benjamin Franklin of Pennsylvania observed that "perjury [is] too easily made use of against innocence."[20] Finally, Mason moved to insert "giving them aid [and] comfort."[21] The Convention agreed.

The text referred to the Committee of Style provided that "[t]reason against the United States shall consist only in levying war against them, or in adhering to their enemies, giving them aid and comfort. The Legislature shall have power to declare the punishment of treason. No person shall be convicted of treason, unless on the testimony of two witnesses to the same overt act, or on confession in open court."[22] No further changes were made.[23]

The framers of the American Constitution took Blackstone's warning seriously and defined treason narrowly. Treason can "only" consist of two offenses: "levying War against" the United States and "adhering to [the] Enemies" of the United States by "giving them Aid and Comfort." The concept of "levying war . . . looks inward, to internal rebellions."[24] Those who "owe allegiance to the United States and rebel against it are not enemies, but traitors subject to prosecution for levying war."[25] The "enemies provision," however, "looks outward; an enemy is always a foreign state, group, or person who owes no allegiance to the United States."[26] These are the *only* ways to commit treason. Conviction requires two witnesses "to the same overt act" or a confession in open court. These elements closely track the English treason acts. Treason is the only crime defined in the Constitution.

Other provisions of the Constitution also reference treason. Representatives and Senators can be arrested while in session for treason,[27] a person can be impeached for treason,[28] the Fugitive from Justice Clause recognizes that states can charge a person with treason,[29] and the President can pardon the offense of treason.[30] (See Essay Nos. 31, 117, 141, and 105.)

THE RATIFICATION DEBATES

During the Constitutional Convention, James Madison thought the definition of treason was too "narrow," but in Federalist No. 43, he defended this provision. Madison warned that "violent factions" could "wreak[] their alternate malignity on each other" through "new fangled and artificial treasons." The Constitution limits these risks by "inserting a constitutional definition of the crime, fixing the proof necessary for conviction of it, and restraining the congress, even in punishing it, from extending the consequences of guilt beyond the person of its author." In Federalist No. 84, Alexander Hamilton mentions the narrow definition of treason as one of the guarantors of rights that make a separate bill of rights unnecessary.

In the Pennsylvania Convention, James Wilson defended the provision, arguing that "Congress can neither define nor try the crime."[31] He observed that in England, a "very great part of their tyranny over the people had arisen from the extension of the definition of treason."[32] It was true that the Constitution defined "only" two types of treason, but some Anti-Federalists warned that Congress could use another label, such as "sedition," to prohibit political speech.[33] At the ratifying conventions, several states favored a bill of rights that would expressly protect free speech to prevent such prosecutions.

EARLY PRACTICE

In *Ex parte Bollman* (1807), the U.S. Supreme Court narrowed the scope of the Treason Clause.[34] Two associates of Aaron Burr were charged with treason for conspiring to levy war against the United States. Specifically, the defendants were alleged to have conspired to subvert the government by force. The allegations were sensational: They recruited troops, procured maps, and drew up plans, and there was an "actual assemblage of men for the purpose of executing a treasonable design."[35] The Court, per Chief Justice John Marshall, held that these acts did not constitute treason. Moreover, the Court rejected the concept of "constructive treason."

Marshall also presided over the treason trial of Aaron Burr.[36] In that case, Burr was not present in the assembly of men but could be found guilty of treason on the testimony of two witnesses if he aided in the levying of war. Conviction required participation in an overt treasonable act. Ultimately, Burr was found not guilty.

The first two convictions for federal treason occurred in Philadelphia in the wake of the Whiskey Rebellion.[37] This uprising in western Pennsylvania arose following a federal excise tax on whiskey in 1791–1794.[38] In these cases, the courts defined treason broadly as people combining to defeat or resist a federal law.[39] President George Washington pardoned both men.[40] Five years later, after Fries's Rebellion, the courts adopted an even broader definition of treason.[41] The legitimacy of designating these acts as treason remains controversial.

LATER CASES

In the wake of World War II, the Supreme Court narrowed the scope of the treason clause. For example, *Cramer v. United States* (1945) held that speeches in favor of the enemy, opposition to government measures, or striking in defense plants failed to constitute "aid and comfort" and that "if there is no adherence to the enemy in this, if there is no intent to betray, there is no treason."[42] Yet *Haupt v. United States* (1947) modified the two-witness standard to permit other evidence of treasonable intent. This decision made intent and an overt act amenable to different standards of proof.[43] *Kawakita v. United States* (1952) found that to convict a dual citizen of treason, he still must have allegiance to the United States. Kawakita, a dual citizen, was found guilty by a jury on the basis of overt acts.[44] He was the last person convicted of treason in U.S. history.[45]

TRIALS FOR TREASON

Since the standards for treason are high, trials for treason have been rare at both the national and state levels. Individuals have been prosecuted instead under laws for conspiracy and sedition. These crimes target activities that undermine the state without directly attacking it. Julius and Ethel Rosenberg, for example, were convicted in 1953 of espionage and were executed.[46] Aldrich Ames, a CIA agent who betrayed American personnel to the Soviet Union, was charged with espionage in 1994.[47] John Walker Lindh, who allowed himself to be captured by the Taliban, was prosecuted in 2002 for conspiracy and aiding the enemy rather than treason.[48] The last person indicted for treason was Adam Gadahn in 2006, who was indicted for aiding and abetting al-Qaeda and appearing in their videos threatening Americans.[49] In 2015, he was killed in a drone attack in Pakistan.

OPEN QUESTIONS

- Is it better to rely on seditious conspiracy and sedition to treat betrayal of the United States and aiding its enemies?
- Section 3 of the Fourteenth Amendment imposes disqualification if a person has given aid and comfort to the enemies of the United States. Does this phrase have the same meaning as similar language in the Treason Clause?[50] (See Essay No. 198.)

Cite as: Joyce Lee Malcolm, *The Treason Clause*, *in* THE HERITAGE GUIDE TO THE CONSTITUTION 505 (Josh Blackman & John G. Malcolm eds., 3d ed. 2025).

Notes

1. 2 Sir Frederick Pollock and Frederic William Maitland, The History of English Law Before the Time of Edward I 523–32 (2d ed. 1898). **2.** 25 Edw 3 Stat. 5 c2. **3.** 26 Henry VIII, c. 13. **4.** 1 Edw. 6 c. 12. **5.** 4 Blackstone 75. **6.** 36 Geo. III. c. 7. **7.** Crime and Disorder Act 1998, https://perma.cc/K5BU-YR7A. **8.** Declaration of Independence. ¶ 21. **9.** Carleton E.W. Larson, *The Revolutionary American Jury: A Case Study of the 1778–1779 Philadelphia Treason Trials*, 61 SMU L. Rev. 1441, 1451–1452 (2008). **10.** *Republica v. Chapman*, 1 U.S. (1 Dall.) 53 (Pa. 1781); Josh Blackman, *Original Citizenship*, 159 U. Pa. L. Rev. PENNumbra 95, 113–116 (2010). **11.** 2 Farrand's 134. **12.** *Id.* at 136. **13.** *Id.* at 137, 144, 168. **14.** *Id.* at 177. **15.** *Id.* at 182. **16.** *Id.* at 345. **17.** *Id.* **18.** *Id.* **19.** *Id.* at 346. **20.** *Id.* at 348. **21.** *Id.* at 349. **22.** *Id.* at 565, 571. **23.** *Id.* at 601, 661. **24.** Carlton F.W. Larson, On Treason: A Citizen's Guide to the Law 134 (2020). **25.** *Id.* **26.** *Id.*; Josh Blackman & Seth Barrett Tillman, *Sweeping and Forcing the President into Section 3*, 28 Tex. Rev. L. & Pol. 350, 531 (2024). **27.** Art. I, § 6, cl. 1. **28.** Art. II, § 4. **29.** Art. IV, § 2, cl. 2. **30.** Art. II, § 1, cl. 8. **31.** 2 Elliot's 487. **32.** *Id.* **33.** Akhil Amar, America's Constitution: A Biography 244–45 (2005). **34.** 8 U.S. (4 Cranch) 75. **35.** *Id.* at 128. **36.** *United States v. Burr*, 25 Fed. (No. 14,692d) (C.C.D. Va. 1807). **37.** Letter to George Washington from "Incog." (June 10, 1795), https://perma.cc/9H9P-46RQ. **38.** Peter Kotowski, *Whiskey Rebellion*, Geo. Wash. Pres. Library Digital Encyclopedia, https://perma.cc/NZ9L-6XH9. **39.** Carlton F.W. Larson, *The Forgotten Constitutional Law of Treason and the Enemy Combatant Problem*, 154 U. Pa. L. Rev. 863, 904 (2006). **40.** George Washington, Proclamation—Granting Pardon to Certain Persons Formerly Engaged in Violence and Obstruction of Justice in Protest of Liquor Laws in Pennsylvania (July 10, 1795), https://perma.cc/SCZ7-9E6P. **41.** *Case of Fries*, 9 F. Cas. 826, 840 (Iredell, Circuit Justice, C.C.D. Pa. 1799) (No. 5126). **42.** *Cramer v. United States*, 325 U.S. 1, 29 (1945). **43.** 330 U.S. 631 (1947). **44.** 343 U.S. 717 (1952). **45.** *The Case for Treason*, CBS News (Dec. 17, 2001), https://perma.cc/M59N-ECRL. **46.** Federal Bureau of Investigation, Famous Cases and Criminals: Atom Spy Case/Rosenbergs, https://perma.cc/H2X7-53NW. **47.** Federal Bureau of Investigation, Famous Cases and Criminals: Aldrich Ames, https://perma.cc/L8HN-88E6. **48.** *United States v. Lindh*, 227 F. Supp. 2d 565 (E.D. Va. 2002). **49.** U.S. Citizen Indicted on Treason, Material Support Charges for Providing Aid and Comfort to al Qaeda, U.S. Dep't of Justice (Oct. 11, 2006), https://perma.cc/8XH3-5GZG. **50.** Blackman & Tillman, *supra* at 521–22.

ESSAY NO. 138: THE PUNISHMENT OF TREASON CLAUSE
ART. III, § 3, CL. 2

The Congress shall have Power to declare the Punishment of Treason, but no Attainder of Treason shall work Corruption of Blood, or Forfeiture except during the Life of the Person attainted.

—Joyce Lee Malcolm

INTRODUCTION

This essay continues from the prior entry on the Treason Clause (see Essay No. 137) but focuses on the punishment for treason. The English punishment for treason was extremely harsh because treason was thought to be especially heinous and to include several crimes, each of which was to be punished.

HISTORY BEFORE 1787

At common law, punishment for high treason in England was especially brutal. A convicted traitor was hanged and cut down before dead. Then his entrails were drawn out and burned, his body was divided into four quarters, and the quarters were posted prominently as a warning to others. This process was known as *hanging, drawing and quartering*. The traitor was also *attainted*. The convicted individual would forfeit his title and property to the Crown, thereby depriving his heirs of the estate. Corruption of blood deprived an attainted person of his property, and he could not inherit or pass on property to his heirs. Thus, the traitor's family was punished for the crime of one of its members.

Before the Revolutionary War, the American colonists insisted that the English acts and punishment for high treason should not apply to them. In 1774, James Duane of New York, a member of the Continental Congress, agreed that the colonies were entitled to the benefits of the English common law and statutes but rejected the authority of English law with regard to treason outside the English realm. These acts were to be in force, Duane insisted, only in remote and foreign parts that lacked tribunals for a legal trial. John Rutledge of South Carolina also rejected these English treason acts.[1]

It is notable that Americans, even in the throes of the American Revolution, were reluctant to charge their fellow citizens with treason. Between September 1778 and April 1779, for example, twenty-four men were tried for treason in Pennsylvania. Of these, only four were found guilty, and even in these cases, the juries asked for leniency from the death penalty. The punishment, unlike punishment under English law, was hanging. Two men tried in Pennsylvania were executed by hanging. This reluctance to bring charges of treason seems to have been general. During the war, Loyalists were banished, and their properties were confiscated and sold at auction. The British also were cautious about bringing charges of treason in America for fear of retaliation against their troops.[2]

THE CONSTITUTIONAL CONVENTION

The Constitution specifies that "Treason against the United States shall consist only in levying War against them, or in adhering to their Enemies, giving them Aid and Comfort."[3] The Constitution is explicit both in defining treason and in mirroring the English requirement that there be two witnesses testifying to the same act or open confession in court. The Constitutional Convention spelled out the definition and standard of evidence to be used in prosecuting treasonable offenses to prevent the power granted in Article III from being used against political opponents. Although this might have been left to the courts, the delegates clearly felt that it was so important that they should fix the definition and rules themselves. The definition they adopted ruled out any treason in thought.

The Constitutional Convention had several debates over two questions related to the punishment for treason: Could the President pardon treason, and who should decide the punishment for treason? The Framers agreed that the legislature should decide the punishment for treason and that punishment must not include corruption of blood except during the life of the convicted individual. They also agreed that the President could pardon treason. (See Essay No. 105.)

THE RATIFICATION DEBATES

In Federalist No. 74, Alexander Hamilton argued that it was safe for the President to pardon treason because he could be impeached if he misused the power. During the Pennsylvania Convention, James Wilson agreed that Congress should decide the punishment for treason but said that punishment must not include "corruption of blood or forfeiture, except during the life of the person attainted."[4] Tench Coxe of Pennsylvania, writing as A Freeman, emphasized that treason against the United States should not involve corruption of blood, which would leave "unoffending families of attainted persons stripped of all hereditary property." He praised the Constitution for that decision. But, he was still concerned about attainder. Coxe wrote that "by the existing laws of all the states, *the unoffending families of attainted persons*, stripped of all hereditary rights, and condemned to the bitter portion of extreme poverty, are left . . . to meet the trials of the world alone."[5]

The Anti-Federalists were in complete agreement with the Federalists on this issue. Brutus, perhaps the shrewdest of the Anti-Federalists, approved the Constitution's declaration that "no bill of attainder shall be passed" and felt it "proper the legislature should be deprived of the exercise of this power, because it seldom is exercised to the benefit of the community, but generally to its injury."[6] (See Essay No. 69.)

EARLY PRACTICE

In 1790, the First Congress passed the Act for the Punishment of Certain Crimes Against the United States.[7] The punishment for treason was death by hanging, not the hanging, drawing, and quartering of English practice. The American statute imposed a lesser punishment for misprision of treason (knowing but concealing the commission of treason): imprisonment not to exceed seven years and a $1,000 fine.

MODERN PRACTICE

Congress has reduced the punishment for treason over the years, even as prosecution for treason has remained rare. Today, the punishment for treason varies from the death penalty to imprisonment of not less than five years, to a fine of not less than $10,000, to being incapable of holding any office under the United States.[8]

The United Kingdom modified its punishment for treason more slowly than the United States. In 1814, Parliament abolished corruption of blood for all crimes except high treason, petty treason, and murder.[9] Petty treason was abolished by the Offences Against the Person Act of 1828. Four decades later, the punishment of corruption of blood for murder and high treason was finally abolished by the Forfeiture Act of 1870.

OPEN QUESTIONS

- Why has punishment for the serious crime of treason been reduced from death to five years in prison and a $10,000 fine?
- Should treason be made easier to prove rather than having the punishment reduced to insignificance?
- Does the Punishment of Treason Clause authorize Congress to impose the death penalty for treason, even if the Supreme Court has held that only murder can be punished with the death penalty?

Cite as: Joyce Lee Malcolm, *The Punishment of Treason Clause, in* THE HERITAGE GUIDE TO THE CONSTITUTION 509 (Josh Blackman & John G. Malcolm eds., 3d ed. 2025).

Notes
1. 1 Letters of Members of the Continental Congress 43–44, 75 (Edmund Cody Bennett ed., 1921). **2.** Carlton F.W. Larson, *The Revolutionary American Jury: A Case Study of the 1778–1779 Philadelphia Treason Trials*, 61 SMU L. Rev. 1441, 1452 (2008); Carlton F.W. Larson, The Trials of Allegiance: Treason, Juries, and the American Revolution (2019). **3.** Art. III, § 3. **4.** 2 Elliot's 469. **5.** *Friends of the Constitution: Writings of the "Other" Federalists 1787–1788*, 99 (Colleen A. Sheehan & Gary L. McDowell eds., 1998). **6.** Storing 2.9.103. **7.** 1 Stat. 112 (1790). **8.** 18 U.S.C. § 2381. **9.** 54 Geo. 3 c. 145.

PART 4

ARTICLE IV

ESSAY NO. 139: THE FULL FAITH AND CREDIT CLAUSE
ART. IV, § 1

Full Faith and Credit shall be given in each State to the public Acts, Records, and judicial Proceedings of every other State. And the Congress may by general Laws prescribe the Manner in which such Acts, Records and Proceedings shall be proved, and the Effect thereof.

—Stephen E. Sachs

INTRODUCTION

The Full Faith and Credit Clause is among the Constitution's few rules of "horizontal federalism" governing relations among the states. At a minimum, it requires states to receive each other's laws and judgments in evidence, while Congress is authorized to impose greater obligations of recognition and enforcement. Modern doctrine, however, attributes substantially more power to the clause as well as to the courts that interpret it.

HISTORY BEFORE 1787

Before the Revolution, the colonies were legally independent of one another. Like foreign governments, they sometimes adopted statutes that recognized each other's public records, such as recorded deeds or judicial judgments.[1] Most states, however, relied on recognition doctrines found in international law and in the common law, which might require that foreign documents be proven by testimony in local courts. Local courts could also revisit foreign judgments, treating their determinations as only *prima facie* evidence of the merits.[2] Judgment creditors in one state might thus face difficulties collecting debts in another—especially if, as James Madison described in Federalist No. 42, "the effects liable to justice, may be suddenly and secretly translated in any stage of the process, within a foreign jurisdiction."

The Articles of Confederation required that each state give "Full Faith and credit . . . to the records, acts, and judicial proceedings of the courts and magistrates of every other State."[3] However, the Articles did not give the Confederation Congress any power to enforce this provision, and state courts soon disagreed

as to what this ambiguous charge meant. One Pennsylvania court, for example, held that this Full Faith and Credit Clause entailed accepting such documents only as full evidence of the original proceedings, not necessarily as binding the parties.[4] By contrast, a South Carolina court gave the clause greater effect by treating parties as bound by the prior judgment of a sister state's court.[5]

By 1781, a congressional committee had proposed amending the Articles to clarify this obligation. Congress would have new powers to declare "the method of exemplifying records" and especially "the operation of the Acts [&] Judicial Proceedings" of one state in another.[6] Congress, however, took no action.

THE CONSTITUTIONAL CONVENTION

The Philadelphia Convention adopted this suggestion. The Committee of Detail's report largely repeated the Articles' version of the clause.[7] James Madison of Virginia suggested that Congress should be empowered "to provide for the *execution* of Judgments in other States."[8] Edmund Randolph, also of Virginia, thought executing other states' judgments would be unprecedented; he offered more specific language for recognizing judgment debts issued with proper jurisdiction.[9]

Gouverneur Morris of Pennsylvania proposed punting the question to Congress, enabling it "by general laws" to "determine the proof and effect of such acts, records, and proceedings."[10] A committee endorsed Morris's proposal as limited to "the effect [of] judgments."[11] James Wilson of Pennsylvania emphasized the proposal's improvement upon the Confederation's clause, which he saw as largely useless: "[I]f the Legislature were not allowed to *declare the effect* the provision would amount to nothing more than what now takes place among all Independent Nations."[12]

Morris again proposed expanding Congress's power to address the "effect" of records and legislative acts as well. William Samuel Johnson of Connecticut and Edmund Randolph objected to this power as too broad,[13] but Morris's motion carried.[14] The final version of the Constitution thus not only extended the Articles' language to cover "public Acts"— apparently with an eye to state insolvency laws[15]—but also added a power in Congress "by general Laws" to "prescribe the manner" of proving public documents "and the Effect thereof."[16]

THE RATIFICATION DEBATES

During Ratification, debate on the clause focused on this new congressional power. In Federalist No. 42, Madison praised the clause as "an evident and valuable improvement," especially as compared to the Articles of Confederation's version, which was "extremely indeterminate" and "of little importance under any interpretation which it will bear." During the Virginia ratifying convention, George Mason worried that Congress might go too far in declaring the effects of state acts in other states; Madison dismissed his objection, and little more was heard of it.[17] The Anti-Federalist Native of Virginia described the Clause's benefits as "obvious,"[18] and another Anti-Federalist, Cassius, agreed that "the benefit to be derived from such a regulation must be great, especially to those who are sometimes obliged to have recourse to law."[19]

EARLY PRACTICE

Unfortunately, the First Congress failed to provide clarity with respect to the effect of state records in other states. A 1790 statute created a detailed process for authenticating state documents but provided only that authenticated "records and judicial proceedings"—and not the acts of state legislatures—would have "such faith and credit given to them in every court" as they enjoyed at home.[20] This language resembled other authentication statutes making a copied record as good evidence as the original.[21]

Soon there would be confusion over whether Congress had prescribed *any* binding effect for these documents at all. As late as 1817, a House committee concluded that Congress had not done so.[22]

JUDICIAL PRECEDENT

In the two decades after the Constitution was ratified, state and federal courts again fell into disarray, particularly when it came to enforcing judgments from courts with doubtful jurisdiction. For example, in *Armstrong v. Carson's Executors* (1794), Justice James Wilson on circuit read the 1790 Act to require a New Jersey judgment to have precisely the same effect in Pennsylvania "as in the Court from which it was taken."[23] In the New York case of *Hitchcock v. Aicken* (1803), Justice James Kent rejected *Armstrong*'s reasoning, arguing that "there is a manifest and essential difference" between "the same *faith and credit*" and "the same *effect*."[24] And in *Peck v. Williamson* (1813), Chief Justice John Marshall on circuit agreed with Justice Kent, holding that "the constitution makes a pointed distinction between the faith and credit, and the effect," of a state record.[25]

In *Mills v. Duryee* (1813), the U.S. Supreme Court sought to settle the issue. *Mills* construed the 1790 Act as determining the effect of state judgments, making them conclusive in other states as to the parties' rights and obligations.[26] This rule eventually took hold with an exception for judgments rendered without jurisdiction.[27] Over time, however, the rule in *Mills* was attributed to the Constitution rather than to the act of Congress. In 1805, for example, Justice Joseph Story wrote that the 1790 Act "seems to provide for" admitting out-of-state documents as "evidence only."[28] By 1833, however, Story read both the statute and the Constitution itself to require conclusive effect for state judgments.[29] Nevertheless, the statute did not prescribe any effect for state "acts"—meaning that for most of the nineteenth century, neither the Constitution nor the statute was read to address the topic of choice of law, whether to mandate or forbid any use of state laws in other states.

That approach changed with a dictum in *Chicago & Alton Railroad v. Wiggins Ferry Co.* (1887).[30] The Court began to use the clause to regulate state choice of law, requiring effect for those and only those laws within the territorial power of each state to enact—as the Court put it, laws "within the legislative jurisdiction of the enacting state."[31]

In the twentieth century, the Court has occasionally employed the clause to insist that states hear tort suits arising from accidents in other states as well as to forbid "special rule[s]" of law "hostile to [their] sister States."[32] But because the clause does not describe the several states' legislative jurisdiction, the Court has largely given up on policing it. Current doctrine permits state courts to employ the law of any state with "a significant contact or significant aggregation of contacts, creating state interests, such that [the choice] is neither arbitrary nor fundamentally unfair."[33]

OPEN QUESTIONS

- In recent years, the clause has been debated most frequently with regard to the interstate recognition of same-sex marriages. Some have focused on its first, self-executing sentence—that "Full Faith and Credit shall be given," which Madison described as "of little importance." They argue that this language automatically requires conclusive effect to other states' laws, even those contrary to local public policy, as anything else would be less than "full."[34] Others have argued that this sentence merely requires accepting sister-state documents as evidence equivalent to the originals, leaving their "effect" wholly up to Congress.[35] Still others have argued that the clause requires some degree of force in between, whether as "prima facie proof of the obligation that the plaintiff claimed" or as requiring other states to treat state acts as conclusive within their own territorial jurisdiction.[36]

- The scope of Congress's power under the second sentence of the clause has attracted less attention. Congress has used this effects power only occasionally, enacting a few statutes on interstate recognition of child custody and child support. Congress has enacted more controversial statutes such as the Defense of Marriage Act (denying mandated effect to same-sex marriages), which was repealed by the Respect for Marriage Act (requiring marriage recognition without regard to sex).[37] In theory, this power could be used to govern both state choice-of-law (by "prescrib[ing] . . . the Effect" of "Acts") and state personal jurisdiction (by doing the same for "judicial Proceedings").[38] Thus far, however, Congress has not yet chosen to test its limits.

Cite as: Stephen E. Sachs, *The Full Faith and Credit Clause*, in THE HERITAGE GUIDE TO THE CONSTITUTION 512 (Josh Blackman & John G. Malcolm eds., 3d ed. 2025).

Notes

1. Act of Assembly 1731, P.L. 129 (S.C.); Stephen E. Sachs, *Full Faith and Credit in the Early Congress*, 95 Va. L. Rev. 1201, 1221–22 (2009). **2.** *Walker v. Witter*, 99 Eng. Rep. 1, 4 (K.B.) (1778). **3.** Articles of Confederation, art. IV, § 3. **4.** *James v. Allen*, 1 U.S. (1 Dall.) 188, 192 (Pa. C.P. Phila. County 1786). **5.** *Jenkins v. Putnam*, 1 S.C.L. (1 Bay) 8, 10 (C.P. & Gen. Sess. 1784). **6.** 1 DHRC 143, 144. **7.** 2 Farrand's 188. **8.** *Id.* at 448. **9.** *Id.* **10.** *Id.* **11.** *Id.* at 483–84. **12.** *Id.* at 488. **13.** *Id.* at 488–89. **14.** *Id.* at 489. **15.** *Id.* at 447. **16.** Art. IV, § 1. **17.** 3 Elliot's 584–85. **18.** 9 DHRC 687. **19.** 5 DHRC 503. **20.** Act of May 26, 1790, ch. 11, 1 Stat. 122. **21.** Act of Sept. 15, 1789, ch. 14, 1 Stat. 68; Process Act of 1792, ch. 36, § 12, 1 Stat. 275, 279. **22.** 31 Annals of Cong. 500 (1817). **23.** 2 U.S. (2 Dall.) 302, 303 (C.C.D. Pa. 1794) (Wilson, J.); *Wade v. Wade*, 1 N.C. 601 (Ct. Conf. 1804). **24.** 1 Cai. 460, 480–81 (N.Y. 1803) (opinion of Kent, J.). **25.** 19 F. Cas. 85, 85 (C.C.D.N.C. 1813) (No. 10,896) (Marshall, C.J.); *Bartlet v. Knight*, 1 Mass. (1 Will.) 401, 404–05 (1805) (opinion of Thatcher, J.). **26.** 11 U.S. (7 Cranch) 481, 484 (1813). **27.** *D'Arcy v. Ketchum*, 52 U.S. (11 How.) 165, 176 (1851). **28.** Joseph Story, A Selection of Pleadings in Civil Actions 296 (1805). **29.** 3 Story's Commentaries §§ 1306–07. **30.** 119 U.S. 615 (1887). **31.** *Id.* at 622; David E. Engdahl, *The Classic Rule of Faith and Credit*, 118 Yale L.J. 1584, 1589 (2009). **32.** *Franchise Tax Bd. of Cal. v. Hyatt*, 578 U.S. 171 (2016); *Hughes v. Fetter*, 341 U.S. 609 (1951). **33.** *Allstate Ins. Co. v. Hague*, 449 U.S. 302, 313 (1981) (plurality opinion); *Phillips Petroleum Co. v. Shutts*, 472 U.S. 797, 821–22 (1985). **34.** Douglas Laycock, *Equal Citizens of Equal and Territorial States: The Constitutional Foundations of Choice of Law*, 92 Colum. L. Rev. 249, 296 (1992); Larry Kramer, *Same-Sex Marriage, Conflict of Laws, and the Unconstitutional Public Policy Exception*, 106 Yale L.J. 1965, 1986 (1997).

35. Sachs, *supra* at 1229–31.   **36.** Engdahl, *supra* at 1597; *id.* at 1588; Jeffrey Schmitt, *A Historical Reassessment of Full Faith and Credit*, 20 Geo. Mason L. Rev. 485, 488–89, 491–92 (2013).   **37.** 28 U.S.C. §§ 1738A–1738B; Pub. L. No. 104–199, § 2, 110 Stat. 2419, 2419 (1996) (repealed 2022); 28 U.S.C. § 1738C(a).   **38.** Art. IV, § 1; Stephen E. Sachs, Pennoyer *Was Right*, 95 Tex. L. Rev. 1249, 1317–18 (2017).

∿

ESSAY NO. 140: THE PRIVILEGES AND IMMUNITIES CLAUSE
ART. IV, § 2, CL. 1

The Citizens of each State shall be entitled to all Privileges and Immunities of Citizens in the several States.

—David R. Upham

INTRODUCTION

On July 4, 1776, the representatives of the "one People" of British America declared that "these United Colonies are . . . Free and Independent States."[1] From the beginning, this *one* people subsisted across *multiple* states, and their representatives sought to safeguard both this unity and this multiplicity. Even before declaring independence, Congress began to draft a charter that promoted both of these ends. The Articles of Confederation guaranteed to the citizens of each state "all privileges and immunities of free citizens in the several states."[2] This interstate guarantee would be readopted, with some modification, in the Constitution's Privileges and Immunities Clause. This provision, also known as the Comity Clause, would pose challenges and then controversies that remained unsettled until the 1870s and beyond.

HISTORY BEFORE 1787

In 1774, the First Continental Congress declared that the American colonists were "entitled to all the immunities and privileges granted and confirmed to them by royal charters, or secured by their several codes of provincial laws."[3] They were also entitled to "all the rights, liberties, and immunities of free and natural-born subjects, within the realm of England."[4] These rights and immunities included certain *civil* rights, such as the right "peaceably to assemble . . . and petition the king" and "the great and inestimable privilege of being tried by their peers of the vicinage."[5] (Both of these rights would be recognized in the First and Sixth Amendments.) Above all, the declaration included the *political*

"right of representation" whereby "the people" might "participate in their legislative council."[6] This right would include the right to vote.

On June 24, 1776, shortly before independence, the Continental Congress announced a broad definition of this people:

> [A]ll persons residing in any of the United Colonies, and deriving protection from the laws of the same, owe allegiance to the said laws, and are members of such colony; and that all persons passing through, visiting, or mak[ing] a temporary stay in any of the said colonies, being entitled to the protection of the laws during the time of such passage, visitation or temporary stay, owe, during the same, allegiance thereto.[7]

With Independence, Congress began to draft what would become the Articles of Confederation, adopted in 1781. The Fourth Article, expressly designed "to secure and perpetuate mutual friendship and intercourse among the people of the different States in this Union,"[8] included the following guarantees:

1. "the free inhabitants of each of these States, paupers, vagabonds, and fugitives from justice excepted, shall be entitled to all privileges and immunities of free citizens in the several States";

2. "the people of each State shall have free ingress and regress to and from any other State";
3. this people "shall enjoy therein all the privileges of trade and commerce, subject to the same duties, impositions, and restrictions as the inhabitants thereof respectively"; but nonetheless,
4. those "restrictions shall not extend so far as to prevent the removal of property imported into any State, to any other State, of which the owner is an inhabitant."

This Article seemed conservative and thus uncontroversial. Its purpose was to "secure and perpetuate" the preexisting unity of the one people. Congress relied on the traditional language of entitlement to "privileges and immunities." This term or some variant thereof had appeared frequently in colonial documents to describe Americans' rights as colonial British subjects. And Congress then specified some of the undeniable civil rights of American membership, which were enumerated perhaps only out of an abundance of caution: the right to travel to every state, the right to enjoy "privileges and immunities" in another state equally with the citizens of that state, and the rights of commerce.

Conversely, the language in Article IV reflected some anomalies or innovations. First, Congress extended these rights of interstate citizenship not simply to "citizens," but to all "free inhabitants" (with "paupers, vagabonds, and fugitives from justice" excluded). Second, Congress added a peculiar exemption: Sojourning citizens could export their property back to their home states even if local laws prohibited such exports. This provision was probably added to exempt traveling slaveholders from local antislavery laws.[9]

Article IV left open at least two questions. First, the term "free inhabitants" undoubtedly included free black persons, but the states were divided on black citizenship. Several southern states regarded freed slaves and their descendants as permanent noncitizens; but northern states generally allowed free blacks the political privileges of citizenship.[10]

Second, the text left a seemingly absurd implication as to voting rights. The traditional "privileges and immunities" of Anglo-American subjecthood had included suffrage. The 1774 resolution had recognized the subjects' "right of representation."[11] Under Article IV, a sojourning citizen, with an entitlement to "all" such privileges, would immediately have the right, in any other state, not only to travel, commerce, and petition, but also to vote despite any local qualification as to durational residence or age, sex, or property. Such fluidity would destroy the political integrity of the distinct states.

To address these concerns, in June 1778, the delegation from South Carolina offered two revisions to the proposed but not yet ratified Article IV. As amended, (1) the provision would embrace only "free *white* inhabitants" and (2) traveling whites would enjoy in other states the rights of citizenship only "according to the law of such states respectively, for the government of their own free white inhabitants." In other words, free blacks would have no interstate rights under Article IV, and white Americans' rights would be defined by local state laws, including suffrage regulations. The Continental Congress rejected these and all other amendments to the proposed Articles.[12]

THE CONSTITUTIONAL CONVENTION

The Founders had another chance to revise this provision during the Constitutional Convention. The earliest proposal was in a Committee of Detail draft prepared by James Wilson of Pennsylvania. It stated that "The free (inhabs) Citizens of each state shall be entitled to all Privileges & Immunities of free citizens in the sevl States."[13] According to Farrand's Records, this provision was added by John Rutledge of South Carolina, and the word "inhabitants" was struck out.[14] In 1820, then-Representative Charles Pinckney of South Carolina claimed "to have introduced this clause into the Constitution."[15] On August 6, Rutledge delivered the Committee of Detail's report, which included this revised, streamlined text: "The Citizens of each State shall be entitled to all privileges and immunities of citizens in the several States."[16]

The proposal was debated briefly on August 28. Pinckney "was not satisfied with it" and "seemed to wish some provision should be included in favor of property in slaves."[17] It seems he preferred to retain the special "property" exemption found in the Articles of Confederation. There was no further recorded debate. The Convention rejected Pinckney's motion and approved the Committee's proposal by a vote of 9 to 1 to 1. South Carolina voted no, and the Georgia delegation was divided. Slaveholders would receive a more limited right to control the travel of their slaves with the Fugitive Slave Clause. (See Essay No. 142.) A draft by the Committee of Style indicated a slight revision, changing "citizens *in* the several States" to "citizens *of* the several States,"[18] but the Committee's report, delivered on September 12, kept the language as "citizens in the several States."[19]

This new streamlined version of the Privileges and Immunities Clause thus (1) replaced "free inhabitants" and "free citizens" with the same word, "citizens," (2) omitted the enumeration of the rights of travel and commerce, and (3) discarded, over some southerners' objection, the special exemption for exportation of "property."

THE RATIFICATION DEBATES

During ratification, there was little recorded discussion about the Privileges and Immunities Clause. In Federalist No. 80, Alexander Hamilton wrote simply that this provision "may be esteemed the basis of the Union." In Federalist No. 42, James Madison praised the revised clause's coherence and simplicity, observing that under the Articles of Confederation, there was "confusion" in the language: "Why the terms *free inhabitants*, are used in one part of the article; *free citizens* in another, and *people* in another, or what was meant by superadding 'to all privileges and immunities of free citizens,'— 'all the privileges of trade and commerce,' cannot easily be determined." However, Madison said nothing about the deletion of the special exception for exportation of property.

Despite these apparent improvements, the revised and ratified Privileges and Immunities Clause arguably left at least three questions unanswered. First, history would suggest that voting was a privilege and immunity of citizenship. Thus, this apparent absurdity as to sojourners' political rights remained.

Second, there was some uncertainty concerning the civil rights of travel, trade, petition, etc. Were these constitutional entitlements absolute rights that the state must respect, state laws to the contrary notwithstanding? Or was a state required only to treat out-of-state citizens equally to the state's own citizens? Nevertheless, as Professor Earl Maltz has observed, "the idea of a state government failing to provide its own citizens" with such rights "was almost unthinkable."[20] Thus, the only evil to be feared was state discrimination against citizens from other states.

Third, the new Constitution did not fully define the term "citizen." The text indicated at least two kinds of citizens. Congress had the power "To establish an uniform Rule of Naturalization" of citizenship,[21] and the President must be a "natural born Citizen."[22] Congress, then, could provide the "uniform rule" for such naturalization, but what provided the "rule" defining native citizenship? Under the common-law rule, the native subject or citizen included any human being born within and under the jurisdiction of a state or nation.[23] Yet, given the facts of American slavery and American racial prejudice, there was doubt as to whether native-born black persons, even if free, enjoyed birthright citizenship.

EARLY JUDICIAL PRECEDENT

In the first half century after ratification, the courts did little to settle the meaning of the Privileges and Immunities Clause. The only matter that was settled was the citizenship status of corporations. *Bank of United States v. Deveaux* (1809) held that corporations were "citizens" for purposes of Article III of the Constitution.[24] Under so-called diversity jurisdiction, a citizen of one state can sue a citizen of another state in federal court. However, *Bank of Augusta v. Earle* (1839) found that such artificial entities were not citizens for the purposes of the Article IV Privileges and Immunities Clause.[25]

The state courts offered widely different interpretations of the clause. The high courts in Maryland and Virginia affirmed that a "limited operation is to be given to these words, and not a full and comprehensive one," because these guarantees could not include the right to vote and to hold office.[26] This approach seemed inconsistent with the text, which secured "*all* Privileges and Immunities."

The Tennessee and Delaware courts found that the clause probably bound only the federal government but not the states.[27] And the Massachusetts Supreme Judicial Court declared that a traveling citizen must become a resident of a new state before enjoying any privileges of citizenship therein.[28] These decisions conflicted with the Framers' original intent: to bind the states to respect the citizens' immediate entitlement to such civil rights as travel, trade, and property in all the states.

Corfield v. Coryell (1823) provided the most widely respected interpretation of the Privileges and Immunities Clause. Justice Bushrod Washington wrote the decision while riding circuit in Pennsylvania. Washington recognized that the clause protected "fundamental" civil rights that were recognized in all free governments, such as the rights to travel, residence, and commerce.[29] The clause also protected an immunity against "higher taxes or impositions than are paid by the other citizens of the state." Washington then added that the clause may also protect the political rights of citizenship, but only "as regulated and established by the laws or constitution of the state in which it is to be exercised." However, Justice Washington left open the question of whether a traveling citizen was exempted from any local law that might abridge a local citizen's rights or was instead entitled only to a freedom from interstate discrimination.

RIGHTS OF TRAVELING FREE BLACKS

In the four decades before the Civil War, slavery and race occasioned the most prominent controversies as to the meaning of the clause. First, there was deep division as to whether free blacks were "citizens," and if so, whether they were entitled to the privileges of travel, residence, and commerce throughout the Union, local racist laws notwithstanding.[30] In 1820, after Congress had approved the admission of Missouri as a slave state, the state's convention adopted a constitution that required the legislature to "prevent free negroes [a]nd mulattoes from coming to and settling in this State, under any pretext whatsoever."[31] In Congress, most northerners charged that this exclusion would violate the Privileges and Immunities Clause. Congress

settled on a "compromise." Missouri had to agree that its constitution "shall never be construed" so as to exclude "any citizen, of either of the states in this Union" from "the enjoyment of any of the privileges and immunities to which such citizen is entitled under the constitution of the United States."[32] This proviso, however, did not resolve who was a citizen and what those rights were.

Afterwards, many courts flatly denied that free blacks were citizens under the Privileges and Immunities Clause.[33] Further, courts held that even if traveling free blacks were citizens, the clause prohibited only interstate discrimination. Thus, incoming black citizens could not complain if they were subjected to the same codes imposed on free blacks native to that state.[34] In the first reported federal case interpreting the clause, Judge William Cranch explained that even if they were citizens, traveling free blacks "can claim only those privileges and immunities which belong to citizens of the latter state, in like circumstances."[35]

Leading jurists endorsed this interstate-equality reading. Justice Joseph Story wrote that the clause "communicate[s] all the privileges and immunities, which the citizens of the same state would be entitled to under the like circumstances."[36] Chancellor James Kent said much the same.[37]

Opponents of these laws, however, insisted that free blacks were citizens. Thus, when these citizens came into a new state, they were entitled to these rights without discrimination on the basis of race. For example, an 1843 report to Congress contended that "the citizens of each State are entitled to" these privileges and immunities "equally, without discrimination of color or condition."[38] The following year, a federal court in Massachusetts observed that a Louisiana law excluding free blacks from the state "wholly ignored" the Privileges and Immunities Clause.[39] In 1864, a federal court in Virginia found that the Clause exempted migrating black citizens from state laws that abridged, on the basis of race, the fundamental rights defined by Justice Washington.[40]

RIGHTS OF TRAVELING SLAVEHOLDERS

Leading up to the Civil War, the courts also had to determine the rights of traveling slaveholders to bring their slaves into free states. Just as slave states became intolerant of traveling free blacks, free states were intolerant of traveling slaveholders. Some southern and western courts affirmed that sojourning citizens were exempt from local antislavery laws.

This issue was addressed in the infamous *Dred Scott v. Sandford* (1857) decision.[41] The central legal question in that case was whether Scott was a "citizen" of a state for purposes of Article III diversity jurisdiction. In his majority opinion, Chief Justice Roger B. Taney held that free blacks could *never* be citizens under Article III. Taney reasoned that if free blacks were citizens under Article III, they would also be citizens under Article IV and therefore entitled to privileges such as the rights to travel, speech, assembly, and arms, as well as an exemption from local racist laws that might infringe these rights.[42] For Taney, that result was intolerable. His opinion thus at once both rejected black citizenship and suggested that the Constitution might entitle a traveling slaveholder to an exemption from local antislavery laws. Justice Samuel Nelson's concurrence explained that this case did not resolve this issue. This question, he explained, "turns upon the rights and privileges secured to a common citizen of the republic under the Constitution of the United States," and "[w]hen that question arises, we shall be prepared to decide it."[43]

In *Lemmon v. People* (1860), the New York Court of Appeals would decide this issue.[44] In this case, a Virginia slaveholder and her husband traveled to New York with her slaves. However, while in New York, she lost custody of her slaves under the local antislavery law. Lemmon claimed that as a sojourning citizen, she was exempt from this law. The divided court held that the Privileges and Immunities Clause entitled the sojourners only to freedom from interstate discrimination. Lemmon would be subject, equally with New York citizens, to local emancipation law. In the lead opinion, Judge Hiram Denio offered a narrow reading of Article IV. He wrote that "in a given State, every citizen of every other State shall have the same privileges and immunities—that is, the same rights—which the citizens of that State possess." However, "where the laws of the several States differ, a citizen of one State asserting rights in another, must claim them according to the laws of the" other state, "not according to those which obtain in his own."[45] In other words, a Virginian could not assert the rights protected by Virginia law in New York.

Southerners were outraged. The South Carolina Declaration of Secession cited this decision as violative of the asserted right of slave transit.[46] This right of slave transit was expressly enumerated in the Confederate Constitution's version of Article IV.[47]

POSTBELLUM SETTLEMENT

In the decade after the Civil War, these antebellum controversies were largely resolved. *Minor v. Happersett* (1875) held that Article IV did not protect political rights, including voting rights. The U.S. Supreme Court held that "the Constitution has not added the right of suffrage to the privileges and immunities of citizenship as they existed at the time it was adopted."[48] As a result, nothing in the Privileges and Immunities Clause would affect the states' authority to restrict the suffrage on any ground, whether sex, age, property, or residence. Suffrage was not "the absolute right of all citizens."[49]

The questions of slave transit and black citizenship were settled by constitutional amendments. The Thirteenth Amendment, ratified in 1865, nullified any alleged right of citizens to hold slaves (see Essay No. 191). The Fourteenth Amendment, ratified in 1868, provided a robust definition of citizenship. The Citizenship Clause (see Essay No. 192) affirmed that every person, without regard to race, would enjoy native birthright citizenship if "born" in the United States and "subject to the jurisdiction thereof."

The Privileges or Immunities Clause of the Fourteenth Amendment also addressed whether the "privileges and immunities" might override state law (see Essay No. 194). This somewhat enigmatic provision specifies that "[n]o State shall make or enforce any law which shall abridge the privileges or immunities of citizens of the United States." The authors of the clause, including Senator Jacob Howard of Michigan, evidently thought that the Article IV Privileges and Immunities Clause and the Fourteenth Amendment's Privileges or Immunities Clause had some close relation to one another.[50] However, the original meaning of the Privileges *or* Immunities Clause and its relation to the Privileges *and* Immunities Clause are questions about which originalist scholars sharply disagree. The Privileges *or* Immunities Clause of the Fourteenth Amendment should not be confused with the Privileges *and* Immunities Clause in Article IV. The different conjunctions (and/or) likely turned on the fact that the Fourteenth Amendment was framed in the negative ("No state shall . . .").

As late as 1868, the Supreme Court had still not interpreted the Article IV Privileges and Immunities Clause. Senator Howard, who served on the Joint Committee for Reconstruction, observed that the Court had not "undertaken to define either the nature or extent of the privileges and immunities thus guaranteed."[51] However, a year after the amendment's ratification, *Paul v. Virginia* (1869) would provide an answer. Writing for a unanimous Court, Justice Stephen Field observed that Article IV "insures to" a citizen of one state when traveling to "other States the same freedom possessed by the citizens of those States in the acquisition and enjoyment of property and in the pursuit of happiness."[52] Field relied on Judge Denio's separate opinion in *Lemmon*, which adopted a federalism-based, interstate-equality reading of Article IV.

MODERN DOCTRINE

Consistent with the postbellum settlement, under modern doctrine, there are three steps in considering a claim under the Privileges and Immunities Clause. First, is the claimant an out-of-state citizen? In-state residents "have no claim under the Privileges and Immunities Clause."[53] Second, per *Paul v. Virginia*, has a traveling citizen been discriminated against on the basis of his or her state of citizenship or residency?[54] In assessing discrimination, the Court focuses on the reason why the state discriminated against traveling citizens. Third, does this discrimination adversely affect "fundamental" privileges or immunities? Pursuant to *Minor*, the Court has found that political rights are not fundamental under this clause. By sharp contrast, political rights *are* considered "fundamental" under the Equal Protection Clause (See Essay No. 196). The Court has held that these "privileges" include certain state-created rights, such as recreational hunting.[55] It has also read the Privileges and Immunities Clause of Article IV, as well as the Privileges or Immunities Clause of the Fourteenth Amendment, to protect a right to travel.[56]

OPEN QUESTIONS

- Under modern doctrine, the Supreme Court limits the Privileges and Immunities Clause to a freedom from interstate discrimination and wholly excludes political rights. Is this doctrine consistent with the original meaning and original intent of the clause?
- Has the acceptance of the interstate-equality reading impaired efforts to recover the original meaning and intent of the Fourteenth Amendment's Privileges or Immunities Clause? This latter provision was arguably adopted to correct the interstate-equality reading.
- Is there a difference between the right to travel protected by the Article IV Privileges and Immunities Clause and the Fourteenth Amendment's Privileges or Immunities Clause?[57]
- Is the so-called Dormant Commerce Clause "more appropriately housed" in the Privileges and Immunities Clause?[58]

Cite as: David R. Upham, *The Privileges and Immunities Clause, in* THE HERITAGE GUIDE TO THE CONSTITUTION 515 (Josh Blackman & John G. Malcolm eds., 3d ed. 2025).

Notes

1. Declaration of Independence, ¶ 32. 2. Articles of Confederation, art. IV, § 1. 3. 1 J. Am. Cong. 21 (Oct. 14, 1774). 4. *Id.* at 20. 5. *Id.* 6. *Id.* 7. *Id.* at 385. 8. Articles of Confederation, art. IV, § 1. 9. Henry Sherman, Slavery in the United States of America 15 (1858). 10. Hanes Walton, Jr. et al., The African American Electorate: A Statistical History 80, 118–20 (2012). 11. 1 J. Am. Cong. 20 (Oct. 14, 1774). 12. 2 J. Am. Cong. 606 (June 25, 1778). 13. 2 Farrand's 173–74. 14. *Id.* at 163. 15. *Id.*; 3 Farrand's 445. 16. 2 Farrand's 187. 17. *Id.* at 443. 18. *Id.* at 577. 19. *Id.* at 601. 20. Earl M. Maltz, The Fourteenth Amendment and the Law of the Constitution 34 (2003). 21. Art. II, § 8, cl. 4. 22. Art. II, § 1, cl. 3. 23. *Lynch v. Clarke*, 1 Sand. 583, 639 (N.Y. Ch. 1844). 24. 9 US 61 (1809). 25. *Bank of Augusta v. Earle*, 38 U.S. 519 (1839). 26. *Campbell v. Morris*, 3 H. & McH. 288 (Md. 1797); *Murray v. McCarty*, 2 Munf. 373, 398 (Va. 1811). 27. *Kincaid v. Francis*, 3 Cooke 49, 53 (Tenn., 1812); *Douglas's Admin. v. Stevens*, 1 Del. Ch. 465, 477 (1821). 28. *Abbott v. Bailey*, 23 Mass. 89, 91–92 (1827). 29. 6 Fed. Cas. 546, 551–52 (C.C.E.D. Pa. 1823) (No. 3230). 30. 16 Albert Bushnell Hart, The American Nation, 1831–1841, at 276–77 (Albert Bushnell Hart ed., 1906). 31. Mo. Const. of 1821, art. III, § 26. 32. Resolution Providing for the Admission of the State of Missouri into the Union, on a Certain Condition, ch. 54, 3 Stat. 645 (1821). 33. *Amy v. Smith*, 11 Ky. 326, 334 (1822). 34. *Id.* at 335. 35. *Costin v. Washington*, 6 F. Cas. 612, 613–14 (C.C.D.C. 1821) (No, 3,266). 36. 3 Story's Commentaries § 1800. 37. 2 James Kent, Commentaries on American Law 71–72 (2d ed. 1832). 38. Committee on Commerce, Free Colored Seamen—Majority and Minority Reports, H.R. Rep. No. 80, at 2 (1843). 39. *The Cynosure*, 6 F. Cas. 1102, 1103 & n.3 (D. Mass. 1844) (No. 3529). 40. *In re Dorsey* (E.D. Va. 1864) (Op. of Underwood, J.), *reprinted in* Edward McPherson, The Political History of the United States of America During the Great Rebellion 442–43 (2d ed. 1865). 41. *Dred Scott v. Sandford*, 60 U.S. 393 (1857). 42. *Id.* at 417. 43. *Id.* at 468 (Nelson, J., concurring). 44. 20 N.Y. 562 (N.Y. 1860). 45. *Id.* at 608. 46. Declaration of the Immediate Causes Which Induce and Justify the Secession of South Carolina from the Federal Union (Dec. 24, 1860), *in* 2 Alexander H. Stephens, A Constitutional View of the Late War Between the States 671, 674 (1870). 47. Confederate Const., art. IV, § 2, cl. 1 (1861). 48. *Minor v. Happersett*, 88 U.S. 162, 171 (1874). 49. *Id.* at 175. 50. Speech of Sen. Jacob Howard on a Proposed Fourteenth Amendment (May 23, 1866), *in* 2 The Reconstruction Amendments: The Essential Documents 185 (Kurt T. Lash ed., 2021). 51. *Adamson v. People of State of California*, 332 U.S. 46, 105 (Black, J., dissenting) (quoting Sen. Jacob Howard, 39 Cong. Globe, 39th Cong., 1st Sess. 2764 (1866)). 52. 75 U.S. 168, 180 (1869) (citing *Lemmon v. People*, 20 N.Y. 562, 607 (1860) (opinion of Denio, J.)). 53. *United Bldg. & Constr. Trades Council v. Mayor & Council of Camden*, 465 U.S. 208 (1984). 54. *McBurney v. Young*, 569 U.S. 221 (2013). 55. *Baldwin v. Fish & Game Comm'n of Mont.*, 436 U.S. 371 (1978). 56. *Saenz v. Roe*, 526 U.S. 489, 501 (1999). 57. *Id.* at 521 (1999) (Thomas, J., dissenting). 58. *Nat'l Pork Producers Council v. Ross*, 598 U.S. 356, 370 (2023) (citing *Tyler Pipe Indus., Inc. v. Wash. State Dept. of Revenue*, 483 U.S. 232, 265 (1987) (Scalia, J., concurring in part and dissenting in part)); *id.* at 408–409 (Kavanaugh, J., concurring).

~

ESSAY NO. 141: THE FUGITIVE FROM JUSTICE CLAUSE
ART. IV, § 2, CL. 2

A Person charged in any State with Treason, Felony, or other Crime, who shall flee from Justice, and be found in another State, shall on Demand of the executive Authority of the State from which he fled, be delivered up, to be removed to the State having Jurisdiction of the Crime.

—Zack Smith

INTRODUCTION

The Fugitive from Justice Clause provides a mechanism by which a person who is charged with a crime and flees from one state to another state can be returned. This process, known as extradition, traces its roots back to antiquity. In 1793, Congress enacted an extradition law that seemed to impose a duty on states to extradite fugitives. In 1861, the U.S. Supreme Court held that the states were not obligated to return fugitives, but the Court reversed that decision more than a century later. Today, most states have adopted the Uniform Criminal Extradition and Rendition Act, which imposes specific obligations on states to extradite fugitives.

HISTORY BEFORE 1787

For millennia, sovereigns have extradited fugitives to other sovereigns. Extradition agreements date back to the Egyptian, Hittite, and Roman empires.[1] In 1174, England and Scotland negotiated a treaty to extradite traitors and felons.[2] This practice carried forward to the colonial era. By 1643, colonial governments in Massachusetts and Connecticut "pledged themselves to each other" to extradite fugitives from justice.[3]

After independence, the Articles of Confederation implemented an extradition process for the new states to follow.[4] This provision applied to "any Person guilty of, or charged with, treason, felony, or other high misdemeanor in any state." If that person "fle[d] from Justice" and was "found in any of the united states," the "Governor or executive power of the state from which he fled" had the ability to "demand" his return. After that demand was made, the fugitive was supposed to "be delivered up, and removed to the state having jurisdiction of his offence."

THE CONSTITUTIONAL CONVENTION

The delegates to the Constitutional Convention adopted the provision from the Articles of Confederation with only minor alterations. The Committee of Detail's report, delivered on August 6, provided that "[a]ny person charged with treason, felony or high misdemeanor in any State, who shall flee from justice, and shall be found in any other State, shall, on demand of the Executive power of the State from which he fled, be delivered up and removed to the State having jurisdiction of the offence."[5] On August 28, "high misdemeanor" was changed to "other crime."[6] The change was made "to comprehend all proper cases," as the former language had a "technical meaning too limited."[7] This proposal was approved without objection.[8] Charles Pinckney of South Carolina noted that the delegates chose to broaden the language because "a State should always be at liberty to demand a fugitive from justice, let his crime be what it may."[9] At that juncture, "high crimes and misdemeanors" had not yet been added to the Impeachment Clause (See Essay No. 117).

Pinckney and Pierce Butler of South Carolina moved "to require fugitive slaves and servants to be delivered up like criminals."[10] Because of various objections, their proposal was withdrawn "in order that some

particular provision might be made apart from this article."[11] This other "particular provision" would later become the Constitution's Fugitive Slave Clause. (See Essay No. 142.)

THE FUGITIVE SLAVE ACT OF 1793

The Fugitive from Justice Clause garnered little attention during the ratification debates, but concerns arose after ratification over whether this provision was self-executing (enforceable by its own terms) or whether Congress needed to act.

In 1791, Pennsylvania Governor Thomas Mifflin demanded the return of Virginians who were indicted for "forcibly remov[ing]" a "colored man" from Pennsylvania with the intent to "enslave him."[12] However, the Attorney General of Virginia determined that "the offence charged in the indictment was not such a crime as, under the constitution, required a surrender."[13] The Virginia Attorney General further ruled that no "positive law," or federal statute, imposed an obligation on the state to extradite fugitives. In other words, the Fugitive from Justice Clause was not self-executing. Rather, Congress needed to enact legislation to implement this clause. As a result, "[t]he governor of Virginia refused to arrest the defendants, and deliver them to the authorities of Pennsylvania."[14] The Pennsylvania governor transmitted these correspondences to President George Washington, "who laid them before congress."[15] Justice John McLean, writing half a century later, observed that "this correspondence, and the forcible removal of the colored person . . . gave rise to" federal legislation.[16]

In February 1793, the Second Congress passed the "Act respecting fugitives from justice, and persons escaping from the service of their masters."[17] This law, which implemented the Fugitive from Justice Clause, is better known as the Fugitive Slave Act. Under the statute, the requesting state must produce "a copy of an indictment found" or "an affidavit made before a magistrate of any state or territory" charging the "person so demanded" with a crime. And that document must be "certified as authentic by the governor or chief magistrate of the state or territory from whence the person so charged fled." It would then be "the duty of the executive authority of the state or territory to which [the fugitive] shall have fled, to cause him or her to be arrested and secured" and to provide notice of the arrest to the demanding state executive or his agent. Further, the apprehending state executive had to "cause the fugitive to be delivered to such agent [of the demanding state] when he shall appear." An agent was "empowered" to transport the fugitive, and it would be a crime to "rescue the fugitive." However, if the agent did not appear for six months, "the prisoner may be discharged." Finally, the state making the request would pay for all costs or expenses.

Almost fifty years later, in *Prigg v. Pennsylvania* (1842), Justice Joseph Story explained that the 1793 act "may be truly said to cover the whole ground of the Constitution, both as to fugitives from justice, and fugitive slaves."[18] He observed that Congress has "discretion" in meeting "the exigencies of the Constitution" and that "the legislation of Congress, if constitutional, must supersede all state legislation upon the same subject; and by necessary implication prohibit it."[19] Story explained in his *Commentaries* that the Fugitive from Justice Clause would "promote harmony and good feelings among the states" and would "give strength to a great moral duty, which neighbouring states especially owe to each other, by elevating the policy of the mutual suppression of crimes into a legal obligation."[20] Story described this principle as both "useful in practice" and "unexceptionable in its character."

IS EXTRADITION MANDATORY?

Nonetheless, *Prigg* also ruled that Congress could not compel states to enforce the Fugitive Slave Act.[21] This holding was a precursor to the modern anti-commandeering doctrine. About twenty years later, in *Kentucky v. Dennison* (1861), the Court reached a similar holding about the Fugitive from Justice Clause: the federal government lacked the power to compel the states to extradite a fugitive.[22] Chief Justice Roger B. Taney, who wrote the majority opinion, observed that the words "it shall be the duty" in the 1793 act "were not used as mandatory and compulsory, but as declaratory of the moral duty which this compact created, when Congress had provided the mode of carrying it into execution." Taney reasoned that there is no clause "in the Constitution which arms the Government of the United States with this power" to compel state officials to take certain actions.[23] Such a "power," Taney wrote, "would place every State under the control and dominion of the General Government, even in the administration of its internal concerns and reserved rights." If the federal government had the power to "compel" a "duty" on a state official, "it might overload the officer with duties which would fill up all his time."[24]

More than a century later, the Court overruled *Dennison* in *Puerto Rico v. Branstad* (1987), holding that the federal courts could compel states to comply with the Fugitive from Justice Clause through writs of mandamus and other mechanisms.[25] Justice Thurgood Marshall, writing for the majority, found that *Dennison* "is the product of another time" and "may stand no longer" because "[t]he conception of the relation between the States and the Federal Government there announced is fundamentally incompatible with more than a century of constitutional development."[26] Marshall made this remark a decade before the Court enunciated its modern anti-commandeering doctrine in *Printz v. United States* (1997).[27]

STATE POWERS OVER EXTRADITION

Dennison and other cases held that Congress possessed exclusive authority to legislate with respect to extradition.[28] But the Supreme Court reversed course in *Innes v. Tobin* (1915) and found that states also could legislate in this area.[29] One scholar described *Innes* as "a somewhat unsatisfying opinion, citing no authority for its reasoning."[30] Later cases helped to explain the limits and contours of the states' power. For example, a state executive who receives an extradition request may make sure that a facially valid charge exists in the state requesting extradition but may not look into the substantive merits of the case against the accused.[31]

Questions also arose over what it meant to "flee from Justice." Initially, some commentators thought that someone involuntarily removed from a state could not be considered a fugitive from justice, and questions also arose over whether someone had to flee with the explicit purpose of avoiding justice. If the person left the state for another reason, is he still a fugitive from justice? The Supreme Court answered in the affirmative and made it clear that a demanding executive must show only that the person had been present in the state when the alleged crime occurred and that he subsequently left the state.[32] But a state may satisfy its own laws before returning an individual to another state to face charges.[33] Furthermore, by its terms, the Fugitive From Justice Clause requires extradition only for criminal matters, including misdemeanors, but not for civil offenses.

Today, most states have adopted some form of the Uniform Criminal Extradition and Rendition Act.[34] One scholar noted that "the need for [these laws] grew directly out of the *Dennison* and *Prigg* opinions and the lack of any enforcement mechanism external to the states for the [Fugitive from Justice] Clause."[35] The purpose of these state laws was to transform the extradition process from one essentially "governed by comity to one governed by compulsion."[36] These Uniform Acts were largely promulgated and adopted before the Supreme Court reversed its earlier decisions and held that the federal government could enforce the constitutional and statutory obligations of state officials in the extradition context, and they allow in some instances for extradition beyond what the Constitution demands.

OPEN QUESTIONS

- Did the Fugitive from Justice Clause, standing by itself, impose obligations on states, or did Congress need to enact enforcement legislation? In other words, was the Clause self-executing?
- In 2023, Florida Governor Ron DeSantis stated that he would "not assist in the extradition" of former President Donald Trump, who was a Florida resident, to New York. DeSantis cited the "questionable circumstances" of the indictment. Would this refusal to extradite have been constitutional?[37]

Cite as: Zack Smith, *The Fugitive From Justice Clause, in* THE HERITAGE GUIDE TO THE CONSTITUTION 521 (Josh Blackman & John G. Malcolm eds., 3d ed. 2025).

Notes

1. Peter D. Sutherland, *The Development of International Law of Extradition*, 28 St. Louis U. L.J. 33, 33 (1984). 2. *Id.* 3. *Kentucky v. Dennison*, 65 U.S. 66, 101 (1861). 4. Articles of Confederation, art. IV, § 2. 5. 2 Farrand's 187–88. 6. 2 Farrand's 443. 7. *Id.* 8. *Id.* at 437. 9. 3 Farrand's 112. 10. *Id.*; 2 Farrand's 443. 11. *Id.* 12. *Prigg v. Pennsylvania*, 41 U.S. 539, 666 (1842) (McLean, J., dissenting). 13. *Id.* 14. *Id.* at 666–67. 15. *Id.* at 667; Letter from Thomas Mifflin to George Washington (July 18, 1791), https://perma.cc/DA6F-YZYL. 16. 2 Farrand's 667; Paul Finkelman, *The Kidnapping of John Davis and the Adoption of the Fugitive Slave Law of 1793*, 56 J. South. Hist. 397–422 (1990). 17. 1 Stat. 302 (1793); 18 U.S.C. § 3182 (current codification). 18. 41 U.S. 539, 617 (1842). 19. *Id.* 20. 3 Story's Commentaries § 1803. 21. *Printz v. United States*, 521 U.S. 898 (1997). 22. 65 U.S. (24 How.) 66 (1861). 23. *Id.* 24. *Id.* at 107–08.

25. *Puerto Rico v. Branstad*, 483 U.S. 219 (1987). 26. *Id.* at 230. 27. 521 U.S. 898 (1997). 28. Christopher N. Lasch, *Rendition Resistance*, 91 N.C. L. Rev. 149, 196 n.289 (2013). 29. *Innes v. Tobin*, 240 U.S. 127 (1915). 30. Lasch, *supra* at 196 n.290. 31. *Michigan v. Doran*, 439 U.S. 282 (1978). 32. *Roberts v. Reilly*, 116 U.S. 80 (1885); *Drew v. Thaw*, 235 U.S. 432 (1914). 33. *Taylor v. Taintor*, 83 U.S. (16 Wall.) 366, 371 (1873). 34. Milton Hirsch, *Midnight Run Re-Run: Bail Bondsmen, Bounty Hunters, and the Uniform Criminal Extradition Act*, 62 U. Mia. L. Rev. 59 (2007); Leslie W. Abramson, *Extradition in America: Of Uniform Act and Governmental Discretion*, 33 Baylor L. Rev. 793 (1981). 35. Lasch, *supra* at 200. 36. *Id.* 37. Shane Goldmacher, *DeSantis Says Florida Wouldn't Aid Trump's Extradition to New York*, N.Y. Times (Mar. 30, 2023), https://perma.cc/332K-67EZ.

⟨~⟩

ESSAY NO. 142: THE FUGITIVE SLAVE CLAUSE
ART. IV, § 2, CL. 3

No Person held to Service or Labour in one State, under the Laws thereof, escaping into another, shall, in Consequence of any Law or Regulation therein, be discharged from such Service or Labour, but shall be delivered up on Claim of the Party to whom such Service or Labour may be due.

—Bradley Rebeiro

INTRODUCTION

Perhaps none of the clauses in the Constitution pertaining to slavery was more nebulous or spurred more contention and violence than the Fugitive Slave Clause.[1] There is little doubt that this provision pertained to fugitive slaves. It was referred to as the Fugitive Slave Clause even though the words *fugitive* and *slave* appear nowhere in the text.[2] The Framers reached a consensus that would protect property in slaves but paradoxically omit lawful recognition of slavery. Still another issue remained: the Fugitive Slave Clause did not carry with it an express grant of power. This omission resulted in significant conflict between the federal government and southern states on one side and northern states on the other. Many of these conflicts, which centered on the proper scope and meaning of the Fugitive Slave Clause and Congress's power to enforce it, were resolved in favor of the federal government and southern states.

HISTORY BEFORE 1787

The origins of the Fugitive Slave Clause lie somewhat counterintuitively with *Somerset v. Stewart* (1772).[3] Stewart, a Virginia slaveholder, brought one of his slaves—James Somerset—with him on a business trip to England. Through the writ of habeas corpus, Somerset claimed he was free by virtue of setting foot on English soil, where slavery was unlawful. In a decision that sent shockwaves through the southern colonies, Lord Mansfield granted Somerset's habeas petition. He reasoned that slavery was so contrary to the nature of law that only positive, or statutory, law could sustain it. Put differently, if a slave was brought to English soil—where slavery was not tolerated—that slave became free.

This pronouncement did not cause significant friction among the colonies and, later, the states. The Articles of Confederation, for example, provided for the return of fugitives from justice but said nothing of slaves.[4] But as more states considered and enacted emancipation laws, the slaveholding states began to appreciate the implications of *Somerset*.[5] The first step these states took to protect their peculiar property was the Northwest Ordinance of 1787. The Confederation Congress banned slavery in the territories but ensured that fugitive slaves could be reclaimed if they sojourned to the territories.[6] No longer would slaveholders have to worry about *Somerset*'s rationale: Positive legislation in a sense would sustain the odious institution for slaveholding states.

THE CONSTITUTIONAL CONVENTION

Although it would later lead to significant tension in interstate relations, the Fugitive Slave Clause prompted surprisingly little discussion at the Constitutional Convention. On August 28, 1787, Pierce Butler and Charles Pinckney of South Carolina introduced a provision to require the return of fugitive slaves.[7] James Wilson of Pennsylvania objected that their proposal would require the executive of each state to deliver fugitive slaves at public expense.[8] Roger Sherman of Connecticut argued that there was "no more propriety in the public seizing and surrendering a slave . . . than a horse."[9]

Butler and Pinckney withdrew their provision from consideration and later reintroduced a revised version that mirrored the Articles of Confederation's fugitive provision but included a provision for the returning of fugitive slaves:

"If any person bound to service or labor in any of the U– States shall escape into another State, he or she shall not be discharged from such service or labor, in consequence of any regulations subsisting in the State to which they escape, but shall be delivered up to the person justly claiming their service or labor."[10] With these deliberations happening so close to the Northwest Ordinance's enactment, Butler and Pinckney were able to rely on plenty of authority; they just needed the right words.[11]

The Committee of Style later changed the proposed clause in several ways. Most notably, "legally" was changed to "under the laws thereof." This change avoided the idea that slavery was morally valid.[12] The resulting clause's plain language, full of circumlocutions, was ambiguous in two ways that would later carry significance: It did not specify *who* would have the responsibility to recover fugitive slaves, and it did not mention the word "slave," although all delegates understood the clause to reference fugitive slaves.[13] What seemed relatively clear at the time, however, was that the clause would ensure that *Somerset* would not have purchase in the wake of northern emancipation.

THE RATIFICATION DEBATES

Viewed in the light of the controversies that would soon follow, it is equally surprising that there was no considerable attention given to the Fugitive Slave Clause during the ratification debates. Perhaps the closest example is Federalist No. 42, where Madison discusses competing claims of citizenship and the need for uniform naturalization rules. The emphasis on "free inhabitants" and the problem of some states conferring citizenship on persons for whom another state might proscribe citizenship might be read to address the problem of free states conferring citizenship on fugitive slaves.

EARLY PRACTICE

During the early Republic, the Fugitive Slave Clause was interpreted to promote slavery. The Second Congress passed the Fugitive Slave Act of 1793 (formally "an Act respecting fugitives from justice, and persons escaping from the service of their masters").[14] This act authorized states to assist in the recapture of fugitive slaves. Perhaps more controversially, it gave slave

owners or their agents authority to enter states into which fugitive slaves had escaped in order to recover them. (See Essay No. 141.) It also provided steep penalties for anyone who helped to harbor or conceal escapees.

Significant opposition to the Act arose in the North. States passed the first versions of what would become known as Personal Liberty Laws, which provided modest protections for free blacks.[15] The first iterations of these laws took the form of anti-kidnapping statutes. These laws heavily penalized or even criminalized the kidnapping of free blacks. They also prohibited slave owners or their agents from seeking to recover alleged fugitives without the involvement of local authorities and generally provided formal procedures to process the return of runaway slaves. On their face, the Personal Liberty Laws seemed to conform to the 1793 Act, but they denied slave holders and their agents what they believed was the full measure of protection to recover fugitive slaves under the federal statute.

PRIGG V. PENNSYLVANIA AND *JONES V. VAN ZANDT*

In 1842, the contest between slaveholders and Personal Liberty Laws finally reached the Supreme Court in *Prigg v. Pennsylvania*.[16] Pennsylvania's Personal Liberty Law prohibited the removal of blacks from the state for the purpose of enslaving them. Margaret Morgan, who was residing in Pennsylvania, was alleged to have escaped from Maryland. Edward Prigg was charged with securing Morgan's return to Maryland. The Pennsylvania Supreme Court upheld Prigg's conviction for kidnapping Morgan. However, on appeal, the Supreme Court declared that the Personal Liberty Law was unconstitutional. Justice Joseph Story's majority opinion found that the state law was preempted by the Fugitive Slave Clause and the 1793 Fugitive Slave Act. But the Northern states also emerged with a small win: Story determined that the federal government could not force states to assist in executing the 1793 Act.

Rather than settling the matter, however, *Prigg* simply presented another possibility among the competing interpretations and increased friction over the Fugitive Slave Clause. In 1837, Salmon P. Chase would be one of the first lawyers to offer a new view of the Fugitive Slave Clause when abolitionists sought his legal expertise in several high-profile cases out of Ohio. The first case involved a fugitive slave named Matilda, who worked for James G. Birney, a well-known abolitionist.[17] Matilda had been seized by slave catchers, and Birney, with very little time to spare, solicited Chase's assistance to provide Matilda with a legal defense. Chase invoked the Northwest Ordinance of 1787 and argued, much in line with *Somerset*, that property claims in slaves could not survive into free territories.[18] Unsurprisingly, Chase's argument did not win the day, and Matilda was sold into slavery.

In *Jones v. Van Zandt* (1847), Chase refined his theory of the Fugitive Slave Clause. Relying in part on Story's reasoning in *Prigg*, Chase posited that the federal government did not have power to enact the Fugitive Slave Act.[19] Chase relied heavily on Madison's Notes from the Constitutional Convention. He argued that Framers intended to ensure that the Constitution—and by extension, the federal government—did not recognize the moral validity of slavery. Rather, the Constitution provided certain protections for the institution. Chase maintained that the Fugitive Slave Clause did not expressly grant the federal government power to enforce it, an omission that he found significant. According to Chase, the clause's enforcement was to be left to the states and the states alone.[20] To Chase's dismay, the Supreme Court rejected his argument and upheld the constitutionality of the 1793 Act.[21]

THE FUGITIVE SLAVE ACT OF 1850

As tension over the future of slavery continued to rise, Congress passed more statutes to assuage the South's concerns. These measures continued to anger the North and contributed to increasingly unapologetic anti-slavery visions of the Constitution. Perhaps nothing brought the conflict to a head more than the Fugitive Slave Act of 1850.[22] *Prigg* had confirmed that state officials could not be forced to carry out the 1793 Act. In response, under the 1850 Act, federal magistrates would adjudicate claims concerning alleged fugitive slaves and would be awarded more money if they determined that an alleged fugitive was indeed a fugitive slave.

The 1850 law also denied the alleged fugitive an opportunity to be heard before the magistrate or present evidence. Northerners found this provision particularly objectionable, as it was tantamount to a denial of the due process of law under the Fifth Amendment (See Essay No. 172). The Wisconsin Supreme Court, for instance, declared the act unconstitutional, but the U.S. Supreme Court overturned that decision in *Ableman v. Booth*.[23] Several states refused to assist in enforcing the Act. In cities with a strong anti-slavery presence, there was an increased resistance to the capture of blacks.[24]

ABOLITIONIST RESPONSES TO THE FUGITIVE SLAVE CLAUSE

Some abolitionists responded with increasingly creative interpretations of the Fugitive Slave Clause. Frederick Douglass, for instance, popularized a theory that the clause did not pertain to slaves at all. Douglass, relying on the omission of the word "slave," argued that the clause could apply only to indentured servants or those who could enter contracts and thus were "held to Service or Labour."[25] Because slaves could not enter contracts, they could not be "held to Service" in any sense. Thus, the federal government had no obligation to ensure the protection of slaveowners' claims to property in slaves. Moreover, the Due Process Clause of the Fifth Amendment, properly understood, imposed an affirmative duty on the federal government to protect the liberty of *all* persons, including the enslaved.

Ultimately, the conflict around the Fugitive Slave Clause—in some measure caused by the Framers' reluctance to make clear what it covered and who could enforce it—could not be solved through the political process or through the courts. Not until ratification of the Thirteenth Amendment, which abolished slavery, was the conflict finally put to rest.

Cite as: Bradley Rebeiro, *The Fugitive Slave Clause, in* The Heritage Guide to the Constitution 525 (Josh Blackman & John G. Malcolm eds., 3d ed. 2025).

Notes

1. Art. IV, § 2, cl. 3. **2.** Sean Wilentz, No Property in Man: Slavery and Antislavery at the Nation's Founding 103–04 (2019). **3.** *Somerset v. Stewart*, 98 Eng. Rep. 499 (1772). **4.** Articles of Confederation, art. IV, § 2. **5.** Wilentz, *supra* at 101–09. **6.** The Northwest Ordinance, Art. VI (1787). **7.** 2 Farrand's 443. **8.** *Id.* **9.** *Id.* **10.** *Id.* at 453. **11.** Wilentz, *supra* at 103–05. **12.** 2 Farrand's 628; Wilentz, *supra* at 111–12. **13.** Wilentz, *supra* at 107. **14.** 1 Stat. 302 (1793). **15.** Thomas Morris, Free Men All: Personal Liberty Laws of the North, 1780–1861, ch. 2 (1974). **16.** *Prigg v. Pennsylvania*, 41 U.S. 539 (1842). **17.** John Niven, Salmon P. Chase: A Biography 50 (1995). **18.** *Id.* at 51–54. **19.** Brief for Defendant, *Jones v. Van Zandt*, 46 U.S. 215 (1847). **20.** *Id.* at 100. **21.** *Van Zandt*, 46 U.S. at 232. **22.** 9 Stat. 462 (1850). **23.** 62 U.S. 506 (1859). **24.** Lawrence Lader, Bold Brahmins: New England's War Against Slavery: 1831–1863, at 203–16 (1973). **25.** Frederick Douglass, Address at Scottish Anti-Slavery Society, Glasgow, Scotland, The Constitution of the United States: Is It Pro-Slavery or Anti-Slavery? (Mar. 26, 1860).

❧

ESSAY NO. 143: THE ADMISSIONS CLAUSE
ART. IV, § 3, CL. 1

New States may be admitted by the Congress into this Union; but no new States shall be formed or erected within the Jurisdiction of any other State; nor any State be formed by the Junction of two or more States, or Parts of States, without the Consent of the Legislatures of the States concerned as well as of the Congress.

—Gary S. Lawson

INTRODUCTION

From the earliest days of the nation, the number of states was expected to increase. Some expected the increase to come at least partly from new territorial acquisitions ranging from Canada to Cuba.[1] Others expected the new states to come from the breakup of original states, several of which had boundaries stretching from the Atlantic Ocean to the Mississippi River. But everyone knew that thirteen was just a starting point.

HISTORY BEFORE 1787

In 1780 and 1781, New York and Virginia ceded the land that came to be called the Northwest Territory. (See Essay No. 144.) At the time, the ceded land was too sparsely populated to become states. On October 10, 1780, the Continental Congress resolved that ceded lands would "be settled and formed into distinct republican states, which shall become members of the federal union, and have the same rights of sovereignty, freedom and independence, as the other states."[2] In July 1787, the Confederation Congress adopted the Northwest Ordinance, which formalized this resolution. It specified that "[t]here shall be formed, in the said [Northwest] territory, not less than three nor more than five States."[3] Even before the Constitution was signed, "statehood was imminent in the American concept of territory."[4]

THE CONSTITUTIONAL CONVENTION

The admission of new states was discussed at the earliest stages of the Constitutional Convention. The Virginia Plan allowed new states to be admitted only from territory "within the limits of the United States."[5] That would exclude Canada, which was expressly allowed to join the Union under the Articles of Confederation.[6] The New Jersey Plan contained no such constraint.[7] The Committee of Detail adopted the broader New Jersey Plan version, which, echoing the 1780 resolution, provided that "new States shall be admitted on the same Terms with the original States."[8]

Gouverneur Morris of Pennsylvania objected to requiring equality for admitted states, fearing that the political power of new Western states would overwhelm the East.[9] James Madison of Virginia countered that new states had to be admitted on an equal footing. He "insist[ed] that the Western States" would not "submit to a Union which degraded them from an equal rank with the other States." Morris's motion to strike out the equality requirement won by a vote of nine to two.[10] Morris also proposed that a state should not be formed out of a previous state without the consent of Congress and the previous state's legislature.[11] This proposal passed by a vote of eight to three.[12]

THE RATIFICATION DEBATES

In Federalist No. 43, Madison noted that the "eventual establishment of *new states*, seems to have been overlooked" in the Articles of Confederation and that "[w]ith great propriety therefore has the new system supplied the defect." He defended "[t]he general precaution that no new states shall be formed without the concurrence of the federal authority and that of the states concerned" as "consonant to the principles which ought to govern such transactions." Madison also suggested that forbidding partition of a state without its consent "quiets the jealousy of the larger states; as that of the smaller is quieted by a like precaution, against a junction of states without their consent."

Some Anti-Federalists, such as Luther Martin of Maryland, argued that Congress should be able to break up states, even over the objection of their state legislatures. For example, large states would straddle the Appalachian mountains or the Ohio and Mississippi rivers. Martin argued that the inhabitants on the "western side" would struggle to "remain connected" with those on the "atlantic side" and that it might "justify even recourse to arms, to free [the Westerners] from, and to shake off, so ignominious a yoke."[13]

FORMING NEW STATES OUT OF EXISTING STATES

The final text of the Admissions Clause has three clauses, separated by semicolons:

> New States may be admitted by the Congress into this Union; but no new States shall be formed or erected within the Jurisdiction of any other State; nor any State be formed by the Junction of two or more States, or Parts of States, without the Consent of the Legislatures of the States concerned as well as of the Congress.

The second clause, standing by itself, seems to suggest that the formation of new states out of existing states is completely prohibited, but the Framers expressly rejected that proposal in the Virginia Plan. The better reading is that the second clause is modified by the third clause: New states may be formed out of an existing state provided the new state, the existing state, and Congress all consent. This text reflects Morris's pro-state-legislature position and Madison's account in Federalist No. 43.

Historical practice supports this reading. In 1791, Vermont became the first state admitted under the Constitution.[14] New York had agreed to cede the land that became Vermont. In 1792, Kentucky was admitted with Virginia's consent.[15] Neither state had been part of a territory.

FORMING STATES FROM TERRITORY ACQUIRED AFTER 1788

The text of the Constitution reflects the New Jersey Plan's approach to admissions: New states were not limited to territory belonging to the United States in 1788. However, this position was not held by some leading figures in the early Republic. Gouverneur Morris, members of Congress, and Thomas Jefferson's Attorney General, Levi Lincoln, interpreted the Admissions Clause to apply only to territory possessed in 1788.[16] Jefferson himself was equivocal on the point. Sometimes he insisted on the need for a constitutional amendment; at other times, he seems to have been influenced by the powerful arguments of his Treasury Secretary, Albert Gallatin.[17] Ultimately, Jefferson would accede to the legality of admitting states formed out of new territory.[18]

Some members of Congress, primarily from New England, maintained that foreign territory could not become a state even if a constitutional amendment purported to allow it.[19] In a realpolitik sense, these concerns were understandable; the admission of numerous new states would dramatically swing the balance of power in Congress away from the New England states. But such concerns had little grounding in the Constitution as written.[20]

Here too, historical practice has rejected this reading. The land acquired in the 1803 Louisiana Purchase, which doubled the landmass of the United States, would be carved into several states. Two decades later, in 1823,

Thomas Jefferson wrote to James Monroe that he had "looked on Cuba as the most interesting addition which could ever be made to our system of states."[21] Most of the other states were formed from territories. Texas and Hawaii, however, were admitted without ever being either federally governed territories or part of pre-existing states,[22] but this distinction does not appear to be relevant to the Admissions Clause.

THE EQUAL FOOTING DOCTRINE

The Constitutional Convention rejected an express requirement that new states would be admitted with an equal status, or on equal footing, with existing states. Nevertheless, Congress admitted states on such grounds. Kentucky, for example, was "received and admitted to this Union, as a new and entire member of the United States of America."[23] Two decades later, Congress admitted Alabama as a state. Following the custom with previous admissions, Alabama was admitted "upon the same footing as the original states, in all respects whatever."[24]

Congress subsequently purported to grant title to some tidelands in Alabama, but *Pollard's Lessee v. Hagan* (1845) held that once Alabama acquired statehood, Alabama was the only governmental body capable of granting title to such lands.[25] The Court's holding could perhaps have been based on the terms of the Virginia and Georgia cessions of the land that ultimately became Alabama.[26] However, *Hagan* set out a constitutional rule: new states have the same rights that the original thirteen states had to land under navigable waters. This principle has come to be known as the *equal footing doctrine*. This holding has since been extended

to guarantee to all new states the same level of sovereignty possessed by original states. For example, Oklahoma had the right to determine the location of the state's capital.[27] Some modern scholarship doubts that the equal footing doctrine reflects original constitutional meaning,[28] especially given the Convention vote to strike an equality requirement, but the doctrine remains settled law.[29]

Even with the equal footing doctrine, Congress can still place conditions on a state's admission. Statutes that authorize states' admissions typically prescribe the process by which the people of a territory may draft and adopt a state constitution.[30] Other federal enabling acts have contained a range of restrictions. Utah, Arizona, New Mexico, and Oklahoma were required to prohibit polygamy,[31] and Nebraska was required to guarantee adult male black suffrage.[32] Congress can refuse admittance until such conditions are met, but it loses the power to impose conditions after a new state is admitted on an "equal footing" with other states. Congress, of course, retains the power to rely on its other enumerated powers to bind the states.[33]

FEDERALLY OWNED LAND IN ADMITTED STATES

The territories often have federally owned land. When those territories are admitted as states, the federal government can retain those federally owned lands. Moreover, Congress can impose conditions on the treatment of the federally owned land after a territory is admitted as a state. The courts have held that these agreements are enforceable.[34]

OPEN QUESTIONS

- Under the Resolution of Annexation, Texas has the option of creating as many as four additional states out of its territory.[35] Can Texas constitutionally possess the unilateral right of creating four additional states, or would those individual entities have to petition Congress independently as well?
- In 1863, during the Civil War, West Virginia was admitted to the Union, but that admission arguably lacked the consent of the official Virginia legislature in Richmond. Is West Virginia constitutional?[36]

Cite as: Gary S. Lawson, *The Admissions Clause, in* THE HERITAGE GUIDE TO THE CONSTITUTION 528 (Josh Blackman & John G. Malcolm eds., 3d ed. 2025).

Notes

1. Articles of Confederation, art. XI; Letter from Thomas Jefferson to James Monroe (Oct. 24, 1823), https://perma.cc/BJF9-XWUD.   **2.** 18 J. Cont. Cong. 915 (Oct. 10, 1780).   **3.** 32 J. Cont. Cong. 342 (July 13, 1787).   **4.** Peter S. Onuf, Statehood and Union: A History of the Northwest Ordinance xxx (2019).   **5.** 1 Farrand's 22.   **6.** Articles of Confederation, art. XI.   **7.** 1 Farrand's 245.   **8.** 2 Farrand's 173.   **9.** *Id.* at 454.   **10.** *Id.*   **11.** *Id.* at 461–62.   **12.** *Id.* at 462.   **13.** Storing 2.4.102.   **14.** 1 Stat. 191.   **15.** 1 Stat. 189.   **16.** Gary Lawson & Guy Seidman, The Constitution of Empire: Territorial Expansion & American Legal History 73 (2004).   **17.** *Id.* at 75.   **18.** Everett S. Brown, The Constitutional History of the Louisiana Purchase 17–29 (1920).   **19.** Lawson & Seidman, *supra*, at 75–77.   **20.** *Id.* at 77–78.   **21.** Jefferson to Monroe (Oct. 24, 1823), *supra*.   **22.** Lawson & Seidman, *supra*, at 91–94, 108–10.   **23.** 1 Stat. 189.   **24.** Act of Mar. 2, 1819, ch. XLVII, § 1, 3 Stat. 489, 490.   **25.** 44 U.S. (3 How.) 212 (1845).   **26.** *Id.* at 224.   **27.** *Coyle v. Smith,* 221 U.S. 559, 573 (1911).   **28.** Roderick M. Hills, Jr., *The Unwritten Constitution for Admitting States,* 89 Fordham L. Rev. 1877 (2021).   **29.** *PPL Montana, LLC v. Montana,* 565 U.S. 576, 591 (2012).   **30.** Eric Biber, *The Price of Admission: Causes, Effects, and Patterns of Conditions Imposed on States Entering the Union,* 46 Am. J. Leg. Hist. 119, 127–29 (2004).   **31.** *Id.* at 129–31; *Society of Separationists v. Whitehead,* 870 P.2d 916, 927–29 (Utah 1993).   **32.** 14 Stat. 391–92.   **33.** *Coyle,* 221 U.S. at 568.   **34.** *Stearns v. Minnesota,* 179 U.S. 223, 243–46 (1900).   **35.** Act of Mar. 1, 1845, § 2, 5 Stat. 797, 798.   **36.** Vasan Kesavan & Michael Stokes Paulsen, *Is West Virginia Unconstitutional?,* 90 Cal. L. Rev. 291 (2002).

~~~

ESSAY NO. 144: THE TERRITORIES CLAUSE
ART. IV, § 3, CL. 2

The Congress shall have Power to dispose of and make all needful Rules and Regulations respecting the Territory . . . belonging to the United States. . . .

—Gary S. Lawson

INTRODUCTION

The United States "is the name given to our great republic, which is composed of States and territories."[1] Today, non-state federal territories include the District of Columbia, Guam, the Virgin Islands, American Samoa, and the Commonwealths of Puerto Rico and the Northern Mariana Islands. Within the boundaries of states, the United States owns and governs more than a quarter of the country's land mass, and the Department of the Interior is one of the world's largest property managers.

Even at the Framing, the United States owned and governed a vast territory. There has long been a broad consensus that Congress can rule federal territory as a government with general rather than specifically enumerated legislative power. The Supreme Court has declared repeatedly that Congress has "general and plenary" power over federal territory.[2] Yet the Territories Clause still became among the most contentious clauses in the Constitution. The issue of territorial governance was at the heart of the Civil War and debates over imperialism.

HISTORY BEFORE 1787

Shortly after independence from England was declared, the former colonies began to plan for the expansion of the United States. In 1776, John Dickinson prepared the initial draft of the Articles of Confederation. Article 19 would have given the Continental Congress extensive power to govern new territories.[3] In 1780 and early 1781, New York, Connecticut, and Virginia granted substantial amounts of land for "the use and benefit of such of the United States, as shall become members of the federal alliance of the said states."[4] The Articles of Confederation, ratified on March 3, 1781, lacked any provision concerning governance of the territories; Dickinson's proposed Article 19 was not part of the final document. Nonetheless, no one raised any serious objections to the Confederation Congress's power to administer territory held by the United States.[5] Everyone assumed that the power must exist.

In 1784, the Confederation Congress enacted a relatively thin framework for local self-government in the territories outside the thirteen states.[6] In 1787, this framework was replaced by a more elaborate structure known as the Northwest Ordinance.[7] The new structure continued to provide for some measure of territorial self-governance, but Congress added several positions appointed by the central government, including a governor, a secretary, and a judiciary.[8] The Northwest Ordinance guaranteed to residents of the territories the rights of trial by jury, property, and contract.[9] Article VI of the Ordinance abolished slavery within the territory but also created a process for the return of runaway slaves that was a forerunner of the Fugitive Slave Clause.[10]

THE CONSTITUTIONAL CONVENTION

On August 30, 1787, Gouverneur Morris of Pennsylvania offered a proposal: "The Legislature shall have power to dispose of and make all needful rules and regulations respecting the territory or other property belonging to the U. States."[11] The provision was approved with no recorded debate.[12] Morris later privately explained that he wrote the provision to address the acquisition of a future territory such as Canada or Louisiana. In that case, "it would be proper to govern them as provinces and allow them no voice in our councils." Morris explained that "[i]n wording the third section of the fourth article, I went as far as circumstances would permit to establish the exclusion" and added that "[c]andor obliges me to add my belief, that, had it been more pointedly expressed, a strong opposition would have been made."[13]

THE RATIFICATION DEBATES

The Territories Clause was not a major issue in the ratification debates. In Federalist No. 43, James Madison observed that this clause grants "a power of very great importance, and required by considerations. . . ." A Massachusetts Anti-Federalist wrote that this provision "surrender[s] into the hands of Congress all the western territory, of larger extent I conceive than the kingdoms of Great Britain and Ireland."[14] He remarked that "so concise, and so ample a conveyance of such a[n] extent of territory, couched in such smooth and easy language I never before read." Once the Constitution was ratified, however, the Territories Clause became central to much constitutional and political discourse.

EARLY PRACTICE

The Constitution was ratified in 1788. The new United States government assumed ownership of the vast Northwest Territory, and further cessions from states were expected. Leading Founding-era figures, including Thomas Jefferson, hoped to acquire additional territory ranging from Canada to Cuba.[15] The Northwest Ordinance of 1787 promised that the Northwest Territory would eventually be formed into three to five states. Moreover, Article VI, Clause 1 of the Constitution guaranteed that the "Engagements" of the old government, such as that promise in the Ordinance, would be "valid" and "fulfilled" (See Essay No. 153). However, some provision needed to be made for the governance of this federally held territory until states were formed. Provisions were also needed for the governance of subsequently acquired federal territory.

CONGRESSIONAL CONTROL OF TERRITORIES

The Territories Clause resembles the Federal District Clause and the Federal Enclave Clause, which give Congress the power of "exclusive Legislation" over both the nation's capital and federal lands acquired from and within states (See Essay Nos. 64 and 65).[16] The Territories Clause also appears to be a plenary grant of power to Congress to govern territory as a general government. The text does not seem to require that each act of legislation must be traced to an enumeration of power beyond the Territories Clause itself. On this understanding, in the territories, Congress could pass a general criminal code, regulate the private law of torts and contracts, provide for rules of marriage and descent, and behave as any state government within its own jurisdiction could behave. This view emerges naturally from the text, which places territories in the same phrase as, and gives Congress the same power over, "other Property," such as inkwells and wagons.

One early debate concerned whether the Territories Clause applied only to territory possessed by the national government in 1788. In *Dred Scott v. Sandford* (1857), Chief Justice Roger B. Taney and a plurality of the U.S. Supreme Court expressed this view when denying that Congress had power to prohibit slavery in the subsequently acquired Louisiana Territory.[17] Albert Gallatin, President Thomas Jefferson's Secretary of the Treasury, had anticipated this argument half a century earlier. He noted that Article IV, Section 3, Clause 2 references both "Territory or other Property." Gallatin explained that "as the words 'other property' follow, and must be embraced by the same construction which will apply to the territory, it would result . . . that the United States could not, after the Constitution, either acquire or dispose of any personal property."[18] In other words, the notion that the Territories Clause does not apply to subsequently acquired territory is wholly implausible. Gallatin's view has prevailed.

Does the Constitution impose any limits on territorial legislation? The answer is obviously that it can. Congress, for example, can pass territorial legislation only by complying with the formalities of Article I, Section 7 for lawmaking. If that is true, however, one must then ask what other parts of the Constitution might also limit the reach of the Territories Clause.

The simple answer would be that *all* parts of the Constitution that limit federal power would also limit regulation of federal territories. However, while that simple answer might well be correct as a matter of original meaning, it has never been the law and is emphatically not the law today.

From the Founding onward, Congress has entrusted the inhabitants of federal territories with as much power of self-governance as has seemed prudent at the time. Congress has long authorized elected territorial legislatures to exercise broad authority. These laws created autonomous lawmaking bodies that act with no "intelligible principle" to guide them. If the Constitution's general separation-of-powers principles apply to territorial governance, this arrangement seems to violate even the weakest form of the nondelegation doctrine. Courts have nonetheless repeatedly and consistently upheld territorial legislatures against such challenges—albeit with little reasoning.[19] The Supreme Court also has held that the Constitution's requirement of uniformity for duties and tariffs throughout the United States does not apply to territories.[20] Judges in federal territories do not have the tenure and salary guarantees that Article III, Section 1 requires for federal judges. Since 1829, the courts have consistently upheld this anomaly[21] in rulings that have been subject to vigorous academic criticism.[22]

Since the middle of the twentieth century, many federal territories have been allowed to elect their own executive officers, such as governors. These elections appear to violate the Appointments Clause,[23] which requires that federal "officers of the United States" must be appointed by the President, executive department heads, or federal courts. In 2020, the Supreme Court held that territorial officials who exercise purely local functions are not federal officers subject to the Appointments Clause.[24] However, the Court did not explain what exactly those territorial officials were.[25] That holding might not extend to high-ranking territorial officials such as governors, who sometimes have authority to execute federal law and not merely territorial law. The bottom line is that for more than two centuries, territorial governance has stood largely, though not quite entirely, outside the Constitution's normal structural rules.

In some cases, the Court has sought to ground federal power to govern territories in sources other than the Territories Clause, such as the treaty power or general notions of sovereignty.[26] In practice, little has turned on these disputes, as the claimed scope of the power has not seemed to vary significantly with the claimed source. As the Court noted in 1880, "[t]here have been some differences of opinion as to the particular clause of the Constitution from which the power [to govern territory] is derived, but that it exists has always been conceded."[27]

CONSTITUTIONAL RIGHTS IN THE TERRITORIES

To what extent do protections of individual rights, such as the Bill of Rights, apply to federal governance of territories? In the early twentieth century, the United States became an empire with territories around the world, and the federal government had to decide whether to impose American legal institutions, such as trial by jury, on cultures that were unfamiliar with such practices. The Supreme Court addressed this issue in a series of cases decided over the course of two decades. These decisions, known as the *Insular Cases*, developed the "doctrine of territorial incorporation,"[28] which distinguishes territories that are likely candidates for future statehood from those that are not. For the former, all provisions of the Constitution apply of their own force to territorial inhabitants. For the latter, those provisions that are "fundamental" apply of their own force to territorial inhabitants; "non-fundamental" constitutional rights apply only if and how Congress chooses to extend them. The requirements of criminal juries and grand jury indictment have been deemed specifically *not* to be fundamental in this sense.

This doctrine has been universally criticized by scholars but has never been overruled. The Court cited the doctrine approvingly in *Boumediene v. Bush* (2008),[29] declaring that this "century-old doctrine informs our analysis in the present matter."[30] In *United States v. Vaello Madero* (2020), the Court declined an invitation to reconsider the doctrine, although Justice Neil Gorsuch vigorously urged its overruling in an appropriate case.[31]

Moreover, the courts have applied federal equal protection principles differently to inhabitants of territories. Courts have upheld, for example, race-based employment preferences and restrictions on land sales in territories.[32] Such regimes would likely be unconstitutional if imposed in states. *Vaello Madero* clarified that congressional distinctions between territorial and non-territorial residents need only satisfy a rational basis standard.[33] Thus, under current doctrine, the Constitution does not apply to territorial governance in a straightforward, uniform, and easily understood fashion.

PRESIDENTIAL POWER OVER THE TERRITORIES

What are the President's authorities in the territories? During times of war, American forces will sometimes occupy foreign land. Under international law principles, an occupying force has both the power and the duty to govern the occupied territory. However, the Territories Clause only empowers Congress to legislate over territory that "belong[s] to the United States," and occupied territory does not belong to the United States. Therefore, the clause does not authorize congressional legislation to govern occupied territory. Instead, the power to govern occupied territory during wartime stems from the President's "executive Power" and role as commander-in-chief of the military.[34]

Territorial governance in that setting is both part of and limited by the international laws of war.[35] It is unsettled whether Congress could take part in that governance pursuant to its own war powers or the Necessary and Proper Clause. In the past, some occupied territories were conveyed to the United States pursuant to a treaty of peace, thereby becoming "Territory . . . belonging to the United States." At that point, the President's wartime powers of governance seem to end and Congress's power to govern under the Territories Clause seems to begin. But what if Congress does not get around to governing?

This sequence of events occurred with respect to California in 1848 following the Mexican–American War. Congress, largely because of gridlock over slavery, did not pass a statute for the governance of California—not even a general statute delegating authority to executive officials. Military officials in California nonetheless, and with no congressional authorization, set up a peacetime military government that included customs offices to collect tariffs. *Cross v. Harrison* (1854) upheld the constitutionality of a peacetime military government in federal territory.[36] That precedent was extended following the Spanish–American War.[37] The precise scope of this presidential authority to erect military governments during peacetime has yet to be fully explored.

OPEN QUESTIONS

- Are the *Insular Cases* still good law?
- Do any structural provisions other than Article I, Section 7 limit Congress's power over territories?
- Can the United States maintain and govern territory indefinitely without making the territory a state or granting it independence? Can the United States unilaterally grant a territory independence without the territory's consent?

- Does United States governance of territories such as Puerto Rico violate international law?[38]

Cite as: Gary S. Lawson, *The Territories Clause, in* The Heritage Guide to the Constitution 531 (Josh Blackman & John G. Malcolm eds., 3d ed. 2025).

Notes

1. *Loughborough v. Blake*, 18 U.S. (5 Wheat.) 317, 319 (1820). **2.** *Late Corp. of the Church of Jesus Christ of Latter-Day Saints v. United States*, 136 U.S. 1, 42 (1890). **3.** 4 Letters of Delegates to Congress, 1774–1789, at 243 (Paul H. Smith ed., 1979). **4.** 19 J. Cont. Cong. 211 (Mar. 7, 1781); Gary Lawson & Guy Seidman, *Are People in Federal Territories Part of "We the People of the United States"?*, 9 Tex. A. & M. L. Rev. 655, 668 (2022). **5.** James G. Wilson, The Imperial Republic: A Structural History of American Constitutionalism from the Colonial Era to the Beginning of the Twentieth Century 73 (2002). **6.** 26 J. Cont. Cong. 276 (Apr. 23, 1784). **7.** Ordinance for the government of the territory of the United States, North West of the river Ohio, 32 J. Cont. Cong. 334 (July 13, 1787). **8.** Gregory Ablavsky, *Administrative Constitutionalism and the Northwest Ordinance*, 167 U. Pa. L. Rev. 1631, 1633 (2019). **9.** 32 J. Cont. Cong. 340 (July 13, 1787). **10.** Steven Gow Calabresi & Gary Lawson, The U.S. Constitution: Creation, Reconstruction, the Progressives, and the Modern Era 913–14 (2020). **11.** 2 Farrand's 466. **12.** *Id.* at 459. **13.** 3 Farrand's 404. **14.** Storing 4.2.6. **15.** Letter from Thomas Jefferson to President James Madison (Apr. 27, 1809), https://perma.cc/8A32-YSS6. **16.** Art. I, § 8, cl. 17. **17.** *Dred Scott v. Sandford*, 60 U.S. (19 How.) 393, 432–43, 448–49 (1857). **18.** Letter from Albert Gallatin to Thomas Jefferson (Jan. 13, 1803), https://perma.cc/KE57-XQUJ. **19.** *District of Columbia v. John R. Thompson Co.*, 346 U.S. 100, 106–09 (1953); *Cincinnati Soap Co. v. United States*, 301 U.S. 308, 323 (1937). **20.** *Downes v. Bidwell*, 182 U.S. 244 (1901). **21.** *Am. Ins. Co. v. 356 Bales of Cotton, Canter*, 26 U.S. (1 Pet.) 511 (1828). **22.** Gary Lawson & Guy Seidman, The Constitution of Empire: Territorial Expansion and American Legal History 149 & n.45 (2004). **23.** Art. II, § 2, cl. 2. **24.** *Fin. Oversight & Mgmt. Bd. for P.R. v. Aurelius Inv., LLC*, 590 U.S. 448 (2020). **25.** Seth Barrett Tillman & Josh Blackman, *Offices and Officers of the Constitution, Part III: The Appointments, Impeachment, Commissions, and Oath or Affirmation Clauses*, 62 S. Tex. L. Rev. 349, 410–12 (2023). **26.** *Sere v. Pitot*, 10 U.S. (6 Cranch) 332, 336–37 (1810). **27.** *National Bank v. Cnty. of Yankton*, 101 U.S. 129, 132 (1880). **28.** *Balzac v. Porto Rico*, 258 U.S. 298 (1922). **29.** 553 U.S. 723 (2008). **30.** *Id.* at 759. **31.** *United States v. Vaello Madero*, 142 U.S. 1539, 1552 (2022) (Gorsuch, J., concurring). **32.** *Wabol v. Villacrusis*, 958 F.2d 1450 (9th Cir. 1992). **33.** *Vaello Madero*, 142 U.S. at 1542–43. **34.** Art. II, § 2, cl. 1. **35.** *Fleming v. Page*, 50 U.S. (9 How.) 603 (1850). **36.** 57 U.S. (16 How.) 164 (1854). **37.** *Santiago v. Nogueras*, 214 U.S. 260 (1909). **38.** Gary Lawson & Robert D. Sloane, *The Constitutionality of Decolonization by Associated Statehood: Puerto Rico's Legal Status Reconsidered*, 50 B.C. L. Rev. 1123 (2009).

ESSAY NO. 145: THE PROPERTY CLAUSE
ART. IV, § 3, CL. 2

The Congress shall have Power to dispose of and make all needful Rules and Regulations respecting . . . other Property belonging to the United States. . . .

—Judge Ryan T. Holte

INTRODUCTION

The original meaning of the Property Clause grants the federal government power to hold and dispose of land. At the time, dispose meant to manage or govern the land, but the clause did not grant unlimited power to retain and keep property in perpetuity. This view of land disposal changed as the country expanded west. Today, the federal government owns roughly twenty-eight percent of the United States: 640 million acres of land with fifty-six percent of those acres in only eleven contiguous western states.[1] This essay contrasts the federal government's original grant of power to hold and dispose of property with its contemporary practice of retaining property.

HISTORY BEFORE 1787

Before the Revolution, some (but not all) colonial charters gave large expanses of land to colonies. After 1776, debates arose surrounding the title, governance, management, and disposal of the western lands claimed by several of the original states. The states with land wanted to retain it, and the landless states argued the colonial charters should instruct the federal government to hold the land for the benefit of all.[2] In *Fletcher v. Peck* (1810), Chief Justice John Marshall wrote this "momentous question . . . threatened to shake the American confederacy."[3] Indeed, these disputes nearly halted ratification of the Articles of Confederation.

In 1780, the Continental Congress attempted to reconcile these disputes. Congress first urged colonies to cede their lands to the United States. Congress next issued a resolution recommending "the unappropriated lands that may be ceded or relinquished to the United States, by any particular states . . . shall be disposed of for the common benefit of the United States."[4] On March 1, 1781, the day the Articles of Confederation went into effect, some states ceded their "western lands" to the United States to act as an "impartial arbiter" over land disputes.[5] The central government then disposed of the majority of the ceded lands through privatization. These sales generated revenue to pay war debts and the expenses of the budding nation.

In 1787, at around the same time the Framers were drafting the Constitution, Congress passed the Northwest Ordinance to govern the land northwest of the Ohio River. The Ordinance facilitated additional land transfers to the United States, created the first federal territory, and established a legislative framework for creating new states.[6] The Ordinance provided: new states would be on an equal footing with the original states; Congress would have a limited governing role over federal land after statehood; and states were prohibited from interfering with federal regulations "necessary for securing title."[7] In a letter to George Washington, Richard Henry Lee explained the Northwest Ordinance was seen as "preparatory to the sale of the lands."[8]

THE CONSTITUTIONAL CONVENTION

On August 18, 1787, the Constitutional Convention referred to the Committee of Detail a list of powers for the legislature, including the power to "dispose of the unappropriated lands of the U. States."[9] On August 30, 1787, Gouverneur Morris of Pennsylvania recommended the Convention consider somewhat different language: "The Legislature shall have the power to dispose of and make all needful rules and regulations respecting the territory or other property belonging to the U. States."[10] This motion was agreed to with only Maryland dissenting.[11] With these changes, the provision gave Congress authority to dispose of or sell property, but not to retain or hold property.

The placement of the Property Clause also provides context to its meaning. The Framers situated the Property Clause in the same provision of Article IV as the Territories Clause, which grants the federal government power over its territories. (See Essay No. 144.) The Clause further follows the Admissions Clause, which requires the consent of both Congress and a ceding state to create a new state from the ceding state's property.[12] (See Essay No. 143.) Finally, the phrase "all needful rules and regulations" mirrors the language of the Necessary and Proper Clause, which gives Congress broader incidental powers.[13] (See Essay No. 66.) Relatedly, the Federal Enclave Clause authorizes federal land ownership within a state only after the state consents to the "Erection of Forts, Magazines, Arsenals, dock-Yards, and other needful Buildings" in furtherance of an enumerated power. (See Essay No. 65.) The Property Clause, read within the broad constitutional structure, therefore gives the federal government power to manage and dispose of acquired property within the boundaries of a state. As Professor Robert Natelson has noted, "'other Property' was land within the boundaries of a state, owned by the federal government."[14]

The Property Clause was initially introduced to permit land ownership with limited control by the federal government. By design, the federal government then served as an "impartial arbiter" to dispose of unappropriated lands within new states. There would now be an express enumerated power that both the Northwest Ordinance and Articles of Confederation lacked.[15]

THE RATIFICATION DEBATES

In Federalist No. 7, Alexander Hamilton observed "[t]erritorial disputes have at all times been found one of the most fertile sources of hostility among nations." In Federalist No. 38, Madison remarked the Northwest Ordinance governed territories "without the least colour of constitutional authority" under the Articles of Confederation. The Ordinance also did not resolve territorial disputes between the states free from federal control of public lands.

But the Property Clause had well-understood limits. Post-ratification correspondences confirm the federal government's power under the clause is directed to the disposal of property.[16] In a May 17, 1788, letter, Madison observed "the establishment of the new Govt. will thus promote the sale of public lands."[17] Madison's letter suggests the federal government would permanently hold land under the Federal Enclave Clause only with the express permission of a state. Indeed, in 1803, Gouverneur Morris noted he originally wished to write the Property Clause to allow future acquisitions of land—such as Canada and Louisiana—to be held in perpetuity as federal provinces.[18] Morris's disappointment suggests the Framers' final language did not permit the Property Clause to empower permanent land ownership by the federal government unless explicitly enumerated in the Constitution—especially given the Founder's skepticism toward the new federal government.[19]

EARLY PRACTICE
As the United States grew in square miles and added new states, disputes arose regarding the title to "unappropriated lands." This history further reflects the original understanding that the Clause never included permanent federal ownership.[20]

In 1790, for example, North Carolina ceded land to the federal government. This land became part of the Southwest Territory and later, in 1796, the State of Tennessee.[21] But there were questions about ownership of the public land in Tennessee: did it belong to the new state, or did Congress retain ownership? In 1796, Tennessee Governor John Sevier wrote to Tennessee Representative Andrew Jackson arguing that without title to the underlying unappropriated land of Tennessee, "we should not equally stand possessed of those free and independent rights the original States enjoy."[22] Jackson agreed ongoing federal land ownership was inconsistent with state equality, writing "the right to the Soil" was "firmly invested in the sovereignty of the State."[23] Later in 1796,

Tennessee declared Congress had no claim to the unappropriated lands, as the acts of admission reserved none.[24]

In 1800, a congressional committee appointed to investigate Tennessee's land claims reported that the regulatory power was ceded to the state, but the title to the land in Tennessee remained with the federal government.[25] Speculators and squatters' rights, however, were already facts of life in the land the federal government retained, making the congressional report effectively meaningless. In 1833, President Andrew Jackson vetoed a bill that "failed to recognize the necessity of permanent disposals of federal public land holdings."[26] Jackson's veto message reaffirmed the federal government was obligated to "dispose[] of [the public lands] for the common benefit of the United States, according to the compacts of cession," and the "remaining unsold [land] shall be abandoned to the States and the machinery of our [federal] land system entirely withdrawn."[27] In 1841, Congress made Tennessee the agent for management and disposal of the land.[28]

JUDICIAL PRECEDENT
Early U.S. Supreme Court cases emphasized the Property Clause's disposal power. *Mayor of New Orleans v. United States* (1836) ruled the treaty ceding the Louisiana Purchase to the United States from France did not authorize the federal government to gain title to and dispose of land claimed by the city of New Orleans.[29] This decision was silent on the federal government's permanent retention of public land under the Property Clause. Instead, early cases emphasized the federal government's temporarily held "power to dispose of" land.

United States v. Gratiot (1840) ruled the Property Clause permits some federal management of public lands for national purposes.[30] The Supreme Court's broader interpretation of the Property Clause justified the government's retention and leasing—not just sale and preparation for sale—of public land.[31] *Pollard v. Hagan* (1845) demonstrated a more limited interpretation of congressional power over federal land within the states.[32] Its holding applied to the ownership of land under navigable waters. Later water-rights cases refused to extend *Pollard* to dry land.[33]

Irvine v. Marshall (1857) and *Gibson v. Chouteau* (1871) reflect a state's inability to interfere with the federal government's disposal power.[34] *Irvine* signified broad authority for the federal government over its property in the territories "to be disposed of . . . as the government may deem most advantageous to the public."[35] By contrast, states are constrained from "interfer[ing] with the government while it owns the public lands or in the legally effective transfer of such lands."[36] In *Gibson*, the Court reasoned any measure a state takes to deprive the transferee of "the right to possess and enjoy the land" constitutes "a denial of the power of disposal in Congress."[37] *Gibson* was more emphatic than *Irvine*, stating that Congress's power to control and dispose of property was "subject to no limitations."[38] Neither case mentions retention powers—only disposal powers.

Camfield v. United States (1897) was a first step in a growing and more expansive view of the federal government's property power. As the Court explained, "[t]he general government doubtless has a power over its own property analogous to the police power of the several States," and a "different rule would place the public domain of the United States completely at the mercy of state legislation."[39] *Camfield* affirmed Congress's broad power as a proprietor, allowing the federal government to

prohibit—and directly punish—trespassing on federal land. Congress could also police conduct on private land when that conduct directly interferes with the federal government's property rights. The Court recognized "[t]he government has the same right to insist upon its proprietorship of [its property] that an individual has to claim [their property]."[40]

The leading modern case is *Kleppe v. New Mexico* (1976),[41] which deviates from the original meaning of the Constitution. The dispute related only to wild burro management on public lands, but the *Kleppe* Court applied the Property Clause broadly to give Congress extensive power over public lands—irrespective of disposal, retention, or use of the lands— "without limitation."[42] The Court expanded the general scope of the Property Clause.[43] Contrary to the Property Clause's original meaning, courts have unjustifiably given this dictum undue weight.

Four months after *Kleppe*, Congress passed the Federal Land Policy and Management Act of 1976 ("FLPMA"). This statute declared "public lands [will] be retained in Federal ownership, unless it is determined that disposal of a particular parcel will serve the national interest."[44] The FLPMA radically shifted public land policy and effectively repealed older public land disposal laws.

OPEN QUESTIONS

- Under modern precedent, the Supreme Court reads the Property Clause broadly to allow the Federal government unlimited disposal and control of property, but it has yet to address any limitations on retention of federal land. The State of Utah challenged the perpetual federal retention of unappropriated lands under the FLPMA as unconstitutional—seeking 18.5 million acres of land currently managed by the Bureau of Land Management with no designated federal purpose. While the Supreme Court denied the original jurisdiction case in 2025, the State of Utah has already commented on other legal options.[45] Will a future Utah land case, or another similar case, elicit a review of the Framers' original understanding of constraints on federal property retention when land is not used in service of an enumerated power, and potentially reintroduce prohibitions on retention of land "without limitation"?

Cite as: Judge Ryan T. Holte, *The Property Clause, in* THE HERITAGE GUIDE TO THE CONSTITUTION 535 (Josh Blackman & John G. Malcolm eds., 3d ed. 2025).

Notes

1. Carol H. Vincent & Laura A. Hanson, Cong. Rsrch. Serv., R42346, Federal Land Ownership: Overview and Data 1, 20 (2020). **2.** Gary Lawson & Guy Seidman, *The American Experience with Territorial Governance, in* EU Law of the Overseas: Outermost Regions, Associated Overseas Countries and Territories, Territories Sui Generis 417 (Dimitry Kochenov ed., 2011). **3.** 10 U.S. 87, 142 (1810); Paul W. Gates, History of Public Land Law Development 49–51, 59–73 (1987). **4.** 18 J. Cont. Cong. 915 (Oct. 10, 1780). **5.** Andrew Jackson, Veto Message of December 4, 1833, *in* 3 A Compilation of the Messages and Papers of the Presidents 57–58 (James D. Richardson ed., 1911); Donald J. Kochan, *Public Lands and the Federal Government's Compact-Based "Duty to Dispose": A Case Study of Utah's H.B. 148—The Transfer of Public Lands Act,* 2013 B.Y.U. L. Rev. 1133, 1153–1157 (2014). **6.** Gregory Ablavsky, *The Rise of Federal Title,* 106 Cal. L. Rev. 631, 643–44 (2018). **7.** *Id.* at 644; Jeffrey M. Schmitt, *Limiting the Property Clause,* 20 Nev. L. Rev. 145 (2019). **8.** *Letter from Richard Henry Lee to George Washington (July 15, 1787), in* The Papers of George Washington, at 258–60 (W.W. Abbott ed., 1st ed. 1997); *Letter from Richard Henry Lee to George Washington (Oct. 11, 1787), in id.,* at 370–71. **9.** 2 Farrand's 321, 324. **10.** *Id.* at 466; Gates, *supra* at 73–74. **11.** 2 Farrand's 466; Gates, *supra* at 74. **12.** Art. IV, § 3, cls. 1, 2; Eric Biber, *The Property Clause, Article IV, and Constitutional Structure,* 71 Emory L. J. 739, 756–61 (2022). **13.** Robert G. Natelson, *Federal Land Retention and the Constitution's Property Clause: The Original Understanding,* 76 U. Colo. L. Rev. 327, 348 (2005). **14.** *Id.* at 359. **15.** Kochan *supra* at 1155 n.91; Biber, *supra* at 771. **16.** Kochan, *supra* at 1159–67.

17. Letter from James Madison to George Nicholas (May 17, 1788), https://perma.cc/42E7-5KZ5. **18.** 3 Farrand's 404; Gates, *supra* at 74; Natelson, *supra* at 368; William Michael Treanor, *The Case of the Dishonest Scrivener: Gouverneur Morris and the Creation of the Federalist Constitution,* 120 Mich L. Rev. 1, 14–15 (2021). **19.** *Id.* **20.** Schmitt, *supra* at 159. **21.** Samuel C. Williams, *The Admission of Tennessee into the Union,* 4 Tenn. Hist. Q., at 291, 293, 303, 309, 312 (1945); Act of Apr. 2, 1790, 1 Stat. 106; Southwest Ordinance, 1 Stat. 123 (1790). **22.** Letter from John Sevier to Andrew Jackson (Dec. 12, 1796), *in* 1 The Papers of Andrew Jackson 102 (Sam B. Smith & Harriet Chappell Owsley eds., 1980). **23.** Letter from Andrew Jackson to John Sevier (Jan. 18, 1797), *in id.* at 116–118. **24.** Gates, *supra* at 54. **25.** H.R. Rep. No. 6-57 at 97–99 (1800). **26.** Kochan, *supra* at 1163. **27.** Jackson, *supra* at 68; Kochan, *supra* at 1163–65. **28.** Gates, *supra* at 54. **29.** 35 U.S. 662, 662 (1836). **30.** 39 U.S. 526, 538–39 (1840). **31.** 39 U.S. at 534; Kochan, *supra* at 1173. **32.** 44 U.S. 212, 220, 224 (1845). **33.** *Scott v. Lattig,* 227 U.S. 229, 244 (1913); *Texas v. Louisiana,* 410 U.S. 702, 713 (1973); *Arizona v. California,* 373 U.S. 546, 597–98 (1963). **34.** 61 U.S. 558 (1857); 80 U.S. 92 (1871). **35.** 61 U.S. 558, 561–62 (1857). **36.** Kochan, *supra* at 1175 (citing *Irvine,* 61 U.S. at 561–62). **37.** 80 U.S. at 100. **38.** *Id.* at 99. **39.** 167 U.S. 518, 525–26 (1897). **40.** *Id.* at 526. **41.** 426 U.S. 529, 539 (1976). **42.** *Id.* **43.** David E. Engdahl, *State and Federal Power over Federal Property,* 18 Ariz. L. Rev. 283, 349–58 (1976). **44.** 43 U.S.C. § 1701(a)(1). **45.** Press Release (Jan. 13, 2025), https://perma.cc/9FTB-U982.

~

ESSAY NO. 146: THE CLAIMS CLAUSE
ART. IV, § 3, CL. 2

. . . [A]nd nothing in this Constitution shall be so construed as to Prejudice any Claims of the United States, or of any particular State.

—Zack Smith

INTRODUCTION

Despite its relative obscurity, the Claims Clause played a crucial role in securing ratification of the Constitution. Land grants by the English monarchs that were less than clear yielded much uncertainty and acrimony. Moreover, there were claims to these same lands by other nations and tribes. The Claims Clause maintained the status quo for western land claims until they could be resolved through the political process or litigation. From ratification until the early twentieth century, the Claims Clause laid dormant. However, it briefly appeared in arguments about the United States granting independence to territories and could make such an appearance again in the future.

HISTORY BEFORE 1787

In 1496, King Henry VII of England granted permission for John Cabot to settle the New World.[1] This decision set off a chain of events with which the Framers of the U.S. Constitution would still be grappling over two centuries later. In those interim years, England would establish thirteen American colonies. Many English settlers laid claim to broad swaths of the unexplored North

American continent. In fact, the land grants provided to seven of the thirteen colonies purportedly gave them control of the land "from sea to sea" within certain definite parallels of latitude.[2] At the time, it was unknown exactly where the Americas met the Pacific Ocean. Spain, France, and various Indian tribes asserted competing claims to many of these same lands, particularly those west of the Appalachian Mountains. The colonies also squabbled among themselves about competing boundary lines that resulted from claims that were less than clear and sometimes overlapping.

After 1776, matters became only more muddied and contentious. Large states like Virginia, North Carolina, and Georgia laid claim to broad tracts of western land, but smaller states had no western land claims; Maryland in particular feared that the large states would use their reserves of western land to increase their own power and prestige at the expense of the smaller states.[3] Maryland refused to ratify the Articles of Confederation until Virginia and other states with western land claims had ceded those claims to the new national government to be used for the benefit of the new nation as a whole.[4] Many states with land claims did cede them, but some did not, and even those that did cede their western claims often did not cede all of them and attached certain conditions for the disposition of the portions they did cede.[5] The 1783 Treaty of Paris formally ended the American Revolution, and Great Britain relinquished its claim to much of the land west of the Appalachian Mountains.[6] However, the treaty did not resolve the competing land claims between and among the new national government and the various states.

THE CONSTITUTIONAL CONVENTION

The disputes over land claims threatened to derail the Constitutional Convention. In fact, the larger states threatened to walk out of the Convention because of suggestions that they could be divided without their consent.[7] On August 30, Luther Martin of Maryland said that it was unreasonable to require the small states to guarantee the western land claims of the large states. Martin argued that small states would also walk out of the Convention unless a reasonable resolution was reached regarding

the land issue.[8] Fortunately, Daniel Carroll, also of Maryland, proposed compromise language. His proposal stated that "nothing in this Constitution shall be construed to affect the claim of the U.S. to vacant lands ceded to them by the [1783] Treaty of peace."[9] In other words, the Constitution would be silent about the status of these lands.

Some delegates, such as James Wilson of Pennsylvania, opposed this addition as unnecessary.[10] James Madison of Virginia generally agreed that the Constitution did not need to say anything on the matter, but he did not see the harm in adding this language as long as it was "neutral and fair" and made clear that "the claims of particular states also should not be affected" by the Constitution.[11] Some versions of this clause proposed later made clear that the U.S. Supreme Court should examine "all such claims," an addition that the delegates rejected as unnecessary.[12] The Convention settled on language that removed any reference to the Treaty of Paris.[13] The Committee of Style shaped the final version of the clause that made its way into the Constitution.[14]

The Constitution would not "prejudice" or affect any claim that the United States or an individual state might have to western land. This provision would simply maintain the status quo until each claim was resolved through political or legal processes. According to Professor Michael Stokes Paulsen, this clause is one of the Constitution's "rule-of-construction" provisions and makes clear "what not to infer from what [has] just been said" preceding it.[15]

RATIFICATION DEBATES

In Federalist No. 43, Madison argued that the Claims Clause "is proper in itself, and was probably rendered absolutely necessary by jealousies and questions concerning the Western territory sufficiently known to the public." In Federalist No. 7, Alexander Hamilton admitted that the "discordant and undecided claims" related to the "vast tract of unsettled territory within the boundaries of the United States" had caused controversy. So far, however, it had "been the prudent policy of Congress to appease this controversy, by prevailing upon the States to make cessions to the United States for the benefit of the whole."

At the state ratifying conventions, debates erupted over what the appropriate disposition of the western lands should be, but there were no extended discussions about the Claims Clause.

COMMENTARY

Well after ratification, commentators recognized the importance of the Claims Clause. In 1833, Justice Joseph Story observed that the disposition of western lands proved to be the "subject of long and ardent controversy."[16] In 1880, Thomas Cooley wrote that under the Claims Clause, "some [claims] were recognized and some disputed, but all . . . were subsequently adjusted amicably."[17] As intended, the Claims Clause maintained the status quo until the competing claims could be resolved through either the political process or litigation.

OPEN QUESTIONS

The Claims Clause has spawned no notable litigation, but it did receive fleeting attention in the early twentieth century. At the time, the United States considered granting independence to the Philippines, a territory it had acquired following the Spanish-American War.

Some legal commentators argued that this proviso prohibited the United States from granting independence to any territory once it had been acquired because doing so would "prejudice" the beneficial interests each state enjoyed in that territory. Independence could be granted only if each state consented to that disposition.[18] Others argued against this reading of the clause, and subsequent practice proved this "prejudice" argument to be a nonstarter.[19] If the United States were ever to consider granting independence to any of its remaining territories, this argument could be raised.

Cite as: Zack Smith, *The Claims Clause*, *in* THE HERITAGE GUIDE TO THE CONSTITUTION 539 (Josh Blackman & John G. Malcolm eds., 3d ed. 2025).

Notes

1. *Johnson v. M'Intosh*, 21 U.S. (8 Wheat.) 543, 576 (1823); 1 Story's Commentaries § 1.   **2.** Paul W. Gates, History of Public Law Land Development 49 (1968).   **3.** *Id.* at 49–58.   **4.** *Id.* at 50.   **5.** *Id.* at 49–58.   **6.** Definitive Treaty of Peace Between the United States of America and His Britannic Majesty, Sept. 3, 1783, 8 Stat. 80.   **7.** 2 Farrand's 464.   **8.** *Id.*   **9.** *Id.* at 465.   **10.** *Id.*   **11.** *Id.*   **12.** *Id.* at 466.   **13.** *Id.*   **14.** *Id.* at 459, 578.   **15.** Michael Stokes Paulsen, *Does the Constitution Prescribe Rules for its Own Interpretation?*, 103 Nw. U. L. Rev. 857, 891 (2009).   **16.** 3 Story's Commentaries §§ 1308–1315.   **17.** Thomas Cooley, General Principles of Constitutional Law in the United States of America 168 (1880).   **18.** F. Harold Smith, *Correspondence: The Right of Congress to Grant Philippines Sovereign Independence*, 19 Ill. L.R. 339, 342–43 (1924–1925).   **19.** Vincente G. Sinco, *The Power of Congress to Relinquish Sovereignty over the Philippines (Concluded)*, 7 Phil. L. J. 60, 70–71 (1927).

⌒〜〜

ESSAY NO. 147: THE GUARANTEE CLAUSE
ART. IV, § 4

The United States shall guarantee to every State in this Union a Republican Form of Government, and shall protect each of them against Invasion; and on Application of the Legislature, or of the Executive (when the Legislature cannot be convened), against domestic Violence.

—Robert G. Natelson

INTRODUCTION

Through the Guarantee Clause, the federal government provides three guarantees to the states: to ensure that every state in the Union has a "Republican Form of Government"; to protect each state against foreign invasion; and, under specified conditions, to protect each state "against domestic Violence." These guarantees necessarily imply that the federal government has sufficient grants of authority to execute these mandates. Generally, the Constitution grants power to individual assemblies such as the House of Representatives or officers like the President, but the Guarantee Clause grants authority directly to the federal government as an entity. The federal courts have declined to review cases involving whether a state has a "Republican Form of Government," and the justiciability of the clause's other protections remains unresolved.

HISTORY BEFORE 1787

The requirement that all states must be republican is traceable to lessons learned from Greek historians who were standard schoolbook fare for the Founding generation. Their discussions of the Achaean and Amphictyonic Leagues—Hellenistic-era Greek confederacies—taught that monarchical members tended to undermine their republican federal partners.

The Founding generation seems to have recognized that republics could be aristocratic as well as democratic in nature. Founders like John Adams were familiar with a number of aristocratic republics, including the Roman, Dutch, and Venetian republics.[1] Baron Montesquieu—an authority cited more often during the constitutional debates than any other—accordingly divided republics into aristocratic and democratic categories: "When the body of the people is possessed of the supreme power, it is called a *democracy*. When the supreme power is lodged in the hands of a part of the people, it is then an *aristocracy*."[2]

During the Revolutionary War, the Continental and Confederation Congresses undertook the defense of the states. The Articles of Confederation codified a duty to defend the states: "States . . . enter into a firm league of friendship with each other, for their common defense . . . binding themselves to assist each other, against all force offered to, or attacks made upon them. . . ."[3] This provision was the immediate predecessor of the Guarantee Clause. However, the Articles did not include a "Republican Form of Government" mandate.

THE CONSTITUTIONAL CONVENTION

The Guarantee Clause emerged from the earliest days of the Constitutional Convention. On May 29, 1787, Governor Edmund Randolph's Virginia Plan provided that "a Republican Government & the territory of each State . . . ought to be guaranteed by the United States to each State."[4]

On June 11, James Madison of Virginia proposed an amendment: "[A] republican constitution, and its existing laws ought to be guaranteed to each State by the U. States."[5] Randolph supported the change "because a republican government must be the basis of our national union; and no state in it ought to have it in their power to change its government into a monarchy."[6] This new form was adopted unanimously.[7]

On July 18, however, this provision became the subject of sharp discussion. Gouverneur Morris of Pennsylvania objected to the notion that "such laws as exist in R[hode] Island should be guaranteid."[8] Morris did not want the federal government to guarantee Rhode Island's government, which was one of which he and other delegates strongly disapproved.

George Mason of Virginia insisted that in the event of rebellions, a federal response would be necessary. "[I]t will be a bad situation indeed," Mason said, if the "Genl Govt should have no right to suppress rebellions agst. Particular States."[9] On the motion of James Wilson of Pennsylvania, the language was changed to "That a republican form of Government shall be guaranteed to each State—and that each State shall be protected against foreign and domestic violence."[10] According to Madison, Wilson's proposal was "well received," and it passed unanimously.[11]

The Committee of Detail further reworked the language: "The United States shall guaranty to each State a Republican form of Government; and shall protect each State against foreign invasions, and, on the application of its Legislature, against domestic violence."[12] The Committee added an enumerated power of Congress "to subdue a Rebellion in any State, on the Application of its Legislature."[13] The Convention did not adopt this enumerated power, perhaps because it was superfluous.

On August 30, the delegates debated whether approval of a state legislature should be required before the federal government could quash domestic violence. John Dickinson of Delaware observed that the rebellion "might hinder the Legislature from meeting."[14] He proposed that a legislative request was sufficient, but if the legislature could not be convened, the state executive could make the request.[15] The Convention approved this proposal.

However, the Committee of Style altered that process. Its draft granted the executive the unconditional power to apply for federal assistance even if the legislature was available.[16] On September 15, two days before the Constitution would be signed, the Convention reversed this change.[17] The final clause provided that "[t]he United States shall guarantee to every State in this Union a Republican Form of Government, and shall protect each of them against Invasion; and on Application of the Legislature, or of the Executive (when the Legislature cannot be convened), against domestic Violence."

THE RATIFICATION DEBATES

During the ratification debates, the Guarantee Clause was not especially controversial. Madison explained its purpose in Federalist No. 43: "In a confederacy founded on republican principles, and composed of republican members, the superintending government ought clearly to possess authority to defend the system against aristocratic or monarchial innovations." Madison added that "[w]henever the States may choose to substitute other republican forms, they have a right to do so, and to claim the federal guaranty for the latter."

In Federalist No. 63, Madison referred to democratic states such as the Athenian democracy interchangeably as democracies or as "republics." Alexander Hamilton used similar terminology in Federalist No. 9. The Founders also referred generally to the American states as democracies as well as republics.[18] In Federalist No. 10, Madison distinguished a "republic" from a "pure democracy." Madison was not suggesting that *all* institutions of direct democracy were inconsistent with a republic; rather, he was apparently criticizing Aristotle's *teleutaia demokratia*. This extreme, or ultimate democracy, was a theoretical form of mob rule that

was unrepublican because it did not respect the rule of law.

Founding-era dictionaries defined the noun *republic* as "a commonwealth, a free state,"[19] or "a state or government in which the supreme power is lodged in more than one."[20] Dictionaries defined the adjective *republican* as "placing the government in the people."[21] With some refinements, the Founders' consensus understanding of the "Republican Form" is consistent with these definitions. In general, they viewed a republic as a state (1) responsible to its citizenry, (2) without a king, and (3) that respected the rule of law.[22] John Adams was seemingly alone among the Founders in considering Great Britain's limited monarchy to be a "republic" because one branch of the British government, the House of Commons, represented the people.

The guarantee of republican government was widely understood as a guard against monarchy. *A Citizen and Soldier,* an anonymous pamphlet published in North Carolina, observed that under the Constitution, a state "could not alter its republican form of government to a monarchy."[23] Another anonymous essay from Plain Truth in the *Philadelphia Independent Gazetteer* observed that the Constitution "shall guarantee [to every state] against monarchical or aristocratical encroachments."[24]

The Constitution's opponents raised a few complaints. Silas Lee of Massachusetts, for example, warned that the Guarantee Clause might empower the federal government to "establish one [particular] republican form, such as they shall chuse, throughout the whole [nation]."[25] The more common objection was that the Guarantee Clause did not go far enough to prohibit aristocracies. Hampden, an Anti-Federalist from Pennsylvania, warned that "under aristocratical republics, there is often less personal freedom and political importance enjoyed by the people at large than under despotic forms . . . ."[26] Agrippa, another anti-Federalist, wrote to the Massachusetts ratification convention that "It is vain to tell us, that the proposed government guarantees to each state a republican form. Republicks are divided into democraticks, and aristocraticks."[27]

Other objections were raised with respect to the Guarantee Clause's scope. During the

New York ratifying convention, John Lansing, Jr., complained that the guarantee of republican government applied only to the states but should also extend to "the Jurisdiction of the Genl Govt." and federal enclaves.[28]

WHAT IS AN INVASION?

Founding-era dictionaries defined "invasion" as "a descent upon a country, an [sic] usurpation, or encroachment."[29] This definition seems to include both formal military operations and peaceful, although unauthorized, in-migrations. Eighteenth-century English usage seems to confirm this definition. For example, before the Constitution's adoption, both Benjamin Franklin and the Pennsylvania legislature referred to peaceful but unauthorized immigration of Connecticut settlers into Pennsylvania as an "invasion."[30] Nevertheless, some commentators have argued that the term "invasion" refers only to formal military operations.[31]

JUDICIAL PRECEDENT

There is not much federal case law on the Guarantee Clause.[32] *Luther v. Borden* (1849) declared that whether a state government has been established and whether it is republican in form are political questions for Congress to decide. In other words, these claims were not *justiciable* issues for the courts to resolve.[33] *Minor v. Happersett* (1874) deviated from this rule, holding that a republican form of government could deny women the right to vote.[34] Apart from that precedent, the Supreme Court has continued to adhere to its non-justiciability position even though the history has not been unambiguous.[35]

In *Kerr v. Hickenlooper* (2015), the U.S. Court of Appeals for the Tenth Circuit questioned whether "Republican Form" cases are always non-justiciable. On appeal, the Supreme Court vacated that opinion on other grounds.[36] The Tenth Circuit also ruled that a subdivision of a state lacks standing to argue that its parent state does not have a republican form of government.[37]

Under settled doctrine, citizens of a state who believe their state government is no longer republican can apply only to Congress for relief rather than to the courts. State courts, by contrast, have been more receptive to Guarantee Clause claims. Some litigants have argued that institutions of direct democracy, like initiatives and referenda, are inconsistent with a republican form of government; republics, they claim, must be entirely representative. Some of these advocates have misread James Madison's comments in Federalist No. 10. The claim that democracy and republicanism are mutually exclusive categories has no Founding-era pedigree.

The Delaware Supreme Court adopted the purported "republic v. democracy" distinction in 1847,[38] but this distinction was rejected by the highest tribunals of Colorado, Washington State, Oregon, and other states.[39] In 2015, the U.S. Supreme Court, citing Madison's reassurance about the ability of states to alter their republican forms of government, declared that voter initiatives were legitimate components of the "Republican Form."[40] In addition, three federal appeals courts have opined in dicta that the Constitution's use of the term "invasion" and its variants refers only to formal military operations.[41]

OPEN QUESTIONS

- *Luther v. Borden* and related cases were brought by individual plaintiffs. Would the outcome have been different if the dispute had been brought by a duly constituted government of a "parent state" against the federal government? A plaintiff state government would be, unlike the individual plaintiffs in prior cases, the direct beneficiary of the Guarantee Clause.
- *Luther v. Borden* and related cases held that judicial disputes about whether a state has a "Republican Form of Government" are not justiciable, but whether courts can hear disputes brought by states that claim the federal government failed to "protect" them "against Invasion" or "against domestic Violence" remains an open question. Can a duly constituted government of a "parent state" maintain a suit against the federal government for failure to comply with the Guarantee Clause's other two mandates?

- What are the original public meanings of the terms "Invasion" and "domestic Violence" in the Guarantee Clause?

Cite as: Robert G. Natelson, *The Guarantee Clause, in* THE HERITAGE GUIDE TO THE CONSTITUTION 541 (Josh Blackman & John G. Malcolm eds., 3d ed. 2025).

Notes

1. John Adams, A Defence of the Constitutions of Government of the United States of America (1787–88). **2.** M. De Secondat, Baron de Montesquieu, 1 The Spirit of Laws 11–12 (4th ed. 1766). **3.** Articles of Confederation, art. III. **4.** 1 Farrand's 22. **5.** *Id.* at 202. **6.** *Id.* at 206. **7.** *Id.* at 202. **8.** 2 Farrand's 47. **9.** *Id.* **10.** *Id.* at 48–49. **11.** *Id.* at 49. **12.** *Id.* at 174. **13.** *Id.* at 168. **14.** *Id.* at 467. **15.** *Id.* **16.** *Id.* at 578. **17.** *Id.* at 628–29. **18.** 9 DHRC 1106. **19.** Nicholas Bailey, An Universal Etymological English Dictionary (25th ed. 1783). **20.** 2 Samuel Johnson, A Dictionary of the English Language (8th ed. 1786); 2 John Ash, A New and Complete Dictionary of the English Language (1775). **21.** Thomas Sheridan, A Complete Dictionary of the English Language (2d ed. 1789) (unpaginated); 2 Samuel Johnson (same). **22.** Robert G. Natelson, *A Republic, Not a Democracy? Initiative, Referendum, and the Constitution's Guarantee Clause*, 80 Tex. L. Rev. 807 (2002). This entry relies on this article unless otherwise stated. **23.** 31 DHRC 543, 546. **24.** 2 DHRC 216, 218 **25.** 5 DHRC 874 **26.** 2 DHRC 663, 668. **27.** Storing 4.6.60. **28.** 22 DHRC 2089 **29.** Nathan Bailey, An Universal Etymological English Dictionary (1783) (unpaginated). Thomas Sheridan, A Complete Dictionary of the English Language (1789) (unpaginated); Samuel Johnson, A Dictionary of the English Language (6th ed., 1785) (unpaginated). **30.** Robert G. Natelson & Andrew T. Hyman, *The Constitution, Invasion, Immigration, and the War Powers of States*, 13 Brit. J. Am. L. Stud. 1, 24 (2024). **31.** Frank O. Bowman III, *Immigration Is Not an "Invasion" Under the Constitution*, Just Security (Jan. 29, 2024), https://perma.cc/KE57-XQUJ. **32.** Tara Leigh Grove, *The Lost History of the Political Question Doctrine*, 90 N.Y.U. L. Rev. 1908 (2015). **33.** 48 U.S. (7 How.) 1 (1849). **34.** 88 U.S. (21 Wall.) 162 (1874). **35.** *Pac. States Tel. & Tel. Co. v. Oregon*, 223 U.S. 118 (1912); *Baker v. Carr*, 369 U.S. 186 (1962); *Rucho v. Common Cause*, 588 U.S. 684, 718 (2019); Grove, *The Lost History*. **36.** *Kerr v. Hickenlooper*, 744 F.3d 1156 (10th Cir. 2015), *judgment vacated by Hickenlooper v. Kerr*, 576 U.S. 1079 (2015). **37.** *Kerr v. Polis*, 20 F.4th 686, 701 (10th Cir. 2021). **38.** *Rice v. Foster*, 4 Harr. 479 (Del. 1847). **39.** *Bernzen v. City of Boulder*, 525 P.2d 416 (Colo. 1974); *Hartig v. City of Seattle*, 102 P. 408 (Wash. 1909); *Kadderly v. City of Portland*, 74 P. 710 (Or. 1903). **40.** *Ariz. State Legislature v. Ariz. Indep. Redistricting Comm'n*, 576 U.S. 787, 817 (2015). **41.** *California v. United States*, 104 F.3d 1086, 1091 (9th Cir. 1997); *Padavan v. United States*, 83 F.3d 23, 28 (2d Cir. 1996); *New Jersey v. United States*, 91 F.3d 463, 468 (3d Cir. 1996).

PART 5

ARTICLE V

ESSAY NO. 148: AMENDMENTS—CONGRESSIONAL PROPOSAL CLAUSE ART. V

The Congress, whenever two thirds of both Houses shall deem it necessary, shall propose Amendments to this Constitution. . . .

—Robert G. Natelson

INTRODUCTION

Article V specifies the Constitution's amendment procedure. Its symmetrical parts exemplify James Madison's observation in Federalist No. 39 that the Constitution is partly national and partly federal (state-based). Four assemblies perform functions in the process: state conventions, state legislatures, an interstate (federal) convention, and the federal legislature (Congress). In the first of two mandatory stages, amendments can be proposed by two-thirds of both houses of Congress or at "a Convention for proposing Amendments" called upon "Application of the Legislatures of two thirds of the several States." Before the second stage, Congress decides which assembly will vote on ratification: the state legislatures or conventions within each state. Article V requires that for an amendment to be ratified, three-fourths of either state legislatures or state conventions must vote to ratify.

Article V also limits Congress and the conventions to "proposing Amendments to this Constitution." These provisions suggest that Article V may not be employed to propose an entirely new Constitution.[1] (See also Essay Nos. 151 and 152.)

HISTORY BEFORE 1787

The period from 1776 to 1787 was a time of intensive state constitution-writing, and the resulting documents displayed various approaches to amendment. The 1776 constitutions of New Jersey, South Carolina, and Virginia had no amendment provisions.[2] However, because the first two were legislative creations, a legislative power of amendment was implicit. The South Carolina document was replaced two years later by a new state constitution that permitted legislative amendment after specified procedures were followed.[3] The constitutions of Delaware and Maryland of 1776 similarly permitted legislative alteration contingent upon compliance with special procedures or super-majority votes.[4] The Massachusetts and New Hampshire constitutions provided for a one-time review by the people of the state after a set interval had passed.[5]

Several other state constitutions created an amendment procedure that reflected the "censorial power," which allowed people outside state government to review the laws. This procedure was based on the recommendation of Jean-Louis De Lolme, a Swiss commentator. The 1776 Pennsylvania constitution authorized the election every seven years of a council of censors, which had the power to propose amendments to be ratified by a popularly elected convention.[6] Vermont copied this approach in its constitutions of 1777 and 1784.[7] Georgia's 1777 constitution permitted a majority of voters in a majority of counties to call a statewide convention to draft amendments specified by the counties.[8]

At the national level, Article XIII of the Articles of Confederation permitted amendment only by unanimous state ratification of a congressional proposal. During the Founding era, a "confederation" was defined as merely a treaty or league, so this unanimity requirement was not surprising. The resulting impossibility of obtaining amendments that almost everyone agreed were necessary promoted interest in simply replacing the Articles.

THE CONSTITUTIONAL CONVENTION

On May 29, 1787, Edmund Randolph presented the Virginia Plan to the Constitutional Convention. Its provision on amendment contained two components: "provision ought to be made for the amendment of the Articles of

Union whensoever it shall seem necessary" and "the assent of the National Legislature ought not to be required."[9] On June 11, the Convention agreed to the first component but reserved decision on the role of Congress, if any.[10] On July 23, the delegates again agreed to the first component and submitted it to the Committee of Detail,[11] which was entrusted with preparing the Constitution's first draft. The committee assigned Edmund Randolph to construct an outline for a constitution, and in that outline Randolph proposed limiting the national legislature's role to calling an amendments convention only on the application of two-thirds of the state legislatures. The Committee's final report presented that formula to the full convention on August 6.[12]

Gouverneur Morris of Pennsylvania suggested that Congress be permitted to call an amendments convention "whenever they please."[13] But on August 30, the convention unanimously approved the Committee's proposal instead.[14]

On September 10, the delegates again debated the issue. Elbridge Gerry of Massachusetts moved to reconsider the amendment procedure.[15] Alexander Hamilton of New York successfully suggested that Congress, along with the states, be empowered to propose amendments. James Madison of Virginia was uncertain about the makeup of a proposing convention and successfully offered language providing that, on the application of two-thirds of the states, Congress rather than a convention would draft amendments. When John Rutledge of South Carolina objected to permitting amendments that might interfere with slavery, the Convention added a provision banning interference with the slave trade before 1808.

The Committee of Style adopted Madison's language allowing Congress to propose amendments and to designate whether ratification would be by state legislatures or state conventions.[16] However, at the insistence of George Mason of Virginia, the federal proposing convention was reinserted.

THE RATIFICATION DEBATES

In Federalist No. 43, Madison defended the congressional proposal. He observed that the Constitution "equally enables the general and the State governments to originate the amendment of errors, as they may be pointed out by the experience on one side, or on the other." The Constitution's opponents did not seriously question the wisdom of allowing Congress to propose amendments. Most of the discussion centered on the prospective role of a federal convention.

SUBSEQUENT PRACTICE

All amendments that have been proposed have originated with Congress. The federal convention route has never been used. For the first 170 years of the Republic, Congress responded preemptively whenever the popular will was strong enough to make a convention likely. For example, in 1789, James Madison, as a member of the House of Representatives, introduced a proposed Bill of Rights. Fearing that an amendments convention might propose more sweeping changes, he emphasized the importance of congressional action to avoid such an eventuality.[17]

Several years later, Congress again responded to the popular will. The decision of the U.S. Supreme Court in *Chisholm v. Georgia* (1793) held that non-consenting states could be sued in federal court.[18] This case caused widespread outrage. Congress promptly proposed the Eleventh Amendment, which effectively reversed the Court's decision. (See Essay No. 189.)

By 1911, nearly two-thirds of the states had applied for a convention to propose an amendment for direct election of U.S. Senators.[19] Congress responded reluctantly by proposing the Seventeenth Amendment on May 16, 1912.[20] (See Essay No. 203.) Similarly, after the fifth state had applied for a convention for an amendment limiting the President to two terms, Congress proposed the Twenty-Second Amendment.[21] (See Essay No. 209.)

JUDICIAL PRECEDENT

In 1981, a federal court in Idaho observed that most Article V issues have been adjudicated, either directly or indirectly.[22] Moreover, there has been a substantial amount of case law since then. A marked characteristic of Article V case law has been its adherence to historical practice, both during the Founding era and in subsequent years.[23]

First, the courts have addressed whether Article V disputes can be resolved in the courts. In other words, are such cases *justiciable*? The courts have held repeatedly that they are, or at least should be, justiciable.

Second, the courts have decided whether a congressional resolution proposing an Article V amendment has to be presented to the President. *Hollingsworth v. Virginia* (1798) held that it does not.[24] *Hollingsworth* was the first in a series of judicial decisions ruling that when legislative assemblies act under Article V, they perform "federal functions" as independent bodies empowered directly by the Constitution rather than as federal or state legislatures.[25]

Third, the courts have analyzed the voting rules for Congress to propose an amendment. The traditional parliamentary common law rule of decision requires a majority vote of those present as long as a quorum is present.[26] Article V altered the traditional rule by requiring a "two thirds" vote of each house. But Article V did not alter the rest of the formula.[27] The common law rules seem to apply to other actions Congress undertakes as part of the amendment process, such as deciding whether to debate a suggested amendment and choosing a mode of ratification.

Fourth, the courts have considered whether Congress must include an explicit finding of necessity in its proposals. Under the parliamentary common law rule, the answer is "no." Accordingly, the Court also has answered "no," despite the fact that Article V includes the phrase "whenever two thirds of both Houses shall deem it necessary."[28] This is one of several judicial decisions applying the ordinary parliamentary common law to Article V procedures where the Constitution does not specify a different rule.[29]

Fifth, the courts also have addressed whether Congress may fix a time limit within which a proposed amendment must be ratified. *Dillon v. Gloss* (1921) ruled that Congress may do so as "an incident of its power to designate the mode of ratification."[30] However, it is difficult to see how a time limit is incidental to the bare choice of whether ratification shall be by state legislatures or state conventions. It makes more sense to consider a time limit adopted at the time of proposal as part of the proposal itself. *Coleman v. Miller* (1939) held that " Congress has the power . . . to fix a reasonable limit of time for ratification in proposing an amendment."[31] This case suggests that the time limit is part of the proposal.

OPEN QUESTIONS

In 1972, Congress proposed the Equal Rights Amendment (ERA) with a seven-year ratification deadline. By 1978, several states had repealed their ratifications, and it was clear that the necessary three-fourths would not ratify the ERA within the original time frame. Congress then passed a joint resolution purporting to extend the deadline for another three years. This resolution was supported only by a simple majority.

If a deadline is adopted by a two-thirds majority of each house of Congress when an amendment is proposed, it is difficult to see how a simple majority or even a two-thirds majority could change that deadline after the fact: The deadline is part of the package weighed by state legislatures and conventions when deciding whether and when to ratify. Extending the deadline should require a new amendment. The Justice Department's Office of Legal Counsel reached this conclusion in 2020.[32] And in 2023, the D.C. Circuit Court of Appeals ruled that Congress likely has the authority "to set deadlines outside of the text of the amendment."[33]

Nevertheless, some politicians and scholars argue that states still may ratify the ERA—although even the purportedly extended deadline has long passed. On January 17, 2025, President Joe Biden stated "that the Equal Rights Amendment has cleared all necessary hurdles to be formally added to the Constitution as the 28th Amendment."[34]

Cite as: Robert G. Natelson, *Amendments—Congressional Proposal Clause, in* THE HERITAGE GUIDE TO THE CONSTITUTION 548 (Josh Blackman & John G. Malcolm eds., 3d ed. 2025).

Notes

1. Robert G. Natelson, *The Founders' Origination Clause (and Implications for the Affordable Care Act)*, 38 Harvard J. L. & Pub. Pol. 629, 682–87 (2015). **2.** N.J. Const. of 1776; S.C. Const. of 1776; Va. Const. of 1776. **3.** S.C. Const. of 1778, art. XLIV. **4.** Del. Const. of 1776, art. X; Md. Const. of 1776, art. X. **5.** Mass. Const. of 1780, art. X; N.H. Const. of 1784, Pt. II. **6.** Pa. Const. of 1776, § 47. **7.** Vt. Const. of 1777, § 44; Vt. Const. of 1786, art. XL. **8.** Ga. Const. of 1777, art. LXIII. **9.** 1 Farrand's 22. **10.** *Id.* at 203. **11.** 2 Farrand's 87. **12.** *Id.* at 188. **13.** *Id.* at 468. **14.** *Id.* **15.** *Id.* at 557–59. **16.** *Id.* at 578. **17.** 1 Annals of Cong. 446 (1789). **18.** 2 U.S. 419 (1793). **19.** 38 Harv. J.L. & Pub. Pol'y 629, 682–87. **20.** George H. Haynes, The Senate of the United States: Its History and Practice 116 (1938). **21.** Article V Library, *Article V Convention Application Analysis: Limit Presidential Tenure*, https://perma.cc/ZJF4-JAAJ. **22.** *Idaho v. Freeman*, 529 F.Supp. 1107, 1126 (D. Idaho 1981), judgment vacated as moot, *Carmen v. Idaho*, 459 U.S. 809 (1982). **23.** Robert G. Natelson, The Law of Article V: State Initiation of Constitutional Amendments (2d ed., 2020). **24.** *Hollingsworth v. Virginia*, 3 U.S. (3 Dall.) 378 (1798); Seth Barrett Tillman, *A Textualist Defense of Article I, Section 7, Clause 3: Why* Hollingsworth v. Virginia *Was Rightly Decided, and Why* INS v. Chadha *Was Wrongly Reasoned*, 83 Tex. L. Rev. 1265 (2005). **25.** Robert G. Natelson, *Federal Functions: Execution of Powers the Constitution Grants to Persons and Entities Outside the Federal Government*, 23 U. Penn. J. Const. L. 193, 197 (2021). **26.** *Oldknow v. Wainright*, [K.B. 1760] 2 Burr. 1017, 97 Eng. Rep. 683. **27.** *Rhode Island v. Palmer* (*National Prohibition Cases*), 253 U.S. 350 (1920). **28.** *Id.* **29.** *Dyer v. Blair*, 390 F. Supp. 1291 (N.D. Ill. 1975). **30.** *Dillon v. Gloss*, 256 U.S. 368, 376 (1921). **31.** *Coleman v. Miller*, 307 U.S. 438, 454 (1939). **32.** Stephen A. Engel, Ass't Att'y Gen., Off. of Legal Counsel, U.S. Dep't of Justice, Memorandum Opinion for the General Counsel, National Archives and Records Administration (Jan. 6, 2020), https://perma.cc/RH4C-2S4N. **33.** *Illinois v. Ferriero*, 60 F.4th 704, 719 (D.C. Cir. 2023). **34.** Statement from President Joe Biden on the Equal Rights Amendment (Jan. 17, 2025), https://perma.cc/3Q66-DGUH.

ESSAY NO. 149: AMENDMENTS—CONVENTION PROPOSAL CLAUSE
ART. V

The Congress . . . on the Application of the Legislatures of two thirds of the several States, shall call a Convention for proposing Amendments, . . .

—Robert G. Natelson

INTRODUCTION

The Convention Proposal Clause provides an alternative route for proposing constitutional amendments for state consideration. Two-thirds of the state legislatures must submit an "Application" to Congress "call[ing for] a Convention for proposing Amendments." In its Founding-era sense, the word "Application" means merely a communication. It does not imply, as modern sense suggests, that an inferior entity is applying to a superior one. It is thus misleading to refer to an Article V application as a petition. Applications on the same topic or topics from two-thirds of the state legislatures trigger a mandatory duty on the part of Congress. Each application is really an order contingent on the two-thirds threshold being reached. A convention for proposing amendments has never been called.

HISTORY BEFORE 1787

For more than a century before independence, Great Britain's North American colonies had a rich convention tradition.[1] The colonists sometimes met in conclaves called "conventions of the people," where they undertook such tasks as the dissolution of King Charles I's "Dominion of New England." Each convention of the people was held within the political boundaries of a single colony, and delegates were elected directly by the voters from towns, counties, and other districts.

Americans also held conventions among the several colonies. These conventions addressed such common issues as defense and relations with the Indian tribes. Among the most famous were the Albany Congress of 1754 and the Stamp Act Congress of 1764. (At the time, "congress" was a synonym for an intergovernmental convention.)

After 1776, the new states continued these traditions. They held conventions of the people to draft state constitutions and to govern states pending adoption of those constitutions. They also held interstate conventions, commonly called "conventions of the states," "conventions of states," or "conventions of delegates from the states." These temporary, ad hoc task forces originated with the issuance of a call, usually from a state legislature but sometimes from the Continental Congress or a prior convention. The call was an invitation to meet at a particular time and place to discuss prescribed topics. State legislatures then decided whether to participate. If the decision was affirmative, each state legislature determined the size of its delegation of "commissioners" and how they were to be chosen and instructed.

At the designated time, the commissioners assembled at the designated place. Once a quorum of states was achieved, the convention elected its officers and, if the convention was large enough, adopted formal rules and formed committees. Each state invariably had one vote. The commissioners then turned to the assigned agenda and continued to work until they either finished or were permanently deadlocked. At that point, they adjourned *sine die* (indefinitely).

The Second Continental Congress (1775–1781) called several conventions of states. For example, the 1777 Yorktown Convention was called to consider common responses to monetary inflation, but it deadlocked and adjourned without proposing a solution. Moreover, the narrow scope of congressional power induced individual states to call most conventions on their own. Most of these were regional ("partial"), but some, such as the 1780 Philadelphia Price Convention, were national ("general"). With varying success, these meetings addressed such issues as price inflation, Revolutionary War defense, and interstate trade.

In 1786, Virginia called a general convention of states to meet in Annapolis, Maryland, to discuss trade issues. The convention recommended to the legislatures of the five states that sent delegates that they invite all states to meet in Philadelphia the following May to discuss ways to strengthen the Union. In response to this recommendation, the Virginia legislature—not

Congress, as commonly believed[2]—called the Constitutional Convention.

THE CONSTITUTIONAL CONVENTION

The Constitutional Convention was itself a convention of states and frequently referred to as such.[3] (See Essay No. 148.) Both the Virginia Plan of May 29, 1787, and the draft Constitution reported by the Committee of Detail on August 6, contemplated that federal conventions would prepare and adopt all amendments. On September 10, the Convention agreed that amendments would be proposed by Congress, either on its own initiative or on demand by two-thirds of the states, and that amendments would be subject to state ratification.[4]

The Committee of Style included this scheme in its penultimate draft of the Constitution. This provoked a strong response from George Mason of Virginia, who "thought the [Committee's] plan of amending the Constitution [was] exceptionable & dangerous."[5] Mason contended that "the proposing of amendments" would "depend . . . on Congress," as "no amendments of the proper kind would ever be obtained by the people."[6] Elbridge Gerry of Massachusetts and Gouverneur Morris of Pennsylvania, who served on the Committee, "moved to amend the article so as to require a Convention on application of 2/3 of the" states at which the states could propose amendments.[7]

James Madison of Virginia "did not see why Congress would not be as much bound to propose amendments applied for by two thirds of the States as to call a Convention on the like application."[8] In other words, Madison thought that Congress would be bound to propose the specific amendments put forward by two-thirds of the state legislatures. Madison "saw no objection however against providing for a Convention for the purpose of amendments" but acknowledged "that difficulties might arise as to the form, the quorum" and other particular issues, which should be avoided "as much as possible" in a Constitution.[9] Despite Madison's doubts, the Morris–Gerry motion was approved unanimously, and the proposing convention was reinserted into the draft Constitution.[10]

Some scholars have claimed that the nature and composition of an amendments convention are mysteries.[11] However, there is no real doubt that the Founders understood an amendments convention to be a convention of the states. This is well established by contemporaneous official and unofficial records from the Founding Era.[12]

The Framers' importation of the "convention of states" mechanism into the Constitution enabled states to participate in the amendment proposal process. The procedure was a familiar one, because there had been at least twenty conventions of colonies between 1677 and 1776 and ten conventions of states between 1776 and 1787.[13] Moreover, convention protocols were well understood. In fact, at least thirteen of the Constitution's fifty-five Framers had served as commissioners at such gatherings, and several had served on multiple occasions.[14] Other Framers had been members of state legislatures that had called conventions or commissioned and instructed commissioners.

The Constitution's Framers also borrowed the in-state "convention of the people" mechanism for ratifying the Constitution and constitutional amendments.

THE RATIFICATION DEBATES

Advocates of the Constitution assured the ratifying public that if amendments should prove necessary, the state legislatures could obtain them readily. They relied heavily on the Convention Proposal Clause and the general understanding that an amendments convention was a convention of the states. For example, in Federalist No. 85, Alexander Hamilton remarked that "whenever . . . ten states, were united in the desire of a particular amendment, that amendment must infallibly take place." At the time, ten out of the thirteen states would meet the two-thirds threshold for calling a convention of the states to propose amendments.

The Constitution's advocates also emphasized that if a sufficient number of states applied, Congress would have no choice but to call a convention. "The words of this article are peremptory," noted Hamilton. "The Congress 'shall call a convention.' Nothing in this particular is left to the discretion of that body."

Another advocate of the Constitution, Tench Coxe, had been Pennsylvania's delegate to the Annapolis Convention. Coxe's published writings were more accessible and perhaps more popular than the Federalist Papers.[15] Yet, his crucial role in ratification debates is often overlooked.[16] Coxe repeatedly resorted to the Convention Proposal Clause to calm public concern. He explained that "two thirds of the states can *always* procure a general convention for the purpose of amending the constitution." Moreover, "three fourths of them can introduce those amendments into the constitution" even when "the President, Senate and Federal House of Representatives, should be *unanimously* opposed to each and all of them." Coxe echoed Mason's argument: The convention procedure was a way to obtain amendments while bypassing any meaningful interference from Congress.

Participants in the ratification debates assumed that most or all amendments conventions would be limited to considering amendments of the kind designated in the state legislative applications. In Federalist No. 85, for example, Hamilton wrote that "every amendment to the constitution, if once established, would be a single proposition, and might be brought forward singly."[17] In modern times, some academics have doubted whether an application or convention can be limited,[18] but there is no record of any such doubt among the Framers or ratifiers.

APPLICATIONS BY STATES FOR CONVENTIONS

The Constitution was ratified on June 21, 1788, when New Hampshire became the ninth of the original thirteen states to ratify it. The first Article V legislative application was issued by the Virginia legislature on November 14, 1788. It demanded a "convention of the states" to consider "the defects of this Constitution that have been suggested by the State [ratifying] Conventions."[19] On February 5, 1789, New York applied for a convention in even broader terms.[20] Because of the expectation that Congress would propose amendments on its own, no other states similarly applied. And the First Congress would propose what would become the first ten amendments.

There were many more legislative applications during the nineteenth and early twentieth centuries. The states sought amendments on subjects as disparate as slavery and polygamy.[21] The applications indifferently referred to an amendments convention as a "convention of the states" or as a convention for proposing amendments. In *Smith v. Union Bank* (1831), the U.S. Supreme Court employed the former term.[22]

The first application campaign that came close to the two-thirds threshold needed to trigger a convention was for direct election of Senators. When Congress finally proposed the Seventeenth Amendment in 1912, twenty-nine of the then-necessary thirty-two applications had been submitted. The twentieth century saw a plethora of state applications on such subjects as congressional term limits, a balanced budget amendment, limiting the scope of the federal government, campaign finance reform, and presidential term limits. The last one resulted in the congressional proposal of the Twenty-Second Amendment.

There also has been a series of non–Article V conventions of states on a range of subjects. The most significant was the February 1861 general convention in Washington, D.C., which was called by Virginia to propose to Congress a constitutional amendment in an attempt to head off civil war.[23] Former President John Tyler presided. The convention produced an amendment, but Congress did not act on it. During the twentieth century, a series of smaller interstate conventions (called "commissions") met to negotiate Western water compacts, the best known of which was the 1922 Colorado River Commission.[24] In 2017, yet another convention of states met in Phoenix, Arizona, and drafted rules for a future Article V convention.[25] In general, all of these meetings followed standard interstate convention protocols.

MECHANICS OF A CONVENTION OF THE STATES

Article V case law clearly and consistently relies on historical practice.[26] Some Article V cases have arisen under the Convention Proposal Clause, but even the cases that have not have effectively settled many questions about the clause. Combining judicial and historical precedent produces several conclusions.

First, when a state legislature applies for a convention, as when any assembly exercises an Article V function, it operates independently of state constitutional and legal standards. The legislature may follow its usual rules, but it may also craft rules for the occasion. An application may be limited to specific subjects. An application may also be plenary—that is, unlimited as to any subject.[27] Applications probably do not expire with the passage of time, but a legislature may impose a termination date or rescind it.

Second, Congress is not obliged to call the convention until two-thirds of state legislatures have applied on the same general topic. Then Congress must issue the call, inviting all states and specifying the time, the place, and the subject matter designated by the conforming applications. Historical application and call practice suggests that loose agreement on the subject matter also is sufficient to trigger a call. Sometimes, however, while overlapping in subject matter, applications feature significant variation. This results in what is called the "aggregation problem." Despite Hamilton's assurance that Congress has no discretion in calling a convention, Congress may have to exercise some threshold discretion on whether the subject matters are generally the same.[28]

Third, each state legislature designates the number of commissioners in its delegation and the mode of selecting them. It also formally instructs them on how to vote. When the convention meets, it elects its own officers and adopts its own rules. Each state presumptively receives one vote, although the convention, by a majority of states present and voting, may alter this formula. The convention is limited to the agenda defined by the legislative applications and the congressional call. Such a limit is uniform practice for conventions of states. In 1933, the North Carolina Supreme Court observed that "those calling an Article V ratifying convention may limit its authority."[29]

Fourth, if the convention decides that additional amendments within the prescribed scope of the application are warranted, it may draft them and vote to propose them. In keeping with parliamentary common law, an amendment is adopted if there is a majority of states present and voting. Recommendations outside the convention's prescribed scope are *ultra vires* and not duly proposed amendments. Congress therefore may not designate a mode of ratification for them.

Finally, once the convention's assigned business is complete, it adjourns *sine die*.

OPEN QUESTIONS

- Can a "plenary" (open subject) application be aggregated with a single-subject application to trigger a call for a single-subject convention?
- Recent commentators generally agree that applications may limit the convention's subject matter, but can an application bind the convention to consider only specific amendment language? Your author thinks that such an application would be invalid. Other scholars argue that specific-language applications are valid and binding on the convention.[30]

Cite as: Robert G. Natelson, *Amendment—Convention Proposal Clause, in* The Heritage Guide to the Constitution 551 (Josh Blackman & John G. Malcolm eds., 3d ed. 2025).

Notes

1. Robert G. Natelson, *Founding-Era Conventions and the Meaning of the Constitution's "Convention for Proposing Amendments"*, 65 Fla. L. Rev. 615 (2013); Robert G. Natelson, *Is the Constitution's Convention for Proposing Amendments a "Mystery"? Overlooked Evidence in the Narrative of Uncertainty*, 104 Marquette L. Rev. 1 (2020). **2.** 40 Harv. J.L. & Pub. Pol'y 61 **3.** Natelson, *Mystery, supra* at 34–35. **4.** 2 Farrand's 559. **5.** *Id.* at 629. **6.** *Id.* **7.** *Id.* **8.** *Id.* at 629–30. **9.** *Id.* **10.** *Id.* **11.** Natelson, *Mystery, supra* at 6–11. **12.** *Id.*; Robert G. Natelson, *List of Additional Founding-era Descriptions of an Article V Convention as a "Convention of States"*, Article V Information Center (Feb. 16, 2025), https://perma.cc/LA8H-Q6FL. **13.** Robert G. Natelson, *List of Conventions of States and Colonies in American History*, Article V Information Center (Aug. 10, 2017), https://perma.cc/N8CW-9LXD. **14.** Natelson, *Founding-Era Conventions, supra* at 691–710. **15.** Tench Coxe, *A Friend of Society and Liberty*, Pa. Gazette (July 23, 1788), reprinted in 18 DHRC 277, 283–84; Tench Coxe, A Pennsylvanian to the New York Convention, Pa. Gazette (June 11, 1788), reprinted in 20 DHRC 1139, 1142. **16.** Jacob E. Cooke, Tench Coxe and the Early Republic (1978). **17.** Robert G. Natelson, *Proposing Constitutional Amendments by Convention: Rules Governing the Process*, 76 Tenn. L. Rev. 793, 723–34 (2011). **18.** Natelson, *Mystery, supra* at 5. **19.** 1 Annals of Cong. 258–59 (1788). **20.** *Id.* at 29–30. **21.** Article V Library, https://perma.cc/5TC6-L5MW. **22.** 30 U.S. 518 (1831). **23.** Robert Gray Gunderson, Old Gentlemen's Convention: The Washington Peace Conference of 1861 (1961); L.E. Chittenden, A Report of the Debates and Proceedings in the Secret Sessions of the Conference Convention, for Proposing Amendments to the Constitution of the United States, Held at Washington, D.C., in February, A.D. 1861 (1864), https://bit.ly/3H2zKTU. **24.** Minutes and Record of the First Eighteen Sessions of the Colorado River Commission Negotiating the Colorado River Compact of 1922, https://perma.cc/3ZT6-MYB4. **25.** Journal of the Balanced Budget Planning Convention, Phoenix, Arizona, September 12, 2017–September 15, 2017, https://perma.cc/63DX-TMKA. **26.** Robert G. Natelson, The Law of Article V: State Initiation of Constitutional Amendments (2d ed., 2020). **27.** Opinion of the Justices to the Senate, 366 N.E.2d 1226 (Mass. 1977). **28.** Robert G. Natelson, *Counting to Two Thirds: How Close Are We to a Convention for Proposing Amendments to the Constitution?*, 19 Fed. Soc'y Rev. 94 (2018). **29.** Opinion of the Justices, 172 S.E. 474 (N.C. 1933). **30.** Michael B. Rappaport, *The Constitutionality of a Limited Convention: An Originalist Analysis*, 28 Const. Comment. 53, 89 (2012); Michael Stern, *Reopening the Constitutional Road to Reform: Toward a Safeguarded Article V Convention*, 78 Tenn. L. Rev. 765 (2011).

ᕫ

ESSAY NO. 150: AMENDMENTS—RATIFICATION PROCESS
ART. V

The Congress, whenever two thirds of both Houses shall deem it necessary, shall propose Amendments to this Constitution . . . [which] shall be valid to all Intents and Purposes, as Part of this Constitution, when ratified by the Legislatures of three fourths of the several States, or by Conventions in three fourths thereof, as the one or the other Mode of Ratification may be proposed by the Congress.

—Robert G. Natelson

INTRODUCTION

After an amendment is proposed, either by Congress or by a federal convention, Congress must decide whether that measure should be considered for ratification or rejection by state legislatures or state conventions. The Constitution does not specify a different rule of decision, so under parliamentary common law, the rule for this congressional decision is a majority of those present and voting (a quorum being present).[1] The Constitution specifies that for an amendment to be declared ratified, it must be approved by three-fourths of these legislatures or conventions, with—absent a convention or legislative rule to the contrary—each convention or legislative chamber deciding by a majority of those present and voting, a quorum being present.

Historical practice, both before and after the Founding, provides additional details. For example, states have rescinded earlier ratifications of an amendment and have reconsidered earlier decisions not to ratify an amendment. Article V grants state legislatures power to ratify amendments (if Congress chooses the legislative ratification procedure) and incidental power to call in-state conventions (if Congress chooses the convention ratification procedure).

THE CONSTITUTIONAL CONVENTION

On August 6, 1787, the Committee of Detail proposed for amendment by a federal convention without any provision for congressional proposal or for a separate ratification procedure. On September 10, Roger Sherman of Connecticut moved to add congressional proposal coupled with a stipulation that "no amendments shall be binding until consented to by the several States."[2] Elbridge Gerry of Massachusetts seconded this motion, and James Wilson of Pennsylvania successfully amended it to specify that ratification would require the approval of two-thirds of the states.[3] The motion was defeated by a vote of six to five. Wilson then renewed his motion with the margin needed for ratification changed from two-thirds to three-fourths. His revised motion was approved unanimously.[4]

James Madison of Virginia then moved a substitute proposal that looked much like what ultimately was adopted.[5] The text granted Congress the option of selecting a legislative or convention mode of ratification. Alexander Hamilton of New York seconded that proposal.[6] John Rutledge of South Carolina insisted on a ban on amendments altering how representatives are apportioned.[7] With that ban inserted, Madison's draft was adopted by a vote of nine to one with one state divided.[8] The Committee of Style's penultimate draft of the Constitution,[9] as well as the final draft, retained the ratification procedure in that form.

THE RATIFICATION DEBATES

The ratification procedure was generally not controversial, and discussions of it by the Constitution's advocates during the ratification debates were brief. In Federalist No. 43, James Madison explained that the ratification threshold was not too high, and not too low, but was just right. Article V, he explained, "guards equally against that extreme facility [or ease], which would render the Constitution too mutable [changeable]; and that extreme difficulty, which might perpetuate its discovered faults."

James Monroe, writing as "A Native of Virginia," observed that "two-thirds of Congress" or "two-thirds of the Legislatures" would "no doubt" propose amendments to address "important defects."[10] The author contended that "the result of such Convention, will [not] be rejected by one-fourth of the States: Since all the States must feel the inconvenience of important defects."

RECONSIDERATION OF NON-RATIFICATION AND RESCISSION OF RATIFICATION

In 1866, the Fourteenth Amendment was sent to the state legislatures for ratification. Some states initially rejected the amendment but later ratified it; others ratified but later rescinded. Congress sought to resolve the issue by a joint resolution, declaring it adopted as of July 9, 1868. In *Coleman v. Miller* (1939), the Supreme Court relied on that precedent to concede to Congress authority to resolve the effect of successive rejections, ratifications, and rescissions.[11]

Eleven states existing during Reconstruction have since ratified the Fourteenth Amendment, rendering academic that specific dispute.

However, *Coleman v. Miller*'s concessions to Congress are of doubtful authority. First, there is no obvious reason why state legislatures should not be permitted to reconsider their amendment-related actions in a timely manner just as they can reconsider their other decisions. Second, allowing Congress to overrule the expressed will of state legislatures gives Congress a far greater weight in the amendment process than the constitutional text or the relevant history justifies. Third, *Coleman* relied on the precedent by which Congress declared the Fourteenth Amendment adopted, but subsequent ratifications of that amendment by additional states rendered Congress's pronouncement unnecessary. Fourth, *Coleman* has been followed by eight decades of contrary practice: States have freely ratified and adopted legislative applications after previously refusing to do so and freely rescinded previous ratifications and applications. Moreover, a federal court has upheld a ratification rescission,[12] and no one seems to have questioned seriously the legitimacy of rescinding applications.[13]

RATIFICATION BY CONVENTION

In 1789, the First Congress opted to send twelve amendments to state legislatures for ratification, ten of which were ratified and became known as the Bill of Rights. It was not until February 1933 that Congress chose to send an amendment to a state ratification convention. In December of that year, three-fourths of the state conventions ratified the Twenty-First Amendment, which repealed the Eighteenth Amendment and ended prohibition. (See Essay No. 208.) Congress apparently chose the convention path because many people believed that legislative ratification of the Eighteenth Amendment did not reflect true popular opinion, and the convention mode was seen as more likely to repeal prohibition.[14]

At one time, courts and commentators expressed doubts about how long a proposed and unrescinded amendment without a time limit remained ratifiable. *Dillon v. Gloss* (1921) suggested that there might be a "reasonable time" limit with reasonableness to be determined by Congress.[15] However, this question seems to have been resolved by the accepted ratification of the Twenty-Seventh Amendment in 1992—203 years after it was proposed. (See Essay No. 216.)

JUSTICIABILITY OF RATIFICATION DECISIONS

Justice Hugo Black concurred in *Coleman v. Miller*. He opined that "[t]he Constitution grants Congress exclusive power to control submission of constitutional amendments."[16] Black reasoned that "[f]inal determination by Congress that ratification by three-fourths of the States has taken place 'is conclusive upon the courts.'" The former senator added that "Congress has sole and complete control over the amending process, subject to no judicial review."[17]

Some scholars argue that this concurring opinion proves that Article V cases are nonjusticiable and cannot be resolved by the courts. However, Black's opinion is in tension with the text and history of Article V. The Constitution does not grant Congress the "exclusive power" over amendment; it balances responsibilities among various assemblies. Moreover, the states can substantively bypass Congress through the federal convention route. Despite Black's concurrence, courts have had no hesitation in adjudicating Article V disputes.[18] Much of the ensuing case law has dealt with ratification issues.[19]

POWERS OF STATE LEGISLATURES TO RATIFY AMENDMENTS

United States v. Sprague (1931) ruled that Congress's power to select among the two "Modes of Ratification"—state legislatures or state conventions—is absolute and not affected by the nature of the amendment proposed.[20] The Court has twice held that a ratifying state legislature acts as an independent assembly, free of state constitutional constraints such as a required referendum or the governor's veto.[21] In this regard, the state legislatures function as Congress functions when proposing amendments. Lower courts have decided that, in accordance with historical practice, ratifying legislatures and conventions may establish their own rules and judge their own members notwithstanding state law or other precedents.[22] A plethora of cases have held that neither Congress nor the states may manipulate or alter the ratification process through ordinary legislation.

Further, *Dillon v. Gloss* (1921) determined that Article V, like other legal texts, creates incidental powers by implication.[23] Thus, lower tribunals have held that when Congress adopts the state convention mode of ratification, state legislatures have implied power and duty to adopt measures necessary to provide for the election of delegates to the convention.[24] In accordance

with historical practice, the courts also have determined that convention delegates should be elected from districts rather than at large.[25]

OPEN QUESTIONS

- Can state legislatures ratify an amendment after earlier refusing to ratify it? Can state legislatures rescind an earlier ratification of an amendment? If legislative reconsideration of ratification is valid, the question of timing remains. One possible solution is to permit states to move in and out of the ratification pool until three-fourths of them have ratified the amendment or the stated time limit has passed. At that point, the legislature's most recent decision should become irrevocable.
- Can Congress subsequently extend a time limit for ratification adopted at the time of proposal?

Cite as: Robert G. Natelson, *Amendments—Ratification Process, in* THE HERITAGE GUIDE TO THE CONSTITUTION 555 (Josh Blackman & John G. Malcolm eds., 3d ed. 2025).

Notes

1. *Oldknow v. Wainright*, [K.B. 1760] 2 Burr. 1017, 97 Eng. Rep. 683. **2.** 2 Farrand's 558. **3.** *Id.* at 558–59. **4.** *Id.* at 559. **5.** *Id.* **6.** *Id.* **7.** *Id.* **8.** *Id.* **9.** *Id.* at 578. **10.** A Native of Virginia, Observations Upon the Proposed Plan of Federal Government (Apr. 2, 1788), *in* 9 DHRC 689. **11.** 307 U.S. 433, 450 (1939). **12.** *Idaho v. Freeman*, 529 F. Supp. 1107 (D. Idaho 1981), judgment vacated as moot sub nom. *Carmen v. Idaho*, 459 U.S. 809 (1982). **13.** *Howard Jarvis Taxpayers Ass'n v. Padilla*, 363 P.3d 628, 650 (Cal. 2016). **14.** Everett Somerville Brown, Ratification of the Twenty-First Amendment to the Constitution of the United States 3–4 (1938). **15.** 256 U.S. 368 (1921). **16.** 307 U.S. 433, 457 (1939). **17.** *Id.* at 459. **18.** *Dyer v. Blair*, 390 F. Supp. 1291 (N.D. Ill. 1975) **19.** Robert G. Natelson, The Law of Article V: State Initiation of Constitutional Amendments (2d ed. 2020). **20.** 282 U.S. 716 (1931). **21.** *Hawke v. Smith*, 253 U.S. 231 (1920); *Leser v. Garnett*, 258 U.S. 130 (1922). **22.** *Dyer v. Blair*, 390 F. Supp. 1291 (N.D. Ill. 1975). **23.** 256 U.S. 368, 373 (1921). **24.** *State ex rel. Tate v. Sevier*, 62 S.W.2d 895 (Mo. 1933); *State ex rel. Donnelly v. Myers*, 186 N.E. 918 (Ohio 1933). **25.** *In Re Opinion of the Justices*, 167 A. 176 (Me. 1933).

ESSAY NO. 151: PROHIBITION ON AMENDMENT—MIGRATION, IMPORTATION, AND APPORTIONMENT
ART. V

. . . no Amendment which may be made prior to the Year One thousand eight hundred and eight shall in any Manner affect the first and fourth Clauses in the Ninth Section of the first Article . . .

—Robert G. Natelson

INTRODUCTION

Article V imposes two express limitations on amendments. First, it prohibits amendments that alter any state's equal representation in the Senate without the consent of that state. (See Essay No. 152.) Second, when Article V came into effect, it prohibited amendments adopted before the year 1808 that "in any Manner affect[ed]" the constitutional scope of three congressional powers: the power to restrict

immigration; the power to regulate foreign commerce (specifically, the slave trade); and the power to impose taxes.

HISTORY BEFORE 1787

Under the Articles of Confederation, individual states decided what persons should be admitted across their borders and what articles should be traded. The Confederation Congress had no authority over immigration or foreign or interstate commerce.[1] When Congress sought to restrict immigration of "convicted malefactors," for example, it had to ask the states to pass legislation rather than adopt its own measures.[2] Similarly, Congress had no taxing authority. Instead, it requisitioned set amounts from the states from time to time, and the state governments decided how the burden should be allocated.[3]

THE CONSTITUTIONAL CONVENTION

On August 6, 1787, the Committee of Detail, chaired by John Rutledge of South Carolina, reported its draft constitution.[4] This draft granted Congress the power to "regulate commerce with foreign nations."[5] Trade with foreign nations was understood to include trade in slaves, because slaves were considered articles of commerce.[6] The draft also granted Congress the power to "declare the law and punishment of . . . offences against the law of nations,"[7] which was understood to include authority over the "Migration" of free persons.[8] Finally, it granted Congress the power to "lay and collect taxes."[9]

However, the Committee of Detail draft also restricted the taxation power. In particular, direct taxes were to be allocated among states according to the total in each state of free citizens plus three-fifths of slaves.[10] In the final Constitution, this became the Apportionment Clause (Article I, Section 2, Clause 3), which is discussed in Essay No. 9. The Committee of Detail draft also imposed a flat ban on prohibiting or taxing immigration and the slave trade.[11]

On August 24, the Committee of Eleven recommended that the ban on prohibiting or taxing immigration and the slave trade expire in 1800.[12] On August 25, the Convention adopted a motion from the floor by Charles Cotesworth Pinckney of South Carolina to extend that date to 1808.[13] Another motion adopted on the same day permitted Congress to impose "a tax or duty . . . on such importation not exceeding ten dollars for each person."[14] This tax would be a capitation because it was imposed on each slave's head. The Committee of Style changed the direct tax apportionment rule to apply only to "capitation[s]."[15] On September 14, the Convention altered the language to "capitation . . . or other direct tax."[16]

The final results were Clauses 1 and 4 of Article I, Section 9: Clause 1 provided: "The Migration or Importation of such Persons as any of the States now existing shall think proper to admit, shall not be prohibited by the Congress prior to the Year one thousand eight hundred and eight, but a Tax or duty may be imposed on such Importation, not exceeding ten dollars for each Person" (See Essay No. 67). Clause 4 provided: "No Capitation, or other direct, Tax shall be laid, unless in Proportion to the Census or Enumeration herein before directed to be taken" (See Essay No. 71).

On September 10, the Convention added a provision requiring that proposed amendments must be ratified by three-fourths of the states.[17] This new provision made it possible for a supermajority of states to alter the migration, importation, and direct tax restrictions in Article I, Section 9, Clauses 1 and 4. John Rutledge of South Carolina responded that he "never could agree to give a power by which the articles relating to slaves might be altered by the States not interested in that property and prejudiced against it."[18] The draft was changed (probably by James Madison of Virginia) to "obviate this objection" by adding new language: "provided that no amendments which may be made prior to the year 1808 shall in any manner affect the [appropriate sections]."[19] In the finished Constitution, this became "no Amendment which may be made prior to the Year One thousand eight hundred and eight shall in any Manner affect the first and fourth Clauses in the Ninth Section of the first Article."

THE RATIFICATION DEBATES

The ratification debates displayed some discontent on the part of both advocates and opponents of the Constitution with respect to the accommodations made to slavery and the slave trade.

ELIMINATION OF THE SLAVE TRADE

On March 2, 1807, Congress voted overwhelmingly to prohibit the slave trade as of January 1, 1808.[20] Congress did not regulate the immigration of free people for many years after that, and it has never exercised its power to impose a capitation on immigrants.

OPEN QUESTIONS

- Why did Congress never exercise its power to impose capitations or other direct taxes on slaves or immigrants?
- May a prohibited amendment be adopted by first ratifying an amendment removing the prohibition and then ratifying the prohibited amendment?

Cite as: Robert G. Natelson, *Prohibition on Amendment—Migration, Importation, and Apportionment, in* THE HERITAGE GUIDE TO THE CONSTITUTION 558 (Josh Blackman & John G. Malcolm eds., 3d ed. 2025).

Notes

1. Articles of Confederation, art. II; 34 J. Cont. Cong. 528 (Sept. 16, 1788).   **2.** 34 J. Cont. Cong. 528 (Sept. 16, 1788).   **3.** Articles of Confederation, art IX, § 5.   **4.** 2 Farrand's 177–89.   **5.** *Id.* at 181.   **6.** Robert G. Natelson, *The Original Understanding of the Indian Commerce Clause: An Update,* 23 Fed. Soc'y Rev. 209 (2022); Robert G. Natelson, *The Meaning of "Regulate Commerce" to the Constitution's Ratifiers,* 23 Fed. Soc'y Rev. 307 (2022).   **7.** 2 Farrand's 182.   **8.** Robert G. Natelson, *The Power to Restrict Immigration and the Original Meaning of the Constitution's Define and Punish Clause,* 11 Brit. J. Am. Leg. Stud. 209, 211 (2022).   **9.** 2 Farrand's 181.   **10.** 2 Farrand's 183.   **11.** *Id.*   **12.** *Id.* at 400.   **13.** *Id.* at 415.   **14.** *Id.* at 417.   **15.** *Id.* at 572.   **16.** *Id.* at 618.   **17.** *Id.* at 559.   **18.** *Id.*   **19.** *Id.*   **20.** 2 Stat. 426 (Mar. 2, 1807).

❧

ESSAY NO. 152: PROHIBITION ON AMENDMENT—EQUAL SUFFRAGE OF THE STATES CLAUSE
ART. V

> *. . . no State, without its consent, shall be deprived of its equal Suffrage in the Senate.*

—Robert G. Natelson

INTRODUCTION

Article V imposes two categories of limitations on constitutional amendments. First, there are limits on Congress's powers over migration, importation, and apportionment. (See Essay No. 151.) Second (and the subject of this essay), an amendment to the Constitution cannot "deprive" a state "of its equal Suffrage in the Senate" without the state's consent. This exception is not quite as broad as it might appear. The language does not prevent an amendment that *expands or reduces* the number of Senators from each state as long as the size of each state's Senatorial delegation remains the same. Every state could have one, three, or ten Senators. Moreover, in the unlikely event that lower-population states consented, an amendment could allocate a different number of Senators to states based on population or other factors.

THE CONSTITUTIONAL CONVENTION AND RATIFICATION

The Confederation Congress met on the principle of sovereign equality: "[E]ach state shall have one vote."[1] The "Great Compromise" in the Constitutional Convention of 1787 apportioned the House of Representatives approximately by population but retained state equality in the Senate: Each state would have two Senators, although they would vote individually rather than by state.[2]

The Great Compromise sometimes is called the Connecticut Compromise because the three Connecticut delegates—Roger Sherman, Oliver Ellsworth, and William Samuel Johnson—were instrumental in brokering it.[3] On September 15, after the delegates had already agreed to the Article V amendment process, Sherman perceived a potential danger and "expressed his fears that three fourths of the States might be brought to do things fatal to particular States as abolishing them altogether or depriving them of their equality in the Senate."[4] Sherman "thought it reasonable that the proviso in favor of the States importing slaves should be extended so as to provide that no State should be affected in its internal police, or deprived of its equality

560

in the Senate."[5] Here, "internal police" referred principally to a state's ability to regulate activities with minimal impact on other states.

James Madison of Virginia responded that if the Convention adopted "these special provisos, . . . every State will insist on them, for their boundaries, exports & c."[6] In other words, inserting protections for parochial state interests into the draft constitution would encourage more demands of the same kind. Sherman's motion was defeated by a vote of eight to three. Sherman then moved to strike Article V "altogether." This motion failed, receiving only two "aye" votes. Gouverneur Morris of Pennsylvania proposed an alternative text: "that no State, without its consent shall be deprived of its equal suffrage in the Senate." "This motion," Madison wrote, "being dictated by the circulating murmurs of the small States was agreed to without debate, no one opposing it, or on the question, saying no."[7]

During the ratification debates, this limitation on the amendment power received no special attention beyond the wider question of the composition of the Senate.

OTHER LIMITATIONS ON AMENDMENTS

Article V provides that Congress may "propose Amendments to this Constitution." This text implies a ban on proposing or ratifying a "complete substitute." In other words, Article V cannot be employed to adopt an entirely new Constitution.

Some have argued that some kinds of constitutional changes—beyond those expressly prohibited by Article V—are too profound to be the subject of amendment. For example, *Leser v. Garnett* (1922) presented a challenge to the validity of the Nineteenth Amendment, which Maryland had declined to ratify.[8] The plaintiffs argued that the "character" of the amendment represented "so great an addition to the electorate" that "if made without the state's consent, [would] destroy [Maryland's] autonomy as a political body."[9] The U.S. Supreme Court, in a decision written by Justice Louis Brandeis, rejected this claim based on historical practice. The Court observed that the Nineteenth Amendment "is in character and phraseology precisely similar to the Fifteenth" and that

both amendments were adopted by "the same method," which meant that "[o]ne cannot be valid and the other invalid."[10] In addition, "That the Fifteenth [Amendment] is valid, although rejected by six states, including Maryland, has been recognized and acted on for half a century."[11]

There is another response to the claim that changes unmentioned in Article V can be too fundamental to be the subject of amendment. It is a textual response and does not depend on prior practice or similar precedents. During the Founding era, as today, a widely repeated rule of documentary interpretation was that the enumeration of certain items implies that items not on the list are excluded. During the Founding era, the rule usually was stated as *Designatio unius est exclusio alterius* (the designation of one thing implies the exclusion of others).[12] Today, it usually is stated as *Expressio unius est exclusio alterius* (the expression of one thing implies the exclusion of others).[13] The same principle holds when the items listed are exceptions to the general rule: "Exceptions strengthen the force of the law in cases not excepted, so enumerations weaken it in cases not enumerated."[14] Thus, the fact that Article V enumerates several prohibited amendments strongly suggests that there are no other exceptions—that all amendments not listed as prohibited are permitted.

AMENDMENTS OUTSIDE OF ARTICLE V

Some scholars have argued that constitutional amendments can be adopted legally by procedures outside of Article V. One contention is that Article V limits only government, so the people can propose and ratify amendments themselves.[15] A second contention posits that "constitutional moments" can effectively amend the Constitution through politics and judicial acquiescence.[16] The 1936 federal election, followed by Supreme Court decisions sustaining ensuing legislation, is said to have been such a "constitutional moment."

The first contention is based on a faulty premise. Article V is not a governmental process: Assemblies operating under Article V—legislatures and conventions—function as independent assemblies representing the people, not as government institutions. *United States v. Sprague* (1931) observed that under Article VI, "Congress must function as the delegated agent of the people in the choice of the method of ratification."[17] That process binds not only the government, but the people as well. Thus, *Dodge v. Woolsey* (1855) stated that by adopting the Constitution, the people "have excluded themselves from any direct or immediate agency in making amendments to it, and have directed that amendments should be made representatively for them."[18]

The "constitutional moment" claim fails to consider major differences between candidate elections and the process of constitutional amendment. Endorsement of a successful candidate's platform in a single election, even if that platform is rubber-stamped by jurists, is not the same as real constitutional change. Voters in candidate elections register their choices in short, heated campaigns involving numerous bundled short-term issues. Ratification of constitutional amendments is a decision involving only one or a few long-term issues, unbundled from others, and taking place over an extended period of time.

Moreover, the hypothesis that the Constitution can be amended outside of Article V clashes sharply with the document's text. Article V enumerates four separate methods of amending: (i) congressional proposal followed by state legislative ratification; (ii) convention proposal followed by state legislative ratification; (iii) congressional proposal followed by state convention ratification; and (iv) convention proposal followed by state convention ratification. This precise enumeration implies that the enumerated items are exclusive. Finally, Article V's enumerations of restrictions on the amendment process cannot be presumed to be nugatory, which they might well be if alternative methods of amendment were available.

OPEN QUESTIONS

- How would a state "consent" to have its suffrage reduced in the Senate? Could consent be provided by the state legislature or a state convention acting alone? (State legislatures and conventions are the assemblies that can perform the "federal function" of ratifying an amendment.) Would adoption of a statute through the normal legislative process be sufficient? Would consent require alteration of the state's constitution?
- States have rescinded proposed constitutional amendments. Could a state rescind its consent to have its suffrage reduced, or is a consenting state forever bound by that decision?
- Could an amendment transfer senatorial powers to the House of Representatives or to another entity? For example, the British have shifted power from the House of Lords to the Supreme Court of the United Kingdom. Could an amendment simply abolish the Senate?

Cite as: Robert G. Natelson, *Prohibition on Amendment—Equal Suffrage of the States Clause,* in THE HERITAGE GUIDE TO THE CONSTITUTION 560 (Josh Blackman & John G. Malcolm eds., 3d ed. 2025).

Notes

1. Articles of Confederation, art. V, § 4. **2.** 2 Farrand's 19–20. **3.** Clinton Rossiter, 1787: The Grand Convention 186, 191 (1966). **4.** 2 Farrand's 629. **5.** *Id.* **6.** *Id.* at 630–31. **7.** *Id.* at 631. **8.** 258 U.S. 130. **9.** 258 U.S. at 136. **10.** *Id.* **11.** *Id.* **12.** Thomas Branch, Principia Legis et Aequitatis 19 (1753). **13.** Antonin Scalia & Bryan Garner, Reading Law: The Interpretation of Legal Texts 107 (2012). **14.** *State ex rel. Chandler v. Main,* 16 Wis. 398, 406 (1863); *Schwartz v. Rhoades,* 6 Pa. C.C. 385, 386 (1889); Anonymous ("A Gentleman of the Middle Temple"), The Grounds and Rudiments of Law and Equity 107 (2d ed., 1751). **15.** Akhil Reed Amar, *Philadelphia Revisited: Amending the Constitution Outside Article V,* 55 U. Chi. L. Rev. 1043 (1988). **16.** 2 Bruce Ackerman, We the People: Transformations (1998). **17.** 282 U.S. 716, 733 (1931). **18.** 59 U.S. 331, 348 (1855).

PART 6

ARTICLE VI

ESSAY NO. 153: THE DEBTS AND ENGAGEMENTS CLAUSE
ART. VI, CL. 1

All Debts contracted and Engagements entered into, before the Adoption of this Constitution, shall be as valid against the United States under this Constitution, as under the Confederation.

—Judge Paul B. Matey

INTRODUCTION

Debt fueled the American Revolution and created lingering obligations as the Framers contemplated a new form of government. Drawing on centuries of classical thought, they understood that the new government must inherit old obligations. The Debts and Engagements Clause honored that tradition and bolstered the creditworthiness of the new American Republic.

HISTORY BEFORE 1776

The duty of a successor government to honor the obligations of its predecessor has deep roots in classical thought.[1] Dutch jurist Hugo Grotius understood the people as the source of sovereignty "whatever the form of government may be," just as the "Roman people" were "the same, whether under kings, consuls, or emperors."[2] So because "it is the same people, possessing all the same rights, and powers, which are now exercised in a different manner," it is "evident that a state, which from a commonwealth has become a regal government, is answerable for the debts incurred before that change."[3] Thomas Rutherforth, a mid-eighteenth-century natural law thinker,[4] wrote that a change in the "civil constitution of a state is" merely "a change of the form of government in a state, and not a change in the essential form of the state itself."[5] And E. de Vattel, an influential Swiss jurist,[6] viewed the state as a moral actor that "has its own affairs and interests . . . deliberates and takes resolutions in common, and . . . thus becomes a moral person . . . susceptible at once of obligations and of rights."[7] Vattel reasoned "[w]hen a person duly authorized contracts in the name of the State[,] his act binds the Nation itself and consequently all future rulers of the social body. . . .

Nothing can release the Nation from the obligation of discharging such debts."[8]

The views of these classical thinkers were echoed in colonial writings. George Mason of Virginia noted that the "Ministry in Great Britain, as well as the Torys here, have indeed constantly accused us of engaging in the War to avoid the Payment of our Debts; but every honest Man has denied so injurious a Charge, with Indignation."[9]

THE ARTICLES OF CONFEDERATION

The Continental Congress grappled with our Nation's soaring war debts.[10] The Articles of Confederation made all debts chargeable to the Continental Congresses enforceable against their successor, the Congress of the Confederation. Article XII provided that "[a]ll bills of credit emitted, monies borrowed, and debts contracted by or under the authority of congress, before the assembling of the united states, in pursuance of the present confederation, shall be deemed and considered as a charge against the united States, for payment and satisfaction whereof the said united states and the public faith are hereby solemnly pledged."[11] That was a sizable obligation stemming from the central government's inability to raise revenue.[12] Congress was forced to rely on credit, often taking loans purely to pay the interest on prior borrowing.[13]

By 1783, citing the "successful termination of the war" and "the critical exigencies of public affairs," Oliver Ellsworth, James Madison, and Alexander Hamilton proposed it was "the duty of Congress to review and provide for the debts which the war has left upon the United States, and to look forward to the means of obviating dangers which may interrupt the harmony and tranquillity of the Confederacy."[14]

THE CONSTITUTIONAL CONVENTION

During the Constitutional Convention of 1787, the Framers debated the need to assure creditors that plans for a new republican government would not erase the existing debts and obligations of the states.[15] The Framers looked to the Articles of Confederation's language; the classical legal theory arising from the European "synthesis" of Roman, canon, and civil law;[16] and the natural law's moral precepts.[17]

The earliest version of the Debts and Engagements Clause appeared on May 29, 1787. Edmund Randolph of Virginia proposed that "provision ought to be made for the continuance of [the Confederation] Congress and their authorities and privileges, until a given day after the reform of the articles of Union shall be adopted, and for the completion of all their engagements."[18] The delegates agreed to this proposal on June 5 by a vote of 9 to 2 without any debate.[19]

The Convention revisited the proposal on July 18. But Gouverneur Morris of Pennsylvania opposed the "assumption of their engagements."[20] Madison contended that the provision would only "prevent[] an interregnum, which must exist in the interval between the adoption of the New Govt. and the commencement of its operation."[21] However, James Wilson of Pennsylvania noted that "some provision on the subject would be proper in order to prevent any suspicion that the obligations of the Confederacy might be dissolved along with the Governt. under which they were contracted."[22]

Ultimately, the Convention rejected the part relating to the continuance of Congress by a 6 to 3 vote and unanimously disapproved of the part about completion of the Congress's engagements. At this point, the provision did not yet address the assumption of debts.

On August 21, William Livingston of New Jersey delivered the recommendation from the Committee of Eleven "respecting the debts of the several States."[23] The proposal stated that "[t]he Legislature of the U. S. shall have power to fulfil the engagements which have been entered into by Congress and to discharge as well the debts of the U– S: as the debts incurred by the several States during the late war, for the common defence and general welfare."[24] Critically, however, this proposal did not make the assumption of debt mandatory. Elbridge Gerry of Massachusetts thought that Congress should be given "the power only, without adopting the obligation," and observed that states that "had done most" to "sink their respective debts . . . would be alarmed, if they were now to be saddled with a share of the debts of States which had done least."[25]

The Convention further debated the proposal the next day. Madison thought this provision was "necessary," noting that after 1776, "Debtors to Brittish subjects" argued that "contracts under the old Government were dissolved by the Revolution which destroyed the political identity of the society."[26] Morris proposed an amendment stating that Congress "*shall* discharge the debts & fulfil the engagements (of the U. States)."[27] The proposal was adopted unanimously.

On August 23, the Convention considered a further amendment that again introduced the idea of mandatory debt assumption: "The Legislature shall fulfil the engagements and discharge the debts of the U. S."[28] This proposal stirred fresh opposition focused on the kinds of debt. Pierce Butler of South Carolina expressed "his dissatisfaction lest it should compel payment as well to the Blood-suckers who had speculated on the distresses of others, as to those who had fought & bled for their country."[29]

The Convention returned to this clause on August 25. George Mason of Virginia thought the obligation was "too strong" and would "beget speculations" because "the Government will be more able to pay them."[30] Randolph urged softer language: "All debts contracted & engagements entered into, by or under the authority of Congs. shall be as valid agst the U. States under this constitution as under the Confederation."[31] Randolph's proposal passed by a vote of 10 to 1 with only Morris voting against it.[32] Notably, this text did not squarely address whether Congress would assume state debts from before ratification.

The Committee of Style, which included Morris, altered the text: "All debts contracted and engagements entered into *before the adoption of this Constitution*"[33] would be valid. Professor William Treanor has observed that Randolph's proposal "[i]mplicitly . . . did not allow assumption of state debts unauthorized by Congress."[34] But the Committee's change "allowed Congress to assume state debts" from the Articles of Confederation government "regardless of whether those debts had been previously authorized by Congress."[35] By contrast, Professor David Schwartz has argued that the change had no substantive effect.[36]

But perhaps there is a more innocuous justification for the change. On August 25, shortly after Randolph's proposal was adopted, the Supremacy Clause was modified. With this revision, the Supreme Law of the Land would include treaties "which shall be made" in the *future* "under the Authority of the United States," as well as "all Treaties made" *prior* to ratification of the Constitution.[37] Madison explained that this change would "obviate all doubt concerning the force of treaties preexisting" the Constitution.[38] Likewise, Article III provides that the "judicial Power" extends to cases concerning "Treaties made" before ratification, "or which shall be made" after ratification.[39] The Committee of Style would separate the Debts and Engagements Clause from Congress's enumerated powers, moving it to Article VI, immediately before the Supremacy Clause.[40] The Committee may have attempted to standardize the language in Article VI such that treaties, as well as debts and engagements, were all valid whether entered into before or after ratification.

THE RATIFICATION DEBATES

During the ratification debates, Madison and Hamilton drew on the classical tradition and its natural law foundation to defend the clause. In Federalist No. 43, Madison claimed that the Clause "can only be considered as a declaratory proposition" built on the natural law moral principle that no "government would *dare*, with, or even without, this constitutional declaration before it, to remit the debts justly due to the public" on the pretext that a change in government erases its obligations. In Federalist No. 84, Hamilton similarly emphasized the "established doctrine of political law that '*States neither lose any of their rights, nor are discharged from any of*

their obligations by a change in the form of their civil government.'"[41]

The Anti-Federalists focused more on the accumulation of federal debt than the Debts and Assumptions Clause. Brutus, for example, wrote that he could "scarcely contemplate a greater calamity that could befal this country, than to be loaded with a debt exceeding their ability ever to discharge."[42] Centinel agreed that the clause protects debts "*against* the United States."[43] Agrippa argued that assumption of state debt was an "[a]ssurance[] of [the] sort easily given, and as easily forgotten," leaving states responsible for their own obligations and those of the new Republic.[44] Related concerns about the tax power were shared by Madison and James Monroe. Monroe wrote to Madison that "No proposition that I have seen removes my objections to [the assumption provision]," which "at best, if it does not compel the industrious & complying States to pay the debts, or a part of the debts, of those who have been less deserving, it prefers the exercise of taxation in the hands of the national to those of the State governments, [which] I cannot approve."[45]

EARLY PRACTICE

In 1790, the First Congress passed Treasury Secretary Alexander Hamilton's financial plan, which assumed states' Revolutionary War debts.[46] Federalists in Congress argued that "the Constitution gave the national government this power."[47]

The French Revolution provided an early test of whether the new government would honor its debt obligations. After King Louis XVI was deposed in 1792, the Washington Administration considered stopping payments on the French loans that financed the American Revolution. Then-Secretary of State Thomas Jefferson wrote that it was an "oblig[atio]n of Contracts" in the "nature of [a] Moral oblig[atio]n" imposed "on individuals" as well as "societies" in the "aggregate."[48] Morris agreed: "The honest Nation is that which like the honest Man 'hath to its plighted Faith and vow forever firmly stood, and tho it promise to its Loss yet makes that Promise good.'"[49] Ultimately, the nation honored its debts.

Justice Joseph Story later concurred that the clause expressed "the doctrine[] that revolutions in government have, or rather ought to have, no effect whatsoever upon private rights, and contracts, or upon the public obligations of nations."[50] Because this doctrine "result[ed] from the law of nations, and the moral obligations of society," it had the effect of reassuring the nation's "public creditors, foreign as well as domestic."[51]

JUDICIAL PRECEDENT

The Debts and Engagements Clause has rarely prompted litigation, probably because the First Congress promptly assumed all state debts, satisfying creditors. The Engagements prong was indirectly raised in antebellum cases concerning slavery. The Northwest Ordinance of 1787, adopted before the Constitution's ratification, prohibited slavery in the territories.

Did the ordinance and its prohibition of slavery remain valid after ratification? In *Strader v. Graham* (1850) and *Dred Scott v. Sandford* (1857), Chief Justice Roger B. Taney reasoned that the Northwest Ordinance's ban on slavery "ceased to be in force upon the adoption of the Constitution."[52] But in his *Strader* dissent, Justice John Catron countered that the Northwest Ordinance was "an 'engagement entered into' before the adoption of the Constitution," making it "equally binding on the one Congress as the other, according to the sixth article of the new Constitution."[53] Justice Henry Baldwin had made a similar point a decade earlier in *Heirs v. Kibbe* (1840).[54]

OPEN QUESTIONS

Scholars have recently cited the clause in debates over secondary issues such as whether Morris used his position on the Committee of Style to alter the substantive meaning of the Constitution.[55] Otherwise, few questions about the Debts and Engagements Clause remain open.

Cite as: Judge Paul B. Matey, *The Debts and Engagements Clause, in* THE HERITAGE GUIDE TO THE CONSTITUTION 564 (Josh Blackman & John G. Malcolm eds., 3d ed. 2025).

Notes

1. Hugo Grotius, The Rights of War and Peace 120–21 (A.C. Campbell trans., 1901) (1625); Andrew Forsyth, Common Law and Natural Law in America 24–25 (2019); John Locke, Some Thoughts Concerning Education §§ 185–86 (1693). **2.** Grotius, *supra* at 120. **3.** *Id.* at 121. **4.** Gary L. McDowell, *The Limits of Natural Law: Thomas Rutherforth and the American Legal Tradition*, 37 Am. J. Juris. 57, 58 (1992). **5.** 2 Thomas Rutherforth, Institutes of Natural Law: Being the Substance of a Course of Lectures on Grotius de Jure Belli et Pacis 673 (1756). **6.** Vincent Chetail, *Vattel and the American Dream: An Inquiry into the Reception of the* Law of Nations *in the United States, in* The Roots of International Law 251–300 (Pierre-Marie Dupuy & Vincent Chetail eds., 2013). **7.** E. de Vattel, Law of Nations or the Principles of Natural Law § 2 (Charles G. Fenwick trans., 1916) (1758). **8.** *Id.* at §§ 215–16. **9.** Letter from George Mason to Arthur Campbell (May 7, 1783), https://perma.cc/E7TY-UQAJ. **10.** David P. Currie, *The Constitution in Congress: Substantive Issues in the First Congress, 1789–1791*, 61 U. Chi. L. Rev. 775, 802 (1994); Edmund W. Kitch & Julia D. Mahoney, *Restructuring United States Government Debt: Private Rights, Public Values, and the Constitution*, 2019 Mich. St. L. Rev. 1283, 1292 (2019). **11.** Articles of Confederation, art. XII. **12.** David Hutchison, The Foundations of the Constitution 94 (1928); Alexander Hamilton, Report Relative to a Provision for the Support of Public Credit (Jan. 9, 1790), https://perma.cc/EZ8T-HLED. **13.** 5 Elliot's 22; 24 J. Cont. Cong. 277 (Apr. 26, 1783). **14.** 24 J. Cont. Cong. 277 (Apr.

26, 1783). **15.** 2 Farrand's 413–15. **16.** Adrian Vermeule, Common Good Constitutionalism: Recovering the Classical Legal Tradition 1 (2022); Norman Barry, *Classical Theory of Law*, 73 Cornell L. Rev. 283, 284 (1988). **17.** Thomas G. West, The Political Theory of the American Founding: Natural Rights, Public Policy, and the Moral Conditions of Freedom (2017). **18.** 1 Farrand's 22. **19.** *Id.* at 121, 227, 237. **20.** 2 Farrand's 46–47. **21.** *Id.* at 47. **22.** *Id.* **23.** *Id.* at 355. **24.** *Id.* at 355–56. **25.** *Id.* at 356. **26.** *Id.* at 377. **27.** *Id.* **28.** *Id.* at 392. **29.** *Id.* **30.** *Id.* at 412; Joseph M. Lynch, Negotiating the Constitution: The Earliest Debates over Original Intent 72 (1999). **31.** 2 Farrand's 414. **32.** *Id.* **33.** *Id.* at 603 (emphasis added). **34.** William M. Treanor, *The Case of the Dishonest Scrivener: Gouverneur Morris and the Creation of the Federalist Constitution*, 120 Mich. L. Rev. 1, 103 (2021). **35.** *Id.* **36.** David S. Schwartz, *Framing the Framer: A Commentary on Treanor's Gouverneur Morris as "Dishonest Scrivener,"* 120 Mich. L. Rev. Online 51, 77–78 (2022). **37.** Art. VI, cl. 2. **38.** 2 Farrand's 417. **39.** Art. III, § 2; 2 Farrand's 432. **40.** 2 Farrand's 569–71, 594–96, 603. **41.** Federalist No. 84 (Hamilton). **42.** Storing 2.9.94. **43.** *Id.* at 2.7.167. **44.** Storing 4.6.33. **45.** Letter from James Monroe to James Madison (July 26, 1790), https://perma.cc/N8XR-KDAU. **46.** Funding Act of 1790, 1 Stat. 138, 142; Max M. Edling, A Revolution in Favor of Government: Origins of the U.S. Constitution and the Making of the American State 206–14 (2003). **47.** Treanor, *supra* at 103. **48.** Thomas

Jefferson, *Notes for Opinion on the Treaty of Alliance with France* (before Apr. 28, 1793), https://perma.cc/WV3R-2JXF. **49.** Letter from Gouverneur Morris to Thomas Jefferson (Dec. 21, 1792), https://perma.cc/JDB7-E3XJ. **50.** 3 Story's Commentaries § 1827. **51.** *Id.* at §§ 1827–28. **52.** *Strader v. Graham*, 51 U.S. (10 How.) 82, 97 (1850); *Dred Scott v. Sandford*, 60 U.S. (19 How.) 393, 438 (1857). **53.** *Strader*, 51 U.S. at 98 (Catron, J., dissenting). **54.** 39 U.S. (14 Pet.) 353, 417 (1840) (Baldwin, J., concurring). **55.** Treanor, *supra* at 103; Schwartz, *supra* at 77–78.

⌒

ESSAY NO. 154: THE SUPREMACY CLAUSE
ART. VI, CL. 2

This Constitution, and the Laws of the United States which shall be made in Pursuance thereof; and all Treaties made, or which shall be made, under the Authority of the United States, shall be the supreme Law of the Land; and the Judges in every State shall be bound thereby, any Thing in the Constitution or Laws of any State to the Contrary notwithstanding.

—Gary S. Lawson

INTRODUCTION

The Supremacy Clause is a conflict-of-laws rule specifying that certain national acts take priority over any state act that conflicts with those national acts. In this respect, the Supremacy Clause represents a choice from among several strategies for dealing with federal-state conflicts that emerged during the constitutional drafting process. Case law has developed a complex body of doctrine for determining when federal-state conflicts arise and for carving out certain immunities that each level of government has against the other.

HISTORY BEFORE 1787

Any federal system needs a strategy for dealing with potential conflicts between the national and local governments, and at least three strategies are available. First, each government could be given exclusive jurisdiction over its respective sphere, which would avoid altogether the possibility of direct conflict. Second, the governments could have concurrent jurisdiction, but one government could be given power to veto actions of the other, either in the event of actual conflict or in general classes of cases. Third, both governments could be allowed to act without mutual interference, but one government's acts could be given primacy over the other's in the event of actual conflict.

In the pre-Revolution era, some colonists urged the first approach to handle relations between the colonies and England: The English Parliament could regulate colonial trade, but local legislatures would have exclusive authority over other matters.[1] The Articles of Confederation tried a version of the third approach. Article XIII provided that "[e]very state shall abide by the determinations of the united states in congress assembled, on all questions which by this confederation are submitted to them." Article II put a limit on this supremacy by ensuring that states retained a broad sphere of authority: "Each state retains its sovereignty, freedom and independence, and every Power, Jurisdiction and right, which is not by this confederation expressly delegated to the United States, in Congress assembled." Moreover, it was not clear whether congressional acts were self-enforcing or required implementing state legislation. If states enacted laws contrary to "determinations of the united states in congress assembled," those subsequent state laws might have prevailed under conventional rules of priority of legal acts.[2]

The federal Constitution would make the supremacy of the national government far clearer.

THE CONSTITUTIONAL CONVENTION

The Constitution proposed a federal system that would separate powers between the central government and the state governments. The

Framers would consider all three strategies for conflict management.

First, the Constitution assigns the federal government exclusive power over certain areas, such as treaties,[3] but it was unclear whether certain other federal powers, such as the bankruptcy or commerce powers, would be exclusive or concurrent.[4] Some Framers favored the second strategy. The Virginia Plan proposed that "the National Legislature ought to be impowered . . . to negative all laws passed by the several States, contravening in the opinion of the National Legislature the articles of Union."[5] That proposal received initial approval from the delegates.[6]

James Madison of Virginia favored an even broader negative.[7] He seconded the motion by Charles Pinckney of South Carolina to give Congress "authority to negative all Laws which they shd. judge to be improper."[8] Representatives from small states vigorously opposed this expanded national veto.[9] Elbridge Gerry of Massachusetts insisted that Pinckney's proposal would "enslave the States."[10] The strong veto was voted down 7 to 3.[11] The delegates also voted it down again later.[12]

The Framers ultimately settled on the third approach with respect to the Supremacy Clause: Certain types of federal law would be given primacy over conflicting state laws.

What eventually became the Supremacy Clause was introduced on June 15, 1787, as part of the New Jersey Plan.[13] Although the New Jersey Plan never progressed, Luther Martin a month later put forth a variant of its supremacy clause, which was adopted unanimously.[14] After some technical changes, the Supremacy Clause emerged in its final form.[15] It was adopted with little debate or dissent.

The clause lists three types of law that are the "supreme Law of the Land": the Constitution, federal statutes enacted pursuant to the Constitution, and past and future treaties. These federal laws are effective even if something in a state law is to the "Contrary," and state court judges are "bound" by this supreme law regardless of what state law, including state constitutional law, provides. In particular, Founding-era state judges were now bound to enforce the 1783 Treaty of Peace with Great Britain, which provided guarantees against the confiscation of Loyalist property.[16]

THE RATIFICATION DEBATES

During the ratification process, some opponents of the Constitution feared that the Supremacy Clause—sometimes called the "Sweeping Clause"—would destroy the states as meaningful entities. For example, at the Pennsylvania ratifying convention, Robert Whitehill asserted that "Article 6, clauses 2 and 3 are concluding clauses that the state governments will be abolished."[17] Others worried about subordinating state laws to treaties that did not require ratification by the House of Representatives.[18] Alexander Hamilton responded in Federalist No. 33 that the Supremacy Clause and the Necessary and Proper Clause were "only declaratory of a truth which would have resulted by necessary and unavoidable implication from the very act of constituting a federal government, and vesting it with certain specified powers." He further explained that unconstitutional federal laws or treaties are not supreme law: "Acts of the larger society which are *not pursuant* to its constitutional powers but which are invasions of the residuary authorities of the smaller societies . . . will be merely acts of usurpation and will deserve to be treated as such."

WHAT IS THE SUPREME LAW OF THE LAND?

The Supremacy Clause does not distinguish among the three named sources of federal law: the Constitution, laws of the United States, and treaties. All three are equally supreme over competing sources of state law. They also are supreme over lesser types of federal law, such as federal common law or federal regulations.[19]

The Supremacy Clause does not itself establish the supremacy of the Constitution over federal statutes or treaties.[20] In *Marbury v. Madison* (1803), Chief Justice John Marshall recognized that the principle of constitutional supremacy can be inferred from the Constitution's structure: "Certainly all those who have framed written constitutions contemplate them as forming the fundamental and paramount law of the nation."[21] As a result, "the theory of every such government must be that an act of the legislature repugnant to the Constitution is void."[22] The Supremacy Clause merely added weight to these primary structural arguments. By "declaring what shall be the *supreme* law of the land, the *constitution* itself is first mentioned, and not the laws of the United States generally, but those only which shall be made in *pursuance* of the constitution, have that rank."[23]

Justice Joseph Story observed that this provision does not grant power to any federal actor. The Supremacy Clause does not preclude other strategies for dealing with potential national and state conflicts. It does not even allocate substantive power between the national and state governments.[24] Rather, the clause is *only* a conflict-of-laws rule. It decides which particular type of law prevails over another type of law.

The Supremacy Clause's sequencing of the sources of federal law is at most modest evidence in favor of constitutional primacy. Marshall recognized this principle in *Marbury*.[25] If the sequencing mattered, it would also suggest that federal statutes must always take precedence over federal treaties. Vasan Kesavan has advanced this position, drawing on, among other things, other instances of the seeming sequencing in the Constitution.[26] But standard law has long been that federal statutes and treaties are equally supreme.[27] If a statute and treaty are in conflict, the latest enactment would control.[28]

Modern law also treats federal administrative regulations as supreme over competing sources of state law.[29] One court of appeals held that a memorandum signed by the President could also override state law.[30] However, some scholars disagree as to whether this doctrine is consistent with the language of the Supremacy Clause. The text refers to "Laws of the United States . . . made in Pursuance" of the Constitution. Such laws are statutes enacted in accordance with the lawmaking procedures of Article I, Section 7. Administrative regulations and executive orders do not go through this process.[31] Other scholars contend that federal "Laws" can include executive actions with binding effect.[32] Whatever the correct originalist answer may be, current doctrine allows at least some administrative regulations to override state law; in fact, federal regulations have emerged as the most frequent source of federal-state conflicts.[33]

WHEN DOES FEDERAL LAW "PREEMPT" STATE LAW?

When a state law conflicts with a supreme federal law, the state law is *preempted*, meaning that the state law cannot be given legal effect in those instances of conflict. Until the early twentieth century, the U.S. Supreme Court would determine whether there was a straightforward conflict between a federal statute and a state law.[34] However, the Court changed course during the New Deal as the locus of reformist legislation shifted from the states to the federal government. The modern doctrine makes it easier to find federal preemption of state law. Even if there is no express conflict based on the text of the law, the Court will find that preemption occurs when Congress intended a federal statute to preempt a state law.[35]

The Court has found evidence of such congressional intent in a federal statute's express provision declaring that it does or does not preempt state law,[36] but such a clear statement of intent is not needed. The Court has held that state law is preempted "[w]hen Congress intends federal law to 'occupy the field'" or "to the extent of any conflict with a federal statute."[37] Conflicts can also result when it is impossible to comply with both state and federal law.[38] State law is also preempted when it "stands as an obstacle to the accomplishment and execution of the full purposes and objectives of Congress."[39] Justice Clarence Thomas, however, has called for the Court to reconsider so-called implied preemption.[40]

The Court has not adopted a clear test by which to determine when a state law sufficiently obstructs federal purposes. Rather, this decision "is a matter of judgment, to be informed by examining the federal statute as a whole and identifying its purpose and intended effects."[41] The Court generally presumes that federal law will not preempt laws that address matters of traditional state concern,[42] although this presumption has proven difficult to apply and has sharply divided the Court.[43]

INTERGOVERNMENTAL IMMUNITY

Under the Supremacy Clause, states cannot regulate, interfere with, or control federal instrumentalities. This doctrine of intergovernmental immunity is generally traced to *McCulloch v. Maryland* (1819).[44] This landmark case held that states could not tax the Bank of the United States. The statute creating the bank did not specifically forbid state taxes, but the Court reasoned that "[i]t is of the very essence of supremacy to remove all obstacles to [the federal government's] action within its own sphere." Under this principle, Chief Justice John Marshall explained, "every power vested in subordinate [state] governments" must be "modified" so "as to exempt [the federal government's] own operations from [the states'] own influence."[45] The intergovernmental immunity found in *McCulloch* was not stated expressly in the Supremacy Clause; the Court inferred it from the broader principle of federal supremacy.

The Supreme Court has since qualified the widest implications of this principle. For example, states can tax the salaries of federal employees.[46] Modern law maintains that "a state law is thus no longer unconstitutional just because it indirectly increases costs for the Federal Government, so long as the law imposes those costs in a neutral, nondiscriminatory way."[47] However, the courts will uphold even state legislation that discriminates against federal instrumentalities where Congress clearly and unambiguously waives its constitutional immunity.[48]

OPEN QUESTIONS

- Under the Supremacy Clause, the "Judges in every State" are "bound" by the "supreme Law of the Land." What about state executive and legislative branch officials?[49]
- Under the so-called doctrine of judicial supremacy, a simple majority of the Supreme Court can declare what constitutes the "supreme Law of the Land" with finality.[50] Can this doctrine be supported by reference to the Supremacy Clause?[51]

Cite as: Gary S. Lawson, *The Supremacy Clause*, *in* THE HERITAGE GUIDE TO THE CONSTITUTION 568 (Josh Blackman & John G. Malcolm eds., 3d ed. 2025).

Notes

1. Christopher D. Drahozal, The Supremacy Clause: A Reference Guide to the United States Constitution 4 (2004). **2.** Caleb Nelson, *Preemption,* 86 Va. L. Rev. 225, 247–50 (2000). **3.** Art. I, § 10, cl. 1; Art. II, § 2, cl. 2. **4.** Steven Gow Calabresi & Gary Lawson, The U.S. Constitution: Creation, Reconstruction, the Progressives, and the Modern Era 595–97 (2020). **5.** 1 Farrand's 21. **6.** *Id.* at 54. **7.** Drahozal, *supra* at 13–14; Michael D. Ramsey, *The Supremacy Clause, Original Meaning, and Modern Law,* 74 Ohio St. L.J. 559, 577 (2014). **8.** 1 Farrand's 164. **9.** *Id.* at 165–68. **10.** *Id.* at 165. **11.** *Id.* at 168. **12.** 2 Farrand's 27–28. **13.** 1 Farrand's 245. **14.** 2 Farrand's 22. **15.** Drahozal, *supra* at 21–24, 68–70. **16.** *Id.* at 8–10. **17.** 2 DHRC 526. **18.** Drahozal, *supra* at 28–30. **19.** Jonathan Mitchell, *Stare Decisis and Constitutional Text,* 110 Mich. L. Rev. 1, 6 (2011). **20.** Gary Lawson, *Rebel Without a Clause: The Irrelevance of Article VI to Constitutional Supremacy,* 110 Mich. L. Rev. First Impressions 33 (2011). **21.** 5 U.S. (1 Cranch) 137, 177 (1803). **22.** *Id.* **23.** *Id.* at 180 (emphasis added). **24.** 2 Story's Commentaries §§ 1836–42. **25.** *Marbury,* 5 U.S. (1 Cranch) at 180. **26.** Vasan Kesavan, *The Three Tiers of Federal Law,* 100 Nw. U. L. Rev. 1479, 1499–1502 (2006). **27.** *Head Money Cases,* 112 U.S. 580, 598–99 (1884). **28.** *Cook v. United States,* 288 U.S. 102, 118–19 (1933). **29.** *Geier v. Am. Honda Motor Co., Inc.,* 529 U.S. 861 (2000). **30.** *Ariz. Dream Act Coal. v. Brewer,* 818 F.3d 901, 915 (9th Cir. 2016). **31.** David S. Rubenstein, *The Paradox of Administrative Preemption,* 38 Harv. J. L. & Pub. Pol'y 267 (2014). **32.** Joshua Hawkes & Mark Seidenfeld, *A Positive Defense of Administrative Preemption,* 22 Geo. Mason L. Rev. 63, 71–75, 77–78 (2014). **33.** David S. Rubenstein, *Delegating Supremacy?,* 65 Vand. L. Rev. 1125, 1128 (2012). **34.** Stephen A. Gardbaum, *The Nature of Preemption,* 79 Cornell L. Rev. 767, 783 (1994). **35.** Nelson, *supra.* **36.** *Arizona v. United States,* 567 U.S. 387, 399 (2012). **37.** *Crosby v. Nat'l Foreign Trade Council,* 530 U.S. 363, 372 (2000). **38.** *PLIVA, Inc. v. Mensing,* 564 U.S. 604, 618 (2011). **39.** *Hines v. Davidowitz,* 312 U.S. 52, 67 (1941). **40.** *Kansas v. Garcia,* 589 U.S. 191, 213 (2020) (Thomas, J., concurring); *Wyeth v. Levine,* 555 U.S. 555, 583 (2009) (Thomas, J., concurring). **41.** *Crosby,* 530 U.S. at 373. **42.** *Rice v. Santa Fe Elevator Corp.,* 331 U.S. 218, 230 (1947). **43.** *Va. Uranium, Inc. v. Warren,* 587 U.S. 761 (2019); *PLIVA,* 564 U.S. 604; *Geier,* 529 U.S. 861. **44.** 17 U.S. (5 Wheat.) 316 (1819). **45.** *Id.* at 427. **46.** *Graves v. N.Y. ex rel. O'Keefe,* 306 U.S. 466 (1939). **47.** *United States v. Washington,* 596 U.S. 832, 839 (2022). **48.** *Id.* **49.** *Printz v. United States,* 521 U.S. 898, 907 (1997). **50.** *Cooper v. Aaron,* 358 U.S. 1, 18–20 (1958). **51.** Josh Blackman, *The Irrepressible Myth of* Cooper v. Aaron, 107 Geo. L.J. 1135 (2019).

ESSAY NO. 155: THE OATH OR AFFIRMATION CLAUSE
ART. VI, CL. 3

The Senators and Representatives before mentioned, and the Members of the several State Legislatures, and all executive and judicial Officers, both of the United States and of the several States, shall be bound by Oath or Affirmation, to support this Constitution. . . .

—Judge Gregory G. Katsas & Andrew W. Smith

INTRODUCTION

There are two oath clauses in the Constitution: Article II provides specific wording of the President's Oath and Article VI requires that a range of federal and state officeholders must be "bound by Oath or Affirmation, to support this Constitution." The Oath or Affirmation Clause in Article VI built upon a long-standing tradition of requiring leaders to take oaths to follow the law in the discharge of their offices. No doubt a careful observer can find some cases where a willful judge found a way to reach an unconstitutional result—something that is doubly true for statutes enacted by Congress—but as the Framers recognized, the oath seeks to provide the essential ingredient in a functional legal system: An officer's loyalties lie foremost with the Constitution.

HISTORY BEFORE 1787

In England, the king swore an oath to govern "according to the Statutes in Parliament Agreed on and the Laws and Customs of the same."[1] English judges similarly saw their oaths as creating a duty to decide cases in accord with the law.[2] Americans inherited this tradition and upon winning their independence further entrenched it. The signers of the Declaration of Independence "mutually pledge[d] to each other our lives, our fortunes, and our sacred honor."[3] Early state constitutions mandated that certain officers take an oath or affirmation,[4] and at least some state courts recognized that these oaths mattered.[5] In North Carolina, judges relied on "the obligation of their oaths" to "give their opinion" that a state law was unconstitutional.[6]

Unlike the state constitutions, the Articles of Confederation lacked a general oath requirement. They prescribed only one oath: A judge who decided disputes between states was required to swear "well and truly to hear and determine the matter in question, according to the best of his judgment, without favour, affection, or hope of reward."[7] The Articles also did not require delegates to the national legislature to take an oath to the Confederation: In this "firm league of friendship," allegiances remained with the states.[8]

THE CONSTITUTIONAL CONVENTION

As part of the Virginia Plan, Edmund Randolph proposed that "the Legislative, Executive & Judiciary powers within the several States ought to be bound by oath to support the articles of Union."[9] This proposal prompted some pushback. Roger Sherman of Connecticut worried that requiring state officers to swear an oath to the federal Constitution would "unnecessarily intrud[e] into the State jurisdictions."[10] But Randolph reminded the Convention that state officers are "already under oath to the States." To avoid partiality among these officers, state officers "ought to be equally bound" to the national government.[11] "If the state judges are not sworn to the observance of the new government," Randolph asked, "will they not judicially determine in favor of their state laws?"[12]

Implicit in the debate between Sherman and Randolph was the understanding that an oath shapes an officer's loyalties in deciding matters before him, but not everyone shared this opinion. James Wilson of Pennsylvania was "never fond of oaths, considering them as a left handed security only."[13] Because the left hand helps the right hand, the oath was only a "secondary security."[14] Wilson explained that a good government "did not need [oaths], and a bad one could not or ought not to be supported."[15]

Luther Martin of Maryland proposed to remove "within the Several states" from the text. Under this proposal, it seems that only *federal* officers would be required to take an oath to the Constitution.[16] That proposal was defeated by a vote of 7 to 4. Randolph's proposal was accepted by a vote of 6 to 5.[17]

The Convention returned to Randolph's proposal on July 23. Elbridge Gerry of Massachusetts proposed that "the Officers of the National Government" should also take an oath to "support . . . the Natl. Govt."[18] Gerry explained that this revised oath would "cure" any perception that the federal and state governments were not part of the same "General System."[19] Gerry's proposal was approved unanimously.[20]

On August 6, John Rutledge of South Carolina delivered the Committee of Detail's report.[21] This report expressly provided that "[t]he Members of the Legislatures, and the executive and judicial Officers of the United States, *and of the several States* shall be bound by Oath to support this Constitution."[22] It also provided a separate oath for the President.[23] However, the Framers did not provide specific wording for the Article VI oath as they had done for the President's oath. Instead, they left that task to Congress.

On August 30, James Madison of Virginia proposed a religious accommodation: An officeholder who could not swear an "oath" could alternatively take an "affirmation."[24] That proposal passed unanimously. The text was referred to the Committee of Style, which made a slight revision: "Members of the Legislatures" was changed to "the senators and representatives before mentioned."[25] The clause now provided that "[t]he senators and representatives before mentioned, and the members of the several state legislatures, and all executive and judicial officers, both of the United States and of the several States, shall be bound by oath or affirmation, to support this constitution."[26] In the end, Randolph prevailed: Both federal and state officers must bind themselves to support the U.S. Constitution.

THE RATIFICATION DEBATES

During the ratification debates, supporters of the Constitution hailed the benefits of the Oath or Affirmation Clause. In Federalist No. 27, Alexander Hamilton noted that the oath worked hand-in-hand with the Supremacy Clause to ensure the "regular and peaceable execution of the laws of the Union." In Federalist No. 44, Madison explained that the Oath or Affirmation Clause was necessary because "members and officers of the State Governments . . . will have an essential agency in giving effect to the Federal Constitution." At the Connecticut ratifying convention, Oliver Wolcott emphasized that the oath filled a void left by the Constitution's elimination of religious tests. Wolcott stated that a religious test was no longer a "necessity" because the Constitution "enjoins an oath upon all the officers of the United States," which amounts to a "direct appeal to that God who is the avenger of perjury."[27]

Conversely, the Anti-Federalists saw these unifying and stabilizing effects of the Oath or Affirmation Clause as bugs, not features. James Winthrop, writing as Agrippa, complained that "state officers are also bound by oath to support this constitution," thereby "binding the state judges and other officers, to execute the continental laws in their own proper departments within the state." When combined with the Supremacy Clause, Winthrop noted, the oath ensured that even "questions between citizens of the same state are to be decided by the general laws and not by the local ones."[28] But both sides shared the view that the oath to the Constitution mattered, displacing a judge's freedom to decide a case however he preferred.

OATHS IN THE FIRST CONGRESS

The House and Senate were supposed to assemble on March 4, 1789, but on that date, they lacked a quorum.[29] Shortly after the House obtained a quorum, the members voted to approve an oath by a resolution.[30] On April 8, the Chief Justice of New York administered the oath to the Speaker and then to the other members present.[31] However, at that point, the Senators and Vice President John Adams had not yet taken oaths of office. Adams also had not participated in the joint session on April 6 when the electoral votes were counted and George Washington was elected President.[32]

On May 6, Congress passed the first oath statute.[33] The oath provided, "I, A. B.

do solemnly swear or affirm (as the case may be) that I will support the Constitution of the United States." Justice Joseph Story related that "a few members" worried about "the constitutional authority of congress to pass such an act" but that, ultimately, "it was approved without much opposition."[34] On June 1, President Washington signed the bill into law.[35] This was the first statute the President signed—a testament to the importance of oaths at the time. Two days later, Vice President Adams took his Article VI oath and then proceeded to issue the oath to the other Senators present and to the Secretary of the Senate.[36] Yet even before taking the oath, Senators and the Vice President had transacted business.[37]

THE OATH AND THE JUDICIARY

Federal judges have long cited their oath as a basis for the power of judicial review. In *Marbury v. Madison* (1803), Chief Justice John Marshall explained that because "a judge swear[s] to discharge his duties agreeably to the constitution of the United States," he may not apply a "law repugnant to the constitution."[38] This duty is binding even when (or maybe especially when) the Constitution points in a direction that diverges from a judge's own preferences. Justice Story defended his decision in *Prigg v. Pennsylvania* (1842),[39] which upheld the Fugitive Slave Act, based on his oath. Story wrote that he had to issue a decision helpful to slaveholders despite his abolitionist convictions because he "cannot forget or repudiate my solemn obligations at pleasure."[40]

The U.S. Supreme Court has also connected the federal judiciary's limited jurisdiction to the oath. *Arizona Christian School Tuition Organization v. Winn* (2011) observed that Article III's limits on jurisdiction exist in part because the "legislative and executive departments of the Federal Government, no less than the judicial department, have a duty to defend the Constitution."[41] The Court added that this "shared obligation is incompatible with the suggestion that federal courts might wield an 'unconditioned authority to determine the constitutionality of legislative or executive acts.'"[42]

The oath may provide an important backdrop in the exercise of judicial review. For instance, the Court has reviewed laws with a "presumption of constitutional validity" in part because legislators "are required to take an oath to support the Federal Constitution."[43] Justice Clarence Thomas has similarly observed that courts should afford the executive branch a "presumption of regularity . . . for a coordinate branch of government whose officers . . . take an oath to support the Constitution. . . ."[44] The oath also informs some jurists' understanding of *stare decisis*. Echoing *Marbury*, Justice Thomas has argued that judges take an oath to support the Constitution—not judicial precedents—and a precedent demonstrably inconsistent with constitutional text should therefore not be followed.[45]

Contemporary judges have explained that the oath holds our legal system together by compelling officers to follow the law, not their personal preferences. When Justice Antonin Scalia spoke at Chief Judge Jeffrey Sutton's investiture, "he did not talk about textualism or originalism," but "instead devoted his remarks to the words of the oath."[46] To Judge Frank Easterbrook, the oath meant that he had made a "contract": "In exchange for receiving power and lifetime tenure I agreed to limit the extent of my discretion."[47] Chief Judge William H. Pryor Jr. has argued that "the oath requires that judges apply the meaning of enacted texts even if doing so, in their view, works against the common good."[48] Putting it simply, Chief Judge Sutton reminds us that "'where there's a will there's a way' is not part of the oath."[49]

THE OATH AND CONGRESS

Members of Congress, like the President and judges, have looked to the oath as a constraint on their power. James Madison argued that the legislator should take "the same view of the official oath . . . as is taken by a Judge."[50] Senator Mike Lee of Utah has stated that Senators, who take an Article VI oath, "are never excused from our responsibility to look out for, protect, and defend the Constitution of the United States."[51] Under this view, members of Congress retain the ability to interpret the Constitution for themselves.[52] Scholars remain divided, however, as to whether the Article VI oath dictates any specific interpretive methodology.[53]

The Article VI Oath Clause has also been seen as the only oath that can be imposed on members. In 1862, during the Civil War, Congress enacted the Ironclad Oath statute.[54] The law required holders of certain federal positions to swear that they did not support people "engaged in armed hostility" against the United States. Taking the oath falsely was a crime, and a convicted person could be disqualified from holding certain positions.[55] In 1863, Senator Charles Sumner of Massachusetts put forward a resolution requiring all Senators to take the newly prescribed loyalty oath.[56] Senator James Asheton Bayard, Jr., of Delaware, however, argued that Congress did not have the power to add additional qualifications for elected positions that are created by the Constitution. Bayard claimed that the Article VI oath, which was imposed by the Constitution, was the only oath that members could be required to take.[57] After a debate, a majority of Senators disagreed with Bayard, and Sumner's resolution was passed. Bayard, a three-term Senator, resigned in protest on a point of principle.[58] The loyalty oath would not last long. Congress repealed the statute in 1868, the same year the Fourteenth Amendment was ratified.[59] Section 3 of the Fourteenth Amendment would disqualify certain people who had taken oaths to the Constitution and engaged in insurrection from holding certain positions.

THE OATH AND STATE OFFICIALS

The Oath of Affirmation Clause applies to specific state officials: members of state legislatures and "all executive and judicial Officers . . . of the several states."[60] In *Printz v. United States* (1997), Justice David H. Souter's dissent argued that the oath requirement showed that Congress has the power to commandeer state officials and mandate that they enforce federal law. Souter, quoting Madison, wrote that "[i]t is appropriate for state officials to make an oath or affirmation to support the Federal Constitution because, as explained in The Federalist, they 'have an essential agency in giving effect to the federal Constitution.'"[61]

The majority disagreed, holding that Congress cannot commandeer state executive officials, despite those officials' federal oath. Justice Scalia's majority opinion explained that state officials are bound only by laws "made in Pursuance [of the Constitution]" and that "laws conscripting state officers [to] violate state sovereignty . . . are . . . not in accord with the Constitution."[62] A textual inference confirmed the point. The oath forces state executive and legislative officers to support "this Constitution," but the Supremacy Clause imposes an additional obligation on state judges: "[T]he Judges in every State shall be bound" by the "Laws of the United States."[63] Scalia wrote that "courts should have been viewed distinctively in this regard; unlike legislatures and executives, they applied the law of other sovereigns all the time."[64] The "anti-commandeering" doctrine has been defended and criticized by originalist scholars.[65]

OPEN QUESTIONS

- The First Congress assembled on March 4, 1789. However, it was not until June 3 that the President, Vice President, and all members of Congress had taken their oath of office. When did the constitutional terms for these elected positions begin? In 1790, the First Congress determined that all of their terms began on March 4,[66] and this date was reflected in the Presidential Succession Act of 1792.[67] How could an officer's constitutional term begin before he took a constitutional oath?

- The President and Vice President are not expressly enumerated in the Article VI Oath or Affirmation Clause, but this provision does refer to "executive . . . Officers of the United States." Do the President and Vice President fall in this category?[68] The first oath statute expressly refers to the Vice President in his legislative capacity as "President of the Senate."[69]

Cite as: Judge Gregory G. Katsas & Andrew W. Smith, *The Oath or Affirmation Clause, in* THE HERITAGE GUIDE TO THE CONSTITUTION 572 (Josh Blackman & John G. Malcolm eds., 3d ed. 2025).

Notes

1. Coronation Oath Act 1688, 1 W. & M. c. 6 (Eng.). **2.** Declaration of Judges on Unlawful Imprisonments (June 9, 1591), *in* 5 W.S. Holdsworth, A History of English Law 495 (1927); Philip Hamburger, *Law and Judicial Duty*, 72 Geo. Wash. L. Rev. 1, 23–24 (2001). **3.** Declaration of Independence, ¶ 32. **4.** S.C. Const. of 1776, arts. VI, XXXIII; N.J. Const. of 1776, art. XXIII; Del. Const. of 1776, art. XXII; Pa. Const. of 1776, § 40; N.C. Const. of 1776, art. XII; Ga. Const. of 1776, art. XXIV; Vt. Const. of 1777, ch. 2, § IX; S.C. Const. of 1778, art. XXXVI; Mass. Const. of 1780, ch. VI. **5.** Jeffrey Sutton, Who Decides? States as Laboratories of Constitutional Experimentation 46–47 (2022). **6.** *Bayard v. Singleton*, 1 N.C. 5, 6 (1787). **7.** Articles of Confederation, art IX, § 2. **8.** *Id.*, art. III. **9.** 1 Farrand's 22, 28. **10.** *Id.* at 194, 203. **11.** *Id.* at 203. **12.** *Id.* at 207. **13.** 2 Farrand's 87. **14.** Roberta Bayer, *James Wilson's Views on Oaths*, James Wilson Inst., Anchoring Truths, https://perma.cc/WF8X-BWN6. **15.** 2 Farrand's 87. **16.** 1 Farrand's 194. **17.** 1 Farrand's 194. **18.** 2 Farrand's 87. **19.** 2 Farrand's 88. **20.** *Id.* **21.** *Id.* at 177. **22.** *Id.* at 188 (emphasis added). **23.** *Id.* at 185. **24.** *Id.* at 468. **25.** *Id.* at 565, 579, 590. **26.** *Id.* at 603. **27.** 2 Elliot's 202. **28.** Storing 4.16.19. **29.** S. Jour., 1st Cong., 1st Sess. 3 (Mar. 4, 1789); H.R. Jour., 1st Cong., 1st Sess. 3 (Mar. 4, 1789). **30.** H.R. Jour., 1st Cong., 1st Sess. 7 (Apr. 6, 1789). **31.** *Id.* at 11 (Apr. 8, 1789). **32.** S. Jour., 1st Cong., 1st Sess. 7–8 (Apr. 6, 1789). **33.** H.R. Jour., 1st Cong., 1st Sess. 29 (May 6, 1789). **34.** 2 Story's Commentaries § 1840. **35.** An Act to regulate the Time and Manner of administering certain Oaths, 1 Stat. 23 (1789). **36.** S. Jour., 1st Cong., 1st Sess. 31 (June 3, 1789). **37.** Seth Barrett Tillman & Josh Blackman, *Offices and Officers of the Constitution, Part III: The Appointments, Impeachment, Commissions, and Oath or Affirmation Clauses*, 62 S. Tex. L. Rev. 349, 428 (2023). **38.** 5 U.S. 137, 180 (1803). **39.** 41 U.S. 539 (1842). **40.** Letter from Joseph Story to Ezekiel Bacon (Nov. 19, 1842), *in* Life and Letters of Joseph Story 431 (1851). **41.** 563 U.S. 125, 133 (2011). **42.** *Id.* (quoting *Valley Forge Christian Coll. v. Ams. United for Separation of Church & State, Inc.*, 454 U.S. 464, 471 (1982)). **43.** *Illinois v. Krull*, 480 U.S. 340, 351 (1987). **44.** *Dep't of Commerce v. New York*, 588 U.S. 752, 792 (2019) (Thomas, J., dissenting in part); Aram A. Gavoor & Steven Platt, *In Search of the Presumption*

of Regularity, 74 Fla. L. Rev. 729, 757–59 (2022). **45.** *Gamble v. United States*, 587 U.S. 678, 716–18 (2019) (Thomas, J., concurring). **46.** NR Symposium, *Antonin Scalia—A Justice in Full* (Feb. 29, 2016), https://perma.cc/3EPE-AVAD. **47.** Frank Easterbrook, *Textualism and the Dead Hand*, 66 Geo. Wash. L. Rev. 1119, 1122 (1998). **48.** William Pryor, *Politics and the Rule of Law*, Heritage Found. Lecture (Oct. 20, 2021), https://perma.cc/WKC6-257S. **49.** Jeffrey Sutton, *A Review of Richard A. Posner, How Judges Think*, 108 Mich. L. Rev. 859, 874 (2010). **50.** Letter from James Madison to Charles J. Ingersoll (June 25, 1831), https://perma.cc/N44S-5YKV. **51.** 159 Cong. Rec. S6771 (2013). **52.** Amy Coney Barrett & John Copeland Nagle, *Congressional Originalism*, 19 U. Pa. Const. L. 1, 28–29 (2016). **53.** Christopher Green, *Is the Oath Argument for Originalism Circular?*, The Originalism Blog (May 11, 2020), https://perma.cc/WU35-6499. **54.** Act to Prescribe an Oath of Office, and for other Purposes, ch. 127, Pub. L. No. 37-127, 12 Stat. 502 (1862) (repealed 1868). **55.** Myles S. Lynch, *Disloyalty & Disqualification: Reconstructing Section 3 of the Fourteenth Amendment*, 30 Wm. & Mary Bill of Rts. J. 153, 165 (2021). **56.** Cong. Globe, 38th Cong., 1st Sess. 31, 37 (1864). **57.** Josh Blackman & Seth Barrett Tillman, *Is the President an "Officer of the United States" for Purposes of Section 3 of the Fourteenth Amendment?*, 15 N.Y.U. J.L. & Liberty 1, 36–39 (2021). **58.** Senator Resigns to Protest Loyalty Oath, United States Senate, https://perma.cc/FLJ8-6WCF. **59.** The Senate's First Act—The Oath Act, United States Senate, https://perma.cc/V9B7-A6VY. **60.** Tillman & Blackman, *supra* at 419 n.324, 421–22. **61.** 521 U.S. 898, 943 (1997) (Souter, J., dissenting). **62.** *Id.* at 924–25 (majority opinion). **63.** *Id.* at 907. **64.** *Id.* **65.** Richard Re, *Promising the Constitution*, 110 Nw. U. L. Rev. 299, 343 (2016); Saikrishna Prakash, *Field Office Federalism*, 79 Va. L. Rev. 1957, 2001 n.231 (1993); Anthony J. Bellia, Jr. & Bradford R. Clark, *The International Law Origins of American Federalism*, 120 Colum. L. Rev. 835, 924–34 (2021); Wesley J. Campbell, *Commandeering and Constitutional Change*, 122 Yale L.J. 1104, 1133–37 (2013). **66.** 1 Annals of Cong. 1010–11 (1790). **67.** 1 Stat. 239, 241 (1792). **68.** Tillman & Blackman, *supra* at 431–33. **69.** 1 Stat. 23.

~

ESSAY NO. 156: THE RELIGIOUS TEST CLAUSE
ART. VI, CL. 3

. . . no religious Test shall ever be required as a Qualification to any Office or public Trust under the United States.

—Gerard V. Bradley

INTRODUCTION

The Constitution as ratified in 1788 contained one explicit reference to religion: Article VI bans religious tests for "any Office or public Trust under the United States." Today this freedom from religious tests may seem to be obviously required by basic principles of religious liberty, but at the time of the Framing, states were free to impose religious tests as they saw fit—and they did. State tests generally limited public offices to Christians or, in some states, only to Protestants. Under the federal constitution, however, national offices were open to everyone, regardless of their faith. There are no judicial decisions construing the religious test ban despite an abundance of constitutional litigation over the boundary between church and state. This lack of precedent does not suggest that the clause has been ineffectual. On the contrary: It has produced its intended effect without the aid of judicial interpretation. Federal offices have been open to believers and non-believers of all stripes ever since the Founding. The Religious Test Clause has been a singular constitutional success.

HISTORY BEFORE 1787

The British colonists who came to America brought with them a long history of legal discrimination against Roman Catholics. This tradition had roots in King Henry VIII's marital meanderings and his establishment of the Anglican Church under the monarch's supreme authority. The matter with Catholicism, then and thereafter, was more jurisdictional and about power than it was about doctrine or ceremony. According to historian Michael Breidenbach, "What made Catholicism so odious to early American Protestants was the pope's claim (and Catholics' apparent acceptance of it) that he had temporal authority over all civil rulers, including even the right to depose a secular authority."[1] In fact, when Pope Pius V excommunicated Queen Elizabeth in 1570, he declared that "Catholics' ultimate allegiance was to the pope, not to their temporal sovereign."[2]

In the colonies, Maryland was an exception. Its proprietary founders, the Calverts, were themselves Catholic. But other states continued this bias against Catholics even after independence. The Massachusetts Constitution of 1780, for example, was reminiscent of the old English oath of supremacy. Candidates had to swear "that no foreign prince, person, prelate, state, or potentate hath, or ought to have, any jurisdiction, superiority, preeminence, authority, dispensing or other power, in any matter, civil, ecclesiastical, or spiritual, within this commonwealth."[3] This provision clearly applied to Catholics. In 1788, the New York legislature enacted a similar oath of abjuration for officeholders, although it stopped short of disenfranchising Catholics.[4] The North Carolina Constitution of 1776 also included a religious test clause that extended to atheists, non-Protestants, non-Christians, and those who "who . . . hold religious principles incompatible with the freedom and safety of the State."[5]

By the time of the Philadelphia Constitutional Convention, states did not discriminate among Protestant sects in eligibility for public stations. Catholics were clearly eligible in Pennsylvania, Delaware, and Maryland. In other states, only Protestants could hold office.[6]

THE CONSTITUTIONAL CONVENTION

On August 20, 1787, the Convention referred a series of proposals to the Committee of Detail.[7] One of them stated that "[n]o religious test or qualification shall ever be annexed to any oath of office under the authority of the United States."[8] On August 30, Charles Pinckney of South Carolina proposed a revised text: "But no religious test shall ever be required as a qualification to any office or public trust under the authority of the United States."[9] Roger Sherman of Connecticut argued that the ban was "unnecessary" because "the prevailing liberality" provided "sufficient security" against restrictive tests, but Pinckney's motion was approved.[10] The Committee of Style later modified the scope of the clause: "office or public trust under the authority of the United States" was changed to "office or public trust under the United States."[11]

THE RATIFICATION DEBATES

Luther Martin of Maryland explained that the Religious Test Clause "was adopted by a great majority of the convention, and without much debate."[12] The "prevailing liberality" was not, however, as prevailing as Sherman believed, and the clause was hotly disputed in some states during the ratification debates. The main objection was that "Jews," "Turks," "infidels," "heathens," and even "Roman Catholics" might hold national office under the proposed Constitution.[13] The times were such that the force of this objection was for many both substantial and nearly self-evident.

Martin observed that some members of the Convention would have distinguished between "the professors of Christianity and downright infidelity or paganism."[14] A Friend to the Rights of the People, an Anti-Federalist from New Hampshire, criticized the ban on religious tests, warning that "we may have a Papist, a Mohomatan, a Deist, yea an Atheist at the helm of Government."[15] A Friend questioned whether it was "good policy to discard all religion" and concluded that "no man is fit to be a ruler of protestants, without he can honestly profess to be of the protestant religion."[16] David, an Anti-Federalist from Massachusetts, wrote that "Papists and Atheists" should be excluded from government: "The latter . . . have no principles of virtue, and the former . . . acknowledge a foreign head, who can relieve them from the obligation of an oath."[17]

Pennsylvania's Benjamin Rush expressed the more restrained view that "many pious people wish the name of the Supreme Being had been introduced somewhere in the new Constitution."[18] The Religious Test Clause was thus a focal point for reservations about the Constitution's entirely secular language.

Some defenders of the Religious Test Clause responded that perhaps a belief in God and a future state of reward and punishment, notwithstanding the ban, could be required of federal officers.[19] On this interpretation, Article VI would have ruled out specifically sectarian tests as well as (possibly) tests that excluded only non-Christians. Some defenders suggested that the constitutional requirement of an "oath" to support and defend the Constitution implied that officers had to affirm at least some tenets of natural religion.[20] It is true that the Constitution specified an alternative to swearing—namely, "affirm[ing]"—but this alternative did not rebut the relationship between an oath and religion. Swearing and affirming were alternative ways to make solemnly clear that one believed. Whether by "oath or affirmation," some defenders of the Religious Test Clause maintained, certain beliefs

about divine matters could and should be prerequisites for federal officeholders.

The plain meaning of the text imposed a clear prohibition on religious tests. This was surely the predominant understanding of the constitutional language. First, various Christian sects feared that if any test were permitted, one might be designed to their disadvantage. No single sect could hope to dominate national councils, but any sect could imagine itself the victim of a combination of the others. Oliver Ellsworth of Connecticut noted that if a religious oath "were in favour of either congregationalists, presbyterians, episcopalions, baptists, or quakers, it would incapacitate more than three-fourths of the American citizens for any publick office; and thus degrade them from the rank of freemen."[21] Second, proponents also argued that the Constitution wisely declined to exclude some of the best minds and least parochial personalities to serve in the national government. In 1787, Tench Coxe of Pennsylvania, observed that "[t]he people may employ any wise or good citizen in the execution of the various duties of the government."[22]

TO WHOM DOES THE RELIGIOUS TEST CLAUSE APPLY?

By its terms, the ban extends to those who hold "any Office or public Trust under the United States." Professors Seth Barrett Tillman and Josh Blackman write that this category includes all appointed and elected federal officeholders, including the President and members of Congress.[23] The text does not apply to state officeholders. However, the U.S. Supreme Court effectively eliminated the clause's limitation to federal officeholders in *Torcaso v. Watkins* (1961).[24] The Justices declared unconstitutional a state-imposed religious test, relying on the Establishment and Free Exercise Clauses of the First Amendment. The holding effectively expanded the scope of the Religious Test Clause to ban even a required profession of belief in God by any public official, federal or state.

OPEN QUESTIONS

In *Kennedy v. Bremerton School District* (2022), the Supreme Court said that it had "abandoned" its oft-criticized *Lemon* test for Establishment Clause violations, substituting for it a "historical practices and understandings" test.[25] Any attempt to revisit the *Torcaso* holding would now raise a series of challenging questions. First, how much does the Free Exercise Clause, as opposed to the

Establishment Clause, contribute to the holding in *Torcaso*? Second, does current Free Exercise doctrine support *Torcaso*? Third, the Justices would have to reckon with the two radically divergent "historical practices and understandings" at the Founding and for decades thereafter at the state and federal levels. Depending on how the Court answers these questions, the Justices might have to consider for the first time explicitly "incorporating" the No-Test Clause and then giving it (for the first time) an authoritative judicial interpretation.

Cite as: Gerard V. Bradley, *The Religious Test Clause, in* THE HERITAGE GUIDE TO THE CONSTITUTION 576 (Josh Blackman & John G. Malcolm eds., 3d ed. 2025).

Notes

1. Michael D. Breidenbach, Our Dear-Bought Liberty: Catholics and Religious Toleration in Early America 116 (2021).　**2.** *Id.* at 10.　**3.** Mass. Const. of 1780, ch. VI.　**4.** John Webb Pratt, Religion, Politics, and Diversity: The Church–State Theme in New York History 107 (1967).　**5.** N.C. Const. of 1776, art. XXXII; Seth Barrett Tillman, *A Religious Test in America?: The 1809 Motion to Vacate Jacob Henry's North Carolina State Legislative Seat—A Re-Evaluation of the Primary Sources*, 98 N.C. Hist. Rev. 1 (2021); Seth Barrett Tillman, *What Oath (If Any) Did Jacob Henry Take in 1809?: Deconstructing the Historical Myths*, 61 Am. J. L. Hist. 349 (2021).　**6.** Gerard V. Bradley, *The No Religious Test Clause and the Constitution of Religious Liberty: A Machine That Has Gone of Itself*, 37 Case W. L. Rev. 674 (1987).　**7.** 3 Farrand's 340–41.　**8.** 2 Farrand's 335.　**9.** 2 Farrand's 461, 468.　**10.** *Id.* at 468.　**11.** *Id.* at 603; Peter K. Rofes, The Religion Guarantees: A Reference Guide to the United States Constitution 12 (2005).　**12.** Storing 2.4.108.　**13.** Storing 4.22.4.　**14.** Storing 2.4.108.　**15.** Storing 4.23.3.　**16.** *Id.*　**17.** *Id.* at 4.24.5　**18.** Letter from Benjamin Rush to John Adams (June 15, 1789), https://perma.cc/4FV4-T5N8.　**19.** Bradley, *supra* at 696–97.　**20.** *Id.*　**21.** Essays on the Constitution of the United States 169 (Paul Leicester Ford ed., 1892).　**22.** Pamphlets on the Constitution of the United States 146 (Paul Leicester Ford ed., 1888).　**23.** Seth Barrett Tillman & Josh Blackman, *Offices and Officers of the Constitution, Part I: An Introduction*, 61 S. Tex. L. Rev. 309, 315 (2021).　**24.** 367 U.S. 488 (1961).　**25.** 597 U.S. 507 (2022).

PART 7

ARTICLE VII

ESSAY NO. 157: THE RATIFICATION CLAUSE
ART. VII, CL. 1

The Ratification of the Conventions of nine States, shall be sufficient for the Establishment of this Constitution between the States so ratifying the Same.
—John P. Kaminski

INTRODUCTION

When the Constitutional Convention met in May 1787, the procedure for ratification of its proposal was a serious concern. Article XIII of the Articles of Confederation stipulated that amendments needed to be approved by Congress and then "confirmed" by all of the state legislatures. Believing that such a procedure was improbable, the Convention delegates debated and devised a unique procedure for ratification that became the last and shortest article of the Constitution.

ADOPTION OF STATE CONSTITUTIONS AFTER INDEPENDENCE

Americans had a long history of written constitutions that provided for the organization and operation of their governments. Before independence, every American colony had a charter granted either by an English monarch or by a proprietor who owned the land, such as William Penn. During the Revolutionary era, Americans wrote more than a dozen state constitutions and many amendments to these constitutions.[1] All but one of these constitutions were declared to be operational by the bodies that wrote them.[2] The exception was Massachusetts. In 1780, the proposed Massachusetts constitution was submitted to the people in town meetings that were followed by a ratifying convention that tabulated the towns' votes and declared the constitution adopted.[3] This uniquely American procedure, which New Hampshire followed in adopting its second state constitution in 1783,[4] set a precedent for future American constitutions.

In May 1776, two months before the Declaration of Independence was signed, the Second Continental Congress resolved that the provincial legislatures should "adopt" new constitutions "under the authority of the people" instead of the Crown that would "best conduce

to the happiness and safety of their constituents in particular, and America in general."[5]

RATIFICATION OF THE ARTICLES OF CONFEDERATION

In response to Virginia's June 7, 1776, call for independence, Congress created three committees—one to draft a declaration of independence, one to seek foreign assistance, and one to draft articles of union. For almost a year and a half afterward, the Second Continental Congress intermittently debated a form of government for the new country.

Congress submitted the Articles of Confederation to the states in November 1777, providing that it needed to be adopted by all of the state legislatures.[6] The New England states submitted the Articles to the people in town meetings, which then instructed their state legislators to ratify.[7] All of the legislatures formally adopted the Articles, submitted their forms of ratification to Congress, and instructed their delegates to Congress to sign the Articles "on the part and behalf of" their particular states.[8] It took three and a half years to achieve this mandatory unanimity: The Maryland legislature adopted the Articles on February 2, 1781, and its delegates to Congress signed the Articles on March 1, 1781.[9]

AMENDMENTS TO THE ARTICLES OF CONFEDERATION

Article XIII of the Articles of Confederation provided that alterations needed to "be agreed to in a congress of the united states, and be afterwards confirmed by the legislatures of every state."[10] Several state legislatures also submitted proposed amendments with their ratifications of the Articles. For instance, the New Jersey legislature proposed nine amendments, the second of which gave Congress the exclusive power to regulate the trade of the United States with foreign countries. Congress rejected all of New Jersey's proposed amendments on June 25, 1778. Indeed, Congress rejected *all* of the states' proposed amendments.

Between 1781 and 1785, Congress proposed several amendments itself. In February 1781 and April 1783, Congress proposed that it should have the power to levy a five percent impost on foreign importations to be earmarked to pay the Revolutionary War debt. In April 1783, Congress proposed that federal expenses should be apportioned among the states based on population with three-fifths of the slaves being counted in this apportionment. However, no amendment was adopted by all of the state legislatures. Other amendments introduced in Congress also never received its approval—including seven that would have remedied some of the most serious defects of the Articles.[11] The first would have given Congress the exclusive power to regulate foreign commerce and levy imposts on foreign importations. The sixth proposed the creation of a federal judiciary. In August 1786, these amendments died in Congress as a result of sectional animosities caused by the negotiations between the United States and Spain over the right of Americans to navigate the Mississippi River.[12]

In view of the repeated failure to adopt amendments, the Virginia legislature in January 1786 appointed eight commissioners to meet in a convention of the states "to consider how far a uniform system in their commercial regulations may be necessary to their common interest and their permanent harmony."[13] The commissioners, who were scheduled to meet in Annapolis, Maryland, in September 1786, were "to report to the several States such an act . . . as, when unanimously ratified by them," would increase Congress's power to regulate commerce.[14] After the arrival of commissioners from only five states, nationalist-minded commissioners such as Alexander Hamilton of New York and James Madison of Virginia seized the initiative. They wrote a report that they sent to Congress and the states calling for another convention to meet in Philadelphia in May 1787 "to devise such further provisions as shall appear to them necessary to render the constitution of the Foederal Government adequate to the exigencies of the Union."[15]

Several states appointed delegates to this proposed convention before Congress acted. On February 21, 1787, without reference to the Annapolis Convention's report, Congress finally resolved that the states should appoint delegates to a convention to meet in Philadelphia. The resolution provided that the convention was called "for the sole and express purpose of revising the Articles of Confederation and reporting to Congress and the several legislatures such alterations and provisions therein as shall when agreed to in Congress and confirmed by the states render the federal constitution adequate to the exigencies of government and the preservation of the Union."[16]

THE CONSTITUTIONAL CONVENTION

On May 29, 1787, at the start of the Constitutional Convention, Governor Edmund Randolph submitted the Virginia Plan. It provided that Congress first approve the proposed Constitution and then submit it to the state legislatures, which in turn should call state conventions to consider ratification.[17] On June 5, Roger Sherman of Connecticut objected to this procedure. Instead, he would use the amendment procedure in the Articles of Confederation.[18] Madison opposed ratification by state legislatures and argued philosophically that the Constitution needed to be adopted directly "by the supreme authority of the people themselves."[19] Elbridge Gerry of Massachusetts was "afraid of referring the new system" to the people who, in New England, "ha[d] at this time the wildest ideas of Government in the world."[20]

From a practical political perspective, Rufus King of Massachusetts favored ratification by conventions because it was simply easier. All but two state legislatures (Pennsylvania and Georgia) were bicameral as opposed to single-bodied conventions.[21] Furthermore, state legislatures would be reluctant to approve a constitution that would reduce their powers. Pierce Butler of South Carolina also preferred conventions because state legislators had taken oaths to support their governments, and the new Constitution was expected to diminish the powers of the state governments.[22] James Wilson of Pennsylvania wanted ratification by a simple majority of the states.[23] States that did not initially ratify could join the Union subsequently. Charles Pinckney of South Carolina suggested that nine states should be sufficient for ratification.[24]

On June 12, the Convention approved the Virginia Plan's ratification provisions by a vote of six states to three with two states divided.[25] Three days later, William Paterson introduced the New Jersey Plan, which included the Articles' amendment procedure.[26] Under this procedure, the unanimous approval of the state legislatures was necessary to adopt any alterations in the Articles.[27]

On July 23, when debate on the ratification procedure resumed, George Mason of Virginia and Nathaniel Gorham of Massachusetts favored ratification through conventions.[28] Oliver Ellsworth of Connecticut and Gerry favored ratification through legislatures.[29] Hugh Williamson of North Carolina then proposed that each state legislature should decide what method its state would use.[30] Alternatively, Gouverneur Morris of Pennsylvania proposed that one general convention of the states "chosen & authorized by the people" should "consider, amend, and establish" the Constitution.[31] No delegate seconded Morris's proposal. The Convention then voted nine states to one that the Constitution be submitted to the Articles of Confederation Congress, which after approving it would send it to the state legislatures for submission to conventions.[32]

On August 30, the Convention considered how many states would be necessary to adopt the Constitution. Wilson again proposed that seven of the thirteen states (a majority) would be "sufficient for the commencement of the plan."[33] Morris suggested that a greater number of states be required if they were not contiguous.[34] Roger Sherman felt that "ten States at least ought to be made necessary."[35] Randolph said that nine states would provide "a respectable majority of the whole" and was "familiar" because the Articles required the approval of nine states for the adoption of several important matters such as declaring war, borrowing money, and ratifying treaties.[36] Wilson now suggested "eight as preferable." Butler favored nine, revolting "at the idea, that one or two States should restrain the rest from consulting their safety."[37] (Several amendments to the Articles had failed of ratification even though they had been ratified by all but one or two of the 13 state legislatures.) Daniel Carroll of Maryland and Rufus King supported all thirteen states for approval because

the Constitution otherwise would "operate on the whole though ratified by a part only."[38]

The next day, King proposed that the Constitution should be implemented only among the states that actually adopted it, which was approved by a vote of nine states to one.[39] Morris then revived Williamson's proposal allowing each of the state legislatures "to pursue their own modes of ratification."[40] A vote on requiring all thirteen states to ratify was rejected unanimously except for Maryland.[41] A proposal for a ten-state requirement was defeated seven states to four, and a vote for nine states was approved eight to three.[42] Then, on motion of Morris and Pinckney, the Convention agreed by a vote of eight to three to delete the requirement that Congress must approve the Constitution before it was transmitted to the states.[43] This feature was known as congressional approbation.

On September 10, Gerry objected to the omission of congressional approbation. He would have required the Confederation Congress to approve the Constitution. Otherwise, he said, there was "an annulment of the confederation with so little scruple or formality."[44] Thomas FitzSimons of Pennsylvania felt that congressional approbation had been stricken "in order to save Congress from the necessity of an Act inconsistent with the Articles of Confederation under which they held their authority."[45] After all, the Articles of Confederation required unanimous consent of all the states to propose a new form of government.

Hamilton wanted congressional approbation but thought that each state convention should decide whether nine states were sufficient to "take effect among the nine ratifying States."[46] Nathaniel Gorham strenuously opposed Hamilton's proposal.[47] Randolph then vowed that he would not sign the Constitution unless the state conventions should "be at liberty to offer amendments to the plan," which "should be submitted to a second General Convention, with full power to settle the Constitution finally."[48] A proposal by Hamilton to require congressional approbation with implementation among nine ratifying states was rejected by a ten-to-one vote.[49]

The Convention then unanimously agreed that Congress would not have to approve of the Constitution, which would be implemented among the adopting states after ratification by nine state conventions.[50] These features were added at the end of the Constitution in Article VII. On September 17, the Convention passed a resolution under which the Constitution would be presented to Congress and then submitted by Congress to the state legislatures, which in turn would call conventions to be elected by the people. The conventions "assenting to, and ratifying" the Constitution were then to notify Congress of their action.

THE CONSTITUTION BEFORE THE CONFEDERATION CONGRESS

On September 18, Convention Secretary William Jackson left Philadelphia carrying the Constitution to Congress in New York City. The Constitution was read in Congress on September 20 and assigned for debate six days later. Congress considered the Constitution for three days between September 26 and 28, primarily debating two issues.

The first issue debated was whether Congress would give the Constitution its approbation when transmitting it to the states.[51] Anti-Federalists in Congress, such as Nathan Dane of Massachusetts and Richard Henry Lee of Virginia, wanted to specify in the transmittal that the Constitutional Convention had violated the Articles of Confederation and Congress's February 21 resolution calling the Convention.[52] With a large majority, Federalists like James Madison and Nathaniel Gorham wanted to send the Constitution to the states with Congress's approbation or at least without any derogatory comments.

The second issue was whether Congress could propose amendments to the Constitution. Richard Henry Lee led Anti-Federalists in proposing amendments that included a bill of rights that should be appended to the Constitution.[53] Federalists, wanting to avoid the appearance of any opposition, agreed to a compromise by which the Constitution was to be sent to the states without congressional approbation and all signs of debate (including Lee's amendments) were to be stricken from Congress's journal.[54]

The transmittal resolution of September 28, 1787, began with the words "Resolved Unanimously," thus implying that Congress had unanimously approved the Constitution. George Washington, responding to James Madison's account of the congressional proceedings, wrote adroitly that "This apparent unanimity will have

its effect.—Not every one has opportunities to peep behind the curtain."[55]

THE RATIFICATION DEBATES

Throughout the public debate over the Constitution, the provision for ratification by the approval of nine state conventions was often considered.[56] Anti-Federalists criticized the ratification procedure provided in Article VII strongly and repeatedly. Richard Henry Lee, Elbridge Gerry, Luther Martin, and Patrick Henry condemned the abandonment of Article XIII's amendment provision as a violation of Congress's February 21, 1787, resolution and the instructions that delegates had received from their state legislatures. John Quincy Adams, who opposed the Constitution before his home state of Massachusetts ratified it in February 1788, viewed the ratification process as "an open and bare-faced violation of the most sacred engagements which can be formed by human beings. It violates the *Confederation*."[57]

Federalists justified abandonment of the Articles' amendment provision both because of the impossibility of achieving a unanimous endorsement of any change and because they preferred to seek the direct approval of the people through state conventions. In Federalist No. 22, Madison argued against the minority controlling government action as well as the inefficacy of basing the existence of any government on the approval of state legislatures instead of the will of the people. By resting on the approval of state legislatures, the Articles of Confederation could also be repealed by state legislatures. Consequently, it was necessary to lay the "foundations of our national government deeper than in the mere sanction of delegated authority." Rather, "[t]he fabric of American Empire ought to rest on the solid basis of the consent of the people. The streams of national power ought to flow immediately from that pure original fountain of all legitimate authority" as expressed by the approval of the people in state ratifying conventions.[58]

On June 21, 1788, the New Hampshire convention became the ninth to ratify the Constitution.

Cite as: John P. Kaminski, *The Ratification Clause, in* THE HERITAGE GUIDE TO THE CONSTITUTION 582 (Josh Blackman & John G. Malcolm eds., 3d ed. 2025).

Notes

1. Willi Paul Adams, The First American Constitutions: Republican Ideology and the Making of the State Constitutions in the Revolutionary Era (2d ed. 2001). 2. *Id.* 3. Samuel Eliot Morrison, A History of the Constitution of Massachusetts (1917). 4. 28 DHRC xli–xlii. 5. 4 J. Cont. Cong. 342, 358 (May 10 & 15, 1776). 6. 1 DHRC 93. 7. *Id.* at 102, 109. 8. *Id.* at 94. 9. *Id.* at 135. 10. *Id.* at 93. 11. *Id.* at 163–68. 12. *Id.* at 163–64. 13. *Id.* at 176–81. 14. *Id.* at 180. 15. *Id.* at 184. 16. *Id.* at 187. 17. 1 Farrand's 22. 18. *Id.* at 122. 19. *Id.* at 122–23. 20. *Id.* at 123. 21. *Id.* 22. *Id.* at 128. 23. *Id.* at 123. 24. *Id.* 25. *Id.* at 214. 26. *Id.* at 242–45. 27. *Id.* at 250. 28. 2 Farrand's 88, 90. 29. *Id.* at 89–91. 30.

Id. at 91. 31. *Id.* at 93. 32. *Id.* at 93–94. 33. *Id.* at 468. 34. *Id.* 35. *Id.* at 468–69. 36. *Id.* at 469. 37. *Id.* 38. *Id.* 39. *Id.* at 475. 40. *Id.* at 477. 42. *Id.* 43. *Id.* at 478. 44. *Id.* at 559–60. 45. *Id.* at 560. 46. *Id.* 47. *Id.* 48. *Id.* at 560–61. 49. *Id.* at 562–63. 50. *Id.* at 563, 579. 51. 1 DHRC 327–40. 52. *Id.* at 327–30. 53. *Id.* at 337–39. 54. *Id.* at 339–40. 55. 13 DHRC 358. 56. Carlos E. Gonzalez, *Representational Structures Through Which We the People Ratify Constitutions: The Troubling Original Understanding of the Constitution's Ratification Clauses*, 38 U.C. Davis L. Rev. 1373 (2005). 56. 14 DHRC 223 (emphasis in original). 57. *Id.* at 444. 57. 14 DHRC 223 (emphasis in original). 58. *Id.* at 444.

~⟋

ESSAY NO. 158: THE ATTESTATION CLAUSE
ART. VII, CL. 2

Done in Convention by the Unanimous Consent of the States present the Seventeenth Day of September in the Year of our Lord one thousand seven hundred and Eighty seven and of the Independence of the United States of America the Twelfth In witness whereof We have hereunto subscribed our Names. . . .

—John P. Kaminski

INTRODUCTION

Near the end of the Constitutional Convention, a number of delegates indicated that they could not sign the proposed Constitution. To alleviate their qualms and present the Constitution as the unanimous proposal of the Convention, Benjamin Franklin suggested that the delegates affix their names to the Constitution as witnesses to the unanimous approval of states. After a brief discussion, the Convention agreed to Franklin's proposed attestation clause.

FINAL OBJECTIONS TO THE CONSTITUTION

On September 15, 1787, two days before the end of the Constitutional Convention and just before the final vote on the draft Constitution, three delegates voiced their objections. Edmund Randolph of Virginia, who had introduced the Virginia Plan, thought the Constitution was not sufficiently republican and moved that there should be another convention to consider amendments proposed by the state ratifying conventions.[1] George Mason, also of Virginia, who had strongly advocated that a Bill of Rights be added to the Constitution, seconded

Randolph's motion for a second convention and predicted that without significant changes, the new government would begin as "a moderate aristocracy" and end in either monarchy or "a tyrannical aristocracy."[2] "With the expedient of another Convention as proposed," Mason said that he would sign the Constitution.[3] Elbridge Gerry of Massachusetts, fearing that the powers of Congress were too broad, thought that "provid[ing] for a second general Convention" was the best that could be done.[4]

At that point, 11 state delegations were present. Rhode Island had not sent a delegation, and two of the three New York delegates had left the Convention two months earlier, leaving New York without a "full representation" and thus unable to cast an official vote.

All of the delegations present voted against a second convention and then voted in favor of the final text of the Constitution.[5] The Convention then ordered the Constitution engrossed on parchment in preparation for signatures. (An "engrossed" document was the final version of a document that often was printed or transcribed on fine paper or parchment to be approved by a final vote.) The Convention also ordered that

500 copies of the engrossed version should be printed.[6]

FRANKLIN'S PROPOSAL

When the Convention reconvened on September 17, after the final reading of the document, Benjamin Franklin, who was feeble at the age of eighty-one, asked James Wilson, a fellow Pennsylvania delegate, to deliver an address he had prepared strongly endorsing the Constitution despite any perceived imperfections.[7] Franklin, hoping to gain the support of critics and create a sense of common accord, moved that the Constitution be signed by the delegates as individual witnesses of "the unanimous consent of the states present."[8]

According to James Madison's notes, "This ambiguous form had been drawn up by G.M. [Gouverneur Morris of Pennsylvania] in order to gain the dissenting members, and put into the hands of Doct. Franklin that it might have the better chance of success."[9] The Articles of Association adopted by the First Continental Congress on October 20, 1774, provided a similar attestation clause stating that "[t]he foregoing association being determined upon by the Congress, was ordered to be subscribed by the several Members thereof and there upon we have here unto set our respective names accordingly." It is perhaps merely coincidental that in June 1777, Morris had served on a committee in the Second Continental Congress that drafted the attestation clause at the end of the Articles of Confederation.

Morris, speaking for himself, said that he would sign the Constitution even "with all its faults" because the signing "form proposed related only to the fact that the *States* present were unanimous."[10] Alternatively, Hugh Williamson of North Carolina suggested that the delegates sign only the transmittal letter to Congress that the Convention had approved on September 12, which would "do nearly as well" and might "be satisfactory to some members who disliked the Constitution."[11] "For himself," Williamson "did not think a better plan was to be expected and had no scruples against putting his name to it."[12] Alexander Hamilton of New York hoped that every delegate would sign. He worried that a few non-signers "of consequence . . . might do infinite mischief by kindling" underlying fears of the Convention.[13] Although most delegates knew that "no man's ideas were more remote from the plan than his own were known to be," Hamilton felt that the choice now lay "between anarchy and Convulsion on one side, and the chance of good to be expected from the plan on the other."[14]

The clause made at least one convert. William Blount of North Carolina said that he was prepared not to sign the Constitution "so as to [not] pledge himself in support of the plan," but the "form proposed" allowed him to sign attesting to "the fact that the plan was the unanimous act of the States in Convention."[15] Randolph and Gerry, however, were unmoved. They reiterated their opposition to the Constitution and regarded "the signing in the proposed form, as the same with signing the Constitution. The change of form therefore could make no difference with" them.[16] Charles Cotesworth Pinckney of South Carolina objected to the ambiguity of the clause. "He thought it best to be candid and let the form speak the substance."[17] Jared Ingersoll of Pennsylvania "did not consider the signing, either as a mere attestation of the fact, or as pledging the signers to support the Constitution at all events, but as a recommendation, of what, all things considered, was the most eligible."[18]

The Convention then approved Franklin's motion by a vote of 10 states to none, with one state (South Carolina) divided.[19] Although Madison's notes indicate that Pinckney and Pierce Butler, two of the four delegates from South Carolina, "disliked the equivocal form of the signing" and voted against the motion, both signed the Constitution.[20]

SIGNING THE CONSTITUTION

Thus, the signers subscribed their names "In witness" to what was "done in Convention" with the names grouped by states with the exception of George Washington, who signed first and separately as President and deputy from Virginia. The states were listed in geographical order, beginning on the right-hand edge of the document and continuing on the left, from north to south. In the right-hand column were New Hampshire, Massachusetts, Connecticut, New York, New Jersey, and Pennsylvania. In the left-hand column were Delaware, Maryland,

Virginia, North Carolina, South Carolina, and Georgia.

The signatures appeared in the same order on the Declaration of Independence and the Articles of Confederation. This was also the order in which all votes were recorded in the Articles of Confederation Congress and in the Convention. On the Declaration of Independence, the signers subscribed the document for themselves individually even though they were grouped together by states. And the Articles of Confederation were signed "on the part and behalf of" their particular state as each state legislature adopted the Articles even though this phrase was attached by a brace to each delegation's signatures.

The engrossed version of the Constitution also has a short errata followed by an "Attest" signed by "William Jackson Secretary," which appears in a third column to the left of the two columns with the delegates' signatures.

In the end, Randolph, Mason, and Gerry did not sign the Constitution. Madison wrote in his notes that they "declined giving it the sanction of their names."[21] The Morris–Franklin arrangement, however, allowed Alexander Hamilton to sign as a witness even though, as the sole New York delegate in attendance, he was ineligible to vote on the substance. The Convention's rule required at least two delegates to make an official delegation.[22] The Convention's rules were incomplete, however. There was no extant reference to requiring the *attendance* of at least two delegates to make an official delegation. Such was the rule in the Confederation Congress, and it was used in all roll call votes in both Congress and the Convention. On May 28, a Convention rule indicated that a majority of a delegation should be recorded for a state "which shall be fully represented."

State legislatures had appointed 65 delegates to the Convention; 55 attended at various times over the course of the sessions, and 39 signed the final document.[23] George Read of Delaware signed not only for himself, but also for John Dickinson, who had left Philadelphia two days earlier because of illness and had authorized Read to sign his name.[24] Although Read signed for Dickinson, the two signatures are separated by the signature of fellow Delawarean Gunning Bedford, Jr.

THE RATIFICATION DEBATES

During the ratification debates, Federalists used the ambiguity of the Attestation Clause to their advantage. Many newspapers alluded to the unanimity of the Convention. For example, on October 1, 1787, Boston's *American Herald* praised the Convention's unanimity as "an auspicious omen of our future concord and felicity."[25] By October 18, this report was reprinted in six newspapers in Massachusetts, Rhode Island, New York, and Pennsylvania. On September 29, 1787, Curtius, in New York's *Daily Advertiser*, praised the Convention for its "most perfect unanimity."[26] Two days later, Caesar, also in the *Daily Advertiser*, continued to praise the unanimity that was "unequalled in ancient and modern story."[27]

Franklin's final speech received widespread newspaper circulation throughout the country. Upon request, Franklin sent copies of the speech to Nathaniel Gorham of Massachusetts and Daniel Carroll of Maryland. The former version was printed in the *Boston Gazette* on December 3 and reprinted at least 26 times by December 21. The latter version was printed in the *Virginia Independent Chronicle* on December 5 and reprinted in ten newspapers by February 16, 1788.

Anti-Federalists also took advantage of that ambiguity of the Attestation Clause. They asserted that Washington did not personally approve the Constitution, but had signed only as a witness to the unanimous approval of the states in attendance. For example, on November 19, 1787, the Boston *American Herald*, asserted that "it is as notorious as it is true, that this Great Man *never gave an opinion upon the subject in Convention*, and honoured it with his Signature merely in his capacity of PRESIDENT of that *Body*."[28] On November 21, 1787, the Philadelphia *Freeman's Journal* reported "that the General, Mr. Franklin, and some others, did only sign as witnesses, and that they had no hand in forming it."[29] Between December 4 and 12, this item was reprinted in newspapers in New York City; Boston; Baltimore; Salem, Massachusetts; and Poughkeepsie, New York.

Seldom was Hamilton's solitary signing mentioned. On January 25, 1788, a paragraph in Philadelphia's *Independent Gazetteer*, denied that the states had unanimously supported the

Constitution in the Convention. "Mr. Yates and Mr. Lansing of New-York gave it a decided opposition, while only Mr. Hamilton gave it his support. There were two delegates from New-York against it, and only one in favor."[30] The *Gazetteer's* paragraph was reprinted in *The Virginia Independent Chronicle* on February 6 and Boston's *American Herald* on March 17.

ENGROSSED CONSTITUTION AND PRINTED CONSTITUTION

The four-page manuscript engrossed version of the Constitution is on display in the National Archives. It was written by Jacob Shallus of Philadelphia, who was the assistant clerk of the Pennsylvania Assembly. The Convention's printers (John Dunlap and David C. Claypoole, the printers of the daily *Pennsylvania Packet*) printed a six-page broadside version that was soon ready for distribution on September 17, 1787. However, a couple last-minute changes made by the Convention delegates required Dunlap and Claypoole to make the necessary changes in the printed Constitution. After adjusting the type for the Preamble, Dunlap and Claypoole also printed the Constitution in the *Pennsylvania Packet* on September 19.

There are some differences between the Attestation Clause in the engrossed Constitution and the clause as it appears in the Convention's official six-page broadside printed Constitution. The wording of the clause is the same, but the punctuation and capitalization are quite different. Both versions have the signatures in two columns. The right-hand column in the engrossed manuscript Constitution starts with George Washington, who signed as President and deputy from Virginia, followed by the delegations from New Hampshire through Pennsylvania. The left-hand column starts with Delaware and ends with Georgia. The printed Constitution sets George Washington's name in large capital letters centered above all the other names and then reverses the two columns: New Hampshire is at the top of the left-hand column, and Delaware is at the top of the right-hand column.

In the engrossed Constitution, Secretary William Jackson's attestation is on the far-left-hand side of the document, below the errata. The errata identifies certain interlineations and erasures in the manuscript Constitution.

However, the errata does not appear in the printed Constitution because the corrections were incorporated into the text of the printed Constitution. In the printed version, Jackson's attestation was centered immediately after the list of the signers. Although attestations and signatures are not normally regarded as part of the substance of a legal document, the Attestation Clause has traditionally been included in printings of the Constitution.

DATE OF THE ATTESTATION CLAUSE

The Attestation Clause includes two dates: "Seventeenth Day of September in the Year of our Lord one thousand seven hundred and Eighty seven and of the Independence of the United States of America the Twelfth." The former date follows the verbiage commonly used in English treaties and American colonial charters, although the contemporary British tradition was to date documents to the reign of the sitting monarch. The reference to years since Independence was also commonly used in post-independence American diplomatic and congressional documents. For example, the Articles of Confederation was dated "the fifteenth day of November in the year of our Lord One Thousand Seven Hundred and Seventy seven, and in the Second Year of the Independence of America."

The Attestation Clause is the one part of the Constitution that expressly mentions God. Recent interpretations of the clause have inferred from the language of the dating either that it was meant to infuse the Constitution with a theistic interpretation based on the language of the Declaration of Independence or that the Constitution is founded on a higher-law system of justice and limited government that was created by the natural law principles embodied in the Declaration.[31] Rather than searching for some veiled meaning in the Attestation Clause, it would seem most likely that the language was commonly used to date documents.

It would seem also that there might be three "official" versions of the Constitution. The engrossed hand-written version and the six-page broadside version printed by Dunlap and Claypoole were both mentioned above. These documents were submitted to the Confederation

Congress sitting in New York City. Congress read the Constitution on September 20, 1787, and after debates on September 26–28 agreed unanimously to submit it to the states for their consideration.

Congress then ordered a new printing of the Constitution, which was prepared as a four-page broadside by John and Archibald M'Lean, printers of New York's *Independent Journal*. This official printed Constitution contains the Attestation Clause and the congressional resolution submitting the Constitution to the states. With a handwritten attestation by Secretary of Congress Charles Thomson, this four-page broadside was sent to the states. It was this version that included the attestation clause that was read, considered, and ratified by the state conventions.[29]

Cite as: John P. Kaminski, *The Attestation Clause*, in THE HERITAGE GUIDE TO THE CONSTITUTION 586 (Josh Blackman & John G. Malcolm eds., 3d ed. 2025).

Notes

1. 2 Farrand's 631, 634. 2. *Id.* at 632. 3. *Id.* at 632, 636–40. 4. *Id.* at 632–33, 635–36. 5. *Id.* at 634. 6. *Id.* 7. *Id.* at 641. 8. *Id.* at 641–43. 9. *Id.* at 643. 10. *Id.* at 645 (emphasis in original). 11. *Id.* 12. *Id.* 13. *Id.* at 645. 14. *Id.* at 645–46. 15. *Id.* at 646. 16. *Id.* at 646–47. 17. *Id.* at 647. 18. *Id.* 19. *Id.* 20. *Id.* 21. *Id.* at 649. 22. 1 Farrand's 11. 23. 2 Farrand's 648–49. 24. *Id.* 25. 4 DHRC 28–30. 26. 19 DHRC 66. 27. *Id.* at 70. 28. 4 DHRC 272–73 (capitalization and emphasis in original). 29. 14 DHRC 163. 30. 15 DHRC 572. 31. Jesse Cross, *"Done in Convention": The Attestation Clause and the Declaration of Independence*, 121 Yale L. Rev. 1236 (2012).

PART 8

THE BILL OF RIGHTS

ESSAY NO. 159: THE ESTABLISHMENT CLAUSE
AMEND. 1

Congress shall make no law respecting an establishment of religion. . . .

—Stephanie Barclay

INTRODUCTION

Scholars generally agree that the Framers viewed the eighteenth-century Church of England as a foil for their vision of the relationship between church and the federal government.[1] The Establishment Clause reflects this historical sentiment. The Framers, however, did not believe that a public role for religion was an evil in itself. Rather, historical practice surrounding ratification of the First Amendment suggests that as long as government action did not reflect certain problematic hallmarks of government action that established churches, the role of religion in public life was often a welcome and important aspect of the early Republic.

HISTORY BEFORE 1787

Before the American Revolution, the Church of England had some day-to-day discretion over religious activities, but the state exercised significant control over the Church's doctrines and personnel, along with participation in various religious activities of the Church.[2] For instance, attendance at Anglican services was mandatory, with nonattendance resulting in fines, and the payment of some tithes were mandatory as a special form of tax.[3] The Church also received preferential public financial support through mechanisms like land grants.[4] Non-members were not allowed to vote or hold public office, and a religious test oath was used to enforce this restriction.[5]

In the colonies, the Church of England was officially established by law in the five southern colonies of Georgia, North Carolina, South Carolina, Virginia, and Maryland.[6] It thus remained the dominant religious institution in many of the colonies, but the restrictions these established legal regimes imposed on citizens varied by colony. The laws related to an established church were not found in one statute, but instead arose from "a web of legislation, common law, and longstanding practice."[7] Professor Michael McConnell has argued that the six historic hallmarks of an establishment included (i) control of church doctrine or leadership; (ii) compulsory religious exercise; (iii) preferential financial support of the established church; (iv) prohibition of dissenting worship or punishments for members of dissenting faiths; (v) use of church institutions for public functions, often in a monopoly capacity; and (vi) restriction of political offices to members of the established church.[8]

Following the Revolution, many newly independent states retained some of these laws, policies, or practices, but not without disagreement. In Virginia, Patrick Henry proposed a tax that would have permitted citizens to choose a Christian church to support or to contribute to a general fund that would be distributed by the state legislature.[9] James Madison vehemently opposed Henry's bill and responded with his famous *Memorial and Remonstrance Against Religious Assessments*.[10] Madison argued that Virginia ought not to pay the salaries of the Anglican clergy. "[R]eligious taxes were equivalent to establishment not because they forced some people to pay for religion they did not like but because they effectively forced *everyone* to engage in a religious observance—namely, tithing."[11] According to Professor Mark Storslee, "the claim about coerced religious observance [of tithing] seems to have defined the scope of that objection" related to funding. Storslee adds that this coercion "offers a plausible explanation as to why Madison and others who opposed church taxes did not oppose . . . the state's repeated funding of religious schools."[12] In other words, the assessment prompted establishment concerns not because it gave funds to religious entities, but because it coerced public participation in a specific religious observance.

Madison raised a second objection to Henry's bill. He questioned why certain groups such as the Quakers and Mennonites should be granted "peculiar exemptions" to the assessments and urged these groups not to be tempted by the offer of privileges to some religious denominations over others.[13] Ultimately, the Remonstrance led to the defeat of Henry's bill and inspired Thomas Jefferson's Statute on Religious Freedom.[14]

DRAFTING THE ESTABLISHMENT CLAUSE

The Constitutional Convention did consider religion, but it was not a major topic of discussion. Ultimately, the text of the Constitution referred to religion only in Article VI, which proscribes religious tests for public office.[15] (See Essay No. 156.) However, Anti-Federalists like Centinel and Federal Farmer objected to ratification because the Constitution contained no protections for religious belief or worship.[16] Federal Farmer described as an "unalienable or fundamental right[]" the proposition that "[n]o man, demeaning himself peaceably, shall be molested on account of his religion or mode of worship."[17] Five states proposed religious freedom amendments to the new Constitution.[18]

During the First Congress, Representative James Madison proposed the following amendment regarding the establishment of religion: "The civil rights of none shall be abridged on account of religious belief or worship, nor shall any national religion be established, nor shall the full and equal rights of conscience be in any manner, or on any pretext, infringed."[19] The amendment was "ordered to be referred to a Committee of the whole."[20] Peter Sylvester of New York was concerned that the clause might be interpreted "to abolish religion altogether," and Roger Sherman of Connecticut thought the clause was "altogether unnecessary" because Congress "had no authority . . . to make religious establishments."[21] Madison understood the proposed amendment to mean "that Congress should not establish a religion, and enforce the legal observation of it by law, nor compel men to worship God in any manner contrary to their conscience."[22] Benjamin Huntington of Connecticut feared that the words of the amendment "might be taken in such latitude as to be extremely hurtful to the cause of religion" and said he desired an amendment that would secure "free exercise of the rights of religion" without "patroniz[ing] those who professed no religion at all."[23]

Madison then suggested adding "national" before religion to prevent the establishment of one sect or prevent two from combining to establish a national religion "to which they would compel others to conform."[24] Elbridge Gerry of Massachusetts raised a semantical objection, observing that the Anti-Federalists "were in favor of a Federal Government, and the others were in favor of a national one."[25] Madison promptly withdrew his motion. Samuel Livermore of Massachusetts would have revised the amendment to read, "Congress shall make no laws touching religion, or infringing the rights of conscience."[26] The House agreed to this amendment and then, five days later, adopted a motion by Fisher Ames of Massachusetts to revise the text so that it now read, "Congress shall make no law establishing religion, or to prevent the free exercise thereof, or to infringe the rights of conscience."[27]

The Senate received a slightly different version from the House: "Congress shall make no law establishing Religion, or prohibiting the free exercise thereof; nor shall the rights of conscience be infringed."[28] The Senate considered various proposals to change this version. One prohibited the establishment of "one religious sect or society in preference to others," and another protected "rights of conscience."[29] Both were rejected. Ultimately, the Senate settled on the following wording: "Congress shall make no law establishing religion, or prohibiting the free exercise thereof."[30] Then, six days later, it changed "religion" to "articles of faith or mode of worship" and added other freedoms that are now found in the First Amendment. The text now provided that "Congress shall make no law establishing articles of faith or a mode of worship, or prohibiting the free exercise of religion, or abridging the freedom of speech, or the press, or the right of the people peaceably to assemble, and petition the government for the redress of grievances."[31]

The Senate and House approved the proposal.[32] A conference committee was appointed to resolve the differences between their respective versions. The committee returned with the final version of the amendment: "Congress shall make no law respecting an establishment of religion, or prohibiting the free exercise thereof; or abridging the freedom of speech, or of the press; or the right of the people peaceably to assemble, and petition the government for a redress of grievances."[33] The amendment was approved by both houses and sent to the states for ratification on September 25, 1789.

RATIFYING THE ESTABLISHMENT CLAUSE

The state ratification debates shed little direct light on the original meaning of the Establishment Clause. However, there was a general desire to avoid an official federal church and prevent the federal government from breaking up state-established religions.[34] Ultimately, the First Amendment was ratified on December 15, 1791. Professor Carl Esbeck has observed that "[t]he absence of popular pushback in the states to ratification of the [First Amendment] is consistent with the understanding that the American public viewed the text as prohibiting any federal involvement in an establishment of religion, be it at the state or federal level."[35]

EARLY PRACTICE

The U.S. Supreme Court has observed that the United States has an "unbroken history of official acknowledgment by all three branches of government of the role of religion in American life."[36] In April and May 1789, shortly after the inaugural session of Congress, both the House of Representatives and the Senate elected official chaplains to offer prayer.[37] On September 22, 1789, Congress passed a statute providing for the payment of various congressional officials, including chaplains.[38]

This practice continued a historical tradition dating back to before independence. In 1774, the First Continental Congress adopted the "procedure of opening its sessions with a prayer offered by a paid chaplain."[39] In 1775, the Continental Congress approved military chaplains.[40] The activities of these government-paid chaplains were accepted under the new Constitution. The First Congress, for example, approved the Bill of Rights only three days after enacting the statute providing for the payment of congressional chaplains.[41]

There is also no record that anyone at the Founding viewed the public display of religious symbols as constituting a religious establishment.[42] To the contrary, such symbols were often viewed as unproblematic and even valuable. For example, in 1776, when the seal for the new nation was being designed, Benjamin Franklin and Thomas Jefferson proposed a biblical scene involving Moses.[43] The seal ultimately adopted by Congress in 1782 features "the Eye of Providence" above the motto Annuit Coeptis: "He [God] has favored our undertakings."[44] In 1789, President Washington's Thanksgiving Day Proclamation referred to "a day of public thanksgiving and prayer" and the role of a "Supreme Being" in "the foundations and successes of our young Nation."[45] As President, Jefferson allowed various religious groups to use federal government buildings for weekly worship services.[46]

There also was significant government funding of religious institutions. In Maryland, a 1776 declaration of rights prohibited the use of taxes to support any particular religion, but the law did permit "a general and equal tax for the support of the [C]hristian religion."[47] When the legislature attempted to enact such a general tax in 1785, some contemporary figures argued that an assessment for the purpose of financing worship "amount[ed] to a coerced religious observance."[48] However, such concerns were not raised in opposition to Maryland's financial support of religious schools throughout the early 1800s.

This practice suggests that historical opposition in Maryland to a general assessment was motivated primarily by a specific opposition to compelled tithes—forcing individuals to contribute to the support of a religious congregation.[49] Conversely, where the government was financing a public good such as education, such concerns were mitigated or altogether nonexistent. This conclusion is supported by evidence from other southern states. For example, North Carolina and South Carolina continued to provide support to religious schools even after passing new state constitutions that put an end to church taxes.[50] Similarly, Georgia eventually prohibited any "'tith[e]s, taxes, or any other rates' in support of religious worship" while continuing its "support for religious academies."[51]

The federal government, even though it was bound by the Establishment Clause, also continued to provide government funds for religious schools.[52] In 1804, President Jefferson assured Catholic nuns in New Orleans, part of the newly acquired Louisiana Purchase, that "the charitable objects of your institution . . . cannot fail to ensure it the patronage of the government it is under."[53] The Jefferson Administration also continued the policy––started under President Washington––of funding priests for Indian tribes.[54] In 1812, the District of Columbia began to use revenues from its education tax to support religious schools.[55] Such government aid seems not to have been controversial at the time.[56] This early history suggests that there was broad cooperation between religion and government.[57]

JUDICIAL PRECEDENT

The Supreme Court has long "looked primarily to historical practices and analogues to guide its analysis" of the Establishment Clause.[58] However, *Lemon v. Kurtzman* (1971) adopted a new history-free tripartite test and "interrupted this long line of precedents" based on history.[59] Over time, however, *Lemon* proved to be an exception rather than the rule in Establishment Clause analysis.[60]

Kennedy v. Bremerton (2022) cemented this shift away from *Lemon*. The Court unequivocally stated that "the Establishment Clause must be interpreted by 'reference to historical practices and understandings.'"[61] Thus, *Lemon* was no longer controlling,[62] but what replaced it?

The Court explained in *Kennedy* that government action that coerced individuals to participate in a religious exercise on pain of legal penalty "was *among* the foremost hallmarks of religious establishments the framers sought to prohibit when they adopted the First Amendment."[63] The Court did not say that coercion, in the abstract, was the *sine qua non* of historical religious establishments.

To underscore that point, the Court concluded its sentence about coercion with a footnote citing Michael McConnell's scholarship that identifies multiple important historical hallmarks of established churches. This footnote also cites approvingly to Justice Neil Gorsuch's concurring opinion from the same term, which summarized and provided some doctrinal guidance relevant to the various historical hallmarks.[64]

Specifically, Justice Gorsuch's concurrence stated that beyond a formal declaration that a religious denomination was in fact the established church, it seems that Founding-era religious establishments often bore certain other telling traits. The government (1) controlled the doctrine and personnel of the established church; (2) mandated attendance in the established church and punished people for failing to participate; (3) punished dissenting churches and individuals for their religious exercise; (4) restricted political participation by dissenters; (5) provided financial support for the established church, often in a way that preferred the established denomination over other churches; and (6) used the established church to carry out certain civil functions, often by giving it a monopoly over a specific function.[65]

Thus, in future cases when the Court is identifying whether a government practice constitutes a violation of the Establishment Clause, it will likely look to whether, at a low level of abstraction, the challenged practice resembles one of these hallmarks in important respects. The Court also will likely apply different types of doctrinal tests, depending on the relevant historical hallmark.

The *Kennedy* Court also analyzed whether the government was mandating participation in a religious exercise and punishing those who fail to comply.[66] The Court emphasized that historically problematic coercion included "mak[ing] . . . religious observance[s] compulsory," "coerc[ing] anyone to attend church,"[67] or otherwise "forc[ing] citizens to engage in 'a formal religious exercise.'"[68] The Court found no coercion in the facts of *Kennedy*, where a football coach willingly ended his practice of post-game religious talks and locker room prayers with his team.[69]

Kennedy also rejects the idea that the Establishment Clause and Free Exercise Clause are conceptually in "direct tension" with one another.[70] Instead, the Court conceives of these clauses as having complementary purposes. There will likely be wide swaths of activity that are protected by the Free Exercise Clause and not prohibited by the Establishment Clause, and vice versa. In some cases, there will be government action that both the Establishment Clause and the Free Exercise Clause together prohibit, speaking with one voice. One could view both clauses as working in tandem to decrease unjustified government control of religion, though from different vantage points.

OPEN QUESTIONS

- Which doctrinal tests will the Court adopt with respect to the various historical hallmarks of religious establishments?
- The Court has indicated that the ministerial exception is one area in which the Free Exercise Clause and Establishment Clause speak with one voice, but questions remain about other areas where this overlap occurs, including in the broader church autonomy context.

Cite as: Stephanie Barclay, *The Establishment Clause, in* THE HERITAGE GUIDE TO THE CONSTITUTION 592 (Josh Blackman & John G. Malcolm eds., 3d ed. 2025).

Notes

1. Stephanie H. Barclay, Brady Earley & Annika Boone, *Original Meaning and the Establishment Clause: A Corpus Linguistics Analysis*, 61 Ariz. L. Rev. 505, 521 (2019). **2.** Michael W. McConnell, *Establishment and Disestablishment at the Founding, Part I: Establishment of Religion*, 44 Wm. & Mary L. Rev. 2105, 2110 2133–38 (2003). **3.** *Id.* at 2144. **4.** *Id.* at 2146–51. **5.** *Id.* at 2176–81. **6.** Barclay et al., *supra* at 511. **7.** McConnell, *supra* at 2110–11. **8.** *Id.* at 2131. **9.** Patrick Henry, A Bill "Establishing a Provision for Teachers of the Christian Religion" (1784), *in* Michael W. McConnell, John H. Garvey & Thomas C. Berg, Religion and the Constitution 49–50 (3d ed. 2011). **10.** James Madison, *Memorial and Remonstrance Against Religious Assessments* (ca. June 20, 1785), https://perma.cc/VAA9-2KY4. **11.** Mark Storslee, *Religious Accommodation, the Establishment Clause, and Third-Party Harm*, 86 U. Chi. L. Rev. 871, 888 (2019). **12.** Mark Storslee, *Church Taxes and the Original Understanding of the Establishment Clause*, 169 U. Pa. L. Rev. 111, 129 (2020). **13.** *Id.* at 908. **14.** Act for Establishing Religious Freedom, January 16, 1786, https://perma.cc/6564-96PN. **15.** Gerard V. Bradley, *The No Religious Test Clause and the Constitution of Religious Liberty: A Machine That Has Gone of Itself*, 37 Case W. Rsrv. L. Rev. 674 (1987). **16.** 2 Storing 2.7.55; *id.* at 2.8.53. **17.** *Id.* at 2.8.86. **18.** Barclay et al., *supra* at 512. **19.** 1 Annals of Cong. 451 (1789). **20.** *Id.* at 468. **21.** *Id.* at 757. **22.** *Id.* at 758. **23.** *Id.* **24.** *Id.* **25.** *Id.* at 759. **26.** *Id.* **27.** *Id.* at 796. **28.** S. Jour., 1st Cong., 1st Sess. 63 (Aug. 25, 1789). **29.** *Id.* at 70 (Sept. 3, 1789). **30.** *Id.* at 77 (Sept. 9, 1789). **32.** *Id.* **33.** *Id.* at 86 (Sept. 24, 1789). **34.** Barclay et al., *supra* at 515. **35.** Carl H. Esbeck, *The Establishment Clause: Its Original Public Meaning and What We Can Learn from the Plain Text*, 22 Fed. Soc'y Rev. 26, 33 (2021). **36.** *Lynch*, 465 U.S. at 674. **37.** Ida A. Brudnick, Cong. Rsrch. Serv., R41807, House and Senate Chaplains: An Overview 1 (2011), https://perma.cc/KT7C-USDP. **38.** *Marsh v. Chambers*, 463 U.S. 783, 787 (1983); Christopher C. Lund, *The Congressional Chaplaincies*, 17 Wm. & Mary Bill Rts. J. 1171, 1184–85 (2009). **39.** *Marsh*, 463 U.S. at 787. **40.** *In re England*, 375 F.3d 1169, 1171 (2004); Richard D. Rosen, Katcoff v. Marsh *at Twenty-Two: The Military Chaplaincy and the Separation of Church and State*, 38 U. Tol. L. Rev. 1137, 1143 (2007). **41.** Michael W. McConnell, *No More (Old) Symbol Cases*, 2019 Cato Sup. Ct. Rev. 91, 109 (2018–19); Lund, *supra* at 1173. **42.** *Shurtleff v. City of Bos., Mass.*, 596 U.S. 243, 287 (2022) (Gorsuch, J., concurring). **43.** James H. Hutson, Religion and the Founding of the American Republic 50–51 (1998). **44.** U.S. Dep't of State, Bureau of Pub. Affairs, The Great Seal of the United States 4–6 (July 2003), https://perma.cc/8KGS-4GYC. **45.** *Van Orden v. Perry*, 545 U.S. 667, 686–87 (2005). **46.** Hutson, *supra* at 84–94. **47.** Maryland Const. of 1776, art. XXXIII; Storslee, *Church Taxes, supra* at 150–51. **48.** *Id.* at 151. **49.** *Id.* at 155. **50.** *Id.* at 155–56. **51.** *Id.* at 156. **52.** *Id.* at 164. **53.** Letter from Thomas Jefferson to the Ursuline Nuns of New Orleans (July 13, 1804), https://perma.cc/QBD8-MVTZ. **54.** Storslee, *Church Taxes, supra* at 168. **55.** *Id.* at 164–65. **56.** *Id.* at 166–67. **57.** *Id.* at 192. **58.** *Shurtleff*, 596 U.S. at 281 (Gorsuch, J., concurring); *Everson v. Board of Education*, 330 U.S. 1, 9–15 (1947); *McGowan v. Maryland*, 366 U.S. 420, 437–40 (1961); *Torcaso v. Watkins*, 367 U.S. 488, 490–91 (1961); *Sch. Dist. of Abington Twp. v. Schempp*, 374 U.S. 203, 294 (1963); *Walz v. Tax Comm'n of N.Y.*, 397 U.S. 644, 678 (1970); Stephanie H. Barclay, *The Religion Clauses After* Kennedy v. Bremerton School District, 108 Iowa L. Rev. 2097 (2023). **59.** *Shurtleff*, 596 U.S. at 282 (Gorsuch, J., concurring). **60.** *Am. Legion v. Am. Humanist Ass'n*, 588 U.S. 19, 68–71 (2019) (Kavanaugh, J., concurring). **61.** *Kennedy v. Bremerton Sch. Dist.*, 597 U.S. 507, 535–36 (2022) (quoting *Town of Greece v. Galloway*, 572 U.S. 565, 576 (2014)). **62.** Barclay, *The Religion Clauses, supra.* **63.** *Kennedy*, 597 U.S. at 537 (emphasis added). **64.** *Id.* at 537 n.5. **65.** *Id.* **66.** *Id.* at 536–44. **67.** *Id.* at 536–37 (quoting *Zorach v. Clauson*, 343 U.S. 306, 314 (1952)). **68.** *Id.* at 537 (quoting *Lee v. Weisman*, 505 U.S. 577, 589 (1992)). **69.** J.A. at 70, 77, 170–72, *Kennedy*, 597 U.S. 507. **70.** *Kennedy*, 597 U.S. at 532–33.

ESSAY NO. 160: THE FREE EXERCISE OF RELIGION CLAUSE
AMEND. 1

*Congress shall make no law . . . prohibiting the free exercise [of religion] thereof
. . . .*

—Vincent Phillip Muñoz

INTRODUCTION

President George Washington's 1790 letter to the Hebrew Congregation of Newport, Rhode Island articulated the Founding Fathers' conception of religious freedom: "It is now no more that toleration is spoken of, as if it was by the indulgence of one class of people, that another enjoyed the exercise of their inherent natural rights."[1] Three interrelated ideas comprise the Founders' understanding of religious freedom as an "inherent" natural right: (1) Individuals possess religious freedom as an endowment from their Creator, not as something granted by the state; (2) when "we the people" ratified the Constitution and the political powers that govern under it, we did not give the government authority over the "inalienable" aspects of our right of religious exercise; and (3) the core meaning of this non-alienated aspect of religious free exercise is immunity from legal sanctions on account of one's religious worship.

To grasp the Founders' understanding, we must recall their natural rights political philosophy and attendant social compact theory of government. The Founders derived the natural right of religious free exercise from the obligation to worship the Creator according to conviction and conscience—an obligation that limits the state's legitimate authority as expressly recognized in the First Amendment's categorical text: "Congress shall make *no law* . . . prohibiting the free exercise [of religion]." The U.S. Supreme Court has floundered in its attempt to articulate a consistent account of the Free Exercise Clause's meaning, perhaps because leading originalist scholars themselves disagree about what exactly the Founders' natural rights philosophy means for First Amendment jurisprudence.

RELIGIOUS LIBERTY AS A NATURAL RIGHT

The Founders articulated their natural rights understanding of religious freedom in their state declarations of rights and constitutions and in documents drafted in early church–state debates.[2] From 1776–1784, eight states drafted declarations of rights. All eight reveal that the Founders held religious liberty to be a natural right possessed by all individuals. Delaware, Pennsylvania, North Carolina, and Vermont, for example, declared with minor variations that "all men" have (or "every individual" has) a "natural and unalienable right to worship God according to the dictates of their own consciences."[3]

In language that encapsulates the Founders' natural rights constitutionalism, the 1784 New Hampshire Bill of Rights declares that "[a]mong the natural rights, some are in their very nature unalienable, because no equivalent can be given or received for them. Of this kind are the RIGHTS OF CONSCIENCE."[4] It goes on to say that "[e]very individual has a natural and unalienable right to worship GOD according to the dictates of his own conscience, and reason" and that "no subject shall be hurt, molested, or restrained in his person, liberty or estate for worshipping GOD, in the manner and season most agreeable to the dictates of his own conscience, or for his religious profession, sentiments or persuasion."

As is true of all natural rights, the Founders held the right of religious liberty to be bounded. New Hampshire's textual proviso recognized this limitation: a person could exercise his rights "provided he doth not disturb the public peace, or disturb others, in their religious worship." The 1777 New York Constitution similarly declared that "the free exercise and enjoyment of religious profession and worship, without discrimination or preference, shall forever hereafter be allowed, within this State, to all mankind."[5] But this liberty was bounded: "*Provided*, That the liberty of conscience, hereby granted, shall not be so construed as to excuse acts of licentiousness, or justify practices inconsistent with the peace or safety of this State." The Founders understood all natural rights to be a part of, and thus limited by, the natural law.[6] Reasonable boundaries on religious exercises could be established because the Founders understood faith and reason to be complementary and compatible.

Many in the Founding generation grounded religious freedom in the Bible and Christianity in a manner articulated by Issac Backus, one of the Founding era's leading preachers.[7] Philosophically, the Founders' natural rights understanding of religious freedom was articulated most powerfully by James Madison in his 1785 "Memorial and Remonstrance."[8]

Madison provided two reasons for the "unalienable" character of the right to religious liberty. First, echoing John Locke's argument in *A Letter Concerning Toleration* and Thomas Jefferson's 1777 draft statute for religious freedom, Madison holds that the opinions of men, including their religious opinions, depend "only on the evidence contemplated by their own minds [and] cannot follow the dictates of other men."[9] Perhaps because of the argument's philosophical thinness,[10] Madison immediately adds a second, more original argument: The right of religious liberty is also inalienable "because what is here a right towards men, is a duty towards the Creator." Moreover, "[i]t is the duty of every man to render to the Creator such homage and such only as he believes to be acceptable to him. This duty is precedent, both in order of time and in degree of obligation, to the claims of Civil Society."

Madison here holds that our right to religious freedom follows from our duty to the Creator to worship in a manner that accords with our "reason and conviction."[11] The ultimate grounding of our natural right to religious freedom is our more fundamental duties to God.

Madison's argument presumes that these truths about the human person and the nature of religious obligation—that we are made to worship freely and according to conviction and conscience—are accessible to reason. They also are the foundation of limited government. Because our duties to our Creator are "precedent, both in order of time and in degree of obligation, to the claims of Civil Society," we recognize that the inalienable character of the natural right to religious freedom places some aspects of religious exercise beyond the authority of government.

THE MEANING OF THE FREE EXERCISE CLAUSE

The recognition in Founding-era state charters of natural rights, including the "unalienable" right of religious free exercise, served as the backdrop for the leading Anti-Federalist criticism of the proposed federal constitution—namely, that it lacked a declaration of rights. Other than the prohibition of religious tests for federal offices, the Constitutional Convention of 1787 devoted almost no attention to matters of church and state or religious liberty. Anti-Federalists' criticisms led Representative James Madison and the Federalist-dominated First Congress to draft what would become the Bill of Rights.

Few firm conclusions can be drawn about the Free Exercise Clause's original meaning from the First Amendment's drafting record. (See Essay No. 159.) During the drafting of what would become the Second Amendment, members of the House of Representatives debated whether to include a provision for conscientious exemption from military service. That religious exemptions were debated in the context of the Second Amendment and after provisional free exercise text had been adopted may indicate that the drafters did not understand the right of free exercise to include a right of exemption; if so, the subsequent conscientious objector debate would have been superfluous.[12] But the drafting record is thin, and conclusions drawn from it are at best only probable. Founding-era state debates and documents seem to be the best available historical records to apprehend the Framers' understanding of religious free exercise.

BELIEF-ACTION V. EXEMPTION

The U.S. Supreme Court's first significant religious liberty case, *Reynolds v. United States*

(1879) held that the Free Exercise Clause deprived Congress "of all legislative power over mere opinion" but left it "free to reach actions which were in violation of social duties or subversive of good order."[13] The case was brought by George Reynolds, secretary to Mormon Church leader Brigham Young, who argued that the clause provided religious believers such as himself with immunity from criminal prosecution for violation of federal laws prohibiting bigamy and polygamy. The Court rejected Reynolds's claim by distinguishing religious *beliefs*, which were constitutionally protected, from religiously motivated *actions* that were subject to governmental regulation.

The belief-action doctrine more or less guided the Court through a number of cases in the 1940s, including *Cantwell v. Connecticut* (1940),[14] in which the Court incorporated the Free Exercise Clause to apply against the states. The Court's most notable case from the era, *West Virginia State Board of Education v. Barnette* (1943), held that the First Amendment prohibited government-run schools from mandating that students must recite the Pledge of Allegiance and salute the American flag. Jehovah's Witness children brought the case, but the Court's reasoning made clear that no student, not just those with religious objections, could be coerced to recite the Pledge or salute the flag.[15]

In *Sherbert v. Verner* (1963), the Court set aside the belief-action distinction and inaugurated its exemption construction of the Free Exercise Clause.[16] Justice William Brennan's sweeping, non-originalist majority opinion held that the First Amendment provides religious believers with a presumptive right to be exempt from otherwise valid laws and administrative actions that they find religiously burdensome. Brennan shifted the focus of judicial inquiry from jurisdictional limits on legislative power to the impact of laws and regulations as experienced by religious believers. *Sherbert* also placed the burden of proof on the state to show that it was advancing a "compelling state interest" if and when a law or application of law burdened religious believers.

Under the *Sherbert* approach, religious litigants won some notable victories, but they did not always prevail. *Wisconsin v. Yoder* (1972) ruled that Amish parents possessed a constitutional right to be exempt from mandatory school attendance laws.[17] But *United States v. Lee* (1982) held that members of the Old Order Amish could be made to pay Social Security taxes against their religious objections.[18] And *Lyng v. Northwest Indian Cemetery Protective Association* (1988) held that the Free Exercise Clause did not prevent the government from building a road through federal lands traditionally used by Native American tribes for religious purposes.[19]

PERMISSIBLE V. MANDATED EXEMPTION

The Court significantly shifted its free exercise jurisprudence again in *Employment Division v. Smith* (1990), curtailing *Sherbert* and its exemption-granting approach.[20] While recognizing that religious accommodations made by the political branches were constitutionally *permissible*, Justice Antonin Scalia's majority opinion held that religious exemptions were not constitutionally *mandated*. The Free Exercise Clause, Scalia wrote, "does not relieve an individual of the obligation to comply with a 'valid and neutral law of general applicability on the ground that the law proscribes (or prescribes) conduct that his religion prescribes (or proscribes).'"[21]

Smith was met with a torrent of criticism. Congress responded by passing the Religious Freedom Restoration Act (1993), which attempted to overrule *Smith* by legislating *Sherbert*-like exemptions. Prominent legal scholars also responded critically. Most notably, law professor Michael McConnell argued in a pair of prominent law review articles against Scalia's *Smith* construction and for Brennan's *Sherbert* construction on originalist grounds.[22]

Three of McConnell's arguments deserve particular emphasis because of their notable influence, including their influence on the free exercise jurisprudence of Justices Sandra Day O'Connor and Samuel Alito. First, McConnell highlights the text of some of the Founding-era state charters, including the New York Constitution of 1777. McConnell contends that the peace and safety "provisos" recognize that religious believers have a right to be exempt from otherwise valid laws, except when the state is acting to prevent "acts of licentiousness" or "practices inconsistent with the peace or safety" of the state.[23]

Second, McConnell interprets Madison's logic in the "Memorial and Remonstrance" to support exemptions. As noted, Madison writes that our duty to the Creator is "precedent, both in order of time and degree of obligation, to the claims of civil society." McConnell reasons that if religious obligations to God are of higher priority than legal obligations imposed by the state, then a Madisonian understanding of religious free exercise is "consonant" with the exemption approach originally adopted in *Sherbert*.[24]

Third, McConnell contends that the Founders' exemption-granting practices, including "the history of oath requirements, military conscription, [and] religious assessments," demonstrate "that religion-specific exemptions were familiar and accepted means of accommodating these conflicts"[25] between perceived obligations of faith and the demands of the law.

Justice O'Connor employed McConnell's scholarship extensively in her dissenting opinion in *City of Boerne v. Flores* (1997), arguing that *Smith* was incorrectly decided. "The practice of the Colonies and early States bears out the conclusion," O'Connor claimed, "that, at the time the Bill of Rights was ratified, it was accepted that government should, when possible, accommodate religious practice."[26] Following McConnell, O'Connor concluded that religious believers generally have a presumptive right to be exempt from burdensome but otherwise valid laws.[27]

In the same case, Justice Scalia defended his no-exemption Free Exercise Clause construction, this time providing the originalist argumentation that his *Smith* opinion lacked. Scalia relied on Professor Philip Hamburger's scholarship[28] arguing that the "provisos" of early American charters communicated that the right of religious liberty did *not* include a right to break the law.[29] Scalia noted that the "Memorial and Remonstrance" was directed against adoption of the law at issue, not a plea for exemptions from it,[30] and that Founding-era exemption-granting practices were legislative rather than judicial in character. However, the fact that "legislatures sometimes (though not always) found it appropriate to accommodate religious practices does not establish that accommodation was

understood to be constitutionally *mandated* by the Free Exercise Clause."[31] According to Scalia, the Free Exercise Clause protects only against legislation taken "for" or "in respect of" religion and not against neutral and generally applicable state actions that indirectly or incidentally burden religious individuals or institutions.[32]

In spite of Scalia's opinions, McConnell's exemption interpretation of the Free Exercise Clause has become the leading originalist understanding, though not all prominent originalists agree with it. As I read Madison, natural rights constitutionalism requires equality before the law, not special accommodations such as exemptions.[33]

Moreover, in my view, the exemptionist construction of the First Amendment is not supported by the Founders' conception of religious liberty as an "unalienable" natural right more generally. In the Founders' social compact constitutionalism, "inalienability" is a jurisdictional concept that defines the limits of the state's power. We the people do not alienate—that is, do not grant government jurisdictional authority over—our inalienable rights. Therefore, the state lacks authority to prescribe, proscribe, or regulate religious exercises as such. But when the legislature adopts laws within the powers we have granted to it, those laws constitutionally can be applied against religious individuals. In this understanding, the First Amendment does not compel exemptions from otherwise valid laws, including the type of laws at issue in *Smith* (welfare eligibility regulations and criminal drug laws) or in *City of Boerne* (land use regulations), even if religious individuals and institutions find them burdensome.

RECENT FREE EXERCISE DOCTRINE
Smith remains the Court's leading Free Exercise Clause precedent, but it does not govern all Free Exercise Clause cases. The Court employs heightened scrutiny when a law is not neutral toward religion or is not generally applicable. *Church of the Lukumi Babalu Aye v. City of Hialeah* (1993) found unconstitutional city ordinances targeting Santerian religious practices.[34] *Masterpiece Cakeshop v. Colorado Civil Rights Commission* (2018) found that a government agency failed to act "neutrally" toward a Christian cakeshop owner who had refused

to design a wedding cake for a same-sex couple.[35] In *Fulton v. City of Philadelphia* (2021), a unanimous Court found that city officials had violated the Free Exercise Clause by refusing to contract with Catholic Social Services because of the latter's policy of not licensing same-sex couples to be foster parents. In an opinion by Chief Justice John Roberts, the Court held that the Philadelphia non-discrimination ordinance in question was not neutral and generally applicable because it provided for exemptions at the sole discretion of the city's civil rights commission.[36]

The Roberts Court, by adjudicating the Free Exercise Clause's requirements of government neutrality and non-discrimination, has abandoned the "separationist" idea that the Establishment Clause requires the government to take proactive steps so as not to advance, endorse, or fund religion. In its place, the Roberts Court has held that the Free Exercise Clause prohibits state discrimination against religious individuals based on religious status or potential religious uses of otherwise available government funds.

In *Trinity Lutheran v. Comer* (2017), the Roberts-led Court found that the exclusion of churches from an otherwise neutral and secular aid program violates the Free Exercise Clause.[37] *Espinoza v. Montana Department of Revenue* (2020) similarly set aside a Montana rule that prohibited recipients of tax-credit scholarships from using them at private religious schools.[38]

Carson v. Makin (2022) found unconstitutional a Maine law that prohibited students from using otherwise available state tuition assistance at religious or "sectarian" private schools.[39] And in *Kennedy v. Bremerton* (2022), the Court found unconstitutional a public high school's policy that prohibited a coach from praying on the fifty-yard line after his team's games.[40] Justice Neil Gorsuch's majority opinion declared that the Free Exercise Clause "does perhaps its most important work by protecting the ability of those who hold religious beliefs of all kinds to live out their faiths in daily life through 'the performance of (or abstention from) physical acts.'"[41]

At the same time the Court has interpreted the Free Exercise Clause to mandate equal treatment of religious individuals in various government aid programs, the Court also has interpreted the Free Exercise Clause's protections to reach beyond the mandate of neutrality for religious institutions. *Hosanna-Tabor Evangelical Lutheran Church and School v. EEOC* (2012) and *Our Lady of Guadalupe School v. Morrissey-Berru* (2020) recognized the "ministerial exception," establishing that the Free Exercise Clause protects churches' autonomy in the selection and employment of their own ministers.[42] The clause thus shields religious institutions from most employment anti-discrimination laws in the hiring and selection of those who are considered "ministers."[43]

OPEN QUESTIONS

In *Fulton*, Justice Alito wrote a lengthy concurring opinion, joined by Justices Clarence Thomas and Neil Gorsuch, calling for *Smith*'s reversal. Invoking McConnell's originalist scholarship, Alito argued that "free exercise" seems to extend protection to all religiously motivated actions, not just legislation that targets religion for unfavorable and unequal treatment. Justices Amy Coney Barrett and Brett Kavanaugh joined Chief Justice Roberts's opinion, declining to overrule *Smith*, but in separate concurrences posed a series of questions about what might replace *Smith*. Whether (or perhaps when) *Smith* will be overturned remains to be seen.

Whatever remaining questions and disagreements persist among originalist judges and scholars, they all now agree that the Free Exercise Clause protects the right of individuals to pray and worship according to conscience and without fear of state-imposed punishment or disabilities. This rule clearly was within the Framers' design and understanding when they declared our "first freedom" to be an inalienable natural right.

Cite as: Vincent Phillip Muñoz, *The Free Exercise of Religion Clause, in* THE HERITAGE GUIDE TO THE CONSTITUTION 597 (Josh Blackman & John G. Malcolm eds., 3d ed. 2025).

Notes

1. Letter from George Washington to the Hebrew Congregation in Newport, Rhode Island (Aug. 18, 1790), https://perma.cc/D3HD-LSNG. **2.** Vincent Phillip Muñoz, *Church and State in the Founding-Era State Constitutions*, 4 Am. Pol. Thought 1 (2015). **3.** Del. Decl. of Rts. of 1776, § 2; Pa. Const. of 1776, Decl. of Rights, art. II; N.C. Const. of 1776, Decl. of Rights, art. XIX; Vt. Const. of 1777, Decl. of Rights, art. I. **4.** N.H. Constitution of 1784, Bill of Rights, arts. IV & V. **5.** N.Y. Const. of 1777, art. XXXVIII. **6.** Alexander Hamilton, *The Farmer Refuted, &C.* (Feb. 23, 1775), https://perma.cc/CLJ2-HFHR; James Wilson, *Lectures on Law, in* 1 Collected Works of James Wilson 639 (Kermit L. Hall & Mark David Hall eds., 2007). **7.** Vincent Phillip Muñoz, Religious Liberty and the American Founding: Natural Rights and the Original Meanings of the First Amendment Religion Clauses 82–86 (2022); John Witte, Joel A. Nichols, and Richard W. Garnett, Religion and the American Constitutional Experiment 35–58 (5th ed. 2022). **8.** James Madison, *Memorial and Remonstrance Against Religious Assessments* (ca. June 20, 1785), https://perma.cc/P7J8-L2AH. **9.** *Id.* **10.** St. Augustine, Letter 93 to Vincentius (c. 408), https://perma.cc/9YLH-H6Y2; Vincent Phillip Muñoz, God and the Founders: Madison, Washington, and Jefferson 92–97 (2009). **11.** Madison, *Memorial, supra.* **12.** Vincent Phillip Muñoz, *The Original Meaning of the Free Exercise Clause: The Evidence from the First Congress*, 31 Harv. J.L. & Pub. Pol'y 1083, 1109–19 (2008); *Fulton v. City of Philadelphia*, 593 U.S. 522, 570–94 (2021) (Alito, J., concurring). **13.** *Reynolds v. United States*, 98 U.S. 145, 164 (1879). **14.** 310 U.S. 296 (1940). **15.** 319 U.S 624, 634–35 (1943). **16.** 374 U.S. 398 (1963). **17.** 406 U.S. 205 (1972). **18.** 455 U.S. 252 (1982). **19.** 485 U.S. 439 (1988). **20.** 494 U.S 872 (1990). **21.** *Id.* at 879 (citing *United States v. Lee*, 455 U.S. at 263 n.3). **22.** Michael W. McConnell, *The Origins and Historical Understanding of Free Exercise of Religion*, 103 Harv. L. Rev. 1409 (1990); Michael W. McConnell, *Free Exercise Revisionism and the* Smith *Decision*, 57 Univ. Chi. L. Rev. 1109 (1990). **23.** McConnell, *Origins, supra* at 1461–66. **24.** *Id.* at 1453. **25.** *Id.* at 1472. **26.** 521 U.S. 507, 557 (1997) (O'Connor, J., dissenting). **27.** *Id.* at 554–55 (O'Connor, J., dissenting). **28.** Philip A. Hamburger, *A Constitutional Right of Religious Exemption: An Historical Perspective*, 60 Geo. Wash. L. Rev. 915 (1992); Philip A. Hamburger, *Natural Rights, Natural Law, and American Constitutions*, 102 Yale L. J. 907 (1993). **29.** *City of Boerne v. Flores*, 521 U.S. 507, 539–40 (1997) (Scalia, J., concurring). **30.** *Id.* at 541–42 (Scalia, J., concurring). **31.** *Id.* at 541 (Scalia, J., concurring) (emphasis in original); Gerard V. Bradley, *Beguiled: Free Exercise Exemptions and the Siren Song of Liberalism*, 20 Hofstra L. Review 245 (1991). **32.** *City of Boerne*, 521 U.S. at 538 (Scalia, J., concurring). **33.** Vincent Phillip Muñoz, *James Madison's Principle of Religious Liberty*, 97 Am. Pol. Sci. Rev. 17, 23–24 (2003). **34.** 508 U.S. 520 (1993). **35.** 584 U.S. 617 (2018). **36.** 593 U.S. 522 (2021). **37.** 582 U.S. 449 (2017). **38.** 591 U.S. 464 (2020). **39.** 596 U.S. 767 (2022). **40.** 597 U.S. 507 (2022). **41.** *Id.* at 524 (citing *Smith*, 494 U.S. at 877). **42.** 565 U.S. 171 (2012); 591 U.S. 732 (2020). **43.** Richard W. Garnett & John M. Robinson, Hosanna Tabor, *Religious Freedom, and the Constitutional Structure*, 2011–12 Cato Sup. Ct. Rev. 307 (2012); Richard W. Garnett, *"The Freedom of the Church": (Towards) An Exposition, Translation, and Defense*, 21 J. Contemp. Legal Issues 33 (2013).

ESSAY NO. 161: THE FREEDOM OF SPEECH AND OF THE PRESS CLAUSE
AMEND. 1

Congress shall make no law . . . abridging the freedom of speech, or of the press . . . .

—Eugene Volokh

INTRODUCTION

Free speech/free press law is sometimes described as the tax code of constitutional law. But no matter how complex this law is, and while some of the complexity may be needless, much of it is inevitable. In many ways, communication is the most complicated of human activities, and no simple rule can deal properly with all the different kinds of harms that it can cause—or all the different kinds of harms that restricting communication can cause.

ORIGINAL MEANING OF FREEDOM OF SPEECH AND PRESS

What exactly did the Framers mean by "freedom of speech, or of the press"? Some recent scholarship offers intriguing arguments. Professor Jud Campbell, for instance, has argued that the original "understanding of Founding Era expressive freedom" focused on the "natural rights" of "speech and press freedom[]."[1] These rights, he explains, "were expansive in scope but weak in their legal effect, allowing for restrictions of expression to promote the public good," although "press licensing" was forbidden.[2] Under that view, "[s]edition laws were thus facially consistent with the freedom of opinion when confined to false and malicious speech" about the government.[3] Historian Wendell Bird, on the other hand, has suggested that the original understanding was that speech critical of the government was broadly protected and that sedition laws were seen as unconstitutional.[4]

To date, no definitive scholarly consensus on this question has emerged. The debates in the First Congress, which proposed the Bill of Rights, are brief and unilluminating.[5] Early state constitutions generally included similar provisions, but there is no record of detailed debate about what those state provisions meant.[6] The Framers cared a good deal about the freedom of the press. This care is reflected in the *Appeal to the Inhabitants of Quebec*, written by the First Continental Congress in 1774. The "freedom of the press," the *Appeal* noted, promotes "the advancement of truth, science, morality, and arts in general." It also advances the "diffusion of liberal sentiments on the administration of Government," facilitates the "ready communication of thoughts between subjects," and "promot[es] . . . union among them." With freedom of the press, "oppressive officers are shamed or intimidated into more honorable and just modes of conducting affairs."[7]

The statement mentions some of the values that the Founders saw as inherent in the principle of freedom of the press: the search for and attainment of truth, scientific progress, cultural development, the increase of virtue among the people, the holding of governmental officials to republican values, the strengthening of community, and a check on self-aggrandizing politicians. But broad statements such as this tell us less than we would like to know about what "the freedom of the press" meant to the Founders as a rule of law. This history also does not provide clear rules about when the freedom would yield to competing concerns. Moreover, these statements do not resolve whether the freedom prohibits a limitation on speech only before it occurs—a so-called *prior restraint*—or whether the government can also punish a person after he engages in speech.

Few reported Founding-era court cases interpreted the federal and state free speech and free press clauses, and few Founding-era political controversies excited detailed discussion of what the clauses meant. The governments of the time were small, and the statute books were thin. Not many states passed laws restricting commercial advertising. There appear to have been no prosecutions for obscenity in the United States until 1815.[8] Some states had blasphemy laws, but they appear not to have been enforced until the 1810s.[9] Apparently, no laws banned campaign spending or anonymous speech.[10]

What inference can be drawn from this lack of regulation? Then, as today, the government did not ban all that it had the power to ban, but the fact that it did not regulate certain types of speech does not necessarily mean that such speech was constitutionally protected. The paucity of such bans meant that few people in that era had occasion to define carefully what the constitutional boundaries of speech and press protections might be.

THE SEDITION ACT

The most prominent free press debate following the Framing concerned the Sedition Act.[11] In 1798, the United States was fighting the so-called Quasi-War with France. President John Adams was a Federalist, and the Federalist Party controlled both houses of Congress. The Democratic-Republican Party was in the minority. Federalists suspected that many Democratic-Republican stalwarts sympathized with France and the French Revolution and thus were fomenting disloyalty. Congress consequently enacted the Sedition Act.[12] This statute made it a crime to publish "any false, scandalous and malicious writing or writings . . . with intent to defame" the government, Congress, or the President. The Vice President was not covered by the statute. It was also a crime "to stir up sedition within the United States, or to excite any unlawful combinations . . . for opposing or resisting any law of the United States." Finally, the law prohibited "aid[ing], encourag[ing] or abet[ting] any hostile designs of any foreign nation against the United States, their people or government." Several publishers who were critical of the Federalist government were convicted under the law, often under rather biased applications of the falsity requirement.

The Federalists' actions likely represented a

serious constitutional judgment, not just political expediency. Malicious falsehoods about Vice President Thomas Jefferson, a leading Democratic-Republican, were not subject to prosecution. The law was scheduled to expire on March 3, 1801, the day before President John Adams's term was to end. But shortly before the law expired and after the Federalists lost the 1800 election, Federalist representatives nonetheless tried to renew the act.[13] Had they succeeded, the act would have punished libels against President Jefferson and the new Democratic-Republican congressional majority. The bill was defeated in the House by a vote of 53 to 49 with all but four Federalists voting for it and all Republicans voting against it.

In 1799, Federalist Congressman John Marshall, who would soon become Chief Justice, defended the constitutionality of the Sedition Act (though he had disapproved of it as a policy matter).[14] The free press guarantee meant "liberty to publish, free from previous restraint," so there could be no requirement that printers must be licensed or that their material must be approved before publication. However, the right did not include "the liberty of spreading with impunity false and scandalous slanders, which may destroy the peace, and mangle the reputation, of an individual or of a community."[15]

Here, Marshall echoed the British law as expounded by Sir William Blackstone.[16] Under this view, criminal punishment of some forms of speech *after* publication was constitutional, at least if the punishment was consistent with the traditional rules of the common law. Other early American political leaders, such as James Madison, the principal drafter of the Bill of Rights, argued the opposite. Madison contended that Blackstone's "idea of the freedom of the press can never be admitted to be the American idea of it." Rather, "a law inflicting penalties on printed publications would have a similar effect with a law authorizing a previous restraint on them."[17]

Likewise, Marshall and some other Federalists argued that freedom of the press must necessarily be limited. Marshall wrote that "government cannot be . . . secured, if by falsehood and malicious slander, it is to be deprived of the confidence and affection of the people."[18] Madison and other Republicans disagreed.

Madison argued that even speech that creates "a contempt, a disrepute, or hatred [of the government] among the people" should be tolerated and that the only way to determine whether such contempt is justified is "by a free examination [of the government's actions], and a free communication among the people thereon."[19]

It was as if half the country read the constitutional guarantee one way and half read it the other way. These debates illustrate that there was little consensus even on such fundamental questions as whether the free press guarantee prohibited prior restraint only on publications critical of the government or also forbade punishment for "seditious" speech once it was made.

The Founding generation undoubtedly believed deeply in the freedom of speech and of the press, but then, as now, these general terms were understood differently by different people. Many people did not think about their precise meaning until a concrete controversy arose—and when a controversy did arise, people disagreed sharply on that meaning.

CONSENSUS VIEWS ON FOUNDING-ERA PRACTICE

On some questions, it is possible to have a good idea of what the Framers thought based on a combination of pre-Framing, Framing-era, and post-Framing evidence. First, traditional libel law was seen as permissible. Several state constitutions also secured "freedom of the press" and "liberty of the press."[20] Under these constitutions, defaming another person was understood to be constitutionally unprotected.

Second, the Free Press Clause covered the press as technology.[21] This right was enjoyed by all who used printing presses to communicate to the public at large. The right was not limited to the press in the sense of a specific industry or occupation. Professional publishers and journalists were not seen as having any more constitutional rights than everyone else had.[22]

Third, Framing-era law treated conventionally symbolic expression as tantamount to verbal expression. For example, the display of paintings, liberty poles, and the like was considered speech. Likewise, a burning effigy was also protected. Such communications could be punishable as libel if they conveyed false and defamatory messages about someone, but symbolic and verbal expression would also be equally covered by the freedom of speech or of the press.[23]

Fourth, Framing-era sources treated civil tort liability for speech the same as it treated criminal liability for constitutional purposes. Decisions from Vermont in 1802 and South Carolina in 1806 were the very first court cases setting aside government action on constitutional freedom of expression grounds.[24] These cases involved civil libel verdicts that were set aside because of the state constitutions' petition clauses. Similar cases from that era applied the same principle to state free speech and free press clauses.[25]

ORIGINALISM, THE FREE SPEECH CLAUSE, AND THE SUPREME COURT

McIntyre v. Ohio Elections Commission (1995) illustrates the continuing debate over the original meaning of the clause on the U.S. Supreme Court.[26] The question presented was whether the government could outlaw anonymous advocacy related to elections. McIntyre distributed an anonymous leaflet opposing a school tax levy. By a vote of 7 to 2, the Court held that the Free Speech Clause protected this anonymous electioneering. The majority dealt with the question based on the Court's twentieth-century case law and twentieth-century First Amendment theories. Justices Clarence Thomas and Antonin Scalia, the Court's most committed originalists, focused on the original meaning and reached different results.

Both Justices recognized that there was "no record of discussions of anonymous political expression either in the First Congress, which drafted the Bill of Rights, or in the state ratifying conventions."[27] Both recognized that much political speech in the time of the Framers, such as the Federalist Papers, was anonymous. Much political speech justifying resistance to Parliament before the Revolution was also anonymous.

To Justice Thomas, the Founders' use of anonymous speech was dispositive. The Federalist Papers reflect that the Framers would have regarded anonymity as a vital aspect of the freedom of speech, particularly political speech. Justice Scalia took a narrower view of what can be accepted as evidence of original meaning

apart from the text of the provision itself. Scalia wrote that "to prove that anonymous electioneering was used frequently is not to establish that it is a constitutional right."[28] Rather, Scalia suggested that the legislatures simply chose not to prohibit the speech even though they had the constitutional power to do so.

Thomas produced evidence that some Founding-era commentators saw anonymous commentary as protected by "the Liberty of the Press."[29] Scalia countered that many of these comments were mere "partisan cr[ies]" that said little about any generally accepted understanding. Thomas found the evidence sufficient to justify reading the First Amendment as protecting anonymous speech. Scalia did not think the historical evidence of what people did necessarily shows much about what people believed they had a constitutional right to do; instead, he turned to American practices of the 1800s and the 1900s, a source that he considered authoritative where the original meaning is uncertain. On this subject, even among originalists, consensus remains elusive.

THE SUPREME COURT'S FREE SPEECH DOCTRINE

The Supreme Court's free speech and free press law has not much been influenced by original meaning. Instead, it stems primarily from the experience and thinking of the twentieth century. The Court first began to hear a wide range of free speech cases only in the late 1910s. This approach has produced several general free speech principles.

First, the free speech/free press guarantee restricts only government action. The clause does not limit action by private employers, property owners, householders, churches, universities, and the like. State statutes may provide protection against privately imposed speech restrictions. For example, about half of the states provide some such protection for speech or other forms of political activity,[30] but those are matters of legislative decision, not constitutional command.

Second, the free speech/free press guarantee applies equally to federal and state governments. It includes local governments as well as all branches of each government. In particular, the civil courts are subject to the First

Amendment. For this reason, libel law and other tort law rules must comply with free speech/free press principles.[31]

Third, the free speech/free press guarantee provides essentially equal protection to speakers and writers. It does not matter whether they are members of the institutional press. Newspapers enjoy no more and no fewer constitutional rights than individuals enjoy.[32] The medium of communication also generally does not matter. Books, newspapers, movies, and the Internet are treated equally. However, the Court has treated differently over-the-airwaves radio and television broadcasting. For historical reasons, these transmissions have been given less constitutional protection.[33]

Fourth, the free speech/free press guarantee extends to any conduct that is conventionally understood as expressive, such as waving a flag, wearing an armband, or burning a flag.[34] The guarantee also extends to conduct that is necessary in order to speak effectively. For example, the First Amendment protects the right to use money to buy a public address system or to buy advertising.[35] In particular, restrictions on independent campaign expenditures generally violate the First Amendment because effective speaking to the broad public generally requires money.[36]

Fifth, the free speech/free press guarantee extends to speech about religion, science, morality, social conditions, and daily life, not just to political speech. The guarantee also extends to art and entertainment because "[t]he line between the informing and the entertaining is too elusive for the protection of that basic right."[37] "What is one man's amusement," the Court has explained, "teaches another's doctrine."[38] The guarantee also extends to low-brow expression (such as jokes or even profanity) as well as high-brow expression.[39]

Sixth, the free speech/free press guarantee extends to all viewpoints, good or evil. There is no exception for Communism, Nazism, Islamic radicalism, or "hate speech," whatever that term may mean.[40] *Gertz v. Welch* (1974) concluded that "[u]nder the First Amendment there is no such thing as a false idea" and that "[h]owever pernicious an opinion may seem, we depend for its correction not on the conscience of judges and juries but on the competition of other ideas."[41]

These rules apply to content-based restrictions, which focus on what the speech communicates—for instance, by persuading people, offending them, or frightening them. Content-neutral restrictions relate to the non-communicative impact of speech—restrictions on noise, obstruction of traffic, and so on—and are easier to justify. The test for content-neutral restrictions is complicated, but the key point is that the government may generally impose content-neutral "time, place, and manner restrictions" as long as those restrictions leave open ample alternative channels for communication. All such restrictions, however, must be neutral as to content: If they treat speech differently based on content, they are generally unconstitutional even if they focus only on the time, place, and manner of the speech.[42]

Finally, these rules apply to restrictions imposed by the government acting as sovereign and backed by the threat of jail terms, fines, or civil liability. They also apply to government control of what is said in "traditional public fora," such as parks, streets, sidewalks, or the post office. But the government has broader (though not unlimited) authority when acting as, for instance, employer, K–12 educator, proprietor of government property other than traditional public fora, subsidizer, speaker, or regulator of the airwaves. The rules for these areas are elaborate.[43]

EXCEPTIONS TO FREE SPEECH PROTECTION

The Court has recognized a small set of rather narrow exceptions to free speech protection:

- **Incitement:** Speech may be restricted if it is intended to persuade people to engage in imminent unlawful conduct and likely to cause such conduct. Outside of this narrow zone, even speech that advocates lawbreaking is constitutionally protected.[44]
- **Libel, Fraud, and Perjury:** Libel, fraud, and perjury may generally be punished if they consist of knowing lies. Such statements are generally protected if they are honest—even unreasonable—mistakes, but libel law may still award

compensatory damages for certain statements about private figures that were honest but unreasonable mistakes.[45] Libel law also may award punitive damages for honest mistakes on matters of purely private concern.[46]

- **Obscenity:** Hard-core pornography is punishable if "'the average person, applying contemporary community standards' would find that the work, taken as a whole, appeals to the prurient interest [i.e., a shameful or morbid interest in nudity, sex, or excretion]"; "the work depicts or describes, in a patently offensive way, sexual conduct specifically defined by the applicable state law"; and "the work, taken as a whole, lacks serious literary, artistic, political, or scientific value."[47]

- **Child Pornography:** Sexually themed live performances, photographs, and movies that are made using actual children may be punished even if they do not fit within the obscenity test. This standard does not cover digitized pictures, drawings, or text materials, which are constitutionally protected unless they are obscene. The Court has reasoned that child pornography is unprotected because it hurts the children involved in its making, so the exception covers

only cases where actual children were involved.[48]

- **Threats:** Speech that is reasonably perceived as a threat of illegal conduct (not just rhetorical hyperbole) can generally be punished as long as the speaker was at least reckless about the possibility that the speech would be perceived as threatening.[49]

- **Fighting Words:** Face-to-face insults that are addressed to a particular person and are likely to cause an imminent fight can be punished. More generalized offensive speech that is not addressed to a particular person cannot be punished even if it is profane or deeply insulting.[50]

- **Speech Owned by Others:** Intellectual property laws, such as copyright law, may restrict people from using a particular expression that is owned by someone else, but the law may not let anyone monopolize facts or ideas.[51]

- **Commercial Advertising:** Commercial advertising is constitutionally protected but less protected than other speech (political, scientific, artistic, and the like).[52]

Cite as: Eugene Volokh, *The Freedom of Speech and of the Press Clause, in* THE HERITAGE GUIDE TO THE CONSTITUTION 602 (Josh Blackman & John G. Malcolm eds., 3d ed. 2025).

Notes

1. Jud Campbell, *Natural Rights and the First Amendment,* 127 Yale L. J. 246, 259 (2017).   **2.** *Id.*   **3.** *Id.*   **4.** Wendell Bird, Press and Speech Under Assault: The Early Supreme Court Justices, the Sedition Act of 1798, and the Campaign Against Dissent (2016); Wendell Bird, The Revolution in Freedoms of Press and Speech: From Blackstone to the First Amendment and Fox's Libel Act (2020).   **5.** David A. Anderson, *The Origins of the Press Clause,* 30 UCLA L. Rev. 455, 477–85 (1983).   **6.** *Id.* at 485–86.   **7.** 1 J. Cont. Cong. 108 (Oct. 26, 1774).   **8.** *The Report of the Commission on Obscenity and Pornography* 300 (1970).   **9.** *People v. Ruggles,* 8 Johns. 290 (N.Y. 1811); Stuart Banner, *When Christianity Was Part of the Common Law,* 16 L. & Hist. Rev. 27, 33 (1998).   **10.** *McIntyre v. Ohio Elec. Comm'n,* 514 U.S. 334, 372–74 (1995) (Scalia, J., dissenting).   **11.** Wendell

Bird, Criminal Dissent: Prosecutions Under the Alien and Sedition Acts of 1798 (2020).   **12.** 1 Stat. 596.   **13.** 10 Annals of Cong. 975–76 (1801).   **14.** Gregg Costa, Note, *John Marshall, the Sedition Act, and Free Speech in the Early Republic,* 77 Tex. L. Rev. 1011, 1026–28 (1999); Kurt T. Lash & Alicia Harrison, *Minority Report: John Marshall and the Defense of the Alien and Sedition Acts,* 68 Ohio St. L. J. 435, 435–46 (2007).   **15.** John Marshall, *Report of the Minority on the Virginia Resolutions, in* 1 Classics of American Political and Constitutional Thought 669, 671 (Scott J. Hammond, Kevin R. Hardwick & Howard L. Lubert eds., 2007).   **16.** 4 Blackstone 151.   **17.** James Madison, *The Report of 1800* (Jan. 17, 1800), https://perma.cc/P933-5GEB.   **18.** Marshall, *supra* at 669–70.   **19.** Madison, *The Report of 1800, supra.*   **20.** Seth F. Kreimer, *The Pennsylvania*

Constitution's Protection of Free Expression, 5 U. Pa. J. Const. L. 12, 15 n.9 (2002).   **21.** Eugene Volokh, *Freedom for the Press as an Industry, or for the Press as a Technology?—From the Framing to Today*, 160 U. Pa. L. Rev. 459, 465–98 (2012).   **22.** *Id.* Compare Floyd Abrams et al., *The Press Clause: The Forgotten First Amendment*, 5 J. Free Speech L. 561, 617–20 (2024) (disagreeing with Volokh, *Freedom for the Press, supra*, with Eugene Volokh, *The Press Clause: Important, Remembered, and Equally Shared*, 5 J. Free Speech L. 659 (2025) (responding to Abrams et al.).   **23.** Eugene Volokh, *Symbolic Expression and the Original Meaning of the First Amendment*, 97 Geo. L. J. 1057 (2009). **24.** Eugene Volokh, *Tort Liability and the Original Meaning of the Freedom of Speech, Press, and Petition*, 96 Iowa L. Rev. 249 (2010).   **25.** *Id.* at 251–54.   **26.** 514 U.S. 334 (1995). **27.** *Id.* at 360 (Thomas, J., concurring in the judgment). **28.** *Id.* at 373 (Scalia, J., dissenting).   **29.** *Id.* at 362–66 (Thomas, J., concurring in the judgment).   **30.** Eugene Volokh, *Private Employees' Speech and Political Activity: Statutory Protection Against Employer Retaliation*, 16 Tex. Rev. L. & Pol. 295 (2012).   **31.** *New York Times Co. v. Sullivan*, 376 U.S. 254, 277 (1964).   **32.** Volokh, *The Press Clause, supra* at 505–21.   **33.** *FCC v. League of Women Voters of Cal.*, 468 U.S. 364 (1984).   **34.** *Texas v. Johnson*, 491 U.S. 397, 404–06 (1989).   **35.** *Citizens United v. FEC*, 558 U.S. 310, 336–37 (2010); *Buckley v. Valeo*, 424 U.S. 1, 16 (1976).   **36.** *Buckley*, 424 U.S. at 26.   **37.** *Winters v. New York*, 333 U.S. 507, 510 (1948).   **38.** *Id.* at 510 (1948). **39.** *Cohen v. California*, 403 U.S. 15 (1971).   **40.** *Matal v. Tam*, 582 U.S. 218, 246 (2017) (lead op.); *id.* at 253–54 (Kennedy, J., concurring in part and concurring in the judgment). **41.** *Gertz v. Robert Welch, Inc.*, 418 U.S. 323, 339 (1974). **42.** *Ward v. Rock Against Racism*, 491 U.S. 781 (1989); *McCullen v. Coakley*, 573 U.S. 464 (2014).   **43.** *Connick v. Myers*, 461 U.S. 138 (1983); *Mahanoy Area Sch. Dist. v. B.L.*, 594 U.S. 180 (2021); *ISKCON v. Lee*, 505 U.S. 672 (1992); *Rosenberger v. Rector & Visitors of Univ. of Va.*, 515 U.S. 819 (1995); *League of Women Voters*, 468 U.S. 364. **44.** *Brandenburg v. Ohio*, 395 U.S. 444 (1969).   **45.** *United States v. Alvarez*, 567 U.S. 709, 717–18 (2012) (plurality op.).   **46.** *Dun & Bradstreet, Inc. v. Greenmoss Builders, Inc.*, 472 U.S. 749 (1985).   **47.** *Miller v. California*, 413 U.S. 15, 24 (1973).   **48.** *Ashcroft v. Free Speech Coal.*, 535 U.S. 234 (2002).   **49.** *Counterman v. Colorado*, 600 U.S. 66 (2024).   **50.** *Chaplinsky v. New Hampshire*, 315 U.S. 568 (1942); *Cohen v. California*, 403 U.S. 15 (1971). **51.** *Harper & Row, Publishers, Inc. v. Nation Enters.*, 471 U.S. 539 (1985).   **52.** *Sorrell v. IMS Health Inc.*, 564 U.S. 552 (2011).

ESSAY NO. 162: THE FREEDOM OF ASSEMBLY CLAUSE
AMEND. 1

Congress shall make no law . . . abridging . . . the right of the people peaceably to assemble. . . .

—Tabatha Abu El Haj

INTRODUCTION

The First Amendment establishes "the right of the people peaceably to assemble." The existence of this right was not controversial at the Founding. As the Supreme Court acknowledged in *United States v. Cruikshank* (1875), "The right of the people peaceably to assemble for lawful purposes existed long before the adoption of the Constitution . . . and always has been, one of the attributes of citizenship under a free government."[1] The original public meaning and historical scope of the right is capacious. From the early Republic through the nineteenth century, Americans entertained and established a conception of the right that was broader and more robust than its English predecessor. However, the Supreme Court's attention to assembly has receded since the 1940s. The right was important in several decisions overturning convictions of African Americans who participated in peaceful civil rights demonstrations, but federal courts have largely ignored it since the close of the civil rights era. The Supreme Court last decided a right-of-assembly claim four decades ago.

HISTORY BEFORE 1787

A right of assembly was not enumerated in the Magna Carta of 1215.[2] Nevertheless, it emerged in English constitutional law as a necessary corollary to the right of petition.[3] The right, while extending to the public streets, was limited by a series of riot acts starting in 1412 and by the common-law crimes of riot and unlawful assembly as enforced by juries.[4]

In 1670, for example, William Penn was

arrested and tried in London for delivering a sermon to Quakers gathered on a public street in violation of the 1664 Conventicle Act, which banned "any Nonconformists" from assembling for religious purposes.[5] A jury ultimately acquitted Penn and his fellow Quaker, William Mead, of these charges arising out of their religious worship on the public street. The incident loomed large in early American law because of the prominence of Quakers in Philadelphia.

The people's right to assembly was enshrined in several state constitutions adopted after independence. By 1789, the constitutions of five states—Massachusetts, New Hampshire, North Carolina, Pennsylvania, and Vermont—provided for the right of the people "to assemble together, to consult for their common good" in provisions separate from those protecting freedom of speech.[6] In Massachusetts and New Hampshire, the right was limited to assembly "in an orderly and peaceable manner." No such limit appeared in the North Carolina, Pennsylvania, or Vermont Declarations of Rights. In all instances, the right of assembly was closely associated with processes for seeking "redress of grievances." Thus, it was understood as a means for achieving popular sovereignty and allowing people to influence governance directly and meaningfully.[7]

ADOPTION OF THE ASSEMBLY CLAUSE

During the Constitutional Convention, there was no significant debate concerning the assembly right, but its importance was referenced by prominent Anti-Federalists during the ratification debates. Federal Farmer declared that "[t]he people have a right to assemble in an orderly manner."[8] Centinel observed that the "grand palladium" of liberty included "the right of the people to assemble peaceably for the purpose of consulting about public matters."[9] Consequently, Virginia, New York, and North Carolina pressed for a bill of rights with explicit recognition "[t]hat the people have a right peaceably to assemble together to consult for the common good . . . ."[10]

The First Congress took up the demand for a bill of rights in 1789. Among the amendments proposed by James Madison was one specifying that "[t]he people shall not be restrained from peaceably assembling and consulting for

their common good; nor from applying to the legislature by petitions or remonstrances for redress of their grievances."[11] On August 15, the House debated a consolidated text: "The freedom of speech and of the press, and the right of the people peaceably to assemble and consult for their common good, and to apply to the Government for redress of grievances, shall not be infringed."[12]

The decision to combine the right of assembly with the freedom of speech and press appears to have been the result of a stylistic change by the select committee.[13] During the ensuing floor debate, Representative Theodore Sedgwick of Massachusetts criticized the proposed right of assembly as redundant with the "freedom of speech," remarking that "[i]f people freely converse together, they must assemble for that purpose; it is a self-evident, unalienable right which the people possess; it is certainly a thing that never would be called in question."[14] Representative John Page of Virginia reminded him that "people have also been prevented from assembling together on their lawful occasions."[15] After Page spoke, the House defeated Sedgwick's motion to strike "assembly" from the draft amendment by a "considerable majority."[16]

The final text of the First Amendment, which is strikingly similar to the House's consolidated text, emerged in the Senate, which introduced a right to petition the legislature, combined these rights with protections for religious freedom, and introduced the specific reference to Congress. While the Senate did not keep a record of its debate, the House debate clarifies that right of assembly was considered a separate and distinct right that encompassed more than meetings to address political grievances and entailed a right of access to public streets and spaces.[17]

EARLY PRACTICE

One of the first questions to arise after ratification was whether the right of assembly protected associations or only temporary gatherings.[18] Although the legality of political associations, such as the Sons of Liberty, went unquestioned by the colonists during the American Revolution, the creation of Democratic-Republican Societies in the spring of 1793 drew the ire of the Federalists. The Societies, which had organized around criticisms of the Washington Administration's apparent alliance with Great Britain, were accused of undermining popular sovereignty by seeking to exercise political power outside of the legislature.[19] Federalists implied that the right of assembly protected only temporary gatherings.[20]

In 1798, a Federalist Congress enacted the Sedition Act, which criminalized speech critical of the government, and also prohibited individuals from "unlawfully combin[ing] or conspir[ing] together, with intent to oppose any measures of the government of the United States."[21] Democratic-Republican Societies maintained they were merely asserting their unalienable right to assemble together in a peaceable manner and participated in a variety of festivities, feasts, and processions in the public streets to demonstrate their continued political opposition to the Washington Administration.[22] Ultimately, Democratic-Republicans argued that the Sedition Act was unconstitutional, a position that is generally viewed to have been vindicated by Jefferson's election in 1800.

NINETEENTH-CENTURY TREATISES AND STATE COURT PRECEDENTS

The First Amendment does not protect all gatherings: Assemblies must be *peaceable*. In 1927, Leon Whipple, the first Chair in Journalism at the University of Virginia, noted that in "its original meaning," the term "peaceable" was not "to be confused with 'legal' or 'permissible.'"[23] In the early twentieth century, the meaning of "peaceable" had not yet been litigated formally in federal courts because of their historically limited jurisdiction and the fact that the First Amendment had incorporated against the states.

Nevertheless, nineteenth-century Americans settled on a capacious understanding of this fundamental right. The mere fact that an assembly was illegal did not deprive its participants of constitutional protection.[24] The constitutional shield evaporated only when an assembly descended into a "riot" or "unlawful assembly"—common-law crimes that turned on the presence of violence or an imminent threat of violence to persons or property. In 1844, an *American Law Magazine* article explained that American law could constitutionally preserve the common law of riot and unlawful assembly because gatherings "which look to violence and not to reason and the influence of a strong expression of public opinion, do not fall within the protection of the constitutional guarantee."[25]

Nineteenth-century legal treatises emphasized that nonviolent illegal actions did not render an assembly outside the scope of the right. Professor Albert Wright, writing about the Wisconsin constitution, observed that under the right of assembly, "any number of people may come together in any sort of societies, religious, social or political, or even in treasonous conspiracies."[26] Wright added that "so long as they behave themselves and do not hurt anybody or make any great disturbance, they may express themselves in public meetings by speeches and resolutions as they choose."[27] John Randolph Tucker took a similar view in his treatise on the U.S. Constitution, declaring that "the right of the people peaceably to assemble . . . does not prevent interference with the riotous assemblages of the people; *where there is no riotous conduct the government cannot interfere.*"[28]

Nineteenth-century American cities did not require citizens to ask permission before assembling.[29] "In Britain, the people were not free to assemble in the streets and parks without official permission," as Professor Michael McConnell has noted, but the American understanding of the freedom of assembly broke with this tradition.[30] In 1867, John Alexander Jameson's treatise on the Constitutional Convention asserted that "wholly unofficial" gatherings and "spontaneous assemblies" were protected by the right of peaceable assembly.[31]

The first ordinances to require advance permission to gather in public were passed in the late nineteenth century to suppress the Salvation Army.[32] These laws were almost uniformly declared void by state supreme courts.[33] Only the Supreme Judicial Court of Massachusetts held otherwise.[34] Outside Massachusetts, state court judges routinely displayed great tolerance for disruptive crowds, absent violence. In 1889, an Illinois appellate court emphasized that "the law allows great latitude to public demonstrations, whether religious, political or social, and it is against the genius of our institutions to resort to repressive measures . . . to encroach on [such] fundamental rights."[35]

EARLY SUPREME COURT PRECEDENT

The U.S. Supreme Court addressed the assembly right for the first time in *United States v. Cruikshank* (1875).[36] This case, which was brought under the Privileges and Immunities Clause of the Fourteenth Amendment, acknowledged the English origins of the right but held that the privilege extended only to assemblies "for the purpose of petitioning Congress . . . or for any thing else connected with the powers or the duties of the national government."[37] A decade later, another privileges and immunities case, *Presser v. Illinois* (1886), suggested that assemblies were protected only when "the purpose of the assembly was to petition the government for a redress of grievances."[38] *Presser* marks the only time that the Court expressly limited the right of assembly in this way.

In *Davis v. Massachusetts* (1897), the Court turned to the question of where Americans were entitled to assemble. In this case, a Massachusetts law required a permit to give a public address on the Boston Common, a public park.[39] The Massachusetts Supreme Judicial Court upheld this statute, finding that the legislature's control of its property is identical to that of a private actor. Therefore, the court found, the legislature may "absolutely or conditionally . . . forbid public speaking in a highway or public park" without infringing on any person's constitutional rights. The U.S. Supreme Court did not discuss the right of assembly, but rather accepted the lower court's position.[40] Here, the Supreme Court accepted the outlying position of Massachusetts's high court without directly analyzing the First Amendment, which at the time did not constrain Massachusetts.

Indeed, as late as 1899, John Randolph Tucker observed that the First Amendment right of assembly "has not been the subject of adjudication."[41] That lack of precedent would, however, change after *De Jonge v. Oregon* (1937) incorporated the assembly right against the states.[42] Two years later, the Supreme Court decided *Hague v. Committee for Industrial Organization* (1939).[43] For the first time, the Court asserted explicitly that "the right peaceably to assemble and to discuss . . . and to communicate . . . whether orally or in writing, is a privilege inherent in citizenship of the United States."[44] Importantly, the *Hague* Court distanced itself from the reasoning in *Davis*, asserting that "[w]herever the title of streets and parks may rest, they have immemorially been held in trust for the use of the public and, time out of mind, have been used for purposes of assembly."[45] Nevertheless, *Hague* implicitly sanctioned an important limit to the right of assembly on the public streets: It could be "regulated in the interest of all; and must be exercised . . . in consonance with peace and good order."[46] This principle was subsequently formalized in *Cox v. New Hampshire* (1941), which held that the government could require a permit for an assembly as long as the law treated all viewpoints equally.[47] The final case from this period, *Thomas v. Collins* (1945), held that the right of assembly guarded "not solely religious or political" causes, but also "secular causes."[48]

MODERN SUPREME COURT PRECEDENT

Since the Warren Court, the federal right of peaceable assembly has been subsumed into a right of free expression. The Court has conflated the rights of peaceable assembly, speech, and association into a single speech right.

Part of the impetus for the neglect of the right of assembly was the Court's recognition of a non-textual right of association in *NAACP v. Alabama ex rel. Patterson* (1958), which held that the state could not compel a civil rights organization to disclose its membership list.[49] The Court could have resolved the case under the freedom of assembly since both *De Jonge* and *Thomas* recognized the close nexus between the freedoms of association and assembly. Instead, *Patterson* recognized a right of expressive association as an extension of the freedom of speech. The Court declared it "beyond debate that freedom to engage in association for the advancement of beliefs and ideas is an inseparable aspect of the 'liberty' assured by the Due Process Clause of the Fourteenth Amendment, which embraces freedom of speech."[50]

Roberts v. United States Jaycees (1984) further split this right of association into two aspects.[51] One line of decisions protect "intimate association" as "a fundamental element of personal liberty."[52] Another set of decisions guard "expressive association," defined as "a right to associate for the purpose of engaging in those activities protected by the First Amendment—speech, assembly, petition for the redress of grievances, and the exercise of religion."[53] Professor John Inazu has criticized these decisions on originalist grounds, contending that the right of peaceful assembly, properly construed, covers not just a gathering, but also the group that precedes the gathering.[54] Inazu further maintains that failure to envision protection through the right of assembly has diminished protection.[55] Inazu pointed to *Christian Legal Society v. Martinez* (2010), which held that a public university could force a student organization to open eligibility to all students as a condition of official recognition and access to funding.[56]

There are hints that the Court may revive the Assembly Clause. *Americans for Prosperity Foundation v. Bonta* (2021) declared unconstitutional California's extensive disclosure requirement for registered charitable organizations as a violation of the freedom of association. Justice Clarence Thomas's brief concurrence speculated that "[t]he text and history of the Assembly Clause suggest that the right to assemble includes the right to associate anonymously."[57]

Cite as: Tabatha Abu El Haj, *The Freedom of Assembly Clause, in* The Heritage Guide to the Constitution 608 (Josh Blackman & John G. Malcolm eds., 3d ed. 2025).

Notes

1. *United States v. Cruikshank*, 92 U.S. 542, 551 (1875). **2.** Kenneth Pickthorn, Some Historical Principles of the Constitution 120 (1925). **3.** Robin Handley, *Public Order, Petitioning and Freedom of Assembly*, 7 J. Legal Hist. 123 (1986) (citing W.S. Holdsworth, A History of English Law x, 700–01 (2d ed. 1937)). **4.** Frederic Jesup Stimson, Popular Law-Making: A Study of the Origin History, and Present Tendencies of Law-Making by Statute 284 (1911). **5.** John D. Inazu, Liberty's Refuge: The Forgotten Freedom of Assembly 24–25 (2012). **6.** Pa. Const. of 1776, ch. I, § XVI; Mass. Const. of 1780, art. XIX; N.C. Const. of 1776, art. XVIII, N.H. Const. of 1784, art. XXXII; Vt. Const. of 1777, art. XVIII. **7.** Nikolas Bowie, *The Constitutional Right of Self Government*, 130 Yale L. J. 1652, 1661, 1695–1713 (2021). **8.** Storing 2.8.86. **9.** *Id.* at 2.7.55. **10.** Bernard Schwartz, II The Bill of Rights: A Documentary History 842, 913, 968 (1971). **11.** *Id.* at 1026; 1 Annals of Cong. 451 (1789) **12.** 1 Annals of Cong. 759 (1789). **13.** Schwartz, *supra* at 1050. **14.** 1 Annals of Cong. 759 (1789). **15.** *Id.* at 760. **16.** *Id.* at 761. **17.** Inazu, *supra* at 25; Michael W. McConnell, *Freedom by Association*, 225 First Things 39–44 (2012). **18.** Jason Mazzone, *Freedom's Associations*, 77 Wash. L. Rev. 639, 733–742 (2002). **19.** *Id.* at 737, 742–43. **20.** *Id.* **21.** An act for the punishment of certain crimes against the United States, 1 Stat. 596–97 (July 14, 1798). **22.** Inazu, *supra* at 26–29; Simon P. Newman, Parades and the Politics of the Street: Festive Culture in the Early American Republic (1997). **23.** Leon Whipple, Our Ancient Liberties: The Story of the Origin and Meaning of Civil and Religious Liberty in the United States 104 (1927). **24.** Tabatha Abu El-Haj, *All Assemble: Order and Disorder in Law, Politics, and Culture*, 16 U. Pa. J. Const. L. 949 (2014). **25.** *Riots, Routs, and Unlawful Assemblies*, 3 Am. L. Mag. 350, 357 (1844). **26.** A. O. Wright, An Exposition of the Constitution of the State of Wisconsin § IV (1888). **27.** *Id.* **28.** 2 John Randolph Tucker, The Constitution of the United States § 326 (Henry St. George Tucker ed., 1899) (emphasis added). **29.** Tabatha Abu El-Haj, *Neglected Right of Assembly*, 56 UCLA L. Rev. 543 (2009). **30.** McConnell, *supra* at 41. **31.** John Alexander Jameson, The Constitutional Convention: Its History, Powers, and Modes of Proceeding (2d ed. 1867). **32.** Abu El-Haj, *All Assemble*, *supra* at 982. **33.** *Anderson v. City of Wellington*, 19 P. 719 (Kan. 1888). **34.** *Commonwealth v. Abrahams*, 30 N.E. 79 (Mass. 1892). **35.** *Trotter v. City of Chi.*, 33 Ill. App. 206, 208 (Ill. App. Ct. 1889), aff'd, 26 N.E. 359 (Ill. 1891). **36.** 92 U.S. 542 (1875). **37.** *Id.* at 552. **38.** *Presser v. Illinois*, 116 U.S. 252, 26 (1886). **39.** 167 U.S. 43 (1897). **40.** *Id.* at 47. **41.** Tucker, *supra* at § 326. **42.** 299 U.S. 353 (1937). **43.** 307 U.S. 496 (1939). **44.** *Id.* at 512. **45.** *Id.* at 515. **46.** *Id.* at 516. **47.** 312 U.S. 569 (1941). **48.** 323 U.S. 516, 531 (1945). **49.** 357 U.S. 449 (1958). **50.** *Id.* at 460. **51.** 468 U.S. 609, 617–618 (1984). **52.** *Id.* at 618. **53.** *Id.* **54.** Inazu, *supra* at 77–96, 118–41. **55.** *Id.* at 144–49. **56.** 561 U.S. 661 (2010). **57.** 594 U.S. 595, 619–620 (2021) (Thomas, J., concurring).

~

ESSAY NO. 163: THE FREEDOM OF PETITION CLAUSE
AMEND. 1

Congress shall make no law . . . abridging . . . the right of the people . . . to petition the Government for a redress of grievances.

—David E. Bernstein & R. Trent McCotter

INTRODUCTION

The Supreme Court has observed that "[t]he right to petition is in some sense the source of other fundamental rights, for petitions have provided a vital means for citizens to request recognition of new rights and to assert existing rights against the sovereign."[1] Modern Supreme Court jurisprudence has almost completely collapsed the right to petition into the freedom of speech, but an analysis of the text and history of the First Amendment suggests that the petition right has independent scope. The right to petition has a long-standing Anglo-American pedigree. The right to present formal written petitions to the king and later to Parliament has long been considered a right independent of general free speech and press rights.

ENGLISH HISTORY

The U.S. Supreme Court has recognized that Magna Carta "itself was King John's answer to a petition from the barons."[2] Chapter 61 of Magna Carta established a multi-step petitioning process as the charter's sole enforcement mechanism. First, twenty-five barons were sworn to uphold Magna Carta. Second, nobles had to demonstrate to four of these barons that the king or his officers had transgressed the king's promises. It is still debated whether any four barons could perform that role, or whether four barons were specifically designated. Third, if the nobles met their burden, then those barons would relay the transgression to the king or his justiciar. The barons would ask, or petition, the king to remedy the transgression without delay. In Magna Carta's Latin, the barons would submit a "petent," which has the same root as "petition."[3] Fourth, the king had forty days to redress the offense in the petition. Fifth, if the king failed to redress the offense, the full contingent of twenty-five

barons had "a legal right to organize rebellion" against the king.[4]

At the time, the king was considered above the law, but petitions were the only method by which to seek redress for illegal royal action, and the king was on notice that ignoring the petitions could directly lead to legalized revolt. Although powerful in theory, this right to petition quickly proved futile in practice, especially after a second committee consisting of those more loyal to the king was appointed to "control" the group of twenty-five.[5]

The right to petition expanded beyond nobles.[6] By 1669, Parliament recognized that "it is an inherent right of every commoner of England to prepare and present Petitions to the house of commons in case of grievance." Moreover, the law prohibited punishing a person for submitting a petition: "no court whatsoever hath power to judge or censure any Petition presented."[7] The 1689 Declaration of Rights established that it is "the Right of the Subjects to petition the King," and "all Commitments and Prosecutions for such Petitioning are Illegal."[8]

By the late seventeenth century, petitioning became "an intrinsic part of English political life."[9] Legislatures referred to petitions and bills interchangeably. Petitions became the leading method for people to interact with their government.[10] Moreover, the king and Parliament generally treated petitions seriously, as they would often set the legislative agenda.[11]

AMERICAN HISTORY

Petitioning naturally spread to the American colonies. The Massachusetts Body of Liberties (1641) was the first colonial charter to provide explicit protection for the right to petition. It secured the right to "present any necessary motion, complaint, petition, Bill or information" at "any publique Court, Councel, or Towne meeting."[12] Colonial governments generally recognized the rights to freedom of speech and press.[13] However, there is little evidence that these rights included the right to petition, which had its own legal pedigree.

In 1774, the *Declaration and Resolves of the First Continental Congress* recognized an even broader right: that the colonists "have a right peaceably to assemble, consider of their grievances, and petition the King; and that all prosecutions, prohibitory proclamations, and commitments for the same, are illegal."[14] This provision emphasized the government's lack of power to punish a citizen for petitioning. In the Revolutionary era, this right to petition was more robust than the more general right to freedom of speech. By 1776, Delaware, New Hampshire, North Carolina, Pennsylvania, and Vermont expressly recognized the right to petition.[15] Other states recognized the right informally.[16]

The Declaration of Independence cited violations of the petition right by King George III as a justification for the American Revolution: "In every stage of these Oppressions We have Petitioned for Redress in the most humble terms: Our repeated Petitions have been answered only by repeated injury."[17]

After independence, most state constitutions expressly adopted a right to petition.[18] In the states, petitions sought redress for public issues and private matters such as estate distributions, divorce proceedings, and criminal sentence reductions.[19] The Articles of Confederation provided that when there were conflicts between two states, "the legislative or executive authority, or lawful agent of any state in controversy with another, shall present a petition to congress, stating the matter in question, and praying for a hearing." At that point, the Congress would serve as "the last resort on appeal."[20]

ADOPTION OF THE PETITION CLAUSE

Despite the significance of the petition right, it was not debated during the Constitutional Convention. However, it was raised during the ratification debates. Centinel, a prominent Anti-Federalist, lamented the "omission of" a "grand palladium" of liberty that would serve as a "barrier between *liberty* and *oppression*."[21] Under "the new plan" of government, Centinel argued, there was "no declaration ... that the right of the people to assemble peaceably for the purpose of ... petitioning or remonstrating to the federal legislature ought not to be prevented" and "that *the liberty of the press be held sacred*."[22] Federal Farmer similarly declared that "[t]he people have a right to ... petition the government for a redress of wrongs."[23]

Several state conventions proposed adding a petition clause tracking their own constitutions. From May through August 1788, New York, North Carolina, Rhode Island, and Virginia proposed an identical "right to petition or apply to the legislature for redress of grievances."[24]

The First Congress took up the issue, and on June 8, 1789, Representative James Madison of Virginia proposed a stronger version of the right: The "people shall not be restrained ... from applying to the Legislature by petitions, or remonstrances, for redress of their grievances."[25] Perhaps to match the language of the state proposals more closely, the House Committee of Eleven softened the language in its July 28, 1789, report: "[T]he right of the people ... to apply to the Government for redress of grievances, shall not be infringed."[26]

On August 15, 1789, the House approved a version stating that the "right of the people ... to apply to the government for redress of grievances shall not be infringed."[27] That same day, representatives from several states proposed that "to instruct their representatives" be added, but this was voted down.[28] A similar addition also failed in the Senate on September 3.[29] The next day, however, the Senate approved modified language that included "petition" for the first time: "Congress shall make no law, abridging ... the right of the People ... to petition the Government for a redress of grievances."[30] This language matched the clause's final form, though with slight changes.

The First Amendment would separate the right to petition from the rights to freedom of speech and press. This differentiation followed the historical roots of the petition right as separate and independent. Madison, however, recognized that each allowed the people to "communicate their will" in a different way:

Freedom of speech let the people "privately advise" their representatives, "liberty of the press" meant that they could "publicly address their representatives," and the right to petition let them "declare their sentiments by petition to the whole body."[31]

EARLY PRACTICE

Even before the Petition Clause was ratified, the First Congress received more than 600 petitions. This right preexisted the Constitution and was merely recognized by the Bill of Rights. Typically, these petitions included a list of grievances and signatures. Under the Constitution, Congress was not obligated to address the grievances, but as a matter of practice, it often afforded a formal response.[32] For example, on August 7, 1789, John White, who had been appointed to settle debts between the United States and several states, filed a petition seeking compensation for his work. The House referred the matter to three representatives to prepare a report on the House's "opinion."[33] Many petitions "proposed statutory language" on public matters like commerce, public finance, and slavery.

This last topic would prove to be the most controversial, as Congress received many petitions on the subject of slavery. In 1836, the House adopted a rule that "no further action" would be taken on "all petitions . . . relating" to "slavery, or the abolition of slavery."[34] Four years later, the House ruled that it would not receive abolitionist petitions at all.[35] In 1844, the House repealed the "gag rule" after a fierce debate over the right to petition.[36]

JUDICIAL PRECEDENT

The text of the Petition Clause expressly protects only the right to submit a formal grievance to the government; it does not require the government to consider that grievance. Nor does the text expressly prohibit the government from punishing a person for submitting such a petition. Yet the Supreme Court has adopted these historic principles as the core of the Petition Clause.[37]

However, over time, other aspects of the petition right have changed. For example, the sovereign is not required to respond to petitions on pain of triggering rebellion, as in Magna Carta. Rather, the Supreme Court has held that the government has no "affirmative obligation . . . to listen [or] to respond" to petitions.[38] Moreover, in England, the right protected only petitions directed to the legislature or executive. There was no common-law right to petition the judiciary. In the United States, the Supreme Court has indicated that the Petition Clause also "protects the right of individuals to appeal to courts . . . for resolution of legal disputes."[39] Justices Clarence Thomas and Antonin Scalia have countered that, historically, the right applies only to requests made to the legislative or executive branches.[40]

PETITIONS AND FREE SPEECH

In modern times, the right to petition has become somewhat anachronistic. Democratic politics gradually replaced petitioning as the primary means for constituents to express their views to their representatives. In turn, lobbying became a common means of direct access to legislators. Today, Congress treats most petitions in a pro forma way. They are ignored unless a Senator or Representative presents them, in which case they are entered into the House or Senate Journal and printed in the Congressional Record.[41]

Beyond changes in the political process, the Supreme Court has consistently interpreted the clause as a guarantee of the freedom of speech.[42] This change has rendered the petition right largely superfluous to speech and assembly rights.

Borough of Duryea, Pennsylvania v. Guarnieri (2011) held that the right to petition provides no protection to government employees that is either greater than or different from the protection they would enjoy pursuant to the right to freedom of speech. In that case, the government employee "just as easily could have alleged" a free speech claim as a petition claim.[43] *Boy Scouts of America v. Dale* (2000) recognized a "right to associate for the purpose of engaging in those activities protected by the First Amendment—speech, assembly, petition for the redress of grievances, and the exercise of religion."[44] The petition right has found its modern home as an aspect of the amalgamated right of "expressive association" rather than as a distinct right with its own scope and privileges.

The most robust modern petition right is in the realm of administrative agency processes. The Administrative Procedure Act (APA) requires that every agency "give an interested person the right to petition for the issuance, amendment, or repeal of a rule."[45] When agencies propose legislative rules, they typically must provide public notice, accept comments from the public, and respond to comments that raise significant arguments on pain of having the regulation set aside or remanded by a court.[46] In this way, the APA harkens back to Magna Carta's harsh enforcement mechanism.

OPEN QUESTIONS

- To what extent does the Petition Clause protect lobbying? Does lobbying even involve submitting a petition to the government?[47] *Citizens United v. FEC* (2010) observed in passing that "Congress has no power to ban lobbying itself."[48] But the Court suggested that certain restrictions, such as requiring lobbyists to register with the government, were legal. Would more expansive restrictions like temporary lobbying bans pass constitutional muster?

- Does the Petition Clause impose a constitutional duty on executive agencies to accept or respond to petitions? As noted, the APA imposes a statutory obligation to accept petitions and respond to those that raise significant arguments.

- The Supreme Court has held that the Petition Clause does not protect a right to petition without risk of prosecution. Nor, the Court held, does it protect a right to receive a petition. Lower courts have questioned these holdings.[49] Are the Supreme Court's precedents consistent with the historical tradition?

- *Hague v. CIO* (1939) incorporated the Petition Clause against the states, but the Court was unclear as to the precise basis for doing so.[50] Given the right's deep historical roots, would the Privileges or Immunities Clause rather than the Due Process Clause be the better vehicle for applying the right to the states?

Cite as: David E. Bernstein & R. Trent McCotter, *The Freedom of Petition Clause, in* THE HERITAGE GUIDE TO THE CONSTITUTION 613 (Josh Blackman & John G. Malcolm eds., 3d ed. 2025).

Notes

1. *Borough of Duryea, Pa. v. Guarnieri*, 564 U.S. 379, 397 (2011). **2.** *Id.* at 395. **3.** William Sharp McKechnie, Magna Carta: A Commentary on the Great Charter of King John 465–70 & n.3 (rev. 2d ed. 1914). **4.** *Id.* at 465–69. **5.** *Id.* at 476. **6.** 1 Blackstone 143. **7.** 4 Parliamentary History of England 432–33 (W. Cobbett ed. 1808). **8.** 1 Wm. & Mary, ch. 2. **9.** Maggie Blackhawk, *Lobbying and the Petition Clause*, 68 Stan. L. Rev. 1131, 1144 (2016). **10.** *Id.* at 1144–45. **11.** *Id.* at 1144. **12.** The Massachusetts Body of Liberties of 1641, cl. 12. **13.** James E. Pfander, *Sovereign Immunity and the Right to Petition*, 91 Nw. U. L. Rev. 899, 935 n.127 (1997). **14.** A Decent Respect to the Opinions of Mankind: Congressional State Papers, 1774–1776, at 49, 55 (James H. Hutson ed., 1975). **15.** Gary Lawson & Guy Seidman, *Downsizing the Right to Petition*, 93 Nw. U. L. Rev. 739, 749 (1999). **16.** *Id.* **17.** Declaration of Independence, ¶ 30. **18.** Del. Decl. of Rts. of 1776, § 9; Md. Const. of 1776, § 11; Mass. Const. of 1780, pt. I, art. XIX; N.H. Const. of 1783, pt. I, art. XXXII; N.Y. Bill of Rights of 1787, § 10; N.C. Decl. of Rts. of 1776, § XVIII; Penn. Const. of 1776, ch. 1, § XVI; Vt. Const. of 1777, § 18. **19.** Stephen A. Higginson, *A Short History of the Right to Petition Government for the Redress of Grievances*, 96 Yale L.J. 142, 146 (1986); *Duryea*, 564 U.S. at 394. **20.** Articles of Confederation, art. IX, § 2.

21. Storing 2.7.54. **22.** *Id.* at 2.7.55. **23.** *Id.* at 2.8.86. **24.** Neil H. Cogan The Complete Bill of Rights: The Drafts, Debates, Sources, and Origins 3.1.2.6. **25.** 1 Annals of Cong. 451 (1789). **26.** *Id.* at 759. **27.** 2 Cong. Register 197 (Aug. 15, 1789). **28.** *Id.* at 198. **29.** S. Jour., 1st Cong., 1st Sess. 117 (Sept. 3, 1789). **30.** *Id.* at 118. **31.** 1 Annals of Cong. 766 (1789). **32.** Blackhawk, *supra* at 1136. **33.** 1 Annals of Cong. 710 (1789). **34.** H.R. Jour., 24th Cong., 1st Sess. 1409 (May 26, 1836). **35.** Cong. Globe, 26th Cong., 1st Sess. 150 (1840). **36.** H.R. Jour., 28th Cong., 2d Sess. 10 (Dec. 3, 1844). **37.** *Duryea*, 564 U.S. at 393. **38.** *Smith v. Ark. State Highway Emp., Loc. 1315*, 441 U.S. 463, 465 (1979). **39.** *Duryea*, 564 U.S. at 387. **40.** *Id.* at 399 (Thomas, J., concurring); *id.* at 403–04 (Scalia, J., concurring in part and dissenting in part). **41.** Rule XII, cl. 3, Rules of the House of Representatives (Jan. 10, 2023). **42.** Higginson, *supra* at 143 n.2. **43.** *Duryea*, 564 U.S. at 387–88. **44.** 530 U.S. 640, 678 (2000). **45.** 5 U.S.C. § 553(e). **46.** 5 U.S.C. § 553(b)–(c). **47.** Blackhawk, *supra* at 1132. **48.** 558 U.S. 310, 369 (2010). **49.** *We the People Found., Inc. v. United States*, 485 F.3d 140, 144 (D.C. Cir. 2007); *id.* at 145–49 (Rogers, J., concurring). **50.** *Hague v. Comm. for Indus. Org.*, 307 U.S. 496, 513 (1939); *id.* at 519–21 (Stone, J., concurring); *id.* at 532 (Hughes, C.J., concurring).

~

ESSAY NO. 164: THE RIGHT TO KEEP AND BEAR ARMS
AMEND. 2

A well regulated Militia, being necessary to the security of a free State, the right of the people to keep and bear Arms, shall not be infringed.

—Nelson Lund

INTRODUCTION

Modern debates about the Second Amendment have focused on whether it protects the right of an individual to keep and bear arms or the right of a state to maintain militia organizations. That question, however, was apparently never even raised until long after the Bill of Rights was adopted. Disputes about the meaning of the amendment arose because of changes in the Constitution and constitutional law and because legislatures began to regulate firearms in ways undreamed of in our early history.

HISTORY BEFORE 1789

In our legal tradition, a right to arms was first constitutionalized in the English Bill of Rights, which guaranteed "[t]hat the subjects which are Protestants may have arms for their defence suitable to their Conditions and as allowed by Law."[1] The recognition of this right reflected a political compromise between the Crown and Parliament over control of the militia, an old institution that imposed a duty on civilians to undergo unpaid military training.[2] The existence of this institution had the effect of forcing the Crown to ask Parliament for funds to finance the creation of armies for foreign wars; it also deprived the Crown of a pretext for establishing standing armies during peacetime. The legal recognition of the right of individuals to have arms prevented the Crown from creating an armed "select militia" and disarming the rest of the population.

This provision in the Bill of Rights, initially characterized as a reaffirmation of the ancient rights of Englishmen, actually transformed the old customary duty of serving in the militia into a new right.[3] By the mid-eighteenth century, however, Sir William Blackstone wrote that this right was rooted in "the natural right of resistance and self-preservation, when the sanctions of society and laws are found insufficient to restrain the violence of oppression."[4] Blackstone drew no distinction between protection against oppression by criminals the government fails to restrain and protection against oppression by the government itself.

After the American Revolution, four states went beyond English law by formally constitutionalizing a general right to arms for "the defence of the state" or "defence of themselves and the state."[5] The Constitution proposed in 1787 gave Congress nearly unfettered authority over both the armed forces (whether state or federal) and the preexisting state-based militias.[6] (See Essay Nos. 59–63, 86.) These provisions were a departure from the English tradition of requiring the Executive to rely on the militia except when armies were raised for specific wars. The English approach had considerable popular appeal, but the Constitutional Convention had good reasons for skepticism.[7]

This massive shift of power from the states to the new federal government was very controversial both at the Convention and later during the ratification debates. The Federalists argued that the change was justified by the need to meet foreign threats. For example, Alexander Hamilton warned in Federalist No. 24 against an "excess of confidence" in the nation's security even in times of peace. And in Federalist No. 29, Hamilton argued that "if a well-regulated militia be the most natural defence of a free country, it ought certainly to be under the regulation and at the disposal of that body which is constituted the guardian of the national security."

The Anti-Federalists were more concerned that the new federal government might use force to engage in domestic oppression. Brutus observed that the power to raise armies during times of peace had historically been exercised by rulers to usurp power and wrest liberties from the people.[8] Federal Farmer worried that Congress could create a "select militia" that would be equivalent to a peacetime standing army.[9]

The Federalists responded that America's armed citizenry was a significant deterrent to potential federal abuse. James Madison argued in Federalist No. 46 that any regular army controlled by a despotic federal government would be opposed by "a militia amounting to near half a million of citizens with arms in their hands, officered by men chosen from among themselves, fighting for their common liberties, and united and conducted by governments possessing their affections and confidence." Anti-Federalists like Patrick Henry countered that if Congress had exclusive and virtually unlimited control of the arming and disciplining of the militia, that institution could easily be rendered useless as a means of resisting federal tyranny.[10]

ADOPTION OF THE SECOND AMENDMENT

In the first Congress, Representative James Madison of Virginia proposed a bill of rights that included a right-to-arms provision: "The right of the people to keep and bear arms shall not be infringed; a well armed, and well regulated militia being the best security of a free country: but no person religiously scrupulous of bearing arms shall be compelled to render military service in person."[11] Madison noted that its English predecessor raised a limited barrier against the Crown alone, whereas this amendment would erect "an impenetrable bulwark against every assumption of power in the legislative or executive."[12] A House Committee, which included Madison, Roger Sherman, and John Vining, proposed a revised version: "A well regulated militia, composed of the body of the people, being the best security of a free state, the right of the people to keep and bear arms shall not be infringed; but no person religiously scrupulous shall be compelled to bear arms."[13]

There were two main points of contention with respect to the right to arms in Madison's proposals: The amendment did not condemn the establishment of peacetime standing armies, and it exempted conscientious objectors from compulsory military service.[14] The Senate deleted the religious exemption clause, streamlined the House's text, and rejected a change that would have specified that this is a right to keep and bear arms "for the common defense."[15] The opening clause of the final text—"A well regulated Militia, being necessary to the security of a free State"—conveyed respect for that institution as an alternative to the establishment of peacetime standing armies, but nothing on the face of the text diminishes the Constitution's broad grant of military power to Congress. Nor does the text qualify the amendment's prohibition on infringing the right of the people to keep and bear arms.[16]

The Second Amendment was ratified without provoking controversies about its meaning or desirability. Notably, nothing in the record suggested that the amendment would reduce Congress's sweeping authority over the militia or authorize the states to keep troops without the consent of Congress. Nor did anyone claim that this "right of the people to keep and bear Arms," unlike those enumerated in the First and Fourth Amendments, was something other than a private right belonging to individual American men and women.

SUBSEQUENT DEVELOPMENTS

Much has changed since the Second Amendment was ratified in 1791. First, the nature of the American militia system has changed. Under the traditional system, most able-bodied men were conscripted into service, but this system fell into disuse.[17] Over time, state-based volunteer militia organizations were incorporated into the federal military structure.[18] State and federal statutes still recognize the existence of an "unorganized militia," but Americans now have virtually no expectation of being summoned for active participation in the militia. For its part, the federal military establishment has become enormously more powerful than eighteenth-century armies. These changes have raised questions about whether a well-armed citizenry remains valuable in the modern world as a check against either foreign invasion or tyrannical oppression.

Second, advancements in firearms technology have complicated the relationship between military and civilian weaponry. In the eighteenth century, civilians routinely kept at home the weapons they would need for service in the militia. There was virtually no distinction between the types of small arms used in combat by soldiers and those commonly relied upon by ordinary civilians for all manner of lawful activities, including hunting and personal defense. Modern soldiers are equipped with some types of weapons that have functions and capabilities designed specifically for warfare in ways that arguably render them inappropriate for use in civilian contexts. The value of an armed citizenry has become controversial, and many people today reject important assumptions that almost everyone accepted when the Second Amendment was adopted.

Third, legislatures have become increasingly aggressive in regulating weapons. In 1791, restrictions on the right of individuals to keep and bear arms appear to have been virtually nonexistent except for laws prohibiting the misuse of weapons.[19] Accordingly, there was little reason for anyone to discuss the constitutionality of hypothetical regulations that Congress had no interest in enacting. But Congress eventually did adopt new restrictions, some of which interfere with the ability of citizens to defend themselves against violent criminals.

Fourth, the Fourteenth Amendment, which was ratified in 1868, imposed restrictions on the state governments that had not previously existed.

UNITED STATES V. MILLER

In 1934, Congress enacted the National Firearms Act, the first federal law to regulate the private possession of firearms.[20] The law's scope was quite limited. Most significantly, it imposed a registration requirement and a then-prohibitive $200 excise tax on certain weapons, including machine guns and short-barreled shotguns, that had become associated with organized crime.[21] Five years later, the U.S. Supreme Court considered a challenge to the provision that regulated short-barreled shotguns. In *United States v. Miller* (1939), the Court concluded unanimously that the purpose of the Second Amendment is "to assure the continuation and render possible the effectiveness of [militia] forces" but left open the factual question of whether short-barreled shotguns could serve that purpose.[22]

Thereafter, the lower federal courts uniformly rejected Second Amendment challenges to gun control laws, often on the ground that the Supreme Court had implied that the Second Amendment protects only a "collective right" of the states to maintain militia organizations. The *Miller* opinion did not say this, and its ruling was based on the nature of the weapon, not on the militia status of the defendants. Nevertheless, the Court declined to review any of these decisions. Although the collective right theory never attracted a consensus among the public, the Second Amendment became a dead letter.[23]

DISTRICT OF COLUMBIA V. HELLER

In the late twentieth century, the judicial consensus was challenged by a small group of practicing lawyers, including Robert A. Sprecher, Don B. Kates, David I. Caplan, Stephen P. Halbrook, David T. Hardy, and Robert Dowlut, who argued that the text and history of the Constitution show that the original meaning of the Second Amendment protects an individual right to have weapons for self-defense.[24] Quixotic as this project may have seemed to some at the time, it eventually bore fruit.

In *District of Columbia v. Heller* (2008), the Supreme Court for the first time found that a gun control regulation violated the Second Amendment.[25] Justice Antonin Scalia's majority opinion for five Justices declared unconstitutional a federal law banning the civilian possession of handguns in the nation's capital. Following the path laid out by the modern commentators, Scalia's opinion provided considerable textual and historical support for the Court's conclusion that the amendment protects a private right to keep and bear arms. The exercise of that right does not require any connection with militia service. The handgun ban was declared unconstitutional on the ground that it "amounts to a prohibition of an entire class of 'arms' that is overwhelmingly chosen by American society for [the] lawful purpose [of self-defense] . . . . [H]andguns are the most popular weapon chosen by Americans for self-defense in the home, and a complete prohibition of their use is invalid."[26]

All four dissenters joined an opinion by Justice John Paul Stevens, who concluded that the amendment protects only "the right of the people of each of the several States to maintain a well-regulated militia."[27] The dissent's response to the majority's arguments was based primarily on the Second Amendment's reference to a well-regulated militia. Justice Stevens also relied on what he considered the idiomatic military sense of the phrase "bear arms."[28] The dissent also pointed to the absence of express historical declarations that the amendment protects a private right of individuals.[29] All four dissenters also joined an opinion by Justice Stephen Breyer, who contended that even if the Second Amendment did protect an individual right to have arms for self-defense, it should be interpreted to allow the government to ban handguns in high-crime urban areas.[30]

McDONALD V. CITY OF CHICAGO

The Bill of Rights, including the Second Amendment, originally applied only to the federal government.[31] This limitation left the states with almost all of their extremely broad preexisting authority to restrict the possession and use of weapons. In 1868, however, the Fourteenth Amendment was ratified. There is significant historical evidence indicating that the amendment's Privileges or Immunities Clause was meant to protect the Second Amendment right from infringement by state governments.[32] (See Essay No. 194.) However, *United States v. Cruikshank* (1876) concluded that the Privileges or Immunities Clause did not make the Second Amendment applicable to the states.[33] The Second Amendment was therefore thought to place no limits on the power of state governments to regulate arms.

During the twentieth century, the Supreme Court began to invoke the Fourteenth Amendment's Due Process Clause to apply most provisions of the Bill of Rights to the states and their political subdivisions. (See Essay No. 195.) The vast majority of gun control laws have been adopted at the state and local levels, so the extension of this due process "incorporation" doctrine to the Second Amendment would have significant practical consequences.

In *McDonald v. City of Chicago* (2010), the Court declared unconstitutional the city of Chicago's handgun ban. The same five justices who had formed the majority in *Heller*

now found that the Fourteenth Amendment made the Second Amendment applicable to the states. Justice Samuel Alito, writing for a four-Justice plurality, found that the right was incorporated under the Due Process Clause.[34] Justice Clarence Thomas, writing separately, relied instead on the original meaning of the Privileges or Immunities Clause.[35]

Justice Breyer's dissent for three members of the Court argued that *Heller*'s interpretation of the Second Amendment should not be extended to cover state laws.[36] Rather, he claimed, the spirit of the Constitution creates a presumption against judicial abridgements of the state's regulatory powers.[37] Justice Stevens's separate dissent argued that the Due Process Clause requires courts to work out the Second Amendment's meaning through a process of case-by-case adjudication.[38] He concluded that the handgun ban should be upheld on grounds of judicial restraint.[39]

NEW YORK STATE RIFLE & PISTOL ASSOCIATION V. BRUEN

The holdings in *Heller* and *McDonald* were technically confined to bans on the possession of handguns by law-abiding civilians in their own homes. Those opinions, however, also included nonbinding remarks approving of (i) bans on the possession of firearms by felons and the mentally ill, (ii) bans on carrying guns in "sensitive places such as schools and government buildings," (iii) laws restricting the commercial sale of arms, (iv) bans on the concealed carry of firearms, and (v) bans on weapons "not typically possessed by law-abiding citizens for lawful purposes."[40] *Heller* and *McDonald* did not offer any legal analysis in support of these endorsements.[41]

In the years after these decisions, lower federal courts upheld almost every regulation they reviewed. Some were sustained because of the favorable comments about certain laws in *Heller* and *McDonald*. Most other regulations were upheld on the ground that an individual's interest in exercising the right to arms must give way to restrictions that are substantially related to an important government interest. Although there were strong dissents in several cases, very few regulations were declared unconstitutional.[42] In case after case, the Supreme Court denied review of decisions that upheld a gun control law. (In one case, the Court rejected a state court's rationale for upholding a ban on stun guns and, without addressing the merits, sent the case back to the state court for reconsideration in light of the binding *Heller* precedent.[43])

More than a decade after *McDonald*, the Supreme Court decided *New York State Rifle & Pistol Association v. Bruen* (2022).[44] Justice Thomas's six-to-three majority opinion found that a New York law giving government officials virtually unlimited discretion to ban the carrying of handguns in public was unconstitutional. For the first time, the Supreme Court found that the Second Amendment protects a right to *bear* arms in public as well as a right to *keep* arms at home. The Court rejected the interest-balancing approach that had been adopted by the lower courts. The *Bruen* majority considered this test excessively deferential to legislative judgments, and instead the Court required the government to "justify its regulation by demonstrating that it is consistent with the Nation's historical tradition of firearm regulation."[45]

Nevertheless, *Bruen* left undisturbed the approving comments from *Heller* and *McDonald* about various forms of gun control, none of which had been supported by any historical or legal analysis. In a concurrence, Justice Brett Kavanaugh, joined by Chief Justice John Roberts, expressly reiterated these endorsements.[46] In addition, *Bruen* approved dozens of licensing regimes that restrict the right to carry firearms in public, although the Court qualified this endorsement by saying that it did not rule out constitutional challenges to permitting schemes that are put to abusive ends.[47] Again, no historical or legal support was offered for these endorsements.

Justice Breyer wrote a dissent for three members of the Court in which he argued that the Second Amendment leaves the states with wide discretion to balance the costs and benefits of restrictions on the public carry of firearms.[48] He also predicted that the majority's nearly exclusive reliance on history will prove impractical.[49]

UNITED STATES V. RAHIMI

Two years after *Bruen*, the Court decided *United States v. Rahimi* (2024).[50] Under federal law, a person subject to certain domestic-violence restraining orders is forbidden to possess a firearm. By a vote of 8 to 1, *Rahimi* upheld this statute. Chief Justice Roberts's majority opinion did not identify any historical laws that disarmed people who had not misused weapons but were considered dangerous by government officials. Instead, the majority pointed to laws that forbade people to terrorize the public by going about with dangerous and unusual weapons. The Court also pointed to laws that allowed courts to require an individual to post a *surety*, or bond, for a short period of time when there was probable cause to suspect future misbehavior by that individual. The Court maintained that these two kinds of laws confirm a principle suggested by common sense: The government may disarm anyone who poses a clear threat of physical violence to another person.

Justice Thomas, author of the *Bruen* majority opinion, dissented.[51] Under *Bruen*, when a modern regulation addresses a social problem that existed at the founding, like interpersonal violence, the government must prove that the problem was addressed by a historical regulation with a comparable burden and justification. The historical regulations cited by the majority did not stop anyone from possessing or carrying a weapon, but the statute at issue in *Rahimi* completely strips individuals of their Second Amendment rights even without evidence that they have ever used or threatened to misuse weapons. Therefore, Justice Thomas concluded, the burdens imposed by the regulations are not remotely comparable.

OPEN QUESTIONS

Two questions especially invite further attention from the Supreme Court. First, what kinds of conditions and qualifications on the exercise of gun rights will the courts permit? Second, what kind of historical evidence and how much of it will be required to justify specific restrictions on the possession, carrying, or use of firearms? Depending on how those questions are answered, the judicial revival of the Second Amendment initiated in *Heller* could either effectively expand our constitutional rights or prove to be a largely symbolic exercise that has little practical effect on the government's regulatory discretion.

Cite as: Nelson Lund, *The Right to Keep and Bear Arms, in* The Heritage Guide to the Constitution 617 (Josh Blackman & John G. Malcolm eds., 3d ed. 2025).

Notes

1. 1 W. & M., ch. 2, sess. 2 (1689) (Eng.).   **2.** Joyce Lee Malcolm, To Keep and Bear Arms: The Origins of an Anglo-American Right 113–21 (1994).   **3.** *Id.*   **4.** 1 Blackstone 144.   **5.** N.C. Const. of 1776, Decl. of Rts., art. XVII; Pa. Const. of 1776, Decl. of Rts., art. XIII; VT. Const. of 1776, Decl. of Rts., art. XV; Mass. Const. of 1780, part I, art. XVII; Eugene Volokh, *State Constitutional Rights to Keep and Bear Arms*, 11 Tex. Rev. L. & Pol. 191, 208–09 (2006).   **6.** Art. I, § 8, cls. 12–16; § 10, cl. 3.   **7.** Nelson Lund, *The Past and Future of the Individual's Right to Arms*, 31 Ga. L. Rev. 1, 30–32 (1996).   **8.** Storing 2.9.99–101; 2.9.105; 2.9.110; 2.9.115–20.   **9.** *Id.* at 2.8.39.   **10.** Storing 5.16.2.   **11.** 1 Annals of Cong. 434 (1789).   **12.** *Id.* at 457.   **13.** *Id.* at 749.   **14.** The Complete Bill of Rights: The Drafts, Debates, Sources, and Origins 169–81, 185–91 (Neil H. Cogan ed., 1997).   **15.** *Id.* at 174–75; Lund, *Past and Future, supra* at 34 n.77.   **16.** Lund, *Past and Future, supra* at 20–29; Nelson Lund, *D.C.'s Handgun Ban and the Constitutional Right to Arms: One Hard Question?*, 18 Geo. Mason U. Civ. Rts. L. J. 229, 236–40 (2008).   **17.** 3 Story's Commentaries § 1890; *Andrews v. State*, 50 Tenn. 165, 184 (1871).   **18.** *Perpich v. Dep't of Def.*, 496 U.S. 334, 341–46 (1990); James B. Whisker, The Rise and Decline of the American Militia System 338–39 (1999).   **19.** *Dist. of Columbia v. Heller*, 554 U.S. 570, 631–35 (2008); Nelson Lund, *The Second Amendment*, Heller*, and Originalist Jurisprudence*, 56 UCLA L. Rev. 1343, 1362–64 (2009).   **20.** National Firearms Act, Pub. L. 73-474, 26 U.S.C. §§ 5801–5872.   **21.** Stephen P. Halbrook, *Congress Interprets the Second Amendment: Declarations by a Co-Equal Branch on the Individual Right to Keep and Bear Arms*, 62 Tenn. L. Rev. 597, 601–18 (1995).   **22.** 307 U.S. 174, 178 (1939).   **23.** Nelson Lund, *The Right to Arms and the American Philosophy of Freedom*, Heritage Found. First Principles No. 62 (Oct. 17, 2016), https://perma.cc/D76Q-5VKE.   **24.** Nelson Lund, *Outsider Voices on Guns and the Constitution*, 17 Const. Comment. 701, 703–07 (2000).   **25.** 554 U.S. 570 (2008).   **26.** *Id.* at 628–29. Stephen P. Halbrook, *Text-and-History or Means-End Scrutiny? A Response to Professor Nelson Lund's Critique of* Bruen, 24 Fed. Soc'y Rev. 54, 56–57 (2023); Nelson Lund, *Stephen P. Halbrook's Confused Defense of* Bruen's *Novel Interpretive Rule*, 31 Geo. Mason L. Rev. Forum 82, 89 (2023).   **27.** 554 U.S. at 637 (Stevens, J., dissenting).   **28.** *Id.* at 646–51.   **29.** *Id.* at 652–80.   **30.** *Id.* at 681–723 (Breyer, J., dissenting).   **31.** *Barron v. City of Balt.*, 322 U.S. 43 (1833).   **32.** *McDonald v. City of Chi.*, 561 U.S. 742, 822–38 (2010) (Thomas, J., concurring in part and concurring in the judgment).   **33.** 925 U.S. 542, 551–53 (1876).   **34.** *McDonald*, 561 U.S. at 780–87 (Alito, J.).   **35.** *Id.* at 805–58 (Thomas, J., concurring in part and concurring in the judgment).   **36.** *Id.* at 912–40 (Breyer, J., dissenting).   **37.** Nelson Lund, *Two Faces of Judicial Restraint (Or Are There More?) in* McDonald v. Chicago, 63 Fla. L. Rev. 487, 514–23 (2011).   **38.** 561 U.S. at 858–912 (Stevens, J., dissenting).   **39.** Lund, *Two Faces, supra* at 514–20.   **40.** *Heller*, 554 U.S. at 625–27; *McDonald*, 561 U.S. at 786 (plurality opinion).   **41.** Lund, *The Second Amendment, supra* at 1356–68.   **42.** Nelson Lund, *The Future of the Second Amendment in a Time of Lawless Violence*, 116 Nw. U. L. Rev. 81, 93 (2021); Nelson Lund, Bruen's *Preliminary Preservation of the Second Amendment*, 23 Fed. Soc'y Rev. 279, 284–89 (2022).   **43.** *Caetano v. Massachusetts*, 577 U.S. 411 (2016).   **44.** 597 U.S. 1 (2022).   **45.** *Id.* at 18 (quotation marks and citation omitted).   **46.** *Id.* at 80–81 (Kavanaugh, J., concurring).   **47.** *Id.* at 38 n.9 (majority opinion).   **48.** *Id.* at 93–102 (Breyer, J., dissenting).   **49.** *Id.* at 107–115.   **50.** 602 U.S. 680 (2024).   **51.** *Id.* at 747.

ESSAY NO. 165: THE QUARTERING TROOPS AMENDMENT
AMEND. 3

No Soldier shall, in time of peace be quartered in any house, without the consent of the Owner, nor in time of war, but in a manner to be prescribed by law.
—Andrew P. Morriss

INTRODUCTION

The Third Amendment is often deemed forgotten or languishing in obscurity. Rarely mentioned by the courts, it has enjoyed a renaissance in the academic legal literature, perhaps foreshadowing future relevance under one or more of the theories put forward in scholarly works. After surveying the historical background of the amendment and its adoption, this entry discusses the amendment's two substantive appearances in judicial opinions and concludes with a summary of the academic speculations about its possible wider future application.

HISTORY BEFORE 1787

English grievances over the quartering of troops began with Norman reforms of the English military system after 1066.[1] By 1130, King Henry I's London Charter contained a prohibition on billeting troops within the walls of the city, and this guarantee was repeated in King Henry II's London Charter of 1155.[2] Dissatisfaction with the quartering of troops continued. This practice featured in several foundational laws: the 1628 Petition of Right, the 1679 Anti-Quartering Act, and the 1689 Declaration of Rights and Bill of Rights.[3] Sir William Blackstone wrote that "no soldier shall be quartered on the subject without his own consent."[4] By the 1760s, the right not to have soldiers involuntarily quartered in one's home was well established at common law.[5]

However, Britain's virtually continuous state of war in the eighteenth century led to growing acceptance of a standing army, and the army's growing size made quartering impracticable in Britain. In the American colonies, reliance on the militia continued for most local defense, but British troops stationed in the colonies were quartered in private homes. The 1765 Quartering Act required the colonists to pay for barracks and provisions for the army and allowed quartering of troops in inns, livery stables, and alehouses when necessary.[6] The colonists vigorously objected to quartering troops. These conflicts over quartering escalated after the end of the French and Indian War made the presence of the Army even less popular with the colonists.[7]

Britain reacted to colonial unrest with the 1774 Quartering Act that authorized quartering soldiers in private homes. This law became known as one of the "Intolerable Acts." American objections both to quartering specifically and to the existence of a standing army more generally featured in the First Continental Congress's Declaration of Resolves in 1774.[8] Two

years later, the Declaration of Independence charged King George III with "quartering large bodies of armed troops among us."[9]

THE CONSTITUTIONAL CONVENTION

During the Constitutional Convention, Charles Pinckney of South Carolina proposed a series of recommendations, one of which dealt with quartering: "No soldier shall be quartered in any House in time of peace without consent of the owner."[10] This proposal was not adopted by the Convention.

THE RATIFICATION DEBATES

During the ratification debates, the Anti-Federalists used the absence of a ban on quartering as an argument against the Constitution. For example, Federal Farmer stated that there was no "provision in the constitution to prevent the quartering of soldiers on the inhabitants."[11] He argued that the right against quartering was "particularly valuable to individuals, and essential to the permanency and duration of free government." Similarly, at the Virginia convention, Patrick Henry contended that "one of the principal reasons for dissolving the connection with Great Britain" was the "quartering of troops" but that under the new Constitution, "we may have troops in time of peace" who "may be billeted in any manner—to tyrannize, oppress, and crush us."[12]

Once agreement on the concept of a Bill of Rights was reached, however, there was little controversy over the inclusion of a ban on quartering. Several states also adopted their own constitutional provisions banning the quartering of soldiers. Maryland, for example, provided "[t]hat no soldier ought to be quartered in any house, in time of peace, without the consent of the owner; and in time of war, in such manner only, as the Legislature shall direct."[13]

EARLY PRACTICE

The First Congress responded to the demands for an explicit ban on quartering. James Madison drafted an early version of the amendment. It provided, "No soldier shall in time of peace be quartered in any house without the consent of the owner; nor at any time, but in a manner warranted by law."[14] This text went beyond what any of the states had proposed "by explicitly giving Congress the power to direct quartering whenever the nation was other than at peace."[15] The select committee to which the amendment was referred replaced this text with what became the Third Amendment: "No Soldier shall, in time of peace be quartered in any house, without the consent of the Owner, nor in time of war, but in a manner prescribed by law." Under this amendment, Congress could authorize quartering only during times of war. Once the text was settled, there appears to have been no controversy over the proposed amendment during ratification.

There was considerable quartering of troops in private homes during both the War of 1812 and the Civil War.[16] Despite the widespread practice of quartering in both conflicts, however, there is no record of any efforts by the property owners to seek relief under the amendment.[17]

JUDICIAL PRECEDENT

Justice Joseph Story observed that the Third Amendment "speaks for itself."[18] Perhaps unsurprisingly, there have been few court opinions discussing the amendment. In the few that have discussed it, a key issue is whether it has been incorporated by the Due Process Clause of the Fourteenth Amendment.

In *McDonald v. City of Chicago* (2010), the U.S. Supreme Court noted in a footnote that the amendment had not yet been "fully incorporated."[19] However, the Second Circuit Court of Appeals found that the amendment *was* incorporated.[20] Other courts have not been receptive to Third Amendment claims. The Tenth Circuit Court of Appeals rejected an assertion that federal approval of military flights through the airspace over one's home violated the amendment as "frivolous."[21]

OPEN QUESTIONS

- Are houses of worship protected against quartering?[22]
- Does the Third Amendment limit the militarization of police and use of excessive force by law enforcement?[23]
- Are there any limits to Congress's power under the Third Amendment to authorize the quartering of troops in wartime?[24]
- Should the Third Amendment be incorporated?[25]
- What would be the process for obtaining consent for quartering during peacetime?[26]

Cite as: Andrew P. Morriss, *The Quartering Troops Amendment, in* THE HERITAGE GUIDE TO THE CONSTITUTION 622 (Josh Blackman & John G. Malcolm eds., 3d ed. 2025).

Notes

1. William S. Fields & David T. Hardy, *The Third Amendment and the Issue of the Maintenance of Standing Armies: A Legal History*, 35 Am. J. Leg. Hist. 393, 395–96 (1991). **2.** 1 W. & M., ch. 2, sess. 2 (1689) (Eng.); Fields & Hardy, supra at 399. **3.** *Id*. at 403–05. **4.** 1 Blackstone 413. **5.** Fields & Hardy, *supra* at 411. **6.** *Id*. at 415. **7.** Tom W. Bell, *The Third Amendment: Forgotten but Not Gone*, 2 Wm. & Mary Bill Rts. J. 117, 125–26 (1993). **8.** IV. The Bill of Rights; a List of Grievances (1774), https://perma.cc /Y4FH-VJEP. **9.** Declaration of Independence, ¶ 16. **10.** 2 Farrand's 341. **11.** Storing 2.8.202. **12.** 3 Elliot's 411. **13.** Md. Const. of 1776, Decl. of Rts. XXVIII; Del. Decl. of Rts. § 21 (1776); Mass Const. of 1780, art. XXVII; N.H. Const. of 1784, art. I, § XXVII. **14.** 1 Annals of Cong. 451 (1789). **15.** Bell, *supra* at 134–35. **16.** *Id*. at 136–40.

17. *Id*. at 136, n.153. **18.** 3 Story's Commentaries § 1893. **19.** 561 U.S. 742, 765 n.13 (2010). **20.** *Engblom v. Carey*, 677 F.2d 957, 961–62 (2nd Cir. 1982). **21.** *Custer Cnty. Action Ass'n v. Garvey*, 256 F.3d 1024 (10th Cir., 2001). **22.** Eric Rassbach, *Are Houses of Worship "House[s]" Under the Third Amendment?*, 82 Tenn. L. Rev. 611, 622–23 (2015). **23.** Elizabeth Price Foley, *The War Against Crime: Ferguson, Police Militarization and the Third Amendment*, 82 Tenn. L. Rev. 583, 590–94 (2015). **24.** William Gill, *Wartime Quartering with and Without Legislative Authorization*, 82 Tenn. L. Rev. 567, 568–72 (2015). **25.** Chad Aronson, *The Third Amendment Incorporated: "Soldiers" and Domestic Law Enforcement*, 67 Case. W. Rsrv. L. Rev. 537, 564–75 (2016). **26.** Mark A. Fulks & Ronald S. Range II, *The Third Amendment's Consent Clause: A Conceptual Framework for Analysis and Application*, 82 Tenn. L. Rev. 647, 657–59 (2015).

~

ESSAY NO. 166: THE UNREASONABLE SEARCHES AND SEIZURES CLAUSE
AMEND. 4

The right of the people to be secure in their persons, houses, papers, and effects,
against unreasonable searches and seizures, shall not be violated . . . .

—Orin S. Kerr

INTRODUCTION

The prohibition of unreasonable searches and seizures appears in the Fourth Amendment, ratified in 1791. The clause regulates a vast array of law enforcement practices that include arrests, entries into homes, traffic stops, telephone surveillance, and looking through cell phone records. This essay examines the history of search and seizure before the Revolution, the enactment of the Fourth Amendment, and the development of modern doctrine.

HISTORY BEFORE 1789

In mid-eighteenth-century England, a series of abuses by King George III and his representatives led to widespread opposition to *general* warrants. These court orders authorized government officials to search and seize evidence that placed few, if any, limitations on where the officials could search and what they could seize. Opposition to general warrants found expression in two famous English cases, *Entick v. Carrington* (1765) and *Wilkes v. Wood* (1763).[1] Both involved pamphleteers who were critics of the government. They were arrested and their books and papers were seized using general warrants. In Wilkes's case, the government also seized the papers of forty-nine of his friends. Both men sued the seizing agents for trespass and won judgments in their favor.

In the colonies, leading figures closely watched and cheered on the challenges to general warrants. In 1761, James Otis argued against these warrants in the Writs of Assistance case in Boston with future Founder John Adams in the audience.[2] Although Otis lost the case, his challenge to general warrants drew significant attention to the threat to civil liberties that general warrants posed. As John Adams later reflected on the oral argument, "Then and there the Child Independence was born."[3]

Following the Declaration of Independence, several state constitutions adopted protections focused on general warrants. Some addressed such warrants exclusively. The Virginia Declaration of Rights of 1776, written by George Mason, defined "general warrants" as authorizing "any officer or messenger . . . to search suspected places without evidence of a fact committed, or to seize any person or persons not named, or whose offense is not particularly described and supported by evidence."[4] The Declaration stated that such warrants "are grievous and oppressive and ought not to be granted."

Other state constitutions introduced the notion that there was a broader right against some kinds of searches and seizures, although their texts continued to link the concept to general warrants. The Pennsylvania constitution of 1776 provided that "the people have a right to hold themselves, their houses, papers, and possessions free from search and seizure, and therefore [general] warrants . . . ought not to be granted."[5] The Massachusetts constitution of 1780 added a provision, drafted by John Adams, that was the first to articulate a specific right against unreasonable searches and seizures: "Every subject has a right to be secure from all unreasonable searches, and seizures, of his person, his houses, his papers, and all his possessions."[6] The provision then linked that right to general warrants, which "are contrary to this right[.]"

ENACTMENT OF THE FOURTH AMENDMENT

During the Virginia convention, Patrick Henry opposed ratification in part on the ground that the Constitution contained no equivalent protections against unreasonable searches and seizures. "Suppose an exciseman will demand leave to enter your cellar, or house, by virtue of his office," Henry queried. "If Congress be informed of it, will they give you redress?"[7] In approving the Constitution, a Virginia commission recommended a bill of rights that included a search and seizure provision providing that "every freeman has a right to be secure from all unreasonable searches and seizures of his person, his papers, and property."[8]

In 1789, during the first Congress, Representative James Madison of Virginia introduced what would eventually become the Fourth Amendment. Madison's initial proposal was focused on general warrants: "The rights of the people to be secured in their persons; their houses, their papers, and their other property, from all unreasonable searches and seizures, shall not be violated by warrants issued without probable cause, supported by oath or affirmation, or not particularly describing the places to be searched, or the persons or things to be seized."[9] The Committee of Eleven, made up of representatives of each state, divided the text into two distinct clauses. The first banned unreasonable searches and seizures: "The right of the people to be secure in their persons, houses, papers, and effects, against unreasonable searches and seizures, shall not be violated . . . ." The second specifically banned general warrants: "[N]o Warrants shall issue, but upon probable cause, supported by Oath or affirmation, and particularly describing the place to be searched, and the persons or things to be seized." (See Essay No. 167.) Unfortunately, there are no records that might explain why these changes were made. The Fourth Amendment was then ratified by the states without any meaningful debate.

At the time of the Fourth Amendment's enactment, the nearly exclusive focus was general warrants; little to no attention was paid to the ban on unreasonable searches and seizures. This history makes the original public meaning of the ban on "unreasonable search and seizures" a source of considerable uncertainty. If that term was specifically discussed or its meaning specifically articulated, apart from the ban on general warrants, no records of those discussions are known.

In the absence of clear evidence from the time of its drafting and ratification, scholars have offered different views about the meaning of unreasonable searches and seizures. Professor Thomas Davies argued that the Fourth Amendment was largely focused on abolishing general warrants.[10] In his view, the text of the Fourth Amendment does not impose a more general requirement of reasonable police practices. William Cuddihy argued that the Fourth Amendment was originally understood both to prohibit general warrants and more generally to guard against abusive law enforcement practices.[11] Professor Akhil Reed Amar wrote that the Fourth Amendment as originally understood was intended to promote reasonableness in government investigations, not the imposition of a default warrant requirement.[12] Your author has argued that modern Fourth Amendment doctrine is consistent both with the constitutional text and with the original public meaning.[13]

WHAT IS A SEIZURE?

The threshold question under the Fourth Amendment is whether a government search or seizure has occurred. Under current precedent, a person's property is "seized" when the government meaningfully interferes with a person's possessory interest in his property.[14] This occurs when the government takes a suspect's property from him, forces a person out of his or her home, or takes a package or letter out of the course of delivery.[15] Similarly, a person is "seized" under the Fourth Amendment when the government terminates or restrains his freedom of movement through means intentionally applied.[16] This happens when a government official places a suspect under arrest.[17] A seizure also occurs when the government temporarily detains a person in circumstances in which a reasonable person would not feel free to terminate the encounter and leave.[18]

WHAT IS A "SEARCH?"

The question of when government conduct is a Fourth Amendment "search" has received an enormous amount of judicial attention. The doctrine recognizes two tests. First, under *United States v. Jones* (2012), government conduct is a search if it is a trespass or physical intrusion directed against a person, his house, his papers, or his effects with the intent to obtain information.[19] The second test was announced in Justice

John Marshall Harlan's concurrence in *Katz v. United States* (1967).[20] Under this test, government conduct is a search if it violates a subjective expectation of privacy and society is prepared to recognize that expectation as objectively reasonable. For the most part, government conduct usually ends up being labeled a search if it is an invasion of a private space such as a home, a car, a package, a letter, or a person's pockets.[21] On the other hand, government conduct is ordinarily not labeled a search if it involves surveillance in public.[22]

Many of the most difficult cases bearing on what constitutes a Fourth Amendment "search" involve technological surveillance. New technologies can allow the government to obtain information that would previously have been unknowable without a physical trespass into a protected area. These new developments often prompt the question: Is the government's use of this tool a search on the ground that it obtained private information, or is it not a search on the ground that it was only public surveillance? The cases are complex and have reached varying results. For example, *Kyllo v. United States* (2001) held that the use of a thermal imaging camera directed at a home to reveal its temperature profile was a search.[23] *Carpenter v. United States* (2018) ruled that collecting several days of historical cell site location records also was a search.[24] On the other hand, *California v. Ciraolo* (1986) found that aerial surveillance from public airspace is ordinarily not a search.[25] And *Smith v. Maryland* (1979) found that obtaining the numbers dialed from a telephone line is not a search.[26]

IS A SEARCH OR SEIZURE "UNREASONABLE?"

Once courts recognize that a search or seizure occurred, the next question is whether the search or seizure was unreasonable and therefore unconstitutional. The standard for reasonableness varies depending on the circumstances, and the doctrine can hinge on very specific distinctions. Under *Terry v. Ohio* (1968), brief seizures of a person, such as pat-downs, are reasonable as long as they are supported by specific and articulable facts that justify suspicion.[27] *United States v. Watson* (1976) imposes a higher burden to arrest a person: probable cause

to believe a crime has been committed and that the arrestee has committed the crime.[28] *United States v. Robinson* (1973) permits the government to search a person who has been arrested incident to that arrest without a warrant.[29] However, *Riley v. California* (2014) held that a warrant is needed to search a person's cell phone incident to his arrest.[30]

There are several exceptions to the warrant requirement: (i) searches when exigent circumstances are present (ii) searches when consent is provided by a party who has authority over the space to be searched; (iii) border searches (iv) special-needs searches; and others. *Horton v. California* (1990) recognized the so-called plain view exception.[31] If the police are lawfully in a position to view evidence that is not described in a warrant but the evidence's incriminating nature is immediately apparent, they can seize that evidence.

On the whole, the rules for searching homes tend to be the most restrictive among Fourth Amendment doctrines. Entrance to a home is constitutionally reasonable (and therefore legal) only pursuant to a valid warrant or an exception to the warrant requirement.[32] The rules for searching and seizing cars tend to give the government significantly broader powers than the rules for homes. Under *Whren v. United States* (1996), a police officer can order a driver to pull over a car based on any traffic violation, thus seizing the car and its occupants.[33] The officer can then arrest the driver based on only a minor violation, even if the crime of arrest does not provide for any jail time.[34] Once the person has been arrested, he can be searched incident to that arrest even if the arrest violates state law.[35] Further, the car can be searched without a warrant if there is probable cause to believe that contraband or evidence is located inside it.[36]

THE EXCLUSIONARY RULE

After a Fourth Amendment violation has been established, the remaining question is whether there is a remedy for the violation in a court of law. Historically, the primary remedy for Fourth Amendment violations has been the exclusionary rule. The exclusionary rule was established very early in the Fourth Amendment's development: It was adopted by the U.S. Supreme Court in *Weeks v. United States* (1914).[37] Under the exclusionary rule, evidence obtained as a result of a Fourth Amendment violation may be subject to exclusion from evidence at trial in any subsequent prosecution.[38]

In general, a defendant can successfully invoke the exclusionary rule only if his own rights were violated and the constitutional violation was the direct cause of the evidence's being discovered.[39] Also, *United States v. Leon* (1984) and later cases developed the so-called good faith exception to the exclusionary rule.[40] Under these precedents, the exclusionary rule is a last available resort. Evidence will not be excluded if the officer was acting in good faith; it will be excluded only when the officer who conducted the search acted in a personally culpable manner, as in the case of a knowing or intentional violation.[41]

Civil suits can be filed against state officers for Fourth Amendment violations under 42 U.S.C. § 1983, subject to the defense of qualified immunity. Under the doctrine of qualified immunity, an officer is immune from suit unless the violation was clearly established in law at the time and a reasonable officer would have recognized that the act violated the Constitution.[42]

OPEN QUESTIONS

- What is the future of the exclusionary rule that the Supreme Court adopted in 1914?
- How should the Fourth Amendment adapt to new technology such as computers and the Internet?[43]
- What is the conceptual basis of the "reasonable expectation of privacy" test, and how is it different (if at all) from the trespass test?

Cite as: Orin S. Kerr, *The Unreasonable Searches and Seizures Clause, in* THE HERITAGE GUIDE TO THE CONSTITUTION 625 (Josh Blackman & John G. Malcolm eds., 3d ed. 2025).

Notes

1. 95 Eng. Rep. 807, 817 (KB); 19 Howell's State Trials 1029, 1063 (KB); 98 Eng. Rep. 489, 498 (KB). **2.** Thomas Clancy, *The Framers' Intent: John Adams, His Era, and the Fourth Amendment*, 86 Ind. L.J. 979, 992–1006 (2011). **3.** Letter from John Adams to William Tudor, Sr. (Mar. 29, 1817), https://perma.cc/JH4H-GGVW. **4.** 4 Blackstone 301. **5.** Pa. Const. of 1776, art. X. **6.** Mass. Const. of 1780, art. XIV. **7.** 3 Elliot's 412. **8.** *Id.* at 658. **9.** 1 Annals of Cong.,1st Cong., 1st Sess. 452 (1789). **10.** Thomas Y. Davies, *Recovering the Original Fourth Amendment*, 98 Mich. L. Rev. 547 (1999). **11.** William J. Cuddihy, The Fourth Amendment: Origins and Original Meaning 602–1791 (2009). **12.** Akhil Reed Amar, *Fourth Amendment First Principles*, 107 Harv. L. Rev. 757 (1994). **13.** Orin S. Kerr, Katz *as Originalism*, 71 Duke L.J. 1047 (2022). **14.** *United States v. Jacobsen*, 466 U.S. 109 (1984). **15.** *United States v. Van Leeuwen*, 397 U.S. 249 (1970). **16.** *Brendlin v. California*, 551 U.S. 249 (2007). **17.** *Dunaway v. New York*, 442 U.S. 200 (1979). **18.** *United States v. Drayton*, 536 U.S. 194 (2002). **19.** 565 U.S. 400 (2012). **20.** 389 U.S. 347 (1967). **21.** *Silverman v. United States*, 365 U.S. 505 (1961); *Arizona v. Hicks*, 480 U.S. 321 (1987). **22.** *United States v. Knotts*, 460 U.S. 276 (1983). **23.** *Kyllo v. United States*, 533 U.S. 27 (2001). **24.** *Carpenter v. United States*, 585 U.S. 296 (2018). **25.** *California v. Ciraolo*, 476 U.S. 207 (1986). **26.** *Smith v. Maryland*, 442 U.S. 735 (1979). **27.** *Terry v. Ohio*, 391 U.S. 1 (1968). **28.** *United States v. Watson*, 423 U.S. 411 (1976). **29.** *United States v. Robinson*, 414 U.S. 218 (1973). **30.** *Riley v. California*, 573 U.S. 373 (2014). **31.** *Horton v. California*, 496 U.S. 128 (1990). **32.** *Payton v. New York*, 445 U.S. 573 (1980). **33.** *Whren v. United States*, 517 U.S. 806 (1996). **34.** *Atwater v. City of Lago Vista*, 532 U.S. 318 (2001). **35.** *Virginia v. Moore*, 553 U.S. 164 (2008). **36.** *Carroll v. United States*, 267 U.S. 132 (1925). **37.** 232 U.S. 383 (1914). **38.** *Mapp v. Ohio*, 367 U.S. 643 (1961). **39.** *Wong Sun v. United States*, 371 U.S. 471 (1963). **40.** 468 U.S. 897 (1984). **41.** *Davis v. United States*, 564 U.S. 229 (2011). **42.** *Anderson v. Creighton*, 483 U.S. 635 (1987). **43.** Orin S. Kerr, The Digital Fourth Amendment: Privacy and Policing in Our Online World (2025).

~

ESSAY NO. 167: THE WARRANT CLAUSE
AMEND. 4

. . . and no Warrants shall issue, but upon probable cause, supported by Oath or affirmation, and particularly describing the place to be searched, and the persons or things to be seized.

—Judge Elizabeth L. Branch, Francis Aul, & Austin Mayron

INTRODUCTION

The Warrant Clause, which follows the Fourth Amendment's protections against "unreasonable searches and seizures," regulates the issuance of warrants—judicial writs that authorize law enforcement officers to make searches, seizures, or arrests. A 1750 legal dictionary, for example, defined a warrant as a "Precept under Hand and Seal to some Officer to bring an Offender before the Person granting it."[1]

The text of the Warrant Clause is straightforward. A warrant must be made upon probable cause, be supported by oath or affirmation, and describe with particularity the place to be searched or the persons or things to be seized. Beyond those three requirements, however, courts and commentators have confronted two important questions about the clause's meaning: What does a warrant require, and when is a warrant required? Given the relative clarity of the text and robust historical evidence, the meaning of the Warrant Clause has largely been settled. However, scholars continue to debate what constitutes "probable cause" and when a warrant is required.

HISTORY BEFORE 1787

During the colonial era, a warrant was not understood to be required for a government official to execute a search or seizure.[2] Nevertheless, an officer ordinarily could be sued by the target of a search and be held liable for money damages in a trespass suit if the search was later found to be unreasonable.[3] A warrant was an absolute defense to such a suit and immunized the officer from liability.[4] Concerns arose, however, from the government's use of so-called general warrants that lacked "specificity as to whom to arrest or where to search" or lacked "a complaint

under oath or an adequate showing of cause."[5] (See Essay No. 166.)

The lack of adequate procedural safeguards in obtaining warrants gained widespread attention during three seminal cases from the 1760s.[6] In the *Writ of Assistance Case* (1761), sometimes referred to as *Paxton's Case*, Boston merchants challenged the renewal of the general warrant empowering Massachusetts customs officers to search "any House" for "prohibited or uncustomed" goods.[7] Although the court ruled against the merchants and renewed the warrant, James Otis famously argued to the court that general warrants violated natural rights and were "against the fundamental Principles of Law."[8]

Wilkes v. Wood (1763) involved a general warrant calling for the arrest of "any person suspected of authoring or publishing" a pamphlet disparaging King George III and the seizure of "any papers revealing [its] authorship."[9] Based on a single general warrant, "English officers searched at least five houses and arrested at least forty-nine people."[10] One of the people searched was John Wilkes, a member of Parliament and author of the pamphlet. Wilkes brought a successful trespass action challenging the general warrant. Lord Camden found that the warrant violated the common law. He observed that "no offenders['] names [were] specified in the warrant," which effectively empowered officers "to search wherever their suspicions may chance to fall." Scholars believe *Wilkes* to be "probably the most famous case in late eighteenth-century America."[11]

Finally, *Entick v. Carrington* (1765) involved a general warrant directed at John Entick, an English author who wrote anti-government pamphlets.[12] Unlike the warrant in *Wilkes*, this warrant specifically named Entick as its target, but it did not specifically describe the papers to be seized from Entick. Lord Camden ruled that the warrant targeting Entick was an illegal general warrant and violated the common law.

These three decisions imposed three clear standards. First, warrants could be issued only upon probable cause, a standard that can be traced back to the early common law.[13] In the seventeenth century, Sir Matthew Hale discussed "probable cause of suspicion" and "reasonable cause of suspicion" as interchangeable standards connoting "a reasonable basis for suspecting the individual and making further inquiry."[14] Second, warrants must be supported by a sworn evidentiary showing by oath or affirmation.[15] At common law, "only a person who had personal knowledge of an offense could swear out a complaint and warrant."[16] Third, warrants must describe with particularity the place to be searched or the persons or things to be seized.

Following independence, many states incorporated protections against the use of general warrants into their constitutions. For example, the Virginia constitution of 1776 declared that "general warrants are grievous and oppressive, and ought not to be granted."[17] With such warrants, "an officer or messenger may be commanded to search suspected places without evidence of a fact committed, or to seize any person or persons not named, or whose offence is not particularly described and supported by evidence."[18] Other states adopted similar constitutional protections, including Maryland, Massachusetts, North Carolina, Pennsylvania, and Vermont.[19] This language would parallel the Fourth Amendment's Warrants Clause: Warrants had to be based on cause or foundation, had to be supported by oath or affirmation, and had to name or describe the place to be searched or the persons or things to be seized.

THE CONSTITUTIONAL CONVENTION

During the Philadelphia Convention, there was no recorded debate on warrants. Near the end of the Convention, however, George Mason proposed that the Constitution be "prefaced with a Bill of Rights" to "secur[e] the rights of the people where requisite."[20] Mason's view did not prevail at the Convention, but the Constitution's absence of a Bill of Rights became one of the Anti-Federalists' principal objections.

THE RATIFICATION DEBATES

During the ratification debates, Anti-Federalists raised numerous concerns about warrants. In the Virginia ratifying convention, Patrick Henry warned that "the necessity of securing our *personal rights* seems not to have pervaded the minds of men; for many other valuable things are omitted." Henry would have prohibited "general warrants, by which an officer may search suspected places, without evidence of the commission of a fact, or seize any person without evidence of his crime. . . ."[21] Similar objections were raised at other state ratification conventions.[22] The New York convention proposed an amendment to the Constitution in its formal ratification document. The amendment guaranteed (1) "[t]hat every freeman has a right to be secure from all unreasonable searches and seizures of his person, his papers, or his property"; (2) prohibited "all warrants to search suspected places, or seize any freeman, his papers, or property, without information, upon oath or affirmation, of sufficient cause"; and (3) ruled "that all general warrants (or such in which the place or person suspected are not particularly designated) are dangerous, and ought not to be granted."[23] Other states included similar ratification statements. They made clear that their votes to ratify were contingent on a Bill of Rights later being incorporated into the Constitution.[24]

In Federalist No. 84, Alexander Hamilton countered that a Bill of Rights was "not only unnecessary in the proposed Constitution, but would even be dangerous." Hamilton warned that such an enumeration "would contain various exceptions to powers not granted." As a result, a Bill of Rights "would afford a colorable pretext [for the Constitution] to claim more [federal powers] than were granted."

THE FIRST CONGRESS

During the First Congress, Hamilton's fellow Federalist, James Madison of Virginia, changed his position. Representative Madison drafted what would become the Bill of Rights. Madison's draft provided that "[t]he rights of the people to be secured in their persons; their houses, their papers, and their other property, from all unreasonable searches and seizures, shall not be violated by warrants issued without probable cause, supported by oath or affirmation, or not particularly describing the places to be searched, or the persons or things to be seized."[25] This original draft thus tied the notion of unreasonableness to the issuance of a general warrant.[26]

However, a committee changed the text to read: "The right of the people to be secure in their persons, houses, papers, and effects, against unreasonable searches and seizures, shall not be violated, and no Warrants shall issue, but upon probable cause. . . ."[27] These substantive changes created two conjunctive clauses, one protecting the individual right against unreasonable searches and seizures and one prohibiting the issuance of any warrant without meeting the specified conditions. The committee's version was adopted by Congress without objection and was later ratified by the states.

Thus, the Warrant Clause as originally understood narrowed the "safe harbor" defense of a warrant by incorporating the procedural requirements for obtaining one that were established in state constitutions. The Warrant Clause says nothing about obtaining a warrant as a precondition to carrying out a lawful search or seizure.[28]

The First Congress, which proposed the Fourth Amendment, also enacted statutes that reflected the probable cause standard. For example, a 1789 statute authorized officials to search any ship if they had "reason to suspect" the concealment of goods.[29] A 1791 statute authorized officials to search for fraudulently concealed distilled spirits wherever such spirits "shall be suspected to be so fraudulently deposited."[30]

JUDICIAL PRECEDENT

In *Locke v. United States* (1813), the U.S. Supreme Court described the "fixed and well known meaning" of probable cause as "circumstances which warrant suspicion."[31] The Court adopted a similar formulation of the standard in *Stacey v. Emery* (1878): "facts and circumstances . . . such as to warrant a man of prudence and caution in believing that the offence has been committed."[32] Accordingly, the probable cause standard has long been understood as a flexible inquiry requiring less than proof but more than mere speculation to convict someone of an offense.

The Court's modern view of the Warrant Clause is best summarized in *Katz v. United States* (1967): "[S]earches conducted outside the judicial process, without prior approval by judge or magistrate, are per se unreasonable under the Fourth Amendment—subject only to a few specifically established and well-delineated exceptions."[33] Originalist scholars have questioned whether this "warrant-preference" construction is consistent with the original understanding of the Warrant Clause.[34] Specifically, scholars have noted the lack of historical support for an "across-the-board warrant requirement" unmoored from the factual context of the search. Instead, the historical record confirms the Founding-era understanding of warrants as defenses to trespass actions for unfruitful searches and seizures, not as prerequisites for a search or seizure.

The modern understanding of the Warrant Clause departs from the historical context in two other ways. First, in a departure from *Wilkes*, warrants came to be issued by judicial officers rather than by executive or administrative officials. This development likely occurred out of a preference for a neutral arbiter and to avoid a situation where the executing authority rubber-stamped its own warrants. Administrative warrants by the executive branch are less common today.[35]

Second, and more important, the Supreme Court has interpreted the Warrant Clause together with the Searches and Seizures Clause to hold that a warrant is required in advance of a search in circumstances that go well beyond the original understanding. Because the "touchstone" of the Fourth Amendment's Searches and Seizures Clause is "reasonableness," the Court has held that warrants are required for searches of places where persons enjoy a reasonable expectation of privacy.[36] The paradigmatic example is a person's home and its surrounding area, or *curtilage*.[37] By contrast, searches and seizures of a person and his effects outside the home may not require a warrant, depending on the context and circumstances.

The Court has also extended this modern composite warrant and search-and-seizure doctrine to new technologies. *United States v. Jones* (2012) held that law enforcement officials must obtain a warrant before attaching a GPS tracking device to a vehicle to monitor its movements for an extended period of time.[38] The Court's analysis relied heavily on the history of trespass law at the Founding with the understanding that the Fourth Amendment, at a minimum, must offer the same degree of protection that individuals enjoyed when it was adopted. *United States v. Carpenter* (2018) held that the government's acquisition of historical cell-site location records was a search under the Fourth Amendment requiring a warrant.[39]

SUMMARY

Police are required to obtain a warrant for most searches and seizures unless a judicial exception applies. The most prominent exceptions include:

- *Arrest*: A warrant is not required, for example, when an officer has probable cause to believe that a suspect committed a crime in the officer's presence.[40]
- *Consent*: A warrant is not required when an individual consents to the search of his person or property.[41]
- *Plain View*: A warrant is not required when an officer has a right to be in a position that affords him "plain view" of the objects to be searched or seized.[42]

- *Exigent Circumstances*: A warrant is not required in an emergency when officers have insufficient time to seek a warrant to prevent the destruction or removal of evidence, a suspect from fleeing, or danger to the public.[43]
- *Incident to Arrest and Inventory*: A warrant is not required for a search incident to arrest. Likewise, officers may conduct an inventory search of a person's belongings after an arrest.[44] However, this exception does not extend to digital information on an arrestee's cell phone.[45]
- *Automobiles*: A warrant is not required to search an automobile if an officer has probable cause to believe that the vehicle contains contraband.[46]
- *Stop and Frisk*: A warrant is not required to conduct a non-intrusive search of a suspect if an officer has reasonable suspicion that a crime has been, is being, or is about to be committed by the suspect.[47]
- *Special Needs*: A warrant is not required in other unique circumstances where there are so-called special needs.[48]

OPEN QUESTIONS
- Administrative agencies often conduct warrantless searches related to health and safety, environmental, revenue, and other regulations.[49] Are these searches consistent with the original public meaning of the Warrant Clause?

Cite as: Judge Elizabeth L. Branch, Francis Aul, & Austin Mayron, *The Warrant Clause*, in THE HERITAGE GUIDE TO THE CONSTITUTION 629 (Josh Blackman & John G. Malcolm eds., 3d ed. 2025).

Notes
1. *Warrant*, Giles Jacob, A New Law Dictionary (6th ed. 1750).   **2.** William J. Stuntz, *The Substantive Origins of Criminal Procedure*, 105 Yale L.J. 393, 409 (1995).   **3.** Akhil Reed Amar, *The Bill of Rights as a Constitution*, 100 Yale L.J. 1131, 1178 (1991).   **4.** Akhil Reed Amar, *The Fourth Amendment, Boston, and the Writs of Assistance*, 30 Suffolk U. L. Rev. 53, 60 (1996).   **5.** Thomas Y. Davies, *Recovering the Original Fourth Amendment*, 98 Mich. L. Rev. 547, 558

(1999).   **6.** *Id.* at 562 n.20; 95 Eng. Rep. 807 (C.P. 1765).   **7.** *Paxton's Case of the Writ of Assistance*, in Josiah Quincy, Jr., Reports of Cases Argued and Adjudged in the Superior Court of Judicature of the Province of Massachusetts Bay Between 1761 and 1772, 51–57 (1865).   **8.** Laurent Sacharoff, *The Broken Fourth Amendment Oath*, 74 Stan. L. Rev. 603, 653–54 (2022).   **9.** 98 Eng. Rep. 498 (C.P. 1763); Wesley MacNeil Oliver, *The Modern History of Probable Cause*,

78 Tenn. L. Rev. 377, 397 (2011); Fabio Arcila, Jr., *In the Trenches: Searches and the Misunderstood Common-Law History of Suspicion and Probable Cause*, 10 U. Pa. J. Const. L. 1, 14 & n.41 (2007). **10.** David E. Steinberg, *An Original Misunderstanding: Akhil Amar and Fourth Amendment History*, 42 San Diego L. Rev. 227, 259 (2005). **11.** Akhil Reed Amar, *Fourth Amendment First Principles*, 107 Harv. L. Rev. 757, 772 (1994). **12.** 95 Eng. Rep. 807 (C.P. 1765). **13.** Joseph D. Grano, *Probable Cause and Common Sense: A Reply to the Critics of* Illinois v. Gates, 17 U. Mich. J. L. Reform 465, 479–80 (1984). **14.** 2 M. Hale, The History of the Pleas of the Crown 91–92 (1736). **15.** *Oath*, Thomas Potts, A Compendious Law Dictionary 465 (1803); *Warrant*, Giles Jacob, A New Law Dictionary (6th ed. 1750). **16.** Davies, *supra* at 651. **17.** Va. Const. of 1776, § 10. **18.** *Id.* **19.** Md. Const. of 1776, art. XXIII; Mass. Const. of 1780, art. XIV; N.C. Const. of 1776, art. XI; Pa. Const. of 1776, art. X; Vt. Const. of 1777, art. XI. **20.** 2 Farrand's 470. **21.** 3 Elliot's 588. **22.** Laura K. Donohue, *The Original Fourth Amendment*, 83 U. Chi. L. Rev. 1181, 1285–98 (2016). **23.** 1 Elliot's 328. **24.** Donohue, *supra* at 1290–92. **25.** 1 Annals of Cong. 452 (1789). **26.** Luis G. Stelzner, *The Fourth Amendment: The Reasonableness and Warrant Clauses*, 10 N.M. L. Rev. 33, 39–40 (1980). **27.** *Id.* at 40. **28.** Amar, *The Fourth Amendment, Boston, and the*

Writs of Assistance, supra at 55–56, 60. **29.** Act of July 31, 1789, § 24, 1 Stat. 29, 43. **30.** Act of March 3, 1791, § 32, 1 Stat. 199, 207. **31.** 11 U.S. 339, 348. **32.** 97 U.S. 642, 645 (1878). **33.** 389 U.S. 347, 457 (1967). **34.** Davies, *supra* at 738–50. **35.** *Camara v. Mun. Ct. of City & Cnty. of S.F.*, 387 U.S. 523 (1967); *Griffin v. Wisconsin*, 483 U.S. 868 (1987). **36.** *Brigham City v. Stuart*, 547 U.S. 398, 403 (2006). **37.** *Payton v. New York*, 445 U.S. 573 (1980); *Florida v. Jardines*, 569 U.S. 1 (2013). **38.** 565 U.S. 400 (2012). **39.** *Carpenter v. United States*, 585 U.S. 296 (2018). **40.** *District of Columbia v. Wesby*, 583 U.S. 48 (2018). **41.** *Amos v. United States*, 255 U.S. 313 (1921); *Schneckloth v. Bustamonte*, 412 U.S. 218 (1973). **42.** *Horton v. California*, 496 U.S. 128 (1990). **43.** *Lange v. California*, 141 S. Ct. 2011 (2021); *Birchfield v. North Dakota*, 594 U.S. 295 (2016). **44.** *South Dakota v. Opperman*, 428 U.S. 364 (1976). **45.** *Riley v. California*, 573 U.S. 373 (2014). **46.** *California v. Carney*, 471 U.S. 386 (1985). **47.** *Terry v. Ohio*, 392 U.S. 1 (1968). **48.** *United States v. Martinez-Fuerte*, 428 U.S. 543, 564 (1976); *Mitchell v. Wisconsin*, 588 U.S. 840 (2019); *New Jersey v. T.L.O.*, 469 U.S. 325 (1985); *Bell v. Wolfish*, 441 U.S. 520 (1979); *Griffin v. Wisconsin*, 483 U.S. 868 (1987). **49.** Geoffrey G. Hemphill, *The Administrative Search Doctrine: Isn't This Exactly What the Framers Were Trying to Avoid?*, 5 Regent U. L. Rev. 215, 216 (1995).

~~~

ESSAY NO. 168: THE GRAND JURY REQUIREMENT CLAUSE
AMEND. 5

No person shall be held to answer for a capital, or otherwise infamous crime, unless on a presentment or indictment of a Grand Jury. . . .

—Judge Julius N. Richardson

INTRODUCTION

Juries sit at the heart of our criminal justice system. Americans are commonly most familiar with the constitutional right to a trial with a small or *petit* jury. Less known is that the Constitution also enshrines a right to a large or *grand* jury. At the end of a prosecution, petit juries decide guilt or innocence and so give the people a check against the state's penal power; grand juries stand as citizen gatekeepers at the beginning of the process. Being prosecuted at all, even if ultimately found innocent, is its own punishment. The grand jury is "a protective bulwark standing solidly between the ordinary citizen and an overzealous prosecutor."[1] In modern practice, about two-dozen grand jurors deliberate in closed proceedings outside the presence of a judge. Only if the government is able to prove that it has a meritorious case, the grand jurors

will sign the *indictment*, which allows the prosecution to begin. Although some have questioned the modern importance of grand juries, the Fifth Amendment's grand-jury guarantee continues to stand "between the prosecutor and the accused."[2]

HISTORY BEFORE 1787

The modern grand jury has its roots in the English presentment process from the twelfth century.[3] In 1166, King Henry II's Assize of Clarendon established a procedure through which ordinary men in each locality would begin legal proceedings—through a "presentment"—against those who were suspected of crimes.[4] As Sir William Blackstone explained, a "presentment, *properly* speaking, is the notice taken by a grand jury of any offense from their own knowledge or observation."[5]

This early grand jury, however, lacked significant procedural protections. For example, rather than hearing witnesses or weighing evidence, grand jurors made charges based on what they personally knew about a suspect's public fame. Grand jurors also could be fined—amerced—for failing to make enough charges. After presentment, moreover, the accused generally faced a trial by ordeal in which they would face significant pain. There was no actual trial by jury.[6] Given these limitations, many scholars view Henry II's Assize as an attempt to consolidate his power over legal proceedings rather than as a guarantee of individual rights.[7]

By the early seventeenth century, the grand jury had evolved and achieved enough independence that it was perceived as a check by the people against their government.[8] Thus, in 1642, Lord Edward Coke declared that Magna Carta's famous guarantee that men may be taken or imprisoned only under "the law of the land" included the right to indictment by a grand jury.[9]

The grand jury's new liberty-protecting role was on full display in 1681 when King Charles II sought to prosecute the Earl of Shaftesbury for treason.[10] The London-based grand jury faced considerable pressure to charge, or indict the defendant. The judge told the grand jurors that if they would not indict upon probable cause, they would be "criminals." Yet the grand jury refused to indict.[11] Shaftesbury was nonetheless forced into exile as Charles maneuvered to select new grand jurors more favorable to him.[12] The lesson was clear: Grand jurors could be a safeguard against unfounded or unpopular prosecutions, at least until the Crown meddled.

This perspective on the grand jury traveled across the Atlantic. Each of the thirteen American colonies used grand juries,[13] which were viewed in America, just as they were in England, as an important check against perceived political prosecutions. For instance, three successive New York grand juries famously refused to indict John Peter Zenger for libeling the royal governor, William Cosby.[14] In Massachusetts, grand juries similarly refused to indict colonists for violating the Stamp Act.[15] Yet in America, just as in England, the Crown circumvented the grand-jury process. Zenger still stood trial. Unable to procure an indictment, the prosecutor chose to charge Zenger by

filing an *information* against him.[16] This formal charge can be brought by the government without a grand jury's approval.

After independence, the new states included grand-jury provisions in their constitutions. North Carolina, Pennsylvania, and Delaware did so expressly.[17] Many other state constitutions provided for grand juries indirectly through a prohibition akin to Magna Carta's "law of the land" guarantee.[18] The states continued to use their grand juries just as they had during the colonial period.[19]

THE CONSTITUTIONAL CONVENTION AND RATIFICATION DEBATES

During the Constitutional Convention, the grand-jury right apparently went unmentioned. Article III included a right to a jury *trial* in criminal cases but no such protection for the right to a grand-jury *indictment*.[20]

The grand-jury right also was not central to the ratification debates. Anti-Federalist Federal Farmer mentioned the right among several that he suggested the Constitution ought to protect explicitly. He proposed "that, except in the government of the army and navy, no person shall be tried for any offence, whereby he may incur loss of life, or an infamous punishment, until he be first indicted by a grand jury."[21]

In the Massachusetts ratifying convention, Abraham Holmes decried that "there is no provision . . . in the Constitution to prevent the attorney-general from filing information against any person, whether he is indicted by the grand jury or not."[22] Accordingly, the Massachusetts convention included a list of proposed amendments, one of which included a grand-jury right with language that was very similar to Federal Farmer's proposal: "That no person shall be tried for any crime, by which he may incur an infamous punishment, or loss of life, until he be first indicted by a grand jury, except in such cases as may arise in the government and regulation of the land and naval forces."[23]

New Hampshire proposed a virtually identical amendment when it ratified the Constitution.[24] And New York proposed a similar amendment: "That (except in the government of the land and naval forces, and of the militia when in actual service, and in cases of impeachment) a presentment or indictment by a grand jury ought to be observed as a necessary preliminary to the trial of all crimes cognizable by the judiciary of the United States."[25]

ADOPTION OF THE FIFTH AMENDMENT

In 1789, Representative James Madison of Virginia drafted what would become the Fifth Amendment. It included language similar to the proposals from the states: "[I]n all crimes punishable with loss of life or member, present-ment or indictment by a grand jury shall be an essential preliminary."[26] Unlike the state propos-als, however, Madison's language was limited to crimes punishable with "loss of life or mem-ber." And while the initial Massachusetts pro-posal required a grand jury before a person was "tried," Madison's text more closely resembled New York's "necessary preliminary" phrasing.

Representative Roger Sherman of Connecticut suggested new language that expanded the proposal's scope and tied it to a person being "tried": "No person shall be tried for any crime whereby he may incur loss of life or any infamous punishment, without Indictment by a grand Jury. . . ."[27] The North Carolina Declaration of Rights used the phrase "put to answer," and the select Committee of Eleven introduced the similar phrase "held to answer": "[N]o person shall be held to answer for a capi-tal, or otherwise infamous crime, unless on a presentment or indictment by a grand jury. . . ."[28]

The First Congress adopted the Select Committee's proposed grand jury requirement with limited discussion.[29] Congress referred the amendment to the states with the text it has today.[30] There appears to have been no mean-ingful discussion of this provision during the ratification debates, and following ratification, the early Republic relied on the grand jury for federal indictments.[31]

MODERN GRAND JURY PRACTICE

Under modern federal practice, a typical grand jury consists of twenty-three citizens.[32] The grand jury is selected, sworn, and given gen-eral instructions by a district judge. Then, for eighteen months, the grand jury meets regu-larly in secret. They are guided by the federal prosecutor,[33] who is present for much of the proceeding but is excused during the jurors' deliberations and voting. Secrecy is a central feature of federal grand juries.[34] Though non-deliberative proceedings are transcribed, mat-ters before the grand jury may not be revealed by the jurors or by the government on pain of contempt, subject to specific exceptions.

The grand jury has expansive investigatory powers.[35] The grand jury often hears testimony from law-enforcement witnesses about the evi-dence independently gathered, but it may also conduct its own investigation. Typically under the direction of the prosecutor, the grand jury may subpoena witnesses and records. Those who refuse a subpoena may be held in con-tempt by the presiding judge absent a valid privilege, including the Fifth Amendment privilege against self-incrimination. Witnesses are questioned by the prosecutor, though grand jurors may also pose questions, and false testi-mony before the grand jury may be criminally punished.

The grand jury also performs an accusa-tory role. After the investigation, the grand jury formally accuses the suspect. In that role, the jury serves as a gatekeeper, deliberating and voting on whether evidence establishes proba-ble cause that the suspect committed the alleged crime.[36]

The grand jury places a check on the executive branch, thus protecting individual liberty. The grand jury has discretion, for it "is not bound to indict in every case where a con-viction can be obtained."[37] In most cases, the grand jury considers only the crimes proposed by the prosecutor—that is, an indictment. The grand jury may independently investigate and indict, but only the executive branch may prosecute.[38]

When the Grand Jury Clause requires an indictment, prosecution cannot proceed without it unless the right is waived by the accused, but an indictment's defect is not jurisdictional.[39] The U.S. Supreme Court has observed that "[a]n indictment returned by a legally constituted and unbiased grand jury . . . if valid on its face, is enough to call for a trial of the charge on the merits."[40] Litigants alleging a Fifth Amendment Grand Jury Clause violation rarely succeed.[41]

OPEN QUESTIONS

- Does the grand jury requirement still serve a meaningful role?[42] Does the grand jury do more to aid prosecutions than it does to protect the accused? Is there any difference between the criminal justice systems in states that have a grand jury requirement and states that do not have such a requirement?

- The grand-jury right is one of the few Bill of Rights provisions that has never been incorporated against the states under the Fourteenth Amendment's Due Process Clause. The Supreme Court expressly refused to do so in *Hurtado v. California* (1884).[43] Justice John Marshall Harlan forcefully dissented in *Hurtado*. He argued that Magna Carta's "law of the land" protection encompassed the grand-jury right, citing Blackstone's *Commentaries*, Hawkins's *Pleas of the Crown*, and Hale's *Historia Placitorum Coronæ*.[44] Should the Court reconsider *Hurtado* as an originalist matter?[45]

- The Grand Jury Clause is limited to a "person." The term "person," unlike the Constitution's use of "citizen," has been broadly understood. Does the Grand Jury Clause apply to entities like corporations?[46]

- The Grand Jury Clause is limited to when one is "held to answer" for a crime. Precisely when does this stage occur? It surely includes being put on trial but also appears to include earlier stages of prosecution.[47]

- A "capital" crime is well understood as one that is punishable by death,[48] but what is an "otherwise infamous crime"? The Supreme Court has noted that "otherwise infamous crimes" are those for which the maximum authorized punishment is considered infamous.[49]

Cite as: Judge Julius N. Richardson, *The Grand Jury Requirement*, in THE HERITAGE GUIDE TO THE CONSTITUTION 633 (Josh Blackman & John G. Malcolm eds., 3d ed. 2025).

Notes

1. *U.S. v. Dionisio*, 410 U.S. 1, 17 (1973). **2.** *Hoffman v. U.S.*, 341 U.S. 479, 485 (1951). **3.** Helene E. Schwartz, *Demythologizing the Historic Role of the Grand Jury*, 10 Am. Crim. L. Rev. 701, 707–08 (1972); Richard H. Helmholz, *The Early History of the Grand Jury and the Canon Law*, 50 U. Chi. L. Rev. 613 (1983). **4.** Richard D. Younger, The People's Panel: The Grand Jury in the United States, 1634–1941, at 1 (1963). **5.** 4 Blackstone 301; Nathan Dane, 7 A General Abridgment and Digest of American Law 261–62 (1823). **6.** Helmholz, *supra* at 616–17; Irwin L. Langbein, *The Jury of Presentment and the Coroner*, 33 Colum. L. Rev. 1329, 1330–33 (1933). **7.** Schwartz, *supra* at 703–10. **8.** *Id.* at 710–11. **9.** Edward Coke, The Second Part of the Institutes of the Laws of England 46 (1817 ed.). **10.** Schwartz, *supra* at 711–19. **11.** *Id.* at 717–18. **12.** *Id.* at 717–18. **13.** Younger, *supra* at 5. **14.** James Alexander, A Brief Narrative of the Case and Trial of John Peter Zenger 17–19 (Stanley Nider Katz ed., 2d ed. 1963). **15.** Younger, *supra* at 28. **16.** Alexander, *supra* at 19. **17.** N.C. Const. of 1776, Decl. of Rts., art. VIII; Pa. Const. of 1790, art. IX, § 10; Del. Const. of 1792, Art. I, § 8. **18.** Md. Const. of 1776, art. XXI; N.H. Const. of 1776, art. XV; Va. Const. of 1776, Bill of Rights, § 8; S.C. Const. of 1778, art. XLI; Mass. Const. of 1780, pt. I, art. XII. **19.** Sara S. Beale et al., Grand Jury Law and Practice § 1:4 (2d ed. 2022). **20.** Art. III, § 2, cl. 3. **21.** Storing 2.8.200. **22.** 2 Elliot's 110. **23.** *Id.* at 177. **24.** 1 Elliot's 326. **25.** *Id.* at 328. **26.** 1 Annals of Cong. at 452 (1789). **27.** The Complete Bill of Rights: The Drafts, Debates, Sources and Origins 412 (Neil H. Cogan ed., 2d ed. 2015). **28.** *Id.* **29.** *Id.* at 413–23. **30.** 1 Elliot's 339. **31.** Younger, *supra* at 46–71. **32.** Fed. R. Crim. Pro. 6(a)(1); Andrew D. Leipold, *Why Grand Juries Do Not (and Cannot) Protect the Accused*, 80 Cornell L. Rev. 260, 265 (1994). **33.** *U.S. v. Sells Eng'g, Inc.*, 463 U.S. 418, 431 (1983). **34.** *Douglas Oil Co. of Cal. v. Petrol Stops Nw.*, 441 U.S. 211, 218 n.9 (1979); *Rehberg v. Paulk*, 566 U.S. 356, 374 (2012). **35.** *U.S. v. R. Enters., Inc.*, 498 U.S. 292, 297 (1991). **36.** *Id.* at 297. **37.** *Vasquez v. Hillery*, 475 U.S. 245, 263 (1986). **38.** *U.S. v. Hill*, 26 F. Cas. 315, 316 (C.A.D.Va. 1809) (No. 15,364) (Marshall, C. J.); *Greenlaw v. U.S.*, 554 U.S. 237, 246 (2008). **39.** *U.S. v. Cotton*, 535 U.S. 625 (2002). **40.** *Costello v. U.S.*, 350 U.S. 359 (1956). **41.** *Kaley v. U.S.*, 571 U.S. 320 (2014) **42.** *In re Kittle*, 180 F. 946, 947 (C.C.N.Y. 1910) (L. Hand, J.); Schwartz, *supra* at 732; *U.S. v. Mandujano*, 425 U.S. 564, 571 (1976) (plurality opinion); Leipold, *supra*. **43.** 110 U.S. 516, 534–35 (1884). **44.** *Id.* at 544–45 (Harlan, J., dissenting). **45.** *Ramos v. Louisiana*, 590 U.S. 83, 156 (2020) (Alito, J., dissenting). **46.** *Wong Wing v. U.S.*, 163 U.S. 228 (1896); Peter J. Henning, *The Conundrum of Corporate Criminal Liability: Seeking a Consistent Approach to the Constitutional Rights of Corporations in Criminal Prosecutions*, 63 Tenn. L. Rev. 793, 856–60 (1996). **47.** *Ex parte Wilson*, 114 U.S. 417, 423 (1885); *U.S. v. McIntosh*, 704 F.3d 894, 903–05 (11th Cir. 2013); Wayne R. LaFave et al., 4 Criminal Procedure § 15.1(b) (4th ed. 2023). **48.** *Fitzpatrick v. U.S.*, 178 U.S. 304 (1900). **49.** *Wilson*, 114 U.S. at 423–27; *Mackin v. U.S.*, 117 U.S. 348 (1886).

~

ESSAY NO. 169: THE GRAND JURY EXCEPTIONS CLAUSE
AMEND. 5

No person shall be held to answer for a capital, or otherwise infamous crime, unless on a presentment or indictment of a Grand Jury, except in cases arising in the land or naval forces, or in the Militia, when in actual service in time of War or public danger. . . .

—Judge Gregory E. Maggs & Robert Leider

INTRODUCTION

The Constitution generally requires that criminal defendants must be subject to a grand jury indictment, but Anglo-American law has long recognized both the necessity of having military law and the need to keep that law cabined to members of the military. The Grand Jury Exceptions Clause recognizes that the ordinary modes of common-law criminal procedure do not apply to cases arising in the military. Courts have decided several constitutional issues about this clause: To whom does military law apply? Does military law extend to traditional civilian crimes? Which constitutional criminal procedure rights, if any, apply to military members?

BRITISH PRECEDENT

In England, the only permanent military court was the Court of Chivalry.[1] The court had broad criminal jurisdiction in wartime.[2] It "administered the permanent Law of Arms," but it was not concerned "with enforcing military discipline."[3] Martial law was also applied to soldiers and rebels during the Middle Ages.[4]

By the end of the fifteenth century, the Court of Chivalry had fallen into disuse.[5] With its effective disappearance, military courts consisted primarily of courts-martial authorized by military commanders operating under martial law.[6] In this context, "martial law" meant "a summary form of criminal justice, exercised under direct or delegated royal authority by the military or police forces of the Crown, which is independent of the established processes of the common-law courts, the ecclesiastical courts, and the courts which administered the civil law in England."[7] Sir Matthew Hale, the English jurist, remarked that martial law "in truth and reality . . . is not a law, but something indulged, rather than allowed, as a law."[8]

Through the early seventeenth century, the people subjected to martial law in England included not only members of the armed forces, but also rebels, rioters, thieves, and other non-military defendants.[9] This practice would change with the Petition of Right (1628). The Crown would apply martial law only to soldiers in the field during war and to rebels in England.[10] Hale justified the continued application of martial law to members of the military by explaining that "[t]he necessity of government, order, and discipline in an army is" the only possible way to justify martial law.[11]

The development of standing military institutions created a need for a more permanent system of military justice. When the standing army became an established institution around 1660,[12] the problems of desertion and insubordination became far more common. But desertion and insubordination were not offenses cognizable in civil and common-law courts. H. St. Clair Feilden observed that it became "impossible to maintain a permanent force in time of peace" without a separate military justice system to address military discipline.[13]

In the late seventeenth century, military law began to separate from martial law. In the middle of the century, Parliament passed the Articles of War to govern the British navy.[14] And in 1689, Parliament began to pass annual Mutiny Acts for the discipline of the army.[15] Over time, a separate body of military law would be developed. Confusingly, however, the term "martial law" would still be used as synonymous with military law well into the eighteenth century.[16]

The new legal regime both aimed to make

the military more efficient and sought to control the danger of professional troops.[17] England mandated that members of the military were subject to both civilian law and military law.[18] Soldiers could not plead that they were following military orders as a defense to criminal prosecution.[19] A soldier could be punished severely for acts that would be not criminal or only a slight offense in the civilian world.[20] A soldier also could be punished by court-martial. This special military court proceeding did not provide a trial by a jury of one's peers, which was guaranteed at common law, but rather a panel of superiors.[21] Scholar A.V. Dicey observed that a soldier, by virtue of his employment, does not have "the same freedom" and "occupies a position totally different from that of a civilian."[22]

The militia, comprised of subjects who performed (or could be called to perform) temporary defensive military service, was a third branch of the military. As nonprofessional soldiers, militiamen were subjected to military law "only when in training or when the force [was] embodied."[23] When not called out to active service, militiamen were subject only to the duties of civilian law.

AMERICAN PRECEDENT

In the American colonies, the traditional British military law regime applied. Professional soldiers were subjected to military law while in service. For example, Virginia passed a Mutiny Act in 1757 that applied to officers who were "mustered, or in pay" and to those who were "[e]nlisted or in pay as a soldier."[24] Pennsylvania passed a Mutiny Act in 1756 that applied to officers "commissioned and in pay" and to soldiers "regularly enlisted" who were "paid and maintained by the Crown."[25] As in Britain, civilian law applied to the military—or at least was supposed to do so. The Declaration of Independence objected that Britain had protected soldiers "by a mock Trial, from punishment for any Murders which they should commit on the Inhabitants of these States."[26]

After independence, many states adopted the traditional British limits for military jurisdiction. The Maryland Declaration of Rights of 1776 provided that "no person, except regular soldiers, mariners, and marines in the service of this State, or militia when in actual service,

ought in any case to be subject to or punishable by martial law."[27] The Massachusetts constitution of 1780 included a nearly identical guarantee.[28]

During the Revolutionary War, Congress adopted Articles of War to govern the Army and Navy. The Articles of Confederation also authorized Congress to "have the sole and exclusive right and power of . . . making rules for the government and regulation of the . . . land and naval forces."[29] (See Essay No. 61.)

MILITARY LAW IN THE CONSTITUTION

The Constitution has two separate provisions concerning military law. First, Congress has the power to make "Rules for the Government and Regulation of the land and naval Forces." This provision applies to the Army and Navy. The second clause grants Congress the power to "provide for organizing, arming, and disciplin-ing[] the Militia, and for governing such Part of them as may be employed in the Service of the United States." (See Essay Nos. 61 and 63.)

During the ratification debates, the Anti-Federalists objected vigorously to the Organizing the Militia Clause. Technically, all able-bodied men were in the militia. Therefore, the Anti-Federalists argued, Congress could impose military law on all men of military age. This argument was raised in Maryland, Pennsylvania, and other states.[30] Federalists responded that the national government's power to govern the militia was limited to times when the militia was in actual federal service. For example, George Nicholas said that because the Constitution permitted the national government to govern only "such part of [the militia] as may be in the actual service of the United States," there was no risk that the militia could be subject to martial law when off duty.[31]

The Anti-Federalists wanted additional assurances. The conventions in Virginia, New York, North Carolina, and Rhode Island proposed constitutional amendments guaranteeing that civilian law and common-law criminal procedure rights would apply to all citizens.[32] Similar proposals were advanced by the Maryland minority and the Richmond Antifederal Committee.[33] These proposed amendments recognized two exceptions for when military law would apply. First, military law would apply to cases involving "the government of the land and naval forces" or some equivalent language.[34] In short, soldiers could be subjected to military law by virtue of their status as soldiers. Some proposals further limited military law so that it would apply only in "time of actual War, Invasion, or Rebellion."[35] Second, military law would not apply to militiamen except "when in actual service in time of war, invasion, or rebellion."[36] As a result, civilian law applied to militiamen when they lived as civilians. These proposals tracked traditional British practice.

ADOPTION OF THE GRAND JURY EXCEPTIONS CLAUSE

In August 1789, the House of Representatives passed an amendment that would guarantee the right to a jury trial in a criminal case. That right, however, would not apply "in cases arising in the land or naval forces, or in the militia, in time of war or public danger."[37] In September 1789, the Senate moved this exception language to the guarantee of a Grand Jury indictment.[38] After a conference committee, the House accepted the changes in the grand jury provision. Other changes in the jury trial right did not provide any explicit exceptions for the military.[39] The grand jury requirement would be ratified as part of the Fifth Amendment, and the jury trial right would be ratified as part of the Sixth Amendment. Under the Fifth Amendment, criminal cases would generally be presented to the grand jury, but military cases were excepted.

Despite its drafting, the Grand Jury Exceptions Clause has been understood to stand for the broader proposition that traditional common-law criminal procedure protections do not apply to proper proceedings under military jurisdiction.[40] Thus, for example, members of the military may be tried by courts-martial and are not entitled to a petit jury of their peers even though the Sixth Amendment contains no similar explicit exception for military trials.[41]

MODERN PRACTICE

Under an originalist understanding, which Fifth and Sixth Amendment rights, if any, should apply in military law cases remains an unsettled question.[42] Courts have applied some provisions of the Fifth and Sixth Amendments in military law cases. The U.S. Supreme Court has applied the Double Jeopardy Clause (or has assumed it applies) to bar successive prosecutions by the same sovereign, whether civilian or military.[43] (See Essay No. 170.) Whether those cases are correct as an original matter is uncertain. Under British law, a civilian acquittal would bar a military prosecution, but a military acquittal would not bar a civilian prosecution.[44] The rule perhaps prevented the military from protecting its own for misconduct committed in the civilian realm. Others have assumed that due process and the right to counsel apply, although the Supreme Court has characterized the latter as "much debated and never squarely resolved."[45] (See Essay Nos. 172 and 181.) And there have been dicta to the effect that none of the provisions apply.[46]

The intersection of originalism and modern practice creates difficult questions about how to apply the Grand Jury Exceptions Clause today. Some of the most difficult of these questions involve how to understand Framing-era rules in light of changed circumstances. For example, the bureaucratic structure of the armed forces has changed beyond the Framers' imagination. At the Framing, there was a sharp distinction between the Army and Navy, which were regular forces, and the militia, which was the nonprofessional force.[47] (See Essay Nos. 59 and 60.) Yet the military now has large categories of servicemen who maintain a military affiliation but are not full-time troops. These include military reservists, both actively drilling and inactive, and military retirees of both the regular and reserve components.

Congress's expansion of the armed forces to include nonprofessional forces raises difficult questions about how far Congress may extend military jurisdiction. Consistent with the original understanding, the Court has held that members of the Army and Navy (the regular forces) are subject to military law at all times, militiamen are subject to military law only while on duty, and civilians are not amenable to military law.[48] But what about military retirees who remain affiliated with the armed forces and draw retired pay but have no active-duty service obligations? May Congress subject them to military law for conduct that occurs in their civilian lives? Originalists have debated the constitutionality of such actions.[49]

Similar disputes have not arisen over the nonprofessional troops in the reserve forces. But that is because Congress has statutorily treated reservists as though they were militiamen by limiting military jurisdiction to when they are on active duty or in training.[50] It is not clear whether Congress could constitutionally apply status-based jurisdiction to reservists and subject them to military law for conduct that occurred in their civilian lives.[51]

Finally, questions have arisen about the extent to which Congress may subject servicemembers to military jurisdiction for traditionally civilian offenses. Until 1969, the Supreme Court did not require that an offense cognizable by court-martial must have any connection to the military. Instead, the Court generally policed only personal jurisdiction, holding that members of the Army and Navy (the regular forces) are subject to military law at all times.[52] Militiamen are subject to military law while on

duty,[53] and civilians are not amenable to military law.[54] Beginning in 1969, the Court required that the offense be service-connected to qualify as "arising" in the armed forces.[55] Still, doubts persisted about whether the service-connected rule was correct, and the rule proved difficult to enforce. As a result, the Court abandoned that rule only eighteen years later.[56]

This holding has been a contested issue because of changed circumstances. At the Founding, military law generally applied only to military offenses, but Congress has vastly expanded the range of offenses cognizable in military courts more recently to include traditionally civilian conduct.[57] There are originalist debates over whether the Constitution imposes any subject-matter limits on the crimes for which servicemembers may be prosecuted in military courts. These debates involve legal questions of constitutional meaning, factual disputes about Framing-era practices, and the legal effect, if any, of past practices and arguably changed circumstances.

OPEN QUESTIONS

- How far may Congress extend military jurisdiction over reservists for conduct that occurs when they are not on military duty?
- Do other provisions of the Fourth and Eighth Amendments, as well as the Ex Post Facto Clause, apply in courts-martial?[58]
- *United States ex rel. Toth v. Quarles* (1955) held that the court-martialing of ex-servicemembers for conduct that occurred during their service was unconstitutional.[59] Was this case correctly decided?[60]

Cite as: Judge Gregory E. Maggs & Robert Leider, *The Grand Jury Exceptions Clause, in* The Heritage Guide to the Constitution 637 (Josh Blackman & John G. Malcolm eds., 3d ed. 2025).

Notes

1. 3 Blackstone 68. 2. 4 Encylopaedia of the Laws of England 157, 158 (A. Wood Renton & Max A. Robertson eds., 2d. ed. 1907). 3. J.V. Capua, *The Early History of Martial Law in England from the Fourteenth Century to the Petition of Right*, 36 Cambridge L.J. 152, 157–58 (1977). 4. *Id.* at 158. 5. *Id.* at 152, 158. 6. *Id.* 7. *Id.* at 152. 8. Matthew Hale, History of the Common Law of England 42 (1713); Capua, *supra* at 152. 9. Capua, *supra* at 153. 10. *Id.* at 172–73; Petition of Right, 1628, 3 Car., c. 10 (Eng.). 11. Hale, *supra* at 42. 12. Correlli Barnett, Britain and Her Army 1509–1970: A Military, Political and Social Survey 115 (1970). 13. H. St. Clair Feilden, A Short Constitutional History of England 316 (3d ed. 1897). 14. 2 Wm. Laird Clowes, The Royal Navy: A History from the Earliest Times to the Present 102–03 (1898). 15. Capua, *supra* at 153. 16. George M. Dennison, *Martial Law: The Development of*

a Theory of Emergency Powers, 1776–1861, 18 Am. J. Legal Hist., 52, 52–60 (1974). 17. Dan Maurer, *A Logic of Military Justice*, 53 Tex. Tech L. Rev. 669 (2021). 18. A.V. Dicey, Introduction to the Study of the Law of the Constitution 276 (3d ed. 1889). 19. *Id.* 20. *Id.* at 282. 21. *Id.* 22. *Id.* 23. *Id.* at 285. 24. An Act for Preventing Mutiny and Desertion, *in* 7 The Statutes at Large; Being a Collection of All The Laws of Virginia, from the First Session of the Legislature, in the Year 1919, at 8 (William Waller Hening ed., 1820). 25. An Act for Regulating the Officers and Soldiers Commissioned and Raised by the Governor for the Defense of This Province, § 1, *in* 5 The Statutes at Large of Pennsylvania from 1682 to 1801, at 220 (James T. Mitchell & Henry Flanders eds., 1898). 26. Declaration of Independence, ¶ 20. 27. Md. Const. Decl. of Rts. of 1776, art. XXIX. 28. Mass. Const. Decl. of Rts. of 1780, art.

XXVIII.   **29.** Articles of Confederation, art. IX, § 4. **30.** Maryland Ratifying Convention (1788), *reprinted in* 2 The Bill of Rights: A Documentary History 729, 734 (Bernard Schwartz ed., 1971); *The Address and Reasons of Dissent of the Minority of the Convention of Pennsylvania to their Constituents*, Pa. Packet & Daily Advertiser (Dec. 18, 1787), *reprinted in* Storing 3.11.54; Foreign Spectator, *Remarks on the Amendments to the Federal Constitution, Proposed by the Conventions of Massachusetts, New-Hampshire, New-York, Virginia, South and North-Caroline, with the Minorities of Pennsylvania and Maryland, by a Foreign Spectator: Number VIII*, Phila. Fed. Gazette (Nov. 14, 1788), *reprinted in* The Origin of the Second Amendment: A Documentary History in Commentaries on Liberty, Free Government, and an Armed Populace During the Formation of the Bill of Rights 567, 569–70 (David E. Young ed., 1991).   **31.** 10 DHRC 1280 (John P. Kaminski et al. eds., 1993).   **32.** The Origin of the Second Amendment, *supra* at 458 ¶ 8, 481, 504 ¶ 8, 734 ¶ 8.   **33.** 2 Elliot's 552 (Maryland); 3 Elliot's 660 (Virginia).   **34.** The Origin of the Second Amendment, *supra* at 359 ¶ 13, 389 ¶ 8.   **35.** *Id.* at 389 ¶ 8.   **36.** *Id.* at 359 ¶ 13, 460 ¶ 11, 481, 507 ¶ 11, 735 ¶ 17.   **37.** H.R. Jour., 1st Cong., 1st sess. 108 (Aug. 21, 1789).   **38.** S. Jour., 1st Cong., 1st sess. 129 (Sept. 9, 1789).   **39.** H.R. Jour., 1st Cong., 1st sess. 152–53 (Sept. 25, 1789).   **40.** *Reid v. Covert*, 354 U.S. 1, 37 n.68 (1957).   **41.** *Ex parte Quirin*, 317 U.S. 1, 40 (1942); *Kneedler v. Lane*, 45 Pa. 238, 261 (Woodward, J., concurring); Gregory E. Maggs, *Judicial Review of the Manual for Courts Martial*, 160 Mil. L. Rev. 96, 147–55 (1999).   **42.** Frederick Bernays Wiener, *Courts-Martial and the Bill of Rights: The Original Practice I*, 72 Harv. L. Rev. 1 (1958); Frederick Bernays Wiener, *Courts-Martial and the Bill of Rights: The Original Practice II*,

72 Harv. L. Rev. 266 (1958); Gordon D. Henderson, *Courts-Martial and the Constitution: The Original Understanding*, 71 Harv. L. Rev. 293 (1957).   **43.** *Wade v. Hunter*, 336 U.S. 684 (1949); *Grafton v. United States*, 206 U.S. 333 (1907).   **44.** Dicey, *supra* at 277–78.   **45.** *Middendorf v. Henry*, 425 U.S. 25, 34 (1976); *Weiss v. United States*, 510 U.S. 163, 176 (1994).   **46.** *Ex parte Milligan*, 71 U.S. (4 Wall.) 2, 138 (1866).   **47.** Robert Leider, *Deciphering the "Armed Forces of the United States,"* 57 Wake Forest L. Rev. 1195 (2022).   **48.** *Johnson v. Sayre*, 158 U.S. 109, 114–15 (1895); *Ex parte Milligan*, 71 U.S. (4 Wall.) 2; *Kinsella v. United States ex rel. Singleton*, 361 U.S. 234, 246 (1960).   **49.** *Larrabee v. Del Toro*, 45 F.4d 81, 83–94 (D.C. Cir. 2022); *United States v. Begani*, N81 M.J. 273., 282 (C.A.A.F. 2021) (Maggs, J., concurring); Robert Leider, *Retiring Military Jurisdiction over Military Retirees*, 68 Vill. L. Rev. 751 (2024).   **50.** 10 U.S.C. § 802(a) (1), (3).   **51.** Leider, *Retiring Military Jurisdiction, supra* at 801; Joseph W. Bishop, Jr., *Court-Martial Jurisdiction Over Military-Civilian Hybrids: Retired Regulars, Reservists, and Discharged Prisoners*, 112 U. Pa. L. Rev. 317 (1964).   **52.** *Johnson v. Sayre*, 158 U.S. 109, 114–15 (1895).   **53.** *Id.* **54.** *Ex parte Milligan*, 71 U.S. (4 Wall.) 2; *Kinsella v. United States ex rel. Singleton*, 361 U.S. 234, 246 (1960).   **55.** *O'Callahan v. Parker*, 395 U.S. 258, 272 (1969).   **56.** *Solorio v. United States*, 483 U.S. 435, 436 (1987).   **57.** Wiener, *Original Practice I, supra* at 10–12.   **58.** Maggs, *supra* at 147–55.   **59.** 350 U.S. 11 (1955).   **60.** Christian Burset, *Advisory Opinions and Military Jurisdiction: New Light on Sackville's Case (1760)*, Volokh Conspiracy (Apr. 1, 2024) (posted by Samuel Bray), https://perma.cc /K5WS-92GM.

~

ESSAY NO. 170: THE DOUBLE JEOPARDY CLAUSE
AMEND. 5

. . . nor shall any person be subject for the same offence to be twice put in jeopardy of life or limb. . . .

—Judge Timothy M. Tymkovich & Adam Steinhilber

INTRODUCTION

The Fifth Amendment's Double Jeopardy Clause embodies an ancient legal principle against government overreach, prohibiting multiple prosecutions for the same crime. This essay examines the clause's origins and its still-developing jurisprudence. Specifically, the essay looks at the clause's pre-Constitution history, role in the ratification debates, adoption as a written federal right, and interpretation by the Supreme Court.

HISTORY BEFORE 1787

The origins of double jeopardy can be traced back to Greek, Roman, Jewish, canon, and, most recently, English common law.[1] Under this principle, a person could not be tried twice for the same offense. Sir William Blackstone observed that it was a "universal maxim of the common law of England, that no man is to be brought into jeopardy of his life, more than once, for the same offence."[2] A defendant could have new criminal charges dismissed by pleading a former conviction, a former acquittal, or a pardon for the same offense.[3] There is evidence that the principle applied only to felonies, which were punished by death.[4]

In colonial America, the Massachusetts Bay Colony promulgated the first written double-jeopardy protection.[5] The 1641 Body of Liberties recognized that "[n]o man shall be twise sentenced by Civill Justice for one and the same Crime, offence, or Trespasse." Courts in other colonies, including Virginia and New York, also recognized the common-law protection.[6] In colonial Virginia, an acquitted defendant "was forever discharged" of the accusation.[7] But the protection applied only if the defendant was tried by a court with jurisdiction; if a mistrial resulted because the jury was convened in the wrong county, the defendant could be tried again.[8] New York courts dismissed charges on multiple occasions because the defendant had already been convicted for the same conduct.[9]

After independence, New Hampshire was the first state to enshrine this protection expressly in its constitution: "No subject shall be liable to be tried, after an acquittal, for the same crime or offense."[10] Other states soon followed.[11]

THE CONSTITUTIONAL CONVENTION

There is no record of the delegates discussing double jeopardy at the Philadelphia Convention. The final Constitution guaranteed the right of trial by jury but did not include a double-jeopardy guarantee.

THE RATIFICATION DEBATES

During the ratification debates, the Anti-Federalists wanted a constitutional double-jeopardy protection. Brutus, for example, noted that under the common law, if a defendant "is acquitted no other court can call upon him to answer for the same crime." However, under the proposed Constitution, the government could appeal an acquittal; thus, "[t]he whole matter may have a second hearing," and the defendant "may be subjected to intolerable oppression."[12]

After Maryland ratified the Constitution, a special committee recommended a constitutional amendment prohibiting a "second trial after acquittal."[13] New York's statement of ratification similarly contained a prefatory

declaration of rights, including "[t]hat no Person ought to be put twice in Jeopardy of Life or Limb for one and the same Offence, nor, unless in case of impeachment, be punished more than once for the same Offence."[14]

ADOPTION OF THE FIFTH AMENDMENT

After the First Congress convened in 1789, efforts to add a bill of rights continued. Representative James Madison of Virginia proposed, along with other provisions, a double-jeopardy amendment: "No person shall be subject, [except] in case of impeachment, to more than one trial or one punishment for the same offence."[15] The public meaning of "offence" was quite broad; it referred to a "transgression" or "an act committed against law, or omitted where the law requires it."[16]

During the ensuing debate, several members objected to limiting the protection to "more than one trial." Representatives Egbert Benson of New York, Roger Sherman of Connecticut, and Theodore Sedgwick of Massachusetts feared this language could deprive a defendant of a beneficial second trial at which the defendant could attempt to "undo" his original conviction.[17] Proponents like Representative Samuel Livermore of New Hampshire believed Madison's language declared the current state of the law and would prevent a retrial after an acquittal.[18] Representative Benson's motion to strike the disputed language failed.[19] Representative George Partridge of Massachusetts moved unsuccessfully to add "by any law of the United States" after "offence."[20]

In the Senate, the provision was substantially modified without any recorded discussion. The text was changed to provide that no person shall "be twice put in jeopardy of life or limb by any public prosecution" for the same offense. The phrase "by any public prosecution" was later dropped. The text then provided: "nor shall any person be subject to be put in jeopardy of life or limb, for the same offence." After further deliberations, the wording was slightly modified, yielding the final version: "nor shall any person be subject for the same offence to be twice put in jeopardy of life or limb."[21] The Senate language, as modified, was ratified in 1791 as part of the Fifth Amendment.

FEDERAL PRACTICE

Over time, the U.S. Supreme Court has identified three protections that the clause encompasses: no second prosecution for the same offense after an acquittal, no second prosecution for the same offense after a guilty verdict, and no multiple punishments for the same offense.[22] The clause has not been read literally to apply only to death penalty cases where a person's "life or limb" is in jeopardy.[23] Rather, the protection applies to any indictment or information charging a person with any statutory or common-law felony or misdemeanor sanctioned by death, imprisonment, or fine.[24] Under modern doctrine, the double-jeopardy protection has been incorporated against the states.[25]

Current double-jeopardy jurisprudence addresses five primary issues. Specifically:

Which sovereign's law applies? The clause protects against "separate prosecutions for the same offense."[26] Because "an 'offence' is defined by a law, and each law is defined by a sovereign," the Supreme Court has held that a defendant may be prosecuted under the laws of separate sovereigns for the same conduct.[27] However, this "separate sovereigns" exception has been called into question as against the original understanding of the protection.[28] Governments are separate sovereigns under the clause if they derive their power to prosecute "from wholly independent sources."[29] Because the federal government and the states are separate sovereigns, the clause does not prohibit a federal prosecution after a state prosecution,[30] and vice versa.[31] The clause also does not prohibit successive prosecutions by different states.[32] But it does prohibit successive prosecutions by the state and a local government within that state or two local governments in the same state, because each derives its sovereignty from a common source—the state constitution.[33] Although Indian tribes are sovereigns, allowing separate prosecutions,[34] American territories are not.[35]

What is the charged "offense?" Modern criminal law is characterized by an "extraordinary proliferation of overlapping and related statutory offenses."[36] Double-jeopardy protection depends on carefully ascertaining what is the "allowable unit of prosecution."[37] Few limits, if any, "are imposed by the Double Jeopardy Clause on the legislative power to define

offenses,"[38] but once a legislature defines that proscription, courts "determine[] the scope of protection afforded by a prior conviction or acquittal."[39] To ascertain whether two statutory offenses are the same "offense" for double-jeopardy purposes, the Supreme Court has instituted a multi-element test that determines whether each "offense" contains an element that is not common to the other.[40]

When does jeopardy attach? In other words, how much of a trial has to occur before a new prosecution becomes impermissible?[41] Jeopardy attaches in a bench trial when the first witness is sworn; it attaches in a jury trial when the jury is sworn.[42] An acquittal—a decision of not guilty on the facts—ends the trial.[43] Whether there is an acquittal turns on whether there is a verdict that the prosecution failed to establish criminal liability.[44] Such a verdict—if accepted by the court—is an acquittal even if it is inconsistent with other verdicts.[45]

What punishment is covered? A sanction only counts for double-jeopardy purposes if it is a criminal "punishment."[46] Generally, whether a sanction qualifies depends on the governing statute.[47] In other words, the statute must define a punitive measure as the punishment for a crime for the sanction to fall under the clause; accordingly, not every punitive measure qualifies. For example, the government may seize property used in furtherance of criminal activity (a process called civil forfeiture) even if the defendant has been prosecuted for—and acquitted of—the same conduct that is the basis for the civil forfeiture.[48] It may do so because Congress has authorized parallel civil forfeiture and criminal prosecutions since the Founding, and civil forfeiture proceeds against the property at issue (because of its role in the criminal conduct), not the individual who used it.[49] By contrast, the government may not specially tax criminal conduct and also prosecute a person for that conduct, because the aim of the tax is purely to punish, not to raise revenue.[50] Because the taxed conduct "is completely forbidden," the tax is another means of criminalizing the same activity that the criminal statute criminalizes, so the government may not bring a proceeding to collect the tax after bringing a prosecution; otherwise, it would violate the clause.[51]

When is a retrial allowed? The clause does

not absolutely prohibit retrials.[52] Retrial is generally permissible when a trial terminates for reasons unrelated to the defendant's criminal culpability.[53] A retrial is permissible when a defendant requests a mistrial or when there is a "manifest necessity."[54] A manifest necessity exists, for example, if the jury deadlocks or is unduly influenced by defense counsel's misconduct.[55] A defendant who successfully appeals his conviction for a lesser charge (such as manslaughter) cannot be retried on a greater charge (such as murder).[56] A new trial is not permitted when a defendant successfully challenges his conviction for insufficient evidence; this appellate victory operates as an acquittal.[57] But a new trial is permitted when an appellate court reverses a conviction for improper venue because the reversal did not resolve criminal culpability.[58]

OPEN QUESTIONS

- *Denezpi v. United States* (2022) held that the clause allowed the same sovereign—the federal government—to prosecute a defendant for violating *federal* law after it prosecuted him for violating *tribal* law.[59] What are the implications of this decision?
- Given the increased attention paid to civil forfeiture in recent years, will the Court revisit the line between civil and criminal punishments?
- Because there is evidence that the original double-jeopardy protection applied only to capital offenses, will the Court revisit *Ex parte Lange* (1873), which held that the clause applied to *all* offenses?[60]

Cite as: Judge Timothy M. Tymkovich & Adam Steinhilber, *The Double Jeopardy Clause, in* THE HERITAGE GUIDE TO THE CONSTITUTION 641 (Josh Blackman & John G. Malcolm eds., 3d ed. 2025).

Notes

1. *Benton v. Maryland*, 395 U.S. 784, 795 (1969); David S. Rudstein, *A Brief History of the Fifth Amendment Guarantee Against Double Jeopardy*, 14 Wm. & Mary Bill Rts. J. 193, 196–204 (2005). **2.** 4 Blackstone 335. **3.** *United States v. Scott*, 437 U.S. 82, 87 (1978). **4.** Stephen N. Limbaugh, Jr., *The Case of* Ex Parte Lange *(or How the Double Jeopardy Clause Lost Its "Life or Limb")*, 36 Am. Crim. L. Rev. 53, 63–64 (1999). **5.** Rudstein, *supra* at 221–22. **6.** *Id.* at 223–25. **7.** Arthur P. Scott, Criminal Law in Colonial Virginia 81–82 (1930). **8.** Rudstein, *supra* at 223–24. **9.** *Id.* at 224. **10.** *Id.* at 223; N.H. Const. of 1784, pt. 1, art. XVI. **11.** Rudstein, *supra* at 223. **12.** Storing 2.9.171. **13.** Address of the Antifederalist Minority of the Maryland Convention (May 1, 1788), *in* 12 DHRC 659, 665. **14.** N.Y. Decl. of Rts., Form of Ratification, and Recommendatory Amendments to the Constitution (July 26, 1788), *in* 23 DHRC 2326, 2327. **15.** 1 Annals of Cong. 781–82 (1789); *id.* at 451–52. **16.** N. Bailey, Dictionarium Britannicum (2d ed. 1736); 2 Richard Burn & John Burn, *A New Law Dictionary* 167 (1792). **17.** 1 Annals of Cong., *supra* at 781–82. **18.** *Id.* at 782. **19.** *Id.* **20.** *Id.* **21.** S. Jour., 1st Cong., 1st Sess. 71, 77 (Sept. 4 & 11, 1789); Rudstein, *supra* at 230–32. **22.** *Monge v. California*, 524 U.S. 721, 727–28 (1998). **23.** Limbaugh, *supra* at 65–66. **24.** *Ex parte Lange*, 85 U.S. (18 Wall.) 163, 168–73 (1873); Akhil Reed Amar, *Double Jeopardy Law Made Simple*, 106 Yale L.J. 1807, 1810–12 (1997). **25.** *Benton*, 395 U.S. at 787. **26.** *Denezpi v. United States*, 596 U.S. 591, 594 (2022). **27.** *Gamble v. United States*, 587 U.S. 678, 683–84 (2019).

28. *Id.* at 745–53 (Gorsuch, J., dissenting). **29.** *Puerto Rico v. Sanchez Valle*, 579 U.S. 59, 68 (2016). **30.** *Gamble*, 587 U.S. at 687–90. **31.** *Bartkus v. Illinois*, 359 U.S. 121, 132 (1959). **32.** *Heath v. Alabama*, 474 U.S. 82, 88 (1985). **33.** *Waller v. Florida*, 397 U.S. 387, 393 (1970). **34.** *Denezpi*, 596 U.S. at 598–99. **35.** *Sanchez Valle*, 579 U.S. at 71–73. **36.** *Ashe v. Swenson*, 397 U.S. 436, 445 n.10 (1970). **37.** *Sanabria v. United States*, 437 U.S. 54, 69–70 (1978). **38.** *Id.* at 69. **39.** *Id.* at 70. **40.** *Blockburger v. United States*, 284 U.S. 299, 304 (1932). **41.** *United States v. Martin Linen Supply Co.*, 430 U.S. 564, 569 (1977). **42.** *Serfass v. United States*, 420 U.S. 377, 388 (1975). **43.** *Fong Foo v. United States*, 369 U.S. 141, 143 (1962); *Smith v. Massachusetts,* 543 U.S. 462, 467 (2005). **44.** *McElrath v. Georgia*, 601 U.S. 87, 96 (2024). **45.** *Id.* at 97. **46.** *Hudson v. United States*, 522 U.S. 93, 98–99 (1997). **47.** *Id.* at 99–100. **48.** *United States v. Ursery*, 518 U.S. 267, 287–88 (1996). **49.** *Id.* at 274–75. **50.** *Dep't of Revenue of Mont. v. Kurth Ranch*, 511 U.S. 767, 781–83 (1994). **51.** *Id.* at 778, 782. **52.** *Oregon v. Kennedy*, 456 U.S. 667, 671–73 (1982). **53.** *Smith v. United States*, 599 U.S. 236, 252–54 (2023). **54.** *Kennedy*, 456 U.S. at 671–73; *United States v. Perez*, 22 U.S. (9 Wheat.) 579, 580 (1824). **55.** *Arizona v. Washington*, 434 U.S. 497, 509–10 (1978). **56.** *Price v. Georgia*, 398 U.S. 323, 326–27 (1970). **57.** *Burks v. United States*, 437 U.S. 1, 18 (1978). **58.** *Smith*, 599 U.S. at 253–54. **59.** 596 U.S. at 615–16 (Gorsuch, J., dissenting). **60.** Limbaugh, *supra* at 66–68.

ESSAY NO. 171: THE SELF-INCRIMINATION CLAUSE
AMEND. 5

. . . nor shall [any person] be compelled in any criminal case to be a witness against himself. . . .

—Paul G. Cassell

INTRODUCTION

In the continental European tradition, suspects were often forced to testify against themselves, sometimes through torture. In England, witnesses were questioned while under oath *ex officio* before the notorious courts of the High Commission and the Star Chamber.[1] The oath required the witness to answer all questions truthfully and was used to persecute political and religious dissenters. These proceedings had the odious effect of forcing devout individuals to choose between admitting crimes, to be followed by hanging, or denying crimes, to be followed by damnation. The privilege against self-incrimination in the Fifth Amendment reflects the Framers' determination to avoid these abuses.

HISTORY BEFORE 1787

The *ius commune* (customary European law) contained a rule against forced self-incrimination, and the earliest clear statement of the privilege in the legal life of England sprang from this continental source.[2] Defense attorneys also played an important role in developing a more adversarial system of justice. Through the eighteenth century, the advent of defense counsel and a reconstruction of the criminal trial as involving adversary criminal procedure laid the groundwork for a privilege against self-incrimination.[3] At the start of the eighteenth century, as a development of English common law, the practice of examining the accused at trial ended in English and, by extension, colonial courts.[4] Around the same time, English common-law developments meant that defendants were prohibited from providing testimony at trial on the ground that they were disqualified to testify as interested parties.[5]

These practices concerned only the defendant's testimony at trial, but the accused remained an important source of evidence because he could be questioned before trial and the results of that questioning could be used at trial. The general practice in both England and the American colonies was that constables who made arrests would bring persons accused of felonies before justices of the peace for questioning.[6] The results of such "preliminary examinations" were important sources of evidence. However, reflecting the understanding of a right against self-incrimination, the judicial officer conducting the questioning could not question a suspect under oath or use means of torture or threats of imprisonment.[7]

In America, codifying the privilege against self-incrimination began in Virginia. Section 8 of the 1776 Declaration of Rights provided that "in all capital or criminal prosecutions a man hath a right [not to] be compelled to give evidence against himself."[8] This provision became the model for other states, many of which adopted comparable declarations of rights essentially tracking the Virginia language.[9]

THE CONSTITUTIONAL CONVENTION AND RATIFICATION DEBATES

The Philadelphia Convention drafted a proposed Constitution without a bill of rights. Accordingly, the proposed Constitution made no reference to (among other things) a right against self-incrimination.

This omission was the subject of attack by Anti-Federalists. At the Virginia ratifying convention, Patrick Henry gave a fiery speech. He objected that, in the absence of a bill of rights, "Congress may introduce the practice of the civil law, in preference to that of the common law. They may introduce the practice of France,

Spain, and Germany—of torturing, to extort a confession of the crime."[10]

ADOPTION OF THE FIFTH AMENDMENT

The First Congress responded to such concerns. On June 8, 1789, Representative James Madison of Virginia proposed language that later became the Fifth Amendment. Madison's draft provided that "[n]o person . . . shall be compelled to be a witness against himself . . . ."[11] The language differed only slightly from the Virginia provision, which barred "giv[ing] evidence" against oneself. Madison's text suggested that the privilege applied in both criminal and civil cases.

Representative John Lawrence of New York addressed the proposal that "a person shall not be compelled to give evidence against himself."[12] Lawrence used the language from the Virginia Declaration of Rights.[13] Lawrence described the proposal as "a general declaration in some degree contrary to laws passed" and argued that it should "be confined to criminal cases."[14] He was likely referring to Section 15 of the Judiciary Act of 1789, which contained provisions requiring civil litigants to produce their books or papers containing evidence.[15] Lawrence proposed an amendment restricting the clause to criminal cases. The House adopted the amendment without discussion and then adopted the clause as amended unanimously.[16] The text provided: "nor shall [any person] be compelled in any criminal case to be a witness against himself." The Senate did not change the clause, and this provision was ultimately adopted.

THE PRIVILEGE IN THE EARLY REPUBLIC

After the Fifth Amendment was ratified, courts began to apply the Self-Incrimination Clause in judicial proceedings. In two foundational cases, Chief Justice John Marshall permitted third-party witnesses, who were not the defendants, to claim the privilege. In *Marbury v. Madison* (1803), Marshall ruled that a witness (Attorney General Levi Lincoln) was not "obliged to state any thing which would criminate himself."[17] In the 1807 treason trial of Aaron Burr, Marshall, while riding circuit, ruled that Burr's secretary was required to answer a government question about the plot but on the ground that the answer to the narrowly formulated question could not incriminate the secretary.[18]

THE PRIVILEGE AND PRODUCTION OF DOCUMENTS

The right against self-incrimination does not attach only to in-person testimony. For a time, the Court extended the privilege to the production of documents. *Boyd v. United States* (1886) held that the privilege protected private books and papers.[19] This decision conceived of the right as a way to promote privacy of property. Somewhat relatedly, *Hale v. Henkel* (1906) rejected the claim that a corporation could assert the privilege and said that it must surrender its corporate records.[20]

Fisher v. United States (1976) departed from *Boyd* and held that the Fifth Amendment does not protect against production of private papers unless official compulsion forced the defendant to create the documents.[21] The Court explained that it could not "cut the Fifth Amendment completely loose from the moorings of its language[]." Justice Byron White's majority opinion would not make the privilege "serve as a general protector of privacy, [a] word not mentioned in its text and a concept directly addressed in the Fourth Amendment."[22] The Fifth Amendment, the Court held, protects against "compelled" testimony, "not the disclosure of private information."[23]

THE PRIVILEGE AND IMMUNITY

Immunity is a promise from the government not to use the compelled information against the defendant. Evidence produced under a court immunity order is not incriminating, and therefore a witness cannot assert the privilege. The government may grant a witness *transactional* immunity or *use* immunity. Transactional immunity bars *any* prosecution for the conduct to which the testimony relates. Use immunity permits the government to prosecute the witness but only after proving that the prosecution has made no use of the compelled testimony or any evidence derived from it. Typically, the prosecution will exhaust all other avenues of investigation before applying for a use immunity order, and the supporting affidavit will describe in detail the evidence the prosecution has assembled before compelling testimony.

Brown v. Walker (1896) upheld a federal law that allowed a court to compel a witness's testimony if the witness was granted transactional immunity.[24] The Supreme Court, however, has held that only use immunity is needed to prevent a witness from invoking the privilege.[25]

THE PRIVILEGE AND *MIRANDA*

During the first half of the twentieth century, the Court decided many cases involving the "voluntariness" of confession based on the Due Process Clause, including *Brown v. Mississippi* (1936).[26] However, the Court did not consider the Fifth Amendment to have relevance to police questioning. This would change with *Malloy v. Hogan* (1964), which incorporated the privilege against self-incrimination against the states.[27]

Two years later, in *Miranda v. Arizona* (1966), the Court departed significantly from historical understandings and applied the Self-Incrimination Clause expansively to regulate police questioning. By a vote of 5 to 4, *Miranda* held that "without proper safeguards the process of in-custody interrogation of persons suspected or accused of crime contains inherently compelling pressures which work to undermine the individual's will to resist and to compel him to speak where he would not otherwise do so freely."[28] Justice Byron White's dissent contended that the majority decision had "no significant support in the history of the privilege or in the language of the Fifth Amendment."[29] Chief Justice Earl Warren's majority opinion

resulted in a warning-and-waiver regime. Under this decision, police must provide the famous *Miranda* warnings in order to use a suspect's confession at trial.

Reaction to *Miranda* was swift. In 1968, Congress "repealed" *Miranda*. The statute made police delivery of warnings to be only a factor in determining whether to admit a confession rather than a requirement as *Miranda* had held.[30] That law fell into desuetude as federal law enforcement agencies routinely delivered *Miranda* warnings to suspects. In *Dickerson v. United States* (2000), the Supreme Court declared the statute unconstitutional, although the majority appeared to concede that the Constitution itself did not require the *Miranda* rule.[31] (Your author argued *Dickerson* as *amicus curiae*.)

The Court has created many exceptions to *Miranda*. *New York v. Quarles* (1984) allowed the police to depart from the *Miranda* regime in "public safety" situations.[32] *Oregon v. Elstad* (1985) held that police were free to use the "fruits" of a confession that had been obtained in violation of the *Miranda* procedures.[33] Where police violated the Self-Incrimination Clause directly by obtaining a coerced confession, the government may not use that confession or any evidence that is the fruit of that confession. If, however, the original illegality is a mere violation of the *Miranda* rule, then the government may use any evidence that is the fruit of the violation. Under current doctrine, violating *Miranda* means violating only a prophylactic rule, not a right secured by the Constitution.[34]

OPEN QUESTIONS

- In light of subsequent, narrowing interpretations of *Miranda*, the net effect of the rules on police effectiveness remains disputed.[35] Might the Court, which is more focused on the original meaning of the clause, overrule *Miranda*?
- Can police compel suspects to assist in unlocking cell phones? Compelling a suspect to use his fingerprint to unlock a cell phone might not be "testimonial" and thus outside Fifth Amendment protection. By contrast, a court order requiring a suspect to disclose a password might be viewed as requiring a suspect to say what is "in his or her mind" and thus is a violation of the Fifth Amendment.

Cite as: Paul G. Cassell, *The Self-Incrimination Clause*, in THE HERITAGE GUIDE TO THE CONSTITUTION 645 (Josh Blackman & John G. Malcolm eds., 3d ed. 2025).

Notes

1. Leonard W. Levy, Origins of the Fifth Amendment: The Right Against-Self Incrimination (1968); John Henry Wigmore, Treatise on the Anglo-American System of Evidence in Trials at Common Law (3d ed. 1940). **2.** R.H. Helmholz, *Origins of the Privilege Against Self-Incrimination: The Role of the European* Ius Commune, 65 N.Y.U. L. Rev. 962 (1990). **3.** John H. Langbein, *The Historical Origins of the Privilege Against Self-Incrimination at Common Law*, 92 Mich. L. Rev. 1047 (1994); Leonard W. Levy, *Origins of the Fifth Amendment and Its Critics*, 19 Cardozo L. Rev. 821 (1997). **4.** Off. of Legal Pol'y, U.S. Dep't of Justice, Report to the Attorney General on the Law of Pretrial Interrogation (Feb. 12, 1986), *reprinted in* 22 Mich. J. L. Ref. 437, 455–57 (1989); E.M. Morgan, *The Privilege Against Self-Incrimination*, 34 Mich. L. Rev. 1, 9–11 (1949). **5.** 22 Minn. J. L. Ref., *supra* at 456. **6.** *Id.* at 457–59. **7.** *Id.* at 458–58. **8.** Virginia Bill of Rights of 1776, § 8. **9.** Mass. Const. of 1780, part I, art. XII; Penn. Const. of 1776, Decl. of Rts., art. IX; N.C. Const. of 1776, Decl. of Rts., art. VII; Levy, *Origins, supra* at 405–07. **10.** 3 Elliot's 447–48.

11. 1 Annals of Cong. 451–52 (1789). **12.** 1 Annals of Cong. 782 (1789). **13.** Levy, *supra* at 424. **14.** 1 Annals of Cong. 782 (1789). **15.** 1 Stat. 73, 82; Charles Warren, *New Light on the History of the Federal Judiciary Act of 1789*, 37 Harv. L. Rev. 49, 95 (1923). **16.** 1 Annals of Cong. 782 (1789). **17.** *Marbury v. Madison*, 5 U.S. 137, 144 (1803). **18.** Orin S. Kerr, *Decryption Originalism: The Lessons of* Burr, 134 Harv. L. Rev. 905, 941–46 (2021). **19.** 116 U.S. 616 (1886). **20.** *Brown v. Walker*, 161 U.S. 591 (1896); *Hale v. Henkel*, 201 U.S. 43 (1906). **21.** *Fisher v. United States*, 425 U.S. 391 (1976). **22.** *Id.* at 401. **23.** *Id.* **24.** 161 U.S. 591 (1896). **25.** *Kastigar v. U.S.*, 406 U.S. 441 (1972). **26.** 297 U.S. 278 (1936). **27.** *Malloy v. Hogan*, 378 U.S. 1 (1964). **28.** 384 U.S. 436, 467 (1966). **29.** *Id.* at 527 (White, J., dissenting). **30.** 18 U.S.C. § 3501. **31.** 530 U.S. 428 (2000). **32.** 467 U.S 649 (1984). **33.** 470 U.S. 298 (1985). **34.** *Vega v. Tekoh*, 597 U.S. 134 (2022). **35.** Paul G. Cassell & Richard Fowles, *Still Handcuffing the Cops? A Review of Fifty Years of Empirical Evidence of* Miranda's *Harmful Effects on Law Enforcement*, 97 B.U.L. Rev. 685 (2017).

ESSAY NO. 172: THE DUE PROCESS CLAUSE
AMEND. 5

. . . nor [shall any person] be deprived of life, liberty, or property, without due process of law . . .

—Gary S. Lawson

INTRODUCTION

The Due Process of Law Clauses in the Fifth and Fourteenth Amendments have emerged as sources of many "hot-button" constitutional cases. That would have surprised Founding-era drafters and ratifiers of the Fifth Amendment. The clause was a technical provision that added little to the constraints on executive and judicial power implicit in those functions in the Constitution of 1788. The U.S. Supreme Court did not decide a case involving the meaning of "due process of law" until 1856. Over the past 150 years, however, the Fifth Amendment's Due Process of Law Clause has become a key source of procedural limits on federal, executive, and judicial action.

HISTORY BEFORE 1789

Article 39 of Magna Carta (1215) proclaimed that "no free man shall be taken or imprisoned or disseised or outlawed or exiled or in any way ruined, nor will we go or send against him, except by the lawful judgment of his peers or by the law of the land." This "law of the land" requirement is sometimes known as the principle of legality. The article imposed limits on the powers of the king and his agents, including judges, who were considered executive agents. These government officials could not take unilateral, arbitrary action against certain protected private interests. Executive deprivations of such interests could take place only pursuant to valid legal authority. This principle of legality remained a bedrock of Anglo-American law for centuries.

The specific phrase "due process of law" made its first appearance in a 1354 statute concerning court procedures.[1] "Due process of law" at that time narrowly meant that judgments could issue only when the defendant was personally given the opportunity to appear in court pursuant to an appropriate writ. Specifically, the defendant was served, or provided with the *process* that was *due* under the *law*. The phrase retained this technical meaning in English law through the colonial era.[2]

In 1642, Sir Edward Coke discussed the Law of the Land in his *Institutes of the Lawes of England*. Coke observed that under Article 29, a person could not be "dispossessed of his free-hold (that is) lands, or livelihood, or of his liberties . . . as belong to him by his free birth-right, unlesse it be by the lawfull judgement, that is, verdict of his equals (that is, of men of his own condition) or by the Law of the Land (that is, to speak it once for all) by the due course, and processe of Law."[3]

After independence, the majority of state constitutions contained clauses that restrained the government from depriving persons of protected interests except pursuant to "the law of the land."[4] For example, the New York constitution of 1777 provided that "no member of this State shall be disenfranchised, or deprived of any of the rights or privileges secured to the subjects of this State by this constitution, unless by the law of the land, or the judgment of his peers."[5] The Massachusetts constitution of 1780 similarly declared that "no subject shall be . . . deprived of his life, liberty, or estate; but by the judgment of his peers, or the law of the land."[6] Other charters included the phrase "due course of law" (describing the procedures employed by the law once process was properly served) and "law of the land" (describing the source and content of legal norms).[7]

In February 1787, Alexander Hamilton discussed the Law of the Land Clause in remarks to the New York Assembly.[8] Citing Coke, he explained that law of the land "mean[s] presentment and indictment, and process of outlawry, as contradistinguished from trial by jury."[9]

ADOPTION OF THE FIFTH AMENDMENT

The federal Constitution did not include a law of the land clause, but the Supremacy Clause in Article VI did provide that certain types of federal law were the "supreme Law of the Land." The absence of a law of the land clause was not a subject of meaningful discussion during the ratification debates. The Minority of the Convention of Pennsylvania, however, proposed such an amendment to the federal Constitution that mirrored language from the Pennsylvania state constitution: "no man be deprived of his liberty, except by the law of the land or the judgment of his peers."[10]

In 1789, the First Congress proposed what would become the Due Process Clause.[11] The proposal tracked the form of the state constitutions but used "due process of law" instead of "law of the land." The reasons for this difference are uncertain. Professor Ryan Williams has observed that the drafting and ratification history of the Fifth Amendment's Due Process of Law Clause is "notoriously sparse,"[12] and "[t]here was no commentary or debate about the text that became the Fifth Amendment Due Process Clause."[13] Nonetheless, "due process of law" was distinct from both "due course of law" and "law of the land."[14] Founding-era figures and state court judges often referred to limits on arbitrary executive, judicial, or legislative power, but it is very difficult to tie those discussions to the specific language found in the Fifth Amendment rather than to these broader concepts of due course of law or the law of the land.

ORIGINAL MEANING OF THE DUE PROCESS CLAUSE

The Fifth Amendment was ratified without any meaningful debate or controversy. It is extremely unlikely that this provision was the source of foundational principles of governmental action. Professors Nathan Chapman and Michael McConnell explain that when "the Fifth Amendment was enacted, everyone agreed . . . that the executive could not deprive anyone of a right except as authorized by law."[15]

Consider a hypothetical: Before ratification of the Fifth Amendment, could the President arbitrarily and without legal authorization seize persons or property, and could federal courts conduct secret *ex parte* trials without notice? There is no evidence that this was the general understanding of the federal government's powers. Instead, basic norms of procedure and separation of powers were implicit in the concepts of "executive Power" and "judicial Power."[16] As with most of the Bill of Rights, the Due Process of Law Clause clarified understandings that were already built into the Constitution's enumerations of institutional powers. For example, courts at the time grounded a notice requirement in "general law" without mentioning the Fifth Amendment.[17]

To the extent that the Fifth Amendment's text rather than background principles of executive and judicial power is a source of rights, due process of law applies only to deprivations of "life, liberty, or property." In 1791, the meaning of "liberty" as a personal right was clear. Sir William Blackstone wrote that the right to liberty meant "the power of locomotion, of changing situation, or removing one's person to whatsoever place one's own inclination may direct; without imprisonment or restraint, unless by due course of law."[18] That definition is quite narrow and focused on freedom of movement. Liberty did not include such interests as bodily integrity or reputation; they were encompassed by Blackstone's definition of "life," which referred not merely to an execution, but to an array of rights lumped together under the general heading of personal security: "a person's legal and uninterrupted enjoyment of his life, his limbs, his body, his health, and his reputation."[19]

The term "property" was more ambiguous. It could have referred to land, land plus chattels, or anything of exchangeable value. Perhaps the best definition was whatever interests a court would have recognized as property. None of these understandings would include government benefits. The law sharply distinguished between property rights and privileges that the government could continue or terminate at its pleasure.[20]

EARLY COMMENTARY AND PRECEDENT

Justice Joseph Story in his *Commentaries* equated due process of law with the law of the land, relying on Coke's *Institutes*. However, Story expanded Coke's account beyond initiation of actions to include "the processes and proceedings of the common law."[21] A quarter-century later, *Murray's Lessee v. Hoboken Land & Improvement Co.* (1856) was the Supreme Court's first case construing "due process of law."[22] The Court essentially adopted and extended Story's broader account of the phrase. The Due Process Clause was read as "a restraint on the legislative as well as on the executive and judicial powers of the government."[23] Moreover,

this provision codified "those settled usages and modes of proceeding existing in the common and statute law of England."[24] The lines among due process of law, due course of law, and law of the land were blurred—and that conflation continues to this day.

In 1868, the Fourteenth Amendment added a due process of law clause applicable to the states almost identical to the Fifth Amendment clause applicable to the federal government. (See Essay No. 172.) It is not obvious that the two clauses, enacted in different contexts eighty years apart, would necessarily have the same meaning. In 1901, the Supreme Court raised the possibility of different meanings.[25] Since then, however, courts have treated the two clauses as having the same meaning.

The Fourteenth Amendment's Due Process of Law Clause was treated originally as a source of procedural restraints on state *administrative* action but was not confined to that context.[26] When the executive and judicial branches deprive people of life, liberty, and property, they must employ fair procedures. Moreover, legislatures cannot create novel forms of adjudication that depart too far from traditional models. Some of these results follow from the unamended text of the 1788 Constitution and the essential meaning of executive or judicial power, but locating them in the Fifth Amendment and conforming that meaning to the interpretation of the Fourteenth Amendment has resulted in a complex doctrinal structure that does not necessarily track original meaning.

MODERN UNDERSTANDINGS OF LIFE, LIBERTY, AND PROPERTY

The modern understanding of "life, liberty, or property" has changed dramatically since 1791. Each term now means something different from the Blackstonian understanding of the Founding era. "Life" has been narrowed to include only governmental killings rather than the full range of Blackstonian interests such as physical integrity and reputation. This change has happened by default rather than by express decision. Because some of those interests are obviously among the clause's concerns, this narrowing of "life" has led to some expansion of "liberty" and "property."

In *Meyer v. Nebraska* (1923), the Supreme

Court understood the concept of "liberty" as "not merely freedom from bodily restraint." Rather, it embraced "the right of the individual to contract, to engage in any of the common occupations of life, to acquire useful knowledge, to marry, establish a home and bring up children, to worship God according to the dictates of his own conscience, and generally to enjoy those privileges long recognized . . . as essential to the orderly pursuit of happiness by free men."[27]

The Court's expansion of the concept of "liberty" reached its apogee in *Planned Parenthood v. Casey* (1992). Three justices declared that "[a]t the heart of liberty is the right to define one's own concept of existence, of meaning, of the universe, and of the mystery of human life."[28] *Casey*, however, was overruled by *Dobbs v. Jackson Women's Health Org.* (2022).[29] The precise contours of the Court's conception of "liberty" remain unsettled. They include, for example, freedom from corporal punishment in schools.[30] But liberty does not include a right to have non-citizen spouses admitted to the country.[31] Special, more restrictive doctrines apply to ascertaining whether prison conditions implicate liberty interests.[32]

Board of Regents of State Colleges v. Roth (1972) ruled that "property" would not be construed in accordance with its original meaning.[33] Rather, the meaning of "property" would include an extended range of interests, including government benefits, that are recognized in prior case law. Specifically, such "entitlements" are constructed through statutes and regulations that specify a clear causal connection between satisfaction of criteria for eligibility and receipt of a benefit. Legislatures can thus control to some extent whether benefits count as entitlements by giving executive agents more or less discretion in their administration. Administrators can also exercise control through their crafting of regulations. Some interests, however, such as an equity interest in a home, count as "property" regardless of legislative or regulatory specifications.[34]

PROCEDURAL DUE PROCESS

What process is due before the government deprives a person of life, liberty, or property?

Mathews v. Eldridge (1976) clarified that this "delicate process of judgment" generally requires consideration of several factors.[35] The Court (1) looks to the significance of the "private interest that will be affected by the official action;" (2) balances the "risk of an erroneous deprivation of such interest through the procedures used, and the probable value, if any, of additional or substitute procedural safeguards;" and (3) weighs the "Government's interest" and the "burdens that the additional or substitute procedural requirement would entail."[36] Subsequent case law treats this *Mathews* framework as the nearly exclusive vehicle for assessing procedural adequacy under the Due Process of Law Clause, though this is likely a misreading of the case.[37] A few areas, such as notice and criminal procedure, are analyzed outside this framework.[38]

LIMITS ON DUE PROCESS

There are several limits on application of the Due Process Clause. First, if an interest does not fall within the meaning of "life, liberty, or property," the Due Process Clause does not mandate any particular procedures for its deprivation. Second, the clause applies only to government action. Private entities are not bound by the Fifth Amendment, although difficult questions can arise when the acting entity is nominally private but involved in some fashion with the government. Third, the word "deprived" in the Due Process Clause refers to an intentional or reckless taking of a protected interest. Losses inflicted by government negligence do not implicate the Due Process Clause.[39]

Fourth—and most important—administrative agencies are responsible for the vast bulk of governmental actions that deprive people of their property, but large classes of agency action fall outside the clause's protection. When agencies make rules and function like a legislature, they are immune from the Due Process Clause.[40] However, when agencies adjudicate cases on a case-by-case basis, they are subject to the Due Process Clause. However, agencies are not subject to the same rules as courts. Procedures that would obviously be inadequate in judicial proceedings are considered constitutionally adequate for agency adjudication.

OPEN QUESTIONS

- Which procedures (if any) must come *before* the government deprives people of protected interests? The law in this area remains unsettled. There is a presumption in favor of pre-deprivation procedures that can be overcome when the value of such procedures would be low, the potential risks to the government or public from delaying the deprivation would be high, and/or the person deprived would have an adequate remedy after the deprivation.

- What counts as "liberty" and "property" for purposes of the Due Process of Law Clause by force of the Constitution itself without regard to legislative or executive specification?

- When is the adequacy of procedures for deprivations judged by something other than the three-part *Mathews* framework?

Cite as: Gary S. Lawson, *The Due Process of Law Clause, in* THE HERITAGE GUIDE TO THE CONSTITUTION 648 (Josh Blackman & John G. Malcolm eds., 3d ed. 2025).

Notes

1. 28 Edw. 3, ch. 3 (1354).   **2.** Max Crema & Lawrence W. Solum, *The Original Meaning of "Due Process of Law" in the Fifth Amendment,* 108 Va. L. Rev. 447, 481–83 (2022).   **3.** 2 The Selected Writings of Sir Edward Coke 849 (Steve Sheppard ed., 2003).   **4.** Robert E. Riggs, *Substantive Due Process in 1791,* 1990 Wisc. L. Rev. 941, 973–74.   **5.** N.Y. Const. of 1777, art. XIII.   **6.** Mass. Const. of 1780, part I, art. XII.   **7.** Crema & Solum, *supra* at 462.   **8.** Alexander Hamilton, Remarks on an Act for Regulating Elections, New York Assembly (Feb. 6, 1787), https://perma.cc /ARH9-UJXR.   **9.** *Id.*   **10.** Storing 3.11.13.   **11.** 1 Annals of Cong. 781 (1789).   **12.** Ryan Williams, *The One and Only Substantive Due Process Clause,* 120 Yale L. J. 408, 445 (2010).   **13.** Nathan S. Chapman & Michael W. McConnell, *Due Process as Separation of Powers,* 121 Yale L. J. 1672, 1723 (2012).   **14.** Crema & Solum, *supra* at 462.   **15.** Chapman & McConnell, *supra* at 1679; Gary Lawson, *Take the Fifth . . . Please! The Original Insignificance of the Fifth Amendment's Due Process of Law Clause,* 2017 BYU L. Rev. 611, 619–22 (2018).   **16.** Lawson, *supra* at 626–37.   **17.** *Hollingsworth v Barbour,* 29 U.S. (4 Pet.) 466, 472 (1830); Gary Lawson, *A Truism with Attitude: The Tenth Amendment in Constitutional Context,* 83 Notre Dame L. Rev. 469 (2008).   **18.** 1 Blackstone 134.   **19.** 1 Blackstone 129.   **20.** Paul J. Larkin, Jr., *The Original Understanding of "Property" in the Constitution,* 100 Marq. L. Rev. 1 (2016).   **21.** 3 Story's Commentaries § 1783.   **22.** 59 U.S. (18 How.) 272 (1856),   **23.** *Id.* at 276.   **24.** *Id.* at 277.   **25.** *French v. Barber Asphalt Paving Co.,* 181 U.S. 324, 328–29 (1901).   **26.** *Spencer v. Merchant,* 125 U.S. 345, 356 (1888).   **27.** *Meyer v. Nebraska,* 262 U.S. 390, 399 (1923).   **28.** *Planned Parenthood of Se. Pa. v. Casey,* 505 U.S. 833, 851 (1992).   **29.** 597 U.S. 215 (2022).   **30.** *Ingraham v. Wright,* 430 U.S. 651 (1977).   **31.** *Dep't of State v. Munoz,* 602 U.S. 899 (2024).   **32.** *Sandin v. Conner,* 515 U.S. 472 (1995).   **33.** 408 U.S. 564 (1972).   **34.** *Tyler v. Hennepin Cnty., Minn.,* 598 U.S. 631 (2023).   **35.** 424 U.S. 319 (1976).   **36.** *Id.* at 335.   **37.** Gary Lawson, Katharine Ferguson & Guillermo Montero, *"Oh Lord, Please Don't Let Me Be Misunderstood!": Rediscovering the* Mathews v. Eldridge *and* Penn Central *Frameworks,* 81 Notre Dame L. Rev. 1, 15–19 (2005).   **38.** Gary Lawson, Federal Administrative Law 985–86 (10th ed. 2025).   **39.** *Daniels v. Williams,* 474 U.S. 327, 333 (1986).   **40.** *Bi-Metallic Inv. Co. v. State Bd. of Equalization of Colo.,* 239 U.S. 441 (1915).

ESSAY NO. 173: THE TAKINGS CLAUSE
AMEND. 5

. . . nor shall private property be taken for public use, without just compensation.
—William Baude & Sarah Leitner

INTRODUCTION

Once an uncontroversial part of the Constitution, the Takings Clause is now one of the Constitution's most important protections for private property rights. On its face, the Takings Clause imposes a simple requirement: If the government takes private property, it must pay for what it takes. Some takings are straightforward, such as when the government condemns a house using its power of eminent domain so that it can widen a road or build a courthouse. But other takings are less obvious, such as when the government changes property rights or passes a property regulation without a physical expropriation. This requires courts to decide what defines "property"; what counts as "taking" property, as well as the purposes for which it may be taken; and what constitutes "just compensation."

ORIGINS OF THE TAKINGS CLAUSE

Though the Takings Clause was in some ways an outlier when added to the Bill of Rights, there were a handful of precedents for the clause before ratification. The colonial charters of Massachusetts and the Carolinas, for example, both provided for some degree of compensation to an owner whose property was taken for public use.[1] Following independence, two states each adopted a proto-Takings Clause in their state constitutions. The Vermont constitution of 1777 provided that "whenever any particular man's property is taken for the use of the public, the owner ought to receive an equivalent in money."[2] And the Massachusetts constitution of 1780 expanded upon the guarantee contained in its original colonial charter by providing that "whenever the public exigencies require that the property of any individual should be appropriated to public uses, he shall receive a reasonable compensation therefor."[3]

In 1787, shortly before the Constitution was signed, the Articles of Confederation Congress adopted the Northwest Ordinance to govern the territories that were northwest of the Ohio River. There, Congress included a provision requiring "full compensation" when "public exigences" made it necessary "to take any person's property, or to demand his particular services."[4]

When it comes to the federal Constitution, however, the origins of the Takings Clause are surprisingly obscure. Most provisions of the Bill of Rights were requested in some form as the states ratified the original Constitution, but the Takings Clause was not.[5] Representative James Madison of Virginia added it for unexplained reasons as he sifted through the requested amendments to propose a slate of them.[6] In Congress and during the ratification debates,

there was virtually no recorded discussion about the Takings Clause itself.[7]

EARLY PRECEDENT

The origins of the Takings Clause are made still more enigmatic by the background of limited federal power. There is a good argument that the Constitution did not grant Congress a general power of eminent domain in the first place.[8] Before the Civil War, Congress generally relied upon the states to exercise eminent domain over land that it needed, and in 1845, the Supreme Court declared that "the United States have no constitutional capacity to exercise . . . eminent domain" in the states.[9] Congress exercised eminent domain only over property in federal territories. The federal government also took personal property under conditions of military necessity, but it is unclear how much can be gleaned from this historical practice.[10]

Meanwhile, in *Barron v. City of Baltimore* (1833), Chief Justice John Marshall held that the Takings Clause applied only to the federal government and not to the states, meaning that the states were not required by the federal Constitution to provide just compensation for takings of private property.[11] *Barron*, combined with limited federal power, meant that the clause did very little work in the century after its ratification.[12]

MODERN JUDICIAL PRECEDENT

Under modern doctrine, the Takings Clause is of much greater importance, and its zone of application is much broader. Beginning with *Kohl v. United States* (1875), the Supreme Court recognized a general federal power of eminent domain within the states.[13] The Court has alternately suggested that the power is granted by the Necessary and Proper Clause; that it is granted by implication of the Takings Clause itself; or that it is an inherent power of sovereignty, the specific enumeration of which is unnecessary.[14] Whatever its source, the power is seated in Congress, not the executive, and only Congress has the power to raise the revenues necessary for just compensation.[15]

Furthermore, *Chicago, Burlington & Quincy Railroad Co. v. Chicago* (1897) held that the Fourteenth Amendment's Due Process Clause requires a state to pay just compensation when it takes private property. The Court stated that "since the adoption of the fourteenth amendment, compensation for private property taken for public uses constitutes an essential element in [the] 'due process of law.'"[16] Although that decision did not expressly mention the Takings Clause, later cases have treated *Burlington & Quincy* as having incorporated the clause against the states.[17] In fact, this right was the first element of the Bill of Rights that was held to be part of the Fourteenth Amendment's Due Process requirement.

WHAT IS "PROPERTY"?

The Takings Clause is triggered only when the thing that was allegedly taken is in fact "property." This of course can include land, that is, *real* property. But it can also include *personal* property, such as bank accounts and raisins, or even *intangible* property, such as trade secrets.[18]

The Takings Clause does not itself define property, so courts draw on "existing rules or understandings" about property rights, including state law, traditional property law principles, historical practice, and precedent to discern the contours of a property interest.[19]

WHEN IS PROPERTY PHYSICALLY "TAKEN"?

There are a range of government actions that affect the value or use of property—some of which are clearly takings, and some of which are not. It is easiest to see that there has been a taking when the government formally "condemns" property and takes legal title to it. Such an exercise of eminent domain is the paradigmatic example of a taking.

But condemnation is not necessary to effectuate a physical taking. *Cedar Point Nursery v. Hassid* (2021) held that, even without formal condemnation, there is still a taking whenever the government physically appropriates private property.[20] The Supreme Court made an analogous ruling as early as 1871, concluding that a government-authorized flooding was a taking of property under Wisconsin state constitutional law.[21] This rule applies even if the government authorizes a permanent physical occupation of only a tiny part of the property, and even if the physical appropriation is only temporary.[22] Finally, the technical source of this kind

of taking is of no consequence: "Government action that physically appropriates property is no less a physical taking because it arises from a regulation."[23]

REGULATORY TAKINGS

Although regulations that physically appropriate property are *per se* takings, other regulations of land pose harder questions. In the early twentieth century, the Supreme Court created the so-called "regulatory takings" doctrine. In *Pennsylvania Coal Co. v. Mahon* (1922), Justice Oliver Wendell Holmes wrote that "while property may be regulated to a certain extent, if regulation goes too far it will be recognized as a taking."[24] This doctrine has been widely criticized for lacking a historical basis.[25]

Nevertheless, under modern doctrine, regulations of property are sometimes held to be takings. When a property regulation is challenged as a taking, the Court must usually engage in the "essentially ad hoc" determination of whether a taking has occurred. Under the framework set out in the landmark decision of *Penn Central Transportation Co. v. City of New York* (1978), courts must place particular emphasis on "the economic impact of the regulation on the claimant," the interference with "distinct investment-backed expectations," and "the character of the government action."[26] In practice, courts rarely find that a regulation qualifies as a taking under this test. And even before *Penn Central*, the Court held that zoning regulations would almost never be held to be takings of property.[27]

However, there are a few specific types of regulation that are categorically considered takings. One such category includes regulations of property that deprive an owner of all economically viable use of his or her land.[28] Another category includes regulations that unfairly condition the grant of a governmental permit upon the forfeiture of a physical property interest or the exaction of inappropriate fees.[29] And, as already mentioned above, a regulation that appropriates a right to invade private property is *per se* a taking.[30]

THE PUBLIC USE REQUIREMENT

So to implicate the Fifth Amendment's Takings Clause, the property at issue must actually be "property," and it must be "taken" within the meaning of the clause. But the Takings Clause imposes a third limitation: that "private property be taken *for public use.*"

As with the rest of the clause, the original meaning of this "public use" requirement is difficult to discern. Professor Richard Epstein has argued that as an original matter, the property taken must be usable by the public—either by a government entity or a private entity obligated to grant access on broad and neutral terms like a common carrier.[31] Many nineteenth-century state courts interpreted the requirement in this fashion. For example, courts allowed eminent domain for railroads to claim a right-of-way, or for mills that served the community to build dams that would flood neighboring property.[32]

Throughout the twentieth century, however, the Supreme Court has adopted a much broader reading of the "public use" requirement. The modern view requires only a public *purpose*, rather than that the property be usable by the public, and the Court has given deference to legislatures in defining that public purpose. For example, *Berman v. Parker* (1954) upheld the use of eminent domain to condemn blighted property for urban renewal. Justice William O. Douglas's majority opinion found that "the legislature, not the judiciary, is the main guardian of the public needs to be served by social legislation."[33] *Hawaii Housing Authority v. Midkiff* (1984) unanimously approved Hawaii's breakup of large, landed estates "to reduce the perceived social and economic evils of a land oligopoly traceable to their monarchs."[34]

More recently, *Kelo v. City of New London* (2005) allowed the government to take a private home to transfer it to a private corporation for purposes of economic development.[35] The majority infamously invoked the "diverse and always evolving needs of society" to conclude that governments have "broad latitude in determining what public needs justify the use of the takings power."[36] *Kelo* was a closely divided and extremely controversial decision, prompting Justice Sandra Day O'Connor to write in dissent: "The specter of condemnation hangs over all property."[37] The negative reaction to *Kelo* resulted in state laws designed to increase protection for property holders throughout much of the country.[38]

JUST COMPENSATION

When property has been taken for public use, the Takings Clause mandates the payment of "just compensation." At bottom, the exercise of eminent domain is a forced sale. The amount of this compensation is necessarily a case-specific inquiry, but as a guiding principle, the Court has said that the owner "is entitled to be put in as good a position pecuniarily as if his property had not been taken."[39] However, the Court has also said that "serious practical difficulties" preclude giving "this principle of indemnity . . . its full and literal force."[40] Instead, the owner is typically awarded the "fair market value" of his property even if that is less than his true loss.[41]

A few kinds of takings, as a matter of law, do not entitle the property owner to any kind of compensation. For example, a person cannot seek compensation if his property is confiscated or destroyed during military hostilities.[42] But when compensation is due, the amount awarded may well depend on whether a judge or jury awards it. The Supreme Court has said that "there is no constitutional right to a jury in eminent domain proceedings."[43] However, in the different context of a "regulatory taking," landowners do have the right to a jury trial.[44]

OPEN QUESTIONS

- What should be made of state court decisions that change the scope of property rights? Should such a "judicial taking" give rise to a claim under the Takings Clause? If so, what is the proper remedy?[45]
- *Cedar Point Nursery* adopted a very broad definition of what constitutes a physical appropriation. What kinds of government regulations will be held to physically appropriate property after *Cedar Point Nursery*, and what kinds will not? Is there a physical appropriation when the government requires access to "a business generally open to the public"?[46] What if a regulation reflects "traditional common law privileges to access private property"?[47] Are legitimate permitting conditions takings?[48]

- How should "just compensation" be calculated in situations where the fair market value does not accurately reflect the value of the taking? For instance, what if a market failure, such as a financial crisis, causes the "fair market value" to understate an owner's true loss?[49] On the other hand, what if the taking also produced collateral benefits to the owner, causing "fair market value" to overstate an owner's true loss?[50]

- Is the regulatory takings doctrine supported by the text and history of the Constitution? Many scholars, including John Hart and William Treanor, have argued that regulations of land at the Founding did not give rise to claims for compensation.[51] Professor Eric Claeys, by contrast, has argued that at least some kind of regulatory takings doctrine is supported by historical evidence, whereby regulations that infringed upon an owner's natural rights allegedly required compensation.[52] Professor Michael Rappaport has argued that the regulatory takings doctrine might be justified under the Fourteenth Amendment even if none was originally established by the Fifth Amendment.[53]

- In *Devillier v. Texas* (2024), the Supreme Court granted certiorari to decide the question of whether a person whose property is taken may seek compensation under the Takings Clause, even if the legislature has not affirmatively provided them with a cause of action.[54] But the Court ended up remanding the case to be decided under a Texas law cause of action. So the question remains: Does the Takings Clause provide a cause of action for compensation? If so, does it abrogate sovereign immunity?

The views and opinions expressed in this article are solely those of the authors. They do not purport to reflect the views or opinions of any entities or individuals with which Sarah Leitner is affiliated or that she represents.

Cite as: William Baude & Sarah Leitner, *The Takings Clause, in* THE HERITAGE GUIDE TO THE CONSTITUTION 652 (Josh Blackman & John G. Malcolm eds., 3d ed. 2025).

Notes

1. Massachusetts Body of Liberties § 8 (1641); Fundamental Constitutions of Carolina art. 44 (1669). **2.** Vt. Const. of 1777, ch. 1, § II. **3.** Mass. Const. of 1780, pt. 1, art. X. **4.** Northwest Ordinance of 1787, art. II. **5.** Edward Dumbauld, The Bill of Rights and What It Means Today 10–33, 53, 162 (item 14) (1957). **6.** *Id.* at 53 n.9. **7.** William Michael Treanor, *The Original Understanding of the Takings Clause and the Political Process*, 95 Colum. L. Rev. 782, 791, 835–36 (1995). **8.** William Baude, *Rethinking the Federal Eminent Domain Power*, 122 Yale L.J. 1738 (2013). **9.** *Pollard's Lessee v. Hagan*, 44 U.S. 212, 223 (1845). **10.** Baude, *supra* at 1780–85, 1799–1800. **11.** 32 U.S. 243 (1833). **12.** Baude, *supra* at 1762–66. **13.** 91 U.S. 367 (1875). **14.** *United States v. Gettysburg Electric Railway Co.*, 160 U.S. 668, 679 (1896); *Kohl*, 91 U.S. at 372–73; *U.S. v. Jones*, 109 U.S. 513, 518 (1883). **15.** Art. I, § 8, cl. 1; *Youngstown Sheet & Tube Co. v. Sawyer*, 343 U.S. 579, 631–32 (1952) (Douglas, J., concurring). **16.** 166 U.S. 226, 239 (1897). **17.** *Palazzolo v. Rhode Island*, 533 U.S. 606, 617 (2001). **18.** *Webb's Fabulous Pharmacies v. Beckwith*, 449 U.S. 155 (1980); *Horne v. Dept. of Agric.*, 576 U.S. 350 (2015); *Ruckelshaus v. Monsanto Co.*, 467 U.S. 986 (1984). **19.** *Tyler v. Hennepin Cnty.*, 598 U.S. 631, 638 (2023). **20.** 594 U.S. 139, 147 (2021). **21.** *Pumpelly v. Green Bay & Miss. Canal Co.*, 80 U.S. 166 (1871). **22.** *Loretto v. Teleprompter Manhattan CATV Corp.*, 458 U.S. 419 (1982); *Cedar Point*

Nursery, 594 U.S. at 151–52. **23.** *Cedar Point Nursery*, 594 U.S. at 149. **24.** *Pa. Coal Co. v. Mahon*, 260 U.S. 393, 415 (1922). **25.** John Hart, *Land Use Law in the Early Republic and the Original Meaning of the Takings Clause*, 94 Nw. U. L. Rev. 1099 (2000); *Murr v. Wisconsin*, 582 U.S. 383, 419 (Thomas, J., dissenting). **26.** 438 U.S. 104, 124 (1978). **27.** *Vill. of Euclid v. Ambler Realty Co.*, 272 U.S. 365 (1926). **28.** *Lucas v. S.C. Coastal Council*, 505 U.S. 1003 (1992). **29.** *Nollan v. Cal. Coastal Comm'n*, 483 U.S. 825 (1987); *Dolan v. City of Tigard*, 512 U.S. 374 (1994); *Koontz v. St. Johns River Water Mgmt. Dist.*, 570 U.S. 595 (2013); *Sheetz v. Cnty. of El Dorado, Cal.*, 601 U.S. 267 (2024). **30.** *Cedar Point Nursery*, 594 U.S. at 162. **31.** Richard Epstein, Takings: Private Property and the Power of Eminent Domain 168 (1985). **32.** Ilya Somin, The Grasping Hand: *Kelo v. City of New London* and the Limits of Eminent Domain 40 (2015). **33.** 348 U.S. 26, 32 (1954). **34.** 467 U.S. 229, 241–42 (1984). **35.** 545 U.S. 469 (2005). **36.** *Id.* at 479, 483. **37.** *Id.* at 503 (O'Connor, J., dissenting). **38.** Somin, *supra* at 135–64. **39.** *Olson v. United States*, 292 U.S. 246, 255 (1934). **40.** *United States v. 564.54 Acres of Land, More or Less*, 441 U.S. 506, 510–11 (1979). **41.** *Id.* **42.** *United States v. Caltex*, 344 U.S. 149 (1952). **43.** *United States v. Reynolds*, 397 U.S. 14, 18 (1970). **44.** *City of Monterey v. Del Monte Dunes at Monterey*, 526 U.S. 687 (1999). **45.** Barton Thompson, Jr., *Judicial Takings*, 76 Va. L. Rev.

1449 (1990); *Stop the Beach Renourishment, Inc. v. Fla. Dept. of Env't Prot.*, 560 U.S. 702 (2010). **46.** *Cedar Point*, 594 U.S. at 156–57. **47.** *Id.* at 160. **48.** *Id.* at 160–62. **49.** Eric A. Posner, Last Resort: The Financial Crisis and the Future of Bailouts 161–64 (2018). **50.** *Horne v. Dept. of Agric.*, 576 U.S. 350, 371–77 (2015) (Breyer, J., dissenting). **51.** Hart, *supra*; Treanor, *supra*. **52.** Eric Claeys, *Takings, Regulations, and Natural Property Rights*, 88 Cornell L. Rev. 1549 (2003). **53.** Michael Rappaport, *Originalism and Regulatory Takings: Why the Fifth Amendment May Not Protect Against Regulatory Takings, but the Fourteenth Amendment May*, 45 San Diego L. Rev. 729 (2008). **54.** 601 U.S. 285 (2024).

ESSAY NO. 174: THE SPEEDY TRIAL CLAUSE
AMEND. 6

In all criminal prosecutions, the accused shall enjoy the right to a speedy . . . trial. . . .

—Judge Andrew Brasher & Jack Tucker

INTRODUCTION

Three questions emerge from the text of the Speedy Trial Clause: (1) When is a person "accused" such that the right attaches? (2) What is meant by a "speedy . . . trial?" (3) What is the remedy for a violation of the right? Anglo-American legal history, the ratification debates, and early practice indicate that the right attaches on arrest, may be invoked by a petition for writ of habeas corpus, and protects against lengthy pretrial detention. Later decisions, especially modern doctrine, give the right broader contours.

HISTORY BEFORE 1787

The right to a speedy trial has ancient common-law roots. In 1166, King Henry II issued the Assize of Clarendon to provide protections for people who were arrested. Under the law, if a judge could not come quickly to try people who are arrested, a sheriff would send word to the nearest judge and bring the defendants to wherever the judge could try them.[1] Five decades later, the 1215 Magna Carta guaranteed that "we will not deny or delay to any man, either justice or right."[2]

The historical origins of the right to a speedy trial are connected to the writ of habeas corpus. Under the 1679 Habeas Corpus Act, on the last day of the court's term, judges were required to release a prisoner awaiting trial unless the delay was due to the inability of the prosecution's witnesses to testify that term. At the start of a second term, if the prisoner asked that he "be brought to his trial" and was not "indicted and tried the second term," the judge was required to "discharge" the prisoner "from his imprisonment."[3] Sir William Blackstone considered the Habeas Corpus Act and this protection to be a "second *magna carta*, and stable bulwark of our liberties."[4] He warned that the "confinement of the person, by secretly hurrying him to jail, where his sufferings are unknown or forgotten, is a less public, less striking, and therefore a more dangerous engine of arbitrary government" than even the arbitrary, but more public, taking of a person's life or property without due process.[5]

Before the Constitutional Convention, these deeply rooted protections from pretrial imprisonment carried over to the states. For example, Pennsylvania and Georgia adopted laws that were materially similar to the 1679 Habeas Corpus Act.[6] And the constitutions of Delaware and Maryland, among others, enshrined the more general right to a "speedy . . . trial."[7]

THE CONSTITUTIONAL CONVENTION AND RATIFICATION DEBATES

Despite the deep roots of a right to a speedy trial, the Framers did not include this protection in the Constitution. Article III guaranteed a right to jury in criminal trials, but the right to speedy trial was apparently not discussed at the Constitutional Convention. (See Essay No. 136.) Yet, the absence of this right was discussed during the ratification debates. At the Virginia ratifying convention, Edmund Randolph conceded that Article III's "defect . . . is, that there is no speedy trial."[8] At the Massachusetts Convention, Abraham Holmes expressed similar concern about Article

III's failure to guarantee the right to a speedy trial. Holmes feared that someone could be arrested and charged with a crime, "whether he is indicted by the grand jury or not," and undergo a "long, tedious painful imprisonment" before trial "until the next session of the court."[9]

The Suspension Clause (Article I, Section 9, clause. 2) implicitly guarantees the privilege of the writ of habeas corpus. (See Essay No. 68.) Given the connection between the right to a speedy trial and the Habeas Corpus Act, the Suspension Clause might explain why the right was not discussed at the Constitutional Convention. But the comments made by Randolph and Holmes suggest that the speedy trial right could have a function beyond protecting people from lengthy pretrial detention. Or perhaps it merely guarantees that the writ should issue in cases where pretrial detention becomes excessive. In any event, these assertions, like pre-convention historical practice, suggest that the right to a speedy trial was well-established by 1787.

In the First Congress, Representative James Madison offered a draft amendment, that began, "In all criminal prosecutions, the accused shall enjoy the right to a speedy . . . trial."[10] This proposal would be adopted and ratified without any modifications.

EARLY PRACTICE AND PRECEDENT

Early practice indicates that the core of the speedy trial right was protection from excessive pretrial detention. A leading precedent is Chief Justice Marshall's 1807 circuit court decision relating to Aaron Burr's arrest and imprisonment for treason. Burr requested that the prosecutor produce certain evidence under the Sixth Amendment right to "compulsory process." (See Essay No. 180.) Marshall held that Burr was entitled to the evidence even before a formal indictment. The right of compulsory process serves "the true spirit of the [Sixth Amendment] provision which secures to the accused a speedy trial, that he should have the benefit of the [evidence] as soon as he is brought into court."[11] Marshall reasoned that speedy access to compulsory process "prevents . . . those delays which are never desirable, which frequently occasion the loss of testimony."[12]

This decision could be read to suggest that the right to a speedy trial protects a defendant from delays that hamper his defense. It could also be read to suggest merely that other Sixth Amendment rights that protect a defendant's ability to present a defense should be glossed by the speedy trial right's emphasis on expediency. Moreover, the Speedy Trial Clause protects "the accused." Marshall distinguished between accusation and indictment. He construed "the accused" to mean a person charged with a crime, regardless of whether formally indicted.[13] Accordingly, *Burr*, like Holmes's argument, indicates that the speedy trial right attaches with a charge and arrest, not an indictment.

Early state court decisions construing state guarantees of a speedy trial might also be instructive for Sixth Amendment purposes to the extent that they reflect the ordinary public meaning of a "speedy trial." In an 1804 South Carolina case, the defendant, who was free on bail, was not tried after a second court term. However, the court refused to discharge the defendant because the state's habeas corpus act guaranteed only "that [the accused] should be discharged from [his] confinement on bail, or on [his] own recognisances."[14] In other words, because he was not in custody, the lack of a speedy trial did not justify his discharge. By contrast, in an 1807 Tennessee case, the defendant was detained before trial, and the court held that a prisoner "ought to be discharged" because the state's failure to find a prosecutor "furnishes no ground to keep the prisoner six months longer in confinement."[15] These state cases suggest that the right to a speedy trial protects against lengthy pretrial detention but would not attach to a defendant on bond.

However, in the decades after ratification, the public understanding of the right seemed to expand. In 1851, a Virginia court ruled that the state's speedy trial right applies regardless of whether the defendant is in custody. The court explained that under the state constitution, this right "enacted no new principle or safeguard of freedom. It was but the re-affirmation of a principle declared and consecrated by the" Habeas Corpus Act and Magna Carta.[16] The court also noted that in 1786, Virginia enacted "a new and additional provision for a discharge from the crime upon" the failure to try the accused in the third court term. This rule differed from the historical practice of merely granting bail or discharging from imprisonment during the first and second court terms.[17]

In 1880, a federal territorial court in Montana construed the Sixth Amendment's speedy trial right "with reference to [its] common-law meaning" at the Founding.[18] The court acknowledged that the Constitution did not set a time within which "a person accused of a crime and imprisoned shall be tried" but still held that the accused, "whether in prison or on bail, has the right to demand diligence on the part of the prosecution to the end that he may speedily know whether he is to be convicted or acquitted."[19]

MODERN PRACTICE AND PRECEDENT

Modern practice and precedent deviate from the original meaning of the right to a speedy trial with their expansion of the right to protect against more than excessive detention due to pretrial delay. The Supreme Court first briefly discussed the right in *Beavers v. Haubert* (1905).[20] The Court explained that what counts as a speedy trial depends on the circumstances. *Klopfer v. North Carolina* (1967) incorporated the speedy trial right against the states.[21] Five years later, *Barker v. Wingo* (1972) established several criteria for analyzing a violation of the right: "Length of delay, the reason for the delay, the defendant's assertion of his right, and prejudice to the defendant."[22] The Court also held that the right offers protection from "oppressive pretrial incarceration," the "anxiety and concern" resulting from an accusation, and "the possibility that the defense will be impaired."[23]

Finally, the Court ruled that "the only possible" remedy for a violation of the right is dismissal of the indictment.[24] The Court provided no analysis of whether these various factors are supported by the original meaning of the Sixth Amendment.

The Supreme Court has also held that the right attaches when a defendant is arrested or indicted but does not apply to delay in indicting or arresting a defendant after a crime. *United States v. MacDonald* (1982) held that a person is "accused" and the speedy trial right attaches when "a formal criminal charge is instituted" by indictment, arrest, or other official accusation.[25] However, *United States v. Loud Hawk* (1986) held that if the government delays indicting or arresting a person after he commits an offense, the Speedy Trial Clause does not provide a remedy.[26] Instead, the defendant must look to the applicable statute of limitations and the Due Process Clause. *Doggett v. United States* (1992) held that the speedy trial right attaches if a person is indicted, even if he is neither arrested nor aware of the indictment.[27]

In modern practice, many speedy trial disputes are resolved by applying a statute or rule. On the federal level, the Speedy Trial Act of 1974 provides that a defendant must be tried within a certain number of days, which may be extended only upon a finding that the extension sufficiently serves the "ends of justice."[28] Most state courts operate under comparable statutes or rules, but some states offer no additional protections.

OPEN QUESTIONS

- Justice Clarence Thomas has suggested that, as an originalist matter, the speedy trial right applies only upon arrest, not upon indictment.[29] Is he correct?[30]
- Does the speedy trial right protect only against excessive pretrial detention, or does it also apply to a mere delay in trial?[31]
- As an originalist matter, is dismissing the indictment the appropriate remedy for a violation of the right to a speedy trial? The text refers to a "speedy trial," not to a "speedy release." Or might it be appropriate to grant bail or discharge the defendant from imprisonment? To the extent that the speedy trial right protects against the anxiety of accusation or prejudice to the accused's ability to mount a defense, could other remedies short of dismissal be tailored to the nature of the harm?[32]

Cite as: Judge Andrew Brasher & Jack Tucker, *The Speedy Trial Clause, in* THE HERITAGE GUIDE TO THE CONSTITUTION 657 (Josh Blackman & John G. Malcolm eds., 3d ed. 2025).

Notes

1. 6 Translations and Reprints from the Original Sources of European History 23 (Edward P. Cheyney ed., 1897).   **2.** The American Republic: Primary Sources 94 (Bruce Frohnen ed., 2002).   **3.** Documents of the Constitution of England and America, from Magna Charta to the Federal Constitution of 1789, 37 (Francis Bowen ed., 1854).   **4.** 1 Blackstone 137.   **5.** *Id.* at §§ 135–36.   **6.** George M. Stroud, A Digest of the Laws of Pennsylvania 571–72 (7th ed. 1852); J. Stockdale, A Collection of the Constitutions of the Thirteen United States of North America 366 (2d ed. 1783).   **7.** Del. Const. of 1776, Decl. of Rts., § XIV; Md. Const. of 1776, Decl. of Rts., § XIX.   **8.** 10 DHRC 1350–51.   **9.** 6 DHRC 1366–67.   **10.** 1 Annals of Cong. 452 (1789).   **11.** *United States v. Burr*, 25 F. Cas. 30, 33 (C.C. Va. 1807) (No. 14,692).   **12.** *Id.* at 32.   **13.** *Id.*   **14.** *State v. Buyck*, 2 S.C.L. (2 Bay) 563, 563–64 (1804).   **15.** *State v. Sims*, 1 Tenn. (1 Overt.) 253, 258 (1807).   **16.** *Commonwealth v. Adcock*, 49 Va. (8 Gratt.) 661, 676–77 (1851).   **17.** *Id.* at 677.   **18.** *United States v. Fox*, 3 Mont. 512, 515 (1880).   **19.** *Id.* at 516–17.   **20.** 198 U.S. 77, 86–87 (1905).   **21.** 386 U.S. 213, 225–26 (1967).   **22.** 407 U.S. 514, 530 (1972).   **23.** *Id.* at 532.   **24.** *Id.* at 522.   **25.** 456 U.S. 1, 6 (1982).   **26.** 474 U.S. 302, 318 (1986).   **27.** 505 U.S. 647, 651–54 (1992).   **28.** 18 U.S.C. § 3161.   **29.** *Doggett*, 505 U.S. at 663 (Thomas, J., dissenting).   **30.** Phyllis Goldfarb, *When Judges Abandon Analogy: The Problem of Delay in Commencing Criminal Prosecutions*, 31 Wm. & Mary L. Rev. 607, 633–39 (1990).   **31.** *Doggett*, 505 U.S. at 663 (Thomas, J., dissenting).   **32.** Akhil Reed Amar, *Sixth Amendment First Principles*, 84 Geo. L. J. 641, 649–77 (1996).

ESSAY NO. 175: THE PUBLIC TRIAL CLAUSE
AMEND. 6

In all criminal prosecutions, the accused shall enjoy the right to a . . . public trial . . . .

—Judge Patrick R. Wyrick & Tyler Shannon

INTRODUCTION

The Sixth Amendment guarantees a criminal defendant's right to a public trial. Little debate surrounded this provision. This scant historical record has generated scholarly debate about the origin of the right, the motivation for its inclusion in the Bill of Rights, and its scope. This essay explores the right's roots in the English common law, the American trend toward enumeration, and the judicial precedents that have shaped the modern scope of the right.

HISTORY BEFORE 1787

The origin of the right of public trial is not entirely clear. This right is not mentioned in the 1689 Bill of Rights, the 1621 Petition of Rights, or the 1215 Magna Carta. Some view the English guarantee of a public trial in criminal cases as a response to the Court of Star Chamber's use of secret proceedings in criminal cases.[1] Others argue that the right had cemented itself in the English common law far earlier and that the Star Chamber was merely an ignominious departure from that tradition.[2] Either way, the omission of the right from England's seminal rights-guaranteeing charters of the times demonstrates its roots in the common law.[3] Sir William Blackstone wrote that the "open examination of witnesses . . . in the presence of all mankind, is much more conducive to the clearing up of truth, than private and secret examination. . . . [A] witness may frequently depose that in private which he will be ashamed to testify in a public and solemn tribunal."[4]

Early American practice, however, trended away from reliance on the common law and toward enumeration of the right. The state constitutions generally guaranteed a criminal trial by jury.[5] Pennsylvania and Vermont, in particular, specifically guaranteed that those trials must be public.[6]

THE CONSTITUTIONAL CONVENTION

On May 29, 1787, Charles Pinckney of South Carolina proposed his draft of the Constitution.[7] Article IX guaranteed that for "All Criminal offenses . . . trials shall be open and public, and shall be by jury."[8] There was no recorded debate on Pinckney's proposal.[9] Article III, Section 2 would require that "[t]he Trial of all Crimes . . . shall be by Jury." (See Essay No. 136.) But there was no requirement that the trials must be public.

The lack of a guarantee of a jury trial in civil matters—and the lack of a bill of rights more generally—became an Anti-Federalist rallying cry.[10] However, there was scant concern over the omission of a public trial guarantee; both Federalist and Anti-Federalist writings lack any extensive discussion of the matter.

RATIFICATION OF THE SIXTH AMENDMENT

In 1788, the New York Convention requested that amendments should be added to the Constitution. One of the proposals was a right to a public trial.[11] One year later, the First Congress sent the proposed amendments to the states for ratification. With little fanfare, the right to a public trial for criminal defendants was included.[12] The Public Trial Clause appears to have drawn no criticism or opposition during the ratification debates, even from states whose constitutions did not yet guarantee the right.

EARLY PRACTICE

Few reported federal and state decisions from the early Republic discuss the right to a public trial.[13] By the middle of the nineteenth century, however, the law of public trials had largely become a law of exclusions. The common law, Justice Joseph Story wrote, dictated that "[t]he trial is always public."[14] However, Thomas Cooley explained that the right to a "public" trial does "not mean[] that every person who sees fit shall in all criminal cases be permitted to attend criminal trials."[15] Rather, in many cases, "the character of the charge, and the nature of the evidence by which it is to be supported" permitted excluding certain members of the public. Nevertheless, the right required that, at a minimum, all of those "whose presence could be of . . . service to the accused" would be permitted to attend.

Cooley's more practical understanding of the right was adopted by many late nineteenth- and early twentieth-century courts,[16] but they were hardly uniform in their approaches. For example, in 1918, the Arizona Supreme Court concluded that courts are far apart as to what constitutes a "public trial," often reaching opposite conclusions based on nearly identical facts.[17]

A handful of nineteenth-century courts also grappled with the question of *when* the public must be present. In 1846, the Ohio Supreme Court declared that "all that can be said or [proffered] against [a defendant], and all that can be said or urged in his favor, shall be in the hearing and presence of the public."[18] This early decision recognized that "witnesses shall give their testimony in public, and the court shall declare the law in public; and the jury are sworn to render their verdict according to the law and the evidence thus publicly given."[19] State high courts would criticize trial court judges for communicating with juries outside of the presence of the public.[20]

MODERN PRECEDENTS

In re Oliver (1948) incorporated the Public Trial Clause against the states.[21] Incorporation has had minimal practical effect, however, because the right was expressly protected by the constitutions of forty-three states.[22] Five states— Maryland, Massachusetts, New Hampshire, North Carolina, and Wyoming—protected the right as a matter of due process or common law, and two—New York and Nevada—protected the right by statute.[23]

Oliver recognized that a public trial serves as a "safeguard against any attempt to employ our courts as instruments of persecution."[24] Justice John Marshall Harlan II explained that "the public-trial guarantee embodies a view of human nature, true as a general rule, that judges, lawyers, witnesses, and jurors will perform their respective functions more responsibly in an open court than in secret proceedings."[25] Public trials also make proceedings known to potential witnesses and help to deter untruthful testimony.

The right to a public trial is a right shared between the accused and the general citizenry. As a result, "a defendant can, under some circumstances, waive his constitutional right to a public trial, [but] he has no absolute right to compel a private trial."[26] In addition, courts can temporarily close proceedings.[27] They can take this extreme step when the "dignity, order and decorum" that are and must be "the hallmarks of all court proceedings in our country" are flagrantly disregarded.[28] For example, judges occasionally will close portions of trials to protect minor victims in sex-offense trials or when necessary to preserve the confidentiality of sensitive information, such as the identity of undercover witnesses.[29]

The guarantee of a public "trial" requires that the impaneling of the jury and return of the verdict must be made in open court. Likewise, certain pretrial proceedings must be public. But the Sixth Amendment does not require that all stages and phases of criminal prosecutions must be open to the public. Grand jury proceedings, for example, are secret. The Supreme Court has adopted a strong presumption in favor of public criminal proceedings, including the selection of jurors during *voir dire*.[30]

OPEN QUESTIONS

- Early courts also seem to have understood that the Public Trial Clause protects the *public's* right of access.[31] However, the Supreme Court's more modern cases place this public aspect of the right in the First Amendment.[32] Would the former approach be more consistent with the original public meaning of the Sixth Amendment?[33]
- At the Founding, for a trial to be public, it was necessary for members of the public to be physically present in the courtroom. In a world of emerging—and indeed pervasive—video-conferencing technology, to what extent does virtual access to a criminal trial serve as a constitutionally adequate substitute for physical presence?[34]

Cite as: Judge Patrick R. Wyrick & Tyler Shannon, *The Public Trial Clause, in* THE HERITAGE GUIDE TO THE CONSTITUTION 660 (Josh Blackman & John G. Malcolm eds., 3d ed. 2025).

Notes

1. Eric J. Walz, Note, *The Star-Spangled Chamber: The Venire's Role in Satisfying the Sixth Amendment to the United States Constitution*, 46 Suffolk U. L. Rev. 701, 704–05 (2013); *Campbell v. State*, 11 Ga. 353, 373 (1852).   **2.** Walz, *supra* at 703–04.   **3.** 3 Story's Commentaries § 1785.   **4.** 3 Blackstone 373.   **5.** Akhil Reed Amar, The Bill of Rights: Creation and Reconstruction 83 (1998).   **6.** Pa. Const. of 1776, ch. I, § 9; Pa. Const. of 1790, art. IX, § 9; Vt. Const. of 1777, ch. I, § 10; Vt. Const. of 1786, ch. I, § 11.   **7.** 3 Farrand's 595.   **8.** *Id.* at 600.   **9.** *Id.* at 595.   **10.** Charles W. Wolfram, *The Constitutional History of the Seventh Amendment*, 57 Minn. L. Rev. 639, 667–73 (1973).   **11.** 1 Elliot's 328.   **12.** 1 Annals of Cong. 451–52 (1789).   **13.** Max Radin, *The Right to a Public Trial*, 6 Temp. L. Q. 381, 384 (1932).   **14.** 3 Story's Commentaries § 1785.   **15.** Thomas M. Cooley, A Treatise on the Constitutional Limitations Which Rest Upon the Legislative Power of the States of the American Union 312 (1868).   **16.** *Reagan v. United States*, 202 F. 488, 490 (9th Cir. 1913); *State v. Brooks*, 5 S.W. 257, 264 (Mo. 1887); *People v. Swafford*, 3 P. 809, 810 (Cal. 1884); *Grimmett v. State*, 2 S.W. 631, 634 (Tex. Ct. App. 1886).   **17.** *Keddington v. State*, 172 P. 273, 275 (Ariz. 1918).   **18.** *Kirk v. State*, 1846 WL 60, at 1 (Ohio 1846).   **19.** *Id.*   **20.** *Id.*; *Holton v. State*, 2 Fla. 476, 498–99 (1849).   **21.** 333 U.S. 257 (1948).   **22.** Kenneth Katkin, *"Incorporation" of the Criminal Procedure Amendments: The View from the States*, 85 Neb. L. Rev. 397, 444–45 (2005) (citation omitted).   **23.** *Id.* at 445 (citation omitted).   **24.** *Oliver*, 333 U.S. at 270.   **25.** *Estes v. Texas*, 381 U.S. 532, 588 (1965) (Harlan, J., concurring).   **26.** *Singer v. United States*, 380 U.S. 24, 35 (1965).   **27.** *Waller v. Georgia*, 467 U.S. 39, 48 (1984).   **28.** *Illinois v. Allen*, 397 U.S. 337, 343 (1970).   **29.** 6 Wayne R. LaFave et al., Criminal Procedure § 24.1(b) (4th ed. 2022).   **30.** *Presley v. Georgia*, 558 U.S. 209, 213–14 (2010).   **31.** *State v. Hensley*, 79 N.E. 462, 463–64 (Ohio 1906).   **32.** *Globe Newspaper Co. v. Super. Ct.*, 457 U.S. 596, 604 (1982) (quoting *Mills v. Alabama*, 384 U.S. 214, 218 (1966)).   **33.** Amar, *supra* at 111–13.   **34.** *United States v. Allen*, 34 F.4th 789 (9th Cir. 2022); *Tarpey v. State*, 523 P.3d 916 (Wyo. 2023).

ESSAY NO. 176: THE JURY TRIAL CLAUSE
AMEND. 6

In all criminal prosecutions, the accused shall enjoy the right to a . . . trial, by an impartial jury. . . .

—Judge Kurt D. Engelhardt, Ian Brinton Hatch, & Greta Gieseke

INTRODUCTION

The right to a criminal jury trial is the only individual right enumerated in both the Constitution and the Bill of Rights. Article III, Section 2, Clause 3 of the Constitution provides that "[t]he trial of all Crimes, except in Cases of Impeachment, shall be by Jury." (See Essay No. 136.) The Sixth Amendment guarantees federal criminal defendants the right to trial "by an impartial jury of the State and district wherein the crime shall have been committed." The Supreme Court has held that these two provisions "mean substantially the same thing."[1]

DRAFTING THE SIXTH AMENDMENT

On June 8, 1789, James Madison proposed to the First Congress two separate amendments pertaining to an accused's right to a trial. The first declared that "[i]n all criminal prosecutions, the accused shall enjoy the right to a speedy and public trial. . . ."[2] Although the full text included additional procedural protections, it lacked an explicit mention of a jury right. The second relevant amendment remedied this oversight by declaring that [t]he trial of all crimes . . . shall be by an impartial jury of freeholders of the vicinage. . . ."[3] Congress ultimately deleted the second of Madison's proposed amendments but incorporated the jury right into the text of the first one.[4] This modified amendment later became ratified as what we know today as the Sixth Amendment.[5]

This survey of the legislative history suggests that the purpose of the Sixth Amendment was to ensure that the jury must be "impartial" and to secure the vicinage requirement (that jurors must be taken from the same vicinage where the crime occurred). These two details constitute the only meaningful difference between the Sixth Amendment jury right and the Article III jury right. The vicinage requirement sparked much debate during the First Congress (see Essay No. 178), but the impartiality requirement does not seem to have generated any discussion. However, the courts have gradually expounded upon its meaning over the centuries.

INCORPORATION

In 1868, the Fourteenth Amendment was ratified, and with ratification came an important new question: Does the Fourteenth Amendment incorporate the Sixth Amendment right to a jury trial? The original Sixth Amendment guaranteed a right to a jury in federal courts but said nothing about a right to a jury in state courts. While the legislative history of the Fourteenth Amendment is famously difficult to decipher, it does provide some clues. During the debate on the amendment's meaning, for example, Senator Jacob M. Howard of Michigan said that "the right to be tried by an impartial jury of the vicinage" was a fundamental right protected by the Privileges or Immunities Clause of the Fourteenth Amendment. Howard further argued that "[t]he great object of the" Privileges or Immunities Clause was "to restrain the power of the States and compel them at all times to respect these great fundamental guarantees."[6] (See Essay No. 194.)

Here, a leading Framer of the Fourteenth Amendment intended to incorporate the Sixth Amendment jury trial right. Under this interpretation, the Fourteenth Amendment protected the "privileges or immunities" of citizens against the states, and the Sixth Amendment was to be counted under this group of privileges.

A hundred years later, the U.S. Supreme Court eventually settled the issue, albeit via an avenue slightly different from the Privileges and Immunities Clause suggested by Senator Howard. In *Duncan v. Louisiana* (1968), the Court held that the Fourteenth Amendment's Due Process Clause "incorporated" the right to a jury trial and made it applicable to the states.[7] (See Essay No. 195.) The Court said that although juries were not essential to fairness and due process in every legal system, they were essential to the U.S. system. *Duncan* held that "[p]roviding an accused with the right to be tried by a jury of his peers gave him an inestimable safeguard against the corrupt or overzealous prosecutor and against the compliant, biased, or eccentric judge."[8]

THE IMPARTIAL JURY

A defendant is entitled not only to a jury, but to an "impartial" one. The Founders understood jury impartiality as stemming, in the words of Richard Henry Lee in a letter to Edmund Randolph, from "the unanimous consent of twelve of [one's] neighbors and equals," as they are free from the "involuntary bias" that the "magistracy" would have "towards those of their own rank and dignity."[9] In other words, they understood impartiality as fundamentally rooted in judgment by one's peers. Lee, quoting Sir William Blackstone, wrote that because any judgments rendered by officials, "in spite of their own natural integrity," would be infected with "involuntary bias" favoring other officials.[10] The Supreme Court, examining the impartiality requirement, observed that "[i]mpartiality is not a technical conception. It is a state of mind. For the ascertainment of this mental attitude of appropriate indifference, the Constitution lays down no particular tests and procedure is not chained to any ancient and artificial formula."[11] While "a juror who has formed an opinion cannot be impartial . . . [i]t is not required that jurors be totally ignorant of the facts and issues involved . . . . It is sufficient if the juror can lay aside his impression or opinion based on the evidence presented in court."[12]

A right to an impartial jury is predicated on an ability to challenge potential partiality. Per Edmund Randolph, "as the trial by jury is established in criminal cases, the incidental right of challenging and excepting is also established, which secures, in the utmost latitude, the benefit of impartiality in the jurors."[13] One must also be able to challenge venue. The Founders understood impartiality as lying, in part, in a juror's proximity to the underlying facts and parties. They expressed concern that an accused could be "carried from one extremity of the state to another, and be tried, not by an impartial jury of the vicinage, acquainted with his character and the circumstances of the fact, but by a jury unacquainted with both, and who may be biased against him."[14] As the Supreme Court recognized, however, the reverse can be true as well: A jury pool can be rendered irreparably partial by a case's publicity to the point that denying a venue challenge violates a party's constitutional rights.[15]

THE SIZE OF THE JURY
Some believe that the Constitution guarantees the right to a twelve-person criminal jury, but the only thing currently guaranteeing it is Federal Rule of Criminal Procedure 23(b)(1). The Constitution itself is silent with respect to a jury's proper size. Perhaps this is because the Founders seemed to take for granted a twelve-person criminal jury. Since before Magna Carta,

there was a common-law history of twelve jurors without any discussion of an alternative size.[16] Yet, the Supreme Court, based on an examination of history, held "that the 12-man panel is not a necessary ingredient of" a jury trial, allowing the number of jurors to be as low as six.[17] "[T]he fact that the jury at common law was composed of precisely 12 is a historical accident[.]"[18]

PEREMPTORY CHALLENGES
At the time of the Framing, litigants could challenge a limited number of prospective jurors *peremptorily*—that is, without the need for a reason or explanation.[19] The traditional purpose of these challenges was to ensure impartiality by excluding biased jurors.[20] The Supreme Court, however, has read the Sixth Amendment and the Equal Protection Clause to limit the use of peremptory challenges. In a series of cases beginning with *Batson v. Kentucky* (1986), the Court has held that litigants may not use peremptory challenges to discriminate on the basis of race, gender, or any other classification subject to heightened scrutiny.[21] The *Batson* Court based its decision on the landmark *Strauder v. West Virginia* decision (1880), which similarly held that racial discrimination in jury selection violates the Equal Protection Clause.[22]

The Supreme Court upheld *Batson* in *Flowers v. Mississippi* (2019).[23] Justice Clarence Thomas dissented. He wrote that *Batson* "requires that a duly convicted criminal go free because a juror was arguably deprived of his right to serve on the jury," thereby "giving a windfall to a convicted criminal who, even under *Batson*'s logic, suffered no injury."[24] Thomas further argued that *Batson* itself should be overruled.[25] According to Thomas, the original purpose of peremptory challenges was to assuage "fears of partiality by giving effect to the parties' intuitions about jurors' often-unstated biases" and that "racial biases, sympathies, and prejudices still exist."[26] Requiring a *Batson* explanation for a peremptory challenge, under Justice Thomas's view, might frustrate a litigant's right to secure a jury free of racial bias.[27]

THE JURY RIGHT AND SENTENCING
After a criminal defendant is found guilty by a jury, the judge will impose a sentence. In many

cases, the severity of the sentence will be determined based on the defendant's conduct. But an evaluation of the defendant's conduct involves a fact-intensive inquiry—a role that historically has belonged to juries, not judges. As early as 1794, the Supreme Court laid down the "good old rule" that "on questions of fact, it is the province of the jury, on questions of law, it is the province of the court to decide."[28]

Under this traditional rule, can a judge still make factual findings that result in an increased sentence, or must a jury alone determine those facts? *Apprendi v. New Jersey* (2000) held that the jury must make these findings. The Court declared that "[i]t is unconstitutional for a legislature to remove from the jury the assessment of facts that increase the prescribed range of penalties to which a criminal defendant is exposed."[29] *Apprendi* required a jury to determine beyond a reasonable doubt every fact other than conviction of a prior offense that increases the *maximum* sentence a defendant faces.[30] Surveying the historical tradition, the Court noted that, according to traditional common-law authorities like Blackstone, the truth of every accusation must be determined by the jury. The Court pointed out that any distinction between an element of a felony offense and a "sentencing factor" was unknown at the time of the Founding.[31] Therefore, the traditional view would also have mandated that sentencing factors, just like elements of the offense, be determined by juries.

Alleyne v. United States (2013) extended the *Apprendi* principle to the context of mandatory minimum sentences. The Court held that "any fact that increases the mandatory minimum [sentence] is an 'element' that must be submitted to the jury."[32]

A UNANIMOUS JURY?

The Sixth Amendment's text is silent about whether a jury must find guilt by a unanimous vote. Perhaps this is because, like the twelve-person jury, a unanimity requirement was simply understood as being so foundational that it did not require explicit inclusion.[33] Decisions from before 1972 seemed to make clear that, at least in federal court, juries needed to reach a unanimous conclusion to convict.[34]

In *Apodaca v. Oregon* (1972), the Supreme Court divided over whether a criminal

defendant can be convicted by a nonunanimous jury.[35] Four justices, using reasoning similar to that in *Williams v. Florida* (1970), concluded that conviction by a vote of 10 to 2 did not violate the Sixth Amendment. Four justices dissented, arguing that the amendment preserved the historic unanimity requirement.[36] The remaining justice agreed with the dissenters on the construction of the Sixth Amendment but rejected the view that "all of the elements of jury trial within the meaning of the Sixth Amendment are necessarily embodied in or incorporated into the Due Process Clause of the Fourteenth Amendment."[37] As a result, nonunanimous verdicts were permitted in state courts but not in federal courts.

The dissenters ultimately carried the day. In *Ramos v. Louisiana* (2020), the Court overruled *Apodaca*. Justice Neil Gorsuch, writing for the majority, ruled that "if the Sixth Amendment's right to a jury trial requires a unanimous verdict to support a conviction in federal court, it requires no less in state court." Here, the Court incorporated the unanimity requirement against the states.[38] The Court also made clear that unanimity was indeed historically supported with a discussion ranging from its origins in fourteenth-century England to precedent that the *Apodaca* court did not cite.[39] As Gorsuch said, "[i]f the term 'trial by an impartial jury' carried any meaning at all, it surely included a requirement as long and widely accepted as unanimity."[40] Notably, *Edwards v. Vannoy* (2021) clarified that *Ramos* does not apply retroactively.[41]

PLEA BARGAINING

Despite the central importance of the jury trial in our justice system, very few federal criminal defendants actually exercise their right to have twelve citizen jurors evaluate their guilt or innocence. In 2022, only about 0.4 percent of federal criminal defendants went to trial and were acquitted; 1.9 percent were found guilty; the cases of 8.2 percent were dismissed somewhere during the pretrial process; and 89.5 percent entered guilty pleas and waived their Sixth Amendment right to a jury trial, seeking a reduced sentence.[42]

This now-dominant practice is, at least in some instances, in tension with historical tradition. For example, Sir William Blackstone observed that courts confronted with prisoners pleading guilty in capital cases were "very backward in receiving and recording [a guilty plea], out of tenderness to life of the subject; and [would] generally advise the prisoner to retract it, and plead to the indictment."[43] Several nineteenth-century American treatises

looked askance at the practice generally.[44] When instances of plea bargaining began to appear in appellate reports in the decades following the Civil War, lower courts generally denounced the practice.[45] However, the Supreme Court made clear in *Brady v. United States* (1970) that plea bargaining is constitutional as long as pleas are made both voluntarily and intelligently.[46]

OPEN QUESTIONS

- Does a criminal court commit a structural error by seating a biased juror?
- Which other sentencing enhancements and factors require submission to the jury? What about restitution?
- What are appropriate remedial actions for a successful *Batson* challenge?
- How can a citizen enforce his or her constitutional right to serve as a juror?

Cite as: Judge Kurt D. Engelhardt, Ian Brinton Hatch, & Greta Gieseke, *The Jury Trial Clause, in* THE HERITAGE GUIDE TO THE CONSTITUTION 662 (Josh Blackman & John G. Malcolm eds., 3d ed. 2025).

Notes

1. *Patton v. United States*, 281 U.S. 276, 298 (1930).   **2.** 1 Annals of Cong. 452 (1789); Francis H. Heller, The Sixth Amendment to the Constitution of the United States: A Study in Constitutional Development 28–34 (1951).   **3.** 1 Annals of Cong. 452 (1789).   **4.** S. Jour., 1st Cong., 1st Sess. 77 (Sept. 9, 1789); 1 Annals of Cong. 948 (1789).   **5.** 1 Annals of Cong. 90, 948 (1789).   **6.** Cong. Globe, 39th Cong., 1st Sess. 2765–66 (1866).   **7.** 391 U.S. 145, 150–51 (1968). **8.** *Id.* at 149, 149 n.14, 156.   **9.** 1 Elliot's 504–05.   **10.** *Id.* (quoting 3 Blackstone 379); *Sec. & Exch. Comm'n v. Jarkesy*, 603 U.S. 109, 121, 127 (2024) (quoting Federalist No. 78 (Hamilton)).   **11.** *United States v. Wood*, 299 U.S. 123, 146 (1936).   **12.** *Irvin v. Dowd*, 366 U.S. 717, 722–23 (1961). **13.** 3 Elliot's 573.   **14.** *Id.* at 447.   **15.** *Rideau v. Louisiana*, 373 U.S. 723 (1963).   **16.** 3 Elliot's 467–70, 544–55; *Williams v. Florida*, 399 U.S. 78, 98–99 (1970); Richard S. Arnold, *Trial by Jury: The Constitutional Right to a Jury of Twelve in Civil Trials*, 22 Hofstra L. Rev. 1, 3 (1993). **17.** *Williams*, 399 U.S. at 89.   **18.** *Id.* at 102.   **19.** *Swain v. Alabama*, 380 U.S. 202, 214 (1965).   **20.** *Lewis v. United States*, 146 U.S. 370, 376 (1892).   **21.** 476 U.S. 79, 89 (1986).   **22.** *Id.* at 85–86.   **23.** 588 U.S. 284 (2019).   **24.** *Id.* at 348–49 (Thomas, J., dissenting).   **25.** *Id.* at 351–52.   **26.** *Id.* at 355–56.   **27.** *Id.*   **28.** *Georgia v. Brailsford*, 3 U.S. (3 Dall.) 1, 4 (1794).   **29.** *Apprendi v. New Jersey*, 530 U.S. 466, 490 (2000).   **30.** *Id.*   **31.** *Id.* at 477 (citing 4 Blackstone 349–50), 478.   **32.** *Alleyne v. United States*, 570 U.S. 99, 99 (2013). **33.** 1 Elliot's 504–05; 3 Elliot's 299; *Apodaca v. Oregon*, 406 U.S. 404, 406 (1972), *abrog. by Ramos v. Louisiana*, 590 U.S. 83 (2020).   **34.** *Andres v. United States*, 333 U.S. 740, 748 (1948).   **35.** *Apodaca*, 406 U.S. at 406–07.   **36.** *Id.* at 414–15 (Stewart, J., dissenting); *Johnson v. Louisiana*, 406 U.S. 380, 381 (1972) (Douglas, J., dissenting).   **37.** *Johnson v. Louisiana*, 406 U.S. 366, 369 (1972) (Powell, J., concurring in judgment).   **38.** *Ramos v. Louisiana*, 590 U.S. 83, 93 (2020).   **39.** *Id.* at 90–93.   **40.** *Id.* at 91.   **41.** *Edwards v. Vannoy*, 593 U.S. 255, 258 (2021).   **42.** John Gramlich, *Fewer than 1% of Federal Criminal Defendants Were Acquitted in 2022*, Pew Research Center (June 14, 2023), https://perma.cc/E9Z9-BPHC.   **43.** 4 Blackstone 329.   **44.** John Frederick Archbold, Pleading and Evidence in Criminal Cases 73–74 (1824); John C. B. Davis, The Massachusetts Justice: A Treatise upon the Powers and Duties of Justices of the Peace 232 (1847); *Hallinger v. Davis*, 146 U.S. 314, 324 (1892); *Green v. Commonwealth*, 94 Mass (12 Allen) 155, 175–76 (1866).   **45.** Albert W. Alschuler, *Plea Bargaining and Its History*, 79 Colum. L. Rev. 1, 19–24 (1979).   **46.** *Brady v. United States*, 397 U.S. 742, 747 (1970).

❧

ESSAY NO. 177: THE VICINAGE CLAUSE
AMEND. 6

In all criminal prosecutions, the accused shall enjoy the right to a speedy and public trial, by an impartial jury of the State and district wherein the crime shall have been committed, which district shall have been previously ascertained by law. . . .

—Brian C. Kalt

INTRODUCTION

The Sixth Amendment's Vicinage Clause requires that jurors in federal criminal trials be selected from the state and district where the crime occurred. Congress can draw judicial district lines as it sees fit, but it can do this only prospectively. *Vicinage* refers to the location from which jurors are drawn. *Venue* refers to where the trial is held. Vicinage and venue are intricately and sometimes confusingly linked. The Vicinage Clause is one of the few provisions in the Bill of Rights that has not been applied against state governments by incorporation into the Fourteenth Amendment.

HISTORY BEFORE 1787

In medieval England, jurors were not originally required to be impartial.[1] Rather, they decided cases based on their firsthand knowledge of the crime and the people involved. But even as the notion of the impartial jury emerged in England, the idea that the jury needed to be local remained important. As Sir William Blackstone explained, because juries from the "immediate neighbourhood" were "apt to intermix their prejudices and partialities," the vicinage was expanded, but jurors were still required to be "*de corpore comitatus*, from the body of the county at large."[2] Thus, a fundamental feature of Anglo-American trial juries is that they are local.

Colonial Americans took the idea of local jury trials seriously. Local jury trials were seen as important institutions to safeguard the rights of criminal defendants. In October 1774, the Continental Congress praised the local jury in its "Address to the People of Great Britain." Without a local jury, defendants might "be tried in a distant land, by a *jury* of strangers, and subject to all the disadvantages that result from want of friends, want of witnesses, and want of money."[3] Local jury trials were also important as a cornerstone of democratic self-government. They allowed the colonists to decide what things would and would not be punished in their own communities.[4] The colonists protested mightily when the Crown violated these norms.[5] The Declaration of Independence, for example, charged the King of England with "transporting us beyond Seas to be tried."[6]

After independence, most state constitutions required local jury trials, but in a range of ways. For example, Maryland simply praised the virtues of "the trial of facts where they arise," and Pennsylvania more explicitly gave criminal defendants the right to trial "by an impartial jury of the country."[7] Other states restricted trials to the county or the "vicinity."[8]

THE CONSTITUTIONAL CONVENTION

The Framers wanted to respect the principle of local jury trials—to a point. Article III provided that all federal criminal trials must be by jury and that the venue must be in the state where the crime was committed.[9] (See Essay No. 136.) Although the text made no express reference to the question, implicit in the state-venue requirement was that jurors would be drawn from the state where the crime was committed as well.[10] These requirements were not controversial and triggered no recorded debate during the Convention.[11]

THE RATIFICATION DEBATES

During the ratification debates, on the other hand, Anti-Federalist essayists and delegates criticized the Constitution for not guaranteeing a right to be tried by a jury of the vicinage.[12] The Anti-Federalists wanted an area much smaller than the statewide zones that Article III provided. Centinel wrote that the requirement that jurors must be "*taken from the vicinage*" was a "precaution which is omitted as to trial of crimes."[13] In the Virginia convention, Patrick Henry appealed to the "ancient common law" right under which "the trial of all facts is decided by a jury of impartial men from the immediate vicinage."[14]

Federalists responded that Congress had the power to establish vicinage rules by statute. Also at the Virginia convention, John Marshall analogized to the common law, in which "the preservation of this [vicinage] right [was] in the hands of Parliament."[15] On this question, the Anti-Federalists would prevail. Many ratifying states produced lists of rights they wished to see added to the Constitution; four states' lists included juries of the vicinage.[16]

THE FIRST CONGRESS

The First Congress responded to the Anti-Federalists' criticism and addressed the vicinage issue. Representative James Madison's proposal of what became the Sixth Amendment guaranteed that federal criminal juries would comprise "freeholders of the vicinage."[17] Madison's proposal also specified that if the crime was committed in a county occupied by enemy forces or experiencing an insurrection, the trial could be held in a nearby county in the same state.[18] The latter provision, which was about venue rather than vicinage, suggested that the earlier vicinage provision envisioned county-level jury pools.

The House approved Madison's language after replacing the word "county" with "place."[19] However, when the Senate approved its version of the Bill of Rights, it struck the entire vicinage provision.[20] Senators apparently felt that "of the vicinage" was too vague. Madison explained in a letter that, given the diversity of practices in the various states, "of the vicinage" could have meant anything from a neighborhood to an entire state and that to the extent that "vicinage" meant something specific like the county level, Senators considered that to be too strict.[21]

The two chambers compromised. The House succeeded in restoring a Vicinage Clause, but its final language was closer to the Senate's sentiments.[22] By saying that jurors would be from the state *and* district where the crime was committed, the Vicinage Clause theoretically allowed Congress to make districts as small as the strictest critics could want, but the reality was that districts were state-sized.

Shortly before this compromise was drafted, Congress enacted the Judiciary Act of 1789, which established the new federal districts.[23] Under the Judiciary Act, each state contained only one district, with two exceptions: Virginia had a district covering the part of Virginia that would become Kentucky, and Massachusetts had a district covering the part of Massachusetts that would become Maine.[24] The First Congress therefore understood that, at least for the time being, the Vicinage Clause would not appreciably narrow the statewide scope provided by Article III. As a general matter, jurors in federal criminal trials could be drawn from anywhere in the state, not just from the county where the crime occurred. However, the Judiciary Act also provided for county-level venue and vicinage rules in capital cases when possible.[25] This reinforced the fact that Congress could provide for

vicinages that were smaller than what was established by their district statutes.

RATIFICATION OF THE AMENDMENTS

The states considering the Bill of Rights appear generally not to have discussed the Vicinage Clause to any significant degree. One exception was Virginia. During the first round of ratification debates, objectors complained that the Vicinage Clause still allowed for statewide vicinage rather than the smaller bounds they preferred.[26]

EARLY PRACTICE

Congress stuck with its initial inclination to keep vicinages on the larger side. In the first few decades following ratification of the Bill of Rights, Congress subdivided only a few states into multiple districts.[27] Moreover, the stricter statutory vicinage requirements that the Judiciary Act of 1789 had provided for capital cases were mostly sidestepped and later repealed.[28]

The Vicinage Clause set the bar for vicinage fairly low, and individual judges had a fair amount of discretion with respect to where they would draw jurors from in a district.[29] Federal judges typically followed the practices of their local state courts.[30] While the clause set the bar low, however, that bar was respected.

JUDICIAL PRECEDENT

The Vicinage Clause requires that a district must be "*previously* ascertained by law." The text suggests that this provision was designed to prevent Congress from retroactively manipulating the vicinage in a particular case. No legislative history suggests the contrary.[31] This issue has arisen when a crime is committed in a place that is subsequently transferred to a newly drawn district. The U.S. Supreme Court affirmed the practice of holding the trial in and drawing jurors from the old district as it was constituted at the time of the crime,[32] but it did not hold that the Vicinage Clause requires this practice. The Eleventh Circuit, for example, allowed the trial in a similar case to proceed in the new district.[33] This holding is consistent with the previous-ascertainment requirement only if "previous" is measured by reference to when charges were filed rather than when the offense was committed.

Some crimes occur outside of any state, which makes it impossible to find jurors "of the state" where the crime was committed. In such cases, the Supreme Court has looked to the Venue Clause of Article III, Section 2, which specifies that when a crime is committed outside of any state, venue is wherever Congress directs by statute. *Cook v. United States* (1891) found that the Vicinage Clause implicitly includes this distinction as well.[34] Thus, the Vicinage Clause does not apply outside of the fifty states. Congress has assigned the territories and Washington, D.C., to districts, and jurors are drawn from those districts. *Cook* even allowed a retroactive assignment to a district, which would have violated the previous-ascertainment requirement if the Vicinage Clause had applied. For crimes committed outside of any district, such as on the high seas, federal law assigns the trial to the district in which the defendant is arrested. Without an arrest, the case is assigned to the district in which the defendant last resided or, failing that, to Washington, D.C.[35]

Often, jury pools are drawn from parts of the district other than the one where the crime was committed. Criminal defendants have challenged these pools as violating the Vicinage Clause. The Supreme Court, however, has found that the clause's plain text does not require that jurors be drawn from a particular place in the district. Rather, jurors must be drawn from *somewhere* in the district.[36]

Rule 21 of the Federal Rules of Criminal Procedure allows for a change of venue, but only if the defendant requests it. In 1944, the Rules Advisory Committee attributed this structure to the Sixth Amendment, saying that it gives defendants "a constitutional right to a trial in the district where the offense was committed"—a right that the defendant can waive by asking for a change of venue.[37] This reflects the way that vicinage has been both inextricably linked with and largely subsumed under venue.[38]

What is the remedy for a violation of the Vicinage Clause? *Smith v. United States* (2023) treated the clause the same as most other Sixth Amendment rights are treated.[39] Under this standard, when a jury's composition violates the Vicinage Clause, the criminal defendant is entitled only to a new trial, not to an outright acquittal.

OPEN QUESTIONS

- The Supreme Court has incorporated almost every other provision of the Bill of Rights to apply against state governments, but not the Vicinage Clause. Does the Vicinage Clause apply to the states as well as to the federal government? Lower courts have split over the question.[40] Significantly, most state constitutions require juries from the county or district where the crime was committed, so the effect of incorporation would be limited.[41]
- To what extent does the Vicinage Clause represent a right of the community as opposed to a right only of criminal defendants?[42]

Cite as: Brian C. Kalt, *The Vicinage Clause, in* THE HERITAGE GUIDE TO THE CONSTITUTION 666 (Josh Blackman & John G. Malcolm eds., 3d ed. 2025).

Notes

1. Thomas A. Green, *A Retrospective on the Criminal Jury Trial, 1200–1800, in* Twelve Men Good and True: The Criminal Trial Jury in England, 1200–1800 (J.S. Cockburn & Thomas A. Green eds., 2014). **2.** 3 Blackstone 359–60; Brian C. Kalt, *Crossing Eight Mile: Juries of the Vicinage and County-Line Criminal Buffer Statutes,* 80 Wash. L. Rev. 271, 296 (2005). **3.** 1 J. Cont. Cong. 85 (Oct. 21, 1774). **4.** Steven A. Engel, *The Public's Vicinage Right: A Constitutional Argument,* 75 N.Y.U. L. Rev. 1658, 1681 (2000). **5.** *Id.* at 1680–86. **6.** Declaration of Independence, ¶¶ 19, 20. **7.** Md. Const. of 1776, Decl. of Rts., art. XVIII; Pa. Const. of 1776, Decl. of Rts., § 9. **8.** Kalt, *supra* at 301–02; Drew L. Kershen, *Vicinage,* 29 Okla. L. Rev. 801, 807, 815 (1976). **9.** Art. III, § 2, cl. 3. **10.** Kershen, *supra* at 830–31. **11.** *Id.* at 808. **12.** *Smith v. United States,* 599 U.S. 236, 248 (2023). **13.** Storing 2.7.43 (emphasis in original). **14.** 3 Elliot's 446–47; *Smith,* 599 U.S. at 248 n.11 (2023). **15.** 3 Elliot's 558; *Smith,* 599 U.S. at 248 n.12. **16.** Kershen, *supra* at 816–17. **17.** 1 Annals of Cong. 435 (1789). **18.** *Id.* **19.** *Id.* at 760. **20.** S. Jour., 1st Cong., 1st

Sess. 77 (Sept. 9, 1789).   **21.** Letter from James Madison to Edmund Pendleton (Sept. 23, 1789), https://perma.cc/ZD6J-XD7C.   **22.** 1 Annals of Cong. 913 (1789).   **23.** Kershen, *supra* at 845, 856–57.   **24.** Judiciary Act of 1789, § 2, 1 Stat. 73, 73.   **25.** *Id.* § 29.   **26.** J. Gordon Hylton, *Virginia and the Ratification of the Bill of Rights, 1789–91*, 25 U. Rich. L. Rev. 433, 455 (1991).   **27.** Erwin C. Surrency, *Federal District Court Judges and the History of Their Courts*, 40 F.R.D. 139, 147–48 (1967).   **28.** Drew L. Kershen, *Vicinage—Part II*, 30 Okla. L. Rev. 1, 56–61 (1977).   **29.** *Id.* at 53.   **30.** *Id.* at 56 n.364.   **31.** *Zicarelli v. Dietz*, 633 F.2d 312, 321–25 (3d Cir. 1980).   **32.** *Lewis v. United States*, 279 U.S. 63, 72 (1929).   **33.** *United States v. Louwsma*, 970 F.2d 797, 801–02 (11th Cir. 1992).   **34.** 138 U.S. 157, 181–82 (1891).   **35.** 18 U.S.C. § 3238.   **36.** *Ruthenberg v. United States*, 245 U.S. 480, 482 (1918).   **37.** Fed. R. Crim. P. 21 (advisory committee note 3 to 1944 adoption).   **38.** Kershen, *Vicinage—Part II*, *supra*.   **39.** 599 U.S. 236 (2023).   **40.** 1 Wayne R. LaFave et al., Criminal Procedure § 2.6(b) (4th ed. Dec. 2023 update).   **41.** Kalt, *supra* at 304–10.   **42.** Akhil Reed Amar, *Sixth Amendment First Principles*, 84 Geo. L. J. 641 (1996).

ESSAY NO. 178: THE INFORMED OF ACCUSATION (ARRAIGNMENT) CLAUSE
AMEND. 6

In all criminal prosecutions, the accused shall enjoy the right . . . to be informed of the nature and cause of the accusation. . . .

—Judge Michael B. Brennan

INTRODUCTION

The Sixth Amendment protects the right of an accused "to be informed of the nature and cause of the accusation" against him so that he can receive a fair trial. This guarantee is intended to ensure (1) that an individual suspected of committing a crime receives proper notice of the specifics of the charges against him so that he can prepare a defense and (2) that the court can evaluate the legal sufficiency of the charges in an indictment during a court hearing. This provision is known as the Arraignment Clause because under modern procedure, the accused is informed during an *arraignment* proceeding.

HISTORY BEFORE 1787

An accused's right to be informed of the charges brought by an accuser derives from early English common law with historical underpinnings before Magna Carta. This right is also consistent with Chapter 39 of Magna Carta, which ensured that a person could not be imprisoned without a specified accusation in an indictment or otherwise in accordance with the common law.[1] The privilege against self-incrimination was accompanied from its inception by a corollary right to formal notice of an accusation.[2] The privilege and its corollary caused many political, religious, and legal battles, including disputes about interrogations based on the "oath *ex officio*."[3] During such questioning, the accused was often not informed of his accuser, and the specific charges were not revealed before the interrogation began.[4]

The common-law courts responded to the oath *ex officio* with new procedures. The accused had to be provided with a substantiated accusation based on specific charges.[5] Further, the accusation could be initiated either by an individual complaint, called an *appeal*, or by an accusing jury.[6] This latter institution was a predecessor of the grand jury. Before an answer was required, an accused was entitled to know the specific accusation, its details, and who was making it.[7]

In 1351 or 1352, Parliament enacted a statute that paid respect to Chapter 39 of Magna Carta.[8] The law provided that the king would not proceed against a free citizen without a specific accusation brought in accord with the common law.[9] In 1533, Parliament guaranteed that the people could not be interrogated unless the government provided a substantiated formal accusation.[10]

Sir William Blackstone's referenced a statute passed under King Henry V in 1418. Under this law, all indictments must set forth the name and town or county to identify an offender as well as the time and place of the offense. The indictment "must also be set forth with clearness and certainty: and in some crimes particular words of art must be used."[11]

The right to be informed of an accusation traveled across the Atlantic. The Virginia Declaration of Rights of 1776, written by George Mason, guaranteed "[t]hat in all capital or criminal prosecutions a man has a right to demand the cause and nature of his accusation. . . ."[12] Several colonies copied that language. The same phrase was included in the Pennsylvania constitution of 1776 and the Vermont constitution of 1777.[13] The Massachusetts constitution of 1780 similarly stated that "[n]o subject shall be held to answer for any crimes or offence until the same is fully and plainly, substantially and formally, described to him. . . ."[14] New Hampshire's constitution adopted the Massachusetts formulation in 1783.[15]

THE CONSTITUTIONAL CONVENTION AND RATIFICATION DEBATES

The Philadelphia Convention did not include a right to be informed of accusations. Several states subsequently proposed that this guarantee be added as a constitutional amendment. In 1788, for example, the North Carolina ratification convention proposed a Declaration of Rights with the same language that was used in the Virginia Declaration of Rights: "a man hath a right to demand the cause and nature of his accusation."[16] Similar proposals were put forward by the ratification conventions in Virginia (1788), Rhode Island (1790), and Pennsylvania (1787).[17]

ADOPTION OF THE SIXTH AMENDMENT

During the First Congress, Representative James Madison of Virginia drafted what became the right to be informed of the nature and cause of an accusation. The text he submitted on June 8, 1789, was identical to the language in the Sixth Amendment's Arraignment Clause.[18] This version was adopted by the House and Senate without recorded comment.[19] The guarantee was adopted as part of the Sixth Amendment.

JUDICIAL PRECEDENT

The earliest decision on this subject by the U.S. Supreme Court is *United States v. Mills*

(1833). Without explicit reference to the Sixth Amendment, the Court held that "the offense must be set forth with clearness, and all necessary certainty, to apprise the accused of the crime with which he stands charged."[20]

The first Supreme Court decision on this topic that was grounded in the Sixth Amendment is *United States v. Cruikshank* (1876).[21] The accused were charged with interfering with the constitutional rights of other citizens, but the indictment used generic terms— "several rights and privileges granted to them by the constitution."[22] This text did not provide adequate notice to the defendants.[23] Because the indictment was insufficiently certain and precise, the accused were not properly informed of the nature and cause of the charges against them.[24]

Cruikshank identified three purposes of the charging instrument: "to furnish the accused with such a description of the charge against him as will enable him to make his defence," to permit him to "avail himself of his conviction or acquittal for protection against a further prosecution for the same cause," and to inform the court of the facts alleged so that it may decide whether they are sufficient in law to support a conviction, if one should be had."[25]

In *Rosen v. United States* (1896), a defendant was indicted for sending obscene material by mail, but the charges did not describe each allegedly obscene image.[26] The Court, drawing on the purposes identified in *Cruikshank*, held that no constitutional violation had occurred.[27] Specific descriptions of the materials were not critical to the defense, and there was no indication that either the defendant or the trial court failed to understand the charges.[28]

In *Cole v. Arkansas* (1948), four defendants were tried and convicted of violating one section of a statute.[29] The state supreme court affirmed their convictions even though the evidence showed that the defendants had violated a different provision of the law.[30] However, the Supreme Court reversed.[31] At this point, the Arraignment Clause had not yet been incorporated and applied to the states, so the Court relied on the procedural protections of the Due Process Clause of the Fourteenth Amendment. The majority opinion ruled that the defendants' right to know all the charges against them and put on a complete defense had been violated: "No principle of procedural due process is more clearly established than that notice of the specific charge, and a chance to be heard in a trial of the issues raised by that charge, if desired, are among the constitutional rights of every accused in a criminal proceeding in all courts, state or federal."[32] In *Herring v. New York* (1975), the Court cited *Cole* in concluding that the Sixth Amendment, including its notice provision, has been "extended to a defendant in a state criminal prosecution through the Fourteenth Amendment."[33]

In *Russell v. United States* (1962), the defendant refused to answer questions put to him by the subcommittee.[34] The Court held that the indictment was insufficient because it failed to identify the subject of a congressional subcommittee's inquiry. *Russell*, in establishing basic notice requirements, viewed the notice protections in nineteenth-century case law and applied the same principles. The Court stated that notice provides two well-known functions: It "apprises the defendant of what he must be prepared to meet" and protects against a second prosecution for the same offense.[35] The Court also reviewed several foundational principles in establishing what constitutes sufficient notice, such as specificity in the offense; reasonable certainty as to the charge, including all of the charge's required elements; and information about the charged facts and circumstances.[36]

MODERN PRACTICE

The Sixth Amendment's requirement that the accused must be informed of the accusation is typically accomplished through a charging document, an arraignment on the charge, or both. In the federal system, an indictment must include the elements of the offense charged, fairly inform an accused of the charge against which he will have to defend himself, and allow an accused to plead guilty or not guilty to bar a future prosecution for the same offense.[37] The Sixth Amendment does not require that the accused receive a copy of the indictment,[38] but in practice, that most often occurs. The notice and specificity requirements are usually accomplished by reading the charges to an accused at an arraignment hearing or by specifying the charges in an indictment. The grand jury right has not been incorporated against the states,[39] but in states where indictments are not required, defendants can be informed of the accusations through a criminal information or complaint. (See Essay No. 168.)

Under the Federal Rules of Criminal Procedure, the notice and specificity requirement has taken on a more ministerial character. Rule 7(c) describes the nature and contents of a charging document. Under Rule 7(f) a defendant may be entitled to a bill of particulars. Such a bill would help an accused obtain information when a charging instrument omits factual details,[40] both to prepare a defense and to avoid surprise at trial. Rule 10 governs arraignments in general, including a defendant's right to waive an appearance. Rule 43(a) specifies the requirements for when a defendant must be present. State criminal rules and procedures have similar requirements,[41] but states' rules vary and use the term "arraignment" to refer to a variety of proceedings.[42]

OPEN QUESTIONS

- Does the Sixth Amendment's Arraignment Clause have stronger roots in the Constitution's text than do the procedural due process guarantees of an accused's right to notice of criminal charges?[43]
- Does the Constitution require an arraignment hearing? *Garland v. Washington* (1914) might be read as holding either that the state's failure to hold an arraignment was harmless error or that the Constitution imposes no requirement of an arraignment.[44] The text of the clause requires only that the defendant must be informed of the nature of the charges in some way, which could be accomplished by the charging document and not necessarily an arraignment hearing. The lower courts have held that such a hearing is not required by the Fifth Amendment's Due Process Clause.[45]

- Do Rules 7 and 10 of the Federal Rules of Criminal Procedure fully encompass the notice and specificity requirements of the Sixth Amendment's Informed of Accusation Clause?

Cite as: Judge Michael B. Brennan, *The Informed of Accusation (Arraignment) Clause, in* The Heritage Guide to the Constitution 670 (Josh Blackman & John G. Malcolm eds., 3d ed. 2025).

Notes

1. 1 Sir Frederick Pollock and Frederick William Maitland, The History of English Law Before the Time of Edward I, 173 n.3 (2d ed. 1903)). **2.** Laurence A. Benner, *Requiem for* Miranda: *The Rehnquist Court's Voluntariness Doctrine in Historical Perspective*, 67 Wash. U. L. Q. 59, 64 (1989). **3.** E.M. Morgan, *The Privilege Against Self-Incrimination*, 34 Minn. L. Rev. 1, at 1 (1949). **4.** Benner, *supra* at 70. **5.** *Id.* at 71. **6.** 1 Pollock & Maitland, *supra* at 151–52; 2 Pollock & Maitland *supra at* 466, 642. **7.** Benner, *supra* at 72. **8.** 1 Statutes of the Realm 319, 321 (25 Edward III, c. 4, 1351–1352). **9.** *Id.* **10.** 3 Statutes of the Realm 454, 455 (25 Henry VIII, c. 14, 1533). **11.** 4 Blackstone 306. **12.** Va. Decl. of Rts. of 1776, § 8. **13.** Pa. Const. of 1790, art. 1, § 9; Vt. Const. of 1777, ch. 1, § 10. **14.** Mass. Const. of 1780, art. XII. **15.** N.H. Const. of 1783, art. 15. **16.** 4 Elliot's 243. **17.** 3 Elliot's 658; 2 Documentary History of the Constitution of the United States of America 354–55, 365 (1894). **18.** 1 Annals of Cong. 452 (1789). **19.** *Id.* at 86, 809. **20.** 32 U.S. 138, 142 (1833). **21.** 92 U.S. 542 (1876). **22.** *Id.* at 557. **23.** *Id.* **24.** *Id.* at 559. **25.** *Id.* at 558. **26.** 161 U.S. 29, 31–32 (1896). **27.** *Id.* at 34. **28.** *Id.* at 41. **29.** 333 U.S. 196, 197–98 (1948). **30.** *Id.* at 197–98. **31.** *Id.* at 198. **32.** *Id.* at 201. **33.** 422 U.S. 853, 857 & n.7 (1975). **34.** 369 U.S. 749, 751 & n.2, 760 (1962). **35.** *Id.* at 763, 764. **36.** *Id.* at 764–65. **37.** *Hamling v. U.S.*, 418 U.S. 87, 117–18 (1974). **38.** *United States v. Duzee*, 140 U.S. 169, 173 (1891). **39.** *McDonald v. City of Chicago*, 561 U.S. 742, 765 & n.13 (2010). **40.** *Will v. United States*, 389 U.S. 90, 98, 101 (1967). **41.** 5 Wayne R. LaFave, *et al.* Criminal Procedure § 19.2(c) (4th ed. 2020). **42.** *Id.* at § 21.4(a). **43.** *Lopez v. Smith*, 574 U.S. 1, 4–6 (2014); 333 U.S. at 201. **44.** 232 U.S. 642, 645 (1914). **45.** *Valenzuela-Gonzalez v. U.S. District Court for D. Ariz.*, 915 F.2d 1276–80 (9th Cir. 1990); *United States v. Coffman*, 567 F.3d 960, 961 (10th Cir. 1977).

ESSAY NO. 179: THE CONFRONTATION CLAUSE
AMEND. 6

In all criminal prosecutions, the accused shall enjoy the right . . . to be confronted with the witnesses against him. . . .

—John F. Bash, III

INTRODUCTION

Few clauses of the Constitution better illustrate the ascendency of originalism in the jurisprudence of the modern Supreme Court than the Confrontation Clause. The seminal decision of *Crawford v. Washington* (2004) overruled precedent that had reduced the clause to little more than a judicial balancing test.[1] Instead, based on the text and history of the clause, *Crawford* restored its original function as a strict procedural limitation on the use of out-of-court statements in criminal trials.

HISTORY BEFORE 1789

The right of a criminal defendant to confront an accuser has antecedents in ancient times. The Book of Deuteronomy states that "[i]f a false witness rise up against any man to testify against him that which is wrong; then both the men, between whom the controversy is, shall stand before the Lord, before the priests and the judges, which shall be in those days; and the judges shall make diligent inquisition."[2] The Roman Governor Porcius Festus, who held the apostle Paul in custody, stated in the Acts of the Apostles that "[i]t is not the manner of the Romans to deliver any man up to die before the accused has met his accusers face-to-face, and has been given a chance to defend himself against the charges."[3]

This ancient practice continued to the English common law. The accused were generally guaranteed a right to cross-examine, or confront, their accusers in open court.[4] In the continental civil-law system, judges were empowered to examine witnesses privately.[5] However, in the mid-sixteenth century, Parliament enacted two statutes that authorized judges to examine witnesses when the accused was not present.[6] The judges could then submit the results of the *ex parte* examinations to courts. Over time, the records of such examinations came to be used as evidence in criminal trials. Perhaps the most infamous case was the 1603 treason trial of Sir Walter Raleigh.[7] In that case, statements were taken from Raleigh's alleged accomplices. That out-of-court testimony was read to the jury, but Raleigh was barred from cross-examining the witnesses in open court. This controversial decision came to be viewed as unjust.

English law gradually developed greater protections for the right to confrontation. Courts would generally admit out-of-court testimony only where the witness was unavailable and the defendant had been afforded a prior opportunity for cross-examination.[8] Nevertheless, that guarantee was not always honored in the American colonies. For example, under the infamous Stamp Act of 1765, admiralty courts would hear cases for violating the revenue law.[9] These courts lacked a jury and followed the civil-law system of *ex parte* judicial examination.[10]

With those abuses fresh in the minds of Americans, new state bills of rights drafted between 1776 and 1780 codified the right of criminal defendants to confront their accusers. The 1780 Massachusetts Declaration of Rights, for example, stated that "every subject shall have a right . . . to meet the witnesses against him, face to face."[11]

ADOPTION OF THE CONFRONTATION CLAUSE

During the Constitutional Convention, there was no meaningful discussion of the confrontation right, which also received little attention during the ratification debates. However, at least one Anti-Federalist objected to the lack of any confrontation right in the Constitution. Federal Farmer wrote that "[n]othing can be more essential than the cross examining [of] witnesses, and generally before the triers of the facts in question."[12] During the First Congress, the confrontation right was ultimately incorporated into what became the Sixth Amendment. No evidence has emerged about the drafters' intentions or understandings with respect to that clause.

EARLY PRECEDENT

In the early Republic, a number of state supreme courts interpreted state analogues to the Confrontation Clause. These cases ruled that out-of-court testimony was inadmissible in a criminal trial unless the defendant had been afforded a prior opportunity to examine the witness.[13] Such decisions provide some evidence about the original understanding of the confrontation right.

Another relevant precedent came during the 1807 treason trial of Aaron Burr. Chief Justice John Marshall, who presided over the trial, excluded out-of-court statements by one of Burr's alleged co-conspirators.[14] Nearly 200 years later, the majority and the dissent in *Crawford* sparred over whether the case shed any light on the Confrontation Clause. Justice Antonin Scalia maintained that the opinion did not meaningfully address the clause, which it mentioned only once in passing, and Chief Justice William Rehnquist read the opinion to have affirmed that courts could recognize new exceptions to the confrontation right.[15]

The first Supreme Court decision construing the Confrontation Clause was *Mattox v. United States* (1895).[16] The Court upheld admission of the testimony of a deceased witness from a prior trial. Critically, the decision relied on the fact that the defendant had been able to cross-examine the witness during the first proceeding. However, the Court would later deviate from that rule.

MODERN PRECEDENT

Ohio v. Roberts (1980) was a significant case concerning the Confrontation Clause.[17] The Court held that out-of-court statements by unavailable witnesses were admissible against a criminal defendant as long as they bore "adequate indicia of reliability." In other words, the court would admit out-of-court testimony if it was reliable enough—even though the defendant could not confront and cross-examine the witness. This decision was in no way grounded in the text or history of the Sixth Amendment.

The *Roberts* rule would be overruled in *Crawford v. Washington* (2004). Justice Scalia's majority opinion distilled from this history a rule: The Confrontation Clause bars "admission of testimonial statements of a witness who did not appear at trial unless he was unavailable to testify, and the defendant had a prior opportunity for cross examination."[18] This rule was consistent with the reaction to the trial of Sir Walter Raleigh and with the meaning of confrontation in contemporaneous dictionaries.[19] Scalia acknowledged that "the Clause's ultimate goal is to ensure reliability of evidence" but explained that the clause "commands, not that evidence be reliable, but that reliability be assessed in a particular manner: by testing in the crucible of cross-examination."[20] Scalia quipped that "[d]ispensing with confrontation because testimony is obviously reliable is akin to dispensing with jury trial because a defendant is obviously guilty."[21]

In the wake of *Crawford*, courts have faced three recurring sets of problems in construing and applying the Confrontation Clause. First, the *Crawford* rule applies only to an out-of-court statement that is "testimonial." *Crawford* acknowledged, for example, that out-of-court statements contained in business records and official records are not testimonial.

In *Davis v. Washington* (2006), Justice Scalia concluded that "[s]tatements are nontestimonial when made in the course of police interrogation under circumstances objectively indicating that the primary purpose of the interrogation is to enable police assistance to meet an ongoing emergency."[22] They are testimonial when "the primary purpose of the interrogation is to establish or prove past events potentially relevant to later criminal prosecution."[23] These latter statements could be admitted only if the witness was subject to cross-examination in court.

Justice Clarence Thomas dissented. The two great originalists disagreed about the historical abuses that the Confrontation Clause was designed to prevent. Justice Thomas would have limited "testimonial" statements to those made with "some degree of solemnity," such as statements "contained in formalized testimonial materials" like "affidavits, depositions, prior testimony, or confessions."[24] Statements made during "informal police questioning" were nontestimonial and could be admitted in court without cross-examination.[25] The Court has also decided a series of cases about whether forensic lab reports are considered testimonial.[26]

Second, *Crawford* recognized or suggested exceptions to the rule. For example, *Crawford* indicated in a footnote that courts may be permitted to admit a person's dying declarations—a circumstance in which the witness cannot be confronted.[27] *Crawford* also permitted the admission of statements where the defendant is responsible for a witness's unavailability.[28] Here, the defendant forfeited the right by his own wrongdoing, but *Giles v. California* (2008) held that the forfeiture exception does not apply when the defendant killed the victim for some reason other than preventing her testimony.[29]

Third, there is the question of how *Crawford* applies to videoconferencing tools. Is the confrontation right satisfied when a witness testifies at a criminal trial over camera, or must the witness appear in person, face-to-face with the defendant and the jury? *Coy v. Iowa* (1988) stated that the Court had "never doubted" that the confrontation right requires in-person, face-to-face confrontation.[30] Two years later, however, *Maryland v. Craig* (1990) reversed course. (Justice Scalia wrote the majority opinion in *Coy* but dissented in *Craig*.) *Craig* upheld a procedure whereby a six-year-old victim of child abuse had been examined by the government and cross-examined by defense counsel outside of the courtroom. The examination was visible to the defendant and the jurors via one-way closed-circuit television, but the victim could not view the defendant. *Craig* deemed it sufficient that the procedure was "necessary to protect a child witness from trauma."[31] The Court found that every element of the confrontation right was satisfied other than forcing the witness to look at the accused: There was testimony under oath, the opportunity for cross-examination, and the ability of the judge, jury, and defendant to observe the demeanor of the witness.

OPEN QUESTIONS

- *Maryland v. Craig* relied on a purpose-based approach to the Confrontation Clause. Was this holding undermined by *Crawford v. Washington*'s more formalist interpretation of the clause? During the COVID-19 pandemic, lower courts permitted witnesses to testify by two-way videoconferencing applications.[32] Were these decisions consistent with *Crawford* and the original meaning of the Confrontation Clause?
- The Supreme Court denied review in *Franklin v. New York* (2024), a Confrontation Clause case.[33] In a statement, Justice Samuel Alito wrote that the Court should "reconsider" *Crawford* in an "appropriate case."[34] He observed that "[h]istorical research now calls into question *Crawford*'s understanding of the relevant common-law rules at the time of the adoption of the Sixth Amendment, and whatever else may be said about that decision, there can be no dispute that it has not produced predictable and consistent results."[35] Should *Crawford* be reconsidered?

Cite as: John F. Bash, III, *The Confrontation Clause, in* THE HERITAGE GUIDE TO THE CONSTITUTION 673 (Josh Blackman & John G. Malcolm eds., 3d ed. 2025).

Notes

1. 541 U.S. 36 (2004).   2. Deuteronomy 19:16–18 (King James); Richard D. Friedman, *The Confrontation Clause Re-Rooted and Transformed*, 2003–2004 Cato S. Ct. Rev. 439, 443 (2004).   3. Acts 25:16 (King James); Friedman, *supra* at 443.   4. Friedman, *supra* at 444.   5. *Id.* at 443–44.   6. 1 & 2 Phil. & M., c. 13 (1554); 2 & 3 *id.*, c. 10 (1555); *Crawford*, 541 U.S. at 43–44.   7. *Raleigh's Case*, 2 How. St. Tr. 1 (1603); *Crawford*, 541 U.S. at 44.   8. *King v. Paine*, 5 Mod. 163, 87 Eng. Rep. 584 (1696); *Crawford*, 541 U.S. at 45–46.   9. 5 Geo. 3, c. 12, § 57 (1765); *Crawford*, 541 U.S. at 47–48.   10. *Sec. & Exch. Comm'n v. Jarkesy*, 603 U.S. 109, 121 (2024) (citing Resolutions of the Stamp Act Congress, Art. VIII (Oct. 19, 1765), *reprinted in* Sources of Our Liberties: Documentary Origins of Individual Liberties in the United States Constitution and Bill of Rights 270, 271 (R. Perry & J. Cooper eds. 1959)); *Crawford*, 541 U.S. at 47–48.   11. Mass. Decl. of Rts. of 1780, § XII; N.H. Bill of Rts. of 1783, § XV; Va. Decl. of Rts. of 1776, § 8; Pa. Decl. of Rts. of 1776, § IX; Del. Decl. of Rts. of 1776, § 14; Md. Decl. of Rts. § XIX; N.C. Decl. of Rts. of 1776, § VII; Vt. Decl. of Rts. ch. I, § X.   12. Storing 2.8.53.   13. *State v. Webb,* 2 N.C. 103 (Super. L. & Eq. 1794); *State v. Campbell*, 30 S.C.L. 124, 1844 WL 2558 (App.L.1844); *Crawford*, 541 U.S. at 49–50.   14. *United States v. Burr*, 25 F. Cas. 187 (No. 14,694) (CC Va. 1807) (Marshall, C.J.).   15. *Crawford*, 541 U.S. at 59 n.9; *id.* at 71–74 (Rehnquist, C.J., concurring).   16. 156 U.S. 237 (1895).   17. 448 U.S. 46 (1980).   18. 541 U.S. at 53–54.   19. *Id.* at 51–52.   20. Id. at 61.   21. Id. at 62.   22. 547 U.S. 813 (2006).   23. *Id.* at 822.   24. *Id.* at 836 (Thomas, J., concurring in part and dissenting in part).   25. *Id.* at 838, 840.   26. *Williams v. Illinois*, 567 U.S. 50 (2012); *Bullcoming v. New Mexico*, 564 U.S. 647 (2011); *Melendez-Diaz v. Massachusetts*, 557 U.S. 305 (2009)   27. 541 U.S. at 56 n.6; *Michigan v. Bryant*, 562 U.S. 344, 349, 351 n.1 (2011).   28. 541 U.S. at 62.   29. 554 U.S. 353, 357, 359–61, 377 (2008).   30. 487 U.S. 1012, 1016 (1988).   31. 497 U.S. 836, 857 (1990).   32. *United States v. Akhavan*, Nos. 21-1678-cr(L) *et al.*, 2022 WL 17825627, at *2–*5 (2d Cir. Dec. 21, 2022).   33. 145 S.Ct. 831, 831 (2025).   34. *Id.* (Alito, J.)   35. *Id.*

~~~~

ESSAY NO. 180: THE COMPULSORY PROCESS CLAUSE
AMEND. 6

In all criminal prosecutions, the accused shall enjoy the right . . . to have compulsory process for obtaining witnesses in his favor. . . .
—Judge Joel M. Carson III & Jefferson F. Serfass

INTRODUCTION

On its face, the Compulsory Process Clause narrowly provides criminal defendants the right to invoke the court's subpoena power to compel otherwise unwilling witnesses to come to court and testify. But there is a rich history underlying the clause's seemingly innocuous language. Early Americans likely understood this provision as enshrining a broader set of common-law procedural guarantees. The Compulsory

Process Clause expressly protects an accused's right to compel testimony from material witnesses, and implicitly protects other rights of the accused: the right to *call* his or her own witnesses; the right not to be tried before those witnesses arrive; the right to question those witnesses under oath; and the right to compel those witnesses to bring with them any documents material to their testimony.

HISTORY BEFORE 1787

The Compulsory Process Clause, like other Sixth Amendment guarantees, arose from the abuses suffered by criminal defendants under the early common-law rules governing witnesses.[1] As recently as the late fifteenth century, English courts refused to hear *any* exculpatory testimony from defense witnesses, even from those present in the courtroom and willing to testify. Judges often concluded that allowing testimony against the Crown would be improper.[2] This prohibition eventually yielded to the practice of allowing defense witnesses to testify, but refusing to swear them in.[3] Of course, criminal defendants still suffered because those same courts would then instruct their juries to give more weight to sworn testimony, which only the Crown's witnesses could provide.[4] Even after the common law finally embraced the idea that defendants should be able both to call and to swear in their own witnesses, the Crown continued to convict and execute innocent defendants because those defendants had no right to compel unwilling witnesses to testify at their trials.[5]

The trial of William Ireland, Thomas Pickering, and John Grove in 1678 illustrates the fundamental unfairness of these early common-law practices.[6] The Crown charged Ireland with high treason, accusing him of conspiring with Pickering and Grove to kill King Charles II.[7] (See Essay No. 137.) The Crown's evidence consisted of only two men's testimony. Oates and Bedloe swore that "in August" they attended a meeting in London where Ireland and the others agreed to assassinate the king.[8] Ireland denied the accusations, contending that he was in Staffordshire, a town roughly 150 miles outside of London, during the alleged meeting.[9]

Although Ireland had the right to call witnesses, the court refused to let him contact anyone until the morning of his trial.[10] Then,

at trial, when Ireland named the witnesses he sought to call and pleaded for time for them to arrive, the presiding judge proceeded without them.[11] All three defendants were convicted and executed.[12] Shortly before his execution, Ireland proclaimed that "a hundred and more saw me in Staffordshire; therefore, how I should be [guilty of treason] I do not well know or understand."[13] The injustice of his conviction and execution became apparent when witnesses ultimately confirmed Ireland's alibi and resulting innocence at Oates's own perjury trial seven years later.[14]

Scholars contend that Ireland's story and others like it drove Parliament to grant criminal defendants the right to call witnesses and compel them to testify under oath.[15] These stories also reached the American colonies in Salmon's *State Trials* (1765) and widely circulated pamphlets.[16] So too did news of the new rules permitting defendants to compel the appearance of favorable witnesses. Sir William Blackstone opined that the accused, at least in high treason cases, "shall have the same compulsive process to bring in his witnesses *for* him as was usual to compel their appearance *against* him."[17]

After independence, nine states included some variation of a compulsory process clause in their constitutions.[18] Three states granted the accused the right "to call for evidence in his favour."[19] Two others provided for the right to produce "all proofs that may be favorable."[20] North Carolina guaranteed the right "to confront the accusers and witnesses with other testimony."[21] Delaware protected the accused's right "to examine evidence on oath in his favour."[22] New Jersey promised that "all criminals shall be admitted to the same privileges of witnesses and counsel, as their prosecutors are or shall be entitled to."[23] Maryland granted the accused both the right "to examine [his] witnesses . . . on oath" and the right "to have process for his witnesses."[24]

ADOPTION OF THE SIXTH AMENDMENT

During the First Congress, Representative James Madison of Virginia drafted the Compulsory Process Clause in language that most closely mirrored Blackstone's.[25] The text provided that "the accused shall enjoy the right . . . to have a compulsory process for obtaining witnesses in his favor...."[26] Congress made no substantive changes and debated it only briefly.[27] The states adopted Madison's draft without much recorded debate.[28] That the amendment was so uncontroversial strongly indicates that there was a wide understanding that the Compulsory Process Clause captured the same common-law rights that the various state constitutions aimed to protect.[29]

THE AARON BURR TREASON TRIAL

The first major Compulsory Process Clause interpretation came in *United States v. Burr* (1807). Chief Justice John Marshall, sitting as a trial judge, presided. The United States charged former Vice President Aaron Burr with treason, alleging that Burr planned to seize the United States' western territories and secede from the federal government.[30] The prosecution relied heavily on General James Wilkinson's oral testimony and a letter Wilkinson sent to then-President Thomas Jefferson that purportedly established Burr's guilt beyond doubt.[31] Burr and his attorneys vigorously denied the charges.

When the trial began, Burr sought to compel the President to produce the Wilkinson letter.[32] The government argued that the Compulsory Process Clause granted Burr only the right to compel the President's oral testimony because the clause referred to "witnesses," not "documents."[33]

Marshall rejected this argument and criticized the government's "literal distinction" as "too attenuated to be countenanced in the tribunals of a just and humane nation."[34] Thus, he held that the accused's constitutional right to compel the attendance of witnesses must extend to "their bringing with them such papers as may be material in the defense."[35]

Ultimately, Jefferson produced only a redacted version of the letter.[36] As it turned out, the letter was a sham—written by Wilkinson to vilify Burr and hide Wilkinson's own treason.[37] The jury acquitted Burr.[38] Marshall's Compulsory Process Clause interpretation remains a seminal source for assessing the clause's original public meaning.

MODERN PRECEDENT

More than 150 years after Burr's trial, the U.S. Supreme Court provided the second major Compulsory Process Clause interpretation and application in *Washington v. Texas* (1967). In that case, Texas charged Jackie Washington with murder.[39] Only Washington and another man, Will Fuller, witnessed the shooting. Texas, not knowing which of them truly committed the murder, arrested and charged both of them.[40] At Washington's own trial, he testified that Fuller murdered the victim and that he (Washington) had tried unsuccessfully to stop Fuller.[41] Washington sought to call Fuller to the witness stand to support his story. However, two Texas statutes barred persons charged or convicted as co-participants in the same crime from testifying in each other's defense.[42] The trial court therefore excluded Fuller's testimony.[43] The jury convicted Washington, and the relevant appellate courts affirmed.[44]

The Supreme Court reversed, holding unanimously that the Texas statutes violated the Constitution.[45] The Court found that the Framers designed the Compulsory Process Clause, in part, to make the testimony of a defendant's witness admissible on his behalf. Therefore, the state could not make all defense testimony inadmissible as a matter of procedural law.[46] The Court concluded that "arbitrary rules that prevent whole categories of defense witnesses from testifying on the basis of *a priori* categories that presume them unworthy of belief" violate the Compulsory Process Clause in the same way.[47]

Washington laid the foundation for modern Compulsory Process Clause jurisprudence, but may be questionable on originalist grounds. Scholars dispute whether Americans at the time of the Sixth Amendment's ratification would have understood the clause to reach the two statutes the Court declared unconstitutional in *Washington*.[48] Moreover, federal courts appear to have enforced similar statutes declaring certain witnesses incompetent well into the nineteenth century.[49] Yet, the Texas statutes, in which the prosecution had the right to call a key witness, but the defense did not, plainly defy Chief Justice Marshall's ruling from *Burr*: "with respect to the means of compelling the attendance of witnesses . . . the prosecution and the defense are placed by the law on equal ground."[50]

To establish a Compulsory Process Clause violation under current law, the accused must show (1) that the witness's testimony the accused sought to introduce would have been "favorable and material," and (2) that the government's exclusion was "arbitrary" or "disproportionate" to the evidentiary purposes advanced by the exclusion.[51] Unlike the accused's right to confront adverse witnesses, the accused must try to call a favorable witness to trigger his or her rights under the Compulsory Process Clause.[52]

OPEN QUESTIONS

- With the increase in remote court proceedings, does the Compulsory Process Clause grant defendants the right to compel in-person testimony?
- Under what circumstances, if any, may a defendant invoke the Compulsory Process Clause to secure the testimony of an expert witness?

This composition is not a statement by the United States Court of Appeals for the Tenth Circuit or by Latham & Watkins LLP. Nor does this essay necessarily reflect the views of the court or the firm.

Cite as: Judge Joel M. Carson III & Jefferson F. Serfass, *The Compulsory Process Clause, in* THE HERITAGE GUIDE TO THE CONSTITUTION 676 (Josh Blackman & John G. Malcolm eds., 3d ed. 2025).

Notes

1. *Washington v. Texas*, 388 U.S. 14, 19 (1967). **2.** Peter Westen, *The Compulsory Process Clause*, 73 Mich. L. Rev. 71, 83 n.40 (1974). **3.** 4 Blackstone 355. **4.** *Id.* **5.** Westen, *supra* at 85. **6.** *Id.* at 85 n.51; William Cobbett, 7 Cobbett's Complete Collection of State Trials 79 (1810). **7.** Sir James Stephen, 1 A History of the Criminal Law of England 388 (1883). **8.** *Id.*; Cobbett, *supra*, at 97, 109. **9.** Cobbett, *supra* at 112, 121; Stephen, *supra* at 388. **10.** Cobbett, *supra* at 121. **11.** *Id.* **12.** Stephen, *supra* at 388; Cobbett, *supra* at 141. **13.** Cobbett, *supra* at 141. **14.** *Id.* at 124; Westen, *supra* at 85 n.15. **15.** Westen, *supra* at 89–90; 4 Blackstone 354. **16.** Irving Brant, The Bill of Rights, Its Origin and Meaning 34–35 (1965). **17.** Westen, *supra* at 76; 4 Blackstone 354; Brant, *supra* at 93. **18.** *Taylor v. Illinois*, 484 U.S. 400, 408 n.13 (1988). **19.** *Id.* **20.** *Id.* **21.** N.C. Const. of 1776, Decl. of Rights, art. VII. **22.** Del. Decl. of Rts. of 1776, art. XIV. **23.** N.J. Const. of 1776, art. XVI **24.** Md. Const. of 1776, art. XIX. **25.** Westen, *supra* at 97–98 n.114. **26.** 1 Annals of Cong. 452 (1789). **27.** Westen, *supra* at 98 n.115. **28.** Stacey Kime, *Can a Right Be Less Than the Sum of Its Parts? How the Conflation of Compulsory Process and Due Process Guarantees Diminishes Criminal Defendants' Rights*, 48 Am. Crim. L. Rev. 1501, 1517 (2011). **29.** Westen, *supra* at 100. **30.** *Id.* at 101; Evan Andrews, *Aaron Burr's Notorious Treason Case*, History (Feb. 19, 2025), https://perma.cc /CA8V-Y3SX. **31.** *United States v. Burr*, 25 F. Cas. 30, 31–32 (C.C.D. 1807). **32.** *Id.* at 30. **33.** *Id.* at 32, 34. **34.** *Id.* at 35. **35.** *Id.* **36.** Josh Blackman, *Symposium: It Must Be Nice to Have John Marshall on Your Side*, SCOTUSBlog (July 10, 2020), https://perma.cc/SE2W-RX3A. **37.** Andrews, *supra*; Matthew L. Harris & Jay H. Buckley, Zebulon Pike, Thomas Jefferson, and the Opening of the American West 212–13 (2012). **38.** Harris & Buckley, *supra* at 213; Westen, *supra* at 107. **39.** *Washington v. Texas*, 388 U.S. 14, 15 (1967). **40.** *Id.* at 16. **41.** *Id.* **42.** *Id.* **43.** *Id.* at 17. **44.** *Id.* **45.** *Id.* **46.** *Id.* at 22. **47.** *Id.* **48.** Westen, *supra* at 113–14; Kime, *supra* at 1502, 1516–21. **49.** *Washington*, 388 U.S. at 21–22 (citing *United States v. Reid*, 53 U.S. 361 (1852)). **50.** *Burr*, 25 F. Cas. at 33. **51.** *Makiel v. Butler*, 782 F.3d 882, 907 (7th Cir. 2015). **52.** *Taylor*, 484 U.S. at 410.

~

ESSAY NO. 181: THE RIGHT TO COUNSEL CLAUSE
AMEND. 6

In all criminal prosecutions, the accused shall enjoy the right . . . to have the Assistance of Counsel for his defence.

—Judge Lawrence VanDyke & Alexandria Overcash

INTRODUCTION

The Sixth Amendment of the U.S. Constitution guarantees that "[i]n all criminal prosecutions, the accused shall enjoy the right . . . to have the Assistance of Counsel for his defense." On the eve of the Revolution, a limited version of this right existed in English common law. Counsel could assist defendants but only in some circumstances. Scholars and legal commentators have long understood the Framers to have rejected that narrow common-law rule in favor of a more expansive right to counsel. That expanded right in turn has been amplified and augmented by the American courts, particularly during the twentieth century, so that its contemporary application extends well beyond its original meaning.

THE COMMON-LAW RIGHT TO ASSISTANCE OF COUNSEL

English common law permitted, and sometimes required, counsel to aid defendants in misdemeanor cases.[1] But for felonies, the common law prohibited counsel from aiding a defendant on issues of fact; counsel could only argue questions of law.[2] This rule had no exceptions until Parliament passed the Treason Trials Act of 1695.[3] That act created a narrow exception for felony-treason cases: Counsel could aid defendants, and courts had to appoint counsel if a defendant requested such.[4] The common-law rule remained unchanged for all other felony offenses.[5] Despite this common-law rule, the court purported to serve as the defendant's counsel.[6]

The limitation on the assistance of non-judicial counsel received wide criticism. Sir William Blackstone, for example, faulted this rule as "not at all of a piece with the rest of the humane treatment of prisoners by the English law."[7] Over time, the courts' practices became more lenient.[8] Judges would allow counsel to instruct defendants on what questions to ask with respect to matters of fact. At times, judges even allowed counsel to ask the questions themselves. Nevertheless, Blackstone remained critical, noting that "this is a matter of too much importance to be left to the good pleasure of any judge, and is worthy the interposition of the legislature."[9]

CREATION OF THE AMERICAN RIGHT TO ASSISTANCE OF COUNSEL

The American colonists, heavily influenced by Blackstone, seem to have shared his concerns. Before independence, at least twelve of the thirteen colonies had rejected the English common-law rule and provided a right to the assistance of counsel.[10] Most of the colonies rejected the common law completely, and a couple limited the right to counsel to capital offenses or more serious crimes.[11] Seven of the colonies also provided a limited statutory right to appointment of counsel for certain types of crimes, such as capital offenses and treason.[12] As the U.S. Supreme Court would observe in *Betts v. Brady* (1942), a "great diversity of policy" existed regarding the appointment of counsel in state legislation, and no state constitution contained a right to appointed counsel.[13]

During the state ratification conventions, seven states requested a bill of rights. Two of them, Virginia and North Carolina, proposed a right to counsel, and New York conditioned its ratification on the assumption that the new government would not abridge certain rights, including the right to counsel.[14]

In 1789, the First Congress proposed what would become the Bill of Rights. James Madison proposed an amendment that contained the right to assistance of counsel.[15] Little discussion of the right occurred before it was ratified as part of the Sixth Amendment on December 15, 1791.[16]

JUDICIAL UNDERSTANDING OF THE RIGHT TO ASSISTANCE OF COUNSEL

Few cases from the nineteenth century addressed the right to assistance of counsel. *United States v. Van Duzee* (1891) sheds some light on what the right to assistance of counsel was originally understood to mean.[17] The Court explained that "[t]here is . . . no general obligation on the part of the government . . . to . . . retain counsel for defendants or prisoners." Rather, the Court observed, "[t]he object of the constitutional provision was merely to secure those rights which by the ancient rules of the common law had been denied to them."[18] The Court stressed that "it was not contemplated that this should be done at the expense of the government."[19] This appears to have been the common understanding of the Sixth Amendment right to assistance of counsel until the 1930s.[20]

The Court changed course in *Powell v. Alabama* (1932), an appeal from a state-court conviction.[21] The Court held that the Due Process Clause of the Fourteenth Amendment entitles a defendant to appointment of counsel in some capital cases.[22] *Johnson v. Zerbst* (1938) held that the Sixth Amendment prohibits a federal court from convicting a criminal defendant of a felony unless he has or waives the assistance of counsel.[23] This rule "require[d] appointment of counsel in all cases where a defendant is unable to procure the services of an attorney."[24] Under *Johnson*, the government had to pay for counsel for indigent defendants. But *Betts v. Brady* (1942) made clear that *Johnson* applied only to defendants in federal courts and did not require state courts to appoint and pay for a criminal defendant's attorney. The Court based *Betts* on a survey of the common law, state constitutions, and statutory provisions that governed the right to assistance of counsel and the right to appointed counsel.[25]

Two decades later, the Supreme Court overturned *Betts* in *Gideon v. Wainwright* (1963). This landmark case held that the Sixth Amendment requirement of appointing counsel to indigent defendants applies to the states under the Fourteenth Amendment.[26] *Gideon* has received strong criticism from those who claim that it is inconsistent with the original meaning of the right to assistance of counsel. Justice Clarence Thomas, for example, has observed that "[t]he Sixth Amendment appears to have been understood at the time of ratification as a rejection of the English common-law rule that prohibited counsel, not as a guarantee of government-funded counsel."[27]

As a historical matter, this criticism seems warranted. The right to assistance of counsel arose as a response to the restrictive common-law rule that prohibited attorneys from aiding defendants on questions of fact in nearly all criminal cases. English common law originally provided appointed counsel only to defendants in treason cases, not to all criminal defendants accused of felonies. By contrast, the right of criminal defendants in the United States to *hire* counsel became pervasive in state constitutions and statutes. However, the right to *appointed* counsel did not gain the same traction. It was not included in state constitutions; instead, when provided by the states, it found its home only in statutory provisions.[28]

Moreover, the states' policies were diverse and fluctuated over time. In some states, appointment was discretionary; in others, it was obligatory.[29] Some states required appointment in all cases; others required it only for certain offenses.[30] Against this backdrop, the best original understanding of the right to assistance of counsel is that it provided the right to retain counsel but not to have counsel appointed. *Gideon* did not attempt to explain how its construction of the right to assistance of counsel is consistent with the original understanding of the right. Nor did *Gideon* attempt to square its conclusion that this right is "fundamental" with the states' inconsistent history of appointing counsel. Even so, *Gideon* remains the law of the land today and serves as the foundation for the modern application of the right to assistance of counsel.

MODERN APPLICATION

Under modern doctrine, the Sixth Amendment right to assistance of counsel arises upon "the initiation of adversary judicial criminal proceedings."[31] Once the right has attached, it applies to all critical stages of the criminal process.[32] The right protects both the defendant's right to be assisted by counsel and the defendant's right to represent himself if he knowingly and intelligently waives his right to counsel.[33] Counsel does not need to be provided in a misdemeanor case if a defendant is not sentenced to a term of imprisonment.[34]

If the defendant chooses to exercise his right to assistance of counsel, the counsel, whether appointed or retained, must provide "*effective* assistance of counsel."[35] *Strickland v. Washington* (1984) explained that counsel violates this requirement if the counsel's performance falls outside the range of professional competence and the counsel's performance prejudices the defendant so as to call into question the reliability of the proceedings.[36] Courts analyze the first prong under the prevailing professional norms and take all circumstances into account.[37] To satisfy the second prong, the defendant "must show that there is a reasonable probability that, but for counsel's unprofessional errors, the result of the proceeding would have been different."[38] The Court has expanded on the modern scope of this standard.[39]

OPEN QUESTIONS

- When, exactly, does the right to counsel attach? Does a person have a right to counsel, for example, in pre-indictment plea negotiations?
- What qualifies as a "critical stage" during which a defendant has a right to counsel? Is bail determination, for example, a critical stage?

Cite as: Judge Lawrence VanDyke & Alexandria Overcash, *The Right to Counsel Clause, in* THE HERITAGE GUIDE TO THE CONSTITUTION 679 (Josh Blackman & John G. Malcolm eds., 3d ed. 2025).

Notes

1. William M. Beaney, The Right to Counsel in American Courts 8–9 (1955). **2.** *Id.* at 9; John Langbein, The Origins of Adversary Criminal Trial 26 (2003). **3.** Langbein, *supra* at 67–68. **4.** *Id.* **5.** Beaney, *supra* at 11–12. **6.** Langbein, *supra* at 28–29; 3 Edward Coke, Institutes of the Laws of England 29. **7.** 4 Blackstone 355. **8.** *Id.* **9.** *Id.* at 355–56. **10.** *Powell v. Alabama*, 287 U.S. 45, 61–65 (1932); *Holden v. Hardy*, 169 U.S. 366, 386 (1898). **11.** *Powell,* 287 U.S. at 61–65. **12.** 316 U.S. 455, 467 (1942). **13.** *Id.* **14.** Beaney, *supra* at 23; Laurie S. Fulton, *The Right to Counsel Clause of the Sixth Amendment*, 26 Am. Crim. L. Rev. 1599, 1604 (1989). **15.** Beaney, *supra* at 23. **16.** *Id.* at 23–24. **17.** 140 U.S. 169, 173 (1891). **18.** *Id.* **19.** *Id.* **20.** *Bute v. Illinois*, 333 U.S. 640, 661 n.17 (1948). **21.** 287 U.S. 45, 49 (1932). **22.** *Id.* at 50, 71. **23.** 304 U.S. 458, 463 (1938). **24.** *Betts,* 316 U.S. at 464. **25.** *Id.* at 465–73. **26.** 372 U.S. 335, 344 (1963). **27.** *Garza v. Idaho*, 586 U.S. 232, 260 (2019) (Thomas, J., dissenting). **28.** *Betts,* 316 U.S. at 467. **29.** *Id.* at 468–69. **30.** *Id.* at 469–71. **31.** *Kirby v. Illinois,* 406 U.S. 682, 689 (1972); *Gideon*, 372 U.S. at 344. **32.** *Iowa v. Tovar*, 541 U.S. 77, 87 (2004). **33.** *Faretta v. California*, 422 U.S. 806, 807, 817 (1975). **34.** *Scott v. Illinois*, 440 U.S. 367, 373–74 (1979). **35.** *McMann v. Richardson*, 397 U.S. 759, 771 & n.14 (1970) (emphasis added). **36.** 466 U.S. 668, 687 (1984). **37.** *Id.* **38.** *Id.* at 694. **39.** *Padilla v. Kentucky*, 559 U.S. 356 (2010); *Lafler v. Cooper*, 566 U.S. 156 (2012); *Missouri v. Frye*, 566 U.S. 134 (2012); *Garza v. Idaho*, 586 U.S. 232 (2019).

❧

ESSAY NO. 182: THE CIVIL JURY TRIAL CLAUSE
AMEND. 7

In Suits at common law, where the value in controversy shall exceed twenty dollars, the right of trial by jury shall be preserved. . . .

—Renée Lettow Lerner

INTRODUCTION

At the time of the Founding, the right to jury trial in criminal cases was well-accepted. The drafters of the original Constitution put that right into Article III, Section 2, and the Sixth Amendment repeated it. (See Essay Nos. 136 and 176.) But the right to jury trial in civil cases was controversial. After much debate, the Seventh Amendment guaranteed the right to civil jury trial, in a provision known as the Civil Jury Trial Clause or the Preservation Clause. The controversy over the clause continues today; the right to civil jury trial is one of the few provisions in the first eight amendments to the Constitution that has not been incorporated against the states.

HISTORY BEFORE 1787

In England, the use of juries in civil cases dates back to the twelfth century. To prevent juror confusion, English judges took care that a civil jury only had to decide one factual issue per case. This narrowing of the case was called "pleading to issue." In the eighteenth century, the single-issue rule had relaxed slightly, but the pleading requirements still ensured that only a few issues of fact per case would go to the jury. English judges forbade the joinder of multiple claims and parties.[1]

This drastic simplification distorted many disputes, even as the English legal system had to decide more complicated cases. The English solved the problem by setting up non-jury courts and procedures for these cases. In effect, England had multiple legal systems. The main non-jury court was the Court of Chancery, whose substantive law and procedure were known collectively as equity.[2] There were other non-jury courts such as the Court of Admiralty. Meanwhile, the jury courts were known as the common-law courts.

Sir William Blackstone lavished praise on the civil jury as the "bulwark of our liberties" and "the glory of English law."[3] Blackstone declared that the civil jury's main advantage was that it helped to counteract the class biases of judges.[4] Judges in Blackstone's time were part of the upper classes. In contrast, jurors, although subject to property qualifications, were generally of the middling sort, such as merchants or yeoman farmers.

In the struggles between the American colonies and Britain leading up to the American Revolution, civil juries, like criminal juries, assumed great importance. Civil juries could nullify hated British laws. "Nullification" is the term for a jury's deciding against the law and the facts of a case. In the eighteenth century, jury nullification often involved defying the judge's comments on evidence and instructions on law. The jury was one of the few means of achieving popular influence on government, as the colonists lacked representation in the British Parliament. In *Erving v. Cradock* (1761), a smuggling Massachusetts merchant sued a customs inspector for trespass and won a large verdict from a jury.[5] The royal governor of Massachusetts warned his superiors in London that such verdicts nullified the customs laws.[6] He wrote that, in effect, juries were overturning the judgments of the Court of Admiralty, which sat without juries.

Colonists viewed the jurisdiction of the juryless admiralty courts as a major grievance. The Stamp Act Congress of 1765 complained about the expansion of admiralty courts.[7] The Declaration of Independence listed "depriving us, in many cases, of the benefits of trial by jury" as a reason for separation from England.[8]

After independence, the new states hastened to put the right to a jury trial, both civil and criminal, into their constitutions or declarations of rights.[9] But civil juries' nullification of laws, which had seemed so beneficial during the conflicts with Britain, began to seem less so once Americans started governing themselves.[10] State juries were sympathetic to debtors; they often nullified the laws of contract. Why should twelve persons be able to nullify laws enacted by a legislature that was elected by the people?

THE CONSTITUTIONAL CONVENTION AND RATIFICATION DEBATES

Debates in the Philadelphia Convention highlighted the difficulties with including a right to civil jury trial in the federal Constitution. Hugh Williamson of North Carolina raised the question of a right to civil jury trial late in the proceedings—five days before the scheduled adjournment.[11] Elbridge Gerry of Massachusetts agreed that a right to civil jury trial in federal court was necessary to protect against corrupt judges. But several other delegates argued that it would be impossible to specify when civil juries should be used and that the question should be left to the legislature. George Mason of Virginia conceded the difficulty of specifying which civil cases should go to juries. He thought that a "general principle" laid down concerning civil juries would be sufficient. Mason took the opportunity to argue for a general bill of rights, which the Convention promptly rejected.[12]

A few days later, Charles Pinckney of South Carolina and Elbridge Gerry moved to insert the following language into Article III: "And a trial by jury shall be preserved as usual in civil cases."[13] Several delegates pointed out that the states had different practices concerning when to use civil juries, so there was no national "usual" practice. One of these delegates, Pinckney's first cousin Charles Cotesworth Pinckney, declared that such a clause in the Constitution would be "pregnant with embarrassments." The Convention voted down the proposal unanimously, and the draft Constitution did not contain a right to civil jury trial.

That omission set off fierce objections among the Anti-Federalists. Both George Mason and Elbridge Gerry refused to sign the draft Constitution, and both gave as a reason the lack of a right to a civil jury.[14] In the Virginia ratifying convention, Patrick Henry warned of the plight of a debtor sued in federal court without a jury.[15] Although Henry did not say so directly, he implied that he approved of civil juries' tendency to sympathize with debtors and to nullify the laws of contract. James Madison, opposing Henry, worried that state civil juries were so hostile to creditors, especially foreign creditors, that they discouraged the investment the new Republic badly needed.[16]

The Anti-Federalists were also concerned about a structural problem: The draft constitution created a powerful and extremely independent judiciary. Brutus argued that the federal judges would wield uncontrolled power. He wrote that the federal judges would be "independent of the people, of the legislature, and of every power under heaven. Men placed in this situation will generally soon feel themselves independent of heaven itself."[17] The Anti-Federalists, fearing judicial tyranny and also wanting to control the executive and legislature through juries, insisted on a right to civil jury trial in federal court.[18]

The Anti-Federalist arguments forced Alexander Hamilton to acknowledge that the most successful objection to the draft constitution was the lack of a guarantee of jury trial in civil cases. In Federalist No. 83, Hamilton undertook to justify why it was not necessary. First, in an objection that echoed those of delegates at the Philadelphia Convention, he argued that the distinction between the common law and equity would make such a provision difficult to draft. Second, he argued that juries could not handle complicated cases. Third, he observed that reform of procedural systems is continuously necessary, and the trend was to reduce the scope of jury trial. Therefore, the question of when to use civil jury trial should be left to the legislature. In Hamilton's view, the best argument for the civil jury was corruption in the judiciary, a circumstance that he described as "foreign to the preservation of liberty." Hamilton implied that the best way to address this evil was to deal with it directly by removing corrupt judges.

Despite Hamilton's arguments, the Anti-Federalists remained adamant about the need for a guarantee of a civil jury trial in federal court. While the Anti-Federalists lacked the political power to block ratification or even to condition ratification on including such a right, a number of state conventions, or minorities within them, recommended an amendment

providing a right to civil jury trial.[19] Several of these drew from the text of George Mason's 1776 Virginia Declaration of Rights: "[I]n controversies respecting property, and in suits between man and man, the ancient trial by jury is preferable to any other and ought to be held sacred."[20] For example, the Pennsylvania ratification convention's minority report proposed this text: "[I]n controversies respecting property, and in suits between man and man, trial by jury shall remain as heretofore, as well in the federal courts, as in those of the several states."[21] The Virginia ratification convention, not surprisingly, also stuck closely to Mason's formulation: "[I]n controversies respecting property, and in suits between man and man, the ancient trial by jury is one of the greatest securities to the rights of the people, and to remain sacred and inviolable."[22]

ADOPTION OF THE SEVENTH AMENDMENT

The political threat was serious enough that James Madison feared that a second constitutional convention would be called.[23] During the First Congress, Representative Madison was determined to draft and introduce a set of amendments that included a right to civil jury trial. He had promised his constituents that he would do so as a condition of being elected to the House of Representatives. More generally, he wanted to reassure Americans whose support for the new Constitution and government was wavering. This concern was especially pressing in North Carolina and Rhode Island, which had not yet ratified the Constitution.[24]

Madison had before him many different suggestions and models for a civil jury right from the states.[25] On June 8, 1789, Madison introduced his proposed amendments to the Constitution in the House of Representatives. His proposal for civil juries stayed fairly close to the model from the Virginia ratifying convention, in which he had been a key participant: "In suits at common law, between man and man, the trial by jury, as one of the best securities to the rights of the people, ought to remain inviolate."[26] Madison's vague formulation of "common law" papered over the many different practices of the states.

At the same time, Madison introduced a separate amendment that ultimately became the

Seventh Amendment's Re-examination Clause. That clause provides that "no fact tried by a jury, shall be otherwise re-examined in any Court of the United States, than according to the rules of the common law." (See Essay No. 183.)

By July 1789, Madison was frustrated with the lack of progress on his proposed amendments. On July 21, he proposed a committee to look into amendments to the Constitution, to be composed of one member from each state represented.[27] The committee thus became known as the Committee of Eleven, and Madison was appointed the member from Virginia.

The Committee of Eleven made its formal report a week later on July 28. It streamlined Madison's original proposed amendment concerning civil juries and kept his vague formulation concerning the common law: "In suits at common law, the right of trial by jury shall be preserved." On August 18, the House of Representatives adopted this language, apparently without debate.[28] It then sent the draft amendments, including the right to civil jury trial, to the Senate.

On September 7, the Senate approved the House language concerning civil jury trial and added the words: "where the consideration exceeds twenty dollars."[29] That $20 threshold has puzzled many. At the time, the Senate's usual practice was to meet behind closed doors, and therefore its records are much less extensive than those of the House. Because the debates in the Senate were not recorded, we do not know exactly why the threshold was added. But now we have a good idea. In England, the long-standing threshold for the jurisdiction of the common-law courts, which sat with juries, was a claim of 40 shillings. That threshold dated back to the Middle Ages and remained constant through the eighteenth century. Legal historian Philip Hamburger has pointed out that American states approximated this threshold using their currency. The state thresholds for jury trial varied according to the differing value of the states' currencies. Twenty dollars seems to have been the Senate's effort to approximate the ancient common-law threshold.[30]

A few days later, on September 9, the Senate combined the House's separate proposed amendments concerning civil jury trial and re-examination of facts into one amendment.[31] The Seventh Amendment took on the precise

wording it has today. Following the report of the Committee of Conference, the House agreed to the Senate's changes without debate.[32]

At exactly the same time, Congress had hammered out a statutory compromise on civil juries. The Judiciary Act of 1789 specified that in federal court, juries would determine facts in all civil cases except equity, admiralty, and maritime cases.[33] A constitutional guarantee of a civil jury right therefore appeared as something of an anticlimax, not disturbing an arrangement already agreed to.

The states adopted the Seventh Amendment without meaningful opposition.

WHAT AND WHEN WAS THE COMMON LAW?

The Seventh Amendment invokes the distinction between the common-law courts, on the one hand, and equity and other non-jury courts, on the other. Madison sought to preserve the civil jury only in common-law cases and not in cases that traditionally used non-jury procedures. But the amendment did not define which jurisdiction's "common law" was meant. As the debates in the Philadelphia Convention and over ratification showed, the states' use of civil juries were all different from one another. Moreover, legal systems constantly change. What was the baseline time for "the right of trial by jury [that] shall be preserved"? These questions would be left to the courts.

In an 1812 circuit court decision, Justice Joseph Story declared that the reference point for the Seventh Amendment was the English common law.[34] However, Story did not specify a time. That baseline time became increasingly important as England curtailed civil jury trials beginning in the nineteenth century and through the twentieth, particularly in an act of 1933.[35] Today, England has virtually abolished the institution. In 1935, the U.S. Supreme Court explained that the Seventh Amendment preserves the practice of trial by jury as it existed at common law in England in 1791, the date of the amendment's ratification.[36]

APPLYING THE SEVENTH AMENDMENT

Applying this historical test has been challenging for several reasons. First, determining the civil jury practice of England as of 1791 is difficult. Courts generally lack the capability to perform painstaking research into manuscript sources. Indeed, courts have made significant mistakes by relying entirely on the scanty body of printed material.[37] As a result, courts have continued to send highly complicated cases to jury trial despite historical English practice to the contrary.

Legal historian James Oldham has shown that in 1791 England, complicated cases were resolved almost invariably in Chancery, by arbitration, or by special juries.[38] A special jury could include a group of jurors with special knowledge of the subject matter of a case, such as a group of experienced merchants deciding a commercial dispute or a group of veteran sea captains deciding a case about marine insurance.[39] Special juries were an important feature of English common-law practice in the eighteenth century, although they have virtually disappeared from American practice. In modern times, some antitrust and mass tort cases, which are tried before a jury, are far more complex than any case in eighteenth-century England. Oldham concludes that complex cases may be decided without ordinary juries consistent with the Seventh Amendment's historical test.[40]

Second, many types of civil cases today did not exist in England in 1791. To accommodate new, mainly statutory causes of action and the explosion of agency adjudication, the Supreme Court created the "public rights" doctrine. The Court has not precisely defined the scope of public rights but has held that in matters arising between the government and others, the jurisdiction of Article III courts, together with jury trial under the Seventh Amendment, is not constitutionally required.[41] *SEC v. Jarkesy* (2024) held that the Seventh Amendment required the Securities and Exchange Commission to bring civil fraud cases in federal court with a jury instead of adjudicating them before its administrative law judges as it had been doing.[42] *Jarkesy* cast doubt on several of the precedents that contributed to the public rights doctrine, although it did not

explicitly overrule them. *Jarkesy* could potentially extend to many agencies and existing agency adjudication.

Third, the civil jury in 1791 comprised a cluster of practices: pleading to issue, jury fees, qualifications and selection of jurors, numbers of jurors, judicial comment on evidence to the jury, unanimity, and confinement of jurors until verdict without food, drink, light, or heat.[43] How many of these practices must be reproduced to preserve civil jury trial as it was known in 1791 England? For example, the Seventh Amendment has not been understood to require twelve jurors. Federal courts permit civil juries of fewer than twelve, contrary to the English practice of 1791.[44] Federal courts severely limit a trial judge's ability to comment on evidence to the jury, again contrary to the English practice of 1791. These and other changes in jury practice have fundamentally altered the character of the institution.[45]

Fourth, and most profoundly, civil jury trial was and is a procedural element embedded in an entire system of procedure. The institution does not stand on its own as a complete system. Changing the procedural system surrounding the jury can drastically change the incidence of jury trials.[46] The introduction of elaborate pretrial discovery in the Federal Rules of Civil Procedure of 1938 has eliminated much of the incentive of parties to go to trial.[47] Before the Rules, parties often had to go to trial to find out what the evidence was. Under the Rules, parties can know the evidence in detail before trial and are generally not inclined to go over it again before an unpredictable jury. The Rules also gave judges a powerful tool with which to avoid jury trial in the form of summary judgment.[48] Rates of settlement have soared, and rates of civil jury trial have plummeted. In 2022, jury trials occurred in only 0.67 percent of federal civil cases (1,348 jury trials out of 201,329 total dispositions after court action).[49] Arguably, the Federal Rules of Civil Procedure in effect repealed the Seventh Amendment. But the influence of the jury is still felt in settlement negotiations; outcomes are based partly on the parties' guesses about what a jury will do.

OPEN QUESTIONS

- The Supreme Court has refused to incorporate the Seventh Amendment against the states while incorporating almost all other provisions of the first eight amendments of the Constitution.[50] Is this refusal due to ambivalence about the importance of civil jury trial, a concern about disrupting state practice, or a combination of the two? Would similar reasoning apply to the Court's refusal to incorporate the Grand Jury Clause of the Fifth Amendment? (See Essay No. 168.)
- Are practices that were fundamental to civil jury trials in England in 1791, such as the use of twelve jurors or judicial comment on evidence to the jury, required by the Seventh Amendment? Justice Neil Gorsuch has urged the Court to revisit the precedent which held that *criminal* juries could have fewer than twelve people.[51]
- What will be the fate of the "public rights" doctrine and agency adjudication following *SEC v. Jarkesy*?

Cite as: Renée Lettow Lerner, *The Civil Jury Trial Clause*, in THE HERITAGE GUIDE TO THE CONSTITUTION 682 (Josh Blackman & John G. Malcolm eds., 3d ed. 2025).

Notes

1. John H. Langbein, Renée Lettow Lerner, & Bruce Smith, History of the Common Law: The Development of Anglo–American Legal Institutions 147–52, 253–57 (2009). **2.** *Id.* at 267–99. **3.** 3 Blackstone 350, 379. **4.** 3 Blackstone 379. **5.** Governor Francis Bernard to the Lords of Trade (Aug. 6, 1761), in Josiah Quincy, Samuel Miller Quincy, & Horace Gray, Reports of Cases Argued and Adjudged in the Superior Court of Judicature of the Province of Massachusetts 553–55 (1865). **6.** *Id.* **7.** Resolutions of the Stamp Act Congress (1765), in C.A. Weslager, The Stamp Act Congress: With an Exact Copy of the Complete Journal 201–02 (1976). **8.** Declaration of Independence, ¶ 20. **9.** Va. Decl. of Rts. of 1776, § 11; N.C. Const. of 1776, Decl. of Rights, art. XIV; PA. Const. of 1776, § 25; N.J. Const. of 1776, art. XXII; S.C. Const. of 1776, arts. XVII & XVIII; Ga. Const. of 1777, art. XL & XLI; MD. Const. of 1776, art. XXI; N.Y. Const. of 1777, art. XLI; S.C. Const. of 1778, art. XLI; Mass. Const. of 1780, art. XV; Renée Lettow Lerner, *The Failure of Originalism in Preserving Constitutional Rights to Civil Jury Trial*, 3 Wm. & Mary Bill of Rights J. 811, 819–21 (2014). **10.** *Id.* at 828–29. **11.** 2 Farrand's 587. **12.** *Id.* at 587–88. **13.** *Id.* at 628. **14.** *Id.* at 633 (Gerry), 640 (Mason). **15.** 3 Elliot's 302; Matthew P. Harrington, *The Economic Origins of the Seventh Amendment*, 87 Iowa L. Rev. 145, 170–74 (2001); Charles W. Wolfram, *The Constitutional History of the Seventh Amendment*, 57 Minn. L. Rev. 639, 673–703 (1973). **16.** 3 Elliot's 487, 489. **17.** Storing 2.9.189. **18.** Renée Lettow Lerner, *The Surprising Views of Montesquieu and Tocqueville About Juries: Juries Empower Judges*, 81 La. L. Rev. 1, 24–27 (2020); Harrington, *supra* at 185–87; Edith Guild Henderson, *The Background of the Seventh Amendment*, 80 Harv. L. Rev. 289, 298 (1966). **19.** Henderson, *supra* at 298. **20.** Va. Decl. of Rts. of 1776, § 11. **21.** Storing 3.11.13. **22.** 3 Elliot's 658. **23.** Harrington, *supra* at 222, 227. **24.** 1 Annals of Cong. 449 (1789). **25.** Harrington, *supra* at 217–22. **26.** 1 Annals of Cong. 453 (1789). **27.** *Id.* at 690–91. **28.** *Id.* at 789. **29.** S. Jour., 1st Cong., 1st Sess. 72 (Sept. 7, 1789). **30.** Philip Hamburger, *The Value of Jury Rights*, 93 Geo. Wash. L. Rev. __ (forthcoming 2025). **31.** S. Jour. 1st Cong., 1st Sess. 77 (Sept. 9, 1789). **32.** 1 Annals of Cong. 948 (Sept. 24, 1789). **33.** An Act to Establish the Judicial Courts of the United States, Sess. 1, ch. 20, §§ 9, 12 (Sept. 24, 1789). **34.** *United States v. Wonson*, 28 F. Cas. 745, 750 (C.C.D. Mass. 1812) (No. 16,750); *Parsons v. Bedford*, 28 U.S. (3 Pet.) 433, 447–48 (1830). **35.** Conor Hanly, *The Decline of the Civil Jury in Nineteenth-Century England*, 26 J. Legal Hist. 253 (2005); Charles S. Bullock, *The Abolition of the Right to Trial by Jury in Civil Cases in England*, 63 Am. J. Legal Hist. 281 (2023). **36.** *Dimick v. Schiedt*, 293 U.S. 474, 476 (1935). **37.** *Markman v. Westview Instruments, Inc.*, 517 U.S. 370 (1996); James Oldham, Trial by Jury: The Seventh Amendment and Anglo-American Special Juries 5–16 (2006); Tomás Gómez-Arostegui & Sean Bottomley, Brief of Amici in Support of Neither Party 14–19, *Oil States Energy Servs. v. Greene's Energy Grp.*, 584 U.S. 325 (2018) (No. 16-712). **38.** Oldham, *supra* at 21–24. **39.** *Id.* at 153–64. **40.** *Id.* at 17–24. **41.** *Oil States*, 584 U.S. 325; *Atlas Roofing Co. v. Occupational Safety & Health Rev. Comm'n*, 430 U.S. 442, 449–56 (1977). **42.** 603 U.S. 109 (2024). **43.** Langbein et al., *supra* at 72–75, 419–20, 431–36; 3 Blackstone 375. **44.** *Colgrove v. Battin*, 413 U.S. 149 (1973); Federal Rule of Civil Procedure 48(a). **45.** Renée Lettow Lerner, *The Transformation of the American Civil Trial: The Silent Judge*, 42 Wm. & Mary L. Rev. 195, 197–99 (2000); Renée Lettow Lerner, *How the Creation of Appellate Courts in England and the United States Limited Judicial Comment on Evidence to the Jury*, 40 J. Legal Prof. 215, 219–21 (2016). **46.** Renée Lettow Lerner, *The Resilience of Substantive Rights and the False Hope of Procedural Rights: The Case of the Second Amendment and the Seventh Amendment*, 116 Nw. U. L. Rev. 275, 302–04 (2021). **47.** John H. Langbein, *The Disappearance of Civil Trial in the United States*, 122 Yale L. J. 522, 544–51, 566–69 (2012); Stephen C. Yeazell, *The Misunderstood Consequences of Modern Civil Process*, 1994 Wis. L. Rev. 631, 632, 637–39 (1994). **48.** Federal Rule of Civil Procedure 56; Suja A.

Thomas, *Why Summary Judgment is Unconstitutional*, 93 Va. L. Rev. 139 (2007).   **49.** Table C-4, Federal Judicial Caseload Statistics (Mar. 31, 2022), Administrative Office of the U.S. Courts, https://perma.cc/9424-DQEX.   **50.** *Minneapolis* *& St. Louis R. Co. v. Bombolis*, 241 U.S. 211, 217 (1916). **51.** *Cunningham v. Florida*, 144 S.Ct. 1287, 1287–88 (2024) (Gorsuch, J., dissenting).

⁓

ESSAY NO. 183: THE RE-EXAMINATION CLAUSE
AMEND. 7

In Suits at common law . . . no fact tried by a jury, shall be otherwise re-examined in any Court of the United States, than according to the rules of the common law.
—Renée Lettow Lerner

INTRODUCTION

The Seventh Amendment has two components. The Civil Jury Trial Clause, also known as the Preservation Clause, preserves the right to a civil jury "in Suits at common law." (See Essay No. 182.) The Re-examination Clause limits the ability of courts to "re-examine" facts tried by a jury. The latter provision is less well-known, but Justice Joseph Story thought it "still more important" than the former. Story observed that "we read [the Re-examination Clause] as a substantial and independent clause."[1]

HISTORY BEFORE 1787

A system of jury trial resists thorough appeals. Unlike judges, lay persons who sit on juries do not provide detailed reasons for their decisions. It is difficult for a court to review a decision without reasons. Moreover, use of juries spared English common-law judges from having to decide facts themselves. Judges prized this insulation from deciding facts.[2] Therefore, English judges developed only limited means of reviewing jury verdicts.

None of the methods for reviewing civil jury verdicts was called an appeal. In England, through the late eighteenth century and beyond, appeals existed only in equity, not at common law. For the most part, common-law courts would review a civil jury verdict after the verdict was given but before judgment was entered. One of these methods was addressed to the trial judge, and three were addressed to the full court sitting *en banc*.[3] There were three distinct English common-law courts: King's Bench, Common Pleas, and Exchequer. Each had about three to four judges. At common law, all trials were before juries. Only one judge presided over each trial,[4] but judgment could be entered only by the full court.[5]

A litigant could move that the trial judge grant a new trial. Before the full court, litigants had other options. First, following a verdict for the plaintiff, a defendant could bring a motion in arrest of judgment. This motion was only for errors of law appearing on the record, but the record was generally very scanty and formulaic, giving no hint of the evidence or conduct of the trial. The record was more fulsome in actions on the case, which often alleged negligent torts, and special verdicts. In those cases, the court could address substantive legal questions more easily.

Second, following a verdict for the defendant, a plaintiff could make a motion for judgment *non obstante veredicto* (judgment notwithstanding the verdict). This motion entailed reviewing the verdict on narrow technical grounds. For example, a successful motion could be brought when the defendant pleaded a defense that was not good in law. Again, the defect had to appear on the scanty record.[6]

The third option before the full court became by far the most powerful: motion for a new trial. It was also the most expensive if successful, as the case had to be tried again before another jury. By the mid-seventeenth century, a new trial could be granted for matters that did not appear on the record. The trial judge could certify that the verdict was contrary to his direction on law, or contrary to the evidence, or that there were affidavits of juror misconduct. By the eighteenth century, a new trial could be granted on additional grounds: for example, if the trial judge gave incorrect directions to the jury on law or made an incorrect ruling on admissibility of evidence.[7] To enable proper decision of the motion by the full court, the trial judge gave his fellow judges a detailed report of the evidence at trial. The common-law courts became increasingly willing to grant new trials for insufficiency of evidence. As a technical matter, whether there was sufficient evidence to support the verdict was a question of law, not fact.[8] However, the sufficiency of evidence was close to fact. Thus, Sir William Blackstone observed that a motion for a new trial was then the only current "method of reversing an error in the determination of *facts*."[9]

Requiring a new trial was formally the only way to reduce or add to damages. In practice, however, the full court could threaten to grant a new trial. This pressure would often cause the plaintiff to accept reduced, or *remitted*, damages to avoid a new trial.[10]

The trial judge could use the "case stated" method to seek help from the full court in deciding a point of law. This method was entirely within the trial judge's discretion and could be used only for questions of law. The trial judge took a verdict from the jury subject to the full court's decision on the law. By the late eighteenth century, the usual practice of "case stated" was for the trial judge to put additional specific questions to the jury to discover the factual basis for the verdict.[11]

All of these methods had to be used before the full court entered judgment. Once judgment had been entered, the only method of review was the writ of error. This was a separate suit between the same parties, alleging an error in the first suit. (Hence the term "plaintiff in error.") The error had to be "manifest" and appear on the record—for example, if an essential step was missing. Otherwise, certain limited new facts that were not inconsistent with the record—for example, the death of a party—could be alleged.[12]

These English methods of review of jury verdicts largely carried over to the American colonies and later states, but there were variations. For example, in Massachusetts, the method of review of a jury verdict was to try the case again before another jury in a superior court.[13] Many state constitutions guaranteed a right to a civil jury trial, but no state constitution had a Re-examination Clause.

THE CONSTITUTIONAL CONVENTION

The Philadelphia Convention assigned appellate jurisdiction to the U.S. Supreme Court "both as to Law and Fact."[14] (See Essay No. 135.) This appellate jurisdiction would include review of any lower federal court decisions as well as review of state court decisions concerning the matters specified. In the English common-law courts, review of a jury's findings of fact formally did not exist, although the question of sufficiency of the evidence was the functional equivalent. The Framers' inclusion of "fact" as a subject of appellate review therefore seemed unusually broad and searching.

The delegates to the Convention believed that searching appellate review, including review of fact, was necessary for several reasons. First, as John Rutledge of South Carolina observed, federal laws should be uniform in their interpretation and application throughout the nation.[15] Second, the delegates believed that, at a minimum, state courts would have concurrent jurisdiction with federal courts in deciding questions of federal law. Some delegates did not believe that lower federal courts should be created at all. Even those delegates who were the most enthusiastic about state power feared that state courts would fail to vindicate the power and rights of the federal government or of litigants raising claims under federal law.

James Madison of Virginia worried explicitly about state judges and juries. He was concerned about "the biased directions" that "a dependent [state] judge" would give to a jury. Madison also feared "the local prejudices of an undirected jury."[16] Biased judges and juries might distort facts so grossly that conventional review, with its remedy of a new trial, would be inadequate. Madison observed that "[t]o remand the cause for a new trial would answer no purpose."[17] A judge and a new jury would still be biased. In response to these concerns, William Paterson's New Jersey Plan specified that there would be appeals to federal judges from state court decisions on federal acts regulating commerce "for the correction of all errors, both in law and fact in rendering judgment."[18]

In late July, the Convention appointed a five-member Committee of Detail to write a draft text based on the deliberations of the Convention thus far. The committee's draft text specified the original jurisdiction of the Supreme Court and declared that in other cases its jurisdiction was "appellate" without further elaboration. When the Convention debated the provisions concerning the judiciary, Gouverneur Morris of Pennsylvania asked whether that appellate jurisdiction "extended to matters of fact as well as law—and to cases of common law [jury trials], as well as civil law [non-jury proceedings]."[19] James Wilson of Pennsylvania was a member of the Committee of Detail. He responded that the committee's intent was to extend appellate jurisdiction to facts and law, as well as common law and civil law.[20] John Dickinson of Delaware attempted to clarify this point. He moved to include the words "both as to law and fact," and the Convention unanimously agreed.[21]

THE RATIFICATION DEBATES

The Anti-Federalists were concerned about the federal judiciary's potential power to review jury verdicts and reverse them. The provision in Article III giving the Supreme Court the power to exercise "appellate Jurisdiction, both as to Law and Fact"[22] alarmed the Anti-Federalists. Brutus declared that this language "has justly been considered as one of the most objectionable parts of the constitution."[23] He believed that a civil jury was of little use if the federal judiciary had broad powers to overturn jury verdicts. If a federal judge presided over a jury trial, the jury's factual findings might be re-examined and overturned on appeal. Worse, Brutus worried, the Supreme Court might overturn a jury verdict from a state court. Other Anti-Federalists, including Federal Farmer, complained about these dangers during the ratification debates.[24]

ADOPTION OF THE
RE-EXAMINATION CLAUSE

The Re-examination Clause was an attempt to limit the scope of federal judges' second-guessing of jury verdicts. During the first Congress, Representative James Madison separately drafted the Preservation Clause and what would become the Re-examination Clause. In drafting the Re-examination Clause, unlike the Preservation Clause, Madison did not have a state constitutional model from which he could draw. The intent was to restrict federal courts' reconsideration of facts found by a jury within limits set by the common law.

On June 8, 1789, Madison introduced the following language: "[N]or shall any fact triable by jury, according to the course of common law, be otherwise re-examinable than may consist with the principles of common law."[25] Madison was appointed to the Committee of Eleven (see Essay No. 182), which altered this language slightly to "the course of *the* common law" and "than according to the *rules* of *the* common law" [emphasis added]. Changing "principles" to "rules" suggested more definite restrictions. And the introduction of the definite article "the" before "common law" made the language seem more precise. (There is some confusion about when the definite article was added.[26]) The House of Representatives approved the committee's language.[27]

As with the use of civil jury trial, however, the states had different practices with respect to review of jury verdicts: in other words, there were different versions of the "common law." The amendment did not specify *which* common law, although the indication of a singular, definite common law suggested the common law of England. By contrast, the Preservation Clause has no such definite article. It refers more generally to "suits at common law." This discrepancy has led one scholar to propose that the common law of England was intended for interpretation of the Re-examination Clause but not for the Preservation Clause.[28]

The Senate revised the language into the exact form we see in the Constitution today: "and no fact tried by a jury, shall be otherwise re-examined in any court of the United States than according to the rules of the common law."[29] The Senate also combined this provision with the civil jury right to form what became the Seventh Amendment.

The Re-examination Clause was adopted by the states without meaningful debate.

JUDICIAL PRECEDENT

Justice Joseph Story made a formative decision about the Re-examination Clause while riding circuit in *United States v. Wonson* (1812). Story explained that this provision should be interpreted according to the common law of England: "Beyond all question, the common law here alluded to is not the common law of any individual state, (for it probably differs in all), but it is the common law of England, the grand reservoir of all our jurisprudence."[30] He declared the same test for the Supreme Court in *Parsons v. Bedford* (1830).[31]

Throughout the nineteenth century and into the twentieth, the Supreme Court consistently quoted and applied Story's *Parsons* analysis.[32] In federal court, the only way to correct errors of fact by a jury was by ordering a new trial. In *Dimick v. Schiedt* (1935), the Court specified a precise baseline time for determining the common law of England under the Re-examination Clause: 1791, the year the Seventh Amendment was ratified.[33] This was the preeminent example of a strict originalist test. This historical test was stricter than any applied by state courts to state constitutional jury provisions.[34] Indeed the Court's precedents for the Re-examination Clause are more restrictive than the Court's precedents for the Preservation Clause.

JUDGMENT NOTWITHSTANDING THE VERDICT

The Re-examination Clause proved vulnerable to procedural reforms. Ordering a new trial was an expensive remedy for error: A case had to be tried again before a different jury. In the late nineteenth century, states developed a new procedure to avoid ordering new trials. Judges were authorized to set aside an erroneous jury verdict and enter a contrary judgment.[35] This procedure is known as judgment notwithstanding the verdict (JNOV). This new American procedure was broader than the limited English JNOV at common law. In *Slocum v. New York Life Insurance Co.* (1913), the U.S. Supreme Court declared that the new JNOV procedure violated the Re-examination Clause. The jury had necessarily found facts in giving a verdict, and entering judgment notwithstanding the verdict meant a judicial re-examination of those facts. The only possible remedy for an erroneous jury verdict in federal courts was a new trial.[36] As a result, federal courts, which sometimes

applied state law, could not grant a judgment notwithstanding the verdict.

The legal profession reacted strongly against this decision.[37] Judgment notwithstanding the verdict made procedure in state courts more efficient: Why should the federal courts not follow? These commentators had forgotten about the Seventh Amendment's unique Re-examination Clause, which had no counterpart in the state constitutions, and the federal courts' strict originalist interpretation of that clause.

Despite these obstacles, a method developed to allow federal courts to grant a judgment notwithstanding the verdict. New state laws permitted a trial court to receive a jury verdict that was contingent on the judge's later making a decision on the law. In 1935, the Supreme Court allowed a federal court to apply such a law.[38] The unanimous Court explained that this practice was in accord with the eighteenth-century English common-law practice of reserving questions of law for the court: the "case stated" procedure.[39] This precedent is reflected in Federal Rule of Civil Procedure 50(b), which declares that a judge is automatically deemed to have submitted the case to the jury subject to the court's later decisions on law. This automatic reservation permits judgment notwithstanding the verdict—now known as judgment as a matter of law—in federal courts. In this way, courts and legislatures have crafted a skillful solution to the problem posed by the Re-examination Clause and its strict historical test.

REMITTITUR AND ADDITUR

Questions concerning the Re-examination Clause arise most commonly with respect to judicial review of juries' damage awards. Federal courts have long held that a federal trial judge may overturn a jury verdict for excessive damages and order a new trial. Alternatively, the trial judge may offer the verdict winner a choice: Either agree to a reduction in damages or have a new trial.[40] This practice is known as *remittitur*. One scholar argues that remittitur violates the Re-examination Clause.[41] As explained above, eighteenth-century English courts had an informal practice of remittitur. The Supreme Court has declared that the practice of *additur* (adding to the damages or facing a new trial) violates the Re-examination Clause.[42] Unlike some state judges, a federal trial judge cannot simply enter judgment for a different amount because of insufficient evidence without offering the choice of a new trial.

DEPARTING FROM THE HISTORICAL TEST

Gasperini v. Center for Humanities, Inc. (1996) moved away from a strict historical test for the Re-examination Clause. Justice Ruth Bader Ginsburg's majority opinion instead considered whether a judicial control on jury verdicts was "necessary and proper to the fair administration of justice."[43] *Gasperini* concerned whether an appellate court could review a trial court's failure to grant a new trial for excessive damages. The Supreme Court had long held that federal appellate courts did not have this power, but federal courts of appeals had begun to engage

in this review.[44] The Court declared that federal appellate courts could constitutionally engage in such review. Justice Antonin Scalia wrote a vigorous dissent, joined by Chief Justice William Rehnquist and Justice Clarence Thomas. Scalia examined eighteenth-century English sources and concluded that appellate review of these rulings violated the Seventh Amendment.[45]

Gasperini, together with the actions of lower federal courts, may signal a weakening of the strict historical test. Considerations of efficiency and accuracy in procedure seem to some courts more important than adhering to the practices of England in 1791. Indeed, Hamilton suggested as much in Federalist No. 83 when arguing against a constitutional right to civil jury trial. Over time, the trend has been to allow federal courts, especially appellate courts, to assume more control of jury verdicts.[46]

OPEN QUESTIONS

- Will the Supreme Court continue to move away from the strict historical test for the Re-examination Clause, as it did in *Gasperini*, or will it return to that test?

Cite as: Renée Lettow Lerner, *The Re-examination Clause*, in THE HERITAGE GUIDE TO THE CONSTITUTION 688 (Josh Blackman & John G. Malcolm eds., 3d ed. 2025).

Notes

1. *Parsons v. Bedford*, 28 U.S. (3 Pet.) 433, 447 (1830). **2.** Renée Lettow Lerner, The Jury: A Very Short Introduction 40–42 (2023). **3.** John H. Baker, An Introduction to English Legal History 135–136, 82–85 (4th ed. 2007). **4.** John H. Langbein, Renée Lettow Lerner, and Bruce P. Smith, History of the Common Law: The Development of Anglo–American Legal Institutions 117–23 (2009). **5.** Baker, *supra* at 135–36. **6.** *Id.* at 82–84. **7.** *Id.* at 84–85; Langbein et al., *supra* at 439–50; *Bright v. Enyon*, 1 Burr. 390, 393, 97 Eng. Rep. 365, 366 (K.B. 1757) (opinion by Lord Mansfield); 2 William Tidd, The Practice of the Courts of King's Bench in Personal Actions 605–608, 610 (1794). **8.** Renée B. Lettow, *New Trial for Verdict Against Law: Judge–Jury Relations in Early Nineteenth-Century America*, 71 Notre Dame L. Rev. 505, 508–515 (1996). **9.** 3 Blackstone 405–06. **10.** R. H. Helmholz, *Damages in Actions for Slander at Common Law*, 103 L. Q. Rev. 624, 629–634 (1987). **11.** Baker, *supra* at 84; James Oldham, Trial by Jury: The Seventh Amendment and Anglo–American Special Juries 10–13 (2006). **12.** Baker, *supra* at 136–37. **13.** William E. Nelson, Dispute and Conflict Resolution in Plymouth County, Massachusetts, 1725–1825, at 22–26 (1981); The Common Law in Colonial America, Vol. III: The Chesapeake and New England, 1660–1730, at 69–74 (2016). **14.** Art. III, § 2. **15.** 1 Farrand's 124. **16.** *Id.* **17.** *Id.* **18.** *Id.* at 243. **19.** 2 Farrand's 431. **20.** *Id.* **21.** *Id.* **22.** Art. III, § 2. **23.** Storing 2.9.169. **24.** *Id.* at 2.8.189; Matthew P. Harrington, *The Economic Origins of the Seventh Amendment*, 87 Iowa L. Rev. 145, 220 (2001); Charles W. Wolfram, *The Constitutional History of the Seventh Amendment*, 57 Minn. L. Rev. 639, 679–82 (1973). **25.** 1 Annals of Cong. 452 (1789). **26.** S. Jour., 1st Cong., 1st Sess. 64 (Aug. 25, 1789); *id.* at 71 (Sept. 4, 1789); *id.* at 77 (Sept. 9, 1789). **27.** 1 Annals of Cong. 784 (17 August 1789). **28.** Stanton D. Krauss, *The Original Understanding of the Seventh Amendment Right to Jury Trial*, 33 U. Rich. L. Rev. 407, 447–51 (1999). **29.** S. Jour., 1st Cong., 1st Sess. 77 (Sept. 9, 1789). **30.** *United States v. Wonson*, 28 F. Cas. 745, 750 (C.C.D. Mass. 1812) (No. 16,750). **31.** 28 U.S. (3 Pet.) 433, 448 (1830). **32.** Renée Lettow Lerner, *The Failure of Originalism in Preserving Constitutional Rights to Civil Jury Trial*, 3 Wm. & Mary Bill of Rights J. 811, 871–72 & n.418 (2014). **33.** 293 U.S. 474, 476 (1935). **34.** Lerner, *Failure of Originalism, supra* at 871–72 & n.418. **35.** Renée Lettow Lerner, *The Rise of Directed Verdict: Jury Power in Civil Cases Before the Federal Rules of 1938*, 81 Geo. Wash. U. L. Rev. 448, 515–18 (2013). **36.** *Slocum v. N.Y. Life Ins. Co.*, 228 U.S. 364, 368, 398–99 (1913). **37.** Lerner, *Failure of Originalism, supra* at 871–72 & n.418. **38.** *Balt. & Carolina Line, Inc. v. Redman*, 295 U.S. 654, 658–60 (1935). **39.** Oldham, *supra* at 10–13. **40.** *Kennon v. Gilmer*, 131 U.S. 22, 27–28 (1889); *Dimick v. Schiedt*, 293 U.S. 474, 486–87 (1935); *Hetzel v. Prince*

William Cnty., Va., 523 U.S. 208, 210–12 (1998).   **41.** Suja A. Thomas, *Re-examining the Constitutionality of Remittitur Under the Seventh Amendment*, 64 Ohio St. L. J. 731 (2003). **42.** *Dimick*, 293 U.S. at 482, 486–88.   **43.** 518 U.S. 415, 435 (1996).   **44.** *Id.* at 434.   **45.** 518 U.S. 451–57 (Scalia, J., dissenting).   **46.** *Cooper Indus., Inc. v. Leatherman Tool Grp., Inc.*, 532 U.S. 424, 437 (2001); Debra Lyn Bassett, *"I Lost at Trial–in the Court of Appeals!" The Expanding Power of the Federal Appellate Courts to Reexamine Facts*, 38 Hous. L. Rev. 1129 (2002).

ESSAY NO. 184: THE EXCESSIVE BAIL CLAUSE
AMEND. 8

Excessive bail shall not be required. . . .

—John F. Stinneford

INTRODUCTION

The Eighth Amendment prohibits imposition of "excessive bail." In its modern form, bail is the payment of money to the court in a criminal case to ensure that the defendant exhibits good behavior and appears at trial. In early times, bail was a system that allowed family, friends, and neighbors to act as guarantee, or *surety*, for the release of a prisoner. Over time, however, bail became a system focused primarily on the posting of bond to ensure the released prisoner's appearance at trial. Under Supreme Court precedent, there is no absolute right to bail. The appropriate amount of bail depends on a variety of factors, including the nature of the offense, the character of the defendant, and the likelihood of flight. If the purpose of bail in a given case is to ensure the defendant's appearance at trial, bail set higher than necessary to fulfill this purpose is "excessive" under the Eighth Amendment.

HISTORY BEFORE 1787

The concept of bail has roots that reach back more than a thousand years.[1] Scholars have traced a form of bail to the pre-Norman period whereby a person could stand as surety for a defendant who was guilty of homicide. The surety would insure that the victim's family would receive the full compensation, or *wergild*, that the defendant owed them.

Something more closely resembling modern bail was instituted after the Norman invasion. In 1066, the crown instituted a formal process of criminal prosecution and had to decide what to do with defendants during the interim between arrest and trial. The earliest statutes providing for bail in certain cases were the Assize of Clarendon (1166) and the Assize of Northampton (1176). In the earliest form of bail, the defendant's lord could act as surety for the defendant's good behavior and appearance at trial. Over time, bail developed into a system allowing monetary payments to assure appearance and good behavior. Some defendants, such as those accused of homicide or arrested by special order of the king, were non-bailable. Even for bailable offenses, the king had the authority to order that the defendant be held pending trial. Initially, there were no formal limits on the amount that could be required for bail, but efforts were made to prevent sheriffs from demanding extortionate sums in exchange for release.

Prohibitions against the imposition of excessive bail began to develop in the seventeenth century.[2] These restrictions arose from ongoing conflicts between Parliament and the Stuart kings concerning arbitrary imprisonment. The Stuart kings developed a practice of imprisoning political enemies without publicly identifying the reason. This meant that courts could not determine whether the prisoner was being held on a bailable or non-bailable offense. As a result, it was impossible to obtain the release of these prisoners.

Parliament responded to this practice with several laws. The Habeas Corpus Act of 1640 required the government to state the cause of imprisonment in its response to the habeas petition. The Habeas Corpus Act of 1679 prohibited jailers from trying to evade a court's jurisdiction in habeas cases. At the time, the judges were appointed by the king and served at his pleasure. Some of those judges undermined the purpose of the Habeas Corpus Acts by setting bail so high that the prisoner could not possibly obtain release.

Parliament once again responded. The prohibition of excessive bail first appeared in the 1689 English Bill of Rights.[3] It provided, in part, "[t]hat excessive bail ought not to be required, nor excessive fines imposed, nor cruel and unusual punishments inflicted." Even after enactment of the English Bill of Rights, however, judges retained significant discretion in setting bail. The question of whether to grant bail and how high to set it involved weighing factors such as the seriousness of the offense, the strength of the evidence, the character of the defendant, and the defendant's financial means.[4] The preference for liberty strongly favored the release of defendants before trial, although certain offenses remained "non-bailable."

The English system of bail continued in the United States. The Founding generation was acutely aware of the seventeenth-century English constitutional conflicts concerning bail. Before the adoption of the Constitution, more than half of the state constitutions contained language prohibiting excessive bail.[5] For example, George Mason included this prohibition in the Virginia Declaration of Rights of 1776.[6] Some states provided, either by constitution or by statute, a right to bail for certain types of offense, and some did not.

ADOPTION OF THE EIGHTH AMENDMENT

As initially proposed, the U.S. Constitution did not contain a bill of rights, although some common-law rights were embedded in the constitutional text. During the state ratifying conventions, delegates complained about this absence. Several state conventions proposed that the Constitution be amended to include a prohibition of excessive bail, but there was no discussion of what this provision meant or how it would work in practice.

During the First Congress, Representative James Madison of Virginia introduced a series of amendments now referred to as the Bill of Rights. One of the proposed amendments included a prohibition of excessive bail.[7] The meaning and application of this provision were not discussed in depth during the debate over these proposals.[8] Congress passed the prohibition of excessive bail, and it was ratified by the states.

The First Congress also adopted the Judiciary Act of 1789. This statute allowed bail for all non-capital offenses: "[U]pon all arrests in criminal cases, bail shall be admitted, except where the punishment may be death."[9] This history suggests that the Excessive Bail Clause was not originally understood to provide a right to bail in every case. Moreover, this statute indicates that the First Congress considered the question of which offenses to make eligible for bail to be a legislative one rather than a judicial question. This approach was consistent with that of most states at that time.

SUPREME COURT PRECEDENT

The text of the Eighth Amendment prohibits only "excessive" bail. Suspects in custody do not have a right to bail at all. *Carlson v. Landon* (1952) held that people awaiting deportation could be denied bail if their release would present a danger to public welfare.[10] Moreover, the U.S. Supreme Court has held that Congress has the authority to declare certain crimes or defendants non-bailable. *United States v. Salerno* (1987), for instance, upheld the constitutionality of the Bail Reform Act of 1984, which denies bail for suspects who "pose a threat to the safety of individuals or to the community."[11] The Court acknowledged that "[i]n our society liberty is the norm, and detention prior to trial or without trial is the carefully limited exception." The provisions of the Bail Reform Act fit within this exception.[12]

The excessiveness of bail is determined by comparing it to the government's asserted interest.[13] For example, when the government's concern is to assure the defendant's appearance at trial, "[b]ail set at a figure higher than an amount reasonably calculated to fulfill this purpose is 'excessive' under the Eighth Amendment."[14] But the question of bail is not limited to concerns over flight risk. Bail can also be set at a higher amount or denied altogether on the ground that the defendant poses a danger to society.[15]

OPEN QUESTIONS

- The Supreme Court has never decided whether the Excessive Bail Clause has been incorporated into the Fourteenth Amendment. However, in two cases, the Court implied in dicta that the right has been incorporated.[16]
- The Court has not foreclosed the possibility that there may be a right to bail per se in certain cases.[17]
- The Court has not decided whether bail is automatically excessive when it is beyond the defendant's capacity to pay.

Cite as: John F. Stinneford, *The Excessive Bail Clause, in* THE HERITAGE GUIDE TO THE CONSTITUTION 693 (Josh Blackman & John G. Malcolm eds., 3d ed. 2025).

Notes

1. Hermine Herta Meyer, *Constitutionality of Pretrial Detention*, 60 Geo. L.J. 1140, 1145–62 (1972).   **2.** *Id.* at 1180–90.   **3.** 1 W. & M., ch. 2, sess. 2 (1689), https://perma.cc/F4VX-4229.   **4.** William F. Duker, *The Right to Bail: A Historical Inquiry*, 42 Alb. L. Rev. 33 (1977); Meyer, *supra* at 1139.   **5.** Duker, *supra* at 82.   **6.** Va. Const. of 1776, § 9.   **7.** 1 Annals of Cong. 452 (1789).   **8.** *Id.* at 762.   **9.** An Act to Establish the Judicial Courts of the United States, 1 Stat. 73, § 33 (1789).   **10.** 342 U.S. 524, 545–46 (1952).   **11.** 481 U.S. 739, 755 (1987).   **12.** *Id.*   **13.** *Id.*   **14.** *Stack v. Boyle*, 342 U.S. 1, 5 (1951).   **15.** *Salerno*, 481 U.S. at 754.   **16.** *McDonald v. City of Chicago*, 561 U.S. 742, 765 n.13 (2010); *Schilb v. Kuebel*, 404 U.S. 357, 365 (1971).   **17.** *Salerno*, 481 U.S. at 754.

ESSAY NO. 185: THE EXCESSIVE FINES CLAUSE
AMEND. 8

. . . nor [shall] excessive fines [be] imposed. . . .

—John F. Stinneford

INTRODUCTION

The Excessive Fines Clause of the Eighth Amendment has roots reaching back at least to the adoption of Magna Carta in 1215. An explicit prohibition of excessive fines first appeared in the English Bill of Rights (1689) and was repeated in many American colonial legal codes and early state constitutions. Historical evidence indicates that the clause requires both a measure of proportionality between the fine and the offense and a consideration of the offender's capacity to pay. The Supreme Court did not decide any cases under the Excessive Fines Clause until 1989. The Court engages in proportionality analysis, but has not decided whether the clause also requires courts to consider the offender's capacity to pay. The clause was formally incorporated against the states in 2019.

HISTORY BEFORE 1787

The prohibition of excessive fines originated in the Magna Carta of 1215.[1] Chapter 14 provided that a "A freeman shall not be *amerced*," or fined, "for a slight offence, except in accordance with the degree of the offence; and for a grave offence he shall be amerced in accordance with the gravity of the offence, yet saving always his 'contenement'; and a merchant in the same way, saving his 'merchandise'; and a villein shall be amerced in the same way, saving his 'waynage'." Chapter 14 required that fines be proportionate both to the gravity of the offense and to the offender's capacity to pay. According to historian William McKechnie, the provision was designed to ensure that "[i]n no case could the offender be pushed absolutely to the wall: his means of livelihood must be saved to him."[2]

Magna Carta was confirmed by Parliament in 1225 and reconfirmed more than forty times between the thirteenth and fifteenth centuries.[3] Its provisions concerning calculation of amercements were also repeated in the Statute of Westminster.[4] The historical evidence suggests that in the centuries following adoption of Magna Carta, judicial officials took account of the defendant's capacity to pay when assessing fines, both by moderating the size of the fine and by allowing payments in installments. This practice would avoid perpetual imprisonment for nonpayment and the total destruction of the defendant's capacity to support himself.[5]

By the seventeenth century, many courts had ceased to honor Magna Carta's restrictions on excessive fines. The U.S. Supreme Court observed that by the 1680s, "the use of fines 'became even more excessive and partisan,' and some opponents of the King were forced to remain in prison because they could not pay the huge monetary penalties that had been assessed."[6] In response to these abuses, the English Bill of Rights (1689) included a provision stating that "excessive bail ought not to be required, nor excessive fines imposed, nor cruel and unusual punishments inflicted."[7] Sir William Blackstone wrote that the prohibition of excessive fines restated the principle governing amercements in Magna Carta.[8] A few months after the English Bill of Rights was adopted, the House of Lords ruled in the Earl of Devonshire's case that a large fine imposed on the earl was excessive because it was both unprecedented for his offense and well beyond his capacity to pay.[9]

Even before the adoption of the English Bill of Rights, legal provisions in many American colonies included language mirroring Magna Carta's prohibition of excessive amercements. There is evidence that this limitation was respected in at least some colonial courts.[10]

After independence, the vast majority of states adopted constitutions either explicitly or implicitly prohibiting excessive fines.[11] Several of these constitutions, instead of listing specific rights, contained a blanket statement protecting the constitutional or common-law rights previously given to British subjects. Both Chapter 14 of Magna Carta and the excessive fines clause in the English Bill of Rights were considered mere restatements of preexisting common-law rights and thus came within the scope of these provisions. George Mason included a prohibition of excessive fines in the Virginia Declaration of Rights of 1776.[12]

ADOPTION OF THE EIGHTH AMENDMENT

The U.S. Constitution, as initially proposed, did not contain a bill of rights, although certain common-law rights were built into the document's text. As a delegate to the Constitutional Convention, George Mason of Virginia refused to vote for the Constitution on the ground that it contained "no Declaration of Rights . . . . Nor are the people secured even in the enjoyment of the benefit of the common law. . . ."[13]

Mason's concerns were taken up by the Anti-Federalists in the various state ratifying conventions. They repeatedly argued that because Congress was not obligated to respect rights established through the long usage of the common law, it might innovate in a manner destructive of individual liberty.

Protests such as these ultimately led Representative James Madison to propose a Bill of Rights in the First Congress designed primarily to protect longstanding common-law rights, including the prohibition of excessive fines.[14] There is no meaningful recorded debate on this provision during the First Congress.[15] The proposed amendment was passed by Congress and ratified by the states.

There was little to no litigation over the Eighth Amendment's Excessive Fines Clause during the early years of the Republic. Litigation concerning state constitutional analogues, however, suggests that excessiveness was originally thought to include questions about both proportionality and the offender's capacity to pay.[16]

SUPREME COURT DOCTRINE

The Supreme Court did not decide any cases under the Excessive Fines Clause until 1989, exactly two centuries after the Bill of Rights was proposed. The Court has also decided only five cases under the clause. The Court has not committed to an originalist approach to the clause, but these cases have relied on history more than Cruel and Unusual Punishments Clause cases have. (See Essay No. 186.)

The Court held in 1989 that the clause does not limit punitive damages in civil lawsuits between private parties.[17] The Court noted that "at the time of the drafting and ratification of the [Eighth] Amendment, the word 'fine' was understood to mean a payment to a sovereign as punishment for some offense."[18] The purpose of the clause in both England and America was to prevent the government from abusing the power to impose fines as a way to ruin its perceived enemies. The clause would prevent the government from imposing a fine so large that the defendant could not pay it and then keeping him in prison until it was paid.[19] Such dangers, the Court concluded, are not present in suits between private parties.[20]

Alexander v. United States (1993) ruled that the Excessive Fines Clause limits criminal asset forfeiture.[21] In such a proceeding, the government seeks to seize property that is connected to the commission of a crime. Such a forfeiture, the Court found, is "a form of monetary punishment no different, for Eighth Amendment purposes, from a traditional 'fine.'"[22] *Austin v. United States* (1993) held that the clause applies not only to criminal cases, but also to any civil monetary penalty exacted by the government that "can only be explained as serving in part to punish."[23]

United States v. Bajakajian (1998) provided a standard for determining whether a penalty violates the Excessive Fines Clause.[24] The Court reviewed the history of the excessive fines clauses in England and America and then borrowed the proportionality standard from its non-originalist cruel and unusual punishments jurisprudence. The Court held that a fine is excessive if it is "grossly disproportional to the gravity of a defendant's offense."[25] On one side of the ledger, it considered Bajakajian's culpability and the harm threatened by his offense; on the other side, it considered the size of the forfeiture. Given this balance, the Court ruled that the fine was excessive.[26]

INCORPORATION

Timbs v. Indiana (2019) held that the prohibition of excessive fines is deeply rooted in our country's history and traditions and is thus applicable to the states by incorporation into the Due Process Clause of the Fourteenth Amendment.[27]

OPEN QUESTIONS

- *Austin v. United States* (1993) held that civil *in rem* forfeitures are subject to the Excessive Fines Clause.[28] Did *United States v. Bajakajian* (1998) implicitly call this holding into question?[29]
- As an originalist matter, does the Excessive Fines Clause contain any limit relating to the financial means of the defendant?[30]
- Although the Supreme Court's proportionality analysis in cases involving the Excessive Fines Clause is borrowed from non-originalist case law concerning the Cruel and Unusual Punishments Clause, can it be justified in light of evidence concerning the clause's original meaning?

Cite as: John F. Stinneford, *The Excessive Fines Clause, in* THE HERITAGE GUIDE TO THE CONSTITUTION 695 (Josh Blackman & John G. Malcolm eds., 3d ed. 2025).

Notes

1. Magna Charta, 9 Hen. III, ch. 14 (1225), 1 Stat. at Large 6–7 (1762 ed.). **2.** William Sharp McKechnie, Magna Carta: A Commentary on the Great Charter of King John 287 (2d ed. 1914); Nicholas M. McLean, *Livelihood, Ability to Pay, and the Original Meaning of the Excessive Fines Clause*, 40 Hastings Const. L.Q. 833, 855 (2013). **3.** 9 Hen. III, ch. 14 (1225), 1 Stat. at Large 6–7 (1762 ed.); Faith Thompson, Magna Carta: Its Role in the Making of the English Constitution, 1300–1629, 10 (1948). **4.** 3 Edw. 1, ch. 6 (1275). **5.** McLean, *supra* at 856. **6.** *Browning–Ferris Indus. of Vt., Inc. v. Kelco Disposal, Inc.*, 492 U.S. 257, 267 (1989) (quoting L. Schwoerer, The Declaration of Rights, 1689, 91 (1981)); *Trial of Thomas Pilkington, and others, for a Riot*, 9 State Trials 187 (1683); *Trial of Sir Samuel Barnardiston*, 9 State Trials 1333 (1684)). **7.** 1 W. & M., ch. 2, sess. 2 (1689), https://perma .cc/F4VX-4229. **8.** 4 Blackstone 378. **9.** 11 State Trials 1353; McLean, *supra* at 861–62. **10.** McLean, *supra* at 865–67. **11.** Beth A. Colgan, *Reviving the Excessive Fines Clause*, 102 Calif. L. Rev. 277, 323 n.238 (2014). **12.** Va. Const. of 1776, § 9. **13.** 2 Farrand's 637, 649. **14.** 1 Annals of Cong. 452 (1789); John F. Stinneford, *The Meaning of "Unusual": The Eighth Amendment as a Bar to Cruel Innovation*, 102 Nw. U. L. Rev. 1739, 1808 (2008). **15.** 1 Annals of Cong. 782 (1789). **16.** McLean, *supra* at 870–71. **17.** *Browning-Ferris Indus. of Vt., Inc. v. Kelco Disposal, Inc.*, 492 U.S. 257 (1989). **18.** *Id.* at 265. **19.** *Id.* at 267. **20.** *Id.* at 268.

21. 509 U.S. 544, 558 (1993).   **22.** *Id.*   **23.** 509 U.S. 602, 610 (1993).   **24.** 524 U.S. 321, 334 (1998).   **25.** *Id.* at 334.   **26.** *Id.* at 337–40.   **27.** *Timbs v. Indiana*, 586 U.S. 146 (2019).   **28.** 509 U.S. 602, 610 (1993).   **29.** *United States v. Bajakajian*, 524 U.S. 321, 347 (1998) (Kennedy, J., dissenting).   **30.** McLean, *supra*; Colgan, *supra*.

ESSAY NO. 186: THE CRUEL AND UNUSUAL PUNISHMENTS CLAUSE
AMEND. 8

. . . nor [shall] cruel and unusual punishments [be] inflicted.

—**John F. Stinneford**

INTRODUCTION

The Supreme Court has had difficulty interpreting and applying the Cruel and Unusual Punishments Clause in a consistent manner. The meaning of "unusual" and the role it is supposed to play in interpreting the clause have been obscure. An objective baseline for determining whether a given punishment is so harsh as to be "cruel and unusual" has been elusive. From the late 1950s through the first part of the twenty-first century, the Court's decisions refused to rely upon the original meaning of the Clause, asking instead whether a punishment violated the "evolving standards of decency that mark the progress of a maturing society."[1] The Roberts Court signaled that it would rely on "the original and historical understanding of the Eighth Amendment."[2] Extensive evidence of the clause's original meaning has recently emerged.[3] Courts have decided cases involving both substantive and procedural limits on imposition of the death penalty, prison sentences and prison conditions, and punishment for "status" crimes.

THE ORIGINAL MEANING OF "CRUEL AND UNUSUAL PUNISHMENT"

The historical evidence reveals that "cruel" originally meant "unjustly harsh" and that "unusual" originally meant "contrary to long usage." Thus, "cruel and unusual" originally meant "unjustly harsh in light of longstanding prior practice."[4] This phrasing reflected the belief, shared by English and American legal thinkers and judges, that the longstanding customs of a free people are the most reliable way to determine whether a punishment comports with natural principles of justice.

These customs were embodied primarily in the common law, otherwise called the law of "long use and custom."[5] For example, Edward Coke praised the customary nature of the common law, which "by many successions of ages" had "beene fined and refined by an infinite number of grave and learned men, and by long experience growne to such a perfection."[6] Similarly, Sir William Blackstone wrote that "our lawyers are with justice so copious in their encomiums on the reason of the common law; that they tell us, that the law is the perfection of reason, that it always intends to conform thereto, and that what is not reason is not law."[7] On the other hand, new practices that violated rights established through the "long usage" of the common law were considered unjust and unconstitutional.[8] Thus, a punishment that was significantly harsher than longstanding prior practice would permit would be deemed cruel and unusual.

HISTORY BEFORE 1787

The phrase "Cruel and Unusual Punishments" first appeared in the English Bill of Rights (1689), which provided in part "[t]hat excessive Baile ought not to be required nor excessive Fines imposed nor cruell and unusuall Punishments inflicted."[9]

In 1690, a disgraced Anglican clergyman named Titus Oates filed a petition in Parliament seeking release from a judgment that had been imposed on him five years earlier for his notorious acts of perjury. Oates had made up a false story about a "popish," or Catholic plot to kill the king and had testified in trials against the "conspirators." His testimony resulted in the execution of numerous innocent people. When the perjury was discovered, Oates was tried and convicted. Because perjury was not a felony, he could not be executed for his crime. Instead, the court sentenced him to two serious floggings, a large fine, life imprisonment, four appearances in the pillory per year, and defrocking.

In response to Oates's petition, a majority of both houses of Parliament agreed that his punishments violated the "cruell and unusuall punishments" clause of the new Bill of Rights. These punishments were deemed "extravagant," "exorbitant," there was "no precedent to warrant" them, and they were "contrary to law and ancient practice."[10] Nonetheless, the House of Lords refused to lift the judgment for "so ill a man" as Titus Oates. The parliamentary debates about Oates show that the primary reason his punishment was cruel and unusual was that it was unprecedentedly harsh for the crime of perjury. In other words, it ran contrary to the long usage of the common law.

"CRUEL AND UNUSUAL" IN AMERICA

The Founding generation in America was, if anything, more devoted than the English to the idea that common-law rights, established through long usage, were inviolable. The American Revolution itself was based on the idea that neither King nor Parliament had the authority to violate fundamental common-law rights. The Declaration of Independence invoked the right to jury trial in the vicinage of the offense and the right not to be taxed without representation in Parliament. In the wake of the Revolution, the newly formed states adopted written constitutions designed in part to preserve the common-law rights of citizens. The Virginia constitution, for example, included a Declaration of Rights, written largely by George Mason, that prohibited (among other things) cruel and unusual punishments.[11]

ADOPTION OF THE EIGHTH AMENDMENT

The U.S. Constitution, as initially proposed, did not contain a Bill of Rights, although certain common-law rights were built into the document's text. George Mason, as a delegate to the Constitutional Convention, worried that the lack of common-law limitations on federal power

would allow Congress to create "new crimes, inflict unusual and severe punishments, and extend their powers."[12] He ultimately refused to vote for the Constitution on the ground that it contained "no Declaration of Rights . . . . Nor are the people secured even in the enjoyment of the benefit of the common law."[13]

Mason's concerns were taken up by the Anti-Federalists in the various state conventions. They argued repeatedly that because Congress was not obligated to respect rights established through the "long usage" of the common law, it might innovate in a manner destructive of individual liberty. For example, Abraham Holmes in Massachusetts and Patrick Henry in Virginia argued that Congress might discard the common-law prohibition of torture and adopt practices like those employed in continental Europe.[14] Henry also worried that Congress would impose "the most cruel and ignominious" punishments on the militia in order to convert it into a tool of despotism.[15]

During the First Congress, these protests led Representative James Madison to propose a Bill of Rights that was designed primarily to protect longstanding common-law rights, including by prohibiting cruel and unusual punishments.[16] There was very little discussion of this prohibition. Representatives Samuel Livermore of New Hampshire and William Smith of South Carolina expressed concern that the cruel and unusual punishments clause was "indefinite."[17] But these comments did not provoke any further discussion. The provision was approved by Congress and ratified by the states.[18]

THE CLAUSE AND THE ROBERTS COURT

Bucklew v. Precythe (2019) signaled that the U.S. Supreme Court would rely on "the original and historical understanding of the Eighth Amendment," but the Court did not fully explicate its understanding of the clause's original meaning.[19] For six decades before *Bucklew*, the Court followed an explicitly anti-originalist jurisprudence. A plurality had held in *Trop v. Dulles* (1958) that punishments would be judged not in light of the original meaning of the clause, but according to "evolving standards of decency that mark the progress of a maturing society."[20] Similarly, *Robinson v. California* (1962) relied on "contemporary" standards to find that a state-imposed punishment violated the Cruel and Unusual Punishments Clause as incorporated into the Due Process Clause of the Fourteenth Amendment.[21]

The original meaning of the clause does contain a principle of legal development, albeit one that operates very differently than the evolving standards of decency test. If a once-traditional punishment falls out of usage for a significant period of time, it might become unconstitutional.[22] For example, the First Congress authorized the death penalty for counterfeiting, but this punishment for this offense has arguably become unconstitutional because it fell out of usage a very long time ago. Similarly, new punishments might become part of the tradition if they establish universal reception over a long period of time. For example, prison was a new form of punishment at the time of the Founding but has been used universally for nearly two centuries. It is now part of the tradition.[23]

SUBSTANTIVE AND PROCEDURAL DEATH PENALTY DOCTRINE

An infinitesimally small percentage of felony offenders are subject to the death penalty. Yet the death penalty still has received the lion's share of attention in recent decades from both the Supreme Court and the media.[24]

The Supreme Court has developed both a "substantive" and a "procedural" approach to the Eighth Amendment. Under the substantive approach, the Court has limited application of the death penalty based on a purported current societal consensus against it for certain crimes. For example, *Coker v. Georgia* (1977) found that the death penalty could not be imposed for simple rape.[25] *Kennedy v. Louisiana* (2008) barred the death penalty for aggravated rape of a child.[26] *Enmund v. Florida* (1982) prohibited executing defendants for certain types of felony murder.[27]

Similarly, the Court has ruled that the Eighth Amendment bars executing certain classes of offenders. *Roper v. Simmons* (2008) held that the death penalty could not be imposed on minors who commit murder.[28] *Atkins v. Virginia* (2002) applied the same rule for the mentally disabled.[29] These holdings are based

directly on the anti-originalist evolving standards of decency test.

Under its procedural doctrine, the Court has sought to limit "arbitrary" imposition of the death penalty by requiring that certain procedures be followed at sentencing. *Woodson v. North Carolina* (1976) declared unconstitutional state statutes mandating automatic imposition of the death penalty for certain crimes.[30] The Court also held that juries cannot be given "unbridled discretion" over death penalty decisions and must instead be given guidance.[31] Under modern practice, juries must find the existence of certain statutory aggravating factors before imposing the death penalty.[32]

On the other hand, *Lockett v. Ohio* (1978) held that death penalty-eligible defendants have a right to "individualized sentencing" and that statutes precluding consideration of "relevant mitigating factors" are unconstitutional.[33] But this principle is not unlimited. *United States v. Tsarnaev* (2022), for example, ruled that the government "may enact reasonable rules governing whether specific pieces of evidence are admissible."[34] As a result, states may exclude mitigating evidence that does not comply with such rules.

The Court has not made any effort to reconcile these procedural cases with the original meaning of the Cruel and Unusual Punishments Clause. A natural home for this line of cases would seem to be the Due Process Clause, at least under modern doctrine.

METHODS OF EXECUTION

The Court has scrutinized methods of execution as well. *Glossip v. Gross* (2015) ruled that a method of execution can be found unconstitutional only if it creates "a substantial risk of severe pain."[35] The Court also imposed obstacles to challenging a given method of execution that appear to be inconsistent with the original meaning of the clause. Specifically, *Glossip* held that a prisoner who wishes to challenge a given method of execution "must identify an alternative that is 'feasible, readily implemented, and in fact significantly reduce[s] a substantial risk of severe pain.'"[36] There is no textual or historical basis for this requirement. *Bucklew* suggested that a prisoner may be required to demonstrate that the government "intended its method to inflict [unnecessary] pain."[37] This possible requirement also lacks a solid foundation in constitutional text or history.[38]

PRISON SENTENCES

Does the Eighth Amendment also limit prison sentences? Would a prison sentence be unconstitutional because it is grossly disproportionate to the offense? Could the state impose a life sentence for a parking violation? The Supreme Court has not taken a consistent position on this issue. *Rummel v. Estelle* (1980) suggested that "overtime parking" could not be made "a felony punishable by life imprisonment,"[39] and *Solem v. Helm* (1983) held that the clause contains a proportionality requirement as part of its original meaning.[40] But *Ewing v. California* (2003) deferred to legislative judgments as to proportionality of criminal sentences so strongly as to make proportionality review seemingly illusory.[41] Nonetheless, *Miller v. Alabama* (2012) held that a mandatory life sentence without possibility of parole for juvenile offenders would be unconstitutional.[42] The Court cited the risk that such a sentence would be disproportionate to the minor's culpability.

In short, there has been little rhyme or reason to the Supreme Court's approach to proportionality. The Court was torn between the obvious fact that a given punishment might be so disproportionate to the offense as to be cruel and unusual and the worry that courts lack a neutral principle of adjudication for deciding proportionality cases.

Evidence from the Founding era shows that the original meaning of the clause does prohibit cruelly disproportionate punishments.[43] The clause also provides a neutral principle of adjudication: In determining whether a punishment is cruelly disproportionate to the offense, the Court should compare it to punishments traditionally given for the same or similar offenses. A punishment that is significantly harsher than those traditionally given for the offense may be held cruel and unusual.

PRISON CONDITIONS

Estelle v. Gamble (1976) applied the Cruel and Unusual Punishments Clause to prison conditions.[44] The state cannot impose an "unnecessary and wanton infliction of pain" if prison officials displayed "deliberate indifference" to that pain.[45] Under *Farmer v. Brennan* (1994), a claim of being subjected to inhuman prison conditions can succeed only if a prison official displays a culpable state of mind amounting at least to recklessness.[46] Under the original meaning of the clause, prison conditions can be found cruel and unusual,[47] but because "cruel" refers to the harshness of the conditions and not government officials' state of mind, the recklessness requirement appears to be unwarranted.[48]

PUNISHMENT FOR STATUS

Finally, *Robinson v. California* (1962) held that it was unconstitutional to punish a defendant for the "status" of being addicted to narcotics.[49] The opinion was based on the evolving standards of decency test rather than the original meaning of the Clause. Indeed, the decision contained virtually no legal reasoning of any kind. *City of Grants Pass v. Johnson* (2024) refused to extend *Robinson*'s holding to anti-camping ordinances that respondents claimed imposed punishment based on the "status" of homelessness.[50] The constitutional status of *Robinson* itself was left unsettled.

OPEN QUESTIONS

- How can the Supreme Court reconcile its older anti-originalist precedents with the newer originalist precedents? What would an originalist Cruel and Unusual Punishments Clause jurisprudence look like?
- Is long-term solitary confinement a cruel and unusual punishment? This practice was used in the nineteenth century but was abandoned because of high rates of insanity, self-harm, and suicide. Justice Clarence Thomas has argued that prison conditions cannot be considered a punishment because they were not ordered by a judge as part of the sentence,[51] but there is substantial evidence to the contrary.[52]
- Does the Cruel and Unusual Punishments Clause cover only punishments inflicted

as the result of a criminal conviction, or does it also cover other kinds of government-imposed coercion such as extra-judicial torture?

Cite as: John F. Stinneford, *The Cruel and Unusual Punishments Clause, in* The Heritage Guide to the Constitution 698 (Josh Blackman & John G. Malcolm eds., 3d ed. 2025).

Notes

1. *Trop v. Dulles*, 356 U.S. 86, 101 (1958).   **2.** *Bucklew v. Precythe*, 587 U.S. 119, 136 (2019).   **3.** John Stinneford, *The Original Meaning of "Unusual": The Eighth Amendment as a Bar to Cruel Innovation*, 102 Nw. U. L. Rev. 1739 (2008); John Stinneford, *The Original Meaning of "Cruel,"* 105 Geo. L. J. 441 (2017); John Stinneford, *Rethinking Proportionality Under the Cruel and Unusual Punishments Clause*, 97 Va. L. Rev. 899 (2011); John Stinneford, *Death, Desuetude, and Original Meaning*, 56 Wm. & Mary L. Rev. 531 (2014); John Stinneford, *Experimental Punishments*, 95 Notre Dame L. Rev. 39 (2019)   **4.** Stinneford, *Cruel, supra* at 464.   **5.** 1 The Works of James Wilson 186 (James DeWitt Andrews ed., 1896).   **6.** Edward Coke, 1 Institutes of the Law of England § 138 (15th ed. 1794).   **7.** 1 Blackstone 70.   **8.** Stinneford, *Unusual, supra* at 1783–85.   **9.** 1 W. & M., ch. 2, sess. 2 (1689).   **10.** 10 H.C. Jour. 228, 249 (1689).   **11.** Va. Const. of 1776, § 9.   **12.** 2 Farrand's 637.   **13.** *Id.* at 649.   **14.** 2 Elliot's 111; 3 Elliot's 447–48.   **15.** 3 Elliot's 412.   **16.** 1 Annuals of Cong. 452 (1789); Stinneford, *Unusual, supra* at 1808.   **17.** 1 Annals of Cong. 782 (1789).   **18.** *Id.* at 783; Stinneford, *Unusual, supra* at 1809.   **19.** 587 U.S. at 136.   **20.** 356 U.S. 86, 101 (1958).   **21.** 370 U.S. 660, 666 (1962).   **22.** Stinneford, *Desuetude, supra*.   **23.** Stinneford, *Experimental, supra*.   **24.** Stinneford, *Proportionality, supra* at 902–03.   **25.** 433 U.S. 584 (1977).   **26.** 554 U.S. 407, 441–45 (2008).   **27.** 458 U.S. 782 (1982).   **28.** 543 U.S. 551 (2005).   **29.** 536 U.S. 304 (2002).   **30.** 428 U.S. 280, 301 (1976).   **31.** *Id.* at 302.   **32.** *Id.* at 303–04.   **33.** 438 U.S. 586, 602–05, 608 (1978).   **34.** 595 U.S. 302, 319 (2022).   **35.** 576 U.S. 863, 877 (2015) (quoting *Baze v. Rees*, 553 U.S. 35, 51 (2008) (plurality opinion)).   **36.** *Id.* (quoting *Baze*, 553 U.S. at 52).   **37.** *Bucklew*, 587 U.S. at 136.   **38.** Stinneford, *Cruel, supra*.   **39.** 445 U.S. 263, 274 (1980).   **40.** 463 U.S. 277, 285–87 (1983).   **41.** 538 U.S. 11, 24 (2003) (plurality opinion).   **42.** *Miller v. Alabama*, 567 U.S. 460 (2012).   **43.** Stinneford, *Proportionality, supra*.   **44.** 429 U.S. 97, 104 (1976) (quoting *Gregg v. Georgia*, 428 U.S. 153, 173 (1976)).   **45.** *Id.*   **46.** 511 U.S. 825, 837 (1994).   **47.** Stinneford, *Cruel, supra*.   **48.** *Id.*   **49.** 370 U.S. 660 (1962).   **50.** 603 U.S. 520 (2024).   **51.** *Helling v. McKinney*, 509 U.S. 25, 37–42 (1993) (Thomas, J., dissenting).   **52.** John Stinneford, *Is Solitary Confinement a Punishment?*, 115 Nw. U. L. Rev. 9 (2020).

‿

ESSAY NO. 187: THE NINTH AMENDMENT
AMEND. 9

The enumeration in the Constitution, of certain rights, shall not be construed to deny or disparage others retained by the people.

—Ryan Williams

INTRODUCTION

During Judge Robert Bork's much-publicized Supreme Court confirmation hearing in 1987, he famously analogized the Ninth Amendment to a constitutional "inkblot." Bork explained that judges could not use the amendment to decide cases "without knowing something of what it means."[1] In the years since Bork's testimony, originalist scholars have uncovered a wealth of information regarding the circumstances that led to the amendment's inclusion in the Bill of Rights and the specific concerns it was designed to address. But these historical excavations have not led to a consensus view among originalists regarding the amendment's proper interpretation.

THE CONSTITUTIONAL CONVENTION AND RATIFICATION DEBATES

The story of the Ninth Amendment's adoption begins with the Constitutional Convention's omission of a bill of rights from the original Constitution. The absence of a bill of rights provided a rallying point for Anti-Federalist opposition during the state ratification debates.[2]

Supporters of ratification quickly converged on a defense of the decision to omit a bill of rights that was first articulated by James Wilson of Pennsylvania. Wilson, who was a delegate to the Convention, defended the Framers' decision to leave even very popular rights, such as the freedom of the press, unprotected. In a public speech in Philadelphia on October 6, 1787, Wilson explained that the "very declaration" of such a right in the Constitution "might have been construed to imply that some degree of power was given" to the federal government to regulate the press "since [the Constitution] undertook to define its extent."[3]

Wilson's argument drew upon a widely accepted interpretive canon providing that the inclusion of one thing in a list or enumeration should ordinarily be read to exclude those things not enumerated.

Federalists in other states quickly rallied to Wilson's argument. They contended that a bill of rights was not only unnecessary but also potentially dangerous.[4] In Federalist No. 84, Alexander Hamilton warned about a bill of rights that "contain[ed] various exceptions to powers which are not granted." Such a limited and almost certainly incomplete enumeration of particular rights, Hamilton wrote, would "afford a colourable pretext" for the government "to claim more [powers] than were granted." Instead, Hamilton and others argued that such rights would be better protected by the limited enumeration of federal powers.

Not everyone was convinced by the Federalists' arguments about the danger of a bill of rights. Multiple state conventions proposed lists of amendments that they wished to see adopted following ratification. These amendments, proponents argued, would better secure individual rights. Although none of these proposals perfectly mirrored the language that was ultimately included in the Ninth Amendment, two sets of such proposed amendments have been identified by modern scholars as potentially relevant to the amendment's original meaning.

The first set of proposals called for an amendment that would expressly recognize the existence of "retained" individual *natural* rights that individuals would have possessed in the state of nature and that they retained

when forming their governments. Sir William Blackstone described "natural liberty" as "consist[ing] properly in a power of acting as one thinks fit, without any restraint or control, unless by the law of nature" but observed that "every man, when he enters into society, gives up a part of his natural liberty."[5] The Virginia convention offered one such proposal. It acknowledged the existence of "certain natural rights, of which men, when they form a social compact, cannot deprive or divest their posterity."[6] These rights included "the enjoyment of life and liberty, with the means of acquiring, possessing, and protecting property, and pursuing and obtaining happiness and safety."[7]

The second set of amendment proposals were targeted more directly at addressing the Federalists' concerns about the potential dangers of enumerating rights. The text of Virginia's proposal, for example, provided that "those clauses which declare that Congress shall not exercise certain powers be not interpreted in any manner whatsoever to extend the powers of Congress."[8]

ADOPTION OF THE NINTH AMENDMENT

Following ratification, Representative James Madison of Virginia became the leading champion of a federal bill of rights.[9] In the First Congress, Madison synthesized several of the proposals from the state ratifying conventions into a list of proposed amendments that would provide an important template for the first ten amendments to the Constitution. One of Madison's texts combined aspects of both sets of proposals from the states, referring both to "retained" individual rights and to the constructive enlargement of federal power. Specifically, Madison's proposal declared that "exceptions" of constitutional powers "made in favor of particular rights" should "not be so construed as to diminish the just importance of other rights retained by the people, or as to enlarge the powers delegated by the constitution."[10] This text eventually evolved into the Ninth Amendment.

Madison's speech introducing his proposals acknowledged the Federalists' objection. He said that "enumerating particular exceptions" to the powers granted to the federal government might be read to "disparage those rights which were not placed in that enumeration" and that "it might follow, by implication, that those rights which were not singled out, were intended to be assigned into the hands of the General Government, and were consequently insecure."[11] Madison conceded that this objection was "one of the most plausible arguments" he had "ever heard urged against the admission of a bill of rights into this system," but he believed that it could "be guarded against" and pointed to this proposed text as his attempt to do so.[12]

Madison's proposals were referred to a committee of the House of Representatives on which he served.[13] Unfortunately, this committee kept no formal record of its proceedings, leaving modern interpreters with limited information regarding the considerations that influenced the amendment's final wording.

A possible clue to the committee's internal deliberations is provided by a handwritten list of proposed amendments penned by one of its members, Roger Sherman of Connecticut. The second proposed amendment listed in Sherman's draft declared that "[t]he people have certain natural rights which are retained by them when they enter into Society."[14] These rights included the "rights of Conscience in matters of religion," "of acquiring property and of pursuing happiness & Safety," and "of Speaking, writing and publishing their Sentiments."[15] The draft further specified that the federal government would be barred from "depriv[ing]" the people of such rights.[16]

A separate proposed amendment in the Sherman draft bears some resemblance to the rule-of-construction proposals urged by several of the state ratifying conventions. It provided that powers not delegated to the federal government nor prohibited to the states should be "retained by the states."[17] It further provided that "the exercise of power by the Government of the united States" in "particular instances here in enumerated by way of caution" should not "be construed to imply the contrary."[18]

In the end, the committee settled on new language that departed both from Madison's initial proposal and from the language reflected in Sherman's draft. This new language closely tracked the language that was ultimately included in the Ninth Amendment. For reasons that are not known, the reference to constructive enlargement of federal powers, which had appeared both in Madison's initial proposal and in proposals submitted by the state ratifying conventions, was dropped from what became the Ninth Amendment. Similar concerns were addressed by what would become the Tenth Amendment. (See Essay No. 188.) Instead, the rule of construction supplied by the Ninth Amendment prohibited "constru[ing]" the "enumeration in the Constitution of certain rights to deny or disparage others retained by the people."

ORIGINAL MEANING OF THE NINTH AMENDMENT

The text of the Ninth Amendment, when read literally, only states a rule about how other provisions in the Constitution should be read. The Ninth Amendment's explicit command does not directly confer rights or constrain the scope of federal powers. Rather, the amendment simply instructs interpreters to reject arguments that seek to use the existence of particular enumerated rights in the Constitution to "deny or disparage" other "retained" rights.

This rule-of-construction function is at the center of the traditional view that the Ninth Amendment was solely a response to the concerns expressed during the ratification debates of 1787 and 1788. Many modern originalist scholars articulate this perspective.[19] Proponents of this traditional view generally agree that the Ninth Amendment's rule of construction comes into play only when particular rights are denied or disparaged, because other rights are enumerated in the Constitution. Proponents of this view further agree that the "retained" rights referred to in the amendment cannot be enforced by the courts; instead, such rights are simply left with whatever legal status they would have possessed if an enumeration of rights had not been included in the Constitution.

This narrow understanding of the Ninth Amendment has been called into question by Professor Randy Barnett.[20] According to Barnett, the Ninth Amendment's "retained" rights are individual natural rights that individuals possessed before the Constitution's adoption and "retained" upon forming their government. Barnett agrees that the traditional interpretation is valid as far as it goes but maintains that these "retained" natural rights should be protected by the courts. The judiciary, he believes, should follow a "presumption of liberty." Under this presumption, the federal government must demonstrate that its regulations are truly necessary to protect the liberties of others and not merely a pretext for the imposition of undue burdens on the rightful exercise of natural rights by individuals.

Professor Kurt Lash has responded to Barnett's theory.[21] Lash emphasizes the similarity between the Ninth Amendment and the calls from numerous state ratifying conventions for a rule of construction that would limit the constructive enlargement of federal powers. Lash argues that the amendment's reference to "retained rights" is best understood as encompassing both individual natural rights and the peoples' collective right to local self-government within their respective states. According to Lash, the amendment should thus be read to support a general interpretive rule that limits the constructive enlargement of federal powers in violation of state authority even where the argument for expanding federal powers does not depend on the fact that any particular rights were enumerated.

JUDICIAL PRECEDENT

The scholarly attention lavished on the Ninth Amendment has not been matched by a similar level of judicial interest. Throughout the nineteenth century and early twentieth century, the U.S. Supreme Court invoked the amendment only sporadically, and these decisions almost always concerned limiting the scope of federal powers. For example, in *Houston v. Moore* (1820), Justice Joseph Story's dissent observed that under the Ninth Amendment, "the states retain concurrent authority with Congress" over matters not exclusively confided to the federal government.[22] A century later, in *Ashwander v. Tennessee Valley Authority* (1936), the Court found that the Ninth Amendment did not limit the scope of federal power to dispose of federal property.[23] Following the New Deal expansion of federal regulatory power, the significance of this interpretation faded, and the amendment fell largely into judicial disuse.

In *Griswold v. Connecticut* (1965), Justice Arthur Goldberg wrote a concurring opinion that signaled a possible revival of judicial interest in the Ninth Amendment. Goldberg wrote that the "language and history of the Ninth Amendment reveal that the Framers of the Constitution believed that there are additional fundamental rights, protected from governmental infringement, which exist alongside those fundamental rights specifically mentioned in the first eight constitutional amendments." Goldberg cited this history to support the Court's decision to declare unconstitutional a state law that infringed on an unenumerated right to marital privacy, but his suggestion that unenumerated rights should be grounded in the Ninth Amendment went unheeded. Justice William O. Douglas's majority opinion in *Griswold* mentioned the Ninth Amendment briefly as part of a laundry list of textually specified individual rights but did not rely on it.

Roe v. Wade (1973) extended the privacy right first recognized in *Griswold* to protect a constitutional right to abortion, but the Court did not rely on the reasoning from Justice Douglas's *Griswold* opinion. Rather, the *Roe* majority simply declared that the right to privacy "whether it be founded in the Fourteenth Amendment's concept of personal liberty and restrictions upon state action, as we feel it is, or ... in the Ninth Amendment's reservation of rights to the people, is broad enough to encompass a woman's decision whether or not to terminate her pregnancy."[24]

The *Roe* Court's subtle suggestion that the Fourteenth Amendment's Due Process Clause provided the proper textual source for the privacy right was firmly embraced in later cases. For example, the controlling plurality opinion in *Planned Parenthood v. Casey* (1992), which reaffirmed key aspects of *Roe*, relied exclusively on Fourteenth Amendment substantive due process. (See Essay No. 195.) *Casey* did not mention the Ninth Amendment at all.[25] Later decisions extending protection to other unenumerated rights, such as a right to same-sex sexual relations and same-sex marriage, similarly avoided any mention of the Ninth Amendment.[26]

Dobbs v. Jackson Women's Health Organization (2022) overruled both *Roe* and *Casey* as inconsistent with the Court's established substantive due process methodology. *Dobbs* required that to be judicially protected, "rights that are not mentioned in the

Constitution . . . must be 'deeply rooted in this Nation's history and tradition' and 'implicit in the concept of ordered liberty.'"[27] Consistent with the trend of the Court's post-*Roe* unenumerated-rights decisions, *Dobbs* did not mention the Ninth Amendment aside from a passing reference in discussing the reasoning of *Roe*.[28]

Cite as: Ryan Williams, *The Ninth Amendment, in* THE HERITAGE GUIDE TO THE CONSTITUTION 702 (Josh Blackman & John G. Malcolm eds., 3d ed. 2025).

Notes

1. *Nomination of Robert H. Bork to Be Associate Justice of the Supreme Court of the United States: Hearings Before the S. Comm. on the Judiciary,* 100th Cong. 248–50 (1987). **2.** Kenneth R. Bowling, *"A Tub to the Whale": The Founding Fathers and Adoption of the Federal Bill of Rights,* 8 J. Early Rep. 223, 225–26 (1988). **3.** Federalists and Antifederalists: The Debate Over the Ratification of the Constitution 167–68 (John P. Kaminski & Richard Leffler eds., 2d ed. 1998). **4.** Randy E. Barnett, *The Ninth Amendment: It Means What It Says,* 85 Tex. L. Rev. 1, 27–28 (2006). **5.** 1 Blackstone 125. **6.** 3 Elliot's 657; The Complete Bill of Rights: The Drafts, Debates, Sources, and Origins 636 (Neil H. Cogan ed., 1997). **7.** *Id.* **8.** 3 Elliot's 661; Creating the Bill of Rights: The Documentary Record from the First Federal Congress 21 (Helen E. Veit et al. eds., 1991); Kurt Lash, The Lost History of the Ninth Amendment, 20–23 (2009). **9.** Bowling, *supra* at 231–35. **10.** 1 Annals of Cong. 452 (1789). **11.** *Id.* at 456. **12.** *Id.* **13.** *Id.* at 467–68. **14.** 1 The Rights Retained by the People: The History and Meaning of the Ninth Amendment app. A, at 351, 351 (Randy E. Barnett ed., 1989). **15.** *Id.* **16.** *Id.* **17.** *Id.* at 362. **18.** *Id.* **19.** Michael W. McConnell, *Natural Rights and the Ninth Amendment: How Does Lockean Legal Theory Assist in Interpretation?,* N.Y.U. J.L. & Liberty 1 (2010); Nelson Lund & John O. McGinnis, Lawrence v. Texas *and Judicial Hubris,* 102 Mich. L. Rev. 1555, 1591–93 (2004); Thomas B. McAffee, *The Original Meaning of the Ninth Amendment,* 90 Colum. L. Rev. 1215 (1990); Raoul Berger, *The Ninth Amendment,* 66 Cornell L. Rev. 1 (1980). **20.** Randy E. Barnett, Restoring the Lost Constitution: The Presumption of Liberty (2004); Barnett, *Ninth Amendment, supra.* **21.** Lash, *supra.* **22.** 18 U.S. 1, 48–49 (1820) (Story, J., dissenting). **23.** *Ashwander v. Tennessee Valley Authority,* 297 U.S. 288, 330–31 (1936). **24.** *Roe v. Wade,* 410 U.S. 113, 153 (1973). **25.** *Planned Parenthood of Se. Pa. v. Casey,* 505 U.S. 833 (1992). **26.** *Lawrence v. Texas,* 539 U.S. 558 (2003); *Obergefell v. Hodges,* 576 U.S. 644 (2015). **27.** *Dobbs v. Jackson Women's Health Org.,* 597 U.S. 215, 231 (2022) (quoting *Washington v. Glucksberg,* 521 U.S. 702, 721 (1997)) (internal quotation marks omitted). **28.** *Id.* at 235 & n.16.

ESSAY NO. 188: THE TENTH AMENDMENT
AMEND. 10

The powers not delegated to the United States by the Constitution, nor prohibited by it to the States, are reserved to the States respectively, or to the people.

—Charles J. Cooper

INTRODUCTION

The Tenth Amendment expresses the fundamental principle that undergirds the entire plan of the original Constitution. As James Madison explained in Federalist No. 39, the national government possesses only those powers delegated to it and "leaves to the several States a residuary and inviolable sovereignty over all other objects." The Constitution was "in strictness, neither a national nor a federal Constitution, but a composition of both." Framed by the First Congress in response to demands by state ratifying conventions for a bill of rights, the Tenth Amendment's central purpose was to establish a rule of constitutional construction reaffirming the nature of the federal system.

THE CONSTITUTIONAL CONVENTION

After the Revolution, the Articles of Confederation created a mere "league of friendship" in which "[e]ach state retain[ed] its sovereignty, freedom and independence, and every Power, Jurisdiction and right, which [was] not by this confederation expressly delegated to the United States, in Congress assembled."[1] Over time, it became increasingly clear that this anemic government was unsustainable.

In May 1787, delegates from the states gathered in Philadelphia for the purpose of strengthening the Union. The delegates to the Constitutional Convention were divided, however, over how strong the national government should be. They were wary of centralized government and protective of the sovereignty of their individual states. At the same time, the failure of the Articles of Confederation to "insure domestic tranquility" and other basic government functions revealed the necessity of vesting greater authority in a national government independent of the states.

The Constitution therefore created a novel system of dual sovereignty. Each government possessed direct authority over the people. The national government exercised its limited and enumerated powers over all persons. At the same time, the states exercised their residual sovereign power over their residents. In addition, the states were made a constituency within the national government's structure. The state legislatures chose Senators, determined how presidential electors should be chosen, and defined who would be eligible to vote for members of the House of Representatives. Critical to this system of dual sovereignty were the limitations on the national government inherent in the scheme of enumerated federal powers. This enumeration of powers allowed the federal government to operate only within defined spheres of jurisdiction where it is acknowledged to be supreme.

During the Constitutional Convention, certain delegates argued that the federal government needed a bill of rights. George Mason was perhaps the most adamant in his insistence that the Constitution was deficient without a bill of rights. James Madison described Mason's work in an October 24, 1787, letter to Thomas Jefferson: "Col. Mason left Philada. in an exceeding ill humour indeed . . . . He returned to Virginia with a fixed disposition to prevent the adoption of the plan if possible. He considers the want of a Bill of Rights as a fatal objection." [2]

Mason's argument would not carry the day. After the Constitution was adopted without a bill of rights, critics continued their opposition in the state ratifying conventions.

THE RATIFICATION DEBATES

The Anti-Federalists feared that the new national government would inevitably exceed its enumerated powers, usurp the powers of the states, and infringe on the liberties of the people. In the Virginia ratifying convention, Mason argued that "the general government being paramount to, and in every respect more powerful than the state governments, the latter must give way to the former." [3] Mason, as noted, had declined to sign the Constitution, in part because it lacked a bill of rights. The Anti-Federalists maintained that a bill of rights would be necessary to prevent such oppression. For support, they pointed to many state constitutions that had bills of rights.

The Federalists argued that the analogy between the federal and state constitutions did not work. State constitutions were not limited to specified enumerated powers. Instead, they conferred a general legislative power on the state governments. Because the states had so much power, there was a risk of oppression. State bills of rights, which limited that authority, were deemed necessary to guard individual rights against the danger of plenary governmental power. Madison explained the difference in Federalist No. 45. "The powers delegated by the proposed Constitution to the federal government are few and defined," he argued, and the powers "which are to remain in the State governments are numerous and indefinite." Congress's powers "will be exercised principally on external objects, as war, peace, negotiation, and foreign commerce." The states' powers "will extend to all the objects which, in the ordinary course of affairs, concern the lives, liberties, and properties of the people, and the internal order, improvement, and prosperity of the state."

The Federalists insisted that a federal bill of rights was unnecessary because the proposed national government's limited regulatory powers could reach only those objects granted to it. In Federalist No. 84, Alexander Hamilton similarly contended that a proposed amendment protecting the freedom of the press was unnecessary because Congress had no power to regulate the press: "Why . . . should it be said that the liberty of the press shall not be restrained, when no power is given by which restrictions may be imposed?"

Moreover, the Federalists argued that a bill of rights was potentially dangerous. Under the normal rules of statutory construction, if a bill of rights expressly forbade the government from acting in certain areas, that would necessarily imply that the government had power to act in all other areas. That implication would risk changing the national government from one of limited powers to one of general legislative powers like those of the states. Hamilton emphasized in Federalist No. 33 that acts beyond government's enumerated powers are "merely acts of usurpation" and "deserve to be treated as such."

The Anti-Federalists could not be persuaded. As the price of ratification in several states, they insisted on assurances that a bill of rights, including a provision reserving to the states powers not delegated to the national government, would be considered by the First Congress.

ADOPTION OF THE TENTH AMENDMENT

Despite Madison's opposition to a bill of rights in The Federalist, he seemed to change his mind during the First Congress. Then-Representative James Madison proposed what became the Tenth Amendment. (For the drafting history of the Tenth Amendment, see Essay No. 187.) This provision established a rule of constitutional construction designed to protect against interpreting the Bill of Rights to imply the existence of powers in the national government that were not granted by the original document.

EARLY PRACTICE AND JUDICIAL PRECEDENT

In 1798, President John Adams approved the Alien and Sedition Acts. These laws criminalized false or malicious statements about the federal government. In response, then-Vice President Thomas Jefferson and James Madison secretly wrote the Kentucky and Virginia Resolutions, respectively. These resolutions declared that the Alien and Sedition Acts exceeded Congress's delegated powers in violation of the Tenth Amendment. In other words, Congress lacked the enumerated powers to enact these restrictions on speech and the press. Jefferson argued that the statutes were "altogether void and of no force."[4] Because the

acts were repealed or expired after Jefferson was elected President in 1800, the question of their constitutionality never reached the U.S. Supreme Court.

The Tenth Amendment had limited judicial application in the nation's first century. No decision turned upon it. In *McCulloch v. Maryland* (1819), Chief Justice John Marshall declined to use the amendment as a vehicle for narrowly construing federal powers.[5] Justice Joseph Story would observe similarly that the Tenth Amendment "is a mere affirmation of what, upon any just reasoning, is a necessary rule of interpreting the constitution."[6] He explained that because the Constitution is "an instrument of limited and enumerated powers, it follows irresistibly that what is not conferred is withheld, and belongs to the state authorities."[7]

THE NEW DEAL COURT

During the New Deal, the Supreme Court upheld sweeping federal laws and countenanced an unprecedented expansion of federal powers far beyond the expectations of those who framed and ratified the Constitution. In doing so, the Court relegated the Tenth Amendment essentially to the status of a nullity. *NLRB v. Jones & Laughlin Steel Corp.* (1937) recognized that the Tenth Amendment provides an "explicit reservation" for the "distinction between what is national and what is local. . . ."[8] Only four years later, *United States v. Darby* (1941) declared that the Tenth Amendment "states but a truism that all is retained which has not been surrendered." Justice Harlan Fiske Stone wrote that "[t]here is nothing in the history of [the Tenth Amendment's] adoption to suggest that it was more than declaratory of the relationship between the national and state governments as it had been established by the Constitution before the amendment. . . ." Its purpose, Stone explained, was to "allay fears that the new national government might seek to exercise powers not granted, and that the states might not be able to exercise fully their reserved powers."[9]

In case after case, the Supreme Court upheld Congress's assertion of power to regulate such local concerns as manufacturing, agriculture, and labor relations. *Wickard v. Filburn* (1942) even upheld Congress's power to regulate a single farmer's production of wheat intended for consumption on his own farm.[10] These New Deal Cases thus largely fulfilled the Anti-Federalists' prophecy that the federal government would inevitably usurp the reserved powers of the states. Congress, with the Court's blessing, has inverted Madison's conception of federalism into one in which states' reserved powers are "few and defined" and the federal government's delegated powers are "numerous and indefinite," extending "to all objects which, in the ordinary course of affairs concern the lives, liberties, and properties of the people."

THE BURGER COURT

In the 1970s, the Burger Court reconsidered the Tenth Amendment. *Maryland v. Wirtz* (1968) ruled that Congress could impose the federal minimum wage on state employees.[11] Justice William O. Douglas, joined by Justice Potter Stewart, dissented. They argued that "what is done here is nonetheless such a serious invasion of state sovereignty protected by the Tenth Amendment that it is . . . not consistent with our constitutional federalism."[12] Eight years later, the Court overruled *Wirtz* in *National League of Cities v. Usery* (1976),[13] holding that the Tenth Amendment limits the federal government's power to regulate state governments. Writing for the majority, Justice William H. Rehnquist found that the Tenth Amendment's reservation of powers to the states barred the federal government from transgressing on traditional government functions essential to "the States' 'separate and independent existence,'" such as police and fire protection and public health facilities.[14]

Nine years later, however, the Court overruled *National League of Cities*. *Garcia v. San Antonio Metropolitan Transit Authority* (1985) held that the federal minimum wage could be imposed on municipal transit workers.[15] *Garcia* reasoned that the states' participation in the national political process would "ensure[] that laws that unduly burden the states will not be promulgated."[16] In other words, the states were adequately represented in Congress to prevent the enactment of burdensome statutes. The Court thus made clear that the federal judiciary would no longer entertain federalism challenges. Rather, Congress would henceforth be the sole judge of the constitutional limits on the reach of its powers. Justice Lewis Powell remarked in dissent that the decision "effectively reduce[d] the Tenth Amendment to meaningless rhetoric . . . ."[17]

The *Garcia* decision provoked a sharply negative reaction by President Ronald Reagan, who promptly formed a Federalism Working Group under the leadership of Attorney General Edwin Meese III. The Group's work led to President Reagan's issuance of an unprecedented executive order on federalism. It directed federal departments and agencies to adhere to nine "fundamental principles of federalism," including the principle that, "in the absence of clear constitutional or statutory authority, the presumption of sovereignty should rest with the individual States." And the Group specified that any "[u]ncertainties regarding the legitimate authority of the national government should be resolved against regulation at the national level."[18]

THE REHNQUIST COURT

During the 1990s, the Supreme Court revived the Tenth Amendment to enforce discrete limits on federal power to regulate state operations. The Rehnquist Court developed the commandeering doctrine. Under this line of cases, the machinery of state government could not be mandated to accomplish federal objectives. *New York v. United States* (1992) prevented Congress from requiring a state legislature to provide for the disposal of radioactive waste.[19] *Gregory v. Ashcroft* (1991) found that a federal law regulating the employment of state judges would raise concerns under the Tenth Amendment.[20] *Printz v. United States* (1997) barred Congress from requiring state executive officials to implement a federal scheme of firearms regulation.[21]

Overall, however, the Rehnquist Court's decisions curbing congressional power are but a modest correction of the federal government's wholesale usurpation of the states' reserved powers during the New Deal and Warren Court eras.

OPEN QUESTIONS

- The *Garcia* decision marks the low point in the Court's abandonment of federalism as a judicially enforceable structural protection of state sovereignty and individual freedom against federal regulatory overreach. Should *Garcia* be overruled? What would be a proper test case to revisit that precedent?

Cite as: Charles J. Cooper, *The Tenth Amendment, in* THE HERITAGE GUIDE TO THE CONSTITUTION 706 (Josh Blackman & John G. Malcolm eds., 3d ed. 2025).

Notes

1. Articles of Confederation, arts. II, III.   **2.** 3 Farrand's 135–36.   **3.** 3 Elliot's 29–30.   **4.** Resolutions Adopted by the Kentucky General Assembly (Nov. 10, 1798), https://perma.cc/VS8C-MDVP.   **5.** *McCulloch v. Maryland,* 17 U.S. (4 Wheat.) 316, 406 (1819).   **6.** 3 Story's Commentaries § 1900.   **7.** *Id.*   **8.** 301 U.S. 1 (1937).   **9.** 312 U.S. 100, 124 (1941).   **10.** *Wickard v. Filburn,* 317 U.S. 111 (1942). **11.** 392 U.S. 183 (1968).   **12.** *Id.* at 201–02.   **13.** 426 U.S. 833 (1976).   **14.** *Id.* at 851.   **15.** 469 U.S. 528 (1985).   **16.** *Id.* at 556.   **17.** *Id.* at 560 (Powell, J., dissenting).   **18.** E.O. 12612, 52 FR 41685 (Oct. 26, 1987), https://perma.cc/7QHR-MSEJ.   **19.** 505 U.S. 144 (1992).   **20.** 501 U.S. 452 (1991).   **21.** 521 U.S. 898 (1997).

PART 9

THE CORRECTION AMENDMENTS

~

ESSAY NO. 189: THE ELEVENTH AMENDMENT
AMEND. 11

The Judicial power of the United States shall not be construed to extend to any suit in law or equity, commenced or prosecuted against one of the United States by Citizens of another State, or by Citizens or Subjects of any Foreign State.

—Ernest A. Young

INTRODUCTION

The Eleventh Amendment's seemingly technical language arose out of some of the oldest controversies in American history. The amendment implements to an extent the principle of sovereign immunity—an ancient rule that generally protects governments from suits by private persons and entities. This principle originated in monarchist notions of royal prerogative. Sovereign immunity has required considerable modification in a democratic republic that endows individuals with constitutional rights against government, and it becomes even more complex in a federal system in which state governments frequently assert their immunity to avoid liability for violations of supreme national law. Although the Eleventh Amendment arose in response to the Supreme Court's first major constitutional decision in 1793, it continues to generate extensive litigation and academic controversy.

BACKDROP OF SOVEREIGN IMMUNITY

The notion of sovereign immunity traces back to the English common law as well as theories of unitary sovereignty associated with thinkers like Thomas Hobbes and Jean Bodin. Those theories held that "there must reside somewhere in every political unit a single, undivided final power, higher in legal authority than any other power, subject to no law, a law unto itself."[1]

Unitary sovereignty gave rise to two distinct legal rules of immunity: "[O]ne rule holds that the King or the Crown, as the font of law, is not bound by the law's provisions; the other provides that the King or Crown, as the font of justice, is not subject to suit in its own courts."[2] The first rule was largely rejected even in England and never found much purchase in this country. As

Professor Louis L. Jaffe has observed, the notion that "the King can do no wrong" did not mean that the king was above the law; it meant that the king's power did not extend to unlawful acts.[3] The Supreme Court would affirm that "[n]o man in this country is so high that he is above the law."[4] The second principle—barring judicial remedies against the government—has proven to be more durable.

Sovereign immunity was part of the legal and intellectual backdrop against which the Framers drafted, debated, and ratified the Constitution.[5] There is little evidence that the Constitution was intended to alter the states' traditional immunity from private lawsuits, but the introduction of the Citizen-State Diversity Clause did raise fears that Article III would strip the states of their immunity and subject them to suit in federal court. (See Essay No. 130.) Those fears took on particular urgency in light of the considerable outstanding debts that state governments owed to creditors for Revolutionary War expenditures, as well as potential suits by persons disputing land titles under state law and by British citizens under the peace treaty of 1783.[6]

Several key Framers and ratifiers denied that the Constitution, of its own force, would deprive the states of this immunity. Hamilton made this point in Federalist No. 81, as did James Madison and John Marshall at the Virginia ratifying convention.[7] The Supreme Court repudiated these assurances, however, just a few years later.

CHISHOLM V. GEORGIA AND THE ELEVENTH AMENDMENT

Chisholm v. Georgia (1793) was the Court's first major constitutional case.[8] Alexander Chisholm was executor of the estate of Robert Farquhar, a deceased South Carolina merchant who had provided war material to Georgia during the Revolutionary War.[9] The federal court's jurisdiction to hear the case depended on Article III's Citizen-State Diversity Clause. The majority of the Court found that the clause did override the state's traditional immunity from suit[10]—just as the Anti-Federalists had feared. The Court's holding sparked widespread outrage, largely because of concerns that enforcement of state Revolutionary War debts and pre-Revolutionary land claims would threaten many states' solvency.[11]

The Court observed a century later that *Chisholm* "created such a shock of surprise throughout the country that, at the first meeting of congress thereafter, the eleventh amendment to the constitution was almost unanimously proposed, and was in due course adopted by the legislatures of the states."[12] The amendment provided that "[t]he Judicial power of the United States shall not be construed to extend to any suit in law or equity, commenced or prosecuted against one of the United States by Citizens of another State, or by Citizens or Subjects of any Foreign State."[13] It plainly rejected the result in *Chisholm*; the question is: What *else* does the language cover?

INTERPRETATIONS OF THE ELEVENTH AMENDMENT

Courts and commentators have offered two primary interpretations of the Eleventh Amendment's text. First, the "diversity reading" reads the amendment as simply removing citizen-state diversity of citizenship as an available ground of federal jurisdiction when a private party sues a state government. If another ground—such as a federal question—is available, the federal court's jurisdiction would be unaffected.[14] Second, under the "plain meaning reading," the presence of an out-of-state plaintiff would always defeat jurisdiction whether or not some other ground is available.[15]

For many years, almost all academics, as well as both the majority and dissenting justices in the Supreme Court's major state immunity cases, agreed that the diversity reading was the correct one with regard to the amendment's actual text.[16] For example, the Supreme Court

recognized that "the terms of [the Eleventh] Amendment address only 'the specific provisions of the Constitution that had raised concerns during the ratification debates and formed the basis of the *Chisholm* decision. . . .'"[17] The Court also conceded that "the text of the Amendment would appear to restrict only the Article III diversity jurisdiction of the federal courts."[18]

Judges and scholars disagreed, however, as to whether some sort of structural or common-law immunity existed alongside the textual one that barred suits in federal-question suits or other situations not covered by the amendment's text. *Alden v. Maine* (1999) explained that "Eleventh Amendment immunity" is "something of a misnomer, for the sovereign immunity of the States neither derives from, nor is limited by, the terms of the Eleventh Amendment."[19] Some justices and academics have sought to revive the plain-meaning reading.[20] These authorities also believe in a broader common-law or structural immunity; the main significance of the textual bar would thus be that it could not be waived by the state or abrogated by Congress under any circumstances. In a dissenting opinion, Justice Neil Gorsuch has written that "States have two distinct federal-law immunities from suit"—one grounded in text and one in constitutional structure.[21] Other commentators, however, have sought to ground a broader notion of immunity elsewhere in the text—for instance, in the original understanding of what it means to be a "state" in light of eighteenth-century conceptions of sovereignty under the law of nations.[22]

Either the diversity or plain-meaning reading of the Eleventh Amendment would have barred suit in *Chisholm*: Chisholm's claim rested on state law such that federal jurisdiction depended solely on diversity of citizenship. But the Amendment's ambiguities left open several more difficult questions that the Framers had not confronted directly: Did the states' immunity apply in suits based on federal law? Was that immunity constitutional in stature, or could Congress abrogate it by statute?

The Supreme Court answered the first question in *Hans v. Louisiana* (1890).[23] Hans sought to recover on a repudiated Louisiana bond, but instead of suing for breach of contract under state law, he invoked the federal Contracts Clause to claim that the state had impaired the obligation of the bond contract. The Court conceded that because Hans was a citizen of Louisiana and rested federal jurisdiction on a federal question, his suit fell outside the Eleventh Amendment's textual bar to suits "by Citizens of another State, or by Citizens or Subjects of any Foreign State." Writing for the Court, Justice Joseph Bradley contended that it would be anomalous to allow Hans—a Louisiana native—to sue in circumstances where out-of-state individuals would be barred.[24] The leading explanation of this holding, relied upon in more recent cases, is that the sovereign immunity enjoyed by the states at the Founding was broadly applicable to all sorts of suits, and the Eleventh Amendment was intended only to fill the specific gap in that preexisting immunity created by the Court's decision in *Chisholm*.[25]

After *Hans*, the Court extended the states' immunity in a number of other ways that are inconsistent with the amendment's text. State immunity bars suits in admiralty (notwithstanding the textual limitation to "suit[s] in law or equity")[26] and by foreign sovereigns and Indian tribes (notwithstanding the textual limitation to "Citizens" of a "State" or "Foreign State").[27] The Court also limited state immunity in ways the text seems to foreclose. The Court allowed states to waive their immunity notwithstanding the amendment's framing as a limit on subject-matter jurisdiction (which is generally unwaivable).[28] And it held in *Ex parte Young* (1908) that state immunity does not bar a suit against a state officer for prospective relief—even when, as in most such cases, the state is the real party in interest.[29]

STATUTORY ABROGATION OF STATE SOVEREIGN IMMUNITY

If the states' immunity extends more broadly than the Eleventh Amendment's text, then it is ambiguous whether that immunity enjoys constitutional status. The Rehnquist and Roberts Courts have thus debated whether Congress may abrogate the states' sovereign immunity by statute. There is little doubt that at the Founding, the states enjoyed the sort of sovereign immunity recognized at common law. Most common-law doctrines, however, are

subject to legislative override. Debates at the Constitutional and ratification conventions focused on whether Article III was intended to override this traditional immunity, but they did not address whether Congress could do so by later legislative enactment.

The Supreme Court first addressed this question in *Fitzpatrick v. Bitzer* (1976).[30] *Fitzpatrick* held that Congress may abrogate state immunity when it acts pursuant to its power to enforce the Reconstruction (Thirteenth, Fourteenth, and Fifteenth) Amendments. Several reasons have been given: Those amendments postdate the Eleventh; they were designed by the Civil War victors to cut back on state sovereignty; and their textual grant of power to Congress to "enforce" their provisions may extend to subjecting the states to monetary remedies for violations.[31] The Court likewise held that Congress could abrogate state immunity using its Commerce Power in *Pennsylvania v. Union Gas* (1989),[32] but no majority agreed on a rationale, and the principle remained uncertain.

Seminole Tribe of Florida v. Florida (1996) overruled *Union Gas* and established general parameters for the state immunity jurisprudence.[33] *Seminole Tribe* held that the states' traditional immunity was not a mere holdover from the common law but rather was a basic principle of the constitutional structure; hence, Congress may not abrogate state sovereign immunity by statute, at least when it acts pursuant to its enumerated powers in Article I.

Alden v. Maine (1999) held that, notwithstanding the Eleventh Amendment's limited application to "[t]he Judicial power of the United States," Congress also lacked power to override state sovereign immunity for suits in state courts.[34] *Alden* frankly acknowledged that no such principle could be gleaned from the amendment's text. The Court relied instead on a structural principle that predated the text and applied much more broadly. "The Eleventh Amendment confirmed, rather than established, sovereign immunity as a constitutional principle," Justice Anthony Kennedy explained for the Court. "[I]t follows that the scope of the States' immunity from suit is demarcated not by the text of the Amendment alone but by fundamental postulates implicit in the constitutional design."[35]

Seminole Tribe reaffirmed that Congress retains power to abrogate state sovereign immunity when enforcing the Reconstruction Amendments. Such abrogation can proceed on either of two tracks.[36] The first track—"prophylactic" abrogation—subjects states to liability whenever they violate the abrogating statute. In such cases, courts apply a test formulated in *City of Boerne v. Flores* (1997) to ensure that the statute is "congruent and proportional" to the underlying constitutional violations it is meant to address.[37]

That standard has proven difficult to meet. *Florida Prepaid Postsecondary Education Expense Board v. College Savings Bank* (1999) rejected Congress's attempt to use Section 5 of the Fourteenth Amendment to abrogate state sovereign immunity in patent suits as a way to prevent deprivations of property without due process of law. The Court noted that patent infringements that were unintentional or remediable under state law would not deny due process.[38] Similarly, *Kimel v. Florida Board of Regents* (2000) and *Board of Trustees of the University of Alabama v. Garrett* (2001) rejected claims that state liability under the Age Discrimination in Employment Act (ADEA) and Americans with Disabilities Act (ADA), respectively, would validly remedy violations of the Equal Protection Clause.[39] In each case, the Constitution forbade a far narrower set of distinctions based on age or disability than did the statutes in question.

Nonetheless, abrogation under the enforcement power is appropriate when a high proportion of statutory violations are also constitutional violations of rights protected by Section 1 of the Fourteenth Amendment. Thus, *Nevada Department of Human Resources v. Hibbs* (2003) held that Congress may subject a state to suits for money damages by state employees in the event of the state's failure to comply with the family-care provision of the Family and Medical Leave Act (FMLA).[40] *Hibbs* and similar cases suggest that narrowly drawn abrogation statutes can pass muster under Section 5 of the Fourteenth Amendment, particularly when the rights being enforced call for heightened judicial scrutiny.

A second abrogation track allows courts to enforce a statute purporting to override state immunities on a case-by-case basis as long as the particular plaintiff can show an actual constitutional violation as well as a statutory one. *United States v. Georgia* (2006) held that a disabled prison inmate who alleged that he was confined under conditions that violated both the Americans with Disabilities Act and the Eighth Amendment and was able to prove those allegations at trial could recover damages against the state government.[41] That was true whether or not the ADA provision at issue satisfied the "congruence and proportionality" test. Although relatively few plaintiffs have taken advantage of this theory successfully since 2006, *Georgia* appears to present an appealing alternative for plaintiffs who may struggle to establish that a federal statute abrogates state sovereign immunity across the board.

The Court has reopened questions about the use of Congress's other powers to override sovereign immunity by developing Alexander Hamilton's suggestion in Federalist No. 81 that states may have waived certain aspects of their immunity "in the plan of the [Constitutional] Convention." That notion of a waiver inherent in the constitutional structure had long been used to justify suits against states by the United States itself or by other states in the original jurisdiction of the Supreme Court.[42]

Central Virginia Community College v. Katz (2006) suggested that certain powers enumerated in Article I might also entail such a waiver of state immunity.[43] *Katz* found that the supposedly unique history, purpose, and nature of the Bankruptcy Clause justified such a waiver. The Court did not explore *Katz*'s potential to support waivers with respect to other powers for nearly a decade and a half. *Allen v. Cooper* (2020) rejected a similar argument under the Copyright Clause.[44]

Notwithstanding *Allen*'s disavowal of any "general, clause-by-clause reexamination of Article I," however, the Court has pursued just such a reexamination. *PennEast Pipeline Co., LLC v. New Jersey* (2021) found a waiver of state immunity inherent in the federal government's eminent domain power,[45] and *Torres v. Texas Department of Public Safety* (2022) found a waiver inherent in Congress's power to raise armies.[46] Such broad implied waivers of immunity have the practical effect of recognizing legislative power to abrogate state immunity under the same provisions. The *Katz* line of cases thus significantly undermines *Seminole Tribe*'s holding that Congress's general Article I

powers include no power to override state sovereign immunity.[47]

OPEN QUESTIONS

Whether or not the *Katz* line of cases leads to a fundamental change in the Court's immunity jurisprudence, Congress retains other important tools with which to hold state actors accountable for violations of federal law.

- Congress can induce the states to waive their immunities as a condition for receipt of federal grants under the Spending Clause (Article I, Section 8, Clause 1).[48] The Court has done little, however, to define the limits on such waivers.
- State sovereign immunity has never been understood to bar suits by the United States itself. Federal enforcement agencies thus may continue to enforce the ADEA and ADA against state governments, and whether Congress may delegate the United States' enforcement power to private parties remains an open question.[49]
- Nor does state immunity bar claims against state officers for injunctive relief under the doctrine of *Ex parte Young* (1908)[50] or (when the officer is sued in his personal capacity) for money damages.[51] It is not always easy to define when relief under *Young* is available, however.[52] As long as these options exist, the sovereign immunity embodied in the Eleventh Amendment and its extratextual background principles will tend to force suits against the states into certain channels without entirely eliminating the possibility of relief.

Cite as: Ernest A. Young, *The Eleventh Amendment, in* THE HERITAGE GUIDE TO THE CONSTITUTION 712 (Josh Blackman & John G. Malcolm eds., 3d ed. 2025).

Notes

1. Bernard Bailyn, The Ideological Origins of the American Revolution 198 (1967). **2.** *Seminole Tribe v. Florida*, 517 U.S. 44, 102–03 (1996) (Souter, J., dissenting) (citing Louis L. Jaffe, *Suits Against Governments and Officers: Sovereign Immunity*, 77 Harv. L. Rev. 1, 3–4 (1963)). **3.** Jaffe, *supra* at 4; *United States v. Lee*, 106 U.S. (16 Otto) 196, 220 (1882). **4.** *Lee*, 106 U.S. (16 Otto) at 220. **5.** Stephen E. Sachs, *Constitutional Backdrops*, 80 Geo. Wash. L. Rev. 1813, 1869–72 (2012). **6.** See William A. Fletcher, *The Diversity Explanation of the Eleventh Amendment: A Reply to Critics*, 56 U. Chi. L. Rev. 1261, 1271 (1989); Clyde E. Jacobs, The Eleventh Amendment and Sovereign Immunity 43–64 (1972). **7.** William A. Fletcher, *A Historical Interpretation of the Eleventh Amendment: A Narrow Construction of an Affirmative Grant of Jurisdiction Rather than a Prohibition Against Jurisdiction*, 35 Stan. L. Rev. 1033, 1045–54 (1983). **8.** 2 U.S. (2 Dall.) 419 (1793). **9.** Jacobs, *supra* at 47; Doyle Mathis, Chisholm v. Georgia: *Background and Settlement*, 54 J. Am. Hist. 19, 20–21 (1967). **10.** 2 U.S. (2 Dall.) at 450–51 (Blair, J.); David P. Currie, The Constitution in the Supreme Court: The First Hundred Years 1789–1888, at 14–16 (1985). **11.** Kurt T. Lash, *Leaving the* Chisholm *Trail: The Eleventh Amendment and the Background Principle of Strict Construction*, 50 Wm. & Mary L. Rev. 1577, 1649 (2009). **12.** *Hans v. Louisiana*, 134 U.S. 1, 11 (1890). **13.** Amend. XI. **14.** Fletcher, *The Diversity Explanation*, *supra* at 1264. **15.** Lawrence C. Marshall, *Fighting the Words of the Eleventh Amendment*, 102 Harv. L. Rev. 1342, 1356–71 (1989). **16.** Vicki C. Jackson,

The Supreme Court, the Eleventh Amendment, and State Sovereign Immunity, 98 Yale L.J. 1, 44 n.179 (1988). **17.** *Franchise Tax Bd. v. Hyatt*, 587 U.S. 230, 243 (2019) (quoting *Alden v. Maine*, 527 U.S. 706, 723 (1999)); *Seminole Tribe*, 517 U.S. at 54; Jackson, *supra* at 44 n.179. **18.** *Seminole Tribe*, 517 U.S. at 54. **19.** *Alden*, 527 U.S. at 713. **20.** *PennEast Pipeline Co., LLC v. New Jersey*, 594 U.S. 482, 509–12 (2021) (Gorsuch, J., dissenting); William Baude & Stephen E. Sachs, *The Misunderstood Eleventh Amendment*, 169 U. Pa. L. Rev. 609 (2021). **21.** *PennEast*, 594 U.S. at 509–10 (Gorsuch, J., dissenting). **22.** Anthony J. Bellia, Jr., & Bradford R. Clark, *The International Law Origins of American Federalism*, 120 Colum. L. Rev. 835 (2020); Bradford R. Clark, *The Eleventh Amendment and the Nature of the Union*, 123 Harv. L. Rev. 1817 (2010). **23.** 134 U.S. 1 (1890). **24.** *Id.* at 15. **25.** *Alden*, 527 U.S. at 722–25. **26.** *Ex parte New York*, 256 U.S. 490 (1921). **27.** *Principality of Monaco v. Mississippi*, 292 U.S. 313 (1934); *Blatchford v. Native Vill. of Noatak*, 501 U.S. 775 (1991). **28.** *Clark v. Barnard*, 108 U.S. 436 (1883). **29.** 209 U.S. 123 (1908). **30.** 427 U.S. 445, 456 (1976). **31.** Ernest A. Young, *State Sovereign Immunity After the Revolution*, 102 Tex. L. Rev. 697, 715 n.119 (2024). **32.** 491 U.S. 1 (1989) (plurality opinion). **33.** 517 U.S. 44 (1996). **34.** 527 U.S. 706 (1999). **35.** *Id.* at 728. **36.** Young, *supra* at 718–20. **37.** 521 U.S. 507, 519–20 (1997). **38.** 527 U.S. 627 (1999). **39.** 528 U.S. 62 (2000); 531 U.S. 356 (2001). **40.** 538 US. 721 (2003). **41.** 546 U.S. 151 (2006). **42.** *United States v. Texas*, 143 U.S. 621 (1892); *Rhode Island v. Massachusetts*,

37 U.S. (12 Pet.) 657 (1838). **43.** 546 U.S. 356 (2006). **44.** 589 U.S. 248 (2020). **45.** 594 U.S. 482 (2021). **46.** 597 U.S. 580 (2022). **47.** Anthony J. Bellia, Jr., & Bradford R. Clark, *State Sovereign Immunity and the New Structuralism*, 65 Wm. & Mary L. Rev. 485 (2024); Young, *supra* at 735– 42. **48.** *Sossamon v. Texas*, 563 U.S. 277 (2011). **49.** *Vt.*

Agency of Nat. Res. v. U.S. ex rel. Stevens, 529 U.S. 765 (2000); Young, *supra* at 762–67. **50.** 209 U.S. 123 (1908). **51.** John C. Jeffries, Jr., *In Praise of the Eleventh Amendment and Section 1983*, 84 Va. L. Rev. 47 (1998). **52.** *Whole Woman's Health v. Jackson*, 595 U.S. 30 (2021).

~

ESSAY NO. 190: THE TWELFTH AMENDMENT
AMEND. 12

The Electors shall meet in their respective states and vote by ballot for President and Vice-President, one of whom, at least, shall not be an inhabitant of the same state with themselves; they shall name in their ballots the person voted for as President, and in distinct ballots the person voted for as Vice-President, and they shall make distinct lists of all persons voted for as President, and of all persons voted for as Vice-President, and of the number of votes for each, which lists they shall sign and certify, and transmit sealed to the seat of the government of the United States, directed to the President of the Senate;—the President of the Senate shall, in the presence of the Senate and House of Representatives, open all the certificates and the votes shall then be counted;—The person having the greatest number of votes for President, shall be the President, if such number be a majority of the whole number of Electors appointed; and if no person have such majority, then from the persons having the highest numbers not exceeding three on the list of those voted for as President, the House of Representatives shall choose immediately, by ballot, the President. But in choosing the President, the votes shall be taken by states, the representation from each state having one vote; a quorum for this purpose shall consist of a member or members from two-thirds of the states, and a majority of all the states shall be necessary to a choice. And if the House of Representatives shall not choose a President whenever the right of choice shall devolve upon them, before the fourth day of March next following, then the Vice-President shall act as President, as in case of the death or other constitutional disability of the President.—The person having the greatest number of votes as Vice-President, shall be the Vice-President, if such number be a majority of the whole number of Electors appointed, and if no person have a majority, then from the two highest numbers on the list, the Senate shall choose the Vice-President; a quorum for the purpose shall consist of two-thirds of the whole number of Senators, and a majority of the whole number shall be necessary to a choice. But no person constitutionally ineligible to the office of President shall be eligible to that of Vice-President of the United States.

—Michael T. Morley

INTRODUCTION

The Twelfth Amendment changed the way presidential electors cast their votes for President and Vice President. Under the original procedure set forth in Article II, Section 1, Clause 3, each elector cast two undifferentiated electoral votes for President, at least one of which had to be for a candidate from a state different from the elector's. The candidate with the most electoral votes became President as long as that total reflected votes from a majority of electors appointed. For example, if 100 electors each cast two valid electoral votes, the leading candidate became President if he received at least 51 of the 200 votes cast.

The Constitution anticipated two possible

contingencies. First, if the leading candidates in the electoral college tied, the House of Representatives would choose the President from between (or among) them. Second, if no candidate received the requisite majority in the Electoral College, then the House chose the President from among the five candidates with the most electoral votes. In either type of contingent election, each state's House delegation collectively cast a single vote. A candidate needed votes from a majority of states to win the Presidency. After the President was chosen, the remaining candidate with the most electoral votes became Vice President, regardless of whether he had received a majority. If two or more candidates tied for Vice President, the Senate chose the winner with each Senator casting a single vote. The mechanics of the Vote Counting Clause were discussed in Essay No. 94.

Under the Twelfth Amendment, electors cast separate electoral votes specifically designated for President and Vice President, respectively. This change makes it easier for presidential and vice presidential candidates to run together on a ticket. The provision has also been interpreted to give Congress the authority to resolve disputes over electoral votes.

PRESIDENTIAL ELECTIONS BEFORE THE TWELFTH AMENDMENT

The Electoral College process worked well following the presidential elections of 1788 and 1792. In each case, George Washington was the clear favorite and secured a majority of votes.[1] Problems arose soon afterwards, however, because the Electoral College had not been designed to accommodate the rise of political parties. In the 1796 election, the two leading candidates were Federalist John Adams and Democratic-Republican Thomas Jefferson. Adams, who received the most electoral votes, became President, and Jefferson, the runner-up, became Vice President.[2] Following that election, proposals were introduced in Congress to require electors to separately designate their votes for President and Vice President.[3] Several states, including New York, Massachusetts, and Vermont, adopted resolutions supporting such measures.[4] Congress did not pass any of these proposed amendments.

The election of 1800 was calamitous.

Thomas Jefferson and his ostensible running mate, Aaron Burr, received the same number of electoral votes,[5] triggering a contingent election for President in the House. In that year's congressional elections, the Federalist Party had suffered tremendous losses but retained its majority during the lame-duck session. Many of those Federalist Representatives threw their support to Aaron Burr to hinder Jefferson's election. As a result, neither Jefferson nor Burr received votes from a majority of states throughout the first thirty-five rounds of voting.

After nearly a week, some Federalists abstained to allow Jefferson to secure a majority and win the presidency. Historians have suggested many possible reasons why those Representatives changed their votes. Some of Jefferson's critics, including Alexander Hamilton, determined that he was the lesser of two evils.[6] Others may have been persuaded by promises of political patronage.[7] Lurking in the background was the potential for violence; at least two states had begun to mobilize their militias to march on Washington, D.C., to resolve the impasse and secure Jefferson's election.[8]

OVERVIEW OF THE TWELFTH AMENDMENT

The Twelfth Amendment was adopted in large part to prevent a recurrence of the uncertainty and political intrigue that followed the 1800 election.[9] It was designed to ensure that the candidate who presidential electors—and, through them, the people—intended to choose as President was actually able to assume that office rather than potentially being relegated to the vice presidency.[10] The amendment made seven principal changes to the Constitution's original presidential election process:

1. Each elector still casts two electoral votes, but one is now designated for President and the other for Vice President. A candidate must receive a majority of electoral votes for President to be elected to that office. The amendment retains the original constitutional requirement that each elector must cast at least one of his electoral votes for a candidate from a state other than his own.

2. The amendment changed the procedures for reporting electoral votes by requiring each state's electors to separately tally the number of electoral votes each candidate for President and Vice President receives. This is primarily a formatting requirement and is most relevant when a state splits its electoral votes for a particular office between multiple candidates.

3. Whenever a contingent election occurs, the House may elect the President from among the candidates who received the three highest numbers of electoral votes for that office. Under the original Constitution, the number of candidates eligible to participate in a contingent election differed based on the circumstances. When two or more candidates received votes from a majority of electors and tied, the House had to choose between (or among) them. Conversely, if no candidate received votes from a majority of electors, the House could choose from among the five candidates with the most electoral votes.

4. The Constitution's original drafting left it unclear how many candidates could be considered by the House when no one received a majority of electoral votes and multiple candidates tied for fifth place in the Electoral College. It stated only that "from the five highest on the List the said House shall . . . chuse the President."[11] The Twelfth Amendment resolved this vagueness by specifying that the House must choose from among "the persons having the highest numbers not exceeding three on the list of those voted for as President." The consensus in Congress appeared to be that this revised language authorized the House to choose from among any candidates receiving "the highest three numbers" of votes in the Electoral College—even if multiple candidates tied for any of those positions—instead of "tying down the House to a choice from five persons."[12] Senator John Quincy Adams and a few other members of both chambers be-

lieved that the provision was ambiguous.[13] Representatives Henry Clay[14] and John Clopton[15] each proposed amendments containing even more specific language concerning ties in the Electoral College. Neither chamber of Congress found such additional specificity necessary, however, and those proposals went nowhere.

5. When a contingent election is held but the House fails to choose a President by Inauguration Day, the Vice President "shall act as President, as in the case of the death or other constitutional disability of the President." The original Constitution failed to address these circumstances. The Twentieth Amendment would later modify and expand this provision.

6. A candidate now must receive a majority of electoral votes for Vice President to win that office. If no one receives a majority, then the Senate holds a contingent election in which it elects the Vice President by majority vote from between (or among) the candidates with the two highest numbers of electoral votes.

7. The amendment extended the Constitution's qualifications for President to the office of Vice President.

The Twelfth Amendment makes it easier for a political party's Presidential and Vice Presidential candidates to run together on the same ticket. It further ensures that both the President and Vice President typically will be from the same party, although a contingent election still may cause political rivals to be elected to those offices.

The amendment also reduces the likelihood of contingent elections in the House because it is now mathematically impossible for two or more candidates to receive votes from a majority of appointed electors. A contingent election may occur only under three circumstances:

1. Only two candidates receive electoral votes and they tie, each receiving votes from exactly 50 percent of electors appointed. Since neither candidate has a

majority, a contingent election between them is necessary.

2. Three or more candidates receive electoral votes, and none of them wins a majority.

3. Congress rejects electoral votes from one or more validly appointed electors, thereby precluding any candidate from receiving votes from a majority of electors.

DRAFTING THE TWELFTH AMENDMENT

In May 1802, near the end of the Seventh Congress, the House approved a constitutional amendment directing electors to cast separate electoral votes for President and Vice President. Insufficient time remained in the legislative session, however, for the Senate to consider the issue.[16]

On October 28, 1803, the House adopted another proposed draft of the Twelfth Amendment by a vote of 88 to 31.[17] The Senate passed its own version on December 2.[18] Though generally similar, they contained some important differences. One major distinction concerned the number of presidential candidates who would be eligible to participate in a contingent election in the House. After debating the issue,[19] a House committee[20] and the Committee of the Whole[21] suggested allowing candidates with the three highest vote tallies in the electoral college to participate. The Committee of the Whole rejected proposals to limit contingent elections to the top two candidates in the electoral college[22] or allow the House to choose from among all candidates who received electoral votes for President.[23] The full House amended the Committee of the Whole's proposal to include candidates with the five highest electoral vote tallies on the grounds that figure was more consistent with the Constitution's original limit.[24] The Senate version, like the Committee of the Whole's initial proposal, set the number at three.[25] The House ultimately approved the Senate's language,[26] rebuffing attempts to change the Senate's figure back to five.[27]

Members who advocated reducing the number of candidates in contingent elections sought to limit the House's discretion. They wanted to ensure that the outcomes of presidential elections reflect the will of the people rather than leaving the House flexibility to choose someone with minimal support in the electoral college.[28] Those defending broader choice for the House maintained that Representatives in the House also express the will of the people and should not be distrusted.[29]

Another substantial difference between the House and Senate proposals concerned the consequences of a deadlock in a contingent election. The Senate proposed allowing the Vice President to exercise the powers of President if the House failed to elect a President by Inauguration Day.[30] Supporters explained that temporarily granting authority to the Vice President would eliminate the possibility of "anarchy" if the House failed to choose a President.[31] The Senate had rejected other proposals that would have empowered Congress to specify by law how the President would be selected if neither a President nor a Vice President are chosen.[32]

The House version did not contain any analogous language addressing incomplete or unsuccessful contingent elections. Opponents of the Senate's proposal argued that the Constitution should not contain such a fallback option because the risk of an "interregnum" without a designated President "must operate as the most powerful inducement [to the House] to make an election."[33] They also claimed that the House might interpret this default provision as authorization to refrain from choosing a President.[34] Moreover, enabling the Vice President to assume power would create an incentive for people–including the Vice President himself–to engage in corruption or intrigue to prevent the House from selecting a President.[35] Critics further warned that the Senate's approach contradicted the rest of the Twelfth Amendment by allowing the person the electors designated as Vice President to serve as President whenever the House failed to make a choice.[36]

On December 8, 1803, the House agreed to the Senate's version of the Twelfth Amendment, including its provision concerning failed contingent elections, by a vote of 83 to 42 and transmitted it to the states for ratification.[37] The amendment was ratified in September 1804, shortly before the 1804 presidential election.[38]

DEBATING THE TWELFTH AMENDMENT

The Twelfth Amendment's supporters in Congress argued that allowing electors to designate a President would help to ensure that election results more accurately reflected the will of the people and prevent a recurrence of the election of 1800. Representative John Clopton of Virginia, for example, explained that an election is not a "complete expression of the public will" if it can end with the "appointment of a different person to an office, than the one originally intended for it by a majority of the Electors."[39] Representative James Holland of North Carolina complained that the original constitutional procedure "takes more of the nature of a lottery than an election" because an elector "must leave the event to blind fate, chance, or what is worse, to intrigue to give him a President."[40]

Senators John Quincy Adams of Massachusetts and John Taylor of Virginia also emphasized that both state legislatures and the general public strongly supported such reforms.[41] Additionally, numerous speakers such as Senator William Cocke of Tennessee contended that requiring electors to cast separate electoral votes for President and Vice President would make contingent elections in the House less likely.[42]

Opponents maintained that reducing the likelihood of contingent elections, in which each state casts a single vote regardless of population, would harm smaller states.[43] Under the Constitution's original system, small states could join forces to choose the President in a contingent election when larger states cast most or all of their electoral votes for the same two candidates (such as Jefferson and Burr).[44] The Constitution's original presidential election process also preserved a voice for members of a minority party by enabling them to choose which of the majority party's top two candidates should be President.[45] Critics further contended that the amendment would promote corruption. States could exchange their votes for Vice President for support for their preferred presidential candidate.[46] Opponents even alleged that the amendment would make it easier for corrupt individuals to bribe their way into the presidency.[47]

RESOLVING ELECTORAL COLLEGE DISPUTES

The Twelfth Amendment did not alter the Constitution's original language governing the process for counting electoral votes. It specifies that the "President of the Senate shall, in the presence of the Senate and House of Representatives, open all the certificates and the votes shall then be counted . . . ."[48] Congress has frequently construed this language as granting it the constitutional authority to resolve disputes over the validity of electors' appointments as well as the validity of their electoral votes.[49] For example, in 1857, Wisconsin's presidential electors cast their votes a day late because of a snowstorm.[50] The Constitution requires all electors to cast their votes on the same day, which Congress has the power to specify.[51] The validity of Wisconsin's votes was questioned during the joint session in which Congress counted electoral votes. The Vice President, as presiding officer, declared that the Senate and House were the "properly-constituted authorities of the country" to determine whether those electoral votes were valid.[52] Both chambers debated the issue, but neither voted to reject the votes and they did not affect the election's outcome.

In 1865, Congress adopted Joint Rule 22, which would govern electoral counts through 1875. This rule gave the chambers of Congress authority to resolve "any question" that arose "in regard to the counting of [electoral] votes" submitted by a state's electors.[53] To bolster Congress's exclusive authority over disputes concerning presidential elections, the Enforcement Act of 1870 denied federal courts jurisdiction over election contests concerning presidential electors based on alleged Fifteenth Amendment violations.[54]

Following the presidential election of 1872, Congress invoked Joint Rule 22 to reject electoral votes from several states. It rejected three votes for President from Georgia because they had been cast after the candidate, Horace Greeley, had died; six votes from Arkansas on the grounds that the people certified as electors had not actually won the election; and eight votes from Louisiana because of the state's failure to choose its electors in accordance with state law.[55]

In the 1876 election between Rutherford B. Hayes and Samuel Tilden, disputes again arose over several states' electoral votes. Congress established an electoral commission with power to decide whether to accept states' officially certified slates of electors, resolve disputes between competing slates of electors, and determine the validity of challenged electoral votes.[56] In 1887, Congress enacted the Electoral Count Act. This law created a permanent framework for resolving disputes concerning presidential elections and generally empowered Congress to reject a state's electoral votes when both chambers determined that a state's electors had not been "lawfully certified." Such review was precluded if the state qualified for "safe harbor" status. The law also empowered Congress to reject a state's electoral votes if they had not been "regularly given."[57] Crucially, however, the statute failed to define the terms "lawfully certified" and "regularly given."

Following the 2020 presidential election, objections were raised during the joint session as to whether certain votes were "regularly given,"[58] but neither was sustained. In 2022, Congress passed the Electoral Count Reform Act (ECRA) to reduce the scope of its statutory authority over certain kinds of disputes concerning presidential elections. Under that statute, the joint session must accept as conclusive a state's certification of its presidential electors' appointments, as modified by any court orders.[59] Congress retains its authority to reject states' electoral votes if both chambers conclude they were not "regularly given"—a term that the law still fails to define.

CONSTITUTIONALITY OF THE ECRA

The ECRA purports to limit Congress's authority to reject electoral votes.[60] The Supreme Court has never determined the constitutionality of either the ECRA or its predecessor, the Electoral Count Act. Some scholars have suggested that the statute may be unconstitutional because it purports to impose substantive restrictions on the power that Article I grants to each chamber of Congress to determine its rules of procedure, or that the Twelfth Amendment confers on Congress to determine the validity of states' electoral votes as an inherent part of the counting process.[61] A variation of this argument is that an earlier Congress lacks the authority to entrench restrictions limiting the constitutional power of subsequent Congresses.[62] Other critics maintain that using a statute to regulate the conduct of the joint session is unconstitutional because it allows the President, through his veto power, to interfere with the power of Congress's chambers to determine their rules of procedure.[63] Still others maintain that the Twelfth Amendment does not permit Congress to "reject electoral votes contained in authentic electoral certificates—even when those electoral votes are unconstitutional."[64] It has even been argued that ECRA provisions allowing Congress to reject electoral votes without giving the President the opportunity to veto its actions violates the Presentment Clause[65] as construed in *INS v. Chadha* (1983).[66]

Congress generally avoids having to rely solely on the rules set forth in federal statutes governing the electoral count such as the ECRA by adopting a concurrent resolution reiterating many of the statute's key provisions in advance of its joint session.[67] The concurrent resolution avoids many of these potential objections to the ECRA because it is adopted by the same Congress that will be counting the electoral votes in that election rather than by a past Congress. Furthermore, because concurrent resolutions are not subject to presidential signature or veto,[68] there is no question of improper executive infringement on Congress's constitutional prerogatives.

In any event, long-standing practice also supports the ECRA. Several other laws regulate congressional procedure and limit Congress's discretion concerning its proceedings,[69] and Congress has passed rules and statutes specifically regulating the electoral count for nearly two centuries. Additionally, as a prudential matter, congressional refusal to follow the ECRA's rules in a way that effectively changes the outcome of a presidential election would likely trigger tremendous public backlash, undermine the legitimacy of the ultimate victor, and create a constitutional crisis of the sort narrowly averted following the election of 1876.

OPEN QUESTIONS

- Even accepting the ECRA as a valid limit on Congress's power to count electoral votes under the Twelfth Amendment, the statute fails to identify the circumstances under which the joint session may—or even must—reject electoral votes on the grounds they were not "regularly given."[70] For example, the Constitution requires electors to cast their votes on the same day.[71] It is unclear whether Congress should reject votes that are cast late. On the one occasion when a state's electors cast their votes one day late due to a snowstorm, Congress counted them, but they were not dispositive to determining the election's outcome.[72] Similarly, the Twelfth Amendment itself prohibits an elector from casting his votes for both President and Vice President for candidates from the elector's own state. It is unclear whether Congress may accept either of those votes. On the one occasion when this occurred following the Twelfth Amendment's ratification, the objection was ruled out of order because it was untimely.[73]

- Uncertainty also exists over whether Congress may reject votes from "faithless electors," which are cast for someone other than the candidate who won the popular vote in an elector's jurisdiction. The answer may depend at least in part on whether the relevant state's law binds its electors to vote in a particular manner.

- Electoral votes for candidates who die before the congressional joint session raise serious issues. Following the 1872 election, Congress rejected three electoral votes from Georgia that had been cast for presidential candidate Horace Greeley after he had died on the grounds that the votes were invalid because a deceased person is constitutionally ineligible to serve as President.[74] Congress's decision did not impact the election's outcome because Greeley's opponent, Ulysses S. Grant, received votes from a majority of electors. If Congress rejects the electoral votes of a deceased candidate who wins such a majority, however, then the only person who receives any electoral votes in that election will generally be the losing candidate from the other major political party. Since that person mathematically cannot have received the constitutionally required majority of votes, a contingent election in the House must occur.

  The Twelfth Amendment specifies that Congress must choose the President from among candidates with the three highest numbers of electoral votes. Under these circumstances, only one person—the ostensibly losing presidential candidate—will generally have received any electoral votes for President that Congress recognized as valid and counted. Accordingly, the ostensibly losing candidate would win the contingent election and be declared President. The far preferable outcome would be for Congress to count the votes for the deceased candidate. On Inauguration Day, the Vice President Elect—the deceased candidate's running mate, presumably from that candidate's political party—would be sworn in as President pursuant to the Twentieth Amendment.[75]

Cite as: Michael T. Morley, *The Twelfth Amendment, in* THE HERITAGE GUIDE TO THE CONSTITUTION 717 (Josh Blackman & John G. Malcolm eds., 3d ed. 2025).

Notes

1. S. Jour., 2d Cong., 2d Sess. 485–86 (Feb. 13, 1793); H.R. Jour., 2d Cong., 2d Sess. 701–02 (Feb. 13, 1793); S. Jour., 1st Cong., 1st Sess. 8 (Apr. 6, 1789); H.R. Jour., 1st Cong., 1st Sess. 7–8 (Apr. 6, 1789). **2.** S. Jour., 4th Cong., 2d Sess. 320 (Feb. 8, 1797); H.R. Jour., 4th Cong., 2d Sess. 685–86 (Feb. 8, 1797). **3.** Annals of Cong., 4th Cong., 2d Sess. 1824 (1797); Annals of Cong., 5th Cong., 2d Sess. 493–94 (1798); Annals of Cong., 5th Cong., 3d Sess. 2919 (1799); Annals of Cong., 6th Cong., 1st Sess. 510 (1800). **4.** Annals of Cong., 8th Cong., 1st Sess. 95–96, 537, 542–44 (1803); Annals of Cong., 7th Cong., 1st Sess. 509 (1802). **5.** H.R. Jour., 6th Cong., 2d Sess. 799–801 (Feb. 11, 1801); S. Jour., 6th Cong., 2d Sess. 124–25 (Feb. 11, 1801); *id.* at 127–28 (Feb. 18, 1801). **6.** Letter from Alexander Hamilton to Gouverneur Morris (Dec. 26, 1800), https://perma.cc/MB3S-64WP. **7.** Bruce Ackerman, The Failure of the Founding Fathers: Jefferson, Marshall, and the Rise of Presidential Democracy 106 (2005); Ron Chernow, Alexander Hamilton 638–39 (2004). **8.** Joanne B. Freeman, *The Election of 1800: A Study in the Logic of Political Change*, 108 Yale L.J. 1959, 1963 (1999). **9.** Annals of Cong., 8th Cong., 1st Sess. 22, 104, 157–58, 201, 420, 493, 701, 727 (1803). **10.** *Id.* at 134, 201,

490–91, 685, 735–36.   **11.** Art. II, sec. 1, cl. 3.   **12.** Annals of Cong., 8th Cong., 1st Sess. 680 (1803); *id.* at 677–78, 725, 739; *id.* at 93.   **13.** *Id.* at 92–93, 125, 677–81, 772.   **14.** *Id.* at 420–21.   **15.** *Id.* at 424; *id.* at 377.   **16.** Annals of Cong., 7th Cong., 1st Sess. 303, 1293 (1802).   **17.** Annals of Cong., 8th Cong., 1st Sess. 515–16, 544–45 (1803); H.R. Jour., 8th Cong., 1st Sess. 422 (Oct. 28, 1803).   **18.** Annals of Cong., 8th Cong., 1st Sess. 209–10 (1803); S. Jour., 8th Cong., 1st Sess. 319–20 (Dec. 2, 1803).   **19.** Annals of Cong., 8th Cong., 1st Sess. 375–77, 420–31, 490–95 (1803); *id.* at 528.   **20.** *Id.* at 380–81, 420.   **21.** *Id.* at 495; H.R. Jour., 8th Cong., 1st Sess. 420 (Oct. 26, 1803).   **22.** Annals of Cong., 8th Cong., 1st Sess., 377, 420–21, 424 (1803).   **23.** *Id.* at 426, 429.   **24.** *Id.* at 496–97 (1803); *id.* at 515–16, 544–45; H.R. Jour., 8th Cong., 1st Sess. 421–22 (Oct. 27, 1803).   **25.** Annals of Cong., 8th Cong., 1st Sess. 203–04, 209–10 (1803); S. Jour., 8th Cong., 1st Sess. 319–20 (1803); Annals of Cong., 8th Cong., 1st Sess. 84–85, 97, 106, 124, 126–27 (1803); S. Jour., 8th Cong., 1st Sess. 314–15 (Nov. 23, 1803); *id.* at 315 (Nov. 24, 1803); *id.* at 317 (Nov. 29, 1803); Annals of Cong., 8th Cong., 1st Sess. 87–88, 97–124 (1803).   **26.** Annals of Cong., 8th Cong., 1st Sess. 775–76 (1803); H.R. Jour., 8th Cong., 1st Sess. 480–81 (Dec. 7, 1803).   **27.** Annals of Cong., 8th Cong., 1st Sess. 675, 681, 683 (1803); H.R. Jour., 8th Cong., 1st Sess. 476 (Dec. 7, 1803).   **28.** Annals of Cong., 8th Cong., 1st Sess. 101, 103, 107, 112–115, 120, 122, 426–29, 702 (1803).   **29.** *Id.* at 426–27.   **30.** *Id.* at 134, 136–37; S. Jour. 8th Cong., 1st Sess. 319 (Dec. 2, 1803).   **31.** Annals of Cong., 8th Cong., 1st Sess. 696, 768 (1803).   **32.** *Id.* at 128, 132, 137, 139; S. Jour., 8th Cong., 1st Sess. 317–18 (Nov. 30, 1803).   **33.** Annals of Cong., 8th Cong., 1st Sess. 174, 671, 739 (1803).   **34.** *Id.* at 669, 693, 706, 764, 772–73; *id.* at 132.   **35.** *Id.* at 670, 671, 710, 732, 739, 754; *id.* at 174.   **36.** *Id.* at 668–69, 686, 693, 773, 754, 766.   **37.** *Id.* at 775–76; H.R. Jour., 8th Cong., 1st Sess. 482 (Dec. 9, 1803).   **38.** Secretary of State James Madison, Circular Letter to the Governors (Sept. 24, 1804), https://perma.cc/WAC5-CM7C.   **39.** Annals of Cong., 8th Cong., 1st Sess., 490–91 (1803).   **40.** *Id.* at 736; *id.* at 131, 760.   **41.** *Id.* at 132, 188–89.   **42.** *Id.* at 151; *id.* at 120, 186.   **43.** *Id.* at 162–64, 516–17, 527–28, 537, 539, 747–48.   **44.** *Id.* at 528–29.   **45.** *Id.* at 536, 537; *id.* at 90, 171.   **46.** *Id.* at 91, 94, 95, 155, 173, 692.   **47.** *Id.* at 164, 170, 518, 539–40, 708–09, 715–16, 750.   **48.** Amend. XII.   **49.** Nathan L. Colvin & Edward B. Foley, *The Twelfth Amendment: A Constitutional Ticking Time Bomb*, 64 U. Miami L. Rev. 475, 524 (2010).   **50.** Cong. Globe, 34th Cong., 3d Sess. 660 (1857).   **51.** Art. II, § 1, cl. 4.   **52.** Cong. Globe, 34th Cong., 3d Sess. 652 (1857).   **53.** Cong. Globe, 38th Cong., 2d Sess. 505 (1865).   **54.** Michael T. Morley, *The Enforcement Act of 1870, Federal Jurisdiction Over Election Contests, and the Political Question Doctrine*, 72 Fla. L. Rev. 1153, 1163–72 (2020) (citing An Act to Enforce the Right of Citizens of the United States to Vote in the Several States of the Union, and for Other Purposes, ch. 114, § 23, 16 Stat. 140, 146 (May 31, 1870) ["Enforcement Act of 1870"] (codified as amended at 28 U.S.C. § 1344)).   **55.** Cong. Globe, 42d Cong., 3d Sess., 505, 1291–94 (1873).   **56.** Electoral Commission Act, ch. 37, § 2, 19 Stat. 227, 228–29 (Jan. 29, 1877).   **57.** Electoral Count Act, ch. 90, § 4, 24 Stat. 373, 373–74 (Feb. 3, 1887).   **58.** Cong. Rec. H77, H98 (Jan. 6, 2021).   **59.** Pub. L. No. 117-238, Div. P, § 109(a), 136 Stat. 4459, 5238 (Dec. 29, 2022) (codified at 3 U.S.C. § 15).   **60.** *Id.*   **61.** Nelson Lund, *The Unbearable Rightness of* Bush v. Gore, 23 Cardozo L. Rev. 1219, 1271 n.162 (2002); Chris Land & David Schultz, *On the Unenforceability of the Electoral Count Act*, 13 Rutgers J.L. & Pub. Pol'y 340, 376 (2016); Kesavan, *supra* at 1784.   **62.** *Id.* at 1780; Colvin & Foley, *supra* at 477, 518–19; Laurence Tribe, Erog v. Hsub *and Its Disguises: Freeing* Bush v. Gore *from Its Hall of Mirrors*, 115 Harv. L. Rev. 170, 267 & n.388 (2001).   **63.** Colvin & Foley, *supra* at 518; Art. I, § 5, cl. 1.   **64.** Kesavan, *supra* at 1779; Jack Beermann & Gary Lawson, *The Electoral Count Act Mess: The Electoral Count Act Is Unconstitutional, and Other Fun Facts (Plus a Few Random Academic Speculations) About Counting Electoral Votes*, 16 FIU L. Rev. 297, 305–06, 309, 317–18 (2022).   **65.** Kesavan, *supra* at 1792; Tribe, *supra* at 278.   **66.** 462 U.S. 919, 923–29 (1983).   **67.** 167 Cong. Rec. H10, S7 (daily ed. Jan. 3, 2021) (corrected version).   **68.** Harold Hongju Koh, *The War Powers and Humanitarian Intervention*, 53 Hous. L. Rev. 971, 1021 (2016).   **69.** Aaron-Andrew P. Bruhl, *Using Statutes to Set Legislative Rules: Entrenchment, Separation of Powers, and the Rules of Proceedings Clause*, 19 J.L. & Pol. 345, 347–48 (2003).   **70.** 3 U.S.C. § 15(d)(2)(B)(ii)(II).   **71.** Art. II, § 1, cl. 4.   **72.** Kesavan, *supra* at 1686.   **73.** Cong. Globe, 42d Cong., 3d Sess. 1299–1300 (1873).   **74.** *Id.* at 505.   **75.** Amend. XX, § 3.

PART 10

THE RECONSTRUCTION AMENDMENTS

ESSAY NO. 191: THE THIRTEENTH AMENDMENT
AMEND. 13

Section 1. Neither slavery nor involuntary servitude, except as a punishment for crime whereof the party shall have been duly convicted, shall exist within the United States, or any place subject to their jurisdiction.
Section 2. Congress shall have power to enforce this article by appropriate legislation.

—Kurt T. Lash

INTRODUCTION

The Thirteenth Amendment to the U.S. Constitution abolished chattel slavery on American soil and prohibited involuntary labor except upon due conviction for a crime. Congress drafted the amendment in the early months of 1864. Secretary of State William Seward officially declared it ratified on December 18, 1865. Although the nineteenth-century Supreme Court narrowly construed Congress's power to enforce the Thirteenth Amendment, more recent Court opinions have upheld enforcement legislation banning discrimination in the making and enforcement of contracts and in the buying and selling of real estate. Of all the liberties protected by the federal Constitution, the most basic is the right that is protected by the Thirteenth Amendment: the indelible human right never to be bought and sold as a piece of property.

HISTORICAL BACKGROUND

Prior to 1776, British policy allowed the practice of slavery in all thirteen American colonies. Following the successful break from British rule, the now "free and independent states"[1] could decide for themselves whether to continue the practice of chattel slavery. Southern slaveholding states maintained and eventually deepened their dependence on enslaved labor. Northern states moved toward abolition.[2]

Thomas Jefferson's original draft of the Declaration of Independence condemned King George III for violating the "most sacred rights of life & liberty" by "captivating and carrying" "a distant people" "into slavery in another hemisphere."[3] The Continental Congress decided to delete this reference and instead added a provision equally condemnatory of slavery that became the battle cry of abolitionists for the next eighty years: "We hold these truths to be self-evident, that all men are created equal, that they are endowed by their Creator with certain unalienable Rights, that among these are Life, Liberty and the pursuit of Happiness."[4]

Like the Declaration, the Articles of Confederation contained no express reference to slavery. In 1784, Thomas Jefferson drafted the Ordinance of 1784, which would have organized the western territories and divided them into states. Section 5 provided that "after the year 1800 of the Christian [Era], there shall be neither slavery nor involuntary servitude in any of the said states, otherwise than in punishment of crimes whereof the party shall have been convicted to have been personally guilty."[5] However, Congress struck out Section 5.[6] Three years later, the Confederation Congress passed the 1787 Northwest Ordinance, which governed the federal territories northwest of the Ohio River. Article VI of the Ordinance included the language originally drafted by Jefferson declaring that "[t]here shall be neither slavery nor involuntary servitude in the said territory, other than in the punishment of crimes, whereof the party shall have been duly convicted."[7]

The 1787 federal Constitution continued the post-Revolution policy of leaving the choice of allowing chattel slavery to the states. In fact, the Constitution did not contain the words "slave" or "slavery." As James Madison of Virginia explained during the Constitutional Convention, it would be "wrong to admit in the Constitution the idea that there could be property in men."[8] Nevertheless, several constitutional provisions impliedly referenced slavery. The Three-Fifths Clause of Article I based representation on a counting of "free persons," "Indians not taxed," and "three-fifths of all other persons." Article I also declared that Congress could not prohibit the "Migration or Importation of such Persons" until 1808. And the "Fugitive Slave" Clause of Article IV prohibited northern states from freeing persons escaping from slavery. (See Essays Nos. 9, 67, and 142.)

Despite these implicit acknowledgements of slavery, soon after the Constitution was ratified, Congress added a Bill of Rights. The Due Process Clause of the Fifth Amendment declared that "nor [shall any person] be deprived of life, liberty or property without due process of law." (See Essay No. 172.) Over the next several decades, abolitionists repeatedly insisted that the Due Process Clause essentially constitutionalized the same human right to "life, liberty and the pursuit of happiness" originally proclaimed by the Declaration.

The growing abolitionism in the North and increasing reliance on slavery in the South guaranteed an unending series of political disputes. *Dred Scott v. Sandford* (1857) ruled that slavery could not be banned in federal territory and that black Americans were not and could not become citizens of the United States.[9] Chief Justice Roger B. Taney's majority opinion further inflamed an already divided nation. Republicans rejected *Dred Scott*'s reasoning. In the 1860 election, Abraham Lincoln and the pro-freedom Republican Party prevailed. Soon after, the slaveholding states of the deep South voted to secede from the Union, and a bloody Civil War followed.

DRAFTING OF THE THIRTEENTH AMENDMENT

On January 11, 1864, in the opening days of the 38th Congress, Senator John Brooks Henderson of Missouri submitted a proposed amendment abolishing slavery.[10] On February 17, Senator Lyman Trumbull of Illinois presented a revised version of Henderson's proposal with the language substantially mirroring Jefferson's language in the Northwest Ordinance.[11] For the next four months, Congress debated the constitutional abolition of slavery.

Supporters of the amendment insisted that slavery violated the country's foundational principles as articulated in the Declaration of Independence and the Due Process Clause of the Fifth Amendment. The Founders, they insisted, had expected slavery to die out quickly. Instead, the invention of the cotton gin and slaveholder avarice had thwarted those hopes. In their efforts to protect the institution of slavery, slave states had increasingly violated the fundamental rights of American citizens, including the rights of speech, press, assembly, and petition. Finally, in an ultimate act of constitutional betrayal, slavery convinced the southern states to secede and instigate a bloody civil war. Unless totally abolished, slavery would trigger another war in the future.[12]

Opponents in Congress insisted that slavery was an essential aspect of the original constitutional compact and could not be removed constitutionally.[13] For example, Representative Fernando Wood of New York argued that such a violation of the original compact would fatally undermine state sovereignty and the federalist nature of the Constitution as declared in the Ninth and Tenth Amendments.[14] (See Essay Nos. 187 and 188.) Even if such an amendment were constitutional, it was wrong to pursue the matter during wartime when so many states remained unrepresented. Democratic Senator Willard Saulsbury of Delaware, for example, argued that the amendment "would not be binding on any State whose interest was affected by it" if their representatives were not present to vote on the matter.[15] Other Democrats like Representative Alexander Coffroth of Pennsylvania expressed concerns about the impact of taking the "property" of loyal slaveowners.[16] Finally, opponents argued during the Civil War that abolishing slavery might prolong the war because the South would have little reason to lay down its arms if doing so meant economic ruin.[17]

Just before the Senate voted on the Thirteenth Amendment, Charles Sumner of Massachusetts objected that the language "seems to imply that 'slavery or involuntary servitude' may be provided 'for the punishment of crime.'"[18] In response, Senator Jacob Howard of Michigan defended the use of Jefferson's language from the Northwest Ordinance, arguing that this "expression . . . has been adjudicated upon repeatedly" and "is perfectly well understood both by the public and by judicial tribunals."[19] Sumner's effort to change the language failed.

Sumner also suggested that the amendment should echo the language of the original Constitution's Necessary and Proper Clause and grant Congress "power to make all laws necessary and proper to carry the declaration into effect." Instead, Congress added a second section to the amendment that granted Congress "power to enforce this article by appropriate legislation." No framer at the time discussed whether the final language paraphrased the Necessary and Proper Clause or communicated a broader (or narrower) principle. The ambiguous language of Section Two became a matter of substantial discussion during the debates on the Thirteenth Amendment's ratification.

PASSAGE OF THE THIRTEENTH AMENDMENT

On April 8, 1864, the Senate voted 38 to 6 in favor of the amendment, clearing the two-thirds majority required for passage.[20] In the Senate, Republicans outnumbered Democrats 33 to 10, but in the House, the Republican majority was only 85 to 72. In order to meet the required two-thirds majority, House Republicans would have to convince a significant number of Democrats to support the amendment or at least abstain from voting. For some time, these efforts failed. On June 15, the House voted 93 to 65 in favor of the amendment with only four Democrats voting in support—thirteen votes shy of a two-thirds majority. At the last minute, Republican James Ashley of Ohio "changed his vote from the affirmative to the negative." This switch would allow him to move for reconsideration at a future, more opportune moment.[21]

That moment came several months later. Over the summer of 1864, Union Army victories, including the fall of Atlanta, fueled northern public support for the war and helped to pave the way for Lincoln's re-election in November 1864. Congressional Republicans, meanwhile, gained fifty congressional seats. These numbers seemed to guarantee passage of the Thirteenth Amendment during the next session of Congress. On November 13, 1864, Frederick Douglass noted in a speech in Rochester, New York that the election results "mean[t] that the Constitution of the United States shall be so changed that slavery can never again exist in any part of the United States."[22] The only question was whether constitutional abolition should be left to the Thirty-Ninth Congress or revisited during the final weeks of the outgoing Thirty-Eighth Congress.

On December 6, 1864, in his annual message to Congress, Lincoln encouraged Congress to hold another vote on the amendment before the end of the Thirty-Eighth Congress.[23] The Republican leadership agreed. On January 6, 1865, Representative Ashley moved for reconsideration of the abolition amendment.[24] Although the same members were voting on the same proposed amendment, the political ground had shifted since June 1864. The people had returned Lincoln and an even greater number of Republicans to national office, so the passage of an abolition amendment by the next Congress seemed guaranteed. Moreover, as the Union's victory now seemed inevitable, it was less necessary to hold out the preservation of slavery as an incentive for the South to come to the peace table. And by that time, the loyal slaveholding border states were already moving toward abolition without waiting for an amendment. Maryland abolished slavery just before the national election, and Missouri did the same in the middle of the second round of congressional debates.[25] Finally, several Democrats had lost their reelection bid in the fall elections, and during this "lame duck" session, they were less subject to pro-slavery political pressure. For a number of Democrats, these changed political circumstances were enough to move them from opposition to support—or at least provide them political cover for doing so.

On January 31, 1865, after a final round of speeches and debate, Ashley called the question. The final tally was 119 to 56, two votes more than needed for passage. In the end, eleven Democrats changed their earlier votes and supported the amendment, and eight members did not vote at all.[26]

THE RATIFICATION PROCESS

Having been passed by two-thirds of both houses of Congress, the amendment would now need to be ratified by three-fourths of the states. At the time, there were thirty-six states, and (at least in theory) twenty-seven states would be required for ratification. However, this precise count was debated. Some Radical Republicans would have required ratification only from states that remained loyal to the Union. The Confederate states, these Republicans argued, committed "state suicide" and were not to be counted. Other members of Congress insisted that Confederate states should also count in the denominator.

Several states, including Massachusetts, Pennsylvania, and West Virginia, quickly ratified the proposed abolition amendment. In Massachusetts, the vote was unanimous. In more politically divided northern states, however, the proposed amendment prompted substantial debate. In New York, for example, Democrats echoed their congressional counterparts. They insisted that constitutional abolition was an "encroachment upon the rights of the States" and warned that immediate emancipation was "dangerous both to the interests of the country and of the blacks themselves." In response, Republicans argued that the Civil War had proven that slavery was "incompatible with a free government [and] should be abolished."[27] Only a simple majority was needed from both chambers of the state legislature. In the end, the New York House voted 70 to 40 in favor of the amendment with the Senate concurring 17 to 8. Both votes indicated significant minority opposition but not enough to defeat adoption.[28] About a week later, a similar debate and outcome occurred in Indiana. Republicans blamed slavery for the Civil War, and Democrats claimed the amendment violated the reserved rights of the states. The Amendment passed 26 to 22 in the Indiana senate and 56 to 29 in the state house. Once again, there was significant opposition but not enough to defeat adoption.[29]

Union states that voted against Lincoln in the 1864 presidential election also rejected the proposed Thirteenth Amendment. In February and March 1865, Delaware, Kentucky, and New Jersey rejected the amendment.[30] Governor Thomas Bramlette of Kentucky encouraged the legislature to ratify the amendment on the condition that the state receive compensation for its emancipated slaves. The legislature instead voted to reject the amendment outright on a vote of 21 to 12.[31] In New Jersey, a congressional committee suggested submitting the amendment to the people in a state referendum. The proposal

was rejected, and the amendment failed to pass in a tied vote of 30 to 30.[32]

Ratification in Virginia came about under unusual circumstances. The vote was cast by the government-in-exile located in Alexandria. Governor Francis Harrison Pierpont claimed that his government represented the "true" (Union-supporting) government of Virginia. Pierpont's Administration authorized the creation of the State of West Virginia and then voted to ratify the Thirteenth Amendment. As a result, one Virginia in Alexandria ratified the Thirteenth Amendment while another in Richmond continued its military struggle against the Union.[33]

On April 9, 1865, Confederate General Robert E. Lee surrendered to Union General Ulysses S. Grant at Appomattox Courthouse in Virginia. On April 11, President Lincoln urged supporters of the Thirteenth Amendment to join him in restoring Louisiana's status as a loyal member of the Union despite the relatively low numbers of Union supporters in the state. Lincoln explained that "if we reject Louisiana, we also reject one vote in favor of the proposed amendment to the national Constitution." It would not be "questionable" to secure ratification of "three fourths of those States which have not attempted secession." By contrast, "ratification by three-fourths of all the States would be unquestioned and unquestionable."[34] On April 14, Lincoln was shot by an assassin's bullet, and died the following day.

Securing ratification of the Thirteenth Amendment now fell to Lincoln's Vice President. Andrew Johnson, a Tennessee Democrat, quickly organized provisional governments in the former rebel states. He advised his newly appointed governors, including Provisional Mississippi Governor William L. Sharkey, to abolish slavery and support ratification of the amendment.[35] Johnson hoped that such actions would overcome Republican congressional opposition and pave the way for readmission of the former rebel states. The governments of the southern states, however, initially resisted ratifying the amendment. However, this was not out of a desire to maintain slavery. The former Confederates recognized that the institution was politically dead. Rather, they were concerned about the grant of congressional power in Section Two.

On November 1, 1865, Provisional South

Carolina Governor Benjamin F. Perry wrote to Secretary of State William Seward regarding the state's progress toward ratifying the amendment. According to Perry, the legislature has "no objection to adopting the first section of the amendment proposed but they fear that the second section may be construed to give congress power of local legislation over the Negroes and white men, too, after the abolishment of slavery."[36] In response, President Johnson asked Seward to draft a letter to Governor Perry that dismissed South Carolina's concerns about Section Two. Seward wrote that the objection to Section Two "is regarded as querulous and unreasonable." That clause, he contended, "is really restraining in its effect, instead of enlarging the powers of Congress."[37] Seward's letter would be widely published.

On November 13, South Carolina ratified the Thirteenth Amendment but added a statement of legislative understanding to its official notice of ratification. The state declared "[t]hat any attempt by Congress towards legislating upon the political status of former slaves, or their civil relations, would be contrary to the Constitution of the United States, as it now is, or as it would be altered by the proposed amendment."[38] Alabama, which ratified the amendment on December 2, included a similar ratification notice: "[T]his amendment to the Constitution of the United States, is adopted by the Legislature of Alabama with the understanding that it does not confer upon Congress the power to Legislate upon the political status of Freedmen in this State."[39]

On December 17, 1865, Georgia became the twenty-seventh state to ratify the Thirteenth Amendment, which cleared the three-fourths requirement. On December 18, a few days after the opening session of the 39th Congress, Seward officially announced the ratification of the amendment.[40] In doing so, Seward rejected Radical Republican theories of "state suicide" and counted the votes of every ratifying state, north and south.

CONGRESSIONAL ENFORCEMENT OF THE THIRTEENTH AMENDMENT

Four months after the Thirteenth Amendment was ratified, Congress passed the Civil Rights Act of 1866, the first congressional effort to enforce the amendment.[41] The act declared that "all persons born in the United States and not subject to any foreign power, excluding Indians not taxed, are hereby declared to be citizens of the United States," and that all such citizens enjoyed the same rights of property and contract as "white citizens."[42] Lyman Trumbull of Illinois, the bill's Senate sponsor, explained that the act exercised Congress's power under the Thirteenth Amendment to "secure to all persons within the United States practical freedom."[43] In 1867, Congress relied on its Section Two powers to pass the Anti-Peonage Act.[44] (Peonage imposed forced labor to work off a debt.)

However, not every Republican shared Trumbull's broad reading of Section Two. These concerns helped to fuel the effort to pass the Fourteenth Amendment.[45] Following ratification of the Fourteenth Amendment in 1868, Congress reenacted the 1866 Act, this time as an exercise of its authority under the Fourteenth Amendment.[46]

JUDICIAL PRECEDENT

There have been only a few Supreme Court decisions interpreting the Thirteenth Amendment. In the *Slaughter-House Cases* (1873), a majority of the Court rejected the idea that a state-granted monopoly amounted to "involuntary servitude" of the kind prohibited by the amendment.[47] In the *Civil Rights Cases* (1883), an eight-justice majority ruled that the Thirteenth and Fourteenth Amendments do not empower Congress to prohibit private racial discrimination in places of public accommodation.[48] According to Justice Joseph P. Bradley's majority opinion, "[i]t would be running the slavery argument into the ground to make it apply to every act of discrimination which a person may see fit to make. . . ."[49] The lone dissenter, Justice John Marshall Harlan, argued that the Thirteenth Amendment "obliterated the race line, so far as all rights fundamental in a state of freedom are concerned."[50]

In the 1960s and 1970s, the Supreme Court held that portions of the 1866 Civil Rights Act were valid enforcements of the Thirteenth Amendment. These cases involved private racial discrimination in the sale of real estate and in the making and enforcement of contracts.[51]

OPEN QUESTIONS

- Does the Thirteenth Amendment protect a right to abortion?[52] In the wake of *Dobbs v. Jackson Women's Health Organization* (2022), this issue has become more relevant.[53] Does the text cut the other way and protect developing human life? For example, would the amendment play a role in preventing the development of artificial wombs for the growing and harvesting of human organs?
- Does the adoption of the Thirteenth Amendment prove conclusively that the original Constitution was pro-slavery (and thus needed amending)? Or does it represent a victory for those who argued that the Constitution was not pro-slavery and thus could be amended without altering its fundamental structure?
- Was it constitutionally necessary to count the ratification votes of the former rebel states? Is it constitutionally permissible for Congress to declare that a state has forfeited its status as a member of the Union?
- Does the Thirteenth Amendment apply to animals? Some animal rights activists have tried to invoke the amendment to free whales and other animals held in captivity?[54] Will developments in robotic artificial intelligence force a rethinking of what counts as an "enslaved person?"

Cite as: Kurt T. Lash, *The Thirteenth Amendment*, in THE HERITAGE GUIDE TO THE CONSTITUTION 726 (Josh Blackman & John G. Malcolm eds., 3d ed. 2025).

Notes

1. Declaration of Independence, ¶ 32.   **2.** Sean Wilentz, No Property in Man: Slavery and Antislavery at the Nation's Founding 31 (2018).   **3.** IV. Revised Report of the Committee, 22 March 1784, Founders Online, https://perma.cc/7CEF-XT3X.   **4.** Declaration of Independence, ¶ 2.   **5.** *III. Report of the Committee, 1 March 1784,* Founders Online, https://perma.cc/TY28-UGBB.   **6.** *V. The Ordinance of 1784, 23 April 1784,* Founders Online, https://perma.cc/A8KA-MXYD.   **7.** 1 The Reconstruction Amendments: Essential Documents 10 (Kurt T. Lash ed., 2021) (hereinafter "RA").   **8.** 2 Farrand's 417.   **9.** 60 U.S. 393 (1857).   **10.** 1 RA 386.   **11.** *Id.* at 390.   **12.** Speeches of James Wilson (Mar. 19, 1864), Lyman Trumbull (Mar. 28, 1864), John Brooks Henderson (Apr. 7, 1864), and Charles Sumner (Apr. 8, 1864), *in id.* at 391, 402, 427, 434.   **13.** *Id.* at 408.   **14.** *Id.* at 450.   **15.** 2 RA 416.   **16.** 1 RA 452.   **17.** *Id.*   **18.** *Id.* at 437.   **19.** *Id.* at 442.   **20.** *Id.*   **21.** *Id.* at 447.   **22.** *Id.* at 465.   **23.** *Id.* at 465.   **24.** *Id.* at 466.   **25.** *Missouri: Emancipation Ordinance Adopted Almost Unanimously,* N.Y. Daily Tribune, Jan. 12, 1865, p. 1, *in id.* at 481.   **26.** 1 RA 492–96.   **27.** *Id.*   **28.** *Id.* at 506–11.   **29.** *Id.* at 516–22.   **30.** *Id.* at 523, 527; *id.* at 498.

31. *Id.* at 523.   **32.** *Id.* at 533.   **33.** *Id.* at 498–99.   **34.** *Id.* at 534.   **35.** *Id.* at 543.   **36.** *Id.* at 545.   **37.** *Id.* at 546.   **38.** *Id.* at 546.   **39.** *Id.* at 558–59.   **40.** *Id.* at 561.   **41.** 14 Stat. 27–30 (Apr. 9, 1866).   **42.** *Id.*   **43.** 2 RA 67.   **44.** Statutes at Large, 39th Cong., 2d Sess., ch. 187, p. 546 (Mar. 2, 1867).   **45.** Speech of John Bingham in opposition to the Civil Rights Act (Mar. 9, 1866), *in* 2 RA 135.   **46.** Act of May 31, 1870, ch. 114, § 18, 16 Stat. 144.   **47.** 83 U.S. 38, 69 (1873).   **48.** 109 U.S. 3 (1883).   **49.** *Id.* at 24.   **50.** *Id.* at 40.   **51.** *Jones v. Alfred H. Mayer,* 392 U.S. 409 (1968); *Runyon v. McCrary,* 427 U.S. 160 (1976).   **52.** Andrew Koppelman, *Forced Labor: A Thirteenth Amendment Defense of Abortion,* 84 Nw. U. L. Rev. 480 (2015); Kurt T. Lash, Roe *and the Original Meaning of the Thirteenth Amendment,* 21 Geo. J.L. & Pub. Pol'y 131.   **53.** Ari Blaff, *D.C. Judge Argues 13th Amendment Prohibiting Slavery May Provide Constitutional Right to Abortion,* Nat'l Rev. (Feb. 7, 2023), https://perma.cc/73YC-469W.   **54.** *Tilikum et al. v. Sea World Parks & Entertainment Inc.,* 842 F. Supp. 2d 1259 (S.D. Cal. 2012); Sheri Flannery, *The Thirteenth Amendment Won't Help Free Willy,* 15 The Scholar 29 (2012), https://perma.cc/7QLV-AD8E.

ESSAY NO. 192: THE CITIZENSHIP CLAUSE
AMEND. 14, § 1

All persons born or naturalized in the United States, and subject to the jurisdiction thereof, are citizens of the United States and of the State wherein they reside.
—Kurt T. Lash

INTRODUCTION

The Citizenship Clause establishes birth-right national citizenship, defines the status of national citizenship, and secures the status of state citizenship. The national citizenship clause formally reversed *Dred Scott v. Sandford* (1857), which held that black Americans could not be citizens of the United States.[1] The state citizenship clause prohibits states from denying resident American citizens their equal status as state citizens. The federal government had long treated the children of illegally present aliens who are born in the United States as citizens by birth, but this issue remains contested.

HISTORICAL BACKGROUND

The original Constitution left both state and national citizenship undefined, but several provisions implied the existence of citizenship. For example, Article II requires the President to be a "natural born citizen," Article III allows "citizens" to invoke a federal court's jurisdiction, and Article IV guarantees that "[t]he citizens of each State shall be entitled to all privileges and immunities of citizens in the several States." (See Essays Nos. 96, 131, and 140.) No provision in the original Constitution, however, explained how one became a citizen of the United States or a citizen of an individual state.

Chief Justice John Marshall addressed this issue in *Gassies v. Ballon* (1832): "A citizen of the United States, residing in any state of the Union, is a citizen of that State."[2] Marshall did not indicate whether he was stating a legal definition or simply noting the common understanding. Justice Joseph Story likewise echoed Marshall's presumption, observing that every person who moves to a state with the intention of establishing residence "becomes, ipso facto, a citizen of the state where he resides." Moreover, "[e]very citizen of a state is, ipso facto, a citizen of the United States."[3] Like Marshall, Story did not indicate whether this was a rule of law or simply the common understanding.

During the antebellum era, states simply assumed that they retained the power to determine who could become a local citizen. For white Americans, local birth and current residency generally sufficed to establish state citizenship. For black Americans, the situation was quite different. Enslaved black Americans

were treated not as persons (much less citizens), but as "property." In slaveholding states, free black Americans faced severe legal disabilities that were not imposed on white state residents. Even in northern free states, state laws frequently denied resident black Americans equal civil rights.[4]

In *Dred Scott v. Sandford*, Chief Justice Roger B. Taney relied on this history of racially discriminatory laws to support his conclusion that black Americans were not "citizens" as the term was used in the federal Constitution. The contrary conclusion, Taney pointed out, would require granting black Americans equal rights throughout the Union. These rights would include all the "Privileges and Immunities of Citizens in the several States" recognized in Article IV—a prospect Taney found self-refuting.[5] Justice Benjamin Curtis dissented from the *Dred Scott* majority's view of national citizenship but conceded that the states retained the power to determine who could become a citizen of the state and to determine "[w]hat civil rights shall be enjoyed by its citizens, and whether all shall enjoy the same."[6]

Abolitionist Republicans rejected Chief Justice Taney's race-based reading of the Constitution and his denial of black citizenship. In 1859, Representative John Bingham, a Republican from Ohio, asked, "Who are citizens of the United States?" Bingham explained that "all free persons born and domiciled within the United States" are citizens of the United States—"not all free white persons, but all free persons." He contended that the word "white" is not in the Articles of Confederation and the Constitution and concluded that "[t]he omission of this word—this phrase of caste—from our national charter, was not accidental, but intentional."[7]

Bingham's view represented the mainstream Republican understanding of citizenship. In 1862, Republican Attorney General Edward Bates published a *Report on Citizenship*.[8] He explained that the laws of the United States did not recognize a category of "denizens" or persons occupying an intermediate status between foreigner and citizen. Instead, "every person born in the country is, at the moment of their birth, prima facia a citizen . . . without any reference to race or color, or any other accidental circumstances." Under this principle of birthright citizenship, "the free man of color . . . if born in the United States, is a citizen of the United States." Bates argued that Chief Justice Taney's suggestion to the contrary in *Dred Scott* was nothing more than dicta "and of no authority as a judicial decision."

THE THIRTEENTH AMENDMENT AND BIRTHRIGHT CITIZENSHIP

In December 1865, the Thirteenth Amendment was ratified. (See Essay No. 191.) The amendment, by its terms, abolished slavery, but many Republicans contended that the amendment also removed an artificial barrier to birthright citizenship and restored the state and national citizenship of the formerly enslaved. The former rebel states, however, had no interest in recognizing black citizenship and enacted the infamous Black Codes. These race-based laws severely restricted the ability of black residents to buy or rent property, contract for labor, or testify in cases involving a dispute with a white employer. Anyone convicted of vagrancy could be imprisoned and sold as convict labor to their former masters. What little legal process was available to freedmen as a formal matter was either rarely or unequally enforced.[9]

Republicans in the 39th Congress knew that the formal abolition of slavery would not be enough to secure the rights of equal citizenship in the southern states. Accordingly, they refused to seat Democratic Representatives from the former rebel states until they had first established a sufficiently protective legal regime.[10] One of their first efforts in this regard was passage of the Civil Rights Act of 1866. The Act's opening sentence declared that "all persons born in the United States and not subject to any foreign power, excluding Indians not taxed, are hereby declared to be *citizens of the United States*" The Act specifically prohibited states from denying any "such *citizens*" equal local civil rights on the basis of race.[11] Although John Bingham questioned congressional power to pass the Act, he believed the clause was "simply declaratory of what is written in the Constitution, that every human being born within the jurisdiction of the United States of parents not owing allegiance to any foreign sovereignty is, in the language of your Constitution itself, a natural-born citizen."[12]

It was debated whether the Thirteenth Amendment had granted Congress the constitutional power to pass this act. The statute's opening statement that recognized national birthright citizenship openly challenged the Supreme Court's ruling to the contrary in *Dred Scott*. And though it did not make any express reference to *state* citizenship, the law involved matters generally viewed as *state*-level civil rights. According to Justice Curtis's dissent in *Dred Scott*, the Constitution reserved to the states the power to define the status and scope of state citizenship.

DRAFTING THE CITIZENSHIP CLAUSE

Three weeks after Congress passed the Civil Rights Act, the Joint Committee on Reconstruction submitted a proposed Fourteenth Amendment, which addressed the rights of national citizenship.[13] Representative Bingham drafted Section One of the proposal. It declared that "no state shall make or enforce any law abridging the privileges or immunities of citizens of the United States."[14] The Committee's draft did not define how one became a citizen of the United States, nor did it say anything about the status and scope of state citizenship.

The House passed the Joint Committee's draft with little debate, but Senate Republicans desired a number of changes. They held a series of private caucuses in which proposed alterations were drafted and adopted. Senator Jacob Howard of Michigan then announced to the full Senate a proposed addition to the opening of Section One of the Fourteenth Amendment: "All persons born or naturalized in the United States, and subject to the jurisdiction thereof, are citizens of the United States and of the States wherein they reside."[15]

According to Howard, the proposal was "simply declaratory of what I regard as the law of the land already." Howard also addressed the phrase "subject to the jurisdiction thereof." He explained that this category would not include "persons born in the United States who are foreigners, aliens, [and] who belong to the families of embassadors [sic] or foreign ministers accredited to the Government of the United States."[16] According to Senator John Conness of California, "children begotten of Chinese parents in California . . . should be regarded and treated as citizens of the United States, entitled to equal civil rights with other citizens of the United States."[17]

During another debate, Senator Edgar Cowan of Pennsylvania asked, "Is the child of a Gypsy born in Pennsylvania a citizen?"[18] Senator John Conness of California answered that the children of Chinese and Gypsy aliens "shall be citizens" and that he was "entirely ready to accept the provision proposed in this constitutional amendment."[19] During the proceedings, no Senator voiced an objection to the arguments advanced by Howard and Connell.

In response to questions regarding the impact of the clause on Native Americans, Sponsor of the Civil Rights Act and Chairman of the Senate Judiciary Committee Lyman Trumbull responded, "What do we mean by "subject to the jurisdiction of the United States?" Not owing allegiance to anybody else.... It cannot be said of any Indian who owes allegiance, partial allegiance if you please, to some other government, that he is "subject to the jurisdiction of the United States."[20] Both houses accepted the new language of Section One and passed the final version of the Fourteenth Amendment on June 13, 1866.[21]

CITIZENSHIP AND THE RIGHT TO VOTE

During the state ratification debates, proponents of the Fourteenth Amendment described the Citizenship Clauses of Section One as establishing the equal rights of citizenship. In Pennsylvania, Carl Schurz explained that Section One "declares citizens all persons born or naturalized in the United States and provides that such citizens shall be protected in the enjoyment of equal civil rights in whatever State they may reside."[22] Democrats charged that the amendment gave black Americans the right to vote, but Republicans in Congress insisted that mere status of citizenship did not by itself secure the *political* rights of suffrage. Women and children, for example, were citizens but did not have the right to vote.[23]

However, it was widely agreed that the freedmen would receive the *civil* rights of citizenship. The *New Orleans Tribune*, a black American newspaper, wrote that "[e]very man of African descent is not only declared to be a

citizen of the state wherein he resides, but he will be entitled to the *same* privileges and immunities as any other citizen." Additionally, "all classifications among citizens must fall" and "[e]very title of citizenship is declared to be of like value, and to confer the same rights."[24]

In 1868, Reverend Elisha Weaver, a black abolitionist, similarly explained that citizenship "carries with it the rights of citizens." He contended that "the evident duty of a liberty loving and a loyal Congress is to see that a Republican form of government is guaranteed to every State" and added that these rights are "not guaranteed while any State is permitted to withhold from citizens, on account of color merely, the rights of citizens."[25]

Civil rights leaders like Weaver believed that the status of citizenship necessarily removed the color bar at the ballot box. Frederick Douglass, for example, insisted that because "the Constitution of the United States knows no distinction between citizens on account of color," Congress should exercise "its power to secure political rights" for black citizens.[26]

This understanding did not prevail when the Fourteenth Amendment was ratified, but two years later, Americans ratified the Fifteenth Amendment. This third and final Reconstruction Amendment declared that "[t]he right of *citizens* of the United States to vote shall not be denied or abridged by the United States or by any State on account of race, color, or previous condition of servitude." (See Essay No. 201.)

JUDICIAL ENFORCEMENT OF THE CITIZENSHIP CLAUSE

The *Civil Rights Cases* (1883) considered the constitutionality of the Civil Rights Act of 1875, which prohibited discrimination in places of public accommodation.[27] The Court held that Section Five of the Fourteenth Amendment did not empower Congress to prohibit racial discrimination by private actors. Justice John Marshall Harlan was the lone dissenter. He would have upheld the Act as an enforcement of the rights of national and state citizenship under the Fourteenth Amendment. Harlan declared that "Citizenship in this country necessarily imports equality of civil rights among citizens of every race in the same State." He added that

"It is fundamental in American citizenship that, in respect of such rights, there shall be no discrimination by the State, or its officers, or by individuals, or corporations exercising public functions or authority."

BIRTHRIGHT CITIZENSHIP

In *United States v. Wong Kim Ark* (1898), the Supreme Court ruled that the children of lawfully resident parents born on United States soil were "persons born in the United States . . . subject to the jurisdiction thereof" and accordingly are citizens of the United States under the Fourteenth Amendment.[28] The Court interpreted the citizenship clauses as following the common law whereby "every child born in England of alien parents was a natural-born subject, unless the child of an ambassador or other diplomatic agent of a foreign state, or of an alien enemy in hostile occupation of the place where the child was born."[29] Chief Justice Melville Fuller dissented, joined by Justice Harlan. They rejected the argument that the Citizenship Clause followed the English model. Rather, they found that children of foreign nationals were not "subject to the jurisdiction thereof."[30]

Wong Kim Ark considered the status of children born to lawfully resident parents; there remains an ongoing scholarly debate about birthright citizenship for the children of aliens in the country unlawfully. Some scholars contend that the Framers of the Fourteenth Amendment did not intend to grant citizenship to such children.[31] Senator Lyman Trumbull of Illinois, for example, said that "subject to the jurisdiction of the United States" referred to a person "[n]ot owing allegiance to anybody else."[32] Scholars, citing Trumbull, contend that the phrase "subject to the jurisdiction thereof" refers to people who are not subject to allegiances, or loyalties, to foreign states. Children of foreign national parents would be subject to such allegiances and therefore would not be "subject to the jurisdiction thereof."

Other scholars contend that "subject to the jurisdiction thereof" simply refers to a person who was subject to U.S. law.[33] Foreigners who visit the United States are required to follow American laws. Under this argument, these aliens are in every sense subject to U.S. "jurisdiction," or control. These scholars also point to Senator Howard's remarks, and the colloquy between Senators Cowen and Conness. If "subject to the jurisdiction thereof" refers to aliens who are subject to U.S. laws, it does not matter whether the parents are in the country legally.

For more than a century, all three branches of government have treated the children of aliens, whether lawfully present or not, as birthright citizens.[34] However, in January 2025, President Trump signed an executive order that purported to limit birthright citizenship.

OPEN QUESTIONS

- Could the executive branch deprive children of illegal aliens of certain benefits reserved for citizens on the grounds that the former are not birthright citizens?[35]
- What is the relationship between the Citizenship Clause of the Fourteenth Amendment and the Presidential Eligibility Clause in Article II? Would a person who is born outside the United States to an American parent and is a citizen at birth by statute be a natural born citizen for purposes of the presidency? (See Essay No. 96.)
- Does the status of equal citizenship have the effect of guaranteeing all local citizens equal civil rights? If so, should the Court in *Brown v. Board of Education* (1954) have relied on the original understanding of the State Citizenship Clause? What about *Bolling v. Sharpe* (1954), which held that segregated schools in the federal enclave of the District of Columbia were unconstitutional. Should *Bolling* have relied on the concept of National Citizenship Clause?

Cite as: Kurt T. Lash, *The Citizenship Clause, in* The Heritage Guide to the Constitution 731 (Josh Blackman & John G. Malcolm eds., 3d ed. 2025).

Notes

1. 60 U.S. 393 (1857). **2.** 31 U.S. 761, 762 (1832). **3.** 3 Story's Commentaries §§ 564–66. **4.** Kate Masur, Until Justice Be Done: America's First Civil Rights Movement, from the Revolution to Reconstruction 151 (2021). **5.** *Dred Scott*, 60 U.S. at 417. **6.** *Id.* at 583. **7.** John Bingham, Speech Opposing the Admission of Oregon (Feb. 11, 1859), *in* 1 RA 155. **8.** Attorney General Edward Bates, *Report on Citizenship* (Nov. 29, 1862), *in* 1 RA 361–63. **9.** Allen C. Guelzo, Reconstruction: A Concise History 25–26, 45 (2018). **10.** *Majority Report of the Joint Committee on Reconstruction* (1866), *in* 2 RA 214–15. **11.** Civil Rights Act of 1866, 14 Stat. 27–30 (Apr. 9, 1866) (emphasis added). **12.** Cong. Globe, 39th Cong., 1st Sess. 1291 (1866). **13.** *Id.* at 2286–87. **14.** *Id.* **15.** *Id.* at 2890. **16.** *Id.* at 2891. **17.** *Id.* At 2891 (remarks of Mr. Conness). **18.** *Id.* at 2890. **19.** *Id.* at 2891–92. **20.** *Id.* at 2893. **21.** *Id.* at 3149. **22.** *Carl Schurz on the Issues of the Day*, Daily Evening Telegraph (Sept. 10, 1866), at 3. **23.** Speech of Schuyler Colfax (Aug. 7, 1866), *in* 2 RA 258. **24.** John Mercer Langston, *Equality Before the Law*, New Orleans Tribune (June 16, 1866), at 1. **25.** Rev. Elisha Weaver, To the Colored Men of the United States: Call for a National Convention, The Christian Recorder (Oct. 24, 1868). **26.** Frederick Douglass, *Reconstruction*, Atlantic Monthly (Nov. 1866), *in* 2 RA 296. **27.** 109 U.S. 3 (1883). **28.** 169 U.S. 649 (1898). **29.** *Id.* at 658. **30.** *Id.* at 705–32. **31.** John C. Eastman, *Born in the U.S.A.? Rethinking Birthright Citizenship in the Wake of 9/11*, 42 U. Rich. L. Rev. 955 (2008); Amy Swearer, *The Citizenship Clause's Original Meaning and What It Means Today*, Heritage Found. Legal Memorandum No. 243 (May 14, 2019), https://perma.cc/EF6E-L73A; Kurt T. Lash, *Prima Facie Citizenship: Birth, Allegiance and the Fourteenth Amendment's Citizenship Clause*, 101 Notre Dame L. Rev. __ (Forthcoming 2025). **32.** Cong. Globe, 39th Cong., 1st Sess. 2893 (1866). **33.** James C. Ho, *Defining "American": Birthright Citizenship and the Original Understanding of the 14th Amendment*, 9 Green Bag 2d 367 (2006). **34.** *Id.* at 377. **35.** Josh Blackman, *Birthright Citizenship Is a Constitutional Mandate*, Wall St. J. (Oct. 31, 2018), https://perma.cc/6VEG-WJC7.

ESSAY NO. 193: THE STATE ACTION CLAUSE
AMEND. 14, § 1

No State shall make or enforce any law which shall abridge the privileges or immunities of citizens of the United States; nor shall any State deprive any person of life, liberty, or property, without due process of law, nor deny to any person within its jurisdiction of the equal protection of the laws.

—Lee J. Strang

INTRODUCTION

The Fourteenth Amendment imposes several restrictions on the states. They cannot violate the privileges or immunities of citizens, they cannot deprive people of liberty without due process of law, and they cannot deny people the equal protection of the laws. It is clear that this amendment restricts government officials and their official actions, but does it impose similar restrictions on private parties? The Supreme Court has held that it does not. Under the state action doctrine, the Fourteenth Amendment restricts only governmental action; it does not apply to private parties. The doctrine's name is drawn from the words that begin Section 1 of the Fourteenth Amendment: ("No State shall . . ."), which, despite its name, applies to state, local, and federal governments. The state action doctrine is generally easy to apply, but the Supreme Court has struggled with borderline cases, and

scholars have criticized the doctrine as being broader than the Fourteenth Amendment's original meaning.

THE STATE ACTION DOCTRINE IN THE ORIGINAL CONSTITUTION

The original Constitution, ratified in 1788, did not have a clause that explicitly articulated the state action doctrine. However, the text limited application of the Constitution to the federal and state governments. Article I, Section 9 imposed restrictions on Congress (see Essay Nos. 67–76). And Article I, Section 10 separately listed similar prohibitions on the states (see Essay Nos. 77–86). The First Amendment similarly restricted the federal government: "Congress shall make no law. . . ."

Other provisions of the Bill of Rights are not so clear. The Takings Clause of the Fifth Amendment simply provides "nor shall private property be taken for public use, without just compensation." (See Essay No. 173.) This text, stated in the passive voice, does not clearly indicate who is prohibited from taking property. In *Barron v. Baltimore* (1833), a property owner argued that the Takings Clause required the state to provide just compensation.[1] On appeal, the U.S. Supreme Court rejected that argument. Chief Justice John Marshall's majority opinion ruled that the Bill of Rights did not apply to the states and restricted only the federal government. There was no suggestion that a *private* party who took property would be required to pay just compensation.

ADOPTION OF THE FOURTEENTH AMENDMENT

During and after the Civil War, Republicans in Congress worked to ensure that the gains made by victory on the battlefield were legally secure, but they recognized that there were two primary obstacles: through the so-called Black Codes, southern states recreated many aspects of slavery, and newly freed black Americans and their Republican allies were subjected to private violence. State officials often did nothing to stop this violence and in some cases actively assisted in these crimes.

The Thirteenth Amendment, ratified in 1865, created the first clear, textual exception to the state action doctrine. It provides that "Neither slavery nor involuntary servitude . . . shall exist within the United States." (See Essay No. 191.) Both the government and private actors were barred from imposing slavery or involuntary servitude. The scourge of slavery was not merely one of government; it was the ownership of human beings by other human beings.

The Fourteenth Amendment was ratified in 1868. Section 1 contained four important provisions: the Citizenship Clause, the Privileges or Immunities Clause, the Due Process Clause, and the Equal Protection Clause. (See Essay Nos. 194, 195, and 196.) Each of these provisions placed an express limitation on the states. Section 5 authorized Congress to pass "appropriate" legislation to enforce Section 1. (See Essay No. 200.)

The debates over the Fourteenth Amendment included little to no discussion of the state action doctrine. For this reason, scholars have focused on the actions of officers implementing the Fourteenth Amendment after ratification to gather information about the Amendment's relationship to the doctrine.

ENFORCING THE FOURTEENTH AMENDMENT

Congress passed a number of civil rights acts pursuant to its Fourteenth Amendment powers. Many of these statutes criminalized private violence occurring in the South. Most clearly, the Civil Rights Act of 1871 targeted the Ku Klux Klan by criminalizing private conduct.[2]

Congress debated whether Section 5 empowered Congress to target non-state actors. Representative James A. Garfield of Ohio, for example, identified the state's failure to enforce its law against groups like the Klan.[3] He recognized that "the chief complaint is not that the laws of the State are unequal." Rather, "even where the laws are just and equal on their face . . . a portion of the people are denied equal protection under them." Garfield pointed to "a systematic maladministration of" the laws by the government, "or a neglect or refusal to enforce their provisions."

One of the most significant enforcement laws was the Civil Rights Act of 1875.[4] This statute provided that "all persons within the jurisdiction of the United States shall be entitled to the full and equal enjoyment of [places of public accommodation]." However, in the *Civil Rights Cases* (1883), the Supreme Court ruled that Congress did not possess the power under Section 5 to enforce the provisions of Section 1 against private parties.[5] The Court ruled that Section 1 prohibited only state action. The Court relied on the structural principles of federalism and limited and enumerated powers. The Court asked: "If this legislation is appropriate for enforcing the prohibitions of the amendment, it is difficult to see where it is to stop."[6] As a result, the state action doctrine would apply to the Fourteenth Amendment. The Civil Rights Act of 1875 was the last major piece of Reconstruction-era civil rights legislation.

EXCEPTIONS TO THE STATE ACTION DOCTRINE

The *Civil Rights Cases* remains good law,[7] but the Court has created several precedent-based exceptions to the state action doctrine. *Nixon v. Condon* (1932) held that a private political party could not exclude black voters.[8] The Court ruled that the exclusion of black voters was authorized by statute and thus was subject to constitutional scrutiny. *Marsh v. Alabama* (1946) found that a company-owned town could not violate a person's free speech and religious exercise rights.[9] *Burton v. Wilmington Parking Authority* (1961) declared that a private restaurant in a public parking garage was a state actor.[10] The Court even held that a private shopping center was subject to the Free Speech Clause.[11] During this period, Professor Charles Black famously argued that the state action doctrine was being submerged by the exceptions.[12]

However, the Burger Court began to narrow the exceptions. The Court reversed its ruling on private shopping centers[13] and held that a private club with a liquor license was not a state actor.[14] *Jackson v. Metropolitan Edison Co.* (1974) articulated the *public functions* exception to the state action doctrine.[15] Justice William Rehnquist's majority opinion explained that activities that were "traditionally the exclusive prerogative of the State" were state action.[16] This exception covered the white-primary cases, the company town cases, and a handful of others but not much else. The Court has invoked other exceptions, though the doctrine is difficult to synthesize.[17] On the Roberts Court, the state action doctrine seems stable. *Manhattan Community Access Corp. v. Halleck* (2019), for example, held that a cable public access channel is not a state actor.[18]

CRITICISM OF THE STATE ACTION DOCTRINE

Originalist scholars contend that the Supreme Court has articulated an overly broad state action doctrine.[19] This criticism essentially reflects two schools of thought advocated by groups of scholars.

The first group argues that the Equal Protection Clause applies to some situations that would be considered state *inaction*. For instance, Professor Christopher Green has suggested that "it is the state's failures with respect to [private] violence, not the violence itself, which produces a constitutional violation."[20] Green supports this conclusion with a detailed study of the remote and immediate history of the Equal Protection Clause.[21]

The second group argues that the Citizenship Clause, typically coupled with the Privileges or Immunities Clause, imposes an affirmative obligation on states to treat all citizens in a manner comporting with their status as citizens in a republic, particularly with regard to public accommodations laws.[22] This view would require, for instance, that state law prohibit (at least) places of public accommodation from treating citizens differently because of such irrational bases as race. This argument builds on the antebellum Republican thought about citizenship that influenced the Reconstruction Congress to pass the Fourteenth Amendment and the various pieces of civil rights legislation.

OPEN QUESTIONS

- Are social media platforms state actors? Are they public utilities?[23]
- What sort of test could the Court apply to determine whether state *inaction* is subject to Section 1 of the Fourteenth Amendment? Would this test undermine the state action doctrine altogether?
- As a general matter, the Constitution limits only state action and does not restrict private actions. It is clear that the Thirteenth Amendment restricts private action and is not limited to state action, but there may be other exceptions as well. The Twenty-First Amendment prohibits the transportation of alcohol in violation of a state law. (See Essay No. 205.) Would being convicted of violating a state liquor law be a violation of the Twenty-First Amendment?[24] The Foreign Emoluments Clause restricts certain government officials from accepting "any present, Emolument, Office, or Title" from foreign governments. (See Essay No. 76.) And the Domestic Emoluments Clause prohibits the President from accepting emoluments from the federal government and the states. (See

Essay No. 100.) If a covered official accepted a prohibited emolument in his *personal* capacity, would that acceptance violate either or both of these clauses?[25]

Cite as: Lee J. Strang, *The State Action Clause, in* THE HERITAGE GUIDE TO THE CONSTITUTION 736 (Josh Blackman & John G. Malcolm eds., 3d ed. 2025).

Notes

1. *Barron v. Baltimore*, 32 U.S. 243 (1833).   **2.** 17 Stat. 13, § 2 (1871).   **3.** Cong. Globe, 42d Cong., 1st Sess. App. 153 (1871); Enforcement Act of 1870 § 6, 16 Stat. 140 (1870).   **4.** 18 Stat. 335, § 1 (1875).   **5.** *Civil Rights Cases*, 109 U.S. 3 (1883).   **6.** *Id.* at 14.   **7.** *United States v. Morrison*, 529 U.S. 598 (2000).   **8.** 286 U.S. 73 (1932).   **9.** 326 U.S. 501 (1946).   **10.** 365 U.S. 715 (1961).   **11.** *Amalgamated Food Emps. Union Loc. 590 v. Logan Valley Plaza, Inc.*, 391 U.S. 308 (1968).   **12.** Charles L. Black, Jr., *Foreword: "State Action," Equal Protection, and California's Proposition 14*, 81 Harv. L. Rev. 69, 84–91, 108–09 (1967).   **13.** *Hudgens v. NLRB*, 424 U.S. 507, 518 (1976).   **14.** *Moose Lodge No. 107 v. Irvis*, 407 U.S. 163 (1972).   **15.** 419 U.S. 345 (1974).   **16.** *Id.* at 353.   **17.** Jordan Goodson, *The State of the State Action Doctrine: A Search for Accountability*, 37 Touro L. Rev. 151, 159–69 (2021); G. Sidney Buchanan, *A Conceptual History of the State Action Doctrine: The Search for Governmental Responsibility*, 34 Hous. L. Rev. 333, 391–424 (1997).   **18.** *Manhattan Comm. Access Corp. v. Halleck*, 587 U.S. 802 (2019).   **19.** Michael Kent Curtis, No State Shall Abridge: The Fourteenth Amendment and the Bill of Rights 158 (1986); Michael P. Zuckert, *Congressional Power Under the Fourteenth Amendment—The Original Understanding of Section Five*, 3 Const. Comment. 123, 142 (1986).   **20.** Christopher R. Green, *The Original Sense of the Equal Protection Clause: Subsequent Interpretation and Application*, 19 Geo. Mason U. Civ. Rts. J. 219, 254 (2009). Evan D. Bernick, *Antisubjugation and the Equal Protection of the Laws*, 110 Geo. L.J. 1, 36 (2021).   **21.** Randy E. Barnett & Evan D. Bernick, The Original Meaning of the Fourteenth Amendment: Its Letter and Spirit 319–51 (2021); Pamela Brandwein, Rethinking the Judicial Settlement of Reconstruction 28–86 (2011).   **22.** John Harrison, *Reconstructing the Privileges or Immunities Clause*, 101 Yale L.J. 1385, 1425–33 (1992); Ryan C. Williams, *Originalism and the Other Desegregation Decision*, 99 Va. L. Rev. 493 (2013).   **23.** *Moody v. NetChoice LLC*, 603 U.S. 707, 766 (2014) (Alito, J., concurring); *Biden v. Knight First Amend. Inst. at Colum. Univ.*, 141 S.Ct. 1220, 1226 (2021) (Thomas, J., concurring).   **24.** Laurence H. Tribe, *How to Violate the Constitution Without Really Trying: Lessons from the Repeal of Prohibition to the Balanced Budget Amendment*, 12 Const. Comment. 217, 220 (1995).   **25.** Josh Blackman & Seth Barrett Tillman, *The Unresolved Threshold Issues in the Emoluments Clauses Litigation: The President Has Three Bodies and There Is No Cause of Action for Ultra Vires Conduct*, 20 Geo. J.L. & Pub. Pol'y 163, 196–98 (2022).

ESSAY NO. 194: THE PRIVILEGES OR IMMUNITIES CLAUSE
AMEND. 14, § 1

No State shall make or enforce any law which shall abridge the privileges or immunities of citizens of the United States. . . .

—Kurt T. Lash

INTRODUCTION

The exact content and scope of the Privileges or Immunities Clause has long been a matter of substantial academic and judicial debate. Although early decisions by the Supreme Court narrowed the clause almost to the point of non-existence, most scholars and some Supreme Court justices now believe that it was meant originally to make the Bill of Rights enforceable against the states. Other scholars are divided over whether the clause requires nothing more than equal treatment or protects substantive rights beyond those listed in the first ten amendments to the Constitution. To date, the Supreme Court has avoided reinvigorating the clause, choosing instead to base its protection of substantive rights on a reading of the Fourteenth Amendment's Due Process Clause.[1]

HISTORICAL BACKGROUND

The Privileges or Immunities Clause (Section 1 of the Fourteenth Amendment) is one of two clauses in the Constitution that refer to the "privileges" and "immunities" of citizenship. The other (Article IV, Section 2) declares that "[t]he Citizens of each State shall be entitled to

ESSAY NO. 194: THE PRIVILEGES OR IMMUNITIES CLAUSE   *The Reconstruction Amendments*

all Privileges and Immunities of Citizens in the several States." (See Essay No. 140.)

Corfield v. Coryell (1823), an influential antebellum circuit court opinion by Justice Bushrod Washington, found that this clause guarantees visiting citizens from another state equal access to a limited set of locally secured "fundamental" rights.[2] Justice Joseph Story similarly explained that "[t]he intention of this clause was to confer . . . a general citizenship; and to communicate all the privileges and immunities, which the citizens of the same state would be entitled to under the like circumstances."[3]

In *Dred Scott v. Sandford* (1857), Chief Justice Roger B. Taney used this clause as an argument against black citizenship. If black people were citizens, he argued, then black citizens from northern free states who travelled to slave states would have the same right to keep and bear arms granted to resident white citizens. But Taney insisted that black people could not be citizens and thus were not entitled to the privileges and immunities of citizenship.[4]

Although Article IV speaks of the "Privileges and Immunities of Citizens in the several States," numerous antebellum sources referred to the "privileges and immunities of citizens *of the United States*." For example, the 1803 Louisiana Cession Act declared that "[t]he inhabitants of the ceded territory shall . . . enjoy[] . . . all the rights, advantages and immunities of citizens of the United States."[5] According to Daniel Webster, such national privileges or immunities were "recognized or communicated by the Constitution of the United States . . . [as] common to all citizens, and are uniform throughout the United States."[6] Abolitionist Joel Tiffany wrote that the privileges and immunities of citizens of the United States included "all the guarantys of the Federal Constitution for personal security, personal liberty and private property" including "the right of petition, the right to keep and bear arms, the right to be secure from all unwarrantable seizures and searches," and other rights listed in the Bill of Rights.[7] Perhaps ironically, *Dred Scott v. Sandford* also listed the right to keep and bear arms as a "right or privilege" of citizenship—a right Taney denied to black Americans because they were not citizens.[8]

In 1859, Representative John Bingham of Ohio argued that the Privileges or Immunities Clause of Article IV impliedly obligated the states to enforce provisions in the Bill of Rights. According to Bingham, Article IV should be read as if it contained an unstated ellipsis guaranteeing "the privileges and immunities *of citizens of the United States* in the several States."[9] Bingham, like most other antebellum Republicans, did not believe the original Constitution empowered Congress to enforce the Bill of Rights (or Article IV) against the states. His views are important because he later became a principal drafter of the Fourteenth Amendment's Privileges or Immunities Clause.

DRAFTING THE PRIVILEGES OR IMMUNITIES CLAUSE

In December 1865, the 39th Congress began to draft a series of statutes and proposed amendments meant to secure basic rights in the southern states. In February 1866, Representative Bingham, a member of the Joint Committee on Reconstruction, drafted a proposed amendment granting Congress the "power to make all laws which shall be necessary and proper to secure to the citizens of each State all privileges and immunities of citizens in the several States."[10] Bingham explained that his amendment would "arm the Congress of the United States, by the consent of the people of the United States, with the power to enforce the bill of rights as it stands in the constitution today" and added that his draft "hath that extent—no more."[11] During debate, both Republicans and Democrats expressed concerns about the wording of the amendment. Bingham then agreed to return the proposal to the Joint Committee on Reconstruction for redrafting.[12]

Two months later, the Joint Committee returned with a new five-sectioned amendment with a revised version of Bingham's proposal serving as Section 1 of the new amendment. Bingham once again authored the opening section: "No State shall make or enforce any law which shall abridge the privileges or immunities of citizens of the United States. . . ."[13]

In May 1866, Senator Jacob Howard of Michigan, also a member of the Joint Committee, introduced the proposed amendment in the Senate.[14] Howard explained that the Privileges or Immunities Clause protected

740

a variety of rights, including those protected by Article IV as interpreted by cases like *Corfield v. Coryell.* Howard added that these "privileges" and "immunities" included personal rights guaranteed and secured "by the first eight amendments of the Constitution."[15] Howard said that without an amendment, these liberties stood "simply as a bill of rights in the Constitution, without power on the part of Congress to give them full effect," and that the states were therefore "not restrained from violating" them.[16] Howard's speech was widely published in newspapers across the country.

Both the House and Senate approved Bingham's language for the Privileges or Immunities Clause as well as the Due Process and Equal Protection Clauses. Just before final passage, the Senate successfully added a provision defining national and state citizenship.[17]

RATIFICATION OF THE PRIVILEGES OR IMMUNITIES CLAUSE

During the Fourteenth Amendment ratification debates, Republican supporters and Democratic opponents did not spend much time exploring the Privileges or Immunities Clause in detail. Democrats generally opposed passing any amendment and warned that Section 1 would open the door to black suffrage.[18] Republicans denied that Section 1 conferred the *political* rights of suffrage. Rather, they generally paraphrased Section 1 as establishing only equal *civil* rights. Senator Lyman Trumbull of Illinois, for example, explained that Section 1 was simply "the declaration that all good citizens were entitled alike to equal rights" that were "set forth in the Civil Rights" Act of 1866.[19]

POST-RATIFICATION COMMENTARY

On July 28, 1868, Secretary of State William Seward declared the formal ratification of the Fourteenth Amendment. One week later, George Washington Paschal of Texas, a Unionist judge and legal scholar, explained that the Citizenship Clause and Privileges or Immunities Clause ensured that "the lines defining American citizenship will no longer be in doubt" and warned readers not to "underrate this national guarantee."[20] The Bill of Rights would now constrain the states. Similarly, in 1872, Judge

Timothy Farrar described the Fourteenth Amendment as having "swept away" antebellum judicial opinions refusing to apply the Bill of Rights against the states.[21]

In 1870, Americans ratified the Fifteenth Amendment, which declared that "the right of citizens of the United States to vote" shall not be denied on the basis of race. (See Essay No. 201.) Some women's rights advocates claimed that the combination of the Fourteenth Amendment's Privileges or Immunities Clause and the Fifteenth Amendment's right-to-vote language should be understood as empowering Congress to give women the right to vote. Victoria Woodhull, a leading women's suffragist, presented a petition to the House Judiciary Committee calling for legislation to give the "female citizen" the right to vote. According to Woodhull's petition, "[t]he Constitution defines a woman born or naturalized in the United States, and subject to the jurisdiction thereof" as a citizen, and "[o]ne portion of citizens have no power to deprive another of rights and privileges such as are possessed and exercised by themselves." Accordingly, the "male citizen" had no right to deprive the "female citizen" of the privilege of voting.[22]

A majority of the House Judiciary Committee voted to reject Woodhull's petition. In a report submitted by Chairman John Bingham, the majority expressly disagreed with Woodhull's reading of the Privileges or Immunities Clause. The Fourteenth Amendment, the committee found, only "refer[red] to . . . those privileges and immunities embraced" in Article IV. The report concluded that the Fourteenth Amendment "did not add to the privileges or immunities before mentioned, but was necessary for their enforcement as an express limitation upon the power of the States."[23]

The committee's report limited the Fourteenth Amendment's "privileges or immunities" to those previously "embraced" by Article IV. The report could also be read as excluding the provisions of the Bill of Rights from those privileges or immunities, but it is not clear that every member of the majority would have agreed that the states were not required to enforce the Bill of Rights. Bingham had previously argued that Article IV impliedly obligated the states to enforce the Bill of Rights.

In any event, Bingham clarified his personal views two months later. He explained that the national privileges and immunities of citizens of the United States were altogether different from the state-secured rights covered by Article IV.[24] Those national privileges and immunities, Bingham explained, included the provisions of the Bill of Rights.

JUDICIAL PRECEDENT

The U.S. Supreme Court first grappled with the meaning of the Privileges or Immunities Clause in *The Slaughter-House Cases* (1873).[25] Justice Samuel Miller's majority opinion rejected a claim by local butchers that a state-granted monopoly violated their Fourteenth Amendment "privilege or immunities" to pursue a trade. The Court held that the "privileges and immunities of citizens of the United States" were altogether different from those described by Justice Washington in *Corfield v. Coryell*.[26] The Fourteenth Amendment's Privileges or Immunities were those that "owe their existence to the Federal government, its National character, its Constitution, or its laws" such as "[t]he right to peaceably assemble and petition for redress of grievances, the privilege of the writ of habeas corpus . . . and [t]he right to use the navigable waters of the United States. . . ."[27] State-secured common-law rights like the right to pursue a trade were not national privileges and immunities even if they might be guaranteed on an equal basis to visiting citizens by Article IV.

Justice Stephen Field dissented. He contended that the majority had reduced the Privileges or Immunities Clause to "a vain and idle enactment, which accomplished nothing, and most unnecessarily excited Congress and the people on its passage."[28] Justice Joseph Bradley wrote a separate dissent insisting that "[the] right to choose one's calling is an essential part of that liberty which it is the object of government to protect; and a calling, when chosen, is a man's property and right."[29] One day after *Slaughter-House* was decided, the Court rejected Myra Bradwell's claim that the Privileges or Immunities Clause guarantees a woman the right to practice as a lawyer.[30]

The Supreme Court subsequently ruled in *United States v. Cruikshank* (1876) that the protections of the federal Bill of Rights did not apply to the states.[31] In this case, the rights to assemble and to keep and bear arms were not "privileges or immunities of citizens of the United States" protected against state abridgment by the Fourteenth Amendment. *Barron v. Baltimore* (1833) had held that the provisions of the Bill of Rights limited only the federal government and not the state governments.[32] The Court ruled that Chief Justice John Marshall's decision in *Barron* remained good law even after ratification of the Fourteenth Amendment.[33]

The Court has never overruled *Slaughter-House* and *Cruikshank*. Instead, it has interpreted the Fourteenth Amendment's Due Process Clause as "incorporating" provisions in the Bill of Rights against the states. For example, *Gitlow v. New York* (1925) held that the Due Process Clause requires the states to protect the freedom of speech.[34] The federal courts still invoke the Privileges or Immunities Clause in limited contexts, such as the right to travel.[35]

A few Justices have occasionally encouraged the Supreme Court to revisit these narrow interpretations of the Privileges or Immunities Clause. For example, Justice Hugo Black described John Bingham as "the Madison of the first section of the Fourteenth Amendment" and argued that Section 1 was "intended to . . . make the Bill of Rights, applicable to the states."[36]

Justice Clarence Thomas presented an extended history of the Privileges or Immunities Clause in his concurring opinion in *McDonald v. City of Chicago* (2010), in which he encouraged the Court to restore Bingham's original understanding of Section 1.[37] Thomas has also cited the Privileges or Immunities Clause as the basis for the right to be free from excessive fines and the regulatory takings doctrine.[38] Justice Neil Gorsuch has acknowledged "[a]s an original matter" that "the appropriate vehicle for incorporation may well be the Fourteenth Amendment's Privileges or Immunities Clause, rather than, as this Court has long assumed, the Due Process Clause."[39] And in Justice Thomas's concurring opinion in *Dobbs v. Jackson Women's Health Organization* (2022), he repeated his call for the Court to abandon its doctrine of substantive due process and instead enforce the original meaning of the Privileges or Immunities Clause.[40]

OPEN QUESTIONS AND SCHOLARLY DEBATES

- Legal scholars remain deeply divided over the meaning of the Privileges or Immunities Clause. Bingham's personal view of Section 1 seems clear, but it remains a matter of scholarly dispute whether the ratifying public shared Bingham's understanding of the clause. Mid-twentieth-century historians like Charles Fairman rejected Bingham's view that the clause made the Bill of Rights enforceable against the states. Fairman's claims were challenged by historian William Crosskey, whose views were then challenged by Raoul Berger, whose views were challenged by Michael Kent Curtis and Akhil Reed Amar.[41] Most scholars agree that the historical record supports reading the clause as making the federal Bill of Rights enforceable against the states,[42] but that view is not unanimous. Professors John Harrison and Ilan Wurman, for example, contend that the Privileges or Immunities Clause does not incorporate the Bill of Rights.[43]

- Whether the Privileges or Immunities Clause authorizes judicial enforcement of unenumerated rights against the states is a matter of even greater scholarly dispute. Some theorists such as Randy Barnett argue that the clause protects a range of unenumerated rights including economic rights.[44] Barnett has called on the Supreme Court to overrule *The Slaughter-House Cases*. Harrison and Wurman contend that the clause prohibits states from discriminating against contract and property rights. Other scholars, such as Akhil Amar and Michael McConnell, read the clause as authorizing judicial identification and enforcement of enumerated rights that emerge in the laws of the states over time, but they do not include the unenumerated economic rights protected by the Court under the Due Process Clause in cases like *Lochner v. New York* (1905).[45] Other scholars, including the author of this essay, have argued that the Privileges or Immunities Clause enforces only textually enumerated rights against the states such as those listed in the Bill of Rights.[46]

Cite as: Kurt T. Lash, *The Privileges or Immunities Clause, in* THE HERITAGE GUIDE TO THE CONSTITUTION 739 (Josh Blackman & John G. Malcolm eds., 3d ed. 2025).

Notes

1. *Gitlow v. New York*, 268 U.S. 652 (1925). **2.** 6 Fed. Cas. 546 (C.C.E.D. Pa. 1823). **3.** 3 Story's Commentaries § 1800. **4.** 60 U.S. 393, 416–17 (1857). **5.** Louisiana Purchase Treaty (Apr. 30, 1803), *in* 1 The Reconstruction Amendments: The Essential Documents 80 (Kurt T. Lash ed., 2021) (hereinafter "RA"). **6.** Daniel Webster, Memorial to the Congress of the United States on the Subject of Restraining the Increase of Slavery in New States (1819), *in* Kurt T. Lash, The Fourteenth Amendment and the Privileges and Immunities of American Citizenship 56 (2014). **7.** Joel Tiffany, *Treatise on the Unconstitutionality of Slavery* (1849), *in* 1 RA 249. **8.** 60 U.S. 393, 450 (1857). **9.** Cong. Globe, 35th Cong., 2d Sess. 984 (1859) (emphasis added). **10.** Cong. Globe, 39th Cong., 1st Sess. 1088 (1866). **11.** *Id*. **12.** *Id*. at 1095. **13.** *Id*. at 2764. **14.** *Id*. at 2765. **15.** *Id*. at 2766. **17.** *Id*. at 2897. **18.** Speech of Senator Thomas A. Hendrick (Aug. 8, 1866), *in* 2 RA 260–61. **19.** Speech of Lyman Trumbull (Aug. 2, 1866), *in* 2 RA 256. **20.** George Washington Paschal, *The Fourteenth Article*, N.Y. Tribune (Aug. 6, 1868), at 2. **21.** Timothy Farrar, Manual on the Constitution of the United States 487 (3d. ed. 1872). **22.** U.S. House, Judiciary Committee, *Petition of Victoria Woodhull on the Subject of Female Suffrage* (Jan. 2, 1871), *in* 2 RA 607. **23.** U.S. House, Judiciary Committee, *The*

Woodhull Report (Jan. 30 & Feb. 1, 1871), *in* 2 RA 609. **24.** Speech of John Bingham on the Privileges or Immunities Clause of the Fourteenth Amendment (March 31, 1871), *in* 2 RA 620, 626. **25.** 83 U.S. 36 (1873). **26.** *Id*. at 74. **27.** *Id*. at 79–80. **28.** *Id*. at 96. **29.** *Id*. at 116. **30.** *Bradwell v. Illinois*, 83 U.S. 130 (1873). **31.** 92 U.S. 542 (1876). **32.** 32 U.S. 243 (1833). **33.** 92 U.S. at 552. **34.** *Gitlow v. New York*, 268 U.S. 652 (1925). **35.** *Saenz v. Roe*, 526 U.S. 489 (1999); *Shapiro v. Thompson*, 394 U.S. 618 (1969); Ilya Shapiro & Josh Blackman, *The Once and Future Privileges or Immunities Clause*, 25 Geo. Mason L. Rev. 1207 (2020). **36.** *Adamson v. California*, 332 U.S. 46, 71–74 (1947) (Black, J., concurring). **37.** 561 U.S. 742, 813–35 (2010) (Thomas, J., concurring). **38.** *Timbs v. Indiana*, 586 U.S. 146, 157–58 (2019) (Thomas, J., concurring); *Murr v. Wisconsin*, 582 U.S. 383, 419 (2017) (Thomas, J., dissenting). **39.** *Timbs*, 586 U.S. at 157 (Gorsuch, J., concurring). **40.** 597 U.S. 215, 332–33 (2022) (Thomas, J., concurring). **41.** Akhil Reed Amar, The Bill of Rights: Creation and Reconstruction 187–206 (1998). **42.** Amar, The Bill of Rights: Creation and Reconstruction, *supra*; Randy Barnett, Restoring the Lost Constitution: The Presumption of Liberty (2013); Michael Kent Curtis, No State Shall Abridge: The Fourteenth Amendment and the Bill of Rights (1990); Lash, *supra*.

43. John Harrison, *Reconstructing the Privileges or Immunities Clause*, 101 Yale L.J. 1385 (1992); Ilan Wurman, The Second Founding: An Introduction to the Fourteenth Amendment (2020). **44.** Barnett, *supra* at 206; Randy E. Barnett & Evan Bernick, The Original Meaning of the Fourteenth Amendment: Its Letter and Spirit 205–23 (2021). **45.** 198 U.S. 45 (1905). **46.** Lash, *supra*.

~~~

ESSAY NO. 195: THE DUE PROCESS CLAUSE
AMEND. 14, § 1

. . . nor shall any State deprive any person of life, liberty, or property, without due process of law. . . .

—Nathan S. Chapman & Michael W. McConnell

INTRODUCTION

The members of the 39th Congress who passed the Fourteenth Amendment would have been astonished by the diversity of constitutional doctrines the Supreme Court has fashioned out of the Due Process Clause. By its terms, the Due Process Clause simply prohibits the states from "depriv[ing] any person of life, liberty, or property without due process of law." This provision guarantees that the government will act according to law and not arbitrary diktat, yet no provision of the Constitution has been the source of more disparate—or more controversial—Supreme Court decisions. The clause has been the source of doctrines that include "procedural due process" guarantees of notice, a hearing, and standards of proof; "substantive due process" rights to contract, abortion, and marriage; state jurisdictional limits; "incorporation" of the Bill of Rights against the states; and rules governing civil litigation, such as personal jurisdiction and choice of law.

HISTORY BEFORE 1791

Magna Carta (1215) required that a freeman may be "taken, imprisoned, disseised, outlawed, banished, or in any way destroyed" only "by the lawful judgment of his peers [and/or] by the law of the land."[1] By the seventeenth century, English jurists equated "due process of law" with this requirement. In English constitutionalism, due process operated principally as a limit on the Crown's authority to deprive persons of rights without the application of law by a tribunal that was at least quasi-independent. In many cases, due process required a jury.[2] Almost all of the original American state constitutions included similar "law of the land" provisions, and some states separately guaranteed "due process of law."[3] The Fifth Amendment, ratified in 1791, guaranteed that the federal government would not "deprive[]" a person of "life, liberty, or property, without due process of law," but that provision did not limit the power of the states.

ANTEBELLUM PRECEDENT

Throughout the antebellum era, state and federal courts treated the due process clauses synonymously with law of the land clauses.[4] American constitutional innovations gave courts greater independence and denied legislatures many of the judicial powers traditionally exercised by Parliament. Due process of law guaranteed that the government could deprive someone of a right to life, liberty, or property only pursuant to standing law and traditional procedures. Moreover, those rights could ordinarily be denied only by an independent tribunal applying that law according to those procedures.[5]

American courts also held that due process was a limit on the legislature in two kinds of cases. First, the legislature could not authorize judicial procedures that did not meet the traditional level of protections for litigants. Second, due process restricted the legislature's power to act like a court by effectively entering judgment against a particular party. Parliament had long exercised the power to enact special bills that operated like judicial decisions. Sir William Blackstone observed that such bills deprived specific parties of rights based on past conduct that may or may not have violated a previously enacted law.[6] American constitutions deprived legislatures of this power.

Blackstone's short treatise on the natural rights of individuals provided antebellum jurists with a comprehensive account of "life, liberty, and property."[7] The meaning of *life* was literal: "[I]t begins in contemplation of law as soon as an infant is able to stir in the mother's womb."[8] Per Magna Carta, the government could not put someone to death without due process of law.

Liberty was a natural right. John Locke wrote that people were born with that "perfect freedom" to "order their actions, and dispose of their possessions and persons, as they think fit, within the bounds of the law of nature."[9] As part of the social compact, Blackstone wrote, the government could restrain liberty, but only "by due process of law," which meant with standing law and according to established procedural protections such as the writ of habeas corpus and trial by jury.[10] The liberty protected by due process was thus capacious. It included both fundamental rights like the freedom of religion and trivial rights like the freedom to wear a hat. All of these rights could be limited by the government, but only with due process of law.

The right of *property* was somewhat different. All people had a natural right to acquire, use, and dispose of property. However, the contours of each species of property were defined by positive law. The natural right to acquire, use, and dispose of such property was subject to generally applicable law. In Blackstone's words, the right amounted to "the free use, enjoyment, and disposal of all . . . acquisitions, without any control or diminution, save only by the laws of the land."[11] The assumption was that the government may define the general boundaries of private property, but it may deprive someone of a "vested" or settled property interest only with due process of law.

Antebellum courts decided a number of cases that tested the limits of this logic. One set of cases involved special bills. Courts concluded that due process of law prohibited legislatures from effectively targeting a specific person or group of persons for deprivation of contract or property rights, but these courts nearly always upheld generally applicable laws that operated only prospectively and that disinterested tribunals (typically judges or juries) could apply later to individual cases.

The glaring exceptions were a brace of laws from the 1850s that prohibited the sale of alcohol. Some courts found that these laws violated due process by effectively eliminating a species of property. Three other state courts, however, quickly came to the opposite, traditional conclusion.[12] These decisions were the backdrop to the notorious decision in *Dred Scott v. Sandford* (1857).[13] Slavery was contrary to the enslaved person's natural liberty. The *Somerset Case* (1772) held that slavery was unlike other forms of property, and the common law tolerated slavery only where it was affirmatively supported by positive law.[14] Contrary to that norm, *Dred Scott* held that Congress lacked the power to prohibit slavery in the U.S. territories. Chief Justice Roger B. Taney's majority decision further held that a slaveholder could not be deprived of his property right simply by taking an enslaved person into a free territory.[15]

The alcohol cases and *Dred Scott* were aberrations. It was common then as now for states to regulate the possession, use, or sale of property for the public good.

FRAMING THE FOURTEENTH AMENDMENT

The Fourteenth Amendment's Due Process Clause generated little discussion in the 39th Congress. This lack of controversy was not surprising. The Fourteenth Amendment did no more than apply to the states a protection that had long applied to the federal government through the Fifth Amendment. (See Essay No. 172.) Asked what due process required, the amendment's chief sponsor, Representative John Bingham of Ohio, replied that "the courts have settled that long ago, and the gentleman can go and read their decisions."[16] No one disputed this.

What was the understanding of due process of law that had been settled by the courts? In 1871, Representative James Garfield, who had been a member of the 39th Congress, explained that the Due Process Clause "realizes the full force and effect of the clause in Magna Charta, from which it was borrowed." Garfield added that "there is now no power in either the State or the national Government to deprive any person of . . . [l]ife, liberty and property, except by due process of law; that is, by an impartial trial according to the laws of the land."[17]

Garfield's summary raises several questions. What exactly was the relationship between the Magna Carta's "law of the land" provision and due process of law? What was the requirement of "an impartial trial according to the laws of the land"? And what were the rights of "life, liberty, and property" protected by due process of law? Senator Lyman Trumbull of Illinois, also a key supporter of the Fourteenth Amendment, defined the "liberty" protected by the U.S. Constitution as natural liberty, or the "[p]ower of acting as one thinks fit, without any restraint or control," "so far restrained by human laws and no further, as is necessary and expedient for the general advantage of the public."[18]

It is highly unlikely that the reasoning of the hated *Dred Scott* case was carried over into the 39th Congress's understanding of due process under the Fourteenth Amendment. The Republicans of the 39th Congress were aiming to undo the effects of *Dred Scott*, not to sustain them.[19]

SCHOLARLY DEBATES ABOUT THE DUE PROCESS CLAUSE

Scholars disagree about many aspects of the Due Process Clause's original meaning. First, does due process apply in any way to the legislative branch? Some scholars point to historical evidence showing that due process of law referred strictly to the procedures of common-law courts. In England, Parliament frequently passed laws depriving individuals of life, liberty, or property.[20] However, this is not the mainstream view. The leading antebellum due process case, *Murray's Lessee* (1856), involved the constitutionality of a statute.[21]

Second, does due process of law prohibit retroactive or targeted laws that deprive persons of rights? If so, that reading would render several provisions of Article I, Section 9—such as the Bill of Attainder Clause, the Ex Post Facto Clause, and the Contracts Clause—redundant.[22] (See Essay Nos. 80, 81, and 82.) The Due Process Clause, enacted after Article I, was broader than any one of those provisions, and to the extent that it overlapped with them, antebellum American courts embraced the redundancy of constitutional protection for life, liberty, and property from arbitrary deprivation.[23]

Third, do the antebellum cases applying due process to the legislature provide support for at least some version of modern "substantive due process"?[24] In our view, the answer is no. Some of these cases adapted the established procedural understanding of due process for the American system of separated powers. Other cases were out of step with the general course of jurisprudence.

Fourth, does due process incorporate natural law limits on legislation? Such limits were forerunners of modern substantive due process rights.[25] American jurists, including Representative Bingham, sometimes connected the requirement of "due process of *law*" or the "*law* of the land" with principles of divine or natural law.[26] However, they believed that those rights were embedded in the basic principles of the common law that protected rights of property, personal security, contract, and freedom of movement. Antebellum courts and commentators occasionally did opine that positive law had to comply with general principles, natural right, or an abstract notion of "reason,"[27] but the closest they came to enforcing these common-law norms was to read a loosely phrased statute narrowly to avoid violating them.[28]

Fifth, does due process include the right to judicial review of whether a state legislature acted in good faith in exercising the state's police power?[29] Under this view, the clause requires courts to review whether the legislature exercised its power in a good-faith attempt to achieve a constitutionally permissible end.

Sixth, is the text of the Due Process Clause sufficiently broad to include the evolving standards of justice and fairness that undergird modern substantive due process?[30] This argument adopts a remarkably expansive view of discretionary judicial authority over democratically enacted law. Moreover, it conflicts with the predominant understanding of the Fourteenth Amendment's framers and ratifiers. They sought to ensure that states would provide the same structural and procedural protections to black Americans that white Americans had enjoyed under state and federal due process and law of the land provisions.[31] The notion that courts had the authority to declare unconstitutional a state statute for failing a highly subjective means–ends test or for infringing on unenumerated fundamental rights was a product of judicial creativity several decades after the Fourteenth Amendment.

MODERN PROCEDURAL DUE PROCESS DOCTRINE

The modern doctrines that most directly continue the antebellum understanding of due process are called "procedural due process." *Carey v. Piphus* (1978) observed that "[p]rocedural due process rules are meant to protect persons not from the deprivation, but from the mistaken or unjustified deprivation of life, liberty, or property."[32] The U.S. Supreme Court has recognized that the bedrock requirements of procedural due process are "notice and [an] opportunity for a hearing appropriate to the nature of the case."[33] Due process may require different procedures for criminal, administrative, and civil cases. For instance, due process permits a criminal conviction only upon a showing of guilt "beyond a reasonable doubt," but it will permit a judgment of civil liability upon the lesser showing of a "preponderance of the evidence."[34]

Traditional courts determined what process is due based on long-established procedures. Modern courts employ a balancing test based on the courts' own intuitions about the importance of the interests and the reliability of the procedures. The Court has spoken of "property interests" and "liberty interests" instead of "rights." *Matthews v. Eldridge* (1976) crafted a three-part balancing test based on (i) the individual's interest in the property; (ii) the risk that the government's proposed procedures would result in error and the probable value of additional procedural protections; and (iii) the costs to the government of additional process.[35] The outcome of this balancing in any particular case is difficult to predict. Often, no more is needed than notice and an opportunity to be heard with no requirement of a disinterested tribunal.

However, certain constitutionally grounded rights require more process. For example, when the state deprives a person of liberty through physical restraint, the government ordinarily must comply with constitutionally specified procedures that include a reasonable seizure and a jury trial with habeas corpus as a backstop. *Hamdi v. Rumsfeld* (2004) departed from this principle by holding that detainees held at the military facility in Guantanamo Bay, Cuba, required only the notice and hearing requirements usually applicable to civil cases involving welfare benefits.[36] Justice Antonin Scalia dissented and would have afforded American citizens held in custody the full protections of the Due Process Clause. Takings of property under the Fifth Amendment require a jury trial to determine just compensation. For deprivations of so-called "new" property, such as welfare benefits, the process varies with context.[37]

Due process also ensures fair notice and procedural protections in a variety of special contexts. A state must comply with the Due Process Clause when it assesses, gives notice, and collects taxes with special taxes typically subject to more procedural protections and general taxes typically subject to fewer such protections.[38] The clause applies to the deprivation of parental rights.[39] The government also must comply with due process before involuntarily committing a person for mental health problems.[40] Due process limits the exercise of state judicial power over defendants who have insufficient contacts with the state.[41] Due process protects defendants from liability for violating overly "vague" laws that do not provide sufficient notice of their coverage.[42] All of these "procedural due process" doctrines protect persons from mistaken deprivations of rights or from deprivations of rights without adequate notice.

THE INCORPORATION DOCTRINE

Under the "incorporation" doctrine, the Supreme Court has applied most provisions of the Bill of Rights to the states through the Due Process Clause. This doctrine is premised on so-called substantive due process. The Court has held that certain rights are protected from any deprivation whatsoever, regardless of how much notice or how many procedural protections the state may provide.

The first eight amendments were originally understood to restrict the federal government, not the states.[43] In our view, the framers of the Fourteenth Amendment meant to protect the civil rights of black Americans against the states, and at least some of those rights overlapped with the rights enumerated in the first eight amendments. The questions are: Which provision of the Fourteenth Amendment was understood to do so, and how far was it understood to go? Many scholars contend that the Privileges or Immunities Clause was the most likely source of those rights.[44] (See Essay No. 140.) By prohibiting any state from "abridge[ing] the privileges or immunities of citizens of the United States," the clause seems to provide more absolute protection for substantive rights of speech and religious liberty and against unconstitutional forms of punishment. However, the *Slaughter-House Cases* (1873), the Supreme Court's first Fourteenth Amendment decision, read the Privileges or Immunities Clause narrowly to exclude the protections of the Bill of Rights.[45]

In the late nineteenth and early twentieth centuries, the Court repeatedly held that the Fourteenth Amendment does not apply those rights to the states,[46] but the Court gradually changed direction. In a series of cases over the course of the twentieth century, the Court held that the Due Process Clause "incorporates" almost all of the individual rights provisions of the first eight amendments against the states. The only exceptions at present are the Fifth Amendment right to a grand jury indictment in criminal cases; the Seventh Amendment right to jury trial in civil cases; and the Third Amendment right against the quartering of troops, which the Court has never interpreted.

One reason the doctrine developed in fits and starts is that the justices have never agreed either on its rationale or on how far it goes. Some justices have written that the clause incorporates only those rights that are "implicit in the concept of ordered liberty."[47] Others have concluded that the Due Process Clause incorporates *all* of the individual rights enumerated in the first eight amendments.[48] The idea of incorporation through the Due Process Clause does not square with the original meaning of due process, yet the Supreme Court has shown little interest either in abandoning the doctrine or in relocating it under the Privileges or Immunities Clause.[49]

FUNDAMENTAL RIGHTS

The Supreme Court has recognized a second kind of substantive due process. Under the "fundamental rights" doctrine, the Court has announced certain unenumerated fundamental rights that cannot be violated regardless of how much process is provided. This doctrine allows judges to infer rights not necessarily grounded in law and render them impervious to government restraint even with due process.[50] These rights are known as unenumerated rights.

Cases from the 1870s rejected the contention that the Due Process Clause protects unenumerated rights,[51] but the Court changed course by the end of the nineteenth century. This approach was first prompted by Justice Joseph P. Bradley's dissent in the *Slaughter-House Cases*. Over time, the courts held that the Due Process Clause protects the liberty of contract. This right required states to show that laws burdening the sale of goods, services, and employment were "reasonable."[52] The paradigmatic decision was *Lochner v. New York* (1905), which declared unconstitutional a limit on the number of hours bakers could work.[53] During the so-called *Lochner* era, the Court invalidated a number of state economic regulations, primarily laws interfering with the rights of employers and employees to contract for labor.

After much political controversy, the New Deal Court largely abandoned the doctrine.[54] Today, challengers of a state economic regulation must show that it is a wholly unreasonable way to achieve any legitimate state interest.[55] Most contemporary jurists and scholars believe that the economic version of substantive due process was inconsistent with the original understanding of the clause.[56]

Two notable *Lochner*-era substantive due process cases have survived. *Pierce v. Society of Sisters* (1925) and *Meyer v. Nebraska* (1923) held that parents, children, and teachers have freedom from state interference in matters of primary and secondary education.[57] The modern Court has interpreted those cases as progenitors of First Amendment rights of religion, speech, and association.[58] The Court has also seen these cases as forerunners of a broader right of familial autonomy. *Griswold v. Connecticut* (1965) found a right to contraception.[59] *Loving v. Virginia* (1967) and *Obergefell v. Hodges* (2015) recognized a fundamental right to marry.[60] *Lawrence v. Texas* (2003) protected a right to engage in consensual, adult same-sex intimacy.[61]

The Rehnquist and Roberts Courts, however, have generally backed away from recognizing unenumerated rights of "substantive due process" that are not grounded in long-standing tradition. *Washington v. Glucksberg* (1997) rejected a right to physician-assisted suicide.[62] *Dobbs v. Jackson Women's Health Organization* (2022) overruled a right to abortion.[63] If the past is any indication, the future of substantive due process, or whatever other label the Court applies to unenumerated rights, will be unpredictable and politically contentious.

Cite as: Nathan S. Chapman & Michael W. McConnell, *The Due Process Clause, in* THE HERITAGE GUIDE TO THE CONSTITUTION 744 (Josh Blackman & John G. Malcolm eds., 3d ed. 2025).

Notes

1. Nathan S. Chapman & Michael W. McConnell, *Due Process as Separation of Powers*, 121 Yale L.J. 1672, 1682 (2012). **2.** *Id.* at 1683, 1692. **3.** *Id.* at 1705. **4.** James W. Ely, Jr., *The Oxymoron Reconsidered: Myth and Reality in the Origins of Substantive Due Process*, 16 Const. Comment. 315, 328 (1999). **5.** *Murray's Lessee v. Hoboken Land & Improvement Co.*, 59 U.S. (18 How.) 272 (1856). **6.** Chapman & McConnell, *supra* at 1729–30. **7.** 1 Blackstone 141. **8.** *Id.* at 129. **9.** John Locke, Second Treatise of Government ch. 1, § 4 (1689). **10.** *Id.* at 135–37. **11.** *Id.* at 138. **12.** Chapman & McConnell, *supra* at 1769. **13.** 60 U.S. (19 How.) 393 (1857). **14.** *Somerset v. Stewart*, (1772) 98 Eng. Rep. 499 (K.B.). **15.** 60 U.S. (19 How.) at 450. **16.** Cong. Globe, 39th Cong., 1st Sess. 1089 (1866). **17.** Cong. Globe, 42d Cong., 1st Sess. app. at 153 (1871); Thomas M. Cooley, A Treatise on the Constitutional Limitations Which Rest Upon the Legislative Power of the States of the American Union 175 (1868). **18.** 2 RA 69. **19.** Chapman & McConnell, *supra* at 1772. **20.** *In re Winship*, 397 U.S. 358, 278–82 (1970) (Black, J., dissenting); Max Crema & Lawrence B. Solum, *The Original Meaning of "Due Process of Law" in the Fifth Amendment*, 108 Va. L. Rev. 447 (2022). **21.** 59 U.S. (18 How.) 272 (1856). **22.** John Harrison, *Substantive Due Process and the Constitutional Text*, 83 Va. L. Rev. 493, 520–24 (1997). **23.** Chapman & McConnell, *supra* at 1718. **24.** Chester Antieau, The Intended Significance of the Fourteenth Amendment 351–55 (1997); Ely, *supra*; Ryan C. Williams, *The One and Only Substantive Due Process Clause*, 120 Yale L.J. 408, 411–12 (2010). **25.** Frederick Mark Geddicks, *An Originalist Defense of Substantive Due Process: Magna Carta, Higher-Law Constitutionalism, and the Fifth Amendment*, 58 Emory L.J. 585 (2009). **26.** Cong. Globe 39th Cong., 1st Sess. 1094 (1866). **27.** *Calder v. Bull*, 3 U.S. (3 Dall.) 386, 388–89 (1798) (Chase, J.). **28.** Stuart Banner, The Decline of Natural Law: How American Lawyers Once Used Natural Law and Why They Stopped (2021). **29.** Randy E. Barnett & Evan D. Bernick, *No Arbitrary Power: An Originalist Theory of the Due Process of Law*, 60 Wm. & Mary L. Rev. 1599, 1631–32 (2019). **30.** Jack M. Balkin, Living Originalism (2014). **31.** Chapman & McConnell, *supra* at 1778. **32.** 435 U.S. 247, 259 (1978). **33.** *Mullane v. Central Hanover Bank & Trust Co.*, 339 U.S. 306, 313 (1950). **34.** *Rivera v. Minnich*, 483 U.S. 574, 577–78 (1986). **35.** 424 U.S. 319 (1976). **36.** 542 U.S. 507, 535 (2004). **37.** *Goldberg v. Kelly*, 397 U.S. 254 (1970). **38.** *Glidden v. Harrington*, 189 U.S. 255 (1903); *Turpin v. Lemon*, 187 U.S. 51, 58 (1902). **39.** *Santosky v. Kramer*, 455 U.S. 745 (1982); *Lassiter v. Dep't of Soc. Servs.*, 452 U.S. 18 (1981). **40.** *Addington v. Texas*, 441 U.S. 418 (1979); *Parham v. J.R.*, 442 U.S. 584 (1979). **41.** *Int'l Shoe Co. v. Washington*, 326 U.S. 310 (1945). **42.** *FCC v. Fox Television Stations, Inc.*, 567 U.S. 239 (2012). **43.** *Barron v. Baltimore*, 32 U.S. (7 Pet.) 243 (1833). **44.** Akhil Reed Amar, *The Bill of Rights and the Fourteenth Amendment*, 101 Yale L.J. 1193 (1992); Randy E. Barnett & Evan D. Bernick, *The Privileges or Immunities Clause, Abridged: A Critique of Kurt Lash on the Fourteenth Amendment*, 95 Notre Dame L. Rev. 499 (2019); Michael Kent Curtis, *Resurrecting the Privileges or Immunities Clause and Revising the* Slaughter-House Cases *Without Exhuming* Lochner: *Individual Rights and the Fourteenth Amendment*, 38 B.C. L. Rev. 1 (1996); Kurt T. Lash, *The Enumerated-Rights Reading of the Privileges or Immunities Clause: A Response to Barnett and Bernick*, 95 Notre Dame L. Rev. 591 (2019). **45.** 83 U.S. 36 (1873). **46.** *Snyder v. Massachusetts*, 291 U.S. 97, 105 (1934). **47.** *Palko v. Connecticut*, 302 U.S. 319, 325 (1937). **48.** *Adamson v. California*, 332 U.S. 46, 71–72 (1947) (Black, J., dissenting). **49.** *McDonald v. City of Chicago*, 561 U.S. 742 (2010); *id.* (Thomas, J., concurring). **50.** *Lawrence v. Texas*, 539 U.S. 558 (2003). **51.** *Davidson v. New Orleans*, 96 U.S. 97 (1878); *Munn v. Illinois*, 94 U.S. 113 (1876); *Slaughter-House Cases*, 83 U.S. (16 Wall.) 36 (1873). **52.** *Allgeyer v. Louisiana*, 165 U.S. 578 (1897). **53.** 198 U.S. 45 (1905). **54.** *W. Coast Hotel v. Parrish*, 300 U.S. 379 (1937). **55.** *Ferguson v. Skrupa*, 372 U.S. 726 (1963). **56.** David E. Bernstein, Rehabilitating Lochner: Defending Individual Rights Against Progressive Reform (2012). **57.** 268 U.S. 510 (1925); 262 U.S. 390 (1923). **58.** *Wisconsin v. Yoder*, 406 U.S. 205 (1972). **59.** 381 U.S. 479 (1965). **60.** 388 U.S. 1 (1967); 576 U.S. 644 (2015). **61.** 539 U.S. 558 (2003). **62.** 521 U.S. 702 (1997). **63.** 597 U.S. 215 (2022).

⌁

ESSAY NO. 196: THE EQUAL PROTECTION CLAUSE
AMEND. 14, § 1

No State shall . . . deny to any person within its jurisdiction the equal protection of the laws.

—Christopher R. Green

INTRODUCTION

During Reconstruction, freedmen and unionists in the South needed protection from private violence at the hands of the Ku Klux Klan. Against that background, it is natural to read the Equal Protection Clause as requiring states to give everyone in the state "protection of the laws": literal protection from violence and the right to seek redress for privately inflicted injuries through the courts. The Supreme Court, however, has interpreted "equal protection of the laws" as encompassing equality of treatment with respect to anything the government does or provides—education,[1] voting,[2] or the regulation of low-alcohol beer.[3] But other clauses in the Fourteenth Amendment, especially the Privileges or Immunities Clause, could also have been interpreted to secure such equality. (See Essay No. 140.) If the Court were to ask whether equality in these fields is a privilege of citizens rather than reading the Equal Protection Clause so awkwardly, it could use the Equal Protection Clause to cover an important constitutional right that it has denied: the right to physical protection from violence.[4]

HISTORICAL BACKGROUND

The concept of protection by the government has deep roots. In paragraph 40 of Magna Charta (1215), King John promised, "To no one will we deny, delay, or sell right or justice." Paragraph 40 does not say what "right or justice" entails—other provisions of law do that. It declares that the king's job is to give people their legal rights immediately and without a bribe. Legions of writers such as Edward Coke, Thomas Hobbes, and John Locke described government as the exchange of protection for citizens' allegiance. "Allegiance and protection are reciprocal" became a common maxim. Sir William Blackstone defined "the protection of the law" as the "method of recovering and asserting those rights, when wrongfully withheld or invaded."[5]

The Declaration of Independence asserted that a lack of protection is a lack of government. Paragraph 25 complains that King George III "has abdicated Government here, by declaring us out of his Protection and waging War against us."[6] State constitutions echoed the same theme. The New Jersey constitution of 1776 noted that "allegiance and protection are . . . reciprocal ties, each equally depending upon the other, and liable to be dissolved by the others being refused or withdrawn."[7] The North Carolina and Pennsylvania constitutions of 1776 and the Vermont constitution of 1777 included similar language.[8]

At the Constitutional Convention, there was no general discussion of protection from violence because the federal government was not given any general responsibility for the control of crime. However, Article II requires that the President "take Care that the Laws be faithfully executed" and Article IV requires that the United States protect states against (presumably large-scale) "domestic Violence." (See Essay Nos. 115 and 147.)

This understanding continued into the early Republic. In *Marbury v. Madison* (1803), Chief Justice John Marshall wrote that "[t]he very essence of civil liberty certainly consists in the right of every individual to claim the *protection* of the laws whenever he receives an injury."[9] Marshall stressed that "[o]ne of the first duties of government is to afford that *protection*."

The phrase "allegiance and protection are reciprocal" was repeated countless times in treatises, arguments, and judicial decisions in the decades before the Civil War.[10]

"Protection of the law" was explicitly distinguished from other rights in cases like *Roberts v. City of Boston* (1850), Charles Sumner's famous attempt to desegregate the Boston schools. The Massachusetts Supreme Judicial Court ruled that all people are "equally entitled to the paternal consideration and protection of the law," but this entitlement was explicitly distinguished from a general freedom from discrimination.[11]

ADOPTION OF THE EQUAL PROTECTION CLAUSE

In 1865, the Civil War concluded and President Abraham Lincoln was assassinated. Between April and December of that year, President Andrew Johnson's Reconstruction regimes governed the South. The following year, Congress passed the Civil Rights Act of 1866 over Johnson's veto.[12] This landmark statute addressed two problems. First, Congress was dealing with the "Black Codes." The southern states engaged in open racial discrimination against the right of freedmen to make contracts to work in occupations reserved for white citizens. Second, Congress was trying to prevent private violence by the Ku Klux Klan and its ilk. The law provided in part that the freedmen would be "citizens of the United States," and these citizens would have the right to "make and enforce contracts, to sue, be parties, and give evidence" as well as the right to own land. They would also have the "full and equal benefit of all laws and proceedings for the security of person and property."

A few weeks after the Civil Rights Act was passed, Representative John Bingham of Ohio proposed the language that became the second sentence of Section One of the Fourteenth Amendment.[13] This draft included what would become the Equal Protection Clause.[14] There were no significant discussions of the meaning of "protection of the laws" except as an aside. Senator Edgar Cowan of Pennsylvania noted that even a visiting traveler "has a right to the protection of the laws," which he illustrated as the right to the enforcement of laws against murder or assault.[15] The text of the Equal Protection Clause fits the maxim from *Marbury v. Madison* perfectly. To be "within a state's jurisdiction" (its "speaking of the law") is to be bound to show allegiance to the state and thus entitled to the protection of its laws.

ENFORCING THE FOURTEENTH AMENDMENT

After the Fourteenth Amendment's ratification in 1868, the Privileges or Immunities Clause was seen as a mandate for the government to treat people equally. For example, during congressional debates, this provision was invoked as the basis for black voting rights.[16] And in *Bradwell v. Illinois* (1873), advocates of gender equality pointed to the clause to support a woman's right to work as an attorney.[17]

In 1870, Congress readopted the Civil Rights Act of 1866. This statute granted non-citizens the right to make contracts but *not* the right to own real estate. In other words, the law overtly discriminated against non-citizens. The Equal Protection Clause, by its terms, covers all persons and not just citizens; it refers to any "person within its jurisdiction." If "equal protection of the laws" were a general ban on discrimination, this type of discrimination would make no sense. Congress itself withheld from non-citizens the right to own land, and there had long been racial discrimination in determining who might become a citizen. If the Equal Protection Clause is a general ban on discrimination, then the discrimination in the Civil Rights Act, if done by a state, would violate the Equal Protection Clause. (Of course, the Equal Protection Clause itself limits only state action, not action by the federal government, but it would be very odd for Congress to violate the very principle it was imposing on states.) In response to a question about whether the Civil Rights Act's reenactment gave non-citizens all the rights of citizens, Senator William Stewart said, "No; it gives all the protection of the laws. . . . [I]t has no reference to inheriting or holding real estate."[18] However, if the Equal Protection Clause is limited to "protection of the laws," Congress's actions make sense.[19]

During debates over what became the Ku Klux Act of 1871, Republican after Republican emphasized "protection" in the Equal Protection Clause.[20] Bingham identified the clause with paragraph 40 of Magna Charta. Section 3 of the act provided that if a "State shall either be unable to protect, or shall, from any cause, fail in or refuse protection of the people in such rights, such facts shall be deemed a denial by such State of the equal protection of the laws to which they are entitled under the Constitution of the United States."[21] Failure to protect against private violence from *any cause*, explicitly including the lack of ability, was the breach of a duty to supply equal protection of the laws.

JUDICIAL PRECEDENT

The U.S. Supreme Court soon rejected this settled congressional understanding. The *Slaughter-House Cases* (1873) rejected an equal-citizenship reading of the Privileges or Immunities Clause.[22] Thirteen years later, *Yick Wo v. Hopkins* (1886) used the Equal Protection Clause to fill the void left by *Slaughter-House*. *Yick Wo* rearranged the text of the clause: "[T]he equal protection of the laws is a pledge of the protection of equal laws."[23] This decision reassigned "equal" from modifying "protection" to modifying "laws."[24]

Since *Yick Wo*, the Court's antidiscrimination law has been rooted in the Equal Protection Clause, and this doctrine applies to non-citizens as well as citizens. *Yick Wo* declared unconstitutional discriminatory regulatory enforcement against Chinese nationals in San Francisco. *Strauder v. West Virginia* (1880) found unconstitutional a West Virginia law that excluded black people from juries.[25] *Gulf Railway v. Ellis* (1897) found that discrimination against railroad corporations was unconstitutional,[26] although *Plessy v. Ferguson* (1896) infamously upheld racial segregation in railroads.[27] Justice John Marshall Harlan made nods to equal citizenship in several majority opinions and solo dissents,[28] but the Court did not overrule *Slaughter-House*.

During the early part of the twentieth century, the Court provided strong protections for economic and other property rights. But in the wake of the New Deal, the Court eventually retreated from its defense of laissez-faire free-enterprise rights.[29] Rather, the Court limited itself to verifying the existence of a "rational basis" for a distinction in the law. However, laws that affected so-called "[d]iscrete and insular minorities," however, would continue to receive special solicitude and heightened review.[30] By the 1970s, the Court had put together a tripartite scheme:

- Laws that make racial, national, or citizenship-based classifications are reviewed under "strict scrutiny" and must be "narrowly tailored" to achieve a "compelling interest." These cases declared unconstitutional segregation, limits on interracial marriage, some forms of affirmative action, and citizen-only welfare benefits.[31] However, citizenship-based occupational limits for police or teachers are not subject to strict scrutiny.[32] Neither are occupational tests or zoning codes that merely produce disparate *impact* on different racial groups.[33]

- Laws that make sex classifications are reviewed with "intermediate scrutiny" and must be "substantially related" to achieving an "important interest." These cases require the drinking age to be the same for men as for women and permit men to attend the Mississippi University for Women and women to attend the Virginia Military Institute.[34] But the Court has upheld sex distinctions in immigration law, draft registration, statutory rape cases, and perhaps sex segregation in schools.[35] Disparate impacts created by a veteran's preference or pregnancy discrimination are not reviewed under heightened scrutiny.[36]

- Laws that make age, disability, wealth, or other classifications must only be "rationally related" to achieving a "legitimate interest."[37] The Court has declared unconstitutional welfare rules that are hostile to "hippies," zoning restriction that are hostile to those with mental disabilities, and a state-level ban on local anti-discrimination laws for gays and lesbians. But the Court has upheld age limits on types of police work and property tax-based education funding.[38]

Before the New Deal, the Court asked *one* difficult question: whether a particular distinction is arbitrary or not. The new system asks at least *seven* difficult questions: how much scrutiny a particular distinction gets and what counts as "narrowly tailored," "compelling," "substantial," "important," "rational," and "legitimate." Several justices have complained that it is a mistake to treat all classifications of a particular type as if they imposed the same discriminatory costs and therefore need exactly the same sort of justification.[39]

The Equal Protection Clause restricts actions by the states, not actions by the federal government. However, the Court has used the Fifth Amendment Due Process Clause to declare unconstitutional federal school segregation and affirmative action policies.[40] By contrast, the Court has upheld citizenship-based classifications in federal immigration law and classifications based on tribal status.[41] Justice Clarence Thomas has argued that this type of analysis is more fitting under the Fourteenth Amendment's Citizenship Clause, agreeing with a protection-based understanding of "protection of the laws."[42]

THE RIGHT OF PROTECTION

In two cases—*DeShaney v. Winnebago County Social Services* (1989) and *Castle Rock v. Gonzales* (2005)—the Rehnquist Court held that the state does not "deprive" people of life, liberty, or property by failing to protect them.[43] The Court mentioned the Equal Protection Clause only in the context of its general scheme of equality and rejected the argument that the clause provides a literal entitlement to "protection of the laws." These holdings have been criticized by originalist scholars.[44] They contend that the "equal protection of the laws" includes what the Civil Rights Act of 1866 describes as the "full and equal benefit of all laws and proceedings for the security of person and property."

OPEN QUESTIONS

- What would be the implications of a state having a duty to protect against private violence? If courts are ill-equipped to decide police budgeting issues, what role would Congress have under Section 5 in making this obligation more precise?
- Could Congress prohibit abortion if the Equal Protection Clause imposes a duty to protect fetuses?
- Can the tiers of scrutiny survive under an equal-citizenship approach? In 1866, Republicans repeatedly said voting was not a right of citizens—a civil right—because women and children were citizens but not voters.[45] Only the Fifteenth Amendment gave freedmen the vote. Racial, sex, and age distinctions get three different levels of scrutiny by the Court despite unified treatment in 1866.
- What would disparate-impact analysis look like under an equal-citizenship approach? One way to reconfigure the law would be to require states to follow the law of trusts, which requires trustees to give "fair and impartial attention" to the needs of all beneficiaries.[46] It would not be enough for the state merely to refrain from purposefully targeting particular groups.
- What would an equal-citizenship approach mean for affirmative action? Senator Lyman Trumbull defended the Civil Rights Act as giving a remedy to those who needed a remedy, which the white majority did not.[47] Does antidiscrimination law apply when a majority discriminates against itself? Equal-citizenship provisions in early state constitutions applied to benefits given even to a single citizen and therefore were not limited to discrimination *against* minorities but would also apply to special benefits given *to* minorities.[48]

Cite as: Christopher R. Green, *The Equal Protection Clause, in* THE HERITAGE GUIDE TO THE CONSTITUTION 750 (Josh Blackman & John G. Malcolm eds., 3d ed. 2025).

Notes

1. *Brown v. Bd. of Educ.*, 347 U.S. 483 (1954); *Grutter v. Bollinger*, 539 U.S. 306 (2003); *Students for Fair Admissions v. President & Fellows of Harvard Coll.*, 600 U.S. 181 (2023). **2.** *Nixon v. Herndon*, 273 U.S. 536 (1927); *Reynolds v. Sims*, 377 U.S. 533 (1964). **3.** *Craig v. Boren*, 429 U.S. 190 (1976). **4.** *DeShaney v. Winnebago Cnty. Soc. Servs.*, 489 U.S. 189 (1989); *Castle Rock v. Gonzales*, 545 U.S. 748 (2005). **5.** 1 Blackstone 55–56. **6.** Declaration of Independence, ¶ 25. **7.** N.J. Const. of 1776, pmbl. **8.** P.A. Const. of 1776, pmbl; N.C. Const. of 1776, pmbl; Vt. Const. of 1777, pmbl. **9.** 5 U.S. (1 Cranch) 137, 163 (1803) (emphasis added). **10.** Christopher R. Green, *The Original Sense of the (Equal) Protection Clause: Pre-Enactment History*, 19 Geo. Mason U. Civ. Rts. L.J. 1, 35–38 (2008). **11.** *Roberts v. City of Boston*, 59 Mass. 198, 206 (1850). **12.** 14 Stat. 27 (April 9, 1866). **13.** Benjamin B. Kendrick, Journal of the Joint Committee of Fifteen on Reconstruction 87 (1914). **14.** *Id.* **15.** Cong. Globe, 39th Cong. 1st Sess. 2890 (1866). **16.** Cong. Globe, 40th Cong. 3rd Sess. 555–61 (1869). **17.** 83 U.S. 130, 136 (1873). **18.** Cong. Globe, 41st Cong. 2d Sess. 1536 (1870). **19.** Christopher R. Green, *Tribes, Nations, States: Our Three Commerce Powers*, 127 Penn. St. L. Rev. 643, 685–87 (2023). **20.** Christopher R. Green, *The Original Sense of the (Equal) Protection Clause: Subsequent Interpretation and Application*, 19 Geo. Mason U. Civ. Rts. L.J. 219, 224–54 (2009). **21.** 17 Stat. 13, 14 (April 20, 1871). **22.** 83 U.S. 36, 101 (1873). **23.** 118 U.S. 356, 369 (1886). **24.** *United States v. Vaello-Madero*, 596 U.S. 159, 178 n.4 (2022) (Thomas, J., concurring); Green, *Pre-Enactment History*, *supra*; Green, *Subsequent Interpretation and Application*, *supra*. **25.** 100 U.S. 303 (1880). **26.** 165 U.S. 150 (1897). **27.** *Plessy v. Ferguson*, 163 U.S. 537 (1896). **28.** *Neal v. Delaware*, 103 U.S. 370, 386 (1881); *Bush v. Kentucky*, 107 U.S. 110, 118 (1883); *Civil Rights Cases*, 109 U.S. 3, 48 (1883) (Harlan, J., dissenting); *Plessy*, 163 U.S. at 555 (Harlan, J., dissenting). **29.** *W. Coast Hotel v. Parrish*, 300 U.S. 379 (1937). **30.** *United States v. Carolene Prods.*, 304 U.S. 144, 152 n.4 (1938). **31.** *Brown v. Bd. of Educ.*, 347 U.S. 483 (1954); *Loving v. Virginia*, 388 U.S. 1 (1967); *Richmond v. Croson Co.*, 488 U.S. 469 (1989); *Gratz v. Bollinger*, 539 U.S. 244 (2003); *Students for Fair Admissions v. President & Fellows of Harvard Coll.*, 600 U.S. 181 (2023); *Graham v. Richardson*, 403 U.S. 365 (1971). **32.** *Foley v. Connelie*, 435 U.S. 291 (1978); *Ambach v. Norwick*, 441 U.S. 68 (1979). **33.** *Washington v. Davis*, 426 U.S. 229 (1976); *Arlington Heights v. Metro Housing*, 429 U.S. 252 (1977). **34.** *United States v. Virginia*, 518 U.S. 515 (1996); *MUW v. Hogan*, 458 U.S. 718 (1982); *Craig v. Boren*, 429 U.S. 190 (1976). **35.** *Vorchheimer v. Philadelphia*, 430 U.S. 703 (1977); *MUW v. Hogan*, 458 U.S. 718, 720 n.1 (1982); *United States v. Virginia*, 518 U.S. 515, 534 n.7 (1996); *Nguyen v. INS*, 533 U.S. 53 (2001); *Rostker v. Goldberg*, 453 U.S. 57 (1981); *Michael M. v. Super. Ct.*, 450 U.S. 464 (1981). **36.** *Pers. Admin'r v. Feeney*, 442 U.S. 256 (1979); *Geduldig v. Aiello*, 417 U.S. 484, 496 n.20 (1974). **37.** *San Antonio v. Rodriguez*, 411 U.S. 1 (1973); *Cleburne v. Cleburne Living Ctr.*, 473 U.S. 432, 460 (1985) (Marshall, Brennan, and Blackmun, JJ., dissenting); *id.* at 451 (Stevens, J., and Burger, C.J., concurring); *United States v. Windsor*, 570 U.S. 744, 793 (2013) (Scalia, J., dissenting); *Bd. of Retirement v. Murgia*, 427 U.S. 307 (1976), *United States v. Skrmetti*, 145 S.Ct. 1816, 1829 (2025). **38.** *Murgia*, 427 U.S. 307; *Rodriguez*, 411 U.S. 1. **39.** *Cleburne*, 473 U.S. at 452 (Stevens, J., Burger, C.J.); *id.* at 460 (Marshall, Brennan, Blackmun, J.J.); *Windsor*, 570 U.S. at 793 (Scalia, J.). **40.** *Bolling v. Sharpe*, 347 U.S. 497 (1954); *Adarand Constructors v. Peña*, 515 U.S. 200 (1995). **41.** *Matthews v. Diaz*, 426 U.S. 67 (1976); *Morton v. Mancari*, 417 U.S. 535 (1974). **42.** *Vaello-Madero*, 596 U.S. at 178 n.4 (Thomas, J., concurring). **43.** *DeShaney*, 489 U.S. at 197 n.3 (1989); *Castle Rock v. Gonzales*, 545 U.S. 748 (2005). **44.** Green, *Subsequent Interpretation and Application*, *supra* at 254; Evan D. Bernick, *Antisubjugation and the Equal Protection of the Laws*, 110 Geo. L. J. 1, 36 (2021); Randy E. Barnett & Evan D. Bernick, *The Original Meaning of the Fourteenth Amendment: Its Letter and Spirit* 319–51 (2021); Pamela Brandwein, Rethinking the Judicial Settlement of Reconstruction 28–86 (2011). **45.** Christopher R. Green, *Incorporation, Total Incorporation, and Nothing but Incorporation?*, 24 Wm. & Mary Bill Rts. J. 93, 122–24 (2015). **46.** Thomas Lewin, *A Practical Treatise on the Law of Trusts and Trustees* 414 (3d ed. 1857); Christopher R. Green, *Citizenship and Solicitude: How to Overrule* Employment Division v. Smith *and* Washington v. Davis, 47 Harv. J.L. & Pub. Pol'y 465 (2024). **47.** Cong. Globe, 39th Cong., 1st Sess. 1758 (1866). **48.** Christopher R. Green, Equal Citizenship, Civil Rights, and the Constitution: The Original Sense of the Privileges or Immunities Clause 137–38 (2015).

~

ESSAY NO. 197: THE APPORTIONMENT OF REPRESENTATIVES CLAUSE
AMEND. 14, § 2

Representatives shall be apportioned among the several States according to their respective numbers, counting the whole number of persons in each State, excluding Indians not taxed. But when the right to vote at any election for the choice of electors for President and Vice-President of the United States, Representatives in Congress, the Executive and Judicial officers of a State, or the members of the Legislature thereof, is denied to any of the male inhabitants of such State, being twenty-one years of age, and citizens of the United States, or in any way abridged, except for participation in rebellion, or other crime, the basis of representation therein shall be reduced in the proportion which the number of such male citizens shall bear to the whole number of male citizens twenty-one years of age in such State.

—Gerard N. Magliocca

INTRODUCTION

Section Two of the Fourteenth Amendment was written to address representation and voting issues following the abolition of slavery. In 1866, because there was insufficient political support for the direct extension of suffrage to the freedmen, the Joint Committee on Reconstruction proposed a constitutional amendment to penalize states that deny or abridge the voting rights of too many male adult citizens. These states would suffer a proportionate representation penalty in the House of Representatives and, by extension, in the Electoral College. But states could still disenfranchise those guilty of participation in rebellion or other crime. This penalty provision proved unworkable and was never enforced. Today, Section Two is the constitutional basis for state laws that disenfranchise convicted felons.[1]

DRAFTING SECTION 2

Under Article I, Section 2, representation in the House of Representatives was apportioned according to the free population of the states (excluding Indians not taxed) and "three-fifths of all other Persons." (See Essay No. 9.) The Thirteenth Amendment, which abolished slavery, eliminated the purpose of the Three-Fifths Clause. (See Essay No. 191.) As a consequence, formerly Confederate states would get more representatives in the House because their freed slaves would now be fully counted, and those states did not intend to let the freedmen vote.

Senator Jacob Howard of Michigan addressed this problem in his speech introducing the Joint Committee's proposed Fourteenth Amendment: "Shall the recently slaveholding States, while they exclude from the ballot the whole of their black population, be entitled to include the whole of that population in the basis of their representation?" And would those states "obtain an advantage [in representation] which they did not possess before the rebellion and emancipation?"[2] Republicans in Congress agreed that this unjust result could not stand, but nevertheless struggled to craft an effective remedy that did not involve some guarantee of black voting rights. Representative John Bingham of Ohio, for example, "support[ed] the proposed amendment" because he "believe[d] it essential and attainable" but did "not dare to say that it could not be improved."[3]

Both the Joint Committee on Reconstruction and Congress considered multiple formulations of what became the penalty provision. One proposal specified that when the "elective franchise shall be denied or abridged in any State on account of race or color, all persons of such race or color shall be excluded from the basis of representation."[4] In other words, rather than being counted as three-fifths of a person, freedmen would not be counted at all for purposes of representation. The Senate rejected this language.

At the time, all states excluded black women from voting, and there was no groundswell for women's suffrage.[5] The Joint Committee then revised its proposal to limit the category of pre-sumptive voters to "male[s]."[6] This was the first and only time that the Constitution used that word. The new proposal further limited the rep-resentation baseline to male adult citizens.[7] Male aliens and minors would not be included. At the time, some states allowed certain aliens to vote, but under this proposal, these states would gain no representation advantage from having that broader suffrage rule.[8] This second formula-tion of Section 2 referred simply to restrictions on "the elective franchise." Later, the Senate replaced this phrase with "the right to vote" and then specified the federal and state elections that were covered.[9]

Four other aspects of the final text merit comment. First, there was a reference to elec-tions for presidential and vice-presidential elec-tors. By 1868, almost all states used that method rather than direct legislative appointment to choose their electors.[10] Were state legislatures to select their electors, their citizens would not be able to cast a vote and the representation penalty would apply. Second, elections for state judicial officers were included. After the Civil War, the election of state judges was a widespread, though not universal, practice.[11]

Third, Section 2 made exceptions for par-ticipation in rebellion or other crimes. Some states, including South Carolina, disenfran-chised some former Confederates without fear of suffering a penalty.[12] Additionally, twenty-nine states permitted or required felon disen-franchisement.[13] Thus, Section 2 gave states an incentive to extend the ballot to loyal black men and withdraw it from disloyal white men with-out requiring either action.

Fourth, the proposal did not specify how the penalty would be enforced. Senator Jacob Howard of Michigan pinpointed this issue in 1866. He said Section 2 gave the census tak-ers "a rule which is so uncertain, so difficult of practical application, as not only greatly to increase the expenses of ascertaining the basis of representation by Congress in procuring the necessary information, but in many cases the

returns must be so inaccurate and unreliable as to be next to worthless."[14] Howard's prediction proved accurate.

IMPLEMENTING SECTION 2

The 1870 Census attempted to gather the infor-mation that Section 2 demanded.[15] Every man otherwise eligible to vote was asked whether his right to vote was denied or abridged except for participation in rebellion or other crime. The Secretary of the Interior was tasked with conducting the census but dismissed the self-reported data as unreliable because it could not be independently verified.[16] There also was no standard for what "denial or abridged" meant for voting rights. Finally, the Census did not ask which elections someone was unable to vote in or whether they were held before or after 1868.

At the time, Rhode Island imposed a $131 real property ownership requirement to vote. As a result, the state should have lost a seat in the 1872 reapportionment,[17] but Congress declined to enforce the penalty against Rhode Island. Members had doubts about the data, were uncertain about which state should gain the seat that Rhode Island would lose, and perhaps felt that enforcing Section 2 against a northern state would be unpopular.

No future census attempted to gather infor-mation pertaining to Section 2. The Fifteenth Amendment, ratified in 1870, provided a less cumbersome method for addressing racial dis-crimination in voting, but that provision went unenforced for nearly a century. Even today, the administrative obstacles to enforcing the pen-alty provision through the Census are sizeable.

MODERN RELEVANCE OF SECTION 2

In the modern era, Congress made few seri-ous efforts to revive Section 2. One of the ten demands made as part of Martin Luther King Jr.'s 1963 March on Washington for Jobs and Freedom was "[e]nforcement of the Fourteenth Amendment—reducing Congressional rep-resentation of states where citizens are disfranchised."[18] Congress took no action.

Section 2 does provide support for state stat-utes that disenfranchise ex-felons. *Richardson v. Ramirez* (1974) held that such a statute did not violate the Equal Protection Clause.[19] The U.S. Supreme Court relied in part on the fact that Section 2 accepted disenfranchisement for participation in "rebellion or other crime." The lower courts have read *Ramirez* to hold that Section 2 "expressly allows States to disenfranchise criminals without having their representation reduced in Congress."[20] Today, nearly all states impose some form of felon disenfranchisement,[21] but there is no federal disenfranchisement statute.

OPEN QUESTIONS

- What does it mean for the "right to vote" to be "denied" or "abridged in any way"?[22]

Cite as: Gerard N. Magliocca, *The Apportionment of Representatives Clause, in* THE HERITAGE GUIDE TO THE CONSTITUTION 755 (Josh Blackman & John G. Malcolm eds., 3d ed. 2025).

Notes

1. Gerard N. Magliocca, *Our Unconstitutional Reapportionment Process*, 86 Geo. Wash. L. Rev. 774 (2018). **2.** Cong. Globe, 39th Cong., 1st Sess. 2766 (1866). **3.** *Id.* at 431. **4.** The Journal of the Joint Committee of Fifteen on Reconstruction 53 (Benjamin B. Kendrick ed., 1914). **5.** Earl M. Maltz, *The Forgotten Provision of the Fourteenth Amendment: Section 2 and the Evolution of American Democracy*, 76 La. L. Rev. 166–68 (2015). **6.** Joint Committee Journal, *supra* at 44. **7.** *Id.* **8.** Minn. Const. of 1857, art. VII; Or. Const. of 1857, art. II, § 2. **9.** Maltz, *supra* at 176. **10.** *McPherson v. Blacker*, 146 U.S. 1, 32 (1892). **11.** *Republican Party of Minn. v. White*, 536 U.S. 765, 785 (2002). **12.** S.C. Const. of 1868, art. VIII. **13.** *Richardson v. Ramirez*, 418 U.S. 24, 48 & n.14 (1974). **14.** Cong. Globe, 39th Cong., 1st Sess. 3039 (1866). **15.** H.R. Rep. No. 41-3 (1870). **16.** Cong. Globe, 42nd Cong., 2d Sess. 66 (1871). **17.** *Id.* at 82. **18.** March on Washington for Jobs and Freedom: Lincoln Memorial Program 3 (Aug. 28, 1963), https://perma.cc/G3QQ-SU7D. **19.** 418 U.S. 24 (1974) **20.** *Jones v. Governor of Fla.*, 975 F.3d 1016, 1029 (11th Cir. 2020) (Pryor, C.J.). **21.** *Id.* **22.** Franita Tolson, *What is Abridgment?: A Critique of Two Section Twos*, 67 Ala. L. Rev. 433 (2016).

ESSAY NO. 198: THE INSURRECTION OR REBELLION CLAUSE
AMEND. 14, § 3

No person shall be a Senator or Representative in Congress, or elector of President and Vice-President, or hold any office, civil or military, under the United States, or under any state, who, having previously taken an oath, as a member of Congress, or as an officer of the United States, or as a member of any State legislature, or as an executive or judicial officer of any state, to support the Constitution of the United States, shall have engaged in insurrection or rebellion against the same, or given aid or comfort to the enemies thereof. But Congress may by a vote of two-thirds of each House, remove such disability.

—Gerard N. Magliocca

INTRODUCTION

Section Three of the Fourteenth Amendment encapsulated President Abraham Lincoln's call for "malice toward none with charity for all" following the Civil War. Instead of imposing criminal punishments on former Confederate officials, it provided that only some military and civilian officers who served the Confederacy were disqualified from returning to federal or state offices unless a supermajority of Congress waived their disqualification. Section Three was enforced for only a brief time and, with a single exception during World War I, lay dormant until the violence at the Capitol on January 6, 2021.

DRAFTING OF SECTION 3

When the Civil War began, many sitting members of Congress left their positions and joined the rebel government. In December 1865, when the Thirty-Ninth Congress convened, the ex-Confederate states sent many of those former members back to Congress.[1] Republicans opposed seating men who had taken an oath to support the Constitution but supported the Confederacy. The Joint Committee on Reconstruction concluded that these individuals "made no secret of their hostility to the government and the people of the United States" and recommended "the exclusion from positions of public trust of, at least, a portion of those whose crimes have proved them to be enemies of the Union, and unworthy of public confidence."[2]

Later, the Joint Committee proposed what would become the Fourteenth Amendment. But that initial proposal did not include an exclusion from officeholding.[3] Rather, the Senate substituted what became Section Three in an amendment written by Senator Jacob Howard of Michigan.[4]

Section Three did not bar all former Confederates from holding all offices. A person could be subject to disqualification only if he had "previously taken an oath, as a member of Congress, or as an officer of the United States, or as a member of any State legislature, or as an executive or judicial officer of any state, to support the Constitution of the United States." If such a person had "engaged in insurrection or rebellion," he would be disqualified from "be[ing] a Senator or Representative in Congress, or elector of President and Vice-President, or hold[ing] any office, civil or military, under the United States, or under any state." Representative John Bingham of Ohio described the provision as "an act of forgiveness on the part of the American people, without a parallel . . . in the history of nations."[5] Section 3 also granted Congress the power to waive a disqualification with a two-thirds vote of each house of Congress.

IMPLEMENTING SECTION 3
Section Three broke with the original Constitution by imposing the first federal constitutional limit on the ability of individuals to hold a state office. In 1868, prior to ratification of Section 3, Congress readmitted five of the ex-Confederate states to the Union on condition that they deem ineligible from holding certain state offices those individuals who would be disqualified by Section 3.[6] The Florida Constitution barred people who would be disqualified by Section 3 from holding state offices.[7]

The Civil Rights Act of 1870, also known as the First Ku Klux Klan Act, established the first general enforcement statute for Section Three.[8] Section 14 directed federal prosecutors to remove from office certain individuals who were disqualified by Section Three, and Section 15 made it a criminal misdemeanor for a person disqualified by Section 3 to hold a covered office.[9] In 1870, the Senate enforced Section 3 to refuse to seat Zebulon Vance, a member-elect who had served as governor of North Carolina under the Confederacy.[10] North Carolina enforced a state statute that incorporated Section 3 to exclude a disqualified person from a state position.[11]

By 1872, public opinion supported granting amnesty to most former Confederates. Over the preceding years, Congress had waived the disqualification provision for individual men through private bills,[12] but this approach was viewed as inconsistent and inadequate. Moreover, white northerners increasingly felt that disqualification was not helping and might be hurting Reconstruction policy. Accordingly, President Ulysses S. Grant called on Congress to grant a general amnesty.[13] Congress responded with the Amnesty Act of 1872. This statute granted a Section 3 waiver for most of the people disqualified by Section 3.[14] In 1898, Congress conferred a waiver on all remaining living ex-Confederates who were subject to Section 3.[15]

During the twentieth century, only one person, avowed socialist Victor L. Berger, was purportedly excluded from office due to Section 3, although the grounds are not entirely clear.[16] Berger was later re-elected to Congress and permitted to take his seat in the House of Representatives.

SECTION 3 AFTER JANUARY 6, 2021
In the wake of January 6, 2021, the House adopted articles of impeachment charging President Donald J. Trump with "incitement of insurrection." Trump was not convicted of those charges. Federal prosecutors did not charge anyone involved with the events of January 6 with insurrection, but there were many efforts to disqualify people from holding certain offices using Section Three.

New Mexico County Commissioner Couy Griffin was at the Capitol on January 6 and was later convicted of trespassing on the Capitol grounds.[17] In 2022, a New Mexico trial court applied Section 3 to remove Griffin from office. His appeal was dismissed on other grounds, and the Supreme Court denied review.[18]

In 2023, litigants in several states sought to disqualify Donald Trump from the presidential ballot. This litigation presented four primary questions on which judges and scholars disagreed: (1) Was Donald Trump's presidential oath an oath to support the Constitution as an "Officer of the United States"? (2) Did Donald Trump engage in "insurrection"? (3) Is the presidency an "Office . . . under the United States" that a disqualified person could not hold? (4)

Could a state enforce Section 3 to remove Trump from the ballot?[19]

A trial court in Colorado answered "yes" to the second and fourth questions but "no" to the first and third. The Colorado Supreme Court later answered each of these questions in the affirmative and removed Trump from the presidential ballot. (Your author served as an expert witness on behalf of the plaintiffs in the Colorado litigation.) However, the U.S. Supreme Court unanimously reversed on the fourth question. *Trump v. Anderson* (2024) held that "States have no power under the Constitution to enforce Section 3 with respect to federal offices, especially the Presidency."[20]

OPEN QUESTIONS

- Is the President an "Officer of the United States" for purposes of Section 3? Is the Presidency an "Office . . . under the United States" for purposes of Section 3?
- What is the original public meaning of "engaged in insurrection or rebellion"?
- Can Section 3 be used to remove a person from the ballot, or can it be used only to remove a person who is currently holding that position?
- Can a joint session of Congress enforce Section 3 when counting electoral votes pursuant to the Twelfth Amendment?

Cite as: Gerard N. Magliocca, *The Insurrection or Rebellion Clause, in* THE HERITAGE GUIDE TO THE CONSTITUTION 757 (Josh Blackman & John G. Malcolm eds., 3d ed. 2025).

Notes

1. Gerard N. Magliocca, *Amnesty and Section Three of the Fourteenth Amendment*, 36 Const. Comment. 87, 91 (2021). **2.** Report of the Joint Committee on Reconstruction, 39th Cong., at x, xviii (1866). **3.** Benjamin B. Kendrick, The Journal of the Joint Committee of Fifteen on Reconstruction 115–116 (1914). **4.** Cong. Globe, 39th Cong., 1st Sess. 2897 (1866). **5.** *The Constitutional Amendment: Discussed by Its Author*, The Cincinnati Commercial (Aug. 27, 1866), at 1. **6.** Act of June 25, 1868, ch. 70, § 3, 15 Stat. 73–74. **7.** Fla. Const. of 1868, art. XVI, § 1. **8.** First Ku Klux Klan Act, §§ 14–15, ch. 114, 16 Stat. 140 (1870). **9.** *United States v. Powell*, 27 F.Cas. 605 (C.C.D. N.C. 1871). **10.** James G. Blaine, Twenty Years of Congress: From Lincoln to Garfield 531 n.1 (1886). **11.** *Worthy v. Barrett*, 63 N.C. 99 (1869). **12.** An Act to relieve certain Persons therein from the legal and political disabilities imposed by the fourteenth amendment of the Constitution of the United States, and for other Purposes, ch. 1, 16 Stat. 607–613 (1869). **13.** Ulysses S. Grant, Third Annual Message (Dec. 4, 1871), *in* 9 A Compilation of the Messages and Papers of the Presidents (James D. Richardson ed. 1897). **14.** Act of May 22, 1872, ch. 193, 17 Stat. 142. **15.** Act of June 6, 1898, ch. 389, 30 Stat. 432. **16.** Note, *The Power of a House of Congress to Judge the Qualifications of Its Members*, 81 Harv. L. Rev. 673, 681 (1968). **17.** *New Mexico ex rel. White v. Griffin*, No. D-101-cv-2202-00473, 2022 WL 4295619 (N.M. 1st Jud. Dist. 2022), *appeal dismissed*, No. S-1-SC-39571. **18.** *Griffin v. New Mexico*, 144 S.Ct. 1056 (2024). **19.** Josh Blackman & Seth Barrett Tillman, *Sweeping and Forcing the President into Section 3*, 28 Tex. Rev. L. & Pol. 350 (2024); Kurt T. Lash, *The Meaning and Ambiguity of Section Three of the Fourteenth Amendment*, 47 Harv. J.L. & Pub. Pol'y 309 (2024); William Baude & Michael Stokes Paulsen, *The Sweep and Force of Section Three*, 172 U. Pa. L. Rev. 605 (2024); Seth Barrett Tillman & Josh Blackman, *Is the President an 'Officer of the United States' for Purposes of Section 3 of the Fourteenth Amendment?*, 15 N.Y.U. J.L. & Liberty 1 (2021); Myles Lynch, *Disloyalty & Disqualification: Reconstructing Section 3 of the Fourteenth Amendment*, 30 Wm. & Mary Bill Rts. J. 153, 206 (2021). **20.** *Trump v. Anderson*, 601 U.S. 100, 110 (2024).

~

ESSAY NO. 199: THE PUBLIC DEBT CLAUSE
AMEND. 14, § 4

The validity of the public debt of the United States, authorized by law, including debts incurred for payment of pensions and bounties for services in suppressing insurrection or rebellion, shall not be questioned. But neither the United States nor any State shall assume or pay any debt or obligation incurred in aid of insurrection or rebellion against the United States, or any claim for the loss or emancipation of any slave; but all such debts, obligations and claims shall be held illegal and void.

—Gerard N. Magliocca

INTRODUCTION

Section Four of the Fourteenth Amendment was written to address economic issues that arose following the Civil War. The Union incurred an enormous debt in order to wage the war successfully, and the Confederacy incurred an enormous debt while waging war against the Union unsuccessfully. Republicans in Congress were concerned that the former Confederate states would refuse to pay their fair share of this debt upon readmission. Additionally, the abolition of slavery raised the question of whether former slave owners would receive compensation for the loss of their former property. Section Four settled all of these issues. It has been litigated only once but could still be relevant to contemporary fiscal measures that impact the national debt.

ADOPTION OF SECTION FOUR

In May 1866, the Joint Committee on Reconstruction proposed a version of what would become Section Four. This provision, however, barred only the repayment of Confederate debt and the compensation of former slave owners.[1] In the Senate, this proposal was amended to add a guarantee of the Union's war debt.[2] Senator Benjamin Wade of Ohio explained that this amendment would prevent "open and hostile rebels" from blocking debt payments when they returned to Congress.[3]

Section Four addressed three primary questions. First, it settled the status of the federal debt incurred to defeat the Confederacy and of the pensions promised to wounded Union soldiers and to the widows and orphans of the dead. Section Four made clear that "[t]he validity of the public debt . . . shall not be questioned" and that this included "debts incurred for payment of pensions and bounties for services in suppressing insurrection or rebellion." This guarantee would prevent the Civil War from being refought in the budget process. Representative John Bingham of Ohio explained that Section Four required the ex-rebel states to "pledge themselves, as evidence of their returning loyalty" to "contribute their reasonable proportion to the discharge of this sacred debt, contracted in the suppression of the rebellion and in support of the maimed heroes of the Union."[4]

Section Four settled a second outstanding issue. It was clear that Union debt would not be questioned, but what about Confederate debt? There were calls in the South for the southern states to pay Confederate bondholders something. In 1866, Robert E. Lee testified before the Joint Committee on Reconstruction that Virginia would do so if it could.[5] The Joint Committee rejected this possibility, and Section Four ultimately declared Confederate debt "illegal and void." Neither Congress nor the states were permitted to "assume or pay any debt or obligation incurred in aid of insurrection or rebellion against the United States." Senator Jacob Howard of Michigan addressed this point in his speech introducing the Fourteenth Amendment. He denounced the "debt contracted in the prosecution of the most wicked war with which the earth was ever cursed" and said that the issue of repaying those securities should not be left to "political squabbling and party wrangling" in the Capitol or in the state capitals of the former Confederacy.[6]

Finally, Section Four resolved an unintended

consequence of the freedom of enslaved people under the Emancipation Proclamation and the Thirteenth Amendment. The Fifth Amendment requires the government to pay "just compensation" for the taking of "private property." (See Essay No. 173.) Since slaves were considered a form of property, it was widely understood that any government emancipation of slaves would be a taking that required the payment of just compensation. For example, when Congress abolished slavery in the District of Columbia in 1862, the former slave owners were compensated.[7] Following the Civil War, there were estimates that the compensation required for all emancipated slaves could exceed $1 billion,[8] which would be more than $20 trillion in present value. In any event, Congress viewed such payments as an immoral reward for slave owners. Section Four made clear that no such compensation was permitted by the United States or by the states. This rule applied even in border states such as Kentucky and Maryland that retained slavery while remaining loyal to the Union.

JUDICIAL PRECEDENT

The U.S. Supreme Court interpreted Section Four for the first and only time during the New Deal. Prior to 1933, Treasury bonds contained a standard clause stating that the bondholder was entitled to payment in dollars that were fixed by the gold standard at the time the bond was issued. These provisions were known as "gold clauses." In 1933, the United States significantly devalued the dollar with respect to gold. Congress invalidated these "gold clauses" and based debt payments on the new monetary standard. The bondholders claimed that they were not receiving what was promised. They argued in court that "[t]he purpose of the fourth section of the Fourteenth Amendment was definitely to prevent any attempt either to repudiate or to scale down the principal of, or interest on, the public debt."[9] The United States countered that Section Four barred only a nullification of debt, not its reduction.[10]

The Court resolved this dispute in *Perry v. United States* (1935).[11] Chief Justice Charles Evans Hughes wrote the plurality opinion, which held that invalidating the gold clauses violated Section Four.[12] Section Four was therefore not limited to the national debt incurred during the Civil War. Yet, the Court found that the bondholders were not entitled to a remedy because Congress had withdrawn all gold from circulation. This conclusion was widely criticized because the gold clauses in the bonds guaranteed a certain level of value rather than payment in gold itself. Robert H. Jackson, who would later serve on the Supreme Court, wrote that the opinions in *Perry* were "a fascinating study in legalistic reasoning."[13]

On the other hand, a ruling that the bondholders were entitled to relief could have caused significant economic distress and President Franklin D. Roosevelt likely would have disobeyed the decision. Roosevelt had a draft radio address ready explaining why he would not obey *Perry* if the Court held that the bondholders must be paid in pre-devaluation dollars. He justified such defiance by quoting President Lincoln's criticism of *Dred Scott v. Sandford* (1857) in his First Inaugural Address.[14] Thus, Chief Justice Hughes's plurality opinion is sometimes compared to *Marbury v. Madison*, in which the Court also found a clever (if highly dubious) way of denying a constitutional remedy to avoid a political crisis.

OPEN QUESTIONS

- In recent years, there have been fiscal standoffs in which Congress refuses to fund the executive branch. Some members of Congress and commentators have argued that the failure to pay off debts would violate Section 4. For example, if the nation hit the "debt ceiling" set by Congress, would that refusal call into question "the validity of the public debt" as construed by *Perry*? If so, would Section Four confer authority on the President to order unilaterally that debt payments continue notwithstanding his ordinary lack of power to spend money without legal authorization?[15] Since *Perry* was not an opinion of the Court, there are no clear answers to any national debt issue that might arise under Section Four.

Cite as: Gerard N. Magliocca, *The Public Debt Clause*, in The Heritage Guide to the Constitution 760 (Josh Blackman & John G. Malcolm eds., 3d ed. 2025).

Notes

1. Cong. Globe, 39th Cong., 1st. Sess. 2545 (1866). **2.** *Id.* at 2769. **3.** *Id.* **4.** *The Constitutional Amendment: Discussed by Its Author,* The Cincinnati Commercial (Aug. 27, 1866), at 1. **5.** Report of the Joint Committee on Reconstruction, 39th Cong., at 129 (1866). **6.** Cong. Globe, 39th Cong., 1st Sess. 2768 (1866). **7.** An Act for the Release of certain Persons held to Service or Labor in the District of Columbia," ch. 54, 15 Stat. 376 (1862). **8.** Richard L. Aynes, *Unintended Consequences of the Fourteenth Amendment and What They Tell Us About Its Interpretation,* 39 Akron L. Rev. 289, 318–19 (2006). **9.** Brief of Claimant at 18, *Perry v. United States,* 294 U.S. 330 (1935) (No. 532). **10.** Brief of the United States at 62–64, *Perry,* 294 U.S. 330. **11.** 294 U.S. 330. **12.** Gerard N. Magliocca, *The Gold Clause Cases and Constitutional Necessity,* 64 Fl. L. Rev. 1243 (2012). **13.** Robert H. Jackson, The Struggle for Judicial Supremacy 102 (1941). **14.** 1 F.D.R.: His Personal Letters, 1928–1945, at 460 (Elliott Roosevelt ed., 1950). **15.** Garrett Epps, *The Constitution's Latest Blaze of Notoriety: Bad for the Republic,* The Atlantic (June 30, 2011), https://perma.cc/JMQ3-WTE3; Neil H. Buchanan & Michael C. Dorf, *How to Choose the Least Unconstitutional Option: Lessons for the President (and Others) from the Debt Ceiling Standoff,* 112 Colum. L. Rev. 1175 (2012), https://perma.cc/GR7Q-KQ63; Al Weaver, *Sanders Calls on Biden to Use 14th Amendment to Raise Debt Ceiling,* The Hill (May 24, 2023), https://perma.cc/4LRA-3EBT.

ESSAY NO. 200: THE ENFORCEMENT CLAUSE
AMEND. 14, § 5

The Congress shall have the power to enforce, by appropriate legislation, the provisions of this article.

—James C. Phillips

INTRODUCTION

Section 5 of the Fourteenth Amendment, also known as the Enforcement Clause, grants to Congress the power to pass legislation directed at effectuating the provisions of Sections 1 through 4 of the amendment. Like the enforcement clauses of the Thirteenth and Fifteenth Amendments, Section 5 constitutes a delegated power granted to Congress in addition to those listed in Article I, Section 8. The scope of what the clause authorizes turns on the meaning of "enforce" and "appropriate." Earlier decisions suggested that Congress might be able to define and even expand the scope of the rights protected by the Fourteenth Amendment, but the Supreme Court has since rejected that interpretation.

CONGRESS'S DELEGATED POWERS

Article I, Section 8 of the Constitution grants Congress a host of enumerated powers, such as the express powers to lay and collect taxes, regulate commerce, and declare war, but Congress also has the power "[t]o make all Laws which shall be necessary and proper for carrying into Execution the foregoing Powers." (See Essay Nos. 39, 44, 56, and 66.) *McCulloch v. Maryland* (1819) held that the word "necessary" can mean

needful, requisite, useful, conducive, or convenient.[1] These authorities are known as implied powers because they are not expressly enumerated. *McCulloch* gave Congress a broad sweep of implied powers to enforce the other powers enumerated in Article I, Section 8. Under *McCulloch,* Congress could do whatever is "convenient" in order to execute its other enumerated powers.

Section 1 of the Thirteenth Amendment, ratified in 1865, abolished slavery, and Section 2 granted Congress the "power to enforce this [amendment] by appropriate legislation." (See Essay No. 191.) This provision delegated to Congress new implied powers, and Congress did not think that authority was limited to the actual abolition of slavery. The Civil Rights Act of 1866 invoked Congress's powers under Section 2 of the Thirteenth Amendment. This statute prohibited the notorious "Black Codes" that denied blacks certain rights afforded to whites, including the power to make and enforce contracts.[2] However, there were some doubts about whether Section 2 could support this sweeping law. One of the Fourteenth Amendment's leading purposes was to ensure that Congress had adequate power to adopt the Civil Rights Act and future similar laws.

ADOPTION OF SECTION 5

In January 1866, Representative John Bingham of Ohio provided an early glimpse of what became Section 5. He laid out his proposal for a constitutional amendment that would correct the defects of Article IV's Privileges and Immunities Clause by "provid[ing] for the efficient enforcement, by law, of these 'equal rights of every man.'"[3] If adopted, Bingham's proposal would ensure that Congress had the authority to enforce it.[4]

In February 1866, the Joint Committee on Reconstruction proposed another forerunner to Section 5: "The Congress shall have power to make all laws which shall be necessary and proper to secure to the citizens of each state all privileges and immunities of citizens in the several states (Art. 4, Sec. 2); and to all persons in the several States equal protection in the rights of life, liberty and property (Fifth Amendment)."[5] This proposed amendment adopted the phrase "necessary and proper" that appeared in Article I based on a proposal by Bingham.[6] Critics opposed this provision on federalism grounds,[7] and the Joint Committee later changed this language to "appropriate" in the proposed Fourteenth Amendment. During the debates, Representative Thaddeus Stevens of Pennsylvania argued that Sections 1 and 5 working in tandem would empower Congress to rectify state laws that were "unjust."[8]

Section 1 of the Fourteenth Amendment includes the Citizenship Clause, Privileges or Immunities Clause, Due Process Clause, and Equal Protection Clause. (See Essays Nos. 192–196.) Section 5 grants Congress "the power to enforce, by appropriate legislation, the provisions" in Section 1.

The text of Section 5 raises several questions. For example, would the courts as well as Congress enforce the Fourteenth Amendment? The Reconstruction Congress may not have trusted the courts and likely anticipated that Congress would be the principal enforcer of the amendment, but the text and history do not support this Congress-only reading.[9] Did Congress have the power both to define the substantive rights protected by Section 1, such as citizenship's "privileges or immunities," and to enforce them under Section 5? There is no evidence that those who framed Section 5 had this understanding.[10] Some thought Section 5 would give Congress the power to remedy violations of the Fourteenth Amendment but not to expand or contract the rights.[11]

EARLY JUDICIAL PRECEDENTS

The U.S. Supreme Court interpreted Section 5 in a few early precedents. *Ex Parte Virginia* (1880) ruled that Congress can use its Section 5 authority to prohibit states from excluding African Americans from juries. Such a law was an "appropriate" means of ensuring the equal protection of the laws.[12] The Court took a broad reading of what it means for legislation to be appropriate.

In *Strauder v. West Virginia* (1880), the Court decided a case in which a black man had been indicted for murder. West Virginia law permitted only white men to serve on juries. Under federal law, a state court case that deprived a person of a constitutional right could be removed to federal court. This removal statute was authorized by Section 5. Strauder argued that a trial with a segregated jury violated the Fourteenth Amendment and tried to remove his case to federal court. The U.S. Supreme Court found that West Virginia's jury law violated the Equal Protection Clause and that the removal statute could be used to remedy this violation of the Fourteenth Amendment. In other words, Congress had the implied power to enact "appropriate legislation" to "enforce" the "equal protection of the Laws."

Three years later, the Court decided the *Civil Rights Cases* (1883).[13] This decision held that the prohibitions of Section 1 reached only actions committed by the state or its agents, which meant that Congress lacked the power to criminalize the discriminatory actions of private individuals. Thus, Section 5 gives Congress no authority to legislate with respect to the private sector. This principle became known as the state-action doctrine and still prevails today. (See Essay No. 193.)

MODERN JUDICIAL PRECEDENTS

Katzenbach v. Morgan (1966) held that Section 5 gives Congress the power to "remedy or prevent unconstitutional actions."[14] *Katzenbach* analogized "appropriate" in Section 5 to "necessary and proper" as interpreted by *McCulloch v.*

Maryland.[15] This reading would give Congress a very broad sweep of power. *Katzenbach* also suggested that Section 5 allows Congress to expand the meaning of Section 1.

Three decades later, the Court expressly rejected this suggestion. *City of Boerne v. Flores* (1997) considered the constitutionality of the Religious Freedom Restoration Act (RFRA) as applied to the states. This federal law permitted people to sue states for substantially burdening the free exercise of religion. (See Essay No. 160.) Congress purported to *expand* the free exercise right as interpreted by the Supreme Court in *Employment Division v. Smith* (1990). *Boerne,* however, held that Congress lacked this power. The Court ruled that Congress can use its Section 5 powers only to "remedy" constitutional violations of Section 1 as interpreted by the Court; the Court cannot change the scope of the amendment. That holding has been both heavily criticized and defended in scholarship on originalist grounds.[16] The *Boerne* Court also declared that there must be a "proportionality" and "congruence" between the statute "and the legitimate end to be achieved." The Court found that RFRA failed this test because Congress did not show evidence of a harm equal to the measure it enacted.[17] *Boerne* rejected the suggestion that Section 5 should be read as the Necessary and Proper Clause is read. The test for the former provision is far more demanding.

The Court would apply the *Boerne* test in several cases. Could Congress use its Section 5 powers to permit a suit against a state for violating the Americans with Disabilities Act? *Board of Trustees of the University of Alabama v. Garrett* (2001) held that the answer was no.[18] Section 5 only grants Congress authority to ban irrational state employment discrimination against the disabled, and because the disabled are not "a suspect classification" under the Equal Protection Clause, state discrimination against them is not "irrational." However, *Tennessee v. Lane* (2004) permitted suits against the states when a court denied access to disabled people.[19] *United States v. Morrison* (2000) considered the constitutionality of the Violence Against Women Act (VAWA), which provided federal remedies for women who suffered private acts of gender-motivated violence.[20] The Court ruled that this statute exceeded Congress's Section 5 authority.

Congress does have another pretext for enacting enforcement legislation. *Oregon v. Mitchell* (1970) recognized that Congress may prophylactically ban state actions that it has found to be generally violative of the Fourteenth Amendment even if they might not be in some instances.[21] For example, a state could impose a literacy test for voting in a constitutional manner. However, Congress determined that these tests were so commonly abused that they should be banned across the board, and the Court upheld this ban. Critically, however, this federal law was aimed at preventing actual and potential violations of the Constitution; it did not change the Constitution's substantive meaning and guarantees.

OPEN QUESTIONS

- To what degree can Congress invoke its Section 5 powers to alter the original Constitution? The Court has allowed Congress, acting under Section 5, to abrogate state sovereign immunity under the Eleventh Amendment.[22] What other provisions of the Constitution could Congress waive?

Cite as: James C. Phillips, *The Enforcement Clause, in* THE HERITAGE GUIDE TO THE CONSTITUTION 762 (Josh Blackman & John G. Malcolm eds., 3d ed. 2025).

Notes

1. 17 U.S. 316 (1819). **2.** Michael W. McConnell, *Originalism and the Desegregation Decisions,* 81 Va. L. Rev. 947, 957–58. **3.** Cong. Globe, 39th Cong., 1st Sess. 157–58 (1866). **4.** Earl M. Maltz, *The Fourteenth Amendment as a Reconstruction Measure,* at 19 (forthcoming Tulsa L. Rev.). **5.** Benjamin B. Kendrick, The Journal of the Joint Committee of Fifteen on Reconstruction 60–61 (1914). **6.** Jaocobus tenBroek, The Antislavery Origins of the Fourteenth Amendment 187–90 (1951); Maltz, *supra* at 36. **7.** Maltz, *supra* at 37–40. **8.** Maltz, *supra* at 62. **9.** *Id.* **10.** McConnell, *supra* at 1110–15. **11.** *Id.* at 1115–17. **12.** 100 U.S. 339 (1880). **13.** 109 U.S. 3 (1883). **14.** 384

U.S. 641 (1966).　**15.** *Katzenbach*, 384 U.S. at 650 (citing *McCulloch v. Maryland*, 17 U.S. 316, 421 (1819)); *Ex parte Va.*, 100 U.S. 339, 345–46 (1879).　**16.** Saikrishna Prakash, *A Comment on Congressional Enforcement*, 32 Ind. L. Rev. 193 (1998); Keith S. Alexander, *Federalism, Abortion, and the Original Meaning of the Fourteenth Amendment Enforcement Power: Can Congress Ban Partial-Birth Abortion After*

Carhart?, 13 Tex. Rev. L. & Pol. 105 (2008).　**17.** *Boerne*, 521 U.S. at 531–32, 534.　**18.** 531 U.S. 356 (2001).　**19.** 541 U.S. 509.　**20.** *United States v. Morrison*, 529 U.S. 598, 627 (2000).　**21.** *Oregon v. Mitchell*, 400 U.S. 112 (1970).　**22.** *Nev. Dep't of Human Res. v. Hibbs*, 538 U.S. 721 (2003); *Tennessee v. Lane*, 541 U.S. 509 (2004); *United States v. Georgia*, 546 U.S. 151 (2006).

ESSAY NO. 201: THE FIFTEENTH AMENDMENT
AMEND. 15

Section 1. The right of citizens of the United States to vote shall not be denied or abridged by the United States or by any State on account of race, color, or previous condition of servitude—

Section 2. The Congress shall have power to enforce this article by appropriate legislation.

—Earl M. Maltz

INTRODUCTION

In April 1866, the Joint Committee on Reconstruction approved a version of the Fourteenth Amendment that would have explicitly embraced the principle of race-blind suffrage.[1] Because many northerners continued to oppose black suffrage in principle, fears of a political backlash led the committee to abandon the issue.[2] Nevertheless, most Republicans quickly became convinced that additional action was needed. Thus, in 1869, Congress passed the Fifteenth Amendment, which banned all racial discrimination in voting rights. The amendment also included a clause vesting Congress with the power to enforce this prohibition. The amendment was ratified in 1870 and became the last of the Constitution's three Reconstruction Amendments. Subsequently, the enforcement clause provided the authority for passage of the Voting Rights Act of 1965, which is now the primary federal mechanism for preventing discrimination against voters on the basis of race.

DRAFTING OF THE FIFTEENTH AMENDMENT

Republicans had a variety of reasons for supporting the Fifteenth Amendment. First, most Republicans believed that allowing blacks to vote was the right thing to do in and of itself. In addition, after the Reconstruction Act of 1867 forced black suffrage on the former Confederate states, Republicans were charged with hypocrisy for not imposing the same requirement on northern states.[3] Moreover, despite passage of the Reconstruction Act, many Republicans worried that black suffrage in the South would be insecure without a constitutional amendment.[4] Some Republicans also believed that enfranchising blacks in the Union states would provide critical support for Republican candidates in some northern states.[5]

By 1869, these considerations had convinced virtually all mainstream congressional Republicans that a constitutional amendment was desirable. At the same time, however, Republicans were deeply divided over the question of precisely what language should be adopted. A proposal adopted by the House of Representatives provided simply that "the right of any citizen of the United States to vote shall not be denied or abridged . . . on account of race, color, or previous condition of slavery." It also would have armed Congress with the power to enforce this prohibition.[6] However, a number of prominent Republicans complained that this narrow language would essentially "legalise the disfranchisement of the vast body of the loyal race of the south." The states would be left free to adopt qualifications that, although neutral on their face, would in practice be impossible for most freed slaves to satisfy.[7]

Seeking to address these and other

concerns, the Senate passed a measure that would have applied to both the right to hold elective office and the right to vote. This proposal would have banned discrimination not only on the basis of race or color, but also because of nativity, property, education, or religious belief and, like the House version, included an enforcement provision.[8]

Given this conflict between the House and the Senate, a conference committee would normally have been convened and charged with the task of crafting a measure on which both houses could agree. However, the Senate did not vote to enter into conference. Instead, the entire drafting process began anew. The House produced a draft that in many ways was similar to the original Senate version.[9] The Senate responded with a simple prohibition on racial discrimination with respect to the rights to vote and to hold office.[10]

At that point, a conference committee was convened. The committee produced the final version of the Fifteenth Amendment.[11] This formulation prohibited racial discrimination with respect to voting rights and, like the Thirteenth and Fourteenth Amendments, included a section that vested Congress with the power to enforce this prohibition by "appropriate legislation." (See Essay Nos. 191 and 200.) However, the committee language made no reference to the right to hold office.

Many Republicans would have preferred more sweeping language, but most reluctantly accepted the compromise. Senator Henry Wilson of Massachusetts concluded that the Republicans should take "what [they] could get."[12] In March 1869, the committee's language received the necessary majorities in both the House and the Senate.[13]

RATIFICATION OF THE FIFTEENTH AMENDMENT

The ratification process for the Fifteenth Amendment was brief but intense. During the ratification debates, both sides reiterated the points that had been made during the congressional debates.[14] In California and Oregon, opponents derailed ratification efforts by arguing that the amendment would enfranchise Chinese immigrants.[15] In addition, some members of the women's suffrage movement opposed the amendment because it did not grant women the franchise.[16]

At the time, there were still three ex-Confederate states that were not yet represented in Congress: Virginia, Mississippi, and Texas. Congressional Republicans required the legislatures of those three states to ratify the amendment in order to regain their status as equal partners in the Union.[17] The three state legislatures promptly complied with this condition and pushed the Fifteenth Amendment over the threshold. On March 30, 1870, the Secretary of State declared that the Fifteenth Amendment had been ratified by the requisite three-fourths of the state legislatures.

VOTING RIGHTS AFTER THE FIFTEENTH AMENDMENT

Even before the Fifteenth Amendment was ratified, the Reconstruction Acts had established a regime that greatly enhanced the political power of African Americans in a number of the former Confederate states. For example, in 1870, Hiram Revels became the first black person to serve in either house of Congress after being selected to serve in the Senate by the state legislature of Mississippi.[18] At the same time, however, these gains were already being threatened. Organizations such as the Ku Klux Klan waged a campaign of terror designed to intimidate black voters and allow white supremacists to regain control of the electoral process.

Immediately after adoption of the Fifteenth Amendment, Republicans in Congress relied on its Section 2 authority to protect the gains that had been made by the former slaves. However, by the early 1890s, federal resolve had faded. During that same period, white supremacists regained control of the state governments throughout the South. Those governments adopted a variety of measures known as Jim Crow laws that were designed to prevent black people from regaining influence in the electoral process.[19]

JUDICIAL PRECEDENT: SECTION 1

The U.S. Supreme Court was called upon to decide the constitutionality of Jim Crow laws that began to disenfranchise the freedmen. *Williams v. Mississippi* (1898) considered the constitutionality of a literacy test. The Court refused to consider the motives of the lawmakers who had adopted the facially neutral test and rejected the constitutional challenge.[20] However, *Guinn v. United States* (1915) declared unconstitutional a grandfather clause that essentially allowed illiterate white people to vote while excluding potential black voters. The Court found that the only plausible explanation for this clause was an intent to discriminate on the basis of race.[21]

More recently, the Court has invoked both the Fourteenth and Fifteenth Amendments in a variety of voting rights cases. Cases declared unconstitutional facially neutral restrictions on voting rights where the legislative history revealed an intention to exclude or hinder African Americans.[22] The Court also blocked gerrymanders that were clearly designed to disenfranchise black voters.[23] In addition, the Court has held that race may be considered in the redistricting process only as long as racial considerations do not predominate and there is no effort to dilute the voting strength of minorities.[24]

JUDICIAL PRECEDENT: SECTION 2

The Court's view of the scope of the enforcement authority granted to Congress by Section 2 of the Fifteenth Amendment has also evolved over time. *Ex Parte Yarbrough* (1884) suggested that Congress could rely on its Section 2 powers to regulate the actions of private actors, such as the Ku Klux Klan, that sought to limit the ability of racial minorities to participate in the political process.[25] Two decades later, the Court reversed course. *James v. Bowman* (1903) held that the Fifteenth Amendment did not allow Congress to regulate purely private activity.[26]

However, in subsequent cases the Court avoided the problem by expansively defining some nongovernmental activities as state action for purposes of the Fifteenth Amendment, particularly in cases involving challenges to the constitutionality of white primaries and the exclusion of people of color from a political caucus that had an outsized influence on the selection of government officials.[27]

THE VOTING RIGHTS ACT

Congress passed the Voting Rights Act of 1965 after committee hearings produced extensive evidence that literacy tests and other devices had been used to systematically deny people of color the right to vote in several Southern states. The statute included provisions of general applicability, and imposed other restrictions on those states that both used literacy tests and similar devices and had either low voter registration in 1964 or low voter turnout in the presidential election that was held in that year. The Voting Rights Act was also construed to subject the electoral apparatus in those states to federal supervision by requiring all changes in existing procedures to be precleared by federal officials. In *South Carolina v. Katzenbach* (1966), the Supreme Court rejected a constitutional challenge to these and other parts of the Voting Rights Act.[28] The Court found that the scope of the power granted to Congress by Section 2 was analogous to that granted to Congress more generally by the Necessary and Proper Clause.

By its terms, the original preclearance requirement under the Voting Rights Act of 1965 would have expired in five years. However, the duration of the requirement was increased on a number of occasions. In 2006, the duration was extended for an additional twenty-five years. But at the same time, the 2006 statute did not change the coverage formula for those states that were made subject to the requirement by virtue of conditions that had existed in 1964. In *Shelby County v. Holder* (2013), the Court held that, in the absence of continuing widespread racial discrimination in those states, Congress could not rely on the original coverage formula to apply the preclearance requirement to some states while not imposing the same requirement on other states. In the decade since *Shelby County*, Congress has not updated its coverage formula or placed any states or local governments under federal supervision.

OPEN QUESTIONS

- The Voting Rights Act outlaws any restriction "which results in a denial or abridgement of the right . . . to vote on account of race or color."[29] *City of Rome v. United States* (1980) held that Section 2 of the Fifteenth Amendment empowers Congress to outlaw restrictions on voting that have a discriminatory effect even absent proof that such restrictions were intended to limit the political power of racial minorities.[30] However, *City of Boerne v. Flores* (1997) narrowly read Congress's power under Section 5 of the Fourteenth Amendment.[31] Did *City of Boerne* undermine *City of Rome*? Does Congress have the authority to restrict state power based on a discriminatory effect?[32]

- Would Congress have the authority to impose a preclearance requirement on all states without exception?

Cite as: Earl M. Maltz, *The Fifteenth Amendment*, in THE HERITAGE GUIDE TO THE CONSTITUTION 765 (Josh Blackman & John G. Malcolm eds., 3d ed. 2025).

Notes

1. Benjamin B. Kendrick, The Journal of the Joint Committee on Reconstruction 99 (1914). **2.** *Id.* at 101. **3.** Cong. Globe, 40th Cong., 3d Sess. 1628 (1869). **4.** *The Platform and the Nominations*, 6 The Nation 425 (May 28, 1868). **5.** Cong. Globe, 40th Cong. 1st Sess. 561 (1869). **6.** *Id.* at 745. **7.** *Id.* at app. 97. **8.** Id. at 1044. **9.** *Id.* at 1428. **10.** *Id.* at 1318. **11.** *Id.* at 1563–64. **12.** *Id.* at 1626. **13.** *Id.* at 1563–64, 1641. **14.** William Gillette, The Right to Vote: Politics and the Passage of the Fifteenth Amendment 79–165 (1965). **15.** *Id.* at 153–56. **16.** *Id.* at 118. **17.** *Id.* **18.** U.S. Senate Historical Office, Hiram Revels: First African American Senator (Feb. 25, 2020), https://perma.cc/N3UJ-LN7Z. **19.** Xi Wang, The Trial of Democracy: Black Suffrage and Northern Republicans, 1860–1910 chs. 2–6 (1997). **20.** 170 U.S. 213 (1898). **21.** 238 U.S. 347 (1915). **22.** *Rogers v. Lodge*, 458 U.S. 613 (1982); *Hunter v. Underwood*, 471 U.S. 222 (1985). **23.** *Gomillion v. Lightfoot*, 364 U.S. 339 (1960). **24.** *Bush v. Vera*, 517 U.S. 952 (1996). **25.** 110 U.S. 651 (1884). **26.** 190 U.S. 127 (1903). **27.** *Smith v. Allwright*, 321 U.S. 649 (1944); *Terry v. Adams*, 345 U.S. 461 (1953). **28.** 383 U.S. 301 (1966). **29.** 52 U.S.C. § 10301. **30.** 446 U.S. 156 (1980). **31.** 521 U.S. 507 (1997). **32.** Luis Fuentes-Rower, *The Future of Section Two of the Voting Rights Act in the Hands of a Conservative Court*, 5 Duke J. Const. L. & Pub. Pol'y 125 (2010).

PART 11

THE PROGRESSIVE ERA AMENDMENTS

ESSAY NO. 202: THE INCOME TAX AMENDMENT
AMEND. 16

The Congress shall have power to lay and collect taxes on incomes, from whatever source derived, without apportionment among the several States, and without regard to any census or enumeration.

—Andy Grewal

INTRODUCTION

The Sixteenth Amendment, approved by Congress in 1909 and ratified in 1913,[1] makes it relatively easy for Congress to pass an income tax.[2] The Supreme Court had ruled in 1895 that an income tax was a "direct tax" that required apportionment under Article I, Section 2 of the original Constitution.[3] The Sixteenth Amendment "overturned" that holding.[4] Income taxes may be laid "without apportionment among the several States, and without regard to any census or enumeration."

If an apportionment requirement applied, Congress could not collect income taxes by setting broadly applicable rates. Instead, it would need to allocate tax obligations to the states according to their populations.[5] For example, if Congress wanted to raise $1 trillion through an income tax and two states each had ten percent of the population, each state would need to individually raise $100 billion. This equal allocation would apply even if the people in the first state had large incomes and the people in the second state had small incomes. So, under this regime, the people in the richer state could raise $100 billion through one income tax rate, but the people in the poorer state would need another, higher income tax rate to raise the same amount. By lifting the apportionment requirement, the Sixteenth Amendment allows Congress to raise income taxes through nationally applicable rates.

HISTORY BEFORE PROPOSAL

In the early Republic, Congress raised most revenue through external taxes like customs, duties, and excises.[6] For example, Congress imposed duties on distilled spirits, carriages, snuff, and sugar.[7] In the early era, internal taxes were relatively limited.[8] One early internal tax, the federal carriage tax, prompted litigation over whether it was a direct tax that required apportionment.[9] *Hylton v. United States* (1796) concluded that the federal carriage tax was not so described. Several opinions in that case suggest that only real estate taxes and capitation taxes qualified as direct taxes.[10]

If a tax is not direct, then it faces a uniformity requirement.[11] An indirect tax must apply uniformly across the United States rather than in a geographically targeted manner.[12] No apportionment requirement applies to indirect taxes.[13] During the Constitutional Convention, Gouverneur Morris of Pennsylvania conceded, "[w]ith regard to indirect taxes on *exports* & imports & on consumption, the rule [of apportionment] would be inapplicable."[14]

Congress first passed an income tax during the Civil War and viewed it as an indirect tax.[15] That is, it established a geographically uniform system rather than an apportioned one.[16] This income tax was challenged in *Springer v. United States* (1881) as a direct tax that had to be apportioned.[17] Citing *Hylton*, the Court rejected that argument.[18]

Not long after the Civil War, Congress let the income tax law expire, but it revived the tax in 1894.[19] Legislators were concerned that heavy reliance on tariffs and excises was unfair.[20] The revived income tax raised only limited constitutional concerns within Congress,[21] but it soon faced a judicial challenge, and unlike the earlier challenge in *Springer*, this challenge was successful.

Pollock v. Farmers' Loan & Trust Co. (1895) held that the 1894 income tax law unconstitutionally imposed a direct tax because it reached income from real property.[22] Taxing income from real property, the Court concluded, was no different from taxing the real property itself. As *Hylton* had earlier intimated, a tax on real property was a direct tax. Thus, the Court concluded that the 1894 income tax law could not reach income from real property.[23] The Court further concluded that a tax on income from personal property, which the 1894 income tax included, also established a direct tax and that the unconstitutional provisions of the 1894 income tax law could not be severed from the rest.[24] Thus, through a five-to-four vote, the entire act fell.[25]

THE CONGRESSIONAL DEBATES
Pollock sparked major controversy. For example, then-President William Howard Taft privately opined that "[n]othing has ever injured the prestige of the Supreme Court more" than *Pollock*.[26] The Court's opinion also prompted sharp public reaction.[27] *Pollock* drew even more contemporaneous debates than *Plessy v. Ferguson* (1896), which established the infamous "separate but equal doctrine."[28] *Pollock* even drew unfavorable comparisons to *Dred Scott v. Sandford* (1857), through which the Court aggressively defended slavery.[29] Justice John Marshall Harlan, who dissented in *Pollock*, wrote that the decision in that case "will become as hateful with the American people as the *Dred Scott* case was when it was decided."[30]

Congress actively debated whether it should propose an amendment to override *Pollock*. Some critics believed that *Pollock*'s plain infirmity meant that no amendment would be necessary. President Theodore Roosevelt stated in his 1901 State of the Union Address that *Pollock* was so "undoubtedly very intricate, delicate, and troublesome" that the Court might itself overturn the decision.[31]

In the end, concerns over economic inequality drove Congress to pass what would become the Sixteenth Amendment,[32] enabling a progressive income tax. Senator Norris Brown of Nebraska sponsored the amendment and adopted a relatively narrow approach to overriding *Pollock*. His proposed amendment would not eliminate the apportionment requirement altogether; that requirement would continue to apply to direct taxes unless the direct tax qualified as an income tax. After a heated debate, the proposed amendment was passed by an overwhelming majority.[33]

THE RATIFICATION DEBATES
Ratification of the proposed Sixteenth Amendment faced few stumbling blocks. Governor Charles Evans Hughes of New York, the future Chief Justice of the United States, expressed concern that the broad power to tax incomes "from whatever source derived" would mean that Congress could tax interest income earned on state government bonds.[34] *Pollock* had held that such interest income was protected from federal taxation because Congress otherwise could infringe on state sovereignty.[35] Once Hughes received assurances that the Sixteenth Amendment would not threaten state sovereignty, he supported ratification.[36] Though Hughes's hesitation delayed the process, the Sixteenth Amendment earned ratification in only four years.

JUDICIAL PRECEDENT
The chief controversy over the Sixteenth Amendment has related to whether Congress has imposed "taxes on income" as described in the amendment. If Congress purports to tax "income" but in fact taxes property, the statute must be stricken as an unapportioned direct tax.

Eisner v. Macomber (1920) stated that income was appropriately defined as "the gain derived from capital, from labor, or from both combined,"[37] but *Commissioner v. Glenshaw Glass Co.* (1955) broadened that definition.[38] Under that case, income is not limited to the gain derived from capital or labor. Rather, income generally includes "undeniable accessions to wealth, clearly realized . . . over which the taxpayers have complete dominion."[39] Under this definition, income can include gains realized without any investment or effort by the taxpayer. Thus, after *Glenshaw Glass*, the taxpayer may have income when he wins a prize or receives punitive damages at trial.

Given the expansive definition of income established by *Glenshaw Glass*, Congress has had little trouble satisfying the Sixteenth Amendment. The Court has not found since *Macomber* that Congress exceeded its authority to impose "taxes on incomes."[40]

OPEN QUESTIONS

- Some Sixteenth Amendment questions linger for "mark-to-market" provisions in the federal tax code. Those provisions assume that income may arise through appreciation in a taxpayer's property in advance of any sale.[41] In this way, mark-to-market provisions deviate from ordinary tax principles[42] and contemplate income without "realization."[43]
- This departure from realization principles raises constitutional concerns. *Macomber* held that Congress could not properly invoke the Sixteenth Amendment when it attempted to tax gains in advance of any realization.[44] *Glenshaw Glass* referred to realization principles even as it expanded *Macomber*'s definition of income.[45] However, *Cottage Savings v. Commissioner* (1991) did not describe realization as a constitutional requirement.[46]
- In *Moore v. United States* (2024), the Court was asked to resolve whether the Sixteenth Amendment mandates realization as a prerequisite to income taxation. The majority ultimately resolved the case without addressing that question. However, the separate concurring and dissenting opinions in *Moore* revealed a sharp debate over realization, and the precise relationship between the Sixteenth Amendment and realization remains unclear.

Cite as: Andy Grewal, *The Income Tax Amendment*, *in* The Heritage Guide to the Constitution 770 (Josh Blackman & John G. Malcolm eds., 3d ed. 2025).

Notes

1. S.J. Res. 40, 61st Cong. (1909); Amend. XVI, 36 Stat. 184 (1913).   **2.** Calvin H. Johnson, *Binding Constitutional History: Reverse* Pollock *and End Fatal Apportionment*, 25 Fla. Tax Rev. 740, 763 (2022).   **3.** *Pollock v. Farmers' Loan & Tr. Co.*, 158 U.S. 601, 637 (1895).   **4.** *Nat'l Fed'n of Indep. Bus. v. Sebelius*, 567 U.S. 519, 571 (2012).   **5.** Art. I, § 9, cl. 4.   **6.** Sean Lowry, Cong. Rsrch. Serv., R43189, Federal Excise Taxes: An Introduction and General Analysis 2 (2013), https://perma.cc/WZ3F-9MZJ.   **7.** Act of Mar. 3, 1791, ch. 15, 1 Stat. 199; Carriage Tax of 1794, ch. 45, 1 Stat. 373; Act of June 5, 1794, ch. 51, 1 Stat. 384.   **8.** Joseph M. Dodge, *What Federal Taxes Are Subject to the Rule of Apportionment Under the Constitution?*, 11 J. Const. L. 839, 879 (2009).   **9.** *Hylton v. United States*, 3 U.S. 171 (1796).   **10.** *Id.* at 175 (1796) (Chase, J.); *id.* at 177 (Paterson, J.); *id.* at 183 (Iredell, J.).   **11.** Art. I, § 8, cl. 1.   **12.** *Taylor v. Secor*, 92 U.S. 575, 611–12 (1875); *Edye v. Robertson*, 112 U.S. 580, 594–95 (1884).   **13.** 1 Farrand's 592.   **14.** *Id.*   **15.** Act of July 1, 1862, ch. 119, §§ 89–93, 12 Stat. 432, 473–75; Edwin R. A. Seligman, Income Tax: A Study of the History, Theory, and Practice of Income Taxation at Home and Abroad 430–35 (1911).   **16.** *Pollock*, 158 U.S. at 663 (Harlan, J., dissenting).   **17.** *Springer v. United States*, 102 U.S. 586, 592 (1881).   **18.** *Id.* at 599–602.   **19.** Revenue Act of 1894, ch. 349, § 27, 28 Stat. 509, 553; Sheldon D. Pollack, *Origins of the Modern Income Tax, 1894–1913*, 66 Tax Law. 295, 301–15 (2013).   **20.** H.R. 4864, 53rd Cong., 26 Cong. Rec. 6634 (1894); Erik M. Jensen, *The Taxing Power, the Sixteenth Amendment, and the Meaning of "Incomes,"* 33 Ariz. State L.J. 1057, 1092 (2001).   **21.** 26 Cong. Rec. 6608–39 (1894);

Jensen, *supra* at 1105–06.   **22.** *Pollock*, 158 U.S. at 637.   **23.** *Id.*   **24.** *Id.*   **25.** Dawn Johnsen & Walter Dellinger, *The Constitutionality of a National Wealth Tax*, 93 Ind. L.J. 111, 128 (2018).   **26.** 1 Archibald Butt, Taft and Roosevelt: The Intimate Letters of Archie Butt 134 (1930); Bruce Ackerman, *Taxation and the Constitution*, 99 Colum. L. Rev. 1, 5 n.12 (1999).   **27.** Alan Furman Westin, *The Supreme Court, The Populist Movement and the Campaign of 1896*, 15 J. Politics 3, 22 (1953); *id.* at 22–23.   **28.** 163 U.S. 537 (1896); Davison M. Douglas, *The Rhetorical Uses of* Marbury v. Madison: *The Emergence of A "Great Case,"* 38 Wake Forest L. Rev. 375, 395–96 (2003).   **29.** 60 U.S. (19 How.) 393 (1857).   **30.** David G. Farrelly, *Justice Harlan's Dissent in the* Pollock *Case*, 24 S. Cal. L. Rev. 175, 180 (1951).   **31.** Theodore Roosevelt, State of the Union Address (Dec. 3, 1901), https://perma.cc/A9UV-P79V.   **32.** Jensen, *supra* at 1123–25.   **33.** Jensen, *supra* at 1114–22; H.R.J. Res. 5, 61st Cong., 44 Cong. Rec. 4440 (1909).   **34.** 45 Cong. Rec. 1694–99, 2245–47, 2539–40 (1910); *Evans v. Gore*, 253 U.S. 245, 260–61 (1920).   **35.** *Pollock*, 158 U.S. at 630.   **36.** Bruce Ackerman, *Taxation and the Constitution*, 99 Colum. L. Rev. 1, 50 (1999) (citing John D. Buenker, The Income Tax and the Progressive Era 255–61 (1985)).   **37.** *Eisner v. Macomber*, 252 U.S. 189, 207 (1920).   **38.** 348 U.S. 426, 431 (1955).   **39.** *Id.*   **40.** Jensen, *supra* at 1131–32.   **41.** 26 U.S.C. § 475.   **42.** *Weiss v. Wiener*, 279 U.S. 333, 335 (1929).   **43.** 26 U.S.C. § 475.   **44.** *Eisner*, 252 U.S. at 211.   **45.** *Glenshaw Glass*, 348 U.S. at 431.   **46.** 499 U.S. 554, 559 (1991).

~

ESSAY NO. 203: THE POPULAR ELECTION OF SENATORS AMENDMENT
AMEND. 17, CL. 1

The Senate of the United States shall be composed of two Senators from each State, elected by the people thereof, for six years; and each Senator shall have one vote. The electors in each State shall have the qualifications requisite for electors of the most numerous branch of the State legislatures.

—Michael R. Dimino

INTRODUCTION

Under the original Constitution, each state's two U.S. Senators were "chosen by the [state] Legislature."[1] The first clause of the Seventeenth Amendment changed that system. Senators, like members of the House of Representatives, would be "elected by the people." The amendment made the Constitution more democratic, but by eliminating the role of the state legislatures, the amendment lessened the protection that states had against measures that were harmful to their interests. The change created by the amendment was not revolutionary, however; even before its ratification, some states gave the people a substantial voice in the selection of U.S. Senators. How much the amendment democratized the Senate is debatable.

HISTORY BEFORE PROPOSAL

Under the Articles of Confederation, Congress was composed of delegates from each state, and each state had equal voting power. The Constitution's "great compromise" created a bicameral Congress. Members of the House of Representatives were chosen directly by the people with seats allocated to states based on population; Senators were chosen by state legislatures with two seats allocated to each state. In Federalist No. 62, James Madison defended this method of apportionment, arguing that because the Constitution would create "a compound republic partaking both of the national and federal character," "the government ought to be founded on a mixture of the principles of proportional and equal representation." Few objected to the state legislatures' power to choose Senators; as Professor Todd Zywicki has concluded, "there was near-universal support

for election of Senators by state legislatures both at the Constitutional Convention and in the state ratifications."[2]

Placing the choice of Senators in the state legislatures made the Senators representatives of the states as institutions; the House represented the people directly. Professor David Schleicher has observed that, whereas direct election of Representatives was a way of ensuring that popular opinion would receive a voice in Congress, election of Senators by the legislatures was viewed as "a means of insulating [the] government from popular opinion."[3] The interests of the two houses of Congress would therefore check each other.

The Senate was viewed as necessary to protect the interests of the states—and especially the small states—against the interests of the nation as a whole. George Mason of Virginia, for example, contended that "states needed the power of self-defense against the federal government"—a power that was to be found in the Senate.[4] In a July 20, 1789, letter to Vice President John Adams, Representative Roger Sherman of Connecticut described the relationship between the Senate and the states: "The senators being eligible by the legislatures of the several states, and dependent on them for reelection, will be vigilant in supporting their rights against infringement by the legislature or executive of the United States."[5]

The original Constitution was thus a compromise between two sides of a debate: those who wanted a national government that was responsible to the people and those who wanted a federation or confederation with a central government responsible to the constituent states. As Madison observed in Federalist No. 62, the election of Senators by state legislatures would "secure the authority" of the federal government and "form a convenient link between the two [state and federal] systems."

By making the two houses of Congress responsible to two very different constituencies, the Framers ensured that proposed legislation would enjoy widespread support before enactment. For example, Article I, Section 7 creates a two-step process to impose taxes: "All Bills for raising Revenue shall originate in the House of Representatives; but the Senate may propose or concur with Amendments as on other Bills." This sequencing was deliberate. Madison explained in Federalist No. 62 that "[n]o law or resolution can . . . be passed without the concurrence first of a majority of the people, and then of a majority of the states." He similarly contended that the risk of corruption was lessened if the lawmaking power was split between two houses constituted in different ways: "the improbability of sinister combinations will be in proportion to the dissimilarity in the genius of the two bodies."

The benefit of a Senate, chosen distinctly from the House, was thought to be especially pronounced in its ability to provide mature reflection and stability to check the "sudden and violent passions" to which the House would be subject. In Federalist No. 63, Madison remarked that the Senate "may sometimes be necessary, as a defence to the people against their own temporary errors and delusions."

SUPPORT FOR POPULAR ELECTION OF SENATORS

Despite this consensus at the Framing, the election of Senators by state legislatures soon became a matter of contention. Between 1826 and 1908, six amendments providing for the direct popular election of Senators were proposed; all six were approved by the House of Representatives, and all six failed in the Senate.[6] With the advent of the Progressive era, the country's desire for democracy became stronger than its desire to represent the institutional interest of states.[7] Proponents of popular election successfully criticized selection by state legislatures as elitist, undemocratic, and subject to corruption or excessive influence from powerful interests.[8]

By the early twentieth century, most states already allowed their voters in effect to elect their Senators.[9] A majority of those states had non-binding primary elections that would select Republican and Democratic nominees for the U.S. Senate.[10] Whichever party had a majority in the state legislature would then (usually) elect the candidate that won that party's primary election.[11] In 1908, Oregon had a popular election to "instruct" the state legislature whom to elect as Senator.[12] Within five years, a majority of states offered some form of popular election.[13]

ADOPTION OF THE SEVENTEENTH AMENDMENT

In April 1911, the House of Representatives approved a version of what would become the Seventeenth Amendment.[14] This text, however, included a race rider. Under the Elections Clause, Congress can "alter [the] Regulations" adopted by state legislatures concerning the "Times, Places and Manner of holding Elections for Senators and Representatives."[15] The proposed amendment would have removed Congress's power to regulate the election of Senators by providing that "[t]he times, places, and manner of holding elections for Senators shall be as prescribed in each State by the legislature thereof." As a result, Congress would not have been able to interfere with Senate election laws that disenfranchised black voters.

Senator Joseph Bristow of Kansas proposed a substitute amendment without the race rider.[16] Bristow referenced the "outside controversy" concerning the rider[17] and argued that the Elections Clause should not "be in any way touched" or "repeal[ed]" by the Seventeenth Amendment. In June 1911, the Senate split 44 to 44 on Bristow's substitute amendment with three Senators not voting.[18] Vice President James Sherman cast the deciding vote in favor of adoption. After a year of stalemate, in May 1912, the House passed the Senate version.[19] The amendment proceeded to the ratification process.

THE RATIFICATION PROCESS

Ratification of the Seventeenth Amendment was quick, and votes in favor of ratification were overwhelming. Fifty-two of the seventy-two state legislative chambers that voted to ratify the Seventeenth Amendment did so unanimously.[20] In all thirty-six ratifying states combined, there were only 191 negative votes, 152 of which came from Vermont and Connecticut.[21] In April 1913, Connecticut's ratification pushed the total over the three-fourths threshold. On May 31, Secretary of State William Jennings Bryan announced the Seventeenth Amendment's ratification.[22]

THE SEVENTEENTH AMENDMENT AND FEDERALISM

The Seventeenth Amendment lessened Senators' interest in advocating for their states and for a limited national government. When Senators were elected by state legislatures, they had an incentive to protect state power.[23] When the Seventeenth Amendment made their continuance in office dependent on the people, however, Senators had less reason to push for limits on national power.[24] As a result, the amendment weakened one of the most important "political safeguards of federalism" built into the original Constitution.[25]

During the debates concerning the amendment, there was not much discussion of federalism.[26] The omission may seem surprising, given that the indirect election of Senators was one of the guarantees of federalism that the Framers built into the original Constitution. Yet, because most states, as a practical matter, already chose their U.S. Senators by some form of popular election, the election of Senators by state legislatures was less significant for federalism than the Framers anticipated. As Professor Akhil Amar has observed, states that supported the Seventeenth Amendment "were voting to constitutionalize rules that were already largely in place or about to be in place."[27]

There is perhaps some irony in the effect that ratification of the Seventeenth Amendment had on federalism. Throughout the nineteenth century, state legislative races tended to focus on national issues because one of the most important responsibilities of state legislatures was to choose U.S. Senators. For example, the 1858 election for the Illinois General Assembly featured the celebrated Lincoln–Douglas debates, which focused on whether slavery should be permitted in new territories, even though the people could not vote for Lincoln or Douglas for the Senate seat. However, after the Seventeenth Amendment, state legislative races would focus on local issues. In this regard, the Seventeenth Amendment may have promoted federalism by freeing state legislative races to focus on state issues.[28]

JUDICIAL PRECEDENT

The U.S. Supreme Court has addressed the Seventeenth Amendment only indirectly. For example, *Garcia v. San Antonio Metropolitan Transit Authority* (1985) upheld federal regulations of state employment.[29] The Court found that the Constitution contained no substantive prohibition on such federal regulation, and held that the states should rely on the "federal political process" rather than judicial intervention "in preserving the[ir] interests."[30] The Court acknowledged that "changes in the structure of the Federal Government have taken place since 1789, not the least of which has been the substitution of popular election of Senators by the adoption of the Seventeenth Amendment in 1913," but maintained "that the fundamental limitation that the constitutional scheme imposes on the Commerce Clause to protect the 'States as States' is one of process rather than one of result."[31]

Other decisions have reflected a greater willingness to find constitutional guarantees of state autonomy. For example, *Seminole Tribe v. Florida* (1996), *United States v. Lopez* (1995), and *Gregory v. Ashcroft* (1991) found that there remained a strong judicial role in protecting the interests of states within our constitutional system, even after the Seventeenth Amendment weakened states' influence in Congress.[32] None of these cases, however, cited the Seventeenth Amendment.

Cite as: Michael R. Dimino, *The Popular Election of Senators Amendment, in* THE HERITAGE GUIDE TO THE CONSTITUTION 773 (Josh Blackman & John G. Malcolm eds., 3d ed. 2025).

Notes

1. Art. I, § 3, cl. 1. **2.** Todd Zywicki, *Beyond the Shell and Husk of History: The History of the Seventeenth Amendment and Its Implications for Current Reform Proposals*, 45 Clev. St. L. Rev. 165, 183 (1997). **3.** David Schleicher. *The Seventeenth Amendment and Federalism in an Age of National Political Parties*, 65 Hastings L.J. 1043, 1050 (2014). **4.** *Id.* **5.** 6 The Works of John Adams 440 (Charles Francis Adams ed., 1851), https://perma.cc/2GYL-GB4T. **6.** Neil MacNeil & Richard A. Baker, The American Senate: An Insider's History 22–23 (2013). **7.** Steven Gow Calabresi & Gary Lawson, The U.S. Constitution: Creation, Reconstruction, the Progressives, and the Modern Era 1733 (2020). **8.** Schleicher, *supra* at 1074. **9.** Zywicki, *supra* at 165. **10.** Jay S. Bybee, *Ulysses at the Mast: Democracy, Federalism, and the Sirens' Song of the Seventeenth Amendment*, 91 Nw. U. L. Rev. 500, 537 (1997). **11.** *Id.*; William H. Riker, *The Senate and American Federalism*, 49 Am. Pol. Sci. Rev. 452, 466 (1955). **12.** Akhil Reed Amar, America's Constitution: A Biography 412 (2005). **13.** *Id.* **14.** H.J. Res. 39, 62d Cong. (May 11, 1911), https://perma.cc/VA7Y-MQ26. **15.** Art. I, § 4, cl. 1. **16.** *17th Amendment to the U.S. Constitution: Direct Election of U.S. Senators (1913)*, Nat'l Archives, https://perma.cc/NHS4-V4S7. **17.** 47 Cong. Rec. 1483 (1911). **18.** *Id.* at 1923. **19.** *Joint Resolution Proposing an Amendment to the Constitution Providing That Senators Shall Be Elected by the People of the Several States, May 13, 1912*, Nat'l Archives, https://perma.cc/V3XB-HMDJ. **20.** Ralph A. Rossum, *Seventeenth Amendment*, Center for the Study of Federalism (2006), https://perma.cc/BL6L-GUU9. **21.** *Id.* **22.** *Notification of the Ratification of the 17th Amendment to the Constitution, by Secretary of State William Jennings Bryan, May 31, 1913*, Nat'l Archives, https://perma.cc/XHK8-WTEL. **23.** Todd J. Zywicki, *Senators and Special Interests: A Public Choice Analysis of the Seventeenth Amendment*, 73 Ore. L. Rev. 961 (1996). **24.** Ralph Rossum, Federalism, the Supreme Court and the Seventeenth Amendment: The Irony of Constitutional Democracy (2001). **25.** Herbert Wechsler, *The Political Safeguards of Federalism: The Role of the States in the Composition and Selection of the National Government*, 54 Colum. L. Rev. 543 (1954). **26.** Riker, *supra* at 469. **27.** Amar, *supra* at 412. **28.** Schleicher, *supra* at 1074–81. **29.** 469 U.S. 528 (1985). **30.** *Id.* at 551. **31.** *Id.* at 554 **32.** 517 U.S. 44 (1996); 514 U.S. 549 (1995); 501 U.S. 452 (1991).

ESSAY NO. 204: THE SENATE VACANCIES AMENDMENT
AMEND. 17, CL. 2, 3

When vacancies happen in the representation of any State in the Senate, the executive authority of such State shall issue writs of election to fill such vacancies: Provided, That the legislature of any State may empower the executive thereof to make temporary appointments until the people fill the vacancies by election as the legislature may direct.

This amendment shall not be so construed as to affect the election or term of any Senator chosen before it becomes valid as part of the Constitution.

—Todd J. Zywicki

INTRODUCTION

Under Article I, Section 3, Clause 1 of the Constitution as originally ratified, Senators were "chosen by the Legislature" of each state (see Essay No. 15); under Clause 2, the state "Executive" could "make temporary Appointments" to fill a Senate vacancy when the state legislature was in "Recess" (see Essay No. 16). Clause 1 of the Seventeenth Amendment, ratified in 1913, removed the legislature's power to elect Senators and replaced it with the popular election of Senators (see Essay No. 203); Clause 2 altered the process by which Senate vacancies would be filled and potentially raises sparsely litigated separation-of-powers, federalism, and partisanship issues. Under Clause 3, the new method for electing Senators did not apply to those who were already in office.

SENATE VACANCIES UNDER THE ORIGINAL CONSTITUTION

Under the original Constitution, the state legislatures elected Senators. If a Senate vacancy arose while the state legislature was in session, the legislature could meet immediately to elect a new Senator. However, if the state legislature was in recess, there would be a period during which the state would lack equal representation in the Senate. The Framers addressed this circumstance through the Senate Vacancies Clause: "[I]f Vacancies happen by Resignation, or otherwise, during the Recess of the Legislature of any State, the Executive thereof may make temporary Appointments until the next Meeting of the Legislature, which shall then fill such Vacancies."[1] House of Representatives vacancies, by contrast, are filled by election: "When vacancies happen in the Representation from any State, the Executive Authority thereof shall issue Writs of Election to fill such Vacancies."[2]

THE CONSTITUTIONAL CONVENTION

The proposal to fill vacancies in this manner generated minimal debate at the Constitutional Convention. James Wilson of Pennsylvania argued that empowering the executive to fill Senate vacancies would "remove[] the appointment too far from the people."[3] At that time, the executive in many states was elected by the legislature; this structure would therefore create a double layer of insulation from the people. Wilson also argued that "it was unnecessary as the Legislatures will meet so frequently."[4]

Edmund Randolph of Virginia defended this provision as "necessary to prevent inconvenient chasms in the Senate."[5] At the time, some state legislatures met only once a year; Senate vacancies would therefore "be of more consequence" because the Senate would "have more power & consist of a smaller number than the other House."[6] Randolph further argued that the state executive could be trusted with the responsibility because the appointment would be for "so short a time."[7]

THE RATIFICATION DEBATES

During the ratification debates, there was some debate between the Federalists and Anti-Federalists over this clause. Cato wrote in his fifth paper that the Constitution gave "the executive the unprecedented power of making temporary senators, in case of vacancies, by resignation or otherwise."[8] In Federalist No. 67, Hamilton suggested that "Cato was arguing the President—that is, the federal 'Executive'— could fill a temporary Senate vacancy pursuant to the Recess Appointments Clause."[9] Hamilton responded that this clause grants "an express power . . . in clear and unambiguous terms, to the State Executives, to fill the casual vacancies in the Senate by temporary appointments."

HISTORY BEFORE PASSAGE OF THE SEVENTEENTH AMENDMENT

According the Congressional Research Service, temporary appointments of Senators by governors occasioned "only minor controversy."[10] Between 1789 and 1913, twenty of the 189 Senators appointed by governors were contested, and the Senate excluded only eight of these appointments.[11] Occasionally, state legislatures would deadlock on electing a Senator, and the seat would remain unfilled, sometimes for an extended period.[12] Governors would attempt to appoint a temporary Senator to ensure that the state's representation in the Senate was not compromised by legislative deadlocks even if the legislature was not technically in recess. The Senate could and often did then exclude the would-be Senator.

By the mid-nineteenth century, voters began to agitate for some degree of popular election of Senators. A majority of states adopted mechanisms for *de facto* direct election of Senators.[13]

ADOPTION OF THE SEVENTEENTH AMENDMENT

The House of Representatives approved the Seventeenth Amendment in 1911. In the Senate, the primary sponsor of the amendment was Joseph L. Bristow of Kansas. Bristow noted that the language of Clause 2 "makes the least possible change in the Constitution to accomplish the purpose" of adopting election of Senators by popular vote.[14] The requirement that the state executive issue a writ of election in the event of a Senate vacancy tracked the process for filling House vacancies almost verbatim.[15]

Clause 3 of the Seventeenth Amendment provided that "[t]his amendment shall not be so construed as to effect the election or term of any Senator chosen before it becomes valid as part of the Constitution." This text made clear that the direct election of Senators was to take place prospectively. It would not displace sitting members of the Senate who had been elected by state legislatures under the original constitutional process.

WRITS OF ELECTION

In the event of a Senate vacancy, Clause 2 provides that the state executive "shall issue writs of election to fill such vacancies." This process is modeled after the House Executive Writs of Election Clause. (See Essay No. 12.) A writ of election is a legal command that an election be held. The Constitution does not specify how quickly the writ must be issued or how quickly the election itself must be held. However, the governor cannot decline to issue the writ.

The courts have recognized that governors will balance two conflicting goals. On the one hand, the people have an interest in a speedy popular election to ensure full representation in the Senate. On the other hand, the state has an interest in conducting elections on a regularized basis to maximize voter participation and minimize administrative expense.

This issue has been litigated following several Senate vacancies. In June 1968, for example, Senator Robert F. Kennedy of New York was assassinated, but New York was permitted to postpone the election of his replacement until 1970 rather than being required to hold both a primary and a general election by the fall of 1968.[16] In 1991, following the death of Senator John Heinz of Pennsylvania, a special election was scheduled, but instead of a primary for the political parties, the conventions of the two major parties could choose the candidates. The courts held that the Seventeenth Amendment did not mandate that party nominees be chosen by popular vote as long as the actual election was by popular vote.[17] In 2008, Senator Barack Obama of Illinois stepped down to become President, but the state did not schedule a special election. Instead, the seat was filled in 2010 following the next regularly scheduled general election. Illinois Governor Rod Blagojevich would later be impeached, convicted, and imprisoned for bribery and corruption charges related to his actions in filling this vacancy. Constitutional amendments have been introduced in Congress to impose federal limits on the Senate vacancies process, but none has passed.[18]

THE EXECUTIVE'S TEMPORARY APPOINTMENT POWER

Almost all of the states authorize their governors to make a temporary appointment in the event of a vacancy,[19] but some states have granted and removed this power for overtly political reasons. In 2004, Democratic Senator John Kerry of Massachusetts was running for President, and Republican Mitt Romney was governor. The Democratic legislature stripped the governor of his power to make a temporary appointment lest Romney temporarily appoint a Republican Senator. Five years later, in 2009, Democratic Senator Ted Kennedy was very ill, and there was a Democratic governor. The Democratic legislature restored the governor's power to make a temporary appointment.[20] In 2024, Republican Senator Mitch McConnell of Kentucky had some health concerns. In response, the Republican Kentucky legislature stripped the Democratic governor of this power so that he could not fill McConnell's seat if it became vacant.[21]

In most of the states that have granted the governor this power, the appointee will serve until the next regularly scheduled statewide election. In a minority of states, the governor is required to call a special election on a strict timeline.

Some states restrict whom the governor can appoint. In several states, this includes requiring that the appointee must be of the same party as the vacating Senator. In Utah, for example, the governor must appoint someone from a list of three prospects recommended by the vacating Senator's party. Some scholars contend that once the governor is empowered to make these temporary appointments, the states cannot impose additional restrictions.[22]

OPEN QUESTIONS

- Is there a Senate "vacancy" when voters elect an ineligible candidate?[23] In October 2000, Missouri Governor and Senate candidate Mel Carnahan died, but state law prohibited removing Carnahan from the ballot at that late juncture.[24] The following month, the majority of Missouri voters knowingly voted for the deceased Carnahan for Senator. After Carnahan's death, Missouri's lieutenant governor became governor. He could have declared the votes to be improper or "spoiled" ballots in support of an ineligible candidate but instead declared that the election had created a vacancy for purposes of the Seventeenth Amendment. He filled the vacancy with Carnahan's widow, Jean Carnahan, and issued a writ of election for 2002. This strategy was not challenged at the time.[25]

- Can a Senator's "incapacity" trigger a "vacancy"?[26]
- The Seventeenth Amendment provides that the "legislature of any State may empower the executive thereof to make temporary appointments." Does the governor have any role in that process, or is that power reserved solely for the "legislature"? Could the governor veto a bill stripping him of the power to make temporary appointments?[27]
- The Ineligibility or Sinecure Clause provides that "[n]o Senator or Representative shall, during the Time for which he was elected, be appointed to any civil Office under the Authority of the United States, which shall have been created, or the Emoluments whereof shall have been increased during such time."[28] In 1936, the governor of Michigan appointed Representative Prentiss Marsh Brown to fill a Senate vacancy.[29] For a brief period, Brown received a Senate salary that was increased during the time he had been elected to the House. Did the Sinecure Clause bar that appointment?[30] Is a vacant Senate seat an "office under the Authority of the United States"? A Senate seat is generally an elected position, but is a temporary Senate seat an appointed position?[31]

Cite as: Todd J. Zywicki, *The Senate Vacancies Amendment, in* THE HERITAGE GUIDE TO THE CONSTITUTION 776 (Josh Blackman & John G. Malcolm eds., 3d ed. 2025).

Notes

1. Art I, § 3, cl. 2. **2.** Art. I, § 2, cl 4. **3.** 2 Farrand's 231. **4.** *Id.* **5.** *Id.* **6.** *Id.* **7.** *Id.* **8.** Storing 2.6.37. **9.** Seth Barrett Tillman & Josh Blackman, *Offices and Officers of the Constitution, Part III: The Appointments, Impeachment, Commissions, and Oath or Affirmation Clauses*, 62 S. Tex. L. Rev. 349, 439–40 (2023). **10.** Thomas H. Neale, Cong. Rsrch. Serv., R44781, U.S. Senate Vacancies: Contemporary Developments and Perspectives 9 (2018), https://perma. cc/79S4-AAHN. **11.** *Id.* **12.** Todd J. Zywicki, *Senators and Special Interests: A Public Choice Analysis of the Seventeenth Amendment*, 73 Or. L. Rev. 1007 (1994); Wendy J. Schiller, Charles Stewart III, & Benjamin Xiong, *U.S. Senate Elections Before the 17th Amendment: Political Party Cohesion and Conflict 1871–1913*, 75 J. of Politics 835 (2013). **13.** Jay S. Bybee, *Ulysses at the Mast: Democracy, Federalism, and the Sirens' Song of the Seventeenth Amendment*, 91 Nw. L. Rev. 500 (1997). **14.** 47 Cong. Rec. 1482 (1911). **15.** *Id.* at 1483. **16.** *Valenti v. Rockefeller*, 292 F. Supp. 851 (S.D.N.Y. 1968), *aff'd* 393 U.S. 405 (1969). **17.** *Trinsey v. Pennsylvania*, 941 F.2d 224 (3rd Cir. 1991). **18.** Neale, *supra* at 14–16. **19.** National Conference of State Legislatures, *Vacancies in the United States Senate* (Sept. 25, 2023), https://perma.cc/4F9F-3FJC. **20.** Louis Jacobson, *Massachusetts Legislature Flip-Flops on Governor's Senatorial Appointment Power*, PolitiFact (Sept. 24, 2009), https: //perma.cc/6KWU-XKCQ. **21.** Bruce Schreiner, Kentucky *GOP Lawmakers Remove Democratic Governor's Role in Filling US Senate Vacancies*, Associated Press (Apr. 12, 2024), https://perma.cc/3YJU-D54Z. **22.** Vikram David Amar, *Doubts About Mitch McConnell's Health Implicate Important Questions Under the Seventeenth Amendment*, Verdict (Aug. 11, 2023), https://perma.cc/7S6V-27PF. **23.** Zachary D. Clopton & Steven E. Art, *The Meaning of the Seventeenth Amendment and a Century of State Defiance*, 107 Nw. U. L. Rev. 1181, 1200–01 (2013). **24.** *All About Missouri History: Elected Officials: United States Senators*, Missouri Secretary of State, https://perma.cc/6VKT-784B. **25.** Michael G. Adams, *Missouri Compromise: Did the Posthumous Senatorial Election of Mel Carnahan and Subsequent Appointment of Jean Carnahan Compromise Federal or State Law?*, 29 N. Ky. L. Rev. 433 (2002). **26.** Clopton & Art, *supra* at 1200–01; Jack Maskell, Cong. Rsrch. Serv., Incapacity of a Member of Congress (2011). **27.** Josh Blackman, *The Kentucky Legislature Removed the Governor's Power to Temporarily Appoint a Senator*, Volokh Conspiracy (Apr. 25, 2024), https://perma. cc/4EK2-XL63. **28.** Art. I, § 6, cl. 2. **29.** Biographical Directory of the United States Congress 1774–Present, https://perma.cc/P47Y-RF5V. **30.** Seth Barrett Tillman & Josh Blackman, *Offices and Officers of the Constitution, Part VI: The Ineligibility Clause*, 64 S. Tex. L. Rev. 209, 239–241 (2025). **31.** Josh Blackman, *A Reply to Peter Keisler and Richard Bernstein, and Michael Luttig, on Section 3*, Volokh Conspiracy (Feb. 7, 2024), https://perma.cc/W2TD-RUCY.

〜

ESSAY NO. 205: THE PROHIBITION AMENDMENT
AMEND. 18

Section 1. After one year from the ratification of this article the manufacture, sale, or transportation of intoxicating liquors within, the importation thereof into, or the exportation thereof from the United States and all territory subject to the jurisdiction thereof for beverage purposes is hereby prohibited.

Section 2. The Congress and the several States shall have concurrent power to enforce this article by appropriate legislation.

Section 3. This article shall be inoperative unless it shall have been ratified as an amendment to the Constitution by the legislatures of the several States, as provided in the Constitution, within seven years from the date of the submission hereof to the States by the Congress.

—Paul J. Larkin

INTRODUCTION

Alcohol's delightful allures and sometimes baleful consequences have enticed and/or repelled people ever since Noah became the first vintner.[1] People have used alcohol to celebrate victory in battle and fallen military comrades as well as international treaties, domestic political agreements, graduations, marriages, anniversaries, childbirths, and a host of other events.[2] America is no exception to that tradition: Peter Stuyvesant noted that one-quarter of the houses in New Amsterdam sold tobacco, beer, and brandy.[3] The vessel that carried John Winthrop and the Puritans in 1630 to settle the Massachusetts Bay Colony held more liquor than water.[4] In 1758, a prominent Virginia farmer spent nearly all of his Virginia House of Burgesses campaign funds to buy brandy, rum, cider, beer, and wine on election day for voters.[5] And so on.[6]

But like almost everything else in life, alcohol also has its downsides. Samuel Johnson observed that "[i]n the bottle, discontent seeks for comfort, cowardice for courage, and bashfulness for confidence."[7] Alcohol has caused imbibers to destroy their health, lose their moral bearings, commit violent crimes, squander their wages, ruin marriages and families, and generate a host of other nasty outcomes.[8] Beginning in the late eighteenth and early nineteenth centuries, advocates for temperance (moderate consumption) and prohibition (complete abstinence) started down a path that culminated in adoption of the second constitutional amendment to prohibit private conduct: the Eighteenth (Prohibition) Amendment. (The first was the Thirteenth Amendment, which outlawed slavery.) Ratified in 1919, the Prohibition Amendment had a short half-life and, having been repealed by the Twenty-First Amendment in 1933, is the only amendment to have passed into history.[9]

RISE OF THE PROHIBITION AMENDMENT

The late eighteenth and early nineteenth centuries saw a great increase in alcohol consumption in America, largely by men. Two principal groups rose to quell that behavior and limit its dangerous consequences: ministers, who saw alcohol abuse as a threat to men's souls, and women, who felt the impact of alcohol abuse on their persons and families.

Individual ministers and religions, such as Methodism, used moral suasion to dissuade Americans from abusing liquor or persuade them to abstain entirely. Women sought to change not only minds, but also laws and, to do so while being denied the right to vote, organized associations such as the Woman's Christian Temperance Union (WCTU). These associations, through presence, prayer, or songs—and sometimes in a less soft-pedaled manner—sought to close individual saloons, supported legislation to restrain the issuance of liquor permits, and demanded enforcement of the laws on the books.

The apex of nineteenth-century prohibitionism was the passage of an 1851 Maine law making that state "dry" (alcohol-free). A dozen other states passed similar laws over the remainder of that decade.[10] This mid-century success, however, was short-lived. Prohibition was a politically divisive issue, and the Democratic and Republican parties were reluctant to add it with slavery as the focus of a national campaign. By 1860, Maine had repealed its alcohol ban, and the other states with similar statutes either followed suit or ignored their prohibition laws.

The Civil War displaced prohibition as a subject of national debate. Afterwards, the so-called Gilded Age proved to be an unfavorable environment for prohibition's rebirth. The century ended with the nation, by and large, remaining "wet."[11]

Popular opinion changed dramatically over the first two decades of the twentieth century for several reasons. Alcohol prohibition movements grew in other nations. The Anti-Saloon League, a politically savvy group, focused on disparaging saloons instead of the men who drank in them and supported any politician, regardless of party, who opposed alcohol. In addition, due to the influence of Progressivism, our societal focus on individual liberty shifted gradually to a focus on aggregate welfare. Patriotic opposition to German beer interests also grew once the United States entered the Great War against Kaiser Wilhelm.

ADOPTION OF THE EIGHTEENTH AMENDMENT

These factors and others enabled prohibition's supporters to persuade two-thirds of the Senate and House of Representatives to pass the Prohibition Amendment in November 1917. Section 1 of the amendment barred the "manufacture, sale, or transportation," as well as the "importation" and "exportation," of "intoxicating liquors" from "one year after ratification." The prohibition applied only to alcohol used for "beverage purposes," which would exclude alcohol used for medicine and other similar purposes. Section 2 granted Congress and the states "concurrent power" to enforce the amendment. Prior amendments, such as the Fourteenth Amendment, gave only Congress an enforcement power. Section 3 provided that the amendment would become inoperative within seven years after it was submitted to the states, but it would not take nearly that long.

By January 1919, three-fourths of the states had ratified the amendment. In fact, ratification before the 1920 census potentially changed the composition of legislatures. Congress enforced the amendment with the National Prohibition Act, also known as the Volstead Act, which created a mechanism to take action against the manufacture, interstate transportation, and sale of alcohol.[12]

REPEAL OF THE PROHIBITION AMENDMENT

The Prohibition Amendment became unpopular after only thirteen years because of internal flaws and external opposition. The amendment and the Volstead Act did not specifically prohibit the possession and use of liquor, and the exception for medical-use alcohol sometimes resulted in pharmacies becoming a town's largest distillers. "Rum runners" smuggled liquor in from other nations, such as the Caribbean Islands and Canada, where it was legal. A large percentage of the population still wanted to be able to drink. Alcohol moved indoors into clubs and "speakeasies" that were frequented by locally prominent parties and political officials and protected by corrupt local law enforcement officers.

The widespread evasion of Prohibition generated disrespect for the amendment and the Volstead Act, which in turn corroded belief in the rule of law. The Great Depression denied the federal, state, and local governments funds they would normally realize from income or business taxes, so liquor taxes became an attractive alternative revenue source. Crime became a considerable national problem, not just as a result of the importation and sale of liquor, but also because of the violence that accompanied black market activities.

By 1933, the nation had had enough of Prohibition. Each house of Congress passed the Twenty-First Amendment to repeal the Prohibition Amendment, and three-fourths of the states agreed. (See Essay No. 208.) Whether liquor should or should not be sold was an issue that was left to the states to resolve as they saw fit.

Cite as: Paul J. Larkin, *The Prohibition Amendment*, *in* THE HERITAGE GUIDE TO THE CONSTITUTION 780 (Josh Blackman & John G. Malcolm eds., 3d ed. 2025).

Notes

1. *Genesis* 9:20.   **2.** *John* 2:1–11; The Iliad Bk. VI; The Odyssey Bk. 9.   **3.** Edward Behr, Prohibition: Thirteen Years that Changed America 9 (2011).   **4.** Daniel Okrent, Last Call: The Rise and Fall of Prohibition 7 (2010); Thomas R. Pegram, Battling Demon Rum: The Struggle for a Dry America, 1800–1933, at 7 (1998).   **5.** Pegram, *supra* at ix.   **6.** *Tenn. Wine & Spirits Retailers Ass'n v. Thomas*, 588 U.S. 504, 520 & n.6 (2019); Behr, *supra* at 9.   **7.** 2 Samuel Johnson, The Lives of the Most Eminent English Poets 399 (1781).   **8.** Bureau of Justice Statistics, U.S. Dep't of Justice, No. NCJ 168632, Alcohol and Crime: An Analysis of National Data on the Prevalence of Alcohol Involvement in Crime iii, vi–vii, 1 (rev. Apr. 28, 1998), https://perma.cc/NG3V-ZCKQ; *Breithaupt v. Abram*, 352 U.S. 432, 439 (1957).   **9.** Jack S. Blocker, Jr., American Temperance Movements: Cycles of Reform (1989);

Joseph R. Gusfield, Symbolic Crusade: Status Politics and the American Temperance Movement (1963). Richard F. Hamm, Shaping the 18th Amendment: Temperance Reform, Legal Culture, and the Polity, 1880–1933 (1995); John Kobler, Ardent Spirits: The Rise and Fall of Prohibition (1973); Lisa McGirr, The War on Alcohol: Prohibition and the Rise of the American State (2016); Pegram, *supra*; W.J. Rorabaugh, The Alcoholic Republic: An American Tradition (1981); Sarah W. Tracy, Alcoholism in America: From Reconstruction to Prohibition (2005); The Prohibition in the United States: A History from Beginning to End (2019); Clark Byse, *Alcoholic Beverage Control Before Repeal*, 7 Law & Contemp. Prob. 544 (1940). For an extensive list of sources, see Pegram, *supra*, at 191–201.   **10.** Pegram, *supra*, at 3–42.   **11.** Pegram, *supra* at 43–108.   **12.** 41 Stat. 305–323, ch. 85.

~~~~~

ESSAY NO. 206: THE SUFFRAGE AMENDMENT
AMEND. 19

The right of citizens of the United States to vote shall not be denied or abridged by the United States or by any State on account of sex.
Congress shall have power to enforce this article by appropriate legislation.
—Judge Edith H. Jones & Jacob R. Weaver

INTRODUCTION

The Nineteenth Amendment very precisely models the Fifteenth Amendment by stating simply that the right to vote shall not be denied or abridged on account of sex and that Congress is empowered to enforce it. Ratification of the Nineteenth Amendment culminated a seven-decade effort to enfranchise American women. Yet the speed with which the amendment moved through Congress to a three-fourths affirmative vote of state legislatures belies the complex and prolonged political struggle behind it.

EARLY HISTORY

The Constitution never impeded women's suffrage or any other rights of women. As adopted in 1788, it embraced "We the People" and was written in gender-neutral language, using such terms as "persons" and "citizens." The word "he," when sparsely used, generically encompassed both sexes.[1] By contrast, the Northwest Ordinance enacted in 1787 authorized one representative per 500 "male inhabitants" in territorial assemblies,[2] and the New York State Constitution referred to the state legislature as

consisting of "two separate and distinct bodies of men."[3] Contemporary legislators knew how to specify males.

A principal support of the federalist framework lay in the requirement that "electors" for the House of Representatives "shall have the Qualifications requisite for Electors of the most numerous Branch of the State Legislature."[4] Madison explained this provision in Federalist Nos. 52 and 57: The states retained exclusive authority to define who could vote for House members, subject to Congress's ability to determine the times, places, and manner of federal elections, in order to ensure members' dependence on their local constituents and curb their appetite to usurp power over the states. The U.S. Supreme Court has routinely acknowledged the rights of states to determine the qualifications of voters.[5]

All but one of the original thirteen states limited the franchise to (usually white) men who also satisfied requirements as to age, residency, and often property ownership.[6] New Jersey, the exception, allowed "adult inhabitants" who owned a certain amount of property to vote between 1776 and 1807, and as a result, thousands of unmarried women voted.[7] (Married women were not eligible to vote due to coverture; because they could not own property, they were not eligible to be electors.) The state's 1790 election law expressly denominated voters as "he or she."[8] However, political maneuvering ahead of the 1808 federal elections led the legislature to extend the franchise to any white male taxpayer but also to withdraw it from women and black men.[9]

SUFFRAGE DURING THE ANTEBELLUM AND RECONSTRUCTION PERIODS

The start of the broad movement for women's rights is generally pegged to the 1848 conference in Seneca Falls, New York.[10] But as the New Jersey experience shows, this was not the first discussion about women's access to the ballot. In Virginia, the debate over women's place in the polity cropped up during the convention of 1829;[11] in 1838, Kentucky became the first state to allow women to vote in school board elections;[12] and in 1846, a group of women petitioned the New York convention for suffrage.[13] But credit is due to Seneca Falls hosts Elizabeth Cady Stanton and Lucretia Mott, who were originally associated with the emancipation movement.[14] Frederick Douglass and several black women attended the Seneca Falls meeting and supported the ladies' work.[15] The conference ultimately called for women's suffrage as well as other, more radical reforms.[16] After Seneca Falls, the women's movement spread nationally, often in conjunction with the emancipation movement.[17]

During the Civil War, leaders of the movement, including Stanton and Susan B. Anthony, supported the Union cause.[18] Afterward, they lobbied the Reconstruction Congress to include women's suffrage in the Fourteenth Amendment. Instead, the women were shocked when Section 2 was drafted to reduce the congressional delegation of any state that denied "male inhabitants" the right to vote according to a formula based on "male citizens."[19] Although the leaders obtained ten thousand signatures on a petition to strike the word "male,"[20] their advocacy failed. They then sought to include women's suffrage in the Fifteenth Amendment,

but its scope was ultimately limited to "race, color or previous condition of servitude."[21] At this point, a bitter rift developed between the women's movement leaders who were determined to oppose the Fifteenth Amendment, often with ugly racist rhetoric, and those who supported the amendment.[22] The rift would last for more than twenty years.[23]

Starting in 1874, suffragists persuaded members of Congress repeatedly to introduce a proposed sixteenth amendment that would enfranchise women.[24] The suffragists also undertook to secure eligibility to vote in court cases founded principally on the Citizenship and Privileges or Immunities Clauses in Section 1 of the Fourteenth Amendment.[25] The Supreme Court rejected their arguments in *Minor v. Happersett* (1874).[26] The Court settled that women are "citizens" of the United States,[27] but Chief Justice Morrison Waite's majority opinion held that because the regulation of suffrage is constitutionally reserved to the states, it is not among the privileges or immunities of national citizenship.[28]

SUFFRAGE IN THE STATES AND TERRITORIES

Through the next several decades, the cause of women's suffrage made slow progress. Even as a constitutional suffrage amendment stalled, the states and territories began to extend the franchise to women. The territories of Wyoming and Utah adopted full women's suffrage in 1869 and 1870, respectively.[29] The 1872 national Republican Party platform mildly endorsed women's rights.[30] Some states and localities enfranchised women in school board and municipal elections.[31] However, adverse state supreme court decisions stymied such efforts.[32] For example, the New Jersey Supreme Court held that only male citizens were entitled to vote for elected officers under the New Jersey constitution,[33] and the Michigan Supreme Court ruled that the Michigan constitution did not give the legislature the authority to create a new class of voters in women.[34] Colorado and Idaho enacted full women's suffrage in the 1890s.[35]

Then, by about 1910, the tide began to turn. Five additional states established full women's suffrage by the end of 1912.[36] That year, the Progressive Party platform became the first to endorse full suffrage for women.[37] A half-dozen other states enacted "presidential suffrage," enabling women to vote for presidential electors.[38] By 1916, both the Democratic and Republican Party platforms supported states' enlarging the franchise to women.[39] President Woodrow Wilson initially supported the states' rights position, which was perceived as critical to the party's Southern electoral base.[40] A few years later, however, he switched to advocate for a constitutional amendment supporting women's suffrage.[41]

ADOPTION OF THE NINETEENTH AMENDMENT

In 1918, a close congressional vote for the Nineteenth Amendment failed,[42] but political and social forces had aligned for final passage the following year. The public recognized women's valiant service during World War I in employment outside the home and in foreign fields.[43] Ongoing economic and industrial changes were vastly increasing the opportunities for women to join the workforce. The liquor industry, which initially feared that women's suffrage would bring about Prohibition, retreated from funding opposition to the movement after the Eighteenth Amendment was ratified in early 1919.[44] Suffragists had mounted widely publicized parades and large demonstrations,[45] and public sympathy was engendered by Washington, D.C., jailers' horrific mistreatment of women suffragists who were arrested for regularly picketing in front of the White House.[46] Nevertheless, a vigorous debate centered on the propriety of a constitutional amendment versus states' exclusive right to determine voter eligibility, on broader social consequences, and on whether women's enfranchisement would encourage divisive social legislation.[47] Congress enacted the amendment by June 1919, and three-fourths of the states ratified by August 1920.[48]

LITIGATION AFTER THE NINETEENTH AMENDMENT

Ratification was followed by a quick series of constitutional challenges. Petitioners argued that the amendment was too significant to be enforced without a particular state's consent, that the ratifying state's legislatures lacked the power to do so, or that they violated legislative procedure in the process.[49] The Supreme Court made short work of these constitutional challenges to the amendment, which the Court interpreted simply to prevent denial or abridgment of the right to vote on account of sex.[50]

However, *Adkins v. Children's Hospital of the District of Columbia* (1923) overturned a minimum wage law for women.[51] Justice George Sutherland, who in his private law practice advised suffragist Alice Paul, wrote the majority opinion.[52] He reasoned that the Nineteenth Amendment culminated revolutionary changes in women's status such that legislative protections of their ability to contract must be viewed with skepticism.[53] The Court later rejected a male voter's challenges to a Georgia poll tax that exempted women who chose not to register to vote.[54] Regarding the Nineteenth Amendment, the Court dryly observed that the poll tax exemption was not intended to "deny" men the right to vote "on account of" their sex.[55]

At the state and federal levels, courts wrestled with whether the amendment implicitly compelled women's eligibility to serve on juries.[56] On the other hand, there was no doubt that women voters could serve in elective offices as a result of the amendment.[57]

OPEN QUESTIONS

- Recent scholars have criticized the Court's "thin," textualist interpretation of the Nineteenth Amendment.[58] One prominent scholar lauds instead the *Adkins* Court's reasoning about the scope of post-Nineteenth Amendment women's rights, although that decision has long been criticized for its roots in the "*Lochner* era."[59] The question is whether proponents of a "thick," or purposivist, approach to the Nineteenth Amendment can find affirmation in the courts—something they have yet to do.[60]

Cite as: Judge Edith H. Jones & Jacob R. Weaver, *The Suffrage Amendment, in* THE HERITAGE GUIDE TO THE CONSTITUTION 782 (Josh Blackman & John G. Malcolm eds., 3d ed. 2025).

Notes

1. Noah Webster, American Dictionary of the English Language (1828); Thomas G. West, Vindicating the Founders: Race, Sex, Class, and Justice in the Origins of America 75 (1997). **2.** Act of Aug. 7, 1789, 1 Stat. 51, n.(*a*) (reproducing the Northwest Ordinance of 1787 enacted by the Confederation Congress). **3.** Robert Natelson, *A Woman as President? The Gender-Neutral Constitution*, Volokh Conspiracy (Oct. 28, 2015), https://perma.cc/S87P -V8EJ. **4.** Art. I, § 2, cl. 1; Art. II, § 1; Act of Jul. 9, 1778, 1 Stat. 4, Art. II. **5.** *Shelby Cnty. v. Holder*, 570 U.S. 529, 543 (2013) (citing *Carrington v. Rash*, 380 U.S. 89, 91 (1965)). **6.** Hayley N. Lawrence, *The Untold History of Women's Suffrage: Voting Rights Pre-Ratification*, 52 Int'l Soc'y Barristers Q. 1, 4–10 (2021). **7.** Judith Apter Klinghoffer & Lois Elkis, *"The Petticoat Electors": Women's Suffrage in New Jersey, 1776–1807*, 12 J. Early Rep. 159 (1992). **8.** *Id.* at 172. **9.** *Id.* at 186–89. **10.** Tracy Thomas, *Reclaiming the Long History of the "Irrelevant" Nineteenth Amendment for Gender Equality*, 105 Minn. L. Rev. 2623, 2627–28 (2021); Joellen Lind, *Dominance and Democracy: The Legacy of Woman Suffrage for the Voting Right*, 5 UCLA Women's L.J. 103, 145–148 (1994). **11.** Proceedings and Debates of the Virginia State Convention of 1829–30, at 55, 66–70, 227, 351 (1830). **12.** Lawrence, *supra* at 19. **13.** Thomas, *supra* at 2628; Report of the Debates and Proceedings of the Convention for the Revision of the Constitution of the State of New York 646 (1846). **14.** Thomas, *supra* at 2627–30. **15.** *Id.* at 2630. **16.** 1 History of Woman Suffrage 67–74 (Susan B. Anthony, Matilda Joslyn Gage, Elizabeth Cady Stanton eds., 2d ed. 1889). **17.** Thomas, *supra* at 2631–32. **18.** Lind, *supra* at 150. **19.** Reva B. Siegel, *She the People: The Nineteenth Amendment, Sex Equality, Federalism, and the Family*, 115 Harv. L. Rev. 947, 968–69 (2002). **20.** *Id.* at 969. **21.** Amend. XV, § 1; Siegel, *supra* at 969 & n.59. **22.** Thomas, *supra* at 2634–36. **23.** *Id.* at 2638. **24.** Siegel, *supra* at 970, 974–76. **25.** *Id.* at 971–72. **26.** 88 U.S. 162 (1874). **27.** *Id.* at 165. **28.** *Id.* at 178. **29.** Lawrence, *supra* at 24. **30.** Siegel, *supra* at 973 & n.71. **31.** Lawrence, *supra* at 17–22. **32.** *Id.* at 15. **33.** *Kimball v. Hendee*, 30 A. 984 (N.J. 1894). **34.** *Coffin v. Bd. of Election Comm'rs*, 56 N.W. 567 (Mich. 1893). **35.** Lawrence, *supra* at 25–26. **36.** *Id.* at 26 n.144. **37.** Richard L. Hasen & Leah M. Litman, *Thin and Thick Conceptions of the Nineteenth Amendment Right to Vote and Congress's Power to Enforce It*, 108 Geo. L.J. 27, 43 (2020). **38.** Lawrence, *supra* at 22–24. **39.** Hasen & Litman, *supra* at 43. **40.** Thomas, *supra* at 2644–46. **41.** *Id.* **42.** Sandra Day O'Connor, *The History of the Women's Suffrage Movement*, 49 Vand. L. Rev. 657, 667 (1996). **43.** Lind, *supra* at 191. **44.** Thomas, *supra* at 2642. **45.** *Id.* at 2643–44. **46.** *Id.* at 2644. **47.** *Id.* at 2642. **48.** *Id.* at 2646–47. **49.** *Lesser v. Garnett*, 258 U.S. 130 (1922). **50.** *Id.* **51.** 261 U.S. 525 (1923). **52.** Thomas, *supra* at 2653. **53.** *Adkins*, 261 U.S. at 553. **54.** *Breedlove v. Suttles*, 302 U.S. 277 (1937). **55.** *Id.* at 284. **56.** *J.E.B. v. Alabama*, 511 U.S. 127, 131–42 (1994); Siegel, *supra* at 1019–22. **57.** O'Connor, *supra* at 670; Nathaniel Moak, *Are Women Legally Eligible in New York as Notaries Public?*, 41 Alb. L.J. 244 (1890). **58.** Siegel, *supra*; Hasen & Litman, *supra*. **59.** Siegel, *supra* at 1012–19. **60.** Hasen & Litman, *supra* at 63–71.

PART 12

THE GOVERNMENT AMENDMENTS

ESSAY NO. 207: THE PRESIDENTIAL TERMS AMENDMENT
AMEND. 20

Section 1. The terms of the President and the Vice President shall end at noon on the 20th day of January, and the terms of Senators and Representatives at noon on the 3d day of January, of the years in which such terms would have ended if this article had not been ratified; and the terms of their successors shall then begin.

Section 2. The Congress shall assemble at least once in every year, and such meeting shall begin at noon on the 3d day of January, unless they shall by law appoint a different day.

Section 3. If, at the time fixed for the beginning of the term of the President, the President elect shall have died, the Vice President elect shall become President. If a President shall not have been chosen before the time fixed for the beginning of his term, or if the President elect shall have failed to qualify, then the Vice President elect shall act as President until a President shall have qualified; and the Congress may by law provide for the case wherein neither a President elect nor a Vice President shall have qualified, declaring who shall then act as President, or the manner in which one who is to act shall be selected, and such person shall act accordingly until a President or Vice President shall have qualified.

Section 4. The Congress may by law provide for the case of the death of any of the persons from whom the House of Representatives may choose a President whenever the right of choice shall have devolved upon them, and for the case of the death of any of the persons from whom the Senate may choose a Vice President whenever the right of choice shall have devolved upon them.

Section 5. Sections 1 and 2 shall take effect on the 15th day of October following the ratification of this article.

Section 6. This article shall be inoperative unless it shall have been ratified as an amendment to the Constitution by the legislatures of three-fourths of the several States within seven years from the date of its submission.

—Brian C. Kalt

INTRODUCTION

The main purpose of the Twentieth Amendment was to change the timing of presidential and congressional terms and of congressional sessions. The amendment also empowered Congress to provide for the handling of two constitutional conundrums: (i) the lack of a President-Elect to take the oath on Inauguration Day and (ii) the deaths of candidates in "contingent" elections in which no presidential or vice-presidential candidate wins a majority of electoral votes and the winners are chosen by Congress.

HISTORICAL BACKGROUND

The original Constitution specified that Congress had to assemble at least once per year on the first Monday in December unless Congress legislated a different day.[1] (See Essay No. 23.) However, the Constitution did not specify a particular day on which congressional and presidential terms would begin. After the Constitution was ratified, the outgoing Articles of Confederation government issued a resolution providing that the new government would start on March 4, 1789.[2] As a matter of practice, March 4 became the day on which future congressional and presidential terms would start.[3]

By the twentieth century, this schedule was causing difficulties. Because elections were held early in November, the new Congress typically would not start its first session until December of the next year, thirteen months after being elected.[4] This delay dampened the force of the electorate's expression of its will. Moreover, voters in an election might cast out members of the old Congress or even change which party held the majority.

Regardless of the sentiments that the voters had expressed, however, the old Congress would convene in December—a month after the election—for a "lame-duck" session that ran until the term ended in March. Presidents who were not reelected also would remain in power as unaccountable lame ducks until March. Aside from this accountability problem, the second session of the term was necessarily short, which made it too easy for obstructionists to block legislation by running out the clock.[5] Congress would look to amend the Constitution to fix these problems.

THE CONGRESSIONAL DEBATES

In 1922, during a contentious lame-duck session, Senator George Norris (R–NE) proposed a constitutional amendment to reform this calendar.[6] In February 1923, the Senate overwhelmingly approved Norris's proposal. The Senate's resolution, with only minor changes, would become Sections 1 and 2 of the Twentieth Amendment. Under the proposal, congressional terms would no longer start on March 4, and sessions would no longer start by default in December. Instead, they would start on the same day in early January. Thus, the first session of a two-year term would begin on the first day of the term, two months after the election, rather than 13 months after the election. The second session of a term would begin nine months before the next election instead of one month after it and would no longer have to be conducted in such haste and with such unaccountability to voters.[7]

The Senate resolution also moved the date for the presidential term up to January, although several days after the congressional term began. This decoupling was directed at reforming contingent elections. The Twelfth Amendment provides that if no presidential candidate wins a majority of the Electoral College, the House of Representatives chooses a President from among the top candidates. Similarly, if no vice-presidential candidate wins a majority, the Senate chooses a winner from among the top candidates. Under the original Constitution, with congressional and presidential terms starting on the same day, the old, possibly repudiated,

lame-duck Congress conducted these contingent elections.[8] By starting the President's term after Congress's term, Norris's proposal was designed to have the new Congress, "fresh from the people," conduct any contingent elections.[9]

The resolution had general support in the House but was opposed by the House leadership, so it was never brought up for a vote.[10] The Senate passed similar versions of Norris's proposal again in 1924, 1926, 1928, and 1929, but each time the House either never voted on the resolution or considered only an objectionably altered version of it.[11] Although final passage in the House was out of reach in those years, the House Committee on Elections enhanced the proposal in its drafts, adding most of what would become Sections 3 and 4.

The House proposal that became Section 3 was designed to reform the Twelfth Amendment's contingent-election provisions. If the presidential election were thrown into the House, the Twelfth Amendment required the House to make its choice before the start of the presidential term. However, if no choice was made when the President's term began, the Vice President would act as President for the entire term.[12]

In 1926, the House committee softened the deadline by proposing that the Vice President would act as President after the term began only for as long as it took the House to make a choice. Once a President was chosen, the Vice President would no longer act as President. The Twelfth Amendment also had a worrisome gap: What if the Senate failed to select a Vice President before the deadline? In that case, who would become Acting President? The House committee's version gave Congress the power to provide for such a double vacancy.

The committee would use those same principles to handle several other situations. First, if the President-Elect died, the Vice President–Elect would replace him. Second, Congress could flexibly legislate a solution if *both* the President-Elect and Vice President–Elect died. During debate on the House floor, this coverage was extended beyond just death. The new language spoke of a *failure to qualify*. This catchall term was meant to encompass disability, an unresolved election dispute, disqualification, or any other scenario that could cause a new term to begin without anybody able to be sworn in as President.[13]

Finally, the House committee added what would become Section 4. This provision empowered Congress to address the death of a contingent-election candidate.[14] At every other point in the election process, a presidential or vice-presidential candidate who died could be replaced by his party, but in a contingent election, if one of the finalists died, the Constitution would not allow him to be replaced, effectively disenfranchising the dead candidate's supporters.[15] With Section 4, Congress was empowered to legislate a solution to this problem.

The logjam in the House was finally broken after Democrats won a majority in the 1930 midterm elections. The Senate again easily passed Senator Norris's simple resolution, and this time the House passed its enhanced version, also by an overwhelming margin. A conference committee set January 3 as the date for Congress's term to start and January 20 for the President's term to begin. The committee also provided under Section 5 that the amendment would become effective on October 15 of the year it was ratified. The Senate readily accepted the House's additions in Sections 3 and 4. The conference committee also included Section 6, a seven-year deadline for ratification similar to one the House's version had included. On March 1 and 2, 1932, the two chambers approved this final version and sent the amendment to the states for ratification.

THE RATIFICATION DEBATES

Ratification of the Twentieth Amendment was swift and uncontroversial. The process was completed less than a year later on January 23, 1933.[16] By April, all forty-eight states had ratified it. Twenty-nine of those ratifications occurred between Election Day 1932 and March 4, 1933. During that period, the Great Depression raged, and the lame-duck government sat paralyzed while the newly elected President Franklin Roosevelt and Congress waited agonizingly for their terms to begin.

THE AMENDMENT IN PRACTICE

As Section 5 provided, Sections 1 and 2 of the amendment became operative on October 15, 1933. Thus, the second session of the 73rd Congress began on January 3, 1934, instead of on March 4; the 74th Congress began on January 3, 1935; and President Franklin Roosevelt's second term began on January 20, 1937. All subsequent congressional and presidential terms have followed Section 1.

In 1934, Congress updated the congressional calendar and compressed the Electoral College timeline so that it would be completed before January 20 instead of March 4.[17]

In 1947, Congress enacted a new Presidential Succession Act that revised the line of succession, placing the Speaker of the House first in line after the Vice President. Like earlier succession statutes, the 1947 law applied if a double vacancy arose in the middle of the term—that is, if both the President and Vice President died. In an innovation, the 1947 act also applied to a double vacancy that arose on Inauguration Day.[18]

Other than these provisions, Sections 3 and 4 have lain mostly dormant. To date, no President-Elect has ever died or failed to qualify, no election has remained unresolved past the start of the term, and Congress has never passed legislation under Section 4 to address the death of a presidential or vice-presidential candidate in a contingent election.[19]

JUDICIAL PRECEDENT

Because the Twentieth Amendment is straightforward and technical, it has generated virtually no litigation. One case, *Lindsay v. Bowen* (2014), dealt with an underaged presidential candidate challenging a state's decision to exclude her from the ballot.[20] She argued that under Section 3, Congress had exclusive power to judge presidential candidates' qualifications; the Ninth Circuit disagreed.[21]

OPEN QUESTIONS

- If neither candidate has an Electoral College majority, the contingent presidential election is conducted "immediately" after the electoral-vote count. Under current law, the votes are counted on January 6, three days after the new congressional term starts on January 3. Could Congress set the counting day before January 3? Nothing in the text of the Twentieth Amendment expressly specifies that the count may not be conducted before the new Congress assembles. However, it is clear that the Framers wanted contingent elections to be conducted by the new Congress instead of the outgoing Congress.[22] To what extent should the Framers' intentions inform a court's interpretation of the text?

- Under Sections 1 and 2, lame-duck sessions of Congress routinely meet after Election Day. When lame-duck Congresses have taken consequential actions, such as impeachment, some have questioned the validity of those actions, citing the spirit of the Amendment.[23] Should lame-duck sessions after Election Day be eliminated?
- When does someone become the President-Elect for purposes of Section 3? Is it as soon as the Electoral College votes in December? Is it only when the electoral votes are officially counted in January? If a candidate dies after the Electoral College has voted but before Congress can count the votes, do those votes count? How does Section 3 apply?

Cite as: Brian C. Kalt, *The Presidential Terms Amendment, in* THE HERITAGE GUIDE TO THE CONSTITUTION 788 (Josh Blackman & John G. Malcolm eds., 3d ed. 2025).

Notes

1. Art. I, § 4, cl. 2.   **2.** 34 J. Cont. Cong. 515 (Sept. 12, 1788).   **3.** Edward J. Larson, *The Constitutionality of Lame Duck Lawmaking: The Text, History, Intent, and Original Meaning of the Twentieth Amendment*, 2012 Utah L. Rev. 707, 716–17.   **4.** David E. Kyvig, Explicit and Authentic Acts: Amending the U.S. Constitution, 1776–1995, at 269–70 (1996).   **5.** Larson, *supra* at 727, 739–44.   **6.** *Id.* at 718–22.   **7.** Kyvig, *supra* at 270–71.   **8.** Larson, *supra* at 744–46.   **9.** S. Rep. No. 72-26, at 4 (1932).   **10.** George W. Norris, Fighting Liberal: The Autobiography of George W. Norris 337–39 (1945).   **11.** Larson, *supra* at 728–29.   **12.** Amend. XII.   **13.** Brian C. Kalt, *A Distinct System for Presidential Succession on Inauguration Day: Getting the Most out of* *Section 3 of the Twentieth Amendment*, 46 Cardozo L. Rev. 307 (2024).   **14.** Brian C. Kalt, *Of Death and Deadlocks: Section 4 of the Twentieth Amendment*, 54 Harv. J. on Legis. 101, 117, 124 (2017).   **15.** *Id.*   **16.** Larson, *supra* at 734.   **17.** Twentieth Amendment Adjustment Act, Pub. L. No. 73-286, 48 Stat. 879 (1934).   **18.** Act of July 18, 1947, 61 Stat. 380, 380–81.   **19.** Kalt, *Of Death and Deadlocks, supra* at 145–47.   **20.** 750 F.3d 1061 (9th Cir. 2014).   **21.** *Id.* at 1065.   **22.** Larson, *supra* at 744–46.   **23.** Bruce Ackerman, The Case Against Lameduck Impeachment (1999); John Copeland Nagle, *A Twentieth Amendment Parable*, 72 N.Y.U. L. Rev. 470 (1997); Larson, *supra* at 709 et seq.

ESSAY NO. 208: THE REPEAL OF PROHIBITION AMENDMENT
AMEND. 21

Section 1. The eighteenth article of amendment to the Constitution of the United States is hereby repealed.

Section 2. The transportation or importation into any State, Territory, or Possession of the United States for delivery or use therein of intoxicating liquors, in violation of the laws thereof, is hereby prohibited.

Section 3. This article shall be inoperative unless it shall have been ratified as an amendment to the Constitution by conventions in the several States, as provided in the Constitution, within seven years from the date of the submission hereof to the States by the Congress.

—Paul J. Larkin

INTRODUCTION

The Twenty-First Amendment made the United States "wet" at the discretion of the states. What repeal did legally beyond that has been a matter of debate. Did Section 2 grant the states independent constitutional authority, exempt from (for instance) the Commerce Clause, to regulate the manufacture, transportation, sale, and possession of alcohol as they saw fit? Or did Section 1 merely repeal the Eighteenth Amendment while Section 2 left the states subject to the restraints elsewhere imposed by the Constitution? Over the past eighty years, the U.S. Supreme Court has changed its position as to how these questions should be answered.

THE REPEAL OF PROHIBITION

The Eighteenth Amendment granted the federal and state governments a "concurrent" enforcement power to regulate alcohol. Section 1 of the Twenty-First Amendment expressly repealed the federal government's power to regulate alcohol, but Section 2 retained the state's enforcement power: "The transportation or importation into any State, Territory, or Possession of the United States for delivery or use therein of intoxicating liquors, in violation of *the laws thereof,* is hereby prohibited." Here, "the laws thereof" refers to state laws. Therefore, the violation of state liquor laws actually violates the federal Constitution.[1]

THE TWENTY-FIRST AMENDMENT AND THE COMMERCE CLAUSE

As written, the Commerce Clause affirmatively empowers Congress to regulate interstate commerce and does not disable the states from doing likewise.[2] Nonetheless, the Supreme Court has interpreted the clause to contain an implicit "negative command" as well.[3] Under the so-called Dormant Commerce Clause, states are disempowered from discriminating against or unduly burdening interstate commerce absent express congressional permission.[4] This doctrine rests on the premise that the Framers adopted the Commerce Clause "to avoid the tendencies toward economic Balkanization that had plagued relations among the Colonies and later among the States under the Articles of Confederation."[5]

A few years after the Prohibition repeal amendment took effect, the Supreme Court had to decide whether the Commerce Clause limited a state's Twenty-First Amendment authority to regulate liquor. In a series of opinions by Justice Louis D. Brandeis,[6] the Court held that a state's greater power to ban alcohol altogether included the lesser power to allow alcohol to be sold under

whatever conditions a state saw fit, even if they would otherwise violate the Commerce Clause.[7] Thus, the Court's case law allowed states to discriminate against liquor produced out of state.[8] The effect of these early cases was to treat the Twenty-First Amendment as an exception to the Commerce Clause.[9] These cases, which came on the heels of Prohibition's repeal, paid little or no attention to the repeal amendment's provenance. Perhaps the justices were intimately familiar with the events of that era.

The tide shifted in *Hostetter v. Idlewild Bon Voyage Co.* (1964), which held that New York could not prohibit the sale of alcohol to international travelers leaving from a state airport.[10] Without affirmatively overruling the 1930s-era precedents, the Court rejected the notion that the Twenty-First Amendment had repealed the Commerce Clause for alcohol regulations.[11] Another case decided on the same day, *Department of Revenue v. James B. Beam Distilling Co.* (1964), held that a state cannot tax the importation of alcohol under the Twenty-First Amendment because the Export-Import Clause of Article I expressly prohibits any such tax absent express congressional approval.[12] Other cases from the 1980s found various state regulations and taxes on out-of-state alcohol to be unconstitutional.[13] Finally, *Granholm v. Heald* (2005) formally overruled the 1930s precedents.[14]

In 2019, after reviewing all of its decisions, the Court concluded that the Twenty-First Amendment is but "one part of a unified constitutional scheme" and does not erase any and all constitutional limitations on a state's authority to regulate alcohol.[15] A contrary ruling, the Court held, would generate "absurd results that the provision could not have been meant to produce."[16] Accordingly, a state cannot justify otherwise invalid alcohol regulations on the ground that the repeal amendment erases any and all federal constitutional restraints on that subject.

THE TWENTY-FIRST AMENDMENT AND INDIVIDUAL RIGHTS

Alcohol does not sell itself, and the states have regulated that business ever since the Twenty-First Amendment took effect.[17] The question arose whether that amendment gave the states an additional, federally based power to regulate the alcohol industry atop the states' police power.[18] Specifically, did the Twenty-First Amendment give the states greater authority to regulate individual rights, such as the First Amendment? Here, too, the Court has done an about-face in its view of the effect of the Repeal Amendment.

Initially, the Court treated that provision as an independent source of regulatory authority. In *California v. LaRue* (1972), the state restricted nude dancing by employees of establishments licensed to serve alcohol.[19] The Court held that the state's Twenty-First Amendment power to regulate alcohol justified restrictions on what might otherwise be considered free expression. The Court also expressly rejected the claim that the state's regulations violated the Free Speech Clause, relying in part on "the added presumption" of constitutionality "that the Twenty-first Amendment requires."[20] This rule, however, would not last.

Over time, the Court has recognized that the Repeal Amendment did not override every other constitutional provision. State alcohol regulations must comply with the Free Speech Clause,[21] the Establishment Clause,[22] the Due Process Clause,[23] the Equal Protection Clause,[24] and the federal spending power.[25] *Tennessee Wine & Spirits Retailers Association v. Thomas* (2019) reaffirmed that line of cases.[26] There is no indication that the Court will walk back the current case law. Accordingly, the Court's 1930s-era precedents interpreting the Repeal Amendment have passed into the same history that holds the Prohibition Amendment.

OPEN QUESTIONS

- What is the original public meaning of the language used in Section 2 of the Twenty-First Amendment? Does it serve as an implicit exception to other limitations of state power?
- What is the original intent of Section 2? Did Congress intend to allow the states to discriminate against interstate commerce? The Supreme Court has suggested that the answer is "no."[27]

Cite as: Paul J. Larkin, *The Repeal of Prohibition Amendment*, in THE HERITAGE GUIDE TO THE CONSTITUTION 791 (Josh Blackman & John G. Malcolm eds., 3d ed. 2025).

Notes

1. Josh Blackman & Seth Barrett Tillman, *The Unresolved Threshold Issues in the Emoluments Clauses Litigation: The President Has Three Bodies and There Is No Cause of Action for Ultra Vires Conduct*, 20 Geo. J.L. of Law & Pub. Pol'y 163, 195–96 (2022). **2.** Art. I, § 8, cl. 3. **3.** *Okla. Tax Comm'n v. Jefferson Lines, Inc.*, 514 U.S. 175, 179 (1995). **4.** *Gibbons v. Ogden*, 22 U.S. (9 Wheat.) 1, 209 (1824). **5.** *Hughes v. Oklahoma*, 441 U.S. 322, 325–26 (1979); *Md. Compt. of the Treasury v. Wynne*, 575 U.S. 542, 548–50 (2015). **6.** *Calif. St. Bd. of Equalization v. Youngs Market Co.*, 299 U.S. 59 (1936); *Indianapolis Brewing Co. v. Mich. Liquor Control Comm'n*, 305 U.S. 391 (1939); *Joseph S. Finch & Co. v. McKittrick*, 305 U.S. 395 (1939); *Mahoney v. Joseph Triner Corp.*, 304 U.S. 401, 404 (1938). **7.** *Ziffrin, Inc. v. Reeves*, 308 U.S. 132, 138 (1939); *Youngs Market*, 299 U.S. at 63. **8.** *Indianapolis Brewing Co.*, 305 U.S. at 394. **9.** *McKittrick.*, 305 U.S. at 398. **10.** 377 U.S. 324, 329–33 (1964). **11.** *Id.* at 331–32. **12.** Art. I, § 10, cl. 2; 377 U.S. 341, 345–46 (1964). **13.** *Healy v. Beer Inst., Inc.*, 491 U.S. 324, 341–43 (1989); *Bacchus, Brown-Forman Distillers Corp. v. N.Y. St. Liquor Auth.*, 476 U.S. 573, 584–85 (1986); *Bacchus Imports, Ltd. v. Dias*, 468 U.S. 263, 274–76 (1984). **14.** 544 U.S. 460 (2005). **15.** *Tenn. Wine & Spirits Retailers Ass'n. v. Thomas*, 588 U.S. 504, 2462 (2019). **16.** *Id.* at 518–20. **17.** Clark Byse, *Alcoholic Beverage Control Before Repeal*, 7 Law & Contemp. Prob. 544 (1940). **18.** *Barbier v. Connolly*, 113 U.S. 27, 31 (1884). **19.** 409 U.S. 109, 113–19 (1972). **20.** *Id.* at 118–19. **21.** 44 *Liquormart, Inc. v. Rhode Island*, 517 U.S. 484 (1996); *Capital Cities Cable, Inc. v. Crisp*, 467 U.S. 691, 711–16 (1984). **22.** *Larkin v. Grendel's Den, Inc.*, 459 U.S. 116 (1982). **23.** *Wisconsin v. Constantineau*, 400 U.S. 433 (1971). **24.** *Craig v. Boren*, 429 U.S. 190 (1976). **25.** *South Dakota v. Dole*, 483 U.S. 203 (1987). **26.** 588 U.S. at 529–537. **27.** *Id.* at 529 & n.14 ((citing Aaron Nielson, *No More "Cherry-Picking": The Real History of the 21st Amendment's § 2*, 28 Harv. J.L. & Pub. Pol'y 281 (2004)).

~

ESSAY NO. 209: THE PRESIDENTIAL TERM LIMITS AMENDMENT
AMEND. 22

Section 1. No person shall be elected to the office of the President more than twice, and no person who has held the office of President, or acted as President, for more than two years of a term to which some other person was elected President shall be elected to the office of President more than once. But this Article shall not apply to any person holding the office of President when this Article was proposed by Congress, and shall not prevent any person who may be holding the office of President, or acting as President, during the term within which this Article becomes operative from holding the office of President or acting as President during the remainder of such term.

Section 2. This article shall be inoperative unless it shall have been ratified as an amendment to the Constitution by the legislatures of three-fourths of the several States within seven years from the date of its submission to the States by the Congress.

—Judge Chad A. Readler & Andy Nolan

INTRODUCTION

Until 1951, Presidents traditionally served for a maximum of two terms. In their attempts for a third term, Ulysses Grant in 1880 and Theodore Roosevelt in 1912 tried unsuccessfully to break that tradition. Franklin Roosevelt circumvented the two-term tradition in 1940 and 1944 with his third and fourth terms. In response, Congress considered a two-term limit for Presidents. Congress eventually approved the proposition and sent the amendment to the states for ratification, which proved to be a slow process. The amendment was ratified in 1951, four years after Congress had sent it to the states. Since the amendment's ratification, there have been calls to repeal and end term limits, but the two-term limit remains, and theorized methods to circumvent the amendment have not been tested.

THE TWO-TERM TRADITION

The two-term tradition began in 1797 with George Washington's decision not to pursue a third presidential term.[1] Washington rejected pressure to return for a third term, emphasizing growing partisanship and a desire to retire.[2] Similar to Washington, Thomas Jefferson did not seek reelection for a third term at the conclusion of his second term in 1808.[3] From 1808 to 1880, the two-term tradition remained unchallenged. Popular Presidents such as James Madison, James Monroe, and Andrew Jackson similarly did not seek reelection at the conclusion of their second terms.

In 1880, Ulysses Grant attempted to break the "no third term" precedent,[4] but his efforts stalled as he lost the Republican nomination.[5] Grover Cleveland stood for election three times, winning his first and third contests,[6] and Theodore Roosevelt famously ran for (and lost) a third term in 1912, his first term having begun following William McKinley's death in office.[7] Some scholars suggest that Calvin Coolidge considered a third term; his initial term had been an abbreviated one following Warren G. Harding's death while in office.[8] These candidates enjoyed the legal right to run for a third term, but there was stiff popular resistance because of the two-term tradition. The public's philosophical opposition to a third term is thought to have played a major role in the electoral defeats of both Grant and Roosevelt,[9] and by the 1930s, the two-term norm was firmly established.

In 1940, as President Franklin D. Roosevelt's second term drew to a close, opposition to a third term stiffened. Eight states passed resolutions calling for limitations on presidential tenure.[10] Ultimately, the issue would break down along partisan lines. Roosevelt was a Democrat, and the Republican Party platform, both in 1940 and 1944, called for limiting a President to two terms.[11] Wendell Willkie, the 1940 Republican nominee, announced that he would seek a ban on third terms if elected.[12] In response, Roosevelt justified his decision to seek a third term as made necessary by an "overriding public danger" prompted by World War II.[13] In the end, resistance to the third term would not be decisive at the ballot box—Roosevelt was reelected in 1940 and 1944—but interest in presidential term limits remained, and current events would keep the issue at the forefront of public attention. In his third term, Roosevelt was perceived as having health concerns that impaired his performance.[14] He would die in 1945, just eighty-two days into his fourth term.

DRAFTING THE TWENTY-SECOND AMENDMENT

In 1947, Republicans regained control of Congress. The 80th Congress considered two proposals that would have imposed term limits: one to limit the President to a single six-year term and one to impose a limit of two four-year terms.[15] Only the latter garnered any consideration.[16] The day it first considered the proposal, a House Judiciary subcommittee favorably reported the idea to the full committee.[17] Just two days later, the full committee approved the proposal,[18] and despite Democratic accusations that the amendment was "anti-Roosevelt," the House overwhelmingly approved the two-term limitation.[19]

The House version, however, raised concerns in the Senate.[20] The language was broad: It provided that no person would be eligible for reelection who served any part of two terms.[21] The Senate Judiciary Committee worried that "[s]imply because a man might hold office or act as president for a few days or months," that person should "not arbitrarily be foreclosed from serving two further full terms of 4 years each."[22] Private meetings between Senators Robert Taft (R–OH) and Millard Tydings (D–MD), among others, brought about a compromise.[23] In this version, someone who "succeeded to the presidency" but served "less than two terms" could be "elected president twice" in his "own right."[24] President Harry Truman would be exempted from the new rule.[25]

Unlike some state constitutions, the text contains no exception for non-consecutive terms.[26] The two-term limit drops to one election if the individual has occupied the presidency for more than two years without having been elected. Such a scenario would arise if the sitting President resigned, died, or was removed from office.[27] For example, President William McKinley began his first term in 1897 and his second in 1901. After McKinley's assassination later that year, Vice President Theodore Roosevelt became President. Roosevelt served the last three years of McKinley's term and was reelected in 1904. Had the amendment been in effect at the time, it would have barred Theodore Roosevelt from standing for a third term in 1912.[28]

When the final language was brought to the floor, it was approved by the Senate.[29] The House followed suit one week later, sending the amendment to the states for ratification on March 21, 1947.[30]

RATIFYING THE TWENTY-SECOND AMENDMENT

Congress set a seven-year time limit for ratification.[31] Ratification required the approval of thirty-six states, but state-level discourse was not robust. Rather, as a contemporary magazine noted, the amendment "slipped through ... state legislatures almost without notice."[32] Within roughly two months of congressional approval, eighteen states ratified the Amendment with very little debate.[33] The amendment's chances were somewhat in doubt from 1948 through 1950. In the first two months of 1951, however, thirteen newly constituted state houses ratified the amendment.[34] On February 27, 1951, Minnesota became the thirty-sixth state to ratify the Twenty-Second Amendment, leading to its adoption.[35] All told, only the Twenty-Seventh amendment took longer to ratify.[36]

The pace of ratification resulted in a limited historical record,[37] but some observations can be gleaned from the ratification debates. For one, the primary drive to ratify came from a desire to curb executive authority. The states were particularly receptive to this view, as many had already term-limited their governors.[38] For another, the push to limit executive power came in the wake of the rise of the modern presidency as well as then-recent American brushes with dictatorships.[39] Politics also played a role. The bulk of the ratifying states had Republican-led state houses, and a handful of conservative Democratic states cemented the amendment's enactment.[40]

Some scholars reviewing the ratifying debates have understood the amendment as both a posthumous rebuke of Roosevelt and an affront to the office's then-occupant, an increasingly unpopular Truman.[41] But nakedly partisan arguments invoking either Roosevelt or Truman appear to be absent from the advocacy favoring the amendment.[42] Rather, the amendment seemingly is better understood as giving "legal effect" to the two-term tradition.[43]

CALLS FOR REPEAL

Calls for the repeal of the Twenty-Second Amendment have surfaced on occasion.

In the 85th Congress, five repeal bills were introduced.[44] At the time, then-President Dwight Eisenhower's popularity was a major motivator,[45] but opponents, echoing sentiments from the nation's Founding, claimed that the amendment's demise would contribute to a harmful culture of irreplaceable Presidents.[46] Others worried that the political effort required to accomplish rescission would distract from other important priorities.[47] Even Eisenhower demurred on the prospect of a third term were one available.[48]

Not all other Presidents have been as circumspect. Ronald Reagan spoke out in favor of ending term limits during his presidential tenure, stressing that he did not seek to take advantage of the potential opportunity for himself but nevertheless sparking renewed energy for repeal.[49] Legislative efforts have been made from time to time ever since then.[50]

OPEN QUESTIONS

As with other constitutional provisions, commentators have questioned the amendment's scope. At least one scholar has asked whether a popular President could circumvent its restrictions by running as Vice President and taking over for a President who would subsequently step down.[51] In so suggesting, it has been emphasized that the amendment bars being thrice "elected" to the office, not serving in it more than twice. That possibility, however, arguably is in tension with the Twelfth Amendment, which provides that anyone ineligible to be President is likewise disqualified from the vice presidency.[52] Professor Derek Muller has observed that the "stronger view may be that once a President has met the term limits of the Twenty-Second Amendment, he is ineligible."[53] Likewise, Article IV's Guarantee Clause has been raised as an obstacle to this proposal.[54] However, until a twice-elected President chooses to test this proposition, these debates remain purely academic.

Cite as: Judge Chad A. Readler & Andy Nolan, *The Presidential Term Limits Amendment, in* The Heritage Guide to the Constitution 794 (Josh Blackman & John G. Malcolm eds., 3d ed. 2025).

Notes

1. George Washington, Farewell Address (Sept. 17, 1796), https://perma.cc/2ZNN-BRHF. **2.** Letter from George Washington to Jonathan Trumbell Jr. (July 21, 1799), https://perma.cc/HB2N-AKQ5. **3.** Thomas Jefferson to the Citizens of Washington, D.C. (Mar. 4, 1809), https://perma.cc/MB2V-UK6X. **4.** Stephen W. Stathis, *The Twenty-Second Amendment: A Practical Remedy or Partisan Maneuver,* 7 Const. Comment. 61, 63–64 (1990). **5.** Willis Thornton, The Third Term Issue: Hot Potato of American Politics 51–57 (1939). **6.** Michael J. Korzi, Presidential Term Limits in American History: Power, Principles & Politics 64–65 (2011). **7.** Bruce G. Peabody & Scott E. Gant, *The Twice and Future President: Constitutional Interstices and the Twenty-Second Amendment,* 83 Minn. L. Rev. 565, 583 (1999). **8.** Earl Spangler, Presidential Tenure and Constitutional Limitation 9 (1977). **9.** Thornton, *supra* at 51–57, 69–71. **10.** Stathis, *supra* at 65. **11.** Peabody & Gant, *supra* at 586–87. **12.** *Id.* **13.** Franklin Delano Roosevelt, Speech to Democratic National Convention (July 19, 1940), https://perma.cc/AG6G-BSH3. **14.** Korzi, *supra* at 113–15, 119–23. **15.** Stathis, *supra* at 66; 93 Cong. Rec. 846 (1947). **16.** Stathis, *supra* at 66. **17.** 93 Cong. Rec. 863–64 (1947). **18.** *Id.* **19.** *Id.* at 872 (1947); Stathis, *supra* at 67; Martin B. Gold, The Twenty-Second Amendment and the Limits of Presidential Tenure: A Tradition Restored 235 (2019). **20.** Stathis, *supra* at 67. **21.** *Id.* **22.** S. Rep. No. 80-34, at 3 (1947). **23.** Stathis, *supra* at 68. **24.** *Id.* **25.** Gold, *supra* at 244–45. **26.** Ga. Const. art. 5, § 1, ¶ 1; Va. Const. art. 5, § 1. **27.** U.S. Const. amend. XXV, §§ 1, 4. **28.** Nathan Miller, Theodore Roosevelt: A Life 350 (1992). **29.** 93 Cong. Rec. 1978 (1947). **30.** *Id.* at 2392 (1947); Stathis, *supra* at 68; Gold, *supra* at 250. **31.** 93

Cong. Rec. 1800 (1947).   **32.** Henry Steele Commager, *To Form a Much Less Perfect Union*, N.Y. Times Mag. (July 14, 1963), at 5.   **33.** Staff of S. Subcomm. on the Const., 99th Cong., Amendments to the Constitution: A Brief Legislative History 72 (Comm. Print 1985).   **34.** *Id.*   **35.** *Id.*   **36.** David Huckabee, Cong. Rsrch. Serv., 97-922 GOV, Ratification of Amendments to the U.S. Constitution 4 (1997), https://perma.cc/ST83-S557.   **37.** J.W. Peltason, Cowin & Peltason's Understanding the Constitution 367 (12th ed. 1991).   **38.** Bernard Lemelin, *Opposition to the 22nd Amendment: The National Committee Against Limiting the Presidency and its Activities, 1949–1951*, 29 Canadian Rev. of Am. Stud. 142 (1999).   **39.** 97 Cong. Rec. 2485–86 (1951).   **40.** Stathis, *supra* at 70.   **41.** *Id.* at 70–71.   **42.** 97 Cong. Rec. 2486 (1951).   **43.** 30 Penn. Legis. J.

1597 (1947).   **44.** Stathis, *supra* at 73.   **45.** *Id.*   **46.** *Id.* at 74; 103 Cong. Rec. app. A2686 (1957).   **47.** 103 Cong. Rec. app. A3075 (1957).   **48.** Dwight D. Eisenhower, *The President's News Conference* (May 13, 1959), https://perma.cc/P33Q-KS56.   **49.** Associated Press, *Reagan Favors Repeal of Ban on Third Term*, N.Y. Times (Sept. 15, 1985), at 33.   **50.** Thomas H. Neale, Cong. Rsrch. Serv., R40846, Presidential Terms and Tenure: Perspectives and Proposals for Change 24–26 (2009).   **51.** Dan T. Coenen, *Two-Time Presidents and the Vice-Presidency*, 56 B.C. L. Rev. 1287 (2015).   **52.** Richard Albert, *The Constitutional Politics of Presidential Succession*, 39 Hofstra L. Rev. 497, 565–66 (2011).   **53.** Derek T. Muller, *Scrutinizing Federal Election Qualifications*, 90 Ind. L.J. 559, 570 (2015).   **54.** Peabody & Gant, *supra* at 620–24.

ESSAY NO. 210: THE DISTRICT OF COLUMBIA ELECTORS AMENDMENT AMEND. 23

Section 1. The District constituting the seat of Government of the United States shall appoint in such manner as the Congress may direct:

A number of electors of President and Vice President equal to the whole number of Senators and Representatives in Congress to which the District would be entitled if it were a State, but in no event more than the least populous State; they shall be in addition to those appointed by the States, but they shall be considered, for the purposes of the election of President and Vice President, to be electors appointed by a State; and they shall meet in the District and perform such duties as provided by the twelfth article of amendment.

Section 2. The Congress shall have power to enforce this article by appropriate legislation.

—Derek T. Muller

INTRODUCTION

Under the original Constitution, the seat of the federal government was not directly represented in that government. The District of Columbia was not a state, so it did not elect members of Congress or participate in the Electoral College. The Twenty-Third Amendment, ratified in 1961, ensured that the District of Columbia could participate in presidential elections. No major legal disputes have arisen over this amendment. Nevertheless, it complicates efforts to make the District of Columbia a state, and proponents recognize that statehood ought to be coupled with repeal of the amendment to avoid electoral difficulties.

HISTORICAL BACKGROUND

The Constitution anticipated a District that would become the seat of government for the United States. States would cede land to the federal government, and Congress would then exercise authority over that territory.[1] Residents of what would become the District of Columbia were unable to participate in federal elections. There is no significant record of the Framers discussing a choice to exclude residents of the District from federal elections. In Federalist No. 43, James Madison observed that the District's arrangement "obviated" "every imaginable objection." Although he did not elaborate on the point, he wrote that "sufficient inducements of interests" would make inhabitants of the District "willing parties to the cession." Madison stressed that the District would "of course" be allowed "a municipal legislature for local purposes."

Congress's proximity to the District seemed

to suggest that it would govern in the District's interest, but, over the decades, indirect representation fell out of favor in both law and practice in federal elections. The Seventeenth Amendment, for instance, took the election of Senators out of the hands of the legislature and into the hands of the people. Likewise, at the Founding, many state legislatures chose presidential electors, but the election of presidential electors now takes place exclusively by popular vote in every state.

This expanding preference for direct election and representation carried over to the seat of government. In 1883, Representative Henry Blair of New Hampshire introduced an ultimately unsuccessful amendment that would have given electoral votes in presidential elections to the District of Columbia.[2] During the first half of the twentieth century, more than a dozen similar amendments were suggested.[3] After World War II, District of Columbia residents were active in advocating for federal representation. The area saw an influx "of young, liberal Democrats" who identified such representation with a larger movement for civil rights.[4]

THE CONGRESSIONAL DEBATES

Formal consideration of what would become the Twenty-Third Amendment began in 1959. Senator Estes Kefauver of Tennessee introduced Senate Joint Resolution 39.[5] The resolution was meant originally to give governors emergency authority to appoint temporary House members in the event that more than half of the House's authorized seats were vacant at a single time; then two amendments were added.[6] The first proposed to eliminate the poll tax in federal elections.[7] The second proposed to grant residents of the District of Columbia electors in federal elections and non-voting delegates in the House of Representatives with the number of electors and delegates to be determined by the District's population just as it was in the states.[8] In 1960, this proposal would have resulted in four electoral votes and two delegates for the District.[9]

On the floor of the Senate, the amendment to grant suffrage to District of Columbia residents was praised as a message to the world about America's commitment to democracy, and the current lack of voting rights in the District was criticized as taxation without representation.[10] On February 2, 1960, the Senate passed the three-part resolution by an overwhelming majority, with minimal objection to the amendment granting suffrage to the District of Columbia, and sent it to the House for consideration.[11]

In April, the House Judiciary Committee held hearings on Senate Joint Resolution 39.[12] Convinced that he would be unable to achieve committee approval of all three parts of the resolution, Judiciary Committee Chairman Emanuel Celler of New York suggested that the portions of the resolution eliminating the poll tax and granting governors emergency authority to appoint representatives be removed and that the amendment granting electors to the District of Columbia be "water[ed] down."[13] The committee approved Celler's proposal. The amendment was altered so that the District would not receive any delegates to the House and its number of electors would be capped at the number given to the least populous state.[14] This compromise in essence would provide the District with three electoral votes, regardless of its population.[15] Just as Article II, Section 1 granted the respective state legislatures plenary power over the manner of selecting presidential electors, a like power was given to Congress to provide the "manner" of appointing electors in the District. This power was not granted to the local District municipal government.

The committee presented the updated resolution to the House as House Joint Resolution 757, which was discussed on the floor on June 14, 1960.[16] Representative John Lindsay of New York supported the resolution but criticized its cap on the number of electors the District could have. He said the cap "serves no useful purpose [and] violates logic," "imposing . . . by constitutional language, a permanent inferior status upon the District's participation in the electoral college."[17] Representative Frank Bow of Ohio also supported District suffrage but regretted that under the resolution, the District would have no delegates in the House.[18]

Ultimately, the House decided, with little to no vocal objection on the floor, to replace the language of Senate Resolution 39 with the updated language of House Resolution 757.[19] The Senate approved the House's changes in

Senate Joint Resolution 39 on June 16, 1960, and the proposed amendment was transmitted to the states.[20]

THE RATIFICATION DEBATES

The requisite three-fourths of the states approved the amendment in less than a year. Only Arkansas rejected it. Arkansas state representative Marion Crank stated that the amendment was an attempt "to create another state" and that "[g]iving [the District of Columbia] electors is the first step."[21]

PRACTICE

The District of Columbia was able to cast electoral votes for the first time in the 1964 presidential election. It participates in presidential elections every four years alongside the 50 states. Perhaps understandably, the Twenty-Third Amendment has seen no major litigation since its adoption. Congress, by statute, adopted a winner-take-all system, which is how most states award presidential electors. The winner of the plurality of votes receives all three of the District's presidential electors.[22]

THE TWENTY-THIRD AMENDMENT AND D.C. STATEHOOD

Efforts to give statehood to the District of Columbia pose problems in light of the Twenty-Third Amendment. If the District were to become a state, the "seat of Government of the United States" would not be eliminated. Instead, it would be reduced to a small federal enclave containing the White House and the federal Mall with only a few dozen residents. These few residents would be entitled to the three electoral votes granted to the seat of government by the Twenty-Third Amendment. Granting three electoral votes to a community of this size is undesirable for obvious reasons.

Recent statehood efforts have included provisions requiring states to allow federal district residents to vote in the last state in which they resided, but it is unclear whether Congress has the power to compel states to do so. Statehood proposals also include an expedited process to repeal the amendment, which might leave a handful of voters unable to vote anywhere. Finally, unless repeal happened simultaneously with statehood, it could create anomalies in elections for at least a short period of time, although scholars have suggested possible work-arounds that remain debated.[23]

Cite as: Derek T. Muller, *The District of Columbia Electors Amendment, in* THE HERITAGE GUIDE TO THE CONSTITUTION 797 (Josh Blackman & John G. Malcolm eds., 3d ed. 2025).

Notes

1. Art. I, § 8, cl. 17.   **2.** John Vile, Encyclopedia of Constitutional Amendments, Proposed Amendments, and Amending Issues 480 (2003).   **3.** *Id.*   **4.** Clement E. Vose, *When District of Columbia Representation Collides with the Constitutional Amendment Institution*, 9 State of Am. Federalism 105, 115 (1979).   **5.** 105 Cong. Rec. 13944 (1959).   **6.** 106 Cong. Rec. 1745 (1960).   **7.** *Id.* at 1758.   **8.** *Id.*   **9.** *Constitutional Amendment on D.C Suffrage*, 16 Congressional Quarterly Almanac 284–287 (1960), https://perma.cc/4P65-BZZ9.   **10.** 106 Cong. Rec 1759 (1960).   **11.** *Id.* at 1765.   **12.** *Id.* at D176; D180.   **13.** *Constitutional Amendment on D.C Suffrage, supra.* **14.** *Id.*   **15.** *Id.*   **16.** 106 Cong. Rec 12552 (1960).   **17.** *Id.* at 12563.   **18.** *Id.* at 12564.   **19.** *Id.* at 12571.   **20.** *Id.* at D360.   **21.** Morton Mintz, *Arkansas Is First to Reject District Voting Amendment: Vote Is 59–26; Opponent Fears Try at Statehood*, Wash. Post, Times Herald (Jan. 25, 1961), https://perma.cc/R327-BXLP.   **22.** Pub. L. 87-389 (Oct. 4, 1961); D.C. Code §§ 1-1001.08(e), 1-1001.10(a)(2).   **23.** Derek T. Muller, *Twenty-Third Amendment Problems Confronting District of Columbia Statehood*, 2021 Harv. J.L. & Pub. Pol'y 2 (2021); Jessica Bulman-Pozen & Olatunde C. Johnson, *Federalism and Equal Citizenship: The Constitutional Case for D.C. Statehood*, 110 Geo. L. J. 1269, 1312 (2022).

⌒⌐

ESSAY NO. 211: THE POLL TAXES AMENDMENT
AMEND. 24

Section 1. The right of citizens of the United States to vote in any primary or other election for President or Vice President, for electors for President or Vice President, or for Senator or Representative in Congress, shall not be denied or abridged by the United States or any State by reason of failure to pay poll tax or other tax.

Section 2. The Congress shall have power to enforce this article by appropriate legislation.

—Derek T. Muller

INTRODUCTION

The Twenty-Fourth Amendment, adopted in 1964, prohibits poll taxes in federal elections, which only a few states still required at that time. The amendment sought to stamp out a qualification that targeted black voters after the end of Reconstruction. Two years after ratification of the amendment, the Supreme Court construed the Fourteenth Amendment's Equal Protection Clause to prohibit poll taxes in state elections as well. Litigation occasionally arises over whether some financial costs that attend voting qualify as a "poll tax."

HISTORICAL BACKGROUND

In the early days of the Republic, property ownership was commonly a prerequisite to voting,[1] but many states replaced property ownership with a requirement that voters had to pay taxes. This change significantly broadened the franchise because far more citizens paid taxes than owned property.[2]

The form of these tax requirements varied. New Hampshire's 1784 constitution, for instance, required that an adult man who desired to vote in the state Senate election could do so only after "paying for himself a poll tax."[3] Massachusetts amended its constitution in 1821 to permit adult men who paid "any state or county tax" in the six months preceding an election to vote unless that voter was "exempted from taxation."[4] States later loosened taxpaying requirements, and by 1855, almost all states had abolished their property and taxpaying qualifications.[5]

During Reconstruction, many southern state constitutions were amended to guarantee race-neutral voting rights. These provisions were often required as a condition for readmission to the Union. However, shortly after Reconstruction ended, the poll tax resurfaced in the South to dilute the effect of these provisions.

In 1889, Florida adopted the first among this new generation of poll taxes, and other southern states quickly followed. Under these laws, citizens who were otherwise eligible to vote (for example, the state's adult male inhabitants) were required to pay a tax, typically between $1 and $2, when registering to vote and then annually thereafter.[6] Some states phased out the poll tax for older voters. Mississippi required voters to pay the tax by several months ahead of an election.[7] The poll tax was cumulative in some states. Until 1953, Alabama had a $1.50 poll tax that could accumulate for up to 24 years. A person who was eligible to vote but did not register for two decades would have to pay a tax of $36 to vote.[8]

These poll taxes were often designed to disenfranchise black voters. During the 1902 Virginia constitutional convention, for instance, one delegate declared that the tax was introduced "with a view to the elimination of every negro voter who can be gotten rid of, legally, without materially impairing the numerical strength of the white electorate."[9]

Poll taxes also had the effect of disenfranchising the poor in general, including white voters.[10] Some states created "grandfather clauses" that exempted voters who had performed military service during the Civil War or whose ancestors had been eligible to vote before the

Civil War. These exemptions were designed to benefit poor white voters.[11]

The U.S. Supreme Court upheld the constitutionality of the poll tax in *Breedlove v. Suttles* (1937).[12] A white twenty-eight-year-old man in Georgia challenged the $1 poll tax, which was assessed each year on men between the ages of twenty-one and sixty but exempted the elderly, the blind, and women. The Court found that poll taxes did not deny any privilege or immunity under the Fourteenth Amendment and that Georgia could make a reasonable exemption for women without violating the Nineteenth Amendment. Instead, the Court held, "the state may condition suffrage as it deems appropriate."

THE CONGRESSIONAL DEBATES

Starting in 1939, legislation to eliminate poll taxes in federal elections was introduced in every Congress. However, these bills were never passed.[13] Members of Congress debated whether the poll tax could be abolished by ordinary legislation or whether ending them required a constitutional amendment.[14]

Over that time, some states repealed their poll taxes. By 1962, only five states—Alabama, Arkansas, Mississippi, Texas, and Virginia—had a poll tax.[15] The taxes were relatively small; in Virginia, for instance, it was $1.50 annually, and a voter must have paid all taxes due in the preceding three years.[16]

In 1962, what would become the Twenty-Fourth Amendment was introduced in Congress. Some members argued that poll taxes were racially discriminatory and that Congress should outlaw them pursuant to the enforcement powers of the Fourteenth and Fifteenth Amendments, which barred racial discrimination.[17] But these powers did not directly reach the disenfranchisement of the poor, and poll taxes also swept in both white and black voters. Congress decided against using its Fifteenth Amendment enforcement power. Rather, an amendment targeting the poll tax was considered the safer constitutional approach.

The amendment's supporters attacked the poll tax as a vehicle for fraud. The tax facilitated political corruption through vote buying. Political machines would make block payments of the tax for their voters. For instance, labor unions would pay poll taxes on behalf of their members to ensure high voter turnout among their membership.[18]

Members of Congress debated whether to abolish the poll tax in all elections or only federal elections. In the end, there was consensus to abolish it in only federal elections, a concession to advocates of states' rights. Senator Spessard Holland of Florida, for instance, argued that "many" Senators "strongly feel that the election of State and local officials and the making of decisions on strictly local matters, such as bond issues, tax millage questions, referendums, recall procedures, and the like, are properly and more effectively handled on the State and local level, and we would strenuously oppose any effort to control such matters by Federal law."[19] The final version of the amendment applied only to "any primary or other election for President or Vice President, for electors for President or Vice President, or for Senator or Representative in Congress." Congress carefully excluded elections for state, local, and municipal positions.

The text prohibited a "poll tax" or "other tax." During the congressional debates, little time was devoted to defining the terms in the amendment, such as what constituted a "poll tax" or "other tax." Instead, the principal subject of debate was whether it was appropriate for Congress to direct states how to run their elections.[20] Southern members also stressed that few states still had poll taxes and that states should retain the authority to decide for themselves what to do. Senator Allen Ellender of Louisiana argued that "[o]nly five States" had poll taxes and that "[e]very State must pass upon this question and decide whether it wants a poll tax or not."[21] Senator J. Lister Hill of Alabama expressed his "unalterable opposition to having the Federal Government interfere with or in any way meddle with the affairs of the States in connection with the matter of the poll tax or any other matter of domestic concern to the people of the States."[22]

The amendment was approved by the Senate on March 27, 1962, after surviving a ten-day filibuster, by a vote of 77 to 16 with seven not voting.[23] On August 27, 1962, the House approved the amendment by a vote of 294 to 86 with 54 not voting and one voting present.[24]

Thirty-eight states ratified the amendment by January 1964. After ratification, President

Lyndon Johnson remarked that "[t]here can now be no one too poor to vote. There is no longer a tax on his rights. The only enemy to voting that we face today is indifference."[25]

JUDICIAL PRECEDENT

The Supreme Court construed the Twenty-Fourth Amendment for the first time in *Harman v. Forssenius* (1965). Ahead of the amendment's ratification, Virginia modified its law to permit voting in federal elections only if, at least six months before each election, a voter had either paid a poll tax or filed a certificate of residence. The Court declared the Virginia law to be unconstitutional. The broad language of the Twenty-Fourth Amendment, the Court stressed, prohibited not only the denial, but also the abridgement of the right to vote. The Court construed the Twenty-Fourth Amendment in parallel with its precedents on the Fifteenth Amendment, which prohibited both denial *and* abridgment of the right to vote on the basis of race, color, or previous condition of servitude. The Court explained that the Twenty-Fourth Amendment "'nullifies sophisticated as well as simple-minded modes' of impairing the right guaranteed"[26] and applies to "'onerous procedural requirements which effectively handicap exercise of the franchise.'"[27]

The drafters of the amendment had limited its scope to federal elections. Two years after its ratification, however, the Supreme Court rejected that distinction. *Harper v. Virginia State Board of Elections* (1966) announced that the use of poll taxes as a requirement for voting in state elections violated the Equal Protection Clause of the Fourteenth Amendment.[28] *Harper* concerned a Virginia statute that required the payment of a poll tax not to exceed $1.50 as a precondition for voting in local elections. Virginia argued that this amount was minimal and thus not a significant burden on the right to vote.

The Court admitted that "the right to vote in state elections is nowhere expressly mentioned" in the Constitution but nevertheless declared the statute unconstitutional because "once the franchise is granted to the electorate, lines may not be drawn which are inconsistent with the Equal Protection Clause of the Fourteenth Amendment."[29] The Court explained that a "State violates the Equal Protection Clause of the Fourteenth Amendment whenever it makes the affluence of the voter or payment of any fee an electoral standard." The majority stressed that "[v]oter qualifications have no relation to wealth nor to paying or not paying this or any other tax."[30]

Justice Hugo Black lamented in dissent that the majority "consult[ed] its own notions rather than following the original meaning of the Constitution." This decision, Black wrote, was "apparently . . . based on the belief" that "be[ing] bound by the original meaning of the Constitution is an intolerable and debilitating evil" and "that our Constitution should not be 'shackled to the political theory of a particular era.'" Rather, "the Court must have constant power to renew [the Constitution] and keep it abreast of this Court's more enlightening theories of what is best for our society."[31] The Court, Black wrote, was on a mission to "save the country from the original Constitution." Justice John M. Harlan also dissented. He pointed out that the political process was the appropriate channel for resolution of the dispute. Most States had already abolished poll taxes in state elections, and the Twenty-Fourth Amendment was recently and quickly ratified.[32]

The judiciary has largely rejected efforts to extend the Twenty-Fourth Amendment to other financial costs associated with voting. For example, the amendment does not forbid making re-enfranchisement of felons contingent on payment of child support[33] or payment of past-due fines.[34] Additionally, the indirect costs associated with obtaining voter identification—such as the cost of obtaining paperwork that is required to obtain an identification card—do not constitute a poll tax.[35]

Nevertheless, there are some outlier cases. In 2005, a federal district court held that Georgia's voter identification law violated the Twenty-Fourth Amendment. Voters were required to provide photo identification to vote, and voters without appropriate identification needed to pay $20 for an identification card that would be good for five years. A court found that this "fee" functioned as a tax, and the Georgia legislature subsequently amended the law to eliminate the fee.[36] In general, however, voting rights claims have received a better hearing from federal courts under other constitutional or statutory bases.

OPEN QUESTIONS

- The Twenty-Fourth Amendment prohibits a poll tax or "other tax" as a requirement for voting. What is the meaning of "other tax"?[37] Are the financial penalties associated with the disenfranchisement of felons considered taxes?[38]
- The Twenty-Fourth Amendment uses the phrase "by reason of." What is the relationship between a cost associated with voting and the predicate phrase "by reason of"? A plurality of the Eleventh Circuit *en banc* concluded that "the Twenty-Fourth Amendment prohibits denials of the right to vote for which the failure to pay a tax is not only the but-for cause, but also the reason for the State's action."[39] In other words, the plurality concluded that "the Twenty-Fourth Amendment prohibits denials of the right to vote motivated by a person's failure to pay a tax."[40]

Cite as: Derek T. Muller, *The Poll Taxes Amendment, in* THE HERITAGE GUIDE TO THE CONSTITUTION 800 (Josh Blackman & John G. Malcolm eds., 3d ed. 2025).

Notes

1. Alexander Keyssar, The Right to Vote: The Contested History of Democracy in the United States 28–29 (2000). 2. Frederic D. Ogden, The Poll Tax in the South 2 (1958); Keyssar, *supra* at 29–30. 3. N.H. Const. of 1784, art. 28. 4. Mass. Const. of 1780, amend. III. 5. Keyssar, *supra* at 29. 6. Ogden, *supra* at 32–33. 7. *Id.* at 34. 8. *Id.* at 33. 9. Keyssar, *supra* at 112. 10. Ogden, *supra* at 20–29. 11. Keyssar, *supra* at 112. 12. 302 U.S. 277 (1937). 13. H. Rep. No. 1821, at 2 (1962). 14. *Anti-Poll-Tax Legislation: Hearings Before the Subcomm. on Elections of the H. Comm. on Admin.*, 80th Cong. (1947). 15. H. Rep. 1821, *supra* at 3. 16. *Harper v. Va. Bd. of Elections*, 383 U.S. 663, 664 n.1 (1966). 17. H. Rep. No. 1821, *supra* at 5; Bruce Ackerman & Jennifer Nou, *Canonizing the Civil Rights Revolution: The People and the Poll Tax*, 103 Nw. U. L. Rev. 63, 79–87 (2009). 18. Ogden, *supra* at 90–91, 100–03. 19. *Abolition of Poll Tax in Federal Elections: Hearings Before Subcomm. No. 5 of the H. Comm. on the Judiciary*, 87th Cong. 25 (1962). 20. 108 Cong. Rec. 17654–70 (1962). 21. *Id.* at 5034. 22. *Id.* at 4364. 23. S. Rep. 99-87, at 80–81 (1985). 24. 108 Cong. Rec., *supra* at 17670. 25. Nan Robertson, *24th Amendment Becomes Official: Johnson Hails Anti-Poll Tax Document at Ceremonies*, N.Y. Times (Feb. 4, 1964), https: //perma.cc/ZE6S-YCZ2. 26. 380 U.S. 528, 540–41 (1965) (quoting *Lane v. Wilson*, 307 U.S. 268, 275 (1939)). 27. *Id.* at 541 (quoting *Lane*, 307 U.S. at 275). 28. 383 U.S. 663 (1966). 29. *Id.* at 665. 30. *Id.* at 666. 31. *Harper*, 383 U.S. at 677 (Black, J., dissenting). 32. *Id.* at 685–86 (Harlan, J., dissenting). 33. *Johnson v. Bredesen*, 624 F.3d 742 (6th Cir. 2010). 34. *Harvey v. Brewer*, 605 F.3d 1067 (9th Cir. 2010) (O'Connor, J., sitting by designation). 35. *Gonzalez v. Arizona*, 677 F.3d 383 (9th Cir. 2012), aff'd on other grounds, *Arizona v. Inter Tribal Council of Arizona, Inc.*, 570 U.S. 1 (2013). 36. *Common Cause/Ga. v. Billups*, 406 F. Supp. 2d 1326, 1366–71 (N.D. Ga. 2005). 37. Allison R. Hayward, *What Is an Unconstitutional "Other Tax" on Voting? Construing the Twenty-Fourth Amendment*, 8 Election L.J. 103 (2009). 38. *Jones v. Governor of Fla.*, 975 F.3d 1016, 1037–40 (11th Cir. 2020) (en banc) (W. Pryor, C.J.). 39. *Id.* at 1045 (plurality opinion). 40. *Id.*

~

ESSAY NO. 212: THE PRESIDENTIAL SUCCESSION AMENDMENT—SECTIONS 1 AND 2
AMEND. 25

Section 1. In case of the removal of the President from office or of his death or resignation, the Vice President shall become President.

Section 2. Whenever there is a vacancy in the office of the Vice President, the President shall nominate a Vice President who shall take office upon confirmation by a majority vote of both Houses of Congress.

—John D. Feerick

INTRODUCTION

The tragic death of President John F. Kennedy on November 22, 1963, called attention to weaknesses and ambiguities in the Constitution's provision for presidential succession. For a brief moment, there was hope the President might survive the assassin's bullet. Vice President Lyndon Johnson's succession to the presidency took place while some wondered what might have been if Kennedy had lived, unconscious and disabled. Incentivized by the risk of such uncertainty, members of Congress proposed the Twenty-Fifth Amendment to the Constitution on July 6, 1965.[1] The amendment was ratified by three-fourths of the States on February 10, 1967, and proclaimed by President Johnson at a White House ceremony thirteen days later.[2] The amendment's four sections address the constitutional effect of specific succession contingencies, provide for the filling of a vice presidential vacancy, and set out procedures for handling presidential inabilities.

HISTORY OF PRESIDENTIAL SUCCESSION

In 1841, shortly after his inauguration, William Henry Harrison became the first President to die in office. When Vice President John Tyler asserted that he had become President, critics argued that Tyler was simply exercising the powers of the presidency but had not assumed the office. Article II, Section 1, Clause 6 provides that "[i]n Case of the Removal of the President from Office, or of his Death, Resignation, or Inability to discharge the Powers and Duties of the said Office, the Same shall devolve on the Vice President. . . ." What "devolve[d] on the Vice President": the "Office of the President" or merely the "Powers and Duties of the said Office"? The text was unclear as to whether the Vice President became President or discharged the powers and duties of the presidency without assuming the office.[3] (See Essay No. 97.)

In the face of this uncertainty, Tyler set what became known as "the Tyler Precedent," which would cause much confusion in the following decades.[4] In 1881, a shooting left President James Garfield incapacitated. The Tyler Precedent was one of several reasons why Vice President Chester A. Arthur resisted succession. Arthur worried that he would become President under this precedent and permanently displace Garfield regardless of whether Garfield recovered.[5] Nearly forty years later, similar concerns about the Tyler Precedent arose after President Woodrow Wilson suffered a stroke.[6] Section 1

of the Twenty-Fifth Amendment would address the Tyler Precedent.

SECTION 1

In 1963, Senator Birch Bayh of Indiana chaired the Senate Judiciary's Subcommittee on Constitutional Amendments. Bayh described Section 1 as the heart of the amendment.[7] It provided that "[i]n case of the removal of the President from office or of his death or resignation, the Vice President shall become President." This text resolved the ambiguity in the Constitution's original succession provision regarding the status of a Vice President. The Vice President would not simply exercise the President's powers; he would displace the former President and assume the office of the presidency.

Section 1 codifies the Tyler Precedent—but only for death, resignation, and removal. In those contingencies, the Vice President becomes President. Sections 3 and 4 deal with inability separately, letting the Vice President serve as Acting President during presidential inabilities. (See Essays Nos. 213 and 214.) The amendment makes clear that the President can return to the office's powers and duties upon recovery. The President remains President for the duration of an inability, just without the office's powers and duties.

Death, resignation, and removal cause permanent terminations of the presidency, in which case it would cause no problems for the Vice President to become President permanently. But inability is a temporary state from which the President may recover, and the Vice President may be seen as too eager to displace the President. In testimony before the House Judiciary committee, Bayh noted that it would be a mistake to include "inability" in the same list as death, resignation, and removal. He explained that the Twenty-Fifth Amendment would make "it easier for the Vice President to assume presidential duties" while allowing the Vice President to "act [temporarily] and not make it look as if he is power hungry."[8]

SECTION 2

Section 2 establishes a method for selecting a Vice President whenever a vacancy occurs in that office: "Whenever there is a vacancy in the office of the Vice President, the President shall nominate a Vice President who shall take office upon confirmation by a majority vote of both houses of Congress." The use of "vacancy" in Section 2 covers the contingencies of the Vice President's death, resignation, and removal. There would also be a "vacancy" when the presidency is vacant, and the incumbent Vice President would become President. In this case, the new President would leave a vacancy in the vice presidency.

A vacancy under Section 2 does not occur when the Vice President has an inability. What happens if both the President and Vice President have an inability? The congressional debates about the Twenty-Fifth Amendment suggest that Section 2 does not apply to such dual inabilities.[9] In this scenario, the person who is next in the line of succession would act as President only, under the Presidential Succession Act, without the power to nominate a Vice President.[10]

NOMINATING A NEW VICE PRESIDENT

When there is a vacancy in the office of Vice President, Section 2 empowers the President to make a single nomination. If that nomination failed, the President would make another nomination.[11] A President is not limited as to whom he nominates for the position. The President is left free to choose the best qualified person for assistance with the burdens of office and international travel.[12] An earlier version of the amendment directed the President to make a nomination within thirty days of a vice presidential vacancy, but this requirement was dropped.[13] The congressional debates indicate that the President should act with dispatch in making a nomination and that Congress will determine the time it needs to exercise its confirmation duty.[14]

CONFIRMING A NEW VICE PRESIDENT

Under Article II of the Constitution, the President nominates officers in executive and judicial branches with the "advice and consent" of the Senate. This simple majority vote by the Senate does not involve the House. However, under Section 2 of the Twenty-Fifth Amendment, both the Senate and the House must approve the new Vice President. This bicameral confirmation process gave the fullest expression to the voice of the people by the inclusion of the House of Representatives.[15]

Senator Bayh said "confirmation" was used instead of "advice and consent" (the language used in Article II) to avoid implications that might come from past precedent involving "advice and consent."[16] The conjunction of "nomination" with "confirmation" makes clear that recess appointments of a Vice President are not permitted under Section 2 of the amendment as they would be under the "advice and consent" processes. The word "confirmation" also excludes the possible use of recess appointments as with presidential nominations requiring the advice and consent of the Senate only.[17] Senator Bayh analogized the nomination and confirmation processes under the Twenty-Fifth Amendment to the existing nomination and election processes for President and Vice President.[18]

THE TWENTY-FIFTH AMENDMENT AND THE PRESIDENTIAL SUCCESSION ACT

Throughout the Twenty-Fifth Amendment's development, reference was made to the importance of keeping the vice presidency filled at all times, subject to gaps when nominations to fill a vacancy were pending before Congress. In making the case for keeping the vice presidency filled at all times, Senator Bayh pointed to the pace of international affairs and military security.[19] Prior to the Twenty-Fifth Amendment, the office of Vice President was vacant for thirty-seven years as a result of eight presidential successions, the deaths of seven Vice Presidents, and the resignation of Vice President John C. Calhoun.[20] But if the presidency and vice presidency were both vacant, the Presidential Succession Act would be available if needed.

Throughout American history, there have been two primary approaches to presidential succession. The first approach placed the presiding officers of Congress—the Speaker of the House and the Senate President Pro Tempore—as first in line after the Vice President. In 1886, Congress changed the line of succession to run to the heads of the executive departments in the order of their creation.

In 1945, President Harry S. Truman asserted that the Speaker of the House was the appropriate official to be the next successor after the Vice President. In Truman's view, the Speaker is an elected official who is chosen for the speakership by representatives of the people.[21] The Presidential Succession Act of 1947, which remains in effect, places the Speaker as first in line, followed by the Senate President Pro Tempore, and then by the heads of the executive departments in the order of their creation.[22]

An earlier version of the Twenty-Fifth Amendment provided a new line of succession in which the heads of the executive departments would be the immediate successors after the Vice President. Filling a vacancy in the vice presidency would have minimized the need to reform existing law and also would have been offensive to the then-Speaker of the House of Representatives.[23] However, Senator Bayh dropped these provisions.[24] Had the Twenty-Fifth Amendment not been in place when President Richard Nixon resigned, under the existing line of succession with a Speaker of the other party first in line, the nation might have undergone a constitutional crisis instead of a peaceful transition.

SECTIONS 1 AND 2 IN PRACTICE
Section 2 was applied on two occasions in 1973 and 1974 but not since then. In October 1973, Vice President Spiro Agnew resigned as part of a plea bargain, nolo contendere, to resolve criminal tax evasion charges. Agnew's resignation created a vacancy in the office of Vice President.

On October 12, President Nixon nominated Representative Gerald Ford, the Republican Minority Leader, to be the new Vice President. Ford testified at hearings in both houses. His nomination was approved by the Senate on November 27, 1973, by a vote of 92 to 3 and by the House on December 6, 1973, by a vote of 387 to 35. Ford was then sworn in by Chief Justice Warren Burger before a joint session of Congress in the House chamber.[25]

On August 9, 1974, President Nixon resigned as a result of the Watergate scandal and impeachment charges brought by the House Judiciary Committee. Vice President Ford immediately succeeded to the presidency under Section 1 of the Twenty-Fifth Amendment.[26] On August 20, President Ford nominated New York Governor Nelson Rockefeller to be his successor as Vice President. Rockefeller went through a lengthy confirmation process that resulted in his being confirmed by the Senate on December 10, 1974, by a vote of 90 to 7 and by the House on December 19, 1974, by a vote of 287 to 128. Rockefeller was then sworn in as the forty-first Vice-President in the Senate chamber by Chief Justice Burger.[27]

For the next two years, President Ford and Vice President Rockefeller effected a successful transition as confirmed by witnesses who testified before Senate review hearings in 1975.[28]

Cite as: John D. Feerick, *The Presidential Succession Amendment - Sections 1 and 2*, in THE HERITAGE GUIDE TO THE CONSTITUTION 803 (Josh Blackman & John G. Malcolm eds., 3d ed. 2025).

Notes
1. John D. Feerick, The Twenty-Fifth Amendment: Its Complete History and Applications 56–104 (3rd ed. 2014). **2.** John D. Feerick, *The Twenty-Fifth Amendment—In the Words of Birch Bayh, Its Principal Author*, 89 Fordham L. Rev. 31 (2020). **3.** Joel K. Goldstein, *Taking From the Twenty-Fifth Amendment: Lessons in Ensuring Presidential Continuity*, 79 Fordham L. Rev. 959, 966 (2010). **4.** *Id.* **5.** *Id.* at 966–67; Candice Millard, Destiny of the Republic: A Tale of Madness, Medicine and the Murder of a President (2011). **6.** John D. Feerick, From Failing Hands: The Story of Presidential Succession 171–72 (1965), https://perma.cc/6QWC-9UBF. **7.** Feerick, *The Twenty-Fifth Amendment—In the Words of Birch Bayh, supra* at 34. **8.** *Presidential Inability: Hearings on H.R. 836 et al. Before the H. Comm. on the Judiciary*, 89th Cong. 80 (1965), https://perma.cc/5X8A-B85F. **9.** Feerick, *History and* *Applications, supra* at 115; 111 Cong. Rec. 3253 (1965); *Presidential Inability, supra* at 86–87. **10.** Feerick, *History and Applications, supra* at 109. **11.** *Presidential Inability, supra* at 50, 54; *Hearings on Presidential Inability and Vacancies in the Office of Vice President Before the Subcomm. on Const. Amends. of the S. Comm. on the Judiciary*, 88th Cong. 62, 205 (1964), https://perma.cc/CC6D-GVSM. **12.** Feerick, *History and Applications, supra* at 109. **13.** *Id.* at 71–74. **14.** *Id.* at 111. **15.** *Id.* at 109–10. **16.** *Presidential Inability, supra* at 45. **17.** *Id.* at 110; Roy E. Brownell II, *Can the President Recess Appoint a Vice President?*, 42 Pres. Stud. Q. 622 (2012). **18.** 109 Cong. Rec. 24,421 (1963). **19.** *Id.* **20.** Feerick, *History and Applications, supra* at 314. **21.** Harry S. Truman, Special Message to the Congress on Succession to the Presidency (June 19, 1945), https://perma.cc/8XQL-4QXF. **22.** Feerick, *From Failing Hands,*

supra at 204–10.   **23.** Feerick, *History and Applications, supra*, at 71.   **24.** *Id.* at 71–75.   **25.** *Id.* at 135–57.   **26.** *Id.* at 158–66.   **27.** *Id.* at 221–52.   **28.** *Examination of the First Implementation of Section Two of the Twenty-Fifth*   *Amendment: Hearing Before the Subcomm. on Const. Amends. of the S. Comm. on the Judiciary,* 94th Cong. (1975), https://perma.cc/23ED-CCKD.

~~~

ESSAY NO. 213: THE PRESIDENTIAL SUCCESSION AMENDMENT—SECTION 3 AMEND. 25

Section 3. Whenever the President transmits to the President pro tempore of the Senate and the Speaker of the House of Representatives his written declaration that he is unable to discharge the powers and duties of his office, and until he transmits to them a written declaration to the contrary, such powers and duties shall be discharged by the Vice President as Acting President.

—John D. Feerick

INTRODUCTION

The Twenty-Fifth Amendment addresses vacancies and succession with regard to the presidency and vice presidency. Section 1 provides that if the President is removed, dies, or resigns, the "Vice President shall become President." Section 2 provides a process by which a vice presidential vacancy can be filled. (See Essay No. 212.) Section 3, the subject of this essay, establishes a mechanism by which the President can temporarily declare in writing his own incapacity. During the President's inability, the Vice President would serve as "Acting President." Section 4 empowers the Vice President and Cabinet to declare that the President is unable to discharge his powers and duties. (See Essay No. 214.)

PRESIDENTIAL INABILITY BEFORE THE TWENTY-FIFTH AMENDMENT

Article II, Section 1, Clause 6 provides that "[i]n Case of the Removal of the President from Office, or of his Death, Resignation, or Inability to discharge the Powers and Duties of the said Office, the Same shall devolve on the Vice President. . . ." The Constitution does not define "Inability." Before the Twenty-Fifth Amendment, several Presidents suffered severe incapacities. In 1881, Vice President Chester A. Arthur resisted succession after President James A. Garfield became incapacitated.[1] President Woodrow Wilson suffered a debilitating stroke, but Vice President Thomas R. Marshall did not

displace him or want to do so. The Constitution did not provide a mechanism for the President to hand off his powers, at least temporarily, during an incapacity; an ailing President's only option was to resign.

In 1955, Representative Emanuel Celler of New York solicited views from jurists, political scientists, and public officials about the idea of the President being able to declare his own inability.[2] In 1956, Celler issued a House Judiciary Committee report summarizing their views, which reflected wide agreement that the President's self-declaration would be proper.[3] Celler put his own proposal into a bill to enable the President to declare his own inability without any check on his ability to do so.

During his tenure, President Dwight Eisenhower suffered three disabling illnesses. The Eisenhower Administration, after studying the subject, joined in Celler's reform effort.[4] In 1958, Eisenhower created as a temporary solution a letter agreement with Vice President Richard Nixon. Under this agreement, the presidential powers and duties would be transferred to Nixon if Eisenhower became disabled.[5] This transfer would occur if the President declared his own inability. If the President was unable to do so, the Vice President could declare the President unable after "consultation" as seemed "to him appropriate under the circumstances."[6] In either case, the President could decide for himself when the inability ended. There was no check on the President's returning to his powers and duties.[7] This agreement would help to form the basis for Section 3 of the Twenty-Fifth Amendment. (Following Eisenhower's example, Presidents John Kennedy and Lyndon Johnson created identical letter agreements with their respective Vice Presidents.[8])

DEVELOPMENT OF SECTION 3

In the late 1950s and early 1960s, Senator Estes Kefauver of Tennessee chaired the Senate Judiciary Committee's Subcommittee on Constitutional Amendments. Kefauver held a series of hearings on the subject of presidential inability with the goal of proposing a constitutional amendment. In August 1963, after Kefauver's death, Senator Birch Bayh of Indiana became the new chairman of the subcommittee. Bayh dedicated himself to continuing Kefauver's initiative.[9] After President Kennedy's assassination, various organizations, including especially the American Bar Association (ABA), were also motivated to find a permanent solution to the disability problem. The state of the world at the time and the threat of nuclear war with the Soviet Union further emphasized the need to prevent any gaps in presidential leadership.[10]

Senator Bayh's initial proposal for a constitutional amendment included (1) a provision empowering a President to declare in writing his own inability and transfer his powers and duties to the Vice President as Acting President and (2) language providing that if the President does not so declare, the Vice President, "if satisfied that such an inability exists, shall, upon the written approval of a majority of the heads of the executive departments in office, assume the discharge of the powers and duties as Acting President."[11] The language empowering the President to declare his own inability followed the model of Eisenhower's agreement with Nixon. Another Bayh provision authorized Congress to resolve the issue in the event of a dispute between the President and other relevant officials with respect to the President's ability to discharge his duties.[12]

In January 1964, the ABA convened a group of twelve lawyers to formulate its position on the subject. Included in this group was Herbert Brownell, Eisenhower's Attorney General, who had helped to develop the Administration's approach to presidential inability.[13] Bayh, who also participated in the meeting, would praise the ABA and the initiative by the Eisenhower Administration.[14]

Hearings on the proposed constitutional amendment on presidential inability and vice presidential vacancy led the Senate Subcommittee on Constitutional Amendments to approve Senate Joint Resolution (S.J. Res.) 139 in May 1964 with changes that included dropping a provision for a Cabinet line of succession. The full Judiciary Committee approved it in August with changes and the issuance of a report.[15] It came up for debate in the Senate on September 28, 1964, and was approved by a voice vote and then again the next day on a roll call vote of 65 to 0.[16]

S.J. Res. 139 was introduced in January 1965 by Senator Bayh as S.J. Res. 1 and by Emanuel Celler in the House of Representatives as House Joint Resolution (H.J. Res.) 1. A one-day Senate hearing followed with several key witnesses, including Attorney General designate Nicholas Katzenbach, former attorney general Herbert Brownell, and ABA President Lewis Powell, appearing in support of the proposed amendment. In February 1964, both the full Senate Judiciary Committee and its Subcommittee on Constitutional Amendments approved the proposed amendment with amendments. It was debated in the Senate on February 19 and approved by a roll call vote of 72 to 0.[17]

House Judiciary Committee hearings began in February 1965, and following their conclusion in March, H.J. Res. 1 was approved by the Committee with changes from S.J. Res. 1 as approved in the Senate. In the House of Representatives, William McCulloch of Ohio and Richard Poff of Virginia successfully pressed the case for time limitations and procedures in the Constitution when cases of presidential inability were declared by the Vice President and Cabinet and challenged by the President. In April 1965, after an extensive debate in the House, the proposed amendment was approved by a vote of 368 to 29.[18] The conference committee appointed to resolve differences between the House and Senate was chaired by Senator Bayh with Representative Poff as vice chairman. The committee issued a unanimous report in June 1965 that was adopted by Congress on July 6, 1965,[19] as the proposed

Twenty-Fifth Amendment. The amendment was finally ratified on February 10, 1967.

Throughout the period from December 1963 to July 1965, members of both major political parties in both houses of Congress supported and urged the adoption of a constitutional amendment to handle presidential inabilities and vice presidential vacancies. President Eisenhower weighed in with his support as did President Johnson in a special message to Congress in January 1965. In the Senate Subcommittee on Constitutional Amendments hearings, Bayh stated that "here we have a constitutional gap—a blind spot if you will. We must fill this gap if we are to protect our Nation from the possibility of floundering in the sea of public confusion and uncertainty, which often times exists at times of national peril and tragedy."[20] In the House, Celler stated that the presidential inability gap "becomes more threatening as the complexity of the domestic and foreign policy grows." He noted that the proposal, while it did not meet every conceivable contingency, did meet "foreseen contingencies," especially the "practical human problems with reference to Presidential inability."[21]

SECTION 3 IN PRACTICE

Presidents can invoke Section 3 whenever they recognize that they are unable to discharge the powers and duties of office. Additionally, declarations of inability under Section 3 can be prospective and conditional in nature. For example, declarations can declare the circumstances under which they become effective, including the hour when the Vice President becomes Acting President.[22] Since the adoption of the Twenty-Fifth Amendment, three Presidents—Ronald Reagan, George W. Bush, and Joseph R. Biden—have invoked Section 3 to transfer their powers and duties to the Vice President as Acting President in circumstances involving general anesthesia.

In March 1981, Reagan was seriously wounded when he was shot. He entered the hospital conscious and underwent emergency surgery. Although Reagan was in the hospital for several days while recovering, he did not invoke the Twenty-Fifth Amendment.[23]

In July 1985, Reagan underwent surgery to remove a large polyp from his colon. Before receiving general anesthesia, he signed a letter that was prepared for him by White House Counsel Fred Fielding. The letter directed Vice President George H.W. Bush to discharge the powers and duties of the presidency,[24] but it also said that Reagan did "not believe that the drafters [of the Twenty-Fifth] Amendment intended [Section 3's] application to situations such as the instant one." The letter asserted that the transfer of power was consistent with a "long-standing arrangement" between Reagan and Bush, and Reagan said he did not intend that the transfer should set a precedent for future Presidents.[25] Reagan appeared to disclaim Section 3's use but nevertheless followed all of the provision's requirements. He sent his letter to the Speaker of the House and the President Pro Tempore of the Senate, notifying them of the transfer of power. Eight hours after the procedure was completed, Reagan sent those officials another letter notifying them that he was reassuming the President's powers and duties. In their respective memoirs, Reagan and his wife Nancy acknowledged that he had used Section 3.[26]

President Reagan's White House Counsel's Office compiled a binder with guidance for using the Twenty-Fifth Amendment. A memorandum in the binder emphasized that Section 3 is "eminently preferable" to Section 4, which provides for involuntary transfers of presidential powers. The memo cites Section 3's simplicity compared to Section 4 and says that its use would be "justly perceived as a voluntary and conscious decision by the President."[27]

In 2002 and 2007, President George W. Bush invoked Section 3 when he underwent colonoscopies. The transfers of presidential powers and duties to Vice President Richard Cheney lasted for about two hours. Before undergoing anesthesia on both occasions, Bush sent letters to the Speaker of the House and Senate President Pro Tempore, and he later sent letters notifying them that he was retaking power as required by Section 3.[28] The Reagan-era binder was updated and passed along from Administration to Administration at least until the Donald Trump Administration.[29] The Obama Administration had comprehensive plans for presidential succession,[30] but it is not known whether those plans included the same binder.

President Donald Trump may have had a

colonoscopy in 2019. The White House Press Secretary at the time strongly implies in her book that he underwent the procedure without telling the public or invoking Section 3.[31] In October 2020, President Trump was hospitalized for several days while he recovered from COVID-19.[32] He did not invoke the Twenty-Fifth Amendment on that occasion. On November 19, 2021, President Joseph R. Biden had a routine colonoscopy under general anesthesia and had a potentially cancerous polyp removed. Following Section 3's protocol, Biden sent letters to the legislative leaders notifying them of his transfer of presidential powers and duties to Vice President Kamala Harris and his resumption of those powers and duties.[33]

Between 1985 and 2021, other Presidents considered using Section 3 without ultimately doing so. They included Jimmy Carter;[34] George H.W. Bush;[35] Bill Clinton, whose doctor saw Section 3 as a possibility for knee surgery;[36] and Barack Obama, who had a "virtual" colonoscopy.[37]

OPEN QUESTIONS

- The Framers of the Twenty-Fifth Amendment understood that its inability provisions did not address every gap in the Constitution. Senator Sam Ervin of North Carolina, a strong supporter of S.J. Res. 1, analogized the comprehensive drafting of the provision to "the old adage that too many cooks would spoil the broth" and described the final product as the "very best possible resolution on the subject obtainable in the Congress of the United States as it is now constituted."[38] The "broth" referenced by Ervin included suggestions concerning inabilities of both a President and Vice President, the inability of a President when there is no Vice President, and the inability of an Acting President.[39] The inability dealt with in the Twenty-Fifth Amendment is that of a President, not a Vice President. Sections 3 and 4 assume there is an able Vice President. If the President and Vice President are disabled, the Amendment does not work. As for a disabled Acting President, when the Vice President is Acting President, for example, there is no vacancy in the Vice Presidency at that point. One then must move away from the Twenty-Fifth Amendment and deal with the line of succession as an aid.
- Since September 11, 2001, congressional hearings, bills, and resolutions, as well as reports of commissions, symposia, law school clinics, articles, and books, have advanced recommendations for possible additions to the Twenty-Fifth Amendment in areas of presidential and vice presidential inability. In the meantime, the Twenty-Fifth Amendment has provided a safety net that set well, as Senator Michael Mansfield of Montana put it on September 28, 1964, "in the building which is this republic."[40]
- What are the different scenarios in which Section 3 could be invoked? The 1985 Commission on Presidential Disability identified "three different medical contingencies: an emergency, a planned procedure, and treatment of chronic ailments."[41] What sorts of guidelines would be appropriate for each contingency? President George H.W. Bush and Vice President Dan Quayle discussed these contingencies.[42]
- What would happen if the Vice President was incapacitated and the President recognized or anticipated his own inability? The President would undoubtedly hesitate to invoke Section 3 when it would result in transferring powers and duties to an incapacitated Vice President. An incapacitated Vice President could not resign, and there is no way to replace an incapacitated Vice President short of impeachment. Section 3 would effectively become inoperable. Could Congress pass a law allowing the President and the Cabinet to declare the Vice President unable, which would make it possible for the President to transfer power to the next person in the line of succession after the Vice President (the Speaker of the House barring a vacancy in that office) in the event of a vice presidential inability?[43] Could Congress pass a law allowing the President, with a majority of the Cabinet, to declare the Vice President unable, thus designating someone else as Acting Vice President?[44]

- Could a President create a "prospective declaration" of inability? This declaration would identify specific situations or ailments that would render the President unable to discharge the office's power and duties. If any of those contingencies occurred, presidential powers would automatically transfer to the Vice President under Section 3.[45] Who would adjudge if one of those situations was triggered? What would happen if the President disagreed and said the situation had not yet occurred?

Cite as: John D. Feerick, *The Twenty-Fifth Amendment - Section 3, in* THE HERITAGE GUIDE TO THE CONSTITUTION 807 (Josh Blackman & John G. Malcolm eds., 3d ed. 2025).

Notes

1. John D. Feerick, From Failing Hands: The Story of Presidential Succession 121–28 (1965), https://perma.cc/6QWC-9UBF; Candice Millard, Destiny of the Republic: A Tale of Madness, Medicine, and the Murder of a President (2011). **2.** Feerick, *From Failing Hands, supra* at 238–39. **3.** *Id.* **4.** *Id.* **5.** *Id.* at 228–29. **6.** *Id.* **7.** *Id.* **8.** *Id.* **9.** *Id.* at 242–44. **10.** Rebecca C. Lubot, *"A Dr. Strangelove Situation": Nuclear Anxiety, Presidential Fallibility, and the Twenty-Fifth Amendment*, 86 Fordham L. Rev. 1175, 1178 (2017). **11.** John D. Feerick, The Twenty-Fifth Amendment: Its Complete History and Applications 71–74 (3rd. ed., 2014). **12.** *Id.* at 299–305. **13.** Feerick, *From Failing Hands, supra* at 243–57. **14.** John D. Feerick, *The Twenty-Fifth Amendment—In the Words of Birch Bayh, Its Principal Author*, 89 Fordham L. Rev. 31, 36–37 (2020). **15.** Feerick, *History and Applications, supra* at 75–78. **16.** *Id.* at 78. **17.** *Id.* at 91. **18.** *Id.* at 100. **19.** Feerick, *In the Words of Birch Bayh, supra* at 44–50. **20.** *Id.* at 63. **21.** *Id.* at 95. **22.** Feerick, *History and Applications, supra* at 198–99. **23.** Fred F. Fielding, *An Eyewitness Account of Executive "Inability,"* 79 Fordham L. Rev. 823, 825–29 (2010). **24.** Feerick, *History and Applications, supra* at 196–99. **25.** Letter from President Ronald Reagan to the President Pro Tempore of the Senate and Speaker of the House of Representatives (July 13, 1985), https://perma.cc/9ZV4-SWPD; Feerick, *History and Applications, supra* at 196–99. **26.** Feerick, *History and Applications, supra* at 198–99. **27.** Office of White House Counsel, Contingency Plans: Death or Disability of the President (Mar. 16, 1993), https://perma.cc/Q84E-DVLD. **28.** Feerick, *History and Applications, supra* at 202–03. **29.** Fielding, *supra* at 828–29; John Rogan, *Improving the White House Plans for Presidential Inability*, Lawfare (May 9, 2018), https://perma.cc/TV3K-H3DA. **30.** Second Fordham University School of Law Clinic on Presidential Succession, *Fifty Years After the Twenty-Fifth Amendment: Recommendations for Improving the Presidential Succession System*, 86 Fordham L. Rev. 917, 934 n.82 (2017). **31.** Stephanie Grisham, I'll Take Your Questions Now: What I Saw in the Trump White House 284 (2021). **32.** Noah Weiland et al., *Trump Was Sicker than Acknowledged with Covid-19*, N.Y. Times (Feb. 11, 2021), https://bit.ly/3TNKPeB. **33.** John D. Feerick & John Rogan, *Invoking the 25th Amendment Should Be* https://bit.ly/4kdd3dH. **34.** Robert J. Lipshutz, Office of White House Counsel, *Documents from Carter's Contemplated Use of Section 3* (1978), https://perma.cc/XK4B-NW84. **35.** Feerick, *History and Application, supra* at 200–01. **36.** E. Connie Mariano, *In Sickness and in Health: Medical Care for the President of the United States, in* Managing Crisis: Presidential Disability and the 25th Amendment 83, 93 (Robert E. Gilbert ed., 2000). **37.** Lawrence K. Altman & Jeff Zeleny, *President in "Excellent Health," Routine Checkup Finds*, N.Y. Times (Feb. 28, 2010), https://bit.ly/3I9e88R. **38.** Feerick, *In the Words of Birch Bayh, supra* at 49–50. **39.** Feerick, *History and Applications, supra* at 93. **40.** Feerick, *In the Words of Birch Bayh, supra*. **41.** Miller Ctr. Comm'n No. 4, Report of the Commission on Presidential Disability and the Twenty-Fifth Amendment (1988), https://perma.cc/6SS4-BGP6. **42.** John D. Feerick, *Remarks, Presidential Succession and Impeachment: Historical Precedents, From Indiana and Beyond*, 52 Ind. L. Rev. 43, 66–67 (2019); Presidential Disability: Papers, Discussions, and Recommendations on the Twenty-Fifth Amendment and Issues of Inability and Disability Among Presidents of the United States (Robert J. Joynt & James F. Toole eds., 2001). **43.** Fordham University School of Law's Clinic on Presidential Succession, *Ensuring the Stability of Presidential Succession in the Modern Era*, 81 Fordham L. Rev. 1, 27 (2012). **44.** Second Fordham Clinic, *supra* at 934 n.82. **45.** First Fordham Clinic, *supra* at 31–32; Second Fordham Clinic, *supra* at 930–37.

⌐✦

ESSAY NO. 214: THE PRESIDENTIAL SUCCESSION AMENDMENT—SECTION 4
AMEND. 25

Section 4. Whenever the Vice President and a majority of either the principal offi-cers of the executive departments or of such other body as Congress may by law provide, transmit to the President pro tempore of the Senate and the Speaker of the House of Representatives their written declaration that the President is unable to discharge the powers and duties of his office, the Vice President shall immedi-ately assume the powers and duties of the office as Acting President. Thereafter, when the President transmits to the President pro tempore of the Senate and the Speaker of the House of Representatives his written declaration that no inability exists, he shall resume the powers and duties of his office unless the Vice Presi-dent and a majority of either the principal officers of the executive department or of such other body as Congress may by law provide, transmit within four days to the President pro tempore of the Senate and the Speaker of the House of Rep-resentatives their written declaration that the President is unable to discharge the powers and duties of his office. Thereupon Congress shall decide the issue, assembling within forty-eight hours for that purpose if not in session. If the Con-gress, within twenty-one days after receipt of the latter written declaration, or, if Congress is not in session, within twenty-one days after Congress is required to assemble, determines by two-thirds vote of both Houses that the President is unable to discharge the powers and duties of his office, the Vice President shall continue to discharge the same as Acting President; otherwise, the President shall resume the powers and duties of his office.

—John D. Feerick

INTRODUCTION

Section 4 of the Twenty-Fifth Amendment allows the Vice President, acting either with a majority of the Cabinet (*i.e.*, principal officers of the executive departments) or with "such other body as Congress may by law provide," to declare the President "unable to discharge the powers and duties of his office." Such a dec-laration would temporarily transfer presiden-tial powers and duties to the Vice President as Acting President. The President can declare that he is able to resume his powers and duties, but the Vice President and a majority of the Cabinet or, again, "such other body as Congress may by law provide" can override that declaration. Ultimately, the decision falls to Congress. A two-thirds vote of each house designates that the Vice President will continue to serve as Acting President. If that vote fails, the President resumes his powers and duties. (Sections 1 and 2 are discussed in Essay No. 212; Section 3 is discussed in Essay No. 213.)

STEP 1: THE VICE PRESIDENT, AFTER DECLARING THE PRESIDENT'S INABILITY WITH THE CABINET, IMMEDIATELY BECOMES ACTING PRESIDENT

Section 4 may be invoked when the Vice President and Cabinet determine that the President is "unable to discharge the powers and duties of his office," but any member of the Cabinet can raise the subject for discussion.[1] The Vice President must join with a "majority of either the principal officers of the executive departments or of such other body as Congress may by law provide." The Vice President and other officials must then send a written declara-tion of inability to the Speaker of the House of Representatives and the President pro tempore of the Senate, at which point the Vice President will "immediately" become Acting President.

This text gives rise to two important ques-tions. First, what is an "inability"? The Framers of the Constitution included "inability" as a succession contingency but left the country no discussion of its meaning and duration.[2] Nor does the Twenty-Fifth Amendment define "inability." However, the provision's framers spoke often of its reach.

In 1965, Senator Birch Bayh of Indiana said that the words "inability" and "unable" in Section 4 "refer to an impairment of the President's faculties" that renders him "unable to make or communicate his decisions of his own competency to execute the powers and duties of his office."[3] Bayh and Senator Robert F. Kennedy of New York, in a long exchange concerning the term "inability," made clear that it meant an inability to perform all of the constitutional duties of the office of President and included both physical and mental inability. Bayh reemphasized that it included a temporary or short inability and that a President "who was unconscious for 30 minutes when missiles were flying toward this country might only be disabled temporarily, but it would be of severe consequence. . . ."[4]

Similarly, Representative Richard Poff of Virginia, another framer of the amendment, said that Section 4 covers two situations: (1) when the President "by reason of some physical ailment or some sudden accident is unconscious or paralyzed and therefore unable to make or communicate a decision" and (2) "when the President, by reason of mental debility, is unable or unwilling to make any rational decision, including particularly the decision to stand aside."[5] In 1965, testifying before the House Judiciary Committee, former Attorney General Herbert Brownell spoke of cases in which a President is "physically ill and his doctors recommend temporary suspension of his normal government activities," "is going to have an operation," or is "going abroad and might be out of reliable contact with the White House for a short period."[6]

The legislative history makes clear that the amendment does not cover cases of a President's unpopularity, impeachable conduct, laziness, or poor judgment. Senator Bayh emphasized that "the inability that we deal with is described several times in the amendment itself as the inability of the President to perform the powers and duties of his office."[7]

A second question raised at the first step is *which* body should declare the President unable to discharge his powers and duties. The body chosen for inclusion in the amendment was "the principal officers of the executive departments." Senator Robert Kennedy of New York stated that "the Deputies or Under Secretaries . . . would, when there clearly are vacancies in the Cabinet, become acting heads of the departments until new principal officers were confirmed, or, if Congress were not in session, until recess appointments were made."[8]

But Congress has the power to select "another body" through a statute to function with the Vice President. The framers of the amendment chose the principal officers of the executive departments, along with the Vice President, in the belief that those close to the President would have a sense of the facts and that a decision by them would engender public confidence. This approach makes some sense because the President would have selected his Vice President and appointed his principal officers. The President exhibited trust in these officials, so they likely could be trusted to determine when the President is unable. There is a consistency between Section 4 and separation of powers principles.

In 1964, the American Bar Association recommended that Congress should be able, by statute, to select another body to invoke the amendment and working collaboratively with the Vice President. This statutory remedy would be necessary if unforeseen circumstances or contingencies made the prescribed method unworkable.[9] Some have suggested that there are also pragmatic reasons for not vesting this power in officials that the President can fire. Robert F. Kennedy expressed reservations about the use of the Cabinet as the determining body. He said there was a need for a continued examination of that provision. Recalling President Woodrow Wilson's disability after suffering a stroke, Kennedy observed that "there was no evidence of any overt attempt to usurp the powers of the President, [yet] the ailing President nevertheless decided to dispose of [meaning fire] any Cabinet member who seemed to present a threat." Wilson had fired his Secretary of State when he heard that he was calling Cabinet meetings in an effort to keep the country functioning.[10] Kennedy worried that a "[m]ore serious . . .

conflict might follow, in a comparable situation, now that a procedure for determining disability is established."[11]

During the first Trump Administration, Congressman Jamie Raskin of Maryland introduced two bills to create "another body" under Section 4. Both proposals involved bodies composed of physicians and former high-ranking executive branch officials who would be appointed by congressional leaders from both parties. Each proposal attracted more than sixty co-sponsors, but neither was ultimately subject to a vote by the full House.[12]

Senator Albert Gore of Tennessee (father of the future Vice President) and other Senators expressed concern that confusion might arise if Congress created another body to work with the Vice President to declare presidential inabilities. These Senators were concerned that Section 4's language authorizing inability declarations by "the Vice President and a majority of either the principal officers of the executive departments or of such other body as Congress may by law provide" could support an interpretation of two co-equal bodies functioning at the same time. Senator Bayh made clear that a congressionally created "other body" would supplant the Cabinet in the Section 4 process.[13]

STEP 2: THE PRESIDENT CAN DECLARE HIMSELF ABLE AND RESUME HIS POWERS AND DUTIES, BUT THE VICE PRESIDENT AND CABINET CAN OVERRIDE THAT DECLARATION

Section 4 allows the President to disagree with an inability declaration. If the President states that no inability exists, the Vice President and Cabinet or other body created by law have four days to reassert their inability declaration. During the amendment's development, the House and Senate had different views on the length of the period for reasserting an inability declaration. The Senate specified seven days, and the House specified two days. Bayh testified before the House Judiciary Committee that the President "would have more than one chance but, having utilized the one chance, I think he would be very careful in making a second appeal to the Congress." He added that frequent appeals to Congress "would certainly reflect the attitude

with which Congress would look on his mental capacity."[14]

During the four-day "waiting period," the President would remain out of power until the Vice President and Cabinet or other body decided whether to reassert their inability declaration.[15] The House and Senate would meet separately and process the issue raised, and if they failed to make a decision within twenty-one days, the President would immediately resume his powers and duties.

STEP 3: CONGRESS MUST CONVENE WITHIN FORTY-EIGHT HOURS

After the declaration is received, Congress must act quickly. The conference committee also accepted a House amendment requiring Congress to convene within forty-eight hours after the Vice President and Cabinet (or other body) had reasserted their inability determination.[16] The forty-eight-hour provision was a suggestion made by House Speaker John W. McCormack to be sure that the resolution of the disagreement was done with speed, especially if Congress was in recess.[17]

STEP 4: FOR THE VICE PRESIDENT TO CONTINUE SERVING AS ACTING PRESIDENT, WITHIN TWENTY-ONE DAYS, TWO-THIRDS OF BOTH HOUSES MUST VOTE THAT THE PRESIDENT REMAINS UNABLE

The conference committee resolved a difference regarding the time that Congress has to consider a dispute over the President's inability. The House proposal gave Congress ten days to decide the issue, and the Senate conferees did not want any limit.[18] The committee settled on twenty-one days.[19] For the President to remain out of power beyond the twenty-one-day review period, two-thirds of both houses of Congress would have needed to affirm the inability determination that resulted in Congress receiving the issue. Lewis Powell, president-elect of the American Bar Association, stated that "[t]he independence of the executive branch must be preserved, and a President who has regained his health should not be harassed by a possibly hostile Congress."[20] It is believed that the recommendation provides appropriate safeguards for a proper balancing of the interests involved.[21]

POTENTIAL INVOCATIONS OF SECTION 4

In 1981, President Ronald Reagan was shot and underwent emergency surgery. Reagan did not invoke Section 3 and thereby declare himself "unable to discharge the powers and duties of his office," and there was some discussion within his Administration about whether Section 4 should be invoked.[22] Absent precedents, there was confusion in the White House over what steps to take. President Reagan's hospital aides (not the Vice President and the Cabinet) decided that it was unwise to transfer the President's powers and duties to Vice President George H.W. Bush at that time.[23] Later in Reagan's term in office, outgoing staff members suggested consideration of Section 4 because Reagan was allegedly "inattentive and inept," but Chief of Staff Howard Baker quickly rejected those concerns as unfounded.[24]

Following the Capitol attack on January 6, 2021, some Cabinet secretaries discussed whether to invoke Section 4 to remove President Donald Trump from the presidency's powers and duties.[25] On January 12, 2021, the House of Representatives passed a resolution calling on Vice President Michael Pence to convene the Cabinet to invoke Section 4. Examples of Trump's supposed "inability to discharge the most basic and fundamental powers and duties of his office" cited by the resolution included Trump's alleged failure to provide for a peaceful transfer of power.[26] Vice President Pence refused to invoke the amendment. He wrote that the Twenty-Fifth Amendment "was designed to address Presidential incapacity or disability," not to provide "a means of punishment or usurpation."[27] Invocation of Section 4 was also a subject of political debate in 2024 during the latter part of the presidency of Joseph Biden.[28]

OPEN QUESTIONS

- Who are the "the principal officers of the executive departments"? Which executive departments are included? Does this group include acting heads of departments?[29] The amendment's legislative history indicates that acting secretaries can and should participate in the process.[30]
- Without the Vice President's agreement, the Cabinet or another body created by Congress cannot use Section 4. Accordingly, Section 4 is inoperable if the vice presidency is vacant or the Vice President is incapacitated. Provisions to cover vice presidential inabilities and dual inabilities of the President and Vice President were excluded from the amendment because of concerns that the added complexity would make passage of the amendment more difficult.[31] Could Congress designate the next person in the line of succession after the Vice President to work with the Cabinet to declare both the President and Vice President unable?[32] Could Congress empower the President and Cabinet to declare the Vice President unable?[33]
- How should Congress resolve a dispute over presidential inability? Could Congress establish a joint committee of both houses to gather information related to the President's capacity?[34]
- Section 4 empowers the heads of executive departments to participate in a decision as to a President's inability. If a vacancy exists in a department, there is evidence in the amendment's legislative history that an acting head of the department would be authorized to participate in making such a determination.[35]
- Can Congress designate someone to act with the Cabinet under Section 4 where there is a vacancy in the office of Vice President? Can Congress declare that a Vice President is disabled?
- During a dispute over presidential inability, can Congress make informational requests of the President or adopt rules?

Cite as: John D. Feerick, *The Presidential Succession Amendment - Section 4,* in THE HERITAGE GUIDE TO THE CONSTITUTION 812 (Josh Blackman & John G. Malcolm eds., 3d ed. 2025).

Notes

1. John D. Feerick, The Twenty-Fifth Amendment: Its Complete History and Applications 117 (3rd ed. 2014). **2.** Art. II, § 1, cl. 6.   **3.** 111 Cong. Rec. 3282 (1965).   **4.** *Id.* at 15,380.   **5.** *Id.* at 7941.   **6.** *Presidential Inability: Hearings Before the House Comm. on the Judiciary,* 89th Cong. 240 (1965).   **7.** Feerick, *History and Applications, supra* at 117; John D. Feerick, *The Twenty-Fifth Amendment—In the Words of Birch Bayh, Its Principal Author,* 89 Fordham L. Rev. 31 (2020).   **8.** 111 Cong. Rec. 15,380 (1965).   **9.** John D. Feerick, From Failing Hands: The Story of Presidential Succession 253 (1965).   **10.** Feerick, *In the Words of Birch Bayh, supra* at 46–47.   **11.** *Id.*   **12.** H.R. 1987, 115th Cong. (2017); H.R. 8548, 116th Cong. (2020).   **13.** Feerick, *In the Words of Birch Bayh, supra* at 48–49.   **14.** *Id.* at 41–42.   **15.** Joel K. Goldstein, *Talking Trump and the Twenty-Fifth Amendment: Correcting the Record on Section 4,* 21 J. of Const. L. 73, 125–49 (2018).   **16.** John D. Feerick, That Further Shore: A Memoir of Irish Roots and American Promise 257–58 (2020).   **17.** Feerick, *History and Applications, supra* at 45–46.   **18.** *Id.* at 192–94; Feerick, *In the Words of Birch Bayh, supra* at 45–46.   **19.** 111 Cong. Rec. 15,379 (1965).   **20.** *Presidential Inability and Vacancies in the Office of the Vice President: Hearings Before the Subcomm. on Const. Amends. of the S. Comm. on the Judiciary,* 88th Cong. 93 (1964).   **21.** Feerick, *History and Applications, supra* at 114–21.   **22.** *Id.* at 195.   **23.** *Id.* at 192–94; Feerick, *In the Words of Birch Bayh, supra* at 45.   **24.** *Id.* at 199; Arthur B. Culvahouse Jr., *A White House Counsel's Perspective on Presidential Health and the Line of Succession,* 80 Fordham L. Rev. Online 79, 80 (2022).   **25.** Jeff Stein, *Treasury Secretary Mnuchin involved in discussions about the 25th Amendment, but is unlikely to pursue Trump's removal,* Washington Post (Jan. 8, 2021), https://perma.cc/UY2P-QXAZ.   **26.** H. Res. 21, 117th Cong. (2021).   **27.** Letter from Vice President Michael R. Pence to House Speaker Nancy Pelosi (Jan. 12, 2021), https://perma.cc/2XTD-U6VG.   **28.** Emily Brooks, *Speaker Johnson: Cabinet Should Consider Removing Biden Through the 25th Amendment,* The Hill (June 28, 2024), https://perma.cc/7244-SG2G; Martin Pengelly, *Republican cites 25th amendment in bid to remove 'too old' Biden from office,* The Guardian (Feb. 27, 2024), https://perma.cc/FCC6 -QLXF.   **29.** James Heilpern, *Acting Cabinet Secretaries & the Twenty-Fifth Amendment,* 57 U. Rich. L. Rev. 1169 (2023).   **30.** Feerick, *From Failing Hands, supra* at 117–18; Yale Law School Rule of Law Clinic, The Twenty-Fifth Amendment to the United States Constitution: A Reader's Guide 13 (2018).   **31.** Feerick, *History and Applications, supra* at 115.   **32.** Second Fordham University School of Law Clinic on Presidential Succession, *Fifty Years After the Twenty-Fifth Amendment: Recommendations for Improving the Presidential Succession System,* 86 Fordham L. Rev. 917, 959–64 (2017); Fordham University School of Law Clinic on Presidential Succession, *Ensuring the Stability of Presidential Succession in the Modern Era,* 81 Fordham L. Rev. 1, 26–31 (2012); Roy E. Brownell II, *What to Do If Simultaneous Presidential and Vice Presidential Inability Struck* Today, 85 Fordham L. Rev. 1027 (2017).   **33.** Second Fordham Clinic, *supra* at 964–68.   **34.** Feerick, *History and Applications, supra* at 120.   **35.** *Id.* at 114–18.

⌒

ESSAY NO. 215: THE MINIMUM VOTING AGE AMENDMENT
AMEND. 26

Section 1. The right of citizens of the United States, who are eighteen years of age or older, to vote shall not be denied or abridged by the United States or by any State on account of age.
Section 2. The Congress shall have power to enforce this article by appropriate legislation.

—Michael R. Dimino

INTRODUCTION

The Twenty-Sixth Amendment prohibits the states and the national government from establishing a voting age higher than eighteen. Before the Amendment's ratification in 1971, nearly all states had a voting age of twenty-one, but Americans were persuaded that people who were old enough to be drafted to fight in Vietnam were also old enough to vote. Beyond raising the minimum voting age, the amendment likely also protects young voters against intentional discrimination, even as a result of laws that make no explicit reference to age.

THE CONSTITUTION AND VOTING RIGHTS

The text of the Constitution contains no affirmative right to vote. To be sure, it declares that members of the House of Representatives shall be chosen by the "people" in "elections," which has been true for Senators as well since the adoption of the Seventeenth Amendment, and requires that voters in congressional races "shall have the Qualifications requisite for Electors of the most numerous Branch of the State Legislature."[1] But nowhere does the Constitution say that any particular class of people shall have the ability to vote for federal representatives.

Instead, the Constitution leaves the question of suffrage "to the states, but prohibits states from denying voting rights based on particular criteria."[2] Those criteria include religion under the Free Exercise Clause; "race, color, or previous condition of servitude" under the Fifteenth Amendment; sex under the Nineteenth Amendment; and "failure to pay any poll tax or other tax" under the Twenty-Fourth Amendment. The Twenty-Sixth Amendment's prohibition of age discrimination in voting rights is the most recent of these limitations on the power of states to determine the qualifications for voting.

MINIMUM AGE FOR VOTING AND *OREGON V. MITCHELL*

For most of the nation's history, states determined the minimum age for voting, and that age limit was set consistently at twenty-one.[3] Some variation was introduced beginning with World War II when Georgia lowered its voting age, but only three other states had followed suit as of 1970.

That year's amendments to the Voting Rights Act purported to require the states to allow eighteen-year-olds to vote,[4] but Congress's authority to impose such a requirement was questionable.[5] The Constitution gives Congress the power to "make or alter" state regulations concerning the "Times, Places, and Manner" of federal elections,[6] but there is no provision explicitly allowing Congress to decide *who* may vote in federal elections.[7]

The statutory amendments were challenged in *Oregon v. Mitchell* (1970).[8] In a 4-1-4 split decision without a majority opinion, four Justices of the U.S. Supreme Court held that Congress had no authority to set a minimum voting age. Another bloc of four Justices opined that Congress could choose to lower the voting

age as a way to enforce the Equal Protection Clause.[9] Justice Hugo Black wrote the controlling opinion, concluding that Congress's power to alter the "Manner" of federal elections gave it the authority to extend voting rights to eighteen-year-olds in federal elections but not in state contests.[10]

The result was that Americans who were eighteen to twenty years old had a right, granted by federal statute, to vote in federal elections but no right to vote in state elections. This situation presented "an administrative and logistical nightmare for state election officials."[11] Only a constitutional amendment could resolve this incongruity and extend voting rights to that age group in both federal and state elections nationwide.

PROPOSAL AND RATIFICATION OF THE TWENTY-SIXTH AMENDMENT

Oregon v. Mitchell was decided on December 21, 1970. The Senate approved the Twenty-Sixth Amendment on March 10, 1971, by a vote of 94 to 0, and the House approved it on March 23, 1971, by a vote of 401 to 19. The text mirrored the language used in the Fifteenth and Nineteenth Amendments: "The right of citizens of the United States, who are eighteen years of age or older, to vote shall not be denied or abridged by the United States or by any State on account of age." The states ratified the amendment a mere 107 days after it was approved by Congress: "by far the most rapid" ratification of a constitutional amendment in the history of the Republic.[12]

The amendment was adopted during the Vietnam conflict. It struck many Americans as unjust that men who were eighteen to twenty years old were being drafted and thousands were dying when they did not have the right to vote in the elections that determined the course of that armed conflict. A similar argument had been made "during or after every major war," but, until Vietnam, "it had little effect on the traditional consensus that twenty-one was the age of political maturity."[13]

The amendment faced minimal opposition, perhaps in part because states did not want the administrative hassle of maintaining two separate lists of voters eligible in federal and state elections. There were some skeptics, however, who argued that people in that age group lacked sufficient judgment to vote and would therefore be swayed more easily by appeals that more mature voters would reject.[14]

SCOPE AND ENFORCEMENT

The Twenty-Sixth Amendment does not require states or the United States to permit every adult to vote, nor does it prohibit states from allowing people to vote before they reach age eighteen. Rather, it prohibits states and the national government from establishing a minimum voting age that is any older than age eighteen. That is, the amendment makes it unconstitutional to deny the right to vote to an adult *because of that person's age*. The states retain the power to deny voting rights based on a lack of U.S. citizenship, lack of residence within the jurisdiction, or felony conviction. Somewhat counterintuitively, it prohibits states from establishing a *maximum* voting age as well. If the government were to deny, for example, people above the age of sixty-five the right to vote, that would be a denial of the right to vote of a person "eighteen years of age or older" "on account of age."

Like several other rights-granting amendments beginning with the Thirteenth, the Twenty-Sixth Amendment has an enforcement clause (Section 2) empowering Congress to "enforce this article by appropriate legislation." That grant of power expands congressional authority, enabling Congress to pass laws to protect the right to be free from age discrimination in voting in federal and state elections even if such a law would not be authorized by any of Congress's other powers. Nevertheless, it remains true that, except as to the kinds of discrimination proscribed by the First, Fifteenth, Nineteenth, Twenty-Fourth, and Twenty-Sixth Amendments, the Constitution leaves to states the determination of who may vote in elections. As the Supreme Court noted in *Arizona v. Inter Tribal Council of Arizona, Inc.* (2013), "[p]rescribing voting qualifications . . . 'forms no part of the power to be conferred upon the national government' by the Elections Clause . . . ."[15]

JUDICIAL PRECEDENT

The Supreme Court has decided only one case under the Twenty-Sixth Amendment. The case was *Symm v. United States* (1979), which held that a voter-registration questionnaire distributed to young college students violated the Twenty-Sixth Amendment.[16] The case was decided without oral argument and without a majority opinion. The Court did not explain its reasoning; it simply affirmed the lower court. *Symm* would appear to indicate that the amendment does more than simply lower the voting age to eighteen. Rather, it protects people ages eighteen to twenty from voting discrimination. This protection would prohibit laws that do not discriminate on their face but that are motivated by a desire to suppress the votes of people in that age group.

Such an interpretation would bring the Twenty-Sixth Amendment into line with the Constitution's other provisions barring discrimination in voting. The Fifteenth and Nineteenth Amendments protect not only against facially discriminatory laws, but also against facially neutral laws that are adopted or applied with a discriminatory purpose.[17]

In 1972, the Colorado Supreme Court held that the amendment prohibited age discrimination not only in voting qualifications, but also in the rules governing eligibility to circulate initiative petitions. The court found that the amendment's restrictions apply "to the entire process involving the exercise of the ballot and its concomitants."[18] However, the Minnesota Supreme Court held that the amendment did not prohibit states from establishing age requirements above age eighteen for holding public office.[19]

The U.S. Supreme Court has noted that "the rights of voters and the rights of candidates do not lend themselves to neat separation; laws that affect candidates always have at least some theoretical, correlative effect on voters."[20] Thus, age limits on candidates affect the rights of voters who support those candidates, and one might suppose that young voters disproportionately support young candidates. Nevertheless, age restrictions on officeholding are included in the Constitution itself.[21] It would be quite remarkable if the Twenty-Sixth Amendment's protection of eighteen-year-olds' right to vote gave them, by implication, the right to run for President or governor as well. Accordingly, the extent to which the amendment permits states and the national government to establish an age requirement above age eighteen for participating in the political process in ways other than voting is unclear.

The lower courts have also addressed laws that relax the voting rules for senior citizens, effectively making it harder for younger people to vote than it is for seniors. During the COVID-19 pandemic, Texas law permitted voters who were at least sixty-five years old to vote by mail. Younger voters, however, were denied that option unless they were disabled or absent from the jurisdiction. In *Texas Democratic Party v. Abbott* (2020), the Fifth Circuit Court of Appeals upheld the distinction.[22] The court recognized that the law facially discriminated on the basis of age but found that the law was constitutional because it rationally sought to

ease burdens that were disproportionately faced by older voters.

The court's holding might be suspect because constitutional rights generally may not be overcome merely because a discriminatory law creates a rational distinction. The courts typically review race-based and sex-based distinctions utilizing strict or intermediate scrutiny, rather than rational basis. As a result, discrimination on the basis of race or sex is not rendered constitutional just because it is a rational way to ease burdens faced by the race or sex benefited by the distinction. Accordingly, it remains to be determined whether other courts will follow the Fifth Circuit's lead in applying the rational-basis test to election laws that apply differently to voters of different ages.

OPEN QUESTIONS

- To what extent does the Twenty-Sixth Amendment prohibit age discrimination in aspects of the political process other than voting?
- Does the Twenty-Sixth Amendment protect against laws that disproportionately harm younger voters even if the laws themselves do not mention age? Would the intent of the legislature enacting such laws matter?
- Would the Twenty-Sixth Amendment be violated if a law limited the voting power of younger voters because of a desire to harm the party or policies favored by younger voters? What if a law sought to *augment* the voting power of younger voters to compensate for their lower rates of turnout or as a way to help interests favored by younger voters?
- Does the Twenty-Sixth Amendment forbid laws that ease voting requirements for older voters if, in so doing, the laws create a disparity between the voting rules applicable to voters of different ages?
- Is the rational-basis test the appropriate standard of review for claims under the Twenty-Sixth Amendment, or does the amendment mirror the protections against race and sex discrimination in the Fifteenth and Nineteenth Amendments? Courts review alleged violations of these other amendments with heightened judicial scrutiny.

Cite as: Michael R. Dimino, *The Minimum Voting Age Amendment, in* THE HERITAGE GUIDE TO THE CONSTITUTION 816 (Josh Blackman & John G. Malcolm eds., 3d ed. 2025).

Notes

1. Art. I, § 2, cl. 1; amend. XVII.   **2.** Michael R. Dimino et al., Voting Rights and Election Law: Cases, Explanatory Notes, and Problems 4 (3d ed. 2021).   **3.** Alexander Keyssar, The Right to Vote: The Contested History of Democracy in the United States 225 (rev. ed. 2009).   **4.** 84 Stat. 314 (1970).   **5.** *Oregon v. Mitchell*, 400 U.S. 112, 117–18 (1970).   **6.** Art. I, § 4, cl. 1.   **7.** *Arizona v. Inter-Tribal Council of Arizona, Inc.*, 570 U.S. 1, 16 (2013).   **8.** 400 U.S. 112 (1970).   **9.** U.S. Const. amend. XIV, §§ 1, 5.   **10.** 400 U.S. at 124 (opinion of Black, J.).   **11.** Keyssar, *supra* at 227.   **12.** *Id.* at 228.   **13.** *Id.* at 225.   **14.** Rebecca de Schweinitz, *"The Proper Age for Suffrage": Vote 18 and the Politics of Age from World War II to the Age of Aquarius, in* Age in America: The Colonial Era to the Present 209 (Corinne T. Field & Nicholas L. Syrett eds., 2015).   **15.** 570 U.S. 1, 16–17 & n.8 (2013).   **16.** 439 U.S. 1105 (1979).   **17.** *White v. Regester*, 412 U.S. 755 (1973); *Gomillion v. Lightfoot*, 364 U.S. 339 (1960).   **18.** *Colorado Project-Common Cause v. Anderson*, 495 P.2d 220, 223 (Colo. 1972).   **19.** *Opatz v. City of St. Cloud*, 196 N.W.2d 298 (Minn. 1972).   **20.** *Bullock v. Carter*, 405 U.S. 134, 143 (1972).   **21.** Art. I, §§ 2, 3; art. II, § 1.   **22.** 961 F.3d 389 (5th Cir. 2020).

~

ESSAY NO. 216: THE CONGRESSIONAL COMPENSATION AMENDMENT
AMEND. 27

No law, varying the compensation for the services of the Senators and Representatives, shall take effect, until an election of representatives shall have intervened.
—GianCarlo Canaparo

INTRODUCTION

Under the original design of the Constitution, the President's compensation could not be increased or decreased during his term in office,[1] and compensation for federal judges could not be decreased during their tenure.[2] However, the Congressional Compensation Clause, also known as the Ascertainment Clause, placed no limits on when Senators and Representatives could give themselves a raise.[3] (See Essay No. 30.) During the ratification debates, several states proposed an amendment that would delay the effect of any law changing compensation until after the next election of the House of Representatives. The Twenty-Seventh Amendment was ratified in 1992, and a federal court held shortly thereafter that automatic cost-of-living adjustments did not run afoul of the amendment.

THE FIRST CONGRESS

During the ratification debates, the Congressional Compensation Clause proved controversial. Anti-Federalists warned that members of Congress could enrich themselves at the public expense. The Virginia, New York, and North Carolina conventions submitted a proposed amendment that would delay the effect of any law changing compensation until after the next election of the House of Representatives. On June 8, 1789, James Madison proposed it to the First Congress.[4] Madison endorsed this amendment because it eliminated the risk of self-dealing. With an intervening election, members could not be sure that they would still be in office when their salaries changed. Madison explained that any raises "cannot be for the particular benefit of those who are concerned in determining the value of the service."[5]

On August 14, 1789, the amendment was briefly debated in the House.[6] Only two members spoke about the provision. Representative Theodore Sedgwick of Massachusetts said that

the amendment would do "little good" because it would not stop "designing men" from lowering their wages to make themselves popular or to exclude poor but worthy challengers.[7] Representative Jacob Vining of Delaware supported the amendment because he did not like the idea of "leaving it in the breast of any man to set a value upon his own work."[8] The Senate did not record any official debates about the amendment and approved it.[9]

RATIFYING THE TWENTY-SEVENTH AMENDMENT

On September 25, 1789, twelve proposed amendments, including the Congressional Compensation Amendment, were sent to the state legislatures for ratification.[10] By December 1791, the amendments numbered three through twelve were ratified by three-fourths of the state legislatures. These ten amendments became known as the Bill of Rights. But the first two proposed amendments did not receive sufficient support. Eleven states were needed for ratification, but the Congressional Compensation Clause was approved by only six states.[11] For most of the next two centuries, it was largely forgotten.

In 1982, Gregory D. Watson, a sophomore at the University of Texas-Austin, wrote a college paper arguing that the states could still ratify the Congressional Compensation Amendment because Congress had not put a time limit on it.[12] By contrast, the Eighteenth, Twentieth, Twenty-First, and Twenty-Second Amendments would be operative only if ratified within seven years after they were submitted to the states. Watson earned a "C" on his paper because his professor believed that the amendment had expired. In response, Watson launched a self-funded mission to secure ratification of the Congressional Compensation Amendment. Thirty-two states were still needed to approve the amendment, as six states had already approved it two centuries earlier.

Watson's efforts were well-timed. Between 1982 and 1991, Congress raised members' salaries from approximately $70,000 to $125,000. These frequent salary increases and apparent self-dealing sparked growing public anger,[13] and the states would soon support the amendment. Colorado, for example, declared that the "present political, social, and economic conditions are the same or even more demanding today than they were when the proposed amendment was submitted for adoption."[14] States rushed to follow Colorado's lead. On May 7, 1992, Michigan provided the decisive thirty-eighth state for ratification.

On May 20, 1992, Congress completed the process of formally adopting the Twenty-Seventh amendment.[15] It provides that "[n]o law, varying the compensation for the services of the Senators and Representatives, shall take effect, until an election of representatives shall have intervened." Soon, litigation would arise over the meaning of the word "law."

JUDICIAL PRECEDENT

As the states considered whether to ratify the Congressional Compensation Amendment, there was some debate about whether the process could be resumed after so many years.[16] In *Dillon v. Gloss* (1921), the U.S. Supreme Court said that "ratification must be within some reasonable time after the proposal."[17] But this dictum was not controlling, and Congress had not included a time limit in the amendment. Moreover, *Coleman v. Miller* (1939) held that disputes about ratification procedures and timing belonged to Congress alone.[18]

Only five months after the Twenty-Seventh Amendment was ratified, members of Congress challenged the constitutionality of the Ethics Reform Act of 1989. This statute provided Senators and Representatives with automatic annual cost-of-living adjustments. The plaintiffs argued that every annual adjustment was a new "law" for purposes of the amendment.[19] As a result, those raises could take effect only *after* an intervening election. In *Boehner v. Anderson* (1992), the district court rejected this argument.[20] The court of appeals affirmed.[21] The panel found that the Ethics Reform Act was a "law" that took effect after an election.[22] Therefore, the pay raise complied with the terms of the Twenty-Seventh Amendment.

OPEN QUESTIONS

- Does the word "compensation" in the Congressional Compensation Clause have the same meaning as the word "compensation" in the Twenty-Seventh Amendment? Would an originalist analysis focus on the meaning of the word in 1789 or its meaning in 1992? Was there any linguistic drift between 1789 and 1992?
- The text of the Twenty-Seventh Amendment draws a distinction between a law "varying the compensation" and the law "tak[ing] effect." At what point does a law vary compensation, when the law is enacted or when it takes effect?[23]

Cite as: GianCarlo Canaparo, *The Congressional Compensation Amendment, in* THE HERITAGE GUIDE TO THE CONSTITUTION 820 (Josh Blackman & John G. Malcolm eds., 3d ed. 2025).

Notes

1. Art. II, § 1, cl. 7.   **2.** Art. III, § 1.   **3.** Art. I, § 6, cl. 1. **4.** 1 Annals 451.   **5.** 1 Annals 458.   **6.** 1 Annals 756–57.   **7.** 1 Annals 756.   **8.** 1 Annals 756–57.   **9.** Richard B. Bernstein, *The Sleeper Wakes: The History and Legacy of the Twenty-Seventh Amendment*, 61 Fordham L. Rev. 497, 528–29 (1992).   **10.** 1 Annals of Cong. 90–91 (1790). **11.** Bernstein, *supra* at 532.   **12.** *Id.* at 537.   **13.** *Id.* at 535, 537–38.   **14.** Colorado House Concurrent Resolution No. 1008, 54th Gen. Assembly, 2d Reg. Sess., at 1152 (1984). **15.** Bernstein, *supra* at 542.   **16.** GianCarlo Canaparo & Paul J. Larkin, Jr., *The Twenty-Seventh Amendment: Meaning and Application*, 2021 Harv. J.L. & Pub. Pol'y Per Curiam 1, 3–4 (2021).   **17.** 256 U.S. 368, 375 (1921).   **18.** 307 U.S. 433, 456 (1939).   **19.** *Id.*   **20.** 809 F. Supp. 138, 139 (D.D.C. 1992).   **21.** 30 F.3d 156 (D.C. Cir. 1994).   **22.** *Id.* at 161; *Shaffer v. Clinton*, 54 F. Supp. 2d 1014 (D. Colo. 1999), *aff'd on other grounds sub nom. Schaffer v. Clinton*, 240 F.3d 878 (10th Cir. 2001).   **23.** Canaparo & Larkin, *supra* at 17; Adrian Vermeule, *The Constitutional Law of Official Compensation*, 102 Colum. L. Rev. 501, 516–21 (2002).